The Translator

Burton Raffel is Distinguished Professor of Humanities at the University of Southwestern Louisiana. He is the translator of many works, including *Gargantua and Pantagruel* (awarded the French-American Foundation Translation Prize), *Père Goriot*, *Beowulf*, and the five romances of Chrétien de Troyes.

The Editor

Diana de Armas Wilson is Professor of English and Renaissance Studies at the University of Denver. She is the author of *Allegories of Love: Cervantes's "Persiles & Sigismunda,"* co-editor of *Quixotic Desire: Psychoanalytic Perspectives on Cervantes*, and author of the forthcoming *Cervantes, the Novel, and the New World*.

A NORTON CRITICAL EDITION

Miguel de Cervantes
DON QUIJOTE

A NEW TRANSLATION

BACKGROUNDS AND CONTEXTS

CRITICISM

Translated by

BURTON RAFFEL

UNIVERSITY OF
SOUTHWESTERN
LOUISIANA

Edited by

DIANA DE ARMAS
WILSON

UNIVERSITY OF DENVER

W • W • NORTON & COMPANY • *New York* • *London*

W. W. Norton & Company has been independent since its founding in 1923, when William Warder Norton and Mary D. Herter Norton first published lectures delivered at the People's Institute, the adult education division of New York City's Cooper Union. The Nortons soon expanded their program beyond the Institute, publishing books by celebrated academics from America and abroad. By mid-century, the two major pillars of Norton's publishing program—trade books and college texts—were firmly established. In the 1950s, the Norton family transferred control of the company to its employees, and today—with a staff of four hundred and a comparable number of trade, college, and professional titles published each year—W. W. Norton & Company stands as the largest and oldest publishing house owned wholly by its employees.

The text of this book is composed in Electra
with the display set in Bernhard Modern.
Composition by PennSet, Inc.
Manufacturing by the Courier Companies—Westford Division.
Book design by Antonina Krass.
Production manager: Diane O'Connor.

Library of Congress Cataloging-in-Publication Data

Cervantes Saavedra, Miguel de, 1547–1616.
    [Don Quixote.   English]
    Don Quijote : a new translation, backgrounds and contexts,
criticism / Miguel de Cervantes ; translated by Burton Raffel ;
edited by Diana de Armas Wilson.
        p.   cm. — (A Norton critical edition)
    Includes bibliographical references (p.   ).

    ISBN 0-393-97281-X

    1. Cervantes Saavedra, Miguel de, 1547–1616.   Don Quixote.
I. Raffel, Burton.   II. Wilson, Diana de Armas.
III. Title.
PQ6329.A2   1998b
863'.3 — dc21   98-8066
                                                                          CIP

W. W. Norton & Company, Inc., 500 Fifth Avenue, New York, N.Y. 10110
www.wwnorton.com
W. W. Norton & Company Ltd., Castle House, 75/76 Wells Street,
London W1T 3QT

67890

Contents

Editor's Introduction

In an endearing appeal to his readers, Sidi Hamid Benengeli — the Arab historian and pseudo-author of *Don Quijote* — asks to be celebrated not for what he wrote but for what he refrained from writing (II.44).[1] To introduce a novel that has generated, down some four centuries, a staggering tradition of multilingual and polycultural commentary, one must cultivate Sidi Hamid's restraint. If *Don Quijote* needs a commentary to be understood — as its own hero suggests in a classic moment of metafiction (II.3) — this is scarcely the place for it. After a brief survey of Cervantes's life, I shall confine my remarks to three aspects of *Don Quijote*: the romance fictions it critiques, its generic transformation of these fictions into the first modern novel, and the connections between this novel and the newly discovered Americas.

The long and tangled history of the modern novel begins in Europe, and it begins with Cervantes. Hailing him as the inventor of a new genre, many critics have categorized *Don Quijote* as "the first great novel of world literature," or "the first modern work of literature," or "the archetypal novel."[2] Two postmodern novelists, their lives and writings continents apart, have tried to account for Cervantes's legacy "to the entire subsequent history of the novel." The Czech novelist Milan Kundera, who regards *Don Quijote* as "the first European novel," celebrates Cervantes for teaching us "to comprehend the world as a question." And the Mexican novelist Carlos Fuentes, who embraces Cervantes as the "Founding Father" of Latin-American fiction, applauds the ethical stance through which he "struggles to bridge the old and new worlds."[3]

The writer who offered us this new way of reading the world, Miguel de Cervantes Saavedra, was born in 1547 and into a lifetime of continuous adversity, privation, and poverty. As the fourth child of a luckless

1. Cervantes himself divided into four parts the volume now called *Don Quijote*, Part I (1605). He titled his 1615 continuation "Segunda parte" [Second Part], but he made no internal divisions there except chapters. Following this nomenclature, most critics traditionally divide *Don Quijote* into Part I and Part II, and they parenthetically cite from the text by part and chapter number, as above. Raffel has translated the two traditional "parts" into "volumes" in order to maintain the "parts" of the 1605 text.
2. Citations, seriatim, from Georg Lukács, *The Theory of the Novel*, trans. Anna Bostock (1971; rpt. Cambridge, Mass.: The MIT Press, 1977), p. 88; Michel Foucault, *The Order of Things: An Archaeology of the Human Sciences*, trans. of *Les Mots et les choses* (New York: Vintage, 1973), p. 48; and Robert B. Alter, "Mirror of Knighthood, World of Mirrors," in *Don Quixote: Miguel de Cervantes*, The Ormsby Translation, rev., ed. Joseph R. Jones and Kenneth Douglas (New York: W. W. Norton & Company, 1981), p. 973.
3. Milan Kundera, *The Book of Laughter and Forgetting*, trans. Michael Henry Heim (New York: Penguin, 1981), p. 237; see also Kundera's "Depreciated Legacy of Cervantes," in *The Art of the Novel*, trans. Linda Asher (London: Faber and Faber, 1990), pp. 3–20. Carlos Fuentes, *Don Quixote, or the Critique of Reading* (Austin: The University of Texas Press, 1976), pp. 9 and 48.

barber-surgeon living at the margins of accepted Spanish society and even, at one point, in debtor's prison, the young Cervantes experienced a rootless childhood marked by repeated Dickensian flights from creditors. Although born in a famous university town near Madrid, Alcalá de Henares, he was never to enjoy a university education. Instead, he joined the military, lost the use of his left hand while fighting against the Turks at Lepanto (1571), was seized by Barbary Coast pirates en route home from the wars, and spent over five years as a captive in an Algerian *bagnio*.

Upon his return to Spain, as a maimed veteran whose ransom had beggared his family, Cervantes soon discovered that his postwar career prospects were grim. In 1580 — the year of Cervantes's liberation from captivity — Philip II annexed Portugal, with all its possessions in Africa, Brazil, and the East Indies, to an unwieldy empire that already included vast New World holdings. Despite the spread of Philip's dominions, stretching from Naples to the Philippines, Spain's imperial glory showed visible signs of fading. The steady flow of gold and silver from the American colonies had produced, in the metropolis, a wildly inflationary economy. The idea of emigrating to the New World took root in Cervantes's mind during these lean years. A document in his own hand — an application to the Council of the Indies in 1582 for a colonial post in America — was found this century in the Spanish archives at Simancas. Evidently nothing came of this application, since Cervantes was forced to accept work as an itinerant tax collector, wringing quotas of wheat and fodder and olive oil from resistant Andalusian villages. Some of these provisions were targeted for Philip's Invincible Armada, scheduled to attack England in 1588. In yet another petition submitted in 1590, Cervantes begged to be considered for any one of various posts then vacant in the Indies: the comptrollership of the Kingdom of New Granada, or the governorship of a province in Guatemala, or the post of accountant of galleys at Cartagena, or that of magistrate of the city of La Paz. This last petition was brusquely rejected: in its margins some functionary wrote the utopian response, "let him look around here for some favor that may be granted him."[4]

Instead of America, Cervantes landed in the Royal Prison of Seville. The innocent victim of a bankrupt financier holding his state funds, he was jailed briefly in 1592 and continued, for a decade, to tangle with the Treasury over a shortage in his tax-moneys. As the Prologue to Part I of *Don Quijote* teasingly suggests, the idea for the novel, though hardly the manuscript, may have been engendered during his incarceration. *Don Quijote* was published in 1605 and was an immediate success, both in Europe and America. Hundreds of documented copies of the first edition crossed the Atlantic the same year of publication. In 1607 — just as Jamestown, Virginia, was struggling to become the first permanent British settlement in the New World — a small mining town in the highlands

---

4. For the whole text of Cervantes's 1590 application, see José Toribio Medina, "Cervantes americanista: Lo que dijo de los hombres y cosas de América [Cervantes Americanist: What He Said about the People and Things of America]," in *Estudios cervantinos* (Santiago de Chile: Fondo Histórico y Bibliográfico José Toribio Medina, 1958), pp. 535–36.

of Peru awarded its first prize, during a festive ring joust, to impersonations of Don Quijote and Sancho.[5]

Blessed with a volcanic vitality during the last decade of his writing life, Cervantes produced — apart from Part Two of *Don Quijote* (1615) — plays, interludes, poems, novellas, and a final novel which he heralded as "the great *Persiles*" and considered his masterpiece. All of this industry, however, brought profit only to his publishers. He died in 1616 — on the same date, if not the same day, as Shakespeare — probably of diabetes. In the prologue to the *Persiles*, written four days before his death, Cervantes apologized to his future readers for the "broken thread" of his writing. Almost four hundred years of novelists have attached themselves to that thread.

Lionel Trilling's notorious claim that "all prose fiction is a variation on the theme of *Don Quijote*" has exercised scholars for decades.[6] Readers chasing variants of the hoary theme of illusion and reality, however, might pause to remember that *Don Quijote* begins as a book about books. In an early modern European world marked by the violent social upheavals of nascent capitalism — and by the kinds of race, class, and gender wars that history seems to be repeating — Don Quijote remained a stubborn captive to the books of chivalry, to plots that serenely replayed the ancient protocol of knight errantry. To understand why Cervantes' hero is represented, throughout his novel, as a "sane madman" requires some knowledge of the medium that led to his madness:

> Don Quijote so buried himself in his books that he read all night from sundown to dawn, and all day from sunup to dusk, until with virtually no sleep and so much reading he dried out his brain and lost his sanity. He filled his imagination full to bursting with everything he read in his books, from witchcraft to duels, battles, challenges, wounds, flirtations, love affairs, anguish, and impossible foolishness . . . (I.1).

The books that "dried out" Don Quijote's brain were the runaway bestsellers of the Renaissance. Published during the childhood of the printing press, these books had their efflorescence between 1508 and 1602, during the century of the conquest and exploration of America.

The same fictions that crazed Don Quijote had enthralled a diverse population of insatiable European readers, from Scandinavia to Sicily. Kings such as Charles V and Francis I, saints such as Ignatius Loyola and Teresa of Avila, and even innkeepers such as Juan Palomeque, the illiterate book-lover in *Don Quijote*, were all intoxicated by the "wild stories" in the books of chivalry (I.32). That their hollow fictions were deeply encoded in fantasy only added to their appeal. Guardians of culture, predictably, regarded these books as deleterious to readers and even harmful to the state. Cervantes's cathedral priest of Toledo (I.47), for example, brings to mind the attack on chivalric romances by such apprehensive humanists as

---

5. Irving A. Leonard, *Books of the Brave* (New York: Gordian Press, 1964), pp. 270–89 and 306–12.
6. Lionel Trilling, "Manners, Morals, and the Novel," in *The Liberal Imagination* (New York: Viking, 1950), p. 203.

Montaigne, the inventor of the essay, who called these books "wit-besotting trash."

The romances of chivalry display a fairly constant repertoire of literary types: knights and squires, lords and vassals, dwarfs and giants, hermits and ogres, phantoms and enchanters, and — most crucial to the genre — damsels in distress. In between jousting in tourneys or questing for grails, chivalric heroes indulge in much violent swordplay. Although amputations are legion, magic potions, a staple of these plots, function like crazy glue to restore limbs to their owners. Trials by ordeal abound, and the virtuous, or at least the virtuous bloodlines, always prevail. Perhaps the key code in romance is the pervasive polarity of good and evil (the good guys versus the bad guys) with little ambiguity of character. Traces of the most popular agents of chivalric romance — either Arthurian (King Arthur and his Knights of the Round Table) or Carolingian (Charlemagne and his Twelve Peers) — still haunt our own best-seller lists. Less well known to Anglo-American readers, however, are knights like Don Quijote's beloved Amadís of Gaul, so popular that he produced a robust crop of generational sequels, of literary sons and even grandsons.

As the opening chapter makes clear, Don Quijote lives by the book. Reinventing himself as a knight-errant, he creates Dulcinea as his supreme fiction, a disembodied woman who becomes "the lady of his thoughts." The naive reading of this otherwise cultivated village gentleman — we might call it his *bibliomania* — leads him to imitate, at every crux, the idealized heroes of his cherished romances. The text presents its hero's magnificent obsession as a kind of addiction. The notion of books as addictive may seem quaint to an age all too familiar with other forms of substance abuse. An assessment of *Don Quijote* as "the first and greatest epic about addiction," however, conjures up a parade of romance addicts like Flaubert's Emma Bovary. In Emma's favorite books, invariably about love affairs between sensitive lovers and their damsels in distress, "there were gloomy forests, broken hearts, vows, sobs, tears and kisses," and, in the high chivalric mode, horses were "ridden to death on every page."[7] Don Quijote anticipates not only Madame Bovary but also, in our day, those legions of readers who devour a volume a day of "bodice-ripper romances," or those masses of television and computer addicts, hooked obsessively on their soap operas or on their ghostly *"affaires des modems."*

But Don Quijote is not *Don Quijote*. Although Cervantes's hero is a credulous reader, the novel he inhabits is a revolutionary book. One of its refrains — "Each man is the child of his deeds" — challenged a Spanish ruling class committed to an ideology of inherited blood. *Don Quijote* displaced, for its age, the aristocratic and authoritarian formulas of traditional stories with the ambiguity and relativity of a new kind of narrative — the novel — what Hegel would call "the epic of the middle-class world." Melville, who in a stirring apostrophe aligns Cervantes with An-

---

7. Susan Sontag made the remark about addiction in *The Boston Globe*, Book Section, March 9, 1986. Gustave Flaubert, *Madame Bovary*, trans. Francis Steegmuller (New York: Modern Library, 1957), p. 41.

drew Jackson, would move that middle-class epic into even more demo-
cratic vistas when he conferred the honors of knighthood upon a simple
crew of fishermen. *Don Quijote*, with its dialogic structures and great range
of innovation, revolutionized the art of narrative. The contemporary novelist Robert Coover claims that Cervantes's stories "sallied forth against
adolescent thought-modes and exhausted art forms, and returned home
with new complexities."[8]

What were some of these complexities? In the Prologue to Part One of
the novel, a fictionalized Cervantes announces his abdication of literary
paternity: *Don Quijote* is not his child but his stepchild. By yielding the
narration of his text to a cry of authors, he debunks both authorship and
authority, allowing himself to be drowned out by numerous surrogates: a
phantom author, editors, translators, censors, an apocryphal novelist attempting to capitalize on the success of Part One, and even ourselves.
Challenging the prevailing norms for citing illustrious authorities, Cervantes returns authority to the subjective reader. Not unlike hypertext today,
Cervantes urges us to participate in authoring his book: "Reader, you decide," is one of the narrator's most engaging imperatives (II.24).

Cervantes even makes Don Quijote participate in these interactive
games. In Part Two, the knight meets characters who recognize him as
the hero of Part One, a text by then enjoying wide circulation in print.
Overnight, Don Quijote becomes the hero of his own chivalric romance.
This, in its day, was truly novel: a fictional character who worried about
his own representation, who wondered whether the author had depicted
his "platonic loves" indecorously, whether he had discredited the purity
of his lady, and — most vertiginous of all as we are reading Part Two
— whether the author had, in fact, promised a Part Two! In the wake of
writers like Pirandello and Borges, critics have applied the term *metafiction*
to this kind of self-conscious narrative, a fiction which exposes its own
techniques. The roots of metafiction do not go back to *Tristam Shandy*,
as critics committed to an English "rise of the novel" sometimes suggest,
but to *Don Quijote*: Laurence Sterne himself invokes his debt to "the easy
pen of my beloved Cervantes."

That easy pen avowed only one aim for itself: "to topple the books of
chivalry" — that is, to undermine the kind of literature that, for centuries,
had underwritten a European aristocracy grounded on feudal institutions.
Don Quijote constitutes a long meditation on the seductiveness, as well as
the perniciousness, of these cognitive structures, most cruelly instanced, as
Nietzsche rightly observed, by the Duke and Duchess in Part Two. In the
Prologue to Part One, Cervantes announces that *Don Quijote* is aimed at
"demolishing the whole false, irrational network of those chivalric romances," a claim repeated, with laborious insistence, throughout the text.
Not all readers take that claim literally: many see it as ironic, as more of
a pretext, in both senses of the word, than an intention. If the degree of
Cervantine irony remains arguable (irony, after all, is in the eye of the
beholder), the text's advertised demolition project cannot be erased. It is
not only the attack on the romances of chivalry that makes *Don Quijote*

8. Robert Coover, *Pricksongs and Descants* (New York: E. P. Dutton, 1969), p. 77.

an antiromance. And it was not only Lord Byron who believed that Cervantes had "smiled Spain's chivalry away" (*Don Juan*, 13.11).

Even while Don Quijote was fruitlessly trying to revive knight-errantry across the arid plains of La Mancha, "Spain's chivalry" was enjoying a crepuscular resurgence in the New World. Cervantes's masterpiece has been widely read as a parody of the moribund romances of Medieval Europe, but the chivalric discourses it parodies were closely linked to the political realities of Renaissance America. As one Argentine scholar puts it, "America was the scene where chivalry rode for the last time."[9] Cervantes parodies — sometimes even satirizes — many of the rhetorical conventions legitimizing Spain's empire-building projects in the New World, conventions that appear repeatedly in the conquest chronicles. Recent attempts of historians to reconstruct early American colonial materials, to challenge the Anglo-oriented institutionalization of American history, may indeed make *Don Quijote* pertinent reading for a whole new generation of Americanists.

Even though he regards all comparisons as "odious," Don Quijote invites comparison with the conquistadors. A modern description of Columbus as "a kind of Quixote a few centuries behind his times," to cite only one of many conflations of these two figures, suggests some curious linkages between Don Quijote at his quirkiest and Columbus at his most chivalric.[1] Both men — the literary construct and the real-life explorer — exhibit a credulous and overstressed imagination; an alertness to the appearances of enchantment; a love for the ceremonies of naming; an ideology of certainties based on prescience rather than experience; a penchant for adjusting the data, as well as challenging the humanity, of informants who pass on any unwelcome intelligence; a fondness for imposing oaths on other people; and, above all, an injudicious bookishness. The Great Admiral conducted much of his "Enterprise of the Indies," in short, in compliance with chivalric formulas.

That the books of chivalry were the favorite reading material of the conquistadors was documented in 1949; that key traits in these books went on to frame many details and descriptions of the New World was articulated some dozen years later.[2] Since then, thanks largely to scholars ready to cross "the high seas, jungles, and deserts of colonial literary production," we have begun to understand more precisely how chivalric romance — the same genre that unhinged Don Quijote — related to the way Europeans wrote about their colonial experiences and even to the way they wrote about the New World peoples.[3] Anxious lest the books of chivalry

9. Valentín de Pedro, *América en las letras españolas del Siglo de Oro* (Buenos Aires: Editorial Sudamericana, 1954), p. 78; translation mine.
1. Tzvetan Todorov, *Conquest of America*, trans. Richard Howard (New York: Harper & Row, 1984), p. 11.
2. See Leonard, *Books of the Brave*, for this documentation. Manuel Alvar cites the earlier work of Stephen Gilman (1961) and Angel Rosenblat (1961) in "Fantastic Tales and Chronicles of the Indies," in *Amerindian Images and the Legacy of Columbus*, ed. René Jara and Nicholas Spadaccini (Minneapolis: University of Minnesota Press, 1992), p. 176.
3. See Rolena Adorno, "Colonial Spanish American Literary Studies: 1982–92," *Revista Interamericana de Bibliografía* 38 (1988), 170; and "Literary Production and Suppression: Reading & Writing about Amerindians in Colonial Spanish America," *Dispositio* 11, 28–29 (1986), 15–19. See also the cross-cultural work of Jorge Albistur, James D. Fernández, Mary Gaylord, Roberto González-Echevarría, Roland Greene, George Mariscal, Walter Mignolo, and James Nicolopulos.

corrupt the natives — who might be unable to distinguish romance from true history — Philip II, even prior to assuming the throne, had issued an official prohibition in the Indies of books "such as those about Amadís."[4] Years later Cortés's chronicler, Bernal Díaz del Castillo, would famously compare the dazzling first sight of Tenochtitlán, today's Mexico City, to the marvels narrated in *Amadís* — that prominent book in Don Quijote's library. As the common cultural referent of the age, in short, chivalric romances like *Amadís* not only dominated Spain's politics of representation but also provided America with some of her most poetic place names, such as California and Patagonia.

An earlier American translator of *Don Quijote*, Samuel Putnam, announced in 1949 that much remained to be done in tracing Cervantes's influence in America, where it seemed to be "less than elsewhere."[5] I would begin, instead, by tracing America's influence on Cervantes. Although earlier scholars had nodded to Cervantes's many references to America — to Mexico and Peru, parrots and alligators, tobacco and cacao, cannibals and Caribs — more generative connections between *Don Quijote* and the New World have been emerging since mid-century. In the 1950s, a Peruvian historian categorized *Don Quijote* as "a benevolent satire of the conquistador of *ínsulas* or Indies." By the sixties, a Colombian scholar was proposing a connection between Don Quijote (in his saner persona as Alonso Quesada) and Gonzalo Jiménez de Quesada, explorer of El Dorado, founder of the Kingdom of New Granada, and governor of Cartagena — places in the Indies where Cervantes applied for work. By the seventies, an Italian scholar had catalogued some of the conquest chronicles that were available to Cervantes. By the eighties, a North American scholar, discussing the "chivalric textuality" being parodied in *Don Quijote*, linked its hero to "the first conquistadors and seekers of new worlds." And by 1992, the Columbian Quincentenary, at least one writer wondered whether the existence of *Don Quijote* would have even been possible "without the Discovery."[6]

To align the first modern novel with the imperial process that produced the conquistadors — men who acted out "the impossible dream" in the New World — will require further study of the Amerindian cultures vanquished by Spain's colonial chivalry. One of these cultures is eulogized in Alonso de Ercilla's *La Araucana* (1569–1589), an epic about Spain's American wars in Chile that Cervantes strategically placed in Don Quijote's library, where it is evaluated, and saved from the bonfire, during the famous scrutiny of the books (I.6). That *Don Quijote* owes much to the chronicles of conquest of America — that it serves, indeed, as a textual manifestation of Spanish imperialism — has begun to take on greater

4. José Toribio Medina, *Biblioteca Hispano-Americana*, 7 vols. (Santiago de Chile, 1898–1907), vol. 6, pp. xxvi–xxvii.
5. "Introduction," *The Portable Cervantes*, trans. and ed. Samuel Putnam (New York: Viking, 1949), p. 27.
6. Cited, seriatim, are Raúl Porras Barrenechea, *El Inca Garcilaso en Montilla* (1561–1614) (Lima: Editorial San Marcos, 1955), p. 238; Germán Arciniegas, "Don Quijote y la conquista de América," *Revista Hispánica Moderna* 31 (1965), pp. 11–16; Stelio Cro, "Cervantes, el 'Persiles' y la historiografía indiana," *Anales de literatura hispanoamericana*, vol. 4 (Madrid: Universidad Complutense, 1975), 5–25; Daniel P. Testa, "Parodia y mitificación del Nuevo Mundo en el *Quijote*," *Cuadernos hispanoamericanos* 430 (April 1986), pp. 63–71; and Pedro Acosta's rev. of Roa Bastos' *La vigilia del Almirante*, in *El Tiempo*, "Lecturas dominicales" (Bogotá, July 4, 1993).

interpretive importance. Cervantes's text is, in many ways, an absorption of and a response to some of these chronicles, whose bravely pretentious and often fictitious exploits have been repeatedly, if preposterously, called "quixotic."

American readers may be surprised at the fair number of promotional references to their continent in *Don Quijote*. These images of economic promise mirrored the popular belief among Golden Age Spaniards that America was the place to become rich and famous. Moved by his master's illusions of omnipotence and delusions of philanthropy, Sancho wants to become both. His continuous talk of personal ennoblement — of being granted islands and governorships, of founding a dynasty, of tapping into the slave trade in order to convert his hypothetical African vassals "into silver and gold" (I.29) — allegorizes the New World even as it parodies the discourse of the conquistador. Sancho's later discovery that governing islands is "dismal" (II.13) echoes the gubernatorial experience of, among others, Columbus in Hispaniola. Don Quijote's famous Golden Age speech to the uncomprehending goatherds (I.11), on the other hand, gestures not only to ancient classical writers — Hesiod, Virgil, Horace, Ovid, Seneca, and Macrobius — but also to early modern Cubans. In a text available to Cervantes, Peter Martyr, the first historian of the New World, explained to an astonished Europe the philosophy of the "golden age" natives Columbus had encountered in Cuba: "they know no difference between Mine and Thine, that source of all evils" (*De Orbe Novo* I.3).

If *Don Quijote* allegorized Spanish exploits in the New World, the novel would soon after be deployed, by New England colonists, to satirize English exploits there. As early as 1637, barely a generation after Cervantes's death, various figures begin to advertise their readings of *Don Quijote*, available to them in English since Thomas Shelton's 1612 translation. Thomas Morton, for example, regards the attack on him by Miles Standish and other Puritan "worthies" as "like don Quixote against the Windmill."[7] And Cotton Mather vilifies Roger Williams — the "first rebel against the divine-church order in the wilderness" — as a violent Don Quijote, a "windmill" whirling in his head with such fury that "a whole country in America" was likely "to be set on fire."

Other, more than quixotic, forces would be setting our country on fire. Mark Twain's reading of *Don Quijote*, a few centuries later, would focus less on rebellion and more on ignorance. Huck Finn's recollection of Tom Sawyer's mocking words — "If I warn't so ignorant, but had read a book called 'Don Quixote' . . ." — offers Cervantes' book as an antidote to literalism, as a way to cope with spiteful enchanters who defraud the imagination. Representing ignorance as curable by the book, a young American protagonist reaches for an old Spanish fiction to help him make sense of a blighting social reality. Don Quijote, the would-be knight-errant whose specialty is "righting wrongs" in Renaissance Spain, takes root in the consciousness of Twain's characters, as they play out a story about racial wrongs in Middle America. Hemingway's claim that "all modern Ameri-

---

7. Thomas Morton, *New English Canaan* (1637), in *The Norton Anthology of American Literature*, vol. 1 (New York: Norton, 1998) 212.

can literature comes from one book by Mark Twain called *Huckleberry Finn*" is both complicated and enriched by that book's Spanish ancestor. At least one major American writer loudly acknowledged that ancestry: Faulkner claimed to read *Don Quijote* once a year — "as some do the Bible."

Burton Raffel's sprightly new translation invites us to do the same. If reading *Don Quijote* in the original Spanish was, for Lord Byron, "a pleasure before which all others vanish" (*Don Juan*, 14.98), reading it in Raffel's version will prove that pleasure need not vanish in translation. In his negotiations with *Don Quijote* — which he considers "the greatest novel ever written" — Raffel operates as a cultural go-between. One anecdote may explain his translating strategy, a far cry from the mechanical "this for that" labor of philologists. After I queried his masculine personification of Death — "but it's always *la muerte* in Spanish," I protested — Raffel explained that when Death knocks in English, she's a he. "*La muerte*," he wrote, "is as emphatically masculine in English as it is in German; sure, French, Italian, Portuguese, and Latin agree with Spanish, but it's an Anglo-Saxon world, this English-speaking one." Death's gender-bending here, however, should not be taken to signal an Anglo-Saxon world in this translation, whose intentions are manifestly Hispanic: "I want this translation to *sound* like it's set in Spain — to *feel* as Spanish as possible," Raffel continued. "It's not a book that could have been written in English — or indeed in any other language. *Don Quijote*'s magnificence is indubitably Hispanic."

Readers may find some jarring exceptions in Raffel's attempts to match, in English prose, what he calls Cervantes's "matchless original." He does not follow, for instance, Golden Age transcriptions of common Arabic names, a practice now widely rejected as forming part of colonialist discourse. The Spanish "Cide Hamete" is accordingly replaced by "Sidi Hamid," a name that readers familiar with Arabic will recognize as the best transcription available of the colloquial (Maghrebi) Arabic. Nor does Raffel follow the Spanish monetary system of Cervantes's day, e.g., *escudos*, *reales*, ducats, or doubloons. His "Translator's Note," however, explains his strategy in this regard.

Although a character in the novel rightly foresees the fame of *Don Quijote* as universal — "There will be no nation on earth," says Samson Carrasco, "and no language spoken, in which it will not have been translated" (II.3) — it is left to the hero himself to discuss the art of translation. When Don Quijote visits the print shop in Barcelona, he remarks, to a profit-minded Italian translator on the premises, that reading most vernacular translations "is rather like looking at Flemish tapestries on the wrong side." This sweeping indictment excludes two historical translators, the hero goes on to explain, whose skill leaves in doubt "which is the translation and which the original" (II.62). Although highly sensitive to his own representation in print, Don Quijote would have surely welcomed Burton Raffel to his visionary company of skillful translators.

I wish to thank the University of Denver for a Graduate Work Study grant that funded an invaluable assistant to my editing labors: the gracious, anticipatory, and superbly efficient Cynthia Kuhn. This project also owes much to the kind counsel and expert reading of Michael McGaha, editor of *Cervantes*, who not only supplied invaluable information about avoiding offensive translations of Arabic names and titles, but also provided a long and useful list of *errata* in the trade edition of this translation. I am deeply grateful to John J. Allen, former president of the Cervantes Society of America, for sharing with me various artistic representations of Don Quijote. I am also grateful to Ralph di Franco, Professor of Spanish at the University of Denver, whose expertise on the *Romancero* clarified for me Don Quijote's imitation of various ballads. I also wish to acknowledge the contributions of my graduate students — too many to thank personally, but, like Don Quijote, you know who you are — in a series of courses on the multiple rises of the novel. Without the timely and confident urging of Carol Bemis, editor of the Norton Critical Series, I would have long ago foundered. The last days of proofreading this volume were graced by the arrival of Amalia Theodoredis, *"prenda querida de mi alma,"* to cite Cervantes on newborns. Finally, let me mark the great debt I owe to my husband, Douglas B. Wilson. Even without professing knight-errantry, he has remained — to borrow Don Quijote's own self-analysis — "magnanimous, gallant, bold, calm, [and] patient" (I.50) — during the various trials and captivities of this editing project.

Diana de Armas Wilson
University of Denver
October 2, 1998

Translator's Note

No one can reproduce Cervantes's style in English. Not only is his prose uniquely magnificent, but the very music of Spanish, its syntactical structures, and the thrust and flavor of its words, are literally untransportable into any other language. Syntactical organization being however the most basic hallmark of prose style — the stamp of a writer's mind — I have made it my special concern to re-create, as closely as possible, the organization of Cervantes's sentences. Neither this nor any other device can adequately capture Cervantes's style, but I have tried to track the movement — the pace; the complexity, or simplicity; the degree of linguistic density; the structural transitions — of *Don Quijote*'s inimitable prose. I have also worked hard to match the rhetoric of that prose, as I have tried, when I could, to find reasonably exact verbal equivalences. I have been scrupulously careful not to mute Cervantes's dazzling irony, nor have I consciously suppressed, bowdlerized, or altered anything.

There have inevitably been dislocations: Spanish is a very different language from English; Spanish culture and social organization are different; and in the almost four hundred years since Cervantes wrote, much has changed in all sorts of way. I have tried to keep these dislocations as small and, relatively speaking, as unimportant as possible. But readers accustomed to Cervantes's Spanish, and especially readers learned in the ways of early seventeenth-century Spain, will inevitably be pained by any loss whatever. I do not blame them. I ask them, however, to remember that straightforward lexical dislocations, though they may often seem deeply objectionable, are in truth a good deal less important than such larger matters as style, pacing, fidelity to authorial intent, and the like. To turn Spanish *canónigo* into the English "canon," e.g., would in my considered opinion betray rather than accurately transmit what Cervantes was in fact saying. Accordingly, in order to faithfully reflect Cervantes's meaning, in the alien context of twentieth-century American English, I have here translated *canónigo* as "cathedral priest." So too the seventeenth-century Spanish *capitán*, which then meant "primary commander" (and had at one time the same meaning in English: think of the phrase "captains of industry"), can no longer be properly translated as twentieth-century "captain," that word now designating a subordinate commander. I have therefore translated *capitán* as "general," that being, again, what in *our* language it actually means. Linguistic history also reveals that the German word *thaler* entered Spanish *before* it entered English, being used both in Spain and in its colonies for the Spanish "piece of eight" coin, called (after the German) a *dolar* and worth eight *reales*. It was then borrowed

— strictly, re-borrowed — as a monetary term, both in Britain and, later, in its North American colonies. (See, *inter alia*, O.E.D., D, p. 589, col. 2, and especially the citation from Barnaby Rich's *Farewell to Militarie Profession*, 1581, and Noah Webster, *An American Dictionary of the English Language*, 1828.) With this largely forgotten history in mind, therefore, the many archaic monetary terms employed by Cervantes have been reduced to one, "dollar," well understood at that time as an English word of Spanish origin. If this is in some senses a linguistic compromise, on the facts it is clearly historically legitimated.

Especially important but utterly untranslatable material has been explained, with the utmost brevity, in square brackets incorporated into the text; there are also, both when absolutely necessary and, admittedly, at moments of sheer desperation, a fair number of footnotes. Spanish names and sounds have been retained whenever possible.

My primary text has been the edition of *Don Quijote* by Martín de Riquer (Planeta, 1980); I have consulted, though less frequently, the edition by Luis Andrés Murillo (Clásicos Castalia, 1978). I have also had constantly in front of me Sebastián de Covarrubias' *Tesoro de la lengua castellana o española*, originally published in 1611 (in the 1943 edition by Martín de Riquer). Whenever contemporary scholars or lexicographers have differed from Covarrubias as to the precise meaning of a word or a phrase, I have invariably deferred to Cervantes's contemporary, who in a sense cannot be wrong, because he — unlike any of us — was there.

Inevitably, my debts to living and breathing sources are too great to list in full. I must however single out Professors Diana de Armas Wilson and Ronnie Apter, who gave me both encouragement and (exactly when I needed it) discouragement, and Philip Ward, editor of *The Oxford Companion to Spanish Literature*, who administered a useful drubbing to an early draft of the Prologue. My colleague at the University of Southwestern Louisiana, Professor James D. Wilson, had no direct hand in the translation, but it was the article on Cervantes which he commissioned from me, for *The Mark Twain Encyclopedia*, which made me acutely aware that I did not feel comfortable recommending any of the existing translations of *Don Quijote*, and thus led very directly indeed to the making of this translation.

Finally, I am deeply indebted to Professor John J. Allen, former president of the Cervantes Society of America, for a sensitive, intelligent, wonderfully detailed vetting of the entire manuscript. Nothing we mortals produce can be perfect, not even Cervantes's *Don Quijote* (though it seems to me the greatest novel any mortal, living or dead, has ever written). But after so thorough a scrubbing as Professor Allen has provided, I take comfort in the thought that whatever weeds may remain are at least well-hidden. They are of course my sole responsibility. Still, to borrow Professor Allen's words, as he finished his large labors of *cervantista* dedication, "I like to think that Cervantes would not be displeased."

Burton Raffel
Lafayette, Louisiana

The Text of
DON QUIJOTE

SPAIN
at the End of the
Sixteenth Century

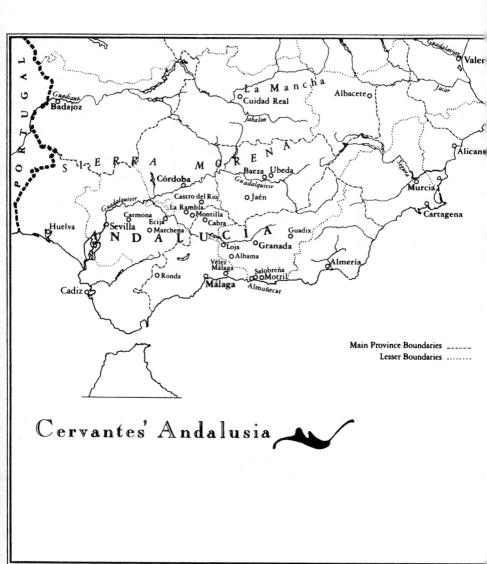

Main Province Boundaries _____
Lesser Boundaries ....

Cervantes' Andalusia

VOLUME ONE

Prologue†

Leisurely reader: you don't need me to swear that I longed for this book, born out of my own brain, to be the handsomest child imaginable, the most elegant, the most sensible. But could I contradict the natural order of things? Like creates like. So what could my sterile, half-educated wit give birth to except the history of a sniveling child, withered, whining, its head stuffed with all kinds of thoughts no one else would even think of, like a man bred in a jail cell, where everything grates on your nerves and every new sound makes you still sadder. Peace, a calm spot, delightful meadows, serene skies, murmuring brooks, and a tranquil spirit — they turn even the most sterile Muses fertile, filling the world with wonderful, delightful offspring. Sometimes a father has an ugly child, utterly unlovely, but love drapes a veil over his eyes so he's blind to its faults and sees them as wit and charm and describes them to his friends as clever and graceful. But though I may seem to be Don Quijote's parent, I'm only his step-father, and I'm not interested in saying things just because everybody else does, or in begging you, dearest reader, with tears in my eyes, to please forgive or overlook my child's faults — because you're neither his relative nor his friend, and your soul sits in its own body, you can make up your mind for yourself, with the best of them, and by God you're the boss in your own house, like a king in charge of his tax-collectors. You know the old saying: whatever I've got under my coat is mine, not the king's. Which means you're under no obligation at all, so you can say anything you like about this history, you don't have to worry about being insulted if you don't like it or rewarded if you do.

But I would have preferred to give it to the world just as it is, plain and simple, not decorating it with a prologue or an endless list of all the sonnets, epigrams, and elegies we put in the front of books. Because, let me tell you, though writing the book was hard work, nothing was harder than this preface you're reading right now. I kept picking up my pen and putting it down, over and over, not knowing what I was supposed to write, and once, when I was sitting like that, just hanging fire, motionless, with the paper in front of me, a pen stuck behind my ear, my elbow on the desk, my hand on my cheek, wondering what I ought to say, one of my friends suddenly came in, clever, smart, and seeing me so buried in thought asked me why, and I didn't hide anything from him, I told him I was worried about the prologue I had to write for Don Quijote's history, and beginning to think I neither wanted to write it nor let that noble knight's adventures see the light of day.

"And why shouldn't I be worried what that time-honored old law-giver we call the Public will say, seeing me, after this long sleep in the silence of oblivion, coming out again, now, with all my years on my back, with reading matter about as juicy as dry grass, totally unoriginal, and a feeble style — a book thin in learned conceits, lacking any erudition or serious

†Four brief preliminary statements by Cervantes have been omitted from this translation.

7

ideas, without a single annotation in the margins and absolutely no footnotes at the back, the way I see other books (even if they're stuffed with
lies and indecencies) crammed full of Aristotle's wisdom, or Plato's, and
the whole mob of philosophers, and then everybody's stunned and says
they're written by really learned men, widely read, truly eloquent.[1] And
Lord, when they cite the Holy Scriptures! All you can say is they're like
some new Saint Thomas or some other holy Church Doctors: just see how
careful they are to stay so delicately proper, one minute describing a lover
so distracted he's out of his head, and the next giving us a nice little
Christian sermon that's sheer joy, a treat to hear, a delight to read. My
book doesn't have that stuff, because I haven't got anything to scribble in
the margins, or anything to annotate at the end, and I haven't any idea
what writers I've borrowed from, or how to set them all out right at the
start, the way the rest of them do, according to the letters of the alphabet,
beginning with Aristotle and finishing with Xenophon or Zoilus or Zeuxis
(though one of them slandered everyone and the other was a painter). And
there aren't any sonnets at the beginning of my book — at least, not
sonnets by noblemen, dukes, counts, bishops, society ladies or celebrated
poets — though if I asked two or three carpenters and plasterers, all
friends of mine, I know they'd turn them out for me, and they'd be poems
the best-known writers in Spain couldn't match.[2] And so, my dear sir, my
good friend — to get on with it — I've made up my mind that Señor
Don Quijote has to stay buried in the archives of La Mancha, until Heaven
sends down someone to adorn him with all the things he needs, because
I know I just can't supply them — I don't know enough, I haven't read
enough, and besides I'm a loafer by nature, I'm too lazy to go hunting for
authors who say what I already know how to say without their help. And
now, my friend, you know how I got into that stupified rapture in which
you found me — and isn't it all more than enough reason to be hung
up by the ears?"

Hearing which, my friend slapped himself on the forehead and, laughing as hard as he knew how, said to me:

"My God, brother, now I begin to see how badly I've misunderstood
you, all this time, thinking you were sensible and prudent, no matter what
you were doing. And now I see that's about as far from the truth as the
sky is from the earth. How can such a trivial matter, something so easy to
fix up, possibly have the power to entrap, to take possession of a ripe,
mature mind like yours — an imagination, a wit, that can chew its way
through problems infinitely tougher than this? By my faith, this doesn't
come from not being in the habit of using your head, but from overwhelming laziness and a shortage of plain hard thinking. You want to know
if I'm right? Pay attention and you'll see how, in just the twinkling of an
eye, I get rid of all your problems and repair every single one of those
difficulties that, according to you, are paralyzing you and keeping you from

1. Cervantes is thematizing here a cultural revolution that took place between 1550 and 1650, when
   Western thinkers had begun to mistrust the writings of antiquity as sources for all important truths.
2. Cervantes is poking fun here at books by his contemporaries (e.g., Lope de Vega) that were
   prefaced with dozens of laudatory poems by socially prominent people, threaded with erudite
   quotations, and capped with alphabetical indexes of classical authors.

bringing before the world the history of your famous Don Quijote — that shining light, that true mirror of knight errantry."

"Tell me," I answered, after hearing what he'd said, "just how you expect to fill in the gaping hole of my fears and turn the chaos of my confusion into clarity?"

To which he replied:

"First of all, the problem of all the sonnets and epigrams and elegies you haven't got at the beginning of your book, which are supposed to be written by important, titled people, simply disappears if you take the trouble to write them yourself. Then you can baptize them and give them any name you like; they can be progeny of Prester John of the Indies or the Emperor of Trebizond, both of whom, I've heard, were famous poets. And if they weren't, and some pedants and university graduates try to stab you in the back, mumbling that it isn't true, just snap your fingers at them, because even if they can prove you're lying, they can't cut off the hand you wrote with. And as for those missing marginal references, the names of all the books and writers where you went hunting for the wit and wisdom quoted in your history, all you have to do is scribble in any bits and pieces of Latin you happen to remember — anyway, whatever scraps it's easiest for you to lay your hands on. Then, when you talk about freedom and bondage, you shove in

> Non bene pro toto libertas venditur auro
> It's a bad bargain to sell freedom, even for all the gold you can get.
> [Walter Anglicus, 12th cent.]

And in the margin you cite Horace, or whoever said that. When you're talking about death's power, let them have

> Pallida mors aequo pulsat pede pauperum tabernas,
> Regumque turres
> Death raps his bony knuckles, bleached,
> Indifferent, on any man's door, a palace or a hut. [Horace]

If you're talking about the friendship and love God tells us to show our enemies, go right to Holy Scripture itself, which you can manage with just a touch of research. Why not quote the very words of God? *Ego autem dico vobis: diligite inimicos vestros,* 'But I say to you, love your enemies.' If you're talking about evil thoughts, give them the Gospel: *De corde exeunt cogitationes malae,* 'Evil thoughts spring forth from the heart.' If your subject is the fickleness of friends, well, you've got Cato, who put it this way:

> Donec eris felix, multos numerabis amicos,
> Tempora si fuerint nubila, solus eris.
> When you're rich, you'll have lots of friends,
> But when the skies darken you'll be alone. [Ovid]

And with a pinch of Latin here, and a pinch of Latin there, they might even think you're a scholar, which isn't a bad reputation, these days. Latin pays. As for annotations at the end of your book, why, it shouldn't be hard to do it like this: if you mention some kind of giant in your book, make sure it's the giant Goliath — and with just that stroke, which will cost you almost nothing, you get a magnificent annotation, because then you can put in: *The giant Golias, or Goliath, was a Philistine whom David killed, in the Vale of Terebinto, with his wondrous slingshot, according to the story in the Book of Kings* — in the chapter where you find all that written.[3] And then, to show your learning in the humanities and in heavenly cosmography, make sure, somehow or other, you get the name of the River Tagus into your history, and you've immediately got yourself another fantastic annotation, like this: *The River Tagus was named for a Spanish King; it originates in such-and-such a place and flows down to the ocean, kissing the walls of the famous city of Lisbon, which is said to be lined with gold, etc., etc.* If you talk about thieves and thievery, let me remind you about Cacus — I know his story by heart; if it's whores, there's the Bishop of Mondoñedo, who'll lend you Lamia, Lais, and Flora, and *that* annotation will really boost your reputation; if you need cruel, wicked women, Ovid will hand over Medea; if it's magicians and witches, Homer's got Calypso, and Virgil's got Circe; for heroic generals, there's Julius Caesar's *Commentaries*: he'll lend you himself — and there are thousands of Alexanders in Plutarch. When it's a question of love, all you have to have is two ounces of Italian and you run smack into Leon the Hebrew [Judas Abravanel], who'll really fill you to the brim. And if you don't want to get into foreign parts, right here at home you'll find Fonseca's *Del Amor de Dios* [*On the Love of God*]: he's packed in everything you or anyone else, no matter how clever, could possibly want on that subject. In short, all you have to do is make sure you manage to get in all these names I've given you, or let your book toll the titles of all these histories, and then let me take care of supplying the annotations and marginal notes: on my honor, I'll fill up all the margins and use up four sheets at the end of the book.

"So: now let's get to the question of all those learned citations other books have but yours doesn't. This is the easiest thing in the world to fix, because all you have to do is find some book that quotes everybody from A to Z, just the way you said they do. Then you take this alphabetical parade and put it into your book, and though it'll be an obvious fake, because all that stuff doesn't make much sense in your pages, that doesn't matter a bit. And who knows? There may even be some people so gullible they'll believe you really used all that stuff in this innocent, straightforward tale of yours — and if it doesn't do anything else, at least that fat catalogue gives your book an immediate air of authority. And what's more, no one's going to investigate whether you really paid any attention to all those writers, because what's in it for them? And that's especially true, if I understand what you were saying, because this book of yours simply doesn't need any of the things you say it lacks, because the whole thing is an attack on romantic tales of chivalry, which Aristotle never heard of, and St. Basil never mentioned, and Cicero never ran across, and your story's fantastic nonsense isn't concerned with precisely how to determine truth or with exact astrological calculations, nor are geometrical measurements important in your story, or showing up rhetorical arguments, and your

3. I Kings 17:48–49.

book doesn't preach anything at anybody, mixing up human things with divine ones (which is the kind of jumble no Christian mind should dress itself up in). All you've done is write about what you see: the better you copy, the better your book. And since all your story tries to do is shatter the authority of all those tales of chivalry, and their influence on people, especially common people, all around the world, you don't need to go begging wise sayings from philosophers, or advice from the Holy Scriptures, or myths from poets, or speeches from orators, or miracles from saints. All you have to do is try, with meaningful words, properly and effectively arranged, to honestly unroll your sentences and paragraphs, clearly, sensibly, just explaining what you're up to as well and as powerfully as you can. Let your ideas be understood without making them complicated or obscure. And see, too, if your pages can make sad men laugh as they read, and make smiling men even happier; try to keep simple men untroubled, and wise men impressed by your imagination, and sober men not contemptuous, nor careful men reluctant, to praise it. In sum: keep yourself focused on demolishing the whole false, irrational network of those chivalric romances, despised by so many, yet adored by so many more — do this, and what you've accomplished will be no small affair."

I listened to my friend in profound silence, and his words so struck me that, without any argument, I said he was right and made up my mind to use his exact words for this prologue, in which, gentle reader, you'll see my friend's good sense, as well as my good luck, at such a moment of need, in finding such a counsellor, and why, finally, much to your own relief, you'll find this history of the famous Don Quijote de La Mancha so plain, so straightforward, and so utterly free of confusion — Don Quijote, who in the opinion of every single inhabitant of the district of Campo Montiel, was the purest, chastest lover and the bravest knight errant seen in those parts for many years. I don't want to exaggerate the service I perform for you, allowing you to make the acquaintance of such a noble and honorable knight; but I think you do owe me thanks for this introduction to the celebrated Sancho Panza, his squire, who virtually encapsulates, it seems to me, every one of the squirely virtues to be found anywhere in the whole flock of useless books about chivalry ever published. And, so saying, may God grant you health, and may He not forget me, either. *Vale*, Farewell.

Part One

Chapter One

— *which deals with the status and way of life of the famous knight,
Don Quijote de La Mancha*

In a village in La Mancha (I don't want to bother you with its name)
there lived, not very long ago, one of those gentlemen who keep a lance
in the lance-rack, an ancient shield, a skinny old horse, and a fast greyhound. Three quarters of his income went into his pot of stew (which
contained a good deal more cow than sheep), the cold salt beef he ate
most nights, Friday's beans and lentils and Saturday's leftover scraps, and
sometimes a slender young pigeon for Sunday. All the rest ended up in a
heavy broadcloth coat, velvet breeches he wore on feast days (with velvet
slippers to match), and the fine quality homespun he wore, with great
dignity, during the week. He lived with a housekeeper who was over forty,
and a niece who hadn't reached twenty, plus a boy for the fields and the
market, who spent as much time saddling the old horse as wielding the
pruning knife. Our gentleman was getting close to fifty, but strong, lean,
his face sharp, always up at dawn, and a devoted hunter. It's said his family
name was Quijada, or maybe Quesada: there's some disagreement among
the writers who've discussed the matter. But more than likely his name
was really Quejana. Not that this makes much difference in our story; it's
just important to tell things as faithfully as you can.

And you've also got to understand that the aforementioned gentleman
spent his free time (which meant almost all the time) reading tales of
chivalry, with such passion and pleasure that he almost forgot to keep up
his hunting, not to mention taking care of his estate, carrying his curiosity
and foolishness so far that he sold acre after acre of good crop land in
order to buy books of these tales. He brought home as many as he could
find, and read them, but none seemed to him as good as those written by
the famous Feliciano de Silva, which he relished for the clarity of their
prose and their complicated arguments, to his mind positively pearl-like,
especially when he read gallant love declarations and letters full of courtly
challenges, like: *The ability to reason the un-reason which has afflicted my
reason saps my ability to reason, so that I complain with good reason of
your infinite loveliness,* or: *The heavens on high divinely drop your divinity
down on you, the stars themselves bringing you strength, thus making you
deserving of the high deserts which your immensity deserves.*[1]

---

1. Although the particular passages quoted are from romances of chivalry by Feliciano de Silva and
Antonio de Torquemada, respectively, they perfectly exemplify the ornate and bloated style of the
books that crazed Don Quijote.

Arguments like these cost the poor gentleman his sanity: he'd lie awake at night, trying to understand them, to puzzle out their meaning, which even Aristotle couldn't have comprehended if he'd come back to life for just that purpose. The incredible number of wounds given and received by Don Belianís troubled him: no matter the great doctors who had cured him, they couldn't have kept his face and indeed his whole body from being covered with scars. But all the same he admired the author for promising, at the end of the book, an even more interminable adventure, and often felt like taking up his pen and supplying it himself, exactly as promised, and someday he surely would have done it, and even done it well, if other ideas, still greater and vaster, hadn't gotten in his way. He was always arguing with the village priest — a learned man, with a degree from a provincial university — about who'd been the better knight, Palmerín of England or Amadís of Gaul. But Master Nicolás, the village barber, said no one could possibly compare with the Knight of Phoebus, but if anyone could it had to be Don Galaor, Amadís of Gaul's brother, who could adapt himself to anybody and anything and wasn't finicky, nor was he a crybaby, like his brother, and as for courage wasn't second to his brother or anyone else.

In a word, Don Quijote so buried himself in his books that he read all night from sundown to dawn, and all day from sunup to dusk, until with virtually no sleep and so much reading he dried out his brain and lost his sanity. He filled his imagination full to bursting with everything he read in his books, from witchcraft to duels, battles, challenges, wounds, flirtations, love affairs, anguish, and impossible foolishness, packing it all so firmly into his head that these sensational schemes and dreams became the literal truth and, as far as he was concerned, there were no more certain histories anywhere on earth. He'd explain that Cid Ruy Díaz[2] had been a very good knight, but simply couldn't be compared to the Knight of the Flaming Sword, who with one backhand stroke had cut in half two huge, fierce giants. He liked Bernardo del Carpio[3] even better, because at Roncesvalles he'd killed Roland the Enchanted, taking advantage of Hercules' clever trick of strangling Antaeus, son of Mother Earth, by hoisting him up in his arms. He thought very well of the giant Morgante because, even though he belonged to that gigantic race, who were all arrogant and rude, he alone was pleasant and well-bred. But the knight he treasured above all others was Reinaldos de Montalbán,[4] especially when he could be found riding out of his castle and robbing everyone he met, or when he traveled across the ocean to steal the idol of Mohammad,[5] which according to chivalric history was fashioned of solid gold. For a chance to kick that traitor, Galalón,[6] he'd have gladly given his housekeeper — and even thrown in his niece, too.

2. Spain's eleventh-century national hero.
3. A legendary figure appearing only in Spanish versions of the story of Roland, Charlemagne's nephew.
4. One of the Twelve Peers of France.
5. The prophet (A.D. 570–632) who founded Islam, a religion that actually prohibits the use of idols, golden or otherwise.
6. Charlemagne's brother-in-law, a legendary figure known in France as *Ganelon*. He was also an archtraitor, responsible for the death of Roland and the Twelve Peers in A.D. 778, in the western Spanish Pyrenees.

Indeed, his mind was so tattered and torn that, finally, it produced the strangest notion any madman ever conceived, and then considered it not just appropriate but inevitable. As much for the sake of his own greater honor as for his duty to the nation, he decided to turn himself into a knight errant, traveling all over the world with his horse and his weapons, seeking adventures and doing everything that, according to his books, earlier knights had done, righting every manner of wrong, giving himself the opportunity to experience every sort of danger, so that, surmounting them all, he would cover himself with eternal fame and glory. The poor fellow already fancied that his courage and his mighty sword-arm had earned him, at the least, the crown of the Emperor of Trebizond. And in a transport of joy over such pleasant ideas, carried away by their strange delightfulness, he hurried to turn them into reality.

The first thing he did was polish up his great-grandfather's suit of armor, which for a century or so had been lying, thrown in a corner and forgotten, covered with mildew and quietly rusting away. He got it as clean and bright as he could, but saw that it had a major deficiency: the helmet was gone, and all that was left was a metal headpiece that would cover just the top of his skull. So he put together, ingeniously, a kind of half-helmet of cardboard that, fitted into the headpiece, looked very much like the real thing. True, when he wanted to test its strength and see if it could stand up under a slashing stroke, he pulled out his sword and gave it a couple of whacks, and the very first blow undid in a second what had taken him a week to put together. He couldn't help but think it a poor sign that he'd destroyed it so easily, so to safeguard himself against that risk he went back to work, lining the inside with iron bars until he was satisfied it was strong enough, after which, not wanting to make any further experiments, he declared it a perfect, finished helmet, ready for use.

Then he went to have a look at his skinny old horse, whose hide had more cracks than a clipped coin and more blemishes than Gonela's nag, which, *tantum pellis et ossa fuit*, was so much skin and bones. But in his eyes neither Alexander's Bucephalus nor El Cid's Babieca could match it. He spent four days trying to decide what name to give the old horse, because — as he said to himself — it would be wrong for the steed of such a celebrated knight, a horse with such merit of its own, not to bear a famous name. What he was after was something to make clear what the animal had been before his master turned to knighthood, and what it had now become. It was clear to him that, the master having changed his state, the horse's name had to reflect the new condition of things — had to be something great and famous, in order to properly indicate the new way of life, the new profession, that the horse too had adopted. After he'd proposed and discarded a huge list of names, wiping out each one, framing another, then getting rid of that one too, dipping over and over again into his memory and his imagination, he finally decided to call the animal *Rocinante* [*rocin* = old horse; *ante* = before], which struck him as a truly lofty name, resonant, and also meaningful, because an old horse was exactly what it had been, before, while now it had risen to be first and foremost among all the old horses in the world.

Having settled on such a fine name for his horse, he turned to himself, and spent eight more days thinking until, at last, he decided to call himself

Don Quijote [*quijote* = thigh armor] — a plain fact which, as we have said, persuades the authors of this highly veracious history that, beyond any question, his family name must have been Quijada, rather than Quesada, as others have claimed. Yet remembering that the brave Amadís was not content to call himself just plain Amadís, but added on his kingdom's name, in order to make it famous, too, thus terming himself Amadís of Gaul, so as a good knight he wanted to add his region's name to his own and finally decided to dub himself *Don Quijote of La Mancha*, which as far as he was concerned neatly explained his lineage and his origins, both of which he thus honored.

Well, with his armor scrubbed clean, and his helmet ready, and then his horse christened and himself confirmed, he realized that all he needed and had to hunt for was a lady to be in love with, since a knight errant without love entanglements would be like a tree without leaves or fruit, or a body without a soul. So he said to himself:

"Now, if for my sins, or by good fortune, I happen to find a giant right here in this neighborhood, which after all is something that usually happens to knights errant, and we have a go at it and I overthrow him, or maybe split him right down the middle, or, however it happens, conquer and utterly defeat him, wouldn't it be a good idea to have someone to whom I could send him, so he could go and kneel down in front of my sweet lady and say, his voice humble and submissive, 'I, my lady, am the giant Caraculiambro, lord of the island of Malindrania, defeated in man-to-man combat by that knight who can never be too much praised, Don Quijote de La Mancha, who has sent me here to offer myself at your pleasure, to be dealt with however your Grace may happen to think best'?"

Oh, how our good knight relished the delivery of this speech, especially once he'd decided who was going to be his lady love! It turns out, according to some people, that not too far from where he lived there was a very pretty peasant girl, with whom he was supposed, once upon a time, to have been in love, although (as the story goes) she never knew it nor did he ever say a word to her. Her name was Aldonza Lorenzo, and he thought it a fine idea to bestow on her the title of Mistress of his Thoughts. Hunting for a name as good as the one he'd given himself, a name that would be appropriate for that princess and noble lady, he decided to call her *Dulcinea del Toboso* [*toboso* = limestone rock], since Toboso was where she came from. To him it seemed a singularly musical name, rare, full of meaning, like all the others he'd assigned to himself and everything that belonged to him.[7]

---

7. The humor of these adopted names may be lost in translation: the gross *Quijote* (thanks to its Spanish suffix *-ote*) clashes with the treacly *Dulcinea*, although both their places-names (La Mancha and El Toboso) are consummately "down home." This is a decided linguistic swerve from chivalric and aristocratic nomenclature.

Chapter Two

*— which deals with Don Quijote's first expedition away
from his home*

Having taken care of these arrangements, he had no desire to postpone his plan for even a moment longer, propelled by the thought of how badly the world might suffer if he delayed, for he intended to undo endless wrongs, set right endless injustices, correct endless errors, fix endless abuses, and atone for endless sins. One morning before dawn, on a steaming July day, without telling anyone what he was up to or being seen by a single soul, he put on all his armor, climbed onto Rocinante, settled his flimsy helmet into place, grasped his shield, picked up his spear and, riding through the back gate, set out for the open fields, wonderfully well content at how easily his noble desire had been set in motion. But he'd barely found himself out in the open when a horrible idea struck him — so awful that it very nearly made him give the whole thing up. And what he remembered, suddenly, was that he had not been officially constituted a knight, so that according to the laws of chivalry he neither could nor should take arms against anyone who had. Even if that ceremony had been performed his shield had to be a bare white, to indicate his inexperience; it could bear his insignia only once his courage had earned that privilege. His determination wavered, he fairly staggered under these realizations — but driven more powerfully by his madness than any rational motive, he decided to have himself properly dubbed by the first knight he bumped into, imitating all the many other knights who had done things just that way, according to what he'd read in the books that so possessed him. As for the matter of the bare white shield, he decided that, as soon as he could, he'd scrub it whiter than ermine, and thus he calmed himself and continued on his way, letting his horse follow its nose, which seemed to him the very essence of knightly adventures.

As our brand-new adventurer jogged along, he kept talking to himself, saying:

"Who could doubt that, in time to come, when the true history of my mighty deeds sees the light, the wise man who composes that narrative, reaching the point in his tale where he describes this my first adventure, bright and early in the morning, might write something like: 'Scarcely had the rubicund Apollo brushed the strands of his lovely golden locks across the face of the broad and spacious earth, no sooner had the tiny, speckled fledgling birds begun to greet the breaking of roseate dawn with the gracious, melifluous harmony of their sweet-toned tongues — that dawn which, slipping from her heavenly husband's soft couch, began to show herself through mortal gates and balconies, at the edge of La Mancha's horizon — when that notable knight, Don Quijote de La Mancha, rising from the inactivity of his feathered mattress, mounted himself on his famous steed, Rocinante, and began to ride across the fabled ancient fields of Montiel.' "

Which was in fact exactly where he was riding. And then he jogged on, declaiming as he went:

"How blessed the era, how happy the time, when the tale of my glorious adventures will see the light — worthy of being engraved in bronze, sculptured in marble, and painted on wooden panels in an eternal memorial. Oh you, wise enchanter, whoever you may be, to whom it shall fall to be the noble chronicler of this extraordinary history! I beg you, do not forget my good Rocinante, unendingly the companion of all my wanderings and my every journey."

Then he began once again, as if he'd really been a madly passionate lover:

"Oh Princess Dulcinea, mistress of this miserable heart! How sorely you have wronged me, driving me out of your presence, spurning me with your harsh, unbending scorn, ordering me never to appear before your surpassing, incomparable beauty. Oh my Lady, remember this your loyally dutiful heart, which has suffered so much for your love."

So he went along, reeling off a whole string of nonsense, all according to the fashion he'd been taught by his books, imitating their language as closely as he could. And being thus totally preoccupied, he rode so slowly that the sun was soon glowing with such intense heat that it would have melted his brains, if he'd had any.

He plodded along almost the entire day, but nothing worth talking about happened, which made him desperately unhappy, because he fairly ached to bump into someone who would prove his courage and the strength of his mighty sword arm. There are writers who say the first adventure which came to him was at Lápice Pass, and others who say it was when he fought with the windmills, but from what I've been able to learn on this point, and from what I've found recorded in the archives at La Mancha, the whole day went by and, by nightfall, he and his horse were both exhausted and dying of hunger. Looking everywhere, high and low, to see if he could find a castle or a shepherd's hut where he could take shelter and satisfy his piercing hunger and other needs, he saw, not far from the road he was on, an inn, which seemed to him like a star guiding him at least to the doorways (if not to the castles) of his salvation. Quickening his pace, he reached it just as darkness fell.

As it happened, two young women stood near the door, of the sort called party-girls, or whores, on their way to Seville with some mule drivers who had decided to call it a day. And since for our adventurer everything he thought or saw or imagined seemed to him to take place exactly as things occurred in the books he'd been reading, the moment he saw the inn he took it for a castle, with four tall towers topped by gleaming silver spires, and even a drawbridge and a deep moat, together with everything else such establishments were described as possessing. Arriving at this inn, which as I say seemed to him a castle, he reined in Rocinante not far from the doorway, expecting that some dwarf would get up on the parapets and signal, with a trumpet blast, that a knight had arrived. But seeing that they were taking a long time about it, and that Rocinante was in a hurry to get to the stables, he rode directly up to the door and saw the two outcast girls, who seemed to him a pair of beautiful maidens or two gracious ladies taking their ease in front of the castle gates. Just then it happened that a swineherd came by, trying to drive a drove of hogs — I won't excuse myself for mentioning them, because that's what they are — out of a stubble field, and as a signal for them to herd together he blew his horn, which Don Quijote immediately took as the sign he'd been waiting for, that the dwarf was announcing his arrival. He approached the inn with a happy bound, which terrified the two women, seeing a man like him, armed as he was, coming rapidly toward them. But Don Quijote, seeing their flight, understood that they were afraid, and raised his cardboard visor, showing them his dry, dusty face. And then he said to them, both his voice and his manner courteous:

"Flee not, noble damsels, nor anticipate the slightest inappropriate behavior. No! The order of knighthood to which I profess allegiance neither troubles nor afflicts anyone, and certainly not such noble virgins as you, by your bearing, clearly show yourselves to be."

Both girls stared at him, trying to make out his face, half covered by the clumsy visor. But when they heard themselves called virgins, something wonderfully unlikely in their profession, they couldn't keep from laughing, which they did so heartily that Don Quijote was insulted and said to them:

"Beauty should carry composure with it, and frivolous laughter is pure stupidity. Nor do I say this in order to give you pain or to demonstrate ill will, for I have no desire except to place myself at your service."

This language, which the women could not understand, and the shabby figure our knight presented, just made them laugh even harder, which made him still angrier, and things might have gotten a good deal worse if, at that point, the innkeeper hadn't come out, a man whose immense corpulence made him extremely peaceable. Seeing what a humbug Don Quijote was, wearing armor as crazily incongruous as were, also, his bridle, spear, shield, and helmet, he wasn't at all disinclined to join the damsels in their amusement. But then, worried by such a display of miscellaneous military apparatus, he decided to treat the man politely, and said to him:

"Sir knight, if it's hospitality your grace seeks, except for a bed (because in this inn there isn't a single one left), here you can find an abundance of everything else."

Seeing how humbly the castle warden spoke (since that was how he saw both the innkeeper and his inn), Don Quijote replied:

"Sir Castle-man, anything at all is quite sufficient for me, because

> All I need is my armor,
> My only rest is war —

And so on."

The innkeeper thought he'd been called a Castilian, having been taken for one of those honest men who come from Castile, although he was in fact not only an Andalusian but one who came from the beach at San Lúcar,[1] at least as accomplished a thief as Cacus,[2] and no less corrupt than a failed university student studying to be a page. He answered:

"In that case,

---

1. A well-known haunt of thieves and swindlers, of picaresque or underworld figures.
2. A legendary Roman giant, son of Vulcan, and famous cattle rustler in antiquity. See page 10 of this translation, where he exemplifies thieves and thievery.

Your bed will be hard boulders,
Your sleep will be on guard — [3]

And that being the way it is, you'll do very well to dismount, because in this hovel you won't have to worry about not sleeping — you'll have enough opportunity to last you a whole year, let alone a single night."

Saying which, he took hold of Don Quijote's stirrup, and our knight dismounted slowly and painfully, exactly like someone who hadn't eaten a mouthful all day.

He immediately told the innkeeper to take special care of his horse, because he was the best grain-eating, man-carrying quadruped in the whole world. The innkeeper looked the animal over, and didn't think he seemed as good as Don Quijote had said — not even half as good — but he led him to the stable, then came back to see what his guest might want. He found him being helped out of his armor by the two damsels, who had already made up their quarrel. But having gotten off the breastplate and the back section, they didn't know how to remove the neck guard, and couldn't get off either it or the helmet, for the guard had been tied on with green ribbons, which would have had to be cut, since the knots couldn't be untied. But Don Quijote wouldn't hear of it, and spent the rest of the night with his helmet on, looking the funniest, strangest figure imaginable. Since he imagined that the wornout sluts who were helping him off with his armor were the foremost ladies of the castle, while they were at work he quoted to them, most suavely:

" — Never was there a knight
Whom ladies served so well
As our famous Don Quijote,
Leaving his native dell:
Maidens, princesses all,
Served knight and horse as well.[4]

Rocinante, dear ladies, is my horse's name, and I am Don Quijote de La Mancha. Although I hadn't intended to reveal myself until that memorable day when the glorious deeds I shall perform in your service can have earned me the right to be known, the necessity of adapting that old poem about Lancelot to the instant occasion has informed you of my name long before you should rightly have known it. But there will come a time when you ladies will command me, and I will obey, and the bravery displayed by my sword-arm will prove my desire to serve you."

The women, not used to hearing such rhetoric, did not respond with a single word, but only asked if he wanted something to eat.

"Whatever I ingest," answered Don Quijote, "will surely, I believe, do me a great deal of good."

Now it happened to be a Friday, so the inn had absolutely nothing to eat but some pieces of a fish called cod, in Castille, and troutlet in Andalusia, and elsewhere known by other names. They asked him if his grace

---

3. Don Quijote recites the first two lines of a poem from a popular sixteenth-century romance; the innkeeper responds with the next two lines [*Translator's Note*].
4. Don Quijote adapts yet another popular poem [*Translator's Note*].

would perhaps be willing to eat troutlet, since they had no other fish they could offer him.

"If there are a lot of troutlets," answered Don Quijote, "they can do quite as well as a whole trout, because I don't care if you give me ten one-dollar bills or one ten-dollar bill. And maybe these troutlets will be something like veal, which is better than beef, just as the flesh of a kid is better than that of a goat. But however it may be, bring it quickly, because the labor and struggle of bearing arms cannot be endured without the belly's guidance."

They set a table at the doorway of the inn, so he could enjoy the cool air, and the innkeeper brought him a portion of troutlet badly marinated and worse cooked, and a chunk of bread so black and greasy that it resembled his armor. What was really funny was watching him eat, for his helmet was still on his head and, since he had to use both hands to raise his visor, he was unable to get anything into his mouth unless someone else put it there, which one of the women obligingly did for him. But giving him anything to drink was impossible, or at least would have been if the innkeeper hadn't punched a hole in a reed stem and, with one end stuck into his mouth, poured his wine in through the other. Don Quijote accepted all this patiently, in exchange for preserving intact the ribbons on his helmet. In the meantime, it happened that a pig-gelder arrived at the inn and, to announce his coming, blew four or five blasts on a kind of reed whistle, which was all it took to complete the picture for Don Quijote: he was at a famous castle, and dining to the sound of music; the codfish was fresh-caught trout, the bread was snowy white; the whores were noble ladies, and the innkeeper was the castle warden — all of which proved that his courage and indeed his day's journeying had been well employed. What truly bothered him, however, was that he still had not been properly constituted a knight. To his mind, he could not properly experience any adventures at all without having been officially received into the order of knighthood.

Chapter Three

— in which we learn how cleverly Don Quijote decided to have himself dubbed a knight

Oppressed by this thought, he hurried through his dull, lodging-house dinner and, when he was done, called for the innkeeper. Leading him off to the stable, where they could be alone, he fell on his knees in front of him, and said:

"Brave knight, I will never rise from this position unless and until, thanks to your chivalric courtesy, you grant me a boon I wish to request of you, a favor which will bring you honor and be of use to the whole of humanity."

Seeing his guest at his feet, and hearing such statements, the innkeeper was completely at a loss, not knowing what to do or say. He tried to persuade him to get up, but Don Quijote again declared that he never would, and at last the innkeeper had no choice but to say that the desired boon would be granted.

"My lord," answered our knight, "I expected nothing less from someone of such magnificence as yourself. Accordingly, I say to you that the boon I have begged of you, and which your great liberality has granted me, is this: on the morning which follows this day you will well and truly dub me a knight. All the rest of this night, in the chapel of this your castle, I will maintain a vigil over my armor, and then tomorrow, as I have said, what I have so much desired can be accomplished, thus enabling me, as it is only right, to travel through all four parts of the world seeking adventures and helping needy persons, which is the task of knightly orders and of all knights errant like myself, who are driven to the performance of heroic deeds."

Now, as I've said, the innkeeper was a pretty sly fox, already suspicious of his guest's sanity, and hearing talk like this fully persuaded him. To have some fun, he made up his mind to humor Don Quijote, so he assured him he was following exactly the right path, and that his desires and the boon he had asked were absolutely correct, for such a plan was both natural and proper for knights as prominent as he seemed to be, and as his gallant bearing proved he in fact was. He told Don Quijote that he himself, in his youth, had given himself up to the same honorable profession, traveling to different parts of the world, seeking adventures, including such notable spots as the Fish Market at Málaga, the Laughing Islands, the Crossroads in Seville, the Marketplace in Segovia, the Olive Warehouse in Valencia, the Bandstand in Granada, the beach at Sanlúcar, the horsetrack in Córdoba, the bars in Toledo,[1] and all kinds of other places, where he'd had lots of practice being light on his feet, quick with his hands, perpetrating injustice, wooing widows, seducing virgins, cheating schoolboys and, to make a long story short, making a name for himself in who knows how many courts and tribunals virtually everywhere in all of Spain. At last, he'd taken himself to this castle, where he lived off his own estate and those of others, offering hospitality to any knight errant who appeared, no matter what his rank or status, simply because of the great affection he felt for all those who followed that profession and, also, so he could share with them whatever they happened to own, in order to repay him for his kindness.

He also told Don Quijote that his castle had no chapel where a vigil could be maintained, because he'd had to have it torn down, though it was soon to be entirely rebuilt. But when necessary, he knew, such a vigil could be maintained anywhere, so that night Don Quijote could make use of the castle courtyard, and then, in the morning, God willing, they would perform the proper ceremonies and confer knighthood upon him — indeed, making him such a knight that no one in the whole world could possibly be more knightly.

Then he asked if Don Quijote was carrying any money. Don Quijote answered that he didn't have a cent, since in none of the chivalric tales

---

1. Well-known meeting places for thieves, vagabonds, gamblers, prostitutes, etc. Cervantes here provides a kind of underworld map of sixteenth-century Spain.

he'd read was there any mention of knights errant carrying money. The innkeeper told him that on this matter he was quite mistaken, because although it was true that the stories omitted such details — for it seemed to their authors unnecessary to write about plain and essential subjects like money and clean shirts — this was no reason to think knights errant didn't need money. In fact, it seemed to him absolutely definite and well-established that every single knight errant, in all the thoroughly attested books which were so full of knights, carried with him an overflowing purse, to take care of any emergency, just as each of them carried shirts and a little pouch full of ointments, so they could treat whatever wounds they received. Out in the fields and deserts where they did battle, after all, and from which they might emerge wounded, there was no guarantee of any-one being available to care for them, unless they had some wise magician as a friend, who could instantly come to their aid, transporting to them a damsel or a dwarf, right through the air, wafting them on a cloud and carrying a flask filled with a liquid of such power that, tasting only a single drop, these knights would be cured of their wounds in the twinkling of an eye, made as whole and sound as if they'd never received an injury. But in case they weren't thus protected, these oldtime knights made very sure their squires were provided with money and everything else they might require, as for example lint and ointments. And when these knights hap-pened not to have squires — which was a rare and uncommon situation — they carried such things themselves, in a very unobtrusive special saddlebag, very nearly invisible, tied on behind their horse and looking for all the world as if it held something far more important than mere money, it being sometimes felt not quite right for knights errant to carry mere saddlebags. So he advised Don Quijote — indeed, as his protegé-soon-to-be he even commanded him — not to ride out again without money or the other supplies referred to, for he would see how useful they were, when he least expected them to be.

Don Quijote promised to do everything he'd been advised to, just as soon as he could. So it was settled that he would keep his vigil in a large courtyard off to one side of the inn and, gathering all his armor, he set it on a trough standing near the well, then took up his shield, grasped his spear, and with unmistakably gallant bearing began to march back and forth in front of the trough. Night was just falling as his promenade began.

The innkeeper told everyone what his crazy guest was doing, telling them all about the vigil over the armor and the ceremonial conferring of knighthood still to come. Amazed at such a strange form of madness, they went to observe it (from a distance), and saw Don Quijote sometimes pacing calmly up and down, sometimes leaning on his spear, his eyes fixed on his armor, staring fixedly at it for a long time. The night had gotten very dark, but the moon shone so brightly that it could have competed with the sun from which it borrowed, and everything the almost-brand-new knight did was easily visible.

Just then, one of the muledrivers staying at the inn decided to water his team, and found it necessary to lift Don Quijote's armor off the trough where it was lying. And, seeing this, Don Quijote said to him, in a loud voice:

"Oh you, whoever you may be, rash knight, who approach and lay hands on the armor of the bravest knight errant ever to wear a sword! Be careful, think what you do: touch that armor only if you wish to surrender your life in return for your impudence."

The muledriver paid no attention to all this babble — though it would have been better for his health if he had. Instead, grabbing the armor by the straps, he tossed it as far off as he could. Seeing which, Don Quijote lifted his eyes toward heaven and fixed his mind — or so it seemed — on his Lady Dulcinea:

"Help me, oh my lady, in this, the first insult offered to a heart you hold in thrall. May your favor and your protection not fail me at this crucial moment."

And speaking these and many other words like them, he dropped his shield, raised his spear with both hands and gave the muledriver such a stunning blow on the head that he fell like a shot: had another such blow been delivered, no surgeon would have been necessary. But Don Quijote just gathered up his armor and went back to quietly pacing up and down, exactly as he had done before. A little later, not knowing what had happened to the first muledriver (because he still lay unconscious), another one arrived, also intending to water his mules, and as he was starting to lift away the armor in order to get at the trough, Don Quijote — neither saying a word nor invoking anyone's protection — dropped his shield yet again, raised his spear and, without quite smashing it into little bits, certainly split the second muledriver's head into more than three pieces, for he laid it open in at least four places. At the noise, everyone in the inn came rushing, including the innkeeper. Seeing which, Don Quijote raised his shield and, with his hand on his sword, declared:

"Oh Lady of Beauty, the courage and strength of my enfeebled heart! Now, Magnificent One, now, turn your eyes toward your miserable knight, who stands here, awaiting such a splendid adventure."

Which declaration so restored his spirits that, as far as he was concerned, he'd never have retreated, not if all the muledrivers in the world came rushing at him. And seeing how it was, the injured men's friends kept their distance, but began to throw stones, from which Don Quijote protected himself as best he could with his shield, not daring to step away from the trough and abandon his armor. The innkeeper yelled at them to leave him alone: hadn't he already told them Don Quijote was crazy? He'd be set free even if he killed every last one of them. Don Quijote was shouting still louder, calling them liars and traitors and the Castle-man a coward and a puffed-up braggart for allowing knights errant to be treated this way: were he himself already received into the order of knighthood, he'd hold him responsible for such cowardice.

"But as for you, you vulgar, worthless scum, you're beneath my notice. Throw anything you want to, come on, attack me, insult me as much as you like: you'll find out what your stupidity and insolence will cost you!"

He said this with such energy and boldness that all those arrayed against him were filled with a terrible fear, and this terror, quite as much as the innkeeper's arguments, actually got them to stop throwing stones. Don

Quijote let them drag off their wounded, then went back to the vigil over his armor, as calm and peaceful as before.

But the innkeeper didn't much care for his guest's games, and made up his mind to cut it all short, giving Don Quijote his damned knighthood before there were any more disasters. So he went and apologized for the insolence shown by that low rabble, about which (he said) he hadn't known a thing, though they'd certainly been nicely punished for their impudence. Then he reminded Don Quijote that, as he'd already explained, the castle had no chapel, nor was one needed for what still remained to be done, since all that was required, according to his knowledge of knightly ceremony, was a whack on the side of the head and a tap with a sword, and all of that could be accomplished in the middle of a field. The vigil over Don Quijote's armor had been well and truly fulfilled, since two hours was all that was necessary — and he'd been out there more than four. Don Quijote believed every word of this, declaring that he stood ready to be obedient in all things and that indeed it was best to have it done with as quickly as possible, for it seemed to him that were he attacked yet again, after he'd been properly dubbed a knight, he wouldn't leave a person alive in the whole castle, unless there were those the castle warden might order not to be killed — and of course, out of respect, they would be spared.

Thus put on guard, and more than a little frightened, the castle warden hurriedly brought out a book in which he recorded the straw and barley he supplied to the muledrivers. Then, along with a boy carrying a stump of candle and the two damsels previously mentioned, he approached Don Quijote and ordered him down on his knees, after which, reading from his book of instructions — as if he'd been pronouncing a prayer of great piety — he suddenly lifted his hand and gave the neophyte a good whack on the neck as well as, with a flourish of Don Quijote's own sword, a tap on the shoulder, all the time muttering between his teeth, as if he were saying Mass. This done, he directed one of the damsels to buckle on the sword, which she did with great poise and tact — of which a great deal was needed, to keep from bursting into laughter at every step in the ceremony. Still, what they'd seen of the brand-new knight's fighting ability kept their laughter in check. When the sword hung at his side, the good lady said to him:

"May God make you a very successful knight, and fortunate in combat."

Don Quijote asked her to tell him her name, so he might know, from that time on, to whom he was obliged for the favor bestowed on him, for he intended to award her a share of the honor he would earn by the strength of his arm. She answered most humbly that she was known as La Tolosa, since she was the daughter of a cobbler who lived in Toledo, near the archbishop's palace in Sancho Bienaya Plaza. But wherever she might be, she would serve and honor him as her lord. Don Quijote replied that, as she loved him, he hoped she would from this moment on title herself Doña Tolosa. She promised she would; the other damsel buckled on his spurs; and he had the same conversation with her as with the sword-lady. He asked her name, and she said she was known as La Molinera, since she was the daughter of a well-known and respected miller of Antequera, after which Don Quijote requested that she too would henceforward title herself Doña Molinera, once again offering her his services and his thanks.[2]

Having thus galloped straight through these never-before-seen ceremonies, Don Quijote couldn't wait to be up on his horse and on his way, seeking adventures, so he quickly saddled Rocinante, mounted, and embraced his host, saying such strange things, as he thanked him for having performed the ceremony of knighthood, that it's impossible to reproduce the exact words. In order to see him gone, the innkeeper replied with rhetoric every bit as elaborate, though a lot shorter, not even bothering to charge him for what he'd been served, letting him go with a simple "goodbye and good luck."

Chapter Four

— what happened to our knight when he left the inn

The sun was just coming up when Don Quijote sallied forth from the inn, so happy, brimming with such self-confidence, such delight at finding himself a fully qualified knight, that his joy seemed to burst right out of his horse's sides. But remembering his host's advice about the supplies he ought to be carrying with him, especially money and clean shirts, he decided to go back home and make arrangements for everything, including a squire, planning to take on a country fellow who lived nearby, a poor man with lots of children, but exactly suited to performing squirely duty for a knight. With this in mind, he steered Rocinante toward his own village, and the horse, realizing where they were heading, began to trot along so briskly that his feet didn't seem to touch the ground.

Don Quijote hadn't gone very far when, just to his right, from a thick wood, he heard the sound of a frail voice, like someone moaning, and immediately declared:

"God be thanked for the grace He has shown me, sending so prompt an opportunity to live up to the oaths I have sworn, and the chance to harvest the fruit of my warmest desires. That voice, without a doubt, is the sound of some needy man or woman, yearning for my protection and help."

And pulling the reins hard over, he headed Rocinante in the direction from which the voice had seemed to come. Just a few paces into the wood, he saw a mare tied to an oak tree, and then a boy of about fifteen tied to another, stripped to the waist, who was the person he had heard crying — and not without reason, because a husky country fellow was whipping away at him with a leather strap, warning him with each stroke, ordering:

"Keep your mouth shut and your eyes open!"

To which the boy answered:

"I won't do it again, master — by the love of God, I won't do it again, I promise from now on I'll take better care of the flock!"

2. Don Quijote tries to ennoble these prostitutes, whose lineage does not entitle them to the honorific title of "Doña." His aristocratic address, however, ironically coincides with the practice of "real life" Spanish Renaissance prostitutes.

Seeing what was going on, Don Quijote called out, angrily:

"Discourteous knight, it is bad to fight with someone who cannot defend himself. Mount your horse and take up your lance" — and in fact there was a long cattle prod propped up against the oak to which the mare was tied — "and I shall make you understand just how cowardly you have been behaving."

Seeing a figure in full armor brandishing a lance in his face, the farmer thought he was as good as dead, and replied as mildly as he could:

"Sir knight, this boy I've been punishing is my servant, who's supposed to take care of a flock of sheep I keep around here, but he pays so little attention that I lose one every day, and when I punish him for his carelessness — his wickedness — he says I do it out of stinginess, to keep from paying him the wages he's earned, but by God and on my soul he's lying."

"You dare tell *me*, you peasant scum, that he lies to *you?*" said Don Quijote. "By the sun that shines down on us, I've half a mind to run you through with this lance. Hurry up and pay him, and without another word, or else by the God who governs us all I'll finish you off, I'll exterminate you on the spot. Quick, untie him."

The farmer lowered his head and, without a word, untied his servant, of whom Don Quijote inquired just how much his master owed him. The boy said for nine months, at seven dollars a month. Don Quijote did his arithmetic and calculated the sum as seventy-three dollars, and told the farmer to pay it then and there, unless he preferred to die instead. The frightened peasant replied that as he lived and breathed and according to the oath he'd sworn — though in fact he hadn't sworn to anything — the sum wasn't that much, because he had to deduct the price of three pairs of shoes he'd given the boy on credit, plus another dollar for two blood-lettings they'd had done for him when he was sick.

"That's all very well," answered Don Quijote, "but let the shoes and blood-lettings be set against the unjust whipping you've given him. If he broke the leather of shoes you paid for, you've broken his own skin, and if the barber drew blood when he was sick, you've drawn it when he was perfectly healthy. As far as that's concerned, then, he doesn't owe you a thing."

"But, sir knight, the trouble is that I don't have any money with me. Let Andrés come home with me, so I can pay him the whole thing, dollar for dollar."

"Go anywhere with you?" said the boy. "That'll be the day! No, sir, I wouldn't even dream of it — because once he gets me alone, he'll skin me the way they did Saint Bartolomé."

"He won't do any such thing," answered Don Quijote. "All that's necessary is that I command him and he'll do as I say, and since he has sworn to me according to the laws of knighthood, to which he owes obedience, I grant him his freedom and guarantee that he will pay you."

"But your grace, sir, just think what you're saying. This master of mine isn't a knight and he hasn't received any kind of orders. He's Juan Haldudo [*haldudo/faldudo* = long-skirted] the Rich, from near Quintanar."

"That doesn't matter," answered Don Quijote. "Long-skirts can be knights, too, especially since each of us is as each of us does."

"That's true," said Andrés. "But this is my master. What's *he* done, when he won't pay me what he owes me for my work and my sweat?"

"Who says I won't pay you, brother Andrés?" answered the farmer. "Be good enough to come along with me and I swear by every order of knighthood that exists anywhere in the world I'll pay you, exactly as I've said I would, dollar for dollar — with perfumed dollars, if you want them."

"Perfumed dollars would be nice," said Don Quijote, "but just pay him in real dollars, and I'll be happy with that. Now be careful that you do exactly as you've sworn, because if you don't, by that same oath I swear I'll hunt you down and punish you — and I'll find you, even if you hide yourself better than a little wall-lizard. And if you want to know who's given you these commandments, so you'll be even more profoundly obligated to obey them, know that I am the brave Don Quijote de La Mancha, the undoer of wrongs and injustices. So may God go with you, and never forget what you've here promised and sworn to, under the penalties here set out."

Declaring which, he spurred his Rocinante and, in just a moment, had left them behind. The farmer watched him go, and when he saw that Don Quijote was both out of the wood and out of sight, he turned to his servant Andrés, saying:

"Come over here, my boy, so I can pay you what you're owed, as that righter of wrongs commanded me to."

"I swear to you," cried Andrés, "your grace, you'd better do exactly what that good knight told you to, may he live to be a thousand! Because as he's a brave man and a good judge, by all that's holy, if you don't pay me he'll come back and do everything he said he would!"

"Oh, I swear the same thing," said the farmer. "But my feelings for you are so warm that I want to pile on more debt, so I can pay you still more."

And he took him by the arm and once again tied him to the oak tree, and whipped him so hard that he left him for dead.

"Now call him, Master Andrés," said the farmer, "this undoer of wrongs. Let's see if he can undo that. Anyway, I don't think I've quite done with you: I feel an urge to really skin you alive, as you were afraid I might."

But, finally, he untied the boy and told him he was free to go look for his judge, so the penalties could be carried out. Andrés slunk away, swearing to go hunt up the brave Don Quijote de La Mancha and tell him, blow by blow, exactly what had happened, and then his master would have to pay him seven times over. But, just the same, he went away weeping and his master stood there laughing.

And thus the brave Don Quijote righted that wrong and with immense satisfaction went jogging on toward his village, exceedingly happy with what had happened and feeling that he'd made a singularly fine and lofty beginning to his knightly ventures. As he rode he said to himself, softly,

"Well may you call yourself, this very day, the most fortunate of all ladies who dwell on this earth, oh most beautiful of all beauties, Dulcinea de Toboso! For it has fallen to you, in good fortune, to hold in humble submission to your sole will and desire a knight so valiant and renowned as is, and will be, Don Quijote de La Mancha, who as all the world knows was just yesterday received into the order of knighthood and today has righted the worst wrong and injury which injustice can invent and cruelty can commit, plucking from the hand of my despicable foe that lash which, without reason, he'd so savagely applied to that gentle child."

Just then he arrived at a place where four roads crossed, and at once remembering all those crossroads where knights errant had paused and pondered which road to take, in imitation of them he too paused for a while. Finally, after long hard thought, he dropped the reins and let his old horse go where he wanted to, and Rocinante did as he'd meant from the first, which was to take the road home to his own stable.

Having traveled about two miles, Don Quijote saw a great crowd of people who, as it turned out later, were Toledo merchants going to buy silk at Murcia. There were six of them, riding along under their parasols, together with four mounted servants and three young muledrivers on foot. As soon as Don Quijote spied them, he imagined some new adventure was coming, one that seemed ready-made for imitating as closely as he possibly could the adventures he'd read about in his books. So he assumed a bold, gallant stance, set himself solidly in his stirrups, gripped his lance, raised his shield in front of him and, placing himself right in the middle of the road, awaited the arrival of these knights errant, as he'd already decided they had to be. Then, when they came close enough to see and hear, he called out to them, and with a haughty look said:

"Let everyone in the world halt, unless the entire world acknowledges that nowhere on earth is there a damsel more beautiful than the Empress of La Mancha, she who has no equal, Dulcinea del Toboso."

The merchants came to a stop, hearing these arguments and seeing the strange figure who had spoken them, and from both his appearance and his words were quickly aware that he was mad. But they wished to unravel, gently, the source of the acknowledgment they were being asked to make, and one of them, who was a bit of a practical joker, and had his wits about him, said:

"Sir knight, we have no idea who this lady you speak of might be. Show her to us. If she is as lovely as you indicate, we will cheerfully and voluntarily acknowledge the truth of that which you have urged upon us."

"Were I to show her to you," replied Don Quijote, "what would you have accomplished by acknowledging so obvious a truth? What's important is that you believe without seeing her, that you acknowledge, affirm, swear, and defend this truth. If not, you'll have to do battle with me, you monstrous, arrogant fellows. Now come on, one at a time, as the rules of knighthood require, or else all at once, which is surely the usual evil usage of people like you: here I await and expect you, trusting in the truth I have proclaimed."

"Sir knight," answered the merchant, "I beg your grace, in the name of this entire company of sovereign princes, that in order to keep us from having on our consciences the acknowledgment of something which in truth we've neither seen nor heard, and what's more, something so prejudicial to the Empresses of Alcarria and Estremadura,[1] that your grace

---

1. The sharp-witted trader plays into the hero's absurdity by conjuring up empresses of rustic and thinly populated regions.

may be pleased to show us some portrait of this lady, even one no larger than a grain of wheat, for a thread can show you what the yarn is like, and we would thereby be fully satisfied and sure, and your grace too will be happy and fulfilled. For I suspect that we are already so much of your view that, even if the portrait you show us reveals that she's blind in one eye and the other runs red and flashes like brimstone, in spite of all that, and simply to gratify your grace, we would say anything you wished in her favor."

"Nothing runs from her eyes, you disgusting rabble," answered Don Quijote, burning with anger, "nothing, I say, nothing but amber and musk-oil in soft cotton, and she's neither one-eyed nor humpbacked, but straighter than a Guadarrama spindle — and now you're going to pay for the great blasphemy you've uttered against a woman as beautiful as my lady!"

Saying which, he aimed his lance at the man who'd been speaking and charged so wildly and angrily that, if Rocinante hadn't had the good fortune to stumble and fall in the middle of the road, it would have gone badly for the quick-tongued merchant. Rocinante fell, and his master rolled along the ground a pretty good distance, and then, wanting to get up, couldn't, all loaded down by his lance, his shield, his spurs, and his helmet, plus the weight of that old armor. And even as he struggled in vain to stand up, he was shouting:

"Don't run, you cowards! Wait, you slave rabble! It's my horse's fault, not mine, that I'm stretched out here."

One of the young muledrivers, who couldn't have had much of the milk of human kindness in him, heard these arrogant words from the poor downfallen knight and couldn't keep from beating an answer on his ribs. Going over to him, he picked up his lance and, after smashing it to pieces, took one of the fragments and began to give our Don Quijote such a whacking that, despite and quite regardless of his armor, he threshed him like a load of grain. His employers called to him not to hit so hard and to leave Don Quijote alone, but the muledriver was pretty well worked up and couldn't leave the game until he'd tossed in the rest of his angry cards, so turning to the other pieces of the lance he finished by cracking them all on the miserable, toppled body of Don Quijote — who, despite the whirlwind of blows falling on him, never shut his mouth, threatening heaven and earth, and the whole pack of scoundrels, which is what they seemed to him.

The muledriver got tired, and the merchants went on their way, talking as they went about what had happened to the poor beaten fellow. And he, as soon as he saw himself alone, went back to trying to stand up, but if he couldn't do it when he was healthy and in one piece, how was he supposed to manage, thoroughly thrashed and exhausted? And yet he thought himself lucky, for it seemed to him that this was a fitting misfortune for a knight errant, and everything was his horse's fault, and still he couldn't stand up, his body was so bruised and battered.

Chapter Five

— which continues the tale of our knight's misfortune

Realizing, finally, that in fact he could not move, Don Quijote decided to fall back on his usual solution, which was to think of some passage from his books, and his madness brought to mind the tale of Valdovinos and the Marqués of Mantua, when Carloto left him wounded up on the mountain — a story all little boys know, young men haven't forgotten, and old men still celebrate and even believe, though for all that it's no truer than the ones about Mohammad's miracles.[1] Don Quijote thought this was exactly the sort of situation in which he now found himself, and so, giving elaborate proof of his immense grief and sorrow, he began to roll around on the ground while declaiming, with all due weakness, exactly what the wounded knight said, as he lay on the wooded hillside:

— Where can you be, my lady,
And be unaware of my sorrow?
Oh, either you know nothing
Or your heart is false and untrue.

And then he went on reciting the ballad, as far as the lines:

— Oh noble Marqués of Mantua,
My uncle, my lord by blood![2]

Now it happened that, as he reached this verse, a farmer from his own village, one of his neighbors, came by, travelling home after bringing a load of grain to the mill. And seeing a man stretched out on the road, he went over and asked him who he was and why he was groaning so miserably. Without any question, Don Quijote believed the farmer was his uncle, the Marqués of Mantua, so his only answer was to go declaiming the exact words of the ballad, which went on to tell of his misfortune and the love story of the Emperor and his wife.

The farmer was amazed, hearing all this nonsense and, removing Don Quijote's visor (already pretty well smashed to bits), cleaned off the dust and dirt that covered his face — and immediately recognized him. So he said:

"Mr. Quijana" — as he must have been known when he'd still had his wits about him, and before he'd transformed himself from a peaceful country gentleman into a knight errant — "who's responsible for doing this to your grace?"

But no matter how often he asked, Don Quijote just went on with his ballad. This being the case, the good man pulled off, as well as he could, the breastplate and the back piece of Don Quijote's armor, to see if there were any wounds, but found neither blood nor any kind of mark at all. Then he struggled to raise him up from the ground and, with a good deal

---

1. This popular story from old ballads tells of Carloto, Charlemagne's son, who wounds Valdovinos and leaves him in a mountain forest in order to have his wife. Valdovinos's uncle, the Marqués of Mantua, finds his wounded nephew while hunting.
2. Deliberately misquoted; the original reads, "My lord, my uncle by blood" [*Translator's Note*].

of effort, got him up on his own donkey, which seemed to him a steadier mount than the horse. He gathered up the military equipment, including the bits and pieces of the lance, and tied them on Rocinante's back, after which he took the horse by the reins and the donkey by its halter and set out toward their village, listening with great thoughtfulness to the nonsense that Don Quijote kept spouting. Nor was Don Quijote any less uncomfortable, because from sheer exhaustion and banging about he couldn't hold himself upright on the donkey, and from time to time he groaned so profoundly that heaven itself must have heard him, which once again led the farmer to ask him what was wrong, at which point the devil alone must have dredged out of his memory tales that matched what was happening. Suddenly forgetting about Valdovinos, he remembered the tale of Abindarráez, the Moor, when the governor of Antequera, Rodrigo of Narváez, captured him and led him as a prisoner to his castle. So now, when the farmer started asking him if he was all right and what was bothering him, Don Quijote replied with the same arguments, and in the same words, used by the captive Moor to reply to Rodrigo of Narváez, exactly as he'd read about it in the history La Diana, by Jorge de Montemayor, where it's all written out, and he made such excellent application of it to his own situation that the farmer walked along cursing his fate for having to listen to such a torrent of rubbish. But all this babbling made it absolutely clear that his neighbor had gone mad, and he hurried toward the village, to keep from going crazy himself, listening to Don Quijote's long-winded harangue.

When Don Quijote got to the end of his history, he said:

"Your grace, Don Rodrigo of Narváez, must surely know that this beautiful Jarifa, of whom I've been speaking, is now the lovely Dulcinea del Toboso, for whom I have performed, and am performing, and will in the future perform the most remarkable deeds of knighthood ever in this world seen, or seeable, or to be seen."

To which the farmer answered:

"Look your grace, sir, sinner that I am, I'm not Don Rodrigo of Narváez, nor am I the Marqués of Mantua, but Pedro Alonso, your neighbor, and you, your grace, aren't Valdovinos, or Abindarráez, but that honorable gentlemen, Mr. Quijana."

"I know who I am," replied Don Quijote, "and I know that I not only can be those of whom I have spoken, but the twelve Peers of France, and even the Nine Worthies, since all their heroic deeds put together or counted up each by each are surpassed by mine."[3]

Exchanging these and other such courtesies, they got to the village just as it was growing dark, but the farmer waited until night had fallen, so the half-dead gentleman might not be seen on so poor a mount. When it seemed to him the right time, accordingly, they entered the village and went to Don Quijote's house, where they found everything in an uproar: the priest was there, and the barber, both of them great friends of Don Quijote, and to whom his housekeeper was loudly proclaiming:

---

3. The "Twelve Peers" were Charlemagne's legendary knights. The "Nine Worthies" were Joshua, David, Judas Maccabaeus, Hector, Alexander, Caesar, Arthur, Charlemagne, and Geoffrey of Bouillon (leader of the First Crusade). Note that this last proverbial list includes three Jews, three pagans, and three Christians.

"As a college graduate, your grace, Señor Pero Pérez" — which was how the priest was usually addressed — "what do you think of my master's misfortune? He hasn't been seen in three days, and neither has his horse, or his shield, or his lance, or his armor. Oh miserable me! I'm afraid it's just the truth, the way it is that I was born in order to die, that it's these accursed books of chivalry of his, he's always reading them, and they've turned his poor brain all topsy-turvy. I can remember him saying, many times, talking to himself, how he'd like to be a knight errant and go all over the world hunting for adventure. Just pack all those books off to Satan and Barrabas! They've ruined the sharpest mind we had in all La Mancha."

Don Quijote's niece said the same thing, and then added:

"Please understand, Master Nicolás" — this was the barber's name — "that, often, my dear uncle would be reading these cruel, inhuman books of miserable adventures for two consecutive days and nights, after which he'd throw them down and take up his sword and walk up and down, slashing at the walls, and when he was good and tired he'd say he had killed four giants as tall as towers, and all the sweat he'd worked up was blood from the wounds he'd received in battle, and he'd gulp down a huge jug of cold water, and then he'd be quiet and peaceful and say that this water was really a rare and precious potion the great Esquife⁴ had made for him, the great magician who was his good friend. But it's all my fault, because I never warned either of you gentlemen what foolish things my dear uncle was up to, which you could have saved him from before we got where we are now, by burning all these wicked books of which he has so many, because they deserve burning every bit as much as heretics do."

"I agree with you," said the priest, "and by my faith the sun will not go down tomorrow without public judgment being passed on them and their being sentenced to the flames, to keep anyone else who might read them from doing as my good friend has apparently done."

Now the farmer and Don Quijote heard all this, which fleshed out the farmer's understanding of his neighbor's illness, and he at once called out, loudly:

"Your graces, open the door to Sir Valdovinos and to the Marqués of Mantua, who come to you sorely wounded, and to the Moor Abindarráez, taken captive by the brave Rodrigo of Narváez, governor of Antequera."

Hearing this, they all rushed out and, some of them recognizing their friend, some their master, and some their uncle, though he hadn't gotten off the donkey, because he couldn't, they hurried to embrace him. Don Quijote stopped them:

"Halt, all of you! It's my horse's fault, but I've been badly wounded. Bring me to my bed and then, if possible, call the wise witch Urganda, who can examine me and cure my wounds."

"Oh my dear Lord!" the housekeeper exclaimed. "I knew right from the bottom of my heart what had happened to my master! You just get into bed, your grace, without calling on this Hurgada [*hurgada* = sexually well-used], and we'll get you well. Curses on these chivalry books — I've said

---

4. A mistake easily made by someone who has heard but not read the name for Alquife, husband of the witch Urganda [*Translator's Note*].

it once and I'll say it a hundred times more — for bringing your grace to this!"

They quickly got him into bed and, trying to examine his wounds, found he had none. He told them that he was bruised all over, having taken a great fall with Rocinante, his horse, while fighting ten giants — the wildest, most insolent anywhere on earth.

"Ah ha!" said the priest. "We've got giants in all this, have we? By my faith, I'll burn them all up before nightfall tomorrow."

They asked Don Quijote a thousand questions, but all he felt like answering was that he wanted something to eat and would they please go away and let him sleep, because that was the most important thing. So that was what they did, and the priest interrogated the farmer at great length as to exactly how he'd come upon Don Quijote. The farmer told him everything, including all the nonsense spouted both when he'd found Don Quijote and when he was bringing him home, which made the priest still more anxious to accomplish what he did the next day, which was to fetch the barber, Master Nicolás, and take him along to Don Quijote's house.

Chapter Six[1]

— the entertaining and thorough inquisition into the library of our ingenious gentleman made by the priest and the barber

The priest asked his niece for the keys to the room where her uncle, who remained asleep through this whole proceeding, kept his books, they being the true authors of all the damage, and she was delighted to hand them over. They went in together, the housekeeper along with them, and found more than a hundred large folio volumes, extremely well bound, plus a good many smaller ones as well, and as soon as the housekeeper saw them she turned and ran out of the room, coming back at once with a great bowl of holy water and a sprinkling brush, and saying to the priest:

"Take this, your grace, sir, and sprinkle the whole room, so none of the magicians who swarm in those books can enchant us, to get even for throwing them out of the world."

The priest had to laugh at the housekeeper's naiveté, and he told the barber to hand him the books, one at a time, so he could see what they were all about, because perhaps he could find some that didn't deserve to be cast into the fire.

"No," said the niece, "none of them are worth pardoning, because

---

1. This chapter — which famously narrates the scrutiny or "inquisition" of Don Quijote's library — is sustained by a running metaphor of books-as-heretics. The personified books are variously sentenced: some are saved and some damned; some are dropped into a dry well; one is sent into exile; and one is even recommended a laxative ("a dose of rhubarb"). The inquisition itself proceeds by genres, moving from the romances of chivalry (Don Quijote's favorite reading) to the pastoral and epic genres. Among the many books mentioned in this chapter, familiar today largely to scholars of Spanish Golden Age literature, the most important is the first to be scrutinized and saved from the bonfire: *The Four Books of Amadís of Gaul*, a revision of a late medieval romance by Garci Rodríguez de Montalvo, published in 1508. As what follows will show, Don Quijote is obsessed with imitating Amadís.

they've all taken part in the damage. It would be better to just throw them out the windows, down into the patio, and stack them up and set them to burning — or else take them to the yard and start a bonfire out there, where the smoke won't bother anybody."

The housekeeper said the same thing, both of them equally eager to see the death of these innocents, but the priest wouldn't agree without at least first checking the titles. And the first that Master Nicolás handed him was *The Four Books of Amadís of Gaul*, seeing which the priest observed:

"Now this one is something of a mystery, because, according to what I've heard, this was the first of the chivalric stories ever printed in Spain, and all those that came after have had their beginning and very origin in this book, so it seems to me that since it's been responsible for spreading the doctrines of such an evil sect, there's absolutely no reason for not throwing it into the fire — we've got to do it."

"No, sir," said the barber, "because I've also heard it said this is the very best book of chivalry ever composed, and so, because it's a unique specimen of the art, it ought to be pardoned."

"Which is true," said the priest, "and for that reason let's grant it its life, at least for now. Let's have a look at the one standing next to it."

"This," said the barber, "is *The Exploits of Esplandián*, Amadís of Gaul's legitimate son."

"Nevertheless," said the priest, "the father's worthiness should not be attributed to the son. Take it, madame housekeeper; open that window and throw it down in the yard, so we can start getting ready for our bonfire."

The housekeeper took it with great pleasure, and the good Esplandián went flying down in the yard, there to await with great patience the fire that threatened him.

"Next," said the priest.

"This next one," said the barber, "is *Amadís of Greece*. Indeed, as far as I can tell, all the ones on this side are of the same Amadís family line."

"So throw them all in the yard," said the priest. "For the chance to burn Queen Pintiquiniestra, and shepherd Darinel and also his pastoral poems, as well as the author's fiendishly complicated and confused arguments, I'd burn my own father too, if I found him acting like a knight errant."

"And I agree," said the barber.

"So do I," added the niece.

"In that case," said the housekeeper, "let's have them, and down to the yard they go."

They gave her the books — so many that she didn't bother with the stairs but just threw them out the open window.

"Who is this big fat one?" asked the priest.

"That," answered the barber, "is *Don Olivante de Laura*."

"Ah," said the priest, "the man who wrote this book also composed *The Flower Garden*, and there's no way of deciding which of the two is more truthful — or, to put it better, less chockfull of lies. All I can say is this fellow goes down to the yard, for being a proud fool."

"This next one is *Florismarte of Hircania*," said the barber.

"We've got Señor Florismarte?" answered the priest. "Then by my faith he's got to go right down to the yard, in spite of his strange birth and all his famous adventures. What else could we do, considering his crabby, barren style? To the yard with him, madame housekeeper, along with the other one."

"With pleasure, my dear sir," she replied, doing his bidding with great delight.

"This one is *Platir the Knight*," said the barber.

"An old book," said the priest, "but its age doesn't entitle it to any mercy. Let it go down with the others, no defense permitted."

Which is what was done. They opened the next book and saw it was *The Knight of the Cross*.

"The title might make you forgive its ignorance, but you know what they say: 'The devil hides behind the cross.' Into the fire with it."

Picking up another book, the barber said:

"This one is *Knighthood's Mirror*."

"Oh I know you, your grace," said the priest. "Here we've got Señor Reinaldos de Montalbán and all his friends and relations, worse thieves than Cacus, and the twelve Peers of France, along with that wonderfully truthful historian, Turpín, but in fact I don't think we ought to condemn them to more than perpetual exile, because they had a hand in our famous Mateo Boyardo's *Orlando Innamorato* [*Orlando in Love*], which also gets them woven into the fabric of that good Christian poet, Ludovico Ariosto, and his *Orlando Furioso* [*Orlando Insane*] — to whom, if I find him here, speaking any language but his own, I'll show not the slightest respect, though if he's speaking his own language I'll bow to him most profoundly."

"I've got him in Italian," said the barber, "but I don't understand it."

"It wouldn't do you any good if you did," replied the priest, "which is why we might have forgiven his translator if he hadn't brought him to Spain and turned him into a Spaniard, thus depriving him of most of his original value, which is what they do to all those poems they try to change into other languages, for no matter how careful they try to be, or how skillful they are, they never bring them to the level quite naturally achieved in their native tongues. So what I say is that this book, and all the others we find that deal with these French subjects, should be dropped into some dry well until we figure out what we ought to do with them, except for *Bernardo del Carpio* and one other called *Roncesvalles*, for if I get my hands on those, they go right to our housekeeper here, and from her to the fire, without any possibility of pardon."

The barber completely agreed, for it seemed to him right and proper that so good a Christian as the priest, such a friend of the truth, wouldn't for the world say anything that wasn't both Christian and true. So, opening another book, he saw that this one was *Palmerín of the Olive Trees*, and standing next to it was another called *Palmerín of England*, of which volumes the priest said:

"Let's turn this olive wood right into kindling, and burn it until even its ashes are consumed, but we ought to take care of that English palm tree, preserving it as something unique, making for it a special case like the one Alexander found among Darius' treasures and saved as a home for Homer's works. This book, my friend, has two kinds of authority: first, because it's very good, and second, because they say it was written by a good, sensible Portuguese king. Every one of the adventures of the Castle of Miraguarda is superb, wonderfully well-written, and their narration, which is both polished and clear, is extremely careful with the voices of those who are supposed to be speaking, presenting them each with great correctness and deep understanding. Accordingly, I say — provided you agree, Master Nicolas — that like *Amadís of Gaul* this book should be kept from the fire. As for the rest, the lot of them, we need make no further inquiries: let them all die."

"No, my friend," answered the barber, "for the one I have right here is the famous *Don Belianís*."

"But that one," replied the priest, "really ought to be given a dose of rhubarb, on account of its second, third, and fourth parts, which need to be purged of their overflowing biliousness, and they also need to get rid of all that stuff about the Castle of Fame and those other even more important irrelevancies, so we'll give them the benefit of an extension and then, depending on how they reform themselves, they'll receive either compassion or just punishment. Considering which, my friend, carry them off to your own house, but don't let anyone read them."

"With pleasure," answered the barber.

And without tiring himself by reading any more books about knighthood, he told the housekeeper to take all the big volumes and toss them into the yard with the others. Nor did he speak to deaf ears, but to someone who took more pleasure in burning these books than in destroying a cobweb, no matter how huge and finely spun it might be, so grabbing as many as eight at a time she threw them out the window. Lugging so many all at once, she happened to drop one at the barber's feet, who, curious enough to pick it up and find out what it was, saw it was titled *The History of that Famous Knight, Tirante the White*.

"God in Heaven protect me!" shouted the priest. "We're in the presence of Tirante the White? Hand him over, my friend: why, I found this story a treasurehouse of delight, a goldmine of pleasure. Here we have that brave knight, Don Kyrie-eleison of Montalbán, and his brother Thomas, and the knight Fonseca, and the battle between Tirante the great and the wolfhound, and the witty chatter of Mademoiselle Pleasureofmylife, along with the love affairs and all the tricks of the widow Peaceful, and My Lady the Empress, who's in love with her page, Hipólito. To tell you the truth, my friend, for its style this is the best book in the world: knights take regular meals, in these pages, and they sleep in their beds, and die in them, and make wills before they die, plus all sorts of other things that don't happen in other tales of this sort. Despite all that, let me tell you, we'll send the man who wrote it, who didn't deliberately perpetrate all those other absurdities, to the galleys for the rest of his life. But take the book home and read it, and you'll see for yourself how justly I've spoken."[2]

"That's what I'll do," replied the barber. "But what are we going to do with all these little books we still have on our hands?"

"These," said the priest, "can't be books of chivalry, but poetry."

---

2. What the priest calls "the best book in the world" is a Castilian translation of *Tirant lo Blanch*, a text written in Catalan by Joanot Martorell (Valencia, 1490).

And, opening one, he saw it was *Diana*, by Jorge de Montemayor, so he explained, expecting the others would be much the same sort:

"These don't deserve burning, like the others, because they aren't as dangerous as tales of chivalry — they never will be. What harm is there in books that exercise the mind?"

"Oh my dear sir!" the niece exclaimed. "You ought to have these burned too, just like the others, because it wouldn't take much, once my uncle is cured of his knighthood sickness, to start reading these books and feel like becoming a shepherd, and then go around in the woods and meadows, singing and playing a flute and, even worse, writing poetry, which everyone knows is an infectious disease for which there's absolutely no cure."

"This young lady's speaking the truth," said the priest. "It would be a very good thing to free our friend of any such future difficulty or danger. So let's begin with Montemayor's *Diana*, which doesn't seem to be a candidate for burning, except we ought to cut out everything about the wise old witch Felicia and all that stuff about the enchanted water, and almost all the long stretches of verse, which happily leaves it the fine prose — plus the honor of being the first book of its kind."

"What comes next," said the barber, "is *Diana*, part two, by that Salamancan doctor, Alonso Pérez, and still another one with the same title, written by Gil Polo."

"The Salamancan one," replied the priest, "should go out the window and swell the ranks of the condemned, down in the yard, but let's save Gil Polo's, as if it had come from Apollo's own pen — and then we need to get on with it, my friend, and hurry things up, because it's getting late."

"Now this book," said the barber, opening another, "is *The Ten Books of Those Lucky in Love*, by Antonio de Lofraso, the Sardinian poet."

"By the holy orders administered to me," said the priest, "since Apollo has been Apollo, and Muses Muses, and poets poets, no one's written a book at once so funny and so foolish — and one that, in its way, is the best, the most singular thing of its kind ever to see the light of day, so whoever hasn't read it had better admit he hasn't read anything truly delightful. Let me have it, my friend: finding this is worth more to me than getting a cassock of Florentine silk."

He set it aside with great pleasure, and then the barber continued:

"These next ones are *The Shepherd of Iberia, The Nymphs of Henares*, and *Jealousy's Home Truths*."

"In which case all we have to do," said the priest, "is hand them over to the secular arm,[3] which is the housekeeper. But don't ask me to explain, or else we'll never be finished."

"This one's *The Shepherd of Fílida*."

"That's no shepherd," said the priest, "but a very knowing courtier. It should be saved, like some precious gem."

"Now this big one here," said the barber, "is called *Anthology of Miscellaneous Poems*."

---

3. A blatant allusion to the Spanish Inquisition, an ecclesiastical tribunal that investigated persons suspected of crimes against religion, who, if condemned, would be handed over to the "secular arm" or ordinary tribunal for sentencing.

"If only there weren't so many of them," said the priest, "they'd be worth more. This book needs weeding, it has to have the vulgarities cleaned out from among its truly fine things. Save it, because the author's a friend of mine, and out of respect for the other more heroic, more elevated books he's written."

"This one," said the barber, "is López Maldonado's *Collection of Poems and Songs*."

"The writer of this book, too," answered the priest, "is a great friend of mine, and when he recites his poems everyone who hears them admires them: his voice is so smooth and sweet that he makes them utterly enchanting. His eclogues are a bit too long — but how can you have too much of a good thing? We'll put it with the others we've set aside. But what's that book right next to it?"

"*Galatea*, by Miguel de Cervantes," said the barber.

"For years, this Cervantes has been a great friend of mine, and he certainly knows a lot more about misfortune than he does about poetry. There are good touches in his book; he starts some things, but he finishes nothing; we can only hope the second part, which he keeps promising, will set matters right and the book will earn the compassion now denied it. So keep him, my friend, locked away at home with all the others."

"That will be fine with me," answered the barber. "And here are three more, all together: Don Alonso de Ercilla's *Araucana*; the *Austríada*, by the Córdoba judge, Juan Rufo; and *Monserrate*, by the Valencian poet, Cristóbal de Virues."

"Now these three books," said the priest, "are the best heroic verse ever written in the Spanish language — they can compare very favorably with the most famous ever written in Italian. Keep them, as the richest jewels in all of Spanish poetry."[4]

The priest was too tired to look at any more books, so he decided that all the rest would be labelled "contents unknown" and then burned, but then the barber picked up one called *Angelica's Tears*.

"I'd have been weeping myself," said the priest, hearing the title, "if I'd ordered that book to be burned, because its author [Luis Barahona de Soto] was one of the most famous poets in the whole world, not just in Spain, and did some superb translations of Ovid's tales."

Chapter Seven

— *the second expedition of our good knight, Don Quijote de La Mancha*

They had just gotten to this point when, suddenly, Don Quijote began to shout:

"Now, now, brave knights! Now is when you need to show the strength of your brave arms! Or else the courtiers will win the tournament!"

Hurrying to respond to this clamorous uproar, they completely forgot

---

4. Ercilla's *Araucana* (1569–1589) stands out among these Spanish poems as the first colonial war epic in America. It addresses, with a remarkable amount of breast-beating, the Spanish conquest of the Chilean Indians.

about examining the rest of the books, and so it seems that Don Luis de Avila's *Carolea*, and *The Lion of Spain*, and *The Emperor's Adventures*, all perished in the flames, without being seen or heard from, although they must have been among those that were left and, conceivably, if the priest had seen them, he'd not have given them such harsh punishment.

When they reached Don Quijote he had gotten out of bed and, still shouting all sorts of foolishness, was slashing back and forth in all directions, as wide awake as if he'd never been asleep. They crowded around and by sheer force got him back to bed; when he was calmer, he turned to the priest, saying:

"Clearly, my dear Archbishop Turpín,[1] it is infinitely to our discredit, we who call ourselves the Twelve Peers, to allow the courtly knights to gain a victory in this tournament. We must exert ourselves, for it is we who have won on each of the last three days."

"Hush, your grace — my friend," said the priest. "Perhaps it will please God to see the tide of fortune change, so that he who loses today may win tomorrow, so for now you must take care of your health, for it seems to me you must be surpassingly tired, if not badly wounded."

"Wounded, no," said Don Quijote, "just exhausted and weak — there's no doubt about it, for that bastard Don Roldán has beaten me half to death with the trunk of an oak tree, and just out of envy, seeing that I, and I alone, stand up to his boasting. But I would not be Reinaldos de Montalbán if, when I rise from this bed, I don't pay him back, in spite of all his magic tricks — and, for now, bring me something to eat, because I know that would be the best thing: let my vengeance rest on my shoulders alone."

Which was what they did. Astonished by his insanity, they gave him food and let him go back to sleep.

That night the housekeeper burned to ashes every book lying out in the yard, and all the ones left in the house, too, and among those that perished in the flames there must have been some which deserved to be preserved forever. But fate was against it, as was the laziness of their inquisitor, thus fulfilling the words of the old proverb about the upright sometimes having to pay for sinners' crimes.

One of the remedies the priest and the barber resorted to, to deal with their friend's illness, was to close up and wall over the room where he'd kept his books, so that when he was on his feet again he would not be able to find them, thinking that if they eliminated the cause perhaps the effect would cease too — and they could say that a magician had carried them off, room and all. So they had it done as quickly as possible. Two days later Don Quijote got up, and the first thing he did was go to consult his books. Not finding the room where it ought to be, he went from one room to another, hunting. At the spot where the door should have been, he groped around with his hands, letting his eyes go this way and that, but without saying a word, until finally he asked the housekeeper which was the room where he kept his books. Having been carefully instructed as to what she should say, she answered:

---

1. Archbishop of Rheims as well as Charlemagne's chaplain.

"What room? What in the world are you looking for, your grace? There's no such room in this house, not now, and no books either, because the devil himself has carried them off."

"Not the devil," replied the niece, "but a magician who swept down out of the sky, one night, that very same day just after your grace rode away, and he climbed down off the great snake he'd been riding and went into that room, and I don't know what he did in there, but finally, before too very long, he flew up through the roof, leaving the house in a cloud of smoke. And when we went to see what he'd been up to, we couldn't find a book or a room or anything. But the housekeeper and I, we remember very well, that as he was leaving, that evil old man, he shouted out — in a very loud voice — that he had some private quarrel with the person who owned those books and that room, and he'd done damage in the house that, soon enough, we would see for ourselves. And he also said his name was Muñatón the Wise."

"He must have said Frestón," said Don Quijote.

"I don't know," put in the housekeeper, "whether his name was Frestón or Fritón, just that it ended with a *ton*."[2]

"So it does," said Don Quijote, "and he's a learned magician, and a great enemy of mine, who bears a grudge against me because, as his magic arts tell him, a time will come when I fight in single combat against a knight he supports, and I will vanquish that knight without the magician being able to stop me, all of which explains why he tries to make as much trouble for me as he can. But I will show him he can neither oppose nor avoid that which has been ordained by Heaven."

"Who could doubt that?" asked the niece. "But my dear uncle, who obliges your grace to be involved in these quarrels? Wouldn't it be better to stay quietly at home and not travel all over the world, hunting for some imaginary bread made without wheat, and forgetting how many go forth looking for wool and come back shorn?"

"Oh my dear niece," answered Don Quijote, "how little you know about such things! Long before I'm ever shorn, I'll have stripped away beards — hair, skin, and all — from anyone who's even thought about touching the tip of a single hair of mine."

The two women didn't want to say anything more, for they saw how angry he was getting.

Well, then, it came about that he stayed very quietly at home for fifteen days, showing no sign of wanting to repeat his original nonsense, and during that time he had lively discussions with his two friends, the priest and the barber, in which he argued that what the world most needed were knights errant and that true chivalry would be resurrected in him. Sometimes the priest would oppose him, sometimes he'd agree, knowing that without this ruse there would be no way at all to lead him toward reason.

During this time, too, Don Quijote sought out a farmer, a neighbor of his and a good man (if we can use that term for anyone who's poor) but not very well endowed from the neck up. To make a long story short, he

2. Don Quijote alludes to a wizard who is the reputed "author" of *Belianís de Grecia*, a romance of chivalry scrutinized in I.6.

piled so many words on him, coaxing him, making him promises, that the poor fellow agreed to ride out with him and serve as his squire. Among other things, Don Quijote told him he ought to be delighted to join the quest because you could never tell when an adventure might earn them, in two shakes of a lamb's tail, a whole island, and Don Quijote would leave him there to be its governor. Because of promises like this, and many more of the same sort, Sancho Panza — which was the farmer's name — left his wife and children and agreed to become his neighbor's squire.

Don Quijote promptly set to work hunting up money and, selling something here, pawning something there, making one bad bargain after another, he managed to put together a fair-sized sum. He also wangled a small shield for himself (borrowed from a friend) and, patching up his helmet as best he could, warned his squire of the exact day and hour at which he planned to ride out, so Sancho could make sure he had everything he was going to need. And above all else Don Quijote advised him to bring along saddlebags, which Sancho said he would do, and he'd bring a very fine donkey, too, because he hadn't had much practice getting places on foot. Don Quijote had some doubts about the donkey, trying to remember if there had ever been a knight errant whose squire rode along on an ass, but couldn't recall a single one. In spite of which he decided to take Sancho with him, intending to arrange a more honorable mount as soon as he had the chance, by seizing a horse from the first ill-mannered knight he bumped into. He got some shirts ready, and as many other things as he could, following the advice the innkeeper had given him, and all of this having been arranged without either Sancho Panza saying goodbye to his wife and children, or Don Quijote to his niece and his housekeeper, one night they rode out of the village without anyone seeing them, and rode so far that, by dawn, they thought it would be impossible to find them, even if a search were made.

Sancho Panza jogged along on his donkey like some biblical patriarch, carrying his saddlebags and his leather wine bottle, wanting very badly to see himself the governor of an island, as his master had promised. Don Quijote had decided to go in the very same direction, and along the very same road, as on his first expedition, which led through the fields of Montiel, which he crossed with less difficulty than the last time, for it was early morning and the sun's rays came slanting down and did not tire them out. Then Sancho Panza said to his master:

"Now be careful, your grace, sir knight errant, you don't forget that island you promised me, because no matter how big it is I'll know how to govern it."

To which Don Quijote answered:

"You must know, Sancho Panza my friend, that it used to be very common, in ancient times, for knights errant to make their squires governor of whatever islands or regions they conquered, and I am resolved not to neglect this gracious custom — indeed, I intend to improve on it, for occasionally, and I suspect most of the time, they waited until their squires had grown old and fed up with such service, enduring bad days and even worse nights, and then gave them a title — count, or more often marquis of some valley or province, more or less. But if you and I both live, it could be that in less than a week I'll have conquered a kingdom to which others pay allegiance, which would be just right for crowning you ruler of one of those subordinate domains. Nor should you think this in any way remarkable, for no one can possibly foresee or even imagine the way the world turns for such knights, so it could easily happen that I will be able to grant you still more than my promise."

"So," said Sancho Panza, "if I become a king, by one of those miracles your grace is talking about, at the very least my old lady, Teresa,[3] would get to be a queen, and my kids would be princes."

"But who could possibly doubt it?" answered Don Quijote.

"I doubt it," replied Sancho Panza, "because it seems to me that, even if God let crowns come raining down all over the earth, none would land on my wife's head. You see, señor, she wouldn't be worth two cents as a queen. She might make a better countess, but it wouldn't be easy, even with God's help."

"Put yourself in God's hands, Sancho," said Don Quijote, "and He will give both you and your wife what it is best you should each have. But don't so lower your spirit that you'll be satisfied with less than a provincial governorship."

"I won't, my lord," answered Sancho, "especially since I've got a master like your grace, who understands just what's best for me and what I can handle."

Chapter Eight

— *the great success won by our brave Don Quijote in his dreadful, unimaginable encounter with two windmills, plus other honorable events well worth remembering*

Just then, they came upon thirty or forty windmills, which (as it happens) stand in the fields of Montiel, and as soon as Don Quijote saw them he said to his squire:

"Destiny guides our fortunes more favorably than we could have expected. Look there, Sancho Panza, my friend, and see those thirty or so wild giants, with whom I intend to do battle and to kill each and all of them, so with their stolen booty we can begin to enrich ourselves. This is noble, righteous warfare, for it is wonderfully useful to God to have such an evil race wiped from the face of the earth."

"What giants?" asked Sancho Panza.

"The ones you can see over there," answered his master, "with the huge arms, some of which are very nearly two leagues long."

"Now look, your grace," said Sancho, "what you see over there aren't giants, but windmills, and what seem to be arms are just their sails, that go around in the wind and turn the millstone."

"Obviously," replied Don Quijote, "you don't know much about adventures. Those are giants — and if you're frightened, take yourself away

---

3. Cervantes later calls her Juana. Even Homer nods [*Translator's Note*].

from here and say your prayers, while I go charging into savage and un-equal combat with them."

Saying which, he spurred his horse, Rocinante, paying no attention to the shouts of Sancho Panza, his squire, warning him that without any question it was windmills and not giants he was going to attack. So utterly convinced was he they were giants, indeed, that he neither heard Sancho's cries nor noticed, close as he was, what they really were, but charged on, crying:

"Flee not, oh cowards and dastardly creatures, for he who attacks you is a knight alone and unaccompanied."

Just then the wind blew up a bit, and the great sails began to stir, which Don Quijote saw and cried out:

"Even should you shake more arms than the giant Briareus[1] himself, you'll still have to deal with me."

As he said this, he entrusted himself with all his heart to his lady Dulcinea, imploring her to help and sustain him at such a critical moment, and then, with his shield held high and his spear braced in its socket, and Rocinante at a full gallop, he charged directly at the first windmill he came to, just as a sudden swift gust of wind sent its sail swinging hard around, smashing the spear to bits and sweeping up the knight and his horse, tumbling them all battered and bruised to the ground. Sancho Panza came rushing to his aid, as fast as his donkey could run, but when he got to his master, found him unable to move, such a blow had he been given by the falling horse.

"God help me!" said Sancho. "Didn't I tell your grace to be careful what you did, that these were just windmills, and anyone who could ignore that had to have windmills in his head?"

"Silence, Sancho, my friend," answered Don Quijote. "Even more than other things, war is subject to perpetual change. What's more, I think the truth is that the same Frestón the magician, who stole away my room and my books, transformed these giants into windmills, in order to deprive me of the glory of vanquishing them, so bitter is his hatred of me. But in the end, his evil tricks will have little power against my good sword."

"God's will be done," answered Sancho Panza.

Then, helping his master to his feet, he got him back up on Rocinante, whose shoulder was half dislocated. After which, discussing the adventure they'd just experienced, they followed the road toward Lápice Pass, for there, said Don Quijote, they couldn't fail to find adventures of all kinds, it being a well-traveled highway. But having lost his lance, he went along very sorrowfully, as he admitted to his squire, saying:

"I remember having read that a certain Spanish knight named Diego Pérez de Vargas, having lost his sword while fighting in a lost cause, pulled a thick bough, or a stem, off an oak tree, and did such things with it, that day, clubbing down so many Moors that ever afterwards they nicknamed him Machuca [Clubber], and indeed from that day on he and all his descendants bore the name Vargas y Machuca. I tell you this because, the first oak tree I come to, I plan to pull off a branch like that, one every bit

---

1. One of the "hundred-handed" (*Hekatoncheires*) giants, sons of Uranus and Gaia.

as good as the huge stick I can see in my mind, and I propose to perform such deeds with it that you'll be thinking yourself blessed, having the opportunity to see them, and being a living witness to events that might otherwise be unbelievable."

"It's in God's hands," said Sancho. "I believe everything is exactly the way your grace says it is. But maybe you could sit a little straighter, because you seem to be leaning to one side, which must be because of the great fall you took."

"True," answered Don Quijote, "and if I don't say anything about the pain it's because knights errant are never supposed to complain about a wound, even if their guts are leaking through it."

"If that's how it's supposed to be," replied Sancho, "I've got nothing to say. But Lord knows I'd rather your grace told me, any time something hurts you. Me, I've got to groan, even if it's the smallest little pain, unless that rule about knights errant not complaining includes squires, too."

Don Quijote couldn't help laughing at his squire's simplicity, and cheerfully assured him he could certainly complain any time he felt like it, voluntarily or involuntarily, since in all his reading about knighthood and chivalry he'd never come across anything to the contrary. Sancho said he thought it was dinner-time. His master replied that, for the moment, he himself had no need of food, but Sancho should eat whenever he wanted to. Granted this permission, Sancho made himself as comfortable as he could while jogging along on his donkey and, taking out of his saddlebags what he had put in them, began eating as he rode, falling back a good bit behind his master, and from time to time tilting up his wineskin with a pleasure so intense that the fanciest barman in Málaga might have envied him. And as he rode along like this, gulping quietly away, none of the promises his master had made were on his mind, nor did he feel in the least troubled or afflicted — in fact, he was thoroughly relaxed about this adventure-hunting business, no matter how dangerous it was supposed to be.

In the end, they spent that night sleeping in a wood, and Don Quijote pulled a dry branch from one of the trees, to serve him, more or less, as a lance, fitting onto it the spearhead he'd taken off the broken one. Nor did Don Quijote sleep, that whole night long, meditating on his lady Dulcinea — in order to fulfill what he'd read in his books, namely, that knights always spent long nights out in the woods and other uninhabited places, not sleeping, but happily mulling over memories of their ladies. Which wasn't the case for Sancho Panza: with his stomach full, and not just with chicory water, his dreams swept him away, nor would he have bothered waking up, for all the sunlight shining full on his face, or the birds singing — brightly, loudly greeting the coming of the new day — if his master hadn't called to him. He got up and, patting his wineskin, found it a lot flatter than it had been the night before, which grieved his heart, since it didn't look as if they'd be making up the shortage any time soon. Don Quijote had no interest in breakfast, since, as we have said, he had been sustaining himself with delightful memories. They returned to the road leading to Lápice Pass, which they could see by about three that afternoon.

"Here," said Don Quijote as soon as he saw it, "here, brother Sancho Panza, we can get our hands up to the elbows in adventures. But let me warn you: even if you see me experiencing the greatest dangers in the world, never draw your sword to defend me, unless of course you see that those who insult me are mere rabble, people of low birth, in which case you may be permitted to help me. But if they're knights, the laws of knighthood make it absolutely illegal, without exception, for you to help me, unless you yourself have been ordained a knight."

"Don't worry, your grace," answered Sancho Panza. "You'll find me completely obedient about this, especially since I'm a very peaceful man — I don't like getting myself into quarrels and fights. On the other hand, when it comes to someone laying a hand on me, I won't pay much attention to those laws, because whether they're divine or human they permit any man to defend himself when anyone hurts him."

"To be sure," answered Don Quijote. "But when it comes to helping me against other knights, you must restrain your natural vigor."

"And that's what I'll do," replied Sancho. "I'll observe this rule just as carefully as I keep the sabbath."

While they were talking, they could see, coming down the road, two Benedictine friars, mounted on a pair of camels — or, at least, the mules they rode on were every bit as big. Like well-bred travelers, they were wearing dust-goggles and carrying parasols. Behind them there was a coach with four or five outriders, mounted on mules, and two young muledrivers on foot. The coach contained, as became clear later on, a Basque lady on her way to Seville to join her husband, who was sailing for the Indies to take up a post of some distinction. The friars were not her traveling companions, although they were on the same road, but as soon as Don Quijote saw them he said to his squire:

"If I'm not mistaken, this is going to be the most famous adventure ever heard of, for those black forms over there must be, and indeed they are, there's no doubt about it, magicians who are spiriting away a princess in that coach, so I need to exert every bit of my strength to undo such wrongdoing."

"This is going to be worse than the windmills," said Sancho. "Now look, your grace, those are Benedictine friars, and the coach has got to belong to some well-bred lady. Listen to me: watch out, you'd better be careful — don't be fooled by the devil."

"But haven't I already told you, Sancho," answered Don Quijote, "that you don't know anything about adventures? What I tell you is the truth, as you'll see in a moment."

Saying which, he galloped ahead and set himself in the middle of the road, right in the friars' path, and as soon as he thought they were close enough to hear what he said, he called out:

"You masked devils,[2] you monsters! Release this very moment the noble princesses you are carrying off against their will, or else prepare yourself to die on the spot, as fit punishment for your evil deeds."

---

2. The Benedictine friars are masked, like most well-to-do Golden Age travelers, to protect their faces from dust and sunburn.

The friars pulled back on the reins and gaped — as much at Don Quijote's appearance as at what he said, to which they responded:

"Sir knight, we're not masked devils nor are we monsters, we're just two Benedictine monks riding down the road, and whether or not there are any kidnapped princesses in that coach, we have no idea."

"Don't waste soothing words on me," said Don Quijote. "I know you, you lying scum."

And without waiting for any further response, he spurred Rocinante and, lance at the ready, rushed at the first friar with such fearless courage that, had the man not dropped off the mule, he would have been thrown to the ground and probably badly wounded, if not already stone dead. The second monk, seeing how his companion had been treated, dug his spurs into his huge mule and began to gallop over the fields, faster than any wind.

Seeing the friar fall, Sancho Panza fairly leapt off his mule, went over to him, and started pulling off his robes. Just then the two young muledrivers, the friars' servants, came up and asked him why he was pulling those clothes off. Sancho told them this was his legitimate prize, as spoils of the battle won by his master, Don Quijote. The muledrivers, who had no sense of humor, and knew nothing about either booty or battle, saw that Don Quijote had already ridden on past and was speaking to the people in the coach, so they jumped on Sancho and knocked him to the ground and, barely leaving a hair in his beard, beat him and kicked him, leaving him stretched out on the ground, senseless and half-dead. Then, without losing a moment, they helped the friar to mount again — terrified, trembling, his face white as a sheet. And as soon as he was up on his mule, he spurred it right after his companion, who was waiting, a good way off, wondering how this sudden violent outburst would conclude. And then, without waiting to see how the whole affair might end, the two of them rode off down the road, making more signs of the cross than if the devil himself had been right behind them.

As we have said, Don Quijote was speaking to the lady in the coach, saying to her:

"My lady, your beauteousness is now enabled to dispose of yourself exactly as you most please, since your proud kidnappers lie in the dust, overthrown by this strong arm of mine. And lest you worry yourself about the name of your liberator, know that I am called Don Quijote de La Mancha, knight errant and soldier of fortune, and captive to the matchless and most beautiful lady, Doña Dulcinea del Toboso. In acknowledgment of the kindness I have extended to you, I ask only that you direct yourself to Toboso and present yourself to that lady on my behalf, telling her what part I have had in your liberation."

One of the mounted pages accompanying the coach, a Basque, had been listening to everything Don Quijote said, and seeing that the knight did not intend to allow the coach to continue on its way, declaring that it must turn around and go back to Toboso, rode over to Don Quijote, took hold of his lance, and said to him, in bad Spanish (and worse Basque), approximately as follows:

"Go away, wrong riding knight. By the God that made me, if you no leave coach, as I am Basque I kill you."[3]

Don Quijote understood him very well indeed, and replied with perfect calm:

"Were you a knight, as to be sure you are not, I would already have punished you for your stupidity and insolence, you miserable creature."

To which the Basque responded:

"I no knight? I swear to God as I Christian you lie. You put down spear and draw sword, and we find out pretty damned soon who get bell onto cat. Basque on ground be gentleman on sea, by the devil, and you liar who think say other thing."

"And so, said the noble knight Agrajes, we shall see," answered Don Quijote.

And tossing his spear to the ground, he drew his sword, raised his shield, and attacked the Basque, determined to kill him. Seeing him come, the Basque would have preferred to get down from his mule, which was a rented animal he could not trust, but had no choice except to draw his own sword. Still, he was lucky enough to find himself near the coach, so he grabbed a cushion to use as a shield, and they had at it, exactly as if they'd been mortal enemies. The others tried to settle the quarrel, but couldn't, because the Basque kept saying in his broken Spanish that if they didn't let him finish his fight he'd kill his mistress and everyone else who got in his way. The lady in the coach, astonished and terrified by what she saw, directed the coachman to drive off a bit, and from that distance prepared to watch the harsh battle — and as that struggle went on, the Basque gave Don Quijote a great blow high on the shoulder, swinging over his shield, and had our knight not been in armor the thrust would have split him down to the waist. Feeling the weight of this colossal blow, Don Quijote cried out, at the top of his lungs:

"Oh lady of my soul, Dulcinea, flower of all beauty, help this knight of yours, who, to please your great goodness, now finds himself in this difficult situation!"

He said all this, and tightened his grip on his sword, and held the shield high in front of him, and attacked the Basque, all at the same time, having made up his mind to trust everything to a single blow.

Seeing him come at him this way, with such determination, the Basque perfectly well understood our knight's courage, and made up his mind to do exactly the same thing. So he held himself ready, behind his upraised coach cushion, but could not turn his mule an inch in any direction, for the animal, totally exhausted and not meant for these particular games, couldn't so much as lift a hoof.

So, as we've said, there came Don Quijote right at the wary Basque, his sword raised high, resolved to cut the man in half, and the Basque awaited him, his sword too lifted high, and sheltering behind his cushion, and everyone around was terrified, waiting to find out what would come of the tremendous blows which each of them was threatening for the other, and

---

3. The broken English here simulates the broken Spanish of Basques, often satirized, and sometimes even compared to Native American languages, in Cervantes's day.

the lady in the coach and all the rest of her servants were saying a thousand prayers and making vows to every holy image and sacred shrine in all of Spain, if only God would save their fellow, and them too, from the immense danger in which they found themselves.

But the trouble with all this is that, at this exact point, at these exact words, the original author of this history left the battle suspended in mid-air, excusing himself on the grounds that he himself could not find anything more written on the subject of these exploits of Don Quijote than what has already been set down. Now it's true that I, your second author, found it hard to believe that such a fascinating tale could have been simply consigned to the dust, nor that there wouldn't be clever people in La Mancha, curious to find out if in their archives, or in other documents, there wasn't something more about this famous knight. And so, with this idea in mind, I was not without hope that I'd dig up the ending of this pleasant story, which, were the judgment of Heaven favorable, I proposed to narrate as, in fact, you may hereafter find it narrated in Part Two.

Part Two

Chapter Nine

— in which is narrated the end of the stupendous battle between the gallant Basque and the brave knight of La Mancha

We left off the first part of this history with the courageous Basque and the celebrated Don Quijote, their swords bared and uplifted, each ready to smash a furious stroke at the other — a stroke so furious, indeed, that were both blows to have landed squarely on target, each man would have been, at the least, split from top to bottom like an opened pomegranate. And at exactly that moment of dire uncertainty the pleasant tale was broken off, and left mutilated, nor did the original author give us the slightest idea where we might find the missing part.

Now this deeply upset me, since the pleasure of reading so abbreviated a narrative was turned into vexation, as I thought of what a hard time I was going to have, trying to find the large section which (or so it seemed to me) had to be missing from this delightful story. It struck me as utterly impossible — totally unlike the way such things are done — that there wouldn't have been *some* learned man who'd make himself responsible for recording the never-before-seen exploits of such a splendid knight, for no such deficiency had ever occurred to any of those knights errant,

> the ones that everyone talks of,
> hunting all over for adventure —

since each and every one of them had one or two learned chroniclers (as alike as if made to order) who not only transcribed their heroic deeds but told us even their silliest thoughts and most childish behavior, no matter how hidden and secret they might have been. It simply could not be that such a fine knight could have been so unfortunate, when Platir and others like him had chroniclers in abundance. Accordingly, I was not persuaded that such a charming history could have been left mangled and in disarray, so I laid the blame on the corrupting touch of time, which devours and consumes all things, and had surely either kept the rest of the story hidden or had destroyed it.

On the other hand, it seemed to me that, since his library had included such modern books as *Jealousy's Home Truths* and *The Nymphs of Henares*, his history too ought perhaps to be a modern one — so that, if it hadn't been written down, it might still remain in the memories of folk from his village and also their neighbors. I found this notion hard to deal with, and I longed to know really and truly everything about our famous Spaniard

50

Don Quijote's life and all his heroic exploits, he who was the light and ornament of La Mancha knighthood, the first in our age, and in this whirling time, to set himself the task of knight errantry, and the righting of wrongs, the succoring of widows, the protecting of damsels — those pure females who rode the land with their cracking whips and their palfreys, and their staggering virginity on their backs, up one mountain and down another, and out of one valley and into another — who, were it not for some vile rascal, some villain with a woodsman's axe and a peasant's clumsy helmet, some monstrous giant, who ravishes them, would (back in those days) turn into damsels of eighty who had never in their lives slept a single night under a roof and would go to their graves as virginal as the mother who'd borne them. I declare, accordingly, that for these and many other reasons our gallant Quijote is worthy of perpetual and very special praise — and even I shouldn't be denied a bit of it, on account of the hard, faithful work I put in, hunting for the conclusion of this pleasant tale, though I am well aware that if Heaven, circumstances, and good fortune had not come to my assistance, the world would have had to do without a diversion and an entertainment that should be able to claim a reader's attention for almost two hours. And this, then, is how it all happened:

One day, when I was in the Alcaná [marketplace] at Toledo, a boy came by, selling some old notebooks and other documents to a dealer in silks, and since I'm always reading, even scraps of paper I find in the street, it was perfectly natural for me to pick up one of the old notebooks the boy was selling, which I saw was written in what I knew to be Arabic characters. But although I recognized the script, I still didn't know how to read it, so I went looking for some Moor[1] who could speak Spanish and read it to me, and it wasn't hard to find exactly the sort of translator I was looking for — in fact, even if I'd been hunting a different language, older and better [Hebrew], I'd have found it. Anyway, fate furnished me with a man who, when I told him what I wanted and put the book in his hands, opened it right in the middle and, reading a bit, began to laugh.

I asked him what he was laughing at, and he told me it was something he'd found written in the margin, as an annotation. I asked him to explain what it was and, still laughing, he said:

"This, as I told you, is written right here in the margin: 'The aforementioned Dulcinea del Toboso, referred to so many times in this history, was said to have the best hand for salting pork of any woman in all La Mancha.'"

When I heard him say "Dulcinea del Toboso," I was stunned, absolutely astonished, for I understood at once that these old notebooks contained the history of Don Quijote. Having made this realization, I quickly asked

---

1. Cervantes uses here the term *morisco*, meaning a descendant of the North African invaders of Spain. The *moriscos* largely continued to speak Arabic and to practice their Islamic religion until their official expulsions between 1609 and 1613. In *Don Quijote* II.54 (page 645 of this volume), a character called Ricote the Moor speaks of "His Majesty's decree threatening such harsh punishment of my people." Philip III's Edict of 1609 commanded the *moriscos*, under pain of death, to be ready to embark for Africa within three days. These royal edicts, coming slightly over a century after Spain's official expulsion of the Jews (1492), were an early modern form of "ethnic cleansing."

him to read from the very beginning, which he did, making a rapid translation from Arabic into Spanish. And this is what he said:

"History of Don Quijote of La Mancha, written by Sidi [señor] *Hamid
Benengeli* [eggplant-shaped], *Arab historian."*

I had to be exceedingly careful to hide the happiness I felt, when these
words came to my ears — and snatching the old notebooks and documents away from the silk dealer, I bought them all from the boy, paying
him half a dollar, though if he'd had the wit, and if he'd understood why
I wanted them, he surely could have asked and gotten more than six dollars
for the purchase. And then I quickly drew the Moor aside, into the church
cloister, and implored him to translate these notebooks into Spanish for
me, every single one of them that had to do with Don Quijote, neither
omitting nor adding a thing, and I offered to pay him whatever he wanted.
He was happy with fifty pounds of raisins and three bushels of wheat, and
promised to translate carefully and well, using no more words than absolutely necessary. But in order to get the business done as easily as possible,
and to keep from letting such a magnificent discovery out of my hands, I
carried him home with me, and in little more than a month and a half
he translated everything, exactly as it's told here.

In the first of the notebooks there was an exceedingly realistic painting
of Don Quijote's battle with the Basque, both of them pictured in exactly
the stances described by the story, both raising their swords, one protected
by a shield, the other by a coach-cushion — and the Basque's mule so
exceedingly lifelike that you could spot him for a rented animal, even
from a long crossbow-shot away. There was a caption just underneath the
Basque, reading: "Don Sancho de Azpetia," which was surely his name,
and underneath Rocinante there was another, reading: "Don Quijote."
Rocinante was marvelously well-painted, so big and boney, so thin and
lean, with such a spine, so obviously tubercular, that he showed very
plainly how wisely and properly he'd been named "Rocin-ante." Near him
was Sancho Panza, holding his donkey's halter, and underneath him there
was another inscription, reading: "Sancho Zancas," and apparently, at least
as far as we can tell from the picture, he was short, with a big belly and
long legs, which is why he must have been given the names *Panza* [belly]
and *Zancas* [long legs], and indeed the history used both names, at one
time or another. There are a few other small points possibly worth mentioning, but they're really not of much importance — and they have
nothing to do with a faithful telling of the story, which can never be bad
if it's truthful.

And if there is any possible objection to the truthfulness of the account,
it can only be that the author was an Arab, since it's very natural for people
of that race to be liars. On the other hand, since they're so very hostile to
us, the author is more likely to have toned down rather than embellished
his tale. Which seems to me, indeed, to have been what happened, since
when he could and should have let his pen go, in praise of such a fine
knight, he seems to have quite deliberately passed over things in silence
— a serious error and an even worse plan, for an historian should be
accurate, truthful, and never driven by his feelings, so that neither self-
interest nor fear, neither ill will nor devotion, should lead him away from

the highway of truth, whose very mother is history, time's great rival — storehouse of men's actions, witness of time past, example and bearer of tidings to the present, and warning for the future. And here in this account I'm sure you'll find everything you may want, presented in the pleasantest way, and if indeed there's anything worthwhile missing, I'd blame it on its dog of an author, rather than on any deficiency in the subject itself.

So this, according to the translation, is how the second part begins:

With the savage swords of the two brave and infuriated combatants raised on high and at the ready, they seemed to be threatening the very heavens, the earth and the fiery gulfs with their boldness. And the first to rain down his blow was the angry Basque, who dealt it with such force and in such a fury that, had the sword not swivelled as he swung, that single stroke would have been enough to end the savage battle — and also the entire career of our knight. But some happy destiny, preserving Don Quijote for better things, twisted the blade around so that, though it struck him on the left shoulder, it did him no more damage than to slice off all the armor on that side, knocking it to the ground along with most of his helmet and half of his ear, all of which clattered down with a horrifying racket, leaving him very badly battered.

Good God, who could easily recount the rage that now filled the heart of our La Manchan, having been dealt such a setback! The best we can say is that he reared up once again in his stirrups, took a two-handed grip on his sword, and swung so savagely at the Basque, hitting him squarely on the coach-cushion and on the head that, though the cushion had offered him first-rate protection, now it was as if a mountain had fallen on him, and blood began to pour out of his nostrils and his mouth, and also from his ears, and it looked as if he would fall off his mule, as indeed without any doubt he would, had he not clutched at the animal's neck. But still, his feet fell out of the stirrups, and in a moment his arms slipped away, and his mule, terrified by the fearful blow, began to run through the fields, and after a few leaps threw his master to the ground.

Don Quijote was watching all this with great calm, and when he saw the Basque fall, he leaped off his horse and ran quickly toward him, then put the point of his sword between the Basque's eyes and ordered him to surrender, or have his head cut off. The Basque was so shaken he could not speak a word, and it would have gone very badly for him, given Don Quijote's blind rage, except that the ladies in the coach, who had to this point been watching the combat in great distress, hurried over and most earnestly begged our knight to show them the great grace, and extend to them the great favor, of sparing the life of their page. To which Don Quijote replied, soberly and with great pride:

"Certainly, lovely ladies: I am deeply pleased to do as you ask of me. But only on one condition, and that is that this knight must promise and agree to journey to Toboso and present himself on my behalf to the peerless Doña Dulcinea, so that she may dispose of him as it best pleases her."

Frightened and miserable, not disputing a word or asking who Dulcinea might be, the ladies promised that their page would do everything that Don Quijote had ordered to be done.

"Accordingly, trusting in your word, I will do him no further harm, though he richly deserves it."

Chapter Ten

— a lively discussion between Don Quijote and Sancho Panza, his squire

By this time Sancho Panza had gotten to his feet, though somewhat abused by the friars' young muledrivers, and had been watching his master Don Quijote's combat and praying, in his heart, that God would grant him victory and thereby win some island where Sancho could be made governor, as he'd been promised. So when he saw the battle had ended, and his master was about to mount Rocinante, Sancho hurried over to hold the stirrup for him and, before Don Quijote could mount, sank down on his knees, grasped his master's hand and, kissing it, said:

"If your grace, Don Quijote my lord, would please give me the governorship of the island you won in this hard fight. No matter how big it might be, I'm sure I'll know how to govern it as well as anyone who's ever governed islands anywhere in the world."

To which Don Quijote replied:

"Be advised, brother Sancho, that this adventure, and any like it, are not island adventures, but crossroads adventures, in which nothing is won except a cracked head or a missing ear. Be patient: in time there will be adventures after which I will be able to make you not simply a governor, but something even more."

Sancho thanked him profusely and, kissing his hand yet again, as well as the skirt of his armor, helped his master mount Rocinante. Then he climbed up on his donkey and began to follow along behind his lord, who kept up a rapid pace. Without either saying farewell or even speaking to the ladies in the coach, he headed directly into a nearby wood. Sancho followed him as well as his donkey could manage, but Rocinante was going so fast that, finding himself being left behind, he had to call to his master to wait for him. Don Quijote obliged him, pulling in Rocinante until his weary squire could catch up. And when he got there, Sancho said:

"It seems to me, señor, that we ought to take refuge in a church somewhere, because the man you were fighting got left in pretty bad shape and it wouldn't take much for them to notify the police and have us arrested, and by God, if that's what they do, before we get out of jail we'll be sweating up to our ears."

"Silence," said Don Quijote. "Where have you ever seen, or for that matter read of, a knight errant being summoned before a court of justice, no matter how many homicides he may have perpetrated?"

"I don't know anything about *hum-asides*," answered Sancho. "I've never even heard one. All I know is that the police are in charge of fighting in the fields. I leave all those other things alone."

"Then don't worry, my friend," replied Don Quijote, "for I will deliver you out of the hands of the Chaldeans,[1] not to mention the police. But tell me, by your life: have you ever seen a braver knight, anywhere in the entire known world? Have you ever read, in all the histories, of anyone who can, or ever could, charge into battle with such vigor? such spirit and endurance? such skill as a swordsman? or more dexterity at unhorsing an opponent?"

"The truth is," answered Sancho, "I've never read any histories at all, because I can't read or write. But what I'd be willing to bet is that I've never served a bolder master than your grace in all the days of my life, and I hope to God that boldness doesn't cost what I said it might cost. All I ask your grace is to let me take care of you, because there's a lot of blood coming out of that ear and I've got bandages right here and some white wax medicine in my saddlebags."

"We wouldn't need any of that," replied Don Quijote, "if I'd remembered to make a vial of that Saracen Fierabrás'[2] balm, one drop of which would save us time as well as medicine."

"What's a vial?" said Sancho Panza. "And what balm are you talking about?"

"A magical balm," answered Don Quijote, "the recipe for which I carry in my memory, because having it I have no need to fear death, nor contemplate dying, no matter what wounds I receive. So when I make it, and give it to you, all you'll have to do, for example, when you see that in some battle I've been cut in half (which happens quite often), is pick up the half that fell to the ground and very carefully — before the blood dries — put it back on top of the other half, which will still be sitting in the saddle, fitting it on very tightly and neatly. Then quickly give me just two drops of that balm and, as you'll see for yourself, I'll be as sound as an apple."

"If that's true," said Panza, "here and now I renounce all claim to that island you promised, because all I want, in payment for the fine service I've given you so freely, is for your grace to give me the recipe of this fantastic liquid. I think it'd be worth more than two dollars an ounce, anywhere, and there's nothing else I need to lead an honest, easy life. But I do need to know, first, if it costs a lot to make."

"For less than three dollars," answered Don Quijote, "you can make a gallon and a half."

"As I'm a sinner!" replied Sancho. "But then what're you waiting for to make it, your grace, and teach me, too?"

"Silence, my friend," declared Don Quijote. "I plan to teach you greater secrets, and to grant you greater gifts. But, for now, let's take care of this ear, which hurts more than I should like it to."

Sancho took the bandages and medicine out of his saddlebags. But when Don Quijote saw his shattered helmet, he nearly lost his mind. Placing his hand on his sword, and raising his eyes toward the heavens, he said:

"I hereby swear by the Creator of all things, and by the four Holy

---

1. An ancient people dwelling in Mesopotamia and mentioned several times in the Old Testament (Ezekiel, Daniel, and Jeremiah).
2. A Saracen giant in the Carolingian legends who, while sacking Rome, stole two containers of leftover embalming fluid used for Jesus.

Gospels which more fully testify to Him, that I will lead my life as did the great Marquis of Mantua, when he swore to avenge the death of his nephew Valdovinos, vowing from that day forth never to eat bread from a tablecloth, nor to lie with his wife, as well as some other matters which, though I don't at the moment recall them, I hereby include here by reference, until I take revenge on the man who has thus wronged me."

Hearing this, Sancho said:

"Now remember, your grace, señor Don Quijote, that if that knight does what you ordered him to do, and goes and presents himself before Lady Dulcinea del Toboso, he'll have completely discharged his debt to you, and unless he commits some other crime he doesn't deserve any other punishment."

"You have thought well and you have spoken well," replied Don Quijote, "and so I annul the oath, insofar as it refers to the taking of any new revenge. But I hereby declare and reaffirm my determination to conduct my life as I have stated, at least until I win by force of arms another similar helmet, of the same quality, belonging to some other knight. Nor should you think, Sancho, that I swear this lightly, for I have a model to follow: this same thing happened, down to the very last detail, in the matter of Mambrino's helmet, and it was Sacripante who paid so dearly for it."[3]

"My lord, send all your grace's oaths and vows to the devil," answered Sancho, "because they're bad for the health and they damage the conscience. If I'm wrong, just tell me: suppose it happens that we go along for a long time and don't bump into a man wearing a helmet — what are we going to do? Are you supposed to fulfill the oath, in spite of all those obstacles and inconveniences, like sleeping in your clothes and not sleeping in a civilized place, and all those thousands of other penances that crazy old fool, the Marquis of Mantua, put in his oath, which your grace now wants to re-validate? Just think about it, your grace: what if we don't meet any armed men on any of these roads, except muledrivers and cart drivers, who not only don't wear helmets, but probably never even heard the word mentioned in all the days of their lives."

"But there you deceive yourself," said Don Quijote, "because by the time we've been at this crossroads two hours we'll have seen more armed men than ever marched against Albraca, when they fought for the hand of Angélica the Beautiful."

"All right, then. Let it be," said Sancho, "and may it please God that we do well and the time comes for winning that island it's costing me so much to earn, and after that let me die."

"I've already told you, Sancho, not to worry about these things. If we don't win an island, there's always the kingdom of Denmark, or that of Soliadisa, both of which would suit you the way a ring fits on the finger, and even better, because you'd be on dry land, which would make you happier. But everything has its time, so let's see if you've got anything we can eat in those saddlebags, because we'll soon be hunting for a castle

---

3. Mambrino was a Moorish king in Boiardo's Italian epic *Orlando Innamorato*. His helmet, won by Rinaldo, allowed Rinaldo to vanquish the pagan Dardinel (not, as Don Quijote mentions, Sacripante). The theme of Mambrino's helmet will recur across *Don Quijote*.

where we can spend the night and make the balm I told you about —
for I swear to you, by God, my ear is really hurting me."

"I've got an onion, and a bit of cheese, and who knows how many crusts
of bread," said Sancho. "But bread crusts aren't proper for such a brave
knight as your grace."

"How little you understand!" answered Don Quijote. "I want you to
know, Sancho, that it is an honor for knights errant not to eat at a table,
and when they do eat that it should be whatever comes to hand. And you
would be clear about this if you had read as many books of knighthood
as I have, for though I have indeed read a great many, I have never in
any of them found any account of knights errant eating, unless it happened
that someone was giving them a sumptuous banquet: the rest of the time
they get by on next to nothing. And even though, plainly, we realize that
they could not manage without eating and doing all those other natural
things — since, really, they were simply men, just as we are — at the
same time we need to understand that, spending most of their lives in the
woods and fields, without a cook, their most usual meal would have to be
simple rustic food, exactly like what you just offered me. Thus, Sancho
my friend, don't be displeased by what pleases me. Don't try to make the
world all over again, or to change knight errantry."

"I beg your pardon, your grace," said Sancho, "but since I don't know
how to read or write, as I've already told you, I've never learned or even
thought about the rules of knighthood. From now on I'll make sure there
are all sorts of dried fruits in my saddlebags, just for your grace and because
you're a knight, and what I'll stock up on for myself, since I'm not one of
your profession, is chickens and more solid food like that."

"I haven't told you, Sancho," said Don Quijote, "that knights errant are
absolutely obliged to eat only these fruits of which you speak, but simply
that such would have to constitute most of their usual meals, augmented
by whatever herbs they could find in the fields, about which they were
well informed and as to which I too have some learning."

"Knowing about herbs," replied Sancho, "is a good thing, and I
wouldn't be surprised if, some day, we'll have use of that knowledge."

At which point he produced what, as he'd said, was still in his saddlebags, and the pair ate their lean, dry meal peacefully and companionably.
But since they much wanted to find their night's lodging, they didn't take
very long about it. They quickly remounted and hurried to locate an inhabited spot before nightfall, but the sun went down, taking with it their
hope of getting what they wanted, just as they arrived at some miserable
goatherds' huts, and so they made up their minds to stop there. And it was
as upsetting to Sancho, not getting to a town or a village, as it was pleasant
to his master to sleep under the open sky, for every time this happened to
him he thought himself more and more conclusively a true knight.

Chapter Eleven

— what happened between Don Quijote and the goatherds

The goatherds agreed most cheerfully to put him up for the night. After Sancho had taken care of Rocinante and the donkey (as well as under the circumstances he was able), he was drawn by the fragrance given off by certain pieces of salted goat flesh, boiling away in a big pot on the fire. He would have liked to determine, then and there, if they were ready to be transferred from pot to stomach, but didn't, because just then the goatherds took them off the fire and, spreading some sheepskins on the ground, quickly set up their rustic table and, with great good will, invited both master and servant to share their food with them. Six of them, who were in charge of that flock, sat down on the sheepskins, not without first inviting Don Quijote, in their best country manners, to take a seat on a small wooden feeding trough, which they turned upside down for him. Don Quijote took the seat, while Sancho, as cup bearer (the cup having been made from a ram's horn), remained standing. Seeing him still on his feet, his master said:

"In order to show you, Sancho, what virtue lies in knight errantry, and how well poised are those who practice it, in whatever walk of life they may be, to swiftly become the honored and respected of the world, I want you to come to my side and, in the company of these good people, to be seated, so that you may be seen as my equal — I who am your master and natural lord. I want you to eat from my plate and drink from my cup, for we can say of knight errantry as one says of love: it makes all things equal."

"A thousand thanks!" said Sancho. "But I've got to tell you, your grace, that when I have enough to eat I can eat just as well, and even better, on my feet and by myself, as sitting next to an emperor. What's more, to tell you the truth, I can eat a lot better in my own corner, without any fussing or show of respect, even if it's just an onion and crusts of bread, than if I get roast turkey at some other table where I have to eat slowly, and not drink too much, and keep wiping my fingers, and not sneeze or cough if I want to, and all sorts of other things that go along with privacy and freedom. So, my lord, let's trade these honors your grace wants to show me, being a practitioner and believer in knight errantry (since I'm your squire), for other things more comfortable and useful to me. So all of this, though I acknowledge it with gratitude, I also renounce from now to the end of the world."

"But in spite of all that, you've got to sit down here, because whoever humbles himself is magnified by God."

And taking him by the arm, Don Quijote made Sancho sit down beside him.

The goatherds understood none of this gibberish about squires and knights errant, but just ate and held their tongues, watching their guests who, with obvious determination and zest, were stuffing down chunks of meat by the fistful. When the meat was all gone, acorn-nuts were poured onto the sheepskins, in a great heap, and at the same time the shepherds set out half a cheese, harder than cement. Nor, all this time, had the wine-horn been lazing about, for it kept going around and around — sometimes full, sometimes empty, like the bucket of a waterwheel — so regularly that, of the pair of wineskins to be seen, one was emptied. After Don Quijote had nicely satisfied his stomach, he picked up a handful of acorns and, staring attentively down at them, spoke more or less as follows:

"Blessed the time, and blessed the centuries, called by the ancients the Golden Age[1] — and not because, then, the gold which we in our age of iron so value came to men's hands without effort, but because those who walked the earth in that time knew nothing of those two words, *thine* and *mine*. All things were shared, in that holy age; to obtain his daily bread, no one had to trouble himself any more than to lift his hand and gather his food from the sturdy oak trees, which freely rewarded them with their sweet, delicious fruit. On every hand there were clear fountains and flowing rivers, offering up their delightful, transparent waters. Wise and careful bees shaped their busy republic in the cleft rocks and the tree-hollows, offering the abundant harvest of their sweet work to whoever might come, freely and even-handedly. Out of sheer natural courtesy, the great cork trees peeled off their broad, airy skin, with which the first houses were roofed, held up by rough and ready posts, defenses against nothing more than the inclement heavens. Everyone was at peace, then, everyone friendly, everyone living in harmony; the heavy, curved plough had still not dared dig open or penetrate the sacred entrails of our original mother, and she, under no compulsion of any kind, offered the children who then possessed her, and from every part of her fertile, spacious bosom, whatever might feed, sustain, and delight them. Simple, beautiful country damsels, their hair braided or worn round their heads, roamed from valley to valley, in that time, and from hill to hill, wearing nothing more than might be necessary to decently cover what decency wants and has always wanted to cover, nor were they adorned with the sort of decorations women use today, who cherish Tyrian purple and all manner of extravagant silk fashions. In that time, women wore a few green burdock leaves or sprigs of twined ivy, and were every bit as magnificently decked out as, in this time, any of our court ladies, parading about in the strange, exotic creations revealed to them by idle curiosity. Then, they spoke their thoughts of love from the soul, simply and unpretentiously, exactly as they thought them, not searching for elaborate verbal circumlocutions to beautify them. Truth and simplicity were unmixed with fraud, deceit, and malice. Justice remained firm and sure, neither troubled nor offended against by patronage and self-interest, as today she is so grievously tainted and troubled and persecuted. Judges did not feel themselves, as they do today, entitled to be tyrants, because in that time there was nothing to judge, and no one to be judged. Damsels and decency both walked everywhere, as I have said, either alone or chaperoned, unafraid that impudence and lust might attempt to menace them; a ruined woman fell of her own will and desire. But now, in our era of abominations, none of them are safe, though we

---

1. The first of four ages delineated by Hesiod in his *Works and Days*: gold, silver, bronze, and iron. Don Quijote identifies his own heroic enterprise as taking place in an age of iron (I.20).

hide them, lock them away in some new labyrinth like that of Crete —
because even there, whether through cracks in the stone, or through the
very air, the amorous plague will make its way to them, achieve its object
in spite of all our sheltering devices, fervent in its cursed busyness. And
for their protection, as time went on and wickedness grew, the order of
knights errant was established, to defend damsels, shelter widows, and succor orphans and those in need. My goatherd brothers, I am one of that
order, on behalf of whom I thank you for the kind welcome and generous
reception accorded to me and to my squire. And nevertheless, though
natural law ordains that everyone alive be of assistance to knights errant,
the fact that you fulfilled your duty, in thus extending your kind hospitality,
without any knowledge thereof, makes me offer you my warmest gratitude,
with all the good will I can muster."

Our knight delivered himself of this copious oration — which could
just as well have been omitted — because the acorn-nuts they'd given
him made him remember the Golden Age, and so he was stirred to address
such a useless harangue to the goatherds, who never said a word, but
simply listened to him, enthralled and astounded. Sancho too remained
silent, eating acorns and making regular visits to the second wineskin,
which, to cool its contents, they had hung from a cork tree.

Don Quijote spent more time talking than in finishing his supper, and,
when the meal was done, one of the goatherds said:

"So your grace can say even more truthfully, señor knight errant, that
we entertained you cheerfully and without hesitation, we're going to make
you happy with the singing of one of our friends, who'll be here pretty
soon. This is a young fellow who knows what he's doing, and he's crazy
in love, and — above all — he knows how to read and write and he
can play a shepherd's fiddle just as well as you'd want."

He'd barely finished these words when they heard the shepherd's fiddle,
and soon they saw the man who was playing it, a young fellow of about
twenty-two, very good-looking. The others asked him if he'd had his supper
and, when he answered that he had, the goatherd who'd promised music
said to him:

"So now you can sing a little and make us happy, Antonio, because you
see this gentleman who's our guest: let him know that even in the mountains and woods there are people who understand music. We've told him
how talented you are, so now we want you to show how truthfully we've
spoken, so we ask you, please, to sit down and sing that song about your
love — the one your uncle, the priest, wrote for you, and everyone in
town liked so much."

"With pleasure," the boy replied.

And without their having to ask again, he seated himself on the fallen
trunk of an oak and, tuning his fiddle, soon began to sing most agreeably,
as follows:

> "Olalla, I know you adore me,
> Though your words have never said so,
> Nor even your lovely eyes,
> Those silent speakers of love.

For I know how wise you are,
And what you want me to know:
Love, when once it's known,
Can never again be sad.

But still it's true, Olalla,
You've sometimes shown me a soul
As hard as bronze, and a breast
White, but cold as rock.

But somewhere in all your frowns,
Your wonderfully modest coldness,
I see a glimmer of hope
Wavering there on the edge.

And my love leaps at the bait,
Though faith is all it owns,
Never discouraged by silence,
Never swollen by smiles.

If love, as I think, is grace,
What you should learn from love
Is that all my hopes will end
Exactly as I've always planned.

And if all that love does for love
Earns love a little kindness,
Some of the things I've done
Must have moved your heart.

For surely you've seen, and more
Than once (if you've wanted to look),
That even on Mondays I wear
Clothes that would honor the Sabbath.

Love and elegance walk
The very same road, so all
I want, whatever the day,
Is to look good in your eyes.

And the dances I've danced for you,
The songs I've written
And sung to you at all hours,
Even in the middle of the night.

Who could count the times
I've told your beauty, and praised it?
And every word was true,
Though some were unhappy to hear them.

Your friend Teresa Barrocal
Heard me describe you, and said:
'You think you're in love with an angel,
But you're really adoring an ape,

Decked out in trinkets and charms,
And that hair — you think it's hers?
All that make-believe beauty
Would catch Cupid himself.'

She was wrong, and she made me angry,
And her cousin came to defend her,
And gave me a challenge — and you know
The rest, what both of us did.

I couldn't hold you cheap:
No word I've said is untrue
Or intended to trap you, deceive you.
I've better things in mind:

· The ties the Church can tie
With silken lovers' knots.
So bow your head to the yoke,
And see how fast I follow.

If you won't, here's what I swear
By the holiest of all the saints:
I'll never come down from these mountains
Unless I come as a monk."

Which was how the goatherd ended his song, and although Don Quijote asked him to sing something else, he got no support from Sancho
Panza, who was more interested in sleeping than in hearing songs. And
so he said to his master:

"You'd better start thinking, your grace, where you're going to rest your
head tonight, because the work these good men have to do, the whole day
long, doesn't let them spend the night singing."

"I understand, Sancho," answered Don Quijote. "It isn't hard to figure
out: all those visits to the wineskin make sleep more attractive than music."

"It made its way down everyone's throats, may God be thanked," replied
Sancho.

"I don't deny it," answered Don Quijote. "Go to sleep wherever you
want to. Men of my profession are happier awake, and watchful, than
asleep. But just the same, Sancho, it would be good to have you tend this
ear of mine, which bothers me more than it ought to."

Sancho did as he was told, and one of the goatherds, seeing the wound,
told him not to worry, because he had a remedy that would cure it nicely.
So he pulled off some rosemary leaves, which grew plentifully right there,
chewed them up, then mixed them with a bit of salt and put the paste on
Don Quijote's ear, tying it on with a bandage and assuring them that no
other medicine would be needed, which was exactly the truth.

Chapter Twelve

— what a goatherd came and told them

Just then, one of the youngsters who fetched supplies from the village came over, saying:

"Do you know what happened in town, my friends?"

"How could we know?" one of the goatherds answered.

"In that case," the young man went on, "let me tell you. Our famous student-shepherd, Grisóstomo, died this morning, and they're whispering he died of love. It's that damned Marcela, Guillermo the Rich's daughter — the one who goes all over the place dressed like a shepherd."

"You mean Marcela?" one of the goatherds said.

"That's who I said," the youngster replied. "And the funny thing is that, in his will, he says he's to be buried out in the fields, as if he were a Moor, and right at the foot of Corktree Fountain Rock, because that's supposed to be the place where he saw her the first time — and they claim he used to say that, too. And there's other stuff in his will, things the bishops down there say can't be done, and shouldn't be done, because it's like the heathens. But his great friend, Ambrosio the student, who dressed like a shepherd, the way Grisóstomo did, says it all has to be done just the way it's written down, without leaving out a thing, and it's got the whole village in an uproar. But in the end, or so they say, it'll be done the way Ambrosio and all his shepherd friends want, and tomorrow they'll bury him just where I said, with a great big show. I think it's really going to be something to see, and me, I'm not going to miss it, even though I'm not supposed to go back down tomorrow."

"We'll all go," answered the goatherds, "and we'll draw lots to see who has to stay and take care of everybody's goats."

"You're right, Pedro," said someone, "but you won't have to do all that, because I'll take care of the whole business. And don't think I'm nice, or not interested. It's just that I stepped on a sharp stick, the other day, and I can't walk."

"In any case, we thank you," answered Pedro.

Don Quijote asked Pedro to tell him more about the dead man, and about the shepherd girl, to which Pedro responded that, as far as he knew, the man had been a rich gentleman's son, who'd lived in a nearby village, and that for many years he'd been a student at the University of Salamanca, and then come back home, with a reputation for both wisdom and scholarship.

"And they say he particularly understood all about the stars, and what they're doing up there in the sky, the sun and the moon, because he knew just when there'd be a clips."

"An *eclipse*, my friend, not a *clips*," said Don Quijote, "meaning an obscuring of those two great heavenly bodies."

But Pedro just went on with his story, not concerned with trivialities:

"And also, he could predict when it would be a good year or an arren one."

"You mean *barren*, my friend," said Don Quijote.

"*Barren, arren,*" answered Pedro. "You end up in the same place. But I can tell you it was his predictions, because they listened to him, that made his father and his friends very rich. They did whatever he told them to. He'd say: 'This year, plant barley, not wheat.' Or: 'This time, you can plant chickpeas and not barley. Next year we'll have a bumper olive crop, but for three years after that you won't get enough to squeeze out a drop of oil.'"

"That's called astrology," said Don Quijote.

"I don't know what it's called," replied Pedro, "but I do know he understood all this, and even more. Anyway, it wasn't more than a few months after he came from Salamanca when, one day, he surprised everyone by dressing like a shepherd, wearing a sheepskin coat and carrying a staff, and giving up those long scholar's robes he used to wear, and at the same time Ambrosio, his old friend, who'd been a student with him, started wearing shepherd's robes, too. I forgot to say that the dead man, Grisóstomo, was a great one for writing ballads and songs — so much so, that he wrote carols for Christmas Eve, and plays for Corpus Christi, and the young fellows from our village acted in them, and they all said they were really good. But when the village people all of a sudden saw these two scholars dressing like shepherds, they were really surprised, and couldn't figure out why they'd done such a strange thing. Now, about then Grisóstomo's father died, and he inherited a big estate, not just in land, plus a lot of cattle — I mean, all kinds, cows and horses and mules and sheep and goats — and a lot of cash, all of it his and nobody else's, and really, he deserved it, because he was a nice man and charitable and he was good to honest people, and just to look at him was like getting a blessing. Pretty soon everyone knew the only reason he'd changed his clothes was so he could wander around these wild places, chasing after that shepherd girl, Marcela — the one our youngster talked about, before — because poor Grisóstomo, may he rest in peace, fell in love with her. So now let me tell you, because you ought to know, just who this girl is, because maybe, or maybe not, you'd never in all your life hear anything like this, even if you lived as long as Sarna."

"You mean, *Sarah,*" replied Don Quijote, who couldn't stand how the goatherd mangled his words.

"Sarna [*sarna* = scabies] lives long enough," answered Pedro, "but señor, if you go on correcting every word I use, I can talk for a year and never get to the end."

"Excuse me, my friend," said Don Quijote. "I only interrupted you because there's such a big difference between *Sarna* and *Sarah*. But your reply is a very good one, since *Sarna* does live longer than *Sarah*, so go on with your story, and I won't contradict you any more about anything."

"Well, then, my very dear sir," said the goatherd, "let me say that there's a farmer in our village who's even richer than Grisóstomo's father, and his name is Guillermo, and besides his huge fortune God gave him a daughter, whose mother died the most respected woman anywhere around here. It seems to me I can see her right now, her face just like the sun on one side and the moon on the other, and on top of all that she was a hard worker and a friend to the poor, and I think this very minute her soul ought to be happy with God, up there in the other world. The loss of such a good wife killed her husband, Guillermo, leaving his daughter, Marcela — who was very young and very rich — in the custody of her uncle, a priest whose pulpit is in our village. The little girl grew so beautiful that we were all reminded of her mother, who'd been very beautiful, but it still seemed the daughter would outdo her. So it happened that, by the time she reached fourteen or fifteen, no one had ever seen her without blessing God for making her so lovely, and most of them were hopelessly in love with her. Very wisely, her uncle kept her carefully hidden away, but in spite of that her reputation grew, as much for her beauty as for her wealth, and it wasn't just among our own people but with everyone for miles and miles around, and some of the very best people, too, and her uncle kept being asked, and begged, and bothered to let them marry her. But he was a very upright man, a good Christian, and though he would have liked to have her married as soon as he could, because he saw she was of age, he didn't want to do it without her consent — and it wasn't that he had one eye on the profits he earned from her estate, while they waited for the girl to get married. And let me tell you, they said the same thing all over the village, praising their good priest — and I'm sure you know, sir knight, that in little villages like these everything is chewed over and people whisper about everything, so you'll realize, as I do, that a priest has to be powerfully good before his parishioners are forced to say good things about him, especially in villages."

"That's true," said Don Quijote, "but go on. This is an excellent tale, and you, my good Pedro, tell it in fine style, most gracefully."

"May I never run out of God's good grace, that's what matters. As for the rest of it, you'll understand that, although her uncle brought forward everyone who wanted to marry her, and told her all about each of them, asking her to pick and choose as she pleased, all she'd ever reply was that she didn't want to get married just then — and besides, since she was so young, she didn't think she was ready for the responsibilities of marriage. All of which seemed to him reasonable excuses, so her uncle stopped bothering her and waited for her to grow a little older, so she'd know how to choose a companion who'd suit her. He said, and quite rightly, that parents have no right to push their children into a way of life against their will. And then, when you couldn't have expected it, suddenly there was fickle Marcela, turned into a shepherdess. And no matter what her uncle and everyone else in town did to talk her out of it, she made up her mind to go out in the fields with the other shepherdesses and take care of her own flocks. And since now she was right out in public, and everyone could see her beauty, I couldn't even begin to tell you how many rich bachelors, gentlemen and farmers, got dressed up like Grisóstomo and went wooing out in those fields. One of them, as I told you, was our late lamented himself, and they say he'd gone beyond loving her: he absolutely adored her. But don't think just because she chose to be so independent, and live such a free life, with so little protection — or none at all — that she gave any sign, not even any appearance, that her virtue and chastity had suffered. No, she was so careful about her honor that, of all those who wooed and courted her, not one ever boasted, and in truth not one of them could have boasted, that she'd given him even the tiniest, smallest prospect of getting what he wanted. She doesn't avoid either the shepherds' company or their conversation, and she treats them courteously and pleasantly, but if she finds they have any designs on her, even if it's as honest and upright as matrimony, she hurls them away like a cannon. And yet, living this way, she does more damage, here on this earth, than if she carried the plague, because her pleasantness and her beauty draw the hearts of those who deal with her, and then they court her, and they love her, but her scorn and honesty drives them to despair, and they don't know what to say to her, except to call her cruel and ungrateful, and other things like that, which is in truth how she acts. And were you to stay around here, señor, some day you'd find these hills and valleys echoing with the moans of disappointed lovers. Not far from here there's a spot with almost two dozen tall beech trees, and there isn't one of them that hasn't had its smooth bark cut into, to write Marcela's name, and on some there's a crown just above, as if her lover wanted to proclaim that her beauty wears, and deserves, the crown of all womanhood in the world. Here, there's a shepherd sighing; over there, one's moaning; down there, you hear passionate love songs, and up there, hopeless dirges. There'll be someone spending the whole night, sitting at the foot of some tall oak tree or steep crag, never once closing his weeping eyes, lost, carried away by his thoughts: the sun finds him there, in the morning. And there'll be another, unable to ease his sighs, unable to find relief, lying stretched out on the burning sand, in the full heat of the most furious summer afternoon, sending his lament to the merciful heavens. And the beautiful Marcela triumphs over this one, and that one, and these, and those, forever free and confident. But everyone who knows her is just waiting to see where her arrogance ends, and who'll be the lucky man to get the job of trying to tame such a fierce temper, trying to enjoy such fantastic beauty. And since everything I've told you is the unquestionable truth, I'm sure what the youngster told us about Grisóstomo's death is equally true. So I advise you, señor, not to miss his funeral, tomorrow, which will really be something to see, because Grisóstomo has a lot of friends, and from here to where they've been told to bury him isn't more than a mile or two."

"I'll have to, indeed," said Don Quijote, "and let me thank you for the pleasure of hearing such a delightful story."

"Oh!" answered the goatherd. "But I don't know even half of what's happened to Marcela's lovers. Maybe tomorrow, on the way to the funeral, we'll bump into some shepherd who'll tell us everything. And for now, I think you'd better sleep indoors, because the night air might hurt your wound, even though the medicine I put on it is so good that you really don't need to worry about anything bad happening."

Sancho Panza, who could have sent all the goatherd's talk straight to the devil, said he thought his master ought to sleep in Pedro's hut. Which his master did, spending the whole night thinking of his lady Dulcinea, in imitation of Marcela's lovers. Sancho Panza settled down between Rocinante and his donkey, and slept — not like some rejected lover, but like a man who'd been kicked and beaten half to death.

Chapter Thirteen

*— in which we reach the end of Marcela the shepherdess' tale,
plus other matters*

Dawn had just begun to show itself in the east when five of the six goatherds rose and came to wake Don Quijote, telling him that if he still intended to go see Grisóstomo's extraordinary funeral, they would go with him. Wanting nothing better, Don Quijote rose and ordered Sancho to quickly saddle Rocinante and the donkey, which he did most obediently, and just as swiftly they all set out down the road. Nor had they gone even a mile when, at a crossroad, they saw six shepherds coming toward them, wearing black sheepskin jackets, their heads crowned with garlands of cypress and bitter oleander. Each of them carried a heavy walking stick, made of holly. And with them there came two handsomely dressed gentlemen, mounted on horses, accompanied by three servants on foot. As they met they exchanged courteous greetings and, when they asked one another where they were headed, they learned that they were all traveling to the funeral, so they rode on together.

Speaking to his comrade, one of the men on horseback said:

"It seems to me, Señor Vivaldo, that delaying our journey, in order to observe so celebrated a funeral, is time extremely well spent, for it cannot help but be a famous event, according to the wonderful things these shepherds have told us of the dead shepherd and also of the murderous shepherdess."

"Exactly how it seems to me," answered Vivaldo, "and I can tell you I'd be willing to delay us for four days, not just one, for the chance to see it."

Don Quijote asked them exactly what it was they had heard about Marcela and Grisóstomo. The traveler replied that, having risen early in the morning, they had met the six shepherds and, observing how sadly they were garbed, had asked them the reason, at which one of them had told them of the wonderful strangeness and beauty of a shepherdess named Marcela, and of all the many lovers who wooed her, and also of Grisóstomo's death and the funeral to which they were going. And then he told everything that Don Quijote had already heard from Pedro.

Then they left this topic and began another, the gentleman named Vivaldo inquiring of Don Quijote why he was journeying, armed as he was, through such a peaceful countryside. And Don Quijote answered:

"The practice of my profession neither allows nor permits that I journey in any other fashion. A life of ease, luxury, tranquillity — all these were concocted for pampered courtiers; while hard work, discomfort, and arms were designed and fashioned solely for those known to the world as knights errant, among whom, however unworthily, I number myself the least of all."

The moment they heard this, they all decided he was crazy, so in order to examine him more closely and find out precisely what sort of madness he was suffering from, Vivaldo asked what he considered knight errantry to mean.

"My dear sirs," answered Don Quijote, "haven't you read the annals and histories of England, which set out the celebrated deeds of King Arthur, who in our Spanish romances is always referred to as King Artús, of whom it is anciently told, and widely understood throughout the realm of Great Britain, that he did not die but, through the devices of enchantment, was transformed into a raven, and that, in time to come, he will return to win back and rule over his land and kingdom? — which is why, from that day to this, you will never find an Englishman killing a crow. Well then, in the days of this good king that famous order of knighthood, the Knights of the Round Table, was created, and it was also the time of the love affair between Sir Lancelot and Queen Guinevere, each and every detail of which, without the slightest omission, you may find recounted in the tales. And the go-between and confidante of that knight and his lady was the honored, honest Mistress Quintañona, from whom derives that well-known ballad, sung all over this Spain of ours, declaring that

> Never was there a knight
> Whom ladies served so well
> As noble Lancelot
> From England's vales and dells — [1]

going on to describe, sweetly and smoothly, Lancelot's love affairs and all his magnificent deeds. And ever since, descending as it were from hand to hand, it has been an order of knighthood spreading and expanding through many and various parts of the world, famous and distinguished for the deeds of the heroic Amadís of Gaul, together with all his sons and his sons' sons, to the fifth generation, as well as the brave Felixmarte of Hircania, and the noble Tirant the White, never praised as he deserves. And — virtually in our own time — we have seen, spoken to, and heard the brave, unconquerable knight, Belianís of Greece. So this, gentlemen, is what it means to be a knight errant, as it is the order of knighthood of which I spoke, and to which, as I have already noted, I have bound myself, sinner as I am. And to everything which the aforesaid knights professed, so I too profess. Accordingly, I journey through these lonely, unpopulated places seeking adventures, my soul intent on volunteering my arm and my very self against the greatest dangers fate can offer me, in the interests of aiding the weak and the needy."

Everything he said further persuaded the travelers that Don Quijote was out of his mind, as also it enabled them to understand the species of madness that had taken hold of him, which astonished them exactly as it did everyone who first made his acquaintance. And Vivaldo, a man of great discretion and lighthearted disposition, decided to give Don Quijote a chance to say even more foolish things, before they reached the site of the funeral, the better to keep the short stretch of road still supposed to be ahead of them from becoming burdensome. Accordingly, he said:

"It seems to me, sir knight errant, that your grace has chosen one of the

---

1. These are the opening lines of a famous Spanish ballad about the arrival of Lancelot at a hospitable castle. Don Quijote had earlier recited these lines in I.2 (page 20 of this text), substituting his own name for that of Lancelot. Given Lancelot's adulterous history, this is a most suggestive substitution.

most rigid professions on earth, for I doubt that even a Carthusian monk[2] is subjected to such austerity."

"To be a Carthusian is perhaps equally severe," answered our Don Quijote, "but I can't believe that, in this world, it's anything like as necessary. Because, to tell the truth, the soldier who does what his captain orders is not of less importance than the captain who gave him the orders. I mean, monks stay in their peace and tranquillity and pray to heaven on the earth's behalf, but soldiers and knights actually execute their prayers, protecting the world by the strength of our arms and the blades of our swords — not from under a roof but under the open sky, in the summer under the unbearable rays of the sun, and in the winter in the sharp-edged frost. What we are, therefore, is the ministers of God on this earth, the arms by which He brings His justice to pass. And since the business of war, and all that concerns war, cannot be carried on without sweat, and drudgery, and plain hard work, it is of course logical that those who practice such a profession labor longer and harder than those who, in calm peacefulness and repose, beg for God's favor toward those who cannot help themselves. Not that I mean to say, or even to think, that a knight errant outranks a cloistered monk. All I mean to deduce, based on what I myself endure, is that knight errantry is without question harder work, more wretched, as well as hungrier, thirstier, meaner, wearier, and more louse-ridden, for there is no doubt that knights errant experience a great deal of misfortune in the course of their lives. And if some, through the might of their arms, have risen to be emperors, by my faith they certainly paid for it by their blood and their sweat, and if, in ascending to such rank, they had not had magicians and enchanters to help them, they would surely have been cheated of their desires and swindled of their hopes."

"On that score I agree with you," said the traveler, "but the one thing about knights errant, among a whole list of other things, which particularly strikes me as wrong, is that at the start of some great and dangerous adventure, in the course of which they clearly may lose their lives, they never even think of placing themselves in God's hands, as every good Christian is supposed to do when in such peril. No, first they entreat their lady loves, and with just as much longing and devotion as if they were praying to the Lord. To my mind, this smacks of paganism."

"Sir," replied Don Quijote, "this is not something that can in any way be dispensed with, and indeed any knight errant who did anything else would be harshly criticized, for since ancient times it has been the rule and custom that the knight errant, as he enters upon any great feat of arms in his lady's presence, should gaze at her softly and lovingly, as if his eyes were begging for her favor and protection at this moment of critical uncertainty, and even if there is no one to hear him he is still obliged to whisper a few words, commending himself to her with all his heart — of which fact the histories of these knights offer us innumerable examples. Nor do we have to take this to mean that they forget to commend themselves to God, for they have time and opportunity for prayer as they go about their work."

---

2. The Carthusian order, founded in France in 1084, was an austere one: its monks lived in cells and never spoke to one another.

"And yet," answered the traveler, "I still have my misgivings, for I've read that, often, two knights errant will insult one another, and so, with one thing and another, they get angry, and wheel their horses around, and find some nice big chunk of field, and just like that, without more ado, they come rushing at each other — and while they're galloping they're commending themselves to their ladies. And it all ends with one of them falling backward off his horse, the other's lance having pierced him right through, and as for the other one, why, to keep from being thrown to the ground he has to hold on for dear life to his horse's mane. I'm afraid I don't see how the dead man could have had the chance to commend himself to God, while everything was happening so fast. They'd be a lot better off if, instead of wasting words on their ladies while they galloped into action, they used the opportunity in the way that, being Christians, they are obligated to do. And what's more, it's my personal opinion that it isn't every knight errant who has a lady he can commend himself to, because they're not all in love."

"That's impossible," replied Don Quijote. "I hereby affirm that there cannot be a knight errant who has no lady, because it is as fitting and natural for them to be in love as it is for the sky to have stars, and I know perfectly well I have never seen the history of a knight errant which shows him without love affairs, which is exactly the reason, too, that were they in fact without ladies, no one would believe they were legitimate knights, but just bastard ones, who hadn't gotten into the stronghold of knighthood through the doorway but by climbing over the wall like a highwayman or a thief."

"Nevertheless," said the traveler, "it seems to me, if my memory doesn't play me false, that I've read how Don Galaor, brother of the brave Amadís of Gaul, never had a particular lady to whom he could commend himself, though all the same he was not thought any the less of, and was a singularly brave and famous knight."

To which our Don Quijote answered:

"Sir, one swallow does not a summer make. Moreover, I happen to know that this knight was secretly very deeply in love, and as for his habit of falling in love with every beautiful woman who appeared, that was simply a natural disposition, which he could not restrain. But, in a word, it's long been settled that he did have one woman to whom he had surrendered his will, and to her he regularly commended himself, but only in secret, for he liked to think of himself as a very private knight."

"So if it's essential that every knight errant be in love," said the traveler, "I must suppose that your grace is too, since that's your profession. And unless your grace thinks as highly of privacy as did Don Galaor, let me entreat you, both in the name of this whole company and in my own, to tell us her name, homeland, rank, and her beauty. She ought to consider herself fortunate, should the whole world know she is loved and served by such a knight as you, sir, seem to be."

At this point Don Quijote heaved a great sigh, and said:

"I cannot say if my sweet enemy would be pleased or not, having the world know I serve her. All I can affirm, in response to what you so civilly ask of me, is that her name is Dulcinea; she comes from Toboso, a village in La Mancha; her rank must at least be that of a princess, since she is my queen and my lady; and her beauty is more than human, for in her one sees realized all the impossible, fantastical characteristics of beauty assigned to their ladies by the poets. Her hair is golden, her forehead an Elysian Field, her eyebrows heavenly arches, her eyes suns, her cheeks roses, her lips coral, pearls for her teeth, her neck alabaster, her breast marble, her hands ivory, her complexion like snow, and all of her that modesty conceals from human sight is, as I think and believe, such that a sensible mind can only praise, not compare."

"We should also like to know her ancestry and lineage," responded Vivaldo.

To which Don Quijote replied:

"She's not one of the ancient Roman Curtii, Gaii, or Scipios, or the modern Colonnas or Orsinos or a Moncada or Requesene of Catalonia, or in any way a Rebellas or Villanovas from Valencia, nor one of the Palafoxes, Nuzas, Rocabertis, Corellas, Lunas, Alagones, Urreas, Foces, or Gurreas of Aragón, or one of the Cerdas, Manriques, Mendozas, or Guzmán from Castile, or the Alencastros, Pallas, and Meneses of Portugal. But she's one of the Tobosos of La Mancha, a lineage which, though it may be modern, is well able to add a fine ingredient to the most illustrious families of future ages. Nor can anyone contradict me about this, except with the stipulation Cervino placed at the foot of the statue erected in honor of Orlando's arms, declaring:

Let no one move this
Who shrinks from combat with Roland."[3]

"My own family is the Cachopins of Laredo," answered the traveler, "but I don't dare set them against the Tobosos of La Mancha — though I must confess that, somehow or other, that name has never before this moment reached my ears."

"Never reached your ears!" replied Don Quijote.

All the others had been listening most attentively to this conversation, and even the goatherds and shepherds could tell that Don Quijote's mind was seriously out of balance. Only Sancho Panza thought his master was speaking the truth, having known him all his life and being aware of who he was. Indeed, the only thing he found it hard to credit was the beautiful Dulcinea del Toboso, because he'd never heard of any such name or any such princess, though he lived so close to Toboso.

They were going along, chatting like this, when they saw, through the pass between two tall mountains, twenty or so shepherds making their way down, all wearing black sheepskin jackets and crowned with garlands which, as they learned later, were some of yew and some of cypress. Six of them carried a bier, covered with all sorts of blossoms and bouquets.

Seeing this, one of the goatherds said:

"What you see, over there, are the men carrying Grisóstomo's bier, and he's having them bury him at the foot of that mountain."

So they hurried to get there, and arrived in time to see the bier set down

3. Ariosto, *Orlando Furioso* XXIV.57.

on the ground, and four of the shepherds, with sharp pick-axes, digging the grave alongside a craggy rock.

The parties greeted one another courteously, after which Don Quijote and those who had come with him began to examine the bier, which contained, all covered with flowers, the corpse of a man about thirty, dressed like a shepherd, and though he was dead he clearly had been, when alive, a handsome and charming fellow. Books and a great many documents were also scattered around the bier, some open, some closed. And everyone there — both those watching and those digging the grave — stayed wonderfully silent, until one of those who had carried the bier said to another:

"Be careful, Ambrosio, that this is the place Grisóstomo mentioned, since you want everything to be exactly as his will directed."

"This is it," replied Ambrosio. "How many times my miserable friend told me, right here, the story of his misfortune. It was here, he told me, that he had his first glimpse of that mortal enemy of the human race, and it was here, too, that he first declared his pure, passionate love, and here, finally, where Marcela that last time so scornfully, so bluntly put an end to it, and drove him to finish off the tragedy of his miserable life. And here, to commemorate so much misery, was where he wanted to be consigned to the bowels of eternal oblivion."

And turning to Don Quijote and the travelers, he went on:

"This body, gentlemen, at which you gaze with compassionate eyes, found its way here from a soul blessed by heaven with an infinite share of its riches. This is the body of Grisóstomo, unique in his talents, unparalleled in his gallantry, the very last word in refinement, perfect friendship reborn, magnificent beyond measure, profound but never pretentious, cheerful without vulgarity and, last but not least, leader in everything virtuous, as well as unmatched in everything unfortunate. He was deeply in love, and was loathed; he adored, and was disdained; he spoke his heart to a wild fiend, he asked for grace from a block of marble, he chased after the wind, he cried to the ears of silence, he paid court to ingratitude, which as his prize gave him to death, to be stolen away in the very middle of his earthly existence, consigned to such an end by a shepherdess he sought to immortalize, to keep alive in the memories of all men, as these documents which you see, here in his bier, could bear witness, had he not commanded me to surrender them to the flames, once his body had been given to the earth."

"You would treat them even more harshly and cruelly," said Vivaldo, "than would their owner himself, for it is neither reasonable nor right to obey the wishes of someone who commands you to do that which goes beyond all reason. Who would have thought it right had Augustus Caesar consented to the divine Virgil's dying wish, and allowed the *Aeneid* to perish? Accordingly, Señor Ambrosio, consign the body of your friend to the earth, but do not consign his writings to oblivion; what he ordered because he had been wronged, you ought not to execute out of imprudence. Rather, by preserving the life of those documents, which bear eternal witness to Marcela's cruelty, let them serve as an example to those who live in future times, to shun and flee from such dangers. Like all who have come here, I already know your impassioned and despairing friend's history, as we also know about your friendship, and how he came to die, and what he ordered be done when his life was ending, which deplorable tale reveals the extent of Marcela's cruelty, Grisóstomo's love, and the steadiness of your friendship, as it also displays their sure fate to the eyes of those who permit themselves a wild gallop down love's delirium. We first heard of Grisóstomo's death just last night, and that he would be buried here, and out of curiosity and pity we rode off our direct route, deciding to see with our own eyes what had so much moved us in the telling. In return for our compassion, and our desire to preserve at least that much, we beg of you, oh wise Ambrosio — at least, I for my part beg you — that you refrain from burning those documents and let me carry some of them away with me."

And then, without waiting for the shepherd to answer, he stretched out his hand and took some of the documents nearest him, seeing which Ambrosio said:

"Let me grant, sir, that you keep what you have taken. But please do not think, vainly, that I will spare the rest from the fire."

Wanting to see what was written there, Vivaldo proceeded to unfold one and saw that it was entitled *Song of Despair*. Hearing these words, Ambrosio said:

"This is the last thing the unlucky man ever wrote, and to show you, my dear sir, how all his misfortunes ended, read it out for all to hear, which you certainly ought to be able to do, in the time required to dig his grave."

"Most willingly," said Vivaldo.

Everyone else being agreeable, they set themselves in a circle around him and, with great care, he read them the following:

Chapter Fourteen

— *in which is set out the despairing shepherd's poem, along with other unexpected events*

GRISÓSTOMO'S SONG[1]

And since you wish, oh cruel one, the power
Of your hard heart proclaimed abroad, in every
Language known, in every nation of men,
I'll take a painful sound from Hell itself,
Change the very voice I sing with.
And then, in addition to my desire, which struggles
To tell my sadness and all the things you've done,
A terrible voice will be heard, proclaiming (for more

---

1. Written (and published) by Cervantes some years earlier, the poem is not always appropriate to the story of Grisóstomo and Marcela. Further, as Cervantes himself said, poetry was *el don que no quiso darme el cielo*, "the gift/talent that heaven did not wish to give me" [*Translator's Note*].

Reliable torment) bits and pieces of broken
Guts, spilled in love's miserable war.
So listen, lend me a pair of civil ears —
Not for the music, but only the ghastly noises
Welling up from my bitter breast, propelled
By an unavoidable madness, sounds of pleasures
Forever lost, and your spite and displeasures.

The lion's roar, the fearful howl of savage
Wolves, the hideous hissing of scaly, wriggling
Snakes, the terrifying screams of dark
And shapeless monsters, the fortune-telling croak
Of hooded owls, and all the rattling clatter
Of the wind, fight with the ocean's tossing waves;
The beaten bull can never hold back a final
Bellow, the turtledove deprived of its mate
Will always coo its sorrow; the eagle owl,
Envied its beautiful eyes, sings sad songs,
Which like the endless weeping heard from Hell
Come pouring out of every sorrowful soul,
Blended with a blast of such a sound
That all the senses swim, and sink, and drown —
All this, because describing my heart's sorrow
Compels my pen to play an unknown role.

Let the sands of Father Tagus' river, the olives
Along the famous Guadalquivir, never
Hear even an echo of such sad confusion:
Let my harsh, unbearable sorrows be scattered
Across high cliffs and down endless canyons,
Sung in dead tongues but living words;
Or through gloomy valleys, or hidden beaches,
Places where human law never reaches,
Or where the sun never shows its light,
Or down among those hordes of savage beasts
Spawned and fed on the flattened plains of Libya —
Let all those empty, barren lands ring
With wild echoes of my wrongs, forever changing,
Clanging harsh, clanging severe, as you
Have tolled my fate, and cut my days — let the brutal
News be carried around the width of the world.

Disdain can kill, and patience be smothered by suspicion —
And neither truth nor falsehood matters a bit.
But jealousy kills a good deal faster, and absence
Prolonged and prolonged deranges life itself;
Even strong belief in coming good fortune
Wilts and dies at the fear of being forgotten.
And death is certain, inevitable, always waiting.
But some incredible magic keeps me alive,
Though jealous, and absent, and fiercely disdained, convinced
Of suspicions I know will bring me death, so sure

Of being forgotten that I burn still more desperately.
And all surrounded with torment, I see not even
A shadow of a shadow of hope — and worse: my heart's
So deeply desperate I never even look,
But like a hopeless penitent I swear what punishes
Best is best to love, and that alone.

Can hope and fear exist together? Could it
Be true — and would it be useful? Fear is forever
More likely: more things bring it blazing to life.
Tell me: if I stand staring directly at jealousy's
Brutal face, should I close my eyes, though I see
The thousand open wounds it has sliced in my soul?
And who would not throw open as wide as hell
The doors of distrust, seeing disdain out
In the open, and every suspicion — oh, what a bitter
Shift! — fully confirmed, and truth turned to lies?
Oh Jealousy, lend me your sharpest blade,
You fiercest tyrant in all the kingdom of love!
And you, Disdain, give me a twisted rope!
But oh, alas, the very worst is this:
Beaten by suffering, I lose all sense of you.

And so I'll die. And knowing that nothing good
Can happen, either in life or death, still
I'll always love you: at least my love will live.
Listen: the wisest man is he who loves
The best, and the freest soul confesses the ancient
Tyranny of love. But listen, too, to this:
My eternal enemy's soul glows like her body,
And I am forgotten because I'm not worth remembering,
And love's dominion is peaceful, is just, precisely
Because of all the wrongs we earn at its hands.
And with this belief, and a hangman's noose,
Hurrying this miserable life to its end,
As your disdain has forced me to do,
I'll offer the wind both body and soul,
Expecting no laurels or palms of future bliss.

You: if I leave this weary life I've come
To loathe, what makes me ready are all the twisted
Wrongs you've done me, all the endless injustice,
Which everyone knows, and everyone's seen. See
For yourself this bleeding heart, and the wounds you gave it,
And how I offer it up, a happy victim
To this your terror, so if your beautiful eyes
Are moved to roil their perfect clarity
Because of my death, don't spoil perfection for me,
Don't atone on my behalf for having
Slaughtered and robbed and stripped my bleeding soul.
No, just laugh as I meet my fate, and make
My death a banquet, a feast for your happy heart.

— But what a fool I am, telling you this,
Knowing as I do that all your fame and glory
Consists in unwinding my life and bringing me death.

Enough, it's time. Let Tantalus carry his burning
Thirst up from the depths of Hell; let Sisyphus
Come, bearing the horrible weight of his stone;
Let Tityus bring his liver-eating vulture,
And Ixion roll on his wheel to all eternity,
And Danus' daughters fill bottomless casks with water,
And all of them shift their death-dealing sorrows into
My breast, and then intone, in bass-like moans
— Assuming a heart so desperate ever deserves them —
Funereal chants, mournful, anguished, over
A corpse unworthy of wrapping in a holy shroud.
Let Cerberus, three-headed dog and guardian of the gate,
With all Hell's monsters, fantastic ancient horrors,
Sing sorrow's fugal counterpoint, and this,
To me, is the perfect pageant for all who die
Of love, exactly the splendor lovers deserve.[2]

Oh desperate song, never complain when once
You lose this unfortunate friend who gave you words,
But realize, instead, that his miserable pain gave you
Life, his sorrow increased your joy, and even
Deep in the tomb sadness belongs to him.

To those who heard it, Grisóstomo's song seemed beautifully done, though Vivaldo said it didn't seem to fit with what he'd heard of Marcela's modesty and virtue, since in these verses Grisóstomo complained of jealousy, suspicion, and the pangs of separation, all of which was unfair to the fine reputation she had in such matters. Ambrosio answered, speaking as someone intimately familiar with his friend's innermost thoughts:

"To satisfy any such qualms, sir, I must tell you that when this miserable man wrote the poem it was he who'd been separated from Marcela — a separation he chose for himself, to see if absence might affect him as it usually does. And since everything worries the absent lover and makes him fearful, Grisóstomo was just as plagued by imaginary jealousies and suspicions as if they'd been real. So Marcela's reputation for virtue, so generally acknowledged, must stand unshaken: even envy neither can nor should find fault with her, no matter how cruel she may be, and prouder than necessary, and a great deal too disdainful."

"You're right," answered Vivaldo.

Then, as he was about to read aloud yet another of the documents he'd saved from the fire, a wondrous vision — and a vision was exactly what it seemed — suddenly rose up and cut him off, and it was the shepherdess Marcela, standing on top of the rock that towered over the grave, and so beautiful that she outdid her own reputation. Those who had never before

---

2. Here concludes a catalogue of mythological figures all tortured by the gods: Tantalus, with fruit and water forever out of reach; Sisyphus, having always to push a stone uphill; Tityus, with his regenerating liver eaten daily by vultures; and Ixion, eternally bound to a turning wheel.

seen her stared in silent amazement, and those who knew her beauty well were no less astonished than if they'd been seeing her for the first time. But when Ambrosio saw her, he cried out, with obvious indignation:

"Perhaps you've come, oh savage stone monument of these mountains, to see if your presence makes blood flow from the wounds of this miserable corpse, whose life was stolen by your cruelty? Or have you come to gloat over the cruel deeds you've wrought, or to gaze down from those heights, like some new and pitiless Nero, at the sight of his Rome burning, or to trample this miserable corpse, like Tarquin's ungrateful daughter?[3] Tell us, here and now, why you've come or what you want — for since I know that Grisóstomo, while he was alive, was always ready to obey you, I will see to it that everyone here, calling themselves his friends, will obey you now that he is dead."

"I come, O Ambrosio," replied Marcela, "for none of the reasons you give, but only for myself, and to explain how utterly unreasonable it is to blame me for everyone's pain and for Grisóstomo's death. So I ask all of you to give me your attention: it won't take long, nor will it waste many words, to convince wise men of the truth. Heaven, you say, has made me beautiful — so very beautiful that you are moved, unable to help yourselves, to love me, and because of the love you show me I am obliged, you say, as also you desire, to love you. I know, by the natural understanding God granted me, that everything beautiful is lovable, but I do not understand how, because it is loved, that which is loved for its beauty is obliged to love whoever loves it. Further: it can happen that he who loves that which is beautiful is himself ugly, and since that which is ugly ought to be hated, it's very wrong of him to say: 'I love you for your beauty; you must therefore love me, even though I'm ugly.'

"But suppose there is no difference and both are equally beautiful: that's no reason for desire to be equal, for everything beautiful does not inspire love. Some beauty is good to see, but does not give rise to affection; and if everything beautiful *did* inspire love, desire would become confused and lose its way, unable to understand where it was going, since an infinity of things beautiful makes for an infinity of desires. And according to what I have heard, true love is not divisible, and must be voluntary, not forced. This being the case, as I believe it is, why do you want my desire to be forced, and for no other reason than that you say you're deeply in love with me? And tell me: if Heaven had made me ugly instead of beautiful, would it be right for me to complain about you, because you did not love me? What's more, please realize I did not choose to be beautiful: whatever I may have, Heaven gave me as an act of grace, not because I either asked for or chose it. And just as the viper should not be blamed for its venom, which has been given it by nature, even though it kills with that venom, so too I should not be reproached for my beauty, for beauty in a good woman is like a remote fire, or a sharp sword, neither of which will burn or cut anyone who stays away from it. Honor and indeed all the virtues

3. That the emperor Nero (A.D. 37–68) fiddled while Rome burned was a topos. And that Tullia desecrated the body of the terrible despot Tarquin (534–510 B.C.) was the subject of a popular ballad.

grace the soul and, whatever else the body may be, without them it cannot claim to be beautiful. And if modesty is one of the virtues that most adorn both body and soul, why does she who is loved for her beauty have to lose her modesty, in order to reward the desire of a man who, just for his own pleasure, strives as hard and as forcefully as he can to make her lose it? I was born free, and I chose the solitude of the fields so I could live free. I find my friends among the trees in these mountains; the clear waters of these streams are my mirrors; I share my thoughts with the trees and the streams, as I share my beauty with them. I am a remote fire, a sword seen from far off. Anyone who has been enchanted by the sight of me has been stripped of all illusions by my words. And if hope continues to feed desire, I have given no hope to Grisóstomo or anyone else — to none of them — so you might better blame their stubbornness than any cruelty of mine for their deaths. And if I am charged that their thoughts were honorable, so that I ought to have repaid them, let me say that when, here in this same place where now you've dug his grave, he told me how virtuous were his aspirations, I told him I meant to live forever alone, and that only the earth would ever possess the fruits of either my mind or my body, so that if he, in spite of all this straightforward explanation, chose to insist, against all reasonable expectations, and to sail right against the wind, is there any wonder that he drowned out in the deepest waters of his own folly? Had I dallied with him, I'd have been a deceiver; had I made him happy, I'd have betrayed what I myself most wanted and strove for. I told him the truth, and he persisted; he fell into despair, but I never hated him. Now think! Can it be right that his sorrow is laid at my door? If you've been deceived, complain; if you haven't had what was promised you, plunge yourself into despair; if you've been enticed, tell your confessor; if I've accepted you, go boast about it. But let no one call me cruel, or a murderess, to whom I've promised nothing, nor ever deceived, nor enticed, nor said yes to. To this very moment, Heaven has not chosen love as my destiny: it's ridiculous to think I would choose it for myself.

"May this public declaration be sufficient for each and every one who courts me on his own behalf, and let it be understood from this day on that, if anyone dies for me, he dies neither of jealousy nor of misfortune, for when you love no one you cannot make anyone jealous. Those who have been told the truth should not be taken for those who have been scorned. He who calls me savage, and a stone monument, should shun me as something dangerous and evil; he who calls me ungrateful should not woo me; if I'm fickle, stay away from me; if I'm cruel, don't come after me; because this savage beast, this stone monument, this ungrateful wretch, this cruel and fickle woman will neither seek them out, nor woo them, nor know them, nor chase after them in any way whatever. If Grisóstomo's impatience and reckless longing killed him, why blame my modest and chaste behavior? If I preserve my purity, living with my friends the trees, why should he want me to lose it in the company of men? You all know that I am rich in my own right and not greedy for what anyone else might have; I live freely, and have no desire to let anyone rule me; I neither love nor hate anyone. I neither entice this man nor court that one; I neither mock this man, nor dally with someone else. Chaste conversation with the shepherdesses I meet, and taking care of my goats, are all the diversions I need. All my desires have their boundaries here in these mountains, and if they ever do go forth, it's only to contemplate the sky's beauty, and the steps the soul takes as it proceeds toward its primal home."

Having said this, and wishing to hear no reply, she turned her back on them and went into the most heavily wooded part of a nearby grove, leaving all who were there dazed, as much by her wisdom as by her beauty. But some — those who had been wounded by the mighty arrows of her beautiful eyes — showed signs of wanting to follow after her, paying no attention to the plain truths they had heard. Noticing this, and thinking it a proper occasion to act chivalrously and assist a maiden who needed help, Don Quijote set his hand on the hilt of his sword and cried, in a loud, clear voice:

"Let no one, no matter what his rank or state, dare to follow after the beautiful Marcela, under penalty of incurring my implacable wrath. She has demonstrated, with clear and sufficient arguments, how little responsibility she bears for Grisóstomo's death, and how utterly unlikely it is that she will yield to the desires of any of her lovers, for which reason it is right that, instead of being followed and persecuted, she be honored and appreciated by all good men in this world, having shown herself to be the only woman alive who can hold to such impeccable modesty."

Whether it was because of Don Quijote's threats, or because Ambrosio told them to remain faithful to their good friend's last wishes, none of the shepherds moved or left that spot until, having finished digging the grave and then burned Grisóstomo's papers, they laid the corpse to rest, not without much weeping among the onlookers. They covered the grave with a great stone, which would stay there until a tombstone had been finished, on which Ambrosio told them he meant to have inscribed an epitaph that would read as follows:

> A lover's cold corpse
> Lies here in this grave,
> A shepherd self-made
> Who died of disdain.
> A beautiful ingrate
> Froze him to death,
> Enlarging the reign
> Of Love's fiery breath.

Then they scattered flowers and branches on top of the grave and, with everyone offering condolences to Ambrosio, they took their leave. So too did Vivaldo and his companion, and Don Quijote said farewell to his hosts and to the travelers, who asked him to come to Seville with them, it being such a splendid place for finding adventures, each street and every corner offering up adventures more abundantly than anywhere else. Don Quijote thanked them for the suggestion and for the kind interest they exhibited, but said that for now he neither wanted nor ought to go to Seville, until he had purged these mountains of all their wicked bandits — with which, according to all reports, they fairly teemed. Seeing how fixed were his intentions, the travelers did not urge him any farther but, saying farewell once more, they left him and went on their way, though as they rode they talked of both the story of Marcela and Grisóstomo and of Don Quijote's madness. As for our knight, he made up his mind to search out the shepherdess Marcela and offer to do whatever he might to assist her. But nothing happened as he thought it would, according to the tale told in this truthful history, which here finishes its second part.

Part Three

Chapter Fifteen

*— wherein is narrated the unfortunate adventure Don Quijote ran into
when he fell in with some heartless Yangüeses*

The wise Sidi Hamid Benengeli tells us that, as soon as Don Quijote
took leave of his hosts, and of all those he'd encountered at the shepherd
Grisóstomo's funeral, he and his squire went into the same wood where,
as they'd seen, the shepherdess Marcela had gone. After proceeding for
more than two hours, searching everywhere but unable to find her, they
stopped at a meadow full of fresh grass, through which ran a gentle, fresh
stream, so very pleasant that it quickly convinced them to stay in that place
all through the afternoon siesta, for the day was growing exceedingly hot.

Don Quijote and Sancho dismounted and left the donkey and Rocinante free to graze on the thick green grass. They turned the saddlebags
inside out and, without any sort of ceremony, sat down together, master
and servant, peaceful and companionable, to eat whatever they'd been able
to find.

Sancho hadn't bothered to hobble Rocinante, confident that the horse
was so tame, and so little inclined to prancing about, that all the mares
in all the pastures of Córdoba couldn't make him do anything troublesome. But it was their luck, and the devil's doing — for Satan isn't always
asleep — that a herd of Galician ponies, who belonged to some muledrivers from Yanguas, came grazing along that valley. It was the muledrivers'
custom to take their siesta, along with their animals, in places where there
was good grass and plenty of water, and the spot Don Quijote had found
was exactly suited to their purpose.

So then it happened that Rocinante decided to have some fun with the
lady ponies. As soon as he sniffed them, he abandoned his usual staid ways
and, never asking his master for permission, broke into a frisky little trot
and began to let them know what he wanted. But since they were more
interested in eating than in other matters, or so it seemed, they gave him
such a welcome with their hooves and their teeth that, pretty soon, his
saddle girths were broken and he was left wearing neither a saddle nor
anything else. But what he felt even worse about was that the muledrivers,
seeing him trying to rape their mares, came running over with cudgels,
and beat him so badly that they stretched him out, bleeding, on the
ground.

By now Don Quijote and Sancho, who'd seen Rocinante being
thrashed, came running up, panting, and Don Quijote said to his squire:

"As far as I can see, Sancho, these aren't knights but vulgar people of a low sort. I mention this because you can perfectly properly help me take revenge for the affront they've given Rocinante, right in front of our eyes."

"What the devil kind of revenge are we going to take?" answered Sancho, "when there are more than twenty of them, and no more than two of us — and maybe we're only one and a half?"

"I'm worth a hundred," replied Don Quijote.

And without any more talk, he took hold of his sword and attacked the muledrivers, and Sancho Panza joined him, led on and excited by his master's example. And to start with, Don Quijote gave one of them such a stroke that he sliced open a leather coat the fellow was wearing, and a good part of his shoulder, too.

But the muledrivers, seeing they were being abused by only two men, while they themselves were far more numerous, took up their cudgels and, surrounding Don Quijote and Sancho, began to whack away at them, eagerly and passionately. The second blow, truth to tell, laid Sancho on the ground, and then the same thing happened to his master, all of Don Quijote's skill and courage proving worthless. His destiny was to fall at Rocinante's feet — for the horse was still lying there, which only goes to show what a pounding you can get from cudgels wielded by angry, rustic hands.

Seeing how much damage they'd done, the muledrivers rounded up their herd just as fast as they could and went on their way, leaving our two adventurers in bad shape and looking even worse.

The first to regain consciousness was Sancho Panza and, finding himself lying near his lord, he said, in a quavering and feeble voice:

"Señor Don Quijote! Ah, señor Don Quijote!"

"What do you want, brother Sancho?" answered Don Quijote in the same sad, weak tones.

"What I'd like, if possible," replied Sancho Panza, "is for your grace to give me two drops of that Folly Blas Balm, if you've got it handy. Maybe it would work for broken bones the way it does for wounds."

"Ah, if I only had it here, unlucky me, what else would we need?" answered Don Quijote. "But I swear to you, Sancho Panza, by my faith as a knight errant, before another two days go by — if fortune doesn't ordain differently — I intend to have it in my possession, unless I've lost every shred of my skill."

"So how long do you think it will be, your grace, before we can move our legs?" replied Sancho Panza.

"All I can say," said our weary knight, "is that I have no idea how long it's going to take. But the whole thing's my fault, for I should never have drawn my sword against men who were not, like me, ordained as knights — which is why, I believe, as a penalty for having disobeyed the laws of knighthood, the god of battles has allowed me to incur this chastisement. Which is why, Sancho Panza, you must pay close attention to what I'm about to tell you, because it's highly significant for our mutual health. And that is, when you see lowborn people like this trying to hurt us, don't wait for me to draw my sword against them, because I won't. But just take your own sword and beat them as much as you like. And if any knights should come to their help and defense, don't worry, I'll know how to stop them for you, and hit them with all my strength — and you've seen by a thousand signals and experiences the power of this my strong arm."

That was how arrogant the poor gentleman had become, since his defeat of the brave Basque. But his master's advice didn't sit well with Sancho Panza, who felt obliged to reply, saying:

"Señor, I'm a peaceful man, gentle, calm, able to overlook any kind of insult because I have a wife and children to feed and raise. So let your grace be told, also, since it's not my place to give orders, that there's no way I'm going to draw my sword, either against a farmer or a knight, and from right now until I appear before God Himself, I hereby pardon whatever injuries have been or are being or will be done to me, whether by anyone high or low, rich or poor, gentleman or commoner, without exception for any rank or status of any sort."

Hearing which, his master replied:

"I could wish I had enough breath to speak a little more readily, and the pain in my ribs would ease up a bit, so I could explain to you, Panza, the mistake you're making. Come closer, you sinner: suppose the winds of fortune, blowing so hard against us at the moment, turn in our favor and puff out the sails of desire, and we're blown safely right into the harbor of one of those islands I promised you, what would happen to you if I conquered it and made you its ruler? Wouldn't you make it all impossible, not being a knight and not wanting to be one, or to show your bravery or any interest in revenging insults and injuries, or in defending your domains? You've got to understand that in newly conquered realms and provinces the natives are never so calm and peaceful, or so devoted to their new lord, that they'll be afraid of making yet another change and once again turning matters on their head — as they say, seeing if they can test their luck — and so the new ruler has to have a good sense for governance and the courage to be aggressive and defend himself, no matter what befalls."

"As for what just now fell on us," answered Sancho, "I could wish I'd had all that sense and bravery your grace is talking about. But I swear, by my faith as a poor man, I'm more in the mood for mustard plasters than conversation. Just you see if you can get up, your grace, and let's try to help Rocinante, even though he doesn't deserve it, since he was the real reason we're lying here like this. I'd never have thought it of Rocinante; I took him for someone chaste and peaceful, like me. So it's true, after all, that it takes a long time to get to know someone, and you can't count on anything, in this life of ours. Who would have thought, after all the heavy whacking your grace gave that miserable knight errant, such a wild storm of blows would come rushing down on our shoulders, following right on their heels?"

"All the same, Sancho," replied Don Quijote, "your shoulders ought to be used to such storms. But mine, clearly, brought up to bear fine hollands and silks, must feel the pain of this roughness far more keenly. And if I did not think — but why do I say 'think'? If I did not know with absolute certainty that all these inconveniences are inevitable counterparts of the bearing of arms, I'd let myself die on this spot, of pure frustration."

To which his squire answered:

"Your grace, if these misfortunes are what you harvest, when you practice knighthood, please tell me if they go right on happening, or if they
take place only at limited times, because it seems to me that two harvests
like this will leave us useless for the third, if God in his infinite mercy
doesn't help us."

"You must know, my friend Sancho," replied Don Quijote, "that the
life of a knight errant is subject to a thousand perils and calamities, but
that the possibility of a knight errant's becoming a king or an emperor is
exactly as great, neither larger nor smaller — as the experience of many
knights of all sorts has well demonstrated, with which histories I am thoroughly familiar. And I could tell you, here and now, if the pain would
permit me, of some who by sheer force of arms have ascended to the high
ranks of which I have previously spoken, and that these same knights, both
before and after, found themselves in all manner of calamities and misfortunes. For example, the brave Amadís of Gaul once found himself in
the power of his mortal enemy, Arcalaus the magician, and it is stated as
a fact that, while he was imprisoned and tied to a pillar in the courtyard,
he was given more than two hundred lashes with the reins of the magician's horse. And further, there is an anonymous writer, one of no small
standing and reputation, who records that, when the Knight of Phoebus
was caught by a certain trapdoor that opened under his feet, in a certain
castle, he found himself fallen into a deep chasm under the earth, bound
hand and foot, and there they gave him one of those enemas, as they're
called, of ice-water and sand, which came close to finishing him off, and
if he hadn't been helped to escape from that sore affliction, by a great sage
who was his friend, it would have gone very badly with the poor knight.
And, like such noble folk, well may I experience these things, for indeed
what they went through was worse than what we are undergoing now. And
what I should like you to understand, Sancho, is that wounds received
from implements that simply happen to be in people's hands are in no
sense humiliating, and this is expressly stipulated in the laws of dueling.
If for example a shoemaker hits a man with the last he's been holding in
his hand, we cannot say, even though the last is made out of wood, that
the man who's been hit has really been beaten. I say this so you will not
think, just because we have been beaten during this quarrel, that we have
been humiliated, since the weapons carried by those men, and with which
they pounded us, were simply their clubs, and none of them, so far as I
can recall, had rapiers, swords, or daggers."

"I had no chance," replied Sancho, "to see that much, because as soon
as I grabbed for my pigsticker they began to really let me have it so hot
and heavy that my eyes couldn't see, and my legs went limp, stretching
me out to rest right where I'm lying now, and where I haven't been worrying whether or not those clubs humiliated me, but just about the pain
caused me by their blows, which made as much of an impression on my
memory as they did on my shoulders."

"In spite of which, brother Panza," answered Don Quijote, "you surely
know that there is no memory which time does not wear away, nor any
pain that death does not remove."

"But could there be a worse misfortune," replied Panza, "than something that has to wait for time to take it away and for death to finish it off? If we'd just taken a tumble that a couple of mustard plasters could cure, it wouldn't be so bad, but I'm beginning to think all the plasters in a hospital might not be enough to put us in good shape."

"Enough of that, Sancho. Summon strength out of weakness," responded Don Quijote, "as I too will do, and we'll find out how Rocinante is, for it seems to me the poor fellow has borne no small share of this mishap."

"There wouldn't be anything surprising about that," answered Sancho, "seeing as how he's such a fine knight errant. What surprises me is that my donkey is still grazing as he pleases, and doesn't even have to pay court costs, while we come out of it paying with our ribs."

"In every disaster," said Don Quijote, "fortune always leaves a door ajar, to offer some relief. And I say that because, now, this little animal will be able to take Rocinante's place, carrying me away from here, to some castle where my wounds may be healed. Nor shall I consider such a mount dishonorable, for I remember having read how splendid old Silenus, tutor to that laughing god, Bacchus, rode into the city of a hundred gates happily mounted on a singularly handsome donkey."

"It could be true that he rode like that, as your grace says," replied Sancho, "but there's a big difference between riding on a donkey and being slung across him like a sack of garbage."

To which Don Quijote replied:

"Wounds received in battle don't deprive you of honor, they give it. And so, friend Panza, let me hear no more answers but, as I've told you, stand up as best you can and place me, however you think best, up on your donkey, and let us leave this place before night falls and catches us in this deserted place."

"But," said Panza, "I've heard your grace say it's fine for knights errant to sleep in wildernesses and deserts most of the year, and they think it's great good luck."

"That," said Don Quijote, "is when they can't do any better, or when they're in love, and then it's so very true, indeed, that there have been knights who have remained up on cliffs, when the sun shines, and when it's dark, and in all the inclemencies of the weather, for two years, and without their ladies even knowing they were there. And one such was Amadís, when, calling himself Beltenebros, he took up lodgings on Barren Mountain, either for eight years or eight months — I'm not very good at counting. Anyway, he was up there as a penitent, for doing something — I don't know what — that bothered Lady Oriana. But let's leave all that, Sancho, and be done with it, before something terrible happens to the donkey, as it did to Rocinante."

"Now that would really be the end," said Sancho.

And emitting thirty moans, followed by sixty sighs, and a hundred and twenty curses and oaths, all directed at whoever was responsible for bringing them there, he got on his feet, standing in the middle of the road, bent over like a Turkish longbow, unable to get himself straightened out, and managed, in spite of all that, to saddle his donkey, who'd been pleasantly led astray by all the incredible freedom he'd enjoyed that day. And then he got Rocinante up on his legs and, if the horse had had a tongue to complain with, you can be very sure that neither Sancho nor his master would have been able to outdo him.

Finally, Sancho hoisted Don Quijote onto the donkey, tied Rocinante behind so he would follow them, single-file, then took the donkey by the halter and started off, heading more or less in the direction he hoped would lead them to the highway. And after only a mile or two Fortune, guiding them from good to better, brought them to the road, on which there turned out to be an inn, which to Don Quijote's delight, and Sancho's regret, his master took for a castle. Sancho argued stubbornly that it was an inn, and his master insisted equally stubbornly that no, it was a castle, and the debate lasted so long that, before it was ended, they had in fact reached the place, and without any further discussion Sancho entered, he and his entire crew.

Chapter Sixteen

— what happened to our ingenious gentleman in the inn which he imagined was a castle

Seeing Don Quijote slung on the donkey's back, the innkeeper asked Sancho what had happened to him. Sancho replied that it was nothing, he'd simply fallen from a high rock and cracked a few ribs. The innkeeper's wife, unlike most such women, was naturally charitable and always sympathized with the misfortunes of those around her, so she immediately busied herself with making Don Quijote well again, and set her young daughter, a very pretty damsel, to help care for their guest. There was also an Asturian girl working in the inn, blessed with a broad face, flat head, stubby nose, one blind eye and the other not entirely functional. But still, her figure was so elegant that it compensated for her other deficiencies: she was about four and a half feet tall, from the top of her head to her feet, and her shoulders, which pretty distinctly weighed her down, made her stare into the ground more than she would have liked. So this charming girl helped the pretty damsel, and the two of them made up a particularly awful bed for Don Quijote, in an attic which showed pretty clear signs that, once upon a time, and for a very long time, it had been used as a hayloft. This spacious chamber also served as lodging for a muledriver, whose bed lay a bit beyond our Don Quijote's. And even though his bed consisted of his saddlebags and the horse blankets used by his mules, it was a great deal better than Don Quijote's, which was composed of four unpainted boards set on a pair of not terribly level carpenter's benches, and a mattress that looked more like a quilt, all full of little lumps of wool, clearly showing through the rips and tears that it was obviously wool, but feeling more like small, sharp pebbles, plus two sheets made of the kind of leather they stretch over archery targets, and a blanket so thin that, had anyone been interested, its threads could have been counted down to the very last one.

They lay Don Quijote on this awful bed, and the innkeeper's wife and her daughter soon had him plastered from top to bottom, while Maritornes — that was the Asturiana's name — held the light for them. And while they were plastering away, the innkeeper's wife noticed a good many bruises all over Don Quijote, and said that looked more like blows than a fall.

"They weren't blows," said Sancho, "but there were a lot of sharp and bumpy places on that rock. — And every tumble gave him a welt." And then he added: "Can you arrange it, your grace, señora, so some of those soft cloths are left over, because there won't be any trouble finding someone who needs them, and in fact my back's hurting me a bit, too."

"So," answered the woman, "you must have fallen down too."

"I didn't fall," said Sancho Panza, "but seeing the somersault my master took, it made me hurt all over, and I felt as if I'd been given a thousand blows."

"That really could be," said the damsel, "because it's often happened to me that I dream I'm falling off a tower, but I never reach the ground, and yet when I wake up I'm as weak and breathless as if I'd really fallen."

"That's exactly it, señora," answered Sancho Panza. "But me, without having dreamed at all, and being even more awake than I am right now, I found myself with just about as many sores as my lord, Don Quijote."

"What did you say this knight's name was?" asked Maritornes, the Asturiana.

"Don Quijote de La Mancha," responded Sancho Panza, "and he's a knight errant, and one of the best, and the strongest, that's been seen in the world for a long time."

"What's a knight errant?" asked the girl.

"You haven't been in the world long enough to know that?" replied Sancho Panza. "Then listen, my sister: a knight errant can see himself, as fast as 'one, two, three,' either beaten with clubs or turned into an emperor. Today he can be the most wretched creature in the world, and the neediest, and tomorrow he can have two or three kingships to give his squire."

"But you, with such a very fine lord," said the innkeeper's wife, "why aren't you — as far as we can tell — even an earl?"

"It's still too soon," replied Sancho. "It's only been a month since we started looking for adventures, and so far we haven't bumped into a thing. That's the way it goes, sometimes: you look for one thing and you find something else. All the same, if my master Don Quijote gets over his wounds — that is, his fall — and I'm not crippled by mine, I wouldn't trade my prospects for the best title in Spain."

Don Quijote, who had been listening very carefully to all this talk, sat up in his bed as best he could and, taking the lady's hand, said to her:

"Believe me, most beautiful dame, you may call yourself fortunate to have me as a guest in your castle, for if I refrain from my own praises it is because, as it is said, he who praises himself degrades himself. But my squire will tell you who I am. Let me only say to you that I will bear, eternally inscribed in my memory, the service you have rendered me, so that while my life endures I may express my gratitude. If only it had not pleased high Heaven that love hold me so closely subject to its laws, and to the eyes of that ungrateful beauty whom I name only in whispers, the eyes of this fair damsel might now be lords of my liberty."

The innkeeper's wife and her daughter and her servant were totally confused, hearing the knight errant's declarations, which as far as they were concerned might have been spoken in Greek, though they quite well understood his words were intended as acknowledgments and compliments, and since they were quite unaccustomed to such language, they stared at him, surprised and thinking him clearly different from the men with whom they usually dealt. So thanking him, as innkeepers do, for his sentiments, mother and daughter left him, while the Asturiana, Maritornes, attended to Sancho, who needed help quite as much as did his master.

Now the muledriver had arranged with her to have some fun together that night, and she had promised that, when the guests were all quiet and her masters were asleep, she'd come and find him and make him happy in any way he wanted. And this pleasant girl had a reputation for never making promises like these without keeping them, even if she'd spoken the words out in the woods, without a witness, because she considered it very much a sign of good breeding, nor did she think herself any less a lady because she was working in an inn; it was bad luck and unfortunate circumstances that had brought her to such a state.

Don Quijote's hard, narrow, rickety, and exceedingly humble bed was the first one you reached, when you entered that starlit room,[1] and then, lying near it, Sancho made his couch, which was only a straw mat and a blanket that looked more like tattered linen than wool. After these, you got to the muledriver's bed, which was made, as I've said, of his saddlebags and all the blankets and other ornaments worn by his two best mules, though in fact he had twelve — gleaming, fat, and famous — because he was one of the richest muledrivers in all Arévalo, according to the author of this history, who makes particular mention of this muledriver, with whom he was personally well acquainted and to whom, some people believe, he was in fact related. But we must also take into consideration that Sidi Hamid Benengeli was in all things a very searching and careful historian, as we can easily see, for whenever he makes reference to something, no matter how small or petty, he never just passes over it in silence — which is an example to be taken to heart by those solemn historians who tell us about things so briskly and briefly that we hardly know what's going on, since the best parts of the book, whether from carelessness or malice, have been left in the inkwell. A thousand blessings on the author of *Tablante of Ricamonte*, and that other book recounting the deeds of Count Tomillas, where everything is carefully described for us!

And so, after visiting his team and giving them their second feeding, he stretched out on his saddlebags and began thinking about his wonderfully punctual Maritornes. Sancho's wounds were already covered with mustard plaster and he was lying down, but though he was trying to sleep the pain in his ribs wouldn't let him, and as for Don Quijote, the way his ribs were aching his eyes were as wide open as a hare's. The inn lay absolutely

---

1. That is, the roof was full of holes [*Translator's Note*].

silent, without any more light than the glow of a single lamp, hung right in the center of the entranceway.

This wondrous stillness, given the fact that our knight's mind was, as ever, full of the things that happened all through those books so directly responsible for his misfortunes, brought into his imagining mind one of the strangest bits of madness anyone could have dreamed of, which was that he had come to a famous castle — since, as I've said, to him all the inns he lodged in seemed to be castles — and the innkeeper's daughter was the lord of the castle's daughter, who, overwhelmed by Don Quijote's gallantry, had fallen in love with him and promised, that very night, to steal away from her parents and play the hussy with him, and believing in the absolute truth of this whole fantasy, which he himself had invented, he began to be concerned about the critical danger his virtue was about to confront, deciding in his heart that he would not betray his lady, Dulcinea del Toboso, even were Queen Guinevere herself, with her Lady Quintañona, to come to him.

While his mind was absorbed by all this nonsense, the hour arrived — and a bad hour it was, for him — when the Asturiana had agreed to make her visit, and so, barefoot, wearing only her chemise, her hair tied up in a cotton net, walking softly and carefully, she entered the chamber where the three men were lodged, seeking the muledriver. But she'd barely gotten through the doorway when Don Quijote became aware of her presence and, sitting up in bed, in spite of all his mustard plasters and the pain in his ribs, stretched out his arms to welcome the beauteous maiden. Walking furtively and half bent over, groping with her hands in front of her, the Asturiana bumped into his arms, and Don Quijote clasped her by the wrist and drew her toward him and, while she did not dare utter a word, made her sit on the bed. Then he felt her chemise and, though it was burlap, to him it seemed the finest and most delicate silk. She wore glass beads on her wrists, but they made him see visions of precious oriental pearls. Her hair, though it was more like a horse's mane, to him was strands of the most magnificent Arabian gold, so radiant that they darkened the sun itself. And though her breath surely smelled of garlic and stale salad, he thought her mouth gave off a delicate, gracious fragrance. In a word, he painted her in his mind as exactly like all the other princesses who, as he had read in his books, would pay visits to badly wounded knights, princesses overcome by love, wearing all the prescribed adornments. And the poor gentleman was so far gone in his fantasy that neither the touch, the smell, nor anything else about the good damsel — which would have made anyone but a muledriver vomit — disillusioned him in the slightest. Indeed, it seemed to him that he was holding in his arms the very goddess of beauty. And so, clasping her tightly, he began to speak in soft, amorous tones:

"Would that I were able, oh lovely and exalted lady, to repay the immense favor you have granted me, by the very sight of your great beauty, but Fortune, which never wearies of persecuting good men, has chosen to place me in this bed, in which I lie so weary and feeble that, no matter how my wishes might long to correspond with yours, it would be impossible. And what makes this impossibility still more impossible, I have

pledged my faith to the incomparable Dulcinea del Toboso, the rare and
and singular lady who occupies my most hidden thoughts. Were this not
an obstacle, I would be a foolish knight indeed if I failed to take advantage
of this fortunate chance granted me by your great kindness."

Deeply upset at finding herself clutched so tightly by Don Quijote,
sweating profusely, and neither understanding nor even listening to his
declarations, Maritornes struggled, in absolute silence, to free herself. The
good muledriver, kept wide awake by his salacious longings, had been
aware of his girlfriend from the moment she came through the door, and
was listening carefully to every word Don Quijote said. Jealous, and fancying that the Asturiana had jilted him for someone else, he crept closer to
Don Quijote's bed and waited to see what came of all this talk, of which
he couldn't understand a word. But seeing that the girl was struggling to
get away and that Don Quijote was trying to hold on to her, he decided
the joke had gone too far, so he hauled back his arm and gave the en-
amored knight such a terrible punch on his lean jaw that Don Quijote's
mouth was swimming in blood, and then, still not satisfied, he climbed
up on the poor knight's ribs and, working his feet as fast as he could,
trampled him from one end to the other.

The bed, weak and set on no very firm foundations, could not handle
the muledriver's added weight and collapsed under him, crashing to the
ground with a noise that woke up the innkeeper, who immediately pre-
sumed this was a quarrel started by Maritornes, because when he shouted
for her she didn't answer. He jumped up, animated by this suspicion, lit
a lamp, and went in the direction from which the racket had come. Seeing
her master coming, and what a state he was in, the girl was frightened and
desperate, and hid in Sancho Panza's bed — he still being asleep —
where she burrowed down and rolled herself up in a ball. The innkeeper
came in, shouting:

"Where are you, you whore? This is your work, damn it!"

At this point, Sancho began to wake up and, feeling some squirming
shape almost on top of him, thought he was having a nightmare, and began
to punch the thing all over, and since his blows landed all over Maritornes,
and hurt like blazes, she threw modesty to the winds and began to give
Sancho as good as she was getting, which jostled him unpleasantly right
out of his dream and, realizing he was being beaten, but not knowing by
whom, he heaved himself up as best he could and tackled Maritornes, at
which point the two of them began the most savagely funny skirmish
you've ever seen.

But then, seeing by the light of the innkeeper's lamp what was going
on with his lady, the muledriver abandoned Don Quijote and went to give
her some much-needed help. The innkeeper ran in the same direction,
but for very different reasons, because he meant to beat the girl, believing
without the slightest doubt that she was the sole cause of all this little
pleasantness. And as it's generally said: The cat got the rat, the rat got the
cord, the cord got the stick — the muledriver gave it to Sancho, Sancho
to the girl, the girl to Sancho, the innkeeper to the girl, and they all
whacked away so briskly that no one was able to stop, and the best part of
it was that the innkeeper's lamp had gone out and, everyone being left in

the dark, they all gave it to each other so mercilessly that you couldn't find an undamaged spot on any one of them.

Now, lodging in the inn that night there happened to be a captain in the local constabulary, and hearing the wild uproar caused by all this fighting, he snatched up his policeman's club and his letters of authority, and went into the dark attic room, crying:

"Stop, in the name of the law! Stop in the name of the law!"

And the first person he bumped into was our well-battered Don Quijote, who was lying in his smashed-up bed, stretched out face up, unconscious, and as his groping hand felt the knight's beard he kept on shouting:

"In the name of the law!"

But seeing that the man he had hold of neither budged nor wiggled, he was convinced the fellow was dead, and that all the other people in the room were his killers, and this suspicion made him shout even louder:

"Lock the inn door! Let no one get out, because they've killed a man!"

This cry scared them all, and they all stopped fighting as soon as they heard it. The innkeeper went back to his bedchamber, the muledriver to his saddlebags, the girl to her own attic room; only our miserable pair, Don Quijote and Sancho, were unable to move anywhere. The constable let go of Don Quijote's beard, and went off in search of a light so he could hunt down and arrest the criminals, but he couldn't find one, because the innkeeper had deliberately snuffed out the single lamp before he retired to his room, so the constable had to make his way to the kitchen fireplace, where with much difficulty, and after a long time, he managed to fill and light another lamp.

Chapter Seventeen

— in which we continue telling the endless troubles experienced by our brave Don Quijote and his squire Sancho Panza, in the inn which, unluckily for him, our knight thought was a castle

By this time, Don Quijote had regained consciousness and, in the same tone of voice he'd used when calling to his squire, earlier, as he lay stretched out in the valley of the clubs, he began to call to him now, saying:

"Sancho, my friend, are you asleep? Are you asleep, friend Sancho?"

"How could I sleep, God help me," answered Sancho, overwhelmed by pain and anger, "when I feel as if all the devils in hell have been after me tonight?"

"I agree with you, most assuredly," replied Don Quijote, "because either I don't know anything about such things or this castle is enchanted. Because, let me tell you — but you've got to swear that what I'm about to say to you will be kept secret until after my death."

"I swear it," answered Sancho.

"I say that," Don Quijote continued, "because I dislike tarnishing anyone's good name."

"And I say I swear to it," Sancho said in his turn, "so I'll hold my tongue until after your grace's death, but I pray to God I can talk about it tomorrow."

"Have I done such terrible things to you, Sancho," replied Don Quijote, "that you long to see me dead so soon?"

"It's not like that," answered Sancho, "but just that I dislike holding on to things, because I don't want them to go bad on me from being kept too long."

"However that may be," said Don Quijote, "I have great confidence in your love, and your politeness, and so let me tell you that, tonight, I experienced one of the strangest adventures I shall ever be able to commend to your attention — and, to make my story as short as possible, you must know that, just a little while ago, the lord of this castle's daughter came to me, one of the most elegant and beautiful damsels you'll find almost anywhere on earth. What can I tell you about how wondrously she was dressed? Or about the nobility of her mind? Or of all those other, more secret matters that, in order to preserve the faith I owe to my lady Dulcinea del Toboso, I will pass over untouched and in silence? Let me tell you only that Heaven may have been jealous, seeing what blessings Fortune had placed in my hands, or perhaps — and by far the most likely explanation — this castle, as I have said, is enchanted, so that just as she and I were engaged in the sweetest, most amorous discourse, there appeared, though I did not see it coming, nor did I know from whence it came, the hand and arm of some colossal giant, which delivered such a blow to my jaw that I was virtually bathed in blood, after which I was beaten so severely that, now, I am in worse condition than when, yesterday, because of Rocinante's impudence, those Galician muledrivers gave us those injuries of which you are well aware. All of which leads me to believe that the treasure of this damsel's beauty must be guarded by some Moorish enchanter, and that this treasure is not meant for me."

"Not for me, either," replied Sancho, "because more than four hundred Moors have been beating me, and so badly that the damage done by those muledrivers' clubs looks like children fooling around. But tell me, señor: what do you call this fine and unusual adventure, which left us as we are now? Your grace wasn't so bad off, getting to hold in your hands that incomparable beauty you talked about. But me, what did I get, except the worst beating I think I've ever had in my life? Oh, how unlucky I am, and my mother who bore me, that I'm not a knight errant, and I'll never be one, either, so the worst of everything always falls on me!"

"Then you were beaten too?" answered Don Quijote.

"Didn't I just say so, damn my whole family tree!" said Sancho.

"Don't be upset, my friend," said Don Quijote, "because now I'm going to make that precious balm which will cure us as fast as you can open and close your eyes."

Just then the constable got his lamp lit and came to see the man he thought had been killed, and when Sancho saw him coming, dressed in his nightshirt, with his nightcap on his head and a lamp in his hand, and scowling darkly, he asked his master:

"Could this be him, señor, that Moorish enchanter, coming back to beat us some more — if he can find someplace that still hasn't been worked over?"

"It can't be the Moor," replied Don Quijote, "because enchanters don't let anybody see them."

"If they don't let you see them," said Sancho, "they certainly let you feel them. If you don't think so, just ask my shoulders."

"Mine could speak just as eloquently," answered Don Quijote, "but that's no reason to think this might be the Moorish enchanter."

The constable came in but, finding them engaged in such a peaceful conversation, stopped short. Truth to tell, Don Quijote was still lying flat on his back, unable to move, beaten and plastered all over. The constable came over to him and said:

"So, how goes it with you, my good fellow?"

"I should speak more politely," responded Don Quijote, "if I were you. Do people in these parts usually talk to knights errant this way, you idiot?"

Finding himself dealt with thus abruptly, by a man who made such a poor appearance, was insufferable to the constable, so he lifted his lamp, filled with oil, and heavy, and hit Don Quijote in the head with it, wounding him badly. Being then in the darkness, he immediately left the room, and Sancho Panza said:

"I'm sure, señor, this is really the Moorish enchanter, who's keeping the treasure for other people, and saving, especially for us, all the heavy fists and banging lamps."

"So it is," replied Don Quijote, "and there's no point making a fuss about their enchantments, or getting all irritated and angry about them, because they're invisible and unreal and we couldn't find anyone to take revenge on, no matter how much we tried. So get up, Sancho, if you can, and summon the governor of this fortress, so we can have them give us a bit of oil, some wine, salt, and rosemary for making the curative balm, since I truly believe it is now very necessary, for I've lost a good deal of blood from the wound this apparition gave me."

Sancho's very bones ached, as he stood up and groped through the darkness to find the innkeeper, and meeting up with the constable, who was trying to find out what had happened to his enemy, Sancho said to him:

"Señor, whoever you may be, please be so kind as to give us a bit of rosemary, some oil, salt, and wine, which are needed to cure one of the noblest knights errant the world's ever seen, who's lying on that bed in there, badly wounded by the Moorish enchanter they've got in this inn."

Hearing this, the constable took Sancho for a brainless fool and, since dawn was now breaking, he opened the inn door and, calling the innkeeper, told him what this good man had asked for. The innkeeper gave Sancho what he wanted, and Sancho carried it to Don Quijote, who was holding his head in his hands, complaining about the pain from the lamp blow, which in fact hadn't done him any more harm than to give him a couple of large welts, because what he thought was blood was only sweat from the anguish and torment he'd just endured.

So he took the herbs, made a paste of them, mixing them all up and cooking them a long time, until the balm seemed ready. Then he asked that a vial be brought, into which he could pour his precious brew, but since there wasn't a vial to be found in the inn, he decided to pour it into an oil jar — really a can of hammered tin — which the innkeeper donated to the cause. And then he said more than eighty Our Fathers over the can, and just as many Ave Marias, and Salve Reginas, and Credos, making a sign of the cross at every word, by way of a blessing, during all of which Sancho was in attendance, as well as the innkeeper and the constable, for the muledriver had already gone peacefully out to take care of his jackasses.

This done, Don Quijote wanted to see if the powers of this precious balm were all that he imagined them to be, so he drank almost half a quart of what he hadn't been able to fit into the oil can, and which was still in the pot where it had all been cooked, and he'd barely gotten it down when he began to throw it back up, so violently that nothing whatever remained in his stomach, and what with the nausea and the upset of his vomiting he began to sweat profusely, at which point he told them to cover him up and leave him. They did this, and after he'd been left sleeping for more than three hours, he woke up and felt immensely better — so much improved, indeed, from his beating, that he considered himself cured, and truly believed that he had found Fierabras' balm, with which remedy he could, from that point on, without any problem whatsoever, confront any form of physical destruction, any battle, any combat, no matter how dangerous it might be.

Sancho Panza, who also attributed his master's recovery to a miracle, asked if he could have some of what was left in the pot, which was no small amount. Don Quijote granted it to him and, in good faith and with an even better feeling, Sancho took the pot in both hands, drew it to his breast, and gulped down not much less than his master had. But since the stomach of a poor man like Sancho could not afford to be as delicate as Don Quijote's, before he chucked it all back up it twisted his guts in such sickness and nausea, with such an intensity of sweating and swooning, that he truly thought he'd come to his last hour, and finding himself thus in such anguish, and struck with such affliction, he cursed both the balm and the thief who'd given it to him. And when Don Quijote saw this, he said:

"I think, Sancho, that you've been so sorely afflicted because you've not been dubbed a knight, for it strikes me that this magic liquid ought not to be employed by those who are not knights."

"If your grace knew that," replied Sancho, " — damn me and all my ancestors! — why did you let me try it?"

Just then the potion went to work, and the poor squire began to pour out liquid at both ends, with such violence that neither the straw mat on which he had flung himself, nor the burlap sheet he'd pulled around him, could ever be used again. He sweated and shook in such a fit and with such paroxysms that not only he himself but everyone else thought he was giving up the ghost. This orgy of misery went on for almost two hours, at the end of which he was left, unlike his master, so drained and weak that he could not stand.

But Don Quijote, feeling, as we have said, restored and healthy, was anxious to be off in pursuit of adventures, for it seemed to him that as long as he tarried he was depriving the world and all those who needed him of his aid and protection — and he felt this especially keenly, having the security and confidence provided by his magic balm. Accordingly, driven by this desire, he himself saddled Rocinante and readied his squire's donkey, then helped Sancho to get dressed and mount the animal. Then he got up on his horse and, as he rode past a corner in the courtyard, saw a short, thin spear standing there, and took it to use as a lance.

Everyone in the inn — more than twenty people — was watching him, including the innkeeper's daughter, and he never took his eyes off her, from time to time emitting sighs that seemed to be wrenched from the very pit of his bowels, sighs which the onlookers thought were caused by the pain in his ribs — or, at least, so thought those who had seen him being bandaged, the night before.

When they reached the gate, Don Quijote called to the innkeeper and, in a calm, sober voice, said to him:

"Señor governor, we have been rendered many and singularly large favors, here in this castle of yours, for which I will remain deeply obliged and grateful all the days of my life. If I am able to repay you by taking revenge, on your behalf, against any arrogant rascal who may in any way have injured you, be advised that my task is none other than to defend those who are little able to take their own revenge for the wrongs done them, and to punish perfidy. Search your recollection, and should you find anything of this sort to entrust to me, you need only say so, and I promise you, by the knighthood with which I have been ordained, to bring you satisfaction and repayment in everything you desire."

The innkeeper replied, just as solemnly:

"Sir knight, there's no need for your grace to revenge any wrongs done me, because I know how to take appropriate revenge when I have to. All I need is that your grace pay me for the expenses you've incurred in my inn tonight, as well as for the hay and barley for your two animals, and also for your meals and your beds."

"Is this then an inn?" replied Don Quijote.

"And a well-respected one," answered the innkeeper.

"Until this very moment," responded Don Quijote, "I have been proceeding under a mistaken assumption, for I truly believed this was a castle, and not a bad one. But since it seems this is not a castle, but an inn, all that can be done, now, is that you waive any question of payment, for I am unable to contravene the rules of knight errantry, which are perfectly clear — and to this moment I have read nothing to the contrary — that such knights have never paid for lodging nor for anything else in the inns where they may have stayed, since by law and custom they are owed whatever hospitality is offered them, in payment for the unbearable hardships they endure as they search for adventures, by night and by day, in summer and winter, on foot and on horseback, experiencing hunger and thirst, heat and cold, and subject to all the inclemencies of the weather and all the discomforts known to earth."

"That's nothing to me," replied the innkeeper. "Just pay me what you owe, and let's hear no talk about chivalry and knighthood. All that matters to me is collecting what I've earned."

"You are a fool and a miserable innkeeper," replied Don Quijote.

Spurring Rocinante, and leveling his lance, he left the inn, nor did anyone detain him, and without bothering to notice if his squire was following him, he was soon a fair distance away.

Seeing him leave without paying, the innkeeper tried to collect his debt from Sancho Panza, who explained, however, that since his lord had not chosen to pay, he was not going to, either, for as a knight errant's squire he was subject to the same rules and regulations as his master, and could not pay bills at inns and taverns. This mightily vexed the innkeeper, who threatened that, if he did not pay the bill, he'd pay in another way that would make him exceedingly unhappy. To which Sancho answered that, according to the laws of knighthood by which his master was bound, he wouldn't pay a single penny, even if it cost him his life, because the fine old customs of knight errantry were not going to be spoiled by him, nor should the squires of future knights errant ever have him to complain about, reproaching him for having violated so just and proper a rule.

But the unfortunate Sancho's bad luck had seen to it that, among the people in the inn just then, were four wool-carders from Segovia, three needle-workers from Córdoba's horseracing district, and a couple of men from Seville's Holiday Market, rollicking fellows, good-hearted, and rough and ready. As if all driven by the same notion, they surrounded Sancho and pulled him off his donkey, and one of them went inside for a blanket from their host's bed. They tossed Sancho into it, but seeing that the ceiling was too low for the job they had in mind, they decided to take him out into the courtyard, where the sky would be the limit. And there, with Sancho in the middle of the blanket, they began to bounce him in the air, having fun with him as if he were a dog at carnival time.

The wretch's cries carried so far that they reached his master's ears, who strained to hear, thinking some new adventure was beginning, until he recognized that without any question the person screaming was his squire, at which point he turned his horse around and, after a hard gallop, arrived back at the inn. Finding the gate locked, he circled about, trying to find a way of getting in, but he hadn't reached the courtyard walls (which were not very high) when he saw the wicked game they were playing with his squire. He saw Sancho rising and then falling through the air so lightly, and so rapidly, that had his anger permitted it, I think he would have had to laugh. He tried to climb from his horse onto the fence, but was still so weak and battered that he couldn't get himself dismounted, and so, sitting high on his steed, he began to pile such insults and abuse on those who were blanket-tossing Sancho that it's impossible accurately to transcribe them — not that his words stopped either their tossing or their laughter, or kept the flying Sancho from his moaning, mixed first with threats and then with entreaties, for nothing was of much use, or in fact accomplished a thing, until out of pure fatigue they finally stopped. Then they brought in the donkey, set Sancho on top of it, and put on his coat. And Maritornes took pity on him, seeing how worn out he was: thinking he'd be helped by a jug of water, she brought him one directly from the well, so it would be cool. Sancho took it and was raising it to his mouth, when he stopped, hearing his master crying out:

"Sancho, my son, don't drink that water! My son, don't drink it, because it will kill you! Don't you understand? I've got the sacred balm right here," and he pointed to the tin can, full of his potion, "two drops of which will cure you at once."

Sancho rolled his eyes, as if crosseyed, and shouted back even louder:

"My God, has your grace forgotten that I'm not a knight, or would you like me to finish vomiting up my guts where I left off last night? Keep your balm for the devils in hell, and let me take care of myself."

And the minute he finished saying this, he began to drink, but discovering with the first swallow that it was water, he broke off and asked Maritornes to fetch him some wine, which she did with great good will, and paid for it herself, for in fact it was said of her that, though she was what she was, she still had a distant resemblance to a Christian.

And then, after Sancho had drunk, he dug his heels into his donkey and, as they were throwing open the gate, he left, well satisfied that he'd paid nothing and stuck to his word, even though he'd had to be ransomed by his usual guarantor, namely, his shoulders. Still, the innkeeper had taken his saddlebags, in payment for what was owed, but Sancho wasn't thinking about anything like that, riding off as hastily as he did. Seeing Sancho go, the innkeeper wanted to bolt and lock the gate, but the blanket-tossers wouldn't let him, for they were the kind who, even had Don Quijote been one of the real Knights of the Round Table, wouldn't have cared two cents.

Chapter Eighteen

— which tells of Sancho Panza's conversation with his master, Don Quijote, and other matters worth recounting

Sancho was so wilted and deeply discouraged, as he rode up alongside his master, that he couldn't hurry his donkey. Seeing which, Don Quijote said to him:

"I have now concluded, my good Sancho, that this castle, or inn, is without any question enchanted, for what otherwise could they be, who so atrociously amused themselves with you, except ghosts and denizens of the other world? And this is corroborated by the fact that, when I reached the courtyard fence, from whence I saw how they played out your sad tragedy, I could not climb it, nor could I get down from Rocinante, so obviously I must have been under a spell, for I swear to you, by my faith as the knight I am, that had I been able to climb, or to dismount, I would have so revenged you that those loafers and rascals would have remembered *that* joke for the rest of their lives, even though it might have contravened the laws of knighthood, which as I have told you many times do not permit a knight to lift his hand against anyone who is not himself a knight, except in defense of his own life, and under circumstances of great and pressing necessity."

"And I would have revenged myself, too, if I could have," said Sancho, "whether or not I'd been dubbed a knight, but I couldn't. Still, I don't think the people who played that game with me were either ghosts or under any magic spells, as your grace says, but just men of flesh and blood like us, and as I heard when they were tossing me up and down, they all had human names. One of them was called Pedro Martínez, and another was Tenorio Hernández, and the innkeeper, I found out, was Juan Palomeque the Lefty. So if you couldn't climb the courtyard fence, señor, or get off your horse, it had to be for some reason other than magic spells. And the pretty clear lesson I learn from all this is that these adventures we're hunting for will only bring us, from beginning to end, such misadventures that we won't know our right foot from the left. And the way my feeble brain sees it, the best and also the proper thing would be to turn around and go right back home, because it's harvest time, now, and we ought to worry about our own affairs and stop traveling from here to there and letting everything go from bad to worse, as they say."

"Sancho," replied Don Quijote, "how little you know about knighthood! Be still, and be patient. The day will come when you will see with your own eyes what a fine and proper thing it is to follow this calling. If you don't think so, just tell me: what greater happiness can a man have on this earth, or what pleasure can equal that of triumphing in a battle and defeating your foe? None. There can be no doubt about it."

"That may be so," replied Sancho, "but I don't know anything about it. All I know is, since we've been knights errant, or your grace has been one (because I don't count myself as one of that honorable number), we've never won any battles, except the one with the Basque, and even that one left your grace with just half an ear and half a helmet, and from then on it's all been beatings and more beatings, punches and more punches, and I had the added pleasure of being tossed in a blanket, which is supposed to have been done by enchanted people, and who can take any revenge on them? So I don't know where the pleasure of conquering your foe, which your grace talks about, is supposed to come from."

"This indeed troubles me, Sancho, and it must trouble you, too," replied Don Quijote. "But from now on I shall try to have at hand a sword so skilfully made that no kind of enchantment can be placed on anyone who carries it with him. And perhaps Fortune will send me the sword carried by Amadís, when he was known as 'The Knight of the Burning Sword,' which was one of the best weapons ever owned by any knight in the world, because not only did it have the power I have already mentioned, but it cut like a razor, nor was any armor, no matter how strong or enchanted, able to stand up to it."

"It would be just my luck," said Sancho, "that, should it ever happen, and your grace finds a sword like that, it'll only be good for full-fledged knights, the way it was with that balm, and as for squires, they can just stuff it."

"Fear not, Sancho," said Don Quijote, "Heaven will look more kindly on you."

Don Quijote and his squire were going along, chatting like this, when down the road Don Quijote suddenly saw, coming right toward them, a great, thick cloud of dust, at which he turned to Sancho and said:

"Oh Sancho, this is the day when you will see all the good things Fortune has reserved for me. This is the day, I tell you, when I will need to show, as never before, the courage of my arm, and the day on which I will work deeds to be written in the Book of Fame, for all future centuries to see. Do you see that cloud of dust, Sancho, rising over there? All that has been churned up by an immense army, come marching here from far and wide and from nations all over the earth."

"If that's what it is," said Sancho, "there must be two of them, because I see another cloud just like that one, coming from the opposite direction."

Don Quijote turned to look and saw it was true, and he was exceedingly happy, because he thought that surely these were two armies, intending to attack and fall upon each other in the middle of that broad plain. His head was always buzzing, night and day, with fantasies about such battles, enchantments, and the like, with such foolishness, with love affairs, challenges, and everything told in his books of chivalry, so that everything he said, thought, or did was concerned with magic spells and all the rest of it. But the dust clouds he'd seen were raised by two large flocks of sheep, with their shepherds, which happened to be traveling down that road in different directions, though because of the dust they could not be clearly seen except from close up. Still, Don Quijote declared they were armies with such fervor that Sancho was ready to believe it, and said:

"Well then, señor, what should we do?"

"What?" said Don Quijote. "Help and protect the needy and the infirm. And understand, Sancho, that the army you see in front of us is led and guided by the magnificent Emperor Alifanfarón, lord of the great island of Trapobana [Ceylon], while that other one, heading at my back, is that of his enemy, the king of the Garamantas [Libya], Pentapolín the Bare Armed, because he always goes into battle with his right arm bare."

"But what are these two lords fighting about?" asked Sancho.

"They're fighting," answered Don Quijote, "because this Alifanfarón is a ferocious pagan, and he's in love with Pentapolín's daughter, a singularly lovely and also charming lady, and a Christian, and her father won't hand her over to the pagan king unless he first foreswears the laws of his false prophet, Mohammad, and converts to her religion."

"By my beard!" said Sancho, "but Pentapolín's really doing the right thing, and I'd like to help him as much as I can!"

"And that's exactly what you ought to do, Sancho," said Don Quijote, "because you don't need to be a knight to fight in a battle of this sort."

"I can see that well enough," answered Sancho. "But where should we put this donkey, so we can be sure to find him after the fighting's done with? I don't think going into battle on such a mount is something anyone's ever done."

"That's true," said Don Quijote. "What you can do with him is set him free, nor does it matter whether he gets lost or not, because after we emerge victorious we'll have so many horses that even Rocinante will run the risk of being traded for another animal. But now pay attention to me, and keep your eyes open, because I want you to understand who are the principal knights in these opposing forces. And so you can see them better, and better focus your mind, let's withdraw to that hill over there, from which we can observe both armies."

Which they did, placing themselves on a slope from which they could easily have seen the two flocks which Don Quijote had turned into armies, if the clouds of dust being whipped up hadn't obscured and indeed quite blocked their vision, in spite of which, seeing in his mind's eye what no eye could see, Don Quijote began to explain, in a loud voice:

"That knight you see over there, in the golden armor, whose shield bears a crowned lion lying at the feet of a damsel, is the brave Laurcalco, lord of Silver-Bridge; the other, whose armor is covered with gold flowers, whose shield displays three silver crowns on a field of blue, is the fearsome Micocolembo, Grand Duke of Quirocia; and that one with huge limbs, just on his right, is the unfrightenable Brandabarbarán of Boliche, lord of the three Arabias, who goes into battle armored in that snakeskin, and carrying a gate as his shield — and it's said that this is in fact a gate from the temple Sampson pulled down, when he turned his death into vengeance on his enemies. Now direct your eyes in the other direction, and you'll see right in the forefront of that other army the ever-victorious and never-defeated Timonel of Carcajona, Prince of New Biscay, whose armor is divided into quarters — blue, green, white, and yellow — and whose shield shows a golden cat on a tawny field, and also a motto, MIAU, which forms the beginning of his lady's name, for she, they say, is the peerless Miulina, daughter of Duke Alfeñiquén of Algarbe. The other one, who squeezes down so heavily on the back of that great, powerful stallion, and whose armor is as white as snow, and his shield a stark white, is an apprentice knight, a Frenchman named Pierre Papín, lord of the barony of Utrique; and that one, clapping his iron heels on the flanks of that striped, graceful zebra, with the blue heraldic bells painted on his armor, is the powerful Duke of Nerbia, Espartafilardo of the Forests, who carries an asparagus on his shield, with a motto, written in Spanish, declaring that *My Luck Grows Straight.*"

And on he went, naming many knights from one or the other cavalry, all of whom he had conjured up out of his own head, and to all of whom he fluently and rapidly assigned armor, colors, devices, and mottoes, swept along by his unparalleled madness, never needing to pause, continuing:

"Now that squadron, in front there, is composed of men from many nations: those who drink the sweet waters of the celebrated Trojan river, Xanthus; the mountaineers who tramp the African plains; those who sieve the finest, purest gold of Arabia Félix; those who relish the famous cool waters of clearflowing Thermodon, in Capodocia; those who operate many sorts of channels for tapping the golden Pactolus, in Lydia; the Numidians, who make more promises than they keep; the Persians, famous archers and bowmen; the Medes and Parthians, who may flee but never stop fighting; the Arabs, who carry their houses with them; the Scythians, as cruel as they are blond; the Ethiopians, with their pierced lips — and a host of other nations, whose faces I see and recognize, though I cannot recall their names. In that other squadron are those who drink the crystaline currents of the olive-rich River Betis; those who smooth and polish their faces with liquid from the eternally rich and golden Tagus; those who are made happy by the useful waters of the divine Genil; those who tramp the Tartesian fields, ripe with good pastures; those who revel in the Elysian meadows of Jerez de la Frontera; the folk of La Mancha, wealthy and crowned with golden tassels of corn; those who wear iron, ancient relics of their Gothic ancestors; those who bathe themselves in the Pisuerga, famous for its gentle currents; those who graze their cattle in the rolling meadows of the winding Guadiana, famous for its hidden course; those who shiver in the cold of the wooded Pyrenees and in the swirling snows of the soaring Apennines; and, in short, all those to be found in Europe."

God help me, but how many provinces he spoke of, how many nations he named, assigning to each, with incredible ease and quickness of mind and tongue, the characteristics it bore, totally entranced, filled to the brim with everything he had read in his lying books!

Sancho Panza hung on his words, unable to speak, from time to time turning his head, trying to see the knights and giants his master was naming; and since he could not see any of them, he said:

"Señor, send me to the Devil if, in spite of all that, there's a man, or a giant, or any of those knights your grace is talking about. Anyway, I can't see them. Maybe it's all enchanted, like the ghosts last night."

"What are you saying?" answered Don Quijote. "You don't hear the whinnying of horses, the blaring of trumpets, the beating of drums?"

"All I hear," answered Sancho, "is the bleating of sheep and rams."

Which was the truth, because the two flocks had now come closer.

"It is the fear you feel, Sancho," said Don Quijote, "which keeps you from either seeing or hearing correctly, for one of the effects of fear is to perturb the senses, so that things no longer seem to be what they are. And if you are so very afraid, go off a bit and let me be solitary, because I am sufficient unto myself to bring victory to whichever side I give my assistance."

Saying which, he spurred Rocinante and, setting his lance in its brace, rode down the slope like a whirlwind. Then Sancho cried out:

"Come back, your grace, señor Don Quijote — I swear to God those are rams and ewes you're attacking! Come back! Oh the miserable father who begot me! What kind of madness is this? Look — there aren't any giants — there aren't any knights, or cats, or armor, or shields divided into quarters, or blue bells gone to the devil. What are you doing? Oh, sinner that I am, oh God!"

But Don Quijote would not turn back; rather, he shouted out, loudly:

"Ho, knights, you who follow and fight under the banners of the brave Emperor Pentapolín the Bare Armed, all of you, follow me! You'll see how easily I avenge him on his enemy, Alifanfarón of Trapobana!"

Saying which, he rode into the middle of a squadron of ewes, and began spearing them as boldly and bravely as if he were really wielding his lance against mortal enemies. The shepherds and drovers who were guarding the flock came running, shouting for him to stop but, seeing that had no effect on him, they pulled out their slings and began to rattle stones as big as a fist around his ears. But he paid no attention to the stones — quite the opposite, he galloped this way and that, shouting:

"Where are you, oh haughty Alifanfarón? Come here to me, a lone knight, who wishes, in solitary combat, to test your strength and pluck away your life, as punishment for what you've done to the brave Pentapolín Garamanta."

Just then a candied almond, drawn from a stream bed, smashed into his side and stove in a pair of ribs. Finding himself so badly battered, he thought he was surely mortally wounded, or even dead, so remembering his magic balm he drew out the tin can and set it to his mouth, beginning to pour the liquid into his stomach, but before he could drink what seemed to him a sufficient amount another sugared almond arrived, hitting him in the hand, and on the tin can, so powerfully that the can was shattered and fell to the road, taking with it three or four of his teeth, molars included, and badly bruising his fingers.

The combination of blows was so powerful that it knocked the poor knight off his horse. The shepherds ran up and thought he was dead, so they quickly collected their flock, loaded up the dead animals (of which there were more than seven), and fled, not bothering with anything else.

All this time Sancho remained up on the slope, watching his master's madness in action and pulling at his beard, cursing the hour and the moment Fate had brought them together. Then, seeing Don Quijote fall to the ground, and the shepherds gone, he came down from the slope and went over to his master, finding him in very bad shape, but still conscious. So he said:

"Didn't I tell you, señor Don Quijote, to come back, that you were not attacking any armies but just flocks of sheep?"

"My enemy, that thief of a magician, works like this, making things disappear and turn into other things. You must understand, Sancho, how easy it is for the likes of him to make us believe whatever they want to, and that this evil creature who so persecutes me, jealous of the glory he saw me about to win from this battle, transformed the ranks of my enemies into flocks of sheep. But if you still do not understand, Sancho, do this one thing, by my life, to undeceive yourself and see how truly I speak: get up on your donkey and follow carefully after them, and you will see how, once they get a little distance away, they will turn back into what they really are and, no longer animals, will be in all respects men, exactly as I first told you they were. . . . But no, don't leave me yet, because I need your kindness and help. Come over here and see how many teeth I'm missing, because it feels as if they haven't left any in my mouth."

Sancho came closer, virtually putting his eyes into Don Quijote's mouth, and that being the moment when the balm had had its chance to work on his master's stomach, his mouth erupted, swifter than any rifle, just as Sancho bent over, and emptied the entire contents of Don Quijote's stomach all over the sympathetic squire's beard.

"Holy Mother of God!" cried Sancho. "What's happening to me? This sinner is surely mortally wounded, because he's vomiting blood from his mouth."

But when he examined it more closely, it became apparent from the color, taste, and odor that it wasn't blood but just the magic balm, which he'd seen Don Quijote drinking, and this so disgusted him that it made his stomach turn over and he vomited out his guts all over his master, which left them both perfectly matched. Sancho went over to his donkey, so he could rummage in his saddlebags for something with which to clean himself, and also his master, and when he found there were no saddlebags he was at the point of losing his mind. Cursing himself once again, he resolved to leave his master and return home, even if he had to lose his wages, plus all his hopes for the promised governorship of an island.

Just then Don Quijote rose and, holding his left hand on his mouth, to keep the rest of his teeth from falling out, took Rocinante's reins with the other hand — for the horse had never moved from his master's side, so loyal was he, and of such a fine disposition — and went over to Sancho, who was leaning on his donkey, face down and with his hand on his cheek, looking wonderfully thoughtful. And seeing him like that, showing such an intensity of sorrow, Don Quijote said:

"Understand, Sancho, that no man is better than anyone else unless he does more. All these storms we've been caught in are signs that soon the weather will turn bright and calm and good things will happen to us, for it's not possible for either good or bad to endure, and from now on, having endured a great deal of bad, the good is already drawing near. So you mustn't be distressed by the misfortunes I've experienced, for you've had no part in them."

"I haven't?" replied Sancho. "Maybe he who was tossed in that blanket, yesterday, was somebody other than my father's son? And the saddlebags I'm missing, today, with all my valuables in them, do they belong to somebody else?"

"You're missing your saddlebags, Sancho?" said Don Quijote.

"They're missing, all right," answered Sancho.

"Then today we'll have nothing to eat," responded Don Quijote.

"But that would only happen," replied Sancho, "if we didn't have, out in these fields, all those herbs your grace said you knew, which Destiny provides for unfortunate knights errant like you."

"Just the same," replied Don Quijote, "I'd take more pleasure, right now, in a chunk of good white bread, or even a loaf of coarser stuff and a couple of sardine heads, than in all the herbs described by Dioscorides, even with Doctor Laguna's explanations.[1] But, in any case, climb up on your donkey, my good Sancho, and come follow me, and God, who provides all things, will not fail us, especially because we're engaged in His work as we are, for He fails not the mosquitoes in the air, nor the worms in the ground, nor the tadpoles in the water, and so merciful is He that He allows His sun to shine on good and bad alike, and His rain to fall on both the just and the unjust."

"Your grace would make a better preacher," said Sancho, "than a knight errant."

"A knight errant knows everything, Sancho, as he must," said Don Quijote, "for in days gone by a knight errant might have to deliver a sermon, or a lecture, right in the middle of the king's camp, as if he were a graduate of the University of Paris, from which we may conclude that the lance has never blunted the pen, nor the pen the lance."

"So, good, let it be as your grace says," responded Sancho. "Let's get away from here and find someplace to stay tonight, and pray God that it

---

1. Dioscorides (A.D. 40–90), a Greek physician, wrote *De materia medica*, a standard pharmacological text for sixteen hundred years. Dr. Laguna's Spanish edition was published in 1555.

be somewhere where there are no horse blankets, nor any blanket-tossers, nor any ghosts, nor enchanted Moors, because if there are, may the devil take the whole lot of them."

"Ask that of God, my son," said Don Quijote, "and guide us where you will, for this time I wish to leave the choice of our lodging entirely up to you. But let me borrow your hand, and see with your finger how many teeth are missing on the upper right side, which is where I feel the pain."

Sancho stuck in his fingers and, after groping about, said:

"How many molars has your grace had on this side?"

"Four," replied Don Quijote, "not counting the wisdom tooth, and all of them whole and healthy."

"Just think carefully what you're saying, señor," responded Sancho.

"I say four, but it may have been five," replied Don Quijote, "because I've never in my life had any teeth extracted, nor have any ever fallen out or been eaten away by cavities or rheumatism."

"Well, on the lower part," said Sancho, "your grace has only two and a half molars, and on the upper, there's not even a half — there's nothing. It's all as flat as the palm of my hand."

"I'm forever unlucky!" said Don Quijote, hearing the sad news his squire gave him. "I'd rather they cut off an arm, except not my sword arm. For you must understand, Sancho, that a mouth without molars is like a mill without a millstone, and a tooth should be considered more valuable than a diamond. But we who profess the harsh rule of knighthood are subject to all this. Up, my friend, and lead on, and I shall follow at whatever pace you like."

Which Sancho did, and directed them to where it looked as if they might find shelter, without leaving the highway, which at that point was a very well traveled road.

They jogged slowly along, because the pain in his jaws bothered Don Quijote and kept him from moving any faster. So Sancho decided to entertain and divert him a bit, and among the other things he told him were the matters narrated in the next chapter.

Chapter Nineteen

— of Sancho's wise remarks to his master, and the adventure with a dead body, along with other remarkable events

"It seems plain to me, señor, that all the calamities happening to us have been punishment for the sin your grace committed against the laws of knighthood, for you've not fulfilled the oath you swore about not eating bread off a tablecloth or embracing the queen, and all the rest of it, which your grace swore you'd do until you'd gotten that helmet from Malandrino, or whatever that Moor's name is, because I don't exactly remember."

"You make a great deal of sense, Sancho," said Don Quijote, "but, to tell you the truth, I'd completely forgotten about it — and you may be sure, moreover, that it's because you are guilty of not having reminded me in time that you had that affair with the horse blanket. But I will make it up to you, for in the order of knighthood there are pathways of restitution for everything."

"Would I have sworn something, maybe?" replied Sancho.

"Your not having sworn is of no importance," said Don Quijote. "It is enough that I understand what shaky ground you're on, and so, whether you are or whether you're not, it won't be a bad idea to furnish ourselves with a way out."

"If that's the way it is," said Sancho, "you'd better be careful, your grace, that you don't forget this, too, the way you forgot the oath, because maybe the ghosts will decide to have fun with me a second time, and maybe even with your grace, if they see you so stubborn."

Night fell on them, right there in the middle of the road, as they were talking about things like this, and before they had reached or even seen a place where they could take shelter. And what was really bad was that they were dying of hunger, since with the loss of the saddlebags they had lost their whole larder and all their stores. And then, to finish off this misfortune, they had an adventure which, without resorting to any ingenious reasoning, really seemed to be an adventure. Night closed down and it grew very dark, but they rode on in spite of that, Sancho believing that since this was a royal highway, just one or two more miles would surely find them in an inn.

Going along in this fashion, the night dark, the squire starving and his master distinctly interested in eating, they saw coming toward them down the road a great many lights, which looked exactly like moving stars. Sancho gaped, nor was Don Quijote unafraid. The squire gripped the donkey's halter, and the master his old horse's reins, and they stopped in their tracks, waiting to see what this could be. And then seeing that the lights were getting closer, and growing larger as they came, Sancho began to shake like someone poisoned by mercury, and Don Quijote's hair stood on end. But then he braced himself a bit and said:

"Sancho, without any doubt this has to be the greatest and most dangerous of all adventures, and I must show all my courage and strength."

"Oh woe is me!" answered Sancho. "If this turns out to be a ghost adventure, as I think it will, how are my ribs going to live through it?"

"Even if it's ghosts," said Don Quijote, "I won't let anyone touch a thread on your back: if they had their fun with you, the last time, it was because I couldn't climb the courtyard fence. But now we're in flat country, where I can wield my sword as I please."

"And if they enchant you, and paralyze you, as they did the other time," said Sancho, "what good will it do us if we're in open country or not?"

"In spite of that," replied Don Quijote, "I beg you, Sancho, to take heart, for this experience will prove to you of what I am capable."

"All right," responded Sancho, "if it's God's will."

Then, withdrawing to one side of the road, they stood watching carefully to see what all those moving lights might be, and from their post they soon saw a crowd of white-robed men, like soldiers garbed for a nighttime attack, which frightful vision completely finished off Sancho Panza's fortitude. His teeth began to chatter like someone freezing with malarial fever, and the clattering got still worse when they could clearly make out what was coming: about twenty men in white robes, every one of them mounted, carrying burning torches, and behind them a litter draped in black mourning, after which came six more mounted men, black-draped down to their mules' feet — for it was easy to see by their slow, steady pace that these were not horses. The white-robed men were murmuring to one another, their voices low and gentle. This strange vision, at that hour and in such an unpopulated place, was more than enough to strike terror in Sancho's heart, and even in his master's, which could very well have been what happened (though Sancho had already as good as given up the ghost). But that was not how Don Quijote reacted, because he immediately began to conjure out of his books of chivalry a vivid adventure.

He imagined that the litter was a bier on which some badly wounded or dead knight must be lying, whose vengeance had been strictly reserved for Don Quijote alone, and so, without a word, he readied his lance, settled himself firmly in his saddle, and with martial bearing posted himself in the center of the road on which the men in white robes would have to pass. When he saw them drawing near, he raised his voice and called out:

"Stop, you knights, or whatever you may be, and inform me who you are, where you're coming from, where you're going, and who you are carrying on that bier, for all appearances indicate that either you yourselves have committed some wrong, or some wrong has been done to you, and it is right and proper, and necessary, that I be told, so that I may either punish you for what you have done, or take fit revenge for the wrong done to you."

"We're in a hurry," replied one of the men in white robes, "and the inn is a long way off, so we can't stop to give you the accounting you've asked for."

And spurring his mule, he began to ride by. This response greatly annoyed Don Quijote and, taking hold of the mule's bridle, he said:

"Either you stop, and behave more politely, telling me what I have asked, or else you'll all have to do battle with me."

The mule, frightened at having her bridle thus pulled at, reared up and threw off her rider, who fell backwards to the ground. A muledriver, who was on foot, saw the white-robed man fall and began to abuse Don Quijote, who flared up and, without waiting any further, couched his lance and attacked one of the men in mourning, throwing him to the ground, badly wounded. And then, turning on the others, it was a sight worth seeing, the quickness and agility with which he charged and utterly routed them. It seemed as if, that very moment, Rocinante had sprouted wings, he wheeled about so lightly and haughtily.

The men in white robes were timid people, and unarmed, and so they took the first opportunity to leave the battle, beginning to run away across the field, still carrying their lighted torches, so that they looked like men at some masquerade ball, during a night of partying and rejoicing, dashing happily here and there. And the mourners, too, scrambling about, wrapped in their flapping formal robes, could not move out of the knight's way, so that in complete safety Don Quijote thrashed them all, driving them, against their will, into the darkness, for they all thought him no human creature but a devil out of hell, who had come to carry off the corpse lying in the litter.

Sancho watched the whole thing, admiring his master's bravery, and saying to himself:

"This master of mine is clearly just as brave and strong as he says he is."

A burning torch was lying on the ground, near the first man who'd been knocked from his mule, and its light enabled Don Quijote to see him, so he went over, put the point of his lance in the man's face, and told him to surrender, or else he'd be killed. To which the fallen one responded:

"I'm already more than surrendered, for I've a broken leg and can't move. I beg your grace, if you're a Christian, not to kill me, for you'd be committing an act of high sacrilege, since I've got a master's degree and have taken my first holy orders."

"Then what the devil brought you out here," said Don Quijote, "if you're a man of the Church?"

"What brought me here?" answered the fallen one. "My bad luck."

"And you're going to have still more," said Don Quijote, "if you don't tell me what I asked you right from the start."

"It won't be hard to answer you, your grace," answered the college man. "So be advised, your grace, that although I told you, before, that I had a master's, I've only received my bachelor's degree. My name is Alonso López, I'm a native of Alcobendas, come here from the city of Baeza, with eleven other men of religion — who are the people carrying torches. We are going to the city of Segovia, accompanying a dead body, which travels in that litter, the body of a gentleman who died in Baeza, where he had been lying in a vault, and now, as I said, we're bringing his bones to his tomb, which is in Segovia, of which he is a citizen."

"And who killed him?" asked Don Quijote.

"God, by means of a pestilential fever which He gave him," answered the bachelor of arts.

"By so doing," said Don Quijote, "God has saved me the trouble of taking revenge for his death, had someone else killed him; since he was killed by Him all we can do is be silent and shrug, as I would do if He killed me. I wish you to know, learned sir, that I am a knight of La Mancha, named Don Quijote, and it is my task and my occupation to travel about the world righting wrongs and undoing injuries."

"I don't see how you could be righting wrongs," said the bachelor of arts, "because you've turned me from right to wrong, leaving me with a broken leg, which I do not think will ever again be right as long as I live, and the injury you have done me thus leaves me so injured that I will remain forever injured, so that it was a colossal misadventure for me, bumping into you as you go hunting adventures."

"All things," responded Don Quijote, "do not follow the same plan. Your injury, my dear Bachelor of Arts López, happened because you were going about at night, with those white surplices and carrying lighted torches, all wrapped in your black mourning and praying, so that you looked, truly, like evil creatures from the other world. And I, I could not help but fulfill my obligation to attack you, and I would have attacked

even had I known for sure that you were indeed demons out of hell —
which is what I in fact thought you."

"Exactly as my destiny wanted you to," said the bachelor of arts. "Now
let me beg of you, sir knight errant (whose errand has turned out so badly
for me), please help me get out from under this mule, which has a tight
grip on my leg, somewhere between the stirrup and the saddle."

"I'd have gone on talking till tomorrow!" said Don Quijote. "How long
did you intend to wait, before telling me what was pressing on you?"

He immediately called to Sancho Panza, but Sancho was not ready to
come, because he was working hard at pilfering, from a pack mule which
had been ridden by one of these fine gentlemen, a good-sized load of
foodstuffs. He'd turned his coat into a sack, and was loading everything he
could carry, and for which he could find room, into his improvised container, after which he loaded it onto his own donkey, and after that he
responded to his master's call, and helped him to pull the dignified bachelor of arts out from under the mule's weight. Then he lifted the injured
man up on the mule and handed him his torch, and Don Quijote told
him to follow in his companions' tracks, and to beg his pardon of them
for whatever damage he had done, for it had all been out of his hands.
Sancho added:

"And if those gentlemen want to know, perhaps, who the brave knight
was who did all this, your grace should tell them it was the famous Don
Quijote de La Mancha, who also goes by the name of 'The Knight of the
Sad Face.' "

So the bachelor of arts rode off, and Don Quijote asked Sancho why
he had all of a sudden decided to dub him "The Knight of the Sad Face."

"I'll tell you," answered Sancho. "I've been examining you for a while,
your grace, by the light of the torch that unlucky fellow was carrying, and
your face really is just about the most awful I've ever seen. It must be
because you're tired from this battle, or else because you've lost all those
teeth."

"That's not it," replied Don Quijote, "but rather, that the learned man,
who will be responsible for writing the history of my exploits, will have
decided it would be good for me to take another name, as all knights
formerly did: so one gets called, 'He of the Burning Sword'; and one, 'He
of the Unicorn'; and this one, 'He of the Damsels'; and that one, 'He of
the Phoenix'; and another one, 'The Knight of the Griffin'; and yet another, 'The Grim Reaper' — names and insignias by which they were
known all across the face of the earth. So it seems to me that it was the
aforesaid learned man who just now put on your tongue, and placed in
your mind, the idea of calling me 'The Knight with the Sad Face,' which
is how, from now on, I think I shall call myself. And so that name may
better describe me, I have decided to have a very sad face painted on my
shield, when I have the chance."

"You don't need to waste time, or money, on a painted face," said
Sancho, "because all your grace has to do is uncover the one you've already got, and turn it towards anyone who's looking at you; that's all it will
take, without any other picture or any painted shield, to make them call
you 'He of the Sad Face.' And, believe me, I speak the truth, because I

tell you, your grace, señor — and I tell you with a smile — hunger and all those missing teeth have made you look really awful, and, as I said, you can do very well without any sad painting."

Sancho put it so well that Don Quijote laughed, but just the same he meant to call himself 'The Knight of the Sad Face' and have his shield, or maybe his practice shield, painted as he had fancied.

Just then, the bachelor of arts reappeared and said to Don Quijote:

"I forgot to warn your grace that you are now excommunicated, for having laid hands, in violence, on a sanctified object — *juxta illud, Si quis suadente diabolo,* 'So too, if anyone, incited by the devil,' and so forth."

"I don't understand that Latin," replied Don Quijote, "but I know perfectly well that I laid no hands, only this lance, and what's more, I had no idea I was injuring either religious persons nor anything belonging to the Church — for which I have the respect and affection due from someone who, like me, is a Catholic and a faithful Christian — but only ghosts and monsters from the other world. But just the same, I remember what happened to Cid Ruy Díaz when he smashed the royal ambassador's chair, right in the presence of His Holiness the Pope, who excommunicated him for it, and I remember how, that very day, the good Rodrigo de Vivar behaved like an exceedingly worthy and courageous knight."

After hearing this the bachelor of arts rode off, as has been noted, without saying another word. Don Quijote wanted to examine the corpse lying in the litter, to see if it was all bones or not, but Sancho wouldn't allow it, saying:

"Señor, your grace has come through this dangerous adventure more safely than in any I've seen. And these people, although they've been defeated and routed, might still be able to figure out that they were beaten by just one man and, feeling ashamed and embarrassed by that, they might turn around and pull themselves together and come looking for us, and give us something to think about. The donkey's right here, the mountain's not far away, we've got hunger to worry about, and all we have to do is leave here, not hurrying ourselves — because as they say, Let dead men look for their graves, and the living look for their bread."

And, leading the donkey, he begged his master to follow along, which, without saying a word in reply, for he saw that Sancho was right, Don Quijote did. Nor had they gone very far, passing between two hills, when they found themselves in a broad, hidden valley, where they stopped, and Sancho unloaded the donkey and, stretching out on the green grass, with hunger as their sauce, they breakfasted and lunched and dined and had supper all at the same time, satisfying their stomachs with more than one lunch pail of what the pack mule had brought for the clerical gentlemen attending the dead man — gentlemen who rarely let themselves do without.

But then another misfortune struck, which to Sancho seemed the worst of all, and that was that they had no wine to drink, nor any water, so — as they were hounded by thirst — Sancho looked around at the meadow, where rich green grass grew in abundance, and said — what you may read in the next chapter.

Chapter Twenty

— *of the never-before seen, absolutely unheard-of adventure accomplished by the brave Don Quijote de La Mancha, with less danger than ever experienced by any famous knight in the entire world*

"Señor Don Quijote, all this grass tells us there has to be, somewhere near here, a spring or brook that waters it, so we ought to go on a little further and find someplace where we can ease this terrible, nagging thirst — which, without any doubt, is more painful even than hunger."

This advice seemed sensible to Don Quijote, so he took hold of Rocinante's reins, Sancho grasped his donkey's bridle (after having loaded onto his back whatever was left from their supper), and they began to walk slowly across the meadow, feeling their way, for it was too dark to see a thing. But they hadn't gone two hundred paces when they heard a loud roaring of water, as if plunging down from some great height. The sound was immensely cheering, so they came to a halt, trying to make sure just where it was coming from, but suddenly they heard a different, clamoring noise that considerably diluted their pleasure — and especially Sancho's, for he was naturally fainthearted and of small courage. What they heard, let me tell you, was something banging rhythmically, with an even, regular clanking of fetters and chains, which together with the tremendous roaring of the water could have brought fear to any heart other than Don Quijote's.

As I've said, it was night, and dark, and they had managed to grope their way between two tall trees, whose leaves, stirring in the faint breeze, made a fearful, delicate sound: what with the solitude, the place, the darkness, the noise of the water and the whispering of the leaves, everything gave rise to fear and dread, especially when they saw that the banging never stopped, and the wind sighed on, and dawn did not come, and on top of everything else they still did not know where they were. But Don Quijote, as fearless as ever, climbed up on Rocinante and, taking up his shield, set his lance and said:

"Let me tell you, Sancho, my friend, that I have been born in this Age of Iron, by the will of Heaven, in order to restore the Age of Gold — or the Golden Age, as they usually call it. I am the man for whom all dangers are expressly reserved, and grand adventures, and brave deeds. I, let me say once more, am the man destined to resurrect the Knights of the Round Table, the twelve Peers of France and the Nine Worthies, and the man who will make the world forget the Platirs, the Olivantes and Tirants, the Phoebuses and Belianises, and the whole mob of once-famous knights errant, by accomplishing such extraordinary things, in this Age in which I find myself, such wonders, such feats of arms, that they will forever darken the brightest of theirs. Take heed, oh God-fearing and faithful squire, of the blackness of this night, its strange silence, the muffled, blurred murmuring of these trees, the fearful sound of that water we have come searching for, which seems to smash down and hurl itself from the lofty mountains of the Moon, and that unceasing banging that grates on and on and offends our ears — all these things, all of them together and each of them separately, are sufficient to fill even the breast of Mars himself with fear, trembling, and dread, let alone anyone unaccustomed to such events and adventures. Yet all these things that I have thus depicted for you do but spur on and whet my soul for more, so that my heart fairly bursts in my chest, longing to rush into this adventure, however difficult it may prove to be. And so, tighten Rocinante's saddle straps a bit, put yourself in God's hands, and wait for me, right here, for exactly three days, no longer, after which, if I do not return, you are free to go back to your village. And from there, to do me a kindness and a good deed, go to Toboso, where you will tell my incomparable lady, Dulcinea, that her captive knight died while undertaking things that might have made him worthy of being called hers."

Hearing these words from his master, Sancho began to cry as if the world were coming to an end, and said:

"Señor, I don't know why your grace wants to attempt this fearful adventure. It's nighttime, there's no one here to see us, we can easily change our route and take ourselves out of danger, even if it *is* three whole days before we get a drink, and since there's no one to see us, how could anyone criticize us for being cowards — especially since I've heard our priest, and your grace knows him very well indeed, preach that anyone who goes looking for danger will die of it. So it's not a good idea to test God, trying to do such an incredible thing, which no one could possibly survive except by a miracle, though Heaven has certainly granted your grace enough of those, keeping you from being blanket-tossed as I was, and preserving you victorious, free, and safe in the midst of so many enemies, all those people who were traveling with the dead man. And if all these things don't stir or soften that hard heart of yours, let it be affected by the thought that, the moment your grace leaves here, I will be so terrified that I will surrender my soul to anyone who wants it. I left my native soil, and my children, and my wife, to serve your grace, believing everything would be better, not worse but, just as greed ruptures a sack, so my hopes have ripped me — for now, just when I think I'm closest to getting that damned, miserable island your grace has so many times promised me, I see that, instead, I'm going to be left all alone in a desolate place where no human beings ever come. In the name of the one God, oh dear señor, do not do me such an outrageously grievous wrong — and if you simply cannot refrain from attempting this deed, at least wait a bit, until morning, which, according to what I learned of such things when I was a shepherd, can't be more than three hours away, since the Little Dipper's spout is right overhead, and you can tell it's midnight by the lefthand line."

"But Sancho," said Don Quijote, "how can you see where that line is, or the spout or the top, when the night is so dark that there isn't a star to be seen in the sky?"

"That's true," said Sancho. "But fear has a thousand eyes, and it sees things under the ground, let alone those up in the sky. Besides, common sense tells you it won't be long till dawn."

"Let it be as long or as short as it likes," replied Don Quijote, "but it shall not be said of me, neither now nor at any other time, that tears and pleas kept me from doing what a knight ought to do. And so, Sancho, let me beg you to say no more, for God, who has stirred my heart into attempting this unprecedented and fearful adventure, will also look after my safety, as He will comfort you in your sadness. Your job, now, is to properly tighten Rocinante's saddle straps, and then remain here, and I, I will soon return, though who knows whether alive or dead."

Seeing how completely determined his master was, and seeing too how little his tears, and advice, and pleas were worth, Sancho decided to rely on his own ingenuity, and force Don Quijote to wait till dawn, if he could. So when he tightened the horse's saddle straps, he cunningly (and without his master being aware) tied Rocinante's legs with the donkey's halter, making it impossible for Don Quijote to leave when he decided to, because all his horse could do was hop. And observing now neatly it had worked out, he said:

"Now, señor, just see how Heaven, touched by my tears and my pleas, has ordained that Rocinante shall not move, and if you decide to be stubborn, and spur him on, and really let him have it, it's Fortune you'll be angry with — you'll be kicking against the pricks, as they say."

This infuriated Don Quijote but, the more he jabbed his spurs into the horse, the less the animal could move, and so, not catching on to the rope trick, he thought he might as well calm himself down and wait either until dawn or until Rocinante began to move again, believing, without much doubt, that something other than Sancho's cunning lay at the root of it. So he said:

"Since Rocinante cannot move, Sancho, I shall be content to wait until dawn smiles down at us, though I shall weep that it takes so long in coming."

"No need to weep," replied Sancho, "because I'll entertain your grace by telling stories the whole time, unless you want to dismount and stretch out for a little sleep, here on the green grass, the way knights errant do, so you can be better rested when day comes, and more fit for this unheard-of adventure which awaits you."

"Who are you telling to dismount or sleep?" said Don Quijote. "Am I, by any chance, one of those knights who look for rest when danger faces them? *You* sleep, since that's what you were born for, or do whatever you want to, and I will do what best suits me."

"Don't be angry, your grace, my dear sir," answered Sancho, "that's not what I meant at all."

And coming close to his master, he put one hand on the front bow of his saddle, and the other on the back, so he was hugging Don Quijote's left thigh, too afraid to venture even a finger's length away, so driven by his terror of the banging noises, which kept right on. Don Quijote directed him to tell a story, as he'd promised, to wile away the time, and Sancho said he would, if his fright at the noises he was hearing would let him.

"But, never mind, I'll try to tell a story which, if I can manage it, and nothing stops me, is really the best story in the world, so pay attention, your grace, and I'll begin. 'Once upon a time — may good things come to everyone, and bad things to anyone who looks for them' — You should know, dear señor, that the ancients didn't start their tales any way they wanted to, which was a saying of Stupid Cato, the Roman,[1] who said: 'Evil to anyone who looks for evil,' which fits this situation like a ring on a finger, showing that your grace ought to stay right where you are, and not go looking for trouble anywhere, and we ought to find another road, because there's nothing forcing us to stay on this one, where so many terrible things keep attacking us."

"Stick to your story, Sancho," said Don Quijote, "and let me worry about what road we take."

"Well, then," Sancho went on, "in a town in Estremadura there was a goat shepherd, that is, a man who took care of goats, and this shepherd, or goatherd, who according to my story was named Lope Ruiz, he was all in love with a shepherdess named Torralba, and this shepherdess named Torralba was the daughter of a very rich cattle dealer, and this very rich cattle dealer — "

"If you tell your story like that, Sancho," said Don Quijote, "saying everything twice, we won't reach the end for two days. Tell it straightforwardly, and tell it like a man of good sense, or don't tell it at all."

"The way I'm telling the story," replied Sancho, "is the way tales are always told where I come from, and I can't tell stories any other way, and you shouldn't ask me, your grace, to tell it some different way."

"Tell it as you please," responded Don Quijote, "since it is Fate's will that I can't avoid hearing it. Go on."

"So anyway, my very dear señor, so dear to my heart," went on Sancho, "as I've already said, this shepherd was all in love with Torralba, the shepherdess, who was a stocky girl, wild and stubborn, and kind of mannish, because she had a little moustache, and I can see it right now."

"You knew her?" said Don Quijote.

"I didn't know her," replied Sancho, "but the man who told me this story said it was so absolutely and exactly the truth that I really could swear, when I tell it to somebody else, that I saw the whole thing. And so, as the days came and went, the devil — who never sleeps, and is always plotting — arranged it that the shepherd's love turned into dislike, which happened because, according to certain wagging tongues, she made him just a little jealous — I mean, she went too far, she went much too far, and then the shepherd hated her from then on and, so he wouldn't have to see her, decided to go away from there to someplace where his eyes would never again encounter her. Now seeing how Lope disliked her, Torralba immediately decided she wanted him, though she'd never wanted him before."

"That's how women are," said Don Quijote, "spurning those who love them and loving those who hate them. But go on, Sancho."

"It happened," said Sancho, "that the shepherd did as he'd intended to and, driving his goats in front of him, set out across the fields of Estremadura, meaning to cross over into Portugal. Torralba, knowing this, went along behind him, following him from far off, barefoot, with a staff in her hand and a knapsack on her back, in which, they say, she carried a sliver

1. *Catón Zonzorino*, "Stupid Cato," instead of *Caton Censorino*, "Cato the Censor." An illiterate's error [*Translator's Note*].

of a mirror and a piece of a comb, and I don't know how many little bottles of pimple medicine, but let her carry whatever she carried, I'm not interested in trying to prove it one way or the other. All I'm going to say is that the shepherd and his flock got to the River Guadiana, and it was the season when the current was high and full and almost overflowing, and at the place he'd come to there wasn't a boat, not even a little one, nor anyone to take him and his flock over to the other side, which he was very anxious to do, because he saw Torralba getting closer, and he knew she was going to give him a lot of grief with her begging and her crying. But he looked around and looked around until he saw a fisherman, who had a little boat with him, such a little tiny boat that all he could carry in it was one man and one goat, so, anyway, the shepherd spoke to him and arranged to have himself and his three hundred goats ferried across. So the shepherd got in the boat and took a goat with him; then he came back and took another one; and he kept coming back, and coming back, and taking another one each time. — But you'd better keep track of how many goats the shepherd carries across, your grace, because if we forget a single one that will be the end of the story, and it won't be possible to tell another word. — Anyway, let me go on. I ought to tell you that the place where they landed, on the other side, was all muddy and slippery, so it took the fisherman a long time to get there and then come back. Anyway, the shepherd came back for another goat, and then another, and then another — "

"Let's say he carried all of them," said Don Quijote. "You don't need to keep coming and going like that, because in a whole year you'll never get them all across."

"How many has he carried over already?" said Sancho.

"How the devil should I know?" replied Don Quijote.

"Now that's just what I was telling you: you had to keep track. Because otherwise, by God, that's the end of the story, because I can't go on."

"What are you talking about?" replied Don Quijote. "Is it so important to the story to know exactly how many goats he carried across, each and every one, so if you miss one goat you can't go on with the story?"

"I can't, señor, no," replied Sancho, "and that's why I asked your grace to tell me how many goats were carried over, and you told me you didn't know, and right there and then I forgot the whole rest of the story, though by my faith it was a very good and pleasant one."

"Do you mean," said Don Quijote, "that's the end of your story?"

"It's as dead as my mother," said Sancho.

"To tell you the truth," replied Don Quijote, "you've told one of the most novel tales, or stories, or histories, anyone in the world has ever thought of, and the way you told it, and then ended it, is something never to be seen, and never ever seen, in the course of a lifetime, though I expected nothing less from your remarkable powers of reasoning. On the other hand, I'm not surprised, for conceivably this banging, which has never stopped, has troubled your brain."

"That may be it," answered Sancho. "But all I know is that there's nothing left to tell of my story: it ends right there, where we get to the mistake in counting how many goats were carried across."

"Fine. Let it end where it wants to," said Don Quijote. "Now let's see if Rocinante can move."

He spurred Rocinante once again, and again he made a few hops and stayed where he was, so well tied were his legs.

Just about then it happened — whether because the cold of morning was on them, or because Sancho had dined on things with a laxative effect, or because it was just a natural phenomenon (which seems much the most likely reason) — he had an urgent need and desire to do that which nobody else could do for him, but his heart was so gripped by fear that he didn't dare move even one dirty fingernail-length away from his master. But to think of not doing what he wanted so badly to do was also impossible, so what he did, to get rid of the problem, was to let his right hand (which had been clutching the rear saddle bow) slide silently and carefully down and untie the slip knot holding up his trousers, keeping his left hand where it was, so that the garment slipped right to the ground and lay around his feet like chains. Then he tucked up his shirt as best he could, and stuck his buttocks (no small and dainty protuberances) out into the air. This accomplished — which he'd fancied would be the worst part of escaping from that terrible trouble and anguish — an even harder problem presented itself, which was: How could he move his bowels without making some sound, some noise? So he began to clench his teeth and squeeze down his shoulders, meanwhile pushing back all the air in his lungs. But no matter how hard he tried he was unlucky enough, in the end, to make just a small noise, not much but significantly different from the sounds fear had produced. Hearing this, Don Quijote said:

"What was that noise, Sancho?"

"I don't know, señor," Sancho answered. "It must be something new, because once they get started these adventures and misadventures don't ever stop."

So he tried his luck again, and did so well that, without making any more noise or fuss, he got rid of the load which had been weighing on him so heavily. But since Don Quijote's sense of smell was every bit as keen as his hearing, and Sancho was snuggled so close to him that the vapors rose almost directly into his nostrils, there was no way to avoid their reaching his nose, and as soon as they did so he sought relief by squeezing his nostrils shut with two fingers. And then he said, rather nasally:

"It seems to me, Sancho, that you're terribly afraid."

"I am," replied Sancho, "but what makes your grace think it's worse now than it was?"

"Because you smell more than you did," answered Don Quijote, "and it's not perfume."

"That may be," said Sancho, "but it's not my fault, but your grace's, for leading me in strange and uncomfortable directions."

"My friend, take three or four steps away from me," said Don Quijote, without taking his fingers from his nose, "and from now on be more careful of your person and of your responsibilities to me — for my friendly manner has led you to forget your place."

"I'll bet," replied Sancho, "your grace thinks I've been doing something natural that I shouldn't have done."

"Let's let sleeping dogs lie, Sancho, my friend," replied Don Quijote.

This sort of talk occupied master and man the rest of the night. But when Sancho saw that dawn was not far off, he very carefully untied Rocinante and tied up his own trousers. And though Rocinante was hardly a lively and spirited steed, finding himself free seemed to spur him on, because he began to paw at the ground — leaping into the air, if he doesn't mind my saying so, was hardly his style. And Don Quijote, seeing that Rocinante was again able to move, interpreted this as a good sign, and felt that, now, he'd be able to undertake his fearful adventure.

Dawn broke, and the world became visible, so Don Quijote was able to see that they were between two tall chestnut trees, which cast a very dark shadow. He heard, too, that the banging had not stopped, though he could not see what was causing it, so without any further ado, he spurred Rocinante and, turning to take leave of Sancho, ordered him to wait there for three days at the most, just as he told him earlier, and if at the end of that time he had not returned Sancho should take it as certain that it was as God had ordained, and his master had ended his days in that dangerous adventure. He restated the message that Sancho, as his ambassador, was to carry to his lady Dulcinea, and told him that, so far as payment of his wages was concerned, he should not worry, because his master had made his will before leaving home, and Sancho would there find himself well satisfied on all matters touching his salary, to be accounted for pro rata from the time he had entered into Don Quijote's service. On the other hand, if God brought him out of this danger safe and sound, and without letting him be bewitched, Sancho could consider himself absolutely certain to have the promised island.

Hearing yet again his master's sorrowful words, Sancho began to weep once more, and decided not to leave him until the whole affair was over and done with.

And from these tears, as well as from Sancho's honorable decision, the author of this history drew the clear inference that he had to have been well born, and at the very least an Old Christian.[2] These sentiments touched Don Quijote, but not so much that he showed any weakness. Indeed, concealing his feelings as well as he could, he began to ride in the direction from which it seemed the noise of rushing water, and the constant banging, were coming.

Sancho followed on foot, leading his donkey by the halter, as he usually did — the perpetual companion of both his good and his bad fortune. Having gone a fair distance, among those tall and somber chestnut trees, they found themselves in a small meadow at the foot of tall cliffs, from which there tumbled an immense flood of water. And right against these cliffs were some badly built houses, which in fact looked more like ruins than dwellings, from which came, it was easy to see, the banging and uproar — which still had not stopped.

Rocinante was agitated by the roaring of the water, and by the banging, so Don Quijote calmed him and, as they came closer and closer to the houses, he commended himself to his lady, with his whole heart, imploring her to aid him in that fearful expedition, and he also, as he rode,

2. I.e., without either Moorish or Jewish ancestry [*Translator's Note*].

commended himself to God, asking that He not forget His servant. Sancho did not leave his master's side, stretching his neck as far as he could, peering as hard as he knew how, right through Rocinante's legs, to see if he could make out what was gripping at him with such tension and fright.

They went another hundred paces and, turning a corner, saw plainly and unmistakably the cause of the incessant banging, the horrible and — to them — frightful clamor, which had held them all night long in such suspense and fear. The answer was absolutely clear. And it was — may you not, oh reader, be angry or upset — six hydraulic hammers, pounding with alternating strokes on newly manufactured cloth.

Seeing what it was, Don Quijote was struck dumb, shocked to the bottom of his boots. Sancho saw this, noting that his master's head was leaning toward his chest, in clear sign of embarrassment. Don Quijote looked over at Sancho, too, and saw that his cheeks were puffed out, and his mouth stuffed full with laughter, obviously ready to burst with it, so despite the intense gloominess he felt, Don Quijote could not keep himself from laughter, and once Sancho saw that his master had begun, he let the dam break so heartily that he had to jam his fists into his sides, to keep from exploding. Four times he stopped himself and then started all over again, and each time just as wildly, all of which fiercely irritated Don Quijote, especially when he heard his squire proclaiming, in mocking tones:

"You've got to understand, Sancho, my friend, that I was born, by the special will of Heaven, in this our Age of Iron, to restore the ancient Age of Gold. I am he for whom all these dangers have been specially reserved — these great deeds, these brave exploits."

And then he repeated everything Don Quijote had said, when they'd first heard the fearful banging.

Seeing Sancho making fun of him, Don Quijote grew so angry that he lifted his lance and gave him two whacks, and so vigorously that, although Sancho took them on the shoulders, had he taken them on the head they would have made it unnecessary to pay any of his salary — except to his heirs. And when Sancho saw that his joking was being taken so seriously, and so badly, he was afraid his master might go on in the same vein, and said, very humbly:

"Take it easy, your grace, for by God I was just joking."

"You may be joking," replied Don Quijote, "but I'm not. Consider this, my merry friend: Do you think, if this had been yet another dangerous adventure, and not just hammers beating out cloth, have I or have I not shown the courage necessary to deal with it, from start to finish? And by any chance am I required — being, as I am, a knight — to be so familiar with the sounds we hear that I can know one from another, and understand whether a particular noise is or is not made by a cloth-hammer? What's more, might it not be the fact — as in truth it is — that I had never in my life seen anything of the sort, as you most surely have, being the vulgar peasant you are, born and raised among such contraptions? Otherwise, just turn these six hammers into six monstrous giants, and send them rushing right at me — whether one at a time or all at once — and if I don't knock them flat on their backs, with their legs sticking up in the air, then you can make fun of me as much as you like."

"That's enough, my dear señor," answered Sancho. "I admit I carried

the joke too far. But tell me, your grace, now that we've made it up —
and may God see to it that every adventure you have, from now on, leaves
you just this safe and sound — wasn't it really something to laugh at, and
wouldn't it make a fine story, that terrible fright we were in? Or, at least,
the terror I felt, because I can see your grace doesn't know what the word
means, neither fear nor trembling."

"I can't deny," responded Don Quijote, "that what happened to us
might be worthy of laughter. But it's not worth telling stories about, because not everyone has the sense to understand the point of a story and
to know what goes where."

"At least," answered Sancho, "your grace knew where the point of your
lance ought to go, aiming it at my head and letting me have it on the
shoulders, for which I thank God (and how quickly I ducked). But never
mind, it'll all come out in the wash, because I've heard it said: 'You always
hurt the one you love' — and also, right after insulting a servant, real
bigwigs always give them a pair of pants — though I don't know what
they do, right after beating them, except maybe knights errant first whack
them and then give them islands, or even kingdoms on dry land."

"Which could be the way the dice fall," said Don Quijote, "for everything might turn out exactly like that. Don't worry about what's been said
and done: you're a sensible man, and you know that what a man does first
isn't always under his control. From now on, however, be warned about
one thing, which is that you check and restrain all this excessive conversation with me, for in all the many tales of chivalry I've read — and their
number is infinite — I've never heard of a squire who talked to his lord
as much as you talk to me. Truly, this seems to me a grievous error, both
for you and for me — for you, because you have less respect for me; and
for me, because I don't command sufficient respect. Consider Amadís of
Gaul's squire, Gandalín, who was the Count of Firme Island, and read
how he always spoke to his lord cap in hand, with his head lowered and
his body bent half over, like a Turk. And what can we say about Gasabal,
Don Galaor's squire, who preserved such a silence that, as proof of his
wondrous taciturnity, his name is mentioned only once in that entire history, which is as long as it is truthful? And from everything I have said,
Sancho, you must conclude that it is essential to make distinctions between
master and servant, between lord and man, and between knight and squire.
And so, from this day on, we must behave with greater propriety, without
teasing and fooling about, because anything that makes me angry at you
is bad for us both. The gifts and favors I have promised you will be yours,
in good time, and if they're not, your salary, at least, cannot be lost, as I
have already explained to you."

"That's all right, just the way you say it, your grace," said Sancho, "but
what I'd like to know, just in case the good time for gifts never comes and
we have to turn to my salary, is this: back in those days, how much did a
knight errant's squire get paid, and did they figure it by the month or by
the day, like bricklayers?"

"I don't think," answered Don Quijote, "those squires were ever on
salary, but just took what they were given. And if I have designated a salary
for you, in the sealed will I left at home, it was in view of what might

happen. For I do not know how knighthood will turn out, in these calamitous times of ours, nor did I want my soul to be troubled by trivial matters, in that other world. Indeed, I would have you understand, Sancho, that there is no profession in this world more dangerous than that of an adventurer."

"And that's the truth," said Sancho, "since just the noise of cloth-hammers can quicken and unsettle the heart of such a brave traveling adventurer as your grace. But you can be sure that from here on I won't spread my lips to mock anything that concerns your grace, but only to do you honor as my master and natural lord."

"And in so doing," replied Don Quijote, "you will endure upon the face of the earth, for only the respect we owe our parents is greater, nor is it unlike, that which we owe our masters."

Chapter Twenty-One

*— dealing with the exalted adventure and golden reward
of Mambrino's helmet, together with other things which happened
to our invincible knight*

Just then, a light rain began, and Sancho wanted to take shelter in the mill that worked the hydraulic hammers, but the annoying joke had left Don Quijote with such a loathing that nothing could make him walk through the door, so they turned off the highway to the right, onto a road like the one they'd taken the day before.

They had not gone far when they spied a mounted man, wearing on his head something that gleamed like gold, and as soon as the rider came into sight Don Quijote turned to Sancho and said:

"It seems to me, Sancho, that there is truth in all our old sayings, for their wisdom is drawn from experience itself, which is the mother of wisdom. And especially this familiar proverb: 'When one door closes, another one opens.' I say this because Fate may have closed one door against us, last night, cheating us with those cloth-hammers, but now she flings open another, by way of a better and more certain adventure, and if I'm not willing to undertake it the fault will be entirely my own, and not something I can blame either on my small knowledge of cloth-hammers or on the intense darkness of night. I say this because, unless I'm much mistaken, he who comes toward us, right now, wears on his head Mambrino's golden helmet, about which I swore the oath you heard me swear."

"You be careful what you say, your grace, and even more what you do," said Sancho, "because I don't want any cloth-hammers beating and scaring the wits out of us."

"What the devil is wrong with you?" replied Don Quijote. "How do you get from a helmet to cloth-hammers?"

"I don't know anything about that," responded Sancho. "But, by God, if I could talk as much as I used to, maybe I could tell you a few things and your grace would see how wrong you are."

"How can I be wrong, you punctilious traitor?" said Don Quijote. "Just tell me: don't you see that knight riding toward us on his dappled grey horse, wearing a golden helmet on his head?"

"What I can see," answered Sancho, "is just a man on a donkey, a drab one like my own, who's wearing on his head something that glitters."

"And that's Mambrino's helmet," said Don Quijote. "Now you go off a little way and leave me alone with him: watch how, to save time, I finish up this adventure without saying a word, and obtain for myself the helmet I've so much wanted."

"I'll get out of the way, all right," replied Sancho. "But may it be God's will — I have to say it again — that this be the real thing, and not cloth-hammers."

"I've already told you, brother, not to say anything to me about those cloth-hammers — not to even think about saying anything to me," said Don Quijote, "or I swear — but I'll just say this: I'll cloth-hammer your soul for you."

Sancho held his tongue, afraid that his master might actually fulfill the vow, which he'd sworn as round as a ball.

Now as far as the golden helmet and the mounted man Don Quijote saw, the true situation was this: there were two villages in that neighborhood, one of them so small that it had neither a pharmacy nor a barber-surgeon, though the other, which was nearby, did, and so the barber from the bigger village also served the smaller one and would come, carrying his brass basin, whenever — as now — a sick person needed to be bled, and another needed a shave. This time, as luck would have it, it began to rain as soon as he started his journey, and because he didn't want to dirty his hat (which was more than likely a new one), he stuck the basin on his head. And being clean, it was visible, gleaming brightly, from half a mile off. He jogged along on a dun-colored donkey, as Sancho had said — and all of this explains how Don Quijote managed to see the donkey as a dapple-grey horse, ridden by a knight wearing a golden helmet. For him, it was the easiest thing in the world to make anything and everything fit into his wild chivalric ideas and all his crazy thoughts. When he saw the poor gentleman drawing near, Don Quijote set his lance and charged straight at him, not bothering to say a word, spurring Rocinante to a full gallop and clearly intending to run him through. But as he charged, Don Quijote cried out — not slowing a bit —

"Defend yourself, base-born creature, or else surrender to me, of your own free will, that which with such justice I am owed!"

Seeing this phantasm coming at him, the barber, who had neither ex-pected nor been imagining anything of the sort, could think of no other way to avoid the thrust of Don Quijote's lance than to throw himself from his donkey — and as soon as he hit the ground he came springing back up and began to run across the plain so fast that the wind itself couldn't have caught him. He left his basin lying on the ground, which satisfied Don Quijote, who said that the pagan fellow had shown a good deal of sense, for he had imitated the beaver, which, finding itself hemmed in by hunters, rips and tears off with its teeth that which, by natural instinct, it knows they're pursuing [namely, its testicles]. He ordered Sancho to hand him the helmet and, lifting it up, the squire said:

"By God this is a good basin, and it's worth a dollar if it's worth a cent."

Then he gave it to his master, who at once set it on his head, rotating it this way and that, trying in vain to find how it was supposed to fit.

"Plainly," he said, "they hammered this famous helmet to fit the pagan for whom it was originally made, and he must have had an immense head — but what's worse, half of it is missing."

Hearing him call the basin a helmet, Sancho couldn't keep himself from laughing, but, remembering his master's anger, he at once stifled it.

"What are you laughing at, Sancho?" asked Don Quijote.

"I'm laughing," Sancho answered, "as I think of the huge head on the pagan who used to own this helmet, which looks exactly like a barber's basin."

"Do you know what I suspect, Sancho? By some strange accident, this wondrous, enchanted helmet must have fallen into the hands of a person who knew nothing about it and could not appreciate its worth, and so, not knowing what he was doing, and seeing that it was the purest gold, he must have melted down the other half, so he could turn it into ready money, and then made the second half into this, which, as you say, looks very much like a barber's basin. But however it happened, for someone like me, who knows just what it is, the transformation is of no importance. I'll have it fixed, in the first village we come to that has a blacksmith, and so carefully that the very helmet Vulcan, god of all blacksmiths, forged for Mars, god of war, won't be a bit better, or worth any more. And in the meantime I'll wear it any way I can, for something is better than nothing — especially since it will be quite good enough to protect me from being stoned."

"Which it will do," said Sancho, "if they're not using a slingshot, the way they did in the quarrel between the two armies, when they tattooed the sign of the cross on your grace's molars, and broke the tin can where you kept that blessed potion which made me throw up my guts."

"It doesn't worry me that I've lost it," said Don Quijote, "because as you know, Sancho, I carry the recipe in my memory."

"Me too," replied Sancho, "but I'll be damned if I ever in my whole life make it, or taste it, because that'll be the end of me. What's more, I'm not going to let myself get to where I might need it, because I'm going to be watching, with all my five senses, to keep myself from wounding, or being wounded by, anyone. I don't say anything about the time when I got tossed in the blanket, because it's hard to stop that kind of bad luck — and, when it happens, all you can do is tuck in your shoulders, hold your breath, close your eyes, and let yourself go wherever Fate, and the blanket, want to take you."

"You're a bad Christian, Sancho," said Don Quijote, hearing this, "because you never forget any insult you've ever received. But men of noble and generous heart do not pay attention to trivialities. Did you get a lame leg? — a broken rib? — a cracked head? — which won't let you forget that joke? Because, if you consider it carefully, it *was* a joke, a bit of fun, and if I didn't so understand it, believe me, I'd have long since gone back there and done more damage, revenging you, than the Greeks did, when their Helen was kidnapped. But you may be sure that Helen, if she walked the earth now, or if my Dulcinea had lived in her day, would not enjoy such great fame for her beauty."

At which point he emitted a sigh, and let it float up to the clouds. But Sancho replied:

"So let it be a joke, because it can't really be revenged. But I know what's real and what's funny, and I also know it isn't going to fade out of my memory, any more than the marks will leave my shoulders. Still, never mind that: just tell me, your grace, what we're going to do with this dapple grey steed (who looks just like a dun-colored donkey) that got left here when your grace tumbled its rider to the ground — because the way old pagan Martín was working his legs and heading for the high country, I don't think he plans on coming back. By my beard, but this is a fine donkey!"

"It has never been my practice," said Don Quijote, "to despoil those whom I conquer, nor is it a knightly custom to take the vanquished's horse and let them go on foot, unless to be sure the conqueror has lost his own horse in the combat, in which case he is allowed to take the defeated one's animal as a lawful prize of war. Accordingly, Sancho, leave this horse — or donkey — or whatever you choose to call it, because when its owner sees we've left here, he'll come back for it."

"God knows I'd rather take it," replied Sancho, "or, at least, exchange it for mine, which I don't think is as good. Really, now, the laws of knighthood must be pretty narrow, if they don't let you trade one donkey for another. Can't I even trade my harness and bridle for his?"

"On that subject I am not perfectly certain," answered Don Quijote, "so this being a doubtful case, and until better information is available, I'd say you may make that exchange, provided the need is truly great."

"So great," responded Sancho, "that it couldn't be greater if I had to put them on myself."

Quickly, once he'd been granted official permission, he performed the ceremony *mutatio caparum* ["change of hoods": newly made cardinals changing into their new red robes], decking his donkey with a thousand bits of finery and vastly improving his looks.

That accomplished, they dined on the spoils of war (or what was left of them) which they'd taken, earlier, from the pack-mule, and drank water from the river that operated the cloth-hammers, but without turning their faces in that direction, so fiercely did they detest the pounding iron that had so terrified them.

Having thus silenced the angry panging of hunger, the rumbling grumbling of their empty stomachs, they mounted and, without deciding what route to follow (because it was much better for knights errant not to choose their own paths), let themselves go wherever Rocinante felt like going, for his master obeyed the horse's decisions, just as the donkey did, always following Rocinante's lead, for sheer affection and comradeship. But, nevertheless, they were soon back on the highway, and down it they went, willy-nilly, without any plan at all.

And as they went along, Sancho said to his master:

"Señor, will your grace grant me permission to talk to you a little? Because ever since you laid that hard order of silence on me, four or five things have been churning around in my stomach, and there's one, right now, here on the tip of my tongue, that's hard to just hold there."

"Say it," said Don Quijote, "but let your conversation be brief. There's no pleasure in long chatter."

"So what I say, señor," responded Sancho, "is that I've been thinking, for days now, how little your grace actually earns from all this hunting for adventures, traipsing through these wildernesses and crossroads, because even if you conquer and finish off the most dangerous adventures in the world, there's no one to see or know about them, so they'll have to be left in perpetual silence, which isn't what you want or they deserve. So it would be better, it seems to me, though your grace knows best, if we were to enlist in the service of an emperor, or some other great prince, who was engaged in a war where your grace could show just how brave and strong you are, and the superior power of your mind, so that when this lord we were serving saw all this, he'd just have to reward us, each of us according to what we deserve, and also so there'd surely be someone to write down your grace's deeds, so they'd never be forgotten. I won't even talk about mine, because they don't go farther than what squires are supposed to do — though I think I can say say that, if histories of knighthood ever record the deeds of squires, I don't see how they can leave out mine."

"That makes a lot of sense, Sancho," replied Don Quijote, "but before a knight gets that far, he has to go roaming all over the world, as if to prove himself, hunting adventures and, when he finishes off a certain number, winning so high a reputation and such fame that, if he arrives at some great monarch's court, he's already known for his deeds, and when the little boys see him coming through the city gate they tag along after him, and run all around him, shouting: 'Here's the Knight of the Sun,' or the Serpent, or whatever sign he rides under and in the name of which he has accomplished great deeds. 'This is the man,' they'll say, 'who all alone fought and beat the mighty giant, Brocabruno, and the man who broke the Grand Mameluke of Persia's nine-hundred-year enchantment.' So they'll all run around proclaiming your exploits, and soon, responding to the yelling and clamoring of the boys and the other good citizens, the king of that realm will come to the window of his royal palace and, the moment he sees the knight, will recognize him by his armor, or perhaps by the device on his shield, and then of course he'll call out, 'Hey there! All you knights of mine, down in the courtyard, come out to welcome the flower of knighthood, who's just arrived!' And at his command they'll all run out, and the king will meet him halfway up the great staircase, and wrap his arms around him, and give him ceremonial kisses on the cheek, and then he'll lead him by the hand to the queen's own chambers, where the knight will find her with her daughter, the princess, who'll of course be one of the most beautiful, polished damsels anyone could unearth, no matter how hard they tried, anywhere in all the known parts of the world. So what will happen, the moment they meet, is that the princess will fix her eyes on him, and he'll fix his on her, and they'll each think the other more divine than human, and without knowing why or why not, then and there they'll be tangled in love's intricate net, and their hearts will swim in sorrow, not knowing how they can give utterance and voice to their

yearning and their love. And then of course they'll take him to some richly
adorned part of the palace, where, having first relieved him of his armor,
they'll fold a long, sumptuous red cloak around him, so that if he had
been handsome in his war clothes, he will seem handsomer still in his
short-coat. That night he'll take his dinner with the king, the queen, and
the princess, never taking his eyes off the damsel, exchanging stealthy
glances with her whenever possible, each of them watching carefully for
their opportunities — she being, as I have said, a wonderfully prudent
young lady. Then, when they take away the tables, an ugly little dwarf will
suddenly come through the door, and right behind him a beautiful lady,
a giant on either side of her, and she will be the bearer of some adventure,
concocted by a very ancient wiseman, the accomplishment of which will
be reserved for the best knight in the entire world. So the king will order
everyone there to attempt it, but nobody will be able to finish it off except
their guest, to the immense enlargement of his reputation, which will
delight the princess, who will consider herself well and truly happy, having
settled her heart in so lofty a style. And the best part of it will be that this
king, or prince, or whatever he is, will be fighting a hard-fought war with
another ruler just as powerful as himself, so the guest will beg him (after
being at his court a while) to be allowed to serve in that war. The request
will be very cheerfully granted, and the knight will courteously kiss the
king's hands, to acknowledge the favor done him. And that night he'll say
farewell to his lady, the princess, through the railing of a garden gate just
below her bed chamber, at which they have many times conversed, the
intermediary and confidante of all this being a lady in whom the princess
places much trust. He will sigh, she will swoon away, the confidante will
fetch her water, much concerned because dawn approaches and, for her
lady's honor, she does not want them to be discovered. The princess will
come around at last, and put her white hands through the railing, to the
knight, who will kiss them thousands and thousands of times, and bathe
them in tears. Then they'll settle on how he's to let her know whether his
fortunes go well or badly, and the princess will beg him to stay away as
short a time as he possibly can, and he'll promise to do that, with many
solemn oaths, and then go back to kissing her hands, and so they'll say a
deeply emotional farewell, a farewell which will seem rather like dying.
He'll go back to his room and throw himself on his bed, unable to sleep
for the pain of parting, then get up early and go to say his formal goodbye
to the king, the queen, and the princess, but only be able to speak to the
king and the queen, for they tell him the princess is indisposed and unable
to receive visitors, and thinking that this indisposition is from the pain of
their parting, the knight feels his heart transfixed, and is just barely able
to keep from revealing his own grief. The princess' confidante is there and
sees everything, then goes to tell it to her lady, who listens in tears, observing to the confidante that one of the most painful things she is experiencing is not knowing who her knight truly is, and whether or not royal
blood flows in his veins. The confidante assures her that such gallantry,
courtesy, and courage could only be manifested if her knight were of royal
and important lineage, which will alleviate the lady's distress, and she will
try to comfort herself, so as not to give her secret away to her parents, and

after only two days she will once again appear in public. By then the knight has gone; contending in war, he conquers the king's enemy, wins many cities, triumphs in many battles, returns to court, sees his lady as he used to see her, they decide he will ask her father for her hand, in return for all he has done. But the king is reluctant to grant the request, because he doesn't know who the knight is, but anyway, whether because he kidnaps her, or by whatever route Fate happens to follow, the princess becomes his wife, and her father comes to think it a stroke of very good luck, because he finds out that the knight is the son of I don't know what brave king, though I don't think his kingdom is likely to be on any map. So the father dies, the princess inherits the throne, and just like that the knight becomes a king. And at this point he turns and shows his gratitude to his squire and to everyone who helped him rise to such great estate: he marries the squire to one of the princess' ladies, who surely will be the intermediary in their love-making, who is herself the daughter of a very powerful duke."

"Let it be just like that, by God," said Sancho. "That's what I'm looking for, because that's exactly what has to happen to your grace the Knight of the Sad Face, down to the last detail."

"You may trust in it, Sancho," replied Don Quijote, "because this is the pathway, and these are the stages in the process — exactly as I have recounted — by which knights rise, and have risen, to be kings and emperors. All we need, now, is to find out which king, Christian or pagan, has both a war and a beautiful daughter — but there'll be time enough to think about that, since, as I told you, first you have to win fame elsewhere, and then you can present yourself at court. And I'm also lacking something else: suppose I find a king with a war and a beautiful daughter, and I've won incredible, universal fame, I still don't see how I can be found to have royal blood, or even be an emperor's second cousin, because the king won't want to let me marry his daughter if he hasn't first got all the information on this subject, no matter how much my famous exploits are worth, so this deficiency may cause me to lose what my arm would well and truly deserve. Now it's true I'm a gentleman of very good family, and I have land and I have money, and I'm entitled to a royal stipend of five hundred *sueldos*,[1] and maybe the learned man who writes my history will trace my relations and ancestors and find that I'm only five or six generations away from a king. Because you must understand, Sancho, that there are two kinds of family histories in this world: one that starts and descends from princes and monarchs, but is ground away by time, little by little, and finally ends in a point, like a pyramid turned upside down; and another that starts with ordinary people, and goes upward, step by step, until it turns into great noblemen. So the difference is that one was, but isn't any more, and the other is, that didn't use to be, and maybe I'll be one of those who, when everything is known, had great and famous beginnings, so my father-in-law the king will have to be satisfied, and if he's not, the princess will have to want me so desperately that, in spite of her father, she'll take me for her lord and husband, even knowing perfectly

---

1. Some authorities identify the *sueldo* (an ancient coin whose value is unclear) as a gift for the military service of an ancestor.

well that I'm the son of a water-carrier — and if she doesn't, that's when I turn kidnapper and carry her off wherever I feel like taking her, because either time or death will surely cure her father's displeasure."

"That also brings us to what certain cold-blooded people say," said Sancho. " 'Don't ask nicely for what you can take for yourself' — though it might be better to say: 'It's better to run away and hide than wait for good men to help.' Which I say because if the king your grace's father-in-law sticks at handing over my lady the princess, all you can do, as your grace says, is resort to kidnapping and carrying her off. But the trouble is that until you make it up with him, and get to have the kingdom for yourself, the poor squire can just go hungry, as far as getting anything out of it. But maybe the confidante will come away with the princess, and he can make up for his bad luck with her, until Heaven ordains differently, because I'd think his own lord would give her to him as his wife, and right away."

"There'd be no objection to that," said Don Quijote.

"Then that being the case," replied Sancho, "all we can do is commend ourselves to God and let Fate do what it pleases."

"May God see fit to have it be," answered Don Quijote, "as I would have it, and as you, Sancho, need it to be, and let it be unworthy to anyone who thinks it unworthy."

"May God bring it to pass," said Sancho. "And since I'm an Old Christian, that ought to be enough to make me a count."

"More than enough," said Don Quijote, "and, if you weren't, it wouldn't make any difference, because I, as the king, can make you a nobleman, and you don't need to pay or do me any services. And when I've made you a count, right then and there you're a gentleman, no matter what anyone says, and by God they'll have to talk to you as you deserve, whether they like it or not."

"Hey, but won't I know how to use the tile!" said Sancho.

"The word is *title*, not tile," said his master.

"That's fine with me," answered Sancho Panza. "I say I'd know how to take advantage of it because, once upon a time, I was usher at union meetings, and the usher's uniform looked so good on me that everyone said I ought to be the president. So how will I look when I throw a duke's cloak, all lined with ermine, over my back, or find myself draped in gold and pearls, the way those foreign counts do? By God, I think they'll come to see me from a hundred miles around."

"You'll look very well," said Don Quijote, "but you'll have to shave your beard more often, because you let it grow like a jungle, so wild and rough, that if you don't trim it every other day — at least — they'll know what you are from a thousand yards away."

"All I need to do," said Sancho, "is hire a barber, and keep him around the house. Besides, if I had to, I could have him follow me around, like a rich man's groom."

"But how do you know," asked Don Quijote, "that rich men have their grooms walking along behind them?"

"I'll tell you," replied Sancho. "I spent a month at court, once, and while I was there I saw a tiny little man going by, who they said was big and important, and there was a mounted man following him everywhere he went, as if he was the rich man's tail. I asked why that man didn't ever walk *with* the little one, and not always follow along behind him. They told me he was the little man's groom, and rich people liked to have their grooms following behind them. So I learned that lesson once and for all, and I've never forgotten it."

"And you're right," said Don Quijote, "and you can lead your barber like that, for customs didn't all start at the same time, nor were they all invented at once, so you can certainly be the first count to have his barber follow him around. Besides, you have to have more confidence in a barber than in someone who merely saddles your horses."

"I'll worry about this barber business," said Sancho, "and you, your grace, keep trying to make yourself a king and me a count."

"So be it," replied Don Quijote.

And then, looking up, he saw what is narrated in the next chapter.

Chapter Twenty-Two

— *how Don Quijote freed many miserable wretches who, most unwilling, were being taken where they did not want to go*

Sidi Hamid Benengeli, the Arab of La Mancha who wrote this lofty, impressive, scrupulously detailed, pleasant and highly imaginative history, tells us that after the conversation between the famous Don Quijote de La Mancha and his squire, Sancho Panza, narrated at the end of chapter twenty-one, Don Quijote looked up and saw twelve men coming down the road toward them, on foot, strung together like beads by chains around their necks, and with shackles on their wrists. And with them came two mounted men and two more also on foot, the mounted men carrying flintlock muskets, and those on foot, daggers and swords. And when Sancho Panza saw them, he said:

"That's a chaingang of the king's galley slaves, heading for the harbor."

"Slaves?" asked Don Quijote. "Is it possible that the king actually enslaves anyone?"

"That's not what I said," replied Sancho, "except that these are condemned criminals going to serve the king in his galleys, whether they like it or not."

"What you mean," responded Don Quijote, "however you put it, is that these people, whether they like it or not, are being compelled to travel this road, against their own free will."

"That's how it is," said Sancho.

"Then," said his master, "it is my obligation as a knight errant to intervene. I have no choice but to undo compulsion and give aid and assistance to all sufferers."

"Your grace must realize," said Sancho, "that Justice — which means the king — is neither compelling nor injuring people like this, but only punishing them for their crimes."

The file of galley slaves reached them, and Don Quijote, speaking most politely, asked the guards to explain to him the reason or reasons why these people were being treated this way.

One of the mounted men answered that these were galley slaves, in His

Majesty's custody, who were being taken to the galleys, and there was nothing more to be said about it, and nothing more to know.

"In spite of which," replied Don Quijote, "I should like to know from each of them personally the reason for his misfortune."

He added additional arguments, sufficiently polite and pressing to oblige them to grant his request, so the other mounted guard said to him:

"Señor, although we carry with us a certified registry, spelling out the sentences of each of these unfortunates, it would not be appropriate to stop, now, either to locate that registry or to read it, but your grace is welcome to approach and query them yourself, if they wish to explain matters to you — and they will, for these fellows like nothing better than acting and talking like the rogues they are."

Given this opportunity — which Don Quijote meant to take, whether or not they offered it to him — he came closer to the chaingang and asked the first in line what sins he had committed, to earn himself so much trouble. The answer was that love had brought him to this.

"And that's all?" replied Don Quijote. "If lovers are to be thrown into the galleys, I would have been rowing in one of them a long time ago."

"But not the kind of love your grace is thinking about," said the galley slave. "I fell passionately in love with a laundry hamper full of white sheets and pillow cases, and I hugged it so lovingly that, if the police hadn't forced me to let go of it, I'd still be clutching it right this very minute. They caught me in the act, so there was no reason to use torture, and to make a long story short, they gave me a hundred stripes on my shoulders and, for good measure, exactly three full years in the *gurapas*, and that was the end of it."

"What are *gurapas*?" asked Don Quijote.

"*Gurapas* are galleys," was the answer.

He was a young fellow of about twenty-four, from Piedrahíta, he said.

Then Don Quijote asked the same question of the next in line, who, sunk in sadness and misery, didn't say a word. But the first one spoke for him, saying:

"This fellow, señor, is here for being a canary — that is, because of his music and singing."

"What?" Don Quijote said once more. "They send you to the galleys for music and singing, too?"

"Oh yes, señor," the galley slave replied. "There's nothing worse than singing, when you've got problems."

"What *I've* heard," said Don Quijote, "is that singing drives your troubles away."

"But here, it's the other way around," said the galley slave. "Anybody who sings even once, cries the rest of his life."

"I don't understand," said Don Quijote.

But one of the guards said to him:

"Sir knight, 'to sing when you're in trouble' means, for these *non sancta* [illicit, impure] fellows, confessing under torture. This silent sinner was tortured and confessed his crime, which was being a rustler — that is, an animal thief — and because he confessed he was sentenced to six years in the galleys, plus two hundred lashes for his shoulders, and now he always walks around silent and dismal, because all the other thieves, the ones back in jail and these fellows here, are constantly making fun of him, abusing and cursing and spitting at him, because, instead of having the guts to say nothing, he confessed. They say there are just as many letters in *no* [no] as in *sí* [yes], and a criminal has all the luck he needs when life or death hangs on his own tongue instead of on the word of witnesses and evidence — and that's pretty much my opinion, too."

"And mine," answered Don Quijote.

Then he asked the third in line the same question he'd asked the others, and was answered readily and confidently:

"I'm making a five-year visit to those fine ladies, the *gurapas*, because I was short ten dollars."

"I'd gladly give you twenty," said Don Quijote, "to get you out of your trouble."

"That," replied the galley slave, "is like a man on the high seas who has plenty of money but is dying of hunger, because he has nowhere to buy what he needs. Let me tell you, if I'd had the twenty dollars your grace now offers me, back when I needed them, I'd have used them to buy off the court clerk's pen and stir up my lawyer's brains, and today you'd see me smack in the middle of Zocodover Plaza, in Toledo, and not out here on this highway, like a greyhound on a leash. But God is Great. Patience — and that's enough."

Don Quijote moved on to the fourth man, who had a white beard down to his chest, and a venerable face. And when asked why he was there, this man began to weep and did not say a word, but the fifth in line spoke up for him, saying:

"This honorable man is off to the galleys for four years, after having been paraded around on a donkey, the way they usually do."

"That means," said Sancho Panza, "as far as I know, being shamed in public."

"That's it," said the galley slave, "and the crime he committed, to deserve this punishment, was being a financial go-between [*corredor de oreja* = "broker" or "pimp"] — anyway, an intermediary for bodies. I mean, this gentleman is being sent up for pimping, and also for a whiff of wizardry."

"If he hadn't thrown in the witchcraft," said Don Quijote, "but left it at being a go-between, he wouldn't deserve just to go rowing in the galleys, but to be their captain or their admiral. For being a go-between isn't so easy; it's a job for tactful people, and extremely important in any well-ordered republic, nor should it be exercised by any but well-born persons — indeed, they ought to have official overseers and examiners, as in other professions, all specified by law and made generally known, as with registered brokers, for this would eliminate all the evils we create, when we allow this task to be performed by stupid people of limited intelligence — silly women, or callow pages, or clowns with little wisdom and less experience, who when good sense is absolutely essential, and significant schemes are afoot, never know whether to push or pull — don't even remember which hand is right and which left. I am tempted to go on and explain the best method for choosing those who, in our republic, ought to perform this essential function, but this is hardly the appropriate place — though, some day, I shall set them out for someone in a position to truly do something about these matters. Let me just say, now, that the pain caused me by seeing this venerable face, crowned by these white hairs, so utterly worn down, and all for being a go-between, has been effectively counter-balanced by the added charge of witchcraft, although I know quite well there are no spells or charms in the world which can make a person do anything against his will, even if simple-minded folk believe there are, for we enjoy freedom of the will, and no herbs or enchantments can take it away from us. What silly women and lying rogues accomplish, with their potions and poisons, is to drive men crazy, which leads people to think they have the power of forcing others to fall madly in love — although, as I say, it's impossible to enslave our free will."

"It's true," said the good old man, "and, in truth, señor, I am not guilty of witchcraft, though I cannot deny the charge of pimping. But I never thought there was anything wrong in it: all I meant was for everyone to enjoy themselves and live peacefully and happily, without quarreling or sorrow. But such benevolence wasn't enough to keep me from going where I have no hope of ever returning, old as I am, and with urinary problems that never leave me alone."

And he started to weep again, as before, which made Sancho feel such pity that he took out one of the four dollars he was carrying and gave it to him.

Don Quijote proceeded to the next in line, inquiring about what he had done to bring him to this pass, and received an even more high-spirited answer:

"I'm here because I fooled around too much with a couple of my cousins, plus two other girls who weren't my sisters, and I had so much fun with all of them that we ended up with a family tree the devil himself couldn't have straightened out. They had no trouble proving I was the one, I didn't get any breaks, and since I had no money I was pretty close to having my neck stretched, but they sentenced me to six years in the galleys, and I didn't fight it; it's my own fault I got punished; I'm still young; if I stay alive it'll all work out. But sir knight, your grace, if you've got anything that could help these poor wretches, you'll be repaid in Heaven, and right here on earth we'll be sure to include your grace in our prayers, wishing you a long life and good health, and may it be as long and as happy as your fine self deserves."

He was wearing student's clothes, and one of the guards said he was a great talker and his Latin was elegant.

Behind these men, there came a singularly handsome fellow of about thirty — though one of his eyes did turn in toward the other just a bit. He was bound quite differently from all the others, with a huge chain, starting at his feet, that was tied all around his body, plus a pair of shackles around his neck, one of them attached to the chain, the other the kind they call a "friendly watchman," or "your friend's foot,"[2] from which shackles two other chains ran down to his waist, where there was yet an-

---

2. Like a yoke, to force a man to hold his head erect [*Translator's Note*].

other pair of manacles, locked onto his wrists by a stout padlock, so he could neither put his hands up to his mouth nor lower his head to his hands. Don Quijote asked why this man wore so many more chains than any of the others, and the guard told him because this fellow had committed more crimes than all the others put together, and because he was so bold and such an incredible scoundrel that, even transported like this, they couldn't be entirely sure of him, but were worried that he might get away.

"Of what crimes can he be guilty," said Don Quijote, "if the worst punishment he deserves is to be exiled to the galleys?"

"He's going for ten years," the guard answered, "which is as good as civil death. The only other thing you need to know is that this fine fellow is the celebrated Ginés de Pasamonte, also known as Ginesillo de Parapilla."

"My dear sheriff," the galley slave said, "let's take it easy and not try to hand out names and nicknames. My name is Ginés, not Ginesillo, and my family name is Pasamonte and not — according to you — Parapilla. Try ploughing your own field, all right? And let that hold you."

"Get off your high horse," replied the guard, "you king of the thieves, or I'll make you shut up, whatever you think."

"Plainly," replied the galley slave, "man proposes and God disposes. But some day someone's going to find out whether my name really is Ginesillo de Parapilla."

"It isn't what they call you, eh, you liar?" asked the guard.

"It's what they call me," replied Ginés, "but I'll make sure they give it up, or I'll skin them alive with my teeth. Now, sir knight, if you've got something to give us, give it to us and be done with it, and goodbye to you, because all this poking into our earlier lives is getting to be a pain. And if it's my life you want to know, let me tell you I'm Ginés de Pasamonte, and I've written my life with these fingers."

"He's telling the truth," said the guard, "because he really has written his own history, which is really something, and he's left the book back in jail, pawned for two hundred dollars."

"And I'll get it back," said Ginés, "if I have to pay twice that."

"It's that good?" asked Don Quijote.

"It's so good," replied Ginés, "that it's going to be too bad for books like *Lazarillo de Tormes*[3] and all those others they've scribbled, or they're still scribbling. All I'll say is that my book has the facts, and they're such fine and fantastic facts that lies just can't compete."

"And what's the book titled?" asked Don Quijote.

"*The Life of Ginés de Pasamonte.*"

"And is it finished?" asked Don Quijote.

"How can it be finished," the galley slave answered, "if my life isn't? What I've written is from my birth up to the last time I escaped from the galleys."

3. The popular and anticlerical first book of picaresque fiction —— the literature of losers, vaga-bonds, and delinquents —— to appear in Renaissance Spain. It was published anonymously in 1554 and translated, within several decades, into French, German, Latin, Italian, Dutch, and English.

"So you've been there before?" said Don Quijote.

"In the service of God, and the king, I was there for four years, so I know all about hardtack biscuits and hard-back whipping," replied Ginés, "so it doesn't bother me a lot, going there again, because I'll have a chance to finish my book, and I've still got a lot of things to say — and in the galleys of Spain you get more time off than I'll need, though I won't need a lot for what I have to write, because I know it by heart."

"You seem a clever man," said Don Quijote.

"Yes, and an unlucky one," replied Ginés, "because bad luck always follows after cleverness."

"It follows after liars," said the guard.

"I've already told you, my dear sheriff," answered Pasamonte, "that you need to take it easy. Your bosses didn't give you that staff so you could mistreat the poor wretches you drive along this road, but just so you could get us where His Majesty commanded. And otherwise, by the life of . . . But enough! Maybe some day it'll all come out in the wash, how you play games with other people's money. Let's all keep our mouths shut, and live well, and talk better — and let's get going: this is getting damned silly."

The guard raised his staff, ready to let Pasamonte have it for threatening him, but Don Quijote got between them and asked him not to mistreat the fellow, for how much did it mean, to let someone whose hands were so tightly tied give his tongue a little freedom? And then he turned and addressed the entire chaingang, saying:

"My dear brothers, from all you've told me I see quite clearly that, though you are being punished for your crimes, the punishments they're inflicting on you are deeply distasteful, and you go to the galleys most unwillingly — indeed, very much against your will. It may very well be that this man's lack of courage, under torture, and that man's lack of money, and that other man's lack of powerful friends and, in the last analysis, the judge's corrupt judging, have been the cause of your downfall, and the reason you did not have the benefit of the fair and just treatment to which you were entitled. And as I rehearse these things in my mind, and reflect on the way it has all been communicated to me, I am persuaded — nay, I am obliged to realize — that your situation fits the goal contemplated by Heaven when it placed me here in this world, and led me to join the order of knighthood to which I belong, and the vow I made, at that moment, to help the needy and those who are oppressed by the strong. But since I am keenly aware that it is the better part of wisdom to do by fair means what need not be done by foul, I wish to ask these gentlemen, your guards, to unchain you and let you go where you will, for they will not lack for others who will serve the king with far better reason. For it seems to me a harsh matter to make slaves of those whom God and Nature have created free. And what's more, gentlemen," added Don Quijote, speaking to the guards, "these poor fellows have done nothing to you personally. Let us each be responsible for our own sins; there is a God in Heaven who will not forget to punish the wicked, or to reward the good, nor is it fitting that honorable men be the executioners of their fellows, who have done nothing to them. I make this request thus gently and calmly, so that, should you see fit to comply, I will have grounds for expressing my gratitude to you. But if you are not willing to do as I have asked, this lance, and this sword, and the strength of my arm, will oblige you to do it against your will."

"What elegant bullshit!" replied the guard. "That's some joke you're pulling on us! He'd like us to free the king's galley slaves, as if we had any such authority, or he had any to order us to! Go on, señor, your grace: follow your sacred road — but straighten out that barber's basin you've got on your head, and don't go hunting for any cats with three legs."

"The cat, the rat, and the rascal are you!" replied Don Quijote.

And as he spoke he attacked the guard so rapidly that, before he could defend himself, he was toppled to the ground, badly wounded by a lance thrust — which was lucky, because he was the one who had the musket. The other guards were stunned and astonished by this sudden development, but then they wheeled toward Don Quijote, the mounted ones drawing their swords, and those on foot their daggers, and rushed at him. Calmly, he waited for them, but it would surely have gone badly for him except that the galley slaves, seeing the chance of obtaining their freedom, managed to break the chain that bound them together. And the melee turned so wild that the guards, first rushing to their prisoners, who had untied themselves, then running back toward Don Quijote, who was attacking them, accomplished nothing at all.

Sancho did his part by helping Ginés de Pasamonte out of his chains, so that Ginés was the first of the galley slaves to jump onto the battlefield, free and unencumbered, whereupon he rushed to the fallen guard and took his sword and his musket, the latter of which he first aimed at one guard and then turned on another, but never fired, all the guards running for their lives, as much because of Ginés's musket as because of all the rocks the freed galley slaves were throwing at them.

Sancho was very worried about this, because he was sure those who had run off would notify the local constabulary, and as soon as the bells began to ring they'd come riding out, searching for the criminals. Which was what he said to his master, begging him to leave there at once and take refuge in the nearby mountains.

"That's all well and good," said Don Quijote, "but I know exactly what has to be done next."

So calling out to the galley slaves, who were rushing wildly about (they had already stripped the guard to the skin), he got them gathered in a circle, to find out what he wanted, and then said to them:

"Well-born people are thankful for the kindnesses they receive, and one of the sins most offensive to God is ingratitude. I say this to you, gentlemen, because you have now seen, at first hand, what I have done for you, and what I should like you to do in return is to take these chains, which I have struck from around your necks, and proceed at once to the city of Toboso, there to present yourselves before Lady Dulcinea del Toboso and inform her that her knight, the Knight with the Sad Face, sent you there with his greetings, in order that you might tell her, blow by blow, everything which took place during this famous adventure, up to the point where you recovered your longed-for freedom. And, having done this, you may go wherever you please, and good luck to all of you."

Ginés de Pasamonte, as spokesman for the rest of them, replied:

"Señor, our dear Liberator, what your grace asks of us is, of all the things in the world, the most impossible of all impossibilities, for we cannot travel down the highway in a body, but only alone and by separate routes, each of us following his own nose and trying to crawl into the bowels of the earth, to keep from being found by the constabulary — which without any question will come searching for us. What your grace can do, therefore, and it is only proper that you do so, is to substitute for this service and tribute to the Lady Dulcinea del Toboso a prescribed quantity of Ave Marias and Credos, which we will say on your grace's behalf, this being something which can be done both by night and by day, whether running or hiding, in peace or in war. But to expect us, now, to turn back the clock to the good old days — asking us to set out, all of us, on a chaingang pilgrimage down the road to Toboso — is like thinking that right now it's the middle of the night, although in fact it's not even ten o'clock in the morning, and your request of us is very like asking an elm tree to give you pears."

"Then damn it all!" said Don Quijote, raging mad. "Don Son of a Bitch, Don Ginesillo de Parapilla, or whatever you're called, you'll have to go to Toboso all alone, your tail between your legs and the whole chain on your back."

Pasamonte, who was not inclined to be long-suffering, had already realized that Don Quijote was not quite right in the head — having first of all undertaken the crazy job of freeing convicted galley slaves, and then begun to treat them as he had — so he winked to his companions and, stepping back a bit, they began to throw such a storm of rocks at Don Quijote that he didn't have enough hands to cover himself with his shield, and poor Rocinante paid no more attention to his master's spur than if he'd been a horse made of brass. Sancho hid behind his donkey, using the animal to protect himself against the shower of rocks hailing down on them. Don Quijote could not so readily take shelter, and God alone knows how many stones struck against his body, thudding down so overwhelmingly that they swept him to the ground — and the moment he fell, the student leaped on him, pulled the basin off his head, and used it to give him three or four whacks on the shoulders — and because he just as often hit the ground with it, the basin was virtually shattered. They pulled off the quilted jacket the knight wore under his armor, and tried to strip off his leg-stockings, too, but the leg-armor got in their way. They stole Sancho's coat and, leaving him in his shirt sleeves, parcelled out the spoils of the battle, then ran off in all directions, considerably more worried about escaping from the constabulary than about carting off their old chains and presenting themselves before Lady Dulcinea del Toboso.

The only ones left were the donkey and Rocinante, and Sancho and Don Quijote — the donkey, sad and very sober, still swivelling his ears around and around, as if he thought the storm of rocks falling on them had not yet ceased; Rocinante, stretched out next to his master, because a stone had knocked him to the ground, too; Sancho, shivering in his shirt sleeves, and from fear of the constabulary; and Don Quijote, furious to find himself badly hurt by the very people for whom he'd done so much.

Chapter Twenty-Three

— what happened to our famous Don Quijote in the Sierra Morena mountains — one of the strangest adventures narrated in this entire veracious history

Finding himself so bruised and battered, Don Quijote said to his squire: "I have always heard it said, Sancho, that doing good for bad men is like throwing water into the ocean. Had I listened to what you told me, I would have avoided this misfortune. But what's done is done. Patience — and let's be more careful, from now on."

"You'll be careful, your grace," replied Sancho, "about as readily as I'll turn into a Turk. But as long as you say you could have avoided all this damage, if only you'd listened to me, listen to me now and let's avoid an even worse one, because, understand me, constables don't pay any attention to the rules of chivalry — all the knights errant in the world don't mean two cents to them — and I can almost hear their arrows whizzing past my ears."

"You're a natural coward, Sancho," said Don Quijote, "but to keep you from saying I'm stubborn and never do as you advise me, this time I want to take your advice and withdraw myself from the violence you so much fear — but only on one condition, which is that never, either in life or death, will you tell anyone that I left and went away from this danger out of fear, but will explain that it was simply to oblige you, and if in fact you say anything different, you'll be lying, and from now to then, and to then from now, I'll deny your explanation and say you lie and will indeed be lying every time you either think or say such things. Don't say another word: because even thinking about my going away from anything dangerous, and especially this situation, which I think is associated with more than just a shadow of fear, makes me feel ready to stay right here and, all alone, wait not only for our brothers the constables, of whom you've spoken and of whom you're afraid, but for the brothers of the Twelve Tribes of Israel, and the Seven Macabees, and for those ancient brothers, Castor and Pollux, and any other brothers and brotherhoods in the whole world."[1]

"Señor," replied Sancho, "to withdraw is not to retreat, nor does hope make any sense, when danger totally outweighs hope, for the wise man is he who takes care of himself today so he is able to fight tomorrow, rather than risking everything on just one day. And you should know that, although I'm crude and lowborn, still I can rise higher than that by being known as a good governor. So don't be sorry you took my advice, but just climb up on Rocinante, if you can, and if not I'll help you, and then just follow me, because something tells me we need our legs, now, more than our hands."

Don Quijote mounted without saying a word and, with Sancho on his

---

1. The Twelve Tribes of Israel, named after the sons and grandsons of Jacob, took possession of the Promised Land after the death of Moses. The Seven Maccabees were martyred brothers who were skinned, mutilated, scalped, and roasted alive in front of their mother (2 Maccabees 7 — the last book of the Apochrypha). Castor and Pollux were mythological twins who, after their deaths, were transformed into the constellation Gemini.

donkey leading the way, they went off into the nearby Sierra Morena mountains, it being Sancho's plan to go completely across and emerge at El Viso, or perhaps at Almodóvar del Campo, concealing themselves for a while in those rugged places in order to keep the constables from finding them, if they came looking. He felt much encouraged, seeing that the store of provisions loaded on the donkey had not been damaged during the fight with the galley slaves, which seemed to him a miracle, after the way the escaped prisoners had ripped and rummaged through everything.

Don Quijote, too, felt his spirits rise as they reached the mountains, for this seemed to him a perfect place for the adventures he was seeking. He rode along, rehearsing to himself all the miraculous things that had happened to knights errant in such solitary and rugged places. He was so absorbed in these encounters, so lost and carried away, that he could think of nothing else. Nor was Sancho worried about anything — now that they seemed to be heading for safer parts — except satisfying his stomach with what was left of their clerical booty, so he jogged along behind his master, sitting side-saddle, pulling food out of a sack and stuffing his gut, nor would he have given a brass penny, going along like that, for *any* adventure.

Just then, he glanced up and saw that his master had halted and was trying to pick up, using the point of his lance, some object that had fallen to the ground, so he hurried up to help, if necessary, and when he got there was just in time to see the point of the lance lifting up a saddle cushion and a small suitcase that was tied to it, both half rotten, or worse, and falling apart, but so heavy that Sancho had to dismount to help get them. His master ordered him to see what was in the suitcase.

Sancho did this as fast as he could, and though the suitcase had been secured by a chain and a padlock, the cracks and tears were so extensive that he could easily make out the contents — four shirts of fine Dutch linen, plus other linen objects equally well-made and clean and, wrapped in a handkerchief, a small hoard of gold coins. And as soon as Sancho saw them, he cried out:

"Blessed be Heaven on high, for finally presenting us with an adventure that's worth something!"

Then, hunting for more, he found a memorandum book, richly decorated. Don Quijote asked to see this, directing him to keep the money for himself. Sancho kissed his hands in gratitude and, removing the linen too from the suitcase, stored it in his food sack. Seeing which, Don Quijote said:

"It seems to me, Sancho, that this cannot possibly be anything but the remains of some lost traveler, obliged to pass through these mountains, where, being attacked by a band of thieving scoundrels, he was killed, after which they brought him to this secret place and buried him."

"It can't be that," replied Sancho, "because if they'd been thieves, they wouldn't have left this money here."

"Now that's true," said Don Quijote, "and so I cannot understand or guess what all this might mean. But wait: let's see if there's anything written in this memorandum book which might furnish us with a clue."

So he opened it, and the first thing he found, written out like a draft, but in a very fine hand, was a sonnet, which he read aloud, so Sancho too could hear it, as follows:

Oh, either Love is deficient in understanding,
Or it overflows with cruelty, or I've been sentenced
To the harshest, hardest of possible punishments for offences
Infinitely smaller than these penalties you've commanded.
    But if Love is a god, there's a line of reasoning no one
Can ignore, a good and sufficient argument: How
Can a god be cruel? And if Love's not the source, who
Ordered this terrible sadness that charms as it stuns?
    It could not be you, Chloe, it could not be you
Who effects such evil, being yourself so good,
Nor could it be Heaven that sends me such misery: it could not.
    But death I know: I have to die, and soon,
For he who suffers from an unknown sickness should not
Expect to be cured by less than a miracle's boon.

"You can't learn anything from that poem," said Sancho, "unless the single clue solves the whole thing."

"Which clue do you mean?" said Don Quijote.

"I thought," said Sancho, "your grace read the word *clue*."

"All I said was *Chloe*," answered Don Quijote, "and there's no question but that's the name of the lady about whom the author wrote this sonnet — and by my faith it's not bad poetry, or I'm no judge of the art."

"Then," said Sancho, "your grace understands poetry, too?"

"Better than you might think," replied Don Quijote, "as you'll find out when you carry a letter, written in verse from start to finish, to my Lady Dulcinea del Toboso. I want you to understand, Sancho, that all — or almost all — the knights errant of the past were great poets and musicians, poetry and music both being skills, or one might better say accomplishments, closely linked to all lovers errant. But it is true that the poems of these knights were distinguished more for their spirit than their beauty."

"Go on reading in that book, your grace," said Sancho, "and maybe you'll find something that tells us what we want to know."

Don Quijote turned the page and said:

"This is prose, and seems to be a letter."

"A letter that was sent, señor?" asked Sancho.

"It begins like a love letter," replied Don Quijote.

"So read it out loud, your grace," said Sancho. "I really like these love things."

"With pleasure," said Don Quijote.

And reading aloud, as Sancho had requested, he found that it went like this:

> *Your false promise and my certain misery have carried me away to where you are more likely to hear news of my death than the sound of my complaints. Oh ungrateful one! You have rejected me in favor of a man wealthier but not better, though if virtue were considered wealth I would not have to be jealous of anyone else's happiness or weep for my own misfortunes. That which your beauty brought into being, your actions have destroyed, because the one made me believe you an angel, while the other shows me you are a woman. May you live in peace, you who gave birth to my war, and may Heaven forever hide your*

*husband's lying tricks, so you will never regret what you have done nor
I have a revenge I do not want.*

After reading this letter, Don Quijote said:

"We can't learn much from this, as compared to the sonnet, except that
it was written by some rejected lover."

Then, leafing through virtually the entire notebook, he found other
poems and letters, some of which he could make out, and others he could
not, but they were all complaints, laments, suspicions, longings and sorrows, moments of kindness and of scorn, some of them celebratory, some
of them mournful.

While Don Quijote looked through the notebook, Sancho — moved
to rapture by the gold pieces he'd found, of which there were more than
a hundred — was looking through the suitcase, poking into every corner,
and into the cushion, too, peering and prying, even pulling seams apart,
unravelling every single thread, to make sure he had overlooked nothing
and done everything he could. And even though he found no more, he
would have sworn, now, that it was all worth it — the blanket-tossing,
the vomiting up his master's magic balm, the blessings pounded into him
by cudgels, the muledrivers' punches, the loss of his saddlebags, his stolen
overcoat and all the hunger, thirst, and weariness he'd experienced in his
grace Don Quijote's service. It all seemed to him more than sufficiently
repaid, now that he'd been rewarded with this treasure.

The Knight of the Sad Face was powerfully interested in finding out
whose suitcase it was, imagining, because of the sonnet, the letter, the gold
coins, and the exceedingly fine shirts, that it must have belonged to some
highborn lover, who had been brought to his despairing end by his lady's
scorn and ill treatment. But since there was no one in that wild and lonely
place who could tell him, all he could do was proceed on his way, letting
Rocinante's feet choose which road to take — which was whatever road
the horse's hooves could find — convinced, as ever, that in such a wilderness he could not help but find some strange adventure.

Proceeding, then, in this frame of mind, he suddenly saw, up on a
mountain peak, a man leaping along, with unusual grace and agility, from
crag to crag and shrub to shrub. He seemed bare-chested, with a thick
black beard, his hair wild and long, his feet bare and nothing on his legs,
his thighs covered by ragged and torn breeches that looked like a kind of
tawny velvet, but in such in state that his skin showed through here, there,
and everywhere. His head was bare, too, and although he moved lightly
and quickly, as we have said, the Knight of the Sad Face was able to
see and take note of all these details, but though he tried he was unable
to follow the man, for in his enfeebled state Rocinante could not scramble
over such steep slopes, and even at his best he was inclined to be slow-
moving and sluggish. Don Quijote immediately thought this was the
owner of the saddle cushion and the suitcase, and decided to find him,
even if it meant spending a year in those mountains, and so, ordering
Sancho to get down off his donkey and cover one area, while he himself
covered another, he hoped that, trying thus diligently, they could perhaps
locate this man who had run away from them so quickly and easily.

"I can't do that," said Sancho, "because as soon as I go away from your grace I get so afraid that a thousand different things scare me, and I imagine I don't know what. So let me warn you: from now on, I'm not going two inches away from you."

"Then that's how it will be," said He of the Sad Face, "and I'm happy you think so well of my courage, which will never fail you, even if your soul leaves your body. So come along just behind me, or however you want to proceed, but let your eyes be like lanterns and let's cover every inch of this mountain range. Perhaps we can locate that man we saw, for without question he must be the owner of your treasure."

To which Sancho replied:

"I'd be a lot happier not finding him, because if we do, and the money turns out to be his, I'll obviously have to give it back, so why bother with all this wasted effort? It's better if I just hold onto it in good faith, until some method involving less snooping and fuss turns up the true owner, and maybe by then I'll have spent it all, and the king will say I don't have to repay it."

"There you delude yourself, Sancho," replied Don Quijote, "because since we've already realized he might be the owner, we have no choice but to look for him and return his property, because, if we don't, that strong suspicion would make us as guilty as if he were in fact the true owner. And so, Sancho my friend, don't let our hunting for him worry you, because finding him will relieve me of any such obligation."

Then, spurring Rocinante, with Sancho, as usual, following along on his donkey, they circled around that part of the mountain and found, lying in a stream, half eaten by dogs and pecked away by crows, a dead mule, saddled and bridled, which discovery confirmed their suspicion that the man who'd run away was the owner of both the mule and the saddle cushion.

As they were staring at the dead mule, they heard something like a shepherd's whistle, and then suddenly, to their left, they saw a large flock of goats and, coming right behind them, over the mountain peak, the old man guarding the flock. Don Quijote called to him, asking him to come down. He shouted back, asking what had brought them to that wild place, where almost nothing but goats, and wolves, and other wild beasts had ever walked. Sancho answered that he should come down and they'd explain the whole thing. So the goatherd came down and, coming over to Don Quijote, said:

"I'll bet you're looking at that hired mule, lying dead in the ravine down there. By God, he's been there six months! So tell me: have you seen his owner around here?"

"We haven't found anyone or anything," replied Don Quijote, "except a saddle cushion and a small suitcase, lying not far from here."

"Oh, I found them too," said the goatherd, "but I never felt like picking them up, or even going close to them, because I was afraid they were bad luck and I might get accused of stealing — the Devil's a crafty fellow, and he makes things come right up under your feet to get you to stumble and fall, without knowing how it happened."

"That's what I say," replied Sancho, "because I found it, too, and I didn't want to get any closer than a stone's throw. I just left it where it's been all along, because I'd pay double to stay out of trouble."

"Tell me, my good man," said Don Quijote, "do you know who might be the owner of these articles?"

"What I can tell you is this," said the goatherd. "Six months ago, more or less, at a shepherd's hut, maybe eight or nine miles from here, a young man showed up, good-looking and well-spoken, riding on that same mule that's lying dead down there, and with that same saddle cushion and suitcase you saw and left lying in the road. He asked us which part of these mountains was the most rugged and hardest to get to, and we told him it was this part, where we're standing right now, which was the truth, because, more than likely, you go maybe another mile further and you won't know how to get back out again, and I'm downright surprised you made it this far, because there isn't a road, or even a trail, to get you here. Anyway, as soon as he heard what we'd said, the young fellow turned his mule around and rode straight to the place we'd told him about, and we were all pretty well struck at how good-looking he was, and puzzled by what he'd asked us and how fast we saw him riding off into the mountains, but from that day on we never saw him again, except a few days later he jumped one of our shepherds, down the road, and without saying a word just punched and kicked him something fierce, and then he went after the pack mule and took all the bread and cheese it was carrying, after which, with that strange quickness, he ran back and hid in the mountains. When the rest of us goatherds found out about this, we spent two days hunting him in the wildest part of these mountains, and we finally found him up in a big old hollow oak tree. He came down to us, all tame-like, his clothes already torn up, and his face all brown and changed by the sun, so we hardly knew who he was, and it was only because of his clothes, ripped as they were — because we'd really noticed them, that first time — we could tell for sure he was the one we were hunting. He greeted us politely, and told us, speaking right to the point, and not wasting any words, that we shouldn't be surprised, seeing him like he was, because this was what he had to do — it was a kind of penance, and he'd been given it on account of all his sins. We asked him to tell us who he was, but we could never get him to do it. We also asked him if, when he needed food, as he surely would, he'd tell us where to find him, because out of sheer kindness and affection we'd be glad to bring it to him — or if he didn't like that idea, at least come and ask us, instead of stealing it from our shepherds. He thanked us for the offer, begged our pardon for his earlier violence, and agreed that, from then on, he would ask in the name of God and not bother anyone. As for his home, he said he had none, but spent the night wherever he could, and then he ended the conversation with such plaintive tears that those of us who heard would have had to be made of stone, if we hadn't wept too, remembering how we had first seen him and how we saw him now. Because, as I said, he was a very gracious, charming young man, and both his manners and his well-phrased speech showed him to be a wellborn and thoroughly elegant person — indeed, though we who heard him were just country people, his refinement was more than obvious, even to us. And then, having gotten to the heart of what he was saying, he suddenly stopped and fell silent, staring down at the ground for a good long time, while we all just stayed quiet and waited, thinking some inward rapture had caught him up, and feeling very sorry to see him like that, because the way he was staring down at the ground, so round-eyed, even his eyelids frozen still, and then sometimes closing his eyes, squeezing his lips together and knitting up his brows, it wasn't hard to understand that some fit of madness had taken hold of him. And then, pretty soon, he showed us just how right we were, because, after first throwing himself to the ground, he jumped up in a great fury and attacked the shepherd who happened to be nearest him, punching and biting him so fiercely and wildly that, if we hadn't pulled him off, he'd have killed the man. And all the time he was saying, "Ah, treacherous Fernando! Now, now you'll pay me back for the injustice you did me — with these hands I'll tear out your heart, the lair and hiding place of all your evil deeds, and especially your lying and cheating!" And he went on like that, everything addressed to this same Fernando, accusing him of being a faithless swindler. We finally dragged him off, though it wasn't easy, and then, without saying another word, he ran off and hid himself in these thickets and brambles, so it was impossible to follow him. So it seems to us he has these mad fits, from time to time, and someone named Fernando must have done him some wrong or other — something serious, if the state he's been reduced to is any indication. And we've seen the proof of all that many times, when he's appeared on the road, sometimes to beg a shepherd to give him the food he's carrying, and sometimes to take it by force, because when the madness is on him, and the shepherds try to give him food, he won't let them, but only punches them and steals it, but when he's right in the head he begs it of them, politely and modestly, for the love of God, and thanks them warmly, weeping as he speaks.

"And I must tell you, gentlemen," the goatherd went on, "that I've decided, with the aid of four young helpers — two who work for me and two of their friends — to find him just as soon as we can, and then, even if we have to do it by force, to take him to the town of Almodóvar, which is about twenty miles from here, and there they can cure him, if his madness can be cured, or else when he's right in the head we can find out who he is and whether he has relatives we can inform of his misfortune. And that, gentlemen, is what I wanted to say in answer to your question, for you must understand that he who owns the articles you came upon is the same man you've also seen, flitting about so agilely and in such a half-naked state."

(For Don Quijote had already told him they'd seen someone leaping about on the mountain.)

And now, struck by what the goatherd had told them, and filled with an even greater longing to know who the unfortunate lunatic was, Don Quijote made up his mind (as indeed his mind had already decided) to hunt for the man all up and down the mountain, overlooking no hiding place and no cave where he might be found. But Fate took care of that even better than he'd imagined or dared to hope, for right at that moment, emerging out of a ravine which led down to where they were standing, out came the young man he wanted to find, talking to himself as he came, and saying things unintelligible even close up, but incomprehensible at a distance. He was dressed as we have said, but when he drew nearer Don Quijote noticed that what was left of a jacket he was wearing still smelled of fine perfume, which told him that such a person could not be lowborn.

The young man greeted them, his voice dull and flat, but his words extremely courteous. Don Quijote returned his greeting no less politely and, dismounting, embraced the madman with cheerful gallantry, holding him tightly in his arms for a long time, as if he were an old and well-known friend. And the madman, who might be called the Knight of the Ragged Scarecrow — as Don Quijote was the Knight of the Sad Face — first allowed himself to be embraced, then drew back a little and, putting his hands on Don Quijote's shoulders, stood staring at him, as if trying to see if he knew who he was, perhaps just as startled to see someone who looked and was dressed like Don Quijote as Don Quijote had been to see him. And, at last, the first to break the silence, after their long embrace, was the Ragged Scarecrow, and you will see in a moment what he said.

Chapter Twenty-Four

— continuation of the adventure in the Sierra Morena mountains

Our historian tells us that Don Quijote listened to the ragged knight of the mountains with the closest attention, and what the madman said was:

"Certainly, my good sir, whoever you may be, though I do not know you, you have amply demonstrated your courtesy and I am deeply grateful for your having extended it to me. I could only wish I found myself better situated to return your compliments with something more than mere good-will, but Fate allows me no other way to repay such kindnesses, except the warm desire to do so."

"What I wish," replied Don Quijote, "is to serve you — so much so that I made up my mind not to leave these mountains until I found you and learned from your own lips if there might be some cure for the sadness and pain that your strange life here seems to demonstrate, and had it been necessary to hunt for you, I would have hunted with infinite care. And if your affliction should be one of those impossible to remedy, it would be my concern to comfort you, as best I could, while you wept and lamented over it, for grief is easier to endure when it is shared. Now if in fact these good intentions deserve any kind of courteous acknowledgment, let me beg you, my good sir, in the name of all the noble feelings of which I plainly see you are capable, as I also implore you, in the name of whatever it may be that you most love, or have loved, in your life, that you tell me who or what it may be that has caused you to live and perhaps to die like a mere animal, here in this wilderness, for both your attire and you yourself show you to be foreign to such a setting.

"And I swear, señor," added Don Quijote, "by the order of knighthood to which I hold fealty, sinner and unworthy as I am, and also by my adherence to the profession of knight errantry, that if you grant me this request I will serve you as faithfully as these oaths bind me to do, either in remedying your misfortune, if remedy there be, or in helping you to lament over it, as I have already promised."

The Knight of the Woods and Forests, having heard these words from the Knight of the Sad Face, simply stared at him, and stood staring, as if measuring him from head to foot, and when at last he was done, he said:

"If you've got any food to give me, for the love of God give it to me, and then, after I've eaten, I'll do exactly as you ask, in gratitude for the warm good will you have shown me."

Sancho immediately rummaged in his sack, and the goatherd in his shepherd's pouch, and the Ragged Man satisfied his hunger, wolfing the food down like someone in a trance, one bite racing after the other so that he seemed simply to gulp rather than swallow, and all the while neither he nor those watching him said a word. When he was finished, he signalled them to follow and led them to a small green meadow, around the corner of a cliff and not very far distant. He lay down on the thick grass, as did the others, still without anyone speaking, until the Ragged Man, having comfortably settled himself, said:

"Gentlemen, if you want me to give you at least the outline of my vast misfortunes, you must promise to ask no questions, nor to say anything, and completely refrain from interrupting the thread of my story, for the moment you do so will be the moment I cease to speak."

The Ragged Man's remarks made Don Quijote remember the story his squire had been telling him, when he hadn't kept track of how many goats had gone across the river, so that the story had been left hanging in the air. — But back to the Ragged Man, who went on as follows:

"I give you this warning because I do not wish to linger over the tale of my miseries, for remembering them only brings me new cause for sorrow, and the less you question me the quicker I can tell it all. But I will omit nothing essential; you will know everything you wish to know."

Don Quijote promised, in the name of the others, to honor the Ragged Man's request and, reassured, the young man began his tale:

"My name is Cardenio; I was born in one of the noblest cities here in Andalusia, and mine is a noble family; my parents are rich, and my misfortune so grave that my parents must have wept over it, and all my kinsmen must have grieved, though all their wealth could not help me; for mere material wealth is worthless, in dealing with sorrows born in Heaven. There lived, in that same place, a heavenly being, so gloriously blessed by Love that I could not have wished for more: that was the measure of Luscinda's beauty, a maiden every bit as noble and rich as I was, but also both more fortunate and less constant than my honorable intentions deserved. I loved, longed for, and adored this Luscinda almost from the moment I was born, and she loved me, with all the innocence and simple good will of childhood. Our parents knew of our plans, nor did they disapprove, for they could easily see that, as time went on, things could only end in our being married, a conclusion that the perfect matching of our families and our wealth made almost inevitable. We came of age, as did our love, at which point Luscinda's father thought propriety required him to deny me the freedom of his house, perhaps imitating the parents of that famous Thisbe,[1] so often sung about by poets. This denial added fuel to the fire and heaped love on love, because although they could silence our tongues they could not muzzle our pens, which, enjoying greater freedom, know very well how to tell a loved one what lies hidden in our hearts, for often the mere presence of the beloved can disturb and silence even the boldest mind and the most daring tongue. Oh Heaven, what reams of letters I sent her! How many pure and delicate replies I received! How many songs I composed and how many impassioned poems, in which my soul poured out and transcribed its feelings, describing its burning desires, cherishing its memories, and relishing its future delights! And then, finally, it became too much for me, and my soul burned to see her, so I decided to do what would most quickly bring me the reward for which I longed and which I deserved, which was to ask her father for her hand in lawful marriage, and I did. He replied that he was grateful for my desire thus to honor him, and he wished to honor me with his treasure, but since my father was still living it was he who by rights should make this request, for if my wish and desire was not shared by my father, he could not permit Luscinda to be wedded in secret or by stealth. I thanked him for his honest response, for it seemed to me he was clearly right, as my father too would say when I told him, so I immediately went to inform him of my wishes. But just as I entered the room, I found him with an opened letter in his hand, and before I could say a word he handed it to me, saying,

'This letter, Cardenio, will show you how the Grand Duke Ricardo wishes to be of use to you.'

"As you surely know, gentlemen, this Duke Ricardo is one of the greatest men in Spain, and his estate is the best in all of Andalusia. I took the letter, and read it, and it was couched so warmly that, even to me, it would have seemed wrong had my father not granted what was asked, which was that I be sent to him immediately, for he wanted me to be his oldest son's companion — not his servant. And he took upon himself, he said, the responsibility for endowing me with a status suitable to the high opinion in which he already held me. I read the letter and could not speak, especially when my father said to me:

'In order to oblige the duke, Cardenio, you'll leave here in two days. Be grateful to God for opening the road on which you'll rise to the heights I know you deserve.'

"And then he gave me some additional words of parental advice. My departure being imminent, I managed to speak to Luscinda, one night, and told her everything that had happened, as I also told her father, begging him to wait a few days, and not give her hand in marriage, so I could find out just what Duke Ricardo wanted of me, a promise he made and which she confirmed with a thousand oaths, weeping and fainting away.

"So then I left for the duke's estate. I was so well received, so well treated, that Jealousy immediately began to rear its ugly head, every kindness the duke extended to me appearing, to his longtime servants, positive injuries to themselves. But my arrival especially delighted the duke's sec-

---

1. Cardenio alludes here to the Asiatic legend of Pyramus and Thisbe, whose parents forbade them to marry. Ovid tells their tragic story in Book IV of his *Metamorphoses*.

ond son, Fernando, a gallant and charming young man, free-spirited and passionate, who soon became so fond of me that everyone was aware of it, for although his older brother thought well of me, and treated me graciously, things never went so far as they did with Don Fernando. And since friends don't keep secrets from one another, and since Don Fernando's kindnesses had grown into friendship, he told me everything, and especially about a somewhat uncomfortable love affair he was having. He'd fallen in love with a farmer's daughter, one of his father's tenants — such a magnificent girl, so beautiful, modest, sensible, and chaste, that no one who knew her could decide in what she excelled most. All the graces and accomplishments of this beautiful farmer's daughter brought Don Fernando's desire to such a pitch that, in order to have her, to overcome her chaste resistance, he decided he had to promise to marry her, for there was no other way. Already bound to him in friendship, I tried as hard as I could to talk him out of it, arguing as forcefully as I knew how and with the liveliest appeals to experience and wisdom, but finding I could not convince him, I determined to tell everything to Duke Ricardo, his father. But Don Fernando, a cunning and far-seeing fellow, anticipated and was afraid of exactly this, knowing that, as a good servant, I would be obliged not to conceal anything that would so damage my employer's honor, so, to distract and deceive me, he told me he'd realized, now, that the very best way to make him forget the beauty which had so long held him in its grip was to take himself away for some months, and he wanted to accomplish this by having the two of us visit my father's house, giving the duke the explanation that this was to be a horse-buying expedition, for there are so many excellent animals in my native city [Córdoba] that its reputation surpasses that of anywhere else in the world. As soon as I heard this I eagerly agreed, as I would have done even had it not been a good idea, for I was moved by one of the most natural forces imaginable, which was that this would provide me with a splendid opportunity to visit my Luscinda. Driven by this notion and desire, I fell in with his plan and actively encouraged the proposed journey — indeed, telling him we ought to leave as soon as possible, because absence really would do the trick, in spite of the very steadiest intentions. I learned, later, that when he suggested this visit he'd already enjoyed a husband's privileges with the farmer's daughter, and was hoping for some safe way of confessing it, afraid of what the duke his father might do when his stupidity was revealed. And it happened, the way it usually does with most young fellows, for whom love is really nothing more than desire and wants nothing greater than delight, so that once delight is achieved desire is ended, and what seemed to be love is forgotten, for there are natural limits to which true love is not subject — but what I meant to say is, as soon as he'd enjoyed the farmer's daughter, Don Fernando's desires were satisfied and his passion quenched, and though he first pretended that going away was intended to dampen his ardor, his departure was really meant to let him escape from the promise he'd made. The duke gave his permission, and ordered me to go with him. We came to my city, where my father received him as the high grandee he was, and I soon got to see Luscinda, and my own desires, which had never been either muffled or dead, sprang back to life, and though it cost me dear I told everything to Don Fernando, for the friendship he showed me was such that I did not think I could conceal anything from him. I extolled her beauty to him, and her grace, her good sense, until my praise for a damsel so wonderfully endowed made him want to see her for himself. I arranged that — and much good it did me — pointing her out to him, one night, sitting with a lighted candle at a window where we used to talk, she and I. He saw her in a loose, flowing gown, and all the beautiful women he'd ever seen were forgotten in a moment. He was speechless, he lost all sense of where he was, entranced and then lovestruck — as you will see in the course of this miserable tale of mine. And what still further kindled his desire (which he concealed from me, and admitted only to Heaven), one day he happened to find one of her letters, begging me to ask her father for her hand — a letter so prudent, so chaste, and yet so passionate that, after reading it, he informed me that in Luscinda, and in Luscinda alone, were joined those graces of beauty and understanding which all the other women in the world possessed only in part. I must confess that, at this point, though I could certainly understand how justly Don Fernando praised her, it troubled me to hear such admiration from his lips, and I began to be afraid and to mistrust him, because he'd never stop talking about Luscinda, and he'd bring our conversation around to her even if he had to drag her in by the hair, all of which began to make me vaguely jealous — not because I had any reason to be afraid that Luscinda's kindness and faithfulness could be turned against me, but, somehow, even though she reassured me, to worry about what my Fate might bring. Don Fernando tried to read everything I wrote to Luscinda, and everything she wrote back to me, claiming that our mutual wisdom delighted him. So it happened, once, that when Luscinda asked me for a book of chivalric romance, one she was very fond of, called *Amadís of Gaul* — "

No sooner had Don Quijote heard the name of this book than he burst out:

"Had your grace told me, at the beginning of your story, that the lady Luscinda was fond of chivalric tales, you'd have had to say nothing more to prove the nobility of her mind, for indeed, señor, she could not have been so fine as you described her, had she lacked the taste for such delightful reading. So as for me you need waste no more words declaiming her beauty, her refinement, or her quick wit, for simply having heard that she is fond of chivalric tales confirms her as the loveliest and most sensible woman in the world. But I could have wished, my dear sir, that together with *Amadís of Gaul* you had sent her *Don Rugel of Greece*, in which I am sure the lady Luscinda would much appreciate Daraida and Geraya, and the wisdom of the shepherd Darinel, with his admirable pastoral poems, both sung and performed by him with such elegance, wit, and easy naturalness. But there may yet be time to remedy the omission, nor would that require anything more than for your grace, at your own sweet will, to come with me to my own village, where I could supply you with more than three hundred volumes, which are my soul's delight and the very solace of my life — though it may well be that they're all gone, thanks to the malice of an evil, jealous sorceror. — But pardon me, your grace, for having broken our promise not to interrupt you as you talked, for at the very mention of anything having to do with chivalry and knights errant I find myself speaking of them every bit as naturally as the sun's rays give heat or the moon's bring down the dew. So pardon me, please, and go on with your story, which is much more to the point."

While Don Quijote was speaking, Cardenio's head had fallen onto his chest, and he seemed profoundly thoughtful. But although Don Quijote twice asked him to continue his story, he neither lifted his head nor spoke a word until finally, after a long silence, he looked up and said:

"I still think, nor could anyone in the world ever persuade me of anything else — whoever believes anything else is an absolute idiot — that that lecherous rascal, Maestro Elisabad, was sleeping with Queen Madásima."

"By God, but that's not true!" answered Don Quijote, suddenly very angry, fairly hurling his denial at the Ragged Man, after his usual fashion, "and it's pure wickedness or, better still, it's pure chicanery, for Queen Madásima was a wonderfully noble lady, and we have no right to assume so lofty a princess would befoul herself with a quack sawbones. Anyone who says anything different is lying in his teeth, and I will make him know it, on foot or on horseback, in armor or not, by night or by day, or however he chooses."

Cardenio sat staring fixedly, for a fit of madness had descended on him and there was no way he was going to continue his story, nor would Don Quijote have listened to it, so angry was he after what he'd heard said about Madásima. What a strange business! To defend her as if she'd actually been his love and his lady — that's what his perverse books had brought him to! Well, as I was saying, the madman Cardenio, hearing himself called a liar and a rascal, and otherwise similarly abused, didn't much appreciate the joke, so he picked up a rock and gave Don Quijote such a violent blow on the chest that he knocked him over. Sancho Panza, seeing his master laid out on his back, tried to punch the lunatic, but the Ragged Man greeted him with a blow that levelled him, after which he jumped up and down on Sancho's ribs to his heart's content. Trying to defend his guest, the old goatherd ran into the same whirlwind. Finally, after beating and trampling on all of them, he stopped and walked calmly and pleasantly off into the mountains, there to hide himself once more.

Sancho jumped up, furious at having been beaten so unjustly, and ran to take vengeance on the goatherd, crying that it was all his fault for not having warned them about the Ragged Man's fits, for had they known they could have protected themselves. The goatherd answered that indeed he had told them, and if they hadn't listened it wasn't he who was to blame. Sancho Panza snapped back at him, and the goatherd at Sancho, and it would have ended in their grabbing each other by the beard and exchanging such fierce blows that they might have smashed themselves to pieces, had not Don Quijote settled the dispute. But Sancho, still clutching at the goatherd, said:

"Leave me alone, your grace, Sir Knight of the Sad Face, because this fellow, he's a country man like me, and not a knight in armor, so it's all right to take it out on him for what happened, fighting on equal terms, like an honest man."

"That may be true," said Don Quijote, "but I know he isn't to blame for what happened."

And so they calmed down, and Don Quijote once more asked the goatherd if it would be possible to find Cardenio, because he had the most intense desire to hear the end of the story. The goatherd repeated what he'd told them at the start, that the Ragged Man had no fixed den, but if the knight roamed widely through the region he'd be sure to find him, whether mad or sane.

Chapter Twenty-Five

— dealing with the strange things that happened to the brave knight of La Mancha in the Sierra Morena mountains, including his imitation of Beltenebros [Amadís of Gaul]'s penitence

Taking leave of the goatherd, Don Quijote mounted Rocinante once more and directed Sancho to follow him, which Sancho did — on his donkey — but not very happily. Slowly, they made their way into the most rugged part of the mountain, Sancho fairly dying to talk things over with his master, but preferring to let Don Quijote begin the conversation, so he didn't break the rule his master had laid down. Finally, unable to endure the silence, he said:

"Señor Don Quijote, your grace, give me your blessing and let me take leave of you, because I want to go back to my house, and my wife, and my children, because at least, with them, I can talk and make as much conversation as I like, and if your grace wants me to travel these wildernesses with you, day and night, and I can't talk when I want to, I might as well be a monk. If Fate would let animals speak, as they used to in Guisopete [Aesop]'s[1] time, it might not be so bad, because I could tell my donkey anything I felt like, and that way I could live with my bad luck, but it's a hard business, and it's impossible to just bear it and not say anything, all this going around looking for adventures and never finding anything but beatings and blanket-tossings, and stones and punches, and in spite of all that to sew your lips together and never dare say anything about what's in your heart, like a deaf and dumb man."

"I understand you very well, Sancho," answered Don Quijote. "You're dying to get rid of the prohibition I placed on your tongue. So consider it removed and say whatever you want to — but with the condition that I lift the restriction only so long as we're traveling through these mountains."

"So be it," said Sancho, "and now I'll speak, because God only knows what's going to happen — and the first thing I want to say, now that you've given me this safe conduct, is this: Why did your grace get so

---

1. Traditional composer of Greek animal fables who, according to Herodotus, lived as a slave in the sixth century B.C.

excited about that Queen Magimasa, or whatever her name was? Who cares whether that Abad [Elisabad] was friendly with her or he wasn't? If your grace had just let that go by — because after all you weren't his judge — I think the lunatic would have gone on with his story, and we could have done without that blow with the rock, and all the kicks and blows and even half a dozen backhands to the head."

"By God, Sancho," replied Don Quijote, "if you knew, as I do, what a respectable and exalted lady Queen Madásima was, I suspect you'd say I'd shown immense patience, not smashing the mouth which uttered such blasphemies. Because it's a very great blasphemy to assert, or even think, that a queen has had an affair with a sawbones quack. What the story really says is that Maestro Elisabad, of whom the madman spoke, was in fact a most sensible fellow who gave very sound advice, and he served as the queen's tutor and her physician. But to think she was his lover is poppycock, worthy of the most serious punishment. All you need to understand, to know that Cardenio didn't realize what he was saying, is that when he said it he was out of his head."

"That's exactly what I say," said Sancho. "There was no need to take a crazy man's words seriously — because if your grace hadn't been lucky, and he'd aimed that rock at your head, instead of at your chest, it would have done us a lot of good to stand up for that lady, may God make her rot. And don't you just think Cardenio wouldn't have gotten off scotfree, for being a lunatic!"

"Whether against sane men or against lunatics, it's the duty of every knight errant to uphold the honor of all women, no matter who they may be, but especially if they're queens as exalted and noble as was Queen Madásima, whose wonderful qualities give me a very special affection for her, she being not only beautiful but extremely sensible and long-suffering about her misfortunes — and there were many of them. And the advice and companionship of Maestro Elisabad were very useful to her, helping her endure her struggles wisely and patiently. But for ignorant and evilly motivated, low and vulgar minds to conclude from this, and to think and say, that therefore she was his concubine, is to lie, I say yet again, and everyone who thinks and says such things is a liar two hundred times over."

"I'm not saying it, and I'm not thinking it," replied Sancho. "It's up to them, and they can live with it; whether they were lovers or not is God's business, not mine. I keep my nose clean, I don't look this way or that; I don't want to know what my neighbors are up to. If you tell lies when you buy, your purse is bound to cry. And since I came into the world naked, I'll leave it the same way: nothing ventured, nothing gained — and suppose they really were lovers? What's it to me? What good is bacon if there's no pot to cook it in? Anyhow, can you put gates around a meadow? And besides, if they criticize God, who *won't* they criticize?"

"My Lord!" said Don Quijote. "What a heap of nonsense you've strung together, Sancho! What does all that have to do with what we were talking about? By all that's holy, Sancho, you be still, and from here on just worry about keeping your donkey moving, and don't get involved in things that aren't your concern. And make sure every one of your five senses understands this: whatever I've done, or I'm doing, or I will do, is exactly what ought to be done and precisely what the laws of knighthood require, for I know more about them than any and all the other knights in the world."

"Señor," replied Sancho, "is it a law of knighthood that we're supposed to be wandering around, lost in these mountains, following no road and no path, hunting for a lunatic who, once we do find him, may perhaps want to finish what he started — and I'm not talking about his story, but just about your grace's head and my ribs, which he may finish by smashing to pieces?"

"Once more, Sancho, I tell you to hold your peace," said Don Quijote, "for you must understand that my desire to find the madman is not the only thing leading me to these mountains but, even more, my plan to accomplish a feat, here, which will win me eternal reputation and fame throughout the known world, for it will be the final touch, the ultimate perfection of all that can bring honor to a knight errant."

"And will it be very dangerous?" asked Sancho Panza.

"No," answered the Knight of the Sad Face, "although who knows? The dice can roll a bad number instead of a good one. But everything will depend on you."

"On me?" said Sancho.

"Yes," said Don Quijote, "for if you return quickly from the place where I plan to send you, my suffering will end quickly and so too will my glory begin. But since it's not fair to keep you in suspense, waiting to find out what I mean, let me tell you, Sancho, that the celebrated Amadís of Gaul was one of the most perfect of all knights errant. But no, I was wrong to say 'was *one* of': he was the only one, the first, absolutely unique, the lord of all those who walked the earth in his time. The devil with Don Belianís and all those who say he was Amadís' equal in this or that, because they deceive themselves, I swear it by all that's holy! And I also say that, just as an ambitious painter, wanting to become famous, tries to imitate the best and most original painters he knows, so too this same principle applies to all the noblest and most important professions which grace our nation, and it's the rule that has to be followed — and *is* followed — by anyone who wants to become known as wise and patient, imitating Ulysses, in whose life and works Homer has painted for us the living portrait of wisdom and patience, just as our master Virgil, in the person of Aeneas, has depicted for us the courage of a pious son and the wisdom of a brave and experienced soldier — in neither case painting and describing them as they actually were, but as they should be, so the example of their virtues may remain as a model for those who come after them. So too was Amadís the True North, the Shining Light, the very Sun of brave and love-struck knights, and all of us who march under the flag of Love and of Knighthood must struggle to imitate him. This being the case, Sancho my friend, as indeed it is, it is my view that the knight errant who most closely imitates Amadís of Gaul will come the closest to achieving knightly perfection. And one of the ways in which this knight most effectively demonstrated his wisdom, courage, boldness, patience, steadfastness, and love was when, rejected by his lady, Oriana, he withdrew to do penance, high on Barren Mountain, changing his name to Beltenebros [Lovely Obscurity] — surely an important and appropriate name for the life he of his own free will had now chosen. And how much simpler for me to imitate him in this, rather than in slicing up giants, beheading serpents, killing dragons, routing armies, smashing armadas, or undoing spells. Further, this location being so admirably suited for such purposes, there's no reason to lose an opportunity offered me by Dame Fortune herself."

"And just what," said Sancho, "does your grace want to do, here in this godforsaken place?"

"Haven't I already explained to you," replied Don Quijote, "that I intend to imitate Amadís, enacting here the role of He Who Despairs, He Who Turns Fool, He Who Rages, so at the same time I can also imitate the brave Don Roland,[2] who when drinking at a fountain came upon proof that Angélica the Fair had been guilty of vile behavior with Medoro, the grief of which discovery drove him mad, so he uprooted trees, muddied the fountain's sparkling water, killed shepherds, butchered flocks, burned down huts, knocked over houses, drove horses wild, and committed a hundred thousand other weird things, eternally worthy to be told and written about? And since I have no intention of precisely imitating Roland, or Orlando, or Rotolando (for Roland is known by all three of these names), item by item, in each and all of the madnesses he perpetrated, and all the wild things he said, and all the furious thoughts he contemplated, I plan to draw up an outline, as best I can, of what seem to me the most important matters. But perhaps I will simply imitate Amadís, who wreaked no insane injuries but, simply through tears and grief, rose to the heights of fame."

"It seems to me," said Sancho, "that the knights who did all these things were driven to them, and had good reason for their foolishness and their penance, but you, your grace, why should you go crazy? What lady has rejected you, or what evidence have you found for thinking Doña Dulcinea del Toboso has committed any kind of stupidity with anyone, Moor or Christian?"

"That's exactly it," replied Don Quijote, "that's just how beautifully I've worked it all out — because for a knight errant to go crazy for good reason, how much is *that* worth? My idea is to become a lunatic for no reason at all, and to ask my lady, seeing what I do without cause, what she imagines I might do if I really had one? Anyway, I've got more than enough reason, considering how long I've kept myself away from my eternal Dulcinea del Toboso, for as you heard that shepherd, Ambrosio, tell us just the other day, when you're far away you feel, and you fear, all kinds of evils. And now, Sancho my friend, don't waste your time advising me to give up an imitation so unusual, so beautifully worked-out, and so utterly original. Mad is what I am, and mad is what I have to be until you return, bringing me the reply to a letter I plan to send, with you as its bearer, to my lady Dulcinea, and if my loyalty merits it, that reply will end my foolishness and my penitence, but if not, then I will be truly mad and, in those circumstances, will be aware of nothing. Accordingly, however the response may go, I shall be free of the discord and trouble in which

2. "Rages" = he who becomes *furioso*, as in Ariosto's *Orlando Furioso* (1532); "Roland," as in the twelfth-century French epic *La Chanson de Roland* [*Translator's Note*].

you will leave me, here — either relishing the pleasure you will bring me, as a sane and sensible man, or unable to feel the evil you will bring me as a lunatic. But tell me, Sancho: have you taken good care of Mambrino's helmet, which I saw you picking up from the ground, after that scoundrel tried to smash it? He couldn't, of course: that simply emphasizes how delicately its steel has been tempered."

To which Sancho replied:

"Good God, Sir Knight of the Sad Face, but I can't stand — I can't even be patient with — some of the things your grace says, and they're beginning to make me think everything you tell me about knighthood, and getting to be kings and emperors, and giving away islands and doing other great and munificent deeds (the way knights used to, in the old days), must all be hot air and lies, all bumbug or humbug or whatever you call it. Because when I hear your grace say that a barber's basin is Mambrino's helmet — and that's what you've been saying for at least four days — what am I supposed to think except that anyone who says and believes such things has gone wrong in the head? I've got the basin in my sack, all dented up, and I'm carrying it around so I can bring it home and fix it and use it for shaving, if God is gracious enough, some day, to let me see my wife and children again."

"Now look, Sancho," said Don Quijote. "I swear to you, by Him to Whom you just finished swearing, that you have the most limited understanding of any squire who lives or has ever lived in this world. Is it possible that, having traveled with me as much as you have, you've still not understood that all the things knights errant have to deal with seem to be mere chimera — foolishness — stupidity, while in fact they're exactly the opposite? And none of this is because that's really what's going on, but just because we're always accompanied by a mob of magicians, changing and twisting everything about, turning things the way they like, and all depending on whether they want to favor us or destroy us. So if that seems to you a barber's basin, to me it looks like Mambrino's helmet, and to someone else it will look like something completely different. Actually, it was singularly wise of the magician who's on my side to make what is really and truly Mambrino's helmet look to everyone else like a barber's basin, because as precious as it is, I'd have the whole world chasing after me to snatch it away, but if they think it's only a barber's basin they won't bother trying to get it, as you could see very well from the fellow who wanted to smash it and finally just left it lying on the ground, and never tried to carry it off, because by God if he'd known what it was he'd never have left it there. Take good care of it, my friend, since I don't need it right now: in fact, if I propose to let my penitence follow Roland rather than Amadís, I'll have to take off all my armor and be as naked as the day I was born."

As they were talking, they came to the base of a tall mountain, virtually a sheer cliff, which jutted out from the other peaks around it. A gentle stream ran along its foothills, creating a meadow so green and luxuriant that your eyes were happy just seeing it. There were groves of wild trees, as well as plants and flowers, all of which made it an exceedingly peaceful place. And it was here that the Knight of the Sad Face decided to perform his penitence, so as soon as they arrived he began to cry out in a loud voice, like a raving lunatic:

"This is the spot, oh heavens, I choose and hereby take in order to bewail the misfortune in which you yourselves have placed me! Here is where the flooding of my eyes will join the waters flowing in this tiny stream, and where, night and day, my deep and unbroken sighs will shake the leaves of these wild trees, in witness to and as symbol of the suffering experienced by my afflicted heart. Oh you, whoever you may be, you rustic gods that dwell in this uninhabitable place, hear the moans of this wretched lover, who by reason of a long absence and fancied jealousies has been brought to this harsh wilderness, here to lament and complain of that ungrateful beauty's cruel disposition, she who is the very end and finality of all human loveliness! Oh you, nymphs and dryads, who love to live in the thick shrubbery of these mountains, may the graceful, lecherous satyrs, who long for you, but always in vain, never ever disturb your sweet rest, so you can help me lament my misfortune, or at least not yourselves grow tired of hearing it! Oh Dulcinea del Toboso, day of my night, glory of my suffering, true North and compass of every path I take, guiding star of my fate, so too may Heaven grant you whatever boons you seek of it, and bring you to reflect upon the place and the condition to which your absence has brought me, and grant me as much delight as my faithfulness deserves! Oh lonely trees, from now on the only companions of my solitude, give me some sign, by the gentle movement of your branches, that my presence here is not disagreeable to you! And oh you, my squire, cheerful companion in both prosperity and adversity, never forget what you shall see me do, here, so you may tell and recite it to she who is the sole cause of it all!"

Saying which, he dismounted, quickly pulled saddle and bridle off Rocinante and, slapping him on the haunches, said:

"He who himself lacks it, gives you your freedom, oh steed as remarkable for your actions as unfortunate in your fate! Go wherever you will, you who carry written on your forehead that neither the hippogryph ridden by Astolfo, nor the celebrated Frontino, who cost the lovely Bradamante[3] so dear, could match your light-footedness."

Seeing this, Sancho said:

"More power to whoever saved us the trouble of unsaddling my old donkey[4] — though by God I wouldn't have set him loose without some love taps, and a few sweet nothings whispered in his ear. But if he were here I wouldn't let anyone unsaddle him: there wouldn't be any reason. No court ever said he was incompetent because love had driven him crazy, or despair, and no one ever said it of his master, either, who was me, as long as God so willed. And to tell you the truth, Sir Knight of the Sad Face, if your madness and my riding off are going to really work, it'd be a good idea to get a saddle back on Rocinante, to make up for my missing donkey, because that would save a lot of time both in my going and my

---

3. Figures from Ariosto's *Orlando Furioso.*
4. Stolen: various editions of the novel contain different accounts, all confused. Either Cervantes, or his printers, or both, seem to have had second — and third — thoughts on this vital subject [*Translator's Note*].

coming back, and if I have to walk who knows when I'll get there or when I'll return, because, in a word, I'm not much of a walker."

"All right, Sancho," said Don Quijote, "let that be how it is, because your plan doesn't sound like a bad one. You should leave here in three days, because during that time I want you to see what I say and do on her behalf, so you can tell her."

"But what else am I supposed to see," said Sancho, "besides what I've already seen?"

"That's how much you know about it!" replied Don Quijote. "Now I have to rip up my clothes, throw away my armor, and beat my head on these rocks, plus other things of the same sort that ought to astonish you."

"For God's sake, your grace," said Sancho, "be careful how you go beating your head, because you might hit on such a sharp rock that the first blow will finish off this whole penitence, and it strikes me that even if your grace has already decided this head-knocking is necessary, and you can't manage without doing it, it might be good enough, since this is all a pretense anyway, a fake, and a game — it might be good enough, it seems to me, to do it in the water, or on something nice and soft, like cotton, and then leave it to me to tell my lady that your grace did it on the point of sharp rocks, harder than diamonds."

"I appreciate your good intentions, Sancho, my friend," replied Don Quijote, "but let me assure you that nothing I'm doing is a joke, but very real, because to do such a thing any differently would be against the laws of knighthood, for they command us never to tell a lie, for that is punishable as heresy, and to substitute one thing for another is lying. Accordingly, when I beat my head against these rocks I must administer real blows, solid and legally binding, and with nothing adulterated or fictitious about them. So you'll have to leave me some bandages for dressing my wounds, since Fate has decreed that we must proceed without the balsam which we lost."

"Losing the donkey was worse," replied Sancho, "because when we lost him we lost the bandages and everything else. And let me ask your grace not to remind me any more of that accursed potion, because just hearing it mentioned makes my soul turn over, not just my stomach. And let me ask another favor: pretend the three days you gave me for seeing all your crazinesses have already gone by, because, really, I've seen them, I know all about them, and I'll tell my lady all sorts of wonderful tales. So just write the letter and send me off, because I can't wait to get back here and rescue your grace from this purgatory I'm leaving you in."

"You call this a purgatory, Sancho?" said Don Quijote. "Call it, rather, hell [*infierno*], or maybe something worse, if there is any such thing."

"*Quien ha infierno*, Whoever's gone to hell," said Sancho, "*nula es retencio*, Can't get it back again,[5] according to what I've heard."

"What do you mean, can't get it back?" said Don Quijote.

"That means," replied Sancho, "that once they've got you in hell, you can never get back out. But it'll be just the opposite for you, your grace,

---

5. An illiterate error for *Quia in inferno nulla est redemptio*, "He who is in hell cannot be redeemed" [*Translator's Note*].

unless my legs won't work — which means, if I've got any spurs for poking Rocinante, because when I get to Toboso, and I'm standing in front of my lady Dulcinea, I'm going to tell her such stories about all the stupidities and crazinesses (which are really the same thing) your grace was doing and will still be doing, that I'll turn her softer than a glove, even if she starts out harder than an oak tree, and then I'll turn around and bring her soft and sweet-toned answer right back through the air, like a wizard, and I'll rescue your grace from this purgatory, which looks more like hell but really isn't, because you can expect to get out of it, which, as I said, those who really are in hell can't do, and I don't think your grace would say anything different."

"That's true," said He of the Sad Face, "but how can we write the letter?"

"And also tell them about the little donkey I'm to have," added Sancho.

"It will all be in there," said Don Quijote, "and since there's no paper, it might be good for us to write on the leaves of trees, as the ancients did, or on wax tablets — although those would be as hard to find, here, as paper. But I've just remembered how we can easily write it, and even more than easily, and that's in Cardenio's notebook, and you'll make sure to have it copied out, in a good handwriting, in the first village where there's a schoolteacher — or if there isn't one, then any churchman will do — but make sure you don't let a court clerk do the copying, because the way they write even Satan couldn't decipher it."

"But what about getting it signed?" asked Sancho.

"Amadís never signed his letters," replied Don Quijote.

"That's all well and good," answered Sancho, "but the order for the three little donkeys has absolutely got to be signed, because if it's just copied out they'll say it's a forged signature, and I'll be left without a donkey."

"The order will be in that same book, signed, and when my niece sees it there won't be any problems. As for the love letter, you can use this signature: 'Yours until death, the Knight of the Sad Face.' And if it comes in someone else's handwriting that won't matter, because as far as I can recall Dulcinea too doesn't know how to write or to read, nor in all her life has she ever seen my handwriting or had a letter from me, because both my love and hers have always been platonic, never involving anything more than a modest glance. Even that, indeed, has been so infrequent that, in the dozen years I have loved her still more than the light of these eyes of mine, which the earth will eventually swallow up, I can honestly swear that I've barely seen her four times, and it may very well be that on none of those four occasions was she ever aware that I was watching her, so chastely and privately has she been raised by both her father, Lorenzo Corchuelo, and her mother, Aldonza Nogales."

"Oh ho!" said Sancho. "Then the lady Dulcinea del Toboso is Lorenzo Corchuelo's daughter, otherwise known as Aldonza Lorenzo?"

"That she is," said Don Quijote, "and she's worthy to be mistress of the entire universe."

"I know her well," said Sancho, "and let me tell you, she can throw an iron ball as far as the strongest boy in the whole village. Praise the Lord!

but she's a damned good girl, well-built and straight as an arrow, and as strong and brave as they come, and she can get any knight errant, or anyone trying to be a knight errant, out of plenty of tight spots, if he takes her for his lady! Oh son of a bitch! but she's a strong one — and what a voice! Let me tell you, one day she got up on the village bell tower, to call some of their boys, working in one of her father's ploughed fields, and even though those fellows were more than a mile off they heard her as if they'd been standing at the foot of the tower. And maybe the best thing about her is that she hasn't got a finicky bone in her body, she knows her way around: she can crack jokes with everyone, and make faces, and tell stories. So as far as I'm concerned, Sir Knight of the Sad Face, you not only can and should go crazy over her, but you're entitled to feel desperate and go hang yourself, and no one who knows anything will say you went too far, even if the devil carries you off. So I wish I was already on my way, just so I could see her, because it's been a long time since I laid eyes on her, and she must have changed: women who are always out in the fields, and in the sun and the air, their faces really take a beating. And I'll confess something to you, your grace, señor Don Quijote: till now I haven't understood a thing, because I really thought the lady Dulcinea you were in love with must be a princess, or someone like that, who'd deserve the grand presents your grace has sent her, like that Basque fellow and all those galley slaves, and all the others there must have been, because your grace must have won lots of battles before I got to be your squire. But when you come to think of it, what good would it do Aldonza Lorenzo — I mean, Lady Dulcinea del Toboso — having all those conquered men your grace will send her, and has already sent her, hunting her up and going down on their knees in front of her? Because it just might be while she was combing out flax, or working in the threshing yard, and they wouldn't know what was going on, seeing her like that, and maybe she'd laugh and get irritated with your present."

"I've told you many times, Sancho," said Don Quijote, "that you're an incorrigible babbler and, though you haven't got much of a brain, you often try to seem clever — but just to show you what an idiot you are, and how wise I am, let me tell you a little story. Once there was a beautiful widow, young, free, and rich, and above all confident and self-assured, who was in love with a laborer who worked at a monastery, a sturdy, well-built fellow, and when the father-superior heard about it he went and spoke to her, by way of giving her some brotherly counsel. 'I'm astonished, my dear lady, and I think I ought to be astonished, to find that so exalted a woman as your grace, so beautiful and so rich, should be in love with such a vulgar fellow, so lowborn, and such a fool, as So-and-So, for here in this house we have so many learned masters, so many fine theologians, that your grace might choose among them as one picks a ripe pear, saying: I'll take this one, but that one I don't want.' But she answered him both gaily and bluntly: 'Your grace, my dear sir, is simply deceiving yourself, and your way of thinking is hopelessly outdated, if you think I've made a mistake in picking So-and-So, though he may seem like a fool, because in what I want him for he's every bit as learned, and more, as Aristotle.' So too, Sancho, for what I want of Dulcinea del Toboso, she's every bit as good as the noblest princess on earth. Indeed, none of the poets who sang so exaltedly of their ladies (using the names they felt like giving them) ever actually had such mistresses. Do you think all the Amaryllises, the Phyllises, the Sylvias, the Dianas, the Galateas, the Phyllidas,[6] and all the others you'll find in the books and romances they sell in the barber shops, or in the tragedies and comedies they put on in theaters, were really flesh and blood women, and in fact belonged to those who sang about them — and who are still singing? Not a bit of it, because most of them are invented so the poets can have something to write poems about, and so they can make people think they're great lovers and build up their own reputations. For me, in the same way, it's enough to think and believe that your good Aldonza Lorenzo is beautiful and modest, and her ancestry doesn't make much difference either, because no one's going to come searching out her pedigree, in order to confer any titles on her, while as far as I'm concerned she's the loftiest princess in the whole world. You've got to understand, Sancho, if you don't understand it already, that two things above all others make people fall in love, and those things are great beauty and a noble reputation, and it's those two things that are perfectly blended in Dulcinea, because no one can equal or even come close to her in beauty or in reputation. And so, to sum it all up, I perceive everything I say as absolutely true, and deficient in nothing whatever, and paint it all in my mind exactly as I want it to be, whether as to beauty or to nobility, so that Helen of Troy can't match her, and Lucretia can't come close, nor can any famous women in all history, whether Greek, Barbarian, or Roman. Therefore, let anyone say what he likes, because if ignorant people are to chide me on this account, those who know anything will not."

"Every word you've said is right, your grace," responded Sancho, "and I'm an ass. I don't know how the word 'ass' got into my mouth, because you shouldn't talk about rope in a house where a man's been hanged.[7] But let's get to that letter, and then, by God, I'll get going."

Don Quijote took up Cardenio's notebook and, going off a bit, calmly began writing the letter, and when he was finished called Sancho over and explained that he wanted to read it to him, so he could remember it in case it got lost on the way, since with his bad luck anything might happen. To which Sancho replied:

"Write it out two or three times, your grace, in that notebook there, and then hand it over, and I'll take good care of it, because it's silly to think I can memorize it: my memory is so bad that lots of times I forget my own name. But anyway, tell it to me, your grace, because I'd really like to hear it: it must be exactly what's called for."

"Then listen, because this is what it says," replied Don Quijote.

DON QUIJOTE'S LETTER TO DULCINEA DEL TOBOSO

Noble, sovereign lady:
He who has been stabbed by the sharp blade of absence, and wounded to the very heart, oh sweetest Dulcinea del Toboso, dispatches

---

6. These paper ladies are all pseudo-shepherdesses in the popular Renaissance genre of pastoral romance.
7. I.e., Sancho's donkey having been stolen, he shouldn't talk about donkeys [*Translator's Note*].

to you the health he himself does not possess. If your beauty looks down on me, if your worthiness is not meant for me, if your scorn remains my destiny, though I may manage to bear this more than bountiful suffering it will be an affliction I can ill support, for in addition to its power it is exceedingly enduring. Oh lovely ungrateful lady, my good squire Sancho will fully recount to you, my beloved enemy, what state I have come to, on your behalf, and if you wish to relieve me, I am yours, but if not, do as you will, for the end of my life will quench both your cruelty and my desire.

    Yours until death,

THE KNIGHT OF THE SAD FACE

"By my father's soul," said Sancho after hearing the letter, "if that isn't the noblest thing I've ever heard. Damn it, your grace manages to say everything just the way you want to — and the way 'The Knight of the Sad Face' works in the signature! I swear your grace is the devil himself, you really are, and there's nothing you don't understand."

"In the profession I follow," replied Don Quijote, "one must know everything."

"Lord!" said Sancho. "Now just turn the page, your grace, and put in the order about the three little donkeys, and make sure you sign it very clearly, so they'll know right away it's from you."

"With pleasure," said Don Quijote.

And after writing, he read it aloud, as follows:

I hereby instruct you, my dear niece, by means of this first directive concerning donkeys, to give Sancho Panza, my squire, three of the five young donkeys I have left at home and in your care. These three donkeys I deliver and pay in return for three others I have already received here, receipt of which I hereby acknowledge, and once you have his receipt your responsibility will be discharged. Given this twenty-second of August in this current year, here in the wilderness of the Sierra Morena mountains.

"That's good," said Sancho. "Now sign it, your grace."

"I don't need to sign it," said Don Quijote. "All I need to do is put in this flourish, which is the same as a signature, and will do for three donkeys, and even for three hundred."

"I trust you, your grace," replied Sancho. "Now let me go saddle up Rocinante, while you get ready, your grace, to give me your blessing, because I plan to leave right away, without watching the stupidities your grace has to do, of which I'll certainly be able to say I've seen you do so many that she won't need to hear any more."

"At least, Sancho, I want you — and also because I think you really need to — I want you, let me say, to see me stark naked and doing a few dozen mad things, which I can accomplish in less than half an hour, so that, having seen them with your own eyes, you can safely swear to all the others you plan to tell her about — and let me promise you, you'll never tell her as many as I plan to perform."

"For the love of God, my lord, don't let me see your grace naked, because it will make me terribly sad and I won't be able to keep from crying, and I've got such a headache from all the tears I shed last night, for my donkey, that I'm just not ready to start any new crying, so if your grace wants me to see some madnesses, do them with your clothes on, your underwear or whatever's most suitable, especially since, as I said, there's no need for that, not for me, and I can get back here so much sooner, when I'll be bringing your grace the news you so want and deserve. And if I'm not, Doña Dulcinea had better get ready for me, because if she doesn't answer the way she should I swear by the most solemn oath in the universe that I'll try to kick and slap the right answer out of her stomach. Because why should such a famous knight errant as your grace have to suffer, and turn himself into a lunatic, and just for a — for a . . . She'd better not make me say it, either, because by God I'll say what I think and I'll upset the whole apple cart, I will, no matter what. That's my style, by God! She doesn't know who I am! But, by God, if she knew me, she'd keep a civil tongue in her head!"

"It would seem, Sancho," said Don Quijote, "that you're no saner than I am."

"I'm not as crazy," replied Sancho, "but I'm a lot madder. But let's leave that: what are you going to eat, your grace, until I come back? Will you jump out on the road, like Cardenio, and steal food from the shepherds?"

"Don't let that worry you," replied Don Quijote, "because even if I had it, I wouldn't eat anything but whatever herbs and fruits this meadow and these trees might give me, for the essence of my scheme requires me not to eat and to accept assorted other hardships of a similar kind. So farewell."

"But, your grace, do you know what worries me? That I won't be able to find this place where I'm leaving you, because it's so hidden away."

"Look around you carefully, and I will try not to go too far from this general area," said Don Quijote, "and, moreover, I will make sure to climb up the very highest of these peaks, to see if I can spy you coming back. Still, to be as sure as possible, in case you miss me and get lost, cut some of the heavy shrubs that grow so plentifully around here and, as you head back out into open country, from time to time lay down a marker of those branches, and they will serve as landmarks for you when you come back to find me, just the way Perseus[8] did with thread, in the labyrinth."

"I'll do that," replied Sancho Panza.

So, cutting some branches, he asked for his master's blessing and, not without many tears on both sides, said his farewells. Then, mounted on Rocinante — entrusted to him by Don Quijote, with repeated injunctions that he take as good care of the animal as of himself — Sancho went down the road toward open country, scattering shrubbery branches at regular intervals, as his master had advised. And thus he rode off, though Don Quijote kept pestering him to stay and see the performance of at least one

8. It should of course be Theseus, not Perseus. Many editors emend, thinking Cervantes made a mistake. But it is Don Quijote, not Cervantes, who makes the mistake [*Translator's Note*]. Theseus, although probably a legendary figure, was believed by the Athenians to have been one of their early kings. Ariadne, the daughter of Minos of Crete, fell in love with him and gave him a thread to find his way out of the labyrinth after killing the Minotaur. After sailing off with Ariadne, Theseus deserted her at Naxos.

or two madnesses. But Sancho was not a hundred paces down the road when he turned and came back, saying:

"Well, your grace is right, and if I'm going to swear with a clear conscience that I saw you doing mad things, I ought to actually see at least one, though I've already seen a great big insanity, because your grace is staying here."

"Isn't that what I was telling you?" said Don Quijote. "Just wait a minute, Sancho, and I'll do one for you, quick as a wink."

And quickly pulling off his breeches, leaving himself in just his shirttails and his skin, without more ado he swiftly jumped as high as he could and did a pair of somersaults, head over heels, uncovering things that, to keep from seeing again, Sancho swung Rocinante around, more than satisfied that, now, he could really swear his master was crazy. Let us leave him to go on his way, until his return, which came sooner than you might think.

Chapter Twenty-Six

— in which we see still more of Don Quijote's splendid testimonials to Love, as performed by him in the Sierra Morena mountains

And so to return to what He of the Sad Face did, once he found himself alone: the history informs us that as soon as Don Quijote performed his leaps and turns, naked from the waist down and clothed from the waist up, and saw that Sancho, not wanting to watch any more of his master's madnesses, had ridden off, he climbed up a very high peak and, as he stood there, went back to debating a point he had argued with himself many times before, without ever resolving the matter, and this was whether it would be better, and more to the point, to imitate Roland's wild madnesses or Amadís' mournful ones. He said to himself:

"If Roland was as good a knight, and as brave as everyone says, is what he did really so remarkable, since he was under a spell, and no one could kill him unless they stuck a pin right in at the tip of his foot, and he always wore shoes with seven iron soles? Still, against Bernardo del Carpio his tricks didn't do him any good, because Bernardo knew all about them and choked him to death with his bare arms, at Roncesvalles. But never mind his bravery: let's deal with his losing his mind, because he certainly did go mad, on account of the evidence he found and also because of the news the shepherd gave him, about Angélica having spent a good many afternoons in bed with Medoro, that curly-haired little Moor who was Agramante's page, and yet if he thought this was the truth, and that his lady had done such an outrageous thing, did he do such a remarkable thing in going mad? And how can I imitate his madness, without imitating the reason for it? I think I can swear that my Dulcinea del Toboso has never in all her life seen a Moor of any kind, the way they really look, wearing their sort of clothes, and I know she's as pure today as the mother who bore her, so I'd clearly be insulting her if, imagining anything else, I made myself go mad with Roland the Raging's kind of madness. On the other hand, I understand that Amadís of Gaul, as a lover who didn't lose his mind and didn't do any crazy things, rose to the very height of Love's fame, and what he did, his story tells us, was simply this — when he saw himself spurned by his lady Oriana, who had ordered him not to show his face before her until she wished him to come, he went off to Barren Mountain, with only a hermit beside him, and there spent his days weeping and commending himself to God, until Heaven came to his aid, there in the middle of his grief and need. So if this is true, as it is, why should I now take the trouble to strip myself naked, or do any harm to these trees, which have never done anything to me? And neither should I disturb the clear waters of these streams, from which I can drink whenever I want. Long live Amadís' memory, and let Don Quijote de La Mancha imitate him in any and every way he can, so it can be said of Don Quijote, as it was once said of another, that if he did not achieve great things, he died trying to achieve them, and if in fact I am neither rejected nor disdained by Dulcinea del Toboso, it is enough for me, as I have already declared, to be obliged to be away from her. So, then, to work! let me remember what Amadís did, and come to understand how I can begin imitating him. But then, I know perfectly well that mostly he prayed and commended himself to God — and what shall I do for a rosary, since I don't have one?"

At this point he suddenly realized what he ought to do, and tore a long strip off his shirttails, which hung down behind him, and tied eleven knots into it, one thicker than the rest, then used this as a rosary the whole time he was there, during which he said thousands and thousands of Ave Marias. But it truly bothered him that there was no other hermit present, to whom he could confess and with whom he could console himself. Accordingly, he kept himself busy, marching back and forth across the meadow, cutting into the bark of the trees and writing in the fine sand near the stream a great many poems, all appropriate to his sadness, and some also praising Dulcinea. But by the time he was found there, the only one that was both complete and legible was as follows:

> Oh trees, and herbs, and plants
> Growing here in this grass,
> So green, so high, so massive,
> If my sickness leaves you passive
> At least hear what I ask.
> My sadness does you no harm,
> No matter how sad it may be,
> For I share myself with thee,
> Weeping tears to the sea
> For the far-off, distant arms
> Of Dulcinea
> from Toboso.

> You see below you here
> The world's most faithful heart,
> Hidden where no love appears
> But only senseless, smarting
> Pain and bewildered tears.

> Love has brought him sorrows
> Of the worst, most bitter sort,
> Enough to fill up barrels
> With his tears, today and tomorrow
> And tomorrow, and all for the loss
>   Of Dulcinea
>   from Toboso.
>
> Searching for splendid deeds
> He found these cursed cliffs,
> And here among rocks and weeds
> Sowed these mournful seeds
> As Love gave him a whiff
>   Of the lash from which all men bleed,
> And no man ever escapes;
> So here he took it on the back,
> And wept, alas and alack,
> For the missing lovely shape
>   Of Dulcinea
>   from Toboso.

Those who found these verses were considerably amused, seeing how Don Quijote had added "from Toboso" to Dulcinea's name, for they suspected him of doubting whether, if he didn't add that information, anyone could understand the poem — and, as he afterwards admitted, this was in fact the truth. He wrote a great many more verses, but as we have noted they could not be deciphered, none of them, but only the three stanzas quoted above. It kept him busy, all this poetic composition, together with a great deal of sighing and calling on the gods and fauns of those woods, and the nymphs in the rivers, and sad, damp Echo, and asking all of them to answer him, and console him, and hear his pleas, plus of course searching out herbs which could keep him alive until Sancho should come back, but had that return been delayed for three weeks, instead of only three days, the Knight of the Sad Face might have been so misshapen that even the mother who bore him would not have known him.

And at this point let's leave him, all wrapped up in his sighs and poetry, and relate what happened to Sancho, riding off on his master's errand — which was that, as he came out on the highway and started toward Toboso, after a journey of only a single day he reached the inn where the unfortunate blanket-tossing had taken place, and he'd no sooner seen it than he felt as if, once again, he was flying up through the air, so he didn't want to go inside, though he could have, and it would have been a good thing, for it was dinner time and he was longing for something hot, since for a long time everything he'd eaten had been cold.

This urge drove him to approach the inn, all the time wondering if he ought to go in or not, but as he hesitated he saw two people coming out of the inn who immediately recognized him. And one of them said to the other:

"Tell me, Father, that man on the horse — isn't he Sancho Panza, the one that our adventurer's housekeeper told us had gone off with her master, to serve as his squire?"

"That's him," said the priest, "and that is our Don Quijote's horse."

They knew him so well because they were the priest and the barber from La Mancha, those who had examined and then condemned to the fire most of Don Quijote's books. And recognizing both Sancho Panza and Rocinante, they wanted to know what had happened, so they approached Sancho, the priest calling to him by name:

"My friend Sancho Panza, where have you left your master?"

Sancho Panza knew them at once, and made up his mind to conceal from them both where and in what state he had left his master, so he replied that his master was doing some important business in another part of the country, which he couldn't really tell them about, not for the very eyes in his head.

"Ah no, no, Sancho Panza," said the barber. "If you don't tell us where you left him, we're going to think — indeed, we already think — you murdered and robbed him, then came riding off on his horse. So you're going to have to give us the old horse's master, or you're in for real trouble."

"There's no reason to go threatening me, because I'm not a man who robs or kills anybody: let everyone die the death Fate, or God, brings him. My master's back in the middle of those mountains, doing penance, and having himself a fine time."

And then, in a nonstop rush of words, he quickly told them what kind of luck he'd had, the adventures he'd experienced, and how he was bringing a letter to Doña Dulcinea del Toboso, who was Lorenzo Corchuelo's daughter, and with whom Don Quijote was in love right up to his ears.

Both men were astonished by what Sancho Panza told them, because even though they knew Don Quijote was crazy, and in what ways, every time they heard about it they were surprised all over again. They asked Sancho Panza to show them the letter he was carrying to Doña Dulcinea del Toboso. He told them it was written in a notebook, and that his master had directed him to have it carefully transcribed in the very first town he came to, to which the priest replied that if Sancho showed it to him, he'd transcribe it in the very finest of handwritings. Sancho Panza stuck his hand under his shirt, but he couldn't find the notebook, nor would he have been able to find it if he'd looked for it from then right down to today, because Don Quijote had kept it and never given it to his squire, nor had Sancho thought of asking for it.

And when Sancho realized that he didn't have the notebook, his face turned deadly pale; he hurriedly felt himself all over, trying again and again to see if he could find it, and then, all of a sudden, plunged both hands into his beard and pulled half of it out, after which, just as frantically, he gave himself half a dozen good punches in the face and on the nose, so that he was covered with blood. Seeing which, the priest and the barber asked him what had happened to make him hit himself so hard.

"What's happened?" replied Sancho. "Just like that, in a second, I've lost three young donkeys, every one of them as big as a castle."

"How's that?" replied the barber.

"I've lost the notebook," cried Sancho, "and the letter to Dulcinea was in there, but also a signed order to his niece, telling her to give me three young donkeys, of the four or five he's got at home."

And then he told them how his own donkey had been lost. The priest comforted him, saying that, when they found his master, he'd get Don Quijote to re-validate the order, and this time write it out properly, the usual way, because orders written out in notebooks were never good enough and wouldn't be fulfilled.

Sancho took some comfort in this, saying that, if this was how it was, he didn't have to worry about the letter to Dulcinea, because he virtually had it memorized, and he could set it out for them whenever and wherever they liked.

"So tell it to us, Sancho," said the barber, "and then we'll write it down."

Sancho Panza hesitated, scratching his head and trying to remember the letter, and then he stood on one foot, and then on the other, sometimes looking down at the ground, sometimes up at the sky, gnawing at his finger tip until he'd bitten it half through, all the while making those who were waiting for him to speak hang on his unspoken words, and finally, after a long silence, declared:

"By God, Father, but the devils have carried off the whole thing. All I can remember is that it began, 'Oh much pawed-over [*sobajada*] lady.' "

"It couldn't say that," said the barber. "Not 'much pawed-over' but 'more than human' [*sobrehumana*] or 'sovereign' [*soberana*] lady."

"That's it," said Sancho. "Yes, and then, if I remember it right, it goes on . . . if I remember it right: 'He who bequeaths and can't sleep, and who is wounded, kisses your lovely hands, you ungrateful and unrecognizable beauty,' and then I don't remember exactly what it said about sending her health and sickness, and then it slid right on until it ended, 'Yours until death, the Knight of the Sad Face.' "

The priest and the barber took great pleasure in Sancho Panza's excellent memory, and praised him for it enthusiastically, asking him to repeat the letter for them twice more, so they too could memorize it well enough so that, later on, they could write it down. Sancho repeated it for them three times, each time saying three thousand more stupidities. And then he told them what was going on with his master — but he was careful not to say a word about the blanket-tossing he himself had experienced, there in that very inn which he still refused to enter. He told them, also, how his master intended, should he receive a favorable reply from Doña Dulcinea del Toboso, to set out to make himself an emperor, or at least a king — something which, as they had both agreed, was a very straightforward matter, especially considering Don Quijote's courage and the strength of his right arm — and, when he became one, he'd marry off Sancho (who would of course have become a widower, by then) to some emperor's daughter, heiress to some great, rich estate, and one that didn't have any sort of island, because he no longer wanted any of those.

Sancho told them all this so calmly, from time to time wiping his nose, and with such utter lack of rationality, that the priest and the barber were astonished all over again, realizing that Don Quijote's madness was so passionate that it had thus swept away this poor man's sanity. Trying to explain the truth to him plainly would make no sense: it seemed to them that, Sancho's conscience not being in any way affected, it was better simply to let him go on believing in this madness — and, besides, it would be more trouble for them, listening to all his nonsense. So they told him to pray for his master's health, because it was indeed a very likely, and not a particularly difficult matter, for Don Quijote to become, in the course of time, an emperor, exactly as he had said, or at least an archbishop or something equivalent. To which Sancho replied:

"Gentlemen, if Fortune spins the wheel so my master decides not to be an emperor, but an archbishop instead, what I want to know is this: what do archbishops errant pay their squires?"

"They pay them," said the priest, "by giving them some church office, with or without a parish, or else they make them a sacristan, and in that case you have to figure in not only a good fixed income but also the altar fees, which add a good bit."

"But in that case," answered Sancho, "the squire can't be a married man, and he's got to know how to help at mass, at least, and if that's the case, oh I'm in for it! because I'm married and I don't know the first letter of the alphabet! What'll happen to me if my master takes it into his head to become an archbishop and not an emperor, the way knights errant are always supposed to do?"

"Don't worry, Sancho my friend," said the barber, "we'll speak to your master about this, and we'll advise him — we'll even make it a matter of conscience — that he be an emperor rather than an archbishop — and besides, it will be easier, because he's braver than he is learned."

"That's what I think," replied Sancho, "though he could do anything. What I think I'd better do is pray to Our Lord to place him where he can do the best for himself and also the best for me."

"You speak like a sensible man," said the priest, "and you'll be acting like a good Christian. But what needs to be done, now, is to arrange your master's rescue from that senseless penitence in which, as you tell us, he's engaged. And to calculate just what we have to do, as well as to eat our evening meal (this being the proper time for that), it makes very good sense for us to walk into this inn."

Sancho told them to go on, but he would wait for them outside and explain, later, why he didn't feel right about going in. Still, he asked them to bring him out something hot to eat and, also, something for Rocinante. So they went in and left him there, and after a while the barber brought him out some food. Afterwards, as the barber and the priest discussed what plan to adopt, in order to bring about the outcome they desired, the priest thought of an approach well-tuned to Don Quijote's tastes and to their own interests, which was this: he'd dress himself up like a wandering maiden, and the barber would do the best he could to seem like a squire, and then they'd go to Don Quijote and pretend this was a damsel in distress and in need, with a boon to beg of him, which as a brave knight errant he couldn't help but grant. And the boon for which he planned to beg would be for Don Quijote to journey with the damsel, to a certain place where she would lead him, there to undo a malicious wrong done her by a wicked knight — imploring him, at the same time, not to command her to raise her veil, nor to ask anything whatever about her, until he had righted the wrong done her by the aforesaid wicked knight. The priest was sure that, in such a cause, Don Quijote would agree to anything,

and so they'd be able to rescue him from the mountains and bring him
back home, where they could try to find some cure for his strange madness.

Chapter Twenty-Seven

*— how the priest and the barber's plan worked out, with other matters
worthy of being included in this magnificent tale*

The barber rather liked the priest's plan — indeed, he liked it so much
that they immediately set about putting it into operation. First, they borrowed a petticoat and a veil from the innkeeper's wife, leaving her as
security one of the priest's new cassocks. Then the barber fashioned a huge
beard out of an old russet and grey donkey's tail, which the innkeeper kept
so he could hang up his comb. His wife wondered why they wanted such
things. The priest gave her a quick summary of Don Quijote's madness,
and explained that they'd thought of this disguise as a way of getting him
out of the mountains, which was where he now was. The innkeeper and
his wife immediately realized this was the lunatic who'd been their guest,
the one who'd made and drunk the magic potion and the master of the
squire who'd been tossed in a blanket, so they told the priest everything
that had happened, not omitting what Sancho had been so careful not to
tell them. And then the innkeeper dressed up the priest fit to kill, in a
flannel skirt with gored velvet stripes eight inches wide, and a green velvet
blouse, trimmed in white satin, the whole outfit probably dating from the
reign of King Wamba.[1] The priest wouldn't let them put a headdress on
him, but he did put on a little quilted linen cap that he usually slept in,
and wound a band of black taffeta around his forehead, using another strip
of the same material as a mask with which to securely cover both his face
and his beard, and then he pulled his hat (which was large enough to
serve as a parasol) way down on his head and, shrouding himself in his
cape, seated himself on his mule, sidesaddle, while the barber, with his
new beard, half white and half reddish brown (and fashioned, as we've
said, from a russet donkey's tail), flowing all the way down to his waist,
climbed onto his mule, too.

They said their goodbyes to everyone, including our old friend Maritornes, who — sinner that she was — promised to pray a rosary of
prayers, that God might grant them success in the difficult but enormously
Christian venture which they were undertaking.

However, they had scarcely left the inn when the priest was suddenly
struck by the thought that it was wrong for him to dress himself up this
way, and that it was an indecency for anyone in holy orders so to be garbed,
even though it might accomplish a good deal, so he turned to the barber
and asked him to exchange costumes with him, since it was a good deal
more proper for the barber to play the role of the needy damsel, leaving
the squire's role for the priest, this being a good deal less of a profanation

---

1. A king of the Gothic line who reigned in the Iberian Peninsula (A.D. 672–680); here a proverbial
figure for antiquity.

of his priestly dignity, and indeed he could have nothing more to do with the scheme on any other terms, even if Don Quijote were to be carried off by the devil himself.

Just then Sancho rode up and, seeing them decked out as they were, could not help laughing. And in the end the barber did exactly as the priest had asked and reversed their roles, the priest explaining to him just how he ought to act and what he had to say to Don Quijote, to coax and even oblige him to go with them, leaving behind the scene he'd chosen for his senseless penitence. The barber assured him he needed no lessons and knew precisely what had to be said. And for the time being, he added, he didn't care to assume his costume, but would prefer to wait until they were near to where they would find Don Quijote, so he folded up his womanly garments, as the priest did his squirely disguise, and they went on their way, Sancho Panza guiding them, and telling them as they rode about the madman they'd met in the mountains — but not telling them about the suitcase they'd found, and what had been in it, because even though he was somewhat stupid, our young friend Sancho was a bit greedy.

The next day they came to the place where Sancho had spread out heaps of bramble branches, to guide him back to where he'd left his master and, recognizing them, he told them this was where they went off into the mountains and it was now time for them to dress themselves for their roles, if that was what his master's deliverance required, and indeed they had already informed him that appearing before him in these guises and costumes was of crucial importance in saving his master from the evil life he had chosen, charging him most strictly not to tell Don Quijote who they were, nor that he knew them, and also that, should his master ask if Sancho had delivered the letter to Dulcinea, he was to reply that, yes, he had, and she, being unable to read or write, had given him an oral reply to transmit to his master, who she ordered under penalty of her disfavor to immediately appear before her, and that this was a matter of the highest importance. And with this, and with the other things they intended to say to him, they could surely bring him to a better way of life, and soon have him well on the way to becoming an emperor or a king (for there wasn't much to worry about, as far as his becoming an archbishop).

Sancho listened to everything, and did his best to remember it all, thanking them warmly for their plan to advise his master to become an emperor rather than an archbishop, because when it came to that, emperors could do a lot more for their squires than archbishops. He also told them that it would be a good idea for him to go on ahead and seek out his master, so he could give him his lady's reply, because that might be enough to rescue him from that place, without their putting themselves to too much trouble. They thought his suggestion made sense, so they decided to wait until he came back with word that he had found Don Quijote.

Sancho rode on into the mountain, through natural openings in the rock, leaving them together at a place where a small, gentle stream flowed, where the other high peaks, and the trees roundabout, created a pleasant, refreshing shade. It was a hot August day, and in those regions very hot indeed; it was about three in the afternoon; and all in all it was an agreeable, nay, an inviting place to rest and await Sancho's return.

So there they were, resting in the shade, when suddenly they heard a sweet, well-trained voice, accompanied by no other instrument, which considerably astonished them, for it did not seem like a place where such accomplished singing was very likely. For though people say that, in the woods and fields, you can find shepherds with remarkable voices, this is more poetic embroidering of fact than bare truth — and especially when the two wonderstruck listeners became aware that what they were hearing were not lines written by some country cattle dealer, but real poems, written by a polished courtier. Indeed, to verify their judgment, let me set out what they heard:

> What makes happiness foreign?
> Scorn.
> And what makes my sadness worse?
> Jealousy's curse.
> And what forces pain to stay?
> Staying away.
> And thus this constant sadness
> Repels all possible gladness,
> And adding its power to scorn and jealousy's scope
> What kills me is staying away, what kills me is hope.
>
> What fed me this painful ration?
> Passion.
> And what turned delight to hate?
> Fate.
> And who allowed me this load?
> God.
> And thus the sovereign breath
> Of these foreign powers brings death,
> And adds its awful power to the heavy weight
> Of faithless love, and heaven, and fickle fate.
>
> What could possibly save me?
> The grave.
> And who can still praise the heart?
> Some world apart.
> And what will cure all sadness?
> Madness.
> And thus it's only fools
> Who play this game by the rules,
> When the only hope for suffering, weeping humanity
> Is death, and endless separation, and insanity.

The time of day, the time of year, the lonely setting, the sound and skill of the singer's voice, made our two listeners happy, as it also filled them with wonder, so they lay perfectly still, waiting to see if they'd hear anything else, but after a long silence they decided to go looking for the musician who had sung so beautifully. But just as they were about to do so, the same voice stopped them in their tracks, singing, this time, the following sonnet:

SONNET

> Sacred friendship, rising on nimble wings,
> You left us, here on earth, only your ghost
> When you rose to heaven and happy angelic things,
> Living eternally blessed with that holy host,
>   Dropping down below, whenever you willed,
> A righteous peace whose face we never see.
> But sometimes jealousy shows us her eyes, filled
> With pleasure and joy that quickly turn mortal, and kill.
>   Come back from Heaven, oh friendship! or at least keep
> This fraud from mocking your very walk and your garb,
> For all he can do is murder everything decent;
>   And if you let this liar stalk our streets
> The world and everyone in it will take up arms,
> And primitive hate will rule us, now your regent.

This song ended in the most profound of sighs, and both men, listening carefully, waited to see if they would hear still more, but finding that the music had now been turned into sobs and tears and moans, they decided to find out who the miserable man might be, with a voice as glorious as his wailing was sorrowful, nor had they gone very far when, coming around a great rock, they saw a man exactly like the one who, Sancho had told them, had told Cardenio's story, and this man, seeing them, did not attack them, but stayed where he was, his head bent onto his breast like someone lost in thought, and after the first unexpected sight not bothering even to raise his eyes.

The priest, who was very well-spoken and had already been informed of Cardenio's unhappiness, recognized him by these signs and approached him, with trenchant yet wise words trying to talk him out of this miserable way of life, for (he said) he might die in that wilderness, which would be a misfortune to end all misfortunes. Cardenio was at the moment completely sane, entirely free of those wild fits which so often swept him out of himself, and observing these two men dressed quite differently from those who usually inhabited the wilderness, he couldn't keep from being somewhat startled, and especially when he heard them speak of his personal sorrows as if they were a well-known affair (as the priest's arguments clearly indicated they were), so he replied as follows:

"I can see perfectly well, gentlemen, whoever you may be, that Heaven, which watches over and helps those who are worthy of its help — and, often, even those who are unworthy — has here in this far-off, desolate spot, so removed from the ordinary life of most men, sent me (who does not deserve it) people who can place right in front of me a variety of forceful arguments, showing me how unreasonably I lead my life, and trying to lead me to some better situation. But since they do not understand, as I do, that in abandoning this injurious life I must fall into a worse one, perhaps it is best if they take me for a man of weak mind — even, still worse, a man not in his right mind. Nor would it be odd if this were the case, for it seems to me that thinking about my misfortunes has such a powerful effect on my mind that it might well bring me to eternal damnation — willy-nilly I turn stone-like, deprived of all my proper senses and understanding, as indeed I perceive very well when, afterwards, people remember for me, showing me signs of what I did while that fearful fit overcame me. Nor do I see how I can do more than feel an empty regret, and vainly curse my fate, excusing the mad things I do by telling anyone who wants to hear what caused me so to act, for once they see what began these things they won't be surprised at what has followed after, and if they bring me no cure at least they will no longer blame me, thus transforming their anger at my boldness into sorrow for my misfortunes. And if you, gentlemen, have come here, similarly motivated, let me first beg you, before you proceed with your wise arguments, to hear the account of those misfortunes (which are uncountable), because it may well be that, having heard them, you can spare yourself the trouble of trying to ease the pain of an evil which no advice can cure."

Wanting nothing more than to hear from his own mouth what had brought his misery upon him, they asked him to please go on, assuring him that they would do nothing, either by way of cure or consolation, except what he liked, and so the sad gentleman began his pitiful tale, employing virtually the same words and gestures with which he'd told it, not many days before, to Don Quijote and the goatherd, when because of Maestro Elisabad and Don Quijote's scrupulous defense of knightly decorum the story had been left unfinished, as this history has already reported. But this time his mad fit held off, most fortunately, and he was able to tell the story to the end. Accordingly, when he got to the point of the letter which Don Fernando had found, in the leaves of the tale, *Amadís of Gaul*, Cardenio said that he remembered it perfectly, and that it ran like this:

LUSCINDA TO CARDENIO

Every day I find more and more in you that compels me to value you more and more highly, and so, if you wish to rescue me from this pressing obligation without levying a tax against my honor, you can do that very well indeed. My father, whom you know and I love, will never force me against my will, and will let you have what it is only right that you have, if you truly think as highly of me as you say, and as I believe you do.

"It was this letter that led me to ask for Luscinda's hand, as I've told you, and it was this same letter which led Don Fernando to take her for one of the wisest and most sensible women of this age, as it was also this letter which led him to the desire to destroy me, before I should obtain what I most desired. I told Don Fernando that all Luscinda's father needed was for my father to ask for her, though I did not dare ask him again, for fear he would not do it — not because he had the slightest doubt about her family heritage, her goodness, her virtue, or her beauty, or that she was such that she would ennoble any other family in all of Spain, but because I knew he did not want me to rush into marriage, before finding out what Duke Ricardo meant to do for me. In a word, I told him I did not dare to risk asking my father yet again, as much for that difficulty as for a variety of others that worried me, without really knowing what they were, except that it somehow seemed to me that what I longed for was never going to happen. Don Fernando's response to all this was to tell me that he would speak to my father for me and arrange for him to go to Luscinda's father. Oh ambitious Marius! oh cruel Catiline! oh Sila, you scoundrel! oh Galalón, you liar! oh treacherous Vellido! oh vindictive Julián! oh greedy Judas![2] Traitor, cruel, vindictive, liar — but what had this sorrowful soul done to you, who so naively revealed his heart and its secrets to you? How had I injured you? What words had I ever spoken to you, what counsel poured into your ear, except what was intended solely to advance your cause and swell your honor? But, wretch that I am, why am I complaining? When heavenly bodies rain misfortunes down on us, they always crash violently, furiously on our heads, and no power on earth can stop them, nor can any conceivable human ingenuity hold them off! And who could have imagined that Don Fernando, a distinguished gentleman, prudent, bound to me by the services I had rendered him, with the power to win whoever his heart yearned for, no matter where he might seek her, would need to steal what was someone else's — to rob me, as they say, of the single ewe in my flock, not yet in fact mine? But enough of such matters, which simply waste our time and accomplish nothing: let us pick up the broken thread of my miserable story.

"Let me say, then, that, seeing my presence as an obstacle to his lying, evil intentions, Don Fernando decided to send me off to his older brother, with the excuse of asking him for funds with which to buy six horses, the purchase of which he had deliberately concluded on that very same day when he had offered to speak to my father, but a purchase he had made for the sole purpose of arranging my absence (to help him in his damnable scheme). He asked to go fetch the money: could I have foreseen his treachery? Could I, by any chance, have even imagined it? No, never: indeed, I was more than happy to offer to go at once, pleased with the fine bargain he had made. That night I spoke to Luscinda, and told her what Don Fernando and I were planning, and how I had good reason to hope that our right and proper desires would finally come to reality. And she — as utterly unaware of Don Fernando's treachery as was I — told me to try to return as soon as possible, for she felt sure our mutual desires would have to wait no longer than the moment when my father spoke to hers. I don't know exactly how it was but, as she told me this, her eyes filled with tears and a lump came into her throat, stopping her from speaking any of the many, many words which, or so it seemed to me, she wanted to say to me. This was something new, and it astonished me, for I had never before seen it: whenever good fortune (and my own attentiveness) had permitted us to talk, we had always spoken easily and happily, without adulterating our conversation with tears, sighs, jealousies, doubts, and fears. I would spend the time thanking the stars for my good luck, heaven having granted her to me as my lady; I would praise her beauty, and say how

2. Marius, Catiline, and Sila were Roman traitors; Galalón betrayed Roland and Charlemagne's peers at Roncesvalles; Vellido betrayed and murdered King Sancho II of Castile; Count Julian, seeking vengeance for the seduction of his daughter Florinda by King Roderick, called upon the Arabs to invade Spain in A.D. 711; and Judas, of course, needs no introduction as a traitor.

dazzled I was by her courage and good sense. And, for her part, she would praise in me what, as my beloved, she thought worthy of praise. And in addition we'd tell each other thousands of unimportant little things, what had been happening to our neighbors and the people we knew, and the most I dared was, almost by force, to grasp one of her beautiful white hands and carry it to my lips — or as close to my lips as, through the low, narrow grille which separated us, I could manage to bring it. But that night, before the sad day of my departure, she wept, she groaned, she sighed, and when she left me I was confused and frightened, terribly worried to have seen in her, for the first time, such signs of grief and regret — but, to keep from destroying all my hopes, I attributed it all to the strength of her love for me, and to the sadness which absence naturally causes in those who truly long for one another. So I left, sadly, thoughtfully, my soul full of worries and doubts, without knowing what it doubted and what it was worried about, though what I had been shown were clear signs of the sad events yet to come. I came where I had been told to go, and gave my letters to Don Fernando's brother; I was received cordially, but I was not sent right back, but ordered to wait — much to my annoyance — eight full days, in a place where their father the duke might not see me, since Don Fernando had written that the money was being sent without his father's knowledge — but the whole thing was a scheme concocted by that liar, Don Fernando, for his older brother had plenty of money and could have sent it immediately. These were commands which I thought of disobeying, for it seemed to me impossible to live that long without seeing Luscinda, especially having left her in the sad state I have already described, but in spite of everything I did obey, as a good and faithful servant, even knowing that it would be at the cost of my own well-being. But on the fourth day of my enforced stay a man arrived, looking for me and bringing a letter the return address of which I recognized as Lucinda's, and the letter was indeed from her. I opened it, fearfully, already frightened, knowing that, to cause her to write to me in my absence, when she wrote to me so seldom even when I was there, it had to be something of great importance. But before reading the letter I asked the man to tell me who had sent him, and how long it had taken him to ride here, and he told me that, one day at noon, he was simply going along a street in my city, and a singularly beautiful woman had called to him from a window, her eyes brimming with tears, and had said to him, hurriedly: 'My friend, if you are, as you seem to be, a Christian, I beg you for the love of God to bring this letter, as fast as you possibly can, to the person and the address written hereon, which is well known and easily located, and in so doing you will perform a great service for Christ our Lord, and for it to be in your own interest to do as I ask, take what you will find wrapped in this handkerchief.'

" 'And as she said this,' he went on, 'she threw a handkerchief to me, in which I found a hundred gold dollars and this gold ring, which I'm wearing, as well as this letter which I've now handed over to you. Without waiting for me to answer her, she quickly left the window, though since she had seen me take both the letter and the handkerchief, and my gestures indicated that I accepted her charge, she knew I would do as she asked. Finding myself so well paid for the trouble of bringing this to you, and knowing by the address that it was you, señor, to whom the letter was to be delivered — for I know you well, señor — and also being obliged by that beautiful lady's tears, I made up my mind not to let anyone else complete the errand but just come and deliver the letter myself. So I got here in just sixteen hours — and as you know it's a ride of over sixty miles.'

"While the newly arrived messenger was telling me this, sympathetically, I hung upon his words, my legs trembling so hard they could barely keep me standing. Well, I opened the letter, and this is what I found:

> Don Fernando promised you to speak to your father, in order that he would speak to mine, and he has done so, but more in his interest than in yours. You must know, sir, that he has himself asked for my hand, and my father, carried away by what he sees as Don Fernando's advantages over you, has agreed — and so enthusiastically that the marriage is to take place in two days, so quietly and secretly that the only witnesses will be the heavens themselves and a few members of this household. You can readily imagine my feelings: if you think you ought to come, come; what comes of all this will show you whether or not I truly love you. May God bring this to your hands before I find myself joined to a man who knows so little about keeping his word.

"These, then, were the explanations contained in the letter and which were sufficient to set me out on the road, no longer waiting for any word or for any moneys from Don Fernando's brother, for it had become completely clear to me that it was not the purchase of horses, but the pursuit of personal pleasure, which had sent me there. The anger I now felt toward Don Fernando, together with my fear of losing the beloved I had won, after so many years of waiting and working and loving, virtually lent me wings, so I reached home the next day, exactly at the hour when it would be possible to speak with Luscinda. I arrived secretly, leaving the mule on which I had ridden at the home of the good man who had brought me her letter, and was lucky enough, at least, that I found Luscinda there at the grille which had witnessed all our loving encounters. I knew her at once, and she knew me — but not as she had known me or I her. But who in all the world can boast that he has plumbed and understood the unintelligible mind and changeable character of a woman? No one, absolutely no one. So as soon as Luscinda saw me, she said:

" 'Cardenio, I am dressed for the wedding. That traitor Don Fernando, and my greedy father, are even now waiting for me in the hall, with the other witnesses, but before they see me married they will see me dead. Don't worry, my friend: just find a way to be there for this sacrifice, for if what I say will not stop it, I have a hidden dagger which can prevent more deliberate violence, ending my life at the same time as it shows you how I have felt and how I feel about you.'

"I answered her at once, wildly, afraid she might not give me the chance to reply at all:

" 'May your deeds be as true as your words, for if you have a dagger to vouch for you, I have here a sword which will either defend you or kill me, if fate goes against us.'

"But I don't think she could have heard me, because I heard them calling to her to hurry: the wedding was waiting. That set the seal on the dark night of my sadness, hurried forward the sunset of my happiness: I stood there, neither seeing nor thinking anything. I could not make myself walk into her father's house, nor could I make myself move at all — but realizing how important my presence was, for whatever would happen in that house, I braced myself as best I could and went in, and since I was well aware of all the entranceways and exits, and the house was full of noise and disorder, I entered unseen and was able to position myself next to a window, in that very hall where she was to be married, so that standing between the long, full curtains which hung there I could see everything without myself being seen. How should I tell you how my heart hammered in my breast, or the thoughts that ran through my brain, the contingencies I tried to plan for, as I stood there? — so many, and of such an order, that I could not tell them if I would, nor is it good that they be told. It is enough for you to know that the bridegroom came into the hall wearing only his everyday clothes, without any additional adornment. The best man was one of Luscinda's first cousins, and there was no one else present, except the servants. After a bit, Luscinda emerged from a dressing room, accompanied by her mother and two of her maids, all of them impeccably dressed and adorned, formally and in full court style and jewelry, as the bride's family and her beauty deserved. Given my excitement, and the trancelike state in which I was waiting, I could not pay close attention to what Luscinda was wearing, except to notice the colors, which were red and white, and the glimmering of all the precious stones set in her head-dress and indeed in everything she wore, the whole effect being to emphasize the rare beauty of her golden hair, which rivalled the gem stones and the four torches set around the hall and shone more brightly than any of them. Oh memory! Mortal enemy to any possible consolation! Why bring back to me, now, this image of my beloved enemy's incomparable beauty? Would it not be better, oh cruel one, to bring back to me what she then proceeded to do, so that, stirred by such a blatant injury, I can at least try, if not to revenge it, at least to surrender this life of mine? But, gentlemen, please don't grow weary of my rambling digressions: my sorrow is not one of those that either can or should be told lightly and succinctly, since each and every aspect of it seems to me worthy of a long, long treatise."

The priest replied that not only were they in no way weary of listening to him, but took great pleasure in all the details with which he had provided them, for these were indeed things that did not deserve to be passed over in silence, and fully merited the same attention as the central facts in his story.

"So let me tell you," Cardenio went on, "how, when everyone was in the hall, the parish priest came in and, taking Luscinda and Fernando by the hand, in order to perform the ceremony, said to them:

" 'Do you, señora Luscinda, take Don Fernando, who stands beside you here, to be your lawful wedded husband, as Holy Mother Church decrees?'

"And I thrust my head all the way out from between the curtains, and strained my ears, my heart pounding, to hear what Luscinda would reply, expecting her words to pronounce either my death sentence or an affir-

mation of my life. Oh, had I dared to come rushing forward, shouting,
"'Ah, Luscinda, Luscinda! Think what you're doing — consider what
you owe me — remember that you're mine and can never belong to
anyone else! And let me warn you that, should you say *yes*, the word will,
then and there, signal the end of my life. Ah, Don Fernando, you traitor,
you thief of all my happiness, you murderer of my very existence! What
do you want? What are you after? How can you possibly hope, as a Christian, to achieve your desire, for Luscinda is *my* wife, and I am her
husband?'

"Oh, what madness! Now, far off and completely out of danger, I say I
should have done what I did not do! Now, having let him rob me of my
beloved, my jewel, I curse the thief, when I could have taken my revenge
on him, if only I had as much heart for vengeance as I have for moaning
and groaning! And, in a word, because, then, I was a coward and a fool,
who could be surprised that, now, I'm dying, shamed, repentant, and mad?
The priest stood waiting for Luscinda's reply, which did not come for a
long time, and just when I was sure she would draw the dagger and let it
speak for her, or else say something blunt and true that would help me, I
heard her saying, in a faint, weak voice,

"'I do.'

"Don Fernando saying the same thing, and putting the ring on her
finger, they were joined forever. The groom turned to embrace his bride,
but putting her hand on her heart she fell fainting into her mother's arms.
And I must tell you how I felt at that moment, for her *I do* made a mockery
of all my hopes, it revealed all Luscinda's words and all her promises to
be false, and it brought me to the impossibility of ever attaining what, at
that instant, I had lost. There was absolutely nothing I could do, I felt
completely helpless, abandoned by Heaven, transformed into an enemy of
the very earth which had nourished me, deprived of the air I needed in
order to breathe my sighs and the moisture required to dampen my eyes.
Only the fire swept higher: I burned with rage and jealousy. They were
all running wildly around, after Luscinda fainted, and as her mother un-
fastened her bodice, so she might breathe, they found there a sealed document, which Don Fernando immediately took and, by the light of one
of the torches, set himself to reading, after which he dropped into a chair
and rested his cheek against his hand, clearly lost in thought, totally unconcerned with what was being done to bring his wife back to herself.
Seeing the general uproar, I took the risk of stepping out, though I did
not care whether or not I was seen, thinking that were my presence noticed
I would do some wild thing which would show the entire world the depth
of righteous indignation in my breast — I would punish my false friend,
Don Fernando, and perhaps even punish the fickleness of the now-
unconscious traitoress. But Fate was saving me for still worse things, if
there can be any, and saw to it that I had more than enough of that
reasoning faculty which, ever since, has left me, and thus kept me from
even desiring to take revenge on my greatest enemies — though, since
any thought of me was the farthest thing from their minds, that would
have been easily accomplished — but, instead, set me to wreaking on
myself the pain and suffering they deserved, perhaps serving myself even

more harshly than I might have served them, if I had killed them then and there, for swift pain is soon done with, but pain which lingers and torments kills and goes on killing, and yet life goes on.

"So I left there and went to the house where I had left the mule, and had the man saddle it for me, and left the city without even bidding him farewell — not daring, as if I had been another Lot, to turn my face and look back. And when I found myself out in the open fields, hidden in the darkness of night, the silence led me to raise my voice and lament, quite unconcerned, and certainly not afraid, that I might be heard or recognized, and I heaped curses on Luscinda and Don Fernando — as if that would soothe the injuries they had done me. I called them cruel, mean-spirited, treacherous, and ungrateful, but more than anything else I called them greedy, for my enemy's wealth had closed my beloved's eyes, letting her abandon me and surrender herself to one with whom Fortune had been far more free and open-handed — and then, in the middle of this out-pouring of curses and accusations, I found myself excusing her, explaining that it was hardly remarkable for a young lady shut away from the world in her parents' house, always obedient to their wishes, to have tried to oblige them when they presented her with such a highborn husband, so rich, and with such a fine presence, for had she not been willing to have him she might have been thought either mad or madly in love with some-one else, something which would not have been useful for her reputation. But then I came back to the argument that, had she declared me already her husband, her parents would have seen that her choice was not such a bad one, and they would have excused her, for before Don Fernando presented himself to them they could hardly, by any kind of reasonable standard, have wanted a better husband for their daughter, and certainly, before saying I do and burning all her bridges behind her, she could have said that her I do had already been spoken, and to me, a fact which I would have more than fully attested to, had she only chosen to try such a deception. And in the end I made up my mind that, when she had chosen to forget the fine words with which she'd deceived me (lost as I was in my steadfast hopes and honest desires), she had acted without much love, without much sense, but with a great deal of ambition and longing for worldly magnificence. Riding restlessly along, I argued aloud all that night, and at dawn found myself at the entrance to these mountains, through which I rode for another three days, following no road and no path, until I came to a meadow (though I do not remember just where it was) and there asked some shepherds where I would find the harshest part of the whole region. They told me it was here, where we are now. So I imme-diately came this way, intending to let my life end here, and as I rode into this wilderness my mule died, perishing of weariness and hunger — or, to my mind more likely, to get rid of such a useless burden as me. So I continued on foot, doggedly, tormented by hunger, having no one and nothing to aid me and not contemplating any request for help. I have no idea how long I remained here, stretched out on the ground, but when I finally got up I was no longer hungry and I found myself among a group of goatherds, and it must surely have been them who cured me of that pressing affliction, because they told me in what state they had found me, and that I'd been saying all sorts of wild and senseless things, showing without much doubt that I'd lost my mind — and indeed I have been aware, since then, that I'm not always sane, but am sometimes split apart and feeble-brained, and doing a thousand crazy things, tearing my clothes, crying out in this desolate place, cursing my fate and pointlessly repeating, over and over, the beloved name of my beloved enemy, with no purpose other than the thought of ending my life in such complaints. And when I'm myself again, I'm so weak and weary that I can barely move. Most of the time I live in a hollow cork tree, thick enough to shelter this miserable body. The cowherds and goatherds who patrol these mountains support me, out of sheer kindness, leaving food out on the roads and up on the rocks, where they know I might come by and find it, so even though I'm sometimes out of my mind, Nature teaches me to understand that food is necessary and quickens in me both the desire to quench this longing and also the will to actually accomplish it. They've told me, when they find me truly sane, that sometimes I jump out on the road and violently steal food from the shepherds who bring it up to them, although they'd gladly give it to me. And this is how I lead these last days of my miserable life, waiting for Heaven to see fit to end it, or else to so change my memory that I can no longer recall either the beauty and treachery of Luscinda or the injury done me by Don Fernando, and if Heaven can accomplish this, and leave me alive, I will turn my mind to better things, but if it cannot, all I can do is pray for the fullness of its mercy on my soul, since I can find neither the courage nor the strength to rescue this body from the straits into which love has made me lead it.

"And this, gentlemen, oh this is the bitter tale of my misfortune! Tell me: could it have been recited less emotionally than you have heard me tell it? But please, neither trouble nor tire yourself with arguments or advice, all meant to assist me, for they can do no more good than what a famous doctor may prescribe for a sick patient who chooses not to listen to him. I do not wish well-being without Luscinda, and she having chosen to belong to another, though she is, or should have been, mine, I prefer to be miserable, having once been able to be happy. She has chosen, by her fickleness, to destroy me once and for all, and I choose, by seeking to die, to satisfy her wish and become an example, for all time to come, of how I alone did without that which all other sufferers have in abundance, for to them the impossibility of having what they wanted was a kind of relief, while for me it brings the most pain and grief, and even in death it seems to me this pain and grief will not end."

And so Cardenio finished his long tale, as miserable as it was loving, and just as the priest was preparing to say some consoling words, he was stopped by a voice, saying in pitiful tones what will be said, momentarily, in the fourth part of this narrative, the third part of which was at this point brought to its completion by that wise and knowing historian, Sidi Hamid Benengeli.

Part Four

Chapter Twenty-Eight

— which deals with an unusual but charming adventure experienced by the priest and the barber in those same mountains

Those were supremely brave and happy days, when that boldest of all knights, Don Quijote, came dashing into the world, for because of his exalted determination to revive and restore for us the long-lost and very nearly moribund order of knight errantry, we now enjoy, in this age of ours — so deficient in cheerful amusement — not only the delight of his own absolutely veracious tale but also all those other stories and narrative digressions which, to some extent, are no less delightful and skilfully told, and every bit as true, as his own history — which, going its own way, twisting and criss-crossing back and forth, now records that, as the priest was getting ready to comfort Cardenio, he was stopped by the sound of a voice that, in melancholy tones, spoke as follows:

"Oh God! Perhaps I have finally found the place where the heavy weight of this body, which I bear so unwillingly, can be laid in some hidden grave! Oh, it may be so, if the loneliness these mountains seem to promise is no deception. Ah, you miserable woman, where could you possibly find better company than these cliffs and brambles, for they permit you to share your misery with Heaven rather than any human creature, there being no one walking the earth from whom you can hope to receive advice for your uncertainties, relief for your sorrows, or cures for anything that ails you!"

The priest, and those around him, heard all this, which seemed to them to have been spoken — as indeed it had been — from somewhere very close by, so they rose to look for whoever had been speaking, nor had they gone twenty paces when, seated at the foot of an ash tree, in front of a craggy rock, they saw a young fellow dressed like a peasant (though because his head was bent forward they could not see his face) washing his feet in the stream that ran by. They stood watching so quietly that he was not aware of their presence, nor was he paying attention to anything except bathing his feet — which looked for all the world like two bits of white crystal lying on the stream bed with the other stones and rocks. The whiteness and beauty of those feet astonished them, for they did not seem fashioned for treading on ordinary ground, nor for walking behind a plow and a pair of oxen (as their owner's clothes would have indicated). So, seeing that their presence had still not been noticed, the priest, who had been leading the way, signalled to the others to crouch down and conceal themselves behind some of the boulders lying about, which they all did, staring attentively to see what the young fellow might do. He had on a short, drab double-cape, belted tightly with a white cloth, dun-colored wool leggings and breeches, and a hat of the same nondescript color. He had the leggings rolled halfway up his legs — which seemed every bit as white as alabaster. After washing his beautiful feet, he wiped them with a small towel which he pulled out from under his hat, at the same time raising his face and showing them its incomparable loveliness — so lovely that, in a low voice, Cardenio murmured to the priest:

"That isn't Luscinda, so it can't be a human being, but perhaps it's an angel."

Then the young fellow took off his hat and, shaking his head from side to side, began to spread out hair so golden that the sun itself might have been jealous of it. And at this point they realized that the apparent peasant was not only a woman, but the most beautiful woman either priest or barber had ever seen — or Cardenio, too, had he not been familiar with Luscinda, for, as he later explained, only Luscinda's beauty could have competed. Her long, golden hair not only covered her shoulders, but as she turned from side to side it fell, if not all the way to her feet, certainly over all the rest of her body, so that only her feet were clearly visible. And then she used her hands as a comb — and if her feet, lying in the water, had looked like bits of pure crystal, her hands moving through her hair seemed like shards of snow. All this left the three onlookers more and more entranced and anxious to know who she was.

And so they decided to show themselves. The sound of them rising to their feet made the beautiful girl lift her head and, with both hands, part the hair in front of her eyes, looking out to see what it was she had heard, and as soon as she saw them she jumped up and, without waiting to put on her shoes or rebind her hair, hurriedly snatched up a bundle lying next to her, which appeared to be clothing, and started to run, obviously frightened and confused, but had not taken six steps when, her delicate feet unable to endure the sharp, harsh rock, she fell to the ground. Seeing which, the three men hurried toward her; the priest was the first to speak:

"Wait, señora, whoever you are, for our only intention is to help you. There is no reason for such an abrupt flight, which neither your own feet nor we will permit."

She did not say a word in reply, astonished and visibly shaken. When they reached her, the priest took her hand and said:

"Señora, that which your garb concealed from us, your hair has revealed: clearly, you must have had powerful cause, to cloak such beauty in so unworthy a guise and venture into this wilderness, where we have had the good fortune to find you — if not to right whatever wrongs have been done you, then at least to assist you with our advice, for while life itself endures no evil can press on us so hard, nor be so utterly devastating, that you should shrink from listening, at least, to well-intentioned counsel directed at your suffering. And so, my dear sir — or my dear madame, whichever you choose to be — put aside the fright caused by our sudden appearance and share with us your fortunes, good or bad, so that jointly, or separately, we may be enabled to help you bear your misfortunes."

The disguised girl stood as if in a trance, while the priest spoke, staring

at them all without moving her lips or saying a single word, as if she'd
been some rustic villager suddenly catching a glimpse of rare and unheard-
of things. But when the priest went on to say something more, though to
the same general effect, she sighed deeply and at last broke her silence:

"Since this mountain wilderness has not been able to conceal me, and
setting free my unruly hair will keep my tongue from telling you lies, what
sense would it make to go on pretending, now, since if you credited my
pretense it would be an act of courtesy and nothing more? Accordingly,
gentlemen, let me say that I am much obliged to you for the offer you've
made, which in turn requires that I grant you all your requests, although
I fear the narrative of my misfortunes will weary you, as much for the
compassion you will feel as for the oppressive weight of the knowledge
that you will be unable either to help or to advise and console me. Still,
so that there may be no uncertainty in your minds about my honor —
you having recognized me as a woman and having encountered me as a
woman young, alone, and wearing such clothing as this, all and indeed
any one of these things being matters which, were they known, could ruin
anyone's reputation — I am compelled to tell you things that, if I could,
I would choose to be silent about."

They had discovered her to be a beautiful woman, but she said all this
so easily and directly, and in such sweet tones, that they found themselves
admiring her good sense no less than her loveliness. And since they proceeded to renew their questions, as well as their promises of help and
support, she quietly and modestly slipped on her shoes, bound up her hair,
and — not obliging them to ask yet again — seated herself on a rock
and, with the three of them sitting around her (but after first stemming
the tears that sprang to her eyes), began to tell them, her voice calm and
clear, the story of her life, which went as follows:

"Here in Andalusia there is a place from which a duke — known as
one of the loftiest in all Spain — takes his title. This duke has two sons,
the oldest being the heir both of his estate and, apparently, of his good
habits, and the younger, who inherits I don't know what, except Vellido's
treachery and Galalón's lies. My parents are this lord's subjects, lowly in
origin but so exceedingly prosperous that, if the riches they won by their
own nature could have been matched by the riches bestowed by birth,
there would have been nothing left for them to desire, nor would I have
had to fear the misery which has, as you can see, now befallen me, for it
may well be that my ill fate stems from their low birth. In truth, their state
is not so lowly that they need be ashamed of it, just as it is not lofty enough
to keep me from thinking that their humble position produced my misfortune. They are peasants, in a word, simple people, of a stock absolutely
untainted by scandal — such Old Christians, as the saying goes, that
there's rust on them — but so exceedingly rich that their wealth, and
their grand way of life, are gradually acquiring for them the reputation of
gentlemen and ladies, and even of aristocrats. But the wealth and nobility
of which they were proudest was having me as their daughter, and since
there were no other children to share in their wealth, and they were af-
fectionate parents, I was one of the most royally indulged daughters who
ever lived. I was the mirror in which they saw themselves, the staff and

support of their old age, and it was toward me, though always as God directed them, that they bent all their desires — and my own desires, because they were indeed such good parents, exactly matched theirs. And just as I was mistress of their hearts, so too I ruled their fortune, for it was I who engaged and dismissed all those who worked for them; all the reports and accounts of those who did their sowing and their harvesting came to me — and all the oil that was pressed, and all the grapes, and every flock of every kind of animal, no matter how large or small, and every beehive. In short, everything an exceedingly rich farmer like my father had or possibly could have came to me for its accounting, and I was steward and lady of it all, on my part so carefully, and on theirs with such delight, that it would be hard to exaggerate our mutual satisfaction. Whatever leisure time was left to me — after having instructed the chief shepherds, the foremen and overseers, and all the other laborers, about what needed to be done that day — I spent in doing what young women ought and need to do, working with my needle and embroidery frame, and often at my spinning wheel. And if, wanting a diversion, I gave over these activities, I sought my entertainment in reading some pious book, or playing the harp, for I had learned from experience that music settles a jangled soul and comforts all manner of spiritual troubles. So that was how I lived in my parents' house, and my reason for telling you all this in such detail hasn't been either ostentation or to make sure you understand that I'm rich, but simply to let you know how, all innocently, I have fallen from so fine a position to the unhappy one in which, now, you find me. And so, living my life in such occupations, and in a retirement that might well be compared to a monk's — never seen, so far as I knew, by anyone other than our servants, for when I went to mass it was very early in the morning, and I was always with my mother and a host of servants, and so well covered and veiled that my eyes scarcely saw anything more than the ground on which my feet were walking — nevertheless I was in fact seen by the eyes of love, or more accurately of idling laziness, keener than the eyes of any lynx, and set in the restless head of Don Fernando, for that was the name of the duke's younger son of whom I've already spoken."

No sooner had the teller of the tale mentioned the name of Don Fernando than Cardenio's face changed color, and he began to sweat so violently that the priest and the barber, watching him, were afraid he was about to have one of those mad fits from which, as they had been told, he suffered from time to time. But though he went on perspiring freely, Cardenio stayed just as he was, staring straight at the girl, for he began to realize who she was. And she, not noticing his reaction, went on with her story, as follows:

"And he had barely so much as seen me when, as he told me afterwards, he fell every bit as madly in love with me as his actions indicated he was. But to keep this account from growing too long, for all it recounts are my misfortunes, let me say nothing of the many, many things Don Fernando did to show me his love. He bribed every servant in the house; he gave my parents gifts, and did them favors, and promised them still more. Every day became a time for feasting and rejoicing, on the street where we lived; no one could sleep at night, for all the music. There was no end to the stream of love letters that, I never knew how, kept falling into my hands, full of impassioned talk and promises, more vows and declarations than I could possibly count. All of this not only did not affect but, indeed, hardened me, as if he were my mortal enemy, so that everything he did to make me amenable to his will had exactly the opposite effect — not that I thought Don Fernando's gallantry objectionable, or his entreaties excessive, for of course I felt some indefinable pleasure in being so desired, so appreciated by such a high-ranking gentleman, nor did his praise seem at all wearisome to me, for I think even the homeliest of women enjoys being called beautiful. But my modesty objected, and also my parents' constant advice, since by this time they were only too well aware of what Don Fernando wanted, for he plainly did not care if the whole world knew it. My parents assured me that their honor and reputation lay entirely in my goodness and virtue, in which they trusted, and considering how utterly unequal Don Fernando and I were, it was not hard for them to see — no matter what he himself might say — that his intention was more to satisfy himself than in any way to benefit me, and indeed if I chose to set some barrier in his way, and oblige him to abandon these tainted solicitations, they would immediately marry me to anyone I chose, whether to one of the leading men in our town or in any of the neighboring communities, for considering my father's wealth and my reputation I could make any marriage I wanted. These plain-spoken promises, and the blunt truths my parents pronounced, helped strengthen my resistance, and I never uttered a word to Don Fernando that even remotely encouraged him. But my determined modesty must have seemed to him mere disdain, and surely still further whetted his lascivious longing, which is what I think his affection truly was — for had it been what it should have been, you gentlemen would not be hearing of it, now, for there would have been no reason to say any of these things. In the end, when Don Fernando learned that my parents were thinking of marrying me off, to keep him from ever having me — or, at least, so I would have even more protectors — that news, or even the suspicion of it, led him to do what, finally, you are about to hear.

"One night, when I was alone in my room, with only my maid for company, having securely locked all the doors for fear that some negligence might endanger my virtue, I suddenly saw — neither understanding nor even able to imagine how it could have happened, in the face of all these precautions and in that apparently secure, solitary silence — there he was, right in front of me, and the sight so shook me that I could neither speak nor even see, so I could not scream, nor did he propose to give me the opportunity, for he immediately came and took me in his arms (for as I have said I hadn't the strength to defend myself, so shocked was I) and began to say such things to me that I cannot fathom how anyone could have such a facility at lying and still make his lies sound like truths. The traitor made his tears vouch for his words, as his sighs proved his longing. And I, young and all alone, still living with my family, totally unfamiliar with such matters, I somehow began — I don't know how — to believe his lies, though all his weeping and his sighing did not stir me to anything more than simple compassion. And then, as I overcame my initial shock, I began to get hold of myself, and to speak more boldly to him than I would have thought possible:

"'If, sir, it were a savage lion clasping me in his arms, instead of you, and I could free myself by doing or saying anything which would endanger my virtue, I could no more do or say any such thing than you or I can turn back time and undo the past. Accordingly, though you clasp my body in your arms, the purity of my desires holds my soul fast, nor can you doubt that my desires are unlike yours — as you will find out if you attempt, by force, to pursue them. I am your subject, sir, but not your slave, and a nobleman of your rank neither has nor should have the right to dishonor and disregard the humbleness of mine, for I think quite as much of myself, lowborn and peasant that I am, as you do of yourself as a gentleman and a lord. Your power is useless against me, as your wealth is worthless, nor can your words deceive me any more than your tears and your sighs can move me. Were I to find, in the man to whom my parents marry me, any of the things of which I've spoken, my will would be his, nor would I ever oppose him; and indeed, were it not for honor, sir, you would readily have, though not with desire, what you are now seeking to obtain by force. I tell you these things so you may know, once and for all, that no one but my legally wedded husband will ever willingly have any part of me.'"

"'If that's all you require, my most beautiful Dorotea' — which is in fact this miserable woman's name — the traitorous gentleman swore to me, 'I hereby pledge you my hand, which is now yours, and let Heaven, from which nothing can be hidden, as well as this image of Our Lady, here in this very room, be our witness.'"

Hearing that her name was Dorotea, Cardenio once again shook with sudden emotion, all but convinced that his initial judgment had been correct. But he did not want to interrupt the tale, so he could find out if it ended as he was almost sure it would, and all he said was:

"And so your name is Dorotea? I have heard of someone else by that name, whose misfortunes may very closely parallel your own. But please go on; later, perhaps, I can tell you some things which will astonish you quite as much as move you."

Dorotea listened closely to Cardenio's remarks, carefully considering his strange, shabby clothing, and then she asked him, in case he knew anything about herself and her family, to tell her at once, for if fortune had blessed her in any respect, it was by giving her the courage to endure whatever blow might descend, feeling as she did that nothing could be worse than what she had already experienced.

"Señora," answered Cardenio, "I would not lose the chance to tell you what was in my mind, were I certain that the truth was what I suspect it may well be, but so far there has been no reason to speak, and in any case what I have to say will not matter much to you."

"So be it," replied Dorotea. "What happened next was that, picking up a statue of the Virgin Mary, Don Fernando called on it to witness the fact of our wedding. With wonderfully compelling words and quite extraordinary oaths, he swore that he would be in truth my husband, for even before he'd finished I told him to consider carefully how angry his father might be, finding him married to a peasant who was one of his own subjects, and I warned him not to be blinded by my beauty, such as it was, for that would not be enough to excuse so grave a fault, adding that if he truly wished me well, then by the love he felt for me he would allow my destiny to more closely match my station in life, for marriages of so pronounced an inequality are never happy, nor does the pleasure with which they begin endure for very long. I told him all this, and much, much more that I can no longer remember — but if you don't intend to live up to the bargain you don't worry about what you've agreed to pay, so when you're arranging a swindle you don't let any inconvenient details bother you. But at the same time I argued with myself, hurriedly: 'All right, but I won't be the first woman whom marriage has raised from a humble to a great position, nor will Don Fernando be the first man led by beauty — or, more likely, by blind passion — to have sought a companion far below his own station. So there'll be nothing new about it, and I ought to accept this honor being pressed upon me by Fate, for if his affection lasts no longer than the achievement of his desires, at least in the eyes of God I will be his wife. And should I try to scornfully repel him, it's plain that, if he can't have it any other way, he'll use force, and then I'll be left dishonored and unable to escape censure from those who can't understand how, unless it was indeed my own fault, I found myself where I now am. How could I possibly explain to my parents, and to others, that this gentleman got into to this locked room without my opening the door to him?' All these questions and responses whirled rapidly around in my brain, and what more than anything else began to lead and bend me toward what, though I did not know it, was in truth my ruin, was all the oaths Don Fernando swore, the witnesses he called on, the tears he shed, and, in the end, the force of his personality and his self-assurance — for, taken together with so many protestations of true love, these could have worn down any heart as un-attached and shy as mine. So I called for my servant, so that there would be someone here on earth, as well as in heaven, to bear witness, and once more Don Fernando repeated and swore each and all of his solemn oaths, summoning fresh hordes of saints to join the heavenly witnesses he'd in-voked the first time, and calling down a thousand curses on his head, should he break the promises he'd given me; then his eyes overflowed and his sighs grew even more profound, and he held me still more tightly in his arms (from which he'd never allowed me to escape), and so I sent my maid back out again, and I was left a maid no more, and he became a traitor and a thief.

"The day that followed after the night of my misfortune did not arrive, I suspect, as rapidly as Don Fernando would have liked, for, once appetite has what it wanted, what it most longs for, thereafter, is to get away from where it achieved its fulfillment. I say this because Don Fernando left me hurriedly and, relying on the cleverness of my maid (who had been re-sponsible for treacherously admitting him), found himself outside in the street before dawn broke. Taking his leave, he assured me I could rely on his good faith (though he did not speak as eagerly or with as much passion as when he came) and on the steadfastness and truthfulness of his vows, and to further confirm his words he drew a costly ring from his finger and put it on mine. And then he went, and I did not know whether I was sad or happy. All I can say is this: I was left confused and profoundly thoughtful and very nearly unable to comprehend what had happened to me, nor did I feel like quarreling with my maid for her treachery in locking Don Fernando into my room — or perhaps I did not so much as think of it, for I could not tell whether what had happened was a good thing or a bad. I had said to Don Fernando, as he left me, that so long as I was now his he might come to me, other nights, in the same way, until the time when he chose to make the matter public. But he did not come again, except the very next night, nor could I so much as catch sight of him, neither in the street nor in church, for more than a month, though I kept trying, in vain, to find him, knowing as I did that he was in the city and, indeed, most days was out hunting, a sport of which he was exceedingly fond. And I can tell you that those days, and those hours, were oppressive and miserable ones, and I remember vividly how I began to doubt, and then to disbelieve in Don Fernando's good faith — and how my maid heard, as at first she had not, bitter reproaches for her impudence — and how I had to be careful of my tears, and of my complexion, so my parents wouldn't ask me why I was unhappy and I didn't have to hunt for lies to tell them. But then came a time when all this was finished, and every such consideration was thrown aside, just as talk about honor was over and done with, and my patience was gone, and my most secret thoughts became public property. And this happened because, a few days later, everyone was saying that, in a nearby city, Don Fernando had married an exceedingly beautiful girl, from an excellent family, though not so terribly rich that her dowry could have led her to hope for so brilliant a match. They said her name was Luscinda, and that, after her marriage, some remarkable things had taken place."

Hearing Luscinda's name, Cardenio did nothing but shrug his shoulders, bite at his lip, wrinkle his brows, and before too long let two streams of tears come rolling from his eyes. But none of this stopped Dorotea from continuing her tale, saying:

"I heard this sad news and, rather than freezing my soul, it fanned such a fire of anger that I very nearly ran through the streets, screaming out the news of my betrayal. All that restrained this wild rage, at least for the moment, was the thought of putting into effect, that very night, a plan I had devised, which was to disguise myself as you see me now, in this outfit which I got from one of the shepherd boys who worked for my father, to whom I told the whole story, begging him to accompany me to the city where I understood my enemy was now staying. After scolding me for my boldness, and criticizing my plan, he saw how utterly determined I was and volunteered to be my companion — as he put it — to the end of the world. I quickly took a pillow case and wrapped up in it a woman's dress and some jewels and money, in case I needed them. And that night, silently and without letting my treacherous maid know, I left my father's house, together with my father's servant and many, many wild ideas, and began to walk down the highway, swept along not by the thought of stopping what I knew had already happened, but at least of making Don Fernando tell me how his conscience had let him do it. It took me two and a half days to reach the city where he was living and, when I asked the first person I met how to find Luscinda's parents' house, I was told much more than I had expected to hear. He told me the address and about everything that had happened at Luscinda's marriage, events so well-known that people there were talking of nothing else. He told me that on the night of the wedding, after saying she would have him as her lawfully wedded husband, Lucinda had fallen into a severe faint, and when her husband unlaced her bodice, to let her breathe, he found a note written in her own handwriting, which declared she could not be Don Fernando's wife because she was already married to Cardenio, who, according to my informant, was an important gentleman of that same city, and she had only said she would take Fernando as her husband so she might be obedient to her parents' wishes. And what the note also indicated, he told me, was that she'd meant to kill herself as she said 'I do,' and explained exactly why — things which were confirmed, he told me, by a dagger they found somewhere in her clothing. And when Don Fernando saw all this, he felt that Luscinda had made a fool of him and he went out of his head and attacked her, even while she was lying there unconscious, trying to stab her with that very same dagger, and would have killed her if her parents and the other people at the wedding hadn't stopped him. And there was even more to the story: Don Fernando, it was said, immediately disappeared, and Luscinda's faint lasted another whole day, and then she'd told her parents she truly was the wife of the man named Cardenio. And I also learned that this Cardenio, who it was said was actually present at the wedding, and had seen her being married — something he had never imagined possible — had fled from the city in despair, after first writing a letter in which he explained the wrong done him by Luscinda, and then declared he would go where no one would ever see him again. All of this was talked about openly and by everyone all across the city, as also was the fact that Luscinda too had then left both her parents' home and the city, and could not be found anywhere, and her parents were out of their minds, not knowing what they could do to find her. And all this news made me more hopeful, because I thought it was better not to find Don Fernando than to find him married, since the doorway to relief no longer seemed completely closed to me and it was possible that Heaven might have created this impediment to his second marriage, thus reminding him what he owed to the first, and what it meant to be a Christian and more responsible for his eternal soul than for any merely human concerns. My mind whirled with all these ideas, and I took what cold comfort I was able, trying to conjure up whatever faint hopes I could imagine for going on with the life that, now, I abhor.

"There I was in that city, not knowing what to do, since Don Fernando wasn't there, when I heard a public proclamation, announcing a great reward to anyone who should find me, and setting out what I looked like and exactly what I was wearing. And I heard, too, that I was said to have run off from my parents' house with the boy who had in fact come with me, which cut me to the quick, seeing how low my reputation had sunk, for they had not thought it enough to tarnish me with my flight, but had to add on the person with whom I had gone — someone so far beneath and so utterly unworthy of me. As soon as I heard this proclamation I left the city, along with my servant — who was already showing signs of becoming less loyal than he had promised — and that same night we reached the wilds of these mountains, for I was in terror of being found. But, as they say, one bad thing leads to another, and the end of one misfortune is likely to be the beginning of a new and worse one, which was indeed how it turned out for me, because my faithful servant — or at least faithful till then — seeing me all alone here, and driven more by his own wickedness than by my beauty, decided to take advantage of the opportunity which, as he saw it, this wasteland offered him and, shame-lessly, without fear of God or any respect for me, demanded that I allow him to make love to me, and when I scornfully and rightly rejected any such brazen proposition, he stopped merely asking, as he had done at first, and began to try to force me. But righteous Heaven, which doesn't often — or perhaps never — let its eyes and its favor slip away from those who live rightly and justly, came to my aid, so that despite my feeble strength I was able, and even easily able, to push him over a precipice, where I left him, not knowing if he was dead or alive, and then quickly, far more quickly than my fright and weariness should have called for, I climbed into these mountains, with only one thought and one idea in my head, which was to hide myself here and flee from my father and anyone who might, on his behalf, be hunting for me. I don't know how many months I've been here, with this sole purpose, having found a shepherd who hired me to help him, at a spot deep in the bowels of this mountain, where I've served as a shepherd boy all this time, trying to stay out in the fields to hide this hair which, now, without even realizing it, I've revealed. But all my care and all my worry has always been useless, for my master discovered I was not a man and, like my own servant, conceived the same base longing, and since Fortune doesn't always provide solutions for every trouble, and there was no precipice or cliff down which I could hurl my master, and kill him, as Fortune had allowed me to do with my servant, I thought it better not to test either my strength or my words against him, but to leave him and hide myself, once more, in this wilderness. So I went into hiding again, trying to find some place where, without fear of human intervention, my sighs and tears might beg Heaven to take pity on me in my misery, and lend me the strength and the grace to be delivered from them, or else to die here in this wasteland, leaving no memory of that sad being who, all innocently, has provided food for gossiping tongues in her own country and in all those surrounding it.

Chapter Twenty-Nine

— dealing with the clever trick used to rescue our love-stricken knight from the harsh penitence he'd undertaken

"And that, gentlemen, is the true history of my tragedy. Now consider and judge for yourselves whether the sighs you've heard, and the words you've listened to, and the tears you've seen flowing from my eyes had good reason to flow even more abundantly — and considering the nature of my misfortune, you will see how pointless all consolation would be, for absolutely nothing can be done. Let me ask of you only — and this you can and ought to do, nor should it be difficult — that you help me find a place where I can pass the rest of my life free of the fear of being discovered by those who are searching for me, for though I understand that my parents' profound love would guarantee me a warm welcome, my shame is so intense, and I am so oppressed by the realization that I cannot come to them as I once was, that rather than look them in the face I would exile myself from them forever, knowing as I do that, in seeing me, they would not see the virtuous daughter they have a right to expect."

And then she fell silent, her face so changed in color that it perfectly reflected the shame she felt in her heart. Those who had been listening were as full of pity as of wonder at her misfortune, and though the priest meant to offer her advice and consolation it was Cardenio who took her hand, saying:

"And so, señora, you're really the beautiful Dorotea, only daughter of that rich man, Clenardo?"

Dorotea was astonished, hearing her father's name from the lips of some-one who seemed so beggarly — for, as I've already said, Cardenio's clothing was extremely shabby — and she said to him:

"And who are you, my friend, to know my father's name? Because unless I'm very mistaken, I never once mentioned it, not once, in telling this whole miserable tale of mine."

"I," answered Cardenio, "am that unhappy man who, as you yourself have told us, Luscinda said was her husband. I am that miserable Cardenio — for the same person whose wrongdoing brought you here, and to this, has brought me, too, to what you now see before you, broken, half-naked, deprived of all human pleasures and, worst of all, deprived even of his senses, for only in those brief intervals when Heaven sees fit to lend them to me am I in my right mind. I, Dorotea, am the one who was there to witness Don Fernando's injustice; I am the one who stood waiting to hear Luscinda pronounce the 'I do' that would make her his wife. I am the one who did not have the courage to see what happened once she fainted, nor what came of the note found in her breast, because I could not bear the pain of seeing so many miseries joined together. And so I gave up and came away from her father's house, and left a letter with my host, asking him to hand it to Luscinda, and then I took myself off to this wilderness, intending to end my life here, for from that moment I loathed that life of mine as if it had been my mortal enemy. But Fate would not take it, satisfied to take my sanity instead, perhaps to keep me safe for the good fortune I have found, now, in meeting you — for if what you have told us is true, and I believe it is, it may well be that Heaven has been hiding a greater happiness in our miseries than either of us had thought possible. Assuming, that is, that Luscinda cannot be married to Don Fernando, since she is already married to me, and Don Fernando cannot be married to her, since he is already married to you, and since Luscinda has so publicly declared these facts, why should we not begin to hope that

Heaven will now give us back what is rightfully ours — since it still exists, neither given to anyone else nor destroyed? And since this newfound expectation comes to us, not from any tenuous, remote hope, nor from any wild fancies, let me beg you, señora, to turn your chaste mind in more courageous directions, as I myself plan to do, and let us adjust ourselves to this new and better fortune that may well await us, for I swear to you, as a gentleman and a Christian, I will never desert you until I see you in possession of Don Fernando, and if persuasion cannot bring him to acknowledge what he owes you, I will take advantage of my position as a gentleman and, knowing that right is on my side, I will challenge him to a duel — without any reference to my own injuries, the vengeance for which I will leave to Heaven, but solely on account of the wrong he has done you, which I will attend to here on earth."

Dorotea was stunned at Cardenio's words and, not knowing how else to thank him for such a noble offer, tried to kiss his feet, but he would not permit it and the priest, speaking for both the lady and himself, said that Cardenio had indeed spoken well. He asked and advised and urged them, above all, to go to his village with him, where they could provide themselves with whatever they might need, and decide whether they ought first to hunt for Don Fernando, or to bring Dorotea home to her parents, or whatever else it might seem to them best to do. Cardenio and Dorotea thanked him, and accepted his gracious suggestion. And the barber, who had been silently hanging on their words, then made a little speech of his own, offering just as willingly as the priest to help them in any way he could.

And then the barber went on, briefly, to explain what had brought them there, and Don Quijote's strange madness, and how they were waiting for the poor knight's squire, who had gone to look for him. Cardenio suddenly remembered, as if it had been a dream, that he had quarreled with Don Quijote, and told the others about it, though he could not explain why it had happened.

Just then they heard cries and recognized Sancho Panza's voice, for, not finding them where he had expected, he was calling out to them. They went to meet him and, when they asked about Don Quijote, he told them he had found his master wearing nothing but his shirt, weak, pale, and half dead of hunger, but still sighing for his lady Dulcinea, and although Sancho had told him that she'd ordered him to leave this place and go directly to Toboso, where she awaited him, he'd replied that he was determined not to appear before her beautyhood until he'd fashioned deeds of such daring that they could be deemed worthy of her grace. If things continued like this, said Sancho, there was a serious danger that his master would not get to be an emperor, as he ought to, nor even an archbishop, which was the very least he could do. And, therefore, they had to see what could be done to make him leave this place.

The priest assured him there was nothing to worry about; they would get his master out of there, no matter what Don Quijote himself intended. Then he explained to Cardenio and Dorotea how they had planned to help the knight, at least as far as getting him back to his own house. To which Dorotea said that she could certainly play the damsel's role better than the barber, and indeed had with her the proper attire to make it thoroughly convincing. They could trust her to know exactly what to say, and to get him to do as they wanted, for she had read many tales of chivalry and knew precisely how damsels were supposed to beg boons of knights errant.

"Then all we need to do," said the priest, "is quickly get it done, for it's plain that Fate is smiling down on us, since," he said to Cardenio and Dorotea, "it has unexpectedly begun to open doors for you, and, for our part, is making it easier to accomplish what we have to do."

Dorotea pulled out of her pillow case a dress of fine, rich wool and a bright green veil, equally delicately woven, and from a small box she took a necklace and other jewels, and in an instant transformed herself into a grand and wealthy lady. She told them she'd taken all this, and more, when she left her home, in case it might be needed, but till now had had no need thus to adorn herself. They were all delighted with her charming transformation, and her grace and beauty, vowing that Don Fernando could not be a man of much taste, to scorn such loveliness.

But the most amazed of all was Sancho Panza, to whom it seemed — and indeed it was true — that in all the days of his life he had never seen such a beautiful creature, so he asked the priest, wonderfully eagerly, to tell him who this lovely lady might be and what she was seeking, here in these out-of-the-way regions.

"Brother Sancho, this beautiful lady," answered the priest, "is no less than the heiress, in the direct male line, of the great kingdom of Micomicón, who has come here hunting your master, in order to beg a favor of him, which is that he un-do some wrong or injury done her by a wicked giant, and this princess has come seeking him all the way from Guinea, because of that great knight your master's immense fame across the entire known world."

"A happy hunt and a happy hunting down," Sancho Panza replied promptly, "especially if my master is lucky enough to un-do that injury and straighten out that wrong, and kill this son of a bitch giant you're talking about, and he'll kill him if he gets to fight with him, unless he's a ghost, because my master can't do a thing against ghosts. But one thing I particularly want to ask you, your grace (though there's more), sir priest, and that's this: in order to keep my master from wanting to be an archbishop, which is really what I'm afraid of, let your grace advise him to marry this princess right away, so then it'll be impossible for him to become an archbishop, and then it won't be hard for him to become an emperor, or for me to get what I most want — because I've really been thinking about this and, the way it looks to me, it wouldn't do me any good if my master becomes an archbishop, because I wouldn't be any good to the Church, since I'm married, and for me to run around trying to get a dispensation so I could have a Church salary, having a wife and children already, as I have, would take forever. So, señor, it all comes down to my master marrying this lady right away — but I haven't been introduced to her, so I can't call her by her right name."

"Call her," replied the priest, "Princess Micomicona, since her kingdom is called Micomicón,[1] so that's obviously what she has to be called."

"That's absolutely right," replied Sancho, "because I've seen a lot of them take their name and their title from the place where they were born, like Pedro from Alcalá, Juan from Ubeda, and Diego from Valladolid, so it must be the same way over there in Guinea, and the queens all take the name of their kingdom."

"Exactly so," said the priest, "and as for seeing your master married, I will do everything in my power."

Sancho was just as happy with all this as the priest was astonished by his stupidity, and at seeing how caught up he was in his master's mad fantasies, for it was obvious that he really believed Don Quijote was going to be an emperor.

Dorotea was now mounted on the priest's mule, and the barber had stuck the oxtail beard onto his face, so they told Sancho to take them to his master, warning him not to say that he knew either the priest or the barber, because Don Quijote's becoming an emperor depended on his not recognizing them. Cardenio and the priest decided not to go with them, the former because he didn't want to remind Don Quijote of their quarrel, and the latter because he simply wasn't needed. So they let the others go on ahead, while they slowly followed on foot. The priest was careful to tell Dorotea what to do, though she told them not to worry about it, because everything would be done exactly right, in every detail, just the way it was supposed to be done, and the way it was always described in the stories.

They'd gone two and a half miles when they suddenly saw Don Quijote among a jagged pile of boulders, dressed, by now, but not wearing his armor, and the moment Dorotea saw him, and was assured by Sancho that this was indeed Don Quijote, she whipped her palfrey into a trot, with the well-bearded barber following along behind. And when they reached the knight, his squire leaped off his own mule and went to lift her down in his arms, but she, dismounting easily, sank to her knees before Don Quijote, and though he tried to get her to rise she refused, and from her prostrate position lifted only her voice, as follows:

"I shall not rise from here, oh brave and mighty knight! unless and until in your goodness and graciousness you grant me a boon, which will redound as much to your honor and renown as to the benefit of the most unhappy and injured damsel on whom the sun has ever shone. And if, truly, the courage of your strong arm matches the accounts of your immortal fame, you surely must aid those unlucky ones who come seeking you from afar, drawn by the promise of your shining name, seeking some remedy for their misfortunes."

"Oh beauteous lady," answered Don Quijote, "not a word shall I say to you, in reply, nor will I deign to hear anything of what you needs must tell me, until you rise from off the ground."

"No, I shall not rise, dear sir," replied the afflicted maiden, "if first, in

---

1. A coinage of Cervantes's, the term *micomicón* combines the Spanish words for monkey (*mico*) and comic (*cómico*).

your great courtesy and kindness, you do not grant me the boon I crave."

"I freely grant and bestow it," answered Don Quijote, "provided only that it does not require me to injure or in any way harm my king, my country, or she who holds the key to my heart and to my freedom."

"There will be no danger and no harm to any of those, oh good sir," replied the sorrowful damsel.

At which point Sancho Panza sidled up to his master and whispered in his ear:

"You can really afford to give her what she wants, señor, because it isn't any big deal: all she wants is to have a giant killed, and the lady who's asking is the noble Princess Micomicona, queen of the great kingdom of Micomicón, in Ethiopia."

"No matter who she is," answered Don Quijote, "I shall do what I am obliged to do and what my conscience requires of me, according to the vows I have taken."

And then, turning to the lady, he said:

"Rise, oh beauteous damsel, for I hereby grant you the boon you ask."

"And what I ask," said the maiden, "is that you, oh most gracious sir, immediately come away with me to where I shall lead you, and that you promise me not to engage yourself in any other adventure nor respond to any other request for your aid until you have revenged me against a traitor who, against every law, human and divine, has usurped my kingdom."

"As I have said, I grant it to you," replied Don Quijote, "and so, my dear lady, from this day forward you may cast aside the gloom which has weighed so heavily upon you and array yourself in the new spirit and strength of your previously exhausted hopes and expectations, for with the help of God and my right arm, you will soon find yourself restored to your throne and in possession, once more, of your ancient, noble realm, in spite and indeed in the very teeth of the rascals who wish to oppose you. And so let us begin, for as they say there is danger in delay."

The needy maiden tried hard to kiss his hands, but Don Quijote, who was in all things a proper and courteous gentleman, would not permit it and, instead, raised her up and, with great gentlemanliness and propriety, embraced her, then commanded Sancho to saddle Rocinante and quickly help him into his armor. Sancho took down the armor from the tree where, like a trophy, it had been hanging and, having quickly saddled the horse, just as promptly armored his lord, who, finding himself fully equipped, declared:

"Let us leave here, in the name of God, and help this noble lady."

The barber was still on his knees, having a good deal of trouble smothering his laughter and keeping his beard in place — for if it had fallen off, that might very possibly have rendered all their efforts useless — but seeing that the boon had been granted, and that Don Quijote was already preparing himself to travel to where his work would be done, the barber rose and took his lady's other hand, so that between them they put her back on her mule. Don Quijote quickly got up on Rocinante, and the barber settled himself on his beast of burden, leaving Sancho on foot, which made him feel keenly all over again the loss of his mule, now so badly needed. But he took it all cheerfully, seeing that his master was well on his way to becoming an emperor, believing without any doubt that Don Quijote would marry this princess and be, at the least, King of Micomicón. The only thing that bothered him was that that country was in a land of black men, and the people he'd be ruling over would also be black, but he soon worked out a plan for getting around that, saying to himself:

"What difference does it make to me if my subjects are black? Do I have to do any more than load them up and bring them to Spain, where I can sell them and get paid in cash, and then I can use that money to buy myself a title or some post that'll support me happily ever after? By God, not unless you're asleep on your feet and you don't know how to sell anything, and you haven't got any idea how to get rid of thirty subjects, or ten thousand, in a flash, just like that! Dear God, but I'll sell them like hot cakes, every god damn one of them, however I can; maybe they're black, but I'll turn 'em into silver and gold! Hey, we'll see how dumb *I* am!"

And then he went along so calm and happy that he completely forgot how unpleasant it was, having to walk.

Cardenio and the priest were watching all this from behind some bushes, and couldn't figure out how to join up with the others, but the priest, who was a genuinely clever fellow, quickly worked out a scheme. Pulling out a pair of scissors, he hurriedly cut off Cardenio's beard and dressed him in a short grey cape he'd been wearing himself, then gave him a black coat: that left the priest in breeches and a jacket and so changed Cardenio's appearance that he wouldn't have known himself if he'd looked in a mirror. Then, though the others had gotten ahead of them while they were thus disguising themselves, it was easy enough to beat them to the highway, because the underbrush and the uneven terrain kept those who were mounted from going as fast as those who were on foot. So they stationed themselves out in the open, near the exit from the mountain, and as Don Quijote and his companions emerged the priest stood staring long and hard, as if indicating he thought he knew them, and finally, after a good long look, he came towards them, throwing his arms wide and shouting:

"How wonderful to see the very model of chivalric gentlemen, my good countryman, Don Quijote de La Mancha, the flower and cream of all gallantry, he who protects and succors the needy, the quintessence of knight errantry!"

As he spoke he clasped Don Quijote by the left knee, and the knight, astonished to see and hear the man, whoever he was, focused all his attention and, at last, recognized the priest, at which point, though still astonished, he struggled to dismount. But the priest would not let him, so Don Quijote said:

"But please, Father, your grace, it would not be right for me to stay mounted while so reverend a person as yourself remains on foot."

"I won't hear a word of it," said the priest. "Your noble majesty must be on horseback, for it is on horseback that you have accomplished the greatest deeds and most magnificent adventures our time has witnessed — and as for me, unworthy priest that I am, it will more than suffice to climb up on the haunches of one of the mules belonging to these gentlemen, traveling with your grace, if that's all right with them. I will pretend I am a knight, mounted on that magic steed, Pegasus, or perhaps on that zebra or that huge stallion on which the famous Moor Muzaraque rode, he who even now lies enchanted on Zulema's great slope, not far from Complutum."

"But I can't agree even to that, my dear Father," replied Don Quijote, "and I feel sure that my lady the princess would be pleased, for love of me, to command that her squire surrender to you his place on the mule, for he can sit on its haunches, if the animal will let him."

"It will let him, I'm sure," answered the princess, "nor do I think it will be necessary to command my dear squire, for he is so perfect a gentleman and a courtier that he would never allow an ecclesiastical gentleman to go on foot, were it possible for him to ride."

"Indeed," said the barber.

And he dismounted at once, inviting the priest to occupy the saddle, which was done with no great fuss. But unfortunately, as the barber climbed up behind, the mule — a rented animal, which is the same thing as saying he was a bad animal — kicked out with both hind legs, and had his hooves landed on Master Nicolás' chest, or his head, the barber would have had good reason to wish he'd never come looking for Don Quijote. But even so, he was tumbled so violently off that he fell headlong, and since he couldn't watch out for his long beard it fell too, but quite separately from him, so finding himself beardless he could think of nothing better than to cover his face with both hands and moan that the mule had half killed him. Seeing such a huge bundle of beard, but no bones and no blood, lying completely detached from the squire's face, Don Quijote exclaimed:

"Praise be to God, what a miracle! His beard's been knocked right off his face, just as if it were sliced away!"

The priest saw that his whole scheme might be discovered, so he quickly grabbed the beard, carried it over to where Master Nicolás was still lying and moaning, and shoving the barber's head down toward his chest re-attached the beard, meanwhile whispering strange words over him, which, he explained, were a magic charm for fastening on beards, as they could see, and when he had it all done he stood up — and there was the squire, just as bushy-bearded and every bit as healthy as he had been before, which powerfully impressed Don Quijote, who begged the priest, when he had the chance, to teach him that charm, for he was sure it was good for more than just re-attaching beards, since, plainly, when the beard was pulled off the skin and flesh would have had to be bruised and torn, and if the charm could have healed all that it was certainly good for a lot more than beards.

"Indeed," said the priest, and promised to teach it to him, the very first chance he got.

Then they arranged that the priest would mount, but the three of them would keep changing places until they got to the inn, which was about seven miles distant. So there were three of them mounted — that is, Don Quijote, the princess, and the priest — and three of them on foot, Cardenio, the barber, and Sancho Panza.

"Your majesty, my lady," said Don Quijote to the damsel, "lead us wherever it best pleases you."

But before she could reply, the priest said:

"To which kingdom do you wish to bring us, my lady? Could it be, perhaps, to Micomicón? I think that must be it, unless I just don't know enough about kingdoms."

Having her wits about her, she knew she ought to agree with him, so she said:

"Yes, señor: that kingdom is exactly where I wish to go."

"Ah, in that case," said the priest, "we'll have to go right through my own town, and from there your grace can take the turn toward Cartagena, where, weather permitting, you'll be able to board ship, and if you have a good wind, a calm sea, and no storms, it shouldn't take you even nine years before you see huge Lake Meona [*meona* = weak-bladdered] — I mean, Lake Meótides — and then you'll be no more than a hundred days journey from your majesty's own kingdom."

"But you're mistaken, my dear sir," she said, "for it's no more than two years since I left there, and in truth we never had good weather — but, in spite of everything, I have succeeded in finding the man I so much longed for, my lord Don Quijote de La Mancha, whose fame reached my ears the moment I set foot in Spain, so that I immediately began to hunt for him, to throw myself upon his immense chivalry and trust to the strength of his invincible arm for justice and right."

"Enough: no more praise of me," said Don Quijote, "for I am opposed to all forms of flattery, and whether it is or is not mere flattery such talk still offends my chaste ears. All I want to say, my lady, is that whatever strength I have, if any, will be devoted to serving you for as long as my life lasts — and so, putting all of this aside for the moment, may I ask the priest to tell me what could have led him to these parts, all alone, with no servants, and dressed so lightly that I worry for him."

"And I can answer you in a few words," replied the priest, "for I must tell you, your grace, señor Don Quijote, that together with Master Nicolás — our friend and barber — I was journeying to Seville, to collect there a sum of money sent me by a relative who went to the Indies many years ago, and not such a little sum, either, for it was more than sixty thousand dollars in gold (and double the gold in a dollar today). Yesterday, as we were coming through here, four highway robbers attacked us and stripped us to our beards, and then they even took those off, too, so the barber had to get himself a false beard, and this young fellow here," he continued, pointing to Cardenio, "well, you wouldn't have recognized him. But the best part of the story is that the people around here say the thieves were galley slaves who were set free, almost on this very spot, by a man so brave that, in spite of a sheriff and his guardsmen, he unchained them all — but there's no question he was either crazy or a scoundrel just like the rest of them, or maybe a man without a soul or a conscience, to let the wolf loose among the sheep like that — the fox in the chicken yard — the fly in the honey jar — for why else would he want to cheat justice and defy his king and natural lord, going against His Majesty's right and proper decrees? He chose to pull the legs out from under His Majesty's galleys, make all kinds of trouble for the police — more than they've seen in a long, long time — and, in short, to endanger his immortal soul without gaining anything for his mortal flesh."

Sancho had told the priest and the barber all about the adventure with the galley slaves, which had brought his master such glory, so the priest really laid it on, wanting to see what Don Quijote might say or do, and our knight changed color at every word and did not dare reveal that it was he who had liberated those fine folk.

"So," said the priest, "that's who robbed us. May God, in His mercy, pardon the man who would not let them serve their rightful sentences."

Chapter Thirty

— which deals with the beautiful Dorotea's wisdom, along with other joyous and entertaining matters

The priest had barely finished when Sancho said:

"By my faith, Father, that deed was done by my master, and it wasn't because I didn't warn him against it, because I told him to think about what he was doing, and it was a sin to free those people, since it was for being great thieves and rascals that they were being marched off to the galleys."

"Fool!" said Don Quijote. "Knights errant are neither concerned nor obliged to interrogate all the afflicted, enchained, and oppressed people they meet with as to why they're in such trouble, or whether they're in distress because they're wrong-doers or because they're unlucky. Our only task is to help them as people in need, concentrating on their suffering, not on their wrong-doing. I came upon a long line of miserable unfortunates, and did for them what my vows require of me, and that's all there is to it. And to anyone who thinks I was wrong, excepting his holiness the honorable priest, I say he doesn't know much about chivalry, and that he lies like a lowborn son of a whore, and I'll let him know it with the edge of my sword, which will spell it out for him in the necessary detail."

And, having said this, he pulled down his helmet (because the barber's basin, which he took for Mambrino's magic helmet, was in his rear saddlebag, waiting to be straightened out after the galley slaves' mistreatment), jammed down on his stirrups, and sat very straight.

Dorotea, a lady who knew what was what, and with an excellent sense of humor, was well aware of Don Quijote's crazy convictions, and that — except for Sancho Panza — they were all teasing the knight, nor did she want to be left out, so seeing his vexation she said:

"Sir knight, do not forget the boon you've promised me, according to the terms of which you are unable to enter into any other adventure, no matter how pressing it may be. So be calm, your grace, for if this worthy man of the cloth had known it was your invincible arm that freed the galley slaves, he'd have sewed three stitches into his mouth, and even bitten his tongue three times over, before speaking a single word that could offend against your grace."

"I'd swear to that," said the priest, "and what's more, I'd shave off half my whiskers, too."

"I shall be still, my lady," said Don Quijote, "and hold back the righteous anger which rose in my breast, and proceed quietly and peacefully until I have indeed fulfilled my promise to you, but, in return for such a good resolve, let me ask that you tell me, if it so pleases you, just what affliction you suffer under, and the names, the numbers, and the natures of those from whom you are to have all that is due you, as well as complete satisfaction and revenge."

"I would be very glad to do so," said Dorotea, "if it would not displease you to hear such lamentations and misfortunes."

"My lady, it could not displease me," answered Don Quijote.

To which Dorotea replied:

"In which case, gentlemen, lend me your ears."

As soon as they heard this, Cardenio and the barber came up beside her, wanting to find out how so knowing a woman would spin her web, and so too did Sancho, who was as bewitched by her as was his master. And Dorotea, after settling herself in the saddle, and taking the time to clear her throat and perform other such preliminaries, gracefully launched herself into her tale:

"First, gentlemen, I must tell you that my name . . ."

And here she hesitated a bit, for she had forgotten the name given her by the priest, but he quickly saw what was needed and came to her aid, saying:

"My lady, who could be surprised at Your Majesty being upset and confused, recounting all your misfortunes? Many mistreated damsels completely lose their memories — so completely they cannot remember even their own names, as we see has happened to you, my lady, who cannot recall that you are the Princess Micomicona, legitimate heir to the great kingdom of Micomicón. Having this in hand, accordingly, Your Majesty can now readily bring back to memory whatever else of your pitiful history you may choose to tell us."

"How true," sighed the maiden, "and now I think I will need to be reminded of nothing, so let me begin at the beginning of my truthful tale. My father the king, whose name was Tinacrio the Wise, was deeply learned in what we call magic, and understood by the practice of this art that my mother, whose name was Queen Jaramilla, was going to predecease him, and that not long thereafter he too was going to leave this life and I would become an orphan. But none of this, he declared, was as hard to deal with as the absolute and certain knowledge that a monstrous giant, lord of a large island that virtually bordered on our kingdom, and whose name was Crosseyed Pandafilando [*pandafilando* = threadspinner] (for it's well known that, although his eyes are in fact perfectly straight, he always likes to look at people backwards, as if he were crosseyed, because it gives him an evil squint and makes everybody afraid of him) — my father, as I said, knew that this giant, when he found out I'd been orphaned, would launch a powerful attack on my kingdom, forcing me to abandon everything, not leaving me so much as a little village in which I could take shelter, but vowing that I could prevent my utter ruin and misery if I would marry him, though as my father also knew I would never willingly enter into such an unequal betrothal, which was of course absolutely true, because I never so much as considered marrying that giant, or indeed any other giant, no matter how huge and wild he might be. My father told me, too, that after his death and as soon as Pandafilando attacked my kingdom, I should not try to defend it, because that would destroy me, but simply let him conquer the kingdom, for that would allow me to prevent the death and utter ruination of my good and loyal subjects, since they could not possibly defend me against the giant's fiendish powers. Instead, I should immediately take some of my people and set out for Spain, where I would find salvation from all my misfortunes in the person of a knight errant, who would by that time be famous all across the country, and whose name, if I remember rightly, was something like Don Azote [*azote* = whip, scourge], or Don Gigote [*gigote* = stewed beef]."

"He would have said Don Quijote, my lady," said Sancho Panza at this point, "or, if he used another name, the Knight of the Sad Face."

"That's exactly right," replied Dorotea. "And he said more: that this knight would be tall, with a lean face, and that on his right side, under his left shoulder, or somewhere thereabouts, he'd have a grey, bristle-haired mole."

Hearing this, Don Quijote said to his squire:

"Here, Sancho my boy, help me take off this shirt, for I need to find out if I'm the knight this wise king foresaw."

"But why take off your shirt, your grace?" asked Dorotea.

"To see if I have that mole your father spoke of," answered Don Quijote.

"You don't need to take off your shirt," said Sancho, "because I know for a fact that your grace has exactly that kind of mole, right in the middle of your back, which is a sign that you're a man of strength."

"Which is quite sufficient," said Dorotea, "because little details don't matter among friends, and whether the mole's on the spine or under the shoulder doesn't matter. All that counts is that there's a mole, no matter where it may be, for it's all one body and my father surely prophesied correctly, just as I have quite properly put myself under Señor Don Quijote's protection, who is obviously the man of whom my father spoke, for this is not only the face of the most famous knight in all Spain, but in all La Mancha, too, and hardly had I disembarked at Osuna[1] when I began to hear his praises sung, and my heart at once told me that this was the man I had come to seek."

"But, my lady, how could you have disembarked at Osuna," asked Don Quijote, "when it's not a port city?"

But before Dorotea could reply, the priest broke in:

"Her majesty the princess should have said that she disembarked in Málaga, but the first place where she heard news of your grace was Osuna."

"That," said Dorotea, "was indeed what I meant to say."

"So go on, Your Majesty," said the priest, "and tell us the rest."

"There's nothing left to tell," replied Dorotea, "except that, in a word,

---

1. Osuna, as we will learn, is Don Fernando's hometown [*Translator's Note*].

by finding my lord Don Quijote I have been so fortunate that I already think of myself as queen and sovereign of my entire kingdom, since his chivalry and his nobility have led him to swear to follow wherever I may lead him, which will simply be to bring him face to face with Crosseyed Pandafilando, so he can kill him and restore what has been so unjustly taken from me, for this is all pre-ordained, as my good father, Tinacrio the Wise, has foretold, having also recorded, in a document written in Chaldean, perhaps, or Greek (neither of which I know how to read), that if this prophesied knight, having cut off the giant's head, asks for my hand in marriage, I'm to marry him at once, without even bothering to say a word, and give him possession both of my kingdom and of me."

"So what do you think, Sancho my friend?" asked Don Quijote. "Are you listening? What did I tell you? See? Now we've got ourselves a kingdom to rule and a queen to marry."

"You're damned right!" said Sancho. "And to hell with any son of a bitch who won't get married by slitting Señor Pandahilado's [*pandahilado* = thread-all-spun] throat! That's some queen! I wish there were fleas like that jumping around in my bed!"

And he leaped into the air, and leaped again, looking hugely delighted, then ran over to Dorotea, seizing the reins of her mule and halting it, and dropping onto his knees begged the lady to let him kiss her hands, to signify that he acknowledged her as his queen and sovereign lady. Who could have helped laughing, seeing the master's madness and his man's absolute innocence? So Dorotea gave him her hands and promised to make him a noble lord of her kingdom, as soon as Heaven should see fit to return it to her. And Sancho thanked her in such a style that everyone laughed all over again.

"And so that, gentlemen," concluded Dorotea, "is my story, and all that remains to be said is that, of all the folk with whom I came away from my kingdom, all I have left is this well-bearded squire, for the others were drowned in an immense storm that blew up just as we spied land, and this squire and I came to shore, miraculously, on two broken boards from our ship, as indeed my entire life has been miraculous and mysterious, as you will have observed. And if my narration has told you more than you wanted to know, or hasn't been as clear as it should be, lay the blame where the priest said it ought to go: unending and extraordinary struggle can affect a sufferer's memory."

"But mine will not fail me, oh brave and noble lady!" said Don Quijote, "no matter what I endure in your service, be it as immense and unheard of as it may, and so I confirm yet again the boon I promised you and swear that I will accompany you to the end of the world, until I encounter your ferocious enemy, whose arrogant head I plan to chop off with the blade of this — but I can't call it my good sword, thanks to Ginés de Pasamonte, who stole mine."

This last he muttered between his teeth, and then went on in his normal voice:

"And when I've chopped it off and put you in peaceful possession of your kingdom, you shall marry entirely as you choose, because as long as my memory holds fast to, and my will is captive and my mind is lost to

— her — but I will say no more, for it is impossible that I marry or even think of being married, were it to the very Phoenix itself."

Sancho Panza was so upset, as his master concluded with this statement about not wanting to be married, that he cried out, in violent indignation:

"In the name of God, damn it, your grace, Don Quijote, you're out of your mind! How can your grace have the slightest doubt about marrying such a fine, noble princess? Do you think Fortune's going to stand around on every corner, offering you luck like this? And is my lady Dulcinea more beautiful? Damn it, no, not even half — and I'll go farther and say she doesn't come up to the shoetops of this one. Lord help me, how can I ever get where I want to go, if your grace keeps chasing the moon? Now you marry her, you marry her right away, may I be damned, and you take this kingdom that's just dropping into your lap, and once you're the king you can make me a count or a governor, and then the hell with the rest of it."

Don Quijote, who could not stand to hear such blasphemy directed at his lady Dulcinea, did not say a word to his squire or to anyone else, but lifted his lance and struck Sancho two blows that knocked him to the ground and, had Dorotea not cried out that he must not strike him again, the knight would without any doubt have killed him on the spot.

"You miserable peasant," Don Quijote said after a moment, "do you think you can always stick your hand into my crotch and I'll just correct you and then forget about it? Well, *don't* think so, you monstrous rascal — and that's what you are, by God, now that you've turned your tongue on my peerless Dulcinea. And don't you understand — you slob, you ditch-digger, you scoundrel — that, without the strength she breathes into my arm, I wouldn't be able to kill a flea? Just tell me, with that lying viper's tongue of yours, who *won* this kingdom, and who cut off this giant's head, and who made you a count — all of which I consider as good as done with, finished, over — except Dulcinea's strength, lent to my arm as the mere instrument of her glorious deeds? She fights through me, and she conquers through me, and I live and breathe in her, I take my life and my very being from her. Oh you wicked son of a whore, what an ungrateful wretch you are, thinking yourself raised from the dust of the earth to become a nobleman, and yet repaying that immense favor by speaking ill of the very one who granted it to you!"

Sancho wasn't so badly hurt that he didn't hear every word his master spoke, and getting up as fast as he could he ran and hid behind Dorotea's mule, and from there he said to his master:

"Tell me, my lord: if your grace is bound and determined not to marry this great princess, it's clear you won't be her king, and if you're not her king, what favors can you do for me? And *that's* what I'm complaining about: just marry this queen, your grace, now that we've got her, as if by the grace of Heaven, and then you can change your mind and go back to my lady Dulcinea. There must have been kings in this world who slept in the wrong beds. As far as her beauty's concerned, it's none of my business — and anyway, when it comes to that, they both look good to me, especially since I've never even seen lady Dulcinea."

"What do you mean, you've never seen her, you lying traitor?" said Don Quijote. "Didn't you just bring me a message from her?"

"I said I didn't really get much chance to see her," said Sancho, "at least, not well enough to pay much attention to how beautiful she was, and all those details, but as far as I'm concerned, in general, I thought she looked pretty good."

"Then you're forgiven," said Don Quijote, "and please forgive me, in turn, for being so angry at you, for what a man is immediately moved to do is not under his control."

"I understand that," replied Sancho, "and the first thing I'm always moved to do is talk, and I can't stop myself from saying, at least once, whatever my tongue wants to say."

"Just the same, Sancho," said Don Quijote, "be careful what you say, because when the pitcher goes to the well too many times . . . but I won't say any more."

"Fine," answered Sancho. "God's up in Heaven, and He sees all this cheating, and He'll decide who's committing a sin: me, because I don't say the right things, or your grace, because you don't do them."

"Enough," said Dorotea. "Hurry over to him, Sancho, and kiss your master's hand, and beg his pardon; and from now on be more careful about what you praise and what you blame; and say nothing bad about this lady Tobosa, of whom all I know is that I am her humble servant; and trust in God, who will not fail to provide you with an estate on which you will live like a prince."

Sancho hung his head and begged his master to let him kiss his hand, which Don Quijote did with quiet grace, and then the knight blessed his squire and told him to come ahead a bit, for there were questions that needed to be asked and important matters to be talked about. Sancho complied and, when the two of them were significantly in front of the others, Don Quijote said:

"I've had no opportunity, since your return, to question you in detail about the message you carried away and the reply you brought back, so now that, fortunately, we finally have both time and opportunity, do not withhold from me the happiness which comes from good news."

"Ask me anything you want, your grace," replied Sancho, "because I can find my way out of anything I get into. But from now on let me beg you, your grace, my lord, not to be so vengeful."

"What makes you say such a thing, Sancho?" asked Don Quijote.

"I say it," the squire answered, "because those blows, just now, weren't so much for what I said about my lady Dulcinea but on account of the quarrel the devil stirred up between us, the other night, because I love and respect my lady Dulcinea like a holy saint, though I know that's not what she is, but just because, your grace, she's yours."

"If you value your life, Sancho, don't go back to that subject," said Don Quijote, "for it bothers me. I have already pardoned you, once, but you know the old saying: a new sin, a new penance."

As they went along, thus conversing, the priest told Dorotea that she had handled herself very well indeed, both as to the brevity of her tale and in its similarity to all the tales of chivalry. She told him she had often amused herself, reading such books, but in truth she didn't know exactly where the various provinces were, nor what cities were ports, which was why she had tried to have herself disembarking at Osuna.

"I knew that," said the priest, "which is why I immediately helped out, saying what I did, which took care of everything. But isn't it strange to see how readily this poor gentleman believes all these fictions and lies, and just because they ape the style and the formulas he finds in his books?"

"Indeed it is," said Cardenio, "and so unusual, not to say unheard of, that I don't think anyone has a sharp enough mind, even if he tried, to be able to invent such a wildly fanciful story."

"And there's yet another thing about it," said the priest, "which is that, no matter how idiotically he talks about matters having to do with his madness, when he talks about other things this good gentleman quite consistently displays a fine intelligence and a clear, calm understanding, so that if you avoid the subject of knighthood you'd have no way of knowing him for anything but a man of great good sense."

And as they went along, talking, so too Don Quijote continued his conversation with Sancho, saying to him:

"Panza my friend, let's bury the hatchet — and now you tell me, without any vexation or ill will, where, and how, and when you found Dulcinea? What was she doing? What did she say? What did you answer? How did she look, as she read my letter? Who copied it out for you? Indeed, tell me everything you think worth knowing about the whole affair, everything worth asking about, and capable of giving me pleasure, neither adding nor inventing anything to please me, nor omitting anything that might in any way leave me in want."

"My lord," said Sancho, "if I'm going to tell you what really happened, nobody copied out the letter for me, because I wasn't carrying a letter."

"You're quite right," said Don Quijote, "because, two days after you left, I found the notebook in which I'd written it, which caused me immense pain, not knowing what you would do, seeing yourself without the letter, and what I expected was that, when you discovered you didn't have it, you'd come right back."

"Which I would have done," replied Sancho, "if I hadn't memorized it when your grace read it to me, so I told it to a priest, and he got it down just point for point, and he said that, though he'd read a lot of letters of excommunication in his time, he'd never seen or read anything as graceful as that one."

"And do you still have it memorized, Sancho?" asked Don Quijote.

"No, señor," answered Sancho, "because after I told it to him I saw there was no need to remember it any more, so I forgot it, but if anything stays in my mind it's that part about 'stubborn' — I mean, 'sovereign lady,' and the ending, 'Yours until death, the Knight of the Sad Face.' But between those I stuck in more than three hundred 'souls,' and 'my life's,' and 'my eyes.'"

Chapter Thirty-One

— *the delightful conversation between Don Quijote and Sancho
Panza, his squire, together with other events*

"None of this displeases me; go on," said Don Quijote. "And tell me:
what was that queen of beauty doing, when you got there? Surely you
found her threading pearls, or embroidering with golden thread some mys-
tic motto for this enslaved knight of hers."

"That wasn't how I found her," replied Sancho, "but out in the yard,
at her house, sifting two or three bushels of wheat."

"Then count on it," said Don Quijote, "those grains of wheat were
grains of pearl, when she touched them with her hands. But if you happened to notice, my friend, was it fine white wheat or the heavy brown
kind?"

"It was just plain ordinary red," answered Sancho.

"Then let me tell you," said Don Quijote, "sifted by her hands, it surely
became the whitest of white flour. But go on: when you gave her my letter,
did she raise it to her lips? Did she put it on her head?[1] Did she perform
some ceremony worthy of such a document — or what *did* she do?"

"When I walked over to give it to her," replied Sancho, "she was working the sieve back and forth, with a lot of wheat in it, so she said to me:
'Just put your letter on that sack over there, my friend, because I can't
read it until I'm done with all this sieving.'"

"Ah, what a sensible lady!" said Don Quijote. "She did that so she could
read it slowly and carefully, all by herself. Go on, Sancho. While she was
doing what she had to do, what did she say to you? What did she ask
about me? And you, what did you answer her? Go on, tell me everything;
don't forget to cross a single 't' or dot a single 'i.'"

"She didn't ask me anything," said Sancho. "But I told her how your
grace, in her honor, was doing penitence, all naked from the waist up,
way out in that mountain wasteland like a savage, sleeping on the bare
ground, not eating bread off a tablecloth or taking care of your beard,
weeping and cursing your fate."

"Now that was wrong," said Don Quijote, "to tell her I was cursing my
fate, because in fact I bless it, and I'll go on blessing it all the days of my
life, since it has made me worthy of loving so high and noble a lady as
Dulcinea del Toboso."

"She's so high," replied Sancho, "that by God she's half a foot taller
than I am."

"What?" said Don Quijote. "Did you measure yourself against her,
Sancho?"

"I measured myself like this," Sancho answered him. "When I was helping her load a sack of wheat onto a donkey, we stood so close together
that I could see she was a good eight inches taller."

"Ah, but isn't it true," replied Don Quijote, "that she links and adorns
this loftiness with a billion spiritual charms! But one thing you'll surely

---

1. A gesture of respect [*Translator's Note*].

admit, Sancho: when you stood so close to her, were you not aware of a delicate odor, an aromatic fragrance, as well as an indescribable something for which I can find no name? I mean, some vapor, some breath of the sort you might find in a fine glovemaker's workshop?"

"All I can say," answered Sancho, "is that there was a kind of human smell, so it must have been because, with all that work, she was hot and sweaty."

"That's impossible," replied Don Quijote, "unless you had a cold, or else you were smelling yourself, for I know the fragrance of that rose among thorns perfectly well — that lily of the fields — that lady of liquid amber."

"Everything's possible," answered Sancho, "because the same odor I smelled, coming from her grace lady Dulcinea, is one I've often smelled coming from me — but there's nothing wonderful about that, because one devil's not much different from another."

"So," Don Quijote went on, "she gets finished with sieving her wheat and sends it off to the mill. But what happened when she read the letter?"

"She didn't," said Sancho, "because I've already explained that she can't read or write, so instead she tore it into little pieces, because she didn't want anybody else reading it, so no one in the village would know her secrets, and she said it was good enough for her, hearing what I could tell her about how much your grace loved her and all the extraordinary penitence you were doing for her sake. And then she told me to tell your grace that she kissed your hands and that she was more anxious to see you right there than she was to write to you, so she asked and directed that, when you heard this, you should go away from all those bushes and brambles and stop doing stupid things, because she wanted so much to see you, you were to get right on the road to Toboso — unless something more important came up — just because she really wanted to see you. She had a good laugh when I told her you were calling yourself 'The Knight of the Sad Face.' I asked her if that Basque fellow, the one you defeated, had been there, and she said that yes, he had, and he was a very good man. I also asked her about the galley slaves, but she told me she hadn't yet seen a one of them."

"So, to this point, everything is going well," said Don Quijote. "But tell me: when you were taking your leave, what kind of costly gem did she present you with, in return for the news you brought her? Because it's an ancient and immemorial custom for knights errant and their ladies to give some rich jewel to their squires, and maids, and dwarves, when they carry messages back and forth, from the ladies to the knights, or from the knights to the ladies, to show their appreciation for the errand thus performed."

"That could be, and I think it would be a fine idea, but it was a long time ago and now all they're used to giving is a piece of bread and cheese, because that's what lady Dulcinea handed me, over the courtyard wall, when she said goodbye, and, to tell you the truth, it was goat cheese at that."

"She is wonderfully generous," said Don Quijote, "so if she didn't give you golden jewelry it could only be because, at the moment, she didn't happen to have anything ready to hand, but mangoes taste good even after

Easter, so I'll talk to her about it, and everything will be taken care of. But do you know what truly astonishes me, Sancho? It seems to me you must have come and gone right through the air, because it's taken you less than three days to get from here to Toboso and back, even though that's more than a hundred miles, which tells me that some magician who's my friend, and watches over me (because there absolutely has to be someone like that, and that's what he has to be, or else I wouldn't be much of a knight errant) — I say, it must be that he helped you travel, without your knowing it, because there have been magicians who picked up a knight errant, sleeping peacefully in his bed and, without him knowing how or anything about it, he wakes up the next day more than a thousand miles away from where he went to sleep. And if it weren't for things like that, knights errant couldn't keep helping each other out of danger, as they're always doing. If one of them happens to be fighting a dragon, up in the mountains of Armenia, or maybe some savage monster, or another knight, and he's getting the worst of the battle and is close to death, and just when you'd never expect it, right out of nowhere, riding on a cloud or a fiery chariot, there comes some other knight errant, his good friend, who just a moment before was way off in England, and helps out and saves him from death, but that very same night back the other knight goes, and then there he is home, eating a good dinner, though it might be four or five thousand miles, or even more, from one place to the other. And this is all accomplished by the knowledge and skill of these learned magicians, who take care of such brave knights. So, Sancho my friend, it's not hard for me to believe that in such a short time you actually traveled back and forth between this place and Toboso, since as I said some magician friend of mine must have carried you through the air, without your even knowing it."

"That must be it," said Sancho, "because by God Rocinante galloped along as fast as a gypsy's donkey with quicksilver [mercury] in its ears!"[2]

"And what quicksilver!" said Don Quijote. "Plus, furthermore, a legion of demons, who can swoop up and down, and take other people with them anytime they want to, without ever getting tired. But let's put that aside for a moment: what do you think I ought to do, now, about my lady Dulcinea's order that I come to see her? Because even though I understand perfectly well that I'm obliged to obey her, at the same time I see how impossible that would be, because of the boon I'm pledged to perform for the princess who's traveling with us, and without any question the laws of knighthood require me to redeem my pledge before I do what happens to best please me. On the one hand, I feel pushed and pulled by the desire to see my lady; on the other, I'm impelled and urged on by having promised to fulfill this pledge, and by the glory that will surely accompany it. But I think the best thing to do is hurry quickly to this wicked giant, and cut off his head right away, and restore the princess to the peaceful possession of her realm, and then, just as soon as I can, come back to glimpse that light which glows throughout my whole being, and so excuse my tardiness to her that she will approve of it, seeing that it all increases her

2. A well-known gypsy trick, to make a donkey more salable [*Translator's Note*].

fame and glory, since every feat of arms I have ever accomplished, and accomplish now, and will accomplish in the future, all stem from the favor she bestows upon me and from my being hers and hers alone."

"My God!" said Sancho. "Your grace just isn't right in the head! Just tell me, señor: are you really thinking of doing all this for nothing — passing up and forever losing the chance for a rich and noble wedding like this, which would bring you a whole kingdom as a dowry, a kingdom that I've heard it said is actually more than a hundred thousand miles around and has in it everything any human being could need, and more, and is even bigger than Spain and Portugal put together? Don't say another word, for the love of God, and be ashamed of what you've said already, and do what I tell you, and pardon me for telling you, but marry her in the very first place where you can find a priest, and if that's not what you want, here we've got our own priest, who can do the whole thing to a tee. And keep in mind that I know what I'm talking about, and what I'm telling you is right on the money, because a bird in the hand is worth two in the bush, and anyone who could have the good and picks the bad instead is trying to make sure that everything doesn't come out all wrong."[3]

"Look here, Sancho," replied Don Quijote, "if you're telling me all this so I can immediately become the king, just as soon as I've killed the giant, so I can grant you favors and give you what I promised, let me tell you that I can easily do exactly what you want without getting married, because I'll make sure it's all spelled out before I fight the battle, so if I win it they'll have to give me part of the kingdom even if I don't marry her, and then I can give it to anyone I want to, and when I do, to whom do you think I'll give it except you?"

"That's fine," replied Sancho, "but be careful, your grace, to take a part near the sea, so if I don't like living there I can pack my black subjects on a boat and do what I said I'd do with them. And don't you worry about going to see my lady Dulcinea right now, your grace: you just go and kill the giant, and let's have this over and done with, because by God I think it's going to be a very honorable and a very profitable business."

"I agree with you, Sancho," said Don Quijote, "you're absolutely right, so I have to take your advice about going with the princess before I visit Dulcinea. But I suggest to you that you, for your part, say nothing about our discussion to anyone, neither to those who are traveling with us nor to those where we will be arriving, for since Dulcinea is so scrupulously modest that she wishes no one to know what's in her mind, it would not be proper for me, nor for anyone else on my behalf, to reveal them."

"If that's the way it is," said Sancho, "why does your grace make all the people you conquer go and present themselves to my lady Dulcinea, because that's just like signing your name to a declaration that you're in love with her and she's your sweetheart? And since they have to kneel down in front of her and say they've come because your grace told them to do whatever she tells them to, how can you possibly conceal what's going on?"

---

3. The proverb in fact declares: "Anyone who could have the good and picks the bad instead shouldn't be angry when everything comes out wrong" [*Translator's Note*].

"Oh, what an idiot, what a fool, you are!" said Don Quijote. "Don't you see, Sancho, that all this just makes her even more famous? You've got to understand that in the knightly way of doing things a lady is deeply honored, having many knights errant in her service, but they can't be thinking of anything more than serving her because she is who she is, not expecting any other reward for all their desires and good intentions than that she be willing to have them as her knights."

"That's the kind of love," said Sancho, "preachers say we ought to have for Our Lord, because He is who He is, without expecting any glory or worrying about any punishment. Me, I'd rather love Him and serve Him because He can do what He can do."

"May the Devil take you, what a peasant you are!" said Don Quijote. "But what wise things you say, sometimes! You'd think you were a learned man."

"But by God I can't read or write," replied Sancho.

At this point Master Nicolás called out to wait a bit, for he and the others wanted to have a drink at a nearby fountain. Don Quijote stopped, which delighted Sancho, weary with all the lies he'd been telling and worried that his master might trip him up, for even though he knew Dulcinea was a peasant from Toboso he'd never in all his life so much as set eyes on her.

By this time, too, Cardenio was wearing the clothes Dorotea had been dressed in when they'd found her, and though they weren't remarkably good they were a great deal better than those he took off. At the fountain they all dismounted, and with what the priest had brought from the inn they managed to at least ease their ravenous hunger.

Which is what they were doing when a young fellow came by, who stared at them long and hard and then rushed toward Don Quijote and, throwing his arms around the knight's legs, began to weep bitter tears.

"Oh, my lord! Don't you even recognize me, your grace? Look at me, please: I'm Andrés, the boy your grace set free when I was tied to an oak tree."

Remembering him, Don Quijote took him by the hand and presented him to all the others, saying:

"So you may see, ladies and gentlemen, how important it is that there be knights errant in the world, in order to right the wrongs and undo the damage done by the haughty wicked folk we find all around us, be advised that, some days ago, passing through a wood, I heard cries and pitiful laments, which sounded as if they came from some needy and afflicted lady. I hurried to her assistance, impelled by my duty as a knight, rushing to where I'd heard the cries of misery, and there I found this young fellow you see in front of you, tied to an oak tree — and I'm delighted to see him now, for he will bear witness that what I tell you is literally and exactly true. He was tied to the oak tree, I say, naked from the waist up, and a farmer — who as I afterwards learned was his master — was giving him a terrible whipping with a horse's reins. And I immediately asked the reason for this ghastly beating, to which the rascal replied that he was beating the boy because he was his employer and the boy's carelessness and neglect smacked more of thievery than of stupidity, at which the boy declared, 'Señor, the only reason he's beating me is because I asked for my pay.' His master answered with a lot of empty words and excuses, to which I listened but to which I paid no attention. In the end, I made him untie the boy and swear he would take him home and pay him every dollar that was owed, and in perfumed gold, to boot. Now, Andrés my son, isn't that the whole and complete truth? Didn't you see for yourself how nobly I commanded him, and how humbly he promised to obey me in every detail, tittle, and jot of what I ordered? Speak up: don't worry or be afraid of anything. Simply tell these gentlemen what happened, so they can understand and appreciate my remarks about the immense usefulness of having knights errant abroad on our roads and highways."

"Everything your grace says is exactly true," answered the boy, "but the end of the business was exactly the opposite of what your grace expected."

"The opposite?" replied Don Quijote. "Didn't he pay you, and at once?"

"Not only didn't he pay me," answered the boy, "but as soon as your grace rode out of the wood, and he and I were alone, he tied me up again to that same oak tree and gave me such a whipping that I looked like Saint Bartholomew, and with every lash he joked and laughed about you, your grace, and if it hadn't hurt so much I would have laughed myself. Anyway, he did such a job on me that from then till now I've been in a hospital, getting cured of everything he did to me. And the whole thing's your grace's fault, for if you'd just ridden on and not interfered where you weren't wanted, and minded your own business, my master would have been satisfied to give me a couple of dozen lashes and then he'd have untied me and paid what he owed. But once your grace insulted him like that, for no good reason, and said so many rude things, he got mad, and since he couldn't take revenge on you, as soon as we were alone he dumped it all out on me, and so hard that I don't think I'll ever be the same again, no matter how long I live."

"The problem was," said Don Quijote, "that I left you there, for I should not have gone until he paid you, because I ought to have realized, after long experience, that no peasant ever keeps his word, if he sees he won't be forced to. But remember, Andrés: I swore to you that if he did not pay you I would come and hunt him down, and I would find him even if he hid himself in the belly of a whale."

"That's true," said Andrés, "but it isn't worth a thing."

"Now we'll see just what it's worth," said Don Quijote.

And as he spoke he sprang to his feet and ordered Sancho to bridle Rocinante, who had been grazing while they ate their meal.

Dorotea asked Don Quijote what he was doing. He replied that he meant to hunt down the peasant and punish him for behaving so badly, and make him pay Andrés to the very last penny, in spite of all the peasants in the world. To which she replied by warning him that he couldn't do any such thing, for he had promised her not to engage in any other adventure until he was done with hers, and since he himself knew better than anyone else the vow he had taken, he should stay calm until he returned from her kingdom.

"That's true," answered Don Quijote, "and so as you say, my lady, Andrés too will have to be patient until I come back, but I swear and promise him yet again that I will not rest until he has been both revenged and repaid."

"I don't believe in all those oaths," said Andrés. "Instead of all the vengeance in the world, I'd rather have something that will help me get to Seville, so if you've got anything I can take with me and eat, give it to me, and you, your grace, you go with God and all the other knights errant, and for their pains may everything work out for them the way they've worked out for me."

Sancho pulled out a chunk of bread and a piece of cheese, and gave them to the boy, saying:

"Take this, brother Andrés, because we all share in your misery."

"And how do you share in it?" asked Andrés.

"God only knows," replied Sancho, "if I'm going to need this piece of cheese and this bread I'm giving you, because you must understand, my friend, that the squires of knights errant have to live with a lot of hunger and a lot of bad luck, and other things, too, that it's better to experience than to have to talk about."

Andrés took the bread and cheese and then, seeing that nobody was going to give him anything more, bent his head and, as the saying goes, picked the road up in his hands. But before he left them, he said to Don Quijote:

"For the love of God, sir knight errant, if you ever meet me again, please, even if you see me being cut into little pieces, don't rush to my aid or try to help me, but just let me be miserable, because no matter what they're doing to me it couldn't be worse than what will happen if your grace helps, so may God curse you and every knight errant who's ever been born into this world."

Don Quijote jumped up and started over to punish him, but Andrés began to run so fast that no one even tried to catch him. His story left Don Quijote deeply embarrassed, so the others had to be extremely careful not to laugh, because that might have pushed the crestfallen knight over the edge.

Chapter Thirty-Two

— which deals with what happened to Don Quijote and his company
in the inn

When they had finished eating their tasty meal, they quickly saddled up and, without encountering anything else worth talking about, the next day reached the inn that Sancho Panza so dreaded, but though he did not want to go in, there was no way to escape. When they saw Don Quijote and Sancho Panza coming, the innkeeper and his wife, their daughter, and Maritornes came out to greet them, all apparently very happy, and Don Quijote acknowledged their welcome with great dignity and composure, telling them to fix him a better bed than the last time, to which the innkeeper's wife replied that if he paid better, this time, she'd give him a bed fit for a prince. Don Quijote said he would, so they made him a reasonably good bed in the same attic room and he lay down at once, feeling very feeble and light-headed.

No sooner had the door been shut behind him when the innkeeper's wife rushed at the barber and, grabbing him by the beard, declared:

"By my faith, you don't need my donkeytail for a beard any more, so let me have my tail back, because it's a shame to keep dragging my husband's old thing around on the ground like that — I mean, the comb I used to keep in that nice tail of mine."

But the barber wouldn't let her have it, although she kept pulling and tugging, until the priest told him to give it to her, since their scheme was no longer needed, for now they could let Don Quijote see who they were, explaining to him that after they'd been robbed by the galley slaves they'd fled to this inn, for if he asked about the princess' squire they could tell him she'd sent the fellow on ahead, to let her people know she was coming and bringing with her the liberator of them all. And at that the barber cheerfully gave the inkeeper's wife her tail and, then and there, they also returned the rest of the equipment borrowed for Don Quijote's deliverance. Everyone in the inn gaped at Dorotea's wondrous beauty, and even at the figure cut by young Cardenio. The priest arranged for them to dine on whatever was available at the inn, and their host, hoping to be better paid, worked hard to fix them an edible meal — while Don Quijote slept on, for they didn't think they ought to wake him, sleep being so much better for him, right then, than food.

Those who sat down to dinner included, first of all, the innkeeper, his wife, his daughter, Maritornes, and all the other travelers who were guests there, and as they ate they talked about Don Quijote's strange madness and how his friends had found him. The innkeeper's wife told them what had happened between Don Quijote and the muledriver and then, looking around just in case Sancho was there, she told the whole story of how he had been tossed up in the blanket, which everyone much enjoyed. But when the priest said Don Quijote's brain had been addled by all the books of chivalry he'd read, the innkeeper said:

"I don't see how that could be true, because, really, as far as I'm concerned there's no better reading in the whole world, and I've got two or three of them, and some more, too, that have meant a lot to me, by God — and not just me, but lots of others. Because when it's harvest time, lots of harvesters come up here on holiday, and there're always some of them who can read, and when they get one of these books in their hands we all gather round them, maybe thirty of us, or even more, and we sit listening with such pleasure that it really takes a load off our minds, and anyway, me, I can tell you that when I hear those wild stories, and about all those smashing blows the knights hand out, I feel like doing the same thing myself, and I know I could listen to them night and day."

"And that's exactly how it is for me," said his wife, "because I never have a good time, here in my own house, unless you're listening to someone read, because then you're so caught up that, for a while, you can't think about fighting."

"That's true," said Maritornes, "and by God I like to hear those things, too, because they're really beautiful, and especially when they tell about some fine lady in her knight's arms, under an orange tree, while the maid who's keeping watch for them is dying with jealousy and fear. And that's sweet stuff, I tell you."

"And what do you think, young lady?" the priest asked the innkeeper's daughter.

"I don't really know, sir," she answered, "but I listen, too, and even though I don't understand I really like hearing it — but what pleases me isn't those terrible blows, in which my father takes such pleasure, but how the knights lament when they have to be away from their ladies, because sometimes, really, it makes me cry, I feel so sorry for them."

"So you'd help them, my dear," said Dorotea, "if it happened to be you for whom they wept?"

"I don't know what I'd do," answered the girl. "All I know is that some of them have ladies who are so cruel that their knights call them tigers and lions and a thousand other horrible names. But, by Jesus! I don't know what kind of people they must be, so heartless, so utterly without a conscience, that rather than give an honorable man so much as a look they'd let him die or go mad. What's the point to being so finicky? If it's an honorable business, why not marry them, if that's all they want?"

"Be quiet, girl," said her mother, "because you seem to know a lot about such things, and girls shouldn't know so much or talk so much, either."

"When this gentleman asked me," the daughter replied, "I couldn't help but answer him."

"All right then, my host," said the priest, "bring me these books, for I'd like to see them."

"With pleasure," the innkeeper answered.

And going into his own room, he brought out an old suitcase, tied around with a light chain, in which the priest found three thick volumes and some documents written in a fine hand. When he opened the first book, he saw that it was *Don Cirongilio of Thrace*; the second was *Felix-marte of Hircania*; and the third was *The History of that Great Commander, Gonzalo Hernández of Córdoba, together with the Life of Diego García of Paredes*.[1] After reading the first two titles, the priest turned to the barber and said:

"We ought to have with us, right now, our friend's housekeeper, and his niece, too."

"Hardly," the barber replied, "because I can carry them out to the yard or over to the fireplace — and there's a very nice fire burning."

"Is your grace planning to burn more books?" asked the innkeeper.

"Only these two," said the priest. "*Don Cirongilio* and *Felixmarte*."

"By any chance," said the innkeeper, "are my books heretics or phlegmatics?"

"You mean *schismatics*, my friend," said the barber, "not *phlegmatics*."

"Whatever," answered the innkeeper. "But if you want to burn one of them, let it be this one, about the Great Commander and Diego García, because I'd rather you burned a son of mine than any of the others."

"Brother," said the priest, "these are two lying books, full of idiocy and

1. The first two books to emerge from the suitcase are romances of chivalry published, respectively, in 1545 and 1556. The history of Gonzalo Hernández de Córdoba addresses the exploits of a Spanish soldier (1453–1515) in campaigns against the Moors in Granada and the French in Naples. Diego García de Paredes (1466–1530) was his companion in both campaigns.

madness, and that one, about the Great Commander, is a true story about the deeds of Gonzalo Hernández de Córdoba, whose many fabulous exploits made him worthy to be called Great Commander by the whole world, a famous and illustrious name no one else deserves, and Diego García of Paredes, furthermore, was a great knight, a citizen of the city of Trujillo, in Estremadura, a brave soldier and so enormously strong that, with just one finger, he stopped a swift-running mill-wheel right in its tracks, and stationed at the entrance to a bridge, with a two-handed sword, he held off an immense army, and no one got past him, and he did things like that all the time, so if he hadn't told his own story, written it himself in his own honor, and with all the modesty of a true knight, but, instead, someone else had written it, really telling the story, and with passion, he'd have made you forget all your Hectors and Achilles and Rolands."

"Now that's really something," said the innkeeper. "That amazes you, eh? — stopping a mill-wheel! By God, your grace ought to read what Felixmarte of Hircania did, cutting five giants in half with a single backstroke, as if they'd been so many friar-dolls carved out of bean pods. And another time he attacked a huge, powerful army that had more than a million six hundred thousand soldiers, every one of them armed from head to toe, and he whipped them all as if they'd been so many sheep. And what can you say about Don Cirongilio of Thrace, who the book tells us was so bold and brave that, once, the story goes, he was sailing down a river and a fiery sea-snake came up out of the water, and just as soon as Cirongilio saw it he threw himself on it and climbed up on its scaly shoulders and squeezed its neck so tight, with both hands, that the snake knew it was going to suffocate, so all it could do was let itself sink to the bottom of the river, taking the knight with it, because he wouldn't let go — what about that? And when he got down there, he found himself in the middle of such elegant palaces and gardens that he was astonished, and just then the serpent changed itself into an old man who told him things no one has ever heard of. Don't say another word, your grace, because if you were to hear all this you'd go out of your mind with happiness. I don't give a damn about the Great Commander or that Diego García of yours!"

Hearing this, Dorotea whispered to Cardenio:

"It wouldn't take much for our innkeeper to play second lead to Don Quijote."

"I agree," replied Cardenio, "because, as far as I can see, he absolutely believes that everything those books say is true and happened exactly the way they say it did, and even the barefooted monks couldn't change his mind."

"But just remember, brother," the priest said once more, "that Felixmarte of Hircania never actually existed, nor did Don Cirongilio of Thrace or any of those knights like them, of whom the tales of chivalry tell so much, because the whole thing's been made up, it's just a fiction spun by lazy imaginations, and woven for exactly the reason you mention — sheer entertainment, just to wile away the time, the way your harvesters do when they read such books. Because I can swear to you that, in fact, this world has never seen a single one of those knights, nor any of their great deeds or their stupidities."

"Sure, tell it to the marines!" answered the innkeeper. "As if I couldn't count to five or tell where my own shoe was pinching me! You can't fool me as easy as all that, your grace, because by God I wasn't born yesterday. Oh, that's a good one, your grace, trying to tell me that everything you can read in all those fine books is just foolishness and lies, when those same books are printed by license of the Royal Council — as if they were people who'd let a pack of lies get put into print, and all those battles and enchantments that just take your breath away!"

"But I've already told you, my friend," the priest replied, "that the purpose of all this is to amuse our lazy minds, and in the same way well-framed governments allow people to play chess, and ball games, and billiards, in order to provide entertainment for those who have no work to do, or don't need to work, or can't, so too they let such books be printed, believing — and surely it's true — that no one could be so stupid as to take any of these books for the literal truth. And if I thought this was the right time, and the right audience, I could tell you what these tales of chivalry would have to be, to become good books, and even useful, and to certain people's taste, but I hope the time will come when I can communicate such things to someone who can do something about them — and in the meantime, my dear innkeeper, you'd better believe what I've told you, and take your books and do the best you can with either their truths or their falsehoods, and much good may it do you, but let it be God's will that you don't suffer from the same affliction that troubles your guest, Don Quijote."

"Not a chance," replied the innkeeper. "I'm not going to be so crazy that I'll turn myself into a knight errant, because I can see perfectly well that things aren't the way they used to be, back in those days, when we're told those famous knights marched through the world."

Sancho had come in, while they were having this discussion, and it left him troubled and deeply thoughtful, hearing it said that knights errant were out-dated, now, and that tales of chivalry were all foolish and full of lies, so he took a silent vow to wait and see what came of this journey his master was making, because if it didn't turn out as well as he expected it to, he'd made up his mind to leave Don Quijote and go back to working the land with his wife and children.

The innkeeper started to carry off the suitcase and the books, but the priest said to him:

"Just a minute, I'd like to have a look at those finely-written documents."

The innkeeper handed them over and the priest saw a work of eight hand-written sheets, the first of which was titled, in large letters, *Story of the Man Who Couldn't Keep from Prying.*[2] He read three or four lines to himself, then said:

"This doesn't strike me as a bad title; I'd be glad to read the whole story."

To which the innkeeper replied:

"Then by all means read it, your reverence, because I can tell you I

---

2. This is Raffel's translation of "El curioso impertinente," an inset story that traditionally appears in English translation, and in literary criticism, with some form of the word "curious": e.g., "The Curious Impertinent," "The Tale of Foolish Curiosity," or "The Story of Ill-advised Curiosity."

had some guests here who read it and liked it so much they tried to get me to give it to them, but I didn't want to, since I plan to give this suitcase back to the man who forgot it here, who might very well come for it some day, and even though I know I'd miss the books I also know I've got to return them, because I may be an innkeeper but I'm still a Christian."

"That's very proper, my friend," said the priest. "All the same, if I like this story you'll have to let me make myself a copy."

"Most willingly," replied the innkeeper.

While they'd been talking, Cardenio had picked up the story and begun reading it, and since it struck him favorably, too, he asked the priest to read it aloud, so everyone could hear.

"Surely," said the priest, "if we wouldn't make better use of our time sleeping than reading."

"It would be enough rest for me," said Dorotea, "to wile away the time listening to a story, for I'm not calm enough to sleep, even if I ought to."

"In that case," said the priest, "I'll be glad to read it, even if only for curiosity's sake — and who knows? Perhaps the tale will be a pleasant one."

The barber too wished to hear the story, and so did Sancho, and when the priest saw that and realized they'd all like to hear it, himself included, he said:

"All right then, pay attention, all of you — and here's how the story begins:"

Chapter Thirty-Three

— which narrates The Story of the Man Who Couldn't Keep from Prying

In Florence, that rich and celebrated city in Italy, in the province they call Tuscany, there lived Anselmo and Lothario, a pair of wealthy, noble gentlemen, and such exceedingly close friends that they'd come to be called *Los Dos Amigos* [The Two Friends]. They were bachelors, young men of the same age and the same habits, which was more than enough to account for their mutual affection. It's true that of the two Anselmo was rather more interested in the amusements of love, and Lothario was fonder of hunting, but when the opportunity presented itself Anselmo would leave his own pastimes and pursue his friend's, just as Lothario would leave his and follow Anselmo's, and so they balanced out their desires so nicely that no clock could have been better regulated.

Now it happened that Anselmo fell in love with a lovely, highborn girl of that same city, the daughter of good parents and so good herself that he made up his mind, if Lothario agreed (and he did nothing to which Lothario did not agree), to ask his father and hers if they could be married. Which was what in fact he did, and his ambassador to her father was Lothario himself, who handled the negotiations exactly as Anselmo wished, so that in a very short time he found himself in possession of the woman he wanted and Camila, who was delighted to be married to Anselmo, could not stop thanking both Heaven and Lothario for bringing her to such happiness. At first, for a wedding is usually the time for happiness and joy, Lothario continued to visit his friend's house, trying to celebrate and honor Anselmo, and to make him as happy as he possibly could, but when all the festivities and celebrations slowed and then were over he deliberately began to come to Anselmo's house less often, for it seemed to him — as indeed it should to anyone with good sense — that one should not continue to visit married friends either as regularly or as often as one had when they were bachelors, for although a good, faithful friend neither can nor should incline a man to suspicion, still, a married man's honor is such a delicate affair that it's capable of being injured even by his brothers, much less his friends.

Anselmo became aware that Lothario was neglecting him, and complained bitterly, saying that had he realized his marriage would have the effect of thus diminishing their friendship, he'd never have gotten married at all, and if the fine relationship they'd had when they were both bachelors had earned them a name so satisfying as *Los Dos Amigos*, Lothario had no business, simply for the sake of caution and propriety, and without any real cause, to throw away such a fine and celebrated name. Accordingly, he begged Lothario — if indeed such good friends could even use such words in speaking to one another — to once again use his, Anselmo's, house as he would his own, and to come and go as he used to, assuring Lothario that Camila, his wife, had no other wish, no other desire, in any way different from his, and in fact Lothario had to understand that, having plainly seen how fond the two friends were of one another, she was puzzled to see Lothario now so aloof.

Lothario listened to these and still more reasons why he ought to be persuaded to use Anselmo's house just as he had before, and replied with such wisdom, good sense, and warnings that Anselmo was thoroughly convinced of his friend's good will and arranged that Lothario should dine with him twice a week, and also on holidays, but though this was their agreement Lothario had no intention of coming any more often than his friend's honor might permit, for he valued Anselmo's reputation even more than his own. It was his opinion, and a wise one, that any married man to whom Heaven had granted a beautiful wife should be every bit as careful of the male friends he brought home with him as he was watchful of the female friends with whom his wife associated, since what cannot be done, or even planned, out on the street, or in church, or even during public holidays or on pilgrimages to sacred sites — opportunities which husbands ought not to always deny their wives — could be easily arranged at some lady friend's house, or at the home of the most proper and innocent of all her female relatives.

And Lothario said, as well, that all married men should have some special friend to warn them about mistakes they were making, because it usually happens that, out of sheer love for his wife, a husband fails to warn her or, because he does not want to make her angry, never tells her at all, that she ought to be doing or not doing some particular things of which either the doing or not doing might well bring him honor or shame, these all being matters as to which, duly warned by his friend, the husband can

easily take care of. But where are we to find friends as sensible, loyal, and
faithful as Lothario here required? I certainly don't know — except that
Lothario himself was clearly one of them, constantly considerate of and
watchful over his friend's honor, trying to ration out, limit, and generally
reduce his regular visits to Anselmo's house, so that your ordinary, lazy
man in the street, with his wandering, suspicious eyes, would see no evil
in the comings and goings of a young, well-born gentleman, blessed with
all the advantages the vulgar would see in him, to a house where there
lived a woman as beautiful as Camila, for although his known kindness
and courage might check all slanderous tongues, nevertheless he had no
wish to stain either his own or his friend's reputation, and so, on most of
the days Anselmo had set for his visits, he managed to be busy elsewhere
and with other matters, which — he explained — he could not avoid,
and this was a procedure which, when the two friends did meet, produced
complaints from one and excuses from the other that took up a good deal
of their time together.

It happened, then, that one day, as the two friends were taking a walk
outside the city, Anselmo turned to Lothario and said:

"Lothario, my friend, you might think, given God's great grace in making me the son of such parents as mine, and in bestowing on me, with
open hands, what are called the blessings of nature as well as those of
fortune, and above all because He has given me you as a friend and
Camila as my wife — two gifts that I may not value as much as I should,
but still as much as I can — that I could not help but be grateful for all
I have received. Yet despite all this, amounting to everything which usually
enables men to lead happy lives, I am the most peevish and disagreeable
man on the face of the earth, and because I can no longer say just when
this mood came over me and I found myself gripped by such a strange,
outlandish desire, I am astonished by myself, and when I'm alone I scold
and argue, trying to stifle this desire and keep it hidden even from my
own mind, but I've been no more able to rid myself of the secret than
I've been to deliberately announce it before the whole world. And since
it will have to come out into the open, I want it to be a secret I share with
you, for I'm sure that, knowing it, and being the accomplished person you
are, as well as my true friend, you will help me, and I'll soon find myself
free of the anguish it's been causing me, just as I'm sure that I'll find
myself as delighted by your thoughtfulness as I've been distressed by my
own irrationality."

Anselmo's words baffled Lothario, for he had no idea what such a long
warning or preamble might lead to, and though he tried to imagine what
strange desire it could be that was so vexing his friend, he could not even
come close to understanding, and so, to end the torment of not knowing,
he told Anselmo he was clearly abusing their close friendship, going
around in circles as he was, trying to explain his most secret thoughts, for
he ought to be absolutely certain his friend's response would be either to
offer the best advice he could or to help accomplish whatever it might be
that Anselmo wanted done.

"That's true," replied Anselmo, "and with exactly such a degree of confidence, Lothario my friend, I must inform you that the desire which so
weighs on me is this: I wonder if Camila, my wife, is really as good and

perfect as I think she is, because I can't truly believe it unless I find some way to test her which will reveal just how good she actually is, the way we test gold by fire. Because, oh my friend! I believe that a woman is no better than the degree to which she either is or is not tempted, and the only safe and secure woman is one who has resisted promises, and gifts, and tears, and all the unremitting advances of devoted lovers. For," Anselmo went on, "why should we be grateful that a woman is good, if no one ever tells her to be bad? What is it worth that she's retiring and timid when no one's given her a chance to cut loose? — when she's well aware that she has a husband who, the very first time he catches her doing anything bold and forward, will kill her? And if she's good only because she's afraid, or because she has no opportunity to be anything else, how can I value a woman as much as if she'd met with temptation and overcome it, emerging crowned with victory? For all these reasons, and many more that I could give you in support of my opinion, I want my wife, Camila, to experience these trials, to be purified, her true worth assayed and known, by the fire of being wooed and tempted, and by someone worthy of inspiring such desires in her. For if she emerges unscathed, as I believe she will, carrying off the palm of victory in this battle, my good fortune will seem to me unmatchable; I will be able to declare that the hollow emptiness of my desires is now filled to the brim; I will affirm that I possess the best woman on earth, she of whom the Psalmist asked, 'Who can find a virtuous woman?' And if things do not go as I expect, I will have the pleasure of having put my judgment to the test, which will keep me from feeling the pain that, quite reasonably, might otherwise have been caused me by so grievous an experience. And since there is absolutely nothing you can say to me, in opposition to this desire of mine, which will be of the slightest use in making me abandon the project, it is my wish — oh Lothario, my dear friend! — that you allow yourself to be the instrument which accomplishes this which means so much to me. I will make every opportunity available to you, omitting nothing I think necessary for tempting a woman who is chaste, pure, retiring, and high-minded. I am inclined to entrust this fearfully arduous undertaking to you because, among other reasons, I feel sure that if it's you who conquers Camila the conquest won't need to be pushed to the final step, but only so far that what could be done may be considered as having been done — out of necessary respect — so that I will be injured only by a desire, and that desire will be hidden by your virtuous silence, which I am well aware will be, in all that concerns me, as eternal as death itself. Accordingly, if you wish me to lead a life that can truly be called living, you will begin this amorous encounter at once, neither lukewarmly nor with any hesitation, but with the zeal and the brisk diligence that my desire asks of you, as well as the good faith of which I am guaranteed by our friendship."

This, then, was what Anselmo said to Lothario, who listened so carefully that, apart from the few words already here transcribed, he did not open his lips until his friend had finished, after which, seeing that Anselmo had no more to say, Lothario stood staring at him for some moments, like a man seeing something he'd never seen before, something that very much surprised and indeed shocked him.

"I can't convince myself, oh Anselmo, my dear friend! that everything you've just said to me is anything more than a joke, for had I thought you were speaking seriously I would not have allowed you to say as much as you have: I would have stopped your long speech by refusing to listen to you. It seems to me utterly clear either that you do not really know me, or I do not really know you. But no: I'm very well aware that you're Anselmo, and you know I'm Lothario; the trouble is that I don't think you're the Anselmo you used to be, and that, for your part, you can't have thought me the Lothario I ought to be, for the things you've said to me aren't the words of my friend Anselmo, and the things you've asked me to do couldn't be asked of the Lothario you know. Even the best of friends have to test their friendship and see how much it's worth — as a poet once said, *usque ad aras* [just as far as the altar], which I take to mean that friendship should never be used for ungodly purposes. And if this was how a pagan felt about friendship, how much more should it be a Christian's feeling, who knows that we should not lose God's friendship for the sake of one merely human? If a friend does in fact ever cross that line, and put aside his reverence to Heaven so he can help his earthly friend, it can't be simply for casual reasons, but only for matters in which that friend's honor or his life are involved. Now you tell me, Anselmo: which of these two dangers threatens you enough to make me willing to undertake anything as detestable as that which you ask of me? Surely neither: rather, as far as I understand, you're asking me to try to do something that will deprive you of both your honor and your life, and at the same time so deprive me, too. Because, plainly, if I try to deprive you of your honor, I deprive you of your life, for a man who has lost his honor is worse than a corpse, and if I am the instrument which does such a wrong to you, as you wish me to be, am I not left dishonored as well and, therefore, equally deprived of my life? Listen to me, my dear friend, and be patient enough not to answer until I have finished telling you how I feel about what this desire of yours wants me to do, for there will be time enough for you to answer me in turn, and for me to hear you out."

"Fine," said Anselmo, "just as you wish."

So Lothario went on:

"It seems to me — oh, Anselmo! — that now you're thinking as the Arabs always do, who can never be made to understand the error of their religion simply from the words of the Holy Scriptures, nor by means of any speculative arguments, nor any based on pure faith, but have to be shown obvious examples — simple, easily understood, palpably demonstrable, unmistakable — with mathematical proofs no one could possibly deny, like: 'If we subtract equal parts from equal parts, the remainder will also consist of equal parts.' And when they cannot understand this verbally, as they usually cannot, you've got to show them with gestures, and put the thing right in front of their eyes — and even then it's never enough to persuade them of the truth of our holy religion. And that's how I'll have to proceed with you, for this desire you've conceived is leading you so far from any semblance of rationality, and pulling you so hard, that I think it would be a waste of time to try to make you see your foolishness, for that is all I can call it — and, indeed, though I'm tempted to abandon you to your folly, as a just punishment for so evil a desire, our friendship will not permit me such harshness, which would leave you in plain danger of perdition. And so you can see this with absolute clarity, tell me, Anselmo: haven't you urged me to tempt a modest woman, seduce a pure woman, press myself on a high-minded woman, woo a woman of good sense? Yes, that's what you've told me. But if you know you have a modest, pure, high-minded, sensible woman, what are you after? And if you believe she'd emerge unscathed from all my attacks, as I have no doubt she would, what better words will you be able to use, in speaking of her, than you can right now? How will she be any better than she already is? Either you don't think she really is what you say she is, or you don't understand what you're asking of me. If it's that you don't think she really is what you say she is, why should you want to tempt her, and not just treat her as already guilty, and then deal with her as you think best? But if she truly is as good as you think her, what an indecent thing it would be to experiment with such a truth, since, once you were done, you'd have to think her exactly what you thought her when you started. Which proves, and proves conclusively, that to attempt to do things more likely to cause harm than good is the act of an irrational, fixated mind, and especially when what we attempt is not something we are forced and compelled to do but can easily be seen as plain madness. We attempt onerous tasks on God's behalf, or the world's, or for both: those who undertake such things for God are saints, trying to live angelic lives while still in human bodies; those who undertake them for the world must travel across the widest seas, through every kind of climate, among the strangest of strange men, in order that they may acquire what we call fortunes. And those who undertake them both for God and for the world are the bravest of brave soldiers, who no sooner see the enemy's wall opened the width of a single cannon ball than, casting fear to the winds, without saying a word or paying the slightest attention to the obvious dangers threatening them, completely swept away on the wings of their desire to fight for their faith, for their country, and for their king, boldly hurl themselves straight at the thousand bristling deaths that await them. These are the things men customarily undertake, and it is honorable, glorious, and supremely good to undertake them, in spite of all obstacles, in spite of all dangers. But what you say you intend to do is neither for the greater glory of God, nor for the sake of fortune, nor for fame among men, for even should you accomplish what you say you seek to, you'll gain no happiness, no pride, you won't be any richer or more honored than you are now, and if it goes badly you'll find yourself steeped in the greatest misery imaginable, because what good will it do you, then, to reflect that no one knows the misfortune you've suffered? Knowing it yourself will be more than sufficient to crush and undo you. To prove this, let me recite a single stanza by the famous poet, Luigi Tansillo, from the conclusion to the first part of his *Saint Peter's Tears*:

Saint Peter's sadness, Saint Peter's shame,
Grew and grew as daylight came,
And alone as he was, with no one to see,
He knew he had sinned and he knew he was he,
For a flowing heart knows its own shame,

Needing no other to mark its blame:
When sin has branded a guilty heart
It burns, though God alone knows it smarts.[1]

"Thus your secrecy, too, will not save you from your sadness; indeed, you'll never stop weeping, if not with tears from your eyes, then with bloody tears from your heart, like that foolish scholar of whom the poet [Ariosto, in *Orlando Furioso*] tells us, who drank from the magic cup which wise Reinaldos carefully shunned — and though this may be a poetic fiction, it contains hidden truths, and moral ones, worth noting, and understanding, and imitating. And let me tell you something more, which should bring you to full knowledge of the enormous error you plan to commit.

"Tell me, Anselmo, if Heaven, or plain good fortune, put you in full and legal possession of a superb diamond, the quality and worth of which had been abundantly attested to, after due inspection, by who knows how many jewelers, all of whom had unanimously declared it to be as fine, noble, and costly as any diamond could possibly be, and you yourself were of the same opinion, would you, if you had no reason to think anything to the contrary — would you, I say, be doing the right thing if you conceived a desire to take this diamond and put it between an anvil and a hammer, so that by pure force you could find out if it was as hard and as fine as everyone said? What's more, suppose you actually did this, and the stone stood up to so foolish a test, it would gain neither in value nor in reputation, while if it broke — which is always possible — wouldn't everything be lost? Surely, everyone would think its owner a fool. Anselmo, my friend, consider Camila that superb diamond, in your opinion as in everyone else's, and that there's no reason for putting her to any risk of being broken, for if she remains intact she'll be worth no more than she is now, while if she falls short and cannot resist, think how your life would be without her, and with what good cause you'll blame yourself for having brought about both her downfall and your own. Reflect that there is no gem in the whole world worth as much as a chaste and honest woman, and that women's honor consists solely of their good reputations, and since you know perfectly well that your wife's reputation could not be better, why try to cast any doubt on it? Remember, my friend, that women are imperfect creatures, and we ought not to put obstacles in their way, to make them stumble and fall, but rather remove obstacles and clear their paths for them, so that they can proceed without difficulty and achieve the perfection they lack, which consists of being virtuous.

"Naturalists tell us the ermine is a small animal with gleaming white fur, so hunters, when they want to catch it, use this trick: knowing where the animal is usually found, and what paths it goes on, they smear those paths with mud, then beat the bushes and make a great racket so the animals run to their usual ground and, when they reach the mud, they just stop and let themselves be caught, rather than walk through slime and

---

1. Luigi Tansillo (1510–1568) was an Italian poet who composed *Le lacrime di San Pietro*. The poem was translated into Spanish by a friend of Cervantes (Luis Gálvez de Montalvo) in 1587, two years after its publication in Italy.

thus stain, or even lose, their shining whiteness, which they value more than freedom or life itself. A chaste and pure woman is like the ermine, and modesty is a virtue whiter and purer than the whitest snow, and he who wishes it not to be lost, but guarded and preserved, must work in a manner quite unlike the ermine, for he must never put in its path the filth of luxuries and all the attentions placed there by importunate lovers, because perhaps (and even if we do without 'perhaps') the woman will not be sufficiently virtuous, sufficiently strong-willed, that she can of herself climb over and make her way through those obstacles, so that what he needs to do is take them away and put in front of her, instead, the purity of virtue and the immense beauty contained in a good reputation. A good woman is like a mirror of clear and shining crystal: she can be dimmed and besmirched by any breath that touches it. A modest woman must be treated like a holy relic — adored, not touched. You must guard and treasure a good woman as you preserve and care for a beautiful garden full of flowers and roses, whose owner lets no one stroll through it or touch its blooms: people have to be content to view it at a distance and savor its scent and its beauties through iron railings. And, finally, let me recite for you some lines I remember hearing in the theater, which seem to me to deal with exactly the matter we've been discussing. A wise old man is giving advice to someone, a young girl's father, telling him to keep her hidden away, watched over and guarded, and among other things this is what he tells the father:

> Women are made of glass,
> But no one needs to know
> If they'll crack or if they'll smash,
> For anything can be so.
>   But breaking them's not hard,
> So a wise man plays no tricks
> Where glass is sure to be jarred:
> What's broken can't be fixed.
>   And no one disagrees,
> And everyone knows why:
> When Danaë's there to be seized
> Gold Jupiters rain from the sky.

"Everything I've said to you thus far, oh Anselmo! has been concerned solely with you yourself, so it's time for you to hear something about what concerns me, and if I must say a great deal, forgive me, for it's all required by the labyrinth into which you've wandered, and by my own desire to rescue you from it. You consider me your friend, and yet you want to strip me of my honor, an act contrary to any notion of friendship, nor is this all you want, for you want me to try to take yours as well. That you wish to deprive me of mine is quite clear, for when Camila finds me trying to seduce her, as you've asked me to do, she'll surely think me a man devoid of honor and worthy of a bad reputation, for what I'd clearly be after would be something completely alien to my real self, and to what your friendship requires of me. Nor is there any doubt that you want me to deprive you of your own honor, for when Camila finds me trying to seduce her, she's

bound to think I've already seen in her some fickleness, some licentious-
ness, which has led me to disclose my wicked desire, and if she considers
herself dishonored, that will rebound on you, for she is yours, and you are
thus yourself dishonored. And this gives rise to a common chain of events:
even though an adulterous woman's husband hasn't been aware of what's
going on, and knows he hasn't given his wife any reason not to be what
she should be, and knows it isn't something he can control, and that his
misfortune doesn't stem from his own negligence and that he had no way
of stopping it, still, for all that, he hears himself called a vile, low name,
and knows that others call him that, and finds that those who know what
his wife has done don't look at him sorrowfully, with pity in their eyes,
but rather with contempt, no matter that they see he's not to blame and
his misfortune comes only from his wicked mate's longing for pleasure.
But let me tell you why an adulterous woman's husband is rightly dishonored, despite the fact that he didn't know about it and isn't to blame,
despite the fact that he's had no part in it and done nothing to bring it
about. But please, don't get tired of listening to me: it's only in your interest
that I speak at all.

"When God created the father of us all, in the Garden of Eden, the
Holy Bible tells us that He put Adam into a deep sleep and, as he lay
there, took a rib from Adam's left side and from that rib formed our mother
Eve, and when Adam woke and saw her he said: 'For this is flesh of my
flesh and bone of my bone.' And God said: 'And for her a man must leave
his father and his mother, and they shall be as two in one flesh.' Which
was how the divine sacrament of marriage was created, a tie so tightly
bound that only death can loosen it. And this miraculous sacrament has
such force and such magical power that indeed it does make two different
persons into one flesh, and especially when two good people marry, for
though they have two souls they have only one will. And so it happens
that, the wife's flesh being the same as the husband's, anything that stains
her, any imperfections for which she strives, fall equally on her husband's
flesh, even though, as I've said, he's done nothing to bring them into being.
For just as pain in a man's foot, or in any part of the human body, is felt
all through that body, all being of one flesh and the head feeling what the
ankle feels, though it has done nothing to create that pain, so too the
husband shares in his wife's dishonor, because he and she are one. And
just as all the honor and the dishonor in the world comes from flesh and
blood, and is of flesh and blood, including a bad woman's sins, the husband inevitably takes his share and, whether he knows it or not, is dishonored. Consider, then, oh Anselmo! into what danger you place yourself,
thus disturbing the calm in which your good wife now dwells; consider
what a hollow, irreverent curiosity leads you to plant such notions in your
chaste wife's peaceful breast; realize that you stand to gain but little, but
may lose so much that I do not want to spell it all out, not knowing the
proper words to say it sufficiently strongly. And still, if everything I've said
is not enough to keep you from this evil plan, you'll have to look elsewhere
for someone to dishonor and disgrace you, for I cannot be the instrument
of your undoing, though I lose your friendship by my refusal — and that
would be a loss greater than any other I can think of."

And having said this, the wise, discreet Lothario fell silent, and Anselmo stood so doubtful, so hesitant, that for quite some time he could not utter a word in reply. And then, finally, he said:

"Lothario, my friend, you've seen how carefully I've listened to everything you've tried to tell me, and all your arguments, your examples, your comparisons have displayed the depth of your wisdom and your truly profound friendship, and I also see, and freely admit, that if I choose not to follow your judgment, and adhere to my own, I will be fleeing from what is good and running toward what is evil. And if that's the case, you must realize that what I'm suffering from, now, is the same disease that often afflicts women when they have a longing to eat dirt, or plaster, or charcoal, or still worse things, nauseating even to look at, but worse to swallow. So something must be concocted to bring me to a cure, which indeed is easily managed, for all you need to do is start, no matter how tepidly, no matter how falsely, your attempt to seduce Camila, who is not likely to be so approachable that she'll surrender at the very first assaults on her virtue — and this bare beginning will be enough for me, and you'll have fulfilled all that you owe to our friendship, not only giving me life but convincing me not to strip myself of my honor. And this much you are obliged to do, and for one very good reason: which is that I, being who and what I am, having made up my mind to put this to the test, you cannot allow me to make this foolishness known to anyone else, which could endanger the honor you seek to keep me from losing — and that yours won't stand as high with Camila as it should, while you're busy trying to seduce her, isn't particularly important, since once she displays the integrity we're expecting, you can pretty bluntly tell her the truth about our trick, which will restore your reputation to what it was before. And because you risk so little, and can please me so profoundly by risking even that, you can't fail to do it, even if you foresee still further drawbacks, since, as I say, if only you'll make a try I'll be able to look at it as a settled and completed matter."

Seeing how fixed and determined Anselmo was, and unable to think of any more examples and arguments to keep him from putting his plan into execution, and understanding as well that Anselmo was threatening to involve someone else, Lothario decided to consent and do what had been asked, if only to avoid anything worse, intending to handle the whole business in such a way that, without disturbing Camila, he could still satisfy her husband, and so he replied that Anselmo should not reveal his thoughts to anyone, that he, Lothario, would take full responsibility for this business, and that he would begin whenever Anselmo wanted him to. Anselmo embraced him tenderly and passionately, thanking him for his offer, exactly as if Lothario were doing him an immense favor, and they agreed to put the plan into execution the very next day; Anselmo would see to it that his friend had an opportunity to be alone with Camila, and the time to speak to her, and he would also furnish Lothario with money and jewels with which to tempt her. He advised Lothario, too, to woo her with music, and to write poems in her praise, adding that if this was too much trouble he, Anselmo, would supply such things himself. Lothario agreed to everything, though with intentions very unlike those in his friend's mind.

And having reached this agreement, they went back to Anselmo's house, where they found Camila awaiting her husband in some anxiety, for he had returned from his walk a good deal later than usual.

Lothario went to his own home, and Anselmo stayed in his, as pleased as Lothario was troubled, for Anselmo's friend couldn't see any way of getting out of this unfortunate business. But that night he thought of a way to deceive Anselmo without insulting Camila, and so the next day he came to dine, and was warmly received by Camila, who welcomed and entertained him with great good will, knowing how much her husband thought of him.

When the meal was over, and the tablecloth removed, Anselmo told Lothario he would be obliged to leave him alone with Camila for a bit, because he had some pressing business, from which he would return in less than a hour and a half. Camila begged him not to go out, and Lothario offered to go with him, but nothing had any effect on Anselmo, and indeed he insisted that Lothario remain and wait for his return, for there was a matter of high importance that needed to be dealt with. Anselmo also instructed Camila not to leave Lothario all alone until he did come back. In a word, he made his necessary — that is, his foolish — absence look so plausible that it would have been impossible to see that it was all a pretense. Anselmo left, and Camila and Lothario were left alone at the table, for the household servants had gone to eat their own dinner. And so Lothario found himself on exactly the dueling ground his friend had chosen for him, and with his opponent facing him, perfectly capable of conquering an entire squadron of well-armed gentlemen with only her beauty as a weapon. Consider, then, whether or not Lothario had good reason to be afraid.

But what he did was lean his elbow on the arm of his chair, and his cheek onto his open palm and, asking Camila to forgive his discourtesy, told her he needed to sleep a bit, until Anselmo came home. Camila replied that it would be better to sleep in the drawing room than in a chair, and suggested he go into the parlor and sleep there. Lothario refused, and remained where he was, sleeping, until Anselmo returned. Finding Camila in her own room, and Lothario asleep, Anselmo (who'd been later than he'd said) thought they'd already had their chance to talk, and even to take a nap, and he couldn't wait for Lothario to wake up so they could go for a walk and Anselmo could ask him how things had gone.

It went as he wished: Lothario woke up, and they went out for a walk, whereupon Anselmo asked his questions and Lothario answered that it had seemed to him unwise to be fully open, this first time, so he'd done nothing more than praise Camila for her beauty, saying that all over the city people were talking of nothing but her loveliness and her good sense, which struck him as a good way to begin, gaining her good will and thus preparing her, the next time, to listen to him with pleasure — working, in short, as the devil works when he wants to trick someone who might be watching out for his coming, changing himself from an angel of darkness into an angel of light, decking himself out in virtue until, finally, he can reveal his true identity and proceed with his evil plans (if his trick goes undetected). All of this delighted Anselmo, who declared that he would provide the same opportunity every day, though not always by leaving the house, but simply by finding things he had to do (for he did not want Camila to see what he was up to).

Many days went by without Lothario saying a word to Camila, though he assured Anselmo that he had spoken to her but had never been able to elicit the slightest indication that she would be in any way responsive to anything improper — not a single flicker of a sign, or anything of the sort; indeed, he reported that she'd threatened to tell her husband, if Lothario didn't give up these wicked thoughts.

"That's very good," said Anselmo. "So far Camila hasn't been won over by your words; now we have to find out if she'll resist actions, too, so tomorrow I'll give you two thousand dollars in gold, and you can offer that to her, or just hand it right over, and I'll give you another two thousand so you can buy jewels to work her up with, for women, and especially beautiful women (no matter how chaste they may be), like to be well dressed and look elegant — but if she resists this temptation I'll be satisfied and you won't have to go to any more trouble."

Lothario replied that, having begun the thing, he would see it through to the end, though he could already see how weary and beaten he was going to be. The next day he got the four thousand dollars in gold, which to him represented four thousand problems, because he had no idea what sort of new lie he ought to invent, but he finally decided to tell her husband that Camila was just as resistant to bribes and pledges as she was to words, and there was no point to trying anything more, because it was all a great waste of time.

But fate, which arranges things its own way, now decreed that, having left Lothario alone with Camila, as he had done many times before, Anselmo this time hid himself in an adjoining room and watched and listened through the keyhole, so he could see what they did, but what he saw was that, in more than thirty minutes, Lothario did not say a single word to Camila, nor would he speak to her if he were there an entire century, which made him realize that everything his friend had told him about Camila's responses had been pure fiction, mere lies. And to confirm this he emerged from his hiding place and, taking Lothario aside, asked him how it was going and what state of mind Camila was in. Lothario replied that he simply couldn't go on with all this, because she had answered him so harshly and unpleasantly that he hadn't the heart to try saying anything more to her.

"Ah!" said Anselmo, "Lothario, Lothario, how badly you've repaid all you owe me, and all I've entrusted to you! I was watching you, just now, through the keyhole, and I saw how you didn't say a word to Camila, which tells me you haven't said anything to her from the very beginning — and if that's true, as it is obviously is, why have you been deceiving me? why are you trying so hard to deprive me of this pathway toward the knowledge I so desperately crave?"

Anselmo said no more, but he had already said enough to embarrass and confuse Lothario, who swore, almost as if it were a matter of honor for him to have been caught telling a lie, that from this point on he would make it his business to do what his friend wanted, without any more lying, as Anselmo would see for himself if he cared to spy on Camila again — though he wouldn't have to worry, because Lothario intended to proceed in a fashion that would render any suspicion unnecessary. Anselmo believed him, and in order to smooth his friend's path decided to leave home for a week or more, to visit another of his friends, who lived in a village not far from the city, arranging for the latter to send him a genuine invitation, so he'd have a reason for leaving his wife alone.

Oh miserable, sorely mistaken Anselmo! What are you doing? What are you trying to do? What are you bringing to pass? Consider how you're acting against yourself, planning your own dishonor, setting up your own damnation. Camila is a good wife to you; you enjoy her in peace and tranquility; your enjoyment has no enemies; her ambitions reach no further than the walls of your house; for her you're the sun shining on high, the center and sum of all her desires, the fulfillment of everything she wants, and the scale by which she measures herself, constantly adjusting her will both to yours and to Heaven's. For if the rich mine of her honor, and her beauty, and her modesty, and the care of her spirit is freely offered to you, and this gift brings you everything you long for, why should you wish to dig still deeper, hunting for new lodes of ore and treasures no man has ever seen, but risking the collapse of everything you already have, since, in the end, it's all propped up by nothing more than the fragile timbers of her natural weakness? Consider that he who hunts the impossible may in perfect justice find himself denied that which is possible, as the poet says, and says better:

> I hunt life in death,
> Sickness is where I seek health,
> I search for freedom in jail,
> Hunt roads where all guides fail,
> Think traitors tell loyal tales.
> So Fate, knowing I expect
> Nothing good or useful, wrecks
> My life, and Heaven smiles,
> Since whatever I want is an idle
> Dream, and nothing I want is real.

Anselmo left for his friend's village the very next day, having told Camila that, while he was away, Lothario would come to take care of the house and to dine with her, and she was to treat him as she would her own husband. Camila was upset at the order her husband had given her, being a wise and modest wife, and told Anselmo that in her opinion no one, if he was absent, should occupy his seat at the head of his own table, and if he spoke thus because he didn't think she could take care of the house herself he ought, at least, to give her a chance to prove that she could, so he could learn from such an experiment if still more supervision were required. Anselmo answered that he had told her what he wanted and what she had to do was bow her head and obey him. Camila said it would be done as he wished, though it would be against her will.

So Anselmo left, and the next day Lothario arrived at the house, and Camila welcomed him with genuine, modest warmth, but managed never to be alone with him, being always surrounded by her maids and other servants, and in particular a young woman named Leonela, of whom she was very fond, because she had grown up with her mistress in Camila's parents' house and, when Camila had married Anselmo, she'd taken Leonela with her. In the first three days of Anselmo's absence Lothario never spoke to his friend's wife, though it would have been possible when the tablecloth was removed and all the servants hurried off to eat their own dinners, as Camila had instructed them to do. Even Leonela, who never left her mistress' side, had been ordered to dine before Camila did, but Leonela was more interested in other things and, needing a few hours and a convenient place to take her pleasure, didn't always do as her mistress ordered; she left them quite alone, as if that was what she'd been instructed to do. But Camila's modest presence, the composure in her face, and indeed her whole bearing was enough to put a brake on Lothario's tongue.

But at the same time, the good that came from Camila's abundant virtue, and which kept him silent, also exposed them to still greater danger, for although his tongue might be silent his mind was free to roam, and it had plenty of opportunity to reflect, item by item, on every aspect of Camila's extraordinary goodness and beauty — truthfully, sufficient to turn a statue, much less a heart of flesh and blood, to thoughts of love.

Given this time and opportunity when he might have been talking to her, Lothario looked at her and thought how worthy of love she was, and this then began, bit by bit, to erode his concern for Anselmo, and he wished a thousand times over he could leave the city and go somewhere where Anselmo would never see him, and he would not see Camila, but the pleasure he took in just looking at her kept him where he was. He tried as hard as he could, struggling with himself to push away this pleasure of looking at her. He blamed no one else for this foolishness; he accused himself of being a false friend, and even a bad Christian; he argued with himself and made comparisons with his friend, and it all ended in the decision that Anselmo's madness and arrogance were worse than his own faithlessness, so that if he could excuse himself for what he was thinking of doing as well before God as among men, he needn't worry about being punished for his sins.

So, finally, the combination of Camila's beauty and her goodness, and the opportunity which her stupid husband had himself placed in their hands, stole away Lothario's loyalty to his friend, and no longer considering anything but where his pleasure led him, and after three days of Anselmo's absence and a continuous struggle against his desires, Lothario began to woo Camila, and so wildly and with such heated words that she was astonished and could do nothing but rise and go to her room without speaking to him. But Lothario wasn't discouraged by her curtness, for hope and love are always born together; it only made him think still better of her. And she, finding in Lothario what she had never expected to find there, didn't know what to do. But since it seemed to her neither safe nor proper to give him another opportunity to speak to her, she decided to send her husband a letter, which she despatched by one of her servants that very night, and which read as follows:

Chapter Thirty-Four

— which continues The Story of the Man Who Couldn't Keep from Prying

Just as it is usually said that an army doesn't look like much without its general, nor a castle without its lord, so I say that it does not look right for a young woman to be without her husband, unless there are good reasons keeping him away. I am so uncomfortable without you, and it is so impossible for me to manage in your absence, that if you don't return at once I will have to seek the shelter of my parents' house, even though I will thus be leaving yours unguarded, for I believe that the guard you have left me — if he merits any such title — is more interested in his own pleasure than in what concerns you: you are a man of too much sense for me to need to say more, nor is it proper that I do so.

Anselmo received this letter and understood from it that Lothario had indeed begun the business, and that Camila must have responded exactly as he would have wished her to, and so, thrilled by the news, he sent Camila an oral reply, informing her that she most certainly should not change her residence, for he would be returning very soon. Camila was surprised at this response, which left her still more perplexed than she had been, because now she dared neither remain in her own home nor go to her parents', since if she remained her virtue was endangered, and if she left she would be going against her husband's express command.

And in the end she decided to do what was in fact the worst thing she could have done, namely, not to flee from Lothario's presence, so she didn't have to say anything to the servants, and she began to regret having written to her husband, worried that he might think Lothario had detected her in some bold behavior, and that this had stirred him to no longer treat her with respect, thinking she did not deserve it. But trusting in her own virtue, she entrusted herself to God and His good will, thinking she could silently resist whatever Lothario might say to her, without needing to say anything further to her husband or causing any dispute or trouble. And she even began to wonder how she might find some excuse for Lothario, when her husband asked her why she'd written him that letter. Thinking such thoughts — more honorable than either accurate or useful — she found herself, the next day, listening to Lothario woo her so ardently that her resistance began to weaken, and modesty began to have trouble controlling her eyes, which longed to give some sign of the loving sympathy his words and his tears had roused in her breast. Lothario saw all this, and it still more enflamed his desire.

It seemed to him, in short, that he had to take the advantage Anselmo's absence had given him and besiege that fortress, and so, wielding praises of her beauty he attacked her vanity, for nothing conquers and brings down beauty's fortified towers, which are bastions of vanity, like vanity itself, pressed forward by flattery's tongue. And, in a word, he worked so skillfully to tunnel through the rock of her integrity, using all the tools at his disposal, that even had Camila been forged of brass he would have brought her to the ground. He wept, he pleaded, he tempted, he adored, he swore, he deceived with such warmth and passion, such proofs of sincerity, that he totally destroyed Camila's virtue and won what he least expected and most wanted.

Camila was conquered, Camila fell, but is it any wonder, since Lothario's friendship too had come toppling down? The proof is clear: passion will always defeat us, unless we flee from it, nor can anyone take up arms against so powerful a foe, for we need divine strength to resist human urgings. Only Leonela knew her mistress' weakness, which the two disloyal friends and new lovers could not conceal. Lothario had no interest in telling Camila about her husband's scheme, nor that it was Anselmo who had brought things to such a pass, for he did not want her to think less of his love and feel that he had seduced her casually, blindly, not knowing what he was doing.

Not too long afterward, Anselmo came home, and never noticed that his house was missing, now, what he had so little regarded and yet so highly valued. He went to see Lothario, and found him at his own house; they embraced, and then Anselmo asked what word his friend would give him: was he to live or was he to die?

"The news, oh Anselmo, my friend," said Lothario, "is that you have a wife worthy to be the model and crown of all good women. Everything I said to her was carried away by the air; my temptations meant nothing to her; she would not accept my gifts; when I pretended to weep, she laughed in my face. In short, just as Camila is the very incarnation of beauty, so too she is a treasurehouse in which chastity dwells alongside modesty and courtesy, and indeed all the virtues which a good woman can enjoy and be praised for. Let me give you back your money, my friend, which I've kept for you, for I had no need of it: your Camila's virtue would never yield to such vulgar things as presents and promises. You can rest content, Anselmo; you need test her no further and, having walked dry and untouched across the sea of troubles and suspicions which women can and do create, you should not once again launch yourself onto that ocean of problems, nor risk, with yet another pilot, the worth and soundness of the barque given you, by Heaven, for your journey across this world, but recognize that you're in a sure harbor and moor yourself with the anchor of clear thought, and stay there, now, until the time comes to pay that debt from which no human generosity can ever be excused."

Anselmo was delighted with what Lothario told him, giving his words as much credit as if they'd been spoken by an oracle. But in spite of that, he begged him not to consider the business concluded, if only out of curiosity and as a diversion, though from now on there was no point to Lothario working quite so hard at it. All Anselmo wanted was for him to write a poem in praise of Camila, calling her Chloris, and he'd explain to Camila that Lothario was in love with a lady to whom he'd given that name, so he could extol her with all the propriety she deserved. But if it was too much trouble for Lothario to write the poem, said Anselmo, he'd do it for him.

"That won't be necessary," said Lothario, "because I'm not on such poor terms with the Muses that they don't visit me, now and then. Tell

Camila this pretense about my being in love, and I'll write the poem —
and if it's not as good as the subject deserves, I'll at least have done my
best."

So the arrogant man and his false friend were agreed and, when Anselmo went home, he asked Camila what she'd already been surprised he
hadn't asked her, namely, why she'd written the letter he'd received from
her. Camila replied that it had seemed to her as if Lothario were looking
at her somewhat more boldly than when her husband was at home, but
she'd been mistaken and decided it had only been her imagination, for
Lothario was avoiding her and trying to keep them from being left alone.
Anselmo told her that she could rest assured, for he happened to know
that his friend was in love with one of their city's noblest young ladies,
whose praises he sang under the name of Chloris — but even were that
not the case, she had nothing to fear from so good and loyal a friend as
Lothario. All the same, if Lothario had not told Camila about this pretended love for Chloris, which he had concocted for Anselmo so he could
go on singing Camila's praises, she would surely have fallen into the desperate pit of jealousy, but being forewarned she took the sudden news
calmly.

The three of them dining together, the next day, Anselmo asked his
friend to recite the poem he'd written to his beloved Chloris — for, since
Camila did not know who she was, it was safe to say whatever Lothario
wanted to.

"And even if your wife did know the lady," replied Lothario, "I would
hide nothing from her, because a lover who praises his lady's beauty and
criticizes her cruelty cannot possibly damage her reputation, but, be that
as it may, here is a sonnet I wrote, yesterday, about Chloris' ingratitude,
and it goes like this:

> In the deep silence of night, when
> Dreams come to mortal men,
> The poor tale of my plentiful woes
> Can be told to Heaven, and to Chloris, who knows
> Them. And when the dawn slowly rises
> Through rosy doors in western skies,
> It will find me here, my broken sighs
> Renewing this battle of ancient foes.
> And when the sun, from his starry throne,
> Beams down his midday rays, my cries
> Will only come harder, and double my moans.
> And even night will find me alone
> And sadly singing my fatal song
> To a blind Heaven and a Chloris without eyes."

Camila liked the poem immensely, but Anselmo liked it even more,
praising it and exclaiming that a lady who failed to respond to such plain
truth-telling was surely wantonly cruel. To which Camila said:

"Then do all these lovesick poets speak the truth?"

"Not as poets," answered Lothario, "but as lovers their words cannot
help but say less than they really mean."

"That's absolutely right," said Anselmo, determined to make Camila listen to Lothario's ideas, for she was as unaware of her husband's trickery as she was now deeply in love with his friend.

And then, taking delight in everything Lothario did, and understanding that his longings, like his poems, were for her, and that she was the real Chloris, she asked him, if he had any other poems in hand, to recite them.

"Yes, I do," answered Lothario, "but I don't think this one is as good as the first — or, to put it more accurately, I think it's somewhat worse. But you can judge for yourself, because this is how it goes:

> My death, I know, is a fact, but whether or not
> You believe this truth, it is true — as true, oh cruel,
> Ungrateful lady! as my corpse stretched on this spot
> At your feet, before I could come to regret your rule.
> And if I were lost in that empty world, forever
> Cold, void of life, and glory, and kindness,
> If my breast were opened you'd see what in life you'd never
> Liked to show me: your beautiful face's likeness.
> And deep in my heart I guard this lovely idol,
> Ready for the hard ending that love leads to,
> And that you, my love, have sown the bitter seed to.
> Oh pity the sailor who gropes through waters wild
> And dark, through unknown seas and perilous ways,
> Knowing no north, no port, but endless haze!"

Anselmo praised this poem just as much as the first one, thus adding link after link to the chain he was winding around his own dishonor, for whatever Lothario might do to betray him, he would declare himself honored and ensure that, with every step Camila took toward the depths of her disgrace, she would hear her own husband declaring that, to him, she was ascending toward the very summit of virtue, the absolute height of a well-deserved good reputation.

There came a day when, finding herself alone with her maid, Camila said to her:

"I'm ashamed to see, Leonela my good friend, how exceedingly little I must have thought of myself, not arranging that Lothario had to wait to enjoy that complete possession which I freely and so quickly gave him. I worry that he'll think me too fast, too fickle, forgetting how strongly he worked to keep me from resisting him."

"Don't worry about that, my lady," replied Leonela, "because it doesn't matter, and a gift isn't worth less when it's quickly given, if you give something good and worthy of being cherished. People say, you know, that 'He who gives quickly, gives twice.'"

"But they also say," Camila answered, "that what doesn't cost much is worth even less."

"That doesn't apply to you," said Leonela, "because, according to what I hear, love sometimes flies and sometimes walks; it runs fast here, but goes slowly there; sometimes it's tepid and sometimes it burns; some people are wounded and some killed; at one and the same time you can begin to feel desire and reach its end; love can encircle a stronghold, in the morning, and by that night have it surrender, for nothing can hold out against it. And that being how it is, what are you frightened of, why are you worried, when everything that happened to you must have happened to Lothario as well, love having chosen my lord's absence as its instrument for conquering us? It was thus forced to finish what it had set out to do, before Anselmo could come back and, simply by being here, leave the task undone. For opportunity is the best agent love can have, in fulfilling its desires: it makes constant use of opportunity, particularly when it first begins its work. I understand this perfectly well, and more from experience than from hearing it talked of, and some day I'll explain it all to you, my lady, for you and I are both women and of the same flesh and blood. And what's more, my lady Camila, you neither surrendered nor gave yourself so quickly as all that, for first you could see his very soul in Lothario's eyes, in his words and his sighs and all the gifts he gave you, and you saw exhibited there, as in his many virtues, just how worthy he was of being loved. And this being so, don't let all these misgivings and finicky notions trouble your mind, but be confident that Lothario values you as you value him, and be happy and well satisfied that, having been caught in love's noose, it's one distinctly worthy of having snared you. Not only do you have the four S's that all good lovers are supposed to have [*solo, solícito, sabio, secreto* = unattached, attentive, sensible, secret], but you have a whole alphabet: just listen, and you'll see how I can recite it by heart. Your lover — as far as I can tell — is

Grateful [*Agradecido*]
Good [*Bueno*]
A Gentleman [*Caballero*]
Generous [*Dadivoso*]
In Love [*Enamorado*]
Steadfast [*Firme*]
Gallant [*Gallardo*]
Honest [*Honrado*]
Distinguished [*Ilustre*]
Loyal [*Leal*]
Young [*Mozo*]
Noble [*Noble*]
Modest [*Onesto*]
Renowned [*Principal*]
Solid [*Quantioso*]
Rich [*Rico*]
— and all the S's I've said already — and then
Close-mouthed [*Tácito*]
True [*Verdadero*]
— and X isn't right for him, because it's a harsh letter —
— and we've already said Y [that is, I]
and Z, Zealous for your honor [*Zelador*]."

Camila laughed at her maid's ABC, understanding that Leonela was more experienced in love's affairs than she'd said, and Leonela admitted as much, informing her mistress that she was engaged in a liaison with a well-born young man from their city, which information upset Camila, who was worried that any such business might well endanger her own honor. She inquired if things had gone beyond mere words. With remarkably little embarrassment, and a good deal of boldness, Leonela replied that indeed they had. Who doubts that, when the mistresses slip, the maids lose all sense of shame, for seeing their ladies stumble why should they worry themselves about wobbling, or about admitting it?

All Camila could do was beg her maid not to tell her lover what her mistress was up to, and then try to manage things as quietly as possible, so neither Anselmo nor Lotario noticed. Leonela assured her she would, but the way she lived up to her promise made reality of Camila's worst fears. For this lewd and insolent Leonela, seeing that her mistress no longer behaved as once she had, was impudent enough to allow her own lover into the house, confident that even if her mistress saw him she would not dare to say a word, and this is only one of the misfortunes ladies bring about when they sin, making themselves into their own servants' slaves, forced to conceal their servants' immorality and infamy, as Camila was, for even though she saw many, many times that Leonela had taken her lover into a room right in her mistress' house, she not only didn't dare scold the maid, but had to help conceal this lover of hers, removing every obstacle, so her husband would see nothing.

But she couldn't keep Lotario from seeing the fellow leaving, once, at dawn, and though at first, not knowing who this man could possibly be, Lotario thought he must be seeing a ghost when he saw him walking off down the street, his cloak up over his face, all muffled up and cautious, Lotario threw off such silly notions — and fell right into another one, which, had not Camila protected them, might have ruined them all. For it was Lotario's idea that the man he had seen making off, so dishonorably, from Anselmo's house, had not been there on Leonela's account, nor did he so much as think of Leonela: all he could imagine was that Camila, who had been so unresistant and fickle with him, had now been the same way with someone else — for when a woman falls, she reaps this misfortune too, that she loses her good name even with the very man to whom, begged and implored, wheedled and coaxed, she's yielded herself, who can now believe even more readily that she's yielded herself to others, and is more than prepared to believe, implicitly, any and every suspicion that crosses his mind. Apparently, whatever good sense Lotario possessed, at this point it deserted him; he could no longer remember any of his clever speeches; for without either hesitation or thought, and in a jealous rage that gnawed at his entrails, he went straight to Anselmo, dying for revenge on Camila (who had done nothing to offend him), and said to his friend:

"I have to tell you, Anselmo, that I've been struggling with myself for days, trying to keep from telling you what it's clearly neither possible nor right that I withhold from you. So understand that Camila cannot hold out against me any longer, she's ready to do whatever I want her to; and if I've taken my time about telling you this, it's been to see if there was anything fanciful about it, or if she was just trying to test me and find out if the amorous attentions I've pressed on her, with your agreement, have been sincere or not. And I also thought that, were she what she ought to be, and what both of us have indeed believed she was, she would have informed you of those attentions, but having now seen how she's kept this from you, I am persuaded she was telling me the truth, promising that the next time you were away she would receive me in the spare room where you keep your valuables" — and it was in fact there that Camila usually did receive him. "But I don't want you rushing into vengeance, since it's only in thought that the sin has been committed, and it might very well be that before the time comes Camila will change her mind, and repentance get the upper hand. And since you've always followed my advice, at least to some extent, please do so now, so there won't be any mistakes and, with proper warning, you'll be able to enjoy whatever revenge you like. Pretend you're going away for two or three days, just as you've done before, but arrange to hide yourself in the store room, where all the tapestries and other things you can cover yourself with will make concealment very easy, and then you'll see with your own eyes, as I will see with mine, what Camila chooses to do, and if it's the wickedness you were so afraid of, once, you yourself can silently, wisely, and sensibly be your own executioner."

Anselmo was completely swept away by his friend's words, which left him stunned and bewildered, for they had fallen on him when he least expected, believing as he had that Camila had triumphantly prevailed over Lothario's pretended seduction; indeed, Anselmo had already begun to glory in her victory. He could not speak, at first, staring down at the ground without moving an eyelash, and then finally said:

"You have done everything, Lothario, that I expected of your friendship; I have no choice but to follow your advice in everything; do as you think best and keep this unexpected development to yourself."

Lothario promised that he would and, as he took his leave, was immediately sorry for everything he'd said, realizing how stupidly he'd acted, for he could have sought revenge on Camila without being thus cruel and dishonorable. He cursed himself for a blockhead, was furious at his fickle, hasty decision, and could not for the life of him figure out how he could undo what he'd done, how he could find some reasonable way out. So, in the end, he decided to tell Camila everything, and since he had plenty of opportunity, found himself alone with her that very day, but she, the moment she saw she could confide in him, spoke up:

"Let me tell you, dear Lothario, that something has happened which so oppresses my heart that, truly, it feels as if it will burst, and it will be a miracle if it doesn't, for Leonela has become so shameless that, every night, she hides one of her lovers right here in this house, and stays with him until dawn, thus putting my reputation at terrible risk, for my good name is at the mercy of anyone who sees him leaving here at such an ungodly hour. And what pains me most is that I can't scold her or even quarrel with her, for her knowledge of our relationship keeps me from saying anything about hers, and I'm afraid something terrible is going to happen."

When she'd first begun to speak, Lothario had thought it a trick to blame Leonela rather than herself for the man he had seen leaving the house, but seeing how she wept, and suffered, and begged him for help, he realized she was telling the truth and, understanding this, became even more confused and sorry about the whole business. All the same, he told Camila not to worry, that he would find a way to check Leonela's insolence. And he also told her what, driven by a wild rage of jealousy, he'd said to her husband, and that Anselmo had agreed to hide in the store room, to see for himself how little faithfulness Camila still retained. He begged her pardon for this madness, asking her what could be done to cure it and how they might escape the complicated labyrinth into which his unfortunate words had plunged them.

Camila was shocked, hearing what Lothario told her, and scolded him angrily as well as wisely and sensibly, criticizing him in strong terms for his unjust thoughts, as well as for the foolish and exceedingly unfortunate decision he had made, but since women are naturally more quick-witted than men, both for good and evil (though not when they deliberately set out to reason things through), Camila immediately came up with a solution to what had seemed an insoluble problem, telling Lothario to go ahead and arrange for Anselmo to hide as he had said he would, the very next day, for she meant to turn all this hiding and seeking to their advantage, making it nicely possible, from then on, for them to enjoy themselves without fear of interruption, and though she did not tell her lover precisely what she had in mind, she warned him, once Anselmo was hidden, to come the moment Leonela called to him, and whatever Camila said to him he must be sure to reply as if he had no knowledge of Anselmo's presence. Lothario protested that she had to come right out and tell him what she was planning, so he could more safely and more sensibly do whatever he might see was necessary.

"I assure you," said Camila, "there's nothing else to worry about, and all you have to do is answer the questions I'll ask you" — for Camila didn't want to explain it all to him in advance, concerned that he might not agree with what seemed to her such a good idea, and might either do or try to figure out how to do something quite different and not nearly as effective.

So off went Lothario, and the next day Anselmo, pretending that he had to visit the friend who lived in a nearby village, set out on his trip and then came back and hid himself, which he was quite readily able to do, because Camila and Leonela deliberately made it as simple as they possibly could.

Anselmo, hiding himself away, felt as edgy as a man expecting to see, right in front of his eyes, a post-mortem performed on the very bowels of his honor, fancying himself on the brink of losing that supreme blessing he had always thought he possessed in his beloved Camila. Having made sure that Anselmo was safely in his hiding place, Camila and Leonela went into the store room and, almost as soon as she crossed the threshold, Camila said, with a great sigh:

"Oh Leonela, my dear friend! Mightn't it be better, before I actually do what, to keep you from trying to stop me, I cannot bear even to describe — mightn't it be better for you to take this dagger of Anselmo, which I had you obtain for me, and pierce my wicked breast? But no, don't, for why should I suffer the punishment for someone else's sin? I must find out, first, what Lothario's bold, dishonest eyes have seen in me, to cause him, thus insolently, to openly declare such a wicked desire as he has now revealed, in flagrant disregard both of his own friend and of my honor. Go to that window, Leonela, and call him, for I have no doubt he's out there in the street, waiting and hoping to carry out his wicked plan. But it will be *my* plan — cruel, but also honorable — that carries the day."

"Ah, my lady!" replied the wise and well-prepared Leonela. "What do you plan to do with that dagger? Are you, by any chance, thinking of departing this life, or of killing Lothario? Whatever you choose will deprive you of your good name and your reputation. How much better to disguise your sense of insult and not give this wicked man a chance to enter this house, where he will find us alone. Consider, my lady, that we are weak women, and he's a man, and determined, and since he would come to us with a purpose so evil, so wildly passionate, it might be that before you could do whatever it is you plan to do, he'd be able to accomplish what would be worse than murder. Oh, curses on my lord Anselmo, who has been so misguided and given this shameless man the run of his house! And my lady, even supposing you do kill him, as I think you mean to, what would we do with him, once he's dead?"

"What, my friend?" answered Camila. "We'll leave him for Anselmo to bury, for it would be only right that he find it rewarding to hide his own shame deep in the earth. Call him, let it be done with, for the longer I wait to exact my well-deserved revenge, the more I offend against the loyalty I owe to my husband."

Hearing all this, Anselmo changed his view of things with every word Camila spoke, but when he understood that she planned to kill Lothario he thought of coming out and revealing himself, for he could not allow such a thing to happen, but he held back, wanting to see where such spirit and determined modesty would take her, intending to appear when she had to be stopped.

Just then Camila fainted dead away and, laying her across a bed that just happened to be there, Leonela began to weep bitterly, and to cry out:

"Oh, what a miserable, unlucky wretch I am, finding myself with the very flower of modesty dying, right here in my arms, the very crown of righteous womanhood, the incarnation of chastity . . . !"

She went on like this, and anyone hearing her could only have taken her for the most compassionate and loyal maidservant in the world, and her mistress for persecuted Penelope reborn. It didn't take Camila long to recover from her swoon and, once she was herself again, she said:

"Leonela, why don't you call that most loyal of all friends ever seen by the sun or covered over by the darkness? Let it be done, swiftly, hurry, run, don't let any delay smother the fire burning in me, or the just vengeance I long for dribble away in mere threats and curses."

"I'm going, I'll call him, my lady," said Leonela, "but first you must give me that dagger so that, in my absence, you won't do something with it that would make all those who hold you so dear spend the rest of their lives weeping."

"I won't do it, oh Leonela my friend," replied Camila, "I promise you, for though you may think me foolish and bold for the sake of my honor,

I don't need to go to extremes the way Lucretia did, who killed herself, they say, even though she'd done nothing wrong, and without first killing the man who'd brought about her downfall. I'll die, if death comes to me, but I must be revenged, I must repay the man whose insolence — for which I am so utterly blameless — has brought me to these tears."

It took a good deal of pleading before Leonela would go and call Lothario, but she finally went, and while she was gone Camila went on speaking, as if to herself:

"Lord help me! Would it have been better to send Lothario packing, as I've already done so many times, than to let him get it into his head (as I've now done) that he can think of me as unchaste and wicked — at least for these moments, while I wait to undeceive him? Yes, surely it would have been better, but simply to let him escape, without any difficulty, after his evil passion has brought us to this, ah, that would have left me unavenged, and my husband's honor unsatisfied. Let the traitor pay with his life for what, lustfully, he meant to do; let the world know (if it ever comes to know anything of this) not only that Camila was faithful to her husband, but that she took vengeance on the man who sought to offend him. Still, after all, I wonder if it mightn't be better to tell all this to Anselmo — but I already let him know about it, when he was off in the village and I wrote him that letter, and if he wouldn't act against the evil, then, I think it must be that, out of sheer goodness and trust, he won't — he can't — bring himself to believe that such an old and reliable friend could even contemplate dishonoring him, because at first I didn't believe it myself, not for a long time, and I wouldn't ever have believed it if Lothario's impudence hadn't reached the point where it was obvious, because he was openly giving me presents and promising me all sorts of things and always shedding tears. But why do I bother saying these things? Does brave determination need to seek advice? Certainly not. Away with traitorous indecision! Rally round me, vengeance! Let my husband's false friend appear, come, stand here, then die, and let it be done with, whatever happens thereafter! I was pure when Heaven entrusted me to Anselmo, and I must leave him pure; at the worst, I will leave him bathed both in my own chaste blood and in that base foulness flowing in the veins of the falsest friend the world has ever seen."

And as she said this she began to walk up and down the room, with the dagger ready in her hand, moving so wildly and unsteadily, and looking so distraught that she seemed to have gone mad and, rather than a delicate woman, to have become a desperate ruffian.

Anselmo watched all this, hiding behind a curtain, and was utterly staggered, thinking he had already seen and heard enough to quench even greater suspicions, and wishing that the final proof of Lothario's appearance could be dispensed with, for he was worried something disastrous might happen, too quickly to be stopped. But as he was about to emerge and show himself, to embrace his wife and end her deception, he held back, seeing Leonela return, leading Lothario by the hand, and Camila, seeing him as well, bent and, with her dagger, marked a deep line on the floor in front of her, exclaiming:

"Listen carefully, Lothario: if by any chance you cross this line, or even come near it, the very moment I see you coming I will pierce my heart with this dagger, here in my hands. And before you say a word to me, I want you to hear something else, too, and then you can say whatever you want to. First, Lothario, I want you to tell me if you know Anselmo, my husband, and what you think of him, and second, whether you also know me. Speak without embarrassment, and don't stand there thinking out your reply, because these aren't hard questions."

Lothario was not so dullwitted that, from the moment she'd instructed him to have Anselmo in hiding, he hadn't been able to figure out what she was up to, and he fell in with her plan so discreetly, so easily, that the two of them made their fabrication look even truer than true. His answer to Camila went like this:

"I never thought, oh lovely Camila, you'd bring me here to inquire about matters so alien to what's filling my own mind. If this is meant to still further delay my promised reward, you might have waited even longer, for what we so much long for becomes wearisome, when its fulfillment comes so tantalizingly close. But to keep you from declaring that I've refused to answer you, let me say that I do indeed know your husband Anselmo, and that we've known one another since we were boys; there's no need to repeat what you know so well of our friendship, for I've no desire to bear witness to the offense which love — that potent excuse for even greater sins — has forced me to commit against it. As for you, you know I think every bit as well of you as he does, and for no jewel less precious would I, otherwise, have had to act thus directly against both my own being and the holy laws of true friendship, which now, under the influence of such a powerful enemy as love, I have broken and violated."

"If you admit that," replied Camila, "you who have become the mortal enemy of everything that rightly deserves to be called love, how can you dare parade yourself in front of me, knowing perfectly well that I am the very mirror in which he sees himself, and in which you too should gaze, to see how little reason you have to injure him? But now I see, oh miserable me! and from the account you've given me, why you've paid so little heed to what you owe yourself, for I see it has to have been some unconscious act of mine, which I ought not to call dishonesty, for it could have been nothing I'd do deliberately, but just some carelessness of the sort women commit, all unknowingly, when they don't think they need to be quite so careful as they usually are. And if that's not it, tell me, oh traitor! when I ever responded to your pleas with a single word, a single sign, which could arouse in you even the shadow of a hope that I intended to gratify your infamous desires? When were all your loving words not rejected and strongly, nay harshly, scorned? When were your multitudinous promises, and your even more bounteous gifts, ever taken seriously or accepted? But since I believe no one can long persevere in such amorous longing without being sustained by some sort of hope, I admit that I must somehow be responsible for your insolence, for clearly some accidental carelessness of mine has kept your hopes alive, which is why I long to punish myself and make myself suffer the punishment your sin deserves. And to let you see that, being thus cruel to myself, I cannot be less cruel to you, I wish you to be here, in witness to the sacrifice I plan to make to my noble husband's injured honor, which you have worked so zealously to injure, and I too have offended against, if in fact I have, by not being careful enough to avoid the opportunity for injury, thus seeming to support and even approve of your wicked designs. Let me repeat that this suspicion of having innocently but carelessly spawned these wild ideas of yours, this is what weighs on me most heavily of all, and I wish to punish myself for it with my own hands, for punishment by any other executioner would perhaps make my sin more public. But before that happens I propose, in dying, to also inflict death, and to take with me someone who, by being dead, can quench my need and my desire for revenge, for wherever my soul may go I will surely see the punishment meted out, unflinchingly, by disinterested justice, on the man who put me in this desperate position."

And as she spoke she leapt at Lothario, with unbelievable strength and agility, her dagger bared, so plainly intent on burying it in his chest that he could hardly tell whether she was play-acting or deadly serious, and had to use all his skill and strength to stop her. She played out this wild hoax so vividly and realistically that, to make it seem truly real, she decided to color herself with her own blood, for seeing that she could not get at Lothario, or perhaps pretending she could not, she declared:

"Since Fate will not let me do everything my just desire dictates, I will at least keep it from taking away my own share of that satisfaction."

Then she struggled mightily to free her dagger from Lothario's grip, and did so, after which she aimed the blade where it could not seriously wound her, burying it high on her left side, near the shoulder, and immediately let herself fall to the ground, as if in a faint.

Both Leonela and Lothario were baffled and astonished by all this, and seeing Camila stretched out on the ground, bathed in her own blood, they were not at all sure what had in fact happened. Lothario quickly, fearfully bent to pull out the dagger, holding his breath in terror, but, seeing how slight the wound was, was immediately at ease, once again admiring his beautiful Camila's wisdom, good sense, and wonderful judgment. To assist her in her splendid performance, he began wailing and weeping over her body as if she were truly dead, with a profusion of curses directed not only at himself but also at the man who had been responsible for bringing her to such an end. Knowing indeed that Anselmo was listening, he said things which would make anyone who heard him feel sorrier for him than for Camila herself, even if she were thought dead.

Leonela put her arms around her mistress and lifted her onto a bed, begging Lothario to go and find someone who could tend to Camila in secret; she also asked him to consider how they could best tell Anselmo about his wife's wound, if he should return home before she was well again. He told her she could say whatever she liked, for he was in no condition to give her any useful advice; all he could say was that she had better try to stop the bleeding, for he was going where no one would ever see him again. And giving every sign of being profoundly sad and shaken, he left the house; but when he found himself alone, and where no one could see him, he kept crossing himself, amazed at how clever Camila was and how effectively Leonela had acted her part. He didn't think Anselmo could help believing his wife a second Portia,[1] and was anxious to see his friend again, so they could both celebrate the deftest jumbling of lies and truths anyone could possibly imagine.

As he had instructed her to do, Leonela took care of her mistress' bleeding, which flowed just strongly enough to validate the hoax, washing out the wound with a bit of wine and binding it up as best she knew how, all the while saying things that, even had nothing been said before, would have been more than enough to persuade Anselmo that, in Camila, he had the absolute model of womanly modesty.

Camila added her own words to her maid's, calling herself a faint-hearted coward, since her courage had failed her just when she needed it most, in order to take her away from this life which she thought so horrid. She asked Leonela's advice: should she, or should she not, tell her beloved husband everything that had happened? To which the maid replied that no, she should not, because Anselmo would feel himself obliged to seek vengeance on Lothario, which would involve him in a terrible risk; a good wife had to be careful not to involve her husband in quarrels, and to keep him out of them to the extent she possibly could.

Camila answered that she thought her maid was right, and she would follow her advice, but in any case it would be useful to decide what to tell Anselmo about how she'd been wounded, for he could not help seeing it, to which Leonela replied that, even in jest, she simply didn't know how to tell a lie.

"How then can I, my sister?" asked Camila. "For to save my life I wouldn't know how to even begin constructing a lie, or keeping one up. If we can't think of some way out of this, it would be better to tell him the bare truth than to get ourselves tangled up in a falsehood."

"Don't worry, my lady," replied Leonela. "Between now and tomorrow I'll think what to tell him, and maybe, the wound being where it is, you can cover it so he doesn't see it, and Heaven may smile on such righteous and honorable ideas as ours. Calm yourself, dear lady, and try to get yourself under control, so my lord won't find you so excited, and leave the rest to me, and to God, who always helps those who mean well."

The performance of this tragedy, in which his honor died, had had an attentive audience in Anselmo, listening and watching a drama performed so wildly and fervently that the actors seemed to have truly become the characters they were in fact only pretending to be. He longed for night to come, so he would have a chance to leave the house and go visit his good friend Lothario, and the two of them could congratulate themselves on the precious pearl he had discovered, while proving his wife's virtue. The two women were careful to make it easy for him to escape and, not neglecting his opportunity, he got out of the house and immediately went in search of Lothario, and found him — and who could adequately describe the embraces Anselmo gave his good friend, the joyous things he said to him, and how extravagantly he praised Camila? Lothario listened to all this, unable to show any satisfaction whatever, for he kept thinking

---

1. The first Portia was the wife of Brutus, who assassinated Julius Caesar in 44 B.C. After her husband's death, she committed suicide by swallowing hot coals.

how utterly deluded his friend was, and how unjustly Anselmo had been wronged. Anselmo could see that Lothario was not overjoyed, but he thought it was because his friend had left Camila wounded and knew he had been responsible, so among the other things Anselmo told him was not to worry about what had happened to her, since the wound was surely not serious, the two women having agreed to try to hide it from him, so there was really nothing to worry about and Lothario could afford to rejoice and be every bit as happy as Anselmo himself was — for was it not entirely due to his good friend's cleverness and ingenuity that, now, Camila's happy husband had been swept to the highest heights of happiness he could ever have dreamed of? Anselmo declared he could think of nothing more fitting than to occupy himself with writing poems in Camila's praise, so future generations would never be able to forget her. Lothario endorsed this noble decision, saying that, for his part, he would be glad to help raise so glorious a monument.

And there was Anselmo, the most delightfully hoodwinked man the world can ever have seen: thinking he was conducting the very instrument of his glorification, he led back to his house, with his own hand, the sole cause of his reputation's ruin. Camila received Lothario with an ostentatiously averted face, though her heart was smiling. This swindle went on for quite some time, until after several months Fortune gave her wheel a spin and brought into the open the evil it had taken so much skill to cover over, and Anselmo's unreasonable curiosity cost him his life.

Chapter Thirty-Five

— the end of The Story of the Man Who Couldn't Keep from Prying

There wasn't much of the story left to read, when Sancho Panza came running wildly out of the room where Don Quijote had been sleeping, shouting:

"Help, gentlemen! Come help my master, who's up to his ears in the fiercest, hardest combat these eyes of mine have ever seen! My God, but he slashed so furiously at that giant, the Princess Micomicona's enemy, that he chopped his head right off, like a turnip!"

"Brother, what are you talking about?" said the priest, looking up from what remained of the story. "Are you sure you're quite right in the head, Sancho? How the devil could such a thing be, when that particular giant is six thousand miles from here?"

Just then, they heard a great racket, and Don Quijote shouting:

"Hold thief! scoundrel! coward! I've got you now, and your sword's of no use to you!"

And then it seemed as if he were slashing away at the walls. So Sancho said:

"Let's not stand here listening, but go in and either break up the fight or else help my master — though there's surely no need for that, because the giant's got to be dead and already trying to explain his past and all his wicked deeds to God — I saw his blood running out on the ground, and his chopped-off head lying there on its side, and it's as big as a huge wineskin."

"Oh lord kill me," said the innkeeper, hearing this, "if that Don Quijote — or Don Devil! — hasn't been slashing away at some of my good red wineskins, stored in there near his bed, and the wine pouring out must be what this fool thinks is blood."

So he dashed into the room, with everyone else behind him, and they found Don Quijote dressed like nothing the world has ever seen. He was wearing his nightshirt, which wasn't long enough in front to cover his thighs, and in back was a full four inches shorter; his legs were long and exceedingly thin, as hairy as a goat's and not very clean; he had a greasy red nightcap on his head (it belonged to the innkeeper); he'd wrapped around his left arm the blanket from his bed, a blanket Sancho had good reason to dislike (as he himself knew very well); and in his right hand he had his bared sword, with which he was slashing in all directions and shouting as if he'd really been fighting some huge giant. But the best part was that his eyes were closed, because in fact he was still asleep and dreaming that he and the giant were locked in battle, for his imagination had been so over-stimulated by the adventure he was about to undertake that he'd dreamed he was already the King of Micomicón, struggling with his enemy. He'd already slashed up the wineskins so thoroughly, believing he was attacking the giant, that the whole room was flooded with wine. And when the innkeeper saw this he got so angry that he attacked Don Quijote, and began punching him so furiously that, had Cardenio and the priest not pulled him off, the war with the giant would indeed have been over, in spite of which the poor knight never woke up, until the barber fetched a great pot of cold water from the well and drenched Don Quijote with it, which woke him up, though he still couldn't understand what was going on.

Seeing what an abbreviated costume he was wearing, Dorotea declined to enter the room and watch the fight between her champion and his antagonist.

Sancho went looking all over the floor for the giant's head and, when he couldn't find it, said:

"And now I see that everything in this house is enchanted, because the last time, when I found myself in this very same place, I was punched and kicked all over and I could never see who was attacking me, and I never did see anybody, and now I can't find that head anywhere, though I saw it cut off with my very own eyes, and the blood running out of the body like a fountain."

"What blood, what fountain are you talking about," said the innkeeper, "you enemy of God and all His saints? Can't you see, you thief, that the blood and the fountain is just these ripped-open wineskins and the red wine that's swimming all over this room? If I could only see, swimming in Hell, the soul of the man who ripped them open!"

"I don't know anything about it," answered Sancho. "All I know is that, since I haven't found the giant's head, I'm likely to see all my land and my title dissolve away like salt in water."

Sancho awake was even worse than his master asleep: that was what his master's promises had done to him. The innkeeper flew into a rage, seeing the squire's indifference and the master's wicked doings, and swore it wasn't going to be like the last time, when they got away without paying, and whatever the privileges of knighthood might be worth they weren't going to keep him from being paid for every damned thing, not this time, right down to the patches he'd have to have sewed onto his broken wineskins.

The priest was holding Don Quijote's hands, for the knight, thinking he had already completed the adventure, and was standing, now, in front of the Princess Micomicona, was down on his knees, saying to the priest:

"Your highness, oh noble, famous lady, now you can live, from this day on, completely safe and in no danger from this ill-born creature, and I too, from this day on, can be free of the pledge I gave you, since with the help of God on high, and with the favor of her for whom I both live and breathe, I have well and truly fulfilled that pledge."

"Didn't I tell you?" exclaimed Sancho, hearing this. "That wasn't wine talking: just see how my master pickled that giant in salt! Oh, there'll be a bullfight today, all right! I'm as good as a count already."

Who could have kept from laughing at their idiocies, master and servant both? They all laughed — except the innkeeper, who consigned himself to hell. But finally, though it was not easy, the barber and Cardenio and the priest managed to get Don Quijote back into bed, where he fell back asleep, looking completely exhausted. Leaving him where he was, they went out to the front gate, to comfort Sancho Panza for not finding the giant's head, though they found it a good deal harder to soothe the innkeeper, who was enraged at the sudden death of his wineskins. Meanwhile, his wife was yelling and screaming at the top of her lungs:

"It was an evil time and an unlucky hour when this knight errant walked into my house, and I wish I'd never laid eyes on him, he's cost me so much! The last time he ran off without paying for the night he spent here, or his supper, his bed, and for barley and straw for the animals, for him and his squire and an old horse and a donkey, because he said he was a travelling knight, and may God curse him and all the traveling knights in the world, and he said that was why he didn't have to pay us a thing, because that was the way it was all written down in the official tariffs for knights errant. And now, on account of this honored knight, here comes another gentleman and goes off with my donkeytail and then he gives it back to me with I don't know how much damage, all skinned and peeled away, so how can my husband use it? And then, to top it all off, they break my wineskins and spill out my wine — and I wish I could see his blood spill out! But that's what *you* think: by my father's bones and my mother's life they'll pay me penny for penny, or my name's not my name and I'm not my father's daughter!"

In her wild fury the innkeeper's wife said all of this, and more like it, and her good maidservant, Maritornes, helped her. But her daughter kept quiet, just smiling now and then. The priest calmed them all down, promising to make good their losses as best he could, for the wineskins as well as for the wine, and especially for the damage to her donkeytail, which was so very important to her. Dorotea comforted Sancho Panza, telling him that, just as soon as it seemed his master had really cut off the giant's head and she was once more peacefully in possession of her kingdom, she promised to give him the greatest countship the kingdom might hold. This made Sancho feel better, though he swore he'd really and truly seen the giant's head cut off, and in fact the giant had a beard that hung all the way down to his belt buckle, and if the head wasn't anywhere to be found it was because everything that went on in that house was caused by magic, as he had proved the last time they'd taken lodging here. Dorotea said she believed him, but he shouldn't worry, and everything would be fine and it would all turn out exactly as he wanted it to.

With calm restored, the priest wanted to finish reading the story, because he saw there wasn't much left. Cardenio, Dorotea, and all the others begged him to read to the very end and he, wanting to please them all, and also enjoying the reading himself, continued the tale, which went on as follows:

So it happened that Anselmo, thrilled with Camila's goodness and virtue, lived a happy, heedless existence, his wife cleverly making sure to frown at Lothario, so her husband understood her inclinations to be the exact opposite of what they really were, and Lothario, to set the seal on what she was doing, asking his friend to allow him to stay away from the house, since Camila so clearly showed how unhappy she was to see him there, but the totally hoodwinked Anselmo said he couldn't allow that at all, and so in a thousand ways he went on weaving the thread of his dishonor, believing all the time that he was ensuring his happiness.

Meanwhile, Leonela felt so confident and free to take her own pleasure that, at last, she got to the point where she paid no attention to anything else and went galloping full speed ahead, trusting that her mistress would not only cover for her but would even tell her how to most conveniently satisfy herself. At last, one night Anselmo heard footsteps in Leonela's room and, wishing to know who was in there, tried to open the door but found it held shut, which of course made him even more anxious to open it, so he pushed so hard that it opened and he entered just in time to see a man jumping out the window, down to the street, and as he quickly ran to catch him, or to find out who it was, he found himself unable to do either, for Leonela threw her arms around him and said:

"Please, my lord, be calm, don't upset yourself running after the man who jumped out. It's my business — and, in fact, he's my husband."

Anselmo refused to believe her; indeed, in a blind rage, he pulled out his dagger and threatened her, commanding her to tell him the truth or else he would kill her. So terrified that she did not know what she was saying, she said:

"Don't kill me, my lord, because I can tell you things more important than you'd ever believe."

"Then tell me, and quickly," said Anselmo, "or else you're dead."

"I can't, not right now," said Leonela, "I'm too upset. Give me until tomorrow and then you'll find out things from me that will surely astonish you — but believe me, the one who jumped out the window is a young man from this city, and we're engaged to be married."

This relieved Anselmo's mind and persuaded him to wait as she had asked, for he never expected to hear anything against Camila, since he was so utterly satisfied and sure of her virtue, so he left the maid's room, locking Leonela inside and telling her she would not be allowed out until she had told him whatever it was she meant to say.

Then he went straight to Camila, telling her, point by point, everything that had gone on with her maid, including Leonela's promise that she had great and important things to tell him. It's hardly necessary to tell you whether Camila was upset, for she was overwhelmed by fear, truly believing, and with reason, that Leonela would tell him everything she knew about her mistress' unfaithfulness; she was far too afraid to wait and find out if this would indeed be the case so, that very night, as soon as she thought Anselmo was asleep, she collected her best jewels and some money and, totally unobserved, left the house and went to Lothario's, to whom she told everything, begging him to find her a hiding place or else to take her away with him, to where they could be safe from Anselmo. All of which so bewildered Lothario that he was unable to say a word, and still less able to make up his mind what ought to be done.

Finally, he decided to bring her to a convent, where his sister was the prioress. Camila agreed, and just as quickly as the situation demanded, Lothario brought her to the convent and left her there, and immediately left the city himself, telling no one he intended to leave.

At dawn, not noticing that Camila was not sleeping at his side, Anselmo was so anxious to hear what Leonela had to say that he slipped out of bed and went to the room where he had confined her. He opened the door and went in, but Leonela wasn't there; all he found were some knotted-together bed sheets tied to the window, clear indication that she'd let herself down and fled. So he turned and went back to give the news to Camila but, not finding her in her bed or anywhere else in the house, became frightened. He asked the servants about her, but none of them knew what to tell him.

As he was hunting here and there for his wife, he found her jewel boxes wide open and most of the jewels gone, which made him realize both the full extent of his misfortune and that it wasn't Leonela who was responsible for it. So just as he was, sad and thoughtful, without completing his toilette, he went to tell his misery to his friend Lothario. But when he couldn't find him, and Lothario's servants told him their master hadn't been at home that night, and indeed had gone off with all the ready money in the house, Anselmo thought he would go mad. And as if to finish it off, when he went back home he found that none of the servants, male and female alike, were there, and the house stood empty and deserted.

He had no idea what to think, what to say, what to do; bit by bit he felt his sanity slipping away. Thinking about himself deprived at one blow of his wife, his friend, and his servants, he felt utterly alone, abandoned by Heaven, and above all stripped of his honor, for in Camila's absence he saw his own downfall.

After long consideration, he made up his mind, finally, to go to the nearby village where his friend lived, which was where he had stayed so this whole miserable affair could be hatched against him. He locked all the doors, mounted his horse and, his spirits sagging, set out on the road, but had barely ridden half the distance when, his mind tormenting him, he had no choice but to dismount and tie his horse to a tree, at the foot of which he let himself fall, moaning in agony, and there he stayed almost till the sun went down, at which point he saw a mounted man riding toward him, coming from the city, and after greeting him Anselmo asked what was the news from Florence. The city dweller replied:

"The strangest news that anyone there has heard in a long, long time, because everyone is saying that Lothario, rich Anselmo's friend of all friends, who used to live at San Giovanni, last night carried off Camila, Anselmo's wife, and the woman too has disappeared. One of Camila's servants told the whole story, after the mayor found her lowering herself down from the windows of Anselmo's house, using bed sheets. I really don't know all the details; all I know is that the whole city is astonished, for no one could have expected such a thing from two such old, close friends, who were so intimate that they were called 'Los Dos Amigos.'"

"Perhaps," asked Anselmo, "you know what road Lothario and Camila took?"

"I have no idea," answered the city dweller, "though I do know the mayor has been trying hard to find them."

"God be with you, sir," said Anselmo.

"And with you," replied the city dweller, riding on.

Such overwhelmingly miserable news was almost the end of Anselmo — and not simply of his sanity, but his very life. He stood up as best he could and reached his friend's house, and though his misfortune had not reached his friend's ears, as soon as Anselmo rode up, pale, exhausted, and withdrawn, it was obvious that something had gone terribly wrong. Anselmo asked if he might immediately go to bed; he also asked for writing materials. Both requests were granted, and he was left to lie down alone, which was what he'd wanted; he'd even asked that the door be locked. When he found himself alone, the full weight of his misery began beating at him, and he understood perfectly clearly that he'd reached the end, so he set himself to setting down a description of the strange death that had overtaken him, but even as he began to write, and before he could record everything, his breath stopped and life left him, victim of the misery which his unwise curiosity had brought about.

The master of the house, finding that it was late and that Anselmo had not called, thought he'd better go in and see if his friend's illness had grown worse, and found Anselmo stretched out, face down, his body half on the bed and half on the writing desk, a partly inscribed sheet of paper open in front of him and a pen still in his hand. He went over to his guest, having first called to him, and when, taking his hand, he found no response, and felt how cold the body was, he realized that Anselmo was dead. Astonished and terribly upset, he called for everyone to come and see the misfortune with which Anselmo had been afflicted, and then he read what Anselmo had written (for he knew his friend's handwriting), which went as follows:

A stubborn, stupid wish has taken my life. Should Camila happen to hear of my death, let her know that I forgive her, because there was no need for her to perform miracles, nor should I have wanted her to, and since I myself fashioned my own dishonor, there's no reason why . . .

Anselmo had written this far, by which it could be seen that it was at exactly this moment, without being able to finish his explanation, that his life had ended. The next day his friend notified Anselmo's relatives (who already knew his misfortune and which convent Camila had gone to) of his death; Camila was almost at the point of accompanying her husband on his inevitable journey — not because she had heard of his death, but because she had heard that his friend had gone away. And it's said that, although she was in fact a widow, she would not leave the convent, and certainly would not become a nun, until, not long after, she heard that Lothario had been killed at the battle of Ceriñola [1503], fought in the kingdom of Naples (to which her tardily repentant lover had taken himself) by Monsieur de Lautrec and the great General Fernández of Córdoba, and when Camila heard this news she did take the veil and, after not very long, she died, wrung by the harsh hands of grief and melancholy. So this was what happened to each of them, united in their deaths by such a wildly willful beginning.

"This strikes me," said the priest, "as a very good story, but I can't convince myself that it's really true, and if it's invented, then the author has made a serious mistake, because I can't believe there's truly a husband who could be as foolish as Anselmo and want to risk anything that could cost him so much. Had this been told as something that happened between a lover and his lady, I could be persuaded, but between husband and wife it smacks too much of the impossible. But as far as style is concerned, I have nothing to criticize."

Chapter Thirty-Six

— which discusses Don Quijote's noble but unusual battle against several wineskins filled with red wine, along with other strange things that took place at the inn

At this point the innkeeper, who had been standing at the gate, called out:

"Here comes a fine band of guests: if they decide to stop here, we can all say *gaudeamus* [let us rejoice]."

"What kind of people?" asked Cardenio.

"Four men," replied the innkeeper, "all mounted, with short stirrups like cavalrymen, carrying spears and shields, all of them wearing black traveling-masks, accompanied by a woman dressed all in white, in a sedan chair, with her face covered too, and some servants on foot."

"Are they close by?" asked the priest.

"So close," replied the innkeeper, "that here they are."

Hearing this, Dorotea covered her face and Cardenio went off into Don Quijote's room, and he'd just barely disappeared when the travelers described by the innkeeper came through the gate and the four men on horseback, who were handsome and well-bred, dismounted and went to help the lady who rode in the sedan chair, one of them lifting her down in his arms and setting her in a chair near the door of the room where Cardenio was hiding. While this was going on, neither the lady nor any of the gentlemen took off their traveling-masks or said a single word, except that when she was seated in the chair the lady gave a profound sigh and let her arms drop at her sides, like someone weak and sick. Their foot-servants took the horses off to the stable.

Watching all this, the priest was anxious to know who these people were, traveling about in such costumes and in such total silence, so he followed after the foot-servants and asked one of them, who replied:

"Excuse me, sir, but I can't tell you who these people are. All I know is they seem to be very important, especially the one who was carrying that lady in his arms, just now, and I can tell you that much because the others are all very respectful to him and do everything exactly the way he tells them to."

"And who is the lady?" asked the priest.

"I can't tell you that, either," said the fellow, "because I haven't once seen her face; she sighs a lot, and you can hear her, and she groans, too, and so deeply that every time you think she's giving up the ghost. But it's no wonder we don't know any more than what I've been telling you, because my friend and me, we've only been with them two days, and that's because we met them on the road and, when they said they'd pay us really well, they talked us into going to Andalusia with them."

"Have you heard any of their names?" the priest asked.

"Not a one," the fellow replied, "because they just ride along in such a deadly silence that it's strange, and all you hear out of them is that poor lady's sighs and sobs, which makes us feel really sorry for her; we're sure she's being forced to go wherever she's going; and as far as we can figure out from her clothes, maybe she's a nun, or she's going to be one, which seems even more likely, and maybe she goes along so sadly because she really doesn't want to take the veil."

"That may well be," said the priest.

So he left them and went back to Dorotea who, having heard the masked lady sighing, was stirred by natural compassion and had gone over to her, saying:

"What's wrong, my dear lady? If it's anything women are familiar with and know how to take care of, I'll be very happy to offer you my services."

But the unfortunate woman did not reply, and though Dorotea repeated her offer even more warmly, there was still no response, at which point the masked gentleman, to whom the foot-servant had said all the others were obedient, came over and said to Dorotea,

"Don't trouble yourself, madame, to offer this lady anything, because it's her habit never to be grateful for what's done for her, and don't bother to make her answer you, because all you'll hear from her mouth is falsehood."

"I have never told a lie," said the lady who had, till then, kept silent. "Indeed, it's precisely because I have been so honest, and so utterly without lying schemes, that I find myself, now, in such a miserable state — as you yourself should bear witness, for my untainted truth has shown you for the false liar you are."

Cardenio could hear her perfectly distinctly, being as close as he was, for only the door to Don Quijote's room stood between them, and the moment he heard her speak he cried out:

"In the name of God! Who do I hear? What voice is that, reaching my ears?"

This cry made the lady turn in astonishment, and not seeing the person who had spoken she stood up and tried to go into the room, but when the gentleman saw this he held her back, not letting her move a step. What with the sudden movement and her agitation, the veil which had covered her face slipped off, exhibiting an incomparable beauty, a face of miraculous loveliness, though pale and staring, her eyes looking this way and that, to every part of the room she could see, with such desperate eagerness that she looked like a mad woman, all of which made Dorotea and everyone who saw her feel enormous pity, though they had no idea what was happening. The gentleman was pressing her down in her chair, holding her so tightly that, although his mask was slipping, he could not hold it up and, finally, it too slipped off and when Dorotea, who'd been embracing the seated lady, looked up, she saw that the gentleman was in fact her husband, Don Fernando, and the moment she recognized him she cried out, from the very depths of her being, a long, wailing "Ay!" and fell back in a dead faint, and only because the barber, who happened to be standing nearby, caught her in his arms, did she keep from toppling to the ground.

The priest quickly came to her assistance, intending to throw water on her face, and as soon as he removed her veil Don Fernando — for that is who it was, holding the other lady — recognized her and stood as if frozen to the spot, though he kept his tight grip on Luscinda, who was struggling to free herself, for she had recognized Cardenio's voice, as he had recognized hers. Cardenio had also heard Dorotea's scream, as she fainted away, and, thinking it was his Luscinda who cried, came bolting out of the room, terrified, and the first person he saw was Don Fernando, who had his arms around Luscinda. Don Fernando knew him immediately, too, and the three of them, Luscinda, Cardenio, and Dorotea,[1] stood in baffled silence, almost not sure what was happening.

They stood there mutely, staring at one another: Dorotea at Don Fernando, Don Fernando at Cardenio, Cardenio at Luscinda, and Luscinda at Cardenio. The first to break the silence was Luscinda, who spoke to Don Fernando as follows:

"Leave me, my lord Don Fernando, in the name of what you owe yourself, being who you are, and even if you have no respect for anything else, and let me hold onto the wall whose ivy I am, the wall whose support you've not been able to pull me away from, no matter how hard you've tried, and despite all your threats, your promises, and your gifts. Take due notice of the fact that Heaven, following strange pathways we are unable to see, has set me here, in front of my true husband. And you know well, after a thousand painful experiences, that only death will ever erase him from my memory. Let these absolutely clear lessons, if you are utterly unable to do anything else, turn your love into fury, your desire into ill-

---

1. Cervantes seems to have forgotten that Dorotea had just fainted away [*Translator's Note*].

will, and thus lead you to take my life, for if I surrender it, here, in front of my noble husband, it will seem to me a life well spent: perhaps my death will show him how I have been faithful to the very last moment."

In the meantime, Dorotea had come back to consciousness and heard everything that was said, which made her aware of who Luscinda was, but seeing that Don Fernando still did not release his captive, nor respond to her words, she summoned up all the courage she possessed and went to kneel at his feet, and shedding an immense quantity of lovely, pitiful tears, she spoke as follows:

"My lord, if the rays of that sun you hold eclipsed in your arms had not dazzled your eyes and deprived you of sight, you surely would have known that the woman who kneels at your feet, luckless unless and until you choose differently, is the miserable Dorotea. I am that humble peasant you raised, whether for your goodness or simply for your pleasure, to the height of being able to call herself yours. I am she who, enclosed by the boundaries of innocence and modesty, was able to live happily until, because you insisted and, so far as I could tell, because you truly and lovingly wanted me, I swung wide the doors of prudence and surrendered to you the keys of my freedom, a gift which you so little appreciated that, as you can clearly see, I have been forced to live here in this place where you've found me, and as I can equally clearly see from the state in which I now find you. In spite of which, please do not for a moment think I came here driven by any sense of dishonor, for all that has brought me here has been my grief and sorrow at finding myself spurned by you. You wished me to belong to you, and wished it in such a way that, even though, now, you wish it were otherwise, you cannot cease to be mine. Consider, my lord, that my unmatchable affection may well offer you compensation for the beauty, the nobility, which you deserted me to obtain, for, being mine, you cannot belong to this beautiful Luscinda, nor can she be yours, since she belongs to Cardenio. And if you think about it, how much easier it will be to bend to your will someone who adores you, rather than trying to guide someone who hates you to love you instead. You wooed my unawareness; you came begging of my honesty; you knew perfectly well I was of peasant blood; you know very well indeed how I surrendered myself to your desire; you cannot appeal to or take refuge in any claim of deception. If this is true, as it is, and you are as much a Christian as you are a gentleman, why do you try, thus elaborately and evasively, to keep from making me as happy and fortunate in the end as you made me in the beginning? And if you do not choose to take me for what I am, your true and lawful wife, at least take me, and let me be, your slave, for in belonging to you I will consider myself both blessed and fortunate. Do not, by casting me off and forsaking me, let my dishonor be publicly debated and discussed; do not bring such a horrid old age to my parents, for they do not deserve such a return on the faithful service that, as good subjects, they have always rendered to you and yours. And if it seems to you that, by mixing your blood with mine, yours will be annihilated, remember that few or even none of the noble families in the world have failed to take exactly this road, and that it is not the woman's heredity which matters in a distinguished blood-line; moreover, virtue is what makes for true nobility, and if this is what you lack, and you deny me the justice you owe me, then I am your superior in nobility. And in short, my lord, my final words to you have to be that, whether you like it or not, I am your wife, the witness thereto being your own words, which ought not — which *must* not — be lies, if in fact you treasure the nobility on account of which you think so little of me; your promise is my witness, a promise which Heaven heard, and indeed you yourself called on Heaven to witness that promise. But should none of this be sufficient, your own conscience should silently scream out at you, in the midst of your pleasures, insisting that what I'm saying to you is true, and ruining your dearest joys, your highest happiness."

The wounded woman said all this, and more, and with such emotion, and so many tears, that even the members of Don Fernando's traveling party, standing there, wept along with her. Don Fernando listened without saying a word, and when she finished speaking she broke into such sobbing and moaning that only a heart of brass could have failed to be moved by such incredible sadness. Luscinda too was watching, no less stirred by Dorotea's feelings than admiring her superb good sense and extreme beauty; but wanting to approach and say consoling words to her, Luscinda was still in Don Fernando's tight grip. Don Fernando, overwhelmed with shame and confusion, stood for a long time, staring down at Dorotea, and then opened his arms and, setting Luscinda free, said:

"You have won, my lovely Dorotea, you have won. How could anyone deny such a weight of truth?"

Luscinda was so weak that, as Don Fernando let her go, she would have fallen to the ground, but Cardenio, who had been standing behind Don Fernando, to keep from being recognized,[2] threw off his fear and, regardless of possible consequences, went to her aid and, taking her in his arms, said:

"If merciful Heaven pleases, and grants you some relief, oh my faithful, steadfast, and lovely lady, I can't believe you'll find any greater safety than in these arms which now receive you, and have welcomed you before, when Fate allowed me to call you mine."

Hearing these words, Luscinda looked at Cardenio and, beginning to understand who he was, at first by his voice, but then satisfying herself by the sight of him, came very close to fainting and, not concerning herself in the least with due decorum, clasped her arms around his neck and pressed her face against his, saying:

"Oh, my lord, you are indeed the true master of this your eternal captive, even should the whims of Fate try to keep us apart, menacing yet again this life which hangs on yours."

This was an exceedingly strange sight for Don Fernando and all those who witnessed it, amazed by something so utterly unexpected. It seemed to Dorotea that Don Fernando had gone pale, and it looked very much as if he wanted to take revenge on Cardenio, for she saw him put his hand on the hilt of his sword, so even as the thought occurred to her, with

---

2. Again, Cervantes seems to have forgotten that Cardenio has already been recognized by Don Fernando [*Translator's Note*].

incredible speed, she clasped him around the knees, kissing them and holding them so tightly that he could not move and, with her tears still flowing freely, said:

"What do you mean to do, oh my sole shelter and refuge, in the face of something so totally unexpected? Your wife is at your feet, and the woman you'd prefer to have as your wife is in her husband's arms. Consider if it would be right, or indeed if it would be possible, for you to undo what Heaven has done, or if it would be proper for you to raise to your own great height a woman who, disregarding all difficulties, strong in her faithful steadfastness, and right in front of your very eyes, can be seen bathing her true husband's face and breast with the waters of love. In the name of God, and in the name of the person you yourself are, I beg you not only not to let these plain and obvious facts rouse your anger, but to let the truth cause your anger to ebb away, allowing this pair of lovers to enjoy one another, in peace and quiet, without any interference from you, for as long as Heaven wishes them to have, and thus demonstrate the generosity of your noble, illustrious heart, so the world may see that you value reason more than passion."

As Dorotea was speaking, Cardenio kept his arms around Luscinda, but never took his eyes from Don Fernando, resolved that, should he see any attempt to attack him, he would do his best to defend himself and injure, for his part, anyone and everyone who showed him hostility, no matter if it cost him his life. But now Don Fernando's friends came forward, along with the priest and the barber, who had been there the whole time (not forgetting our good Sancho Panza), and they all gathered around Don Fernando, begging him to take Dorotea's tears seriously and, if as they suspected her statements were the truth, not to let himself cheat her of her just expectations. They urged him to consider how it could not be mere accident, though it might seem so, that they had all come together at this place where no one could have predicted any such occurrence, but that it had to be a special decree of Heaven, and he himself had to understand, as the priest warned him, that only death could separate Luscinda from Cardenio, and even should the sharp edge of a sword divide them one from the other they would rejoice in their deaths, and since the very acme of wisdom was revealed when a man was confronted with things that could not be helped, he should restrain and overcome himself, and display a generous heart, and of his own free will allow these lovers to enjoy what Heaven had already granted them, and at the same time turn his eyes toward Dorotea's beauty and see how few or none could match her, much less surpass her, for her beauty was joined both to humility and an overwhelming love for himself — and above all, warned the priest, if he took pride in being a gentleman and a Christian he had no choice but to fulfill the promise he had given, and in fulfilling it would keep his faith with God and meet with the approval of all wise and sensible people, who well know that, provided it is accompanied by modesty, it is beauty's privilege — no matter how low its estate — to be able to rise and accommodate itself to any height whatever, without in any way staining the reputation of the man who raises it to be his equal. And when the powerful laws of love are at work (provided sin plays no part), obedience to those laws cannot be blameworthy.

And so, with these arguments piled on top of all the rest, one after the other, Don Fernando's worthy heart — nurtured, after all, by illustrious blood — let itself be cooled down and conquered by truth, which in any case he could not have denied had he wanted, and to show that he had yielded and made his submission to the excellent advice pressed upon him, he bent and embraced Dorotea, saying to her:

"Rise, my lady, for it is wrong for what I treasure in my heart to kneel at my feet, and if, till now, I have not lived up to those words, perhaps it has been Heaven's doing, to let me discover the true faith with which you love me, and learn to value you as you deserve. Let me ask only that you not chide me for my wrong-doing and my abundant neglect, since the same power and the same reasons that drove me to take you for my own also forced me to seek not to be yours. And to see how true this is, simply turn and look, there, into the eyes of that newly happy Luscinda, and you will see the source of all my errors, but now that she has found and attached herself to the man she truly wants, and I have found in you that which fulfills me, let her live long and happily, in peace and happiness, with her Cardenio, as I will pray to Heaven to let me live with my Dorotea."

Saying which, he turned to embrace her and set his face against hers, so tenderly that he had to be careful not to offer unmistakable proof of how truly he had spoken, and how deeply he repented his mistakes, by weeping tears of love. Neither Luscinda nor Cardenio held back theirs, nor did virtually anyone who was there, for the tears rained down so plentifully — some for their own happiness, some for the happiness of others — that it looked for all the world as if some dark tragedy had occurred. Even Sancho Panza wept, though later on he said he was only crying because he realized that Dorotea was not, as he had thought, Queen Micomicona, from whose hands he had expected such free-flowing rewards. The general astonishment, and the general weeping, lasted a very long time, but before too long Cardenio and Luscinda were on their knees before Don Fernando, thanking him for his compassion in such courteous language that Don Fernando did not know how to answer them, so he raised them up and embraced them both, with a great show of affection and graciousness.

Then he asked Dorotea to tell him how she had come to be in that place, so far from her home and family. Speaking sensibly and briefly, she told him exactly what, previously, she had said to Cardenio, which so much pleased Don Fernando and all those with him that they wished the tale had taken longer to tell, so charmingly had Dorotea narrated the story of her misfortunes. And then, when she'd finished, Don Fernando explained what had happened, back in the city, after he had found, in Luscinda's breast, the document in which she had declared herself Cardenio's wife and unable to be his. He said he had wanted to kill her, and indeed would have, had her parents not stopped him, after which he had swept out of their house in violent disgust, determined to avenge himself however he could. He'd learned, the next day, that Luscinda was missing from her parents' house, and no one knew where she had gone, and finally, some months later, he learned she'd gone into a convent, intending to stay there the rest of her life if she could not live that life with Cardenio, and as soon as he'd come by that information he took three gentlemen and went to the convent, but never said a word to Luscinda, fearful that, were it known he was there, she'd be even more closely guarded, so, waiting and watching for a day when the gate might be left open, he set two of his men to guard it while he and the other man went in and looked for Luscinda, whom they found in the cloister, talking to a nun, and without giving her a chance to do anything about it they carried her away, taking her to a place where they furnished themselves with whatever they might need to keep her with them. They were able to do all this with impunity, since the convent was out in the country, a long way from the city. And he told them that, as soon as Luscinda saw she was in his power, she'd fainted away, and once she'd come to herself all she'd done was weep and sigh, never saying a word, and in that fashion, traveling in silence and in tears, they'd reached the inn — which for him, he said, was like arriving in Heaven, where all earthly sorrows are ended forever.

Chapter Thirty-Seven

— which continues the tale of the famous Princess Micomicona, along with other pleasant adventures

Sancho listened to all this, his heart distinctly heavy, for he could see his hopes for a noble title turning into smoke and vanishing, as the beautiful Princess Micomicona turned into Dorotea, and the giant into Don Fernando, and his master slept on peacefully, blissfully unaware of what was happening. Dorotea herself could not be sure her good fortune was nothing more than a dream; Cardenio felt exactly the same way, and so too did Luscinda. Don Fernando thanked Heaven for its grace in rescuing him from that convoluted labyrinth in which he'd come so close to losing both his reputation and his immortal soul; and, in a word, everyone in the inn was well satisfied, rejoicing at the happy resolution of such a troublesome, hopeless business.

The priest, in his wisdom, summed it all up, congratulating each of them for their good fortune — but the jolliest and happiest of them all was the innkeeper's wife, now that Cardenio and the priest had promised to pay her for all the damage Don Quijote had done and for every single thing he had destroyed. Only Sancho, once again, was upset, downcast, and gloomy, and so, his master having just woken up, he went to him with a hangdog face, saying:

"It's fine for you, your grace, Sir Knight of the Sad Face, to sleep as long as you want, without having to worry about killing any giants or getting the princess' kingdom back, because that's all over and done with."

"I should think it was," replied Don Quijote, "because I've had the wildest and most extraordinary battle of my life with that giant, and with one swift backhand stroke — whack! — I sent his head rolling to the ground, and so much blood poured out of him that it ran all over like so much water."

"Your grace might better say: as if it were so much red wine," answered

Sancho, "because you've got to understand, your grace, just in case you don't already, that the dead giant is a sliced-open wineskin, and the blood is twenty gallons of red wine that were stored in its belly, and the chopped-off head is the whore who gave birth to me, and to hell with everything."

"What are you talking about, you lunatic?" replied Don Quijote. "Are you right in the head?"

"Get up, your grace," said Sancho, "and see what great things you've accomplished, and how much they're going to cost us, and have a look at the queen turned into an ordinary lady named Dorotea, plus some other doings which, even if you don't understand them, you'll find quite astonishing."

"None of that's going to surprise me," replied Don Quijote, "because, if you remember it right, I told you, the last time we were here, that everything going on in this place is the work of magic, and why would I be astonished if the same thing were happening again?"

"And I could believe all that," responded Sancho, "if my getting tossed in the blanket was the same kind of thing, but it wasn't, it was real and it really happened, and I saw the innkeeper, the same one who's right here today, holding one end of the blanket, and he bounced me up in the air with all the energy and enthusiasm in the world, and he laughed as hard as he threw me, and when it comes to recognizing people, it seems to me — foolish as I am, and a sinner — that there's no magic involved, but just a lot of exhaustion and even more bad luck."

"Well now," said Don Quijote, "God will find a way to fix everything. Bring me some clothes and let me get out there: I want to see all these things you've been telling me about — all these transformations."

Sancho brought him clothing and, while he was getting dressed, the priest explained Don Quijote's madness to Don Fernando and the others, and the trick they'd used to get him down from Barren Mountain, where he thought he had to be, for failing in his duty to his lady. At the same time the priest narrated virtually all the adventures about which Sancho had told him, which much surprised and delighted them, for they thought (as did everyone else) that this was surely the strangest kind of insanity a deranged mind could possibly conceive. And the priest said more: now that the lady Dorotea's good fortune made it impossible to go on with their earlier plan, they had to work out and design another one, so Don Quijote could be brought home. So Cardenio suggested that they go on with the same plan, except that Luscinda could now play Dorotea's part.

"No," exclaimed Don Fernando, "you don't have to do that: I want Dorotea to go on with this fairy-tale, because we can't be very far from where the good gentleman lives, and I'd be glad to do whatever I can to help him get better."

"It's not more than two days' journey from here."

"And even if it were longer, I'd be glad to make the trip, in exchange for doing such a good deed."

At this point Don Quijote came out, in full military gear, with Mambrino's helmet (rather battered) on his head, carrying his shield, and leaning on the stick he was using as a spear. His strange appearance enthralled Don Fernando and the others — a lean, yellow face, a mile long; a grab-bag collection of weapons and armor; a composed, intensely civilized bearing — and they all remained silent, waiting to hear what he would say. Immensely serious, wonderfully calm, Don Quijote looked at lovely Dorotea and said:

"I am informed by my squire, oh beautiful lady, that your majesty has been stripped away from you, and you have been undone, since you have been transformed from the queen and great lady you were into a most ordinary young lady. If this has been accomplished by your father, the magician king, for fear I would not provide you with the assistance you require, I must say that he neither knew nor knows what he is up to, and surely must be but little versed in the history of knighthood, since had he read those pages as attentively and for as long as I have read them, he would have found that, at every stage of an adventure, knights of less fame than mine have surmounted far more difficult obstacles, for killing an overgrown giant doesn't amount to very much, no matter how arrogant they may be, and indeed just a few hours ago I myself encountered one, and — but I will say no more, so no one can call me a liar, though Time, which uncovers all things, will reveal it all to them when they least expect to hear it."

"You met up with two wineskins," the innkeeper put in. "That was no giant."

But Don Fernando commanded him to be silent and completely desist from interrupting Don Quijote, after which our knight continued:

"In short, oh high and for the moment disinherited lady, I say that, should this be the reason your father has thus transformed you, think nothing of it, for there is no danger on earth through which my sword cannot cut a path, and with that sword it will not be long before I topple your enemy's head to the ground, and place once more on yours the crown that belongs there."

Don Quijote said no more, waiting for the princess to answer, and she, knowing that Don Fernando wanted her to go on with their deception until they had brought Don Quijote home, replied with great poise and politeness:

"Whoever may have told you, oh brave Knight of the Sad Face, that I have been changed and transformed away from my true self, has told you what is not true, because I am today exactly what I was yesterday. It is true, to be sure, that certain fortunate occurrences have produced some alteration in me, for I have been granted more than I could have hoped for, but there is nothing in this to make me anything other than what I have been all along or to cause me to give up the same high opinion I have always held of the strength and courage of your brave and unconquerable right arm. Accordingly, my lord, think once more, in your goodness, just as well as you have done before of the father who begot me; consider him a prudent and well-aware man, for it has been his skill and wisdom that have found me so straightforward and simple a road to the cure for my misfortune, for it is my opinion that if not for you, my dear sir, I should not have been so blessed as I now am, and these gentlemen will bear witness that I speak nothing but the truth. All we need do is set out on our journey, tomorrow, for by this point in the day we could not travel very far; for the rest, and for the happy ending to which I look forward, I must trust in God and in your brave heart."

So spoke wise Dorotea, and when he had heard her, Don Quijote turned to Sancho and said, very angrily:

"Now let me tell you, my little Sancho, that you're the biggest pint-sized idiot in all of Spain. Didn't you just finish telling me, you loose-footed thief, that this princess had been changed into an ordinary lady named Dorotea, and that the head I still think I cut off a giant was the whore who gave birth to you, plus other nonsense that confused me more desperately than I've ever been in my life? By God . . ." — he swore, looking up at Heaven and grinding his teeth — "I'm tempted to make an example of you that, from this day on, would put a little salt on the lying squire-brains that afflict the knights errant of this world!"

"Calm down, your grace, my lord," replied Sancho, "because maybe I've been tricked into all that about the Princess Micomicona's transformation, but as far as the giant's head is concerned, or, at least, cutting open the wineskins, and the blood being red wine, nobody was fooling me, in the name of God, because the wounded wineskins are right there at the head of your bed, and the red wine has turned the room into a lake, and if you don't think so, just wait till the chickens come home to roost — I mean, you'll see for yourself when his grace the innkeeper here asks you to pay all the damages. But it's all right with me if my lady the queen is still what she was — it cheers me up, because I've got as much stake there as anybody around."

"Let me tell you once more, Sancho," said Don Quijote, "that you're an idiot — forgive me — and that's enough."

"Enough," repeated Don Fernando, "let's say no more about this, for since the princess tells us that we should not journey on till tomorrow, because it's too late today, that's precisely what we will do, and tonight we'll spend our time chatting amiably, and when the new day dawns we'll all accompany my lord Don Quijote, for all of us wish to see for ourselves the brave and unheard of deeds he will be called upon to perform, in carrying out this great enterprise which he has undertaken."

"It is I who will serve and accompany you," replied Don Quijote, "and I am deeply grateful for the favor you thus show me, and the good opinion of me which you hold, which I shall try to prove correct, even at the cost of my life — and at any greater cost, if such a thing is possible."

Don Quijote and Don Fernando exchanged an abundance of courtesies and mutual promises, but this was all cut short by a traveler just then entering the inn, from his garb apparently a Christian newly returned from Moorish lands, for he wore a blue woolen jacket, cut short, with half-length sleeves and no collar; his shoes, too, were of blue canvas, with a cap of the same color; he wore dull-brown half-boots and a Moorish scimitar, slung from a strap across his chest. Coming right behind him, mounted on a donkey, was a woman in Moorish clothing, her face hidden by a veil; she had on a small brocade cap and a long Moorish robe that covered her from her shoulders to her feet.

The man was handsome and strongly built, perhaps a little more than forty years old, his face almost as dark as a Moor's, with a great long moustache and a fine beard, and, in short, his bearing showed that, had he been well dressed, he'd have been taken for a well-born man of high rank.

He asked for a room but was told there were none left in the inn, which visibly bothered him; going over to the woman who, by her dress, seemed to be a Moor, he lifted her off the donkey. Luscinda, Dorotea, the inn-keeper's wife and her daughter, and Maritornes, all gathered around her, drawn by clothing the like of which they had never seen, and Dorotea, as ever gracious and sensible, noticing that the man with her was upset by the room shortage, said to her:

"Don't worry about all the conveniences you'll miss here, my dear lady, for our inns simply don't have them — in spite of which, if you'd care to stay with us," and she gestured to Luscinda, "it may be that as you journey down these roads you'll find still worse accommodations."

The veiled woman made no reply, only standing up and, folding her arms across her breast, bowing with both her head and her body, as a sign of appreciation. Her silence led them to believe, without the slightest doubt, that she had to be a Moor and unable to speak a Christian tongue. At that point the captive[1] came over, having been occupied with something else, and seeing them all gathered around the woman who was with him, and that she had not replied when they'd spoken to her, said:

"My dear ladies, this young woman scarcely speaks my language, and knows indeed none but her native tongue, which is why she could not have responded, nor did she, to whatever you asked her."

"We asked nothing of her," replied Luscinda, "but only offered her, tonight, both our company and a share of the room we occupy here, in which she will be made as comfortable as these surroundings permit, according to the good will which we are required to show to all strangers in need but particularly to women."

"I kiss your hands, my lady," the captive said, "on both her behalf and mine, and very properly treasure the favor you have bestowed on us, for at such a time, and coming from such a person as you seem clearly to be, it is easy to see that this is a very great favor indeed."

"Tell me, sir," said Dorotea, "if this lady is a Christian or a Moor? Because by her clothing and her silence we have been led to believe that she is, in fact, what we wish she were not."

"She is dressed like a Moor, and her body is that of a Moor, but her soul is that of a very genuine Christian, for she has an immense desire to be one."

"Then she hasn't been baptized?" said Luscinda.

"There has been no opportunity," the captive replied, "since she left her native city of Algiers, and to this point she has not been in such immediate danger of death that it seemed necessary to baptize her without first instructing her in all the ceremonies commanded by Our Mother the Holy Church, but may it please God that she be baptized, and soon, with all the dignity that her rank deserves, for she is in truth a lady of higher standing than either her clothing or mine might indicate."

---

1. A Christian in Moorish dress, newly arrived from Moorish lands, would have been assumed to be either a captive who had been ransomed or one who had escaped [*Translator's Note*].

With these observations he made everyone who was listening anxious to know who the Moor and the captive might be, but just then no one wanted to ask, because clearly it was more appropriate to find them shelter than inquire into their life histories. Dorotea took the Moorish lady by the hand and brought her to a chair next to her own, then asked her to remove her veil. Speaking to her in Arabic, the captive told her she was being asked to remove her veil, and that indeed she should, which she then did, revealing a face so lovely that Dorotea thought she was more beautiful than Luscinda, and Luscinda that she was more beautiful than Dorotea, and everyone who was watching knew that if anyone could match the two of them it was the Moorish lady, and some of them even felt that she had something of an advantage. And it being beauty's privilege and charm to warm all hearts and attract all affection, everyone was immediately anxious to serve and shower attention upon the lovely Moor.

Don Fernando asked the captive to tell him the lady's name, and he replied that it was Zoraida, but as soon as she heard this, having understood the question, she said with considerable urgency, registering both distress and a good deal of liveliness:

"No, not Zoraida: María, María" — clearly indicating that her name was María and not Zoraida.

These words, and the strong feeling with which the Moorish lady spoke them, made more than one tear fall from those who were listening, especially the women, who are naturally tender and compassionate. Luscinda then embraced her with great affection, saying:

"Yes, yes, María, María."

To which the Moorish lady responded:

"Yes, yes, María; Zoraida *macange!*" — meaning "No."

Night was coming, and, as Don Fernando's companions had directed, the innkeeper had done his best to prepare for them the very finest supper of which his establishment was capable. The time to dine came, and they seated themselves around the kind of long, rectangular table at which servants eat, in noble houses (because the inn boasted no table either round or square), and seated at the head of it, in the chair of honor, Don Quijote, though he tried to decline, and he asked that the Lady of Micomicona sit at his side, he being her protector. Luscinda and Zoraida were seated next, with Don Fernando and Cardenio opposite them, after whom came the captive and the other gentlemen, while the priest and the barber sat next to the ladies. So they dined most happily, their pleasure heightened still farther when they saw Don Quijote stop eating and, stirred by an impulse like that which had moved him when he'd spoken as he had, dining with the goatherds, begin to declaim as follows:

"Truly, my dear gentlemen, if we think about it properly, those who adhere to the order of knight errantry come to behold great and quite incredible things. Consider: would any living man, walking through the gates of this castle right this minute and, by pure chance, seeing us here, be able to appreciate and understand that we are who we are? Who among them would be able to say that this lady, seated beside me, is the great queen we all know she is, and that I am that Knight of the Sad Face whose name is always in Fame's mouth? There can be no doubt, now, that this art, this profession, is superior to any and every calling ever invented by men, and must be still further esteemed because it is so subject to high danger. Away with those, I say, who argue that literature and learning take precedence over arms! I say to them, nor do I care who they may be, that they simply don't know what they're talking about. The argument they usually mouth, and the one on which they mostly rely, is that the labors of the soul are superior to those of the body, and that arms are concerned only with the body — as if any clod could wield them, and only sheer brute force was required, or as if what those of us who do wield them call 'arms' did not include acts that require strength, yes, but also acts that require infinite understanding, or as if the warrior's soul, when he has the responsibility for an army, or for the defense of a besieged city, did not function every bit as much via the mind as via the body. Consider: can one use mere bodily strength to understand or puzzle out what an enemy means to do — all his plans, his stratagems, all the difficulties, or how to foresee and forestall dangers with which he threatens you? These are all of them mental activity, with nothing of the body about them. And since, therefore, it is clear that the bearing of arms is as intellectual an activity as is learning, let us then see in which of the two, arms or learning, the intellect must work harder, which we can discover by considering the goal, the end-point, toward which each strives, for, plainly, whichever seeks the nobler end must be valued higher. Now the end-point, the goal of learning — I do not speak, here, of divine learning, which aims at shepherding souls along the road to Heaven, for that is the goal of all goals with which no other can compare — but I speak, rather, of human learning, which seeks to ensure that every man receives exactly the justice he deserves, understanding and guaranteeing that good laws are obeyed. And without any doubt this is a noble, magnanimous goal — but arms strive for that which is a great deal higher still, for their goal and purpose is the attainment of peace, which is the very best thing humans can desire in this life. Accordingly, the very first good news brought to the world and received by humankind was that given us by the angels, on that night which was our day, when their heavenly voices sang: 'Glory to God in the highest, and peace on earth to men of good will,' and the greeting which the great master of Heaven and earth taught His followers and disciples to say, whenever they came into a house, was 'Peace be on this house,' and many other times He told them, 'I give you my peace; I leave you my peace; peace be with you' — a gift and a jewel and a promise offered and extended by a hand such as His — a jewel without which there can be nothing good, neither on earth nor in Heaven. This peace is the true goal sought by war, and when we say war we say arms, for they are the same thing. Granting this truth, then, that the goal of war is peace, and that in this respect it is clearly superior to learning, let us turn to the body's role in both learning and the profession of arms and see which has the advantage here."

Don Quijote had been speaking so logically and eloquently that, to this point, no one could possibly have thought him addled; indeed, since most of those who heard him were gentlemen, who quite naturally bear arms, they listened with genuine pleasure. He went on:

"Now, this is what being a student requires: first of all, poverty, not because all students are in fact poor, but simply to state the case as bluntly as possible — and then, having said the student must endure poverty, we need say nothing more as to his worldly fortune, for he who is poor possesses nothing worth having, he suffers poverty in everything — hunger, cold, nakedness — and in everything all at once. In spite of which, the student's poverty is not so complete that they never eat at all, but just not as seasonably as other people, and perhaps only from the scraps off the rich man's table — and the worst of it, the student's keenest misery, is what they themselves call 'living off the monastery soup-kitchen.' They can always find somebody's chimney or fireplace, and if it doesn't get them warm it at least makes them less cold and, in any event, they don't have to sleep out in the open. I don't want to talk about all the many other little things, all of them easy enough to understand — like having no shirts, and barely enough shoes, and never enough clothing (which is always threadbare), or how they make themselves sick with eating, whenever good fortune provides them with a banquet. This is the harsh and difficult road, exactly as I have been describing it for you, that they must travel toward their academic goal — slipping here, falling there, then getting up again, only to fall once more — though often, once they do arrive, having gotten by these sandbars, having been swept safely past Scylla and Charybdis[2] as if carried on Fortune's wings, we find them, I say, governing and ruling over the world, perched on a throne, their hunger transformed into satiety, their cold turned into comfort, their nakedness become splendid clothing, and the straw mat on which they once slept transmuted into sheets of fine Dutch linen and silk, all of which is the fair and proper prize won by their virtue. But when we compare and contrast their labors with those of the active warrior, we see that they fall far, far short, as I shall now explain."

Chapter Thirty-Eight

— dealing with Don Quijote's unusual speech about arms versus learning

Then Don Quijote went on, as follows:

"Just as we began our consideration of student life in terms of poverty, and the various aspects thereof, let us now see if the soldier's life is any richer. And what we will find is that there is no one whose poverty is deeper or more profound than his, for he is dependent on his wretched salary, which he receives either late or not at all, and sometimes must forage and steal for, at high risk both to his life and his conscience. And sometimes Fate leaves him so naked that a tattered jacket serves simultaneously as shirt and dress uniform, and in the middle of winter he's in open country, having to fight off all the rigors of the weather, armed only with the breath out of his mouth — and as I can tell you from experience,

---

2. These two sea monsters were the dread of mariners sailing through the Straits of Messina. The peril was either being devoured by Scylla or being sucked into the whirpool of Charybdis. See Homer's *Odyssey* (XII.85ff.).

coming as it does from an empty place, that breath can't help but emerge cold, though this may seem against the laws of nature. He's looking forward to nightfall, when the bed that's awaiting him will renew and refresh him against all these miseries, and — unless he's guilty of some mistake — he doesn't have to worry about that bed being too narrow, because he can measure out the ground as far as he wants to, in any direction, and roll around as much as he likes, without fear of ruining the sheets. So then there comes, in spite of all this, the day and the hour when he's awarded his degree, the time for battle, and maybe he gets an academic hat of bandages, because he's taken a bullet right in the head, or maybe his arm's been crippled, or his leg. And when that doesn't happen, when merciful Heaven protects him and keeps him alive and healthy, perhaps he'll still be just as poor as he was before, and he'll have to go through battle after battle, one after another, and be the victor in all of them, before things get any better; but we don't see many such miracles. For tell me, gentlemen, if you've thought about it: how many fewer men have profited by war than have died in it? Unquestionably, you can only answer that there is absolutely no comparison, for the dead are utterly uncountable and those who have profited, and are still alive, will never total even as much as a thousand. And it's exactly the opposite with men of learning, for what they earn — without counting what they're given — will always be enough to keep them alive: the soldier must work harder, but he receives much less. You can answer, of course, that it's easier to reward two thousand learned men than thirty thousand soldiers, because they can be given offices which simply have to be awarded to those of their professions, while soldiers can only be rewarded out of the wealth and property of the lord they serve. Yet this impossibility only further strengthens my argument. But even setting this to the side, as a labyrinth through which it is hard to make one's way, let us come back to the superiority of arms as opposed to learning, a subject long in dispute and debated this way and that from each side of the question, and among other arguments that have been put forward, learning insists that, without its help, arms cannot endure, since warfare too has its laws, which must be obeyed, and laws fall under their jurisdiction. To this, arms replies that, without it, laws cannot endure, because it is with arms that republics defend themselves, and kings maintain their thrones, cities protect themselves, highways are kept safe and open, the seas are cleared of pirates, and, in short, without arms, all republics, kingdoms, monarchies, cities, and all highways both on land and on sea would be subject to the severities and disturbances that, so long as it lasts and is free to exercise its powers and privileges, always accompany war. And, clearly, whatever costs the most *is*, and *must* be, most highly valued. One rises to learned eminence at the cost of time, sleeplessness, hunger, nakedness, tired brains, weak indigestions, and other such matters, which I have to some extent already discussed, but to achieve a good soldier's goals costs everything required of the student, but so much more intensively that comparisons are impossible, for at every step the soldier is at risk of losing his life. And what constraint of necessity or poverty can the student experience, or be vexed by, to compare with that endured by the soldier, finding himself in a besieged fortress, and standing guard on the walls, or in some outlying watchpost, or high in some tower, when he senses that his enemies are tunneling underground, straight at the place where he is standing, but he cannot under any circumstances withdraw or flee from the danger he knows is drawing ever closer? All he can do is inform his commanding officer, who can perhaps save the situation by digging a counter-tunnel, but then he must stay where he is, waiting for, and fearing, the moment when, without warning, he will suddenly be obliged to fly up into the clouds, without wings, and then come crashing down, whether he likes it or not. And if this strikes you as a trivial risk, consider whether it is matched, or perhaps exceeded, by a situation where two galleys come smashing together, bow to bow, out in the middle of the vast ocean, jammed tightly together, and for the soldier standing out on the battering ram the world is limited to the boards on which his two feet are planted, while at the same time he sees himself facing precisely as many ministers of death as there are yawning cannons aiming at him from the enemy ship, barely a spear length away, and though realizing that his first careless step will take him on a visit deep into Neptune's bosom, yet, in spite of all this, his heart feeling no fear, sustained by the sense of honor that urges him on, he sets himself up as a target for all that artillery and struggles to cross that narrow bridge and get onto the other ship. And what's even more remarkable is that, no sooner has one fallen down so far that he will not rise while the world endures, but another steps right into his place, and if this one too falls into the sea, which is waiting there as if it too were his enemy, another and yet another will come after him, so rapidly that the interval between their deaths is nonexistent: the noblest heroism, the greatest daring, to be found in any of war's supreme moments. Those were indeed blessed times which knew nothing of demoniacal cannonading's ghastly fury, the inventor of which must be in Hell, receiving his due reward for so fiendish an invention, which allows a vile, cowardly arm to pluck the life out of a brave knight, who without knowing how it happens, or from whence it comes, and in the full sway of that courage and energy which burn in brave hearts, is struck by a wandering bullet, fired, perhaps, by someone who fled in panic at the roar and glare when he touched off his cursed machine, thus cutting short and forever ending every thought, and indeed the very life, of one who deserved to live through all the long ages. And when I think of this I must say that my heart is heavy, having taken on this profession of knight errantry, in an age as loathsome as that in which we now live, because although I am myself afraid of nothing, nevertheless it makes me regretful to think that gunpowder and tin may deprive me of the chance to acquire fame and great reputation, across the known world, for the courage of my arm and the keenness of my sword. But Heaven's will must be done; and I will be thought even better of, if I can achieve what I seek to, since I will have confronted far more serious perils than any of the knights errant of ancient times."

Don Quijote gave this long, wandering speech while the others were consuming their dinners, completely forgetting to put anything in his own mouth, although Sancho Panza kept telling him to eat, because afterwards he could say as much as he wanted to. Those who sat listening to this speech experienced a fresh wave of pity, seeing a man who seemed so wonderfully sound in the head, and who spoke so eloquently of every subject he raised, so hopelessly lost when it came to the pitch-black darkness of his unfortunate knight errantry. The priest declared that Don Quijote was quite right in what he'd said about the superiority of arms, and that he himself, notwithstanding he was a man of learning and a college graduate, shared those same opinions.

Dinner over, they took away the tablecloths, and while the innkeeper's wife, and her daughter, and Maritornes, were readying Don Quijote's attic room (in which it had been decided that all the women would spend the night), Don Fernando asked the captive to tell them the story of his life, for it could not help but be odd and interesting, from what he had already let them know, since his arrival with Zoraida. The captive replied that he would gladly do as he'd been commanded, and all that worried him was that the tale might not please them as much as he'd like it to; still, for all that, he would certainly tell it, rather than disobey. The priest and all the others thanked him, and renewed their queries, and, seeing himself so besieged by questions, he told them there was no need to ask at all, when so weighty a command had been given.

"Accordingly, should your graces be pleased to listen to me, you will hear a true tale that may well be superior to those lying narratives framed by strange and labored tricks and artifices."

When he'd said this, they all settled into their places, in profound silence, and he, seeing that they were quiet and waiting for whatever he might say, began to speak as follows, his voice pleasant and calm.

Chapter Thirty-Nine

— in which the captive tells the story of his life

"My family has its roots in a village in the León mountains, where Nature has been kinder and freer than Fortune, though in that poverty-stricken region my father was considered a rich man, and in fact he might really have been so if he'd had as much of a knack for holding onto property as he had for squandering it. And this tendency to be open-handed and extravagant came from having been a soldier, when he was younger, for soldiering is a school where the stingy learn to be generous, and the generous learn to be lavish, because if there truly are any skinflint soldiers to be found, they're like monsters, few and far between. My father went well over the boundary lines of generosity and came very close to prodigality, not a terribly useful trait in a married man with children destined to take his name and his position in the world. My father had three, all male and all of an age to choose themselves a profession. Finding that, as he said himself, he could do nothing to restrain his extravagance, my father decided to remove the very instrument and reason for his wasteful generosity, namely, his property, without which Alexander himself would have seemed tight-fisted. Accordingly, one day he called all three of us into his room and spoke to us approximately as follows: 'My sons, all that needs to be said to tell you I love you is that you're my sons, and all that needs to be known, to understand that I don't love you, is that I'm utterly unable to hold on to the property intended to be yours. And to let you see that from now on I want to love you as a father, rather than ruin you like a stepfather, I plan to do something for you that I have thought about for a long time and, after mature consideration, have decided should be done. You are all old enough to marry — or, at least, to choose a profession which, as you grow older, will prove both useful and honorable. So I have decided to divide my property into four equal parts, three of which I will give you — to each exactly the share that is properly his — and the last of which I will keep myself, to sustain and feed me for however long Heaven wishes to keep me alive. But I want each of you, after you come into possession of your share, to follow the paths I will now indicate. Here in this Spain of ours, we have a saying, and it seems to me absolutely true (as indeed all proverbs are, for they are compressed wisdom drawn from long and knowing experience), which goes: Church, sea, or the king's house, or in clearer terms: 'Whoever wants to be somebody, and be rich, must choose the Church, the sea — that is, the merchant's art — or the king's personal service,' for as they say, 'Better the king's crumbs than a lord's favors.' And I say this, and I wish this, because I want one of you to become a learned man, another a merchant, and the third to serve as a soldier to the king, for it's hard to enter his personal service and, though there's not much profit in war, it is a way of showing great courage and acquiring great fame. Eight days from now I will hand you each your inheritance, in cash, not cheating you out of a single penny, as you will see for yourselves. But tell me, now, if my plan pleases you and you're willing to do as I have suggested.' He ordered me, as the oldest, to answer him, and after telling him that he should not deprive himself of his own property, but do with it exactly as he pleased, for we were young men and well able to earn our way, I finished by saying that I would do as he wished and that my own choice would be the profession of arms, thus serving God and my king. My second brother similarly pledged himself to travel to the Indies, where he would put to good use the money that had come to him. The youngest of us (and in my opinion the wisest) said that he would either become a Churchman or go finish his studies at the university in Salamanca. Once we had made our promises, and chosen our professions, my father embraced us all, and then, in exactly the short time he had promised, fulfilled his part of the bargain, giving each of us his rightful share — which as far as I can recall was three thousand dollars apiece, in cash (for one of our uncles bought my father's estate and paid for it in cash, to keep it in the family) — and on that very same day we each took leave of our beloved father. At the same time, since it seemed to me positively inhuman for my father to be old and have so little to live on, I made him take two thousand of my three thousand dollars, for the remainder was more than enough for a soldier's needs. Both my brothers, moved by my example, each gave him back a thousand, so that my father had four thousand in cash, plus another three thousand in the land he'd retained as his own share, which he apparently did not want to sell. So, as I said, we said farewell to him and to the uncle I mentioned, all of us much moved and weeping, and my father and my uncle asking us to let them know, any time we conveniently could, what had happened to us, for good or for bad. We promised, and they embraced us and gave us their blessings, after which one of us started out for Salamanca, another for Seville, and I for Alicante, where it was said there was a Genoese vessel taking on a cargo of wool bound for its home port.

"It has now been twenty-two years since I left my father's house, and in all that time, though I've written letters, I've never had any news of him or of my brothers. Let me then tell you, briefly, what happened during that time. Taking ship at Alicante, I sailed successfully to Genoa, then went from there to Milan, where I provided myself with the necessary weapons and dress uniforms, for I planned to begin my military service in Piedmont, but as I was heading down the highway to Allesandria della Paglia I heard that the great Duke of Alba was on his way to Flanders. So I changed my plan and went with him, serving in his campaigns, finding myself present at the deaths of Count Egmont and Count Horne, becoming a lieutenant under Diego de Urbina, a famous general from Guadalajara; some while after I came to Flanders, we heard news of the alliance between His Holiness Pope Pius the Fifth, of blessed memory, and Venice and Spain, to combat the common enemy, the Turks, whose fleet had just then captured the famous island of Cyprus, which had been Venetian territory and was indeed a sad and unfortunate loss. We knew for certain that the commanding general of this alliance was going to be His Highness Don Juan of Austria, our good King Philip's natural brother; we also heard of the huge forces he would be directing; and it all made me so excited and anxious to take part in the promised campaign that, though I had good reason to believe (indeed, I had virtually certain promises) I was about to be promoted from lieutenant to captain, and at the very first opportunity, nevertheless I decided to throw it all up and, just as I was, go to Italy. It was my good fortune that Don Juan of Austria was just then arriving in Genoa, and was going on to Naples to join up with the Venetian armada, as in fact he later did, though at Messina. In any case, I found myself part of that most glorious of all campaigns,[1] having already been commissioned a captain in the infantry (an honorable promotion for which luck rather than my own merits was largely responsible). And on that very same day, so blissful for all of Christianity, for then the whole world, and every nation in it, learned how wrong they had been, believing that on the sea no one could beat the Turks — on that day, again, when Ottoman pride and arrogance were shattered, and among the many, many overflowing with joy (for the Christians who died at Lepanto were happier than those left victorious and alive), only I was miserable, because instead of the naval crown I might have hoped for, in the days of old Rome, on the night that followed that celebrated day I found myself with chains on my legs and shackles around my wrists. And this was how it happened: the King of Algiers, Uchalí [Uluj Ali],[2] a bold and successful pirate, had

---

1. The Battle of Lepanto, October 7, 1571, at which Cervantes himself fought and was seriously wounded [*Translator's Note*].
2. A captured Italian who had converted to Islam [*Translator's Note*].

attacked and captured the Maltese flagship, only three badly wounded
knights being left alive, so Admiral Giovanni Andrea Doria came to their
aid, and I and my company were on board his ship. Doing what was
required, I leaped onto the enemy vessel — but veering suddenly away
from Admiral Doria's ship, the Algerians prevented my men from following
me, thus leaving me completely alone, surrounded by so many of my
enemies that, wounded all over, I had no choice but to surrender. And as
you know, gentlemen, Uchalí and all his squadron got away, I was left his
captive, the only sad Christian among so many who were happy, and the
only prisoner among so many who were now free — for fifteen thousand
Christians gained their liberty, that day, all of them galley slaves in the
Turkish armada.

"They took me to Constantinople, where the Grand Turk, Selim, made
my new master lord high admiral of his fleet, both for having done his
duty in the battle and also for having carried off, by his valor, the flag of
the Order of Malta. The next year, which was 1572, I found myself at
Navarino, rowing in the lord high admiral's flagship. And I saw and took
careful notice of how we lost a chance to capture the entire Turkish fleet,
as it lay in port: all the marines and the other elite troops on board were
convinced we were going to attack them right then and there, and they
had their gunny sacks and their *passamaques*, their running shoes, all
ready, because they were going to jump ashore and flee for their lives even
before the Christians came after them — which was how terrified they
were of our fleet. But Heaven decreed differently — not that our commanding general was careless, or that it was his fault — but for Christianity's sins, and because it is God's will that we should always have
scourges to punish us. So Uchalí took shelter at Modón, an island near
Navarino, where he sent his men ashore and fortified the harbor mouth,
then waited until My Lord Don Juan turned back. It was on this voyage
that the Christians captured *The Prize*, a galley captained by the son of
that famous pirate, Barbarossa. The capture was made by the Neapolitan
flagship, *The She-Wolf*, captained by that military thunderbolt, forever fortunate and never defeated, Don Álvaro of Bazán, Marquis of Santa Cruz.
And I must tell you what happened when *The Prize* was taken. That son
of Barbarossa was so cruel, and so savagely mistreated his captives, that
when the oarsmen saw *The Sea-Wolf* bearing down on them, and getting
closer and closer, they all dropped their oars and, seizing the captain,
who'd been standing on the gangway near the poop deck, screaming at
them to row faster, they passed him from bench to bench, all the way
from the stern to the prow, every one of them biting and tearing at him,
so before he'd gotten much further than the mast his soul was down in
Hell: as I said, that was how cruelly he'd treated them, and how much
they hated him.

"Well, we went back to Constantinople, and the next year — that was
1573 — Constantinople found out that My Lord Don Juan had conquered Tunis and taken it away from the Turks, giving it to Mulé Hamet
and thus frustrating the ambitions of Mulé Hamida, his brother, the cruelest and bravest Moor in the world, who'd wanted to return and rule
there. The Grand Turk took this loss very much to heart, so, drawing on

the wisdom his family is famous for, he quickly signed a peace treaty with the Venetians, which was something Venice wanted even more than he did, and, a year later, in 1574, he attacked La Goleta, which commanded the gulf, and the nearby fort My Lord Don Juan had left only half built. Meantime, I kept on rowing, not expecting ever to be free again; in any case, there was no chance of my being ransomed, because I'd made up my mind never to write and tell my father what had befallen me. So La Goleta was taken, and then the fort fell, too, for they had seventy-five thousand Turkish regulars and more than four hundred thousand Moorish and Arab irregulars from the whole of Africa, and this huge horde had with it such a store of munitions and supplies, and so many sappers and diggers, that they could have covered La Goleta and the fort too, using nothing more than handfuls of dirt. La Goleta was the first to fall, though until then it had been considered impregnable, nor were its defenders at fault, for they did everything that could and should have been done: the problem was simply that it turned out, in that desert area, to be infinitely easier to raise up high embankments than anyone had expected, for usually one finds water after digging down only eight or ten inches, but the Turks could go a full five feet and find nothing, so they piled sand bag on top of sand bag, so high that, finally, they stood higher than the walls of the fort, and it was like shooting ducks — no one could do a thing or muster any kind of defense. It was generally agreed that our people shouldn't have closed themselves up in La Goleta, but gone out into the open, down at the landing place, but those who say such things weren't there, nor are they people with much experience in such matters — because if La Goleta and the fort, put together, held barely seven thousand soldiers, how could such a small force, no matter how powerful it might be, venture out in the open and hold its own against so huge an enemy army? And how can you help losing a fort when it's not well supplied, and especially when it's surrounded by a stubborn and very numerous enemy, and on his own ground? Yet many people thought, and myself among them, that Heaven showed Spain a very special grace and favor, permitting the destruction of that criminals' workshop and refuge, that sponge and guzzler, that wastebasket of so much money, all thrown away to no purpose, except that it was supposed to help preserve the blessed memory of its capture by the invincible Charles the Fifth — as if his memory required those stones to keep it eternal, as it surely will be. The fort fell too, but the Turks had to take it bit by bit, because the defenders fought so valiantly and fiercely that they killed more than twenty-five thousand of their enemies, in the course of the Turks' twenty-two attempts to storm their way in. None of the three hundred survivors was unwounded — a clear sign of their strength and courage, and how well they'd defended themselves and remained at their posts. A small stronghold or tower in the middle of a lake surrendered only after bartering for terms; it was commanded by Don Juan Zanoguera, a gentleman from Valencia and a famous soldier. Among the other captives was Don Pedro Puertocarrero, La Goleta's commanding officer, who had done everything he could to defend his fort and who was so overcome by having lost it that he died en route to Constantinople, to which they were bringing him as a prisoner. At the same time they also captured the fort's commanding officer, Gabrio Cervellón, a gentleman from Milan, a splendid engineer and one of the bravest of soldiers. Many important people died in both those fortifications, among whom were Pagano Doria, a knight of the Order of Saint John and a man of notable generosity, as he showed in his open-handedness to his brother, the celebrated Giovanni Andrea Doria; and the worst part of his death was that he was killed by some Arabs to whom he'd entrusted himself, once he saw the fort was going to fall, who promised to dress him like a Moor and take him to Tabarca, a little port or freight station run by Genoese in the coral-fishing business, but the Arabs cut off his head and took it to the high admiral of the Turkish fleet. But he made them living proof of our old Spanish proverb: 'Treason may be delightful, but the traitor is detestable,' and had them hanged, it's said, for not bringing him Pagano Doria alive.

"One of the Christians who was captured when the fort fell was an officer named Don Pedro of Aguilar, a native of some place in Andalusia, I don't know exactly where — a well-respected soldier and unusually intelligent, and in particular a gifted poet. I mention him because Fate brought him to the same galley and the same bench where I was rowing, and made him a slave to the same master, and before we sailed out of that port this gentleman composed two sonnets, in the style of epitaphs, one about La Goleta and the other about the fort. And I'd like to recite them for you, because I know them by heart and I think they'll make you happy rather than sad."

The moment the captive spoke of Don Pedro of Aguilar, Don Fernando looked at his friends and all three of them smiled, and when the captive mentioned the sonnets one of them said:

"Before you go any further, your grace, tell me, please, what happened to this Don Pedro of Aguilar."

"All I know," replied the captive, "is that after two years in Constantinople he disguised himself like an Albanian and escaped, together with a Greek double agent, but whether he made it to freedom or not I don't know, though I think he must have, because about a year later I saw that same Greek in Constantinople, though I couldn't ask him what had happened."

"He did indeed," the gentleman answered, "because this Don Pedro is my brother, and he's at home right now, alive and prosperous, married and with three children."

"May God be thanked," said the captive, "for all His mercies, because as far as I'm concerned no happiness on earth can compare to recovering your freedom."

"And what's more," the gentleman went on, "I too know those sonnets my brother composed."

"Then," said the captive, "you recite them, your grace, because you'll do it better than I can."

"With pleasure," the gentleman answered, "and here's the one written about La Goleta:

Chapter Forty

— which continues the captive's tale

SONNET

Oh fortunate souls, freed from this mortal disguise,
Exempt from flesh, because of the good you've done,
Lifted up from this lowly earth to the wondrous
Beauties, the better life, of Heaven on high,
    You fought for truth and honor, burning with pride
In the power of your hands, while your hearts could guard this ground,
And dyed this sea, this sandy soil around,
From your own rich veins, and with enemy blood. You died
    Unbroken, your glowing courage never bent,
Your sword arms heavy, and as you fell the crown
Of victory was wreathed across your bloody brows.
    This downfall was your blessing, Heaven-sent;
This glorious fame you won in toppling down,
At sword-point, behind those walls, redeems your vows."

"That's the very same poem," said the captive, "that's it exactly."
"And the one about the fort, if I remember it right," said the gentleman,
"goes like this:

SONNET

From this blasted, sterile spot, this ground
Pounded and flattened out by Fate, three thousand
Blessèd Spanish souls, soldiers all,
Flew happily up to dwell in Heaven's hall,
    But only after three thousand strong right arms
Had tried, and failed, to keep this fort from harm,
Three thousand swords grown fewer, three thousand blades
Grown heavy and blunt, till death came where they stayed —
    This very same place where thousands of mournful memories
Have always roamed, through every century known
To man — every century, including our own —
    But soil that never before surrendered any
Souls so righteous to Heaven's shining hands,
Soil never trod by such brave bands."

Everyone thought these weren't bad sonnets, and the captive, delighted
with the news they gave him of his comrades, went on with his tale: "So,
with the fall of both the town and the fort, the Turks gave orders to demolish La Goleta — the fort was already in such shape that there was
nothing left to pull down — and, to get this done as quickly as possible,
and with as little difficulty, they dug three blasting tunnels, but they simply
couldn't blow up what had seemed the weakest part, namely the old walls,
while everything the Little Monk [Giacome Paleazzo, the Spanish kings'
Italian engineer] laid down for the new fortifications was easily levelled to
the ground. Then the fleet returned to Constantinople, triumphant, vic-

torious, and there, a few months later, my master Uchalí died; they called him *Uchalí Fartax*, which is Turkish for 'the scabby-headed [*tiñoso*] renegade,' which is what he was, and the Turks always pick peoples' names either on the basis of some defect or some special quality, because they only use four family names, all of them descending from the direct Ottoman line [Mohammed, Mustafa, Murad, Ali], which leaves everyone else, as I said, to take both their first and their last names either from some physical defect or from some special aspect of their personality. And this Tiñoso, who'd been one of the Great Turk's slaves, had spent fourteen years rowing in the galleys, and didn't become a renegade until he was more than thirty-four years old, because he wanted to get back at a Turk who'd slapped him in the face while he was rowing, which was why he was willing to abandon his faith — and he was such a brave man that, without relying on the indecent methods and schemes used by most of the Great Turk's confidantes, he rose to be King of Algiers and then Lord High Admiral, which is the third highest rank in the whole empire. He'd been born in Calabria, and was a highly moral man who treated his slaves most humanely; there were over three thousand of them, and when he died his will provided that they be divided between the Grand Turk (who always shares equally with the deceased man's children) and the renegades who'd been in Uchalí's service. I was given to a Venetian renegade who'd been captured while a ship's cabin boy, and of whom Uchalí was so fond that he became one of the man's pampered favorites, and indeed turned into one of the cruelest renegades I ever saw. His name was Hassan Pasha [*Azán Agá*], and he rose to be a very rich man and himself King of Algiers; I accompanied him there from Constantinople, more or less happily, because it was so much nearer Spain — not that I planned to write to anyone about the misfortune I'd experienced, but just to see if my luck would be any better in Algiers than in Constantinople, where I'd tried a thousand ways of escaping but none had ever worked out, and I hoped that, in Algiers, I might find some other way of achieving what I so desperately longed for, because I never gave up hoping to be free again, and, each time, when the plans I concocted didn't do the trick, I refused to give up but immediately started hunting and calculating something different, so I could keep going, even if what I was planning was feeble and useless. So I kept on, locked up in a prison or sometimes in a building the Turks call a *baño* [dungeon], where they keep their Christian captives, the ones belonging to the king and also to private individuals, as well as the ones they call *almacén*, which means 'town slaves' — those who work on public projects for the city, and that sort of thing — and getting free is hardest of all for these captives, because they're owned in common and not by any particular person, which means there's no one to arrange a ransom with, even when the money's available. As I said, there are some private individuals who bring their slaves to these *baños*, especially when they're arranging for ransom, because they can safely let them stay there until the ransom money arrives. But the king's slaves, when they're going to be ransomed, don't get sent out to work with the rest of them, unless their ransom money is late coming, in which case, to make the captives write and urge that the money be sent faster, they force them to work with

the others, on public jobs and gathering firewood — which is no picnic.
I was one of those who was supposed to be ransomed, because when they
found out I was an officer, even though I explained that I had no money
and no property either, nothing could stop them from putting me with all
the gentlemen and the others who were sure to be ransomed. I wore a
chain, though it was less for safekeeping and more as a way of marking
me as ransom property, and that was how I spent my time in the *baño*,
along with all the gentlemen and fine people, all of us marked and waiting
for ransom. Hunger and the shortage of clothing were bothersome, sometimes — really, almost all the time — but nothing troubled us as much
as the continual, incredible cruelties my master practiced on Christians.
Every day he'd hang or impale someone, or maybe cut off someone's ears,
and for so little reason, or no reason at all, that the Turks admitted he did
it just because it pleased him, and because he was naturally disposed to
be murderous to any and all human beings. And the only person he treated
well was a Spanish soldier named Saavedra,[1] who'd done things those
people will remember for a long time, always trying to win his freedom,
and this man he never beat or ordered beaten, nor ever said a cross word
to, though for just the least of the things he did the rest of us would have
been afraid of being impaled — and more than once even he was afraid
of exactly that. If it weren't that we haven't the time, I'd stop and tell you
some of the things this soldier did, which would amuse and astonish you
far more than my own tale. But, in any case, let me note that all around
our prison yard were the windows of a rich and noble Moor's house and,
as is the Moors' custom in such things, not only were these more like
holes in the wall than what we call windows, but they were covered over
with heavy, tightly-coiled iron grillwork. Well, one day, as I was standing
on a square out in the yard, alone with three of my companions — all
the other Christians having been sent out to work — just to pass the time
we began to see how far we could jump, wearing our chains, and happening to look up I saw there was a stick protruding from one of those
round holes, with a handkerchief tied to the end, and the stick was waving
up and down, almost like a signal for us to go over and take it. We stood
watching for a moment, and then one of my companions walked over and
positioned himself right underneath it, to see if it would be dropped down,
or what, but as soon as he got there the stick was lifted up and then moved
from side to side, like someone saying 'no' by shaking their head. So the
Christian came back, and the stick was lowered and set to jiggling just the
way it had been doing earlier. So another of my companions went over
and the same thing happened. And then the third went over, and the same
thing happened once again. So I figured I ought to try my luck, too, and
as soon as I stood under the stick they let it fall, and it landed right at my
feet. I immediately untied the knot which I could see in the handkerchief,
and found ten *cianiís*, this being a coin of unrefined gold that the Moors
use, each of which is worth about ten dollars in our money. I need hardly
tell you this was a delightful discovery indeed, but my happiness was
matched by my wonder at who could have given us such a fine present

---

1. That is, the author of *Don Quijote*, Miguel de Cervantes Saavedra [*Translator's Note*].

— but really, given *me* such a present, for they'd plainly indicated they wanted to drop the stick to no one but me, so I was clearly the one they meant to reward. I took that lovely money, broke the stick, and then went back to the square where we'd been standing, looked up toward the window, and saw a singularly white hand quickly opening and then shutting the window. This told us, or at least led us to think, that some woman living in that house must have given us the present, and as a sign that we appreciated it we made a deep bow, or salaam, in the Moorish fashion, bending the head and the body low and crossing our arms on our chests. A little later a small cross, fashioned of sticks, was pushed out through the same little window, and then quickly pulled in again. This seemed to us proof that some Christian lady was a prisoner in that house, and it was she who had given us the money, but the intense whiteness of the hand we'd seen, and the jewelry we'd seen on it, made us reconsider and think, instead, that it had to be some renegade Christian woman, for their Moorish masters often take them as legitimate wives, and think it a very good arrangement, for they like Christian women better than their own. But we really had very little idea what the true situation might be, so from that moment on we spent all our time staring up to the north, where the star of the lady's stick had appeared to us, though it was two weeks before we saw it or her hand again, or any other sign. And though we tried as hard as we could, all during that time, to find out who lived in that house, and if it might contain some renegade Christian lady, all we ever learned was that a highborn and rich Moor named Hadji Murad lived there, a man who'd been in charge of the fort at La Pata, which among the Moors is a singularly noble post. By the time we'd stopped thinking there'd be any more gold coins raining down from that window, we suddenly saw the stick again, with another handkerchief and an even bigger knot tied in it; it was when we were out in the yard again, as we'd been the time before, all alone and by ourselves. We performed the same test, each of the three others going over before I did, but the stick responded only to me and, when I approached, it fell at my feet. I untied the knot and found forty Spanish gold doubloons, and a document written in Arabic, at the end of which a large cross had been drawn. I raised the cross to my lips, picked up the doubloons, and returned to the square, where we all made our deep bows, and then I saw the hand reappear, so I indicated I would read what had been written, after which the hand once again closed the window. We were all baffled and happy at what had happened, but since none of us understood Arabic, we were terribly anxious to understand what the document said, and only too well aware that finding someone to read it to us was a grave difficulty. But finally I made up my mind to confide in a renegade from Murcia, who'd said he was a true friend and made promises that would require him to keep any secret I entrusted to him, for many of these renegades, when they think about returning to the Christian world, take with them sworn statements from notable captives, testifying, in whatever form they can manage, that this particular renegade is a good man who has always been kind to Christians and who has been trying to escape just as soon as he can. Some of them seek such affidavits in good faith; others obtain them quite deliberately and whenever they can, because if they go raiding in Christian lands and either lose their way or are taken captive, they pull out their affidavits and argue that such documents clearly show why they returned to Christian soil, which was because they meant to remain there, and that was the reason they'd joined the pirating Turks. This allows them to soothe the Christians' natural fury, and to make their peace with the Church, without suffering any consequences, and then when they get the chance they return to Barbary and go back to being what they'd been before. There are others, as I say, who seek such testimonials in good faith, to let them truly return to Christianity. In any event, my friend was one of these renegades, carrying affidavits from everyone in the *baño*, all saying as many good things about him as they could; had the Moors found these documents, they'd have burned him alive. I knew his Arabic was excellent, and not just in spoken form, for he could write it, too, but just the same, before I explained the whole situation to him, I asked him to read me the document, saying I'd found it, by pure chance, lying in a hole in my hut. He unfolded it, then stood a long time staring, considering, and muttering between his teeth. I asked if he understood it; he said he understood it perfectly and, if I wanted him to explain it for me, word for word, I should fetch him pen and ink, so he could do it better. We immediately brought him what he wanted, and he sat translating it, bit by bit, until he'd finished, at which he said:

" 'Everything you see here in European writing, without a letter omitted, is exactly what's in this Moorish document, though I must warn you that wherever it says *Lela Marién* it means "Our Lady the Virgin Mary." '

"We then read the document, which went as follows:

> When I was a little girl, my father had a woman slave who taught me, in my own language, how to say Christian prayers, and told me a great deal about Lela Marién. But the woman died, though I know she did not burn in eternal flames, but went with Allah, because since then I've twice seen her, and she's told me to go to the Christian world to see Lela Marién, which I would dearly love to do. But I don't know how: looking out this window I've seen many Christians, but you're the only one who's looked like a gentleman. I am very beautiful and very young, and I have a lot of money I can bring with me: try to arrange it so we can go together, and when we get there you shall be my husband, if you wish to, but if not, I won't care, because Lela Marién will find someone who'll marry me. I've written this myself; be careful who you let read it; don't trust a Moor, because they're all liars. This worries me a lot, because I don't want you to tell anybody: if my father found out, the first thing he'd do is drop me down a well, and then he'd cover me over with rocks. I'll put a thread on the stick: tie on your answer but, if you can't find anyone who writes Arabic, answer me with signs, and Lela Marién will help me understand. May She and Allah watch over you, and also this cross, which I kiss over and over, because that's what the captive woman told me to do.

"Consider, gentlemen, if what we read in this document justly astonished and delighted us all — so obviously, indeed, that the renegade realized we hadn't found it by accident, and that it had in fact been written to one of us, so he asked us, if his suspicions were correct, to trust him and tell him everything, for he would risk his life for our freedom. And as he said this, he drew from his bosom a metal crucifix and, weeping freely, swore — in the name of the God represented by that image, in whom he well and truly believed, though he was a sinner and a wicked man — that he would loyally and faithfully keep any secrets we might want to confide, for to him it seemed and, indeed, was virtually prophesied, that the woman who had written these words was to be the means by which he, and us as well, were to attain our freedom, which would let him bring himself, as he deeply desired, back into communion with the Holy Church, his Mother, from whom he had been separated and cut off, like a putrid limb, and all because of his own stupidity and sinfulness. He said all this with so many tears, and such signs of repentance, that we were all of the same mind and agreed to tell him the entire truth, which we proceeded to do, holding back not a single detail. We showed him the window through which the stick had appeared, which allowed him to take careful note of which house we were dealing with, so he could make a very special effort to find out just who lived there. We all agreed it would be a good idea to answer the young lady's letter, so, having someone who could write Arabic, we immediately had the renegade write out what I dictated to him, which was exactly what I shall repeat to you, here — for nothing significant that happened to me throughout this entire business has ever left my memory, nor ever will, so long as I live. What we said to the Moorish lady, then, was as follows:

> May the true Allah protect you, my lady, and also that Blessed Marién who is God's own Mother and who, because She loves you, has put in your heart the desire to journey to the Christian world. Call on Her to show you how to bring to pass what you have been commanded, for Her mercy is such that She will help you. As for myself, and all the Christians who are here with me, we promise to do whatever we can for you, though we die for it. Don't fail to write to me, letting me know what you decide to do, and I will always reply, for the Great Allah has furnished us with a Christian captive who can speak and write your language as well as you yourself, as you can see by this reply. Accordingly, we can without fear be as helpful to you as you wish. As for what you say might happen when we reach Christendom, that you become my wife, I promise you as a good Christian to do exactly that — and, as you know, Christians keep their promises far better than the Moors do. May Allah and Marién, His Mother, watch over you, my lady.

"The reply having been written and sealed, I waited for two days, until the *baño* was once again deserted, and then went directly to our usual square, to see if the stick would appear, which it very soon did. As soon as I saw it (though I could not see who was holding it), I held up the sheet of paper, indicating that the thread should be lowered to us, but it was already tied in place, so I attached the paper — and it wasn't long before our shining star reappeared, bearing the little bundle that was its white flag of peace. It came dropping down, and I picked it up, and there in the cloth were more than fifty silver doubloons of all sizes and shapes, which heightened our happiness by more than fifty times, and convinced us that we were well on the way to freedom. That very same night, our renegade came back, informing us that he'd learned the house was inhabited by just the Moor we had been told of, Hadji Murad, rich as rich could be, who had just one daughter, heiress to his entire estate and generally considered, all over town, to be the most beautiful woman in all Barbary, and indeed many of the viceroys who'd visited that house had sought her as their wife, but she refused to be married. He'd also learned that she'd owned a Christian woman slave, now dead, which was all exactly as her letter had explained. So we immediately tried to decide, with the renegade's help, the best way to get the Moorish lady out, and bring the whole lot of us to Christian soil, but soon realized that we had to wait for Zoraida's next letter (Zoraida, of course, being she whom you now know as María), for we could see perfectly well that she, and only she, would have to find a path through all our difficulties. After we came to that decision, the renegade told us not to worry, for he'd either see us free or die.

"For the next four days the *baño* was full of people, which was why it took four days before we saw the stick reappear, but once the *baño* was again empty the stick returned, its tied-on handkerchief sagging so heavily that we expected a singularly joyous birth. Stick and handkerchief came down to me, containing another letter and a hundred gold doubloons — and no other kind of money. The renegade was in the hut with us, so we gave him the letter, which he read and told us went as follows:

My lord, I have no idea how to get us to Spain, nor has Lela Marién told me how, though I've asked her. All I can think of is to give you a lot of money, all in gold, as much as I possibly can, so you can use it to ransom yourself and your friends, after which one of you can go to some Christian land and there buy a boat, and then come back for the others. And me you'll find at my father's summer estate, which is near the Babazón gate, near the sea, where I'm to be all summer, together with my father and my servants. From there, in the darkness, you should be able to find me without any trouble and take me to the boat — but remember, you've got to marry me, because if you don't I will ask Marién to punish you. If there's no one you can trust to go for the boat, ransom yourself and go, for I'd rather trust you to come back than anyone else, since you're a gentleman and a Christian. Try to learn about our summer estate; when you walk under this window I will know there's no one else in the *baño*, and I'll give you piles of money. May Allah protect you, my lord.

"This was how the second letter read, and as soon as we'd all read it everyone, including myself, was eager to be the one who got to be ransomed, promising to go and return as fast as possible, but the renegade rejected any such idea, saying that he would not under any circumstances agree that anyone was to go free until we were all freed together, experience having taught him that free men rarely did what they'd said they would surely do, while they were still captives, because certain highborn captives had tried that plan, ransoming someone who was to go to Valencia or Mallorca, with a full purse, to equip a boat and come back for those who had bought him his freedom, but none had ever returned — for, as he explained, once a man was free, the fear of going back and again becoming a captive absolutely wiped out of his mind all memory of worldly obligations. To prove he was telling the truth, he gave us the outline of what had just recently happened to one of the Christian gentlemen — the strangest tale ever heard in those parts, where incredibly astonishing, wondrous things happen all the time.

"What he therefore thought he'd suggest, and we ought to do, was give him the money we had for ransoming one of us Christians, and he'd buy us a boat right there in Algiers, pretending he meant to become a trader and merchant in Tetuán and all along the coast there, for once he had a boat to command it wouldn't be hard to work out some way of getting us all out of the *baño* and safely on board the ship, especially if the Moorish lady furnished, as she'd said she would, enough money to ransom the whole lot of us, because once we were all free it would be the easiest thing in the world to take ship right in the middle of the day. The real problem would be that the Moors didn't let renegades buy or even use boats, except the huge vessels they take on pirating expeditions, because they were worried that anyone who bought a boat — especially a Spaniard — wouldn't want it for anything but a journey back to Christendom. But he could take care of this little problem by having a Moor from old Aragón buy the vessel with him, and also share in buying the merchandise, which would be excuse enough to let him become captain of the ship — and then everything else would of course follow. Even though my friends and I thought buying the boat at Mallorca was a better idea, as the Moorish lady had suggested, we didn't dare contradict him, for fear that, if we didn't do as he wanted, he'd betray us and, if he revealed Zoraida's part in all this, we'd be in serious danger of death, thus ensuring that we'd exchanged our lives for hers, so we decided to put ourselves in God's hands, and in the renegade's. We also composed our answer to Zoraida, explaining that we were doing everything she had advised, for she had counseled us quite as well as if Lela Marién herself had told her what to say, and it would have to be up to her, and only her, whether we held back or went forward with the business. I promised once again that I would marry her; thereafter, at various times when the *baño* happened to be empty, she employed the stick and handkerchief to give us two thousand gold doubloons, plus a letter in which she explained that the next *jumá* (that is, Friday) she'd be leaving for her father's summer estate, and if she were able, before then, she'd give us more money, and if we didn't have enough we should let her know, and tell her just how much we needed, for her father was so exceedingly rich that he wouldn't miss it and, what's more, the keys to everything were in her hands. We immediately gave the renegade five hundred doubloons, to buy us a ship; with eight hundred more I ransomed myself on the pledge of a merchant from Valencia, who happened to be in Algiers at the time, giving him the money and arranging that he'd pay it after the next boat arrived from Valencia, for if the money were handed over at once the king might suspect that it had been in Algiers a long time and that the merchant had kept it for himself, to turn a profit. And further, my master was so difficult that under no circumstances would I have dared to pay him off in a hurry. On the day before the beautiful Zoraida was to go to the summer home she managed to give us another thousand doubloons and to let us know she was in fact leaving, asking that, if I did ransom myself, I should quickly make an effort to study her father's estate and, no matter what, find a way to actually go there and see her. I replied, briefly, that I proposed to do exactly as she had indicated, and that she needed to commend us to Lela Marién, in the words of whatever prayers the captive woman had taught her. Then I arranged to ransom my other three comrades, so leaving the *baño* would create as little difficulty as possible; I was also concerned lest, seeing me ransomed and themselves not, though the money was available, they might create a fuss — the devil might even talk them into doing something that would injure Zoraida; and though I might not have had to be thus concerned, considering the kind of men they were, all the same I wanted to take no chances with this business, so I had them ransomed the same way I'd arranged it for myself, giving the merchant the whole sum, so he could assume our bond with perfect safety and certainty. All the same, I told him nothing of what we were really up to, because that might have been dangerous.

Chapter Forty-One

— the captive's tale continues

"Before another two weeks the renegade had bought a very fine ship, able to hold more than thirty passengers, and to protect himself, making everything look realistic, he thought he ought to make, and in fact made, a voyage to a place called Cherchell [an Algerian port], which was just over a hundred miles distant, towards Orán, where there was an active trade in dried figs. Indeed, he made this trip two or three times, along with the Moor from Aragón, the 'partner' I've already mentioned. (The Barbary Moors call the ones from Aragón *tagarinos*, as they label those from Granada *mudéjares*, though in Fez what they call the *mudéjares* is *elches*, and they're the people the king makes most use of, as soldiers.) Anyway, each time he made the trip he anchored his boat in a cove, within gunshot of the estate where Zoraida was staying, and very deliberately stationed himself there, along with the young Moorish fellows who handled the oars, saying his prayers or rehearsing what, afterwards, he meant to actually do, for which purposes, too, he'd go to the estate and ask for fruit, which Zoraida's father would give him, quite unaware of who he was. But though he'd have liked to speak to her, as he told me later, and tell her I'd arranged that he'd be the one to carry her to Christian soil, thus making her happy and confident, he could never manage it, for no Moorish woman is permitted to be seen by any Moorish or Turkish man, unless her husband or her father so orders. They're allowed to deal, and to speak freely with, Christian captives, sometimes even more than they ought to be, yet I would have regretted it, had he been able to speak to her, for perhaps she'd have been upset, finding her personal affairs discussed by a renegade. But God, who was arranging matters differently, didn't let our renegade fulfill his thoroughly honorable intention. Meanwhile, seeing how easily he could go back and forth to and from Cherchell, and anchor the boat when and where and how he pleased, and that his partner, the *tagarino*, had no interest in doing anything except what he was ordered to do, and that I had been ransomed and all we still needed was some Christians to man the oars, the renegade told me to keep an eye out for some I might like to take with me, aside from those who'd already been ransomed, and arrange things with them for the very next Friday, for that was when he had decided we ought to sail. Accordingly, I spoke to a dozen Spaniards, good oarsmen all, and all of them available for the trip — not that there were many of them to be found, just then, for there were fully twenty ships gone pirating, and most of the oarsmen had gone with them, nor would I have found these men if it hadn't been that their master had decided, that summer, not to try his hand at piracy, so he could finish building a galley he had under construction. All I told these oarsmen was that, the next Friday afternoon, they should slip out, one at a time, and be near Hadji Murad's garden, waiting for me when I came. I gave these instructions to each of them individually, directing that, should they see other Christians there, they were to say only that they'd been told to wait there. Having taken care of this, I still had something else to do, and this was the most important thing of all, namely, to let Zoraida know exactly how far along our plans were, so she might be on notice and well-prepared, rather than being taken by surprise if, unexpectedly, we had to come for her before she might have expected the boatload of Christians to arrive. So I made up my mind to go to her father's summer estate and see if I could talk to her, and exactly one day before we were scheduled to leave I in fact went there, pretending I was collecting certain herbs, and the first person I met was her father, who spoke to me in that lingua franca employed all across Barbary, and even in Constantinople, which neither is nor isn't Moorish or Spanish, or any other language for that matter, but a jumble of all languages, thus allowing us to communicate. And using this lingua franca he asked me what I was doing on his estate and from whom I had come. I told him I was Arnaute Mamí's[1] slave (because I knew this man was one of his very closest friends) and I was looking for all kinds of herbs, to make a salad. He went on to ask me whether or not I was destined to be ransomed, and if so how much was being asked for me. We were thus engaged when my beautiful Zoraida came out of the house, being well aware who I was, and since as I've said Moorish women don't worry about showing themselves to Christians, nor about avoiding them, she didn't have to worry about coming over to where her father and I were standing; indeed, as soon as her father saw her slowly approaching, he called to her to join us. How can I tell you, now, with what beauty, what elegance, and wearing what magnificent, rich jewels my beloved Zoraida first showed herself to my eyes? All I can say is that more pearls hung from her lovely neck, her ears, and her hair than she

---

1. The pirate captain who had captured Cervantes himself [*Translator's Note*].

had hairs on her head; on her ankles — bare, in the Moorish style — she wore two *carcajes* (which is what they call ankle bracelets and bangles) of the purest gold, set with so many diamonds that she told me, afterwards, her father had said they were worth ten thousand doubloons, and the ones she had on her wrists were worth just as much more. She wore many, many pearls, and very fine ones, because Moorish women take special pride and pleasure in adorning themselves with all kinds of pearls, big and small, which is why the Moors own more pearls than the people of any other nation on earth, and Zoraida's father was famous for having not only a great many but also some of the very best pearls in Algeria, as he was also renowned for the possession of more than two hundred thousand Spanish doubloons, all of which were at the command of her who, now, commands only me. Whether or not she was beautiful, thus adorned, you can imagine, seeing how much of the loveliness of her prosperity she has retained, after so many trials and tribulations. Who does not know that, for some women, beauty has its days and seasons, waxing and waning as circumstances dictate? The gusts of emotion naturally lift and drop it back, and more often than not destroy it. In short, that day she was beautifully adorned and fantastically beautiful, and — or at least so she seemed to me — the loveliest woman I had ever seen. And if you add to her loveliness my awareness of all I owed her, you can understand that she appeared before me like some heavenly goddess, descending to earth to aid and delight me. As she came toward us, her father told her, in their own language, that I belonged to his friend Arnaute Mamí, and that I had come seeking salad herbs. She acknowledged my presence and, in that lingua franca[2] I spoke of, asked me if I was a gentleman and why I had not been ransomed. I told her I had indeed been ransomed, and from the price one could tell how highly my master had valued me, for I had brought him fifteen hundred gold *zoltanís*. To which she replied:

" 'Ah, but had you belonged to my father, I would have seen to it that he wouldn't take twice as much for you, for you Christians always lie to us about how much you're worth and, to cheat the Moors, pretend you're all poor.'

" 'That may be, my lady,' I answered her, 'but I was honest with my master, as I am and as I will be with everyone in the world.'

" 'And when do you leave?' asked Zoraida.

" 'Tomorrow, I think,' I said, 'because there's a French boat sailing tomorrow, and I think I'll take it.'

" 'Wouldn't it be better,' replied Zoraida, 'to wait for Spanish boats, and sail with them, rather than go with the French, who aren't your friends?'

" 'No,' I answered, 'although if I had heard that a Spanish boat were indeed coming, I'd wait for it — but it seems clear that I'll be leaving tomorrow, for my longing to be home again and to see those I love is so strong that I simply can't wait for anything more convenient but slower, no matter how much better it might be.'

---

2. The lingua franca the captive alludes to is a mixture of languages [mezcla de lenguas]: Spanish, French, Italian, Portuguese, Greek, and Arabic. Below, the captive will call this lingua franca "the bastard tongue" [la bastarda lengua] used throughout Algiers.

" 'Surely you're a married man, then,' said Zoraida, 'and anxious to be with your wife.'

" 'I'm not married,' I answered, 'but I have promised to marry when I get there.'

" 'And is she beautiful, the lady to whom you've pledged yourself?' asked Zoraida.

" 'She is so exceedingly beautiful,' I replied, 'that to properly and truthfully describe her, I'd have to say she much resembles you.'

"At this her father laughed heartily, saying:

" 'By Allah, my Christian friend, she must be really beautiful, if she looks like my daughter, for this is the most beautiful woman in the entire kingdom. If you don't think so, just look for yourself, and you'll see I'm telling the truth.'

"Her father had been helping me understand what Zoraida was saying, for although she spoke the bastard tongue that, as I've explained, everyone there uses, in that language she spoke more eloquently with signs than words. As we were thus conversing, a Moor came running up, shouting loudly that four Turks had climbed over the walls and were gathering fruit, which wasn't even ripe. The old man was frightened, as was Zoraida, because it's universal and almost automatic for the Moors to be afraid of the Turks, and particularly the Turkish soldiers, who are so arrogant and haughty with their subjects that, in truth, they treat them worse than if they'd been slaves. So her father said to her:

" 'Go in the house, my daughter, and lock yourself in, while I go talk to these dogs, and you, Christian, go find your herbs, and may Allah see you safely home again.'

" 'I bowed, and he went looking for the Turks, leaving me alone with Zoraida, who began to do as her father had directed. But as soon as he was out of sight among the trees, she turned back to me, her eyes filled with tears, and said:

" 'Amexi, oh Christian, amexi?'

"Which meant, 'Are you leaving, oh Christian, are you leaving?'

"I answered:

" 'Yes, my lady, but under no circumstances without you: watch for me this next Friday and don't be frightened when you see us. Have no fear: we are going to Christendom.'

"I said this in such a way that she understood perfectly what had been said, and putting her arm around my neck she began to walk languidly toward the house, but it was just my luck — and could have been exceedingly bad luck, had Heaven not looked after me — that her father, returning after having chased away the Turks, saw us walking in the intimate way I have described. But my quick and clever Zoraida, instead of withdrawing her arm, drew still closer and laid her head on my breast, letting her knees sag a bit, thus clearly showing how weak she felt, and I, simultaneously, made it abundantly clear that I was holding her up whether I liked it or not. Her father came running over to us, and seeing his daughter so apparently feeble asked her what was wrong, and when she did not answer, said,

" 'Obviously, it's those dogs climbing in here that has frightened her.'

"As he took her from my breast and leaned her, now, against his, she sighed and, though her eyes remained dry, said once more,

" '*Amexi*, Christian, *amexi* — Go, Christian, go.'

"To which her father replied,

" 'The Christian need not leave, my daughter; he's done you no harm, and the Turks have gone away. Don't be afraid of anything, for there's no one here to bother you, and as I said the Turks have gone back where they come from, as I asked them to.'

" 'It was indeed the Turks who frightened her, *señor*,' I said, 'but since she says I ought to leave, I have no desire to disturb her. May peace be with you and, with your permission, I will return here for herbs, if I need to, for my master insists there are none to equal yours.'

" 'Come back for as many as you like,' Hadji Murad assured me, 'and please understand that my daughter didn't say what she did because she disliked you or any Christian, but was just indicating that those Turks ought to go away, or perhaps that it was time for you to go looking for your herbs.'

"So I said goodbye to them both, and she, looking as if her heart would break, went off with her father, as I, pretending to hunt for herbs, went up and down all over the estate, exactly as I pleased, carefully examining its entrances and exits, and how well the house was guarded, and in general the best way of handling our whole business. Then I went back and told the renegade and my friends everything that had happened, finding it hard, now, to wait until I might safely possess all the delights offered me, by Fate, in the person of my good and beautiful Zoraida.

"But the time passed, and we finally reached the day and the moment we all longed for: at last executing the plans which, following on judicious thought and much long discussion, we had first formulated and then rehearsed over and over again, we found ourselves exactly as successful as we had hoped, and on the very next Friday after my conversation with Zoraida, as night fell, our renegade anchored the boat almost at her very door. The Christians who were to do our rowing had all been alerted, and were hidden here and there, all around, tensely and excitedly awaiting my coming, anxious to storm on board the boat they could see in front of them, for they had no idea of the arrangement with the renegade and thought they'd have to win their liberty by force of arms, killing the Moors on board the vessel. So as soon as my companions and I arrived, and they saw us there, all those hidden men came running to us. It was already past curfew time, and the whole city was deserted. Once we were all together, we hesitated, not sure whether it was better first to carry off Zoraida or to take care of the hired Moorish oarsmen who'd been plying the boat's oars. As we debated, the renegade appeared and asked what was holding us back, because, he said, it was time; all his Moorish oarsmen were relaxing at their ease and, for the most part, were in fact asleep. We told him what was causing our delay, and he replied that the most important thing was to take control of the ship, which could be done with the greatest ease and without any danger, after which we could go after Zoraida. Everyone approved of what he said, and, without any further hesitation, and with him leading us, we approached the boat and he

jumped right on board, put his hand on his scimitar, and declared in their
Moorish tongue:

" 'None of you move, unless you want to die.'

"Almost all the Christians had now boarded the ship. Seeing how their
captain had spoken, the Moors were frightened and had no appetite for
fighting, so not one of them laid a hand on a weapon — almost none of
them in fact having anything to fight with — and surrendered without a
word, after which the Christians very quickly tied them up, warning that
if they made any sort of noise they'd all be put to the sword at once. That
done, roughly half of us stayed as guards, while the others, with the renegade once more in the lead, went to Hadji Murad's estate and were lucky
enough, when we tried to unlock the gate, to find that it opened as easily
as if it had never been shut, so that, in absolute and complete silence, we
reached the house without anyone seeing us. My beautiful Zoraida was at
a window, waiting for us, and as soon as she sensed our presence she
asked, in a whisper, if we were *nizarani* — that is, if we were Christians.
I told her we were, and that she should come down. As soon as she
recognized me, she did not hesitate a moment, and without saying a
word came down, opened the door, and showed herself more richly
and beautifully dressed than I can possibly tell you. As soon as I saw her
I took her hand and began to kiss it, as did the renegade and my two
friends, and all the others, who didn't know what was happening, followed
suit, so they would not seem ungrateful or unwilling to acknowledge the
lady who was setting us all free. The renegade asked her, in the Moorish
tongue, if her father was there. She replied that yes, he was, and that he
was asleep.

" 'Then we'll have to wake him up,' said the renegade, 'and carry him
off with us, along with everything of value on this entire estate.'

" 'No,' she declared, 'I do not want my father so much as touched, nor
anything else in the house except what I shall take, which will be enough
to make all of you rich and happy, as you shall see in a moment.'

"And as she said this, she turned and went in, saying she'd return at
once, so we stayed there, not making a sound. I asked the renegade what
they'd been saying, which he repeated for me, and I told him that nothing
should be done except what Zoraida wanted, by which point she returned,
bearing a box so full of gold doubloons she could barely carry it. But luck
turned against us, and her father had woken up, meanwhile, heard that
something was going on and, putting his head out a window, immediately
knew that everyone out there was Christian, so he began to cry out in
Arabic, as loud and rapidly as he could,

" 'Christians, Christians! Thieves, thieves!'

"His shouts terrified and, for a moment, completely confused us. But
the renegade, seeing our danger, and knowing how important it was that
we finish this business before we were discovered, quickly went up to
where Hadji Murad stood, with some others of us right behind him,
though I myself did not dare leave Zoraida, who had fallen into my arms,
as if in a swoon. But those who'd gone into the house handled matters so
well that, in another moment, they came back down with Hadji Murad,
carrying him, his hands tied, and a handkerchief stuffed into his mouth,

so he could not utter a word, and warning him that should he speak he would be killed. Seeing him, his daughter covered her eyes, to block out the sight, and her father was completely stunned, having not the slightest idea how willingly she had put herself in our hands. Since what was most necessary, just then, was that we get moving, we went back to the boat just as fast as we could, where those we had left behind were anxiously waiting for us, fearful that something bad had happened. It was barely two hours after nightfall when we all got back to the ship, where we untied Zoraida's father and took the handkerchief out of his mouth, although the renegade made sure to tell him not to say a word, at the risk of his life. Seeing his daughter there, he began to sigh very softly, and especially when he saw how tightly I embraced her, and she lay there quietly, making no attempt to stop me, neither protesting nor pulling away. But in spite of all this, he remained silent, so as not to bring down on himself the many threats uttered by the renegade.

"Finding herself now on board, and seeing that we wanted to set the oarsmen to work, Zoraida was keenly aware that her father was there too, and the other Moors we had tied up, so she spoke to the renegade and asked him to seek a favor from me, namely, that we release the Moors and set her father free, for she'd rather throw herself into the sea in front of his eyes than see a father who had shown her so much love carried off as a captive, and all because of her. The renegade repeated her words to me, and I told him I'd be glad to comply, but he answered that it couldn't be done, because if we set them free right there they'd immediately raise a hue and cry and rouse the whole city, and they'd set out after us with their fastest boats, and on land as well as at sea, so we wouldn't have a chance of escaping, but what we could do was set them free as soon as we reached any Christian soil. Everyone agreed, and Zoraida, too, when it was explained to her, along with our reasons for not immediately doing as she wished, was well satisfied, so in silent joy and happy, brisk earnestness, our brave rowers took up their oars and, commending us to God with all their hearts, began to steer us toward the island of Mallorca, the closest Christian land. But because the north wind blew up a bit, and the sea became somewhat choppy, we couldn't make way directly toward Mallorca, but had to stay near the coast and beat our way around toward Orán, which gave us much cause for concern, because we might be spotted from Cherchell, located sixty miles away. We were also worried that, along the way, we might meet up with one of those Algerian galleys that came back and forth with merchandise from Tetuán, though each and every one of us thought that, encountering a merchant ship, rather than one of the pirate vessels, not only would we not be lost but we'd be able to capture a ship that would let us complete our voyage even more safely. As we sailed along, Zoraida kept her head between my hands, so she should not see her father, and I was sure she was imploring Lela Marién to help us. We'd gone about thirty miles down the coast when it began to grow light and we found ourselves perhaps three rifle shots distant from land, which we saw was all deserted, with no one who could have spotted us, but all the same we rowed hard and got a bit further out to sea, for the wind had let up and it had gotten calmer, and once we were six or seven miles out the rowers were told to work in shifts, while we took something to eat (the boat having been very well provisioned), but they protested it was no time to be resting and, though those who were not rowing might very well be fed, they would not under any circumstances take their hands off their oars. So that was what we did, but just then a crosswind blew up, which forced us to hoist our sails and stop rowing, setting our course for Orán, for no other direction was possible. We did all this exceedingly quickly, and went along under sail at more than eight miles an hour, our only fear being that we might meet a Moorish pirate vessel. We fed the captive Moorish rowers, and the renegade tried to cheer them up, telling them they were not going to remain captives and we would free them the very first chance we got. He told Zoraida's father the same thing, to which the old man replied:

" 'I might anticipate, and trust in, virtually anything else from your liberality and decency, oh Christians, but as for granting me my freedom, don't think me so foolish as to believe *that*! You'd never have taken the risk of kidnapping me simply to let me go thus generously, especially knowing who I am and how much you can expect to get for me, so name your price and I expressly offer you whatever you may want for me and my miserable daughter — or, if not for us both, then for her alone, she who is the best and the largest part of my soul.'

"As he spoke, he began to weep so bitterly that we were all stirred with pity, and Zoraida herself was obliged to look at him and, seeing him crying, was so touched that she rose from her position at my feet and went to embrace her father, putting her face against his, the two of them weeping so passionately that many of us joined them. But when her father saw how gaily she was dressed, and how many jewels she was wearing, he said to her in their language:

" 'What is this, my daughter? Yesterday night, before this terrible misfortune came to us, I saw you dressed in your ordinary, everyday clothing, and now, without there having been any opportunity to dress yourself, and without there having been any joyous news you might want to celebrate by adorning yourself and putting on your best garments, I see you wearing exactly that fine clothing I know so well, and with which in our happier days I was able to furnish you. Answer me, for I find this more startling, and it makes me even more anxious, than this disaster which has struck me.'

"The renegade translated every word of this for us, but she did not say a word. But when he saw, off to the side of the boat, the money box in which she'd kept her jewels, which he knew perfectly well had been left in Algiers city, and had not been taken to his summer estate, he was deeply perplexed and asked her how this box came to be in our hands, and what was in it. And then the renegade, not waiting for Zoraida to answer, told him:

" 'There's no point, sir, in exhausting yourself, asking her all these questions, because the one I'll answer for you will take care of all the others, and so let me tell you that she's a Christian, and it's she who has filed off the chains of our captivity and restored our freedom. She's with us of her own free will, and as happy, I suspect, to see herself here, as someone who emerges out of darkness and into light, from death to life, and from punishment to glory.'

" 'Is he telling the truth, my daughter?' the Moor asked.

" 'He is,' answered Zoraida.

" 'So then,' replied the old man, 'you're a Christian, and you've consigned your father to the power of his enemies?'

"To which Zoraida answered:

" 'That I'm a Christian, yes, but that I've put you in this position, no, for it was never my desire to leave you or to hurt you in any way, but only to do good for myself.'

" 'And what good thing have you accomplished for yourself, my daughter?'

" 'As for that,' she replied, 'seek an answer from Lela Marién, for she can tell you better than I can.'

"No sooner had the Moor heard this when, with incredible quickness, he threw himself headfirst into the sea, and certainly would have drowned had the long, full robes he was wearing not kept him floating just out of the water. Zoraida screamed for us to save him, and we all quickly lent a hand, snatching at his robes and pulling him out, half drowned and unconscious, which so wracked Zoraida that she wept over him as passionately and miserably as if he'd been dead. We turned him face down; he threw up a great deal of water; and two hours later he came back to consciousness, by which time the wind had turned and we had to make for land, rowing as hard as we could to keep from being driven up on the shore, and perhaps it was our kind fortune, once again, that we came to an inlet alongside a small promontory, or cape, known to the Moors as *La Cava Rumía*, meaning in our tongue 'The Wicked Christian Woman,' for it is their tradition that La Cava,[3] who was responsible for the fall of Spain, is buried there — *cava* in their language meaning 'wicked woman,' and *rumía* 'Christian woman' — and they still believe it's bad luck when they're forced to anchor there, which they never do unless they absolutely have to, but for us it wasn't the inlet of a wicked woman, but just a safe harbor from the truly angry sea. We posted sentries, and kept our hands ready on the oars, then ate what the renegade had provided for us and prayed to God and to Our Lady, from the bottom of our hearts, to help us and protect us and give us an ending to match this very fine start. As Zoraida requested, we put her father ashore, along with all the other Moors who, still bound, had come with us, for she could not stand to see, right in front of her eyes, her father and others of her countrymen bound and in captivity; her heart was far too tender to endure it. We had already promised to do this, when we'd first set sail, and there was no danger in setting them down in that uninhabited place. Nor did Heaven turn a deaf ear to our prayers, for the wind soon turned in our favor, and the sea became calm, and it was time for us to happily continue the journey we had started. So we untied the Moors and set them ashore one by one, which vastly surprised them, but when it was Zoraida's father's turn he declared, now in full command of his senses:

" 'Christians, do you know why this wicked woman is happy to see me

---

3. Later known as Florinda, daughter of Count Julián, seduced by Rodrigo, last of the Gothic kings, in consequence of which Spain fell to the Moors [*Translator's Note*].

set free? Do you think it's because she feels any tenderness for me? No, certainly not, it's just that I interfere with her evil passions and she wants me out of her way. And don't think she's changing religions because she believes yours is any better — no, it's just that she knows how much easier it is to practice indecency, in your lands, than it is in ours.'

"And then, turning toward Zoraida — while another Christian and I each held him by an arm, to keep him from doing anything foolish — he said to her:

" 'Oh, you dirty slut, you misguided wench! Where do you think you're going, you wild, blind creature, in the clutches of these dogs, our natural enemies? I curse the hour when I begot you, I curse the pampered luxury in which I raised you!'

"But I saw he was likely to go on like this for a long time, so I quickly got him onto land, and there, in the loudest voice he could muster, he went on cursing and lamenting, begging Mohammad to intervene with Allah and have us destroyed — confounded — killed. And when we could no longer make out his words, because we had raised our sail, we could still see what he was doing, how he was tearing out his beard and his hair and crawling along on the ground — but just once his voice rose so loud that we could understand what he was saying:

" 'Come back, oh my beloved daughter, come back, I forgive everything! Let those men have all this money, it's already theirs, and come back to comfort your miserable father, who will die here in these barren sands, if you abandon him!'

"Zoraida heard it all, and felt it all, and wept, unable to say anything or to answer, except:

" 'Oh my father, pray to Allah that Lela Marién, who made me become a Christian, will console you in your unhappiness. For He knows perfectly well that I could do nothing but what I've done, and that these Christians bear no responsibility for any of it, for even had I not wanted to come with them, but stay at home, it would have been impossible, my soul so cherished this deed that seems every bit as good to me, my beloved father, as it seems evil to you.'

"But her father could not hear her, as she said this, nor could we see him any longer, and as I tried to comfort Zoraida we turned our attention to our voyage, which a right-blowing wind was now making so much easier that in just one more day, we were convinced, we'd see the sun coming up over Spain's shores. But Fortune is rarely, or ever, pure and simple, but either brings with it or else is followed by some bad luck that shakes or even overturns it, and whether it was just Fate, or the curses hurled at his daughter by the Moor (and you have to take them seriously, no matter what kind of father utters them), whatever the reason, about three hours after nightfall, when we were well out at sea, moving along under a taut sail and with oars pulled in and lashed tight (for the right-blowing wind had made it unnecessary to work them), going along in the gleaming moonlight, we saw a square-rigged ship hard by us, under full sail, bearing a little to larboard and directly in our path — so close, indeed, that we had to haul down our sail to keep from ramming her, at which they swung hard over to let us pass. Then they bore down alongside and asked who we were, where we were from, and where we were headed, but since they spoke in French our renegade said:

"'Don't answer, for these have got to be French pirates, who will rob us blind.'

"So no one said a word and, having moved a bit ahead of them, so they were just to the larboard of us, they suddenly fired two cannons, both apparently loaded with chain-shot, for one cut our mast in half, dropping the sail into the ocean, and the second, fired immediately afterward, struck us dead amidships and split our boat open, though it did no other damage, but seeing that we were rapidly sinking we all began to shout for help, begging them to take us on board or we would drown. They promptly lowered their sails and launched their skiff, or small boat, carrying about a dozen well-armed Frenchmen, rifles at the ready; it came alongside and, seeing how few of us there were, and that our boat was going down, they took us in, explaining that it was all our own fault for not having been courteous enough to answer their questions. Our renegade, without anyone seeing what he was up to, took Zoraida's money box and quietly dropped it overboard.

"So there we were, sailing with the Frenchmen, who first got all the information they wanted from us, and then, as if we'd been their worst enemies, stripped us of everything we had, even taking the bracelets Zoraida wore on her ankles. But what happened to Zoraida didn't worry me so much as the fear that, having stolen her richest and most precious jewels, they'd also take the jewel that was worth more than all the others, the one she most dearly treasured. But all those people lusted after was money, and it was a longing nothing could satisfy: their greed was so intense that, had our prisoners' clothing been worth anything, they'd have stolen that from us, too. And there were obviously some of them who wanted to wrap us in a spare sail and throw us into the sea, because they planned to do some trading in Spanish ports, pretending to be from Brittany, and if we were found on board, they'd be punished just as soon as their robbery came to light. But the captain — it was he who had plundered my beloved Zoraida — said he was satisfied with the prize he'd taken, and though he wouldn't land at any Spanish port he would go through the Straits of Gibraltar, at night, or however he could best manage, heading for La Rochelle, which was where he had started from, so it was agreed they'd let us have their skiff, and whatever we needed for the short voyage we'd still have to make, and the next day, in sight of Spanish soil, they did as they'd promised — and, having actually seen Spain, all our cares and our poverty dropped right away from us, forgotten as if they'd never existed, so wonderful is the pleasure of freedom regained.

"It was about noon, probably, when they put us off their ship, having given us two barrels of water and some biscuits, and as my beautiful Zoraida left his vessel the captain, prompted by who knows what feeling of compassion, gave her almost forty gold doubloons, and kept his soldiers from taking the very clothes in which you see her now. So we got in the little boat, letting them know how grateful we were for their kindness, and showing ourselves more thankful than whining; they went back to sea, sailing straight for Gibraltar, and we, steering only by the land we saw in front of us, set ourselves to rowing so hard that, by sundown, we were so close we were sure we could make land before it got really dark, but since it was a cloudy night, and the moon never appeared, and we had no idea exactly where we were, it didn't seem to us entirely safe to try for the shore, though many among us wanted to, saying we ought to make a run for it even if we hit rocks and found ourselves far from any inhabited place, because at least we wouldn't have to worry, as indeed we properly did, about pirate ships from Tetuán, which would set out from Barbary at nightfall and reach Spain at dawn, taking what prize they could, and then turning around and sleeping, the next night, in their own beds, but of all the conflicting opinions put forward the one we finally settled on was to ease ourselves gradually toward the shore and, if the sea was calm enough, to land wherever we could. Which was what we did — and it was probably just before midnight when we came to the base of a towering, squat mountain, which reared up considerably inland from where we were, offering us just enough room to land quite comfortably. So we steered into the sand, jumping out and kissing the ground, happy, with tears of sheer joy, to thank God, Our Lord, for the incomparable grace He had shown us. We took out the provisions we still had, then pulled the boat up on the shore and climbed a long, long way up the mountain, for even there where we were we could not be entirely sure — indeed, we could scarcely believe — that we in fact stood on Christian soil. As far as I was concerned, dawn came far more slowly than we liked. We climbed the rest of the way and, at the top of the mountain, tried to find some populated spot, or at least some shepherds' huts, but found nothing, neither dwellings, nor people, nor even a path or a road. But we were determined to go further, no matter what, sure that we would eventually meet with someone who could tell us where we were. But what bothered me the most was seeing Zoraida have to walk over such harsh ground, and even though for a while I carried her on my back, my weariness made her wearier than any rest could refresh her, so she wouldn't let me do it any more, and with extraordinary patience, and every sign of pleasure, she walked along, letting me lead her by the hand, and we hadn't gone as much as a mile when the sound of a little cow bell reached our ears, plainly indicating that there had to be a herd close by and, all of us looking around, we saw a young shepherd boy, near the foot of a cork-oak tree, very quietly and unconcernedly whittling at a stick with his knife. We called out and, raising his head, he jumped right up and, as we afterwards learned, the first thing he saw was our renegade and Zoraida and, since they were wearing Moorish clothing, was convinced that all of Barbary was after him and went running through the nearby wood, leaping like a rabbit and screaming, with the wildest yells ever heard,

" 'Moors, the Moors have landed! Moors, Moors! To arms, to arms!'

"This frantic shouting completely confused us, and we didn't know what to do, but reflecting that the shepherd's screams would surely raise a hue and cry, and the coast guard would immediately come to see what was going on, we decided that the renegade had better take off his Turkish clothes and put on a captive's jacket that, though it stripped him to his shirt, somebody quickly gave him, and then, commending ourselves to

God, we went down the same road the shepherd had taken, constantly on the alert for the coast guard. Nor were we disappointed, for in less than two hours, as we came out of the underbrush and onto level ground, we saw perhaps fifty mounted men coming toward us, moving rapidly at a brisk half-gallop, and the moment we saw them we stopped and waited, but when they reached us and saw, instead of the Moors they were hunting, a crowd of poor Christians, they were deeply perplexed, and one of them asked if it was we who had caused the shepherd's call to arms.

" 'Yes,' I said, and meant to go on and explain what had happened, and from whence we'd come and who we were, when one of the Christians who'd traveled with us recognized the cavalryman who'd asked the question and, without letting me speak another word, said:

" 'God be thanked, gentlemen, for having brought us to such a fine place! For unless I'm mistaken, the soil we walk on is that of Vélez Málaga — and, unless the years of captivity have robbed me of my memory, you, sir, who've just questioned us, are Pedro de Bustamente, my uncle.'

"The Christian captive had barely finished speaking when the cavalryman jumped off his horse and ran to embrace the young fellow, crying:

" 'Oh my dear, dear nephew, I recognize you, I do — and how I've wept for your death — as has my sister, and everyone in your family, all of whom are still alive — and God will give them the pleasure of seeing you again! We knew you were in Algiers, and judging from your clothing, and the dress of everyone with you, I can see your freedom has been a miracle!'

" 'Exactly,' replied the young man, 'and there'll be time to tell it all.'

"When the other cavalrymen realized we were Christians who'd been in captivity, they all dismounted and invited us to ride their horses to the city of Vélez Málaga, which was eight or nine miles distant. After we'd told them where we'd beached it, some of them went back down the mountain, to bring our boat to the city, and we climbed up behind the others, on their horses, while Zoraida was given the animal our friend's uncle had been riding. The whole city came out to greet us, for someone had gone ahead, bearing the news of our coming. They weren't surprised to see freed prisoners, or captive Moors, for everyone who lived on that coast had long since seen both, but they were stunned by Zoraida's beauty, which at that moment was at its absolute zenith, heightened by our fatiguing journey and by her happiness at finding herself on Christian soil, all of which had lent her face such color that I'll swear, unless my love was bewitching me, nothing to match it was ever seen on this earth — at least, nothing I ever saw. We were taken straight to church, to thank God for His mercies, and the moment Zoraida passed through the door she said she saw faces exactly like Lela Marién's. We told her these were indeed likenesses of the Virgin, and the renegade explained to her, as best he could, what such paintings and statues meant, and that she could pray to them, each and all, as if they were each of them the same Lela Marién who had spoken to her. She had a quick mind, naturally clear-sighted and perceptive, so she immediately understood everything he'd told her. After church, we were all brought to different houses throughout the city, and given hospitality among them, but the young Christian who'd come with us took the renegade, Zoraida, and myself to his parents' home, who were reasonably well-to-do people and welcomed us just as affectionately as they did their own son. We stayed in Vélez six days, and then the renegade, having found out what he ought to do, set out for the city of Granada, where the Holy Inquisition could bring him back into communion with the Church; the other freed Christians went their own ways, leaving only Zoraida and me, furnished only with the doubloons given her by the French pirate, with which I bought the donkey on which she's been traveling, and for the moment I've been serving as her father and her squire, not her husband, for we're going to see if my father's still alive, or if any of my brothers' luck has been better than mine: Heaven having already given me Zoraida, I doubt that anything so good can ever happen to me again. Her patience with all the inconveniences of poverty, and her overwhelming desire to become a Christian, continually astonish me, and will make me her servant as long as I live, though my delight at seeing myself hers, and she mine, is troubled and undercut because I still do not know where I can find shelter for her, here in my country, and whether Time and Death may have so changed my father's and my brothers' estate, and also their lives, that, if they're gone, I could conceivably find no one who still knows me.

"Gentlemen, there's nothing else I can say about my life's story. Whether it's pleasing or unusual you'll have to judge for yourselves; all I can say is that I'd rather have told it more concisely, even though, as it is, my concern that it might be too much for you has led me to omit three or four curious episodes."

Chapter Forty-Two

— what happened next, along with a good many other things well worth knowing

The captive had finished. Don Fernando said to him:

"The way you've told this extraordinary story, my dear sir, beautifully matches its unusual strangeness. Every bit of it is interesting, and distinctly uncommon, and full of episodes that astonish and captivate anyone hearing it, and we've listened to you with such delight that, even should you begin it all over again, and tomorrow find us occupied with exactly the same tale, we would be equally delighted."

As he said this, Cardenio and all the others volunteered to help Zoraida and the captive in any way possible, speaking so warmly and honestly that there could be no doubt of their sincerity. And Don Fernando in particular vowed that if the captive would come with him, he'd fetch his brother, the count, to be Zoraida's sponsor at her baptism — and he himself would undertake to make sure the captive could return to his homeland in easy circumstances and as impressively as he deserved. The captive was cordially grateful for all their generous offers, though he would accept none of them.

Night was falling, and as it grew dark a coach drew up at the inn, followed by some gentlemen on horseback. They asked for rooms, but the innkeeper's wife told them there wasn't a square inch that hadn't already been taken.

"That may very well be," said one of the mounted gentlemen, who'd come inside, "but you've got to find a place for His Honor the Judge."

The innkeeper's wife was visibly upset.

"Señor, the long and the short of it is that I haven't got any beds, but if His Honor the Judge happens to have a bed with him, as surely he does, then by all means let him come in, and my husband and I will let His Honor have our own room."

"That will do very well," the attendant replied.

Just then a man stepped out of the coach, his clothing immediately identifying the office and responsibilities he bore, for his long robe, with its ruffled, gored sleeves, clearly showed that, as his servant had said, he was a judge. Following him out of the coach, holding his hand, was a young lady of about sixteen, in traveling clothes, and so stunning, so lovely, so elegant, that everyone was struck by the sight — and had they not already encountered Dorotea, Luscinda, and Zoraida, all of whom were right there in the inn, they would have been convinced that finding anyone to match her would be exceedingly difficult. Don Quijote saw the judge coming in with her, and immediately announced to him:

"Your grace can enter this castle, and rest yourself here, in perfect confidence, for though it is cramped and poorly fitted out, there is nowhere in the world so cramped and uncomfortable that it cannot find room for arms and learning, especially when both arms and learning enjoy loveliness as their guide and leader, as we see your grace's learning does, in the person of this beautiful young lady, for whom not only should castles open wide their gates, but the very cliffs ought to make way, and mountains split themselves apart and bow themselves down, to properly welcome her. So enter this paradise, your grace, for here you will find suns and stars to glow alongside the firmament you bring with you; here, I say, you will find arms at their very height of perfection, and beauty at its absolute rarest."

Don Quijote's eloquence astonished the judge, who stared fixedly at our knight, no less struck by his appearance than by his words — and then, unable to think how to answer him, the newcomer was stunned yet again by the sight of Luscinda, Dorotea, and Zoraida, who, having heard of the new arrivals, and of the young lady's beauty, had come to see and to welcome her. Don Fernando, Cardenio, and the priest greeted him with more usual courtesies. But in a word, His Honor's entrance was all a jumble, as much because of what he saw as what he heard, though the beautiful women already in attendance gave the lovely young lady a handsome welcome.

The judge could see perfectly well that everyone in the inn was of high, not to say noble birth, but Don Quijote's appearance, face, and bearing, completely confused him. Once all the proper greetings had been exchanged, as well as information about the inn's facilities, everything was arranged just as it had been earlier — that is, all the women would go into the attic already referred to, and all the men would remain outside, as if on guard duty. The judge was more than satisfied that his daughter (which the young lady was) should go off with the other ladies, which she did very cheerfully. And by taking part of the innkeeper's narrow bed, as well as half of the bed the judge had with him, he and his daughter fared better, that night, than they had expected.

The moment he saw the judge, the captive's heart had leaped within him, for he was sure this was his brother, so he asked one of their servants to tell him their names and, if he knew, what part of the country they were from. The servant replied that this was His Honor Juan Pérez de Viedma, and it was said that he was from somewhere up in the mountains of León. This information, coupled with what his own eyes had told him, assured the captive that this was indeed his brother, who, according to their father's advice, had taken the road of learning, and, excited and happy, he drew to one side Don Fernando, Cardenio, and the priest, and told them what was going on, explaining that this judge was surely his brother. The servant had also informed him that the judge was traveling to a post in the Indies, where he was to serve on the High Court of Mexico, and that the girl was his daughter, her mother having died when she was born, and the judge having become a very rich man, what with the dowry and the daughter his wife had left him. The captive asked for their advice on how best to make himself known, or if he ought to find out, first, if, once he revealed himself, his brother would think himself humiliated by such a poor relation, or would welcome him wholeheartedly.

"Let me find out for you," said the priest, "though there is no reason for thinking, my dear sir, that you won't be given a warm welcome, for the good sense and upright bearing easily observable in your brother make it highly unlikely he'd be either arrogant or standoffish, or that he wouldn't understand how to justly estimate the turns of Fortune's wheel."

"Just the same," said the captive, "I'd rather he found out bit by bit who I was, and not all of a sudden."

"As I've assured you," the priest replied, "I'll handle this to everyone's satisfaction."

Dinner was then announced, and they all seated themselves around the table, except the captive and the ladies, who were to dine by themselves in their own room. In the middle of the meal, the priest suddenly said to the judge:

"Your Honor, I had a friend in Constantinople, where I spent some years in captivity, who bears the same name you do; he was one of the bravest soldiers and officers in the whole Spanish army, but just as unlucky as he was gallant and courageous."

"And what was this officer's name, my dear sir?" asked the judge.

"He was called Ruy Pérez de Viedma," answered the priest, "and he came from a village up in the mountains of León. He told me, once, something that had happened between his father and his brothers and himself, and had I heard it from anyone but so truthful a man, I'd have taken it for the kind of fable old ladies spin in winter, in front of the fire. What he told me was that the father had divided his estate among his three sons, at the same time giving them advice better than anything we have from Cato.[1] And I know enough of the story to report that the brother who chose the road of war did so well that, in a very few years, thanks to his bravery and his courage, and with nothing to help him but his extraordinary virtue, he rose to the rank of captain and was thought well on the way to becoming a true commander of men. But Fortune proved fickle, for just as he had every reason to expect his reward, he lost everything, including his freedom, at the battle of Lepanto, just when so many others were recovering theirs. I was taken captive at La Goleta, and then later on, as things worked out, we found ourselves comrades in Constantinople. He went from there to Algiers, where I happen to know he experienced one of the strangest adventures this world has ever seen."

The priest then proceeded, in as few words as possible, to tell the judge what had happened between Zoraida and his brother, and the judge listened more attentively then he had ever before listened[2] to anything. But the priest took the tale only as far as the appearance of the French pirates, and the poverty and deprivation in which the captive and the beautiful Moorish woman had been left, indicating that he had never learned what happened thereafter, nor whether the pair had ever gotten to Spain, or whether the pirates had carried them off to France.

The captive had been listening to every word the priest said, though from concealment, carefully watching every movement his brother made, and the judge, when he saw the priest had finished his tale, gave a deep sigh and, his eyes full of tears, said:

"Oh, sir, if you knew what news you've told me, and how much it means to me — just see these tears rolling from my eyes, which no judicial wisdom or reserve can keep me from shedding! This gallant captain of whom you speak is my older brother, a stronger and nobler-minded man than either my younger brother or myself, who chose the worthy, honorable profession of arms, that being one of the three paths our father suggested to us, exactly as your comrade told you in the fable you may have thought you were hearing. I chose the path of learning, in which, by the grace of God and my own hard work, I have risen to be what you see before you. My youngest brother is in Peru, and so rich that, with what he's sent my father, and me as well, he's easily fulfilled his share of the bargain — indeed, putting so much into my father's hands that he's been able to satisfy his natural generosity — while I've been able to apply myself, comfortably and decisively, to my studies, and to reach the point at which you behold me. My father is still alive, though dying for news of his oldest son, and constantly praying to God not to let death shut his eyes until he looks into his son's eyes once again. What truly surprises me, my brother being the wise man he is, is that through all his struggles and afflictions, or his rich successes, he never thought of communicating with his father, for had *he* known — had any of us known — there would have been no need to wait for the miraculous reed to descend and bring my brother his ransom. But what worries me, right now, is wondering if

1. The allusion here is to Cato the Censor (234–149 b.c.), who had been considered, since the Middle Ages, an authority on maxims and proverbs — the discourses of admonition.
2. *Oidor* = judge; it also means "listener." The pun is subtle, pointed, and untranslatable [*Translator's Note*].

those Frenchmen set him free, or whether they killed him to conceal their crime. And now I will continue my journey, not with the same pleasure I began it, but with a deep melancholy and distress. Oh my good brother, if only I knew where you were, right now! If only I could find you and free you from your struggles, though it should bring them down on my own head! Oh, how shall I tell our old father you're still alive, but perhaps locked into the deepest dungeons in all Barbary, for our money could rescue you, our father's, and my brother's, and mine! Oh beautiful, open-handed Zoraida, if only we could repay what you did for my brother! If only we could witness the re-birth of your soul, and see you married, ah, what a delight it would be!"

The judge said this, and much more like it, all filled with such sympathy and pity for the news about his brother that everyone who heard him joined in his tears.

Accordingly, seeing that he'd accomplished both his and the captive's objective, the priest had no desire to prolong their sadness and promptly rose from the table, went to the chamber where Zoraida was, and led her away by the hand, with Luscinda, Dorotea and the judge's daughter following after. The captive had been waiting to see what the priest was up to, and the priest took him, too, by the hand, and conducted both him and his lady to where the judge and the other gentlemen were sitting, and declared:

"Weep no more, Your Honor, and let all your good longings be herewith fulfilled, for you have in front of you your excellent brother himself and your good sister-in-law as well. This man you see here is Captain Viedma, and that lady is the beautiful Moor who did so much for him. The Frenchmen of whom I told you have left them in the poverty you can see for yourself, so your warm generosity can be permitted to show itself."

The Captain immediately stepped forward to embrace his brother, and the judge put both hands against the other's chest, to examine him at some little distance, but having once established who this was that hugged him so tightly, shed passionate tears, and most of those who were there wept with him. What the brothers said to each other, the emotions they exhibited, can scarcely be imagined, much less recorded on paper. Each offered a hasty summary of what had happened in their lives; they freely displayed the perfect love of two true brothers; the judge embraced Zoraida, offered her all he owned, and had her embrace his daughter; and the sight of the lovely Christian and the infinitely beautiful Moor made everyone start weeping all over again.

And there was Don Quijote, watching, not saying a word, contemplating these strange goings-on and crediting each and all of them to the fantastic paths followed by knight errantry. There were the Captain and Zoraida arranging to return to Seville with his brother the judge, and to inform their father that his oldest son had been found and was free, so that, if he were able, he could attend both Zoraida's wedding and her baptism, it being impossible for the judge not to complete the journey on which he was embarking, for he had learned that, in just a month, the fleet would be leaving Seville and sailing to New Spain, and to miss such an opportunity to take passage would be exceedingly troublesome.

In short, they were all well satisfied and happy with how things had turned out for the captive, and, the night being already two-thirds gone, it was agreed they should retire and, in the time left to them, seek some rest. Don Quijote volunteered to stand guard outside the castle, in case some giant or other evil-doing rascal should assault its walls, lusting after the enormous treasure of female beauty enclosed therein. His friends thanked him warmly, and informed the judge (who was much amused) of the knight's strange cast of mind.

Only Sancho Panza was upset at how tardily they were seeking their beds, and he made himself the best bed of all, throwing himself down on his donkey's harness blanket — which, as will be explained in due course, turned out to be a singularly costly mistake.

So the ladies were finally at rest in their room, and the others lying down in as little discomfort as possible, and Don Quijote left the inn and went out, as he had promised, to post sentinel around the castle.

And then, just before dawn, the ladies heard someone singing so beautifully, in such a striking voice, that they all were obliged to listen closely, especially Dorotea, for she was still awake, lying next to Doña Clara de Viedma, the judge's daughter. No one could think who might possibly be singing so magnificently, and without the accompaniment of any instrument whatever. Sometimes he seemed to be singing in the yard; sometimes in the stable; and as they were listening in this attentive uncertainty, Cardenio came to their door and said:

"Anyone who's not asleep, listen, and you'll hear some young muledriver singing like a nightingale."

"We're already listening, señor," Dorotea answered.

So Cardenio went away and, listening as carefully as she could, this was what Dorotea heard:

Chapter Forty-Three

— which narrates the pleasant tale of the young muledriver, along with the other things that took place in the inn

> — I sail the sea of love,
> crossing its mighty waves
> without the slightest hope
> of finding a port that's safe.
>   I set my course by a star
> I've only seen from afar;
> it gleams brighter in the sky
> than stars Aeneas sailed by.
>   It takes me where it wills,
> and I sail around and around,
> carefully watching its face,
> but careless enough to drown.
>   For why should it be so modest
> that it hides what must not be lost,
> covering itself with clouds
> exactly when I need it most?

> Oh bright and shining star
> whose rays light up my soul,
> if I never know where you are
> I will die: you have my all.

As the singer got to this climax, it seemed to Dorotea unfair not to let Clara hear such a delightful voice, so she shook the girl gently and woke her, saying:

"Forgive me, my dear, for waking you, but I have to, so you can listen to the most perfect voice you're likely ever to hear in your life."

It was hard for Clara to shake off sleep, and at first she did not understand what Dorotea was saying, so she asked her to say it again and then she listened carefully. But she'd heard barely two lines when she began to tremble violently, as if she'd been struck by a sudden sharp fever, and throwing her arms tightly around Dorotea she cried out,

"Oh my God, señora! Why did you wake me? The greatest gift Fortune could give me, right now, would be to close my eyes and my ears, and not let me see or hear this miserable musician."

"What are you talking about, girl? They say it's a young muledriver who's singing."

"No, no, he's a noble lord," answered Clara, "and the place he holds in my heart is so secure that, unless he chooses to give it up, he will hold it forever."

Dorotea was struck by the girl's highly emotional speech, for clearly she was far wiser than her years might have indicated, and so she replied:

"My dear Clara, it's hard to understand exactly what you're saying: I wish you'd be more open and tell me what you mean by talking about your 'heart' and some 'noble lord,' a 'miserable musician,' whose voice so upsets you. But don't tell me anything right now, for I've no wish, in responding to your shock, to lose the extraordinary pleasure of hearing his singing — for it seems to me he's turning his song in a new direction, with different words and a whole new approach."

"Then let him!" Clara answered.

And, to keep from hearing the song, she covered her ears with her hands, which also startled Dorotea — who nevertheless listened carefully as the song continued:

> Oh, hope, sweet hope, you make
> impossibles possible, you take
> the brambles out of the road
> your longing helps to shape,
> so never worry, afraid
> that death is always close.
> Lazy folk can't celebrate
> victories, or gain success,
> and no one's ever blessed
> when Fortune gets its way —
> no sighing, or moaning, or aching,
> or turning away your face.
> Love must sell itself high,
> its glories are worth the world;

no jewel can ever vie
with love's favor earned:
whatever you're able to buy
for nothing ought to be spurned.
So love must go on trying,
reaching for moons and stars;
and I, instead of sighing,
hold hope burning hard,
convinced my heart will be smiling
if I keep my faith unmarred.

And at this the voice ceased, and Clara's sobs began all over again, making Dorotea wonderfully anxious to know what could have caused such a delicate, loving song and such sad weeping. So she asked the girl, once more, to explain what she'd meant to explain before. Worried that Luscinda might be listening, Clara hugged Dorotea as hard as she could and, with her mouth right against her ear, whispered (so softly that no one else could possibly have heard):

"My sweet lady, the singer you heard is the son of a gentleman from Aragón, lord of two villages, whose house in Madrid was right opposite my father's, and even though my father closed the windows with curtains, in winter, and in the summer with shutters, somehow or other, maybe in church, or maybe someplace else — I don't know — this young man, who's a student, saw me. Anyway, he fell in love with me, and without being able to say a word told me so from the windows of his house, using gestures and so many tears that I simply had to believe him, and even love him, though I didn't know exactly what he wanted of me. One of the signs he made was folding one hand into the other, as if to say he wanted to marry me, and I'd be delighted if that could happen, but since I'm half an orphan, without a mother, I had no idea who I should tell, so I just didn't do anything to make him happy except, when my father and all his people were away from the house, I'd pull open the curtain or the shutter, just a little, and let him have a good look at me, and he'd make such a fuss you'd think he was going out of his mind. So then it came time for my father to leave Madrid, and my young man knew about it, though not from me, because I was never able to tell him. He fell sick with grief, I heard, so the day we left I couldn't get to say goodbye to him, following him with my eyes. But two days after we set out, as we arrived at an inn, just a day's journey from here, I saw him at the tavern door, dressed like a muledriver and looking the part so well that, if I didn't always carry his image in my heart, it would have been impossible to recognize him. But I knew him at once, and it amazed me, and made me very happy; he watched me, unknown to my father, from whom he always conceals himself when he walks past me on the streets or in the inns we come to; and when I think who he is, and that it's for love of me he's going along behind us, and putting himself to so much trouble, I feel as if I'll die of sorrow, so I always look at his feet when he's walking. I don't know what he's planning, nor how he was able to get away from his own father, who's terribly fond of him, both because he's the only heir and also because he deserves it, as you'll find out for yourself, madame, when you get the chance to see him. And I can tell you something else: everything he was singing comes out of his own head, because I've heard he's a great student and a poet, too. And there's more: every time I see him, or hear him sing, I shiver all over, and it's like a shock, I'm so afraid my father will realize who he is and understand what we want to do. I've never said a word to him in my life but, just the same, I love him so much I couldn't live without him. Which is all I can tell you about that musician, my dear lady, whose voice pleased you so much — and from that alone you can easily see he's no muledriver, as you said, but a nobleman of standing, as I've said."

"My dear Doña Clara, don't say another word," Dorotea replied, kissing the girl a thousand times, "there's no need to say anything else, not now; let's just wait for tomorrow to come and then, perhaps, if God pleases, we can take care of this business of yours and find it the happy ending such chaste beginnings deserve."

"Oh my dear lady!" sighed Doña Clara, "how else can it all end, when his father's so noble and rich and I'm not even fit to be his son's servant, much less his wife? And as for marrying without my father's consent, I wouldn't do it for anything in the world. All I can ask is that the young man turn around and go home, and leave me, and maybe, when I can no longer see him, and when I'm so far, far away, the pain I feel right now will go away a little, too, though I must admit this isn't a remedy I expect to help me very much. I don't know what sort of devilish plot this was, or how I came to love him as I do, since I'm so young, and he's so young, and in fact I think we're exactly the same age, and I'm still not even sixteen, and I won't be, my father says, until next Michaelmas Day."

Dorotea couldn't help laughing at Doña Clara's childish prattling, then said to the girl:

"Let's rest, my dear, in what little time we still have, and then God will bring back the sun and we'll take care of everything, or else I've lost my touch."

So they went to sleep, and the whole inn fell completely silent — except the innkeeper's daughter and her servant, Maritornes, who were very well aware which way Don Quijote's brain was tilted and, knowing the knight was outside, fully armed and mounted, having posted himself on guard duty, had made up their minds to play a trick on him, or at least amuse themselves, listening to more of his insanities.

Now it happened there wasn't a window in the whole inn that opened out on the meadow, except a kind of straw hole, through which they got rid of dirty straw. So the two young ladies stationed themselves at this hole, and saw Don Quijote on his horse, leaning on his spear, and from time to time emitting such profoundly miserable sighs that, each time, he seemed ready to tear the very soul out of his body. And they also heard how softly and tenderly he uttered a lover's sweet nothings:

"Oh My Lady Dulcinea of Toboso, most beautiful of the beautiful, summit and highest peak of discretion, rich repository of noblest grace, storehouse of pure modesty and, lastly, platonic model of everything useful, modest, and delightful in the entire world! What is Your Grace doing, at this very moment? Do you perchance ever think of your captive knight, willingly exposing himself to so many dangers, and only to serve you? Oh lunar luminary with three faces, send me news of her! Even now, perhaps, you are staring down at her, enviously, as she moves along the corridors of her sumptuous palace, or as she leans her sweet breast against some balcony, pondering how, while still preserving her modesty and infinite nobility, she may soothe the anguish from which, all for her sake, my sad heart suffers, what glorious reward she ought to bestow upon my pain, what repose she should grant my conscientious service and, in the end, what life my death is owed, and what prize all my services. And you, oh Sun, who even now must be swiftly harnessing your glorious steeds, ready to hurtle into the sky and look down on my lady, I beg you, when you see her, to greet her on my behalf — but be careful that, in lavishing your glance and your greeting on her, you keep from kissing her cheek, for I will be more jealous of you than you were, once, of that fleet-footed ungrateful girl[1] who made you huff and puff across the sands of Thessaly or the banks of the River Peneus — for I cannot remember just where it was, so jealous and filled with love, that you went running."

Don Quijote had just gotten to this point in his sorrowful oration, when the innkeeper's daughter began to call to him, coyly:

"Oh sir, your grace, come over here, if you please."

Hearing this, Don Quijote turned his head and saw, by the light of the full moon, the straw hole which, to his eyes, seemed a castle window, covered by the gilded grille found on the windows in all splendid castles (as he fancied the inn to be), and his lunatic mind immediately recalled that earlier time when the beautiful maiden, daughter of the lady of the castle, overcome by love, had come wooing him, and so, not wishing to seem discourteous or ungracious, he tugged Rocinante's reins around and went over to the straw hole, and when he saw the two girls, said to them:

"How I regret, oh beauteous lady, that you should have turned your amorous thoughts in a direction from which it is impossible there can come anything to match your great worth and high nobility. But you should not blame this miserable knight errant, who cannot willingly surrender himself to any love but she who became for him, the moment he saw her, the absolute mistress of his heart. Forgive me, good lady, and go back to your chamber, and do not make it necessary, by telling me what you long for, that I show myself still more disagreeable — and if, perchance, the love you bear me can find any source of satisfaction, other than that which can never be, only ask it of me, and I swear in the name of that sweet, absent enemy of mine to grant it to you at once, even should you seek of me a lock of Medusa's hair, every strand of which is a snake, or even the rays of the sun itself, locked up in a vial."

"My mistress doesn't need anything like that, sir knight," said Maritornes at this point.

"Then what does your lady need, oh wise lady's maid?" answered Don Quijote.

---

1. Daphne; in Greek mythology, a nymph loved by Apollo, who pursued the "fleet-footed" maiden until, at her own entreaty, she was changed into a laurel tree.

"Just one of your handsome hands," said Maritornes, "to help her master the great longing which brought her to this straw hole, at such risk to her honor — for if the lord of the castle, her father, knew anything about this, the smallest thing he'd cut off her would be her ear."

"I'd like to see *that!*" replied Don Quijote. "But he'll keep his anger to himself, unless he'd like to meet the most disastrous end of any father in the world, for raising his hands against the delicate limbs of a lovesick daughter."

Maritornes was sure Don Quijote would proffer his hand, so, having decided what she should do, she turned away from the straw hole and went to the stable, where she picked up the halter rope Sancho Panza used for his donkey, then hurried back to the straw hole, just as Don Quijote was standing up on Rocinante's saddle to reach the window where he imagined the stricken young woman would be. Giving her his hand, he said:

"Accept this hand, my lady — or, to put it more accurately, this scourge of those who do evil in the world; take this hand which, I may tell you, has never touched another woman, not even she who enjoys complete possession of my whole body. I do not give it to you so you may kiss it, but rather so you may see how its sinews are structured, its muscles knitted together, the breadth and capacity of its veins, from all of which you should be able to calculate the strength of the arm which has such a hand."

"So now we'll see," said Maritornes.

And tying a running bow knot in the halter rope, she threw it over his wrist, then dropped the rope back through the straw hole and, with a firm knot, attached it to the door bolt. Feeling the coarse rope against his wrist, Don Quijote said:

"Your grace would seem to be grating rather than greeting my hand. Don't treat it so badly, for after all it can't be held responsible for the ill turn my affection has done you, nor is it right to vent all your anger on so small a part. Remember that she who truly loves ought not to exact so severe a revenge."

But all Don Quijote's words went unheard, for as soon as Maritornes had him tied, she and the innkeeper's daughter ran off, choking with laughter, leaving him rigged up so it was impossible to set himself free.

He was standing, as I've said, on Rocinante's back, his entire arm stuck into the straw hole, tied at the wrist and fastened to the door bolt, and he was standing very anxiously and carefully, for if the horse so much as shifted from one spot to another he'd be left dangling by his arm, so he didn't dare move a bit (though Rocinante's patience and calm might well ensure the horse standing motionless for a whole century).

So there was Don Quijote strung up, and when he became aware that the ladies had vanished he began to imagine the whole business had been managed by magic, just like the time before, when he'd been beaten, there in that same castle, by an enchanted Moor of a muledriver, and he silently cursed his own bad judgment in venturing into the same place a second time, after having fared so poorly at first, for he should have known from what had happened to other knights errant that, once an adventure had been attempted and failed, it was a clear sign of an adventure not meant for them but for someone else, and so there'd been no need to attempt this one again. In any case, he tried to pull down his arm, to see if he could free himself, but he was so neatly trussed up he couldn't do a thing. To be sure, he pulled on the rope very carefully, to keep Rocinante from moving, but still, no matter how hard he tried to lower himself into the saddle, all he could do was stay standing where he was, unless he pulled off his hand.

Then he longed for Amadís' magic sword, over which no enchantment had any power whatever; then he cursed his bad luck; then he tormented himself by thinking how the unfortunate world would miss him, while he hung there, enchanted, as he was convinced, of course, he had been; then he thought of his beloved Dulcinea del Toboso; then he set to calling for his good squire, Sancho Panza, but Sancho was so deep in dreams, stretched out on his donkey's blankets, that right then he couldn't have told you his mother's name; then he called on those wise magicians, Lirgando and Alcife, to come and help him; then he invoked the name of his good friend, the witch Urganda, to bring her to his side; and, in the end, he hung there until morning, so discouraged and bewildered that he began to bellow like a bull, believing that daylight would bring him no relief, and he would have to hang there for all eternity, magically entrapped. What made him even more convinced of this was that Rocinante scarcely moved at all, so he believed both he and his horse would have to remain in this state, neither eating nor drinking nor sleeping, until the evil flux of the stars had waned away, or until some other more powerful magician disenchanted him.

In which belief he was quite wrong, for dawn had barely arrived when four mounted men, well dressed and equipped, and with rifles hung from their saddle bows, appeared at the inn. They banged furiously on the door, which was still locked, and Don Quijote, seeing this, assumed the role of sentinel and called out to them, arrogantly and boldly, even hanging where he was:

"Gentlemen — or squires — or whoever you may be: you've got no business knocking at this castle door, for surely it is perfectly plain that, at this hour, either those inside are still asleep or else it's not their habit to throw open their gates until the sun has spread out all across the earth. Step back, and let the day break, and then we can see whether you ought to be admitted or not."

"What the hell kind of fortress or castle is this?" said one of them, "that makes us have to be so damned formal? You: if you're the innkeeper, tell them to open the door for us, because we're travelers and all we want is to feed our animals and get going again, and we're in a hurry."

"Does it seem to you, gentlemen, that I look like an innkeeper?" answered Don Quijote.

"I don't know what you look like," replied the other, "but I know you talk like an idiot when you say this inn is a castle."

"It is a castle," answered Don Quijote, "and one of the greatest in the whole region, and there are folk inside who have held scepters in their hand and worn crowns on their head."

"It would be better the other way around," said the traveler — "scepters on their heads and crowns on their hands. And maybe that's the way it'll be, if it comes to it, because there's got to be some kind of acting troupe in there, who always use these crowns and scepters you're talking about: in an inn this small, and as quiet as this one is, I don't believe you'd find people who really merit crowns and scepters."

"You know remarkably little of the world," replied Don Quijote, "and you're totally ignorant of what usually happens in knight errantry."

But the other three men got tired of this discussion between their friend and Don Quijote, and started to really bang furiously on the door, which finally woke up the innkeeper, as well as everybody else in the inn, and he got up to find out who was there. Just then, it happened that one of the men's horses sniffed out the presence of Rocinante, who was standing motionless, downhearted and sad, his ears drooping, supporting his haughty master, and since, after all, Rocinante was flesh and blood (though he may have looked like wood), he couldn't help but act a little like a horse and turn to sniff back at an animal who'd made such an approach, and so, though he didn't move very much, Don Quijote's legs slipped out from under him and he went skidding off the saddle, and would have fallen to the ground if he hadn't still been hanging by the arm — which hurt so excruciatingly that he was sure either his wrist would be cut through or else his arm would be pulled out, because he was so very, very close to the ground that, with just the tips of his feet he could lightly graze the earth, which made matters even worse, for once he realized how little more was needed to get his feet planted firmly on the ground he began to kick and struggle as hard as he could to reach terra firma, very much like someone being tortured by the block-and-pulley *strappado*, almost able to touch the ground, but not quite touching it and, the harder they kick and turn, making their own punishment worse, constantly deceiving themselves with the hope that, with just a little more effort, they really can and will reach the ground.

Chapter Forty-Four

— in which these extraordinary events are continued

In the end, Don Quijote yelled so loudly that, abruptly throwing open the doors, the innkeeper came out, terrified who he might find emitting such cries, and others came rushing over too. The same anguished screams had woken Maritornes, as well, and, knowing quite well what was going on, she ran to the straw loft and, without anyone seeing her, untied the halter rope by which Don Quijote had been hanging, so that he immediately fell to the ground, right in front of the innkeeper and the four travelers, all of whom, coming up to him, demanded what he'd been doing, screaming like that. Without answering with a single word, he pulled the rope off his wrist, jumped to his feet, leaped onto Rocinante, took up his shield and, setting his spear, galloped in a wide circle around the meadow, coming back a bit more slowly, and calling out:

"If anyone says I've been justly enchanted, and my lady the Princess

Micomicona grants me her permission, I hereby give him the lie and challenge and dare him to engage me in single combat."

Don Quijote's words astonished the new arrivals, but the innkeeper put their surprise to rest, explaining that this was Don Quijote and they didn't have to pay any attention to him, because he was out of his head.

The travelers then asked the innkeeper if, by any chance, a boy of about fifteen, dressed like a muledriver, had been seen at the inn, proceeding to give an exact description of Doña Clara's lover. The innkeeper replied that there were so many people in the inn that, no, he hadn't noticed anyone like the boy they were asking about. But one of them, having seen the coach in which the judge was traveling, said:

"He's got to be here, because this is the coach they said he was following. Let's somebody stay here at the gate and the rest go in and look for him — and maybe one of us better go on around back of the inn, so he doesn't get away over the fence."

"That's just what we'll do," said another.

So two of them went inside, one stayed at the gate, and the other went around back — and the innkeeper watched all of this and didn't have the faintest idea what they were up to, since as far as he knew they were looking for the young fellow they'd described to him.

It was already full daylight, for which reason, as well as for all the noise Don Quijote had been making, everyone in the inn was up and about, and in particular Doña Clara and Dorotea, both of whom had gotten very little sleep that night, the girl excited at being so close to her lover, Dorotea anxious to see what he looked like. Finding that none of the four travellers paid the slightest attention to him, Don Quijote was furious, half dying with mortification and rage, and had he been able to find any justification, in the rules and regulations of his order, for a knight errant taking on and pursuing any additional business, after having sworn and promised not to take on anything else until he'd finished the business on which he'd already started, he'd have attacked all four of them and made them respond to his challenge whether they wanted to or not, but he knew it would be unseemly and inappropriate to start anything new until he'd gotten Micomicona's kingdom back for her, so he had to bite his tongue and say nothing, waiting to see what these travelers accomplished with all their maneuvers — and one of them indeed found the young fellow they were hunting, sleeping side by side with a real muledriver, totally unaware that anyone might be looking for him and suspecting even less that he might be found.

"Wonderful, Señor Don Luis! Your clothes nicely match what you usually wear — and this bed is every bit as comfortable as the one in which your mother brought you up."

The boy opened his sleepy eyes and stared blankly at the man who had hold of him, and then realized it was one of his father's servants, which so startled him that he couldn't either take it in or utter a word. The servant continued:

"So there's no help for it, Señor Don Luis, but to give in quietly and go back home — unless you want to send my lord your father to the next world, because the pain of your absence can't produce any other result."

"But," said Don Luis, "how did my father know I'd come this way, and dressed like this?"

"You told your plan to another student," answered the servant, "and he was the one who revealed it all, moved to pity when he saw how your father was affected, after finding out you were gone. So your father sent four of his servants to look for you, and here we are, at your service, happier than you'd believe to be returning so quickly, and bringing you to those eyes which so long to see you."

"If I so choose, or if Heaven so decrees," replied Don Luis.

"Have you any other choice, or could Heaven decree anything except your agreement to return? Nothing else is possible."

The young muledriver who'd been lying next to Don Luis heard all this, and slipped away, reporting everything to Don Fernando and Cardenio, and to all the others who were already up and about, telling them how the man had called the boy "*Don*," and exactly what had been said, and that they wanted him to go back to his father's house and the boy didn't want to. Hearing this, and knowing what a beautiful voice Heaven had granted the youngster, they were all anxious to find out exactly who he was and perhaps to help him, if he was going to be forced to obey, so they proceeded at once to where he and his servant were arguing away at one another.

Dorotea came out of her room, just then (with Doña Clara, all upset, just behind her), and, calling Cardenio aside, quickly told him the story of the musician and Doña Clara, he in his turn telling her how servants of the boy's father had come looking for Don Luis, but not softly enough to keep Clara from hearing, who promptly became so beside herself that, had not Dorotea hurried over, she'd have fallen to the ground. Cardenio suggested that Dorotea take the young lady back to their room, and he would try to solve the whole problem, which was what was done.

The four men who'd come hunting for Don Luis were now all in the inn and had congregated around him, trying to convince him not to waste any more time but just come home and relieve his father's mind. His reply was that he could not consider any such thing until he had completed a piece of business involving his life, his honor, and his heart. The four servants would not relent, saying they would not go back without him and, like it or not, they were taking him with them.

"No, you won't," replied Don Luis, "unless you carry me off as a corpse — and if you do carry me off, there'll be no life in me, anyway."

By now, everyone in the inn had gathered around the disputants, notably Cardenio, Don Fernando and his companions, the judge, the priest, the barber, and Don Quijote, the latter being of the opinion that there was no longer any need to guard the castle. Knowing the boy's story, Cardenio asked those who wanted to carry him off why they proposed to take him against his will.

"Why?" asked one of the four. "To save his father's life, because this young fellow's absence has almost killed him."

To which Don Luis replied:

"I don't have to account to anyone. I'm a free man, and I'll go back if I want to, and if not, then none of you is going to force me."

"But reason will compel you, your grace," said his father's servant, "and if that's not enough for you, then it's certainly enough for us, and we'll do what we came for and what we have no choice but to do."

"Tell us what's going on here," the judge interposed.

But the servant, knowing him as a neighbor, answered:

"Doesn't Your Honor recognize this young fellow, your neighbor's son, who has run away from his father's house in these clothes, so unfitted to his station, as you yourself, your grace, can perfectly well see?"

Then the judge looked at the boy more closely and, recognizing him, embraced him and said:

"Why, what silliness is all this, Señor Don Luis, and what mighty reason could have caused you to come here like this, dressed as you are, for it is certainly not clothing which befits your station?"

The boy's eyes filled with tears, and he could not say a word. The judge told the four servants to be calm, and all would be well; and then, taking Don Luis by the hand, he drew him aside and asked him what had brought him there.

But just as he was asking these and other such questions, they heard a huge uproar out at the gate, caused by two guests who had lodged in the inn the night before and, seeing everyone busy with the four hunters, had gotten the idea of leaving without paying their bill. The innkeeper, however, paying more attention to his own affairs than to other people's, grabbed them as they were going through the door and asked them to pay up, using such nasty language about their wicked plan that they, in turn, were moved to respond with blows, and began to pummel him so hard that the poor innkeeper had to bellow for help. The innkeeper's wife and daughter could see no one more at leisure to provide assistance than Don Quijote, to whom the daughter said:

"Help my poor father, sir knight, your grace, in the name of the goodness God gave you, for those two wicked men are thrashing him like wheat."

To which Don Quijote replied, slowly and with grand indifference:

"Lovely lady, I couldn't possibly concern myself with your request, right at the moment, for I've given my word not to take on any other adventures until I've finished the one that's occupying me. But I can do this for you: run and tell your father to fight this battle as well as he can, and to be absolutely sure he doesn't allow himself to be vanquished, and in the meantime I'll go and ask the Princess Micomicona to let me relieve his distress, and if she consents, you may be quite certain I'll rescue him."

"Mother of God!" cried Maritornes, who was standing right there. "Before your grace gets any such permission, my master will long since have gone to the next world."

"Allow me, madame, to seek the permission I have mentioned," answered Don Quijote, "for if I obtain it, what matter if he be in the next world? For should he be there indeed, I will draw him back, despite any objections that world may have — or, at least, I will wreak such vengeance for you, against those who sent him there, that you will be more than moderately satisfied."

And without another word he went and knelt before Dorotea, requesting in elaborately courtly and knight-errantryish language whether Her Mightiness would be pleased to let him aid and assist the warden of this castle, who was seriously in need of such help. The princess agreed most willingly, and he at once took up his shield, buckled on his sword, and proceeded to the gate of the inn, where the two defaulting lodgers were still beating up the innkeeper — but as soon as he got there he stopped in his tracks and stayed where he was, even though Maritornes and the innkeeper's wife asked him why he was taking so long to help their husband and master.

"I have restrained myself," said Don Quijote, "because I am not permitted to lift my sword against people of low condition. You will need to call my squire, Sancho, because this sort of assistance and vengeance is strictly and exclusively his business."

Which was how things were going at the gate of the inn, where punches were landing right and left, the innkeeper was getting very much the worst of it, and Maritornes, the innkeeper's wife, and also his daughter, were practically foaming at the mouth, wild with anger at Don Quijote's cowardice, and at all the damage being done to their husband, master, and father.

But let's leave the poor fellow there, for surely he'll find someone to help him, or maybe not, in which case let him who tackles more than his strength can achieve endure his suffering in silence — and let us move some fifty feet off, to see what Don Luis told the judge, after we left them for a moment, when the boy was asked why he'd made this journey on foot and dressed in such clothing. Holding the judge's hand very tightly, as if to indicate how some great sadness was wrenching his heart, and shedding tears freely, the boy answered:

"My lord, all I can say is that once Heaven decided, and our living so near one another made possible, that I behold my lady Doña Clara — your daughter, and my belovèd — from that very instant she took entire possession of my heart, and if you, my true lord and father, have no objections, I will this very day take her to be my wife. It was for her that I left my father's house, and it was for her that I put on this clothing, so I could follow her wherever she went, as the arrow seeks the center of the target or the sailor the true north. All she knows of my love is what she may have been able to understand, sometimes, seeing me from a distance, my eyes full of tears. You are aware, my lord, of my father's wealth and his eminence, and that I am his sole heir, and if these considerations can persuade you to risk making me blissfully happy, then welcome me, here and now, as your son, for then, should my father, moved by different motives, not wish this supreme good which I have sought for myself, time will be better able to change and re-arrange things than our mere human wills."

Having said this, the lovesick boy fell silent, and the judge was left in bewildered confusion, having heard how wisely and eloquently Don Luis spoke what was on his mind, but finding himself quite unable to deal with so sudden and unexpected a business, so all he said was that the boy should remain calm and arrange with his father's servants not to return that day, so there would be time to consider what might best be done. Don Luis kissed the judge's hands passionately — indeed, he bathed them in his tears, which might well have melted a heart of marble, let alone that of a judge, who as a sensible man was well aware what an advantageous match this would be for his daughter, but who would have liked, if he could, to bring it about with the father's consent, for he was also aware that the father wanted his son to marry into a title.

In the meantime, the departing lodgers and the innkeeper had made things up, more because Don Quijote had talked them into paying their bill in full than because of any threats, and Don Luis' servants had agreed to await the judge's decision (and their young master's), but just then the devil, who never sleeps, arranged that the barber from whom Don Quijote had taken Mambrino's helmet, and whose donkey Sancho Panza had stripped in favor of his own, came walking into the inn, and as this barber was leading his donkey to the stable he caught sight of Sancho Panza, who was adjusting something or other on his saddlebag, and knew at once who it was, and came rushing at Sancho, crying:

"Ah-ha, Mr. Thief — now I've got you! Hand over my brass basin and my saddlebag, and everything else you stole from me!"

Seeing himself so suddenly attacked, and hearing all the curses being flung at him, Sancho grabbed the saddlebag with one hand and, with the other, gave the man a punch in the face, bathing his teeth in blood, but this didn't stop the barber from seizing the harness and, indeed, from yelling so loudly that everyone in the inn hurried over to the fuss and fighting:

"Police, police! Justice! Just because I'm trying to get my property back, this thief, this highway robber, is trying to kill me!"

"You're a liar," replied Sancho, "I'm no highway robber, and my lord Don Quijote won this booty fair and square."

Don Quijote was already there, mightily pleased to see how well his squire was defending himself (and carrying the war to the enemy), and from that moment on thought Sancho a highly creditable fellow, deciding in his heart that, the first chance he got, he'd dub Sancho a knight, for the order of knighthood could use a man like him. Now, among the other things the barber said, during this quarrel, was the following:

"Gentlemen, this saddlebag is just as surely mine as the death I owe God, and I know it as well as if I'd given birth to it, and here's my donkey, right here in the stable, and he wouldn't let me tell a lie. Just try it on him, and if it doesn't fit him as if it were made for his back, then let me be disgraced. What's more, the very same day they stole this from me, they also stole a brand new brass basin, that I hadn't even used, and it was worth a pretty penny."

Don Quijote couldn't listen to this sort of thing without responding, so he got between the two combatants and separated them, then put the saddlebag on the ground, where, until the truth had been unraveled, everyone could plainly see it, and said:

"Here, then, your graces, you can see perfectly clearly how wrong this good man is, giving the name 'basin' to what was, is, and forever shall be Mambrino's Helmet, which I indeed took from him in a fair fight, and of which I made myself the true and lawful possessor! I won't meddle with this business of the saddlebag, except to say that my squire Sancho asked me if he could strip the trappings from this vanquished coward's horse, and place them on his own, and I said he could, and he took them, and as to those trappings being transformed into an ordinary saddlebag, all I can say is that this is how these things usually happen, for such transformations are always taking place, in knightly adventures — and to prove the point, Sancho, hurry and fetch the helmet which, according to this good man, is really a brass basin."

"By God, my lord," said Sancho, "if we haven't got any better proof than you've just claimed, Mambrino's helmet is just as much a brass basin as this good man's harness is a saddlebag!"

"Just do as I tell you," replied Don Quijote, "for it can't be that everything in this castle is bewitched."

So Sancho went to fetch the basin and brought it back, and when Don Quijote saw it he took it in his hands, declaring:

"Behold, your graces, how shamelessly this fellow can call this a basin, and not the helmet I know it to be, and I hereby swear by all the laws of knighthood to which I have vowed obedience that this is indeed the same helmet I took from him, and that nothing has been added to it and nothing taken away."

"That's it, there's no doubt of it," said Sancho, "because from the time my lord won it until right this minute all he's done with it is fight one battle, which was when he freed those miserable people in chains, and if it hadn't been for this basin-helmet things wouldn't have gone very well, because there was a lot of damage done by stones, in that fight."

Chapter Forty-Five

— in which the investigation into the helmet and the saddlebag is concluded, along with other events of an equally veracious nature

"So what do you think, gentlemen, your graces," said the barber, "of what these noble gentlemen are saying, and especially their insistence that this is not a basin but a helmet?"

"And anybody who says it isn't," said Don Quijote, "I will call him a liar, if he's a knight, and a liar a thousand times over, if he's a commoner."

Now our barber, who'd been watching all this, and knew Don Quijote's madness, decided to encourage him in his folly, so he could keep the joke going and amuse everyone, and so he said to the other barber:

"Mr. Barber — or whatever you are — please understand that I too ply your trade, and I've been licensed for more than twenty years and have a detailed knowledge of all the instruments of the barber's profession, without any exception whatever, and so too, when I was younger, was I a soldier, and I'm equally well aware of what an ordinary helmet is, and a peaked and crested helmet, and a light helmet with a brim, or with a visor and, let me say, all other military matters having to do with a soldier's equipment and armor, and I must declare — subject to more learned correction, for I will always bow to superior knowledge — that this object

we see in front of us, and which this worthy gentleman holds in his two
hands, not only is not a barber's basin but is, indeed, just as far from being
one as white is from being black, or the truth is from being a lie, and I
also affirm that, although this is a helmet, it is not a complete helmet."

"Certainly not," said Don Quijote, "because half of it's missing, namely,
the visor."

"Exactly," said the priest, who understood what his friend the barber
was up to.

And Cardenio said the same thing, and also Don Fernando and his
companions, and even the judge, if he hadn't been so preoccupied with
the whole business about Don Luis, probably would have done his part
in keeping the joke alive, but his thoughts were so earnestly traveling
elsewhere that he paid little or no attention to any of these witticisms.

"Good God!" said the barber they were teasing. "Can so many honorable gentlemen actually be saying this is a helmet and not a basin? Something like this could absolutely stun an entire University, no matter how
wise its professors. All right: if this basin is really a helmet, then this plain
old saddlebag must also be some fancy harness, as this other gentleman
says it is."

"It looks like a saddlebag to me," said Don Quijote, "but I've already
said I won't interfere."

"Whether it's a saddlebag or a harness," said the priest, "no one can
better tell us than my lord Don Quijote, for in such knightly matters all
these gentlemen and I are agreed that he knows best."

"By God, gentlemen," said Don Quijote, "so many extraordinarily
strange things have happened to me in this castle, both times I've been
lodged here, that I don't dare speak confidently about anything in this
place, whenever there's any sort of question, because it seems to me that
everything here is subject to enchantment. The first time I had serious
difficulties with an enchanted Moor, and Sancho didn't do much better
with the Moor's helpers, and just last night I was forced to stay hanging
by this arm for almost two hours, without knowing how or why I was
suffering any such misfortune. So for me to give a straightforward opinion
about such a tangled web of confusions would be reckless indeed. And
I've already told you what I can say about this, right here, being a helmet
or a basin — but I simply can't say with certainty whether this other
object is a plain saddlebag or an ornamental harness: I simply have to
leave it to you, gentlemen. Conceivably, since you, your graces, have not,
like me, been dubbed a knight, you may not be obliged to see the enchantments practiced here, so your minds may well be free of all such
entanglements, and you can understand the things that go on in this castle
as they really and truly are, rather than as they appear to me."

"Surely," said Don Fernando at this point, "my lord Don Quijote has
spoken extremely well, and it's up to us to resolve this matter; accordingly,
so that we can proceed most soberly and sensibly, I will take your votes in
secret, gentlemen, and then announce the result clearly and comprehen-
sively."

Those who knew Don Quijote's madness found all this excruciatingly
funny, but those who didn't thought it the stupidest thing they'd ever seen

— notably Don Luis' four servants, and their young master too, as well as three other travelers, just arrived at the inn, who looked like the policemen they in fact were. But the most upset was the barber, whose basin had been transformed, right in front of his eyes, into Mambrino's helmet, and whose saddlebag seemed similarly to have been turned into a rich harness. Those in the know were vastly amused, watching Don Fernando going up and down, taking people's votes, with much whispering in ears so they could declare, in secret, whether the hotly disputed jewel was really a saddlebag or a decorative harness. Having taken the votes of those who knew Don Quijote, Don Fernando called out to the barber-complainant, in a firm, loud voice:

"My good man, this is a terrible bore, collecting all these opinions, because everyone to whom I've put the question tells me it's ridiculous having to declare whether this is an ordinary saddlebag or a decorative harness, for it is plainly decorative, they say, and meant for a horse, not a donkey, and not only that, but for a fine thoroughbred horse, so you'll simply have to resign yourself — you, and your ass, too — to the sad fact that this is indeed a decorative harness and not a saddlebag, and your case has been singularly badly argued and substantiated."

"May I never get to Heaven," said the barber-complainant, "if every one of you gentlemen is not mistaken, and may the Good Lord in Heaven see my soul as clearly as I see my saddlebag, which is no decorative harness — but 'laws are enforced . . .'[1] etcetera, etcetera — so that's all I have to say, except that no, I'm not drunk — indeed, I haven't taken on a thing so far today, except maybe a sin."

The barber's foolish remarks made them laugh just as hard as Don Quijote's mad ones — and just then Don Quijote declared:

"So there's nothing to do, now, but let everyone take what's his, and may Saint Peter bless whatever God has given."

But one of the four servants spoke up:

"If this isn't just a bad joke, I can't believe that men with such good minds as those I see here — or such apparently good minds — can solemnly say this isn't a barber's basin, and that isn't a saddlebag, but since I see they do solemnly say such things, by God, when men insist that plain truth isn't true and ordinary knowledge isn't knowledge, there's got to be a mystery behind it all, because, Jesus Christ!" — and he swore a fat oath — "even if every man jack in the world says it, I won't believe this isn't a barber's basin and that isn't a donkey's saddlebag!"

"But perhaps a female donkey rather than a male one," said the priest.

"Who cares?" said the servant. "That doesn't make any difference at all, but just whether it is or it isn't a saddlebag, as your graces have been saying."

Hearing this, one of the policemen who'd come in and listened to the argument, and then heard the judgment rendered, called out, very hot under the collar:

"It's a saddlebag, or my father's not my father, and anyone who's said anything else, or who says it now, has got to be blind drunk."

1. "Laws are enforced the way kings want them enforced" [*Translator's Note*].

"You lie like a lowborn scoundrel!" shouted Don Quijote.

And raising his spear, which had in fact never left his hands, he aimed such a whack at the man's head that, had the policeman not ducked away, he'd have been stretched out on the ground. The spear shattered, and the other policemen, seeing their friend so badly treated, started shouting for help.

The innkeeper, who was a deputy sheriff, ran to get his nightstick and his sword, and then joined the others; Don Luis' servants made a circle around their young master, to keep him from getting away from them, in all the racket; the barber-complainant, seeing the brawl, went over and grabbed the saddlebag, and Sancho did the same thing; and Don Quijote drew his sword and charged at the policemen. Don Luis was shouting at his servants to go and help Don Quijote, and also Cardenio and Don Fernando, who were at Don Quijote's side. The priest was shouting, too, the innkeeper's wife was screaming, her daughter was caterwauling, Maritornes was weeping, Dorotea couldn't understand what was going on, Luscinda stood there gaping, and Doña Clara had fainted. The barber banged away at Sancho, and Sancho at the barber. Don Luis, as one of his servants clutched at his arm to keep him from getting away, punched the man so hard that his teeth were washed in blood; the judge was keeping everyone at a distance; Don Fernando, who'd gotten one of the policemen under his feet, was having a fine time measuring out the man's body; the innkeeper kept shouting for help — and the whole inn was a jumble of weeping and yelling and crying and stumbling and quaking and trembling and disasters and slashing and punching and banging and kicking and blood pouring out all over. And then suddenly this vast uproar, this chaotic mess, this labyrinth of disorder, took shape in Don Quijote's mind, and he thought he'd been plunged smack into the middle of the famous argument in Agramante's camp,[2] and he bellowed, in a voice that smashed like a hammer:

"Stop, all of you! Put up your swords, calm yourselves — and listen to me, if you want to stay alive."

This huge shout stopped everything, and he went on:

"Didn't I tell you, gentlemen, that this castle was enchanted, that it must be inhabited by a band of demons? The proof, please note, can be seen with your own eyes, for what we have witnessed, here, is nothing more than the argument in Agramante's camp, now transported among us. Just see how, over there, they're fighting over a sword, and here for a horse, and over there for a banner, and there for a helmet, and everyone fighting, fighting, and no one knowing why. So please come forward, your grace, Your Honor our judge, and you, your grace, our priest, and one of you be King Agramante, and the other be King Sobrino, and let there be peace made among us, for by Almighty God what an astonishing bit of wickedness it would be for so many highborn folk as we have gathered here to kill one another for such trifling reasons."

The policemen, who couldn't understand what Don Quijote was saying,

---

2. *Orlando Furioso* XXIV; Agramante and (see below) Sobrino = Muhammadan kings [*Translator's Note*].

but knew they were suffering at the hands of Don Fernando, Cardenio, and their friends, had no interest in making peace; the barber was willing, because in the fighting he'd lost both his beard and his saddlebag; like a good servant, Sancho obeyed at the mere sound of his master's voice; Don Luis' four servants were also willing to give it up, seeing how little they had to gain by continuing. But the innkeeper clamored that this insolent lunatic, who was constantly causing riots in his inn, had to be punished. In the end, the uproar ebbed away, for the time being; the saddlebag remained a rich horse's harness, until the day of judgment; and — in Don Quijote's mind — the barber's basin continued to be a helmet and the inn a castle.

So everything being quiet and, thanks to the efforts of the judge and the priest, everyone now on friendly terms, Don Luis' servants came to him and insisted that he had to leave with them at once, and, while he tried to reason with them, the judge, along with Don Fernando, Cardenio, and the priest, to all of whom the judge communicated what the young man had told him, discussed what ought to be done. In the end, they agreed that Don Fernando should inform the servants of his name and rank, and that it was his pleasure to have Don Luis join him in Andalusia, where his brother the marquis would fête the young man as he deserved, for they plainly foresaw that, just then, Don Luis would utterly refuse to return to his father's supervision, even were he to be torn to pieces. And when the four servants understood who Don Fernando was, and that Don Luis was adamant, they in turn decided that three of them should go back to the young man's father and explain what had happened, while the fourth remained with Don Luis, to serve and not to leave him until either the others returned to claim him or the father sent specific orders.

And so, by Agramante's authority, and King Sobrino's wisdom, the bristling network of disputes was calmed — but the enemy of all agreement, and hater of peace and quiet, feeling himself scorned and mocked, and seeing how little he had gained by creating this whole labyrinth of confusion, decided to try his hand once again, stirring up new quarrels and fresh troubles.

So, when the policemen had calmed down (because they found out they'd been fighting with noblemen and aristocrats) and withdrawn from the quarrel, reflecting that, whatever happened, they were going to get the worst of it, one of them, the man Don Fernando had kicked and beaten, remembered that among the assorted warrants he was carrying — arrest orders for a number of criminals — was, exactly as Sancho had feared, one for someone named Don Quijote, who'd been ordered to be taken in for setting galley slaves free.

Wondering, then, if this arrest order described a man matching Don Quijote's appearance, he carefully drew out his sheaf of documents, found the one he was looking for, and began to slowly read it through (not being a very proficient reader), looking up after each word and checking every description in the warrant against Don Quijote's face, finding that without the slightest doubt this was the man the warrant specified. As soon as he'd established this, he gathered up his documents, grasped the warrant in his left hand, and with his right took Don Quijote by the collar, so tightly that our knight could not breathe, and began to shout:

"In the name of the law! Anyone who wants to see if I mean business, read this warrant, which orders the arrest of this highway robber."

The priest took the warrant and saw that the policeman was speaking the truth, and the wanted man's description matched Don Quijote — who, finding himself so roughly handled by this lowborn scoundrel, flew into a rage and, straining every bone in his body, grasped the policeman by the throat with both hands, and with all the strength he could muster, so that, had there not been help from the other officers, the man would surely have been dead before Don Quijote let him go. The innkeeper, obliged by law to help a fellow officer, came running to lend his support. His wife, seeing her husband once more involved in a fight, started to scream, and her soaring shrieks brought her daughter and Maritornes rushing to the scene, begging the help of Heaven and of all those who happened to be present. Seeing what was going on, Sancho said:

"In the name of God! How truly my master speaks of this castle's being enchanted, because you can't spend a peaceful hour in here!"

Don Fernando separated Don Quijote and the policeman, relieving them both by pulling away both sets of clutching hands — one pair locked onto a coat collar, the other gripping a neck — but nevertheless the policemen would not back off, urging in the name of the law, and of the king, that they be assisted in securing their prisoner, this notorious robber and highwayman, this menace to every street and road, and that they have him in their hands, bound and delivered. Don Quijote laughed in their faces, saying quite calmly:

"Now look here, you vulgar, lowborn wretches: Do you call it highway robbery to free people from their chains, to release them from captivity, to help the miserable, lift up the fallen, and protect the needy? Ah, you're vile, disgusting people, and it's because of your low, despicable minds that Heaven has concealed from you the treasures hidden in ancient knighthood and kept you from knowing what ignorance, what sinfulness you dwell in, knowing nothing and caring less about the ghost, let alone the living presence, of a knight errant! Just look here, you uniformed thieves, who aren't true police officers but highway robbers with official licenses — just tell me: what illiterate peasant signed an arrest warrant against a knight like me? What kind of ignoramus is he, unaware that knights errant are exempt from the application of all laws and statutes, that for them law is their sword, statutes are their spirit, and edicts and proclamations are their will and desire? Tell me, I say, who was the idiot who had no idea that, on the day a man's dubbed a knight errant and devotes himself to his rigorous profession, he acquires privileges and exemptions surpassing anything granted by charters of nobility? What knight errant has ever paid taxes — rent-tax, king's wedding-tax, land-tax — or paid a highway toll or a ship toll? When did a tailor ever charge for making a knight's clothes? What warden, giving him lodging in his castle, ever charged a knight for his bed? What king ever denied him a seat at his table? What lovely maiden could keep herself from loving him and humbly surrendering herself to his will and his desire? And, finally, what knight errant has there ever been or will there ever be, in all the world, without the spirit to deliver four hundred blows, single-handed, against four hundred policemen, if they happen to get in his way?"

Chapter Forty-Six

— more about our worthy knight Don Quijote's remarkable encounter with the policemen, and his incredible ferocity

While Don Quijote was saying these things, the priest was busy persuading the policemen that our worthy knight was out of his head, as they should be able to see by both his actions and his words, and there was no point to proceeding any further because, even if they arrested him and took him off, he'd immediately be set free again, as a madman, to which the policemen replied that it wasn't their business to determine Don Quijote's sanity, but just to do what they'd been commanded to do, and after he'd been arrested once he could be set free three hundred times, as far as they were concerned.

"Nevertheless," said the priest, "you don't need to take him, this time, nor, so far as I understand it, is he willing to let you."

In the end, the priest argued so forcefully, and Don Quijote himself did such mad things, that they'd have had to be madder than he was not to see his madness, so the policemen decided it was better to calm down and even to help make peace between Sancho Panza and the barber, who were still furiously pressing their quarrel. So, as officers of the law, they arbitrated the quarrel and indeed settled it in such a way that both parties were, if not completely satisfied, at least satisfied in part, for they directed that the saddlebags be exchanged but not the saddle girths or the halter ropes — and as far as Mambrino's helmet was concerned, the priest paid the barber (without Don Quijote knowing anything about it) eight dollars for the basin, and the barber gave him a receipt and a disclaimer of any and all further interest, for ever and ever, amen.

Thus the two principal and weightiest quarrels were settled, leaving it up to Don Luis' servants to agree that three of them should return without him, and that the one who'd go with the young man would accompany him wherever Don Fernando chose to take him, and good luck and better fortune having thus begun to turn swords into ploughshares, and to make things easier for the inn's lovers and its brave men, they decided to finish the job up and make everyone happy, so the servants agreed to do as Don Luis wished — and this clearly so pleased Doña Clara that no one seeing her face could have failed to see the joy in her soul.

Zoraida, though she didn't entirely understand what she'd been seeing, swung from sadness to excited pleasure, according to what she thought was happening at the time, and particularly what she could tell from her Spaniard, whom she watched closely and on whom her soul fairly hung. The innkeeper, who'd carefully noted the priest's generous payment to the barber, presented his bill to Don Quijote, including the damage to his wineskins and the wine that had been spilled, vowing that neither Rocinante nor Sancho Panza's donkey would leave the inn until every penny had been paid. The priest quieted him down, on all these scores, and Don Fernando paid the bill, though the judge, too, had cheerfully offered to pay it, and everything was so peaceful and quiet that the inn no longer seemed like the argument in Agramante's camp, as Don Quijote had described it, but more like the calm tranquillity of Augustus Caesar's days, for all of which, it was generally agreed, they were indebted to the priest's wisdom and eloquence and to Don Fernando's extraordinary generosity.

Don Quijote, finding himself free and clear of all his many disputes and entanglements, and of Sancho Panza's as well, thought it would now be best to continue the journey that had been begun and finish up the great adventure for which he had been chosen and to which he had been summoned, and so, with fixed resolve, he presented himself in front of Dorotea, and went down on his knees, though she would not permit him to say a word until he rose again, which, obediently, he did, and then declared:

"Beautiful lady, it is a common saying that diligence is the mother of good luck, and experience has shown, in many great and weighty affairs, that a determined advocate can bring a doubtful lawsuit to a successful conclusion, but in nothing is this clearer than in war, where swift, timely action gives the enemy no time to think, and achieves victory before the opponent has readied his defense. I say this, oh noble and supreme lady, because it seems to me that there is no longer any point to our remaining in this castle, and to stay here might well be costly, in ways we will only come to understand at some point in the future, for who knows if, by means of stealthy, busy spies, our enemy the giant has not already learned that I'm coming to destroy him? — thus granting him time and opportunity to fortify himself in some impregnable castle or stronghold, against which my best efforts, and the strength of my untirable arm, will be of little use. And so, my lady, as I've said, let us employ our swiftness to block his plans, and sally forth at once toward our good fortune, for all that keeps your majesty from happiness is the delay in my meeting your enemy."

Don Quijote had finished, and he said no more, waiting in perfect calm for the lovely princess' reply; and she, in a lordly style well adapted to Don Quijote's, answered him as follows:

"I thank you, sir knight, for your demonstrable determination to aid me in my great distress, fully appropriate to a knight whose obligation and concern it is to assist the orphaned and the needy: may Heaven grant the fulfillment of your desire, and mine, so you may see that, indeed, there are grateful women left in the world. And as for my departure, why, let it be immediate, for in this matter I have no will but yours: do with me entirely as you wish and want, for she who has entrusted to you the defense of her person and placed in your hands the restoration of her kingdom should desire nothing that runs contrary to what your wisdom dictates."

"In the name of God," said Don Quijote, "when a lady thus bows her royal head to me, how can I possibly forego the opportunity to raise her up again and return her to her hereditary throne? Let us leave at once, then, for the common saying that 'there is danger in delay' lends spurs to my desire to be on our way. Heaven never having created, nor Hell ever having seen, anyone or anything that can frighten or worry me, saddle up

Rocinante, Sancho, and ready your donkey and the queen's steed, and let us say farewell to the castle warden and to all these gentlemen, and be out of here."

Sancho, who had heard every word of this, stood shaking his head from side to side, and said:

"Oh, señor, señor, there's more wickedness in the village than you might think, and may all the honorable ladies forgive me for saying so."

"You peasant, what wickedness in what village — nay, in all the cities in the world — can be leveled against me?"

"If you're going to get angry, your grace," replied Sancho, "I'll stop talking, and just say that I said what I said because I owe it to you, as a good squire and a good servant."

"Say whatever you want to," answered Don Quijote, "as long as you don't try to frighten me, for if you're afraid, that's who you are, and if I'm not, that's who I am."

"In the name of God!" cried Sancho, "that's not it — it's just that I consider it absolutely certain and proven that this lady, who says she's queen of the great kingdom of Micromicón, is no more a queen than my mother is, because, if she really was what she says she is, she wouldn't be nuzzling with one of the gentlemen around here, every time you turn your head and behind every outhouse she passes."

Dorotea colored, at these words, for it was true that, when no one was looking, her husband, Don Fernando, had on occasion picked with his lips a portion of the prize his desire had earned him — seeing which, Sancho had thought it a boldness that smacked more of the elegant whore than the queen of a great kingdom — but Dorotea neither could nor wanted to say a word in reply, so she let him speak as he pleased, and Sancho went on:

"I say this, my lord, because after we've gone up this road and down that one, enduring wretched nights and worse days, if it turns out that the fruits of all our labors get picked by a man who's just staying here in this inn — well, why should I hurry to get a saddle on Rocinante, and a saddlebag on my donkey, and make the lady's horse ready, when it'd be better to stay right where we are, so 'all the whores can do their thing,'[1] and we can eat our dinner?"

Oh, dear God, what a temper Don Quijote flew into, hearing his squire saying such rude things! He was so wild with anger that, in a hoarse voice, half stuttering, fire gleaming in his eyes, he said:

"Oh, you lecherous oaf, you contemptible fool — you boor! you idiot! you dumb ox! you foul-mouthed babbler! — you insolent, gossiping, slanderer! You dare say such things, in my presence, with these distinguished ladies all around us? You dare let that muddled mind of yours even *think* such lewd impertinences? Leave me at once, oh you twisted monster, treasure trove of lies, storehouse of deceit, you dark cave of wickedness, creator of evil, fountain of stupidity, sworn enemy of the respect due to all royalty! Go, go! and never let me see you again, or you will have to deal with my anger!"

Saying which, he arched his eyebrows, swelled out his cheeks, stared

---

1. The refrain of a popular song [*Translator's Note*].

wildly this way and that, and with his right foot stamped fiercely on the ground, all in token of the anger boiling inside him. His words, and his furious gestures, left Sancho so shrinking and trembling that, at that moment, he wished the earth would open under his feet and swallow him. All he could think of was turning and fleeing from his master's wrathful presence. But clever Dorotea, who by this point knew Don Quijote very well indeed, soothed his anger, saying:

"We should not, oh Knight of the Sad Face, resent this nonsense uttered by your squire, for quite possibly he does not speak without reason, since, otherwise, neither his fine understanding nor his Christian conscience would let him bear false witness against anyone, so I think we must remember that, since in this castle, as you yourself, sir knight, have said, it is plain that everything is driven by magic, it may well be, let me say, that in this diabolical fashion Sancho has in fact seemed to see what he says he saw, insulting to my modesty though it may be."

"By the omnipotent God on high," Don Quijote replied at once, "I swear your majesty has hit the nail on the head, and some evil vision appeared to this sinner of a Sancho, making him see what he could not possibly see in any way but by enchantment — and, indeed, I'm very well aware of this miserable fellow's goodness and innocence, and that he couldn't tell lies about anyone."

"That surely is and will continue to be true," said Don Fernando, "for which reason you, Señor Don Quijote, ought to pardon him, and return him to the protection of your favor, *sicut erat in principio* [as it was in the beginning], before such visions distorted his good sense."

Don Quijote replied that, indeed, he did forgive him, and the priest went to fetch Sancho, who approached his master most humbly, kneeling and begging for his hand, which Don Quijote allowed him to take, and when Sancho was done kissing it, the knight blessed him, saying:

"So now you'll finally see, Sancho my son, that what I've told you so many times is true, and everything that happens in this castle is caused by enchantment."

"And I believe it," said Sancho, "except for the blanket-tossing business, which really happened in the usual way."

"And that you should *not* believe," replied Don Quijote, "for had that been the case I would have revenged you on the spot, and would do so even now, but neither then nor now could I find anyone to take revenge upon."

Everyone wanted to know what blanket-tossing business they were talking about, so the innkeeper told them the tale of Sancho Panza's flying expedition, blow by blow, which made everyone laugh heartily, and would have just as deeply embarrassed Sancho, except that his master swore, once again, that it was all an enchantment — though Sancho's foolishness never got to the point where he believed it wasn't the plain and simple truth, unadulterated by any kind of magic, that he'd been blanket-tossed by real, flesh and blood people, and not by illusions and fanciful apparitions, as his master believed and kept insisting.

This entire illustrious company had now spent two days at the inn and, all of them thinking it was time to leave, they cooked up a scheme which, without making it necessary for Dorotea and Don Fernando to go all the way back to his village with Don Quijote, under the pretense of freeing Queen Micomicona, would enable the priest and the barber to carry off the knight, as they very much wanted to, and thus have the madman cared for at home. What they arranged was that an ox-cart driver, who happened to be going that way, would take Don Quijote under the following circumstances: they had a kind of crate-like box built with wooden slats, large enough to hold Don Quijote quite comfortably, and then, pursuant to the priest's instructions, Don Fernando and his companions, along with Don Luis' servants and the four policemen, plus the innkeeper, covered their faces and disguised themselves — some of them this way, and some of them that — so that Don Quijote would think them anything but the folk he'd seen in the inn.

That accomplished, in complete silence they crept into the room where he lay sleeping, exhausted from his recent skirmishes. He slept comfortably, totally unaware of what was going on, as they came over to his bed, laid violent hands on him and tied him so tightly, hand and foot, that when he woke with a start he was completely unable to move or, indeed, to do anything but stare and gape, seeing weird faces all around him, which immediately led his perpetually unbalanced mind to see as phantasms of the enchanted castle, who had clearly succeeded in enchanting him (since he could neither move nor defend himself), all of which was exactly as the priest, who had designed the whole scheme, had expected. Of those present, only Sancho was both in his right mind and in his own form, and, even though he wasn't a great deal saner than his master, he had no trouble telling who all of these disguised people really were, but he didn't dare open his mouth until he found out what this attacking and capturing of his master was all about; Don Quijote, too, remained quiet, waiting to see what this unlucky business was leading to; and what did happen was that, bringing in the crate, they locked him inside and nailed the slats so firmly shut that it wouldn't be any joke, prying them open.

As they lifted the crate on their shoulders and started out of the room, there came a dreadful voice (as dreadful as the barber could manage — not the saddlebag barber, but the other one), saying:

"Oh Knight of the Sad Face! Don't be distressed by this captivity into which you've been taken, for it is necessary in order to most speedily accomplish the adventure your great spirit has undertaken. And this will be achieved when the wild lion of La Mancha and the white dove of Toboso are become one, having bowed their noble necks to the easy yoke of matrimony, from which astonishing union will emerge fierce cubs whose claws will be modeled on those of their brave father. This will come to pass before the sun god [Apollo], pursuing the fleeing nymph [Daphne], has on his swift, natural course swept twice through the starry heavens. And you, oh noblest and most obedient squire who ever buckled on a sword, or bore a beard on your face, or possessed a nose with which to smell! Be neither concerned nor unhappy to see the flower of knight errantry thus borne off, before your very eyes, for very soon, if the Creator of this world so wills it, you will find yourself raised to such heights and so exalted that you will hardly know yourself, nor will the promises made you by your good master prove untrue. And be assured, in the name of the wise Mentironiana [*mentir* = to lie], that all your wages will be paid, as you will soon see for yourself, so follow in the footsteps of your brave and enchanted master, for it is better that you too journey where both of you are being sent. Now go with God, for I am allowed to tell you no more, and must return there where only I know."

And as this prophecy came to its end, the unseen voice first rose and then died away, in such affecting tones that even those who were in on the joke were ready to believe they were hearing the truth.

Don Quijote was comforted by the intonement of this prophecy, perceiving immediately what it meant, and that he was to be united in holy, lawful wedlock with his beloved Dulcinea del Toboso, from whose happy womb there would come cubs — that is, his sons — who would lead to La Mancha's eternal glory, and believing this devoutly and contentedly, he sighed deeply, then raised his own voice, declaring:

"Oh you, whoever you may be, who thus happily have prophesied to me! I beg you to ask, on my behalf, that the wise magician who has taken my affairs in charge not allow me to perish in this prison in which now I lie, but let me live to see the fulfillment of those wondrously happy, incomparably glorious promises made to me here, and, should this come to pass, the sufferings of my incarceration will seem to me like glories, and I will take comfort in these chains which bind me, and consider this litter in which I am lying to be a soft and blessed nuptial bed rather than a hard field of battle. And as for the consolation of my squire, Sancho Panza, I trust that being virtuous and moral he will not forsake me, neither in good nor in ill fortune, for should it happen, because of his lack of luck or mine, that I am unable to give him the island I promised, or something equivalent thereto, he will at least not have to give up his wages, for in my last will and testament, which I have long since executed, I have directed that he is to be paid — not pursuant to all his good service, but pursuant to my limited means."

Sancho Panza bowed his head most courteously and kissed both his master's hands, for he could not kiss only one, they being tied so tightly together.

Then the phantasmic figures lifted the crate onto their shoulders, and deposited it in the ox-cart.

Chapter Forty-Seven

— all about Don Quijote de La Mancha's strange enchantment, along with other celebrated events

Finding himself thus crated and hoisted onto a cart, Don Quijote said:

"I have read many profound accounts of knight errantry, but never have I read, or seen, or heard, of enchanted knights being carried off in this way, and so ponderously as these sluggish, slow-moving beasts seem to be doing, for knights are usually swept off through the air, with extraordinary lightness, wrapped in some dark and gloomy cloud, or in some chariot of fire, or on some hippogryph or such-like beast — but here I am, being taken away in an ox-cart, and dear God! it confuses me terribly. But perhaps, in our time, knighthood and enchantments have to proceed down different roads; things were different, in the old days. Or maybe it's that I, as a brand-new knight, and the first to have restored to this world the forgotten profession of knight errantry, have to be dealt with by the magicians via new forms of enchantment and new methods of transportation. What do you think, Sancho, my son?"

"I don't know what I think," answered Sancho, "because I'm not as well read as you are in the old books — but just the same, I can say, and I do say, that these visions walking around here aren't quite what they ought to be [*católicas* = true, right]."

"Aren't Catholics! Oh my Lord!" replied Don Quijote, "how could they be Catholics if they're all demons who have taken on fantastic shapes to do these things and to reduce me to this? And if you want to see if I'm correct, just touch them, feel them, and you'll see they have no bodies, they're just air, just shadows."

"By God, señor," answered Sancho, "I've already touched them, and that devil walking so carefully, right over there, has a good stock of flesh, and he's not at all like the demons I've heard described, because they say demons stink of sulfur and brimstone and things like that, but this one smells like perfume from a mile away."

(Sancho was speaking about Don Fernando, here, because as a nobleman he could be expected to be perfumed, as Sancho had said.)

"Ah, don't be so surprised, Sancho, my friend," said Don Quijote, "because you've got to understand that these devils are terribly clever, and even if they bring smells with them they don't themselves have any smell at all, because they're spirits, and if they *did* have a smell it couldn't help but be evil and stinking, certainly not anything pleasant. And this is because, wherever they go, they carry Hell with them, nor can they ever find any relief from their torments, and a fragrant odor being a source of pleasure and happiness, it's impossible for them to smell of anything like that. So if this demon you're talking about seems to you to smell of perfume, either you're mistaken, or he wants to trick you into thinking he's not a demon."

Master and servant went on talking like this, and Don Fernando and Cardenio, worried that Sancho might not keep quiet about their scheme (as he was already showing significant signs of doing), decided to make a rather hurried departure, so they took the innkeeper aside and ordered him to saddle up Rocinante and throw the saddlebag onto Sancho's donkey, which was promptly done.

While this was going on, the priest arranged for the officers of the law to accompany them as far as La Mancha, offering them a day's pay. Cardenio hooked our knight's shield over one end of Rocinante's saddle-bow, hung the basin from the other and, using only gestures, directed Sancho to mount his donkey and take Rocinante's reins, putting two of the policemen, armed with their rifles, on each side of the cart. But before the cart started off, the innkeeper's wife came out, along with her daughter and Maritornes, to say farewell to Don Quijote, pretending to weep over his misfortune, and our knight said to them:

"Weep not, good ladies, for all such misfortunes are part and parcel of the profession I have chosen, and, indeed, if these disasters did not happen to me I would not consider myself a famous knight errant, for knights of lesser reputation and fame never encounter these things, since there's nobody in the whole world who pays any attention to them. But these things do happen to brave knights, who are much envied, for both virtue and courage, by many princes as well as by many other knights, who try to destroy them by all sorts of evil methods. But in spite of all this, virtue is so powerful that, in and of itself, and despite even the magical powers discovered by the first of the great magicians, Zoroaster, virtue will triumph in every battle, shedding its light all over the world, just as it lights up the sun in the sky. Forgive me, lovely ladies, if I have inadvertently offended against you, for neither knowingly nor willingly have I ever offended a lady, but pray to God to deliver me from this captivity, into which I have been thrust by some evil-minded magician, and should I find myself free once more, rest assured I will not forget the kindnesses rendered me in this castle, that they may be responded to, rewarded, and repaid as they deserve."

While this was taking place between the ladies of the castle and Don Quijote, the priest and the barber were saying their farewells to Don Fernando and his companions, and to the captain and his brother, and to all the well-satisfied ladies, in particular Dorotea and Luscinda. They all embraced one another, promising to keep in touch; Don Fernando telling the priest he had to write and let him know what happened with Don Quijote, and that nothing would please him more than such news; and adding that he, for his part, would take just as much pleasure in letting the priest know all about his own wedding, and Zoraida's baptism, and what happened to Don Luis, and Luscinda's return to her father's house. The priest promised to do exactly as Don Fernando had requested, and without delay. So then they all embraced once again, and once again repeated all their promises and vows.

The innkeeper came over to the priest and gave him some documents, explaining that they'd been found in the lining of the trunk where he'd found the *Story of the Man Who Couldn't Keep from Prying* and, since their owner hadn't come back for them, the priest ought to take them, because he himself could not read and had no use for them. The priest thanked him, and immediately beginning to look them over, saw that the first was entitled *Rinconete and Cortadillo*[1] and was apparently a story of some sort, and since the *Man Who Couldn't Keep from Prying* had been good, perhaps this would be too, for it was possible they were all by the same author, so he held onto them, intending to read them when he had a chance.

The priest and his friend, the barber, mounted and put on their masks, so Don Quijote wouldn't promptly recognize them, and started off, following the ox-cart. The order of march was like this: first came the ox-cart, driven by its owner; the policemen, armed with their rifles, rode alongside, as has been said; then came Sancho Panza on his donkey, leading Rocinante by the reins. Behind all the others came the priest and the barber,

---

1. One of Cervantes's *Novelas ejemplares* [*Model Tales*], published in 1613 [*Translator's Note*].

riding on their mighty mules, their faces covered, as we've noted, plodding slowly and calmly along, never going faster than the sluggish pace required of them by the oxen. Don Quijote stayed seated in his crate, his hands tied, his feet stuck out in front of him, leaning back against the wooden slats as silently and as patiently as if he'd been a stone statue rather than a creature of flesh and blood.

And thus, slowly and silently, they traveled perhaps five miles, and then came to a valley, which the ox-driver thought was a good place to let his animals feed and rest, and he so informed the priest, but the barber thought they'd better go a bit farther, because he knew that, just the other side of a slope now beginning to rise in front of them, there was another valley, with more grass, and much better grass, than the one where they wanted to stop. They followed the barber's advice and continued along the road.

Just then, happening to turn his head, the priest saw six or seven mounted men, on good steeds and well-dressed, riding up behind them, who soon caught up, for they were not plodding on slowly and calmly, like the oxen, but like hot-blooded priests' mules, anxious to take their ease in the inn, which they could see only a couple of miles distant. So the brisk came up to the sluggish, and courteous greetings were exchanged, and eventually one of the newcomers, who was a cathedral priest from Toledo and lord of those who were traveling with him, seeing the carefully arranged order of march (ox-cart, policemen, Sancho, Rocinante, priest, and barber) and especially Don Quijote, boxed up and tied, couldn't help asking why they were transporting the man in this strange way — even though he had already understood, seeing the policemen's uniforms, that the prisoner had to be some truly wicked highway robber, or some other equally infamous criminal wanted by the authorities. One of the policemen, to whom he addressed this query, replied as follows:

"Sir, let the gentleman tell you for himself why he's traveling this way, because we don't know."

Don Quijote heard their conversation, and said:

"Your graces — gentlemen — are you perhaps learnèd and well-versed in matters of knight errantry? Because, if you are, I'll tell you my misfortune; but if you're not, then there's no reason to weary myself with words."

By then the priest and the barber had come riding up, seeing that the newcomers were talking to Don Quijote de La Mancha, wanting to make sure questions were answered in such a way that their trick would not be revealed.

The cathedral priest, to whom Don Quijote had spoken, replied:

"Truthfully, my brother, I'm better versed in books of chivalry than I am in Villalpando's *Summa summularum* [*The Essence of Everything*].[2] So if that's all there is to it, you can with perfect confidence tell me anything you like."

"As God wishes," answered Don Quijote. "Accordingly, my dear sir, you must know that I am being carried in this crate under an enchant-

---

2. Logic textbook, published in 1557 [*Translator's Note*].

ment, brought about by the envy and deceit of evil magicians, for virtue is more persecuted by the wicked than it is loved by the good. I am a knight errant, nor am I one of those whose names are never noted by Fame, to render them eternal in her memory, but rather one of those who, despite and in defiance of that same envy, and in the face of who knows how many Persian Magi, or Indian Brahmans, or Ethiopian Gymnosophists, has carried his name straight into the temple of immortality, to serve as a model and example for all time to come, from whose deeds knights errant will see the footsteps they have to walk in, if they long to attain the summit and highest honors that war and weaponry can bestow."

"My lord Don Quijote de La Mancha speaks the truth," said the priest at this point, "for he is indeed traveling in this cart under an enchantment, not for anything he has done wrong or any sins he has committed, but only because of the spite and malice of those to whom virtue is an irritant and courage a vexation. This, my dear sir, is in fact The Knight of the Sad Face, if you have ever heard that name mentioned, whose courageous exploits and great deeds will be inscribed in imperishable bronze and eternal marble, in spite of envy's untiring efforts to hide them away and malice's labors to obscure them."

Hearing the man who was imprisoned and the man who was at liberty both speak in the same fashion, the cathedral priest was ready to cross himself in astonishment, utterly unable to comprehend what was going on, and those who accompanied him were equally puzzled. Sancho Panza, who had come closer, so he could hear what the gentlemen were saying, decided to set the record straight and said:

"Well now, gentlemen, you may approve or disapprove of what I tell you, but the fact is that my master Don Quijote is traveling under an enchantment just as much as my mother is. He's absolutely right in the head, he eats and he drinks and he does everything he has to, just the way other men do — and as he was doing yesterday, before they locked him up in that crate. And that being the case, why do they want me to believe he's traveling under an enchantment? Because I've heard a lot of people say that people who are bewitched don't eat, or sleep, or speak — and my master, if you don't rein him in, will talk more than any thirty lawyers."

And then, turning to look at the priest, Sancho went on:

"Oh, your reverence, your reverence! Did you think I don't recognize you, your grace, and do you think I haven't figured out and understood just where all these new enchantments are taking us? So understand, please, that I know perfectly well who you are, in spite of that mask on your face, and also understand that I understand, in spite of the way you've covered up your scheme. So, in a word, where envy is in charge, virtue can't survive, nor can it endure when generosity is in short supply. Down with the devil! If it weren't for you, your reverence, right now my master might be marrying the Princess Micomicona, and I might be a count — at least a count, because I could certainly expect that, as much because of my master's generosity as because of all I've done for him! But what they say around here is true, I see it now: the wheel of Fortune spins faster than a mill wheel, and those who went soaring yesterday, today they're back down on the ground. I'm sorry on my children's account, and my wife's, for just when they thought they'd be seeing their father walk in through the door as governor of some island, or viceroy, or maybe a king, they'll see him come walking in as a stable hand. And what I've been saying, your reverence, is meant to lean on your conscience as a priest and make you regret the bad things you've done to my master, because remember, in the next life maybe you'll have to account to God for my master's captivity, and maybe you'll also be responsible for all the good deeds and the other mercies my master Don Quijote can't be doing while you've got him locked up."

"Holy cow!" exclaimed the barber at this point. "So, Sancho, you march under the same banner as your master? God be praised, now I can see he's going to have company in that crate, because you've been bewitched just as surely as he has, by contact with his madness and all that knighthood stuff! Oh, you made a mistake when you got seduced[3] by his promises and let that island you want so much get into your head."

"No one's gotten me pregnant," answered Sancho, "and I'm not the kind of man who lets himself get pregnant, not even by the king, and though I may be poor, I'm an Old Christian, and I don't owe anything to anybody, and if it's an island I want, other people want worse things, and everybody is what he does, and being a man I could get to be Pope, let alone governor of an island, and my master could win so many islands he wouldn't know which one to give me. You'd better watch what you say, Mr. Barber, because shaving beards isn't everything, and you can't tell a book by its cover. And I'm telling you this because we all know who we are, around here, and no one's going to load the dice against *me*. And as far as this enchantment my master's supposed to be under, God knows what's the truth; so let's leave it alone, because it only makes it worse when you stir it up."

The barber thought he'd better not answer Sancho, because all that foolish talk might uncover what the priest was trying so hard to keep hidden, and that same concern led the priest to ask his cathedral colleague to ride on ahead a bit, so he could explain the mystery of the crate as well as other amusing things he wanted to pass along. His clerical colleague obliged him, and he and his servants moved up ahead, anxious to learn everything possible about Don Quijote's condition, his life history, his madness and his strange garb, so the priest quickly told him how and why the madness had begun, and everything that had happened right up to the knight's incarceration in the crate, and the scheme they had devised for bringing him home, to see if they could find a doctor to cure him. Both the servants and their master were astonished all over again, hearing Don Quijote's rambling history and, when this tale was told, the cathedral priest said:

"Truly, your reverence, I myself hold these so-called books of chivalry to be a danger to our country, and though I have read at least the first pages of almost all that have been published, impelled by an idle and treacherous whim, I've never been able to read a single one from begin-

---

3. *Empreñastes*, "seduced, fooled," can also mean "got pregnant by," which is how Sancho understands it [*Translator's Note*].

ning to end, for they seem to me — some more, some less — pretty much all of a piece, one just like the other, and there's nothing more to this one than that one. So this sort of writing seems to me to belong to the genre of tales and fables they call Milesian,[4] which are wildly nonsensical stories seeking only to give pleasure, and not to teach anything — exactly the opposite of moral fables, which both delight and teach at the same time. And since the chief purpose of such books is to give pleasure, I don't understand how they can possibly do that, filled as they are with so much wild nonsense, when what the soul conceives of as delight must be the beauty and harmony presented to it by the eyes, or by the mind, either in what it sees or in what it can imagine, and anything that contains ugliness and disorder cannot possibly give pleasure. For what beauty, what harmony of one part with the whole, and the whole with all its parts, can there be in a book or a tale in which a sixteen year old boy can cut a giant as tall as a tower right in half, with one blow, and as easily as if the giant were made of sugar paste? And when they try to describe a battle for us, after having said the enemy forces consist of a million armed men and, if the book's hero happens to be on the other side, tell me why, sure enough, whether we believe it or not, we have to assume that one such knight carries the day just by the strength of his mighty arm. And then what can we say about how easy it is for a queen, or the heiress to an imperial crown, to fall into the arms of a knight who's not only errant but also unknown? What kind of a mind, unless it's completely coarse and barbarous, could possibly be satisfied, reading how a tall tower full of knights goes sailing off to sea, like a boat on a good wind, and tonight it will be in Lombardy and the next day in the land of Prester John of India — or somewhere else that Ptolemy never wrote about and Marco Polo never saw? And to anyone who answers by saying that people who write such books are creating fictions [*cosas de mentira* = lying things] and therefore aren't obliged to worry about fine points or truth, I say to them that the best lies are those that most closely resemble truth, and what gives the most pleasure is what seems most probable or possible. We have to wed these fantastic fictions to the understanding of those who read them; we have to write them so that impossibilities become possible, and great things become comprehensible, so spirits are enraptured — astonished — dazed — elated — and also entertained, so that pleasure and wonder go hand in hand; and he who shuns realism and imitation can't accomplish such things, which represent writing at its absolutely highest point. I've yet to see a single book of chivalry which truly holds together, with the middle matching the beginning, and the end corresponding to both the beginning and the middle; instead they're composed in so many scattered pieces that they seem to be meant as puzzles or monstrosities rather than balanced entities. And in addition they're written in crabbed styles; their heroic exploits simply aren't credible; their love affairs are pornographic; they don't know much about true courtly manners; their battles are long-winded, their speeches stupid, their journeys ridiculous and, to sum it all up, they bear no resemblance to wise, artful writing, and so

---

4. Erotic adventure tales like the *Satyricon*, the *Golden Ass*, and the *Decameron* [Translator's Note].

deserve to be banished from any Christian nation, exactly like all useless people."

The priest had been listening carefully, and thought this a man with an excellent head on his shoulders, who was making very good sense indeed, so he noted that, being of exactly the same opinion himself, with serious objections to books of chivalry, he had burned Don Quijote's entire library, which had been a large one. And he told of the intense scrutiny he had given these volumes, and just which he had condemned to the fire and which he had allowed to survive, the whole account making the cathedral priest laugh heartily; he then remarked that in spite of all the bad things he had said of such books, they did have one redeeming feature: they dealt with matters upon which a first-rate mind could truly flex its muscles, for knighthood was a subject offering a large, roomy field across which a fluent pen could run freely and as far as it liked, describing shipwrecks and other disasters, furious storms, skirmishes and battles, drawing the picture of a brave general and explaining what it took to become one — showing such a general anticipating the enemy's stratagems, and as a powerful orator, either exhorting or checking his soldiers, and as a man of mature counsel, able to make quick decisions, every bit as able to hold back as to attack; then depicting some pathetic, tragic event, or else something happy and totally unexpected; giving us, here, a ravishing beauty, virtuous, wise, reserved, and there, a true Christian gentleman, brave and courteous; in that corner, a wild, barbarous braggart; over here a gallant prince, courageous and considerate; showing us the goodness and loyalty of vassals, the nobility and generosity of lords. And an author of such books could write about astrologers, and first-rate astronomers, and musicians, and men well versed in diplomacy — and, whenever he wanted to, could show himself an adept at black magic, if he felt like it. He could show us Ulysses' tricks, Aeneas' piety, Achilles' courage, Hector's misfortunes, Sinon's[5] treachery, Euryalus' great friendship,[6] Alexander's open-handedness, Caesar's bravery, Trajan's mercifulness and veracity, Zopyrus'[7] faithfulness, Cato's wisdom, and, in short, everything that can raise a famous man to supreme heights, now displaying such traits in one man alone, now exhibiting them among many.

"And if he does these things in an easy style, intelligently [*con ingeniosa invención* = with inventive skill], sticking as close to the truth as he possibly can, he can without question create a fabric woven out of such variegated and beautiful yarn that, when he's done, it will glow with a loveliness and a perfection of finish that will achieve the highest goal any writing can aim for, namely, to teach and delight at the same time, as I've already said. For the unbuttoned scope [*escritura desatada* = loosened literary writing] of these books allows the author to work in epic modes, as well as lyric, tragic, and comic, with all the accompanying possibilities of poetry

---

5. The man who persuaded the Trojans to take the wooden horse into Troy. In earlier eras, Sinon was viewed as a mistaken Trojan, but in Cervantes' time, he was thought to have been in the pay of the Greeks [*Translator's Note*].
6. See Virgil's *Aeneid* [*Translator's Note*].
7. Persian nobleman who mutilated himself in order to help Darius, his emperor, capture a besieged city [*Translator's Note*].

and rhetoric's sweetness and persuasiveness, for one can just as well write epics in prose as in verse."

Chapter Forty-Eight

— in which the cathedral priest continues to discuss the subject matter of books of chivalry, along with other matters worthy of his intelligence

"It's exactly as you say," said the priest, "which is why those who have been writing such books are all the more to be censured, for they've written without ever once stopping to think, paying no attention to either the art or the rules which one should obey, to make oneself famous as a writer of prose, just as those two princes of Greek and Latin poetry[1] are celebrated in verse."

"I myself," said the cathedral priest, "was once tempted to write a chivalric book, keeping in mind all the points I've been making, and, if I must confess the truth, I actually wrote more than a hundred large sheets of paper. And to see if it was what I wanted it to be, I showed these pages to men who are passionate readers of tales of knighthood, some of them learned and wise, and others ignorant folk who only care about the pleasure of hearing nonsense, and they all thought my book easily passed muster — but, in any case, I didn't go on with it, quite as much because I didn't want to occupy myself with matters so alien to my proper profession as because I realized that there are many more fools than wise men; it's better to be praised by the smaller company of wise men than mocked by the larger crowd of idiots, nor do I have any interest in subjecting myself to the jumbled judgment of the haughty mob, which is exactly what most of the people who read such books are. But what especially compelled me to leave off, and even to give up all thought of ever finishing my book, was a line of reasoning I worked out, in contemplating the plays we see, these days, on our stages, which went like this:

"If these dramas we see — both those with invented plots and those based on historical events — are all, or for the most part, famous nonsense, monstrosities with neither heads nor feet and, nevertheless, the crowd listens to them with great pleasure, and considers and speaks of them as good, though they're immensely far from being anything of the sort, and the authors who write them as well as the actors who appear in them say that's how they have to be, because these plays and nothing else are what the crowd wants, while those who work out a careful plan and trace out an artful plot won't be appreciated except by a few wise men who understand what they're up to, and all the rest are blind to such artful cleverness, and they're better off earning their living from the vulgar many rather than from this precious few — then, I say, that's how it will happen with my book, too, after I've sat up to all hours, trying to observe all the rules I've been talking about — and I'll end up just like the tailor on the corner.[2]

1. Homer and Virgil [*Translator's Note*].
2. Proverb: "Like the tailor on the corner, who sewed for nothing — and then threw in the thread" [*Translator's Note*].

"And although I've sometimes tried to persuade the actors that they're wrong, and that more people will come to see, and much greater fame will be won by, artful rather than ridiculous plays, they're so set and settled in their opinions that they can't be shaken by reason or evidence. I can recall saying to one of these stubborn fellows, one day:

" 'Tell me: don't you remember, just a few years ago, when we put on, here in Spain, three tragedies by one of our famous poets, which astonished, delighted, and enthralled everyone who heard them, fools and wise men alike, the crowd just as much as the cognoscenti, and just these three plays alone brought in more money for the people putting them on than any thirty of the most profitable plays ever before staged?'

" 'To be sure,' this theatrical man said to me, 'you must be talking about [Lupercio Leonardo de Argensola's] *Isabela, Phyllis,* and *Alejandra.*'[3]

" 'Exactly,' I told him, 'and then remind yourself that these plays observed all the rules of the art — and then ask yourself if, by keeping to those rules, they in any way lessened either their worth or their appeal to everyone in the whole world. So the problem isn't with the crowd, which wants nonsense, but with those who don't know how to give them anything else. By God, [Lope de Vega's] *Ingratitude Avenged* wasn't nonsense, and I wouldn't say [Cervantes'] *Numantia* was, or that you'd find any in [Gaspar de Aguilar's] *The Merchant Lover,* and even less in [Francisco Augustín Tárrega's] *My Smiling Enemy,* nor in other plays written by any number of intelligent poets, which have brought them fame and reputation, and been profitable for those who staged them.'

"And I told him a good deal more — and, so far as I could see, I had him pretty well confused, but not enough to convince him to change his mistaken ideas."

"One of the points you've raised, my dear sir," the village priest observed, "reminds me of an old grudge I bear against the plays we see today, which is just as strong as my feelings about books of chivalry, because if drama,[4] as Cicero says, must be the mirror of human existence, founded in the way people actually act and look, what we're seeing today are reflections of poppycock, examples of stupidity, and images of lewdness. For can there be anything more foolish, in this matter we're discussing, than to bring out a little boy in swaddling clothes, in the first act, and then show him in the second as a grown man with a beard? What could be stupider than to depict brave old men and cowardly young fellows, or highly rhetorical flunkeys, cabin boys dispensing wisdom, dishwasher kings and kitchenmaid queens? And what should I say about their treatment of the classical unities, the times and places in which things either happen or can happen, except that I've seen plays where the first act begins in Europe, the second in Asia, and the third ends in Africa — and if there had been four acts, the fourth would have taken us to America, so the thing would have been set in all the four corners of the globe? And if the

3. Although these three plays by Lupercio Leonardo de Argensola (1559–1613), a contemporary of Cervantes, were highly praised, *Isabela* and *Alejandra* were not published until 1772, and *Filis* as late as 1889.
4. *Comedia* can mean "comedy, play, theater"; in *Don Quijote* it usually has the broader rather than the narrower meaning [*Translator's Note*].

mirroring of reality is what a play must be about, how can any ordinary intelligence be satisfied if they pretend that, though something is happening in the reign of King Pepin and [his son] the Emperor Charlemagne [742–814], the chief character in this same drama is supposed to be Emperor Heraclius [575–641], who's supposed to carry the cross into Jerusalem and win the Holy Sepulcher, the way Godfrey of Bouillon [1060–1100] did — with the time gaps between and among them being infinitely large? And suppose the play is just fiction, but they drag in historical realities and jumble up all kinds of bits and pieces of things that happened to different people in different times — and they don't make it even look realistic, but just let the mistakes glare out at you, without any excuse whatever? But the worst is when foolish people who don't know any better say this is absolute perfection and to want anything better is to go hunting for humming birds.

"And what about sacred drama? Oh, what ridiculous miracles they concoct, what strictly legendary [*apocrifas* = apocryphal], half-baked stuff — even attributing one saint's miracles to some one else! They even stick miracles into secular plays, without paying the slightest attention to whether such wondrous stage-business (as they call it) happens to belong there, but just so ignorant people will be astonished and come to see the play — all of which seriously compromises truth and discredits history, as well as disgracing the Spanish mind, since the people in other countries, who are strictly punctilious about dramatic laws, see the absurdities and foolishness we put into our plays and think us ignorant barbarians. And it's not a good enough excuse to say that, in tolerating the existence of a public stage, well-ordered governments chiefly intend to provide their people with some seemly recreation, giving them a chance to dissipate the nasty moods idleness can generate; and since this can be accomplished by any kind of play, good or bad, there's no need for laws regulating the theater, nor for forcing those who write and stage plays to make them what they ought to be, because — as I say — whatever comes along will do the trick. But I would counter by pointing out that the same goal can be a great deal better accomplished, and with no compromises whatever, by good rather than bad plays, because once having heard artful, well-structured theater, an audience will be pleased with its jokes, educated by its truths, caught up in its plot, made more alert by its arguments, put on their guard by its deceptions, made wiser by its examples, angered by its vices, and charmed by its virtues, for a good play produces all these feelings in the souls of those who hear it, no matter how rough and slow-witted they may be: the most impossible of all impossibles is a play that has all these qualities failing to amuse, entertain, satisfy, and generally please better than a play that doesn't have them — and most of the plays put on, these days, don't have them. Nor are the poets who write these plays basically to blame, because some of them are very well aware of their mistakes, and have a very precise knowledge of what they ought to be doing, but since plays have become a salable commodity, they say, and they say truly, that producers won't buy them if they're not the kind they want, so the poets try to please the hand that feeds them by giving it what it wants. You can tell just how true this is from the many, many plays written by one of the finest talents in this kingdom,[5] displaying such charm, such wit, such elegant verse, such brilliant dialogue, such impressive wisdom and learning and, to sum it up, so brimful of eloquence and soaring rhetoric, that the whole world knows his fame, but because he's written his plays to please those who stage them, most of them haven't — though some of them have — been as perfect as they ought to be. There are others who write plays virtually without looking down at the page, so after they've been staged the actors have to run and hide, because they're afraid of being punished, as indeed they often have been, for depicting scenes that slander a king or dishonor some noble family. But all these absurdities would stop, plus many more I won't bother mentioning, if there were some official at Court, wise and sensible, to inspect all these plays before they're acted — and not just those they perform at Court, but all of them, all over Spain, and without his approval, signed and sealed, no one would be authorized to stage a play anywhere, and that way the players would be careful to send their plays to Court, and then they could safely put them on, and what was written for them would be done far more carefully and thoughtfully, because the poets would be worried about their work having to undergo a rigorous, informed inspection — and thus we'd have good plays, which would accomplish exactly what they set out to do, entertaining the people at the same time as they advance the reputation of Spanish wit and talent, in addition to making money for the actors without jeopardizing their personal safety (for there'll be no need to worry about punishing them). And if somebody else, or even this same person at Court, were to inspect whatever new books of chivalry may be written, I'm certain we'd get some that were in fact as perfect as your grace has indicated they could be, thus enriching our language and literature with pleasant, priceless treasures of eloquence, and also letting the old books fade away in the bright light of these new ones, designed for the decent, reasonable amusement not just of the idle but also of the busiest among us, for it's impossible for the bow to be bent forever, and we humans have neither the ability nor the strength to sustain ourselves without some lawful recreation."

The priest and his cathedral colleague had gotten to this point in their conversation when the barber rode up and said to the priest:

"Now this, your reverence, is the place where I said it would be good to take our rest, because here there's lots of good, fresh pasture for the oxen."

"That's how it looks to me," answered the priest.

He told the cathedral priest what he and his company planned to do and, enticed by a lovely valley and a splendid view, the cathedral priest decided to join them. And so he could continue to enjoy the priest's conversation, for he had become fond of him, as well as to find out more or less what Don Quijote had been up to, he ordered some of his servants to go to the inn, from which they hadn't traveled very far, and bring back supper for everyone; he'd decided to take his siesta, that afternoon, right there. One of the servants replied that their pack-mule should have reached the inn by now and would be coming along with more than

5. Lope de Vega [Translator's Note].

enough food for all, so what they'd have to fetch from the inn, now, would only be feed grain for the animals.

"Fine," said the cathedral priest. "Bring all the animals there, and let the pack-mule come here."

While this was going on, Sancho, who had grown suspicious of the priest and the barber, suddenly seeing he'd be able to speak to his master without them being present, went over to the crate and said:

"Señor, to relieve my conscience I want to tell you what's going on about this enchantment of yours, and what I want to say is that those two over there, who've been riding with their faces covered, are our village priest and our barber, and I think they've cooked up this scheme for carrying you off out of pure envy, seeing your grace get so far ahead of them in the doing of famous deeds. Now if I'm right, then you're not enchanted at all, just bamboozled and made fun of. And to prove this, I want to ask you one thing, and if you answer me as I think you have to, you'll have your finger right on this trickery and you'll see you're not enchanted at all, but just turned upside down in the head."

"Ask whatever you want to, Sancho my son," replied Don Quijote, "and I'll try to tell you whatever you want to know. And as far as what you say about those two, who traveled with us, and are still traveling with us, being our priest and our barber, our neighbors and people we both know well, it may very well be that they *look* just like them, but that they really and truly *are* them you shouldn't believe for a minute. What you've got to perceive and understand is that if they seem to be them, as you say, then it's got to be that those who have enchanted me have taken on their appearance and likeness, because it's easy for these magicians to assume any shape they feel like, and they'll have made themselves look like our two friends to make you think just what you're thinking and thus get you into such a labyrinth of thinking and wondering that you'll never get out of it, even if you had hold of Theseus' thread. And at the same time, they'll have managed to make my mind uncertain and unable to figure out who could be doing this to me — because just see, on the one hand you tell me that our priest and barber are traveling with me, and on the other I can see for myself that I've been locked up in a crate, and I don't need anyone to tell me that mere human powers, which aren't supernatural, wouldn't be strong enough to lock me up like this — so what do you want me to think or say except that I've been enchanted far more powerfully than anything I've read about in all the books that tell the tales of knights errant who've ever been enchanted? So you can rest assured about this idea of yours that those two are who you say they are, because they're as much our priest and barber as I'm a Turk."

"Our Lady protect me!" shouted Sancho, in reply. "How can your grace possibly be so pig-headed and stupid that you don't understand that I'm telling you the plain truth, and there's a lot more malice than magic in this captivity and misfortune of yours? But never mind, I want to prove to you beyond a doubt that you're not enchanted. And if I'm wrong, then tell me, as God may free you from this suffering, and as I may see you in my lady Dulcinea's arms, when you least expect it — ."

"Stop promising me things," said Don Quijote, "and ask your question, because I've already told you I'll answer you right away."

"This is what I want to know," replied Sancho. "And that is, that you tell me, without adding or leaving out anything at all, but just the plain truth, the way we can expect those who are knights, like your grace, to speak, and the way they do in fact speak, given the name of knight errant — .''

"I tell you I won't lie about a thing," answered Don Quijote. "Now ask your question, because to tell you the truth, Sancho, I'm getting tired of all these oaths, and vows, and pledges."

"And I can say I'm completely convinced of my master's goodness and truthfulness — so, to get to the point, what I ask, speaking with all due respect, is this: since your grace has been shut up in that crate and, so far as you're concerned, enchanted, have you felt the need and the desire to make what they call, you know, big water or little water?"

"I don't understand this 'big water or little water,' Sancho, so speak more plainly, if you want me to answer you plainly."

"You really can't understand, your grace, what I mean about big water and little water? Little boys all learn that in school. Well, what I'm trying to say is, have you felt like doing what no one can keep from doing?"

"Ah, ah, now I understand you, Sancho! Oh yes, lots of times, and I feel it coming right now. Get me out of this pickle, because it's already pretty messy in here!"

Chapter Forty-Nine

— dealing with Sancho Pancho's perceptive conversation with his master, Don Quijote

"Ah-ha!" said Sancho. "Now I've got you: this is exactly what I wanted to know, with all my heart and my life! So come on, señor: Can you deny what everyone around here says, when somebody's feeling bad? 'I don't know what's the matter with so-and-so — he won't eat, or drink, or sleep, or answer when you ask him a question — he acts as if he's enchanted.' Which shows us that people who don't eat, or drink, or sleep, or do any of the natural things I'm talking about, are people who've been enchanted — but not those who still feel the urge to do what your grace feels like doing, or those who drink when they can, or eat when they can, or answer whatever you ask them."

"That's true, Sancho," replied Don Quijote. "But I've already told you there are many different kinds of enchantment, and it could be that, over time, they've changed from one kind to another, and people who are enchanted these days still do everything I'm doing, although in the old days they didn't. So it doesn't do any good to argue about what's going on today, using evidence about what used to happen. I think and believe that I'm enchanted, and this satisfies my conscience, for it would weigh heavily upon me, if I believed I wasn't enchanted and had let myself be locked up in this crate like a lazy coward, cheating the many poor and needy of the help and protection I ought to be giving them, all those who must at this very moment be in urgent need of my assistance."

"In spite of which," answered Sancho, "I say that, for your own best satisfaction, it would be good if your grace tried to get out of this prison-cell, and it's my duty to help you as much as I can, and maybe even get you out myself, and see if you can mount, once more, on your good Rocinante, who looks as if he's enchanted too, he's going along so sad and gloomy — and once that's done, let's try our luck at more adventures, and if we don't do well, there'll still be time to get back into the crate, in which I promise, as a good and faithful squire, I'll lock myself up along with your grace, if things do work out so badly, or if I'm so stupid I can't do what I say I will."

"I'll be happy to do as you say, brother Sancho," replied Don Quijote, "so when you see a chance of getting me out of here, I'll do anything and everything you tell me. But, Sancho, you'll find out just how mistaken you are about this misfortune of mine."

The knight errant and his reluctantly errant squire kept up their conversation until they arrived at the place where, already dismounted, the priest, his cathedral colleague, and the barber were waiting for them. The cart-driver unyoked his oxen and let them graze as they pleased on that green and pleasant spot, whose luxuriance fairly invited enjoyment — not from enchanted folk like Don Quijote, but certainly from sane and sensible people like his squire, who asked the priest to let his master out of the crate for a while, because, if he weren't allowed out, his place of confinement couldn't be kept as clean and decent as such a respectable gentleman deserved. The priest took his point, and said he'd very gladly do as he'd been asked, except for his fear that, once set free, Don Quijote might very well go back to doing exactly as he'd been doing and vanish who knows where.

"I'll guarantee he won't run off," replied Sancho.

"And so will I, most certainly," said the cathedral priest, "especially if he gives me his word as a gentleman not to leave without our permission."

"You have it," said Don Quijote, who had been listening to everything they'd said, "and do remember that a man under an enchantment, as I am, is not free to do as he pleases, for the magician who cast the enchantment might bind him in place, immovable, for three entire centuries — and even should such a man run off, the magician could bring him back right through the air." That being the case, he added, they might just as well let him out, and especially since it would clearly prove useful for all of them, since if they did not he would surely offend against their noses, unless they kept from coming too close.

The cathedral priest clasped our knight's hand, bound as he was, and, given Don Quijote's solemn oath, they released him from the crate — and how it overjoyed him to find himself out of his cage! The first thing he did was stretch himself all over, and then he bounded over to Rocinante and, clapping him on the haunches, said:

"In the name of God and His Blessed Mother, I still believe, oh flower and model of all horses, that before too long we'll both have what we want — you, your master up on your back, and I, mounted on you, once more doing the work for which God put me into the world."

Don Quijote then walked a good distance away from the others, along with Sancho; he returned vastly relieved and even more anxious to do what his squire had planned.

The cathedral priest watched him, astonished at how strangely his extraordinary madness operated, for so much of what Don Quijote said and did demonstrated perfect understanding; he was out of control, as I've said many times before, only when he got involved in knightly matters. And so, once they were all seated on the grass, waiting for their supper to arrive, the cathedral priest said to our knight, stirred with pity:

"My dear sir, is it possible that such pointless, bitter reading as tales of chivalry could have so possessed you and upset your mind that you've actually come to believe in this business of being enchanted, and all the rest of such stuff, all of it just as far from reality as a lie is from the truth? How can anyone with a functioning human brain possibly believe that the world has ever seen an infinity of Amadíses, and all that horde of famous knights, all those Emperors of Trebizond, that Felixmarte of Hircania, and all those soft-footed ladies' horses, those damsels-errant, those dragons and monsters and giants, those incredible adventures, all those enchantments and battles and immense encounters, those magnificent costumes, and all those lovesick princesses, those squires turned into noblemen, those witty dwarves, and all those love-letters and wooing, so many, many incredibly noble-hearted women and, in a word, all those stupidities that tales of chivalry are composed of? Myself, I know I can find them pleasant enough reading, if I don't let myself think about all their lies and silliness, but once I start realizing what they're all about I throw away even the best of them — and I'd even toss them into the fire, if I had one handy, because that's what cheats and liars deserve; you can't deal with them in the usual way, because they create new sects and whole new ways of life, and let the ignorant masses take their nonsense as truth and reality. Indeed, they're so bold they even dare to attack the minds of sensible, well-born gentlemen — as it's easy enough to see they've done with you, carrying you to the point where you had to be shut up in a crate and dragged about in an ox-cart, like some lion or tiger, going from place to place so people can pay to see him.

"Ah, señor Don Quijote! Take pity on yourself, let yourself return to the ranks of the sane and sensible; make use of the fine mind Heaven has been pleased to give you, and let your happy talents occupy themselves with some different reading, from which your conscience can benefit and your honor increase! And if your thoughts still turn to books of grand deeds and the knights who perform them, read the Book of Judges, in the Holy Bible, for there you'll find magnificent truths and deeds as brave and noble as they are truthful. Portugal had its Viriatus [2nd-cent. A.D. freedom fighter], Rome had its Caesar, Carthage its Hannibal, Greece its Alexander, Castille its Count Fernán González [c. 930–970, nationalist leader]; Valencia had El Cid; Andalusia, Gonzalo Fernández [1453–1515, general]; Estremadura, Diego García de Paredes [15th-cent. man of immense strength]; Jerez had its Garci Pérez de Vargas [13th-cent. knight], Toledo, its Garcilaso [battle of Granada, 1492], Seville, its Manuel de León [who entered a lion's cage for a lady's glove] — and reading all their courageous deeds can inform, educate, delight, and astonish even the very loftiest of minds. This would be reading worthy of your own fine mind, my dear Don Quijote, and you would rise from it learned in history, devoted to virtue, disciplined in goodness, improved in your habits, fearless in your bravery, bold without a trace of cowardice — and all this, to the greater glory of God, and highly beneficial both to you and to La Mancha, from whence, I am informed, your grace traces your lineage."

Don Quijote listened to the cathedral priest attentively, and when it was clear he had said all he meant to, our knight sat silent for some time, reflecting, and then said:

"It seems to me, my dear sir, that what you have sought to persuade me is that knights errant have never existed, and that all books of chivalry are lies and untruths, dangerous as well as useless to our country, and that I've done wrong in reading them, and still worse in believing them, and worst of all in imitating them, taking on myself the harsh profession of knight errantry in which they offer instruction, for you deny that there have been any folk such as Amadís (neither Amadís of Gaul nor Amadís of Greece) nor any of the other knights of whom these books say so much."

"Exactly — word for word, just as your grace has said," the cathedral priest declared.

To which Don Quijote replied:

"And your grace has also said these books have done me a great deal of harm, for they've deranged my mind and brought me to be locked up in a crate, and that it would be better for me to mend my ways and take to a different course of reading — books that were more truthful and would better please and instruct me."

"Quite so," said the cathedral priest.

"Then it seems to me," said Don Quijote, "that it's your grace who's not right in the head, and is under enchantment, for you have uttered so many blasphemies against something so well accepted all over the world, and so universally believed to be true, that anyone who denies it, as your grace plainly does, deserves the same punishment your grace says you would give such books, when you've read and been annoyed by them. Because saying there's never been anyone in this world named Amadís, or any of the other knights of whom the books are full, is like saying that the sun doesn't shine, or ice isn't cold, and the earth neither nourishes nor feeds us — because who in the world could be clever enough to convince us that there's no truth to the tale of Princess Floripes and Guy of Burgundy, or the story of Fierabrás and the bridge at Mantible, which happened in Charlemagne's time and is as true, by God, as it is that it's daylight right now? And if *that's* a lie, then there never was any Hector, or Achilles, and there was no Trojan War, no Twelve Peers of France, or King Arthur of England, who lives on in the shape of a crow and is expected to return to his kingdom at any moment. And you'd also have to claim that Guarino Mezquino's history [Spanish translation, 1548] is a lie, and the Quest for the Holy Grail, and the love story of Tristan and Isolde is a fabrication, like that of Guinevere and Lancelot — even though there are people still alive who can almost remember seeing Lady Quintañona, who poured the meanest glass of wine in all England. And that's so true I can remember being told, by my grandmother on my father's side of the family, when she saw a lady with a headdress like a cowl, 'Grandson, that lady over there looks just like Lady Quintañona' — from which I deduce that my grandmother either knew the lady or, at least, must have seen a portrait of her. And who could deny the truth of the story of Pierres and the lovely Magalona [Spanish translation, 1519], since to this very day you can see, in the royal armory, the very rod with which the brave Pierres steered the wooden horse that carried him up into the air, which is only a little bigger than an ordinary steering stick? And right next to that rod there's Babieca's saddle, just as, in Ronscevalles, they've got Roland's horn, as big as some great girder, and from all of which we're entitled to believe the Twelve Peers of France had to be real, and also Pierres, and El Cid, and the other knights like them,

> the ones that everyone talks of,
> hunting all over for adventure.

If not, then tell me there wasn't any such knight errant as that brave Portuguese, Juan de Merlo, who journeyed to Burgundy and fought the famous lord of Charny, a certain Monsignor Pierre, in the city of Ras, and then afterward fought Monsignor Henri de Remestán, in the city of Basle, triumphing in both encounters and emerging from them covered with honor and fame — and what about the adventures and challenges experienced in Burgundy by those brave Spaniards, Pedro Barba and Gutiérrez Quijada (from whom I trace my own descent, in the direct male line), who were victorious over the sons of Count San Polo? Tell me, too, that Don Fernando de Guevara never went hunting adventure in Germany, where he fought with Lord George, a gentleman related to the Duke of Austria, or that Suero de Quiñones's jousting was just a joke, like Mosén Luis de Falces' battles against Don Gonzalo de Guzmán, the Spanish knight, or all the many, many glorious deeds performed by Christian knights from this and other countries, every one of them authenticated and truthful — for, let me say once more, he who denies such things denies himself any rationality and good sense whatever."

The cathedral priest was stunned by Don Quijote's jumbling of truth and fiction, and to see how devotedly our knight had studied deeds of ancient knighthood, so he replied:

"My dear Don Quijote, I cannot deny there is some truth in what your grace has said, especially about the Spanish knights errant, and I am also quite prepared to admit the existence of the Twelve Peers of France, but I am not willing to concede that they did everything Archbishop Turpín says they did, for the truth is they were knights chosen by the kings of France and known as 'peers' because they were each other's equals in strength, in rank, and in courage — at least, if they weren't, they should have been — and theirs was a kind of military-religious order, like those of Santiago and Calatrava, today, which expect that their members are, or ought to be, worthy knights, brave and well-born. And just as, today, we speak of a Knight of Saint John, or a Knight of Alcántara, in those days they'd speak of a Knight of the Twelve Peers, because the twelve knights chosen for that order were all equals. As far as El Cid is concerned, there's of course no doubt of his existence, nor of Bernardo Carpio's, but whether they did what people say they did is I think much more doubtful. As for Count Pierres' rod, of which your grace made mention, saying it could be found next to Babieca's saddle, in the royal armory, I have to confess I'm at fault, though I don't know whether I'm badly informed or just short-sighted, yet having seen the saddle I've not seen the rod, though it may be as large as your grace indicates."

"But it's most certainly there," replied Don Quijote, "and, what's more, it's said to be wrapped in a calf's-hide covering, to keep it from rotting."

"That may very well be," replied the cathedral priest, "but by the vows I've taken I can't remember having seen it. But even if it's there, I still don't have to believe the stories of all those Amadíses, nor the whole mob of knights those books tell us about, nor is that any reason for a man like your grace — so upright and distinguished, and blessed with such a fine mind — to treat the strange and wild goings on of these foolish books as if they were really true."

Chapter Fifty

— of the learned discussion between Don Quijote and the cathedral priest, as well as other events

"Oh, that's a good one!" answered Don Quijote. "Here we have books printed by royal license, after careful inspection — books read with universal pleasure by high and low alike, poor and rich, the learned as well as the ignorant, plebians and knights — indeed, books read by people of every rank and level — and how can they be mere lies, how can they only seem to be true, when they tell us who these knights' fathers were, and their mothers, what country they came from and who their relatives were, and of what rank, and where they were born and just what they did, every exploit, blow by blow, day by day? You should hold your peace, your grace, and not speak such blasphemy, and — believe me, this is advice you as a sensible man need to have — just read those books, and see how much pleasure they give you. Could there be anything more satisfying than to see, as it were, right in front of our eyes, an immense lake of bubbling, boiling pitch, crawling with hordes of wriggling serpents, and snakes, and lizards, and all sorts of fierce and terrifying animals — and then, right out of the middle of that lake, there comes a doleful voice, saying: 'You, knight, whoever you may be, staring out at this fearful lake, if you yearn for the treasure hidden under these black waters, show the strength of your brave heart and hurl yourself into the middle of this black and burning tide, for otherwise you cannot be worthy to set eyes on the noble wonders hidden here, nor will you ever behold the seven castles of the seven enchantresses who lie under this blackness.' And then the knight, barely waiting for the doleful voice to finish, and not bothering to stop and consider the fearful danger into which he's putting himself — not pausing even long enough to strip off the heavy weight of his armor — commends himself to God and to his lady and throws himself right into the boiling lake, and without knowing what to expect or where he will come to, suddenly finds himself on a flowery meadow, incomparably lovelier than the Elysian Fields themselves. The sky in that place shines clearer, and the sun glows with a new brightness, and the knight sees spread out in front of him a peaceful forest, trees so luxuriantly green that just seeing them is sheer delight, and he hears the sweet, innocent singing of multitudes of brightly colored small birds, flitting through the inter-twined branches. Here there's a small stream, whose cool fresh waters flow like liquid crystal over the fine sand and polished white stones, looking for all the world like powdered gold and the purest of pearls, and there is a fountain beautifully crafted in multi-colored jasper and smooth marble, and over there yet another fountain, more crudely fashioned, on which are clustered tiny mussel shells and the spiralled white and yellow dwell-ings that snails carry on their backs, all set so wildly and profusely, and so intermixed with bits of gleaming crystal and imitation emeralds that it forms a shape of such wild elaboration that art, in the process of imitating nature, seems to have overwhelmed it. And suddenly the knight sees a mighty castle, or king's bright palace, with solid gold walls, parapets of diamond, and gates of topaz — and so fantastically constructed that, even built as it is out of diamonds, garnets, rubies, pearls, gold, and emeralds, the workmanship is still more remarkable. And after seeing all this, what could be better than to find a crowd of lovely maidens coming through the gates? so charmingly and beautifully dressed that, were I now to de-scribe them as they are described in these books, there would be no end to what I might say. And then she who seems to be the leader of all these damsels takes the bold knight who threw himself into the burning lake by the hand and conducts him, without saying a word, into the rich castle, or palace, and there strips him as naked as the day his mother bore him, and bathes him with warm water, and then anoints him with scented salves, and dresses him in a sweet-smelling, perfumed shirt of the finest sheer silk, and another damsel appears and drapes a cloak over his shoul-ders (which surely can't be worth less than an entire city — and perhaps more). And how wonderful when we're told that, once these things have been done, they lead him to another room where he finds tables so marvellously laid that he's left astonished and wondering! How wonder-ful to see him bathing his hands in liquid distilled from amber and sweet-smelling flowers! How wonderful that they seat him in an ivory chair! And how all the maidens serve him, preserving their magical silence! How they bring him so many wonderful dishes, so skilfully prepared, that appetite cannot know which to reach for! How the music flows on as he eats, though he has no idea who is singing or from where! And when his meal is done, and the tables have been removed, how the knight leans back in his chair, perhaps picking his teeth as he usually does, and then suddenly a maiden far lovelier than any of those he has seen comes through the door and seats herself next to him, and starts to tell him all about that castle, and how she is held there by an enchantment, plus much, much more that fascinates the knight and absolutely amazes those who are read-ing his story!

"I've no wish to draw this out any further, for it should already be clear that, at every point in any and all of these tales of knight errantry, a reader — any reader whatever — will be delighted and astonished at what he finds. Just believe me, your grace, as I've already told you, and read these books, for you will see how they drive away melancholy and, for those who may be ill, will improve their condition. I can say for myself that, since I've been a knight errant, I've been brave, courteous, open-handed, well-behaved, magnanimous, gallant, bold, calm, patient, one who can endure severe trials, captivities, enchantments — and although I've just recently been shut up in a crate like a madman, in not very long I expect, by the might of my arm, and if Heaven smiles on me and Fortune does not oppose me, to see myself king of a realm and able to exhibit the graciousness and generosity held here in my heart. Because, my dear sir, by God, a poor man is unable to practice the virtue of generosity with anyone, although he possesses it to the very highest degree, and gracious-ness which is merely abstract is a dead thing — as dead as belief without good deeds. Which is why I hope Fortune will give me the chance to become an emperor, to show what love and goodwill I have for my friends, and especially for this poor Sancho Panza, my squire, who is the best fellow in the world, and on whom I'd much like to bestow a count's title, as I long ago promised him I would — except that I fear he hasn't the ability to take charge of such an estate."

As soon as Sancho heard his master's last words, he said:

"Your grace, señor Don Quijote, you certainly ought to give me that countship you've been promising me for so long, the way I've been waiting for your grace to do, because I promise your grace there won't be any problem about knowing how to govern it, and if I do have any problems I've heard there are people in this world who rent gentlemen's estates and pay them so much a year, and then they take care of the govern-ing and the owner just stretches out his legs and enjoys the rent he's getting, and doesn't worry about anything, and that's what I'll do, and I won't haggle and baggle with them, I'll just walk away from the whole business and enjoy my rent like a duke, and that's how it'll all go."

"Ah, brother Sancho," said the cathedral priest, "but that only takes care of enjoying the rent, and the lord of an estate has to be responsible for administering justice, and this requires ability and common sense, and especially a determination to do the right thing, and if you start without that, then everything will go wrong, and end wrong — which is why God helps carry out the simple man's good wishes, just as He sets His face against the wise man's evil intentions."

"I don't know anything about those philosophies," answered Sancho. "All I know is that as soon as I get to be a count, I'll know how to act like a count, because I've got just as much soul as the next man, and maybe even more body, and I'd be just as much the ruler of my estate as anyone else is of his, and when I'm in charge I'll do what I want to do, and doing what I want to, I'll make myself happy, and making myself happy, I'll be satisfied, and when I'm satisfied, that's all I could ask for, and having all I could ask for, that'll be the end of it, so let the estate come and we'll leave the rest to God and then, as one blind man said to the other, we'll see what we'll see."

"That philosophy makes a lot of sense, Sancho — but just the same, there's a lot to be said about this business of governing estates."

At which point Don Quijote said:

"But I don't know what else can be said, except that I'll be guided by the example set for me by the great Amadís of Gaul, who made his squire

Count of Firme Island — and so, with a clear conscience, I can make Sancho Panza a count, for he's one of the best squires any knight errant ever had."

The cathedral priest was astonished by what beautifully organized nonsense Don Quijote had spoken, how well he had described the Knight of the Lake's adventure, and what a profound effect the lies he'd read in his books had produced on his mind and, what's more, by Sancho's folly in longing so desperately for the title and estate his master had promised him.

By this time the cathedral priest's servants, who'd gone to the inn to fetch the pack-mule, had returned and, to allow the ox-cart driver to take advantage of the spot, as we've said, they used a small rug and the green grass of the meadow as their table, seated themselves in the shade of a tree, and ate their meal. And as they were eating, they suddenly heard, from a nearby grove, a great clamor and the rattling of a sheep bell, and immediately saw a beautiful she-goat, its hide all spotted black, white, and yellow, come bursting out from among the bushes and brambles. And right behind her there came a goatherd, shouting as he scrambled along, saying all the things goatherds usually say to stop runaway animals, or to get them back to the flock. The fugitive she-goat, plainly terrified, ran over to the seated people, as if seeking their protection, and then stopped. The goatherd came over and, taking her by the horns, began to talk to her, like someone capable of both reason and speech:

"Ah, you wild little Spotty, you wild little Spotty, how you've been limping along these last few days! Tell me, daughter, was it wolves that frightened you? Won't you tell me, pretty little one? But of course! It's just that you're a female, and there's no keeping you calm — the devil with that fickle nature of yours, and all those other females you're copying! Come back, come back, my little friend, and even if you're not completely happy, at least you'll be safer, back in your pen, or with your other friends — because if you, who are supposed to protect and lead them, go running off so unprotected, and so completely lost, what will happen to them?"

The goatherd's words pleased his audience, and especially the cathedral priest, who said to him:

"For your own good, brother, calm yourself a bit and don't be in such a hurry to get this she-goat back to her pen, because, after all, she's a female, as you say yourself, and she can't help herself, she'll do as nature compels her, no matter how you try to get in her way. So here, take this mouthful and drink a glass with us, and that will quiet you down and, at the same time, give your goat a chance to rest."

As he spoke, he held out his knife, with a cold loin of rabbit on it. The goatherd took it, and thanked him; he ate, and he drank, and then he said:

"Please, your graces, just because I talked to this animal as if she had a brain, don't think I'm an idiot, because, really, there's a special mystery in the words I used. I'm a peasant, but I'm not so stupid that I don't know how to deal with people and animals."

"I believe every word of it," said the priest, "because I know from experience that mountains make men learned and shepherds' huts hold philosophers."

"In any case, señor," replied the goatherd, "they shelter men who've learned what they know the hard way, and to show you how true this is, gentlemen, and to let you understand it at first hand, if it wouldn't bore you, and if it doesn't look as if I'm inviting myself without waiting for an invitation, and you want to hear it, let me take a little of your time and tell you something absolutely true that will back up what this gentleman," and he gestured toward the priest, "has just been saying, and what I say too."

Don Quijote replied:

"Since this seems to be brushed with a touch of knightly adventure, for my part I will listen to you most willingly, brother, just as all these gentlemen will do, because they are exceedingly sensible folk and well disposed to all odd tidbits and tales capable of interesting, pleasing, and generally entertaining the human mind — as, I have no doubt, your tale will do. So begin, my friend, and we will all listen."

"But I'll pass," said Sancho, "because I'm going down to that little stream with this meat pie, and I'll stay there and stuff myself for the next three days — because I've heard my master, Don Quijote, say that anyone who's squire to a knight errant has to eat whenever he gets the chance, until he can't eat any more, since sometimes it happens that they wander into a wood so thick they can't get out of it for six days, and if the man isn't well-stuffed, or his saddlebags aren't filled to the top, he can just as well stay in there, the way they often find people, dried up like mummies."

"That's absolutely right, Sancho," said Don Quijote. "You go where you want to, and eat as much as you can, for I have eaten all I need and the only food I require, now, is for my soul, which this good man's story will provide."

"As it will for all of us," said the cathedral priest.

And he asked the goatherd to begin the tale he'd promised them. The goatherd released the she-goat's horns, gave her a couple of slaps on the rump, and said:

"Now you lie near me, Spotty. We've got plenty of time to go back to the other animals."

The she-goat seemed to understand, for as her master seated himself, she lay down next to him, very peacefully, and looked up into his face, as if to show she was all ears, and just waiting for whatever her goatherd might say, and so he began as follows:

Chapter Fifty-One

— what the goatherd told all those who were bringing
Don Quijote home

"In a village eight or nine miles from this valley — small, but one of the wealthiest in the whole region — there lived a farmer so well-respected that, although people who are rich are always highly regarded, this man was better thought of for his virtue than for the wealth he'd attained. But the best part of it all, according to him, was that he had a daughter so exquisitely beautiful, so incredibly sensible, graceful, and virtuous that everyone who saw her marveled at the wondrous qualities Heaven and Nature had bestowed on her. She was beautiful even as a child, grew lovelier as she grew older, and by the time she was sixteen had reached the peak of her beauty. They began to talk about her in all the villages around — but why just mention these nearby places? Word of her loveliness spread to the most distant cities, and even reached the royal parlors, as well as the ears of people of every rank and level, so that they came flocking to see her, like some rare, precious object, or some sacred miracle, from all over the country. Her father looked after her, but she took care of herself, too, for no padlocks, or watchmen, or locked doors can guard a girl as well as her own modesty. The father's money and the daughter's beauty made many men seek her hand in marriage, suitors from her own town and from other places, too, but her father, having such a splendid jewel in his care, could not make up his mind, could not decide who among all those who sought her should carry her off. And I was one among all those who came courting such a desirable wife, hopeful, even confident I could win the prize, for her father knew who I was, knew I came from the same town, and of spotless ancestry, and that I was in the prime of life, a young man materially well endowed and just as rich in understanding [*ingenio* = mind, wit, cleverness, creativity, etc.].

But she had another suitor from that same town, just as well endowed, and this made her father hesitate, unable to make up his mind which of us deserved his daughter — so, to end the uncertainty, he decided to tell Leandra (for that was the name of the rich girl who has made me so miserable) that, the two of us being equally deserving, she ought to be free to choose whoever she liked best — an idea worth imitating by all fathers who want to marry off their children, not so they're left to choose ruinously and wickedly, but so the children can choose what best pleases them, and from more than just a single good choice. I have no idea how Leandra chose; all I know is that her father put both of us off with talk of her extreme youth, and a lot of vague generalities, none of which either committed him or turned us away. My competitor's name is Anselmo, and I am Eugenio, just so you can know the names of the characters in this tragedy, though it still isn't over — but it's bound to end in a disaster.

"Just then Vincente de la Rosa came home. He was the son of a poor farmer, and had been off in Italy, and other places, as a soldier. When he'd been just a twelve year old boy, an army officer passing through our village with his company had taken this Vincente with him, and after another twelve years Vincente came back, decked out in all sorts of military finery, splashed with a thousand different colors, covered with a thousand crystal trinkets and hammered steel chains. He wore one uniform today and another tomorrow, but all fancy, gaudy, without much weight and worth even less. Now, farmers and peasants, who are nasty by nature, are even worse when they have nothing to do, so they watched him and, one by one, counted up all his uniforms and trinkets, and found that in fact he had a total of three uniforms, in different colors, with matching garters and stockings, but had worked out so many styles and fashions of wearing them that, without actually counting, you'd have sworn he wore more than a dozen uniforms, with more than twenty feathered caps. But please don't think all this about his clothing is irrelevant or excessive, because his clothes play a large role in this story. He'd sit himself down on a stone bench, just under a tall poplar tree in our village square, and he'd make us all stand around gaping, listening to all the big doings he told us about. There wasn't a country in the whole world he hadn't seen, or a battle he hadn't fought in; he'd killed more Moors than you could find in Morocco and Tunisia and, according to him, he'd had more hand-to-hand fights than Gante and Luna,[1] Diego García of Paredes, and a thousand others whose names he reeled off, and he'd won every single one of them, without ever losing a single drop of blood. On the other hand, he showed us the scars of wounds which, though of course no longer visible, he told us had come from musket wounds received in various skirmishes and forays. And to sum it all up, he had the incredible arrogance to use the familiar form of 'you' with everyone, even those who knew his family, saying that his paternity rested in the strength of his arm, that he'd created his kinsmen by his deeds, and that, being a soldier, he didn't have to concede anything to anyone, not even the king. And to add to all this arrogance, he was something of a musician and strummed his guitar so swaggeringly that there were people who claimed he made it speak — and that wasn't the end of it, because he also fancied himself a poet, so whatever stupid stuff anyone did, he composed a poem about it, three or four miles long.

"So this soldier I've described for you, this Vincente de Rosa, this braggart, this ladies man, this musician, this poet, had lots of chances to see and be seen by Leandra, through a window in her father's house that opened right on the town square. She fell in love with all the tinsel he wore; she was charmed by his poems (because he distributed twenty copies of every one he wrote); she heard about all the great and noble deeds he'd performed (as he himself had narrated them); and, in a word, as the devil must have arranged it, she fell in love with him even before he got the idea of trying to win her. And since no love affairs ever go smoother than those the lady herself wants, Leandra and Vincente had no trouble getting together, and before any of her many suitors knew which way she was leaning, she'd already fallen, having deserted her dear, beloved papa's house (for she had no mother) and gone off with the soldier, who came out of this encounter more triumphantly than any of the others he'd talked about. The entire village was stunned, as was everyone else who heard the news; I was baffled, Anselmo astounded, her father miserable, her relatives humiliated; the authorities being appealed to, the police went into action: they went up and down the roads, searched all the woods, and hunted everywhere, and after three days found our fickle Leandra in a mountain cave, stripped to her underclothes, and without the large sum of money and the heaps of precious jewels she'd taken from home. They brought her back to her poor father; they questioned her about the whole miserable affair; she immediately admitted that Vincente de la Rosa had deceived her, convincing her to flee from her father's house by his promise to marry her and take her to the richest and most depraved city in the whole world, which of course was Naples, and she, stupidly, completely hoodwinked,

---

1. Both unknown [*Translator's Note*].

had swallowed the whole tale and, after robbing her father, she'd handed all the loot over to him, the same night they'd fled together; he'd taken her up a steep mountain and closed her up in the cave where they'd found her. And she also told them that the soldier had robbed her of everything she had except her honor, then just left her in the cave and gone away — and this astonished everyone all over again. It was hard for us to believe the fellow hadn't taken advantage of her, but she affirmed it so earnestly that it was a sort of consolation for her unhappy father, not concerned with the riches that had been stolen, once he found that his daughter had not been deprived of that jewel which, once lost, cannot ever be recovered.

"The very same day on which Leandra re-appeared, her father made her disappear once more, taking her off to a convent in a town near here, hoping that time would wear away some of the bad reputation his daughter had brought upon herself. The fact that she was so young made her less blameworthy, at least to those who didn't care whether she acted badly or well, but those who knew her better, and knew her good sense and her sharp mind, could not attribute her fall to ignorance but, rather, to boldness and to the natural tendencies of women in general, which are usually, for the most part, wild and unsettled. And once Leandra was thus shut away, Anselmo's eyes could no longer see anything — or, at least, nothing that pleased him, and mine too were darkened, with not a gleam of light to brighten them; Leandra's absence increased our sorrow, diminished our patience, made us curse the soldier's damned uniforms and be disgusted by her father's carelessness. In the end, Anselmo and I agreed to leave the village and come to this valley, where he pastures a large flock of sheep, which he owns, and I a good-sized herd of goats, which are mine as well, and we pass our lives among the trees, seeking what relief we can find for our passions, sometimes singing duets praising, or damning, our lovely Leandra, sometimes lying alone and sighing our sorrows to the heavens. A good many more of Leandra's suitors have come to these rugged mountains, following after us, and practicing the same occupations — so many, indeed, that this place almost seems to have been transformed into a pastoral Arcadia, so overflowing is it with shepherds and sheep folds, nor is there anywhere in these woods where you cannot hear our beautiful Leandra's name. In one place there'll be fiery curses mixed with wild passion and an outcry against her lewdness; in another, she'll be pardoned and absolved, and still elsewhere condemned and reviled; someone will sing praises to her beauty, someone else says she's worthless — and, to make a long story short, everyone loathes Leandra, and everyone adores Leandra, and everyone raves so wildly that we have men whining disdainfully about her who've never even spoken to her, and others mourning, insane with jealousy, whom she's never even met — because, as I said, everyone found out about her fall before they learned about her falling in love. There isn't a rocky hollow, or a stream border, or a spreading tree shadow without its sad shepherd, breathing out his misfortunes; wherever you can hear an echo, it's repeating Leandra's name; the mountains ring out 'Leandra,' the brooks murmur 'Leandra,' and we all wait on some word from her lips, bewitched, hoping against hope and afraid without knowing what we're afraid of. Of all these madmen, the one who displays both the most and the least good sense is my rival, Anselmo, because having so many more things to complain about than he ever so much as mentions, all he complains about is being kept away from her, and as he accompanies himself on the rebec[2] — which by the way he plays extremely well — he sings his one complaint in remarkably well-crafted verses. I've taken an easier road, which also seems to me better justified, and that is to criticize the fickleness of women, their inconstancy, their double-dealing, their broken promises, the good faith they can't and won't keep, and — to sum it all up — the lack of good sense they display in directing their thoughts and desires. And that, gentlemen, was the reason behind everything I said to this goat, when I found her here, because she's a female and so I can't think well of her, though she's the best animal in my herd.

"This then is the story I promised to tell you, and if I've been too long-winded about it, I won't be brusque about serving you, either — for my corral is close by, and I've got fresh milk and the finest cheese, and different kinds of the best fruit available, just as delightful to look at as to eat."

Chapter Fifty-Two

— Don Quijote's fight with the goatherd, as well as his strange
adventure with the flagellants, which with great effort he
brought to a happy ending

The goatherd's tale pleased everyone in his audience, and especially the cathedral priest, who noted with puzzled interest that the narrative did not seem to have come from a peasant goatherd, but rather a polished courtier, and he observed that the priest had spoken quite properly, claiming that mountains and woods spawned learned men. They all offered Eugenio whatever assistance they could, but the most generous of all was Don Quijote, who said:

"By God, brother goatherd, if there were any possibility of my beginning another adventure, I'd take to the road this very minute and set things right for you — I'd rescue your Leandra from that convent, where she's plainly being held against her will, in spite of the abbess and anyone else who tried to stop me, and I'd return her to you, for you to do with as you chose — but, mind you, keeping strictly to the laws of knighthood, which stipulate that no young damsel may ever be treated improperly — for I still trust in Our Lord on High not to endow a wicked magician with more power than a good one, and in the meantime I pledge you my succor and assistance, as my vows require that I do, for they expressly command me to help those who are helpless and protect those in need."

The goatherd stared at him, and seeing Don Quijote's unprepossessing face, and how badly dressed he was, turned with some surprise to the barber, sitting beside him, and asked:

---

2. Two- or three-stringed, pear-shaped ancient instrument, played with a bow [*Translator's Note*].

"Sir, who is this man, looking the way he looks and talking the way he talks?"

"Who could it be," replied the barber, "but the celebrated Don Quijote de La Mancha, who rights wrongs, sets injustices straight, protects damsels in distress, terrifies giants, and triumphs in all battles?"

"Now that strikes me," said the goatherd, "as the kind of stuff you read in books about knights errant, who are supposed to do all these things your grace was saying, but in my opinion either you're pulling my leg or this gentleman must have holes in his head."

"And you," cried Don Quijote, "are the greatest rascal in the world, and a coward with holes in *your* head, because there's more in my skull than there ever was in the whoring bitch whose belly you came out of."

And, acting as he spoke, Don Quijote grabbed a loaf of bread and threw it right in the goatherd's face, flattening his nose. But finding himself so palpably manhandled, the goatherd, who had a limited sense of humor, immediately forgot all about the fine rug, the tablecloth, and the diners clustered around them, and leaped at Don Quijote, clutched him around the neck with both hands, and very likely would have strangled him, except that at that point Sancho Panza grabbed him by the shoulders and threw him backward onto the table, smashing dishes, breaking glasses, and spilling and scattering everything in all directions. Finding himself set free, Don Quijote tried to climb up on the goatherd, who, with his face all bloody, was being kicked by Sancho as, on all fours, he groped about for one of the table knives, intending a truly sanguinary revenge, which, however, the priest and his cathedral colleague kept him from accomplishing — but the barber managed to get Don Quijote down under the goatherd, who proceeded to pummel away at our knight until his face was as bloody as the goatherd's own.

Both clerical gentlemen were bursting with laughter, the policemen were jumping up and down with delight, urging first this one and then that one of the combatants on, exactly like people at a dogfight, and only Sancho Panza was seriously angry, because he couldn't get away from one of the cathedral priest's servants, who wouldn't let him go to his master's aid.

Finally, everyone was having a grand old time, except for the two combatants, who were pounding away at each other, when they heard a trumpet blowing such a melancholy blast that, without exception, they turned in the direction from which the sound seemed to come — but the most excited of all was Don Quijote, who even though he was being kept most reluctantly under the goatherd, and being more than mildly pummeled, managed to say:

"Brother devil — and you can't be anything else, since you were brave and strong enough to vanquish me — let me beg you for a brief truce, no more than a hour, because the sad sound of that trumpet we just heard seems to me to mean that some adventure is calling me."

The goatherd, by this time weary of punching and being punched, immediately agreed, and Don Quijote stood up, craning to see from whence the trumpet had sounded — and saw, all of a sudden, many men coming down a slope, dressed in white as if they were penitents.

Now that year, as it happened, the clouds had been denying their showers to the thirsty earth, so all over the region they were conducting public prayers, holy processionals, and parades of self-scourging flagellants, begging God in His mercy to open His hands and let it rain down on them, and to this effect the people of a nearby village were making a pilgrimage to a venerable hermitage located in that valley.

Seeing the penitents' strange garb, Don Quijote did not stop to think how many times he had seen men dressed exactly like that, but fancied himself caught up in an adventure — something into which only he, as a knight errant, could sally forth, a notion he confirmed by imagining that a statue the men were carrying, all covered in black mourning, was in fact some noble lady being forcibly kidnapped by this band of wicked good-for-nothings and brutes, and the moment that thought came to him he ran quickly to Rocinante, who had been peacefully grazing, yanked the bit and his shield off the saddle-bow, and had the horse saddled in an instant, after which he swiftly mounted and, commanding Sancho to hand him his sword, he lifted his shield and shouted to all those around:

"Now, my brave friends, now you will see how important it is that the world be furnished with knights errant — now you will see, as I liberate that noble lady being kidnapped over there, just what knights errant are worth."

And as he spoke he squeezed Rocinante with his thighs (since he had no spurs) and dashed at a brisk trot — for nowhere in this truthful history is it ever recorded that Rocinante managed a true gallop — straight at the penitents, although the priest and his cathedral colleague and the barber did their best to stop him; but it was impossible, even for Sancho, who was shouting at his master:

"Where are you going, señor Don Quijote? What demon's gotten into you, making you attack our Catholic faith? Watch out, damn it, because that's a procession of penitents, and the lady they're carrying on a pedestal is a statue of our pure Holy Blessed Mother. Watch out, señor, be careful, because this time they can say you're crazy, you don't know what you're doing."

But Sancho exhausted himself for nothing, because his master was so anxious to get to the white-robed men, and liberate the veiled lady, that he didn't hear a word, and even if he had wouldn't have turned back, were it the king himself commanding him. So he reached the procession, pulled up his horse (Rocinante being already interested in something rather less active), and in an angry, threatening voice, declared:

"You, there, with your faces covered, who may not be decent men, listen to me carefully."

The first to stop were those carrying the statue, and one of the four priests who'd been chanting prayers, seeing Don Quijote's strange look, and how lean a horse he was riding, as well as other ludicrous aspects of our knight's manner and appearance, replied:

"Brother, if you have something to say, say it quickly, because here are all these good men whipping open their skin, so we can't stop, nor would it be right, to listen to anything, unless it's something so brief you can say it in two words."

"I can say it in one," said Don Quijote, "and this is it: here and now, set free that beautiful lady, whose tears and sad face clearly show that you're taking her against her will and that you've committed some plain outrage, and I, who was born into this world expressly to undo such wrongs, will not allow anyone to take another step until and unless she has the freedom she longs for and deserves."

Hearing all this, none of them could doubt he was a madman, so they began to roar with laughter, which ignited Don Quijote's quick temper and, without saying another word, he drew his sword and attacked those carrying the platform on which the statue rested. One of them, leaving his comrades to hold up the statue, stepped forward to meet Don Quijote's charge, lifting on high a kind of forked stick on which the bearers rested the platform when they were tired, and, after Don Quijote's slashing blow cut this in two, he took the part still in his hands and hit our knight so hard, right on the shoulder of his sword arm (which the shield could not protect against such a discourteous blow), that poor Don Quijote fell to the ground, very much the worse for wear.

Sancho Panza, who was running up, huffing and puffing, saw his master fall and screamed at the fellow who had levelled Don Quijote not to hit him again, because he was an unfortunate bewitched knight, who had never in all the days of his life done any harm to anyone. But what stopped the peasant was not Sancho's shouting but, rather, the sight of Don Quijote lying there, not moving hand or foot, at which, thinking he'd killed the man, he promptly tucked his tunic into his belt and started running across the fields like a buck in heat.

And now all the others who'd been with Don Quijote arrived on the scene, and most of the penitents, seeing them running up, with armed policemen among them, were afraid something bad was about to happen and, gathering around the statue, they threw back their hoods, clutched their whips — as the priests among them gripped their long candlestick holders — and waited for the attack, determined to defend themselves and even, if they could, take the offensive against their attackers, but their luck was better than they could have thought, because all Sancho did was throw himself on Don Quijote's body and begin the most woeful, ridiculous wailing in the world, thinking his master was dead.

Our priest was known to one of the priests participating in the procession, which fact soothed the fears of the drawn-up squadrons. The first priest then told the other one, in very few words, who Don Quijote was, and then he and the whole group of penitents went to see if the poor knight was dead; Sancho Panza was just saying, with tears in his eyes:

"Oh, flower of knighthood, why should one blow from a stick end such a well-spent life! Oh, honor of all your noble ancestors, honor and glory of all La Mancha, and of the entire known world, which will now have to do without you and so will be full of evil-doers, unafraid of being punished for their wicked deeds! Oh, more generous than any Alexander, because for only eight months of service you would have given me the best island the seas encircle and the waves wash upon! Oh, you who were humble to the haughty and proud with the humble, you who rushed into danger, who endured insults and shame, who loved for no reason, who imitated the good and beat up the bad, oh enemy of everyone mean and wicked, in short, oh knight errant! — which says everything anyone can say."

Sancho's shouting and moaning revived Don Quijote, and the first word he said was:

"He who must live away from you, sweetest Dulcinea, is subject to worse miseries than these. Help me, Sancho, my friend, to get myself back into the enchanted ox-cart, because this shoulder of mine is smashed to pieces and I'm in no mood to weigh down Rocinante's saddle."

"I'll do that most, most willingly, my dear lord," replied Sancho, "and let's go back home with these gentlemen, who only want to help you, and there we'll get ourselves ready for more adventures, which will do better things for us and for our reputations."

"Well said, Sancho," answered Don Quijote, "and since the stars are now exerting such an evil influence, it would be a good idea to give them a chance to change."

The priest, his cathedral colleague, and the barber all agreed this would be a very good idea indeed, and so, still chuckling over Sancho Panza's artlessness, they put Don Quijote back on the ox-cart. The penitential procession got ready to go on its way; the goatherd said farewell to everyone; the policemen decided not to go any farther, so the priest paid them what they were owed. The cathedral priest asked to be informed how things went with Don Quijote, and whether he was cured of his madness or persisted in it, and then took his leave as well. And, in short, everyone went his own way, leaving the priest and the barber, and Don Quijote and Panza, and our good Rocinante, who was quite as patient as his master about everything he'd seen.

The ox-cart driver yoked up his animals and made a place for Don Quijote on a bundle of hay, and then they plodded slowly along, as usual, in the direction the priest pointed out, until after six days they arrived at Don Quijote's village, which they reached just at mid-day, and as it happened on a Sunday, so that everyone was out in the village square, Don Quijote's cart crossing right through the middle of it. All the people came over to see who was in the cart, and were astonished to see their neighbor; a small boy ran to tell the knight's niece and his housekeeper that their uncle and master was coming home, weak and pale, stretched out on a pile of hay and travelling in an ox-cart. It was pitiful, hearing the two good ladies' screaming and crying, and seeing how they slapped their own faces and, once they'd seen Don Quijote coming through the gate, they hurled new curses at all wicked books of chivalry.

When Sancho Panza's wife heard of Don Quijote's arrival, she came running, for she had learned that her husband had gone journeying as the knight's squire, and the first thing she asked, when she saw her husband, was whether the donkey was in good health. Sancho replied that the donkey was doing a lot better than Don Quijote.

"Thanks be to God," she answered, "who has granted me this. But now tell me something, my friend: What good has all this squiring done you?

Have you brought me any new dresses? Have you brought shoes for your children?"

"I haven't brought anything like that, wife," said Sancho, "although I've brought home bigger and more important things."

"I'm very happy to hear it," his wife replied. "Let me see these bigger and more important things, my friend, because I'd like to have a look at them, so they can cheer up this sad heart of mine, which has been so miserably unhappy all the time you've been away."

"Wait till we get home, and I'll show you, wife," said Sancho. "For now, just be happy, because if it pleases God we'll go hunting adventures again, and pretty soon you'll see me turned into a count, or the governor of a whole island — and not one of those little islands you see around here, but one of the best there is."

"May Heaven bring it to pass, my husband, because we can really use it. But tell me: what's all this about islands? I don't understand."

"You don't put honey in a donkey's mouth," replied Sancho. "You'll find out in good time, woman, and some day you'll be surprised to hear all your subjects calling you 'My Lady.' "

"But what are you talking about, Sancho — what's all this about 'My Lady' and islands and subjects?" answered Juana Panza (which was Sancho's wife's name, although she wasn't related to him: it was just the custom in La Mancha for a wife to be known by her husband's name).

"Juana, don't be in such a hurry to find out everything all at once. It's enough that I'm telling you the truth, so now shut your mouth. But come to think of it, there's one thing I can tell you, which is that there's nothing better in the world than to be the honored squire of a knight errant who's out looking for adventures. Now it's true most adventures don't turn out as well as you'd like, because if you have a hundred of them, ninety-nine go wrong and get all tangled up. And I know that from experience, because in some of them I've been tossed in a blanket, and in some of them I've been beaten up — but just the same, it's a great thing to go looking for things to happen, crossing mountains, investigating forests, climbing up peaks, getting to visit castles, stopping at inns whenever you want to, and without offering to pay the devil a red cent."

Which was what Sancho Panza and Juana Panza, his wife, said to one another while Don Quijote's niece and his housekeeper were getting the knight into the house, and undressing him, and laying him down in his old bed. He just squinted up at them, trying to understand where he was. The priest instructed the niece to take extremely good care of her uncle, and to watch out that he didn't escape again, telling her all they'd had to do to bring him home. At this point the two women cried out to Heaven all over again, and once more cursed all tales of chivalry, begging God to consign the authors of all that nonsense and stupidity to the very center of the infernal abyss. In a word, they were worried sick that their uncle and master, as soon as he felt a bit better, would be up to his old tricks — and what they were worrying about was in fact what happened.

But the author of this history, though he searched carefully and diligently for some record of what Don Quijote did when he left home and sought adventures for the third time, was unable to find anything — at least, not in authentic sources. All that's left is the report, preserved in La Mancha's memory, that their famous knight did leave his home for a third time, and went to Zaragosa, where he was present at some of the famous tournaments held in that city, and where he did things worthy of his courage, strength, and noble mind. Nor was our historian able to learn how Don Quijote came to die, nor would he have known a blessed thing if, by sheer good fortune, he hadn't gotten hold of an old, old doctor who happened to have in his possession a lead strongbox, which, as he explained, had been found in the rubble of an ancient hermitage, which was being rebuilt, and in this strongbox they'd found some moldy sheets of parchment, covered with Gothic letters that turned out, however, to be Spanish poems, which poems contained a good deal about Don Quijote's glorious deeds and also about the beauty of Dulcinea del Toboso, and what Rocinante looked like, and how faithful Sancho Panza had been, and even about Don Quijote's funeral, along with a number of epitaphs and elegies on his life and ways.

Those verses which could still be clearly deciphered here follow, set out by our trustworthy author in this new and unheard of history. And all said author asks of those who read these poems, in return for the immense labor it cost him, in bringing them to light, hunting and tracking through La Mancha's archives, is that they take all this exactly as seriously as sensible people always take tales of chivalry, which the world loves so dearly, and with that he will consider himself well satisfied, and well paid, and will be encouraged to go hunting new and different ones — perhaps not as truthful, but in any case as ingenious and entertaining.

The first words written on these parchment sheets, found in the lead strongbox, were:

THE ACADEMICIANS OF ARGAMASILLA,[1] A VILLAGE IN LA MANCHA, HEREBY RECORD [*HOC SCRIPSERUNT*] THE FOLLOWING, ABOUT THE LIFE AND DEATH OF THE BRAVE DON QUIJOTE DE LA MANCHA

Academician Monicongo [black man from the Congo] *at
Don Quijote's tomb*

EPITAPH

La Mancha's beloved lunatic, who gave us
more booty than Jason brought Crete,
had a brain that blew in the breeze,
though something more weighty might have been braver,
    and an arm whose strength and power were famous
from China to faroff Baís,
and the awesome Muse we all strive to please
carved sheets of bronze with his praises —

---

1. There are in fact two Argamasillas in La Mancha; it may however be worth noting that, just as *La Mancha* means "spot, stain, blemish," so *argamasa* = cement/mortar, and *silla* = seat/backside/rear end [*Translator's Note*].

all Amadíses he left in the dust,
and Amadís' brother looked small,
for his fame came from love and from valor;
    no Belianís could make a fuss
when he rode Rocinante to his brawls —
he who lies here, cold and pallid.

Paniaguado ["supporter, follower" but also "bread-and-watered"],
    Academician of Argamasilla, in praise of Dulcinea del Toboso

SONNET

She whose fat and flabby face you see,
tubby-breasted, looking down her nose so,
is Dulcinea, queen of El Toboso,
whose love inspired the great knight Don Quijote.
    For her he rode his famous Rocinante
across the great Sierra Morena rows of
hills, the vast plain of Montiel, sought foes of
Aranjuez (all flat), grew tired and weary.
    Because his horse failed him. Oh harsh hard stars,
to fix so sore an end for this great dame,
and that triumphant knight — oh tender beauty,
    how sad that death could cut you off! Oh Mars:
your warrior, too, fell in spite of fame,
and left this stone to say he did his duty.

Whimsy, the Wittiest Academician in all Argamasilla, in praise of
    Rocinante, Don Quijote's steed

SONNET

High on that adamantine throne
where Mars trods, and trods alone,
this furious knight planted his flag
and watched it wave, and never sag.
    And there he hung his armor and the razored
blade he hacked and slashed and tore
his noble deeds with — deeds so rare
that Art now needs new arts for declaring
    his fame. Whatever Gaul may sing
of Amadís and his descendants,
proclaiming their victories till Fame's head rings
    with their cries, today the crown of regnant
glory rests on Quijote's head,
but the songs are sung in La Mancha instead.
    We'll never forget what he's done,
or the fame his horse has won —
the greatest of horses the sun
    has shone on.

Practical Joker, Argamasillianian Academician, to Sancho Panza

SONNET

Here lies Sancho Panza, not much of a man
in body but large of heart — Wonder of wonders!
the plain and simplest squire, with no artful thunders,
in all the world. I swear it; believe me, I can.
He almost became a count. That was the plan,
but not the least of a miserly age's blunders
kept him down — a niggardly time, that under-
values even donkeys. Oh, God damn
an era when such a mild and obedient squire,
could jog along behind a horse as mild
as Rocinante, which bore his lord, and never
prosper! Oh bold, oh human hopes, forever
foiled! Oh broken dreams of relief, oh wild-
eyed fancies, doomed to shadows and funeral pyres!

The Devil's Own, Academician of Argamasilla, on viewing
Don Quijote's tomb

EPITAPH

Here lies a gentle knight
beaten at beatings, lost in war.
Rocinante the horse that bore
him, day and sometimes at night.
Silly Sancho Panza
lies here too, beside him,
faithful, loyal squire, riding
along in death's extravaganza.

Ticky-Tocky, Academician of Argamasilla, on Dulcinea of
Toboso's tomb

EPITAPH

Dulcinea lies here,
plump when she lived on earth,
now ashes and powdered dirt,
in the arms of that Death we all fear.
Born to a decent name,
you might have thought her a lady.
Quijote loved her like crazy,
and her village shared her fame.

These were the legible verses; the others, with letters eaten away, were
handed over to an academician, to figure out what they'd probably said.

We understand that he has in fact accomplished this task, after enormous effort and labor, and plans to let his work see the light of day, hoping we'll soon be reading about Don Quijote's third expedition.

Forsi altro canterà con miglior plectio [Maybe a different poet could sing it better][2]

2. This is a slightly garbled line from Ariosto's *Orlando Furioso* XXX.16.

VOLUME TWO

VOLUME TWO

Dedication:
To the Count of Lemos[1]

Not too long ago, when I sent Your Excellency my plays (sooner printed than staged), I declared, if I remember correctly, that Don Quijote was putting on his spurs, almost ready to come kiss Your Excellency's hand, and now I tell you his spurs are in place and he's on his way — and if he gets there, I think I'll have been of some service to Your Excellency, because people from literally everywhere have been urging me to send him forth, to get rid of the disgust and nausea caused by this other Don Quijote, who has stolen the name, called himself the second part of my book, and in that disguise gone running all over the world; and the most urgent plea of all has been from the great Emperor of China, who just a month ago sent a courier with a letter, in his own language, requesting — or, more accurately, begging — that I send him the real Don Quijote, because he intended to create a college [*colegio*=school, academy] where Spanish would be taught, and the book he wanted the students to read was Don Quijote's history. He also said he wanted me to be the head-master.

I asked the courier if His Majesty had entrusted him with funds to help defray the costs of my journey. He told me the thought had never crossed anyone's mind.

"Then, brother," I told him, "you can go right back to China, at ten o'clock, or twenty o'clock, or whenever you want to, but my health isn't good enough for such a long voyage, and what's more, in addition to being ill, I'm terribly short of cash, and emperor or no emperor, king or no king, I've already got the great Count of Lemos, in Naples, who supports and protects me without any college diplomas or headmasterships, and has been more gracious to me than I could ever wish."

And so I sent him off, and so I send this off, promising Your Excellency *The Trials of Persiles and Sigismunda*,[2] a book I plan to complete within four months, *Deo volente* [God willing], which has to be either the worst or the best ever written in our language — that is, among books written as entertainment; though I'm sorry I called it "the worst," because my friends say it's as good as it could possibly be. May Your Excellency return to Spain in the good health I wish you, and *Persiles* will be ready and waiting to kiss your hands, and I your feet, like the humble servant of Your Excellency that I am.

From Madrid, the last day of October, sixteen hundred and fifteen, Your Excellency's humble servant,

MIGUEL DE CERVANTES SAAVEDRA

---

1. Don Pedro Fernández Ruiz de Castro y Osorio (1576–1622), Cervantes's patron, 1613–1616 [*Translator's Note*].
2. Cervantes's last book, published (posthumously) in 1617 [*Translator's Note*].

Prologue: To the Reader

Oh Lord, distinguished (or even plebian) reader, how you must be eagerly awaiting this prologue, expecting to watch me take revenge on, laugh at, and spit in the face of whoever wrote that second *Don Quijote*,[1] the one they say was conceived in Tordesillas and born in Tarragona! But the fact is, I'm not planning to give you any such satisfaction: it's true, insults may make even the humblest hearts thirst for vengeance, but the rule will have to let me be an exception. You want me to call him an ass, tell him he's a liar, and impudent, but the idea has never so much as occurred to me: his own sin can punish him, he can eat it with his bread, and that's that. It hurts, of course, that he calls me "old," and "one-handed," as if I could have stopped Time and kept it from affecting me, or I'd lost my hand in some tavern brawl, rather than in the noblest battle ever seen by past ages, or this age, or any age still to come.[2] My wounds may not glow when you look at them, but they're worthy enough, at least, to those who know where I got them; the soldier looks a lot better killed in action than alive because he ran away — and this means so much to me that, if anyone were right this minute to suggest and even make possible that which is impossible, I'd rather have been at that wonderful battle than, here and now, be cured of my wounds but never have been there. The marks you can find on a soldier's face, and on his body, are stars, guiding other men to that Heaven which is Honor, and to a longing for well-deserved praise. It should also be said that you don't write with your gray hair but with your mind, which usually gets better as it gets older.

I am offended, too, that this author-impostor calls me jealous and, what's more, makes a great show of telling me (as if I were too stupid to know) just what jealousy is, when in point of fact there are two varieties and I am acquainted only with the holy, noble, and well-intentioned sort, and that being the case, as it is, I have no interest in attacking priests, and especially nobody who, in addition, is a servant of the Holy Office,[3] and indeed if he said what he seems to have said he's completely mistaken, since I worship that person's mind [*ingenio*=mind, imagination, wit, etc.] and have immense admiration for his work, his unwearied virtuous activity, and his sheer virtuosity. But, really, I'm grateful to this impostor-author for observing that my *Model Tales* [*Novelas ejemplares*], though they're more satirical than exemplary, are still good,[4] because how could they be good if they didn't contain a bit of everything?

I suspect you'll tell me I'm making a very limited response and modesty is restraining me, understanding as I do that a man who is down ought not to be kicked and this gentleman is surely suffering great pain — or why else would he be afraid to come out in the open, under a clear sky? Why else would he hide his name and disguise his birthplace, as if he

---

1. The impostor-author was one Alonso Fernández de Avellaneda [*Translator's Note*].
2. The battle of Lepanto, 1571 [*Translator's Note*].
3. The reference is to Lope de Vega, who became a servant of the Holy Office in 1608 and a priest in 1614 [*Translator's Note*].
4. Avellaneda had in fact said Cervantes's *Model Tales* [*Novelas ejemplares*] were "no poco ingeniosas" [not inconsiderably ingenious] [*Translator's Note*].

were guilty of betraying the king? If you happen to meet him, please tell him I'm really not angry, since I know all about the devil's sly temptations, one of the worst of which is to make a man imagine himself capable of writing and publishing a book that will do as much for his reputation as for his pocketbook, and as much for his pocketbook as for his reputation — to prove which, do tell him, in your own witty, eloquent style, this little tale:

A madman in Seville conceived one of the most amusing obsessions ever dreamed up by any madman in the world. He made a reed pipe, tapering to a point at one end, and then, catching a dog out in the street, or wherever he could find one, he'd hold down one of its hind legs with his foot, lift the other leg with his hand and, as best he could, shove the reed in where, by blowing into it, he could make the dog round as a ball, after which (still holding on) he'd give it a couple of good slaps on the belly, and then he'd let it go, explaining to those who'd gathered around, and there were always a lot of people watching:

"You think it's easy, your graces, swelling up a dog like that?" — Do you think it's easy, your grace, making a book?

But if that little tale doesn't do the trick, my dear reader, tell him this one, which is also about a madman and a dog:

There was another madman, in Córdoba, who used to go around with a slab of marble on top of his head, or some other heavy rock, and, when he found a dog that was busy thinking about something else, he'd get right up next to it and let his load drop right down. This would drive the dog wild and, barking and howling, it would run for three blocks without stopping. So it happened, one day, that one of the dogs he dumped on like this belonged to a cap-maker, who was exceedingly fond of the animal. Down came the rock, right on its head, and the wounded dog started to howl and, seeing the whole thing, his master grabbed a measuring rod and came after the madman, beating him until there wasn't a sound bone in his body — and at every stroke he'd shout:

"My *whippet*, you son of a bitch! Can't you see, you monster, my dog's a *whippet*?"

And, repeating the word *whippet* over and over, he drove the mad- man off, broken to bits. The madman learned his lesson and stayed out of sight, not reappearing for more than a month, after which he came back, carrying an even heavier load and up to the same trick. He'd come up to a dog and, staring hard, neither wanting nor daring to drop the stone, would exclaim:

"It's a whippet. Watch out!"

To make a long story short, every dog he bumped into, wolfhounds, pekingese, they were all whippets, and so he could never again drop a thing. Maybe this same fate will befall our historian, and he won't dare drop his clever load into any more books, because when they're bad, books are even harder than stones.

Tell him, too, that I don't care two pennies for his threats: that book of his can't cheat me out of any profit on mine. I answer him in the words of that famous farce, *The Beautiful Bauble*,[5] "Long live His Honor the

---

5. *La Perendenga*, a play about which nothing whatever is known [*Translator's Note*].

Mayor, and the peace of Christ be upon you." Long live the great Count
of Lemos, a profoundly Christian gentleman famous, also, for his generosity, who will keep me on my feet no matter what blows my scanty fortune
deals me, and long life to the extraordinary charity of His Eminence,
Cardinal Don Bernardo de Sandoval y Rojas, of Toledo — even were
there no printing presses left in the world, and even were I attacked by
more books than there are letters in all the satirical poems of Mingo Re-
vulgo![6] These two princes, enticed by no adulation from me nor by any
other form of flattery, but entirely of their own free will, have taken it upon
themselves to help and assist me, making me think myself luckier and
even richer than I would have been had Fortune, by more ordinary means,
lifted me to its very crest. A poor man can keep his honor, but a depraved
man cannot; poverty can darken and dim true nobility, but cannot completely blot it out; and just so virtue can cast a light of its own, even if
only through the inadequacies, the chinks and cracks of want, and can
come to be valued by such high and noble spirits and, in the natural course
of things, be favored by them.

But don't tell him anything else, nor do I have anything more to say to
you, except to assure you that this second volume of *Don Quijote*, hereby
offered to you, is cut by the same craftsman and from the same cloth as
the first, and what I give you, here, is more Don Quijote, until, in the
end, Don Quijote too is dead and buried, so no man will dare raise any
new accusations against him, for those already levied will be quite enough
— and it will be good, too, that some man of honor give you these final
words about such a wise lunatic, never intending ever to mention the
subject again, for too much of a good thing isn't worth anything, but a
scarcity, even if it's bad, is always worth something. I almost forgot to
mention that you can look forward to the *Persiles*, which I'm just finishing,
and also the second part of *Galatea*.

Chapter One

*— conversations about our knight's illness, between and among the
priest, the barber, and Don Quijote himself*

Sidi Hamid Benengeli tells us, in the second half of this history (which
is also Don Quijote's third sally out into the world), that it was almost a
month before the priest and the barber saw our knight again, because they
did not want to remind him of the past, or refresh his memory — though
this was no reason not to visit Don Quijote's niece and his housekeeper,
advising them to indulge him, to let him dine on comforting but invig-
orating foods, good for both the heart and the brain, since any reasonably
sharp mind could see it was from those regions that his sickness stemmed.
They were assured this had been done, and would be done, with as much
affection and care as possible, for they could already see signs that, at
moments, their lord was in his right mind again, which news much pleased
the priest and the barber, who were convinced they'd been right to bring

---

6. Thirty-two poems, published anonymously in the fifteenth century [*Translator's Note*].

him home, all enchanted as he was, on the ox-cart — exactly as recounted in the first volume of this history (as weighty as it is well-documented), in its final chapter. So they decided to pay him a visit and find out just how much better he was, though they considered it virtually impossible he had in fact improved, agreeing between themselves not to so much as mention any aspect of his knight errantry, for fear of re-opening wounds that were still so tender.

They paid him a visit, accordingly, and found him sitting on his bed, dressed in a short-sleeved flannel jacket, and wearing a red Toledo cap, looking so lean and dried-out that he might well have been mummified. He made them very welcome; they inquired into his health; and he answered them very sensibly, and in elegant, very well chosen language; and their conversation turned to the subject known as diplomacy and methods of government, in the course of which they corrected this abuse and utterly denounced that one, reforming one practice and banishing another, each of them constituting himself a new lawgiver, a modern Lycurgus or Solon reborn, and so reconstructing the entire state that they seemed to have thrust it into a forge and pulled it out, entirely changed — and, on every topic they touched, Don Quijote spoke with such wisdom that his two examiners thought him unquestionably cured and completely in his right mind.

Don Quijote's niece and his housekeeper were listening to this conversation and, seeing their lord's mind so exceedingly clear, couldn't stop thanking God, but the priest, wanting to find out if this was truly a complete return of sanity, or merely the appearance of one, changed his original plan of avoiding any mention of chivalry and, moving from one subject to another, finally began to talk about news from the court at Madrid, saying, among other things, that it was held to be absolutely certain that the Turks would be descending on Spain with a mighty armada, though it was not known where they would land their huge armies or what would be their military goal, and adding that this fear, which led us to mobilize our forces almost every year, had fallen across all of Christendom, and His Majesty the King of Spain had already reinforced the coasts of Naples and Sicily, and also of the island of Malta. Hearing this, Don Quijote replied:

"His Majesty has acted like a prudent governor, in thus seasonably reinforcing our coastline, to keep the enemy from catching us unprepared, but if he'd take my advice I'd suggest a precautionary measure that, alas, I'm afraid His Majesty is still very far from even contemplating."

No sooner had the priest heard this, when he said to himself:

"May God's grace go with you, poor Don Quijote, because I think you're plunging from the very peak of your madness down into the profound depths of your foolishness!"

The barber, who'd been thinking exactly the same thing, asked Don Quijote just what precautionary measure he'd recommend, for it might, he said, belong on that long list of senseless suggestions kings are always receiving.

"Mine, Sir Scraper and Shaver," said Don Quijote, "would be sensible, not senseless."

"That's not what I mean," replied the barber. "It's just that experience proves most projects people suggest to His Majesty are either impossible, or nonsensical, or actually dangerous to king and country."

"But mine," answered Don Quijote, "is neither impossible nor nonsensical, but quite simply the easiest, the most appropriate, and both the most feasible and the most basic plan anyone could possibly think of."

"But my dear Don Quijote, your grace is certainly taking your time about telling it," said the priest.

"I have no intention of telling it, here and now," replied Don Quijote, "so that, first thing tomorrow morning, it will be in the ears of the king's advisors, and someone else will have both the thanks and the reward for my labors."

"I give you my sworn word," said the barber, "here in the sight of Our Lord, that I won't repeat what your grace says to a king or a rook, or to any man on earth — and that's an oath I learned from that ballad about a priest, which begins with the priest explaining to the king that a thief stole his hundred dollars and his hot-footed mule."

"I don't know the story," said Don Quijote, "but I know this is a valid oath, because I know the barber is an honest man."

"And if he weren't," said the priest, "I'd vouch for him in this matter and guarantee, under penalty of paying anything assessed against me, that he'll say no more than a dumb mute."

"But you, your priestly grace," asked Don Quijote, "who will vouch for you?"

"My profession," the priest said, "which is the keeping of secrets."

"Then by God!" Don Quijote immediately declared. "What else should His Majesty do but issue a general proclamation that, on such-and-such a day, all the knights errant now roaming across Spain must gather at his court, and, even if no more than half a dozen appear, might it not be that just one among them would be sufficient to completely destroy the Turks' power? Pay attention, gentlemen, and follow my argument. Is there anything new, by any chance, in a single knight errant destroying an army of two hundred thousand men, as if all of them put together had only one throat to slit, or as if they'd all been made of sugar paste? If there is, tell me, please, how many histories are there, chock full of just such marvels? If only our celebrated Don Belianís were alive right now — and it would be an evil hour for me, if he were, though I speak only for myself — or some of Amadís of Gaul's countless descendants, and any one of them faced the Turks, then by God, I wouldn't bet against his chances! Yet God will watch over His people; He will provide them with someone, perhaps not so magnificent as the knights errant of old, but at least not their inferior in spirit; and God knows exactly what I mean, so I won't say anything more."

"Oh my God!" said his niece at this. "May I die if my lord doesn't want to become a knight errant all over again!"

To which Don Quijote replied:

"I will be a knight errant until the day of my death, and may the Turks descend or ascend, exactly as they please, and in whatever strength they can muster — and I repeat, God knows exactly what I mean."

At this point the barber said:

"Gentlemen, will you let me tell you a little story of something that happened in Seville? It fits our situation so perfectly that I'd like you to hear it."

Don Quijote told him to proceed, and the priest and the women gave him their attention, and he began as follows:

"In the lunatic asylum in Seville there was a man put there by his family because he'd gone insane. He'd graduated, as a student of canon law, from the University of Osuna,[1] but even if he'd studied at Salamanca most people would have considered him crazy. After years of being locked away, this university graduate got it into his head that he'd become sane, completely right in the head, and with this conviction he wrote to the archbishop, begging him most earnestly, and with very logical arguments, to let him be released from the misery in which he'd been living, since by the grace of God he'd recovered his lost sanity; it was only because his family coveted his rightful share of their wealth that he was still locked away, and they would go on with that pretence until he was dead and buried. The archbishop, persuaded by such a sensible and well-organized letter, ordered one of his chaplains to find out from the director of the asylum if what the university graduate's letter said was true, and also told the chaplain to speak to the lunatic himself and, if he indeed appeared to be sane, to let him go free. The chaplain did as he'd been told, but the director assured him the man was indeed still insane; although he often managed to speak like a man of large understanding, sooner or later he'd start babbling such quantities of incredible nonsense that he completely nullified all the sane things he'd said before, which anyone could see when they talked to him. The chaplain decided to make the attempt and, going to the madman, talked to him for an hour, and even longer, in the whole of which time not a crooked or foolish word was spoken; on the contrary, the madman talked so very sensibly that the chaplain couldn't help but believe him sane; and, among other things, the madman told him that the director of the asylum was the very farthest thing from impartial, because he didn't want to give up the presents the madman's family gave him to keep him saying that their kinsman was still out of his mind, despite lucid moments, so that the most serious obstacle to getting out of this misery was in fact exactly that great wealth: in order to continue their enjoyment of what was rightfully his, his enemies fraudulently called into question Our Lord's infinite mercy in having returned him from a state of bestiality and made him once more a man. And, in short, he made the director seem highly suspect, his kinsmen greedy and cold-blooded, and himself so exceedingly sensible that the chaplain made up his mind to take the madman away with him, so the archbishop could see for himself what was really going on in this whole affair.

"Acting in good faith, the pious chaplain asked the director to return the clothes this university graduate had been wearing, when he'd entered the asylum, to which the director replied that he'd better watch out, because beyond any doubt this particular university graduate was still crazy.

1. Osuna was a minor and ill-regarded university; Salamanca was extremely highly regarded [*Translator's Note*].

But the director's cautions and warnings had no effect: the chaplain remained determined to take the madman away, and so, in obedience to the archbishop's orders, the madman was dressed in his original clothing, which was clean and new, and when he saw himself dressed like a sane man, and the garments of his insanity removed, he asked the chaplain to be charitable and let him go say farewell to his mad friends. The chaplain said they would both go and see whatever madmen the asylum was sheltering. So they went upstairs, along with some others who happened to be there, and came to a cage which held a wild lunatic, though at that moment he was calm and quiet, and the university graduate said to him:

" 'My brother, tell me if there is anything I can do for you, because I'm going home, God having been pleased, through His infinite goodness and mercy, and not for any merit of mine, to have returned me to my senses. I'm now sane and sound, for nothing is impossible to God's great power. Never lose your hope and trust in Him, for, having returned me to my original condition, He may also restore you, if you truly believe in Him. I will be sure to send you some good things to eat, so eat them, for I want you to know that I, as someone who has been through it, am convinced that all our madness comes from keeping our stomachs empty and our heads full of air. Be brave, be brave — for to be melancholy in our misfortunes is to damage health and spur on death.'

"Another madman, in a cage just opposite, listened to all of this and, rising from an old mat on which he'd been lying, bare naked, he called out, in a very loud voice, to find out who it was that was going home, all sane and sound. The university graduate answered:

" 'It's I, brother, I'm the one who's going, for I need stay here no longer, and I am infinitely thankful to Heaven for having granted me such a great gift.'

" 'Watch your words, university man, so the devil doesn't deceive you,' answered the madman. 'Don't make a fuss; stay at home and be quiet, and you'll keep yourself from having to come back.'

" 'I'm sane and sound, and I know it,' said the university graduate, 'so I don't have to suffer for my sins all over again.'

" 'You're sane and sound?' said the madman. 'All right, fine, we'll see what we'll see. May God be with you. But I swear to you by Jupiter, I, who represent his majesty here on earth, that for this one sin that Seville is committing, today, in thus releasing you and dealing with you as with someone sane and sound, I shall have to levy such a punishment on this city that it will be remembered for centuries and centuries, amen. Don't you understand, you miserable idiot of a university man, that this is well within my power, since, as I've told you, I am Jupiter the Thunderer, and in my hands I hold scorching bolts with which I can, and I do, threaten and destroy the earth? But I choose to administer only one punishment to this stupid city, which is that there will be no rain here, nor anywhere near here, for three whole years, beginning today, at this very moment when I have commanded this scourge. *You* free? *You* sane? *You* cured? And *I* a madman, *I* disabled, *I* under lock and key . . . ? Hah! I'd as soon let it rain as I would hang myself.'

"Everyone was listening to the madman's shouting and ranting — but our university graduate, turning to the chaplain and grasping his hands, exclaimed:

" 'Don't worry, my lord, pay no attention to anything this lunatic says, because if he's Jupiter and won't let it rain, I, who am Neptune, father and god of all waters, will have it rain anytime I feel like it, and anytime it's needed.'

"To which the chaplain replied:

" 'All the same, my lord Neptune, we don't want to irritate my lord Jupiter. You stay right where you are, your grace, and some other day, when we have more time and can do everything at our leisure, we'll come back for you.'

"The director of the asylum laughed, as did everyone else, which embarrassed the chaplain. They took the normal clothing off the lunatic, and he stayed in the asylum, and I've finished my story."

"And *this*," said Don Quijote, "*this* is the story, my dear barber, you thought so appropriate to the occasion that you couldn't help but tell it? Ah, my razor-stropping friend, how blind is the man who can't see what's right under his nose! Do you really not understand that comparisons between one man's wit and another's, or one man's courage and another's, or one woman's beauty and breeding with another's, are always odious and unwelcome? I, my barbering friend, am not Neptune, god of waters, nor do I try to make anyone think me wise, when clearly I'm not. All I keep trying to do is make the world see its error in not resurrecting for itself that happiest of times, when the order of knight errantry roamed valiantly up and down its roads. But our depraved age does not deserve that blessing, as former ages did, when knights errant shouldered and took on themselves the defense of kings, the protection of damsels, the succoring of orphans and wards of court, the punishment of the proud, and the rewarding of the humble. With most of our knights, today, it's the damasks, brocades, and other rich fabrics they wear that rustle as they go, rather than any coats of armor; knights no longer sleep out in the fields, open to all the rigors of the heavens, lying there, armed and armored head to foot; no longer do they try to snatch forty winks, as it's called, without pulling their feet out of the stirrups, but only leaning on their lances, as the knights of old used to do. No longer do they sweep out of a wood, here, and up a mountain, there, and then tramp along a barren, deserted seashore, usually in stormy, angry weather, and then find themselves, right at the water's edge, a tiny boat without oars or a sail or a mast or any rigging or tackle whatever, but with intrepid hearts launch themselves out onto the waves, abandoning themselves to the implacable waves that break across the bottomless sea, on which, one moment, they are borne up toward the sky, and, the next, are pulled deep into the abyss; and setting their breasts against the invincible tempest, find — though they could never have expected it — they're suddenly twenty thousand miles and more from where they set sail, and leaping out onto that distant, unknown land, they experience things worthy of being recorded not simply on paper or parchment, but on bronze. But today sloth triumphs over exertion, laziness over labor, vice over virtue, arrogance over bravery, and the theory of combat over its practice, which lived and shone only in the Age of Gold, the Age of Knight Errantry. And if I'm wrong, tell me: who was ever truer and braver than the famous Amadís of Gaul? Who wiser than Palmerín of England? Who more easy-going and sweet-tempered than Tirant the White? Who more gallant than Lisuarte[2] of Greece? Who more often stabbed and stabbing than Don Belianís? Who more fearless than Perión of Gaul, or more willing to hurl himself into danger than Felixmarte of Hircania, or more forthright than Esplandián? Who more dashing than Don Cirongilio of Thrace? Who fiercer than Rodamonte? Who more sensible than wise King Sobrino? Who bolder than Reinaldos? Who more invincible than Roland? And who more courtly and more courteous than Ruggiero, from whom our dukes of Ferrara are descended, according to Turpín's *Cosmography*?[3] All these knights, and many more that I could recall for you, dear Father, were knights errant, light and glory of knighthood itself. It's these, or men like them, I'd want to carry out my plan, and, with them, His Majesty would find himself well served and, also, saved a good deal of expense, and the Turks would be left pulling out their beards — and I, for all that, will stay in my asylum, if there's no chaplain to take me out of it, and if that Jupiter, as the barber tells us, won't rain, well, here I am, and I'll rain whenever I want to. Which I say because I want Mr. Barber-Basin to know I understand him."

"Now really, my dear Don Quijote," said the barber, "that's not at all what I meant, and I swear to God I meant well, and your grace should not be offended."

"I can decide for myself whether I'm offended or not," replied Don Quijote. "I understand these things."

At this, the priest said:

"Although I've said next to nothing, thus far, I'd like to be rid of a misgiving, born of what Don Quijote has been saying, that bothers me and troubles my conscience."

"You're entitled to speak of a good deal more than that, Father," replied Don Quijote, "so by all means tell us your misgiving: dealing with a troubled conscience is not pleasant."

"With your consent, then," answered the priest, "let me say that my misgiving is that, no matter how I try, I cannot persuade myself that this whole assortment of knights errant you've referred to, Don Quijote, have really been creatures of flesh and blood in this world of ours; I'm inclined to think they're all invented, fictional, fables and lies, dreams narrated by men just roused from sleep — or, more accurately, still half in dreamland."

"This," replied Don Quijote, "is yet another error into which many men have fallen, not believing that such knights have truly walked the earth, and I have often tried, with many people and on all sorts of occasions, to cast the light of truth onto this quite usual mistake. Admittedly, there have been times when I've not succeeded, but on other occasions I have managed to make the shoulders of truth bear the load, for the truth is so

---

2. Lisuarte = Esplandián's son, Amadís's nephew [*Translator's Note*].
3. Neither Turpín nor this book, invented by Cervantes, ever existed. The false lineage of the dukes of Ferrara comes from Ariosto's *Orlando Furioso* [*Translator's Note*].

perfectly clear I can almost declare that my own eyes have actually seen Amadís of Gaul, who was a tall man of fair complexion, with a fine beard (though a very black one), appearing neither quite mild-mannered nor quite severe, not given to saying a great deal, slow to anger but quick to let his anger cool — and in the same way I have described Amadís I think I could also depict all of the many knights errant who appear in all the tales of chivalry the world has ever seen, because it seems to me they were in fact as their histories tell us they were, and by knowing what deeds they did, and what sort of people they were, sound thinking enables us to deduce their features, their complexions, and their stature."

"My dear Don Quijote," asked the barber, "just how tall does your grace think the giant Morgante must have been?"

"In this matter of giants," replied Don Quijote, "opinions vary as to whether or not they are or are not real, but the Holy Scriptures, which cannot fail to be true down to the smallest detail, prove to us they were indeed real, telling us the tale of that Philistine, Goliath, who stood seven and a half cubits [roughly twelve feet] tall, which is certainly an inordinate height. So too, in Sicily they have found arm and shoulder bones so huge that their sheer size proves they belonged to giants who were as tall as the tallest towers; geometry proves this beyond the slightest doubt. Still, for all this, I can't be certain just how big Morgante may have been, though I suspect he couldn't have been exceedingly tall — an opinion which I think finds support in his history, where it is recorded that he often slept indoors, and since there were houses that could hold him, clearly he couldn't have been remarkably big."

"Indeed," said the priest.

And then, deeply enjoying such nonsense, the priest asked what Don Quijote thought Reinaldos de Montalbán had looked like, and Don Roland, and the other Twelve Peers of France, for all of them had been knights errant.

"As for Reinaldos," replied Don Quijote, "I venture he was full-faced, quite florid, with dancing, rather jutting eyes; prickly, with a very quick temper; fond of thieves and all other lost souls. Roland, or Rotolando, or Orlando — for the books use all of these names for him — was to my mind, and I will declare, of middling height, broad shouldered, a bit bow-legged, with a dark complexion and a red beard, covered with hair all over, of a menacing appearance, sparing of words, but for all that very courteous and well-bred."

"If Roland didn't look the part of a gentleman any better than you've said, your grace," answered the priest, "it's no wonder that Lady Angélica the Beautiful spurned him, preferring the charming, elegant, and witty little fledgling of a Moor to whom she surrendered herself. She showed herself wise in the ways of love, choosing Medoro's sweetness instead of Roland's tart severity."

"Now this Angélica, Father," responded Don Quijote, "was a flighty girl, restless and rather fickle, and she filled the world with her boldness as well as with the fame of her beauty; she scorned a thousand good gentlemen, men of courage and wisdom, and was satisfied with a beardless little page, who had neither wealth nor reputation, aside from his well-known gratitude to that best of friends, Darinel. He who sang so wonderfully of her beauty, the great Ariosto, either because he didn't dare or because he didn't care to sing of what happened to her, after her despicable surrender — because they couldn't have been particularly creditable matters — simply dropped her, saying:

> And how she became the Queen of China,
> Maybe a better poet could sing it better.

And this was surely very like a prophecy, for poets are also known as *vates* [seers, soothsayers], which means 'prophets'. You can see how true this was, indeed, from the fact that, later, here in Spain, a celebrated Andalusian poet sang and lamented over her tears, and another famous, not to say unique Spanish poet sang of her beauty."[4]

"But tell me, Don Quijote," said the barber, "hasn't there been a poet, among all those who have praised her, who has satirized this Lady Angélica?"

"It's easy enough to believe," replied Don Quijote, "that if Sacripante or Roland had been poets, they'd have given the damsel what for, for it's both appropriate and quite natural for poets who've been scorned and rejected by the false-hearted ladies — whether imaginary or real — they've chosen as the mistresses of their thoughts, to take revenge with satires and lampoons, though that's an unworthy vengeance for a generous heart, but as yet I have never seen any poems that slander the Lady Angélica, who turned the world on its head."

"Very strange!" exclaimed the priest.

But just then they heard Don Quijote's niece and his housekeeper, who had drifted away some time ago, shouting in the courtyard outside, and they all ran toward the sound.

Chapter Two

— which deals with Sancho Panza's remarkable quarrel with Don Quijote's niece and housekeeper, together with other delightful matters

Our historian tells us that the shouts and cries which Don Quijote, the priest, and the barber heard came from the niece and the housekeeper, and that they were hurled at Sancho Panza, who was struggling to get in to see Don Quijote, while the two women were holding the door against him.

"Vagabond — what are you doing here? Go home, brother, because you're the one, not anyone else, who's been wheedling and coaxing my lord and carrying him off on these trips to nowhere."

To which Sancho replied:

"You Devil's housekeeper, you — the only one who's been wheedled

---

4. The Andalusian poet was Barahona de Soto; his poem was *Las Lágrimas de Angélica* [Angelica's Tears], 1586; the Spanish poet was Lope de Vega, whose poem was *Hermosura de Angélica* [Angelica's Beauty], 1602 [Translator's Note].

and coaxed and carried off to nowhere is me, not your master. He's dragged me all over the world, and you've got the wool pulled right over your eyes, because he tricked me, he promised me a whole island, and I'm still waiting to get it."

"Go choke on those holes and eyes,"[1] answered Don Quijote's niece, "you good for nothing Sancho. What do you mean, holes and eyes? Is that something you eat, you guzzling tub of lard?"

"It's nothing you eat," answered Sancho. "You govern it and you rule it, and it's better than four cities and four judges put together."

"That doesn't matter," said the housekeeper, "because you're not getting in here, you bag-full of evil, you sack of deceit. Go govern your own house and dig in your own garden, and stop chasing after other people's holes and eyes."

The priest and the barber were thoroughly enjoying this conversation, but Don Quijote, worried Sancho might blurt out and let everyone know all sorts of nasty foolishness, including some things that wouldn't be much to his master's credit, called to Sancho and told the two women to be still and let him in. He entered, and the priest and the barber took leave of Don Quijote, feeling quite hopeless about his ever being cured, for they saw how fixed were his crazy ideas, and how utterly steeped he was in his damned chivalry's stupid notions, as to which the priest said to the barber: "You'll see, my friend, how our gentleman will be flying off again, hunting adventure — and maybe sooner even than we think."

"No question about it," answered the barber, "but I'm not as astonished at the master's madness as the squire's stupidity, because Panza believes so devoutly in all that stuff about governing an island that, no matter how many times he's disillusioned, he'll never get it out of his head."

"May God have mercy on them both," said the priest, "and let's be watchful: we'll have to see where all this knightly and squirely craziness leads them, because it seems to me they've both been hammered on the same forge, and the master's madness without the squire's stupidity wouldn't be worth a cent."

"Absolutely," said the barber — "and it would be worth a pretty penny to know what those two are talking about, right now."

"Don't worry," answered the priest. "The niece and the housekeeper will tell us the whole story, because they're not the sort who won't be listening with both ears."

Meanwhile, Don Quijote took Sancho into his room and closed the door and, once they were alone, said:

"It troubles me a good deal, Sancho, that you've said, and still say, I took you away from your hut, since you're well aware that I too did not remain at home. We sallied forth together, we rode together, we journeyed together, and the same fate and the same chance came to us both. And if you were blanket-tossed, once, I've been beaten a hundred times — and that's the only thing in which I've come out ahead."

"That's just how it ought to be," replied Sancho, "because, as you your-

---

1. For "island," Sancho uses the Latinate and poetic *ínsula*, learned from Don Quijote, instead of the more common *isla*. This confuses the two women [*Translator's Note*].

self always say, your grace, knights errant have a better claim to misfortune than squires do."

"You're quite wrong, Sancho," said Don Quijote, "because, as it's been said, *quando caput dolet . . .* [2] and so on."

"The only language I understand is my own," replied Sancho.

"What that means," said Don Quijote, "is that when the head suffers, the limbs suffer too, so that, I being the master and you the servant, I'm your head, and you're a part of me, you being my servant, and therefore, whenever anything bad happens to me, or ever will happen to me, you have to suffer too, just as I have to suffer your misfortune."

"Maybe so," said Sancho, "but when this limb was being tossed in the blanket, my head was on the other side of the fence, watching me fly up into the air, and not feeling any pain at all, but if the limbs have to suffer whenever the head suffers, then the head has to suffer for them, too."

"Are you saying, Sancho," replied Don Quijote, "that I did not suffer when they blanket-tossed you? If that's what you said, don't say it — don't even think it, because at that moment my spirit was feeling more pain than your body did. But let's leave this subject, now, because we'll have plenty of time for debating it, and resolving it. So tell me, Sancho, my friend, how do they talk about me, around here? What do ordinary people think of me? — and gentlemen? and noblemen? What do they say about my courage, and my great deeds, and about my gallantry? What do they say about my taking it on myself to resurrect and bring back to the world the forgotten order of knighthood? In a word, Sancho, I want you to tell me everything you've heard on these subjects — and you must tell me all this without adding a single favorable comment or omitting anything whatever that may be negative, for the task of a loyal vassal is to tell his lord the plain truth, exactly as it happens to be, just as it comes to him, not permitting flattery to swell it or any other empty respect to lessen it — and I want you to know, Sancho, that if princes were always told the plain, unvarnished truth, without any puffing and huffing, things would be very different, and other times would be considered iron ages, not ours, for I personally take this one to be a true age of gold. Please heed this injunction, Sancho, and wisely, and with due deliberation, tell me exactly what you know on these matters about which I've inquired."

"My lord, I'll be very glad to do as you ask," replied Sancho, "on condition that your grace doesn't get angry at me for what I say, since you want me to tell it in its bare skin, without putting clothes on anything I've heard."

"I won't be angry at all," answered Don Quijote. "Please, Sancho: speak absolutely freely and without any beating around the bush."

"Then the first thing I say — that's being said — is that ordinary people think your grace is crazy as a loon, and I'm not any less nuttier. Gentlemen are saying your grace isn't satisfied just to be one of them, but you've added *Don* to your name and thrown yourself headfirst into knighthood on the basis of four grapevines and a scrap of land, and with nothing

---

2. *Quando caput dolet, caetera membra dolent* = When the head suffers, the limbs suffer too [Translator's Note].

but rags on your back and more rags to come. And what the noblemen say is they don't want ordinary gentlemen competing with them, and especially gentlemen who have to take care of themselves and polish their own shoes and patch up their black stockings with green thread."

"But that," said Don Quijote, "has nothing to do with me, since I'm always well dressed, and never patched. Now, *worn*, yes, that may be — but worn more by the effects of war than by time."

"As far as your courage, your grace," continued Sancho, "your gallantry, your great deeds, and the burden you've taken on yourself, there's a variety of opinions. Some say, 'He's crazy, but funny,' and others say, 'He's brave, but unlucky,' and still others, 'He's gallant, but he's got a lot of gall,' and then they go tearing into so many things about us that neither your grace nor I are left with a sound bone in our bodies."

"Remember, Sancho," said Don Quijote, "that wherever lofty virtue arises, it is persecuted. Very few, and perhaps none, of the famous men of the past have escaped malicious slander. Julius Caesar, the boldest, wisest, and bravest of generals, was criticized for his ambition, and for not being scrupulously clean about his person, or his clothes, or even about his habits. Alexander, whose great deeds led him to be called the Great, is said to have been quite a drunkard. Hercules, who performed so many titanic labors, has been called lustful, a real voluptuary. They gossiped about Don Galaor, Amadís of Gaul's brother, saying he was fantastically irritable, and of his brother they whispered that he was a cry-baby. So you see, oh Sancho, when you consider them among all the calumnies levelled against great men, mine shouldn't be hard to bear, as long as they're not worse than you've said."

"On my father's grave, but there you've hit the nail on the head!" exclaimed Sancho.

"So there's more?" asked Don Quijote.

"The tail still has to be skinned," Sancho replied. "It's all been child's play, so far, but if your grace really wants to know all the slanders they're laying on you, I'll go right now and fetch someone who'll tell you the whole story, without leaving out a crumb, because just last night Bartolomé Carrasco's son came home from Salamanca, where he's been a student and took a degree, and when I went to say hello he told me your grace's story is already being told in a book, called *The History of that Ingenious Gentleman, Don Quijote de La Mancha*, and he says I'm in there, too, under my right name, Sancho Panza, and they've got Lady Dulcinea del Toboso, and all kinds of things we went through when no one could have been there to see us, so I was crossing myself in terror, wondering how the historian could have known them."

"Let me assure you, Sancho," said Don Quijote, "that he who writes our history will have to be some wise magician, because nothing is hidden from those men, when they want to write about someone."

"But," said Sancho, "if he's supposed to be a wise man and a magician, then why — according to Samson Carrasco, the college graduate I told you about — is the author of that history named Sidi Hamid Eggplant!"[3]

---

3. Sancho, knowing no Arabic, says *berenjena*, "eggplant," instead of *Benengeli* [*Translator's Note*].

"That is a Moorish name," replied Don Quijote.

"That may be," said Sancho, "because I've heard that most of them really like eggplant."

"You've surely made a mistake, Sancho," said Don Quijote, "in the man's surname, because in Arabic 'Sidi' means 'sir' or 'lord'."

"It could be," replied Sancho, "but if your grace wants me to bring the young man here, I'll hurry right up and get him."

"That will be very pleasant indeed, my friend," said Don Quijote, "for I'm quite astonished at what you've told me, and I won't touch a bite of food until I know all about it."

"Then I'll go and get him," replied Sancho.

And, taking leave of his master, he went looking for the college graduate, and in not too long came back with him, after which the three of them had a thoroughly amusing conversation.

Chapter Three

— all about the absurd conversation among Don Quijote, Sancho Panza, and Samson Carrasco, the college graduate

Our knight sat in deep thought, while waiting for the young college graduate, Carrasco, from whom he expected to hear whether the history of Don Quijote had indeed been put into a book, as Sancho had said, for he could not convince himself that any such book could really exist, seeing that there had not been time for his enemies' blood to dry on his sword-blade. How could he believe his high and noble doings were already in print? Nevertheless, he thought that some magician — though whether a friend or an enemy he did not yet know — might well have used his magic arts to get the story into print. If it had been a friendly magician, the object would have been to extol our knight's deeds, raising them higher than those of the very noblest of knights errant. If it had been an enemy, the object would have been to stamp down his deeds, setting them below the lowest, vilest things ever done by the lowest, vilest squire — although, he told himself, the deeds of squires were never recorded at all. In any case, if any such history really did exist, it had to be the story of a knight errant, and so of necessity it had to be grandiloquent, noble, distinguished, magnificent, and — of course — truthful.

This made him feel a bit better, though it still bothered him that the author was a Moor, to judge by the name "Sidi," for truth simply could not be expected from the Moors, because they were all cheats, swindlers, and wild-eyed troublemakers. He was worried that his lovemaking might have been treated indecently, damaging his Lady Dulcinea del Toboso's modest reputation. He would have liked the tale to set forth the loyalty and propriety he had always maintained toward her, disdaining queens, empresses, and damsels of all ranks and stations, holding back the force of his natural passions. And thus he sat, wrapped in these and many other musings, turning them over and over in his mind, until Sancho and Carrasco appeared.

Don Quijote received the young man with great politeness. Although his name was Samson, Carrasco was not a big man, though he had a large reputation as a wit. His complexion was pale, but his brains were very good. He was twenty-four years old, round-faced, with a flat nose and a large mouth — all of which clearly labeled him a natural trickster, a friend of well-turned phrases and well-pulled legs, as indeed he demonstrated when he caught sight of Don Quijote, for he went down on his knees before our knight, declaring:

"Your magnificence, let me kiss your hands, Lord Don Quijote de La Mancha, for by the garments of Saint Peter that I as a university student wear (although I have taken only the first four orders), you are one of the most famous knights errant ever known or that ever will be known, oh your grace, anywhere on the round surface of this earth. Blessings on Sidi Hamid Benengeli, who has left us your magnificence's history, and even more blessings on the inquiring mind responsible for translating that history from Arabic into our native Castilian, for the universal entertainment of all peoples."

After making him rise, Don Quijote said:

"I gather, from what you say, that a history of me really exists, written by a Moorish wise man?"

"It is so very true, my lord," said Samson, "that I think more than twelve thousand copies of the book have been printed, as you may see for yourself in Portugal, Barcelona, and Valencia, where there have been printings, and there is even a rumor that it's been printed in Antwerp, and I'd guess there will be no nation on earth, and no language spoken, into which it will not have been translated."

At this point, Don Quijote said:

"One of the things most pleasant to a virtuous and distinguished man is to see himself, while he is still alive, go out among the nations and languages of the world, printed and bound, and bearing a good reputation. 'A good reputation,' I say, because, should it be the opposite, no death can be worse."

"As far as a good reputation and a good name is concerned," said the college graduate, "you, your grace, carry away the palm in comparison to all other knights errant, because the Moor in his language, and the Christian in his, have been exceedingly careful to vividly depict your grace's gallantry, the lofty spirit with which you encounter all dangers, your patience in adversity and when you suffer from such misfortunes as wounds, and the modesty and purity of the infinitely platonic love between your grace and My Lady Doña Dulcinea del Toboso."

And here Sancho Panza put in:

"I've never heard My Lady Dulcinea called *doña*, only *Lady Dulcinea del Toboso*, so the history's already made one mistake."

"That's hardly an important objection," replied Carrasco.

"Certainly not," said Don Quijote. "But tell me, your grace, señor university graduate, which of my famous exploits are the most impressive, in this history?"

"On this score," answered the college graduate, "there are differences of opinion, just as there are in matters of taste. Some favor the adventure with the windmills, which appeared to your grace to be Briareus and other many-armed giants; others lean toward the episode of the hydraulic hammers; this person favors the account of the two armies which, afterwards, seemed to be two flocks of sheep; while that one praises the encounter with the corpse being brought to Segovia for burial; one says best of all is when the galley slaves were liberated; another says nothing equals the encounter with the two Benedictine giants, followed by the battle with the brave Basque."

"Tell me, Mister college graduate," said Sancho, "does this book tell about the muledrivers from Yanguas, when our fine friend Rocinante decided to shoot for the moon?"

"This wise man," replied Samson, "left nothing in his inkwell; he tells everything and writes it all out — even Sancho's jumping around in a blanket."

"I didn't do any jumping in the blanket," responded Sancho. "It was all in the air, and more than I wanted."

"As far as I know," said Don Quijote, "no history of humankind hasn't had its highs and its lows, especially histories of knighthood, which can't possibly be filled only with successful adventures."

"All the same," the college graduate went on, "some who have read the book say they wish the author had quietly forgotten a few of the endless beatings Señor Don Quijote receives, in various encounters."

"But there's where historical truth comes in," said Sancho.

"Still, they could in all fairness have stayed silent about such things," said Don Quijote, "since matters which neither change nor affect a history's truthfulness do not need to be recorded, if they tarnish the book's central figure. I dare say Aeneas was not quite so pious as Virgil painted him, nor was Ulysses as wise and cautious as Homer makes him."

"True," replied Samson, "but it's one thing to write as a poet, and very different to write as a historian. The poet can show us things not as they actually happened, but as they should have happened, but the historian has to record them not as they ought to have been, but as they actually were, without adding or subtracting anything whatever from the truth."

"Well, if this Moor's determined to tell the truth," said Sancho, "you're certainly going to find my beatings mixed in with my master's, since they never measured his shoulders without going after my whole body — but I shouldn't be surprised by that, because this same master of mine says that when the head's suffering the whole body has to take its share."

"You're a sly fox, Sancho," replied Don Quijote. "By God, you haven't got a bad memory, when you feel like having one."

"If I felt like forgetting the whacks I've been given," answered Sancho, "the bumps and bruises wouldn't let me, because they're still fresh on my ribs."

"Be quiet, Sancho," said Don Quijote, "and don't interrupt a college graduate, who I ask to please continue telling what this history says of me."

"And about me," said Sancho, "because it also says that I'm one of its main presonages."

"*Personages*, not *presonages*, Sancho, my friend," said Samson.

"Oh ho: have we got ourselves another speech teacher?" said Sancho. "If you keep going down that road, we'll spend our whole lives and never get anywhere."

"May God strike me dead, Sancho," replied the college graduate, "if the second most important person in the whole story isn't you, and there are even people who'd rather hear you talk than the cleverest man in the book — though there are also some who say you were much too simple-minded, believing you really could become governor of that island Don Quijote, sitting right over there, promised to give you."

"It's never too late," said Don Quijote, "so when Sancho gets a bit older, and acquires the experience that age confers, he'll be better fitted to be a governor, and more skillful than he is now."

"By God, señor," said Sancho, "if I can't govern an island, as old as I am now, I couldn't govern one if I got to be as old as Methuselah.[1] The trouble with this blessed island isn't that I'm not smart enough to govern it, but that nobody knows where it is."

"Leave it to God, Sancho," said Don Quijote, "and all will be well, and perhaps even better than you think, for not even a leaf on a tree moves unless God wants it to."

"Exactly," said Samson, "and if it's God's will, Sancho might have a thousand islands to govern, instead of just one."

"I've seen governors around here," said Sancho, "who, as far as I'm concerned, couldn't hold a candle to me, but just the same they get called 'my lord' and they eat with silver spoons."

"But they're not governors of islands," replied Samson, "and they're in charge of easier things — because, at the very least, people who govern islands have to know something about grammar."

"I can take care of the *grama* [*grama* = Bermuda grass]," said Sancho, "but I'll have nothing to do with the part about *mar* [*mar* = sea], because I don't know anything about it. But let's leave all this governor stuff in the hands of God, who can put me wherever He thinks I'll do the most good, and let me tell you, Mister College Graduate Samson Carrasco, that I take really deep pleasure in the fact that the author of this history talks about me in such a way that what he tells doesn't make anyone angry, because let me tell you, by my faith as a good squire, if he'd said anything about me that wasn't fit to be said about an Old Christian, which I am, even the deaf would have heard about it."

"That would be a miracle," answered Samson.

"Miracle or no miracle," said Sancho, "let people watch out how they talk and write about other people, and not just put down, helter-skelter, the first thing that gets into their head."

"One of the problems with this book," said the college graduate, "is that the author puts into it a novella called *The Story of the Man Who Couldn't keep from Prying*, which isn't a bad tale, or badly told, except that it has no business being where it is, and it doesn't tell us anything about your grace, Don Quijote."

1. One of the biblical patriarchs, said to have lived 969 years (Genesis 5:27), Methusaleh is ritually used as a type of longevity.

"I'll bet," said Sancho, "the son of a bitch has dragged in all sorts of silly stuff."

"In which case," said Don Quijote, "the author of this history can't have been a wise man, but some ignorant, senseless blabberer, who started to write it without knowing what he was doing, letting everything go however it wanted, the way Orbaneja, the painter from Úbeda used to do, because when they asked him what he was painting, he'd reply, 'Whatever comes out.' Like the time he painted a rooster, and it was so strange, so bad a likeness, he had to write right next to it, in big Gothic letters, 'This is a rooster.' And that's how it will have to be with my history: there'll have to be footnotes before anyone can understand it."

"Not at all," replied Samson, "because there isn't anything difficult about it, it's so beautifully clear: children turn those pages, young boys read them, grown men understand them, and old men applaud them — and, in a word, the book is so popular and so widely read and understood by people of all sorts, that as soon as they see some flabby old horse they say, 'There goes Rocinante.' And the ones who read it most devotedly are the pages: you won't find a lordly ante-chamber without its *Don Quijote*; one of them picks it up as soon as another sets it down; this one rushes to get it, and that one begs for his chance. Really, this history is the best-liked and least harmful entertainment ever seen, because through the whole length of it you won't find anything even remotely resembling an immodest word or an irreligious thought."

"To write it any differently," said Don Quijote, "would be to set down lies, not the truth, and historians who tell lies deserve to be burned, like people who counterfeit money — and I have no idea why the author relied on novellas and irrelevant stories when there was so much to be written about me. He must have been thinking of the old proverb, 'With straw and with hay, Fill my belly all the way.' Because, really, all he had to do was show my thoughts, my sighs, my tears, my honest desires, and my battles, and he'd have a big fat book, just as big as, and maybe even bigger than, a book holding all of Tostado's[2] work. Really, it seems to me, my dear college graduate, that in order to write histories and other such books, no matter of what sort, you have to have a good head and a mature understanding. To write graciously, wittily, you have to be clever [*ingenio* = cleverness, ingenuity, wit, skill, talent, genius]: the wisest character in a play is the fool, because he who pretends to be a simpleton must never be one. History is a sacred art, because it must be truthful, and where truth is, provided it really is true, there God is also — though, all the same, there are still people who scribble books and toss them out like doughnuts."

"There isn't a book so bad," said the college graduate, "that it hasn't something good in it."

"That's surely true," replied Don Quijote, "but how often it happens that those who have earned fine reputations by their writing, and acquired great fame, lose everything — or at least seriously damage themselves — when they put their work into print."

2. Alfonso Tostado Ribera (d. 1450), author of countless devotional books [*Translator's Note*].

"But that," said Samson, "is because we read what's in print with slow, deliberate care, and see its faults all too easily — especially when we're scrutinizing the work of celebrated writers. Men famous for their genius [*ingenio*] — great poets, illustrious historians — are always (or at least very often) envied by people who take special pleasure and find quite remarkable satisfaction in judging other men's writing, though they've sent none of their own out into the light of the world."

"That's hardly surprising," said Don Quijote, "because there are many theologians who are disasters in the pulpit, but superb when it comes to spotting the faults of those who preach."

"You're absolutely right, Señor Don Quijote," said Carrasco, "but I could wish all these critics had more mercy and fewer scruples, instead of focussing on the specks of dust they find in the clear, bright light of the book they're critiquing, for if *aliquando bonus dormitat Homerus* ["even Homer nods": Horace, *Ars Poetica*], they ought to stop and think how wide-awake he had to be, most of the time, to make his book cast so much light and so little shade, for it may well be that what seem to them terribly serious defects are nothing more than beauty spots, which frequently heighten the loveliness of any face that bears them. Indeed, he who puts a book into print takes an enormous risk, for the most impossible of all impossibilities is that it can please and satisfy everyone who reads it."

"A book about me," said Don Quijote, "can't have pleased very many."

"On the contrary: just as *stultorum infinitus est numerus* [of fools we have an infinite number], so too the number of those who've liked that book is infinite, though there are some who think the author was forgetful, or playing tricks, when he left out the name of the thief who stole Sancho's donkey, because it's not even expressly stated, but only left to be inferred, that the animal was stolen at all, and a little later we see Sancho riding on a donkey that, so far as we know, still hasn't reappeared. People also complain that the author forgot to tell us what Sancho did with those hundred gold pieces he found in that suitcase, up in the Sierra Morena mountains; the money's never mentioned again, but a lot of people would like to know what Sancho did with it, or what he wasted it on, because this seems to them one of the book's most serious omissions."

Sancho replied:

"I'm in no mood, Mister Samson, for explaining and calculating anything, because I've got a real sinking feeling in my stomach and if I don't take care of it with a couple of swigs of nice aged wine my bones are going to melt. I've got wine and my old lady waiting for me, so when I've had my dinner I'll come back and tell you, your grace, and everyone in the world who wants to know, all about losing my donkey and spending that money."

And without waiting for a response, or saying another word, he went right home.

Don Quijote urged the college graduate, most civilly and politely, to stay and do culinary penance [i.e., dine] with him. Carrasco accepted the invitation; a pair of plump young pigeons were added to the menu, and over their meal they talked about knights and knighthood, the college graduate following Don Quijote's lead; the banquet over, they took their siesta, Sancho came back, and they resumed their earlier conversation.

Chapter Four

— in which Sancho Panza satisfies Samson Carrasco's doubts and answers his questions, together with other matters well worth noting and recounting

Returning to Don Quijote's house, Sancho re-opened their earlier conversation:

"As for Mister Samson wanting to know by whom, or how, or when I was robbed of my donkey, let me say that, the same night we ran away from the police, after that miserable adventure with the galley slaves and then the one with the corpse they were carrying to Segovia, we got to the Sierra Morena mountains and my master and I went right into a deep, dark thicket and, my master leaning on his lance, and me sitting on my donkey, all sore and tired from the battles we'd just been through, we fell asleep just as if we'd been lying on four feather mattresses — and, in particular, I slept so heavily that, whoever the thief was, he was able to sneak in and get four sticks under the four corners of my saddle and prop me up so I was still mounted, and then take my donkey out from under me so I never felt a thing."

"Not at all a hard thing to do," said Don Quijote,[1] "nor the first time it's been done, because the same thing happened to Sacripante, at the siege of Albraca, when that famous thief, Brunelo, used this same exact trick to steal the horse from right between his owner's legs."[2]

"Dawn came," Sancho went on, "and I'd barely shaken myself out of sleep when the sticks came loose and I fell to the ground like a shot; then I looked around for the donkey, but couldn't see him; tears came to my eyes and I launched into such a lament that, if the author didn't put it into our history, he'd better understand he's missed out on a damned good thing. And then, after I don't know how many days, when we were going along with the Princess Micomicona, I saw my donkey, and the man who was riding him was dressed like a gypsy, but it was Ginés de Pasamonte, that lying crook, that notorious thug, who my master and I freed from his chains."

"No, no, that's not the mistake," Samson interrupted. "Before the donkey reappears, the author says Sancho is riding on him again."

"I don't know what to say to that," said Sancho, "except maybe the historian got confused, or maybe it was the printer."

"That must be it," said Samson. "But what happened to the hundred gold pieces? Did they get lost?"

"I spent them on myself and my wife, and my children, too, and that's why my wife's been so patient about all these comings and goings in my

---

1. Cervantes does not indicate whether Don Quijote or Samson Carrasco speaks these words; Don Quijote seems the most likely speaker [*Translator's Note*].
2. Narrated both in Boyardo's *Orlando Innamorato* and Ariosto's *Orlando Furioso* [*Translator's Note*].

lord Don Quijote's service, because if I'd come back after all this time, without a red cent, and without my donkey, I'd have had a black home-coming — so if there's anything else anyone wants to know about me, here I am, and I'll say the same thing to the king if he wants to ask, because it's nobody's business whether I kept them or didn't, or whether I spent them or didn't, and if all the beatings I got on these trips had to be paid for in hard cash, at the rate of four cents a blow, another hundred gold pieces wouldn't pay half the bill, so let everybody take care of their own business and not try to see if white is black or black is white, because we're all the way God's made us, and a lot of times we're even worse."

"I'll make sure," Carrasco said, "to explain this to the author, so, if there's another printing, what our good Sancho has told us won't be for-gotten, because it'll raise the book's reputation a good half foot."

"Are there other things in this book that need correcting?" asked Don Quijote.

"There must be," the college graduate replied, "but nothing as impor-tant as the matters we've already discussed."

"Has the author, by any chance," said Don Quijote, "promised a second volume?"

"He has," replied Samson, "but he says he hasn't found it yet, and doesn't know who might have the original manuscript, so nobody's sure if the continuation will ever appear or not — and since some people say, 'Continuations are never as good as the original,' and others say, 'There's more than enough been written about Don Quijote,' maybe we'll never see that second volume — but still, those who are naturally sunny rather than sour-faced, cry, 'Let's have more about Don Quijote! Let him keep rushing around, and Sancho Panza go on jabbering, and we'll see what we'll see — and be happy no matter what.'"

"So what's the author doing?"

"As soon as he finds the manuscript," replied Samson, "and he's really hunting very hard, he'll rush it right into print, because the money he can make interests him a lot more than whatever praise he'll receive."

At which point Sancho said:

"So the author's interested in turning a profit? Good luck to him! It's going to be all hop-hop and slop-slop, like the tailor the night before Easter: whatever gets turned out in a hurry is never finished the way it ought to be. Let this Moor, or whoever he is, pay attention to what he's doing, because my master and I will supply him with so many adventures and all sorts of goings-on that he won't be able to just write a second part, but a hundred of them. I'll bet he thinks we're not up to much, right now, but let him hold our feet up for the blacksmith to take a look at and he'll find out if there's anything wrong with *our* hooves. All I can say is, if my master would take my advice, we'd be out there this very minute, righting wrongs and undoing injustices, the way good knights errant are supposed to."

Sancho had just said this when they heard Rocinante neighing, which Don Quijote took as a very good omen, and then and there made up his mind to leave home in no more than three or four days and, saying as much to the college graduate, he asked for advice as to where they ought to begin their new expedition. Carrasco replied that he'd favor the kingdom of Aragón, and the city of Zaragosa, where, in honor of Saint George, they'd soon be having a singularly solemn tournament, and where Don Quijote might triumph over all the Aragonese knights, who were the most celebrated in the entire world. Don Quijote's decision was supremely brave and honorable, he said approvingly, but warned our knight to be less incautious about encountering peril, since his life did not belong to himself alone but to all those who might have need of his help and protection in their misfortune.

"That's what I really don't like, Señor Samson," said Sancho, "because my master attacks a hundred armed knights like a hungry boy going after half a dozen watermelons! Oh, by all that's holy! — sure, there's a time to attack and a time to retreat; it doesn't always have to be 'Charge! Finish them off, Spaniards.' Besides, I've heard it said (and I think by my master himself, unless my memory's playing tricks) that courage lies somewhere between the two extremes of foolhardiness and cowardice, and if that's the way it is, not only don't I want him running away for no reason, but I don't want him plunging right in when it's better to do something else. Anyway, no matter what, I want my master to know that, if he's taking me with him, it has to be on condition that he has to do all the fighting, and I won't have any responsibility for anything except keeping him clean and comfortable, and I'll work at that just as hard as I can, but if he expects me to go swinging a sword, even against crooked peasants with an axe in their hands and a hood over their heads, he's just wasting his time. I'm not trying to get myself any reputation for bravery, Mister Samson; all I want to be is the best, the most loyal squire that ever served a knight errant, and then if my lord Don Quijote is grateful for all my good work, and wants to give me an island, just one of all those islands he's always saying you can fall into out there, I'll be very grateful — and if he doesn't give me one, I'm still a man, and God knows I am who I am, and I don't have to count on anybody — and what's more, my bread's going to taste just as good if I'm not a governor as it will if I am one, and who knows if maybe, in all this governorshipness, the Devil won't have rigged up some trap for me to stumble into and break my teeth? I was born Sancho, and I expect to die Sancho — but all the same, if Heaven were to decide, all by itself, without my asking, to offer me an island, or something like that, and there was no risk involved, I'm not such an idiot that I'd throw the chance away, because, you know, they also say, 'When someone gives you a cow, go run for a rope,' and 'When something good comes along, get it right into your house.' "

"Spoken, brother Sancho," said Carrasco, "like a professor. But in spite of that, trust in God and in My Lord Don Quijote, who'll surely give you a kingdom, not just an island."

"It's all the same, either way," replied Sancho, "though I can tell you, Señor Carrasco, that if my master does give me a kingdom, he won't be tossing it into a sack full of holes, because I've taken my pulse, by God, and I'm strong enough to rule over kingdoms and govern islands, as I've told my master often enough."

"Watch out, Sancho," said Samson. "Power can change people, and maybe, when you become a governor, you won't even recognize the mother who bore you."

"Say that about low-born people," answered Sancho, "but not about those, like me, who have the Old Christian spirit two inches thick all over their souls. No! Just remember who I am: do you think I could give people the back of my hand?"

"May God watch over you," said Don Quijote, "and, when you're a governor, that's when we'll know. But I think I can almost see it, right now."

Then he asked the college graduate, if he happened to be a poet, to compose a poem for him, about how he'd have to say farewell to his Lady Dulcinea del Toboso, explaining that the first letter in each stanza should spell out her name, so that, scanning only the first letters, you'd read: *Dulcinea del Toboso.*

The college graduate answered that, though to be sure he was not one of Spain's most famous poets (and there weren't more than three and a half of them, anyway), he would certainly compose just such a poem, no matter how difficult it might prove, since there were seventeen letters in the lady's name, and if he wrote four stanzas, each of four lines, he'd have an extra letter on his hands, whereas with five stanzas of what they called *décimas* [here, 5 octosyllabic lines] or *redondillas* [rhyming a-b-b-a], he'd need three more letters. But it didn't matter, because he'd do the best he could to drop a letter, and get the name "Dulcinea del Toboso" into four stanzas.

"However you do it, it has to be done," said Don Quijote, "because if the name isn't completely, unmistakeably clear, there won't be a woman alive who'll believe the poem was written for her."

This was settled, as it was that they would set out in eight days. Don Quijote cautioned the college graduate to keep this to himself, and especially not to reveal it to the priest or to Master Nicolás, or to his niece or his housekeeper, to keep them from blocking his honorable, valiant course. Carrasco promised. And then he said farewell, requesting that Don Quijote keep him informed of everything that happened, whether bad or good. Sancho, too, said his farewells and went to ready things for their journey.

Chapter Five

— the wise and witty conversation between Sancho Panza and his wife, Teresa Panza, along with other matters worth felicitous commemoration

(The translator of this history, when he comes to this fifth chapter, records that he considers it apocryphal, since Sancho Panza speaks, here, far beyond his limited abilities, saying things of such extraordinary subtlety that he couldn't possibly have understood them, but our translator felt professionally obliged to translate this material, and so he continues as follows:)

———

Sancho came home so excited and joyful that his wife could see his happiness while he was still a bowshot away — so extremely exuberant, indeed, that she simply had to ask him about it:

"What's going on, Sancho my friend, that you're hopping along so happily?"

To which he answered:

"Listen, wife: if it were God's will I'd be glad not to look as pleased as I am."

"Husband, I don't understand what you're talking about," she replied, "and I don't know why you say you'd be glad not to be glad, if that was what God wanted — because I may be stupid, but I know you can't find happiness by not having any."

"Look, Teresa," said Sancho, "I'm happy because I've made up my mind to go back into my master Don Quijote's service, and he's decided to go adventure-hunting for the third time, and I'm going with him, because I need the money and also because I'm hoping — which really makes me happy! — I might be able to find another hundred gold pieces just like the ones we've already spent, and I'm sad about being away from you and my children, but if God would let me stay at home, with my feet dry, and still eat, without dragging me through wild places and crossroads — because He could do it without any trouble, just by willing it to happen — then, clearly, I could be happy all the time and with good reason, but as it is I've got happiness all jumbled up with the sadness of parting — and that's why I say that I'd be glad if it were God's will that I shouldn't be happy."

"Now watch out, Sancho," replied Teresa, "because ever since you got to be a member of a knight errant you talk around and around and around in such circles that *nobody* can understand you."

"Woman, it's enough that God understands me," replied Sancho, "because it's His job to understand everything, and so that's that, and for the next three days you have to be really careful to take good care of the donkey, so he's ready to go to war. Give him twice as much hay, and check the packsaddle and all the other gear, because we're not going to a wedding, but right around the world, and we're going to be tangled up with giants and dragons and all kinds of monsters, and we'll be listening to hissing, and roaring, and howling, and whooping and screaming, and all that would be just French lavender if we didn't have to deal with enchanted Moors and shepherds from Yanguas."

"Well, husband," said Teresa, "I know squires errant don't earn their keep just sitting around, so I'll keep praying Our Lord to get you right out of all that trouble."

"Let me tell you, wife," replied Sancho, "if I didn't expect to pretty soon find myself governor of an island, I'd fall over dead, right here and now."

"No, husband, no," said Teresa. "You don't kill the chicken because it catches cold. You go on living, and devil take all the governorships in the world, because you came out of your mother's womb without one, and you've lived all your life without one, and you'll go — or you'll be carried — to your grave without one, whenever God wills it. Lots of people live their whole lives without governorships, and they don't stop living or being counted up along with everybody else. The best sauce in the world is hunger, and because poor people never run out of it, they always enjoy what they eat. But you remember, Sancho: if you're lucky, and you see you've got some kind of governorship, don't forget about me and your children. Remember that little Sancho's already reached fifteen, and he ought to go to school, or else his uncle the abbot won't be able to bring him into the Church. And remember: Mari Sancha, your daughter, won't drop dead if we get her married, because I've got a hunch she's as anxious to have a husband as you are to have a governorship — and, to make a long story short, it's better to have a daughter badly married than living in sin."

"By all that's holy, wife," said Sancho, "if God gives me even a little governorship, I'm going to get Mari Sancha married so well you won't be able to come near her without saying *señora*."

"No, no, Sancho," answered Teresa, "let her marry someone who's just like her, that's the best way, because if you take off her wooden clogs and set her up on high heels — if you pull her out of her plain brown skirt and wrap her up in fancy hoops and toops, with silk skirts on over top of them — if you change her from 'Marica' and 'hey, you,' into 'my lady so-and-so' and 'señora this-and-that' — she's going to be completely lost, and every time she turns around she'll make a thousand mistakes, and keep showing all the homespun yarn and the plain stitching and the rough cloth she's got on underneath."

"Shut up, you fool," said Sancho. "It'll take her two or three years to get the hang of it, and then being dignified and having fancy manners will be second nature to her — and if not, who cares? She'll still be 'my lady,' no matter what."

"Go easy, Sancho, with all this stuff about rank and titles," answered Teresa. "Don't try to be more than you really are; remember the old saying: 'Put your arm around your neighbor's son, and wipe his nose, and take him home with you.' What a wonderful idea, marrying our Mari to some bigshot count, some fathead lord! He could insult her anytime he felt like it, make fun of her as a peasant, with a country bumpkin for a father and a spinning-woman for a mother! Not while I'm alive, husband! By God, I haven't been raising my daughter for *that*! You just bring home your money, Sancho, and let me take care of marrying her off. There's Lope Tocho, Juan Tocho's son, a good solid boy, and someone we know, and I can already see he's got his eye on the girl, and she'd be well married to someone like him, someone like us, and we'd be able to see her all the time, and everybody would live together, fathers and sons, and the grandsons and the sons-in-law, and God's peace and blessing would be on all of us — so don't you go marrying her off into these courts and these grand palaces, where they won't know who she is, and she won't, either."

"Now, just a minute, you idiot, you fool of a woman," answered Sancho. "Why should you try to stop me, for no reason at all, from marrying my daughter to someone who'll give me grandchildren everyone will have to speak to like *gentlemen*? Look here, Teresa: when I was a kid I always heard the adults say anyone who didn't know how to grab good luck, when it came calling, had no business complaining if it passed him by. And here it is, right now, knocking at our door, and it wouldn't be right to shut the door in its face — no, let's let this good wind blow us wherever it wants to."

(It's this kind of talk, and what Sancho then goes on to say, that makes our history's translator call this chapter apocryphal.)

"Don't you see, you dumb beast," Sancho went on, "how good it would be to get myself into some juicy governorship, so I can pull us up out of the mud? And I'll marry Mari Sancha to anyone I want to, and you'll see how everyone will call you 'Doña Teresa Panza,' and you'll sit in church on a rug and cushions, with curtains, and never mind all the fancy ladies in town — the hell with them. — No, you stay the way you are! Don't get any bigger, and don't get any smaller: I don't want you painted like some kind of decoration. And that's that: Sanchica's going to be a countess, no matter what you say."

"Are you listening to yourself, husband?" replied Teresa. "Never mind all that: I'm just afraid you'll ruin my daughter, making a countess of her. You go on and do whatever you want to — make her a duchess, make her a princess — but let me tell you, not with my help, and I won't agree to any of it. I've always been a believer in equality, brother, and I can't see people getting all puffed up for no good reason. When I was baptized they called me Teresa, a plain, simple, everyday name, without anything else tacked on, no red ribbons and fancy laces, no Don-this and Doña-that. My father's name was Cascajo, and since I'm married to you they call me Teresa Panza, though they ought to call me Teresa Cascajo. But kings have to do what the law tells them to, and I'm satisfied with the name I've got, without sticking any Don on top of it and making it heavier than I can carry, because I don't want people saying, when they see me going around dressed like some kind of countess or governor's wife, 'Hey, look at that stuckup slut! She was happy enough to spin up a spool, yesterday, and trot off to mass with her skirt flapped over her head, instead of a shawl, and here she is, today, strutting around in a hoopskirt, with her brooches and her stuckup airs, as if we didn't know her.' If God lets me keep my seven senses — or five — or however many I have — I'm not going to let myself in for anything like *that*. You go be a governor, brother, or an islander, and act as big as you like, but my daughter and me — I swear by my mother — we're not going one step away from this village of ours, because both an honest woman and a broken leg belong at home, and when a good girl is busy doing something she's having herself a holiday. You go have your adventures with your Don Quijote, and we won't venture anything and just let God give us whatever He wants to — and, by God, I don't know where your gentleman got his *Don* from, because his parents didn't have one, and neither did their parents."

"Let me tell you," replied Sancho, "you must have swallowed a demon. My God, woman! What a big fat mess you've strung together, running off in every direction! What the devil has Cascajo got to do with anything I've been telling you? Or brooches, or proverbs, or being stuck up? Just look here, you idiot, you absolute ignoramus — and what else should I call you, when you don't understand a word I'm saying and try to run away from good luck? If I said my daughter ought to throw herself down out of a tower, or go wandering around the world like Princess Urraca,[1] then you'd be right not to give in to me, but if I can stick a *Don* on your back, quick as a wink, and a *Señora* on her, and pick you up out of the dirt, and put you on a pedestal, under a canopy, up on a dais with more velvet cushions than there are cushy Moors in all Morocco, then why don't you agree with me and want what I want?"

"You want me to tell you why, husband?" answered Teresa. "Because there's a proverb that says, 'Whoever conceals you, reveals you.' Nobody gives a poor man more than a quick glance, but you look long and hard at a rich man, and if he's a rich man who was once a poor man, then everybody says nasty things and slanders him, and poor people keep talking like that, and there are poor people all over the place, around here, swarming like bees."

"Look, Teresa," said Sancho, "you just listen to what I'm going to tell you. Maybe this is something you've never heard in your whole life, but it's not my words, because everything I'm trying to tell you comes from that preacher we had here, at Lent last year, and what he said, unless my memory's playing me false, is that whatever we actually see with our own eyes stays in our memory a lot better, and a lot more vividly, than other things that have happened."

(And everything Sancho went on to say, here, is our translator's other reason for calling this chapter apocryphal, because all this is quite beyond Sancho's capacity. And what he goes on to say is this:)

"Which is why, when we see someone nicely dressed, in rich clothing, and with a whole parade of servants, it's almost as if we can't stop ourselves from acting deferentially, even if, at the same time, we can vaguely remember having seen him in some lowly situation — but whether that was a matter of poverty, or perhaps of birth, it's all history, now, dead and buried, and the only thing that matters is what we see right in front of us. And if this person who's been fortunate enough to be lifted out of the muck and mire of poverty (and those were the preacher's exact words), up to the very heights of prosperity, if he behaves himself, and he's open and generous with others, and he doesn't try to compete with those whose families have been noble forever and forever, mark my words, Teresa, there won't be anyone who remembers him as he used to be: they'll just respect him as he is, unless of course they're the jealous type, and no one's good fortune is safe from them."

"I don't know what you're talking about, husband," answered Teresa. "You do what you want to, and don't bother my head any more with all this speechifying and fancy words. Because if you're revolved to do what you said you'd do — "

---

1. She had been leading a licentious life, to punish her father for leaving her out of his will. To restore her to a more moral existence, he changed his will [*Translator's Note*].

"You've got to say *resolved*, woman," said Sancho, "not *revolved*."

"Just don't pick a quarrel with me, husband," replied Teresa. "I speak as God wills, and I don't mind anybody else's business, and what I say is if you've made up your mind you're going to be a governor, no matter what, then take our son Sancho with you, so you can start to teach him to be a governor, too, because it's good for children to inherit and learn how to practice their fathers' trade."

"When I get to be a governor," said Sancho, "I'll send a letter for him to come to me, and I'll send you money, because I won't be short of that: there's never any problem finding people to lend governors money, when they haven't got it handy. And you be sure to dress him up so he doesn't look like what he is, but what he's going to be."

"You send the money," said Teresa, "and I'll dress him up for you like a Christmas tree."

"So then we're agreed," said Sancho, "that our daughter has to be a countess."

"The day I see her a countess," replied Teresa, "will be like the day I bury her — but let me tell you, again, you do whatever you want to, because women are born with this responsibility: we have to obey our husbands, even if they're stupid fools."

And then she began to weep so hard that it was as if she could already see her Sanchica dead and buried. Sancho comforted her, saying that even though he'd have to make the girl a countess, he'd wait to do it just as long as he could. And that finished their conversation, and Sancho went back to see Don Quijote, to make arrangements for their departure.

Chapter Six

— what took place between Don Quijote and his niece and his housekeeper: one of the most important chapters in this entire history

While Sancho Panza and his wife, Teresa Cascajo, were engaged in the aforesaid hopelessly irrelevant conversation, Don Quijote's niece and his housekeeper were not just marking time, because they saw by a thousand signals that their uncle and master was planning on running off for the third time, to resume what they thought of as the evil profession of knight errantry, so they tried in every way possible to lead him away from so wicked an idea — but it was all like preaching in the wilderness and hammering on cold iron. All the same, during one of the many, many arguments they had with him, the housekeeper told him:

"I tell you, my lord, if your grace won't stay home, nice and peaceful-like, and you're going to let yourself wander around all those mountains and valleys like a tormented soul, looking for these things you call adventures, but I call disasters, I think I'm just going to scream and wail to God and the King to help us."

To which Don Quijote replied:

"Housekeeper, I have no idea what God will say, when you complain to Him, nor what His Majesty will say, either, because all I know is that, if I were king, I wouldn't bother replying to all the infinity of irrelevant petitions I'd receive every day — indeed, one of the most serious problems kings have to deal with, and they have a lot of them, is being obliged to listen to everyone and reply to everyone, so I'd rather my affairs didn't have to trouble him at all."

To which the housekeeper answered:

"Tell us, my lord: aren't there any knights at His Majesty's court?"

"Yes," responded Don Quijote, "and a lot of them, which is only right and proper, for they serve as embellishments of a prince's magnificence, befitting His Royal Majesty."

"In which case," she replied, "why can't your grace be one of those who stand around and serve his lord and king, as one of his court?"

"Consider, my friend," responded Don Quijote, "that all knights can't be courtiers, nor need all courtiers be — nor are they capable of being — knights errant; the world requires knights of all sorts; and though we're all knights, there's a great deal of difference between and among us, for courtiers, without leaving their chambers or stepping through the court's doorways, can travel all over the world by simply looking down at a map, without any problems whatever, suffering neither from heat nor cold, hunger nor thirst, while we, the true knights errant, range all across the world, in sunshine, in cold, in the open air, in every kind of bad weather, by night and by day, on foot and on horseback, and it's not simply painted enemies we have to encounter, but real ones, and we must fight them no matter what and no matter when, without worrying about all sorts of silliness, and rules about challenges — whether the spear you carry, or you don't carry, has to be shorter, or the sword; whether you ought to be carrying religious relics or any secret contrivances; whether the glare of the sun ought to be evenly allocated — or maybe chopped up into little pieces; plus all sorts of other such protocols, which they used to enforce in man-to-man challenges, things you don't know about, but I do.[1]

"And you also have to realize that a real knight errant, even if he finds himself facing ten giants so tall that their heads not only touch the clouds, but reach right through them, each of them with legs like the heaviest stone towers ever built, and arms like the masts of great powerful ships, and eyes as big around as immense millwheels and flaming hotter than a furnace for melting glass, still, he can't let himself be the least bit frightened, but nobly and bravely must charge directly at them and, if he possibly can, instantly conquer and completely rout them, even though they be covered with armor fashioned from the shells of a certain fish, said to be harder by far than diamonds, and they carry, instead of mere swords, razor-sharp knives of Damascus steel, or iron-plated clubs studded with steel points — as, more than once, I have seen them do. And I've told you all this, my dear housekeeper, so you can understand the differences between these various kinds of knights — and, indeed, it would be better if princes were all wise enough to set this second kind more highly than the first — or, to put it more accurately, to understand that this second

---

1. Don Quijote partially records and partially burlesques actual medieval rules for knightly combat [*Translator's Note*].

kind, the true knights errant, is in fact the first, for, as we read in their histories, some among them have been the saviors not just of one kingdom, but of many."

"Oh, my dear lord!" cried Don Quijote's niece, hearing this. "Your grace must understand that everything you've said about these knights errant is pure fiction and lies, and all their so-called histories — the ones that aren't burned at the stake — should each and every one of them be draped like a penitent who's confessed to the Inquisition, or at the very least be branded with some mark to label them worthless corrupters of good morals."

"In the name of the Lord who gives me breath," said Don Quijote, "if you were not my niece by blood, my very own sister's daughter, I would be obliged to mete out to you, for this blasphemous statement, such a punishment that its echo would resound all over the world. Can a girl barely able to waggle a dozen lace bobbins dare to discuss, and to criticize, histories of knight errantry? What would My Lord Amadís say, could he hear of it! But he'd pardon you, surely, because he was the humblest and most courteous knight of his time and, what's more, a famous protector of maidens. Yet there are others, who might have overheard such remarks, who were not such good men, neither so courteous nor so wise, some of them rude good-for-nothings. For not everyone known as a knight and a gentleman fully deserves those titles; some are golden, but others only base metal transformed by alchemy, though all may seem alike; assay some of them, and they will not ring true. There are low, vulgar men who are bursting to seem gentlemen, and noble knights who are apparently dying to turn themselves into mere vulgar men; the former rise, either on the wings of ambition or of ability, and the latter sink from weakness or indifference, or from sheer depravity; and we need to look with a knowing eye to know which kind we're seeing, for though they're much the same on the outside they're very different within."

"God bless me!" said his niece. "How can you be so learned, my dear uncle, that, if you had to, you could take to the pulpit or preach in the streets, and still, all the same, be so blinded and taken in by such a common foolishness that you think you're brave and courageous, when you're really old; you think you're strong, when you're really feeble; you think you can go righting wrongs when age has bent you in half — and, above all, that you're a knight, when you're not, because even though gentlemen can become knights, poor ones can't . . . !"

"Niece, you're making a good deal of sense," replied Don Quijote, "though there are things I could tell you about ancestries which would astonish you — but, to keep from mixing that which is divine and that which is human, I won't say a thing. But consider, both of you: listen carefully: all the family trees in the world can be reduced to four sorts, as follows. Some begin humbly, but grow and stretch until they reach the heights of nobility; others, which have magnificent beginnings, stay that way, and continue as they have begun; still others, which start magnificently, but — like a pyramid — end in a point, after diminishing and destroying their beginnings until it all turns into nothing, just like the apex of a pyramid, which in comparison to its base, or foundation, is indeed nothing; and then there are some, the majority, which neither start well nor make any progress, and come to a nameless end, like all ordinary, plebian people. The first category, which begins humbly but rises to a mightiness, and then maintains it, can be illustrated by the Ottoman line, which stems from a humble, lowly shepherd, but has attained the summit where now we see it. The second sort, which starts nobly and remains at that level, can be illustrated by many hereditary princes, who pass on what they have inherited, neither adding nor subtracting, perfectly content to stay within their own peaceful borders. There are millions of families which begin great and end in a point, for all the Pharaohs and Ptolemies of Egypt, and the Caesars of Rome, and that whole endless mob (if we're allowed to use such a word) of princes and kings and lords, Medes and Assyrians and Persians, Greeks and Barbarians, all those noble lineages and all that majestic power have ended in a point and come to nothing, along with everyone who partook of their greatness, for today we cannot trace a single one of their descendants and, even if we could, they would be men of low, humble station. Of the fourth and last category, men of plebian family, the only thing I have to say is that they serve to swell the number of people who are alive, deserving neither any special notice nor any particular praise. And from everything I've told you, my dear, silly ladies, it's easy enough to see that all family trees are jumbled together, and the only ones which seem truly great and illustrious are those which display those qualities in their virtue, as well as in the wealth and generosity of those who bear their names. I've spoken of virtue, and of wealth, and of liberality, because a nobleman of vicious temperament will do vicious things, and a rich man without generosity will be nothing but a greedy beggar, for he who possesses wealth is not fortunate simply in its possession, but in its use — not simply spending it for his own pleasure, but understanding how to spend it properly. The poor knight has no way to prove his knighthood except by being virtuous, by being gracious, well-mannered, courteous, by being polite and attentive, and neither proud, nor arrogant, nor a rumor-monger but, above all else, charitable, because two cents cheerfully handed over to a man in need shows us someone quite as generous as anybody clanging a bell and distributing alms, and no one, seeing a poor knight adorned with all these virtues, can help but think and believe him — even without any direct personal knowledge — a man of good breeding, which is after all hardly strange, since praise has always been virtue's reward, nor can one help but praise those who are virtuous.

"My daughters, there are two roads a man can take, to become rich and honored: one is learning, and the other is war. There is more of war than of learning in me: I was born under the influence of the planet Mars, which leads me to take war as my way of life, and since I am virtually compelled to follow this road, and follow it in the face of no matter what opposition, or from whom, there's no point to your wearying yourselves, trying to persuade me not to do what Heaven itself desires, and Fate ordains, and Reason requires, and toward which — above all else — my own will inclines, for knowing as I do the endless pains associated with knight errantry, I also know the infinite blessings it confers, as I know how narrow is virtue's path and how broad and ample the road to ruin, and as I know, too, the enormous difference in their ends and means, for vice, being spacious and vast, finishes in death, while virtue, being cramped and difficult, culminates in life, and in life eternal, unending, since as our great Spanish poet says:

> Those who climb to immortality
> Come up these harsh and rugged roads that no one
> Ever reaches, who weakens here below."[2]

"Oh Lord, what a shame!" said his niece. "My uncle's a poet, too! He knows everything; he can do everything. I'll bet he could build a house as easily as you'd turn out a bird cage, if he decided to be a bricklayer."

"Let me assure you, niece," replied Don Quijote, "that if my entire being were not absorbed in these knightly matters, there would indeed be nothing I could not do, and nothing I could not make, especially bird cages and toothpicks."

Just then they heard someone at the door and, when they asked who was there, Sancho Panza said, "It's me," and the housekeeper had no sooner heard this than she ran out of the room, to keep from seeing him: she hated him that much. But Don Quijote's niece let him in; his master received him with open arms; and then the two of them shut themselves into Don Quijote's room, where they conducted a conversation fully the equal of the last one they'd had.

Chapter Seven

— Don Quijote's conversation with his squire, along with other notable occurrences

The housekeeper, seeing Sancho Panza closeted with her master, had no trouble figuring out what they were up to, and suspecting their conversation would end in a decision to sally forth a third time, she snatched up her shawl and, in despair and anguish, went looking for Samson Carrasco, the college graduate, thinking that as a well-spoken man, and her master's new friend, he might be able to dissuade Don Quijote from any such wild intention.

She found him walking up and down in the inner courtyard and immediately threw herself at his feet, dripping with sweat and half distracted. Seeing her so frightened and miserable, he said:

"What's going on, Madame Housekeeper? What's happened to you? You look ready to give up the ghost."

"It's nothing, nothing, dear Señor Samson, except my master's breaking out. He's off, he's off again!"

"And just where is he off to?" asked Samson. "Where is he breaking out?"

"He's off," she answered, "right through the gate of his madness. I mean,

---

2. Garcilaso de la Vega, *Elegía 1*, ll. 202–204 [*Translator's Note*].

oh my dear, beloved sir university graduate, he's breaking out again, and this will be the third time, hunting all over the world for what he calls 'lucky ventures,'[1] though I don't know why. The first time he came home stretched out on a donkey's back, half beaten to death. The second time he came in an ox-cart, all shut up in a crate and convinced he'd been enchanted, and in such a state the mother who bore him wouldn't have recognized him: thin, and weak, and yellow, with his eyes shrunk way up into the attic storerooms of his skull, and to bring him even a little bit back to himself cost me more than six hundred eggs, as God knows very well, and the whole world, too, and my chickens, who wouldn't let me tell a lie."

"I can certainly believe that," replied the college graduate, "because they're plump and luscious, and so well-bred they wouldn't tell a falsehood if it killed them. But what you're saying, my dear housekeeper, is that nothing's happened, and there's been no disaster except the one you're afraid your master Don Quijote is contemplating?"

"No, sir," she answered.

"Then don't worry," he replied, "but go happily home, and fix me something nice and hot for breakfast, and as you go you just say the prayer to Saint Apolonia,[2] if you know it, because I'll be right over and then there'll be wonders to behold."

"Oh my God!" exclaimed the housekeeper. "Your grace is telling me to say the prayer to Saint Apolonia? That would be fine, if my master had a toothache, but the problem's in his brains."

"My dear housekeeper," replied Carrasco, "I know what I'm talking about. You just go on and don't try to argue with me, because, remember, I'm a university graduate, and from Salamanca, too, and you can't have a better degree than that."

So the housekeeper left, and our college graduate immediately went hunting for the priest, to tell him what you, reader, will be told when the time comes.

Now while Don Quijote and Sancho were alone they had a conversation, faithfully and precisely recorded by our history, as follows.

Sancho said to his master:

"My lord, I've evinced my wife to let me go with your grace anywhere you want to take me."

"You mean *convinced*, Sancho," said Don Quijote, "not *evinced*."[3]

"Unless I remember wrong," replied Sancho, "I've already asked your grace, once or twice, not to correct my words if you can understand what I'm trying to say, but when you don't understand, just say, 'Sancho, god damn it, I can't understand you,' and then if I don't explain you can go ahead and correct me, because I'm so focile . . ."

"I don't understand you, Sancho," Don Quijote interrupted, "because I don't know the meaning of 'so focile.'"

1. She says *venturas* [good luck] instead of *aventuras* [adventures] [*Translator's Note*].
2. Popularly believed to cure toothache; it plays an important role in the celebrated and widely read *La Celestina* [*The Procuress, Bawd, Madame*] (1499) of Fernando de Rojas [*Translator's Note*].
3. Sancho uses *relucir*, "glitter, shine, bring out," instead of *reducir*, "convert, subjugate, convince" [*Translator's Note*]

" 'So focile,' " replied Sancho, "means 'that's exactly the way I am.' "

"Now I understand even less," said Don Quijote.

"Well, if you can't understand me," answered Sancho, "I just don't know how to tell you, because, may God help me, I don't know any better."

"Ah, ah: I've got it," replied Don Quijote. "You mean you're so *docile* — so mild-mannered, so easy — that whatever I tell you, you'll pay attention and be guided by me."

"And I'll bet," said Sancho, "you got it right away, and knew what I meant, but you wanted to get me all bothered, so you could hear me make a couple of dozen more mistakes."

"That's possible," replied Don Quijote. "So: what did Teresa say?"

"Teresa says," answered Sancho, "I'd better watch out for you, your grace, and keep my mouth shut and let documents talk instead, because whoever gets to cut the cards doesn't need to shuffle them: one 'I take' is worth two 'I give.' And what I say is: women don't go to school, but if you don't take their advice then you're the fool."

"Which is exactly what I say," replied Don Quijote. "Go on, Sancho, my friend — go on, because today your words are like pearls."

"So this is the way it is," Sancho went on. "As you know even better than I do, your grace, we're all of us liable to die, so we're here today and gone tomorrow, and a lamb can go just as fast as a sheep, and nobody can tell himself he'll be alive any longer than God wants him to be, because Death doesn't have any ears, so when he comes knocking on the door of our lives he's always in a hurry, and we can't slow him up by begging or blustering, and everybody says he doesn't care about crowns or mitres, and every day they tell us the same thing from the pulpit."

"All of which is perfectly true," said Don Quijote, "but I have no idea where you're heading."

"Where I'm heading," said Sancho, "is for your grace to tell me exactly how much I'm supposed to get paid every month, for just as long as I'm in your service, and to tell your estate it has to pay me that much salary, because I don't want a lot of good will that's maybe not worth much, or comes too late, or never at all — and let God help me have what I'm supposed to. So I want to know what I'm earning, however much or little it is, because a hen can sit on only one egg, and a lot of little ones make a big one, and as long as you're making something you're not losing anything. Now it's true that if it happens — and I say this because I don't expect or believe it will — but if it happens your grace finally gives me that island you keep promising, I'm not so ungrateful, and I wouldn't carry things so far, that I wouldn't want to figure out just how much the island brings in, and then let my salary be discounted that much, *pro gata* [*gata* = cat]."

"Sancho, my friend," replied Don Quijote, "sometimes it's just as good to have a *gata* as a *rata* [*rata* = rat]."

"I get it," said Sancho. "I'll bet I should have said *rata*, and not *gata*, but that doesn't matter a bit, because your grace knew what I meant."

"And knew it so well," replied Don Quijote, "that I've penetrated right to the bottom of your thoughts, and I understand the target you've been shooting at, with your unending hail of proverbial arrows. Look here, Sancho: I'd be happy to set you some precise salary, if only I were able to find one single precedent anywhere in all the histories of knight errantry, even strictly in passing, something to let me know, to show me, just how much you ought to earn each month, but I've read every one of those books, or at least most of them, and I can't remember reading where any knight errant ever told his squire just how much he was going to be paid. All I know is that every single one of them served at his master's will, and then, when they least expected it, if Fortune happened to favor their masters, they'd suddenly find themselves rewarded with an island, or something just as good, or at least would come out of it with land and a title. So if these kinds of extras and expectations make you want to return to my service, Sancho, it will be well done, but if you think I have to go where no knight errant has ever gone before, and push over ancient rules and customs, then you're wasting your time. So, my friend, you go back to your house and tell your Teresa what I'm willing to agree to, and if she's happy to have you come with me, waiting to see what I do for you, and you're happy, too, then *bene quidem* [well and good], and if not, well, we'll remain friends, just as we were, because if there's pigeon food in the pigeon house, then there'll be pigeons, too. And remember, my son, that a good bird in the bush is worth more than a bad one in the hand, and good complaints are better than bad payments. I'm speaking to you this way, Sancho, so you'll see that I can make it rain proverbs, just as you do. And, finally, what I mean, and what I hereby say, is that if you don't want to come with me, and trust to what may come your way, and take your chances with Fate, as I do, may God be with you and keep you, because I won't have any problem finding squires who are more obedient, more attentive, and nowhere near so clumsy — or so talkative."

When Sancho heard how steady and determined his master was, the heavens grew dark overhead and his heart drooped, because he'd never thought his lord would go without him, not for all the wages in the world, and as he stood there, baffled and concerned, in came Samson Carrasco, along with Don Quijote's niece [and his housekeeper], for the ladies wanted to hear how the young man would try to talk Don Quijote out of his hunt for still more adventures. Samson, sly dog that he was, approached Don Quijote and, embracing him as if they were meeting for the first time, declared in a loud, clear voice:

"Oh, flower of knight errantry! Oh, warfare's resplendent light! Oh, glory and model for the entire Spanish nation! May Almighty God, Who holds the reins of the universe, keep any person or persons from blocking or stopping you, as you go forth on your third sally into the world, and may He entangle them in the labyrinth of their schemes, and never grant them their wicked desires!"

And then, turning to the housekeeper, he said:

"May Madame Housekeeper here leave off her recitation of the prayer to Saint Apolonia, for I know it is the fixed decision of the spheres that My Lord Don Quijote once more put into practice his noble, novel plans, and it would much trouble my conscience if I did not urge this knight not to delay a moment longer, holding back the might of his powerful arm and the goodness of this bravest of souls, because for him to dally is to defraud the world of its righter of wrongs, its protector of orphans, its preserver of virginal chastity, its patron of all widows and supporter of women still married, and many other matters of the same sort, all of which involve, concern, pertain and are annexed unto the order of knight errantry. Ah, my brave and handsome Lord Don Quijote, why wait till tomorrow? Why not start today, Your Majesty, for if there is anything lacking, I stand here ready and willing to make it good, either by myself or at my expense — and even if I had to serve as squire to Your Magnificence, I would consider that the luckiest day of my life!"

Hearing this, Don Quijote turned to Sancho:

"Didn't I tell you, Sancho, I'd have all the squires I wanted? Just see who's after the job — none other than that celebrated university graduate, Samson Carrasco, long the darling and delight of every classroom in Salamanca, a healthy young man, nimble, able to keep his mouth shut, able to bear heat as easily as cold, not to mention hunger and thirst, wonderfully capable of being everything a knight errant's squire ought to be. But Heaven forbid that, simply to satisfy myself, I weaken or break such a pillar of learning, such a repository of knowledge, that I shatter this glory of the fine and liberal arts. Let this new Samson of ours remain here in his own country, and shed honor upon it, thereby bringing honor to the grey-sprinkled heads of his venerable parents, for I shall be satisfied with whatever squire I find, now that Sancho won't condescend to journey with me."

"But I will condescend," replied Sancho, deeply moved, tears flowing from his eyes. "No one's going to say of me, my lord, that I took your bread and then showed you my back, by God, because I wasn't born into some ungrateful family, and the whole world knows — and especially the people in my hometown — what the Panzas, from whom I'm descended, have always been like — and what's more, I can tell from all the good things you've done for me, your grace, and all the good things you've said to me — I can see you want to make it worth my while, so if I've made a big fuss about this business of my salary, it's only been to humor my wife, because, once she makes up her mind to argue about anything, there isn't a mallet in the world that can bang the hoops on a barrel the way she can keep going after what she wants — but, in the end, a man's got to be a man, and a woman's got to be a woman, and since I'm a hundred percent man, because how could I deny it, I'm going to be a man in my own house, no matter what anybody says, so all your grace has to do is fix up your will with that little codicil, so it can't be repoked,[4] and let's leave here right away, so Señor Samson's soul doesn't have to suffer, because he says his conscience is absolutely all over him, trying to get him to talk your grace into going out into the world a third time, so I hereby offer all over again to serve your grace faithfully and loyally, and just as well and maybe better than all those squires who've ever served and still are serving however many knights errant there were or are or ever will be."

Sancho Panza's manner of speaking, and his vocabulary, astonished the

4. Sancho uses *revolcar*, "to trample, knock down," instead of *revocar*, "to revoke" [*Translator's Note*]

university graduate, because even though he'd read the first volume of Don Quijote's history, he'd never believed the man could really be as funny as the book made him seem, but having now heard Sancho talk of a will and a codicil that couldn't be *repoked*, instead of *revoked*, he realized that every single thing he'd read was true, and Sancho was without a doubt one of the most thoroughgoing fools who'd ever lived, and he said to himself that two such idiots as this master and his man had never been seen anywhere in the whole world.

And so, in the end, Don Quijote and Sancho embraced and made it up, and with the consent and approval of the great Carrasco — who had now become their delphic oracle — it was arranged that they'd leave in three days, which would give them time to get everything ready for the journey, and to hunt up a proper helmet, without which Don Quijote insisted he simply could not leave. Samson volunteered to take care of this, because one of his friends had a helmet and would never deny it to him, though it might be all rusty and moldy, rather than bright and shining like polished steel.

Don Quijote's housekeeper and his niece heaped a stream of curses on the university graduate's head; they pulled out their hair, and clawed at their faces, like the hired mourners who used to weep and wail at funerals, exactly as they might have done had Don Quijote suddenly died. But in persuading our knight to sally forth yet again, Samson had a plan, completely worked out in consultation with the priest and the barber (with whom he had been in close communication), the consequences of which will be narrated in subsequent pages of this history.

Finally, after Don Quijote and Sancho had spent their three days making what seemed to them necessary preparations, and Sancho had mollified his wife, and Don Quijote his niece and his housekeeper, they set out on the road to Toboso, one evening, unseen by anyone except the university graduate, who chose to accompany them for a mile or so — Don Quijote mounted on his good Rocinante, Sancho on his old donkey, saddlebags stuffed to the brim with comestibles, purse filled with money given him by his master, to take care of whatever might come to them. Then Samson gave our knight a farewell embrace, begging him, as the laws of friendship required, to send news of his luck, whether good or bad, so the one could be rejoiced in and the other be grieved over. Don Quijote gave his word, Samson turned homeward, and our two travelers turned their faces toward the great city of Toboso.

Chapter Eight

— which tells what happened to Don Quijote, as he was going to visit his lady, Dulcinea del Toboso

"Blessed be Allah the All-Mighty!" says Hamid Benengeli at the beginning of this eighth chapter. "Blessed be Allah!" he repeats three times, noting that he utters this benediction because Don Quijote and Sancho are now back in action, and from this point on the readers of his pleasant

history can count on hearing our hero's heroic deeds and graceful observations, not to mention those of his squire. And he suggests that his readers
forget all the past exploits of our Ingenious Gentleman, fixing their eyes
on those still to come: these will occur on the road to Toboso, as those
began in the fields of Montiel. Nor is this a great deal to ask, considering
how much he promises in return — and so he continues his tale:

Don Quijote and Sancho were now alone, and no sooner had Samson
left them than Rocinante began whinnying and the donkey braying, which
both knight and squire considered a good sign and a happy omen —
although, to tell the truth, the donkey's wheezing and snuffling was louder
than the horse's, from which Sancho deduced that his good fortune was
to surpass his master's, basing this judgment on God only knows what
astrological knowledge, though the history tells us nothing on this subject:
indeed, all we can say is that when he slipped or stumbled he could be
heard wishing he'd never left home, because all you could get from slipping or stumbling was a broken shoe or a cracked rib, and though he was
a fool, this wasn't wide of the mark. Don Quijote said to him:

"Sancho, my friend, night is settling around us as we go, and it's growing
considerably darker than it ought to, if we're to reach Toboso by morning
— but I've made up my mind to journey there before I attempt any new
adventure, to receive the blessing and to take leave of my matchless Dulcinea, for with her authorization I feel sure I can conclude any dangerous
venture happily and well, there being nothing to instill such courage in
knights errant as to see themselves smiled upon by their ladies."

"You're right," replied Sancho, "but I think it's going to be hard for
your grace to see her or speak to her, at least anyplace where you can
receive her blessing, unless she throws it over the courtyard wall, because
that's where I saw her, the last time, when I brought her the letter about
all those crazy, stupid things I left your grace doing, up in the heart of the
Sierra Morena mountains."

"Do you imagine those were mere courtyard walls, Sancho," said Don
Quijote, "near which, or through which, you caught sight of that noble
beauty which no one can ever sufficiently praise? They must have been
the balconies or corridors or porticos, or whatever they may have been, of
her rich and royal palace."

"Maybe," answered Sancho, "but to me they looked like walls, if my
memory serves me right."

"No matter, Sancho: let us hurry onward," replied Don Quijote, "because no matter how I see her, whether through walls or windows, or
chinks and cracks, or through a garden fence, any beam which reaches
my eyes from the glowing sun of her beauty will illuminate my mind and
fortify my heart, and render me utterly unmatched in both wisdom and
courage."

"But the truth is, my lord," replied Sancho, "when I saw this glowing
sun of Lady Dulcinea del Toboso, it wasn't bright enough to cast any rays
at all, which must have been because her grace was busy sifting that wheat
I told you about, and the cloud of dust she raised was hanging in front of
her face and blocking the light."

"Sancho! Can you still seriously maintain," said Don Quijote, "and think, and believe, and stubbornly insist, that my lady Dulcinea was actually sifting wheat, that being a task and an occupation which flies in the face of everything truly important people do, and are required to do, they being created and reserved for far different occupations and amusements, activities which display their lofty status to any eye no matter how distant?! Ah, how badly you've kept in mind, Sancho, those verses of our immortal poet,[1] depicting how those four lovely nymphs behaved, emerging from their crystal home in the beloved River Tagus and seating themselves in a meadow, there to embroider the rich fabric which our poet's fertile invention paints for us, all spun and interwoven of gold and silk and pearls. And this or something like it must have been how my lady was occupied when you saw her, although the jealous spite of some evil enchanter seems to have interfered in all my affairs, changing and inverting that which, by rights, should give me pleasure, into forms wholly unlike those they truly possess, which makes me worry whether, in that history of my deeds, said now to be in print, if its author was by any chance a magician who is my enemy, he might not have substituted one thing for another, blending every truth with a thousand falsehoods and amusing himself with the narration of events totally unlike those which ought to be reported in the sequel to any truthful history. Oh Jealousy, seed of infinite evil and virtue's gnawing destroyer! Sancho, all vices carry with them some pleasure, but not Jealousy, which brings only bitterness, disgust, and rage."

"And I agree with you," responded Sancho, "and I think the saga or history about us the college graduate told us he'd seen must have tumbled my honor in the pig pen, rolly-polly, every way which way, like they say, here and there, all up and down the street. But by God I've never said a word against any enchanter, and I'm not rich enough so they'd be jealous — although it's true I'm pretty clever, and I'm something of a rascal, but all that's well hidden under this always easy and natural disguise of behaving like a fool. And even if all I was good for was my firm, fast, truthful belief in God and all the holy teachings of the Sacred Roman Catholic Church, because I do believe, plus the fact that I'm a mortal enemy of the Jews, as I am, all historians ought to be merciful and treat me well whenever they write anything. But let them say whatever they feel like, because I was born naked and that's what I still am: I don't lose anything, I don't win anything; and even if I see myself stuck into a book and passed all through this world, from one hand to another, I don't give a fig if they say whatever they want to about me."

"Now that reminds me, Sancho," said Don Quijote, "of what happened to a famous poet,[2] who's still alive, when he wrote a witty satire about all the courtesans and didn't mention a certain lady, who either was or wasn't, nobody knew, but when the lady saw that she hadn't been attacked along with the others she complained to the poet, asking him what it was about her that had led him to exclude her from the list, and telling him he had to revise the satire and put her in the new version, or else he'd better

---

1. Garcilaso de la Vega, in Égloga [Eclogue] III, ll.57ff [Translator's Note].
2. Uncertain; perhaps Vicente Espinel, who in 1578 published Sátira contra las damas de Sevilla [Satire on the Ladies of Seville] [Translator's Note].

watch out. So the poet did as she wanted, saying things about her that even a lady's maid wouldn't deserve, and she was perfectly satisfied to see herself famous for her infamy. They say the same thing about the shepherd who set fire to the famous Temple of Diana, considered one of the Seven Wonders of the world, and burned it to the ground, just so his name would live on through all time to come, and even though it was ordered that no one should ever repeat his name, either in speaking or in writing, so his wish would never be granted, everyone knew his name was Erostratus. I might also mention the great Emperor Charles the Fifth's Roman experience with a certain gentleman. He was anxious to see the celebrated Temple of the Rotunda — called in ancient times the Temple of All the Gods [Pantheon], and today by a far better name, All-Saints Church — which is the best-preserved of all the structures the pagans erected in Rome, as it is also the building which, today, best embodies its builders' grand splendor, and best merits its great fame, being shaped like half an orange, extraordinarily large, and beautifully brightly lit, although there is no light but that which comes through a window (better called a round skylight) set at its apex — and it was from this lofty vantage point that the Emperor gazed down at the building, with a Roman gentleman at his side, explaining the exquisite workmanship of that great structure and architectural wonder. When they'd come back down again, this gentleman said to the Emperor:

" 'Your Sacred Majesty, I thought a thousand times of clasping my arms around your Highness and throwing myself down from that skylight, leaving behind me a name the world would never forget.'

" 'I'm grateful to you,' replied the Emperor, 'for not having turned such a wicked idea into reality, so I will make sure that, from this day forward, you'll have no further need to test your loyalty, and I hereby order you never to speak to me again, nor ever to be anywhere when I am there.'

"And he supplemented these words with a handsome gift.

"What I mean, Sancho, is that the desire to become famous is a singularly powerful one. Why else do you think Horatius jumped off that bridge, right down into the depths of the Tiber, wearing a full suit of armor? What scorched Mucius's hand and arm?[3] What drove Curtius to throw himself into the fiery, yawning abyss that suddenly opened, right in the middle of Rome? What — in the face of all the signs and omens he'd seen, every one of them against him — made Caesar cross the Rubicon? And, to choose more modern examples, what swept away gallant Cortés' ships, out in the New World, and left him and his brave Spaniards high and dry, totally cut off? All these and a host of other magnificent exploits of all sorts are and were and always will be famous, longed for by men as a reward — their share of the immortality which famous deeds deserve — though Christians, Catholics, and knights errant are more concerned with eternal glory in ethereal and celestial realms, through all time to come, than in the vanity of a fame earned in this present, wholly finite day and age, a fame that, no matter how long it may last, must finally perish along with this world, the end of which has already been

---

3. C. Mucius Scaevola, who burned off his own right hand when his attempted assassination of King Porsena, then besieging Rome, failed [*Translator's Note*].

foretold. Thus, oh Sancho! whatever we do must not cross the boundaries set for us by the Christian religion, to which we adhere. By killing giants, we must also kill pride; so too we must kill jealousy with kindness and generosity; anger with tranquil actions and peace of mind; gluttony and laziness with abstinence and careful attention to duty; lechery and lewdness with devoted loyalty to those we have made mistress of our thoughts; and sloth by journeying all over the globe, seeking opportunities to act and then acting, not just as Christians, but as famous and worthy knights. And thus you see, Sancho, how we attain those heights of praise which carry us to fame."

"I've understood every word your grace has said," replied Sancho, "but just the same, I wish you'd smear up a doubt that, this very moment, has just popped into my head."

"You mean, *clear up*, Sancho," said Don Quijote. "But speak your piece, and I'll answer as best I can."

"So tell me, señor," Sancho went on, "these Julys and Augusts, and all those brave knights you've talked about, all of them dead — where are they now?"

"The pagans," answered Don Quijote, "are surely in Hell; the Christians, if they were good Christians, are either in Purgatory or in Heaven."

"That's fine," said Sancho, "but now tell me: in the tombs where the bodies of these great lords are lying, are there silver lamps burning in front of them, or are the chapel walls all lined with crutches, and shrouds, and locks of hair, and cut-off legs, and all kinds of wax eyes?"[4] And if not, what *are* they lined with?"

To which Don Quijote responded:

"Pagan tombs were usually magnificent temples: Julius Caesar's ashes were set on an immense stone pyramid, known in Rome, in our time, as 'Saint Peter's Needle'; Emperor Hadrian's tomb was a castle as vast as a large village, called in those days '*Moles Hadriani*' [Hadrian's Pile], and now known as the Castle of St. Angelo, in Rome; Queen Artemis buried her husband, Mausolos, in a tomb that was said to be one of the seven wonders of the world — but none of these tombs, and indeed none of all the many tombs built by the pagans, were ever lined with shrouds or the other offerings and signs we use to indicate that the bodies buried therein belonged to saints."

"I follow that," replied Sancho. "So now tell me: which is worth more, bringing a corpse back to life or killing a giant?"

"That's not hard to answer," responded Don Quijote. "Surely, bringing a corpse back to life."

"Ah-ha," said Sancho. "Now I've got you. So the fame of those who bring back the dead, and make the blind see, and straighten the lame, and cure the sick, and have lamps burning in front of their tombs, and have their chapels swarming with devoted people, all down on their knees, praying to these holy remains, has got to be a better fame — both in this world and in the next one — than that of all the pagan emperors and knights errant who are or ever have been in the world."

"Which is true, I admit it," replied Don Quijote.

---

4. Typical commemorative offerings [*Translator's Note*].

"Then all this fame, these honors, these privileges, or whatever they are," Sancho continued, "they all belong to the corpses and the holy remains of saints, who with the approval and license of our Holy Mother Church, have lamps, holy candles, shrouds, crutches, paintings, locks of hair, eyes, legs, all of which swell devotion and magnify their Christian fame; kings carry these corpses and these holy remains on their backs, and kiss broken bits of their bones, and use them to adorn and make magnificent their chapels and their most cherished altars — "

"Where is all this leading, Sancho?" said Don Quijote. "What are you trying to tell me?"

"What I want to say," answered Sancho, "is that we ought to try to be saints, because it won't take us as long to get the fame we're after: remember, señor, just yesterday, or maybe the day before, or anyway not so long ago that you couldn't put it that way, they canonized or beatified two barefooted little friars, and now it's good luck just to kiss and touch the iron chains they wound around their bodies, to torture themselves, and they're more worshipped, I hear, than Roland's sword, in the King's armory, may God keep him. So, my lord, it's better to be a humble little friar of whatever order you please than a brave erranting knight; God values two dozen whippings more than two thousand wounds from a lance, whether you give them to giants, or monsters, or some half-human beast."

"That's all absolutely true," replied Don Quijote, "but we can't all be friars, and God provides many roads for His chosen to ascend to Heaven. Knighthood too is a religion; there are saintly knights among the angels."

"Yes," answered Sancho, "but I've heard there are more friars in Heaven than knights errant."

"True," responded Don Quijote, "because there are many more in religious orders than there are in knightly ones."

"There are lots who go traveling," said Sancho.

"Lots," replied Don Quijote, "but not many who deserve to be called knights."

And in such conversations, and others like them, they passed that night and the following day, without experiencing anything worth telling, which much bothered Don Quijote. To make a long story short, at dawn the next day they saw the great city of Toboso, a sight which raised Don Quijote's spirits and lowered Sancho's, because he didn't know where Dulcinea lived, having never in his life seen her, any more than his master had. So they were both apprehensive, the one to see her, and the other because he hadn't ever seen her, nor could Sancho think what he would do when his master sent him into Toboso. In the end, Don Quijote decided to enter the city at night, so while waiting for their time to come they lingered in a nearby grove of oak trees, and then, when the hour had finally struck, they rode into Toboso, where adventures came to them that can indeed be considered adventures.

Chapter Nine

— which tells what it tells

"The hour of midnight had come,"[1] more or less, when Don Quijote and Sancho left the wood and entered Toboso. The whole town was serenely silent, because all its inhabitants were asleep and, as they say, snoring like logs. The night was reasonably clear, though Sancho wished it were totally dark, so he'd be able to use darkness as an excuse for his stupidity. The only sound to be heard was dogs barking, which deafened Don Quijote and worried Sancho. From time to time a donkey brayed, pigs grunted, cats miaowed, all of which cacophony of sounds, plus the night's deep silence, seemed ill omens to the lovestruck knight, but just the same he said to Sancho:

"Sancho, my son, take us to Dulcinea's palace, for who knows, perhaps we may find her still awake."

"What palace am I supposed to take us to, in the name of Heaven," replied Sancho, "when I saw the noble lady in a very tiny house?"

"She must have withdrawn, just at that moment," answered Don Quijote, "into one of her castle's small chambers, so she could entertain herself, alone with her attendants, as noble ladies and princesses so frequently do."

"Señor," said Sancho, "since your grace keeps insisting, in spite of me, that my lady Dulcinea's house is a castle, do you really think, at this hour, you're going to find the door open? And would it be a good idea to keep on knocking until finally they hear us and let us in, setting the whole place on its ears? Are we a pair of young fellows come calling on our mistresses, no matter how late, and expecting to be let in?"

"In any case, let's first find the castle," replied Don Quijote, "and then I'll tell you, Sancho, what we ought to do. But notice, Sancho, up ahead there a little: either that huge shape in the darkness must be Dulcinea's palace, or I'm not seeing straight."

"Then you lead the way, your grace," said Sancho, "and maybe that's what it'll be — though even if I see it with my eyes and touch it with my hands I'd just as soon believe it's her palace as I believe, right now, we're in broad daylight."

Don Quijote led the way and, after they'd gone roughly two hundred paces, and reached the great dark bulk, they saw a high tower and immediately realized the building was not a castle but the town's main church. So our knight said:

"We've hit upon the church, Sancho."

"I see it," answered Sancho. "And praise be to God we haven't hit on our own tombs, because it's not good to be walking near cemeteries at this time of night — and I've already told you, your grace, that unless I remember it wrong this lady's house has got to be in a dead-end street."

---

1. Proverbial first line of the enormously popular "Ballad of Count Claros of Montalbán" [*Translator's Note*].

"Damn you, you idiot!" said Don Quijote. "Where have you ever seen castles and royal palaces in dead-end streets?"

"Señor," replied Sancho, "to each its own. Maybe it's the custom, here in Toboso, to build palaces and grand buildings in dead-end streets, so please, your grace, let me hunt through these streets and alleys and see what I can find, because maybe in some odd corner I'll bump into this castle, which I'd just as soon see eaten by dogs, since it's been leading us up and down and all around the town."

"Speak respectfully, Sancho, when you speak of my lady's property," said Don Quijote. "Let's not spoil the party; let's not throw the baby away along with the bath water."

"I'll rein myself in," replied Sancho. "But how can I stand it, when your grace wants me to find our lady's house at midnight, and in the dark, when I've only seen it once in my life, and you yourself can't find it after seeing it, surely, millions and millions of times?"

"You'll drive me crazy, Sancho," said Don Quijote. "Now look, you heathen: haven't I told you a thousand times that never in all my life have I seen my matchless Dulcinea, nor ever crossed the threshold of her palace, and that I've fallen in love because of what I've heard of her celebrated beauty and wisdom?"

"I hear it now," responded Sancho, "and I tell you that, if your grace has never seen her, neither have I."

"That's impossible," replied Don Quijote, "because you told me you'd at least seen her sifting wheat, when you brought me her answer to the letter I sent you here to deliver."

"Don't pay any attention to that, señor," said Sancho, "because I have to tell you that my seeing her, and my bringing you her reply, is all hearsay, too, because I can recognize Lady Dulcinea just as easily as I can punch the sky."

"Sancho, Sancho," answered Don Quijote, "there are times for joking, and times when joking is a very bad idea indeed. Just because I say I've never seen or spoken to the lady who rules my heart is no reason for you to say you've never seen or spoken to her either, since the truth is, as you well know, exactly the opposite."

They were exchanging these observations when they saw, just passing by, a man with two mules, who, judging by the scraping sound of his plough as it dragged along the ground, had to be a peasant who'd gotten out of bed long before dawn, so he could get to work. Which turned out to be the case. He walked along, singing the ballad that says:

— It didn't go well, you Frenchmen, you Frenchmen,
When you came to Roncesvalles.[2]

"Oh Lord, Sancho," said Don Quijote, hearing this. "Will anything good ever happen to us, tonight! Don't you hear what this country fellow is singing?"

"I hear him," replied Sancho. "But what does our business have to do

2. The peasant is singing a version of one of the most popular ballads in the Carolingian cycle, "The Ballad of Count Guarinos."

with the hunt at Roncesvalles? He could just as well be singing the ballad of Calaínos,[3] for all the good or the harm in can do us."

Just then the peasant reached them, and Don Quijote asked:

"Can you tell us, my good friend, and may God be good to you, where we may find the matchless Princess Dulcinea's palace?"

"Sir," answered the young fellow, "I'm a stranger here myself, and I've been in this town only a few days, working in a rich farmer's fields. This house opposite is where the town priest and the sexton live: I'm sure either of them could tell you where you'd find this princess, because they have a list of all Toboso's inhabitants — though it seems to me there isn't a single princess anywhere around here. There are lots of ladies, yes, from fine families, and I suppose each of them might be a princess in her own house."

"The princess I asked about," said Don Quijote, "must be one of those ladies."

"Maybe so," answered the young man. "But goodbye to you, because I see the dawn coming."

And whipping up his mules, he waited for no further questions. Sancho could see how baffled and unhappy his master had become, so he said:

"My lord, it won't be long before dawn, and it wouldn't be right for the sun to find us still out in the street. It would be better to go back out of the city and for your grace to hide yourself in some nearby forest; I will return here during the day, and there won't be a corner in this whole town where I don't go hunting for my lady's house, or castle, or palace, and it would be a great shame if I don't find it — and when I do find it, I'll speak to her grace and tell her where and under what circumstances you're waiting for her to arrange some plan for seeing her, without risking her honor and good name."

"Sancho," said Don Quijote, "you've compressed much wisdom into a few brief words: I have been longing for just such advice as you've now given me, and I accept it with great pleasure. Let us go then, my son, and find a place where I may conceal myself, and you will come back here, as you have said, to find, to see, and to speak with my lady, from whose wisdom and courtesy I expect rewards which amount to far more than mere miracles."

Sancho was fairly bursting to get his master out of the city, so Don Quijote would not discover that the reply supposedly carried back to the Sierra Morena by his squire was in fact a pretense. He hurried them off, and two miles down the road found a convenient wood, almost a forest, in which Don Quijote hid himself while Sancho went back to the city, intending to speak to Dulcinea, in the course of which mission things happened which require renewed attention as well as a new chapter.

---

3. The Moor Calaínos killed Valdovinos, but was killed by Roland [*Translator's Note*].

Chapter Ten

*— in which we are told how skillfully Sancho enchanted
the lady Dulcinea, along with other events quite as
ridiculous as truthful*

As the author of this great history reaches the events narrated in this chapter, he records that he would have liked to pass over them in silence, afraid that no one would believe him, for here Don Quijote's madness reaches almost unimaginable levels, and then goes still farther. But, in the end, although haunted by this fear, this self-mistrust, he wrote it all down exactly as it happened, neither adding nor subtracting from his history a single atom of truth, utterly indifferent to the possibility of being called a liar — and he was right to do so, for although truth may be stretched and grow thin, it does not break, flowing along over any and all lies like oil on water.

And so, continuing his story, he records that as soon as Don Quijote concealed himself in the wood, or oak grove, or forest, near the great metropolis of Toboso, he ordered Sancho to return to the city and not return to his presence without having first spoken, on his master's behalf, to his master's lady, begging her to allow her captive knight to see her and to deign to give him her blessing, after which Don Quijote would be able to look forward to the highest degree of success in every encounter and difficult task he might undertake. Sancho promised to do as he had been commanded, and to come back bearing as fine a response as he had brought the first time.

"Go now, my son," said Don Quijote, "nor quail when you find yourself standing in the full unimpeded light of that beauty which you go to seek. Luckiest of all squires in the world! Fix in your mind, and let no detail slip away, just how she receives you, whether her face changes color when you're giving her my message; whether she is disturbed and disquieted, hearing my name; whether she rests uneasy on her cushion, should you chance to find her seated on the rich dais suitable to her rank; and, if not, if she is standing, note whether she shifts back and forth from one foot to the other; whether or not she repeats her reply for you, two or even three times over; whether she swings from tenderness to harshness, from sharpness to loving-kindness; whether her hand reaches up to tidy her hair, although it suffers from no disarray; and, in a word, my son, note her every action, her every movement, for if you tell them to me exactly as they were I will understand how, in the hidden depths of her heart, she feels about my love for her, for you must realize, Sancho, if you don't already, that it is by their exterior actions and movements, when their love is at issue, that lovers truly reveal the innermost feelings of their hearts. Go, my friend, and may you be guided by better fortune than I possess, and may you return after better success than I dare to anticipate, fearful and yet expectant in this bitter solitude in which, now, you leave me."

"I'm going, and I'll come right back," said Sancho, "so let that little heart of yours take a couple of good breaths, your grace, even though, right now, it's more the size of a hazel nut than a heart, and keep in mind that they always say a good heart wins out over bad luck, and when there's no pig, there's no fence, and they also say that just when you don't expect it, you find a hare jumping out. I say this because we didn't find my lady's palace or castle, tonight, but now it's daytime and I expect to find it, maybe just when I don't expect to — and once I find it, you just leave her to me."

"Indeed, Sancho," said Don Quijote, "since you always bring in those proverbs of yours right on the mark, no matter what we're talking about, maybe God will grant me better fortune in attaining what I desire."

This said, Sancho wheeled around, whipping up his donkey, and Don Quijote stayed where he was, mounted on Rocinante and leaning down against the stirrups and his spear, his head full of melancholy, uncertain ideas, and there we will leave him and travel on with Sancho Panza, who had ridden off no less confused and pensive than his master — so much so that, barely out of the wood, he turned his head and, having made sure that Don Quijote was not in sight, he climbed down from his donkey, seated himself at the base of a tree, and began to conduct the following conversation with himself:

"So: inform us, please, brother Sancho, where your grace is going. Are you hunting for some lost donkey?"

"No, certainly not."

"Then, what is it you're looking for?"

"I'm hunting — and, God help me, there's nothing funny about it — a princess, the shining sun of beauty and of all Heaven, too."

"And where do you expect to find this princess you're talking about, Sancho?"

"Where? In the great city of Toboso."

"But tell me: on whose behalf are you hunting her?"

"On behalf of that famous knight, Don Quijote de La Mancha, who undoes wrongs, and provides food for the thirsty and drink for the hungry."

"Oh, that's wonderful, wonderful. And do you know where this princess lives, Sancho?"

"My master says it must be some royal palace, or maybe a magnificent castle."

"Have you, by any chance, ever seen this lady?"

"I haven't ever seen her, and neither has my master."

"So do you think it would be right and reasonable if the people in this city, knowing you'd come here, intending to fool around with their princesses and upset their ladies, came after you and beat in your ribs with big thick sticks, till you hadn't a sound bone in your body?"

"They'd in fact have every right to do exactly that, unless they knew I was here under orders, and that

> You're just a messenger, my friend,
> And nothing's your fault — nothing."[1]

"Don't be too sure about that, Sancho, because these Manchegan people are just as hot-tempered as they are proud, and they won't stand for

---

1. From a ballad about Bernardo del Carpio, the legendary Spanish hero who killed Roland.

anything from anybody. By God, if they sniff you out, it isn't going to be much fun: Get out of here, you son of a bitch! Back where you came from, halfwit!"

"No! Why should I buy into so much trouble, just to please someone else? And looking for a lady named Dulcinea, here in Toboso, would be like looking for one Marica out of all the Maricas in Ravenna, or maybe for a college graduate in Salamanca. It's the devil, by God, the devil himself who's gotten me into all this! It can't be anybody else!"

Which was how Sancho held his soliloquy with himself, and it led him to declare:

"Okay: there's a cure for everything — except death, because he gets to throw his yoke on all of us, no matter what, when we get to the end of the road. Now this master of mine has proved a thousand times over he's a raving lunatic, and me, I'm not much better — in fact, when I follow along after him, and I serve him, I'm a worse fool than he is, if the old saying still holds true: 'Tell me who you hang out with, and I'll tell you what you are' — and that other one, 'Your father doesn't count as much as your fodder.' So if he's crazy, and he is, and if craziness makes you look at one thing and see another, and it makes you say white is black and black is white — the way he did when he said those windmills were giants, and those monks' big mules were camels, and those flocks of sheep were enemy armies, and all kinds of nonsense like that — it shouldn't be hard to convince him that some peasant girl, the first one I bump into around here, is his Lady Dulcinea — and if he doesn't believe it, I'll swear it's true — and if he swears she isn't, I'll swear she is — and if he's stubborn, I'll be stubborner, and that's the way I'll come out on top, no matter what happens. Who knows? Maybe if I beat him, this time, he'll stop sending me out like an errand boy. Or maybe, when he sees what awful stuff I come back with — and this is really what I expect will happen — he'll think some wicked magician, one of those he's always saying have it in for him, has transformed his beautiful lady into the dog I bring him, out of sheer spite."

This thought put Sancho Panza's mind at ease, and he considered his business as good as done with; he lingered right where he was until morning had passed into afternoon, so Don Quijote would think he'd had time to go to Toboso and come back again; and things worked out so nicely that, when he finally stood up and started to mount his donkey, he saw not one but three peasant girls riding out of Toboso on three jackasses, or maybe three she-asses (our author isn't entirely clear on this point, and though we can logically suspect they were she-asses, since that's what village girls usually ride, we won't go into the subject any more deeply, because there's no need to completely nail it down). And as soon as Sancho saw these three girls, he was off like a shot, after his master, and found Don Quijote sighing and murmuring a thousand amorous laments. Seeing Sancho, our knight called out:

"What's up, friend Sancho? Is this a day I'll have to mark with a white stone or a black one?"

"Your grace ought to mark it in red, the way they write winners' names on the wall at the university, so no one can miss the news."

"If that's how it is," said Don Quijote, "you must be bringing good tidings."

"So good," replied Sancho, "that all your grace has to do is spur Rocinante and ride out in the open and you'll see your Lady Dulcinea del Toboso, who's coming, with two other damsels, expressly to see your grace."

"Mother of God! What are you saying, Sancho, my friend?" said Don Quijote. "Now, don't play any tricks on me — don't try to relieve my very real sadnesses with false happinesses."

"What good would it do me to trick your grace," replied Sancho, "especially when it won't take you long to find out if I'm telling the truth or not? Go on, my lord, spur your horse and come, and you'll see the princess, our mistress, all dressed up and hung with jewels — or, in other words, like the princess she is. She and her damsels are a glowing golden ember, all clusters of pearls — all diamonds, all rubies, all folds of brocade worked to ten layers deep;[2] their hair hangs loose down their shoulders, like so many sunbeams playing in the wind; and, most impressively of all, they're riding on three spotted palsies — the best ones you've ever seen."

"You mean *palfreys*, Sancho."

"What's the difference?" replied Sancho. "Palsies, palfreys: whatever they're riding, they're the most elegant ladies you could ask for, especially the Princess Dulcinea, my lady, who's absolutely overwhelming."

"Let's go then, Sancho, my son," answered Don Quijote, "and to celebrate such unexpected good news, I hereby promise you the best booty I win in the very first adventure I have, and if that's not what you want, I'll promise you, instead, all the foals dropped by my three mares, which as you know are at home, grazing on our village common."

"Let it be the foals," replied Sancho, "because who can be sure the spoils of the first adventure will be any good?"

So they rode out of the wood and saw the three village girls close by. Don Quijote looked up and down the road to Toboso and, since he could see nothing but the three girls, became confused and asked Sancho whether he'd left Dulcinea and her damsels outside the city.

"What are you talking about, outside the city?" Sancho answered. "Are your grace's eyes by any chance in the back of your head? Don't you see them coming, right here, glittering like the sun at high noon?"

"All I can see, Sancho," said Don Quijote, "is three village girls on three donkeys."

"God save me from Satan's grip!" replied Sancho. "Is it really possible that three palfreys, or whatever you call them, all white as snowflakes, look like donkeys to your grace? In the name of God, I'll pull out my beard if that's what they are!"

"But I'm telling you, Sancho, my friend," said Don Quijote, "that they're as truly jack-asses, or she-asses, as I'm Don Quijote and you're Sancho Panza. At any rate, that's what they look like to me."

---

2. Sancho knowingly exaggerates, three layers being the absolute (and most costly) maximum [*Translator's Note*].

"Be quiet, my lord," said Sancho, "don't say such a thing, but get your eyes screwed on right and come and show the respect you owe to the lady of your thoughts, for here she comes."

And as he spoke, he rode out to meet the three girls: he dismounted from his donkey, took one of the three donkeys by the halter and, as he knelt on the ground, declared:

"Queen and princess and duchess of beauty, may your high and mightiness be pleased to acknowledge, in graciousness and kindly feeling, your captive knight, who greets you, there, as if turned to stone, confused and breathless at finding himself in your glorious presence. I am his squire, Sancho Panza, and he is that wondrous knight, Don Quijote de La Mancha, also known as the Knight of the Sad Face."

By this point, Don Quijote had dismounted and fallen to his knees alongside Sancho, his eyes bulging and his face contorted as he stared up at the girl Sancho was calling a queen and a princess, and since all he could see was an ordinary village girl, and not a very pretty one, with a pug face and a stubby nose, he was considerably perplexed and uncomprehending, though he did not dare open his mouth. The girls were quite as astonished as he was, seeing two such different-looking men kneeling in the road, stopping one of them from riding on, but the girl who had been chosen broke the silence, both coarsely and crossly, saying:

"God damn it, get out of the road and let us alone — we're in a hurry."

To which Sancho replied:

"Oh mighty princess and noble lady of Toboso! Is your merciful heart not softened, seeing before you and on his knees, in your exalted presence, the very pillar and support of all knight errantry?"

When the other two heard this speech, they cried out:

"Hey, go soak your head, you horse's ass! You think you can come pull the wool over our eyes, on account of we're country girls? Well, we know all about you smart-asses! Get out of the road, and let us alone, or else watch out."

"Rise, Sancho," said Don Quijote, hearing this, "for it's easy to see that Fortune, unwearied in its persecution of me, stands blocking every road by which this wretched soul of mine may experience any shred of worldly happiness. But you, Dulcinea! Oh most precious of all, absolute height of womanly nobility, sole and solitary solace of this sorrowful heart which utterly adores you! How this savage magician persists in harassing me, beclouding my eyes with cataracts which transform — as they and nothing else could do! — your matchless beauty, your peerless face, into that of a poor peasant girl, and perhaps changed me, too, into some horrible monster, to make me loathsome in your eyes! But please: give me a gentle and loving look; see, in this submissive posture I have assumed before your disguised and undone loveliness, with what perfect meekness I adore you from the very depths of my soul."

"Hey, try that on my grandpa!" answered the girl. "You can really spin out a line! So now get out of the way and let us by, and we'll say thank you and pretty please."

Sancho stepped aside to let her pass, satisfied that he'd gotten himself out of trouble.

The girl to whom he'd assigned the role of Dulcinea no sooner saw herself free than, spurring her *palsy* with a pointed stick, she sent the animal running across the meadow. But since she'd jabbed the donkey unusually hard and painfully, it began to buck so violently that it flung our lady Dulcinea to the ground, and Don Quijote immediately ran to help her up, while Sancho busied himself tightening her packsaddle, which had slid under the donkey's belly. When this had been accomplished, and Don Quijote went to take his enchanted lady in his arms and lift her onto her donkey, said damsel scrambled to her feet unaided and made his intended labor unnecessary, stepping back a bit and then, running rapidly forward, setting her hands on the donkey's haunches and dropping onto its back as lightly as a hawk, sitting astride like a man, at which Sancho exclaimed:

"By all that's holy, but our lady's lighter than a falcon: she could teach the best Cordoban or Mexican riders a thing or two about getting up on a horse! She jumped right over the saddle-hump, and even without spurs she's got that palfrey galloping like a zebra. And those damsels of hers aren't wasting any time, either — they're all racing like the wind."

Which was the truth: the moment they'd seen Dulcinea up on her donkey, the others dashed along behind her and all of them galloped out of sight, covering a good two miles before they so much as turned their heads to look behind them. Don Quijote watched them go, and when he could no longer see them turned to Sancho and said:

"So now do you understand, Sancho, how passionately these magicians hate me? Just think the malicious lengths they go to, carrying out their grudge — even cheating me of the chance to see my lady as she really is. Truly, I was brought into this world to show what real misery can be, to serve as target practice for the arrows of evil fortune. And I must also point out to you, Sancho, that for these traitors it was not enough to have utterly transformed my Dulcinea — no, they had to turn her into someone as ugly and vulgar as that village girl, and at the same time deprive her of that prime characteristic of all noble ladies, namely their lovely scent, which they acquire naturally, spending so much of their time among perfumes and flowers. Because I have to tell you, Sancho, that when I went to help Dulcinea back onto her palfrey — which is what you say the animal was, though to me it looked like a plain she-ass — I was struck by a blast of raw garlic that almost snuffed me out and poisoned my heart."

"What swine!" Sancho exclaimed. "Oh, you fateful, wicked enchanters, if only I could see every one of you strung up by the gills, like sardines on a stick! You know so much; you can do so much; and you possess even more. It ought to be enough for you, you scoundrels, to have turned my lady's pearl-like eyes into cork-tree nuts, and the pure gold of her hair into the red bristles on a pig's tail, without messing with her smell, too — for that could have led us to what lay underneath all that ugly bark. And yet, to speak truthfully, to me she did not seem ugly, for all I could see was her beauty, which was perfected and made transcendent by a mole just to the right of her mouth, moustache-like, from which grew seven or eight red hairs almost a foot long, like strands of gold."

"Since moles on the face must correspond to those on the body," said

Don Quijote, "Dulcinea must have another mole of the same size on her thigh, and on the same side, though the hairs you speak of are distinctly longer than usual."

"Well, all I can tell you, your grace," answered Sancho, "is they looked as if she'd been born with them."

"I'm sure they did, my friend," replied Don Quijote, "for by her very nature Dulcinea could have nothing imperfect or unfinished, so that even if she had a hundred moles like the one you describe, on her they would not be mere moles but veritable moons and resplendent stars. But tell me, Sancho: that thing you tightened, which to me seemed like a packsaddle, was it actually a saddle or a ladies' sidesaddle?"

"Neither," answered Sancho, "but a high-backed, short-stirruped saddle, covered by a cloth so richly made it must be worth half a kingdom."

"And I could not see a bit of it!" said Don Quijote. "I must repeat, and I will say it a thousand times over, that I am surely the most unfortunate of men."

Our cunning Sancho had a hard time smothering his laughter, hearing what nonsense his deftly deceived master was babbling. Finally, after a good deal more talking, they remounted their animals and went down the road toward Zaragoza, which they planned to reach in time for a high festival celebrated every year in that famous city. But things happened to them — many things, both important and unique — before they got there, which are worthy of being recorded and read, as you will soon see.

Chapter Eleven

— Don Quijote's strange adventure with a cart, or wagon, belonging to Parliament of Death

Don Quijote rode along, deeply absorbed in reflections about the savage joke played on him by the magicians, in thus turning his lady Dulcinea into an ugly village girl, and trying, unsuccessfully, to think of some way to transform her back to her proper shape, and these thoughts so gripped him that, not knowing he did so, he dropped Rocinante's reins and the horse, suddenly aware of his new freedom, kept stopping to graze on the green grass so abundant in those fields. Seeing his master so carried away by his thoughts, Sancho turned and said:

"My lord, melancholy was made for men, not animals, but men who give way to it turn themselves into animals. Get hold of yourself, your grace, and be yourself, and take up Rocinante's reins, and wake up, take heart, and show the spirit that all knights errant must possess. What the devil is this? Why such a fit of sadness? Are we here where we are, or somewhere off in France? Let Satan carry off all the Dulcineas in the world, for the well-being of any knight errant is worth more than all the spells and enchantments on earth."

"Be still, Sancho," replied Don Quijote, his voice not at all faint-hearted. "Be still, I say, and speak no blasphemy against that enchanted lady, for her misfortune and mischance are strictly my responsibility: her bad luck stems directly from those wicked magicians' hatred of me."

"I agree," replied Sancho. " 'Who could keep from tears, who has seen her before, and must see her now?' "[1]

"Ah, you can indeed say that, Sancho," answered Don Quijote, "since you saw her in the fullness of her beauty, nor was the magician concerned to cloud your vision or cover her beauty from your eyes: the power of his venom was directed solely at me, and against my eyes alone. But, in any case, I've thought of one way in which, surely, you inaccurately painted her beauty for me, because unless I remember it wrongly you said her eyes were like pearls, and eyes that resemble pearls belong on a sea bream, not on a lady, and it seems to me that Dulcinea's eyes must be more like green emeralds, almond-shaped, with two heavenly arches for eyebrows, so let's take those pearls away from her eyes and confer them upon her teeth, which was surely a mistaken exchange on your part, Sancho, taking her eyes for her teeth."

"That may very well be," answered Sancho, "because her beauty confused me just the way her ugliness did you, your grace. But let's leave everything in God's hands, for He knows what is meant to happen, in this vale of tears, this world of ours, where there's almost nothing untainted by evil, deception, and wickedness. There's one thing that bothers me too, my lord, more than anything else, which is what happens when your grace conquers some giant, or some other knight, and has to make him present himself before our beautiful Lady Dulcinea — and where can this wretched giant, this poor, miserable knight, expect to find her? I can almost see them wandering up and down, all over Toboso, looking for Lady Dulcinea, and even if they bumped into her, right in the middle of the street, they'd no more know who she was than they would my father."

"Perhaps, Sancho," responded Don Quijote, "perhaps the enchantment doesn't extend that far, and wouldn't deprive conquered giants, or knights, of the true sight of Dulcinea, and to be sure of this we'll have to make an experiment and order the first couple of them I conquer and send off to her to come back and tell me what they found when they got there."

"Now that," said Sancho, "seems to me an extremely good idea, your grace, because this plan will get us exactly the information we want, so if it's really just you, your grace, that's enchanted, your misfortune will be lots greater than hers, and, just as long as Lady Dulcinea stays happy and healthy, we'll keep on doing the best we can, hunting for adventures and letting Time do what he wants to — because Time's the best doctor for these maladies, and for worse ones, too."

Don Quijote was intending to reply to Sancho Panza, but he was stopped by a cart that was coming out across the road, loaded with the wildest, strangest shapes and figures anyone could ever imagine. Guiding the mules, and serving as the driver, was an ugly demon. (It was an open cart, without a canopy or any other covering on the top or sides.) The first figure Don Quijote's eyes encountered was no less than Death himself, though with a human face, and next to him an angel with great painted wings; next to him was an emperor wearing his crown, which looked exactly like gold; at Death's feet was the god called Cupid, not blindfolded but carrying his bow and his quiver full of arrows. There was also a knight,

---

1. Sancho bends to his purposes here an old Spanish proverb.

armored all in white but wearing neither crest nor helmet, only a hat covered with vari-colored feathers, plus others wearing different costumes and with their faces differently painted. Seen so unexpectedly, this sight upset Don Quijote and terrified Sancho, but our knight immediately took heart, thinking that here was a new and dangerous adventure, so with this in mind, and a spirit ready to deal with any peril, he set himself in the cart's path and declared, his voice loud and menacing:

"Cartman, coachman, or devil, or whatever you are, tell me here and now who in fact you are, and where you're going, and who are these people you're carrying in your wagon, which looks a good deal more like Charon's ferry than the carts employed by men."

The Devil meekly stopped his cart and answered:

"Sir, we are actors in Angulo el Malo's company. This morning, today being the eighth day after Corpus Christi, we've been in a village just over that hill, putting on a play called *Las Cortes de la Muerte*[2] [Parliament of Death], which we have to present, again, in that village right over there, and since it's already very nearly time, to save ourselves the trouble of undressing and dressing all over again, we are traveling in the costumes in which we'll be acting. This boy plays the role of Death; that one, an Angel; that woman, who is our director's wife, plays the part of the Queen; that fellow acts the Soldier's role; that one, the Emperor; and I play the Demon, one of the leading parts, for in this company I always do lead roles. If your grace wishes to know anything else, you have only to ask me, and whatever I know I will tell you right away, for being, as I am, a Demon, I know everything."

"By my faith as a knight errant," replied Don Quijote, "when I saw this cart I thought I was about to have some grand adventure, but now I must say that a man needs to touch mere appearances with his hand, to keep from being deceived. Go with God, good folk, and put on your play, and keep in mind that, should there be anything useful I can do for you, please command me and I will do it most willingly, for I have been all my life a devoted play-goer, and indeed as a young man I was particularly fascinated by everything theatrical."

As they were talking, Fate led one of the company, dressed as a clown, wearing many jingling bells and carrying three inflated ox-bladders at the point of a stick, to come over to Don Quijote and begin to perform, waving his rod and banging the ground with the ox-bladders, leaping up and down, shaking his bells — an unpleasant spectacle for Rocinante who, before Don Quijote could stop him, took the bit between his teeth and began to dash across the fields, running far more swiftly than his old bones had ever suggested he could. Thinking his master in danger of being thrown, Sancho jumped off the donkey and ran to save him, but by the time the squire got there the knight lay on the ground, with Rocinante alongside him, horse and master having come toppling down — the usual outcome and stopping-point, when Rocinante began frisking about and acting particularly dashing and bold.

But no sooner had the squire leaped off his donkey than the dancing

2. Perhaps the play, so titled, by Lope de Vega. Andrés de Angulo was a late-sixteenth-century theatrical manager [*Translator's Note*].

demon who'd been wielding ox-bladders took Sancho's place on the animal's back and, banging away with the bladders, set the animal dashing across the fields — driven more by fear, and the noise, than by the pain of the blows — toward the village where the company was to perform. Sancho saw both what was happening to his donkey and what had happened to his master, and couldn't decide which one of these problems he should tackle first, but as a good squire, and a good servant, in the end his love for his master prevailed over his fondness for the donkey — although he not only felt it keenly, but thought he would die, every time he saw the bladders lift up and crash down on his donkey's haunches, for he'd rather have had those blows landing on the very apple of his eyes than on the smallest hair in his donkey's tail. Beset by such a confused jumble of concerns, he reached the spot where his master lay — in considerably worse shape than he could have wished — and, helping him up on Rocinante, declared:

"My lord, the devil's carried off my donkey."

"What devil?" asked Don Quijote.

"The one with the ox-bladders," replied Sancho.

"Then I'll get him back," said Don Quijote, "even if he locks himself up in the deepest, darkest dungeons in Hell. Follow after me, Sancho: the cart is moving slowly, and I'll take one of its mules, to make amends for the loss of your donkey."

"You won't need to take the trouble, my lord," responded Sancho. "Stay calm, because I can see the devil's gotten off the donkey, who's coming back where he belongs."

Which was indeed what was happening, because the devil and the donkey had fallen down, in imitation of Don Quijote and Rocinante, and now the devil was making the rest of his journey on foot, while the donkey was returning to his master.

"That's all very well," said Don Quijote, "but some of those people in the cart should pay for that devil's rudeness — by God, I'd punish the emperor himself."

"Don't even think about it, your grace," answered Sancho. "You just listen to me, and don't get involved with actors, because they've got connections. I've seen an actor arrested for a pair of murders, who got off scot free and didn't even have to pay court costs. Remember, your grace, these are cheerful people who make everybody happy, so everybody takes care of them, everybody protects them, and helps them, and thinks well of them, especially when they're a royal company, or officially licensed, in which case all of them — anyway, most of them — dress and strut around like princes."

"Just the same," replied Don Quijote, "I don't have to let that actor devil go off boasting, even if the whole human race is on his side."

So saying, he swung Rocinante around toward the cart, which was by this point approaching the village. And riding rapidly in that direction, he called out:

"Halt, wait, all you happy, laughing fellows, because I'm going to teach you how you have to treat donkeys and any other animals that the squires of knights errant ride on."

Don Quijote was shouting so loudly that the people in the cart heard and understood him, and judging from the knight's words what he had in mind, Death jumped right out of the cart, and the Emperor right behind him, and then the Devil driver, and the Angel, nor did the Queen and the god Cupid remain behind, and all of them took up rocks and stones and set themselves in a line, ready to welcome Don Quijote with the points of their pebbles. Seeing them in such a gallant formation, arms cocked to hurl their stones with as much force as possible, Don Quijote pulled back on the reins and began to consider how the business could be managed with the least risk to himself. As he sat there, Sancho came up and, seeing that his master was preparing to attack so well-formed a defensive position, said:

"It would be the height of folly to even attempt such a business. Just consider, your grace, my lord, that when stones are coming down in showers there's nothing in the world that can protect you, except crawling under a big brass bell and hiding inside. And you should also keep in mind that it's foolhardy, not brave, for a single man to attack an army in which Death is a soldier, and Emperors themselves fight, and both good and bad Angels stand ready to help — and if this isn't enough to make you back off, perhaps it will be if you note that, without any question, among all of those arrayed there, though they may look like kings, and princes, and emperors, there's not a single knight errant to be found."

"Now there," said Don Quijote, "you've raised an issue that can, and which should, make me change my mind. I neither can nor should raise my sword, as I myself have often told you, against anyone who has not been dubbed a knight. So then, Sancho, if you want to take revenge for the injury done to your donkey, it's entirely up to you, though I can remain here and assist you with cries of encouragement and with advice."

"I don't need to take revenge on anyone, my lord," replied Sancho, "because good Christians don't need vengeance for the wrongs done them, especially since we've agreed, me and my donkey, that any insult done him is for me to decide about, and as far as I'm concerned all that matters is living peacefully for as long as Heaven lets me."

"If that's your decision," answered Don Quijote, "my good Sancho, my wise Sancho, my Christian Sancho, my honest Sancho, let's turn our backs on these actors and go in search of better, more suitable adventures, because from what I've seen around here, there won't be any shortage of them — and marvelous ones, to boot."

He swung his steed around, Sancho went and got his donkey, Death and his whole squadron climbed into their cart and went on their way, and the adventure with Death's cart thus came to a happy ending, thanks to the sensible advice Sancho Panza gave his master — who proceeded, the very next day, to experience yet another adventure, with an impassioned knight errant, which was no less dramatic than the one just completed.

Chapter Twelve

— *the strange adventure experienced by our valiant Don Quijote with the brave Knight of the Mirrors*

The day after the encounter with Death had turned into night, and Don Quijote and his squire were sitting under a group of tall, dark trees, Sancho having persuaded his master to dine off some of the supplies carried by the donkey, and as they ate Sancho said to his lord:

"Señor, what an idiot I'd have been, to take the spoils of your grace's first adventure as my reward, instead of the three foals! It's true, you know, that a bird in the hand is worth two in the bush."

"All the same," replied Don Quijote, "if you'd let me attack them, Sancho, as I wanted to, you'd have had as your spoils, at the very least, the Emperor's gold crown and Cupid's painted wings, because I'd have wrenched them off and placed them in your hands."

"Emperors' crowns and sceptres, when the emperors are actors," replied Sancho Panza, "are never made of real gold, but only tin and tinsel."

"Which is true," responded Don Quijote, "because it would be improper for the stage props to be real, rather than make-believe and mere semblances of reality, as the plays themselves are — and I should like you, Sancho, to feel well disposed to the drama, just as I should like you to be toward those who stage and act in plays, as well as those who write them, because they are all united in contributing highly useful things to our country, constantly holding a mirror in front of us, wherein we may see vivid images of our human existence, for nothing so clearly presents us to ourselves the way we really are as do plays and players. And if you don't agree, then tell me: haven't you seen plays showing us kings, emperors, and popes, knights, ladies, and all sorts of other people? One actor plays the villain, another a liar; this one acts the part of a shopkeeper, and that one portrays a soldier; this one is a wise fool, and the other one is a foolish lover; and then the play is over, and they all take off their costumes — and they're all just actors, each every bit as good as the other."

"I've seen that," replied Sancho.

"Well, exactly the same thing happens," said Don Quijote, "in that comedy which is the way of the world, where some of us play at being emperors, others at being popes, and, to make a long story short, at all the different roles there can be, in a comedy. But when that comedy comes to its end — that is, when life is over — death takes away the costumes by which we tell one from another, and in the grave everyone is equal."

"A wonderful comparison," said Sancho, "though not so novel that I haven't heard it many, many times, just as I've heard life compared to a chess game: before the game's completed, each piece has its own role to play, but once it's over all the pieces are dropped into the same bag and jumbled together, which is just the way life comes to its end in the grave."

"Sancho," said Don Quijote, "with every day that passes you're becoming less like a fool and more like a wise man."

"Yes, some of your grace's wisdom has got to rub off on me," replied Sancho, "for land that's dry and unfruitful will give you good crops, if you put on enough manure, and weed it, and till it. I mean, your grace's words have been like manure spread on the barren ground of my dry and uncultivated mind; all the time I've spent in your service, and in contact with you, has been like weeding and tilling; so I hope, in the end, I can sprout blessed fruits which, God willing, will neither be unworthy nor fall away from the pathways of good breeding which your grace has created in my dry and dusty mind."

Don Quijote smiled at Sancho's affected speech, realizing that what he'd said about his improvement was true, because from time to time our knight was astonished at things his squire said — though most of the time, when Sancho tried to talk like what he wasn't, and appear to be a gentleman courtier, sooner or later his words rolled him down from the heights of simplicity to the depths of ignorance, for he showed himself most elegant, and most learned, when he made use of sayings and proverbs, whether or not they had anything to do with the matter at hand — exactly as we have seen and will continue to see in the narration of this history.

They spent most of the night discussing these and other matters, but then Sancho felt the need to close the hatches over his eyes (as he used to say when he wanted to sleep), so he took everything off the donkey's back and turned him loose to graze as he pleased. He did not remove Rocinante's saddle, because his master had expressly ordered that so long as they were in the field, or not sleeping under a roof, Rocinante should not be disburdened: from time immemorial, knights errant had removed their horse's bridle and hung it from the saddlebow — but unsaddle the horse? Heaven forbid! So Sancho did as he'd been told, and let Rocinante too go grazing at will, for between the two animals there existed so strong and special a friendship that, according to rumor, it was a tradition passed down from father to son, and indeed the author of this truthful history penned a number of chapters specifically on the subject, but in the name of the dignity and decorum due to such a heroic tale he felt himself obliged to exclude them — though at times he forgets this resolve and tells us how close the two animals were, each helping the other to properly scratch himself, and how, when they were tired and well-fed, Rocinante would lay his neck across the donkey's (and it stuck out a foot and a half on the other side) and the two of them would stand there, contemplating the ground, sometimes for three days on end, or at least for as long as they were allowed to, or they weren't driven apart by hunger.

They also say that our author penned a comparison between their friendship and that of Nisus and Euryalus, and Pylades and Orestes,[1] and if that is true it's easy enough to see, and for all the world to admire, how unwavering was the friendship between these two peaceful animals, much to the embarrassment of human beings, who keep their friendships so very badly. Which is why it was said:

> Friends are friends no longer:
> Sticks have now become spears.

---

1. From Virgil's *Aeneid* and Greek legend, respectively [*Translator's Note*].

And as someone else has sung:

> Friends have to be careful of friends, etc.[2]

Nor should anyone think our author guilty of digressing, in thus comparing these animals' friendship to that of human beings, for animals have frequently put humans on notice and taught them a great many important things, as for example: enemas, taught us by storks; vomiting and gratitude, taught us by dogs; watchfulness, taught us by cranes; foresight, taught us by ants; chastity, taught us by elephants; and loyalty, which we learned from horses.

So there was Sancho, sleeping at the foot of a cork tree, and Don Quijote dozing beneath a tall oak, but it was not long before our knight was awakened by a noise coming from behind them, at which he leaped up with a start and stood looking and listening to find out what it was, and saw two mounted men, one of whom flung himself out of the saddle, saying to the other:

"Dismount, my friend, and let the horses roam free, because I suspect there's plenty of grass for them, here, in addition to the silence and solitude my lovesick thoughts require."

He was stretching out on the ground even as he spoke, and as he dropped down his armor rattled and shook, clearly indicating to Don Quijote that he must be a knight errant, so going over to Sancho, who was still asleep, our knight took him by the arm and, with no little difficulty, managed to wake him, then said, in a low voice:

"Brother Sancho, we've got ourselves an adventure."

"God give us a good one," replied Sancho. "And where, my lord, your grace, is My Lady Adventure right now?"

"Where, Sancho?" answered Don Quijote. "Just turn your eyes and look, and you'll see a knight errant stretched out over there — and I don't think he's a particularly happy knight errant, because I saw him throw himself off his horse and stretch out on the ground with a considerable show of displeasure — indeed, he made his armor positively rattle."

"Then," said Sancho, "what makes your grace think this is to be an adventure?"

"I don't mean," responded Don Quijote, "that this will necessarily be a full-scale adventure, but only that it is the beginning of one, for this is exactly how adventures begin. But pay attention: as far as I can tell, he's tuning a lute, or perhaps a guitar, and from the way he's spitting and clearing his throat, he must be getting ready to sing something."

"By God, you're right," said Sancho. "He must be a lovesick knight."

"There isn't a knight errant who isn't," answered Don Quijote. "So let's listen to him, for, if he does sing, it will be a thread that leads us to the spool of his thoughts: an overflowing heart always speaks through the tongue."

Sancho was about to reply to his master, but was stopped by the voice

---

2. The first quotation is from a ballad included in Ginés Pérez de Hita's *Guerras civiles de Granada* [*Granada's Civil Wars*]; no source is known for the second, though the phrase seems to have been in popular use [*Translator's Note*].

— neither bad nor good — of the Knight of the Wood, and they listened with no little surprise, and heard the following sonnet:

> "Show me, my lady, some sign of the road
> I can follow to follow your will;
> I swear I'll do as I'm told
> In every detail, over vale and hill.
>   If you wish me dead, silent and still,
> Consider me long since cold;
> If you'd rather love than kill
> I'll sing you love in an antique mode.
>   My heart can show you the world's wide poles,
> Diamonds for hardness, softness like wax:
> The laws of love determine my heart,
>   Which is soft or hard, just as you ask,
> Printed, embossed, with all your art,
> Eternally yours, forever enscrolled."

And then, with an "Ah!" and an "Oh!" that seemed wrenched from the very bottom of his heart, the Knight of the Wood finished his song, but after a moment he declared, in a sorrowful, piteous voice:

"Oh most beautiful, most ungrateful woman in all the world! How can you, oh Your Highness Casildea de Vandalia, how can you allow your captive knight to waste away and perish in this endless wandering, in these harsh and rugged chores? Isn't it enough that I have forced all the knights of Navarre, and of León, and of Andalusia, and of Castille, and, finally, of La Mancha — forced each and all of them to acknowledge you as the most beautiful woman in the world?"

"Not a bit of it," said Don Quijote, hearing this, "because I'm from La Mancha, and I've never admitted anything of the sort, and I neither could nor should admit to anything so prejudicial to my own lady's loveliness — so you can easily see, Sancho, how this knight of ours is speaking absolute nonsense. But let's keep on listening, and perhaps he'll tell us something more."

"He will," replied Sancho, "because I think he plans to go on complaining, non-stop, for at least a month."

Which was not the case, for hearing people speaking from no great distance, the Knight of the Wood broke off his lamentation, got to his feet and, in a loud but civil voice, said:

"Who goes there? What manner of man? Are you perchance one of the happy or one of the sad?"

"One of the sad," replied Don Quijote.

"Then approach," said the Knight of the Wood, "for you may be sure that he whom you find here is both sadness and misery themselves."

Finding himself addressed so gently and politely, Don Quijote went over to him, and Sancho followed along.

The lamenting knight took Don Quijote by the arm, saying:

"Be seated, sir knight — for all I need to know, to number you among the ranks of those who are sworn to knight errantry, is to have found you here in this place, where loneliness and the clear night air, being the natural bed and the proper chamber of all knights errant, keep us company."

To which Don Quijote replied:

"I am indeed a knight, and of the order you mention, and though my heart has been occupied by its own sadness, misfortune, and misery, it has not chosen to banish compassion for the sorrows of others. From the little I have heard you say, I gather that your troubles come from love — that is, from your love for that ungrateful beauty you named in your lament."

And then they seated themselves side by side, peacefully and companionably, on the hard ground, just as if, when dawn broke, they were not intending to break each other's heads.

"By any chance, sir knight," he of the Wood asked Don Quijote, "are you in love?"

"By mischance, yes, I am," replied Don Quijote, "although the penalties of well-placed longings should really be considered blessings rather than misfortunes."

"How very true," replied he of the Wood, "provided that rejection does not disturb our minds and unsettle our reason, for when it is unreasonably harsh it seems more like vengeance."

"My lady has never rejected me," answered Don Quijote.

"Certainly not," said Sancho, who was standing close by, "for my lady's as gentle as a lamb — she's as soft as butter."

"This is your squire?" asked he of the Wood.

"It is," replied Don Quijote.

"I've never before seen a squire," said he of the Wood, "who dared to speak when his master was speaking. At any rate, you couldn't prove that this fellow of mine — who's already as tall as his father — has ever opened his mouth when I was talking."

"By God," said Sancho, "I did speak, and I am entitled to speak in the presence of someone other than — but never mind — let sleeping dogs lie."

The Knight of the Wood's squire then took Sancho by the arm, saying:

"Let's us go where we can talk like squires, to our heart's content, and leave these gentlemen, our masters, to argue, telling each other the tales of their loves, for you can be sure that, when daylight catches up to them, they'll still be at it."

"A fine idea," said Sancho, "and I'll tell you, sir, who I am, so you can see if I belong on that list of the most talkative squires."

At which the two squires withdrew, and had a conversation every bit as funny as that of their masters was sober and serious.

Chapter Thirteen

— continuation of the adventure of the Knight of the Wood,
along with the wise, novel, and mellow conversation
between the two squires

They divided themselves, accordingly, into two groups, one of knights and one of squires, the former retelling their loves, the latter their lives, but our history first narrates the squires' conversation and then follows it with the masters', reporting that, once they had withdrawn a bit, the Knight of the Wood's squire said to Sancho:

"We suffer and endure a hard life, my friend, we who serve as squires to knights errant. Truly, we eat our bread in the sweat of our faces, which is one of the curses God cast upon our original ancestors."

"You can also say," added Sancho, "that we eat it in the icy coldness of our bodies, because who knows more about heat and cold than a knight errant's miserable squire? And even then it wouldn't be so bad if we did eat, because there's less pain when you have food, but there are times when we go for a whole day, or even two, without a bite to eat — except a good taste of the wind."

"And we can endure all that, we can tolerate it," said the Knight of the Wood's squire, "because we look forward to what we'll earn, for unless the master he serves is exceedingly unlucky, after a few go-arounds a knight errant's squire finds himself rewarded with the nice fat governorship of an island, or maybe a good solid countship."

"I've already told my master," said Sancho, "I'll be satisfied with the governorship of an island, and he's so generous, and so good-hearted, he's promised me many times that's what I'll have."

"I," said the other, "will be content to have a canonry in return for my services, and my master has already promised me one — and what a whopper!"

"Your master," said Sancho, "must be some kind of Church knight, so he can reward his squire with that sort of thing, but mine is just a layman — still, I can remember when some pretty knowing people (though I never thought they had anything good in mind) tried to talk him into becoming an archbishop, but all he wants is to be an emperor, and I was scared the whole time he might decide to go into the Church after all, because I wouldn't be good enough to hold that kind of job, and I have to tell you, my good sir, I may look like a man, but as far as being in the Church is concerned I'm just an animal."

"But you're wrong, my good sir," said the Knight of the Wood's squire, "because governorships of islands aren't always what they're cracked up to be. Some of them are bent out of shape, and some are just plain poor, and some are dismal, and, to sum it all up, the ones that stand tallest and look the best bring you a heavy load of problems and worries, and the man unlucky enough to bear them gets beaten to the ground. It would be a lot better if those of us who have undertaken this damned servitude just went back home and kept ourselves busy with milder tasks, maybe hunting, let's say, or fishing, because is there a squire in the whole world so dirt-

poor that he doesn't have an old nag, and a couple of hunting dogs, and
a fishing rod, so he can keep himself busy in his own village?"

"I've got those things," replied Sancho, "although I admit I don't have
a horse — but I've got a donkey that's worth two of the horse my master
rides. God send me the worst Easter I've ever had, and send it right away,
if I'd swap with him, even if he threw in half a dozen bushels of barley.
You'll make fun of me, my good sir, for thinking so highly of my little
greybeard — because that's my donkey's color, he's gray all over. But I've
got more than enough dogs — my village is full of them. Anyway, hunting
is more fun when someone else is picking up the bill."

"Really and truly, señor," responded the Knight of the Wood's squire,
"I've made up my mind to give up this stupid knight-errantry stuff, and go
home to my village, and raise my children, because I've got three of them,
as fine as oriental pearls."

"I've got two," said Sancho, "and they're good enough to present to the
Pope Himself, especially the girl, because I'm raising her to be a countess,
may it please Our Lord, in spite of her mother."

"How old is this little lady you're raising up like a countess?" asked the
Knight of the Wood's squire.

"Fifteen, give or take a couple of years," answered Sancho, "but she's
as tall as a spear, as fresh as an April morning — and as strong as a long-
shoreman."

"Why, she could be a nymph in the green wood," said the Knight of
the Wood's squire, "not just a countess. Oh, the little whore, I'll bet that
little bitch is a strong one!"

To which Sancho replied, somewhat peeved:

"She's no whore, and neither is her mother, and neither of them are
going to be, either, God willing, as long as I'm alive. And you'd better talk
more politely: for a man raised around knights errant, sir, who are the very
soul of courtesy, that kind of language doesn't sound right."

"But you misunderstand the very language of compliments, sir," replied
the Knight of the Wood's squire. "Don't you know that when a knight gets
a good lick at the bull, in the arena, or anytime something's done really
well, the crowd always calls out, 'Oh, you whore you, that was a good
shot!' And what might seem to be a curse is in fact a term of high praise,
so you ought to disown your sons or your daughters, sir, if what they do
isn't good enough to earn their parents such tribute."

"I'll disown them, all right," replied Sancho, "because in the same way
and for the same reasons you've given, sir, you might as well call my
children and my wife whores of all whoredom, because everything they
do and everything they say is worth that kind of praise, and so I can go
home soon and see them I pray God deliver me from mortal sin, and by
mortal sin I mean this dangerous business of being a squire, in which I've
gone and gotten myself involved for the second time, on account of I was
all dazzled by a bag with a hundred gold pieces in it that I found one day
up in the heart of the Sierra Morena mountains, so the Devil is always
setting that in front of my eyes, over there, and over there, and everywhere
except right here, a bag stuffed fat with gold, so I always think the very
next step I'm going to have it in my hands, and I'll hug it like a baby, and

I'll carry it home, and I'll use it to make loans and collect rent and live like a prince, so while I'm thinking like this it's no problem dealing with whatever foolishness my master's up to, because I know perfectly well he's more lunatic than he is knight."

"Which is why," replied the Knight of the Wood's squire, "they say that being greedy breaks the bag — and if we're going to discuss that sort of thing, well, there's no one in the world worse than my master, and what they say about men like him is, 'Other people's problems are what kill the donkey,' because to help another knight who's gone out of his head, he's been turning himself into a crazy man, and what he's running around looking for, if he ever finds it, might just let him have it right on the nose."

"Is he lovesick, by any chance?"

"Oh yes," said the Knight of the Wood's squire, "and over a certain Casildea of Vandalia, who's the roughest, toughest lady you'll ever find, but that's not the leg he's limping on, right now — he's got other fish frying, as you'll see for yourself pretty soon."

"There isn't a road so level," replied Sancho, "that it hasn't got rocks sticking up or holes sticking down; if they cook beans, in other houses, in mine we cook them by the potful; madness gets a lot more attention than good sense. But if it's true, what they say, that it helps to have friends when you're in trouble, then you can make me feel better, sir, because you're serving a master just as stupid as mine."

"Stupid — but brave," said the Knight of the Wood's squire, "and even trickier than either stupid or brave."

"That's not the way it is with mine," answered Sancho, "because he's not a bit tricky, he's got a heart like gold — there's nothing mean about him, he wants to be nice to everybody, and he's got no grudges at all: if it's high noon, a little boy could talk him into thinking it was nighttime, and it's because he's so good-hearted that I love him with all my soul, so I can't talk myself into leaving him, no matter what nonsense he gets himself involved in."

"All the same, sir, my brother," said the Knight of the Wood's squire, "if the blind go leading the blind, everybody's in danger of falling into the ditch. Better for us if we get out while the going is good, and go home where we belong, because those who go hunting adventures don't always find pleasant ones."

Sancho kept clearing his throat and spitting out a kind of thick, dry saliva, which the kindly Knight of the Wood's squire noted and understood:

"It seems to me," he said, "we've talked enough to make our tongues stick to the roof of our mouths — but I've got a pretty good unsticker, hanging from my saddlebow."

He went off and, in another moment, came back with a huge wineskin and a meat pie almost two feet across — which is absolutely no exaggeration, because it had been made of a white rabbit so fat that Sancho, when he hefted it, thought it must be at least a goat, and not a kid, either.

"You brought this with you, sir?" he asked.

"What do you mean?" responded the other. "Do you think I'm some kind of bread-and-water squire? I carry a better supper thrown across my horse's back than do most generals, when they set off on a campaign."

Nobody had to ask Sancho to fall to: right there in the dark he began to shovel in mouthfuls as big as bowknots. And he said:

"Sir, you're a real good squire, as good as they come, first-rate, magnificent, and this banquet proves it, because if it wasn't magic that produced this, it certainly seems like it. All I carry in my saddlebags, unlucky, dirt-poor me, is a chunk of cheese so hard you could break a giant's head with it, with four dozen carob beans to keep it company, and about as many hazelnuts and walnuts, because my master's pretty rigorous, and he believes in knights errant having nothing to keep them going but dried fruits and herbs of the field."

"By God, brother," replied the Knight of the Wood's squire, "you won't catch me eating thistles, or wild pears, or the roots of bushes. Our masters can follow all the knightly laws they like, and eat anything they think they ought to. I take my own lunch-pail, and this wineskin hangs on my saddle-bow, whether they like it or not, and I'm such a pious worshipper, and I love it so dearly, that you'll usually find me giving it a thousand hugs and a thousand kisses."

As he spoke, he handed the wineskin to Sancho, who tilted it back, pointed it straight into his mouth, and stood there staring up at the stars for a good quarter of an hour, and when he was finally done drinking he leaned his head to one side and sighed a great, long sigh, and then said:

"Oh you whore, you son of a bitch, oh you're a good one!"

"Ah, you see?" said the Knight of the Wood's squire, hearing Sancho's exclamation. "You praised this wine by calling it a whore."

"You're right," responded Sancho, "and I admit there's nothing wrong in calling anybody a whore, if it's understood you mean it right. But tell me, sir, by all that's holy, isn't this wine from Ciudad Real?"

"You know what you're drinking!" replied the other. "That's just exactly what it is, and it's done a little aging, too."

"That's right up my alley!" said Sancho. "It doesn't take me long to figure out where wine comes from. Seriously, sir squire: Would you believe I've got such a fine-tuned natural instinct, when it comes to wines, that all you have to do is let me smell it a little and I'll tell you where it comes from, and what kind of grapes it was made from, how it tastes, how long it's been aged, how it's going to ripen, and everything else you'd want to know about a wine? But that's no surprise, because on my father's side I'm descended from the two best wine-tasters anyone's seen in La Mancha in a long, long time — which I can prove, here and now, by telling you what happened to those ancestors of mine, once upon a time. They gave them some wine from a barrel, once, and asked them what condition they thought it was in, whether it was any good, or whether it had gone bad. One of them just touched it with the tip of his tongue; the other only waved it under his nostrils. The first one said there was an iron flavor; the second said he thought it was more like leather. The owner said it was an absolutely clean barrel, and nothing had been put in the wine that could make it taste either like iron or like leather. In spite of which, the two famous winetasters insisted they were right. So after a while the wine was sold, and when they cleaned out the barrel they found a little key, hanging by a little leather strap. You can pretty well see, sir, whether someone who comes from people like that is entitled to say what he thinks about wines."

"Which is why I say," said the Knight of the Wood's squire, "we should stop hunting for adventures: when we've got good country loaves, why go looking for cake? Just go home to our huts: God will find us there, if He wants us."

"I'm going to stay with my master until he gets to Zaragoza, and after that — we'll see what we'll see."

In the end, after a good deal of talking and a good deal of drinking, the two good squires found it necessary to tie up their tongues and put a hold on their thirst, because there was no way they could satisfy it, so they both fell asleep, each of them clutching the almost empty wineskin, and we will now leave them there, and tell what happened between the Knight of the Wood and the Knight of the Sad Face.

Chapter Fourteen

— continuing the adventure of the Knight of the Wood

Among the many things discussed by Don Quijote and the Knight of the Wood, our history records that the Knight of the Wood said:

"In short, sir knight, please understand that it was my destiny — or, to put it more precisely, it was my own choice — to fall in love with my matchless Casildea of Vandalia. I call her matchless because in fact there is none to match her, there being no lady as big as she is, nor any of such exalted standing or such beauty. Now in return for all my yearning, and my gallant thoughts, this Casildea of whom I speak made me take on all sorts of dangerous tasks, just the way his stepmother [Juno] did with Hercules, always promising me that, when I'd completed each one, I only had to finish one more to achieve that end toward which all my hopes have been directed, but the chain of my labors has gone on growing, link after link, until by now my tasks have mounted up past all counting and I have no way of knowing which will be the last, which will bring me to the beginning of desire's fulfillment. Once she ordered me to challenge that famous female giant, Giralda of Seville,[1] who is as fierce and strong as if she'd been made of bronze and who, without ever moving from the spot, manages to be the most changeable, fickle woman in the world. I came, I saw, and I conquered; I made her stay quiet and right where she was, and so for more than a week we had nothing but north winds blowing. Another time she ordered me to weigh the ancient boulders of those huge Guisando Bulls,[2] a job better suited to porters than knights. Still another time she ordered me to rush all the way down into the great Cabra abyss — really, an extraordinary and fearfully risky business — and come back with a detailed account of everything to be found in those profound depths. I made Giralda sit still; I weighed the Guisando Bulls; I hurled myself

---

1. A huge brass statue mounted on a globe and serving as weathercock for the Cathedral of Seville [*Translator's Note*].
2. Pre-Roman statues of bulls, provenance and purpose unknown [*Translator's Note*].

into the abyss and brought to light what had been hidden in those depths; but my hopes remain deader than dead and her commands, like her spurning of me, remain livelier than ever. So, finally, she's ordered me to go roaming through every province in Spain, and make all the knights errant wandering around admit that she and she alone is the most beautiful woman alive, just as I am the bravest and the most impressively lovesick knight, and in pursuance of her directive I have already traveled through most of Spain, defeating many, many knights who had the temerity to contradict me. But what I'm most proud and satisfied about is having conquered, in hand-to-hand combat, that famous knight, Don Quijote de La Mancha, making him concede that my Casildea is lovelier than his Dulcinea — a conquest that counts as much as having defeated every knight in the entire world, for this Don Quijote, you must know, has himself defeated them all, and now that I've beaten him his glory, his fame, and his honor have all been taken away and conferred upon me.

> The better the man you put in the dust,
> The greater the fame you wear on your breast.[3]

So now all the uncountable deeds of Don Quijote can be chalked up to me; they're all mine."

Don Quijote was stunned to hear what the Knight of the Wood was saying; a thousand times he was on the verge of saying it was a pack of lies, and the declaration sat ready on his tongue; but he held himself back as best he could, intending to make the liar confess his lie with his own lips; and so he replied, calmly:

"I can say nothing of your grace's having conquered most of the knights errant in Spain, and even in the whole world, but I rather doubt that you've defeated Don Quijote de La Mancha. Perhaps it was someone else who resembled him, although there aren't many who do."

"What are you talking about?" answered the Knight of the Wood. "By the very Heavens above I fought with Don Quijote, and I defeated him, and he surrendered to me — and he's rather tall, with a lean face, long, thin arms and legs, and a gray beard, his nose aquiline and a bit hooked; he's got a full, drooping moustache, very black. He uses the name Knight of the Sad Face, and for a squire he has a farmer called Sancho Panza; he's carried about on the back of a famous steed named Rocinante, wonderfully obedient to the reins; and, to make a long story short, the lady of his heart is a certain Dulcinea del Toboso, who used to be known as Aldonza Lorenzo — the way I call my lady Casildea of Vandalia, because her name was Casilda and she comes from Andalusia. If all this doesn't prove my case, here's my sword, and *that* will make you give over your doubts."

"Gently, gently, sir knight," said Don Quijote, "and listen to what I'll tell you. Understand, please, that this Don Quijote happens to be my best friend in the world — so much so that, in truth, I think of him as I think of myself — and from all the plain and unmistakeable evidence you've

---

3. From Alonso de Ercilla's *La Araucana* [Araucania = region in central Chile], a Spanish epic about the conquest of Chile [*Translator's Note*].

given me it's impossible not to believe you have indeed conquered him in battle. On the other hand, the sight of my eyes and the touch of my hands tells me it cannot have been him — although, of course, since he has many magician enemies, and one in particular who perpetually persecutes him, it may well be that one of them assumed his shape specifically to allow you to defeat him, in order to cheat him of the fame he has won, throughout the whole known world, by his noble deeds of knighthood. In confirmation of which, let me tell you that, no more than two days ago, these same hostile magicians transformed the beautiful Dulcinea del Toboso into an ugly, vulgar country girl, which must have been what they did to Don Quijote himself — and if none of this can persuade you of the truth of what I've said, here you have before you Don Quijote himself, who will defend that truth on foot, or on horseback, or in any fashion that best pleases you."

So saying, he rose and gripped his sword, waiting to see how the Knight of the Wood would respond; the reply was both prompt and calm:

"If you acknowledge a debt, you pay it: my dear Don Quijote, a man who has already defeated you, in your transformed shape, seems quite likely to do the same against you yourself. Since, however, it would be unbecoming for true knights to work their feats of arms in the darkness, as if they were highway robbers and thieves, let us wait for daylight, so the sun may shine on our deeds. And let it be a condition of our combat that the vanquished shall do whatever his conqueror directs, no matter what it may be, provided only that what may be commanded must be fitting and proper for a knight."

"I am more than happy with this condition and these terms," replied Don Quijote.

At this point they went looking for their squires, and found them lying snoring, in exactly the same position in which they'd fallen asleep. They woke them up and ordered them to ready the horses, because when the sun rose they were going to fight a bloody, harsh, hand-to-hand combat, which news stunned and dumbfounded Sancho, who had heard a long list of heroic exploits from the Knight of the Wood's squire and was worried for his master's safety. But without a word being said, the two squires went to fetch their small herd — for by now the three horses and the donkey had caught each other's scents and were all in the same place.

Along the way, the Knight of the Wood's squire said to Sancho:

"I must tell you, brother, that it is the custom among the warriors of Andalusia, when they serve as seconds in a quarrel, not to just stand watching while their principals fight it out. I explain this because you ought to know that, while our masters are having at it, we too need to be whacking away at each other."

"My dear sir squire," replied Sancho, "this custom may well prevail among the thieves and fighting cocks you speak of, but it would be unheard of among the squires of true knights errant. Anyway, I've never heard my master tell of any such custom, and he knows all the rules of knight errantry by heart. And even if it were a valid rule that squires had to fight while their masters were fighting, I won't do it: I'll just pay whatever penalty is required of peaceful squires, because I'm sure it can't be more than a couple of pounds of candle-wax, and I'd much rather pay that, knowing as I do it would cost me less, that way, than paying for the bandages to patch up my head, which already feels as if it were broken in half. And another thing: it would be impossible for a man without a sword to fight a duel, and I've never in all my life owned a sword."

"I've got just the thing to take care of that," said the Knight of the Wood's squire. "I have a pair of canvas bags, just the same size. You take one, and I'll take the other, and we can have a sort of pillow fight, each of us equally well armed."

"Now that sounds fine," replied Sancho, "because, doing it that way, instead of hurting each other, we'll just give each other a good dusting."

"No, it doesn't have to be exactly like that," answered the other, "because, to keep the wind from blowing the bags away, we'll have to throw in half a dozen nice smooth rocks, all the same weight, and then we can whack each other without doing a lot of damage."

"By my father's body," exclaimed Sancho, "just see what nice soft fur and wads of cotton he's stuffing into those bags, so we won't crack our skulls and break our bones! But my dear sir, even if you fill them full of silkworm cocoons, I'm not fighting. Let our masters fight, that's up to them, but we ought to just drink and live: time will come and take away our lives soon enough, without encouraging him to finish us up before we're all ripe and it's the right season for being plucked."

"All the same," answered the Knight of the Wood's squire, "we've got to put in at least half an hour of fighting."

"Not at all," replied Sancho. "I won't be so discourteous, nor so ungrateful, as to fight about anything — not even the least little thing — with a man, when I've eaten and drunk with him, and especially when I'm not angry at him. Who the devil can bring himself to fight in cold blood?"

"In that case," said the Knight of the Wood's squire, "I'll fix that soon enough. Before we start fighting, I'll just slip over to you, my good sir, and give you three or four good stiff raps in the face, which will lay you out at my feet, and that will wake up your anger for you, even if it was sleeping like a dormouse."

"I can match that," replied Sancho, "with an idea that's just as good. I'll get myself a club, and before you, sir, can wake up *my* anger I'll put yours to sleep with blows that will keep it asleep from here to the next world, in which it's well known that I'm not a man to let anybody mess up his face. So let's everybody take care of his own business — though it would be even better just to let everybody's anger stay asleep, because nobody knows what's in another man's heart, and you can go looking for wool and come home properly sheared yourself, and God blessed peace and cursed quarreling, because if you chase a cat and get it cornered, with its back against the wall, and it turns into a lion, God alone knows what I, since I'm a man, might turn into, so let me inform you, my good sir squire, that your shoulders will have to bear the responsibility for any wrong or injury resulting from a quarrel between us."

"Fine," said the Knight of the Wood's squire. "God will bring us His light, and then we'll see what we'll see."

Just then a thousand kinds of speckled birds began to warble in the trees, their many happy songs seeming to greet and welcome the fresh dawn, already showing her lovely face along the windows and doors of the East, shaking down from her dewy locks myriad drops of liquid pearls, which sweet and gentle liquor bathed the meadows, so they too seemed to gush forth a sweet, shining rain of pearl-like mist; willow trees exuded their delightful manna, streams and fountains bubbled and laughed, brooks murmured, woods swayed happily, and the fields adorned themselves at dawn's arrival. But it was hardly light enough to tell one thing from another when the very first thing Sancho Panza saw was a nose, the Knight of the Wood's squire's nose, which was so huge that it almost seemed bigger than the rest of his body. Our history records, in fact, that this nose was incredible, immense, hooked in the middle and covered with livid, eggplant-colored warts; it hung an inch or two lower than the squire's mouth; and its size, color, warts, and hooked shape made Sancho begin to shake all over, like a child having an epileptic fit, and he resolved in his heart to let himself be given two hundred blows in the face before he'd let his anger be roused and throw himself into combat against this monster.

Looking over his opponent, Don Quijote saw he was already helmeted, with the visor down, so his face could not be seen; our knight also noted that his adversary was a husky man, though not terribly tall. He wore a loose-fitting outer coat over his armor, of a fabric that seemed to be the finest gold, decorated with gleaming little moon-shaped mirrors, making him look quite extraordinarily splendid; there were plumes fluttering all over his helmet, green and yellow and white; his lance, which had been set against a tree, was stout and exceedingly long, with a steel tip almost half a foot in length.

Don Quijote saw and took due note of all this, his inspection leading him to judge the aforesaid knight a man of great strength — not that this conclusion made Don Quijote's heart quake, as it did Sancho Panza's; indeed, with an air of composed, courtly courage, he said to the Mirrored Knight:

"If, sir knight, your great thirst for battle has not dried up your capacity for courtesy, I beg you, in the name of our gallant profession, to lift your visor a bit, so that I may see if your face is as noble as your manner."

"Whether you emerge from this business conquered or conquering, sir knight," replied the Mirrored One, "you'll have plenty of time and opportunity to see me, so that if, now, I do not satisfy your request, it is simply because it seems to me that, were I to delay by pausing to lift my visor, without having first made you admit what you are already well aware that I want you to admit, I would commit a significant offense against the beautiful Casildea de Vandalia."

"Then as we mount our horses," said Don Quijote, "tell me at least if I am the same Don Quijote you claim to have already vanquished."

"My answer to that," said the Mirrored One, "is that, much as one egg resembles another, you do indeed seem to be the same knight I defeated in battle, but since you yourself tell me that you are persecuted by enchanters, I do not dare affirm whether you are or are not the aforesaid same Don Quijote."

"That is sufficient," replied Don Quijote, "for me to think you clearly deceived. Still, so you may be totally undeceived, let our horses now be brought and, in less time than the lifting of your visor would have taken, only provided that God, my lady, and my own right arm defend me, I will see your face, and you will see that I am not the conquered Don Quijote you think me."

Then they gave over their exchange of words, mounted their horses, and Don Quijote wheeled Rocinante hard around, with a tug of the reins, so he could measure off the proper distance from which to turn back and charge at his adversary, and the Knight of the Mirrors performed the same maneuver. But Don Quijote hadn't gone more than twenty paces when he heard the Mirrored One calling to him, so they both returned to their starting points and the Knight of the Mirrors said:

"Keep in mind, sir knight, that the terms of our combat provide that, whoever may be conquered, as we said before, he must place himself at his conqueror's disposal."

"Agreed," replied Don Quijote, "as before, provided only that whatever the conquered one is commanded to do must not transgress against the laws of chivalry."

"That goes without saying," replied the Mirrored One.

Just then Don Quijote caught sight of the other squire's strange nose, which he found no less amazing than Sancho had — so surpassingly strange, indeed, that he thought the fellow must either be a monster of some kind or a new species of man, never before seen on this earth. Seeing his master retreating, to prepare for his galloping assault, Sancho had no interest in remaining alone with Big Nose, afraid that if those gaping nostrils took one swipe at his own nose, it would be the end of the fight for him, leaving him stretched out on the ground, either with the blow or in sheer fright, so he followed along behind Don Quijote, clutching one of Rocinante's stirrup straps, and when it seemed time for his master to wheel around and charge, Sancho said to him:

"Let me beg you, your grace, my lord, that before you turn and fight, you help me climb this cork tree, because from up there I'll be much better able to see the brave and stirring combat you and that other knight are about to have."

"What I suspect, Sancho," said Don Quijote, "is that you'd rather be up in the grandstand, so you can watch the bulls without any danger."

"The truth is," replied Sancho, "I'm absolutely terrified of that squire's huge nose, so I don't dare go anywhere near him."

"It is indeed a phenomenon," said Don Quijote, "that, were I not what I am, would frighten me, too, so come on, I'll help you climb up where you want to be."

While Don Quijote stopped to help Sancho climb up in the cork tree, the Mirrored One had measured off the distance he thought appropriate and, in the belief that Don Quijote had been similarly occupied, tugged his horse's reins around — the animal seemed no less heavy-footed or any better than Rocinante — and without waiting for a trumpet blast or any other cautionary signal came galloping (or, at least, briskly trotting) across the field, straight at his enemy. But then, at about the midpoint, seeing that Don Quijote was helping Sancho climb the tree, he pulled up his steed — for which the horse was grateful, because it was already almost too exhausted to keep moving. But Don Quijote, thinking his enemy was flying at him, dug his spurs as far into Rocinante's skinny flanks as they would go, which made the horse leap so violently that, as our history tells us, this was the first and only time he was ever known to move at a true gallop (for on every other occasion his best speed was no better than a trot), so it didn't take him long to get to where the Mirrored One was frantically digging in his spurs, absolutely unable to move his horse so much as a finger-length from the spot on which it had stopped.

At this splendid moment Don Quijote swept down on his adversary, as the other knight struggled with both his horse and his lance — which he was never quite able, or never had the time, to set in its socket. But Don Quijote, not focussing on such minor details, smashed into the Mirrored One with utter impunity, completely without risk to himself, and tumbled him willy-nilly backwards off his horse, bringing him to the ground with such force that he lay motionless, apparently dead.

Sancho had no sooner seen him fall than he slid down from the tree and hurried over to his master, who had dismounted and was standing over the Mirrored One, undoing his helmet laces to see if he was in fact dead and, if he was alive, to give him some air, and what Don Quijote saw . . . But who can really say what he saw, and not produce absolute shock and wonder and astonishment in everyone who's listening? According to our history, what he saw was the precise face, the exact body, the identical appearance, the same profile, a perfect likeness of, and indeed the very outward show of the university graduate, Samson Carrasco, and as soon as our knight saw him he began to shout:

"Come here, Sancho, and you'll never believe what you'll see! Hurry, my son, and find out just what magic can do, and of what wizards and enchanters are capable!"

Sancho arrived and as soon as he saw the university graduate's face began to cross himself a thousand times and say another thousand prayers. The whole time, there was no sign of life from the fallen knight, so Sancho said to his master:

"It looks to me, my lord, as if — whether you want to or not — your grace ought to shove your sword right up to the teeth of this fellow who looks like the university graduate, Samson Carrasco, and maybe that way you can kill one of those enchanter enemies of yours."

"Not a bad idea," said Don Quijote, "because the fewer enemies, the better."

He was drawing his sword to put into effect Sancho's advice and counsel, when the Mirrored One's squire got there, now quite without the nose that had made him so hideous, and crying as loud as he could:

"Be careful what you do, Señor Don Quijote, because lying right there at your feet you've got the university graduate, Samson Carrasco, your good friend, and I'm his squire."

Then Sancho, seeing him without the hideousness he'd had to start with, said:

"And the nose?"

To which the other responded:

"I've got it right here, in my pocket."

And with his right hand he pulled out a nose fashioned of paste and varnish, a pasteboard construction in the shape already described. Then, looking at him more and more closely, Sancho cried out, in a loud, astonished voice:

"Mother of God, bless me! Aren't you Tomé Cecial, my neighbor and my good friend?"

"Sure I am!" answered the now de-nosed squire. "I'm Tomé Cecial, your friend and companion, Sancho Panza, and pretty soon I'll tell you just how I came to be here, all the tricks and tangles that brought me — but in the meantime, please, beg your lord and master not to touch, harm, wound, or kill this Knight of the Mirrors, who's lying at your feet, because without any doubt whatever he is that rash and reckless university graduate, your friend, Samson Carrasco."

Just then, the Mirrored One recovered consciousness, and when Don Quijote saw this, he set the bare point of his sword right above his face, declaring:

"You're as good as dead, knight, unless you admit that the matchless Dulcinea del Toboso is lovelier than your Casildea of Vandalia, and what's more, you must promise, if you come out of this battle and defeat with your life, that you will go to the city of Toboso and present yourself to her, on my behalf, so that she can do with you whatever she pleases, and if she releases you, you must also come back and seek me out — and the traces my deeds leave behind me will serve to guide you to where I am — so you can tell me about your meeting with her, these being conditions that, as we agreed before our combat, are entirely in conformity with the laws of knighthood."

"I admit," said the fallen knight, "that the Lady Dulcinea del Toboso's worn-out, dirty shoe is worth more than the uncombed but clean beard of Casildea, and I promise to return from her presence to yours, and tell you every single detail you want to hear."

"You must also admit, and declare that you believe," added Don Quijote, "that the knight you defeated could not possibly have been Don Quijote de La Mancha, but someone else who looked like him, just as I admit and believe that, although you indeed resemble the university graduate, Samson Carrasco, you are not him, but someone else who looks like him, who has been put here in Samson Carrasco's shape in order to temper and restrain my fierce anger, and so I may make only gentle use of this glorious victory."

"I admit and declare and assert everything you believe and declare and assert," answered the injured knight. "Just allow me to stand, I beg you, if, that is, the force of my fall will let me, because it's left me all battered and bruised."

Don Quijote and Tomé Cecial, the knight's squire, helped him stand, Sancho never taking his eyes from the said Tomé, but continually asking him questions the replies to which clearly indicated he really was the Tomé Cecial he said he was. Yet Sancho's notion, based on his master's remark that magicians had changed the Knight of the Mirrors into Samson Carrasco, would not allow our knight's squire to believe what in fact his eyes were seeing. In short, both master and man were still bemused and deceived, while the Knight of the Mirrors and his squire, angry and miserable, left Don Quijote and Sancho, intending to find some place where the injured man's ribs could be patched and splinted. Don Quijote and Sancho went back toward Zaragoza, where for the moment our history leaves them, in order to record the Knight of the Mirror and his squire's true identities.

Chapter Fifteen

— which records and explains the true identities of the Knight of the Mirrors and his squire

Don Quijote went down the road wonderfully satisfied, deliriously happy, and quite extravagantly proud of himself for having been victorious over a combatant so gloriously valiant as he imagined the Mirrored One to be, and he fancied that the vanquished knight would surely tell him whether the enchanted transformation of his lady Dulcinea still endured, since he'd obliged the defeated one to return and tell him everything, under penalty of forfeiting all claim to be a knight. But Don Quijote was thinking one thing and the Mirrored One something very different indeed, for right then all the wounded man wanted, as we have noted, was to get his bruises taken care of.

Our history records, accordingly, that when the university graduate, Samson Carrasco, advised Don Quijote to resume his knightly activities, it had been on the basis of a plot, cooked up with the priest and the barber, and intended to oblige Don Quijote to stay peacefully and quietly at home, rather than banging around the world in search of insane adventures, which plan had been formulated by a unanimous vote of all concerned, and strongly urged by Carrasco, to allow Don Quijote to sally forth yet again, since it was patently impossible to hold him back any longer, but then to set Carrasco himself on the road as a knight errant too, there to engage Don Quijote in knightly combat, on some grounds or other, and to defeat him — manifestly, they thought, an easy matter — it having first been agreed that the defeated knight would place himself entirely in the hands of the victor. Having thus vanquished Don Quijote, the university graduate would be able to command him to return to his own village and his proper home, and to remain there for — say — two years, or perhaps until his conqueror directed differently, for it seemed to them absolutely clear that Don Quijote would consider himself completely bound by the laws of chivalry, and perhaps, during this time of imprisonment, he would either forget all his silliness or the others would be able to find some effective cure for his madness.

Carrasco agreed to undertake this responsibility, and Tomé Cecial, Sancho Panza's friend and neighbor, a cheerful, easygoing fellow, volunteered to be Carrasco's squire. So Samson equipped himself in the style already indicated and, to prevent his old friend from recognizing him, Tomé Cecial set the painted, artificial nose on top of his natural one, after which they set out in the same direction Don Quijote had taken, almost catching up to him in time to be present at the adventure with Death's cart. They finally did meet up with Don Quijote and Sancho in the wood, where everything the judicious reader has already read about took place, and if it had not been for Don Quijote's wild fancies, convincing himself that the university graduate was not the university graduate at all, said graduate would have been rendered incapable of proceeding to any advanced degrees, because although he'd been sure he would find birds and to spare, he hadn't even found a nest.

When Tomé Cecial saw how badly their plan had worked out, and what a disaster their journey had ended in, he said to the university graduate:

"By God, Mister Samson Carrasco, we're certainly getting what we deserved, because it's easy enough to plan and try to do a job, but lots of times it's harder to actually accomplish it. Don Quijote's crazy, and we're both right in the head, but he comes out all in one piece, and smiling, and you, your grace, are beaten to a pulp and not smiling a bit. I think we have to stop and ask ourselves: who's crazier — the lunatic who can't help himself, or the one who's crazy of his own free will?"

To which Samson answered:

"The difference between the two is that he who can't help being crazy will stay crazy, and he who chooses to seem mad can walk away from it whenever he wants to."

"In which case," said Tomé Cecial, "I was downright crazy when I agreed to turn myself into your grace's squire, and now I make the choice to give it up and go on home."

"You do whatever you want to," replied Samson, "but you're wasting your time if you think I'm going back home before I give Don Quijote a good beating — and what's motivating me, now, isn't that I want to unscramble his brains, but a longing for revenge, because the pain in my ribs won't allow me any more merciful thoughts."

They went along, conversing in this fashion, until they reached a town where, luckily, they found a bone surgeon, who set the unfortunate Carrasco to rights. Tomé Cecial turned around and went home, and the university graduate was left to contemplate his revenge: our history will come back to him, in due time, so it can now go back to rejoicing along with Don Quijote.

Chapter Sixteen

— what happened when Don Quijote met a sensible gentleman from La Mancha

Don Quijote traveled along as happy, self-satisfied, and proud as we've said, fancying that his conquest made him the bravest knight errant currently walking the earth, and thinking that, no matter how many adventures occurred to him from then on, all of them were already as good as brought to a happy conclusion. He no longer set any great stock in enchantments or enchanters, and had quite forgotten all the beatings he'd been given, in the course of his knightly activities — gone, the stone-throw that knocked out half his teeth; gone, the affair with the ungrateful galley slaves; gone, the impudent shepherds who had almost clubbed him to death. He assured himself, in short, that if only he could find some trick or technique that would disenchant his lady Dulcinea, there'd be no need for him to be jealous of the greatest good fortune ever attained, or capable of being attained, by the bravest knight errant who'd ever lived. These fancies had completely taken over his mind, as he jogged along, until Sancho said:

"Isn't it funny, my lord, that I keep seeing in front of my eyes that monstrous, incredible nose, stuck on my friend Tomé Cecial?"

"And do you fancy, Sancho, by any chance, that the Knight of the Mirrors was in fact Samson Carrasco, the university graduate, and that his squire was really your friend Tomé Cecial?"

"I don't know how to answer that question," replied Sancho, "except that, from the things he told me about my own house, and my wife, and my children, he couldn't be anybody else, because once the nose was off it was Tomé Cecial's face, just the way I've seen it so many times, back home, right next door to my own house, and he sounded exactly like himself."

"Let's stop and think about this, Sancho," replied Don Quijote. "Consider: why on earth would Samson Carrasco, a university graduate, set out as a knight errant, fully armed both offensively and defensively, in order to pick a fight with me? Have I by any chance been his enemy? Have I ever given him any reason to bear me a grudge? Am I his rival, or did he decide to take up the profession of knighthood because he was jealous of the fame I'd acquired in its exercise?"

"Yes, but then what do we say, my lord," answered Sancho, "about how much that knight, whoever he was, looked just like the university graduate, Carrasco, and his squire looked just like my friend Tomé Cecial? And if all this was magic, as your grace says, couldn't they choose to look like other people than these?"

"The whole thing," replied Don Quijote, "is a trick, a scheme, concocted by those evil magicians who've been persecuting me, because they would know that I'd of course be the victor in our combat, so they made sure the defeated knight would have my friend the university graduate's face, so my friendship for him would intervene against the blade of my sword and the power of my arm, and would also moderate the righteous anger in my heart, and thus cause me to grant his life to the wicked and traitorous being who had been trying to deprive me of mine. And to prove this, oh Sancho! remember that you yourself have plainly and unmistakably seen, with your own eyes, how easy it is for these enchanters to substitute one face for another, turning beauty into ugliness and ugliness into beauty, for it's scarcely two days since you've seen, with those very same eyes, the matchless loveliness and elegance of Dulcinea, exactly as she truly and naturally is, while I saw her as an ugly, vulgar, coarse peasant farm girl, with cataracts in her eyes and a stink in her mouth. Well! When this depraved enchanter dared to effect so wicked a transformation, why should he hesitate to do what he did with Samson Carrasco and your friend, so he could snatch the glory of conquest right out of my hands? But just the same, I really don't mind, because no matter what he assumed, it was I who emerged victorious over my enemy."

"God only knows what the real truth is about all this," answered Sancho.

Since he knew that Dulcinea's transformation had been his own fraud and deception, his master's fantastic ideas didn't convince him; on the other hand, he had no interest in arguing, for fear he would say something that would give away his trick.

They were conversing about these matters when a solitary rider caught up to them, mounted on a singularly handsome dapple mare; the man was wearing an overcoat of the best green wool, with red velvet facing and a cap of the same material; the mare's harness trappings were country-style, short-stirruped and colored a matching green and purple. A Moorish scimitar hung from a broad green and gold belt, and the rider's short boots were of leather embroidered in the same colors; his spurs were not gilded, but lacquered green, so glossy and well-polished that, in the way they blended with the rest of his outfit, they looked even better than spurs of pure gold. Coming up to our knight and his squire, he saluted them courteously and urged his horse right on past, but Don Quijote said:

"My gallant friend, if your grace is traveling the same route, and your business is not hurrying you on, we should be pleased to have you ride along with us."

"In point of fact," said the newcomer, "I'd not have ridden by so rapidly except for fear that my mare might disturb your horse."

"There's no need, señor," said Sancho at this point. "You can ease up your mare, because this horse of ours is the most modest and well-behaved in the whole world. He's never been guilty of lewdness, except just once, and that time his misbehavior made my master and me pay seven-fold for his mistake. So let me say, too, that your grace can ride along with us safely, if you want to: even if you served him your mare on a platter, you can be sure this horse wouldn't even look at her."

The rider pulled in his horse, fascinated by Don Quijote's appearance and bearing. Our knight rode bare-headed, Sancho carrying his master's helmet hung from the saddlebow behind him, like a suitcase. And much as the man in green stared at Don Quijote, Don Quijote stared even more penetratingly at him, for the newcomer seemed clearly to be someone both judicious and sensible. He appeared to be about fifty years old, with very little gray hair, a knowing face, and a look neither somber nor merry — and, furthermore, both his bearing and his garments indicated that he was a man of some considerable substance.

The Man in Green's opinion of Don Quijote de La Mancha was, similarly, that here was someone the like of whom he had never before seen. He was struck by Don Quijote's lean horse, by the knight's own height as well as the thin yellowish cast of his face, and by his armor, his manners, and his intense sobriety: this was both a person and an image not seen in that part of the world for a long, long time. Don Quijote was well aware of the attention with which the traveler was considering him, and easily able to perceive the interest behind the silent examination; as a gentleman of great courtesy, and one fond of pleasing others, our knight took the bull by the horns, even before the newcomer could frame a single question:

"My appearance, your grace," said Don Quijote, "being distinctly novel and highly unusual, I could hardly be surprised if you were somewhat astonished, but I think you will be reassured when I tell you that I am, as they say, a knight,

> one of those that everyone talks of,
> hunting all over for adventure.

I have gone forth from my native land, mortgaged my estate, left all luxury behind me, and put myself in the hands of Fortune, who will lead me wherever she pleases. My wish has been to revive the moribund profession of knight errantry, and in that cause I have been spending my days, sometimes stumbling, sometimes falling, sometimes plunging headlong and then rising once more, and much of what I wished to do I have in fact done, assisting widows, aiding damsels and protecting married women, orphans, and wards of tender years — all being the natural and fitting tasks of knights errant, and accordingly, because of my numerous and Christian acts of courage and valor, I have made my way into print in virtually all, or almost all, the nations on earth. Thirty thousand volumes of my history have been printed, and thirty thousand thousand more are likely to be printed, unless Heaven puts an end to it. To make a long story as short as possible, or perhaps to sum up the whole story in a single word, let me say that I am Don Quijote de La Mancha, also known as the Knight of the Sad Face, and although praise of oneself is despicable, there are times when I am obliged to become self-laudatory — namely, when there is no one else to speak for me — and thus, my dear sir, you should no longer be astonished at my horse, my lance, my shield, or my squire, nor all of my arms and armor, nor the yellow pallor of my face, nor the lean lankiness of my person, for now you know who I am and the profession to which I am sworn."

Saying this, Don Quijote fell silent, and the Man in Green, judging by how long he waited before replying, seemed uncertain just what to say, but after a longish time he spoke:

"You were quite correct, sir knight, to understand my interest from my surprised silence, but you've by no means cured the shock of your appearance, for in spite of the fact that you, señor, say that simply knowing who you are ought to put an end to astonishment, it in fact does nothing of the sort — indeed, I must say that, instead, it gives rise to even more surprise and amazement. How can there possibly still be knights errant left in the world, and how can there be true histories printed about real live knights? I cannot believe that, today, there still are those who protect widows, succor damsels, or provide for married women, or take care of orphans, nor would I believe it had I not seen it in your grace with my own eyes. Blessed Heavens! This history of yours, which you tell me has been printed, and which narrates your true and noble acts of chivalry, will soon have driven into oblivion all those tales of make-believe knights errant, of which the world has been so full, much to the injury of sound morals and to the discredit of decent, truthful books."

"Much could be said," replied Don Quijote, "as to whether the histories of knights errant are indeed simply make-believe."

"But who doubts, surely," responded the Man in Green, "that such books are anything but lies?"

"I, for one," answered Don Quijote. "But let us put that to the side, for if our journey together lasts long enough I hope God will allow me to show your grace how wrong you are, siding with the common opinion of those who hold such histories not to be truthful."

These remarks led the traveler to suspect Don Quijote had to be somewhat crazed, so he waited to hear more and have his suspicions confirmed, but before they could get off into other matters Don Quijote asked him to say who he was, since our knight had already given an account of his own rank and way of life. To which the Man in the Green Overcoat replied:

"Sir Knight of the Sad Face, I am a gentleman who lives in the village where we shall be dining, today, if God so wills it. I am more than moderately wealthy and my name is Don Diego de Miranda; I lead my life with my children and my wife, and with my friends; I practice hunting and fishing, though I keep neither hawks nor hounds, except for some tame partridges[1] and sometimes a bold ferret. I have a library of approximately six dozen volumes, some in Spanish, some in Latin, some historical, others devotional, but tales of chivalry have never so much as crossed my threshold. I do more reading in the secular than in the holy volumes, for they provide honest entertainment, their language delightful and their originality diverting and captivating — though here in Spain we don't have very many of these latter. I sometimes dine with my neighbors and friends, and quite often I invite them to my house; the entertainment I offer is proper and inoffensive, nor do I stint in anything. I take no pleasure in gossip, nor do I permit it in my presence; I don't go prying into other people's lives, nor do I keep a sharp eye on what others are doing; I go to mass every day; I share what I own with the poor, without making a great show of my good works, for I have no wish to let hypocrisy and pride creep into my heart — those enemies that ever so gently infiltrate and then take control of the most modest souls; I try to make peace between those I know to be quarreling; I am devoted to Our Lady, and I trust, now and forever, in the infinite mercy of the Lord our God."

Sancho listened to this recitation of the gentleman's way of life with passionate attention, and since it seemed to him a holy and sanctified existence, and that anyone who lived in such a fashion ought to be a miracle-worker, he leaped off his donkey and ran to grasp the man's right stirrup, then devotedly and almost in tears kissed his feet over and over again. Seeing this, the gentleman asked:

"What are you doing, brother? Why are you kissing me?"

"Permit me these kisses," replied Sancho, "because your grace seems to me the first saint in short stirrups I've ever seen in my life."

"I'm no saint," answered the gentleman, "but a great sinner — but you, brother, you must be the holy man, since you display such faith."

Sancho turned and climbed back onto his packsaddle, having drawn an open laugh from the depths of his master's melancholy, and astonishing Don Diego all over again. Don Quijote asked the Man in the Green Coat

---

1. Used by Andalusian hunters as decoys [*Translator's Note*].

how many children he had, observing at the same time that one of the things considered supremely important by the ancient philosophers, though they lacked the true knowledge of God, were the gifts of Nature and of Fortune, in bringing men as many friends and as many good children as possible.

"But I, my lord Don Quijote," replied the gentleman, "I have but one son, and perhaps, if I did not have him, I would be a happier man — and not because he's wicked, but only because he's not quite as good as I would like him to be. He's eighteen years old, and has been for the last six of those a student at Salamanca, learning Latin and Greek, and when I sought to have him turn to the study of other matters, I found him so steeped in his knowledge of poetry (if one can call that truly any sort of knowledge at all) that he couldn't be brought to deal either with law, which I wished him to pursue, or even that queen of all knowledge, theology. I have wanted him to be an honor to his family, for we live in an age when our kings proffer rich rewards to virtuous, well-deserving knowledge — for knowledge without virtue is like pearls on a dungheap. But he spends every waking minute trying to find out if Homer was correct in this or that verse of the *Iliad*; if Martial had or did not have an obscene meaning, in such and such an epigram; if such and such a line in Virgil should be understood this way or that. In a word, the only things he talks about are the works of these poets, as well as those of Horace, Persius, Juvenal, and Tibullus, for he has little or no interest in our modern Spanish writers — and yet, despite all his disdain for Spanish verse, right at the moment he's lost in the construction of a poem on some lines sent him from Salamanca, I suspect for some literary competition."

To which Don Quijote responded:

"My dear sir, children are bits of their parents' entrails, and must therefore be loved, however good or bad they may be, as we love the very souls which give us life; their parents' task is to help them, from the time they are little, to walk in the pathways of virtue, good manners, and sound Christian practices, so that, when they have grown up, they may be the staff and comforter of their parents' old age and the glory of their posterity; nor do I think it proper to oblige them to study this or that branch of knowledge, though there can be no harm in persuading them in one direction or another; and when they are not obliged to study *pane lucrando* [to earn their bread], a student lucky enough that Heaven has given him parents who can allow it should, I believe, be permitted to seek whatever form of knowledge he feels most drawn to, and though poetry is, to be sure, less practical than it is pleasurable, that does not make it anything which it is dishonorable to know. So far as I am concerned, my dear sir, poetry is like a tender young maiden, marvelously lovely, who has been given over to the care of many other young maidens, so that they may enhance, refine, and adorn her, those other young maidens being all the other forms of knowledge, all of whom, deriving their authority from her, must serve and cherish her — yet this maiden does not care to be much handled, nor dragged through the streets, nor broadcast at every street corner or even in the nooks and crannies of palaces. She is framed by an alchemy so rare that whoever knows its secrets can turn her into the purest and most precious gold; but if you possess her, you need to keep her within her proper bounds and not let her run off into clumsy satires or icy-cold sonnets; she should only be marketed in the form of heroic poems, mournful tragedies, or happy and artful comedies; buffoons should be kept away from her, as well as the ignorant mob, all of whom are incapable of understanding or appreciating the treasures she can offer. And you must not think, sir, that when I speak of the 'ignorant mob' I am referring only to humble working people, for all those who know nothing of poetry, whether they be lords or princes, can and should be thus classified. Accordingly, anyone who applies himself to poetry, and fulfills the requirements I have set out, can make his name famous and praised in all the civilized nations of the world. And from what you tell me, my dear sir, about your son not particularly valuing poetry written in our native tongue, I must conclude that, in this respect, his conclusions are not entirely sound, for the following reason: the celebrated Homer did not write in Latin, because he was a Greek, nor did Virgil write in Greek, because he was a Roman. In fact, all the classical poets wrote in the language they drank along with their mothers' milk, nor did they go hunting other tongues better suited to their noble sentiments. This being the case, it makes good sense to carry the practice into the affairs of all nations: we ought not to deprecate German poetry because it is written in German, nor Spanish poetry, and not even Basque, simply because each has been written in its own mother tongue. I suspect, however, that your son, my good sir, does not so much dislike Spanish poetry as poets who are merely Spanish, who do not know other languages and possess none of the other knowledge which can embellish and quicken and support their natural impulses — though even here it may well be that he errs, because the best opinion holds that poets are born, emerging from their mothers' wombs already poets, so that with neither study nor art, but only that with which Heaven has been pleased to endow them, they can compose works of which it has been truly said, *est deus in nobis* [Ovid, "There is a God in us"] . . . , etcetera. It must also be said, of course, that the natural poet who assists himself with art will be all the better for it, and will have the advantage over a poet who knows only what he has learned, since natural talent takes precedence over art: art can only perfect nature. Thus, blending art with nature, and nature with art, produces the best of all possible poets. Let me conclude by saying, my dear sir, that you ought to allow your son to follow his star wherever it leads him and, being as good a student as he apparently is, with the first steps already well behind him (I refer to the study of languages), he should with their assistance be able to ascend to the very summit of the humane arts, which are as eminently suitable to a cape- and sword-bearing gentleman, and adorn, honor, and dignify him, quite as much as a mitre does a bishop or long black robes do a judge. Reprimand your son, your grace, should he pen satirical verses impugning other people's honor — correct him, and destroy the verses; but if his satires are such as Horace wrote, attacking vice in general as elegantly as Horace attacked it, then praise him, since it is entirely legitimate for a poet to compose an assault on envy, and for his poems to criticize the envious, and so too other vices, so long as he does not single out particular individuals, for there are poets who, so long as they can say something truly malicious, are more than prepared to risk banishment to the outer islands of Pontus.[2] A chaste poet will produce chaste poems, for the pen speaks for the soul; whatever ideas a soul spawns will be the ideas it commits to paper; and when princes and kings find the miraculous gift of poetry at work in wise, virtuous, and serious subjects, they honor them, and esteem them, and they confer wealth upon them, and indeed even crown them with the leaves of that tree which thunderbolts never strike,[3] as if to signify that no one ought to offend against those who, being thus crowned, find themselves so honored and adorned."

The Man in the Green Overcoat was astonished at Don Quijote's speech — so much so that he began to abandon his earlier opinion that our knight was somewhat touched in the head. But Sancho, who did not much like this discourse, wandered off the road, as Don Quijote was delivering it, in order to ask some nearby shepherds, who were milking their animals, for something to drink, and then, just as the gentleman was about to respond to Don Quijote's wise and well-considered words, our knight raised his head and saw, coming down the road in the direction they'd been taking, a cart displaying two or three royal flags, which led Don Quijote, sure that a new adventure was in the offing, to shout to Sancho to bring him his helmet. Hearing this summons, Sancho turned away from the shepherds and, just as fast as he could, spurred his donkey back to where his master waited, after which there occurred an adventure which was both astounding and quite insane.

Chapter Seventeen

— which exhibits for us the absolute height and furthest extreme to which Don Quijote's unheard of courage soared or ever could soar, along with the happily concluded adventure of the lions

Our history records that when Don Quijote shouted to Sancho to bring him his helmet, our knight's squire had been in the act of purchasing some cottage cheese from the shepherds and, overwhelmed by the urgency in his master's voice, could not think what to do with his purchase, or how to carry it, and so, to keep from losing what he had already paid for, he decided to drop it into his lord's helmet. His mind put more at ease by this decision, he hurried back to see what his master wanted, and as he arrived Don Quijote said to him:

"Hand me my helmet, friend — because either I don't know much about adventures or what we see coming over there is one for which I will need, and will now proceed to, take up arms."

Hearing this, the Man in the Green Overcoat looked this way and that, but could see only the cart approaching, marked with two or three small royal flags, indicating that this was a vehicle transporting moneys belonging

---

2. The allusion here is to Ovid, who was banished to Tomis on the Black Sea (Pontus).
3. The laurel [*Translator's Note*].

to His Majesty the King, and he said as much to Don Quijote. But our knight would not believe him, always profoundly convinced that everything which came his way had to be one adventure after another, and so what he replied to the gentleman was:

"Forewarned is forearmed. Taking precautions costs me nothing, because I know from experience that my enemies may be either visible or invisible, nor can I be sure when, or where, nor at what moment, nor even in what forms and shapes they will attack me."

Turning to Sancho, he again asked for his helmet, and the squire, having no chance to remove the cottage cheese, had to hand it over as it was. Don Quijote took it and, without looking to see if there was anything in it, hurriedly stuck it on his head — and as the cheese was squashed down and then wrung out, the liquid began to run all down our knight's face and beard, so startling Don Quijote that he called out to Sancho:

"What's going on here, Sancho? It seems as if my skull's going soft, or my brains are melting, or else I'm suddenly sweating from top to bottom! But if I'm sweating, it can't be from fear, though I've no doubt that the adventure I'm about to experience will be a fearsome one. Please: give me something to clean myself with, if you've got anything, because all this perspiration is blinding me."

Without a word, Sancho handed him a rag, silently thanking God for His mercy in keeping Don Quijote from realizing the truth. Our knight wiped himself clean, then pulled off his helmet to see what had so drastically cooled his head — and seeing white pasty stuff all over the inside of the helmet, held it up to his nose and, after taking a good sniff, said:

"By the life of my lady Dulcinea del Toboso, this is cottage cheese you've put in here — traitor! scoundrel! oh, you worst of all worthless squires!"

But Sancho only replied, immensely (and falsely) calm:

"If that's really cottage cheese, your grace, just give it to me, please, and I'll eat it . . . or let the Devil swallow it, because it must have been him that put it in there! You think I'd have the nerve to dirty up your grace's helmet? You've found a bold scoundrel, you have! By my faith, señor, and the small understanding God gave me, it looks as if I must have enchanters who persecute me, too, just for being your grace's creature and right-hand man, and they've stuck that filthy stuff in there to try your patience and make you angry and get you to beat in my ribs, the way you always do. But this time, damn it, they've jumped right into nowhere, because I can trust in my master's good sense, and I know he knows I haven't got any cottage cheese, or any milk to make cottage cheese with, or anything at all like that — and if I did, I'd be putting it in my stomach, not in your grace's helmet."

"Well, who can say?" said Don Quijote.

The Gentleman in the Green Coat had been watching all this, completely astonished, and most especially when, after having cleaned his face, beard, and helmet, Don Quijote put it over his head once more and, setting himself firmly in his stirrups, proceeded to check his sword and take up his lance, saying:

"Now, whatever happens, I'm ready to take on Satan himself!"

The cart flying the royal banner reached them, just then, carrying only the driver, riding on a mule, and a single man seated behind him, in the front of the cart. Don Quijote stationed himself in their path and declared: "Where are you going, brothers? What are you carrying in there, and under what flag are you traveling?"

The driver answered:

"It's my cart, and what's in it is a couple of lions in a cage, and the Governor of Orán's sending them to court, as presents for His Majesty. The flags belong to our lord the king, to show that what's in here is his."

"Are they big lions?" asked Don Quijote.

"They're so big," said the man sitting in the front of the cart, "that Africa has never before sent bigger ones over to Spain, or even any as big as these, and I'm the lions' keeper, and I've shipped a lot of lions, but never any like these. These are a lioness and her mate; the male's in that first cage, and the female's in the one behind him, and they're pretty hungry, right now, because they haven't been fed yet today, so, if your grace will just get out of the way, we need to hurry up and get to where we can feed them."

Don Quijote smiled faintly.

"Lion cubs against me? Against me — lion cubs? and right when they're hungry? Well, we're going to show the gentlemen who sent them here whether I'm the man to worry about a couple of lions! Out of your cart, you, and since you're the lion keeper, open those cages and let these animals come out against me, and right here in the middle of this meadow I'll let them know just who Don Quijote de La Mancha is, and the devil with all the enchanters who sent them here after me."

"Ho ho," said the Gentleman in Green to himself, hearing this. "Now we know what's what with this good knight of ours. It must be the cottage cheese: it's softened his skull and made his brains go bad."

Just then Sancho came over to him, and said:

"Señor, in the name of God, do something to keep my lord Don Quijote from taking on these lions, because if he goes after them they'll tear every one of us to pieces."

"So you really think," replied the gentleman, "your master is crazy enough to take on these savage beasts?"

"He's not crazy," answered Sancho. "Just reckless."

"I'll make sure it doesn't happen," replied the gentleman.

Going over to Don Quijote, who was urging the lion keeper to hurry up and open the cages, the gentleman said:

"My dear sir, knights errant ought to engage in adventures which have at least some chance of succeeding, not those which cannot possibly end well. Courage which verges on rashness smacks more of madness than of fortitude — and especially when these lions have not attacked you — have not even dreamed of any such thing, for they come as presents to His Majesty the King, which means it would be wrong to delay or in any way interfere with their journey."

"My very dear sir," replied Don Quijote, "your grace would do well to tend your tame partridge and your bold ferret, and not mind other people's business. This is my affair, and I know perfectly well whether these lions have come after me, or whether they've not."

And turning to the lion keeper, he said:

"By God, you scoundrel, if you don't open those cages as fast as fast can be, I'll stick you to the side of the cart with this lance!"

The driver, seeing how determined this weapon-wielding apparition was, replied:

"My lord, your grace, please — in the name of charity — let me unyoke my mules and get them and myself someplace where we'll be safe, before the lions are let loose, because if they kill my mules for me it'll be the end of my life, because all I own is this cart and those mules."

"Oh ye of little faith!" responded Don Quijote. "Dismount, then, and do your unyoking, and whatever you will, but you'll soon see that it's a waste of your labor and you might just as well have saved yourself the trouble."

The driver dismounted and unyoked the mules as fast as he could, and then the lion keeper announced in a loud voice:

"Let everyone here bear witness that I open the cages and let loose the lions against my will and only because I have been forced to, and that I hereby declare to this gentleman that whatever damage and injury these animals may cause will be his responsibility and his alone, as well as my salary and everything else I'm entitled to. Please, gentlemen, all of you take cover before I throw open the doors, for I am perfectly confident they'll do me no harm whatever."

The Gentlemen in Green tried once more to persuade Don Quijote not to perpetrate such a piece of lunacy, for he was testing the Lord's patience to attempt such foolishness. Don Quijote replied that he knew exactly what he was doing. The gentleman, knowing our knight was laboring under a delusion, warned him to be very careful.

"Now then, sir," answered Don Quijote, "if your grace has no desire to be a witness to what, according to your view, is bound to be tragedy, just spur that mare of yours and ride to safety."

Hearing this, Sancho, with tears in his eyes, begged his master to give the business up, for in comparison to this affair the adventure with the windmills had been mere child's play, like the dreadful encounter with the hydraulic hammers, and, in a word, all the heroic deeds he had ever accomplished in the whole of his life.

"Remember, señor," said Sancho, "there's no magic at work, this time, and nothing at all like that, because I've seen an honest to God lion claw between the bars and cracks in those cages, which leads me to think a claw that big has got to belong to a lion bigger than a mountain."

"In any event," responded Don Quijote, "fear will certainly make him seem to you even bigger than half the world. Go away, Sancho, and let me be, and if I should die here, just remember our old agreement, and present yourself to Dulcinea — and that's all I need to tell you."

He went on, however, to make some additional comments which left no one in the slightest doubt that he fully intended to proceed with his lunatic scheme. The Man in the Green Overcoat would have liked to actively resist him, but knew he was clearly overmatched, nor did he think it sensible to exchange blows with a madman, for he was now fully convinced that a madman was exactly what Don Quijote had to be. Don Quijote turning, then, to hurry the lion keeper on, and repeat his threats, gave the gentleman in green a chance to whip up his mare, and Sancho his donkey, and the cart driver his mules, thus putting as much distance as they could between themselves and the cart, before the lions were freed.

Sancho was already weeping for his lord's death, by now convinced that this was what the lions' claws would bring, and he cursed his own ill fate, bewailing the moment when he'd decided to serve such a master, but neither his tears nor his lamentations kept him from whipping the donkey as far away from the cart as he could get. Then, seeing that those who were fleeing had gotten well away, the lion keeper turned and once more explained and announced to Don Quijote what he had already explained and announced to him, our knight replying that indeed everything that had been said had been heard and the lion keeper need not bother explaining and announcing anything more, because it was all just a waste of time — and would he please hurry matters up?

The lion keeper's delay in opening the first cage, indeed, had given Don Quijote a chance to wonder whether he would do better to fight on foot than on horseback, and he had decided that he would do better on foot, concerned that Rocinante might be frightened, seeing the lions. So he dismounted, threw his lance aside, took up his shield and, drawing his sword, went forward, step by step, with incredible courage, and set himself in front of the cart, commending himself to God with all his heart, and then to his lady Dulcinea.

Now it must be understood that, having arrived at this point, the author of this truthful history could not help exclaiming:

"Oh strong and infinitely praiseworthy spirit of Don Quijote de La Mancha, mirror in which every courageous man in the world may see himself, Second and New Coming of Don Manuel de León,[1] the honor and glory of all Spanish knighthood! How shall I relate this staggering, frightfully heroic deed? What words and arguments can make it believable to times still to come, and what praise could conceivably not be appropriate, though it be only hyperbole piled onto hyperbole? You — on foot, alone, intrepid, magnanimous, armed only with your sword (and that not of particularly distinguished manufacture), bearing a shield neither gleaming nor fashioned of burnished steel — you, awaiting and watching for a pair of the fiercest lions ever bred in the jungles of Africa! May you be praised, then, by what you were able to do, oh brave man of La Mancha! For I can say no more — I can no longer rely on words."

Here the author's aforesaid exclamation came to an end, and he went forward once more, picking up the skein of his history, relating that, once the lion keeper saw Don Quijote in his posture of readiness, and that there was nothing for it but to release the male lion (under penalty of incurring the bold and indignant knight's displeasure), the keeper threw wide the door of the first cage, in which, as has been noted, there was a lion who seemed the most incredibly large and frightful and monstrous of monsters. The first thing this beast did was turn itself around in the cage, and flex its claws, and stretch itself all over; then it opened its mouth and yawned an exceedingly lazy yawn, and stuck out a tongue almost a foot and a half

---

1. Who had entered a lion's cage to recover a lady's glove: see I.49 [*Translator's Note*].

long and cleaned off its eyes and washed its face; and then it poked its head out of the cage and, with its burning red eyes, stared this way and that — a vision capable of striking fear in even the rashest of hearts. But Don Quijote just stood there, watching carefully, and hoping the animal would leap down from the cart and come where our knight could get at it, planning to chop it to pieces.

His absolutely unparalleled madness actually went this far. But the noble lion, a good deal more civil than it was haughty, didn't pay any attention to childish foolishness or boasting: after staring this way and that, as we've said, the lion turned its back on Don Quijote and, with its hindquarters facing him, slowly and calmly stretched out on the floor of its cage. Seeing this, Don Quijote ordered the keeper to prod it with a stick and irritate it until it came out.

"No, I won't," replied the keeper, "because if I make it angry, the first one it'll tear to pieces is me. Sir knight, your grace, be satisfied with what you've done, which is all courage can be asked to do, and don't tempt Fate a second time. The lion's door is open; it's up to him whether he comes out or doesn't; and since he hasn't, you can wait all day and he still won't. You have proved what a great heart you have, your grace: as I understand these things, no brave combatant need do more than challenge his enemy and wait for him to appear; and an opponent who does not appear accepts all the dishonor, while he who stood and waited for him carries off the crown of victory."

"That's true," answered Don Quijote. "Shut the door, my friend, and write out for me, as best you can, an affidavit of what you've seen me do, to wit, when you set the lion free I stood and waited for him; he wouldn't come out; I stood and waited, but he still wouldn't come out; and then he lay down again. I need do no more — and so much for magic and enchantments! May God be forever on the side of reason, and truth, and true knighthood! Shut the door, as I said, while I signal those who have fled, so they can hear this glorious tale directly from your lips."

The keeper complied and, putting the point of his lance through the rag he'd used to clean cheese from his face, Don Quijote waved it back and forth, summoning those who had fled — and were still fleeing, the whole group of them together, the Gentleman in Green in the lead, all of them looking back over their shoulders at every step. But it was Sancho who noticed the waving white cloth:

"May I die and go to Heaven," he said, "if my master hasn't beaten those fierce beasts, because there he is, calling us back."

They all stopped, and saw that it was indeed Don Quijote who was signaling, which drained away at least some of their fear and allowed them to slowly come close enough to hear our knight calling loudly to them. So they came back to the cart and, as they arrived, Don Quijote said to the driver:

"Come back, brother, and hitch up your mules and go on your way — and you, Sancho, give him two gold pieces, one for him and one for the lion keeper, in return for the delay I caused them."

"I'll hand them over very cheerfully," replied Sancho, "but what's happened to the lions? Are they dead or alive?"

Then, in great detail, and with suitably dramatic pauses, the lion keeper told them how the combat had ended, exaggerating as much as he could Don Quijote's bravery, explaining that the very sight of that noble warrior had frightened the lion, so it didn't dare come out of its cage, though the door had been left open for a long time, and adding that it was he, the keeper, who had assured the knight that it would have been simply testing God to annoy the lion and make it come out, as Don Quijote had asked him to do. The knight had only reluctantly and very much against his will allowed the cage door to be shut.

"What do you think of that, Sancho?" said Don Quijote. "Are there enchantments worth anything against the truly valiant? Those magicians can deprive me of good fortune, but strength and spirit? Never."

Sancho handed over the two gold pieces, the driver yoked up his mules, the lion keeper kissed Don Quijote's hands in gratitude and promised to tell this glorious deed to the king himself, when he got to court.

"If His Majesty asks who performed this feat, tell him it was *The Knight of the Lions*, for from now on I wish to exchange, convert, alter, and transform the fashion by which I have hitherto been known, to wit, *The Knight of the Sad Face*, according to the ancient custom of knights errant, who regularly changed their names whenever they so desired, or had some good reason."

The cart went off in its direction, and Don Quijote, Sancho, and the Man in the Green Overcoat in theirs.

During this entire episode, Don Diego de Miranda had not uttered a word, completely absorbed in observing everything Don Quijote did and everything he said, convinced that our knight was a sane lunatic and a lunatic leaning toward sanity. He had never come across the first volume of this history, for had he read it, Don Quijote's actions and words would no longer have astonished him, knowing as he would exactly the sort of craziness involved — but not knowing, one minute he saw a sane man and the next a lunatic, because what Don Quijote said was harmonious, elegant, and well-phrased, while his actions were insane, rash, and idiotic. Don Diego said to himself:

"Is there anything crazier than to put on a helmet full of cottage cheese and persuade yourself that magicians have been softening your skull? And what could be wilder or more reckless than to deliberately pick a fight with lions?"

Don Quijote interrupted his silent musing:

"I'm sure, Don Diego de Miranda, that your grace can only think of me as a wild lunatic. It would hardly be surprising, for what else could explain what you have seen me do? All the same, I should like your grace to be aware that I am neither so mad nor so foolish as I must seem. A gallant knight looks wonderfully well, in the middle of a great arena, with his king gazing on, as he launches a fine lance stroke against a brave bull; wearing his gleaming armor, a knight makes a splendid appearance at some joyful tourney, parading in front of the ladies; and all knights come off well in military exercises, or what may seem to be military exercises, entertaining and cheering and, if one can phrase it this way, honoring their kings' courts; but every single one of them is surpassed by the knight

errant, who trods along, seeking dangerous adventures in deserts and solitary places, at crossroads and in forests and on mountains, determined to
bring each such adventure to a happy, successful conclusion, concerned
only with achieving glorious and enduring fame. To my eyes, let me say,
a knight errant in some unpopulated part of the earth, offering his assistance to a widow, seems nobler than a knight at court, in the great metropolis, flirting with some damsel. But all knights have their set tasks: let
the courtier attend to his ladies; let his uniform legitimate his king's court;
let his splendid table sustain all manner of poor knights; let him stage
tournaments, conduct tourneys, and show himself grand, open-handed,
and magnificent and, above all, a good Christian, and thus fulfill to the
letter all his obligations. But the knight errant scours the far corners of the
earth, penetrating into the narrowest, most elaborate labyrinths, adjusting
himself at every step to the impossible, enduring out on the unpopulated
frontiers the hot summer sun and the harsh winds and snows of winter,
not startled by lions, not frightened by monsters, not afraid of dragons, for
it is these after which he goes hunting, and to attack and conquer them
all is his principal and also the most profound of his tasks.

"When it fell to my lot to become one of this group of knights errant,
I could not keep from taking on all the obligations which, it seemed to
me, fell under the jurisdiction of my profession, so that my encounter with
these lions was something I was absolutely obliged to attempt (even understanding, as of course I do, that it was the very extreme of rashness),
because I also know that courage is a virtue that necessarily oscillates
between two prejudicial extremes, one of which is cowardice, and the
other recklessness. But it is the lesser of two evils for a brave man to ascend
to the very edge of rashness, rather than risk falling into the pit of cowardice: just as it is easier for a wastrel than for a miser to be generous, so
too is it easier for a reckless man to be truly courageous than for a coward
to ascend to true valor. In this business of taking on adventures, Señor
Don Diego, your grace, believe me: it is better to lose by playing too many
cards than by playing too few, for I would rather have it said of me 'That
knight is reckless and excessively bold' than 'That knight is timid and a
coward.' "

"And let me say, my lord Don Quijote," replied Don Diego, "that everything your grace has said, and everything your grace has done, is
touched with the same consistent and correct logic: if ever all knowledge
of the rules and regulations of knight errantry should be lost, they could
be found, as if in their fit and proper depository and archive, right in your
grace's breast. Let us hurry, now, because it is growing late, and come to
my own village and my own house, where your grace can rest, after your
recent labors — which have not been simply physical, but also of the
spirit, which can frequently produce bodily fatigue as well."

"I am very grateful for your very kind invitation, my dear Don Diego,"
replied Don Quijote.

Picking up their pace, accordingly, it was about two in the afternoon
when they arrived at the village and home of the man Don Quijote now
dubbed "The Knight of the Green Overcoat."

Chapter Eighteen

— what happened to Don Quijote in the castle (or house) of the Knight of the Green Overcoat, along with other odd and unusual things

Don Quijote found Don Diego de Miranda's house a large rural-style dwelling; but the family coat of arms, though fashioned in rough stone, hung over the main door, which faced out on the street; the inner court-yard served as a storeroom, and the front hall as a wine cellar, and there were great wine jugs all over — and since they'd been manufactured in Toboso,[1] our knight was reminded of his now enchanted and transformed Dulcinea, so that, sighing, and without reflecting on what he was saying or in front of whom he might be saying it, he declaimed:

> "Oh sweet jewels, which I see once more,
> God let you be sweet and happy, once![2]

"Oh jars of Toboscan lineage, how you have brought to my mind the sweet jewel of my greatest sorrow!"

Don Diego's son, the student poet, who together with his mother had emerged to greet them, heard these words, and both he and his mother were astonished at the strange figure of Don Quijote, who, dismounting from Rocinante, came forward with great courtesy to kiss the lady's hands. Don Diego said:

"My lady, please welcome, with all your usual grace, Don Quijote de La Mancha, who stands now before you, a knight errant and the bravest as well as the wisest knight anywhere in the world."

His wife, known as Doña Christina, thereupon welcomed Don Quijote with great warmth and courtesy, and the knight presented himself to her with an abundance of well-chosen and polite words. He said virtually the same things to the student, who thereupon took Don Quijote to be a man of discretion and intelligence.

The author of our history, at this point, supplies an elaborate description of Don Diego's house, showing us what is likely to be found in a rich gentleman farmer's house, but the author's translator decided to pass over these and other very similar trifles in silence, since they don't comport well with the main themes of this history, the strength of which comes more from its truth than from such dull digressions.

Don Quijote was taken to a chamber, where Sancho took off his armor, leaving our knight in Walloon-style[3] knickers and a suede jacket, badly stained by his armor; the collar was soft and broad, student fashion, unstarched and without any lace or other trimming; his undershoes were brown and his overshoes were waxed. His good sword hung from a sealskin shoulder-strap (for it is said that for many years he'd suffered from kidney disease),[4] and he wore a plain, collarless short cape of good grey wool. But

---

1. Famous for such manufacture [*Translator's Note*].
2. Garcilaso de la Vega, Sonnet X, universally known; the poet is said to have been inspired by coming upon a lock of his dead mistress's hair [*Translator's Note*].
3. Walloons were the inhabitants of the southeastern provinces of Belgium.
4. And was therefore unable to wear the more usual waist-belt [*Translator's Note*].

the most important thing was that, with five, or perhaps six pots of water (for there is some disagreement as to the exact quantity employed), he washed both his head and his face — though the water, instead of coming out clean, persisted in looking like curds and whey, thanks to Sancho's having lusted after cottage cheese and then having bought the damned stuff, which had turned his master white. And so adorned, with polished grace and elegance, Don Quijote went into the next room, where the student awaited him, charged with entertaining the guest while the table was being set — for the arrival of such a distinguished visitor made Doña Christina anxious to show that she not only knew how to properly receive a guest, but also had the proper wherewithal.

Now while Don Quijote's armor was being removed, Don Lorenzo (for that was Don Diego's son's name) took the opportunity to speak to his father:

"Sir, how are we to take this knight you've brought home with you? His name — his appearance — the way he says he's a knight errant: my mother and I don't know what to make of him."

"I'm not sure what I should tell you, my son," replied Don Diego, "except that I've seen him do some of the craziest things in the world, but also say such wise things that they completely erase and wipe out what he's done: speak to him, find out what he knows about what you know and, since you've good judgment, see whether wisdom or foolishness prevails in his speech. But in all truth I must say that I'd be more inclined to think him mad than sane."

Accordingly, Don Lorenzo set out to entertain Don Quijote, as we have noted, and among other things they said to one another was this remark of Don Quijote's:

"Lord Don Diego de Miranda, your good father, has informed me of your grace's unusual skills and subtle intelligence, and in particular that you're quite a considerable poet."

"I can say I'm a poet," replied Lorenzo, "but I have no claim to any real merit. I'm certainly deeply devoted to poetry and to reading good poets, but my father's praise can't in any way be justified."

"Such humility strikes me as a very good thing," said Don Quijote, "because poets have a way of being arrogant and thinking themselves the very best in the world."

"All rules have their exceptions," answered Don Lorenzo, "for there must be some who deserve such praise but don't themselves think so."

"Not many," replied Don Quijote. "But tell me, your grace: what kind of poem are you working at, right now, for your father has told me it made you somewhat restless and preoccupied? And if it's a poem written in response to someone else's lines, I know something about such work and would be pleased to learn more; if it's for a poetry competition, you ought to aim at the second prize, your grace, because the first prize is always awarded as an act of patronage or in recognition of social standing, but second prize strictly on merit, so that third prize really amounts to second, and what's called first prize, if you calculate matters this way, has to be truly the third — much in the fashion that universities award advanced degrees. All the same, to win first prize is worth a good deal."

"Well," said Don Lorenzo to himself, "as far as we've gotten, I certainly couldn't call you crazy. But let's proceed."

So he said:

"I should think your grace has pretty clearly attended lectures at a university. In what field?"

"Knight errantry," replied Don Quijote, "which is quite as noble an undertaking as poetry, and even a bit more."

"I have no idea what branch of knowledge that might be," said Don Lorenzo, "because till now I've never heard of it."

"It's the kind of study," said Don Quijote, "which embraces within itself all, or most, of the world's knowledge, since he who takes up that profession must have mastered the law, including the laws of both distributive and equitable justice, so he can give every man that to which he is rightly entitled; he must also be a theologian, in order to clearly, distinctly, and correctly understand the Christian law to which he professes obedience, whenever its applicability is invoked; he must be a physician, and in particular an herbalist, so he knows what plants and roots can heal his wounds, even in the middle of uninhabited lands and deserts, for a knight errant cannot forever be stopping to hunt for people who can cure him; he must be an astrologer, so that the stars will tell him the time, even at night, and so he can know what part of the world, and in what climate, he finds himself; he must know mathematics, because he'll find himself constantly in need of it; and above and beyond the necessity that he be adorned with all the theological and primary virtues, we must descend to all sorts of other, minor requirements — for example, that he be able to swim as well, according to legend, as the Italian half-man, half-fish, Nicolas; that he be able to shoe a horse and mend his saddle and bridle; and — to return to loftier matters — that he keep faith with God and with his lady; his thoughts must be chaste, his words modest, his actions generous, his labor patient; he must be charitable to the needy and, to sum it all up, a defender of the truth, though he lose his life in the process. A good knight errant is composed of all these parts, large and small, from which your grace can judge, Don Lorenzo, whether the knowledge a knight errant must acquire, and study, and profess, is or is not the equal of the most elaborate matters taught in our colleges and universities."

"If it's as you say it is," answered Don Lorenzo, "I should have to say that this is the highest of all forms of knowledge."

"Why 'if I say it is'?" asked Don Quijote.

"What I mean," replied Don Lorenzo, "is that I very much doubt there has ever been, or there now is, anyone we can properly call a knight errant, adorned with all of those virtues."

"I have often said," responded Don Quijote, "what I will now say once again, which is that most people do not in fact believe that knights errant ever existed; and since I see that, by some miracle, Heaven has not brought them to the realization that there have been and still are knights errant, no matter how hard I may struggle to convince them I am bound to struggle in vain — as my experience has demonstrated, over and over — I therefore have no desire, now, to stop to correct an erroneous belief which you share with so many others. All I can do is pray that Heaven may enlighten you, letting you understand how beneficial and necessary knights errant have been, in the past, and how useful they might be to the world, today, if we cared to make use of them — though, for our sins, what now triumphs are sloth, indifference, gluttony, and pampered luxury."

"Here's where our guest gets away from us," Don Lorenzo said to himself, at this point, "but just the same he's a wonderful lunatic, and I'd be a lamebrained fool not to realize it."

And so their conversation ended, for they were summoned to dinner. Don Diego immediately asked his son what he'd learned of their guest's mind, to which the young man answered:

"All the learned doctors in the world will never come to a clear understanding of his madness, because he's plainly an off-again on-again madman, shot full of lucid streaks."

They sat down at table and, just as he'd told them, en route, the meal was exactly the sort Don Diego always furnished his guests: well-arranged, plentiful, and delicious. But what most pleased Don Quijote was the marvelous silence which pervaded the entire house, which seemed for all the world like a Carthusian monastery. When, in due course, the tablecloth had been removed, God had been thanked for their meal, and water brought so they could wash their hands, Don Quijote pressed Don Lorenzo to recite what he had written for the literary tournament, and the young man replied that, not wishing to be one of those writers who refused to recite his poems, if asked, but always belched them forth when not asked to:

" — to avoid which, I will recite my poem about a poem for you, though I expect it to win me nothing: I wrote it simply and solely to challenge myself."

"A good friend of mine, and a wise man," responded Don Quijote, "takes the position that no one ought to bother himself with making poems about other people's poems, his argument being that the second poem can never equal the first one, and often, or even most of the time, the second poem wanders away from the original's purpose and plan — and, what's more, the second poet finds himself far too restricted, because he's not allowed to use any interrogative constructions, or 'he said' or 'I will say', and he can't use the nominal forms of verbs, and he can't change the meaning, plus all sorts of other limitations and requirements built into the rules of the contest, as your grace knows only too well."

"Truly, Señor Don Quijote," said Don Lorenzo, "I wish I could catch your grace making mistakes,[5] but I can't, because you slip out of my hands like an eel."

"I'm afraid I have no idea," answered Don Quijote, "what your grace means about my slipping out of your hands."

"I'll come back to that," replied Don Lorenzo. "For now, just listen to the poem we were supposed to respond to, and my response:

5. The word for "mistake," here, is, significantly, *mal latín*, "incorrect Latin" [*Translator's Note*].

ORIGINAL POEM

If all that *might* should turn to *is*,
There'd be nothing more *to be*:
If only what my eyes could see
Were what my heart has wished!⁶

RESPONSE

Just as everything fades away
In the end, so Fortune's favors
Ebbed and died, trickled slowly
To nothing, shaded
And forever old.
I've groveled here at Fortune's feet
For centuries, praying for grace;
Oh let me see some newborn sweetness
Shine in her face,
Rise up complete.
I long for nothing more, no glory,
No joy, no other victory,
No burning triumph, no eternal story,
But only the history
That was, and destroyed me.
Fortune, oh let me be there again,
And soon, and this searing heat,
This pressing pain, will be soothed, and the end
Will be endlessly sweet
And all complete.
But I want too much, for nothing and no one
Can restore what's disappeared;
Time never turns, it's never been done;
No past reappears,
No history draws near.
Time runs and leaps, flies quickly by,
And never turns back, and we're wrong
To beg it to stop, to return: the sky
Of yesterday is gone
Like yesterday's song.
My life is perpetual confusion, hoping
And fearing, first hope, then fear,
Forever believing that Death's stern joke
Is better than tears
Over long-dead years.
But still, as I long for this life to be done,
I know that what I possess
Is better than anything yet to be won
In that unknown emptiness
Still to come.

---

6. Murillo notes that these graceful lines are not by Cervantes [*Translator's Note*].

As Don Lorenzo finished his poem, Don Quijote rose up and, his voice so loud it was almost a cry, shook the young man's hand, declaring:

"In the name of all that's holy, my noble young fellow, you're the best poet alive, and you deserve to be the laureate not just of Cyprus or Gaeta[7] (as a poet once said, may God forgive him)[8] but of the Academies of Athens itself, if they still existed, and of today's Academies in Paris, Bologna, and Salamanca! And if the judges fail to award you first prize, I pray to Heaven that Phoebus Apollo pierce them with his arrows and none of the Muses ever condescend to walk through their doorways. Please, my dear sir, please recite for me something written in a longer-breathed meter, so I can feel the full pulse of your amazing mind."

Need it be said how much Don Lorenzo relished Don Quijote's praise — even though the young man considered our knight a lunatic? Ah, Flattery, how powerful your reach, how vast the boundaries of your pleasant realm! Don Lorenzo promptly proved your potency by granting Don Quijote's request and reciting for him the following sonnet, written about the fable of Pyramus and Thisbe:

SONNET

A pretty girl once cracked a fence
And tore a hole in Pyramus' breast;
Then Love flew in from Cyprus, impressed
To find such a gaping, tiny rent.
But all was silent, for words never went
Across such a narrow bridge: yet the rest
Was done; hearts can fly with the best
In the world, once Love has made his entrance.
Desire works too fast; a careless
Virgin outruns good sense, uncovers
Death instead of the pleasure she sought:
The strangest story! A tiny, airless
Crack turns into death, but lovers
Live and die, over and over and over.

"My thanks to God," cried Don Quijote, after having heard Don Lorenzo's sonnet, "for having shown me, among all the worn-out poets we can find all around us, one truly worthy poet like you, your grace — for the powerful art of this sonnet proves what a poet you are!"

Don Quijote stayed four days in Don Diego's house, royally entertained, and at the end of that time asked his host for permission to leave, explaining that although he deeply appreciated Don Diego's favor, and the superb hospitality to which he had been treated, it seemed to him inappropriate for a knight errant to allow himself too much rest and ease, so he meant to fulfill the requirements of his knightly office, which necessitated that he seek adventures — and since he had heard they would not be hard to find, in that neighborhood, he hoped to keep himself profitably busy until the time came to ride off to the tournaments at Zaragoza, which had

7. On the southern coast of Italy, about halfway between Rome and Naples [Translator's Note].
8. Juan Baustista de Bivar, praised in Cervantes's *Galatea* [Translator's Note].

all along been his intended destination, though he planned first of all to have a look at Montesinos' Cave, about which so many incredible tales were told for miles around, and also to find and explore the spring said to be the true source of the seven lakes of Ruidera.

Both Don Diego and his son praised our knight's honorable resolve, inviting him to take, either from the house or the estate surrounding it, anything that might be of use to him, for they would be delighted to be of assistance, so compelling did they find his personal courage and the worthiness of his profession.

So the day of Don Quijote's departure came — as cheerful a day for our knight as it was a sad and gloomy one for Sancho Panza, who had felt completely at home in the flowing abundance of Don Diego's house, and was deeply disinclined to return to the constant hunger he'd experienced out in the woods and to rummaging as best he could in his poorly stocked saddlebags. Still, he stuffed them to overflowing with everything he thought it best to bring.

"I'm not sure," said Don Quijote to their host's son, as they were saying farewell, "whether I've previously mentioned to your grace that, should you wish to save yourself all the difficulty and trouble to be found along the inaccessible pathways which lead to Fame's great heights, all you need do is turn aside, for a bit, from the highways of Poetry, narrow as they are, and try the even more torturous path of knight errantry, which are however sufficiently wide to make you an emperor in two shakes of a lamb's tail."

These words were quite sufficient to settle the question of his madness, but he strengthened the case against himself by adding:

"God knows I should have liked to take Don Lorenzo with me, to teach him how he must forgive those humbler than himself, just as he must trample and bring down the haughty and arrogant, these being virtues which are part and parcel of the profession I uphold, but even apart from his youth, and the prior claims of his own worthy profession, it is enough for me to recall to you, young man, that, being a poet, you are more likely to win fame if you allow yourself to be guided more by other people's opinions than by your own, for no father and no mother ever see their children as worthless and ugly, and this tendency to self-deception is nowhere stronger than with the children of one's mind."

Father and son both marveled yet again at Don Quijote's jumbled brain, one minute wise and the next foolish, just as they were again struck by the obsessive tenacity with which he pursued his misadventures, thinking them the very height and culmination of all his desires. Everyone repeated compliments and courtesies and then, with the permission of the lady of the castle, Don Quijote and Sancho took their leave, the one mounted on Rocinante and the other on his donkey.

Chapter Nineteen

— which tells the adventure of the lovesick shepherd, along with other truly charming matters

Don Quijote had not gone very far from Don Diego's village when he met two men who might have been either priests or students, traveling with a pair of peasants, and all of them riding on animals that were definitely donkeys. One of the students was carrying, wrapped in green linen (as if it had been a suitcase), what seemed to be a small piece of scarlet cloth and two pairs of homemade wool socks; the other was carrying only a pair of brand-new fencing foils, both sheathed with leather buttons. The peasants were carrying all sorts of things, which seemed to indicate that the lot of them were heading back to their village, having gone shopping in some good-sized town. Quite as startled as were most people, seeing Don Quijote for the first time, students and peasants alike burned with curiosity to find out just who this man, so utterly unlike other men, might be.

Don Quijote greeted them and, after learning that he and they were all going in the same direction, offered to ride along with them, but requesting that they slow their pace, for their donkeys were considerably faster than his horse; and then, to be obliging, he briefly explained to them who he was and the nature of his profession, that he was a knight errant who went all over the world in search of adventures. He told them that his proper name was Don Quijote de La Mancha, but that he was also known as *The Knight of the Lions*. As far as the peasants were concerned, all this might have been spoken in Greek or Gibberish, but not so the students, who immediately understood that Don Quijote was weak-brained — though all the same they thought him something quite wonderful and deserving of respect. One of them said to him:

"If, sir knight, your grace is following no set path, which is usually the case with those who seek adventures, you might well come along with us, and you'll see one of the most splendid, glorious weddings ever celebrated anywhere in La Mancha or, for that matter, for many miles around."

Don Quijote inquired if this was to be the wedding of some prince, for it to be praised in such grand terms.

"No," answered the student, "it's just a farmer and a farmer's daughter, but he's the richest farmer around here and she's the most beautiful girl anyone's ever seen. And it's going to be an extraordinary celebration, as well as a novel one, because they're going to be married in a meadow near the bride's village; she's always called Quiteria the Beautiful, and her husband's known as Camacho the Rich; she's eighteen years old, and he's twenty-two; they're absolutely birds of a feather, though some busybodies who know everything about who's related to whom claim that the lovely Quiteria's lineage is better than Camacho's; but nobody pays any attention to those things any more: if you've got enough money, that takes care of a lot of problems. Anyway, this Camacho doesn't mind spending money, and he felt like turning the whole meadow into one huge covered bower, so the sun's going to have a hard time if it wants to peep in on the green grass growing all over. He's also supplying sword-dancers and bell-ringing dancers, because where he comes from they've got people who really know how to handle bells — and I won't even mention toe-and-heel dancers, because he's got them coming from all over.

"Still, what makes this a remarkable wedding is none of that, nor any of the other things I'm leaving out, but our angry, jealous Basilio, and what he's likely to be up to. This Basilio's a young shepherd who comes from the same village as Quiteria; his house is right next door to hers, so Love decided to repeat the same little game it played, a long time ago, with those forgotten lovers, Pyramus and Thisbe, because Basilio fell in love with Quiteria almost before he could walk, and she responded to his affection with a thousand modest tokens of love, so that the village people were always talking about the games of those two little children, Basilio and Quiteria. But as they grew older, Quiteria's father decided that Basilio should no longer come and go at will in their house, and indeed, to free himself of lingering doubts and suspicions, the father arranged for his daughter to marry Camacho the Rich, for he did not think a marriage to Basilio would be particularly advantageous, Fortune not having been as generous to that young man as Nature had — because to tell the plain, unvarnished truth, Basilio is the nimblest, strongest young fellow we've ever seen, able to toss the weighted bar mighty distances, a first-class wrestler, and a magnificent handball player; he also runs like a deer, jumps higher than a goat, and plays bowls like a magician; and he sings like a lark, plays the guitar so well you can almost hear it speaking and, most impressively of all, he can fence with the best of them."

"That accomplishment alone," said Don Quijote, hearing this, "makes this young fellow a worthy husband not just for Quiteria, but for Queen Guinevere herself, if she were still alive — and never mind Lancelot and all those others who might try to stop him."

"Go tell that to my wife!" exclaimed Sancho Panza, who had been jogging along in silence, listening. "She wants everybody to marry people like themselves, the way they say 'birds of a feather flock together.' But what I want is for this good Basilio — because I'm already starting to like him — to marry this lady Quiteria, and let everyone who tries to get in the way of people who really want to get married live peacefully and prosperously — I mean, just the opposite!"

"If all those who really wanted to were able to get married," said Don Quijote, "parents would no longer have the right to choose when and with whom their children ought to marry, and if girls were allowed to pick their own husbands there'd be some who'd choose their parents' servants, and some who'd choose anyone they saw going by, out in the street, who looked gallant and magnificent to them, though in fact he was a good-for-nothing bully, because love and affection have a way of blinding the understanding, which is so important in choosing your way of life, and marriage is so peculiarly liable to that kind of error that you need Heaven's blessing and infinite care to make a proper choice. Anyone starting off on a long trip, if he's sensible, will first try to hunt up some safe and pleasant companions for the road — and why shouldn't you do exactly that, when the trip you're taking is your whole life, right down to the moment when Death ends it, and even more when the companion you're choosing will have to share your bed, and your table, and every other part of your life, as a wife does with her husband? Your wife's companionship isn't some kind of merchandise you buy and then decide you don't want, so you trade it for something else, or you exchange it for a new one, because marriage is indivisible, and lasts as long as life itself; it's a bond that, once you tie it around your neck, turns into a Gordian Knot that only Death's sharp scythe can ever cut. And I could say much, much more on this subject, were I not so interested in hearing what else our university graduate may have to tell us about Basilio."

To which the university student — or university graduate, as Don Quijote called him — replied:

"All I have left to say is that, from the very moment Basilio learned Quiteria the Beautiful was to marry Camacho the Rich, no one has ever seen him smile or laugh or speak a sensible word; he walks around, sad and thoughtful, talking to himself, all of which pretty plainly indicates that he's lost his mind; he hardly eats or sleeps, and when he does eat he only eats fruit, and the only place he sleeps, when he does sleep, is out in the fields, right on the hard ground, like a wild animal, sometimes looking up at the sky, and sometimes staring into the earth in such a fit of who knows what enchantment that he'd look like a statue wearing clothes if the wind didn't blow his garments this way and that. He shows such clear evidence of lovesickness that everyone who knows him is afraid that, when the priest questions Quiteria, tomorrow, and she says 'I do', for him it will be a death sentence."

"God will take care of everything," said Sancho, "because God, who inflicts wounds, also provides remedies, and no one knows what will happen: there are a lot of hours between now and tomorrow, and in any one of them, even at any single moment, the roof may fall on your head. I've seen it be rainy and sunny at the same time, and sometimes people lie down at night, perfectly healthy, and never move again. And tell me, who's ever boasted he could shove a nail into its spokes and stop the wheel of Fortune? No one, by God, and I wouldn't try to stick the point of a pin between a woman's 'yes' and her 'no,' because it wouldn't fit. Just tell me Quiteria really loves Basilio, and really wants him, and I'll give you a whole sack of good luck, because, from what I've heard, love looks through colored glasses that can make copper seem like gold, and poverty like wealth, and bleary eyes shine like pearls."

"What on earth are you trying to say, Sancho, damn you?" said Don Quijote. "Once you start reeling off proverbs and tittle-tattle, no one but Judas himself can figure out where you're heading. Now tell me, you idiot, what do you know about nails, or wheels and spokes, or anything else?"

"Ah," replied Sancho. "If you don't understand me, then no wonder you think I'm gabbling nonsense. That's all right: I understand me, and I know there's enough good sense in what I said. It's just that you, your grace, my lord, you're always intestigating what I say — and what I do, too."

"You mean *investigating*," said Don Quijote, "not *intestigating*, you corrupter of good speech — may the good Lord confound you."

"Don't get all excited with me, your grace," responded Sancho, "because you know I wasn't brought up at court, and I've never studied at Salamanca, so I could figure out whether I ought to add or subtract a letter from what I say. In the name of God, you can't expect a country bumpkin to talk like a man from Madrid — and I'll bet there are people who've lived in Madrid all their lives and still couldn't handle all this fancy talk."

"That's true," said the university student, "because if you're brought up around the tanneries, or out on the street, you're not going to talk like those who spend every day deep in the Cathedral, but you're all from Madrid, just the same. Good speech — pure and accurate, elegant and clear — comes from good, sensible courtiers, even if they were born in Majalahonda, and I say 'sensible' because many of them aren't, and good sense is the very structure of good language, and goes along with good usage. For my sins, gentlemen, I've studied canon law at Salamanca, and I like to think I can speak my mind in simple, precise, meaningful terms."

"If you didn't prefer wagging those fencing foils to wagging your tongue," said the other student, "you'd have been first in your class, instead of hanging out the rear."

"Look here, Corchuelo, my friend," was the answer. "If you really think fencing skill is nothing but a waste of time, you're about as wrong as you could be."

"As far as I'm concerned, that's not an opinion," replied Corchuelo, "it's the well-established truth, and if you'd like me to prove it to you, first hand, well, you've got a pair of foils, we've got the time, and I'm strong, my hands are steady — and if you add in my courage and energy, which are considerable, I'll make you admit I'm not fooling myself. Dismount; use all the mathematical principles of this so-called science of fencing;[1] and I expect that, with my own rough, modern skills — and next to God I put my trust in them — I can make you see stars at noontime, because I don't think the man's been born who can force me to give up, and I don't think there's anyone in the world I can't force to give ground."

"Whether you'll give up or not, I don't know, and I don't care," replied the swordsman, "though it could very well be that wherever you first set your back foot might also be where we'll have to dig your grave — by which I mean that right on that spot you might well be lying dead, on account of your scorn for the science of fencing."

"So now we'll see," replied Corchuelo.

And jumping nimbly off his donkey, he angrily pulled out one of the fencing foils his friend was carrying.

"No, it can't be done that way," said Don Quijote at once. "I wish to be in charge of this match, as well as the judge of this much-discussed controversy."

Accordingly, he too dismounted and, holding his lance, set himself in the middle of the road, just as the swordsman, moving gracefully and almost like a dancer, came at Corchuelo, who threw himself into combat, as they say, with fire in his eyes. The two peasants who'd been accompa-

---

1. The utility or nonutility of scientific fencing was at this time in hot dispute [Translator's Note].

nying them stayed on their donkeys, mere spectators of this mortal tragedy. Corchuelo attempted a rapid series of slashes and thrusts, downward strokes, backhand sweeps and fierce, two-handed blows, which fell heavier than hail. He charged like a furious lion, but all he got for his pains was a slap on the mouth from the leather button at the tip of his friend's sword, which brought him up short, forcing him to kiss the tip of his opponent's sword like some holy relic, though not quite so devoutly as relics ought to be and usually are kissed.

And then the swordsman proceeded to tick off, one by one, the buttons on the short cassock Corchuelo was wearing, and turned the flaring hem of the cassock into neat, short strips, much like an octopus' tentacles; he twice knocked off his friend's hat, and so wore down Corchuelo that in a fit of wild anger he took his foil by the hilt and threw it so high and so far that one of the watching peasants (who happened to be a notary), who went to fetch it, afterwards declared it had been thrown almost two miles — which testimony will show very nicely, as indeed it has, how very true it is that skill will always defeat strength.

Corchuelo then sat down, exhausted; Sancho went over to him, saying:

"By God, mister university student, if your grace will take my advice, from now on don't challenge anybody to a fencing match, but only to wrestling or throwing the heavy weight, because you're young enough, and strong enough, for that sort of thing, and I've heard that these people who talk about scientific fencing can thread a needle with the point of their sword."

"Enough," said Corchuelo. "I've been knocked off my donkey, and the experience has shown me that what I thought was nonsense is really truth."

So he got up, embraced the swordsman, and they became faster friends than ever, and without waiting for the notary (who'd gone to fetch the sword), because they could see it was going to take him a long time, they decided to ride on, so they could reach Quiteria's village, where all the others had gathered, before it grew late.

The swordsman talked to them, the rest of the way, about the joys and sublimities of fencing, using such evocative language and employing such mathematical diagrams and proofs, that every one of them became well-educated in the pleasures of the science, and Corchuelo's obstinacy was completely cured.

They were almost there, as it grew dark, but before they actually arrived it seemed to each and every one of them that, spread out in front of the village, they saw a canopy of millions of gleaming stars. They also heard a jumble of sweet-toned sounds coming from all sorts of different instruments — flutes, drums, hand-held harps, shepherds' pipes, great tambourines, and timbrels — and as they arrived they saw that the pillars of an arbor, constructed at the entrance to the village, were full of steady-burning lights, untroubled by the wind, which just then was blowing so gently that it could not so much as stir the leaves in the trees. What they had heard were the wedding celebrants, divided into bands that wandered up and down that pleasant spot, some dancing, some singing, and others playing all the different instruments just mentioned. Indeed, peace and happiness seemed to be leaping and frolicking all over the meadow.

There were a good many people putting up scaffolding, from which, the next day, they would be better able to watch all the dancing and the performances scheduled to take place, in honor of the rich Camacho's wedding and poor Basilio's funeral. Don Quijote would not enter the village, though both the peasants and the university students begged him to, but excused himself (more than sufficiently, to his way of thinking) by explaining that knights errant customarily slept in the fields and forests, rather than in populated places and under gilded roofs. So he rode a little way off the road (much against Sancho's better judgment, who could not help remembering how well he'd been accommodated in Don Diego's luxurious house, which might well be called a castle).

Chapter Twenty

— the story of Camacho the Rich's wedding, and what happened to poor Basilio

The fair white Dawn had barely given gleaming Phoebus the time, with his burning rays, to dry away the liquid pearls in her golden hair, when Don Quijote, shaking the sleepiness out of his limbs, jumped up and called to his squire Sancho, who still lay there, snoring; seeing which, our knight declared, before waking him:

"Oh you, blessed above all those living on the face of the earth, for you live both unenvied and without envy, and you sleep with your spirit at ease, with no sorcerers chasing after you, and no enchantments to leap up at your face! Sleep on, I say, and I will say a hundred times more, with no unceasing, devoted vigils over your lady, your rest undisturbed by thoughts of how you will ever pay the debts you owe, not wondering how, tomorrow, you'll be able to feed yourself and your tiny, anxious family. No ambitions trouble you, nor are you wearied by the world's vain shows, for your worries run no farther afield than caring for your donkey: you have laid your burdens on my shoulders, where such responsibilities are naturally and customarily placed. The servant sleeps, and the master lies awake, thinking how to carry the loads he has assumed, and even improve his servant's life, and find the means to reward him. The servant feels no anxiety when the sky turns to bronze and the earth receives none of the moisture it needs; he leaves such worries to his master, who in times of barrenness and hunger must find ways of feeding those who served him when the earth was fertile and food was abundant."

Sancho made no answer to any of this, because he kept on sleeping, and would have stayed asleep had not Don Quijote brought him awake with the butt handle of his lance. He woke up, at last, still heavy with sleep, and then, turning his face this way and that, said:

"Unless I'm much mistaken, there's a scent, a fragrance blowing from that arbor over there, which breathes more of fried bacon than of reeds and rushes and thyme: weddings which begin with such perfume ought to be heaped-up and free-flowing occasions, by my soul."

"That's enough, you glutton," said Don Quijote. "Come, let's go and see these marriage vows, and find out what that rejected Basilio does."

"Just let him do whatever he wants to," replied Sancho. "He can't be a poor man and marry Quiteria. Isn't it enough not to have a dime and still want to fly up in the clouds? By God, señor, it seems to me poor people have to be satisfied with where they find themselves, not go asking for the moon. I'd bet my right arm that Camacho could just pack Basilio in gold, and if that's the case, as it has to be, what a dumbbell Quiteria would be, if she turned her back on all the gowns and jewels Camacho must have given her, and he can go on giving her, so she could pick, instead, Basilio's weight-throwing and fencing. No tavern gives you a pint of wine for a good weight-toss or a fine sword-show. You can't get anyone to buy tricks and fun, so let Count Dirlos[1] have them, but when people with hard cash have talents like that, I just wish my life looked like theirs. You can build a fine building on a good foundation, and the best foundation in the world is money."

"In the name of God, Sancho," said Don Quijote, interrupting him, "that's enough speechifying. If you were allowed to follow every path you start down, I dare say you'd have no time left to eat or sleep, because you'd spend every minute of it talking."

"Now if you'll just think back, your grace," replied Sancho, "and remember the agreement we made, before we started out this last time: one of the specifications was that I had to be allowed to talk as much as I wanted to, just as long as I didn't say anything against my fellow man or your grace's authority, and it seems to me that, to this point, I haven't broken that agreement."

"I don't remember any such agreement," said Don Quijote, "and even if there was one, I want you to stop talking and come along, because the musical instruments we heard last night have begun brightening up the valley again, and before too long, surely, the wedding vows will be exchanged, while the morning's still fresh, rather than in the heat of the afternoon."

Sancho did as his master commanded; he saddled Rocinante, put on the donkey's saddlebags, and then they both mounted and went slowly along, into the arbor.

The very first thing Sancho saw was a young bull, spitted on the trunk of an elm tree, and in the fire where it was to be roasted a small mountain of wood was already burning; the six kettle pots set around the bonfire weren't the usual sort, but six huge wine jars, each one big enough to hold a wholesale meat market: you could easily have shoved a whole sheep into any one of them and hidden it from view like a pigeon. Countless hares already skinned, and chickens already plucked, were hanging from the trees, ready to be popped into the kettles; there was an infinity of birds of every sort, strung up on the branches so the air could keep them cool.

Sancho counted more than sixty wineskins, each holding six gallons, and each, as it later turned out, full to bursting with first-rate wine. There were stacks of the finest white bread, piled up like heaps of wheat on the threshing floor. There were cheeses set one on top of the other, like a wall

---

1. Hero of a popular ballad about the Carolingian kings [*Translator's Note*].

of bricks, and two vats of oil, bigger than the cauldrons in a dyer's shop, for frying crullers and fritters that would then be pulled out with two huge poles and plunged into yet another vat, standing right alongside, which contained a honey mixture.

There were more than fifty cooks, male and female, all of them spotlessly clean, all of them quick-moving, all of them pleased to be there. The bull's huge belly was stuffed with a dozen tender little suckling pigs, sewn into place, one on top of the other, to add flavor and help tenderize the meat. All the different spices and herbs looked as if they hadn't been bought by the pound but by the gallon; they were lying in a great chest, for everyone to see. In short, it was clearly a rustic wedding, but so plentifully supplied that it could have fed an army.

Sancho Panza looked around at everything, and considered everything, and liked everything. He was primarily enthralled by the huge kettle pots, from which he'd loved to have helped himself to a medium-sized dinner; but then he turned to doting on the wonderful wineskins; and finally to the fritters and crullers popping out of the skillets (if it's proper to use such a petty name for such deep-bellied cauldrons); and then, unable to contain himself, or to think about anything else, he went up to one of the attentive cooks and, in courteous, famished terms begged to be allowed to dip a crust of bread into one of the kettle pots. To which the cook responded:

"Brother, today hunger has no power over anyone, thanks to our rich Camacho. Get off your donkey and find yourself a ladle, and skim yourself out a chicken or two, and may they tickle your stomach."

"I don't see any ladles," said Sancho.

"Just a minute," said the cook. "By God, you're a finicky good-for-nothing!"

And as he spoke he picked up a ladle and stuck it into one of the half-sized vats, pulling out three chickens and a pair of geese, then said to Sancho:

"Eat, friend, and let this little skimming be a bit of breakfast and hold you until dinner's served."

"I haven't got anything to carry it in," said Sancho.

"In which case," said the cook, "take the whole thing, ladle and all, because today Camacho's wealth, and Camacho's happiness, are providing everything."

While Sancho was conducting this piece of business, Don Quijote was watching as twelve peasants in their best Sunday clothes came into the arbor, mounted on twelve gorgeous mares wearing rich, colorful harnesses, with breastbands hung with tiny bells. Clustering together, they ran up and down the meadow, over and over, whooping and crying:

"Long live Camacho and Quiteria, he as rich as she is beautiful, and she the most beautiful in the world!"

Hearing this, Don Quijote said to himself:

"It's clear these people have never seen my Dulcinea del Toboso, because, if they had, they'd talk a bit more sensibly about this Quiteria."

Soon, from all sides of the arbor, all sorts of dances began, and among them a sword dance with perhaps two dozen gallant, high-spirited young fellows, all dressed in the finest white linen, and carrying handkerchiefs embossed in multi-colored silk thread, and one of the men mounted on the mares asked their leader, a singularly light-footed fellow, if any of the dancers had been wounded.

"God be praised, so far nobody's been wounded — no one's suffered even a scratch."

And he and his companions immediately launched into a complicated maneuver, with so much spinning and twirling, and such consummate skill that, although Don Quijote had seen many such dances, none had ever seemed as fine.

He was equally impressed by another group of performers, pretty girls so young that, so far as he could tell, all of them were between fourteen and eighteen; they were dressed in fine green wool, their hair partly braided and partly loose, but all so fair and golden it could have rivalled sunbeams, and over their hair they wore wreaths woven of jasmine, roses, crimson amaranth, and honeysuckle. Leading them were a venerable old man and an ancient matron, both of them lighter-footed and more agile than their years suggested. To the sound of a Zamoran bagpipe, modesty in their faces and their eyes, and their feet nimble, they proved themselves the best dancers in the world.

Next came a carefully choreographed dance of the sort that includes speaking roles. It consisted of eight nymphs, divided into two rows: one was led by the god Cupid and the other by Money, the former arrayed with wings, a bow, a quiver, and arrows, and the latter, dressed in rich, particolored gold and silk fabrics. The nymphs who followed Love wore their names on their backs, inscribed in large letters on thick white paper. The first was called *Poetry*, the second *Wisdom*, the third *Good Family*, and the fourth *Courage*. Those who followed Money were labeled in the same way, the first being *Generosity*, the second *Gifts*, the third *Treasure*, and the fourth *Peaceful Possession*. A wooden castle came in front of the whole troupe, drawn by four wild men covered with ivy and green hemp and looking so realistically savage that, for a moment, Sancho was terrified. On the front and four sides of the castle were the words, *Castle of Sensible Modesty*. These dancers were accompanied by four skillful drummers and flute-players.

Cupid began their dance and, after performing two sets of steps, raised his eyes and aimed his bow at a young lady standing between the castle battlements, then spoke to her as follows:

> I am the potent god
> of earth and the skies above,
> obeyed by the rolling flood,
> heard in the darkest groves
> and in horrible hell itself.
> I'm afraid of nothing and no one;
> I please only myself
> and can do what can't be done:
> I command the world, I make,
> I break, I give, I take.

After reciting the poem, he shot an arrow high over the castle and went back to his place. Money immediately came forward, performed two sets of steps and then, silencing the drums, said:

I am stronger than Love,
though Love leads me along;
I spring from roots stronger
than anything on earth or above;
I'm better known and beloved.
I'm Money, and there aren't many
who know how to use or refuse me,
but he who can't raise a penny
does nothing. Worship me
forever, and wealthy be.

Then Money stepped back, Poetry came forward, and after performing two sets of steps, like the others who'd come before her, looked straight at the young woman in the castle and said:

Poetry works with the sweetest
ideas, and becomes the sweetest,
the noblest, most sober and wise.
Oh lady, delighting all eyes,
accept my soul in these lines,
and by letting my earnest praise
enfold you, you earn yourself
envy for the rest of your days,
and find your fortune raised
higher than the moon in the skies.

Poetry went back, and from Money's ranks Generosity stepped forward, did her little dance, and said:

Generosity's my name,
and the wise are neither famous
for piled-up gifts and treasures
nor giving too little; they measure
as they give, and give at their leisure.
But lady, to praise you, today,
I need to heap up words —
I sin honorably and in aid
of love, which always confers
its gifts as they must be paid.

All of the figures in the two groups came forward and retired in this same fashion, each of them first dancing and then reciting their verses — some elegant, some ridiculous, but the only ones Don Quijote could remember (and he had a good memory) were those cited. Then the two groups blended into one, creating figures and dissolving them, gracefully and easily; each time Love passed in front of the castle he shot his arrows high over head, while Money broke gilded cash boxes against the walls and parapets.

Finally, after they'd performed for quite some time, Money pulled out a purse, made from the skin of a whole striped cat and apparently stuffed full of coins, and threw it at the castle, which immediately fell apart, all its boards falling away and leaving the young woman utterly unprotected.

Money and his followers went over and, placing a great golden chain around her neck, made as if to carry her off, helpless and in captivity, but when Love and his band saw this they got ready to free her, making their preparations to the sound of furious drumming, to which they all danced. But the wild men first arranged peace between the two factions and then swiftly gathered up and replaced all the castle boards, so the young woman was once again ensconced within — and this concluded the dance, leaving all the onlookers immensely satisfied.

Don Quijote asked one of the nymphs to tell him who had choreographed and directed their performance. She replied that it was a parish priest, who had a fine sense for such productions.

"And I'll bet," declared Don Quijote, "that any such university graduate or priest is more likely to be a friend of Camacho than of Basilio, and must know more about plays than prayers: he's certainly worked Basilio's talents and Camacho's wealth into that dance of his!"

Listening to all this, Sancho Panza observed:

"I bet on the king of trumps, so I'm sticking to Camacho."

"In other words," said Don Quijote, "it looks as if you're one of those peasants who go around shouting, 'Hurrah for the winner, whoever he is!'"

"I don't know what kind I am," replied Sancho, "but I know for sure I'll never skim such good stuff off Basilio's kettles as I got from Camacho's."

And he pointed to the pot full of chickens and geese, then took one and began to eat it with obvious pleasure, exclaiming:

"Let's see if Basilio's talents can pay for this! Whatever you're worth is whatever you've got, and whatever you've got is what you're worth. There are only two kinds of people in the world, my old grandmother used to say, the *haves* and the *have nots*, and she went with the *haves*, and I can tell you, my lord Don Quijote, it's better to take the pulse of *having* than of *knowing*: a donkey with a gold harness looks a lot better than a horse with a packsaddle. So I just keep betting on Camacho, whose kettles are bubbling with chickens and geese, and rabbits and hares, but if Basilio's kettles ever turned up, and I don't expect they will, all you'd get out of them would be watered-down wine."

"Is that the end of your speech, Sancho?" asked Don Quijote.

"It had better be," replied Sancho, "because I can see it bothers your grace — but let me tell you, if it hadn't, I could have gone on for three days."

"Dear God," said Don Quijote, "may I see you dumb, Sancho, before I die."

"At the rate we're going," responded Sancho, "I'll be chewing on mud long before you're dead, your grace, and by then maybe I'll be so dumb that I won't say another word until the end of the world — or, at least, until the day of judgment."

"Sancho! Even if that were to happen," answered Don Quijote, "your silence couldn't ever pile up as high as all you've said, and are saying, and will surely go on saying your whole life long — and what's more, it's in the natural order of things that my death will come long before yours, so

I don't think I'll ever see you dumb, not even when you're drinking or sleeping — and what else can I possibly say?"

"Dear God, señor," said Sancho, "don't go trusting Death — no, no, because it gobbles up the lamb just as soon as the sheep, and I've heard our priest say that 'Death raps his bony knuckles, bleached, indifferent, on any man's door, a palace or a hut.'[2] Death's too powerful to be finicky, and he has a strong stomach: his mouth opens, and in we go, and his sack holds all kinds of people, no matter how old they are or how important. Death's no tiller who sleeps on the job, he just goes right on reaping and never looks at the clock, and cuts down the dry grass as well as what's fresh and green. And he doesn't bother chewing — just gulps us down and swallows everything he can, because he's as hungry as a starving dog and nothing ever fills him up. And even though he hasn't got a belly, he knows he's a bottomless pit and so he's thirsty for everything living, and guzzles us all down like a jug of cold water."

"That will do, Sancho," said Don Quijote at this point. "Be content with what you've accomplished, and don't risk its undoing, because in sober truth what you've just said, in your own rustic language, is all that any good preacher could say. I tell you, Sancho, if your learning were a match for your good sense, you could stand in the pulpit and go around the world preaching first-rate sermons."

"Good preaching means good living," said Sancho, "and that's all the theology I know."

"Nor do you need any more," said Don Quijote, "though I don't think I'll ever understand how, the fear of God being where all wisdom starts, you can possibly know so much, because you're more afraid of any little lizard than you are of Him."

"My lord, your grace," replied Sancho, "judge what you do as a knight, but don't make yourself the judge of other people's fears, or their courage, because my fear of God is as tremendous as any man's. But let me take care of these skimmings of mine, your grace, because everything else is just empty words, which we'll have to account for in the next world."

As he spoke, he once again attacked the contents of his pot, and so furiously that he roused Don Quijote's appetite — and our knight would surely have come to his squire's aid, in this culinary combat, had he not been stopped by what I'm now obliged to tell you.

Chapter Twenty-One

— which tells more of Camacho's wedding, along with other pleasant events

While Don Quijote and Sancho were having the conversation narrated in the previous chapter, they heard great shouts and a huge rumpus, all coming from a thousand musical instruments, and a whole host of performers, and especially from the twelve men mounted on mares, who

2. Horace — quoted, once before, in the prologue to volume 1 [*Translator's Note*].

came racing by, welcoming at the top of their lungs the bride and groom, just then arriving along with the priest and the families of both young people, as well as the leading citizens of towns and villages all around, every one of them dressed for the festival. As soon as he saw the bride, Sancho declared:

"By God, she's not dressed like a farm girl, but some elegant palace lady. And oh my Lord, that's not peasant-girl jewelry she's wearing, but big fat coral necklaces, and instead of good green wool she's got on velvet three layers thick! Oh Jesus, but that gown's trimmed with pure white linen! No, I swear to God, it's satin! And just look at her hands, will you? They're dripping with jet rings! Oh, let me rot if those aren't gold rings, real thick gold, all covered with pearls, for Christ's sake, white ones, like fresh cottage cheese, and every god damned one of them worth as much as the eyes in your head. Oh, son of a bitch! what hair! If that's not a wig, I've never seen hair longer or blonder in my whole life! Hey, tell me if she's not stacked, if she's not built — like a swaying palm tree loaded with dates: and that's just what they look like, all those jewels hanging from her hair and her throat! Oh, if she isn't a hell of a girl: damned if I'd kick her out of bed!"

Don Quijote laughed at Sancho Panza's crude country compliments, but all the same it seemed to him, too, that aside from his lady, Dulcinea del Toboso, he'd never seen a more beautiful woman. The lovely Quiteria looked distinctly pale, probably because, the night before their weddings, brides always have trouble sleeping.

Camacho's party walked toward a stage, built to one side of the meadow, covered with rugs and strewn with bouquets; this was where they were to exchange their vows, and from which they could look out at the dancers and other performers; and just as they reached the stage, they heard loud shouts from behind them, and some one calling:

"Wait, wait a moment — you're just as thoughtless as you are hasty, all of you."

The wedding party all turned their heads and saw that these cries came from a man dressed, as far as they could tell, in some kind of loose black coat, splashed with streaks of fire red. They had no difficulty making out his crown of funereal cypress, or his heavy walking stick. And as he drew closer they could see that this was valiant Basilio, which discovery left them all uneasy, wondering what his cries and his words were leading up to, and fearing that, making such an appearance, he meant to do something unfortunate.

He came up to them, finally, weary and breathless, and stood directly in front of the bridal pair, digging the steel tip at the bottom of his staff deep into the ground, and then, his face changing color, his eyes fixed on Quiteria, and his voice trembling and hoarse, he declared:

"You know perfectly well, oh ungrateful Quiteria, that according to the sacred law we all believe in you can not marry anyone else as long as I'm alive, nor can you fail to be aware, also, that while I've been waiting for time and hard work to swell my fortune, I've neglected none of the respect and deference your honor deserves — but you, turning your back on everything you owe to my love and good will, you intend to give what is rightly mine to someone else, whose wealth will now bring him not only good fortune but the greatest happiness in the world. And so, to fill his cup to overflowing — not that I think he deserves it, but just because Heaven has chosen to give it to him — I, with my own hands, will do away with that impossibility, that obstacle, which might otherwise stand in his way: I will not come between you. A long, long and happy life to rich Camacho and ungrateful Quiteria! Now die, die, you poor Basilio, for your poverty has clipped the wings of your happiness and laid it in its grave!"

And as he spoke he took hold of the staff he'd driven into the ground and, leaving half of it still planted there, revealed it as the sheath for a medium-sized sword, which had been hidden inside, point upward; the hilt, as it were, being buried in the ground, he quickly, deftly, and with great determination hurled himself onto the blade, the point and perhaps half of the sword immediately emerging, bloodily, from his back, covering the poor fellow in his own blood and stretching him out on the ground, run through by his own weapon.

His friends quickly ran to his aid, weeping for his misery and pitiful misfortune. Don Quijote leapt off Rocinante and also ran to help him, taking him in his arms and finding him not quite dead. They prepared to pull out the sword, but the priest, standing directly beside them, thought it better not to do so before he had heard the dying man's confession, for surely Basilio would die as soon as the blade was pulled free. But Basilio struggled back to consciousness and, his voice heavy and weak, said:

"Oh cruel Quiteria, if only you would grant me, at this last, this final, fleeting moment, your hand in marriage, I might still be able to hope my rashness could be forgiven, since it will have blessed me with the good fortune of making you mine."

Hearing this, the priest advised him to worry about the fate of his soul rather than the desires of the flesh, and to earnestly beg of God to forgive his sins as well as his wild, hopeless deed. But Basilio answered that he would not utter a word unless Quiteria first gave him her hand in marriage, for that would soothe his spirit and let him find the strength to make his confession.

Hearing the wounded man's request, Don Quijote pronounced in a loud voice that it was exceedingly just and reasonable, and furthermore very easy to accomplish, for Camacho would be just as honored to have as his wife the widow of a brave man like Basilio as he would have been to receive her directly at her father's hands.

"This is all a matter of a simple 'yes'," he said, "which will have no other effect than just pronouncing the word, since for this wedding the nuptial bed can only be the grave."

Camacho listened to all this, uncertain and confused, not knowing what he ought to say or do, but Basilio's friends (and there were many of them) insisted so forcefully that Quiteria should give the dying man her hand in marriage, thus preserving his immortal soul — by keeping it from leaving this life in a state of desperation — that they impelled and even compelled him to say that, if Quiteria wanted to do it, he wouldn't mind, since the net effect would only be to delay for a moment or two the fulfillment of his own desires.

Then they all ran to Quiteria, and some of them fell on their knees, and some of them wept, and some of them tried to reason it all out for her, each of them trying to convince her to give poor Basilio her hand, while she, harder than marble, and less moveable than a statue, stood frozen, with no idea what to say, unable to speak, and not knowing what she felt, nor would she have responded at all had the priest not told her to make up her mind quickly, because Basilio's soul had crept up to his teeth and there was no time for standing around, hemming and hawing.

Still silent, seeming visibly shaken, melancholy, and regretful, the beautiful Quiteria walked over to where Basilio lay, his eyes already beginning to roll back in his head, his breath short and quick, mumbling her name between his clenched teeth, and showing every sign of dying, not like a Christian, but like a heathen. Quiteria came over, knelt beside him, and still without speaking indicated that he should give her his hand. Basilio's eyes were wild, as he stared fixedly at her:

"Oh Quiteria!" he said. "You've come to me, mercifully, just when the only thing your compassion can do is serve as a knife blade cutting my soul loose, for I no longer have the strength to relish the bliss you give me, choosing me to be your husband, nor can I hold back the pain that, oh so swiftly, will cover my eyes with Death's ghastly shadow! What I beg of you, oh my fatally gleaming star, is that this hand you ask of me, and now wish me to have, not be given merely as a polite formality, nor to enchant and deceive me yet again, but because you want to confess and declare that you surrender it to me of your own free will, giving me your hand as your own true husband — because at a moment like this it would not be right to deceive me, nor use any deceit with someone who has always so truly treated you."

He kept swooning away, between words, so that everyone present thought each fainting spell would be the last and carry off his soul. Abashed and modest, Quiteria reached out her right hand and took Basilio's, and said to him:

"There is no force powerful enough to bend my will, and so as freely as I possibly can I give you my hand as your lawful wife, and receive yours as my husband, if you too give it to me of your own free will, neither motivated nor swayed by the disaster your wild mind has brought upon you."

"I so give it," answered Basilio, "neither uncertain nor confused of mind, but with whatever clarity of mind Heaven has been pleased to bestow on me, which is how I hereby deliver and acknowledge myself your lawful husband."

"And I your wife," responded Quiteria, "no matter whether you live for many years or they carry you from my arms to your grave."

"For someone as badly wounded as this young man," Sancho Panza murmured, "he certainly talks a lot. He should be advised to take care of his soul, instead, because as far as I can tell it's crept past his teeth and is sitting right on his tongue."

Basilio's hand being joined with Quiteria's, the weeping priest, greatly affected, blessed them, begging Heaven to grant peace to the new husband's soul — but as soon as the marriage had been solemnly blessed, Basilio leaped nimbly to his feet and, with quite incredible boldness, pulled out the sword for which his body had been serving as a sheath.

The onlookers were stunned, and some, more credulous than clever, began to cry:

"A miracle! A miracle!"

But Basilio answered them:

"Not a miracle, no, no! Pure skill, a clever trick!"

Befuddled and amazed, the priest reached out both hands and groped for Basilio's wound, only to find that the blade had not pierced him through and through, but had only gone through a hollow iron tube that, filled with blood, had been neatly set in place — the blood, as they afterwards discovered, having been carefully fixed not to congeal.

In a word, the priest, and Camacho, and everyone standing close by, realized they'd been mocked and made fools of. The new bride did not seem upset by the trick; quite the opposite, for hearing it said that such a marriage, having been a deceitful fraud, could not be considered valid, she declared she affirmed it yet again, which led everyone to conclude that the two of them, Basilio and Quiteria, had known the whole thing in advance, which so embarrassed Camacho and his friends that they took the matter of vengeance into their own hands, many of them drawing swords and charging at Basilio, in whose support a host of other weapons were immediately drawn. Don Quijote, back up on his horse, led the way, well protected by his shield and with his lance in his hand, so that no one could stand up to him. But Sancho, who took no pleasure in and never went looking for such deeds, hid himself among the great wine jars (from which, earlier, he had taken his savory skimmings), thinking that such a sanctuary would be universally respected. Don Quijote shouted:

"Hold, gentlemen, hold! It is wrong to seek vengeance for damage that Love commits, for you should be aware that love and war are one and the same, and just as tricks and stratagems for overcoming one's enemy are legal and accepted in war, so too those who oppose and rival one another in love can surely employ deceit and scheming to attain their desires, so long as they neither injure nor dishonor the beloved. Quiteria was Basilio's, and Basilio was Quiteria's, because Heaven rightly and graciously so ordained. Camacho, being rich, can satisfy his tastes when and where and how he pleases. But all Basilio possesses is this one ewe, and no one is going to take her away from him, no matter how powerful he may be, for two people joined together by God may not be sundered by mortal man, and anyone who plans to try it will first have to get past the point of this spear."

And at this he brandished his lance with such force and agility that all those who did not know him were terrified. Camacho had been so powerfully affected by Quiteria's spurning him that, in an instant, he wiped her out of his mind, and so he accepted the priest's counsel, since it came from a wise and well-intentioned, God-fearing man, and allowed himself and his supporters to be pacified and calmed, in testimony to which they re-sheathed their swords, more vexed at Quiteria's opportunism than at Basilio's trick, and indeed Camacho observed that if Quiteria as an unmarried woman was so very fond of Basilio, she'd still have been fond of him after she was married, so he ought to be even more grateful to Heaven for being rid of her than he had been, in the first place, for getting her.

Once Camacho and his people were resigned and calm, Basilio's supporters too regained their serenity — and Camacho the Rich, to show he was not only not offended by the trick, but didn't give a hoot one way or the other, directed that the celebration go on just as if he himself had really been married, but neither Basilio nor his wife nor any of his partisans wanted to remain, so they all left and went to Basilio's village, for there are virtuous and wise men among the poor, as well as the rich, and they too have followers who honor and protect them, just as wealthy folk have those who flatter and follow along behind.

And they took Don Quijote along with them, thinking him a brave man with a stout heart. Only Sancho felt his spirits darken, finding himself unable to stay and enjoy Camacho's magnificent food and entertainment, which would be going on until nightfall, so he trailed along, wearily and sadly, behind his master, who had gone off with Basilio's crowd, forcing himself to leave the fleshpots of Egypt, though he still longed for them in his heart, and the virtually consumed skimmings, which he carried in their nearly empty pot, kept reminding him of the magnificent abundance he was losing. So, sorrowing and thoughtful, but not hungry, he sat on his donkey's back and followed in Rocinante's tracks.

Chapter Twenty-Two

— which tells of the great adventure of Montesinos' Cave, right in the heart of La Mancha, which adventure the brave Don Quijote de La Mancha brought to a happy conclusion

The newly-weds showered attentions on Don Quijote, in acknowledgment of all he had done to defend their cause, and they singled out his good sense as well as his courage, calling him an El Cid for his feats of arms and a Cicero for his eloquence. For three days our good Sancho had fun at their expense; they admitted that the pretended suicide had not been planned in advance, as far as the beautiful Quiteria was concerned, but had been strictly Basilio's scheme, for he had hoped the outcome would be exactly what it was. Basilio confessed that he had let some of his friends in on the deception, so that, if and when it became necessary, they could help by vouching for his trick.

"You really can't call it a trick, nor should you," said Don Quijote, "for how can there be deceit when the ending is virtuous?"

And he said that the marriage of true lovers was the best of all possible endings, noting that love's principal adversary was hunger and pressing necessity, since love is all happiness, rejoicing, and satisfaction, especially when the lover is in full possession of the beloved object, against which union love's enemies set up and proclaim necessity and poverty. All of which Don Quijote said in order to persuade Basilio to give up his clever accomplishments, for although they could bring him fame they could not bring him money, and he ought to set himself to winning wealth by legitimate means, for these were skills that would never desert the wise and the industrious.

"A man who is poor and honorable," he said, "if indeed it is possible to be both poor and honorable, wins a rare prize when he has a beautiful wife, for should she be taken away from him, then honor too will be gone, murdered. And a beautiful woman with a poor husband, who retains her virtue, deserves to be crowned with the triumphant laurels and palm-leaves of a conqueror. For beauty, simply because it is what it is, draws toward itself the desires of everyone who sees and recognizes it: royal eagles and other high-flying birds come swooping down exactly as they dive at well-made decoys — but beauty coupled with poverty and need also attracts hawks, crows, and carrion-hunters generally, and a woman who can resist such assaults truly deserves a crown at her husband's hands.

"Consider, my wise friend Basilio," added Don Quijote. "A sage whose name I cannot at the moment remember has said that there can never be more than one good woman in the entire world, and he suggested that every man should be firmly convinced that his wife is indeed that woman, for he will then live in peace and happiness. I am not married, nor indeed have I ever contemplated marriage, but just the same I would risk giving the following advice to anyone who asked me how to find the right woman to marry. First: I'd tell him to consider her reputation more than her wealth, for a good woman never earns that title simply by being good, but also by letting her virtue be visible, and women's reputations are far more seriously damaged by public familiarities and boldness than by actual but concealed misdeeds. When you bring a good woman into your house, it's easy enough to keep her good, and even make her better, but when you take in a bad woman it's hard work to improve her, because going from one extreme to another is no simple matter. I'm not saying it's impossible, but I certainly consider it difficult."

Listening to all this, Sancho said to himself:

"Any time I say something smart and solid, this master of mine likes to tell me I could take a pulpit and go around the world preaching fancy sermons — but whenever he starts stringing wise sayings together, and giving people advice, he couldn't just stand in one pulpit but in two at the same time, and parade through the streets and say anything he wants to! God damn him for a knight errant, knowing all this stuff! Deep down in my heart, I used to think all he knew about was knighthood and all that, but damn it if there's anything he hasn't put his pecker into or stirred around with his spoon."

Sancho mumbled a bit of this, and hearing him Don Quijote asked:

"What are you mumbling about, Sancho?"

"I'm not saying anything," replied Sancho, "and I'm not mumbling anything, but just saying to myself I wished I'd heard what your grace was saying, just now, before I got married, because maybe what I'd be saying is 'An ox without a rope can lick himself just fine.'"

"Is your Teresa as bad as all that, Sancho?" asked Don Quijote.

"She could be worse," responded Sancho, "but she could be better, too. Anyway, she isn't as good as I wish she was."

"That's wrong, Sancho," said Don Quijote. "You shouldn't say bad things about your wife, because after all she's your children's mother."

"We're birds of a feather," answered Sancho, "because she says bad things about me anytime she feels like it, and especially when she's jealous — and Satan himself couldn't stand her, then!"

So they stayed with the newlyweds for three days, and were treated and feted like kings. Don Quijote asked the Master of Arts in fencing to find them a guide, so they could go to Montesinos' Cave, because he'd made up his mind to see for himself whether it truly contained all the wondrous things everyone was always saying it did. Basilio said he'd get one of his own cousins to take them, a celebrated scholar and a devoted reader of tales of chivalry, who'd gladly lead them right to the mouth of that famous cave; he'd also point out the lakes of Ruidera, just as well-known in La Mancha — and even throughout Spain. Basilio said Don Quijote would enjoy his cousin's company, because this was a young fellow who knew how to write books worth printing and dedicating to princes. The cousin came, finally, riding a pregnant donkey whose packsaddle sat on a thick particolored mat. So Sancho saddled Rocinante and loaded up his own donkey, saddlebags all stuffed to the brim (as were the cousin's), and then, taking farewell of the others and commending themselves to God, they set out on the road, heading for Montesinos' famous cave.

As they rode along, Don Quijote asked Basilio's cousin what profession he intended to follow, and what fields his studies dealt with, to which the cousin replied that he meant to be a Humanist, and what he worked at as well as what he studied were books for publication — highly useful volumes, all of them, and (for the populace at large) no less entertaining than they were useful. One of them, for example, was entitled *How to Dress and Be Dressed*, in which he described seven hundred and three uniforms, giving details as to their colors, emblems, and monogrammed devices, so that knights and courtiers could find the right ones for festivals and celebrations, without having to go begging for them, or racking their cerebellum (as the saying goes) to hunt up exactly what they wanted and needed.

"Because what I give the jealous, the spurned, the forgotten, and the exiled is exactly what suits them, and makes them juster than the just. I've got another book, too, which I've entitled *Metamorphoses, or the Spanish Ovid*, which is really novel and witty, because I do a burlesque imitation of Ovid: just the way he explained Greek and Roman names and legends, I tell who Giralda of Seville really was, and the Angel Magdalena, and all about the Great Sewer of Vecinguerra at Córdoba, and the Guisando Bulls, and the Sierra Morena Mountains, and the Leganitos and Lavapiés Fountains in Madrid (without of course forgetting the famous Piojo Fountain, and the one in the Golden Sewer, and the one at Priora)[1] — and all of this, along with the necessary allegories, metaphors, and translations, done in a style that's bright and dramatic and educational all at once. And I've got still another book, which I call *The Supplement to Polydore Vergil*,[2] which describes the origin of everything and is really very erudite, very learned, because I look into all the truly important things Polydore left out, and I do it in a lovely high style. For example, Vergil forgot to tell us

---

1. For Giralda and the Guisando Bulls, see II.14, above. The Angel Magdalena is a cathedral spire, in Salamanca; except for the Sierra Morena Mountains, the other references are to well-known Madrid landmarks [*Translator's Note*].
2. A sometimes uncritical, encyclopedic Italian historian, Polydore Vergil (1470–1550), whose *De inventoribus rerum* [*The Inventors of Things*, 1499] was translated into Spanish, in 1550, as *Libro de Polidoro Virgilio que tracta de la invención y principio de todas las cosas* [*Polidoro Virgil's Book*, dealing with the creation and beginning of everything] [*Translator's Note*].

who was the first man in the world to catch a cold, and the first to use mercury ointment to cure the French pox [syphilis], and I tell it all, I dot the i's and I cross the t's, and I use more than twenty-five writers as my authorities — so you can see, your grace, whether or not I've performed an honest, serious labor and given the world, with such a book, something truly useful."

Sancho, who had been listening to the cousin with rapt attention, said to him:

"May God bless these books of yours, sir, and can you tell me, if you know — and since you know everything — who was the first man who scratched his head, because I think it surely must have been Adam, the father of us all?"

"It surely would have been him," replied the cousin, "because there's no doubt that Adam had a head, and hair, and that being the case, and being the first man in the world, some time or other he would have scratched himself."

"I agree, I agree," said Sancho. "But now tell me: who was the first acrobat, the first tumbler?"

"Truthfully, brother," answered the cousin, "I can't tell you that right now, because I haven't yet looked it up. When I get back to where I keep my books, I'll make a point of finding out for you, and I'll let you know, the next time we meet — because there's no reason for this to be both the first and the last time."

"No, wait a minute, sir," Sancho went on. "Don't bother yourself with that, because I've just now understood how to answer the question I asked you. I should have known that Lucifer must have been the first acrobat in the world, because they threw him out of Heaven and he went tumbling down into the abyss."

"That sounds right to me, my friend," said the cousin.

And then Don Quijote said:

"You didn't think up that question and answer by yourself, Sancho. You heard them from somebody else."

"Don't say that, my lord," said Sancho, "because, by God, if I really got started with questioning and answering, we wouldn't be finished from here till tomorrow. I tell you, when it comes to asking stupid questions and giving crazy answers, I don't need to go looking for help from my neighbors."

"You've said even more than you know, Sancho," said Don Quijote, "because there are people who exhaust themselves, investigating matters that, after all their learning and all their investigations, don't add a speck to our understanding and aren't worth remembering."

They spent the day in such pleasant chatter, and took shelter, that night, in a little village, from which to Montesinos' Cave, the cousin explained to Don Quijote, was no further then six or seven miles; if our knight was truly determined to go into the cave, it was necessary to supply themselves with rope, so he could tie it around himself and be lowered into the depths.

Don Quijote declared that, even if the cave reached down to the bottom of the world, he had to find out how far it went, so they bought almost six hundred feet of rope and, the next day, at two in the afternoon, they reached the cave, the mouth of which was spacious and wide, but full of thorn bushes and wild fig trees, brambles and dense growths of weeds, all so thick and densely interwoven that it choked and hid everything. Seeing this, the cousin, Sancho, and Don Quijote dismounted, and the other two at once tied the ropes tightly around our knight, and while they were wrapping and girdling him, Sancho said to him:

"Be careful, your grace, my lord; watch what you're doing. Don't bury yourself alive, and don't hang yourself down into any kind of place where you might look like a bottle somebody was trying to cool off a little. Yes, and it's not your business, your grace, messing around down there where it's got to be worse than a dungeon."

"Be quiet and keep tying," replied Don Quijote, "because this kind of affair, Sancho my friend, was expressly intended for me."

Then the guide said to him:

"I beg your grace, Señor Don Quijote: be careful, keep watch with a hundred eyes on everything you find in there. Who knows? There may be things I can put in my book of *Transformations*."

" 'This drum's in the hands of a drummer who really knows how to bang on it,' "[3] replied Sancho Panza.

This said, and the rope tied tightly around Don Quijote (though tied over the jacket he wore under his armor, and not over the armor itself), Don Quijote said:

"We were careless, not providing ourselves with some sort of little cowbell, which could have been tied right next to me, on this same rope: the tinkling would have told you whether I was still going down, and whether I was still alive — but since that's no longer possible, we'll have to trust in God, and may He guide me."

And then he dropped down on his knees and, his voice subdued, prayed that God might help him and make him successful in what, for all he could tell, might well be a dangerous, unheard-of adventure, after which, in a loud, clear voice, he immediately declared:

"Oh Lady of everything I do and every movement I make, brightest-shining, matchless Dulcinea del Toboso! If somehow the prayers and petitions of this your most fortunate lover should happen to reach your ears, I beg you in the name of your extraordinary beauty to heed them, for all they ask is that you deny me not your favor and your protection, now when I so badly need them. In a moment I shall hurl myself, throw myself, submerge myself in the abyss standing right here, and all I intend is that the world may learn how, with your assistance, there is nothing I cannot attempt and accomplish."

As he spoke, he drew near the cave mouth and saw it was impossible to get down that way, or make himself a pathway, except either by sheer force or by cutting a path, so he drew his sword and began to chop his way through the thick underbrush, making such a clamorous racket that he startled a huge flock of rooks and crows, who fairly roared out in such a dense flurry that they knocked Don Quijote over, and had he been as

3. A proverb, says Covarrubias [*Translator's Note*].

much a superstitious pagan as he was a good Catholic Christian, he would have interpreted it as a bad omen and refused to descend into such a place.

But after a time he stood up, and seeing that there were no more crows or other nocturnal birds flapping out at him (like the bats that had flown out with the crows and rooks), the cousin and Sancho let out the rope a bit and he lowered himself right down to the bottom of the dreadful cave — and as he dropped out of sight Sancho sent his blessing after him, making a thousand signs of the cross:

"May the Lord guide you, and Our Lady of the Mountain of France, and the Holy Trinity of the harbor of Gaeta, oh flower, froth, and cream of all knight errantry! Down you go, oh greatest braggart in the world, oh man with a heart of steel and an arm of brass! May God guide you yet again, and let you come back to the light of this world as free, as healthy and absolutely innocent as when you left us in order to bury yourself in that darkness you've gone to seek!"

The cousin uttered virtually the same prayers and entreaties.

And as Don Quijote dropped farther and farther down, he called to them to keep letting out the rope, which they did, bit by bit, and by the time they could no longer hear his shouts funneling up from the cave mouth they had given him the full six hundred feet and wondered if they shouldn't pull him back up, because they could not drop him down any farther. But in spite of that, they decided to wait half an hour, after which they started reeling in the rope, which came up very easily, and weightless, which made them think Don Quijote had decided to stay where he was, and Sancho, believing this to be the case, shed bitter tears and hauled furiously at the rope, to learn the truth — but then, with about another hundred feet left to pull in, they felt a weight, which absolutely delighted them. And then, after hauling in about sixty feet more, they could clearly see Don Quijote, to whom Sancho began to shout:

"Welcome home, my lord. We were thinking you were going to stay down there and start a family."

But Don Quijote did not say a word, and when they had him completely out they saw that his eyes were closed and he seemed to be sleeping. They laid him on the ground and untied the rope, but he still did not wake up, so they kept turning him first this way and then that, shaking him and poking at him, until finally, after a long time, he began to come to, stretching and yawning as if he'd just woken from some hard, deep sleep, and then looking around him in wonder he said:

"God forgive you, my friends, for you have deprived me of the most delightful existence, and the sweetest sights, that any human being has ever seen or experienced. As a matter of fact, I now truly understand that all the happiness we know, in these lives of ours, goes by like shadows and dreams, or simply withers like the flowers of the field. Oh miserable Montesinos! Oh sorely wounded Durandarte! Oh luckless Belerma! Oh tearful Guadiana, and you, Ruidera's miserable daughters, whose flowing waters show the tears pouring from your lovely eyes!"

The cousin and Sancho stood listening to Don Quijote, who spoke as if, in immense pain, he was pulling the words right out of his very entrails.

They begged him to explain what he meant, and tell them what Hell he had seen.

"You call that Hell?" said Don Quijote. "Do not, for it does not deserve such a name, as you will soon see."

He asked them for some food, for he was ravenously hungry. They stretched the cousin's particolored mat on the green grass and offered Don Quijote the treasures of their saddlebags, after which they sat in great good fellowship, eating some of this and some of that, all of them dining most companionably. And when they took away the mat, Don Quijote de La Mancha declared:

"Let no one get up, and pay close attention to me, my sons."

Chapter Twenty-Three

— the remarkable things the incomparable Don Quijote said he had seen in the depths of Montesinos' Cave, the sheer implausibility and magnificence of which make this adventure seem distinctly apocryphal

It was four in the afternoon when the sun, obscured behind clouds, its light dimmed and its rays moderated, allowed Don Quijote, untroubled by heat and discomfort, to tell the story of what he had seen in Montesinos' Cave to his two distinguished listeners. He began as follows:

"About seventy or eighty feet down into this dungeon, on the right-hand side, there's a large hollowed-out space, big enough to hold a cart and a team of mules. A bit of light filters into it, through some cracks and holes, which run all the way up to the surface of the earth. When I saw this place I was already tired, and fed up with dangling at the end of a rope and descending slowly into the darkness below, not knowing where I was going, so I decided to climb in and rest a bit. I shouted to you, saying you shouldn't let out any more rope until I told you to, but you must not have heard me. So I pulled in the rope you were sending down and made a thick, coiled heap of it, and then I sat down on that, tremendously absorbed in thought, wondering what I had to do to reach the very bottom, since I had no one to help me, and as I was musing, thus uncertainly, all of a sudden, and without trying to, I fell into an incredibly deep sleep, and then, totally unexpectedly, not in the least understanding what was going on, I awoke and found myself in the loveliest, most charmingly delightful meadow nature has ever created or the liveliest human imagination has ever conceived. I rubbed my eyes, and cleaned them, and saw that I was no longer sleeping but was really and truly awake — in spite of which I felt my head and my chest, to make sure this was really me, and not some empty and counterfeit ghost of an illusion, but the touch, the feeling, and the logical things I was thinking assured me it was really me, exactly as I am this minute.

"And then I saw a sumptuous royal palace or castle, with walls that seemed to be fashioned of some clear, absolutely transparent crystal. I saw its two great gates open and an old man in a long cloak of purple flannel emerge and start toward me, the hem of his cloak dragging along the ground; there was a green satin sash, indicating academic rank, across his shoulders and chest, and on his head he wore a black, stiffly wired Milanese cap; his beard, gray as gray could be, came down below his belt; he carried no weapons, but in his hand there was a rosary fashioned of good-sized walnuts, every tenth bead as big as a good-sized ostrich egg. His bearing, his walk, the solemnity and solidity of his very presence, each and all of these things, and all of them together, struck me as enthralling and wonderful. He came over to me, and the first thing he did was clap me in a tight embrace, after which he immediately declared:

" 'For a long time, oh brave knight, Don Quijote de La Mancha, those of us consigned by magic to this lonely wilderness have hoped and waited to see you, so you might let the whole world know what is shut in and covered away by this vast subterranean chamber, known as Montesinos' Cave, into which you have now come — a feat reserved exclusively for someone with your invincible heart and magnificent courage. Come with me, illustrious sir, so I may show you the wonders hidden within this transparent castle, of which I am the warden and perpetual guardian, for I am that very same Montesinos[1] from whom this place takes its name.'

"He had no sooner told me that he was Montesinos than I asked if it were true that, as they said out in the world above, using a tiny dagger he had cut his great friend Durandarte's heart right out of his chest and brought it to Durandarte's mistress, the Lady Belerma,[2] as Durandarte himself had ordered, as he lay at the point of death. He told me that that was indeed what was said, except for the dagger, for it was said to have been neither a dagger nor tiny but a knife sharper even than a carpenter's awl."

"That must have been a knife," said Sancho at this point, "made by Ramón de Hoces, from Seville."

"I have no idea," Don Quijote went on, "but it couldn't have been that knife-maker, because Ramón de Hoces lived just yesterday, and everything that happened at Roncesvalles, which is when this unfortunate business took place, was many many years ago and, furthermore, this is not an important question, for it neither disturbs nor in any way changes the truth or the substance of the story."

"Quite true," responded the cousin. "So please go on, Señor Don Quijote, for I find it sheer delight to listen to you."

"Nor do I tell you this with any less pleasure," replied Don Quijote, "and so: as I said, the venerable Montesinos brought me into the crystal palace, in which, in a lower chamber (built of alabaster, and exceedingly cool) there was a marble tomb, intricately carved, upon which there lay stretched out the figure of a knight, shaped neither of bronze, nor marble, nor jasper, as we find in other tombs, but entirely of bones and flesh. His right hand — which seemed to me distinctly hairy and muscular, usually

---

1. The hero of some half-dozen Spanish ballads, where he features as one of the Twelve Peers. He does not appear in any of the French romances.
2. Belerma and Durandarte are figures peculiar to the Spanish ballad tradition about the legends of Charlemagne and are unknown in the French Carolingian tradition.

a signal of its owner's great strength — lay across his heart. Seeing me
staring in astonishment, before I could ask him anything, Montesinos said:
  " 'This is my friend Durandarte, the very flower and model of brave and
lovestruck knights of his time. He lies here, along with me and many others
besides, enchanted by Merlin,[3] that French magician who's said to be the
devil's own son, and what I think is that, though he wasn't really the devil's
son, he knew (as they say) a bit more than the devil did. No one knows
how or why he cast this enchantment on us, but I suspect the time is not
too far off when this will be revealed. But what astonishes me is that I
know, every bit as certainly as I know that at this moment the sun is
shining, that Durandarte ended his life in my arms, and that after his death
I cut out his heart with my own hands — and by God it must have
weighed two full pounds, for as those who study nature tell us, men with
large hearts also have more courage than those with smaller ones. But this
being the case, and my friend having in fact died, how can he be lying
here and, from time to time, sighing and moaning as if he were still alive?'
  "And no sooner had Montesinos said this, when Durandarte called out
in a loud voice:

> 'Oh my cousin Montesinos!
> The last thing I asked you
> Was to tear out my heart
> As soon as I died,
> Cut it out of my breast
> With your knife or your dagger,
> And carry that heart
> To my Lady Belerma.'

"Hearing this, the venerable Montesinos fell on his knees in front of that
sorrowing knight and, with tears in his eyes, said to him:
  " 'My lord Durandarte, dearest cousin, I did exactly as you commanded,
on that fateful day of your death. I cut out your heart as best I could,
leaving not a particle behind; I cleaned it with a lace handkerchief; I set
out with it, on the road to France, having first placed you in the bosom
of the earth, with so many tears that they could have washed from my
hands the blood that covered them, after I had plunged them into your
entrails, and oh cousin of my soul, as a further sign, I took some salt, in
the first village we came to once we'd left Roncesvalles, and sprinkled it
over your heart, to keep it from stinking and so I could present it to the
Lady Belerma, if not precisely fresh, then at least well dried and preserved;
but she, and you, and I, and Guadiana your squire, and Lady Ruidera and
her seven daughters and two nieces, and many more of your friends and
acquaintances, have for years and years been kept here, enchanted, by the
magician Merlin, and though half a century has passed none of us has
died. The only ones missing are Ruidera and her daughters and nieces,
whose tears must have moved Merlin, because he turned them all into
lakes, which now, out in the world of the living and in the province of La
Mancha, are known as the lakes of Ruidera, seven of which belong to the

---

3. Merlin is in fact British, not French, and from the Arthurian tradition [*Translator's Note*].

kings of Spain, and the other two, being the nieces' lakes, belong to the knights of the Holy Order of Saint John. Your squire, Guadiana, who was similarly mourning your misfortune, was turned into a river which bears your name, but when he came to the earth's surface and saw the sun of another day shining in the heavens, he was so oppressed by the sense of your loss that he plunged right back into the bowels of the earth, but since he can't help flowing where he is supposed to flow, from time to time he returns to the surface and shows himself where the sun and human beings can see him. The lakes I spoke of pour their waters into him, and these, together with the waters of many others which come to him, let him flow into Portugal as a great and mighty stream. All the same, he shows his sad gloominess everywhere he goes, not at all concerned with breeding luxurious, valuable fish, but only coarse and tasteless species, utterly unlike those of the golden River Tagus — and everything I'm now telling you, oh my beloved cousin! I've told you many times before, for since you never answer me, I think you don't believe me, or perhaps you can't hear me, which causes me infinite pain, as God well knows. But this time I have news for you, and though it may not help cure your grief, at least it will not make it worse. Know, then, that you have here in your presence, and if you open your eyes you will see him, that great knight of whom the wise Merlin predicted so many great things: here is Don Quijote de La Mancha, who has brought the forgotten profession of knight errantry back to life, and made it better than it was in ancient times, and with his help and intervention perhaps we may become disenchanted, since the greatest deeds are always reserved for the greatest men.'

" 'And if not,' replied the sorrowful Durandarte, his voice low and weak, 'if not, oh my cousin, what I say is: patience, and shuffle the cards.'

"Then he turned on his side, resumed his usual silence, and said not another word. Just then I heard loud crying and wailing, along with profound moans and sobs, so I turned my head and saw two lines of the most beautiful girls in the world passing along the crystal wall opposite, all of them wearing mourning, and with white turbans on their heads, in the Turkish style. Right after them came a lady, important-looking in spite of being, like the others, dressed all in black, with a long white veil that brushed the ground. Her turban was twice the size of any of the others; she was thick-browed, with a flattish nose; her mouth was large, her lips rouged, and her teeth, when they could be seen, seemed sparse and irregular, though white as peeled almonds; she carried a bit of fine linen in her hands, in which there lay, so far as one could tell, an embalmed heart, all dried and shrunken. Montesinos told me that the procession consisted of Durandarte and Belerma's servants, enchanted exactly like their lord and lady, and that she who brought up the rear, carrying the mummified heart in her hands, was the Lady Belerma herself. They were obliged to conduct this procession four times a week, singing — or, more accurately, wailing — dirges over the corpse, as well as the sorrowful heart, of Montesinos' cousin. If the lady struck me as somewhat ugly, or at least not so lovely as her reputation, this was due to the terrible nights and even worse days she led, in this enchantment — as one could see in the great dark rings under her eyes, as well as her sickly color.

" 'Nor,' said Montesinos, 'is this pallor, and these rings under her eyes, caused by the monthly sickness common to women, because it has been a great many months, not to say years, since she's had any periods or they've so much as shown themselves at her door. It's simply the sorrow her heart experiences, carrying what she carries in her hands, for it keeps reminding her of her unfortunate lover, dead so young, and indeed, had things gone otherwise, even the magnificent Dulcinea del Toboso, so celebrated hereabouts and even in the rest of the world, would be hard put to it to equal her in beauty, charm, and spirit.'

" 'Just a minute, Señor Don Montesinos!' I said, hearing this. 'You are obliged to tell your story as it happened, but you must know that all comparisons are odious and so there's no point to comparing anybody to anybody else. My matchless Dulcinea del Toboso is who she is, and My Lady Doña Belerma is who she is, and who she has been, and let's leave it at that.'

"To which he replied:

" 'My Lord Don Quijote, please forgive me, your grace, for I admit my error, for I was wrong to say the Lady Dulcinea could hardly match the Lady Belerma, since I should have known very well indeed, from who knows how many signs and indications, that you, your grace, are her knight, and I would sooner bite off my tongue than compare her with anything but the heavens themselves.'

"This apology from the great Montesinos calmed me; my heart had been given a sharp shock, hearing my lady compared to Belerma."

"All that surprises me," said Sancho, "is that your grace didn't leap on the old coot and jump up and down on him until you broke every bone in his body, and pulled out his beard to boot, down to the very last whisker."

"Ah no, Sancho my friend," replied Don Quijote, "that would not have been the right thing to do, because we're all bound to respect our elders, whether they're knights or not, and especially when they've been enchanted. I know perfectly well that after all the questions and answers we exchanged so freely, neither one of us owed the other anything."

At this the cousin spoke up:

"What I don't know, Señor Don Quijote, is how, in the comparatively short time your grace was down there, you could have seen so much, and heard so much, and said so much."

"How long was I down there?" asked Don Quijote.

"Less than an hour," answered Sancho.

"That's impossible," replied Don Quijote, "because while I was there night fell, and dawn came, and then it grew dark once more and it dawned no less than three times, so that, so far as I can tell, I must have spent three days in those places so secret and hidden from our sight."

"My master must be speaking the truth," said Sancho, "because since everything that happened was caused by magic, maybe what seemed just an hour to us must have seemed, down there, three days and three nights."

"That may be," replied Don Quijote.

"But did you eat anything in all this time, your grace?" asked the cousin.

"I never swallowed a mouthful," answered Don Quijote, "nor was I ever hungry, and I never so much as thought of food."

"Do enchanted people eat?" asked the cousin.

"They don't eat," answered Don Quijote. "Nor do they move their bowels, though it is thought their nails and beards and hair do grow."

"By any chance, my lord, do enchanted people sleep?" asked Sancho.

"No, certainly not," said Don Quijote. "At least, in the three days I was with them, not one of them ever closed his eyes, and no more did I."

"This is where the proverb comes in," said Sancho. " 'Tell me who you hang out with, and I'll tell you who you are.' Your grace spends his time with enchanted people who never eat and are always on guard: is it any wonder you neither eat nor sleep while you're with them? But now my lord, may your grace forgive me if I just add that, so help me God, and may I go straight to the Devil, if I believe a single word of all you've been telling us."

"Why not?" said the cousin. "Wouldn't Don Quijote have to be lying, in that case? Even if he felt like it he didn't have time to just make up so many millions of lying details."

"I don't think my master was lying," replied Sancho.

"If you don't," Don Quijote asked him, "then what do you think?"

"I believe," Sancho replied, "that this Merlin, or some other magician who put a spell on that whole crowd of people your grace says you saw and spoke to down there, stuck all this crazy business you've been telling us, and all the rest you're going to tell us, right into your head."

"Which might very well be the case, Sancho," answered Don Quijote, "except that it isn't, because I've only told you what I saw with my very own eyes and touched with my very own hands. But what would you say if I tell you, right now, that among all the many other wonderful things Montesinos showed me, which I'll tell you bit by bit and in the proper time, as we continue on our journey, because I simply can't tell all of them here and now, he pointed out three peasant girls cavorting through those same fields, down there, like so many she-goats, and I'd no sooner seen them when I recognized one as the matchless Dulcinea del Toboso, and the two others as the same girls who in fact accompanied her, when we spoke to them just outside of Toboso? I asked Montesinos if he knew them; he replied that he didn't, but he thought they must be some high-born ladies under an enchantment, because they'd just recently appeared in the meadows down there, and I shouldn't be surprised by any of that, because they had a lot of celebrated ladies down there, from all the centuries, past and present, enchanted in all sorts of strange and different ways, and he'd recognized among them Queen Guinevere and Lady Quintañona, who poured out the wine for Lancelot, when

he from Britain came."[4]

Hearing his master say this, Sancho Panza thought he'd either lose his mind or else burst with laughter, for knowing as he did all about Dulcinea's pretended enchantment, in which he had been both the magician and the fabricator of the whole story, he now understood beyond the

---

4. The same ballad quoted by Don Quijote about himself, in slightly adapted form, in I.2 [Translator's Note].

shadow of a doubt that his master was clean out of his mind and as crazy as a loon. So he replied:

"It was an evil hour, in an even worse season, and a truly terrible day, your grace, my cherished patron, when you went down to the other world, and a terrible moment when you met my lord Montesinos, which has brought you back to us like this. You went down there, your grace, with your head sitting straight on your shoulders, the way God put it there, speaking sensibly and giving good advice at every step, but not any more — now you're talking the biggest nonsense anyone could ever imagine."

"Knowing you as I do, Sancho," replied Don Quijote, "I won't pay any attention to your words."

"And I won't pay any attention to yours," responded Sancho, "not even if you knocked me down, not even if you killed me for what I've said, or for what I intend to say unless you start talking more sensibly. But tell me, your grace, now that we're not quarreling, how did you recognize our lady Dulcinea? What proved to you who she was? And if you spoke to her, what did you say, and what did she answer?"

"I knew her," answered Don Quijote, "because she was wearing the same garments she wore when you pointed her out to me. I did speak to her, but she never answered a word, just turned her back on me and ran off so rapidly you couldn't have caught her with a bow and arrow. I wanted to follow her, and I would have, if Montesinos hadn't advised me not to waste my time, because there'd be no point to it, and in particular because it was getting close to the time when I'd need to return from the abyss. He also told me that, in good time, he'd explain how to break the enchantments on him, and Belerma, and Durandarte, and all the rest of them down there. But of all the things I saw while I was there, the most painful happened during this conversation with Montesinos, when one of my luckless Dulcinea's two companions came over to me, without my noticing it, and with tears in her eyes, and her voice shaking and soft, said to me:

" 'My lady Dulcinea del Toboso kisses your hands, your grace, and begs me to return and tell her how you are, and also, because the need is great, she also wants me to beg your grace, as urgently as I know how, if you can lend her six dollars, or however much your grace happens to have with you, against the security of this brand-new cotton petticoat which I have right here, and she promises to pay you back very soon.'

"These words absolutely struck me dumb, so I turned to Montesinos and asked him:

" 'My lord Montesinos, is it possible for people of high rank, who have been enchanted, to suffer from want?'

"To which query he replied:

" 'Believe me, your grace, my lord Don Quijote de La Mancha, that the condition we term want is to be found everywhere, knowing no boundaries and in no respect limited, nor does it spare those who have been enchanted, so that if the lady Dulcinea del Toboso has sent you this request for six dollars, and the security she offers is sound, it would seem to me that you should lend her the stipulated sum, for without any question she must need it very badly indeed.'

" 'I will accept no security from her,' I answered him, 'but I am obliged to give her less than she seeks, because all I have with me is four dollars.'

"So I handed over the four dollars (this was the money you gave me the other day, Sancho, as alms for the poor we meet with on our journey), and said to the woman:

" 'Tell your lady, my friend, that her troubles give me great pain, and that I wish I were a Fugger[5] and could instantly cure them. Tell her, too, that I neither can nor ought to be in good health, suffering as I am for lack of her charming presence and sensible conversation, and that I most earnestly beg her, whenever it may suit her gracious convenience, to allow this her captive servant and travel-worn knight, to see and speak to her. And tell her, also, that when she least expects any such news, she will hear that I have sworn a vow, after the fashion of the Marqués of Mantua, who swore to avenge his nephew Baldovinos after finding him, high up in the mountains, lying at the point of death, which oath obliged him never to eat off a tablecloth, along with other assorted trivial matters he appended thereunto, until that vengeance had been effected — even so will I spare no pains, and will journey to the seven ends of the earth, even more faithfully than ever did Prince Don Pedro of Portugal,[6] until I have succeeded in disenchanting her.'

" 'Your grace owes that, and more, to my lady,' she told me. Then she took the four dollars and, instead of curtsying, she whirled herself into a cartwheel, spinning a full six feet in the air."

"Oh in God's name!" cried Sancho loudly. "Is this possible? Can there really be magicians powerful enough to transform my master's fine mind into such wild craziness as this? Oh my lord, my lord, for God's sake just listen to yourself, think of your good name and stop believing in this empty foolishness which turns all your senses weak and feeble!"

"I know you say such things, Sancho, out of love for me," said Don Quijote, "and since you have very little knowledge of the world, anything that strikes you as difficult is, for you, an outright impossibility, but time marches on, as I've told you before, and when I've told you some of the other things I saw down there, you'll have no choice but to believe what I've told you just now, the truth of which admits neither retort nor argument."

---

5. International bankers and merchants, of German origin, who had strongly backed and were subsequently ennobled by Charles V (Holy Roman Emperor, 1519–1558, king of Spain, 1516–1556) [Translator's Note].
6. Drawn from *Libro del infante don Pedro de Portugal, que anduvo las cuatro partidas del mundo,* [*The Book of Prince Don Pedro of Portugal, who traveled to the four ends of the earth,* 1547]. "Seven" rather than "four" was common parlance in the medieval era and persisted into Cervantes' time [Translator's Note].

Chapter Twenty-Four

— which narrates a thousand trifles, each and all of them as irrelevant as they are also necessary to any proper understanding of this great history

He who translated this great history from its Arabic original, written by its primal author, Sidi Hamid Benengeli, tells us that, when he got to this chapter about the adventure in Montesinos' Cave, he found, written in the margins, and in Sidi Hamid's own handwriting, the following remarks:

"I cannot persuade myself nor quite believe that the valiant Don Quijote in fact experienced literally everything written about in the aforesaid chapter, because everything else that has happened to him, to this point, has been well within the realm of possibility and verisimilitude, but I find it hard to accept as true all these things that supposedly happened in the cave, for they exceed all reasonable bounds. But it's not possible to believe Don Quijote was lying, he who was the most truthful as well as the noblest knight of his time, someone who would not tell a lie if you killed him. All the same, when I consider in what detail he told his story, it seems to me he could not have fabricated such a vast chain of nonsense in so short a time. Accordingly, if this adventure seems apocryphal, do not put the blame on me: I've simply recorded it, and I say nothing as to its truth or falsity. You, reader, as a sensible man, are perfectly capable of making up your own mind; I neither can nor am required to decide — though it is considered certain that there are those who allege that, on his deathbed, he took back every word of it, explaining that he had invented the entire thing, because it seemed to him it very nicely matched the adventures he had read about in his books."

And then our author goes on with his tale, as follows:

The cousin was as shocked at Sancho Panza's daring as at Don Quijote's patience, explaining to himself that such mildness must have stemmed from the pleasure Sancho's master had received, seeing his lady Dulcinea del Toboso, even in her enchanted state, for otherwise the things Sancho had said would surely have earned him a well-deserved beating; in point of fact, the cousin thought Sancho had been insolent. Turning to Don Quijote, he said:

"And I, My Lord Don Quijote de La Mancha, I consider this journey I have made in your company to have been of the very highest utility, for it has brought me four things. The first is to have come to know your grace, which makes me very happy indeed. The second is to know what lies buried, here in Montesinos' Cave, and to learn of the transformations of Guadiana and the lakes of Ruidera, which will be highly useful to me in *The Spanish Ovid* I'm at work on. The third is to understand just how ancient playing cards truly are, for clearly they were already in use in the days of the Emperor Charlemagne, as we can see from what your grace reports Durandarte said, when after that long spell of silence he spoke to Montesinos, waking up and declaring, 'Patience, and cut the cards.' For he could not have learned this way of speaking while he was under enchantment, but only when he was not enchanted, in France during the time of the aforesaid Emperor Charlemagne. This is precisely the kind of information I need for the other book I'm putting together, my *Supplement to Polydore Vergil, on the Inventions of Antiquity*. It seems to me that Polydore Vergil forgot to include playing cards in his book, as I'm now going to do, which will be a matter of large import, especially coming from so serious and truthful a source as Lord Durandarte. And the fourth is to have learned the true source of the Guadiana River, which has been unknown until now."

"Your grace is quite right," said Don Quijote, "though I would like to know — if, by God's good blessing, you're given a license to print these books of yours, which I think unlikely — to whom you plan to dedicate them."

"There are lords and noblemen enough in Spain, to whom I might dedicate them," said the cousin.

"No, not many," replied Don Quijote. "Not that they wouldn't deserve such dedications, but rather that they wouldn't permit them, not wanting to oblige themselves to reward authors for all the work they've put in, not to mention for the courtesy in making the dedication. But I know one prince who makes up for all the others' deficiencies, and does so to such great advantage that if I ventured to speak of it, here, it might quicken envy in rather a lot of generous breasts,[1] but I'll leave that for another and more appropriate time. And now, let's hunt up a place where we can spend the night."

"Not far from here," said the cousin, "there's a hermitage, and one of the hermits who dwells there, who is said to have been a soldier, has the reputation of a good Christian, a singularly wise man, and exceedingly charitable. There's a small house, next to the hermitage, which this hermit constructed at his own expense, and, though it's tiny, it's capable of holding guests."

"Does this hermit keep chickens, by any chance?" asked Sancho.

"There aren't many hermits who don't," answered Don Quijote, "because today's hermits aren't like the ones who used to live in the deserts of Egypt, wearing palm leaves and eating roots they dug out of the ground. Nor by praising those old ones do I mean to say our hermits aren't any good, but just that the penitence practiced by today's hermits isn't as harsh and severe — which doesn't mean they're not good men, or, at least, that I don't think they are, because no matter how bad things may look, a hypocrite pretending to be a good man does less harm than an open sinner."

Just then they saw a man coming rapidly toward them, on foot, whacking away at a jackass loaded with spears and halberds.[2] He greeted them and started past, but Don Quijote said to him:

"Wait, wait, my good man. You seem to be going faster than this jackass likes."

---

1. I.e., the Count of Lemos, dedicatee of this second volume, and Cervantes's patron [*Translator's Note*].
2. An axelike blade with a spiked tip [*Translator's Note*].

"I can't stop, sir," replied the man, "because these weapons I've got here have to be used tomorrow, and so I have no choice but to hurry on, may God bless you. But if you want to know why I'm carrying this load, I plan to spend the night in the inn just past the hermitage, so if we're traveling the same road you'll find me there, and I'll tell you some wonderful things. And, once again, may God bless you."

And he so spurred on his jackass that Don Quijote had no time to ask him what kind of marvels he proposed to tell them about, but since he was distinctly curious and forever driven by the desire to learn new things, he arranged right then and there that they'd go and spend the night at the inn, instead of at the hermitage where the cousin had wanted them to go.

So they all three of them mounted and took the straight road toward the inn (where they arrived a little before dusk). However, the cousin told Don Quijote they could stop at the hermitage for a drink. Sancho no sooner heard this than he swung his donkey around and headed toward the hermitage, and the cousin and Don Quijote followed suit, but as Sancho's bad luck would have it, the hermit wasn't home, as they were informed by a female servant.[3] They asked her for wine, but she answered that her master had none, but if they'd settle for water she'd be very glad to give them some.

"If water would do for me," replied Sancho, "there are wells all up and down the road, which would have done fine. Oh, Camacho's wedding — and Don Diego's overflowing table — oh, how often I miss you!"

So they left the hermitage and spurred on toward the inn, and after a bit met up with a young fellow, walking at no very great speed, which is why they caught up to him. He carried a sword over his shoulder, and suspended from it there was a bundle of what looked like clothing, which as far as they could see had to be trousers or pantaloons, and a cloak, and some shirts, since what he was wearing was a loose velvet jacket, vaguely satin-like, and a shirt which hung out; he had on silk stockings and square shoes of the kind worn at court; he looked eighteen or nineteen years old, cheerful and apparently quite nimble. He was singing *seguidillas*[4] as he went, to make his plodding journey more bearable. As they came up to him, he had just finished one that the cousin immediately memorized, which went like this:

> I'm taking my nothing
> off to war,
> but if I had anything
> I wouldn't go far.

The first to speak to him was Don Quijote, who said:

"Sir gallant, you're traveling very light, I see. Where may you be going? We'd like to know, if you'd care to tell us."

The young man replied:

---

3. Cervantes here uses the term "a subhermitess" [una sotahermitaño], suggesting that the absent hermit keeps a concubine.

4. A folklike verse form of four lines, employed from the sixteenth century to today [*Translator's Note*].

"I'm footloose because it's hot and I'm poor, and where I'm going is to war."

"What do you mean by 'poor'?" asked Don Quijote. "I can certainly understand what you say about the heat."

"My lord," replied the young fellow, "in this bundle I'm carrying a pair of velvet pantaloons, which match the jacket I'm wearing. If I wear them out, here on the road, I won't be able to wear them in the city, and I have nothing to buy more with, which is why you see me strolling along like this — until I catch up to several infantry companies that aren't more than about forty miles from here, and that's where I'll sign myself up. There won't be any shortage of pack trains, from there to the port we'll sail from, which they say is to be Cartagena. I'd much rather serve our lord the king, and fight in his wars, than work for some idiot at court."

"And did they send your grace any travel money, by chance?" asked the cousin.

"If I were serving some Spanish nobleman, or somebody highborn," the young man replied, "I certainly would have gotten some, because that's what comes to you when you work for the right people, and you go right from the servants' mess hall to being a lieutenant or even a captain, or maybe you leave with a fat pension, but — unlucky me — I've always worked for people who were looking for jobs themselves, upstarts and such, the kind who pay you and feed you so badly that it takes half your salary to keep your collars starched, and everyone would call it miraculous if a servant going off to try his luck ever got anything halfway decent."

"Now tell me this, and tell me the truth, my friend," asked Don Quijote. "Is it really possible, after working all those years, that you never got yourself any sort of uniform?"

"I got two of them," replied the young fellow. "But just the way they take away your habit, when you leave a religious house, and hand you back your ordinary clothes, my masters gave me back mine, because just as soon as they'd finished the business that brought them to court, they went straight home again and took the uniforms — which were strictly for show — with them."

"Remarkable *spilorceria* [stinginess], as the Italians say," said Don Quijote. "But, just the same, count yourself lucky for having left court with such a fine plan in mind, because there's nothing on earth so honorable, or so useful, as serving God, in the first place, and, next, serving your king and natural lord, especially by bearing arms, which are capable of raising you, if not necessarily to wealth, then at least to greater honor than can the humane professions — as I've said many times. More great families may have been founded on the humane professions than on the practice of war, but, all the same, those born of war have a certain something, a kind of splendor about them, which marks them out as superior to all others. Remember, young man, what I'm about to tell you, for it will be wonderfully useful as well as helpful, and in all your labors: and what I say is do not think about the bad things which might happen to you, for the worst of all is death, but if you die well, then death is the best of all. Julius Caesar, that noble Roman emperor, was asked which death was the best, and he answered, death which comes unexpected, precisely because

it's sudden and unforeseen, and though he spoke as a pagan, totally unaware of the true God, all the same he spoke well, in terms of sparing our
human feelings, for suppose you're killed in the first skirmish of the first
battle, perhaps by an artillery shell, perhaps blown up by a land mine —
it makes no difference. Death is everything, and it finishes us, and as
Terence says, a soldier killed in battle comes off better than a soldier who
saves himself by running,[5] and a good soldier earns his reputation insofar
as he obeys his generals and all those in command. And be aware, my
son, that it's better for a soldier to smell of gunpowder than of musk
perfume; if by any chance you grow old in this honorable profession,
though much wounded and worn down, or even lame, at any rate you'll
never have gotten there without honor — and honor of the sort that
poverty cannot threaten, especially now that they're helping and taking
care of old and enfeebled soldiers, because it's wrong to treat them the
way people do, who set their black slaves free and drive them off, when
they're too old to work, pretending to grant them liberty when you're really
making them slaves, now, to hunger, a master from whom they can only
be liberated by death. But, for the moment, let us say no more, except
that you should climb up behind me on my horse, until we reach the inn,
and there you must dine with us, and then, tomorrow, you can follow
your road, and may God give you everything you deserve."

The young man would not climb up on the horse, though he accepted
the invitation to dine with them at the inn — and it's reported that, just
then, Sancho said to himself:

"God bless you for a master! Is it really possible for a man who can talk
like that, who can deal with so many things, and so wisely, to also declare
he's seen the crazy impossibilities he says he saw in Montesinos' Cave? So
now we'll see."

Then they arrived at the inn, just at dusk, and Sancho was not unhappy
to see that his master took it for a genuine inn, and not for a castle, as he
usually did. They'd hardly come through the door when Don Quijote
asked the innkeeper about the man with the spears and halberds, and was
told that he was taking care of his jackass. The cousin and Sancho did the
same thing for their donkeys, though Rocinante got the best manger and
the best stall in the stable.

Chapter Twenty-Five

*— which sets out the donkey-braying adventure and the puppeteer's
charming tale, along with the remarkable prophecies of the
prophetic monkey*

Don Quijote couldn't keep his pants on, as they say, until he'd heard
all the wonders promised by the man with the load of weapons. He went
looking for him, in the place the innkeeper had indicated, and found him,

5. Not in fact from Terence; if a quotation, its origin remains obscure [*Translator's Note*].

and asked him to tell, finally, what he'd said he could tell when Don Quijote had questioned him, on the road. The man answered:

"Marvels like mine have to be told slowly, leisurely, and not while standing up. My good sir, your grace, let me finish taking care of my animal, and then I'll tell you things that will astonish you."

"Let's not wait," replied Don Quijote, "because I'll help you with everything you need to do."

Which he did, sifting the barley and cleaning out the feedbox, a humble helpfulness which made the other man feel cheerfully obligated to grant Don Quijote's request, and so, seating himself next to our knight on a stone bench, with an audience and a listening senate composed of the cousin, the prospective soldier, Sancho Panza, and the innkeeper, he began as follows:

"You gentlemen must understand that, in a village some fifteen miles from this inn, one of the aldermen, because of the cleverness and deceit of a serving maid (the whole story would take too long to tell), lost a donkey, and though he tried as hard as he could to find the animal, it was impossible. Two weeks after the donkey's disappearance, according to the story, this alderman was in the public square and another alderman from the same village said to him:

" 'You owe me a reward, colleague: your donkey's turned up.'

" 'I do indeed, colleague, and I'll very gladly pay it,' replied the first alderman, 'but tell me: where was he found?'

" 'Up in the mountains,' answered the second alderman, who had found the animal. 'I saw him this morning, minus his packsaddle or any kind of harness, and looking so lean and feeble he was a pitiful sight. I wanted to round him up and bring him back, but he's already so wild and skittish that, when I went over to him, he ran away, right into the densest part of the forest. We can both go back and look for him, if you like: just let me leave this she-ass at my house and I'll come right back.'

" 'That would be very nice indeed,' said the donkey's owner, 'and I'll do my best to repay you in the same coin.'

"Now, all of these details, told in exactly the way I've been telling them to you, are reported by everyone who knows what really happened in this matter. So after a bit the two aldermen, on foot and side by side, went up the mountain, but when they got to the place where they expected to find the donkey he was nowhere to be found, and even though they looked all around the neighborhood they still couldn't find him. Realizing, finally, that the donkey simply wasn't there, the second alderman said to the first:

" 'Look, colleague: I've just thought of a scheme that will surely let us locate this animal, even if he's stuck down in the bowels of the earth, let alone up here on the mountain. I know how to bray exactly like a jackass, so if you're any good at it, too, it's all as good as done.'

" 'Any good at it, colleague?' said the first alderman. 'By God, I don't play second fiddle to anybody, not even one of these jackasses himself.'

" 'Let's find out, then,' replied the second alderman, 'because this is what I've decided: you go to one side of the mountain, and I'll go to the other, and we'll go all around it in a great circle, and you'll bray, and I'll bray, at regular intervals, and if he's still on the mountain the donkey can't help but hear us and bray back.'

"The donkey's owner replied:

" 'Let me tell you, colleague, that's a first-rate scheme and worthy of someone with your brains.'

"So the two of them separated as they'd planned, but it happened that they each brayed at almost exactly the same time, so they were both deceived into thinking they'd found the donkey. The donkey's owner called out:

" 'That was surely my donkey braying, wasn't it colleague?'

" 'It was just me,' answered the other.

" 'Let me tell you, then,' said the donkey's owner, 'that there's absolutely no difference between you and a donkey, as far as braying's concerned, because in all my life I've never seen or heard such a perfect imitation.'

" 'Such warm praise,' replied the second alderman, 'really belongs to you, colleague, because by God who made me you can bray better and more professionally than the best brayer in the world. The sound you send forth is good and loud; you sustain the tone so well, and just exactly on the beat, and then let it die away just right, swelling and urgent, so, in a word, you clearly win the prize and, for such unusual skill, I hand you the flag of victory.'

" 'Well then,' said the donkey's owner, 'from now on I'll think a lot better of myself than I ever did before, since I have such ability, because even though I always thought I could bray pretty well, I never thought I'd gotten as good at it as you say.'

" 'Now let me tell you something else,' responded the second alderman. 'The world's wasting some rare talents, and those who possess them aren't being made use of as they ought to be.'

" 'Our talents,' said the donkey's owner, 'wouldn't do us much good except in cases like this, because we couldn't use them for anything else, but may God grant that, for this purpose, they'll really prove useful.'

"After this exchange, they went back to their stations, and to their braying, and every time they let loose they fooled each other again, and came back together, until, as a kind of password to let each other know they were hearing human brays, not donkey ones, they agreed to bray twice, one right after the other. So off they went around the mountain, emitting their brays in pairs, and the lost donkey never said a word, and they found not a sign of him anywhere. But how could the poor, unlucky donkey have answered them, when they finally did find him, in the deepest part of the forest, eaten by wolves? Seeing this, the donkey's owner said:

" 'I was astonished that he didn't answer, if he was still alive, because if he didn't bray back when he heard us he couldn't have been a real donkey. All the same, I feel well rewarded, colleague, by having heard how beautifully you bray, so all the effort spent hunting for him wasn't wasted, even though we found him dead.'

" 'You sang the lead, colleague,' said the second alderman, 'because when the abbot sings well, the altar boys have to keep up with him.'

"And then, unhappy and very hoarse, they went back to their village, where they told their friends and neighbors and acquaintances what had happened on their donkey hunt, each one extravagantly praising the other's talents at braying, and eventually everyone for miles around heard the tale. And the Devil, who never sleeps, because he's so fond of seeding and sowing quarrels and disagreements anywhere he can, blowing mischievous gossip into the wind and puffing up arguments out of nothing, saw to it that people from other towns, whenever they saw anyone from our village, would make donkey noises, mocking our aldermen's braying. And then the little boys started doing it, which was just like putting it into the hands and mouths of all the devils in hell, and the whole thing spread from one village to another, and we got to be as easily identified as citizens of the braying village as black men can be distinguished from white ones, and this unfortunate joke has reached such proportions that, often, those being mocked have sallied out in squadrons to fight with the mockers, weapons in hand, and neither king nor castle, nor fear nor shame, can do anything about it. So tomorrow, or some other day soon, I expect the people of my village (and we're the ones who did the braying) will fight a pitched battle against the people from a village six or seven miles from ours, who are some of our worst persecutors, and I bought the spears and halberds you saw so we can fight them properly prepared. And these are the wonders I told you you'd hear, and if you don't think that's what they are, well, I don't know any other ones."

So the good man finished what he had to say, and at the very same time there came through the door of the inn a man dressed all in chamois — his stockings, his breeches, his jacket — who immediately called out:

"Innkeeper, have you got a room? Because here comes the man with the prophetic monkey and the puppet show about setting Melisendra free."

"Mother of God!" said the innkeeper, "but here's Maestro Pedro! Get ready for a good time tonight."

I should have mentioned that this Maestro Pedro wore a huge green taffeta patch over his left eye, and halfway down his cheek, a sign that something was wrong all across that side of his face.

The innkeeper continued:

"Welcome, welcome, your grace, Maestro Pedro! But where's the monkey? and the puppet show? Because I don't see either of them."

"They're not far away," said the man in chamois. "I came on ahead, to see if you had room."

"I'd toss out the Duke of Alba himself, to make room for Maestro Pedro," replied the innkeeper. "Go get the monkey and the puppet show, because we've got people in the inn, tonight, who'll pay to see the puppets and that clever monkey of yours."

"That's fine with me," replied the man with the patch, "and I'll lower the price, and be satisfied to break even. So now I'll get the cart with the monkey and the puppet show rolling on its way."

And he turned and left the inn.

Don Quijote promptly asked the innkeeper who this Maestro Pedro was, and what sort of monkey and puppet show he had with him. The innkeeper replied:

"He's a very famous puppeteer, who for quite a while has been going around eastern La Mancha, putting on a puppet show about Melisendra, who was set free by the celebrated Don Gaiferos, and it's one of the best, and the best acted performances, that anyone in this part of the kingdom has seen in a long, long time. He's also got with him a monkey that has a wonderfully unusual talent, rare enough among monkeys but even, I suspect, among men, which is that Maestro Pedro asks him something, and the monkey listens and then jumps up on his master's shoulders and, bending down to his ear, tells him the answer, and Maestro Pedro calls it right out. The monkey talks a lot more about things that have happened than those still to come, and even if he doesn't always hit the bull's eye he's usually right — which makes us think there's a devil somewhere in him. He gets two dollars for every question, if the monkey answers it — I mean, if his master answers it for him, after the monkey whispers in Pedro's ear, so I think this Maestro Pedro's a very rich man, and *un hombre galante* [a gallant man], as they say in Italy, and *un bon campaño* [good company], and he leads the best life in the world — he can talk for six and drink for a dozen, all thanks to his tongue and his monkey and his puppet show."

Just then Maestro Pedro returned, and right behind him came a cart carrying the puppet show, and the monkey, who was large and had no tail, but felt smooth bare buttocks; his face seemed friendly. The moment Don Quijote saw him, he inquired:

"Tell me, your grace, sir Prophet: *¿qué peje pillamo?* [what kind of fish will we catch?] What's going to happen to us? And here are my two dollars."

He directed Sancho to hand the money over to Maestro Pedro, who replied, on the monkey's behalf:

"Señor, this animal doesn't bother with things still to come; he knows a bit about the past, and more or less the same about the present."

"So help me Hanna," said Sancho, "but I wouldn't give you a penny to tell me about my past! Because who knows it better than I do? And paying you to tell me what I already know would be dumb, and then some. But since he knows the present, here are my two dollars, and let my lord monkeyface tell me what my wife Teresa Panza is up to, right now, and how she's keeping busy."

Maestro Pedro refused to take the money, saying:

"I don't like receiving my wages before I've done my work."

Then, after he'd tapped his shoulder twice, with his right hand, the monkey hopped up, bent to his ear and chattered rapidly away with its teeth, and then, keeping this up for as long as it takes to say the Credo, hopped right back to the ground again — and suddenly, with great urgency, Maestro Pedro fell on his knees in front of Don Quijote and, hugging his legs, declared:

"I embrace these legs as I would embrace the twin columns of Hercules, oh worthy resuscitator of long-forgotten knight errantry! Oh knight not yet praised as you deserve to be, Don Quijote de La Mancha, inspirer of the downhearted, prop of those who totter and are ready to fall, strong right arm and staff for those who have fallen, and counselor of all those who have been unfortunate!"

Don Quijote was utterly dumbfounded, Sancho entranced, the cousin astonished, the man from the braying village stupefied, the innkeeper bewildered and, finally, all those who heard the puppeteer were amazed. Maestro Pedro went on:

"And you, oh good Sancho Panza! Rejoice, best squire to the best knight in the world, for your good wife Teresa is well, and is at the moment combing out a bundle of flax and, to provide you with yet additional detail, has near her left hand a pitcher, with its spout broken off, holding a fair amount of wine, with which she cheers herself as she works."

"I have no trouble believing that," replied Sancho, "because she's a blissfully good one and, if she weren't so jealous, I wouldn't trade her for the giantess Andandona,[1] who according to my master was a whole lot of woman. My Teresa isn't the kind who does without, even if her heirs have to pay for it."

"Let me just say," Don Quijote put in at this point, "that he who reads and travels widely, sees a lot and knows a lot. And I say this because who could possibly have persuaded me that the world contains prophetic monkeys, as I've just this minute seen with my own eyes? For I am indeed the very same Don Quijote de La Mancha of whom this animal has spoken, though his praise has been vastly exaggerated — but whoever and whatever I am, I am thankful to God for the gentle and compassionate heart with which He has endowed me, always desiring to do good to everyone, and harm to no one."

"If I had the money," said the prospective soldier, "I'd ask Mister Monkey what's going to happen to me, in the journey I'm making."

Maestro Pedro, who had now risen to his feet, answered him:

"As I've said, this little animal has nothing to say about the future, though if he could see what is still to come, your having no money would not matter, for to be of any service to Don Quijote, who we have with us, I would forego all the money in the world. So now, because I owe it to him, and to give him pleasure, I will set up my puppet show for the entertainment of everyone in the inn, absolutely free of charge."

The delighted innkeeper, hearing this, pointed out a place where the puppet show could be put, and quick as a wink Maestro Pedro had it ready.

Don Quijote was not particularly pleased with the monkey's conundrums, not thinking it quite proper that a monkey should prophesy at all (whether about the future or the past), so while Maestro Pedro set up his puppet show, Don Quijote and Sancho withdrew to a corner of the stable, where (without fear of anyone else hearing him) our knight observed:

"Now look, Sancho: I've been thinking about this monkey's strange talents, and it seems clear to me that this Maestro Pedro, his master, must have made some kind of compact — whether tacit or explicit I don't know — with the Devil."

"If this outdoor theater of his is compact enough for devils," said Sancho, "it's got to be a pretty dirty thing, all right. But why would Maestro Pedro want such a compact theater?"

"You don't understand what I'm saying, Sancho. All I mean is that he must have made some kind of agreement with the devil, who then breathed this gift into the monkey, for the sake of making money, but in the end the rich man will have to give the devil his soul, which is of

---

1. A character in *Amadís of Gaul* [Translator's Note].

course what that enemy of us all is always after. What convinces me of this is seeing that the monkey can only answer questions about the past or the present, which is as far as the devil's knowledge can go, because the only way he could know anything about the future would be by guessing, and that wouldn't always work: knowledge of time's movements is reserved for God, and God alone, and for Him there is no such thing as past or future, for to Him everything is present. And this being the case, as it is, clearly this monkey must be speaking at the devil's dictation, and it astonishes me that this Maestro Pedro hasn't been brought before the Inquisition and questioned about exactly from whence came this prophetic power of his, because it's absolutely certain that this monkey's no astrologer, and neither he nor his master casts horoscopes, or knows how to — though it's so common in Spain, these days, that there's no little serving girl, or boy, nor even any old shoemaker who won't dare to prognosticate, as if it were some simple card trick — and all their lies and stupidities are completely contaminating the true wonders of astrological science. I know a lady who asked one of these fortune tellers if her lapdog, a tiny little bitch, would get pregnant and have puppies, and how many there would be and what colors. And this great master of heavenly knowledge, after working out the horoscope, told her that, yes, the little bitch would get pregnant, and would bear three pups, one green, one red, and one particolored — on condition, however, that the little bitch would have to be impregnated between eleven and twelve o'clock (either twelve midnight or twelve noon would do), and also that it had to be either a Monday or a Saturday — and what actually happened was that the little bitch died of indigestion, caused by overfeeding, and our master astrologer immediately achieved local prominence as a superbly accurate prognosticator, the way it happens with all, or at least most, of these quacks."

"Just the same," said Sancho, "I still wish your grace would have this Maestro Pedro ask his monkey if what happened to your grace in Montesinos' Cave actually happened or not, because as far as I'm concerned, and I beg your pardon, your grace, *that* was a lot of lies and tricks, or anyway a lot of dream stuff."

"That may very well be," replied Don Quijote. "But I'll do what you suggest, though I have some reservations about it."

Just then Maestro Pedro arrived, looking for Don Quijote, to tell him that, if his grace cared to see it — and it was worth seeing — the puppet show was ready. Don Quijote explained what he'd been thinking and asked if Maestro Pedro could immediately inquire of his monkey whether certain things, supposed to have happened in Montesinos' Cave, were nothing but dreams, or whether they were real, because to Don Quijote himself they seemed both dreamlike and real. Without saying a word, Maestro Pedro went to fetch his monkey and, setting him down in Don Quijote and Sancho's presence, said:

"Mister Monkey, do you see this gentleman? He wants to know if certain things supposed to have taken place in something called Montesinos' Cave really happened or if they didn't."

Then he gave the usual signal, the monkey jumped up on his left shoulder, and seemed to speak in his ear, after which Maestro Pedro declared:

"The monkey says that some of the things you saw, or experienced, in the aforesaid cave, your grace, were false, and some were true, but this is all he knows, and no more, about what you've asked. But if your grace really wants to know more, then on Friday next he'll be able to tell you, because right now he's used up his power and he won't get it back until Friday, as I've already explained."

"Didn't I tell you, my lord," said Sancho, "that I couldn't accept the truth of everything your grace said about what happened in that cave — and not even half of it?"

"Time will tell, Sancho," replied Don Quijote, "for it reveals all things and there is nothing it fails to bring out into the light of day, though it may have been hidden in the earth's bosom. But enough of this, for now, and let's go see our good Maestro Pedro's puppet show, which I suspect must be somewhat novel."

"Somewhat?" responded Maestro Pedro. "This puppet show of mine has sixty thousand novel things in it, so let me tell you, your grace, my dear Don Quijote, it's one of the things most worth seeing anywhere in the world, for *operibus credite, et non verbis* [Believe my works, not my words: John, 10:38] — and now let's get to work, because it's getting late, and there's a lot still to be done, and said, and shown."

Don Quijote and Sancho obeyed him, following along to where the puppet show was set up and ready, surrounded on all sides by tiny burning candles, which made it seem attractive and even brilliant. When they got there, Maestro Pedro put himself inside, for he had to work the puppets; a boy, Maestro Pedro's servant, stood outside, to serve as guide and interpreter of the mysteries performed within, using a small wooden stick, which he held in his hand, to identify each of the characters who appeared.

Everyone in the inn being ready for the performance, some of them standing right up in front, next to the puppet show, and the best seats reserved for Don Quijote, Sancho, the prospective soldier, and the cousin, the commentator began to say what, if you read or hear the next chapter, you too will see and hear.

Chapter Twenty-Six

— continuation of the puppeteer's charming tale, along with other truly first-rate things

Everyone was quiet, Tyrians as well as Trojans[1] — that is, all those watching the puppet show and anxiously waiting to hear their guide and interpreter tell them its wonders, when suddenly, from inside, they heard the sound of many drums and trumpets, and the firing of many cannons, the noise of which did not last very long, after which the boy began to speak, saying:

"This true tale which we will here perform for you gentlemen is abso-

---

1. Quoted from canto 2 of Gregorio Hernández de Velasco's translation of the *Aeneid* (1555) [*Translator's Note*].

lutely faithful to both the French chronicles and the Spanish ballads that everyone knows by heart, even little boys in the streets. It tells how Señor Don Gaiferos freed his wife, Melisendra, who'd been held a captive by the Moors, in Spain, in the city of Sansueña, which is what in those days they called the city which, today, we know as Zaragoza. And now, gentlemen, there you see Don Gaiferos himself, playing chess, as the ballad says:

> Don Gaiferos sits at his chess board,
> Melisendra long since forgotten.

Now the personage appearing over there, wearing a crown on his head and with a scepter in his hand, is the Emperor Charlemagne, who's supposed to be Melisendra's father, and he's annoyed to see how lazy and negligent his son-in-law is being, so he comes out to tell him off, and scolds him with such vehemence, not to say pleasure, that it looks as if he'd really like to give him half a dozen whacks with his scepter — and there are writers who say he really did, and pretty good whacks, too. And then, after saying a lot of things about Don Gaiferos risking his honor, by not arranging to have his wife set free, the Emperor declares:

> That's enough words: now do it!

Watch, gentlemen, how the emperor turns his back and leaves Don Gaiferos so very angry that, see how he knocks over the chessboard and throws the chess pieces all over the place, his anger making him impatient, so he hurriedly calls for his armor, and tries to borrow his cousin Don Roland's sword, named Durindana, but Don Roland won't lend it to him, though he offers to join Gaiferos in this difficult undertaking, but the brave Gaiferos, who's really very angry, won't let him come, saying instead that he'll rescue his wife all by himself, even were she buried in the deep center of the earth, so then he gets into his armor and prepares to start on his journey. Now, gentlemen, look at that tower, appearing over there, which is supposed to be one of the towers of the fortress of Zaragoza, now known as the Aljafería, and that lady, appearing out on the balcony, dressed in Moorish style, is the matchless Melisendra, who often stands out here, looking at the road that leads to France, and thinking of Paris, and of her husband, to console herself in her captivity. Note also a new thing happening, which quite possibly you've never seen before. Now watch — see that Moor, silently and softly stealing up behind Melisendra, his finger across his lips? Watch, now, how he kisses her squarely on the lips, and how she immediately spits and cleans herself with the loose white sleeve of her dress, and then bewails and pulls out her beautiful locks, as if the crime had been their fault. Note also that the somber Moor you see walking up and down, over there, is King Marsilio of Sansueña; having seen the first Moor's insolence, the king at once orders him, even though he's a close kinsman and a great personal favorite, to be arrested and carried through the streets of the city, being given two hundred strokes of the lash as he goes

> with town criers in front of him
> and soldiers walking behind.[2]

---

2. Quoted from a ballad by Francisco de Quevedo [*Translator's Note*].

And here you see the sentence being carried out, even though the crime had barely been committed, because the Moors don't worry about 'formal notice and summons,' or 'orders for arrest and incarceration,' the way we do."

"Boy, boy," called out Don Quijote loudly, at this point, "let your story move in a straight line, and don't detour us into sideways and byways, because of course it takes a lot of evidence to establish the real truth."

And from inside, Maestro Pedro also declared:

"Just stick to the business at hand, my boy, exactly as this gentleman has directed, because that's the very best way. Give us plain song and don't mess with counterpoint, which is apt to collapse under its own weight."

"That's exactly what I'll do," replied the boy, going on as follows:

"This figure you now see, on horseback, wearing a cloak with a hood, is Don Gaiferos once again, and his wife, who's now been avenged for the lovesick Moor's impudence, and feels a lot calmer, is out on the castle balcony chatting with her husband, but thinking he's just some passerby, so she talks to him just the way it says in the ballad,

> Oh knight, if you're off to France,
> ask for Gaiferos —

but I won't stop to recite the ballad, because I don't want to bore you with too many words. All you need is to see how Gaiferos reveals himself, and Melisendra's happy looks and gestures, showing us she's recognized him. So now we see her sliding down from the balcony, so she can sit behind her good husband on his horse. But, oh, unlucky woman! the edge of her petticoat gets stuck on one of the balcony railings, so she's just hanging in the air, unable to reach the ground. But see how merciful Heaven sends us help when we most need it, for Don Gaiferos comes forward and, without worrying whether that rich petticoat gets ripped to shreds or not, he just grabs her and yanks, and like it or not, he brings her down to earth and immediately, with a flourish, puts her on the horse, right behind him, sitting astride like a man, ordering her to hold on tight and put her arms over his shoulders, so they're crossed on his chest, to keep her from falling, because Lady Melisendra isn't used to riding like a man. And you can also see, from the way the horse is neighing and carrying on, that he's happy to be carrying the brave and beautiful burden of both his master and his mistress. Now you see how Gaiferos swings around and rides out of the city, and how joyfully he starts out on the road to Paris. May you travel in peace, oh truest of true lovers! Come safely home to your own beloved country, without fortune placing any obstacles in your happy path! May the eyes of your friends and kinsmen see you enjoying your days in peace and tranquillity, and may your lives last as long as Nestor's!"

Maestro Pedro raised his voice, again at this point, saying:

"Keep it simple, my boy; don't get carried away, because affectation is always a bad thing."

The commentator made no reply, but simply went on, saying:

"But there were more than a few idle eyes, for lazy people manage to see everything, watching Melisendra descend from the balcony and get right up on the horse, and they warned King Marsilio, who ordered the call to arms sounded. And now see how fast they do as he said, for the city's already flooded with the ringing of bells, pealing forth from the towers of every mosque."

"No, no!" Don Quijote exclaimed at this point. "Maestro Pedro has this bell business all wrong, because the Moors don't use bells, just tambourines and drums, and a kind of flute that's very like ours, so all this stuff about the bells of Sansueña pealing out is really quite silly."

When Maestro Pedro heard this, he stopped the ringing and said:

"Don't worry about little details, your grace, My Lord Don Quijote, and don't expect everything to be exactly the way it ought to be, because that's not how the world works. Aren't we always seeing, all around us and almost as a matter of course, a thousand theatrical pieces shot full of a thousand out-of-place, nonsensical things — and in spite of everything they go merrily on their way, and they're greeted not just with applause, but with admiration and all the rest of it? You go on, my boy, and never mind: as long as I fill my money bag, it doesn't matter if we make as many mistakes as there are dust specks in a sunbeam."

"Well, that's true," replied Don Quijote.

And then the boy continued:

"See how many magnificent knights come pouring out of the city, following after the two Christian lovers, and how many trumpets blow, and how many drums are drumming and booming, and hear all the tambourines rattling away. I'm afraid the fugitives won't get away, and they'll be brought back to the city, tied to their own horse's tail, which would be a ghastly spectacle."

But seeing and hearing such a swarm of Moors, and such a banging and general uproar, Don Quijote felt he simply had to help those who were fleeing, so he stood up and shouted:

"They'll never play such tricks on such a famous knight and bold lover as Don Gaiferos, not right under my eyes, not while I'm alive! Hold, you lowborn scoundrels! Don't you dare go after him, don't you dare chase him, or you'll have to fight with me first!"

And as he spoke he pulled out his sword and sprang toward the puppet show, and with swift and incredibly savage strokes began to rain blows on the Moorish puppets, knocking some of them over, beheading others, crippling some and absolutely demolishing others, and along with all the rest slashing one furious overhand blow which, had Maestro Pedro not crouched and cowered to the ground, would have cut through his head even more easily than if it had been made of almond sugar-paste. Maestro Pedro was shouting:

"My Lord Don Quijote, stop, stop! You're not killing and maiming and breaking real live Moors, but cardboard puppets. Oh my God, as I'm a sinner, just look how you're smashing and ruining everything I own!"

But none of this kept Don Quijote from slashing away, forehand, backhand, stabbing and slicing until, in less time than it takes to say two Credos he'd brought the whole puppet show to the ground, and smashed the puppets and props to little pieces: King Marsilio was very badly wounded indeed, and Emperor Charlemagne's crowned head, crown and all, was split in two. The listening senate was in an uproar, the monkey ran out the window and up onto the roof, the cousin was frightened silly, the prospective soldier was thoroughly intimidated, and even our own Sancho Panza was good and scared, because (as he swore once the storm had blown over) he'd never seen his master in such a wild fury. But having pretty much destroyed the puppet show, Don Quijote grew a bit calmer, declaring:

"I wish I had here in front of me, right this minute, all those who do not believe — who refuse to believe — how important knights errant are, in this world of ours. Just consider, if I had not been here, what would have happened to good Don Gaiferos and his beautiful Melisendra: by now, surely, these dogs would have caught them and perpetrated some outrage upon them. So long live knight errantry, the greatest thing our world will ever see!"

"Live and let live," replied Maestro Pedro, his voice weak, "and let me die, because I'm so unlucky that well may I say, with King Don Rodrigo:

> Yesterday I was the lord of Spain . . .
> But today I haven't even a crack
> In a castle wall to my name.[3]

Not half an hour ago — no, not even half a minute ago, I was the lord of kings and emperors, and my stables, and my treasure chests, and my money sacks were full of horses and jewels past all counting, and now, here I am, plucked and beaten down to the very ground, poor, a beggar, and above all else my monkey's gone, and before I get him back, by God, I'll have to sweat blood — and all this because of the utterly irrational anger of this gentleman, who is said to protect orphans, and right wrongs, and accomplish all sorts of charitable acts, but only I have failed to benefit from his generosity, may Heaven be blessed and praised, where the angels live on high. In short, this Knight of the Sad Face has certainly made my face sad!"

Moved by Maestro Pedro's words, Sancho Panza said:

"Don't cry, Maestro Pedro — don't: you're breaking my heart, because you've got to understand that my lord Don Quijote is such a good Catholic, and such a scrupulous Christian, that if he realizes he's done you wrong, he won't deny it, he'll want to pay you back — and then some."

"Just let Don Quijote pay me for even part of the damage he's done me, and I'll be satisfied, and his grace's conscience will feel better, because no one can save his soul if he keeps something against the owner's will and refuses to give it back."

"That's true," said Don Quijote, "but so far as I know I haven't got anything of yours, Maestro Pedro."

"Oh no?" replied Maestro Pedro. "And all these corpses, lying here on the cold hard ground, what threw them down, what absolutely annihilated them, but the invincible fury of your strong right arm? And who but me owned these corpses? And who but them earned me my living?"

"Ah, now I really and truly believe," said Don Quijote, "what I've often

3. Verses from a very popular ballad of Rodrigo, last of the Gothic kings of Spain, beginning "Ayer era rey de España . . ." [*Translator's Note*].

thought and wondered: all they have to do, these enchanters who are always persecuting me, is to put puppets like these where I can see them, and then they immediately change and transform them into whatever they like. Let me tell you, you gentlemen who may be listening to my words: I really and truly thought everything being acted up here was actually happening: to me, this Melisendra *was* Melisendra, and Don Gaiferos *was* Gaiferos, and Marsilio *was* Marsilio, and Charlemagne *was* Charlemagne — and that's why I got so angry and, obliged by my oath as a knight errant, tried to aid and assist those who were fleeing, and with that noble intention did what you have seen me do. If what happened was the exact opposite of what I meant to do, don't blame me, but only the evil men who persecute me — but all the same, this being my mistake, although I was acting in complete good faith, I wish to make myself responsible for any and all charges. Tell us what you want for these broken puppets, Maestro Pedro, and let me hereby agree to pay you at once, in good, legal coin of the realm."

Maestro Pedro bowed and said:

"I expected no less from the brave Don Quijote de La Mancha's extraordinary Christianity, he who is truly the shield and protector of all needy, wandering vagabonds, so let you, Mister Innkeeper, and the great Sancho Panza, be the arbitrators and appraisers for myself and your grace, Don Quijote, as we determine the probable worth of these broken puppets."

The landlord and Sancho agreed, and Maestro Pedro immediately plucked from the ground, minus his head, King Marsilio of Zaragoza, saying:

"See how impossible it will be to restore this king to his original state, and so it seems to me, with all due deference to your better judgments, that on account of his death, decease, and termination, I ought to be paid the sum of four and a half dollars."

"Continue!" said Don Quijote.

"And then, for this top to bottom cleavage," continued Maestro Pedro, picking up the neatly divided Emperor Charlemagne, "I don't think it's too much to ask five dollars and a quarter."

"That's not exactly too little," said Sancho.

"But it's not a lot, either," answered the innkeeper. "Let's split the difference and say exactly five dollars."

"Give him the full five and a quarter," said Don Quijote, "for what's a quarter more or less, in the sum total of this remarkable disaster? But let's finish this up, Maestro Pedro: it's getting close to dinner time, and I'm starting to feel the first rumblings of hunger."

"Now for this puppet," said Maestro Pedro, "who's missing a nose and one eye — and this is the lovely Melisendra herself — I think I should have, and I think this perfectly fair, two dollars and twelve cents."

"Still, it'll be the devil's fault," said Don Quijote, "if by now that Melisendra and her husband aren't at least across the border into France, because the horse they were riding seemed to me more apt to fly than gallop — so you can't sell me a cat instead of a hare, showing me this noseless Melisendra, when the real one, if it comes to that, is now back in France, enjoying herself with her husband. May God help everyone to his own, Maestro Pedro, and let's get it over with and proceed on the straight and narrow as best we can."

Seeing that Don Quijote was wavering, and that he was heading back where he'd just come from, Maestro Pedro was determined not to let him get away, so he said:

"This can't be Melisendra — it's just one of her serving girls, so give me sixty cents for her and I'll be satisfied and well paid."

He quickly set the prices for many more mangled puppets, the two arbitrators adjusted them to the satisfaction of both parties, and the total came to forty dollars and seventy-five cents, and in addition to this, which Sancho immediately paid him, Maestro Pedro sought two dollars for the trouble of having to catch his monkey.

"Give it to him, Sancho," said Don Quijote, "not for catching his monkey, but for tying one on. And I'd give two hundred, right this minute, to anyone who could tell me for certain that Doña Melisendra and Don Gaiferos were already safely back in France."

"There's no one who could tell us about that better than my monkey," said Maestro Pedro, "but just at the moment the devil himself couldn't catch him. Still, I expect that affection and hunger combined will make him look me up, later tonight — and God will bring us the dawn and we'll see what we'll see."

And so the puppet show tempest passed over, and they all dined together in peace and harmony — at Don Quijote's expense, for he was generous to the extreme.

Before dawn broke, the man and his cart full of spears and halberds left the inn, and shortly after daybreak the cousin and the prospective soldier came to say farewell to Don Quijote, the one to return home, the other to continue on his way, and to make that easier for him Don Quijote put a dozen dollar coins in the young man's purse. Maestro Pedro thought it best not to have any more arguments with Don Quijote, with whom he was by now very well acquainted, so he rose before the sun did and, collecting what was left of his puppet show, as well as his monkey, he too went in search of adventures. The innkeeper, who knew nothing at all about Don Quijote, was as astonished at his madness as at his openhandedness. Sancho paid him very well indeed, at his master's orders, and then just before eight that morning they took their leave of the inn and resumed their journey just where they had broken it off — which will suit us fine, giving us the chance to record certain other matters relevant to the narration of this famous history.

Chapter Twenty-Seven

— in which it is explained who Maestro Pedro and his monkey were, together with the unfortunate outcome of the braying-adventure, which did not end as Don Quijote had expected or wanted it to

Sidi Hamid, this great history's chronicler, begins this chapter with the following declaration: "I swear, as a Catholic Christian . . . ," to which the translator adds that when Sidi Hamid swore as Catholic Christian, being as he surely was a Moor, all he meant was that he was swearing in precisely the way that a Catholic Christian would swear, or is supposed to swear, that he is being truthful in saying whatever he says, just as Sidi Hamid, swearing as a Catholic Christian, was verifying his own truthfulness in what he recorded about Don Quijote, and in particular in explaining the identity of Maestro Pedro, as well as the identity of the prophetic monkey whose riddling divinations so astonished all the villages in the whole region.

Sidi Hamid writes, accordingly, that all the readers of the first part of this history will surely remember a certain Ginés de Pasamonte, set free, up in the Sierra Morena Mountains (along with other galley slaves), by Don Quijote, a kindness which was later most unthankfully acknowledged (and repaid in still worse style) by those wicked, habitual evil-doers. This Ginés de Pasamonte, known to Don Quijote as Ginesillo de Parapilla, had then stolen Sancho's donkey — and since, strictly because of the printer's errors, neither the how nor the why of this was set out in the first part, many people conceived the notion that the author's faulty memory was responsible for this confusion. So, to set matters straight: Ginés had stolen the donkey right out from under Sancho Panza, who was sitting there fast asleep, adopting the plan employed by Brunelo at the siege of Albraca, when he stole the horse from between Sacripante's legs; and then, later on, Sancho got the donkey back, as has already been explained.[1] Now this Ginés, trying to keep from being found by the police, who were trying to catch him so he could be punished for his innumerable swindles and other crimes (so many indeed that he himself wrote a fat book, relating them all), decided to wander over to the kingdom of Aragón, put a patch across his left eye, and go into business as a puppeteer, a profession at which, like sleight of hand tricks generally, he was extremely accomplished.

He'd bought his monkey from some Christians, newly liberated from Barbary, and taught him that, at a certain signal, he was to jump up on his master's shoulder and murmur, or seem to murmur, in his master's ear. Then, before he'd take his monkey and his puppet show into a place, he'd find out, either in a neighboring town or from the best source he could locate, what had been going on there, and to whom, and then, keeping all this carefully in mind, he'd first put on his puppet show (sometimes telling a historical tale, sometimes not, but always using jolly, joyful, and familiar material). When that performance ended, he'd talk up his monkey's skills, telling everyone that the monkey knew all about both the past and the present, though he had no knack for seeing into the future. He'd charge two dollars to answer a question, though sometimes he'd discount that a bit, according to how he read his questioners, and whenever he came to a house, and knew what had been happening to those who lived there, even if they asked no questions (to keep from having to pay him) he'd give the monkey the special signal and immediately declare that he'd just been informed of this and that, all of it exactly as things had actually happened. Thus he earned himself an incredible reputation, and everyone sought him out. And since he was a crafty fellow, at other times

1. See II.4, above [Translator's Note].

he'd concoct answers that precisely suited the questions he'd been asked, and since no one bothered to check his responses, or tried to find out how the monkey knew all these things, he made monkeys of them all, and filled his pockets in the process.

He'd recognized Don Quijote and Sancho the moment he walked into the inn, and his prior acquaintance made it easy to absolutely astonish not only Don Quijote and Sancho Panza, but everyone else who was there — but, just the same, it would have cost him dear, had Don Quijote's hand swung just a bit lower, when he was cutting off King Marsilio's head and destroying that king's cavalrymen, as we saw in the preceding chapter.

This, then, is what needed to be explained about Maestro Pedro and his monkey.

Now, getting back to Don Quijote de La Mancha: after leaving the inn, our knight decided to first visit the banks of the River Ebro, and all the countryside around, before going on to Zaragoza; indeed, there was still a very long time before that city's tournaments were scheduled to begin. With this plan in mind, he jogged along for two whole days without meeting anything worthy of being recorded, but on the third day, as he was coming up a rise, he suddenly heard a great racket of drums and trumpets and guns being fired. His first thought was that an army regiment might be passing through, and to see them better he spurred Rocinante up to the top of the hill, but when he got to the summit and looked down, what he saw was, so far as he could make out, more than two hundred men carrying all sorts of weapons — as for example spears, crossbows, halberds (small and large), pikes, along with a few guns and a great many shields. He rode down the slope and drew near enough to these squadrons so that he could clearly make out their banners, distinguishing their colors and reading what they had printed on them, and in particular one flapping pennant of white cloth, on which was painted a very lifelike picture of a donkey standing, like a Sardinian pony, with its head raised, its mouth open, and its tongue stuck out, looking as if it were just in the act of braying. In huge letters, straight across this banner, there was written the following lines:

> Their braying was pointed,
> Our magistrates jointed.

This inscription showed Don Quijote that these were the inhabitants of the braying village, as he explained to Sancho, telling him what was written on the banner. He also said that the man who'd told them it was two aldermen who'd been braying was wrong, according to this banner, which asserted the two had been magistrates. To which Sancho Panza replied:

"My lord, that's no problem, because it could very well be that after a while the aldermen he was talking about became magistrates, so you can call them by both titles — and in any case it doesn't affect the truth of the story, whether they're aldermen or whether they're magistrates, as long as they're the ones who were braying, because a magistrate is just as liable to bray as an alderman is."

In a word, they recognized that these were troops sallying forth from their village to fight those from a neighboring village who had been taunting them more than was fair or neighborly.

Don Quijote rode over to them, making Sancho distinctly uncomfortable, for he was never fond of finding himself involved in this kind of situation. The warriors gathered around our knight, thinking he was one of them. Raising his visor, Don Quijote went over to the bearer of the donkey banner, his manner restrained and dignified, and all the leading combatants clustered nearby, wanting to see him, as astonished as people usually were, seeing him for the first time. Seeing how carefully they were watching him, though no one had as yet spoken or asked him any questions, and wanting to make good use of this silence, Don Quijote himself broke it, declaring in a loud, clear voice:

"Good sirs, let me ask you, as urgently as I know how, not to interrupt a statement I wish to make to you, unless and until you find yourselves annoyed or angered — and should this happen, the very moment you so indicate I shall seal my mouth shut and put a clamp on my tongue."

They all told him to say whatever he wanted, for they'd be more than glad to hear him. Given this permission, Don Quijote went on as follows:

"My dear sirs, I am a knight errant, and war is my business, just as my profession is both protecting those who require protection and also helping the needy. I first heard of your misfortune some days ago, and your reasons for continually taking up arms to wreak vengeance upon your enemies, and after time and again mulling over your problem I find that, according to the laws of chivalry, you're mistaken in considering yourselves to have been insulted, for no private individual can insult an entire village, except by challenging it, collectively, as guilty of treachery — for who can know which particular individual is supposed to have been thus guilty? A good example of this can be seen in Don Diego Ordóñez de Lara, who challenged the whole village of Zamora, not knowing that it was only Vellido Dolfos who had been guilty of treachery, in killing his king, and so he challenged them all, so that everyone was involved both in the matter of vengeance and in the formulation of the reply to the challenge, although it's true that Don Diego went farther, indeed a good deal farther, than the laws of chivalry permit, for there was no need to challenge the dead, and the village water supply, and its stocks of grain, or those as yet unborn, or any of the other details specified in his challenge, but that's the way it goes! Once anger rears its head, the tongue permits no father, no uncle, and no restraint whatever to rein it in. It being the case, therefore, that no one person can insult the king, or any province, city, republic, or any entire group of people, it becomes as clear as day that there's no need to take up arms, to avenge the insult of any such challenge, because no insult exists. What a mess it would be if the people of Clock Town were always trying to kill anyone who called them Clocktowners, and the same thing with Casserolers, Eggplanters, Whalers, Soapmakers,[2] or any of the other nicknames so commonly heard from the mouths of boys and God only knows who else! It would certainly be something, would it not, if every town thus designated got upset and sought vengeance, and they were all forever slashing at each other with swords over every disagreement, no matter how small! No — no: God neither permits nor desires such a state

2. Actual nicknames then in common use for, respectively, the towns and cities of Espartinas, Valladolid, Toledo, Madrid, and either Seville or Torrijos [Translator's Note].

of affairs. Sensible people, and well-regulated governments, take to arms
and draw their swords, and risk their bodies, their lives, and their property,
for four valid reasons: the first, to defend the Catholic faith; the second,
to defend their own lives, which is both natural and divine law; the third,
in defense of their honor, their family, or their property; and the fourth,
in the service of their king, in a just war; and if we perhaps wish to add a
fifth (though it can be included under the second reason, listed above),
in the defense of their country. These five fundamental reasons can of
course be supplemented by others, which might well be just and reasonable, and which could oblige us to take up arms, but to fight over silly
trifles and things that are far more laughable and amusing than they are
insulting, can only suggest that the combatants are utterly unable to think
rationally. Moreover, he who takes an unjust vengeance (and how, indeed,
can there be a just one?) goes directly against the holy laws in which we
all believe, which command us to do good to our enemies and to love
those who hate us, commands which, though they may seem hard to obey,
are in fact difficult only for those for whom the world is more important
than God, and are more fleshly than they are spiritual, because Jesus
Christ, both man and God, and the giver of all laws, He who never told,
or would tell, or could tell a lie, said to us that His yoke was a gentle one,
and His burden easy to bear, so that we need not worry about commandments which it might be impossible to obey. Accordingly, gentlemen, laws
both divine and human oblige you to calm yourselves."

"May the devil carry me off," Sancho said to himself at this point, "if
this master of mine isn't a tologian — because if he isn't, he's as much
like one as one egg is to another."

Don Quijote paused for breath and, seeing that the silence remained
unbroken, was about to continue his oration, and would have so continued
it had not Sancho, seeing his master pause, come jumping in with both
feet and, with his usual keen wit, taking his master's side:

"My Lord Don Quijote de La Mancha, who at one time called himself
The Knight of the Sad Face, and now styles himself The Knight of the
Lions, is a remarkably sensible man, who knows Latin as well as Spanish,
and both every bit as well as a university graduate, and deals with everything and gives others advice after the fashion of an excellent soldier, has
all the laws and regulations of this chivalry business right at his fingertips,
so the only thing you can do, really, is whatever he tells you to do, and
you can blame me if that's bad advice. And, besides, since this silliness
got started just because donkey-braying bothered you — well, I can remember, as a boy, that I went around braying whenever I felt like it, and
no one ever lifted a hand against me, and I brayed so gracefully, and so
naturally, that every time I brayed all the donkeys in our village would
start braying too, and just the same I was still my parents' child, and they
were all respectable people, and even though more than four of the big-
shots in my village were jealous of me, because of my skill, I didn't give
a damn. And just to let you see I'm telling the truth, you just wait a minute,
and listen, because this is like swimming: once you learn how, you never
forget it."

And then, putting his hand to his nose, he began to bray so vigorously that the echo boomed back from all the surrounding valleys. But one of the villagers, thinking Sancho was making fun of them, lifted up the long pole that was in his hand and gave Sancho such a whack that he fell to the ground, absolutely unconscious. Seeing how badly Sancho was being treated, Don Quijote raised his lance and attacked the man who'd toppled his squire, but so many villagers immediately crowded around the assailant that vengeance was impossible — indeed, finding showers of rocks and stones raining down, and a thousand guns and at least as many crossbows leveled at him, Don Quijote swung his horse around and, at the best gallop Rocinante could manage, got away from them as fast as he could, passionately praying that God would save him from this danger and afraid, at every step, that a bullet would slam into his back and come out his chest, and constantly breathing in and out, to see if his lungs were still whole.

But the villagers were satisfied to see him running, and did not fire. And they lifted Sancho, still only half conscious, back onto his donkey, and let him go after his master, which he could not have managed by himself, but the donkey automatically followed in Rocinante's tracks, for he felt completely at a loss without him.

The villagers stayed on the battlefield until darkness fell, and then, because their enemies made no appearance, they went back to their village, happy and rejoicing — and, had they been aware of the ancient Greek custom, they would have erected a monument on the spot.

Chapter Twenty-Eight

*— what Sidi Hamid Benengeli says his readers can learn,
if they read carefully*

When a brave man takes to his heels, look for treachery or deceit; and wise men know that he who turns and runs away lives to fight another day. So it was with Don Quijote, who backed away from the villagers' fury and their clearly felonious intent and ran for his life, not thinking about Sancho or the danger his squire had been left in, but putting distance between himself and the angry foot soldiers until he felt safe. Sancho came after him, as we have said, lying across his donkey. Slowly returning to his senses, Sancho finally caught up with his master and let himself drop off the donkey at Rocinante's feet, deeply gloomy, desperately exhausted, and half beaten to death. Don Quijote dismounted, to have a look at the scars of battle, but finding his squire sound, from top to bottom, angrily turned on him:

"What in God's name made you show off your braying, Sancho? How could you think it a good idea to talk about rope in a hanged man's house? When you supply braying music, what other counterpoint can they give you but a beating? Just be thankful to God, Sancho, that they sanctified you with a club, instead of marking you, *per signum Crucis* [with the sign of the Cross], with a scimitar."

"I can't answer you," replied Sancho, "because I feel as if I'm talking out of the back of my head. Let's just ride away from here, and I'll shut up about my braying — but I won't keep quiet about knights errant who go running off, leaving their good squires beaten to pieces, and threshed like wheat, and in their enemies' power."

"He who retreats is not running," answered Don Quijote, "because let me tell you, Sancho, courage which isn't solidly based on wisdom is called rashness, and anything that rashness accomplishes can be traced to good luck rather than to bravery. So I'll grant you that I retreated, but not that I fled — and I was only following in the footsteps of a host of valiant warriors, who thus preserved themselves for better occasions, as the histories abundantly prove. But those references won't help you, and I don't feel like rehearsing them, so I'll refrain."

So Sancho got up on his donkey, with Don Quijote's assistance, and our knight mounted Rocinante, and proceeding slowly along they took shelter in a wooded grove perhaps half a mile distant. From time to time Sancho emitted profound groans and doleful wails, and when Don Quijote asked the reason for such intense distress, Sancho answered that that was how he felt, from the bottom of his spine to the nape of his neck, and it was driving him crazy.

"Without any doubt," said Don Quijote, "the cause of this pain must be that you were struck by a long, wide stick, which got you all down the back, where all the parts that are giving you pain are located, and if the area struck were wider, so too would be the area which hurts."

"By God!" said Sancho. "You've really taken a load off my mind, your grace, by providing me with such neatly phrased conclusions! Mother of us all! Do you think the reason for my pain is so obscure that you really have to tell me I hurt where that stick struck me? Now if my ankles were hurting, maybe there'd be some point to trying to understand why, but when I'm hurting where I was hit, it doesn't take much to figure it out. By God, my lord and master, other people's bad luck never much hurts us, and it becomes clearer and clearer to me every day how little I can expect from staying with your grace, because if this time you let them beat me, the next time — the next hundred times — we'll be having more of those blanket-tossings and other stuff just as funny, and if this time they got me on the back maybe next time they'll get me right between the eyes. I'd do a lot better, especially being such a barbarian, and incapable of doing anything worth much with my life — I'd do a *lot* better, let me repeat, to go back home to my wife and my children, and raise and support them with whatever God chooses to give me, instead of dragging along after your grace, over roads that aren't even roads, and paths and cart tracks that don't go anywhere, drinking almost nothing and eating even worse. And as far as sleeping! Measure out six feet of ground, brother squire, and more if you like, take as much as you want, because it's all up to you, just suit yourself. I wish I could take the first man who ever thought of knight errantry and throw him on the fire, and burn him down to dust — or at least the first man who ever thought of becoming squire to any of the idiots those oldtime knights errant must have been. I say nothing about our own time, because I respect today's crop, being that your grace is one of them, and since I know your grace understands better than the devil, any time you open your mouth and anything you think about."

"I'd be willing to bet, Sancho," said Don Quijote, "that right now, jabbering away without anyone to stop you, nothing anywhere in your whole body is hurting you. So go on and say, my son, whatever pops into your head and finds itself in your mouth, because in exchange for having nothing hurt you I gladly accept the annoyance I feel at all your impertinences. And if you really want so badly to go back to your home and your wife and your children, the Lord won't let me hold you back. You have my money: count up how long we've been away, on this our third expedition, and think about what you ought to be earning every month, and then pay yourself off."

"When I worked for Tomé Carrasco," replied Sancho, "father of the Samson Carrasco your grace knows well, I was paid two ducats a month, plus my food, but with your grace I don't know what I ought to earn, though I do know a knight errant's squire works a lot harder than anybody working for a farmer, because when we work for a farmer, you know, no matter how hard we work during the day, that night, come hell or high water, we eat out of a pot and we sleep in a bed — and I haven't slept in a bed once, since I started working for your grace. Except for the few days we stayed in Don Diego de Miranda's house, and the regular picnic I had with the skimmings out of Camacho's kettle-pots, plus what I ate and drank in Basilio's house — except for those, all the rest of the time I've slept on the hard ground, under the open sky, a perfect target for what they call the inclement heavens, keeping myself alive with chunks of cheese and crusts of bread, and drinking water, sometimes out of wells, sometimes out of rivers, or whatever we find in these God-forsaken places where we go traveling."

"I must admit, Sancho," said Don Quijote, "that everything you say is true. So how much more than Tomé Carrasco paid you do you think you ought to earn?"

"To my way of thinking," said Sancho, "if your grace would add two ducats more a month, I'd consider myself well paid. I mean, as far as salary's concerned, but when it comes to fulfilling the promise, the solemn word, you gave me about making me governor of an island, I think your grace ought to add in another six ducats, which would make it thirty in all."

"Fine," replied Don Quijote. "So, since it's been twenty-five days since we left home, Sancho, take into account the salary you've set for yourself and figure out what proportion of a month's salary I owe you, and then pay yourself, as I've told you to, with what you have in hand."

"Oh my God!" said Sancho. "What a mess your grace is making of that accounting, because as far as the island's concerned we have to count from the day your grace made me that promise right up to today."

"Well, then, how long has it been, Sancho," said Don Quijote, "since I made you that promise?"

"If I remember it right," replied Sancho, "it must have been more than twenty years ago, give or take maybe three days."

Don Quijote gave himself a great slap on the forehead, and began to laugh with gusto, saying:

"But all the time I was in the Sierra Morenas, and even the whole time we've been away from home, hardly adds up to two months — so how can you say, Sancho, it's been twenty years since I promised you that island? I think you'd really like to have all the money you've got in your pocket for your salary, and if that's the way things are, and that will make you happy, I hereby give it to you, and may it serve you well, because in exchange I'll be rid of the worst squire in the world, and I'll be delighted to be poor and penniless. But just tell me, oh you corrupter of all the squirely laws of knight errantry, where you've ever seen, or read, that any knight errant's squire ever bargained with his lord the way you've been doing with me, saying he had to get so much a month? Go look, go look, you rascal, you thief, you monster, because you're all of that and more — go look, I say, through the whole *mare magnum* [great sea] of those histories, and if you find that any squire ever said, or even thought, what you've said to me here, I want you to blazon it right on my forehead and, what's more, slap me full in the face four times. Swing around your donkey's reins, or his halter, or however you direct him, and go home, because you're not going one step further with me. Oh, the bread ungratefully broken! Oh, the promises misplaced! Oh, you man more beast than human being! Now, now, when I was planning to elevate you so high that, in spite of your wife, they'd have to call you 'my lord'? Now you leave me, when I'd absolutely made up my mind to make you lord of the biggest island in the whole world? So it's just the way you've always said, over and over: honey isn't meant for a donkey's mouth. You're a donkey, and you have to be a donkey, and when your life is over you'll end up a donkey — because I know for a fact you'll be dead long before you ever realize and really understand what a donkey you are."

Sancho kept staring at Don Quijote, the whole while his master was pouring out this bitter reprimand, and felt such intense sorrow that the tears came to his eyes, and at last, his voice low and sad, he said:

"My lord, it's true: all I need to be a complete donkey is a tail. It's all right with me, your grace, if you want to stick one on me, and I'll serve you the rest of my life as the donkey I am. Please forgive me, your grace, and take pity on my ignorance, and remember how little I really know, and that even though I may talk all the time, there's more brainlessness than bad temper in it — but the man who stumbles and then walks straight, walks in the sight of God."

"I'd have been amazed, Sancho, if you hadn't found room in there for a proverb. Fine: I forgive you, as long as you mend your ways, and as long as, from now on, you're not always worrying about yourself, but try to open your heart and be cheerful and optimistic that I'll keep my promises — because even if it takes a long time, that could be just what happens."

Sancho answered that he'd certainly try, though he'd have to find strength in weakness.

So they went into the grove, and Don Quijote settled himself at the foot of an elm tree, and Sancho under a beech — because these trees, and all the others like them, always seem to have feet, but no hands. The darkness brought Sancho more pain than peace, because the night air made his bruises ache all the more. As usual, Don Quijote spent the night reliving events in his mind, but all the same they both got some sleep and, when morning came, rode on toward the banks of the famous River Ebro, where they experienced what you'll find in the chapter just ahead.

Chapter Twenty-Nine

— the famous adventure of the enchanted boat

Jogging leisurely along, Don Quijote and Sancho reached the River Ebro two days after leaving the grove, and Don Quijote was delighted to see the great stream, because the sight of its pleasant banks, the limpid clarity of its waters, the calm flowing of its massive crystalline liquid, shaped a happy landscape that brought a thousand amorous thoughts into his head. And, in particular, what came to his mind were the things he had seen in Montesinos' Cave, because even though Maestro Pedro's monkey had declared part of those things real and part false, the real meant far more to him than the false (though for Sancho it was just the opposite, for he thought the whole thing a lie).

Going along, as I've said, they saw a small boat near the bank, having neither oars nor sails nor rigging, but tied to the trunk of a tree growing right at the edge of the river. Don Quijote looked in all directions, but saw no one, and thereupon, without further ado, he got down from Rocinante, ordered Sancho to climb off his donkey and tie both animals, very securely, to the trunk of a nearby poplar. Sancho asked why they were dismounting thus abruptly, and then tying up their animals. Don Quijote replied:

"Know, Sancho, that this boat which you see here is plainly and without any possibility of mistake summoning and inviting me to step into it, letting it take me to the aid of some knight, or some needy, noble lady, who must be facing some immense affliction, because this is precisely how these things are done in tales of chivalry and by the magicians who meddle and speak in those books. When a knight gets into trouble, and can't escape except with the help of some other knight, even if that other knight is thousands and thousands of miles away, they'll either send down a cloud to carry him off, or else furnish him with a boat he can get into and then, in less time than it takes to open and close your eyes, he's carried — perhaps through the air, perhaps on the waters — right where he wants and needs to be. And this boat, Sancho, as truly as right now it is daylight, has been put here for the same reason! And so, come, before this day has come and gone, tie your donkey and Rocinante together — and may the hand of the Lord show us the way, for I would not refrain from embarking in this vessel even if barefooted monks begged me not to go."

"If that's the way it is," replied Sancho, "and your grace intends to keep giving in to these — what am I supposed to call them? foolishnesses? — then I just have to bow my head and obey, remembering the proverb, which says 'Do what your master tells you to do, and then sit down and eat his food.' But just the same, and to ease my conscience, I want to warn your grace this doesn't seem to me any kind of enchanted boat, but one that belongs to the fishermen on this river, because along here they catch the best shad in the world."

Saying this, Sancho tied up the animals and, his heart sad to overflowing, left them to the enchanters' protection and shelter. Don Quijote told him not to worry about deserting the animals, because those who were about to convey the masters down such remote highways, into such distant regions, would certainly take good care of the beasts.

"I don't know anything about *re-boats*," said Sancho. "I've never in all my life heard such a word."

"*Remote*," replied Don Quijote, "means 'far away,' and I'm not surprised you don't understand it, because you're not supposed to know Latin, like certain people who boast about their knowledge, but haven't got any."

"They're tied," answered Sancho. "What are we supposed to do now?"

"What?" responded Don Quijote. "Cross ourselves and raise the anchor — I mean, get in the boat and cut the rope that's holding it."

He jumped in, followed by Sancho, and cut the rope, and slowly the boat slipped away from the bank. Finding himself out on the river by a good two yards, Sancho began to tremble, afraid he was lost — but nothing bothered him more than hearing the donkey braying and seeing Rocinante struggling to untie himself.

"The poor donkey's braying," he said to his master, "because he's unhappy we're gone, and Rocinante's trying to get himself free, so he can come running after us. Oh, be calm, my dearest friends! Oh, may the madness taking us away from you be turned into sanity, and let us return!"

And he began to weep so bitterly that Don Quijote, his temper flaring, said:

"What are you afraid of, you cowardly creature? What are you crying about, you and your buttery heart? Who's persecuting you — who's chasing after you, you tame mouse? What do you need, you beggar sitting on a pile of gold? Are you trudging barefoot through the Riff Mountains or, as it happens, merely resting on a flat board, like an archduke, and floating along on the calm current of this pleasant river, from which, in not too long, we'll emerge out on the broad sea? Because we've surely already traveled at least seven or eight hundred leagues, and if I had an astrolabe with me, to measure the pole, I could tell you exactly how far we've gone, though unless I'm badly mistaken we've already crossed, or are about to cross, the equatorial line that divides the world in half."

"And when we get to this line your grace is talking about," asked Sancho, "how far will we have gone?"

"A long way," replied Don Quijote, "because the globe is divided into three hundred and sixty degrees, water and land together, according to Ptolemy's computations (and he was the greatest cosmographer the world has ever seen), and when we reach the line I mentioned we'll have gone exactly halfway around."

"Mother of God," said Sancho, "that's some authority your grace is quoting, ptomaine and complications, the greatest cousin-grabber, or whatever he is."

Don Quijote chuckled at Sancho's mangling of Ptolemy's name and his accomplishments, and said:

"Listen, Sancho: when the Spaniards, and all those who sail out of Cádiz, head out toward the East Indies, one of the things that tells them they've passed over the equatorial line is that all the lice on board the ship suddenly die, to the very last one, and they can't find a single louse anywhere on the boat, not for its weight in gold — so run your hand down your thigh, Sancho, and if you find anything living we'll have settled the whole business, and if you don't, then we've already crossed over."

"I don't believe any of this," replied Sancho, "but just the same I'll do what your grace says, even though I know the experiment's a waste of time, because I can see with my own eyes that we haven't gone five yards from the bank, or moved more than two yards downstream from those groves over there, because there's Rocinante and my donkey, right where I left them, and when I take a sight on something on land, as I'm doing this very minute, I swear by all that's holy we're neither moving, nor have we moved, as fast as an ant can crawl."

"Make the test I told you about, Sancho, and don't pay attention to anything else, because what do you know about great polar circles, equatorial lines, zodiacs, ecliptics, poles, solstices, equinoxes, planets, astrological signs, geographical bearings, and measurements, which are what the celestial spheres and the earth are made of? If you knew these things, or any part of them, you'd see perfectly clearly how many parallels we've cut, which signs we've glimpsed, what constellations have come and gone and are even now disappearing behind us. And I tell you, again, feel around and see what you can find, because I suspect you'll discover you're cleaner than a sheet of smooth white paper."

With a practiced hand, Sancho groped down his leg as far as his knee, then looked up at his master.

"Either the experiment isn't a good one," he said, "or else we haven't gotten to where your grace said, not by a long shot."

"Ah?" asked Don Quijote. "Then you found something?"

"Lots of somethings!" replied Sancho.

And pulling out his hand, he proceeded to carefully wash it in the river, down which, in the fullness of the smooth, gentle current, the boat was gently slipping, not impelled by any hidden intelligence, or any secret enchanter, but moving simply with the force of the slowly moving water.

Just then they noticed a number of large water wheels set out in the stream, powering floating flour mills, and as soon as Don Quijote spied them he declared, raising his voice excitedly:

"You see? There, oh my friend, there is the castle city, the fortress where some oppressed knight must be lying, or some queen, some king's daughter, some mistreated princess, to whose assistance I am being carried."

"What the devil city, or fortress, or castle are you talking about, your grace?" said Sancho. "Can't you see these are just flour mills for grinding grain?"

"Be quiet, Sancho," said Don Quijote. "They may look like flour mills, but that's not what they are. Haven't I told you that these magicians change everything and make it look like something else? That is, they don't *really* change things, but just their appearance, as we saw with Dulcinea's transformation — oh sole sanctuary of my dearest hopes!"

By this point the boat had gotten out into the middle of the river, and began to travel a good deal less slowly than it had before. The mill workers, seeing the craft coming down the river, and that the swift current was carrying it straight into the mill wheels, came rushing out with great poles, to stop it, and since they emerged all covered with flour, their faces and their clothing powdered white, they created a distinctly malevolent appearance. They were shouting and screaming:

"You crazy devils! Where do you think you're going? Are you out of your heads? Do you want these wheels to drown you and then break you into little pieces?"

"Didn't I tell you, Sancho," said Don Quijote at this, "that we've reached the place where, here and now, I must show the strength of my sword arm? Do you see what miserable scoundrels have rushed out to attack me? Just look at the monsters ready to fight! What ugly folk, grimacing and scowling at us! . . . Well, now you'll find out, you rascals!"

And standing up in the boat, he began to hurl loud threats at the mill workers:

"Wicked, ill-advised ruffians, release and set free whoever you have enchained in this fortress, this prison of yours, no matter who it may be, someone noble or someone common, because I am Don Quijote de La Mancha, also known as The Knight of the Lions, and high Heaven itself has brought me here to bring this adventure to its happy conclusion!"

And as he spoke he drew his sword and began slashing at the air, intending to do combat against the mill workers, who, hearing but not understanding a word of this nonsense, were frantically trying to push away the boat, which had already been sucked into the mill wheel channel.

Sancho fell on his knees, praying passionately to Heaven to save him from this plain and certain danger — and he was, but only through the devoted skill and alertness of the mill workers, who finally managed to head off the boat with their poles, though in the process they couldn't help overturning it and pitching Don Quijote and Sancho headfirst into the river. Don Quijote, who could swim like a duck, came out of it perfectly well, even though the weight of his armor twice pulled him down to the bottom, because the mill workers jumped in and hauled them out of the water: otherwise, it would have been a Trojan battle for both our brave warriors.

Once they were safe on dry land, soaked to the skin and not exactly dying of thirst, Sancho dropped to his knees, his hands clasped together and his eyes raised to Heaven, and sent God a long, solemn prayer, begging to be released, from this moment on, from any more of his master's wild yearnings and reckless undertakings.

Up came the fishermen who had owned the boat, which the mill wheels had by now smashed to little bits, and seeing it destroyed they proceeded to strip Sancho and demand that Don Quijote pay them for their loss, and with infinite calm, as though nothing whatever had happened to him, he assured the mill workers and the fishermen that he would most cheerfully pay for the smashed-up boat, on the condition that they would immediately and straightforwardly grant freedom to whatever person or persons they were holding prisoner in their castle.

"What castle, what prisoners, are you talking about, you lunatic?" one of the mill workers responded. "Maybe you want to carry off people who bring us grain to be ground?"

"Enough!" said Don Quijote to himself. "Trying to petition or persuade these mongrels would be like preaching to the sands of the desert. What must have happened, in this adventure, is that two powerful magicians clashed, and each of them blocked what the other was up to. One of them sent the boat to fetch me, but the other threw me into the river. May God have mercy: this whole world is nothing but tricks and schemes, each one set against the other. I can do no more."

Raising his voice, then, and looking out at the flour mills, he declared:

"My friends, whoever you may be, locked up in that prison, forgive me, because it is my misfortune, as it is yours, that I am unable to free you from your afflictions. This adventure must be meant for some other knight."

Having said this, he made his arrangements with the fishermen, paying them fifty dollars for their boat, and Sancho paid it out most unwillingly, saying:

"Two boats like this, and we'll have thrown every last penny into the river."

The fishermen and mill workers were absolutely amazed, seeing this pair of strange fellows, so utterly unlike other human beings, and having absolutely no idea what Don Quijote's questions and arguments were all about, they concluded these were nothing but a couple of lunatics and left them, the mill workers going back to their mills and the fishermen to their huts. Don Quijote and Sancho went back to their animals, and to living like animals, and that was the end of the adventure of the enchanted boat.

Chapter Thirty

— *Don Quijote meets a lovely huntress*

They were both in a foul mood, and deeply depressed, when they got back to their animals, and especially Sancho, for anything that happened to their treasury afflicted his very soul; every dollar he had to pay out felt like the absolute apple of his eyes. So without saying a word they mounted and rode away from the famous river, Don Quijote buried in amorous reflections, Sancho deep in thoughts of bettering himself, which seemed at the moment to be a very distant possibility: he may have been a fool, but he had no doubt that everything, or almost everything his master did was crazy, so he began to look for an opportunity when, without making any explanations or even saying farewell to his master, he could just leave and go home. But Fortune arranged for things to go in exactly the opposite direction.

It happened, then, that the next day, as the sun was going down and Don Quijote was riding out of a wood, he saw a green meadow and, off on the far side of it, a group of people, and as he drew closer he became aware that they were hunting with hawks and falcons. Riding up, he saw among them a lively, elegant lady seated on a silver side-saddle and riding a small palfrey, dazzlingly white and hung with green trappings. The lady too was dressed in green, so richly and magnificently that she herself seemed almost to glow. A falcon was perched on her left arm, indicating to Don Quijote that this was a very great lady indeed, and one of the hunters, as was in fact the case. So he said to Sancho:

"Sancho, my son, run over to that lady on the palfrey, holding that hawk, and let her know that I, The Knight of the Lions, kiss her lovely hands and, if her highness grant me that permission, will kiss them in person, and that I will be pleased to serve her in any way I can and in any way her noble self may direct. And watch how you speak, Sancho, and be careful you don't stick any of your proverbs into my message."

"Me, go around *sticking!*" responded Sancho. "How can you say such things to me? As if this were the first time in my life I'd ever carried a message to an important, highborn lady!"

"Except for the one you brought to my lady Dulcinea," answered Don Quijote, "I can't think of any others you've carried — not, at least, since you've been in my service."

"Well, that's true," replied Sancho, "but a man with good credit doesn't mind leaving a deposit, and in a well-stocked house you can expect to smell supper cooking. What I meant was you don't have to warn me and give me instructions, because I can handle everything, I can manage a little of this and a little of that."

"I believe you, Sancho," said Don Quijote. "So go, and may God guide you."

Sancho hurried off, spurring his donkey faster than usual, and, reaching the lovely huntress, dismounted and fell on his knees before her, declaring:

"Beautiful lady, that knight you see over there, known as The Knight of the Lions, is my master, and I'm his squire, known under my own roof as Sancho Panza. This Knight of the Lions, who not long ago was known as The Knight of the Sad Face, sent me over here to say that if your highness might be pleased to allow it, he himself proposes, and is agreeable to, and promises to do what he wishes to do, which is only — according to what he says and I think he means — to serve your lofty highness and beautyness, and if you say yes it will be something that will redound to your nobility's favor, and it will make him very very satisfied and happy."

"Good squire," replied the lady, "you've certainly delivered your message exactly as such messages are supposed to be delivered. Rise, for the squire of such a great knight as He of the Sad Face, of whom we have heard a great deal, should not be down on his knees — rise, my friend, and inform your lord that he is most welcome to be my guest, and that of the duke, my husband, in a pleasure home we maintain here."

Sancho rose, as much impressed by the good lady's beauty as by her noble bearing and courtesy, and especially by what she had said about having heard of his master, The Knight of the Sad Face, for if she hadn't called him The Knight of the Lions it must have been because he'd so recently taken on that title. Then the duchess (though duchess of what remains unknown)[1] asked him:

"Tell me, brother squire: isn't your lord he of whom there has been a book printed, called *That Ingenious Gentleman, Don Quijote de La Mancha*, and whose lady is a certain Dulcinea del Toboso?"

"That's exactly who he is, my lady," answered Sancho, "and that squire who goes along with him in that book, or is supposed to, and whose name is Sancho Panza, is me, unless they got me changed in the cradle — I mean, in the printing press."

"All this pleases me immensely," said the duchess. "Go, brother Panza, and tell your lord he's most welcome at my estate, most welcome indeed — in fact, nothing could have happened that would please me more."

Bearing such a cheerful response, Sancho went back to his master most happily, telling him everything the great lady had said to him, and praising to the heavens, in his own rustic language, the lady's beauty, her charm, and her courtesy. Don Quijote drew himself up in the saddle, settled his feet firmly in the stirrups, arranged his visor to perfection, set Rocinante in motion, and with his spirits high came forward to kiss the duchess' hands, while she, having called the duke, her husband, to her side, explained to him, as Don Quijote drew near, what our knight's message had been, and the two of them, having read the first volume of this history and having learned from that book exactly what form of lunacy afflicted Don Quijote, awaited their introduction to him with the greatest pleasure, determined to indulge his madness and go along with whatever he said, dealing with him as a full-fledged knight errant for however long he might stay with them, with all the formalities set forth in the books of chivalry, which both of them had read and were extremely fond of.

Don Quijote arrived, his visor raised. As he indicated his intention of dismounting, Sancho started over to hold the stirrup, but was unlucky enough, as he began to climb off his donkey, to catch one foot in a saddle-bag rope so tightly that he could not get himself free — indeed, he simply hung there, his mouth and his chest dangling down to the ground. Don Quijote, who never dismounted without Sancho holding his stirrup, and thinking his squire had surely by now assumed that position, came leaping off and brought his entire saddle (which could not have been properly buckled) down with him, he and the saddle both tumbling to the ground, to his great embarrassment, so that he was muttering curses between his teeth at his unlucky squire, though Sancho remained dangling as if his foot were in a shackle.

The duke ordered his huntsmen to help both the knight and his squire, and they assisted Don Quijote, battered by his fall, onto his feet. Limping over as best he could, he fell on his knees in front of the noble pair, but the duke would have none of it: dismounting, he came forward and embraced Don Quijote, saying:

"I'm so sorry, Sir Knight of the Sad Face, that the first thing your grace did, here on my estate, turned out so unfortunately as what we have just

---

1. The favored candidates are Don Carlos de Borja and Doña María Luisa de Aragón, Duke and Duchess of Luna and Villahermosa [*Translator's Note*].

seen. But I dare say squires' carelessness has been responsible for still worse things."

"Whatever may have happened to me, on this occasion, great prince," replied Don Quijote, "cannot possibly have been anything but good, even had I plunged straight to the very bottom of the abyss, since the glory of having met you would raise me back up and rescue me. My squire, may God curse him, is better at setting his tongue loose and saying wicked things than he is at fastening and buckling a saddle so it stays where it's supposed to. But however I make my appearance, whether toppling over or standing straight on my feet, whether walking or mounted, I remain forever at your service, you and my lady the duchess, your worthy consort, worthy queen of beauty and universal princess of courtesy."

"Be careful, My Lord Don Quijote de La Mancha," said the duchess. "Anywhere we may find My Lady Doña Dulcinea del Toboso, it would be wrong to praise others for their beauty."

By this time, Sancho Panza had been untied from his lasso, and was standing nearby, so before his master could answer he said:

"It can't be denied, because it has to be said, that My Lady Dulcinea del Toboso is very beautiful, but the hare jumps out just when you least expect it, and I've heard it said that what we call Nature is like a potter making clay bowls, and he who makes a handsome bowl can also make two of them, or three, or a hundred, and I say all this because, by God, my lady the duchess doesn't have to take a back seat to my mistress the lady Dulcinea del Toboso."

Don Quijote turned to the duchess and said:

"I doubt that your highness has ever conceived of any knight errant in the world having a more talkative or more amusing squire than mine, and he will prove me correct, if your excellency wishes to have my services for a few days."

The duchess replied:

"That our good Sancho should be amusing seems to me a very good thing, because it also indicates that he is wise, for humor and wit, as your grace, Don Quijote, perfectly well knows, can never be found in dull minds, so that our good Sancho being humorous and witty simply confirms that he is also wise."

"And talkative," Don Quijote added.

"So much the better," said the duke, "for you can't really be amusing and be a man of very few words. But rather than waste our time this way, please come, noble Knight of the Sad Face . . ."

"You should really say Knight of the Lions, your majesty," said Sancho, "because there isn't any Knight of the Sad Face any more — or sad figure, either."

"Knight of the Lions it shall be," the duke continued. "I was about to say that the Knight of the Lions should come with me, now, to a castle I own nearby, where he shall be lodged as so lofty a personage must properly be lodged, and of course as the duchess and I regularly lodge every knight errant who comes to our doors."

By this point Sancho had fixed and properly tightened the saddle on Rocinante's back, so Don Quijote remounted, and the duke got back onto his handsome steed and, with the duchess riding between them, they set out for the castle. The duchess commanded Sancho to stay beside her, for she loved to hear his wise observations. She did not need to ask him twice, and Sancho, placing himself with the three others, made himself the fourth in their conversation, which utterly delighted the duchess and her duke, who considered themselves wonderfully lucky to be able to lodge such a knight, and such a squire, in their castle.

Chapter Thirty-One

— dealing with many important matters

Sancho was ecstatic, finding himself, as it seemed to him, in favor with a duchess, because as a fond devotee of the good life he expected her castle would offer him what he had found in Don Diego's and in Basilio's houses, and he would seize the occasion by the forelock, as he always did when feasting and a good time were being offered.

Our history reports that, even before they'd gotten to the summer house, or castle, the duke rode on ahead and explained to all his servants exactly how they were supposed to treat Don Quijote, so that the moment the duchess and our knight arrived at the gates, out leaped two footmen, or grooms, dressed from head to foot in dressing gowns of the finest red satin, and before Don Quijote had either seen or heard them, they took him in their arms and said:

"Your highness, help our lady the duchess dismount."

Which Don Quijote promptly tried to do, he and the lady exchanging a vast stream of mutual compliments, but in the end the duchess carried the day, determined that she would not descend from her palfrey except in the arms of her duke, for (as she said) it would be a shame to entrust so slight and unnecessary a responsibility to so great a knight. So the duke finally came out and helped her dismount — and then, as they walked into a huge courtyard, two lovely young ladies appeared and draped over Don Quijote's shoulders a long cape of the finest red wool, and suddenly all the entrances to the courtyard were crowded with male and female servants, crying in loud voices:

"Welcome to the flower and very cream of knight errantry!"

And then all of them, or at least most of them, lifted small flasks and sprinkled perfumed water on Don Quijote, as well as on his host and hostess, much to Don Quijote's astonishment: finding himself treated exactly as he had always read that knights were treated, in ancient times, it was the first time he was ever fully convinced that he was a real rather than, somehow, an imaginary knight errant.[1]

Deserting his donkey, Sancho stayed close behind the duchess, so he too walked through the gates and into the great courtyard, but then his conscience stung him for leaving the animal all alone, so he approached

---

1. As Riquer notes, "Los servidores del duque conocen a la perfección la literatura caballeresca" [The duke's servants are perfect connoisseurs of the knightly literature] [*Translator's Note*].

a rather prim lady in waiting, who had come out with the others to welcome the duchess home, and in a low voice said to her:

"Señora González, or whatever your honorable name happens to
be . . ."

"My name is Doña Rodríguez de Grijalba," replied the lady in waiting.
"What is it you wish, brother?"

Sancho answered:

"I'd like your grace to do me a favor and go out the castle gate, where
you'll find my silver-gray donkey, and just see to it, your grace, that he's
properly stabled, or stable him yourself, because the poor little fellow's
kind of timid and he's not used to being left alone, not a bit of it."

"Hah!" replied the lady in waiting. "If the master's as clever as the man,
we've got a fine mess on our hands! The devil with you, brother, and
whoever brought you here. You just take care of your donkey yourself,
because the ladies in waiting in *this* house simply don't do that sort of
thing."

"Really?" answered Sancho. "Because I've heard my lord say, and he's
a wizard when it comes to stories, that the way they tell it of Lancelot:

> when he left his native dell
> and came to Britain, all
> the ladies served him well,
> and ladies in waiting took care of his horse,

and especially when it comes to this donkey, well, I wouldn't trade him
for Lord Lancelot's horse."

"You may be a silly prankster," responded the lady in waiting, "but keep
your stupid jokes where they belong, and where they'll gladly pay you for
performing them, because all you're going to get from me is a fig."[2]

"Ho ho!" answered Sancho. "Okay, as long as it's a ripe one — and if
we were playing 'Old Maid' I guess you'd win hands down."

"You son of a bitch," exclaimed the lady in waiting, now flaming mad,
"whether I'm old or not is between me and God; it's none of your business,
you rascal, you with your stinking garlic breath!"

She said this so loudly that the duchess heard her. Turning and seeing
the lady in waiting so upset that her eyes were bloodshot, the duchess
asked with whom she was quarreling.

"With this fellow right here," replied the *dueña*, "this right good man,
who has earnestly asked me to go and stable his donkey, which is just
outside the castle gate, assuring me that things were done this way, somewhere or other, where there were ladies taking care of someone named
Lancelot, and ladies in waiting took care of the fellow's donkey, and then,
to top it all off, he called me old."

"Now that," replied the duchess, "would have struck me as the nastiest
thing he could have said."

So she turned to Sancho:

"You must know, Sancho my friend, that Doña Rodríguez is in fact a

---

2. "To give someone a fig" = in modern English, "to give someone the finger" [*Translator's Note*].

very young woman, and she wears that headdress because it's dignified, and because it's the fashion, and not because of her years."

"May all the rest of my years be miserable," replied Sancho, "if that was what I meant. I only spoke to her, in the first place, because I love my donkey so much, and I didn't think I could find the little animal anyone as kind and good-hearted as My Lady Doña Rodríguez."

Hearing all this, Don Quijote said:

"Is this the place for that kind of talk, Sancho?"

"My lord," responded Sancho, "people have to say what they have to say, wherever they are, and I was standing right here when I remembered my donkey, so I talked about him right here, and if I'd thought about him when I was in the stable, I would have talked about him there."

At which the duke said:

"Sancho's quite right; he's done nothing wrong. The donkey will be fed all he can hold, so Sancho has nothing to worry about, because the donkey will be treated every bit as well as its master."

After this discussion, which pleased everyone except Sancho's master, they went up the stairs and Don Quijote found himself in a room all hung with cloths of the richest gold and brocade, where six damsels took off his armor and served as his pages, all of them carefully coached and instructed by the duke as to how they should act toward Don Quijote, so he might think himself and actually see himself treated as a true knight errant. His armor removed, Don Quijote was left in his tight-fitting breeches and his chamois vest, a tall, dry, lean figure with jaws that, inside his mouth, were constantly kissing each other — such a figure that, if the young women waiting on him had not been careful to smother their laughter (that being one of the explicit orders their lord had given them), they might have burst with it.

They wanted to strip him, so he could be dressed in a shirt, but he would not allow it, explaining that modesty was as important to knights errant as bravery in battle. He told them, all the same, to give the shirt to Sancho, and then, shutting himself into a sleeping room with a richly carved bed, he in fact undressed himself and put on the shirt. And finding himself alone with Sancho, he said to his squire:

"Tell me, you brand-new buffoon and thoroughly ancient pest: do you think it was decent and proper to insult and offend such a venerable and dignified lady in waiting? Was that the right time to be thinking about your donkey, and do you think these are folk who allow animals to be badly treated, while they're paying such respect to those animals' owners? In the name of God, Sancho, get a hold on yourself, so these people don't have to deal with the coarse threads woven into the fabric of a lowborn peasant like you. Be careful, you sinner, because they'll think a lot better of the master when his servants are modest and well-behaved: one of the greatest advantages that princes enjoy, in comparison with ordinary men, is that their servants are as good as they are. Can't you understand, you miserable wretch (because you're likely to make me as miserable as you are), that if they take you for a vulgar peasant, or a laughable fool, they're going to take me for a fraud, a make-believe knight? No, Sancho, no: avoid such surly, inappropriate remarks, for he who stumbles into becomes a chatterbox and a buffoon, falls flat on his face the first time he's kicked and becomes a very unhappy, very unfunny buffoon. Curb your tongue: consider your words, chew them over and over, before you let them out of your mouth, and keep in mind that we have now come to a place from which, should God smile on us, and my arm be strong enough, we can emerge three or four or five times as well-known, and as wealthy, as we have been."

Sancho promised most earnestly to seal up his mouth or bite his tongue before he uttered a word that wasn't appropriate and well-considered, exactly as his master had commanded, and said that Don Quijote could rest easy on that score, for if they were found out it wouldn't be because of him.

Don Quijote dressed himself, buckling on his sword belt and taking up his sword, then threw the scarlet cloak over his shoulders, put on a green satin cap the young women had given him, and thus adorned went back into the larger room, where he found the young ladies waiting, drawn up in a double line, all prepared to furnish him with water for washing his hands, which ceremony they performed with great care and respect.

Twelve pages then arrived, together with the butler, to escort him to table, where his hosts awaited him. They formed a kind of honor guard around him and, with much pomp and ceremony, brought him to another room, where a rich table had been set for exactly four diners. Both the duke and the duchess came to the door to greet him, and with them came a solemn priest of the sort who usually guide princes' households — that is, one of those who, not born princes themselves, have no idea how to teach those who have been so born to be what they are; men who would like the nobleness of the nobility to be limited by the narrowness of their own minds; men who, desiring to show those they guide how to be provident, make them mean-spirited instead; and the solemn cleric who came forward, with the duke and duchess, to greet Don Quijote, was, as I say, one such man. A thousand graceful compliments were exchanged and then, with the duke on one side of Don Quijote and the duchess on the other, they proceeded to seat themselves.

The duke pressed Don Quijote to sit at the head of the table, and though our knight tried to refuse, the duke's importunities were such that he finally had to accept. The priest sat opposite, with the duke and duchess on the two sides.

Sancho was present the whole time, absolutely stupefied to see the honor these princes were doing his master; finally, seeing the multiple courtesies and infinitely polite requests passing back and forth between Don Quijote and the duke, on the subject of sitting at the head of the table, Sancho said:

"If your graces will allow me, I'll tell you the story of what happened in my village, once, with this business of who sits where."

Sancho had no sooner spoken than Don Quijote began to tremble, convinced that his squire was about to spout forth some idiocy or other. But Sancho saw this, and understood quite well, so he said:

"Don't worry, your grace, my lord, that I'll just ramble around or say something that isn't just right, because I haven't forgotten the advice your grace gave me, a little while ago, about talking a lot or saying bad things."

"I remember nothing of the sort," replied Don Quijote, "so say whatever you want to, but make it quick."

"Well, what I want to say," said Sancho, "is so true because my lord Don Quijote, who's sitting right here, won't let me tell lies."

"Lie as much as you want to, Sancho," said Don Quijote, "because I'm not going to rein you in, but just think before you speak."

"I've thought about it, and then thought about it some more," said Sancho, "so I know I'm in no more danger than the bell ringer high up in the church tower, as you'll see from what I say."

"It would be just as well," said Don Quijote, "if your highnesses had this idiot removed from our presence, for his is not exactly a gifted or a well-schooled tongue."

"By the life of my beloved duke," said the duchess, "no one's going to separate me from my Sancho, not one little bit. I'm deeply attached to him, because he's so exceedingly wise."

"May your holiness live on in wisdom," said Sancho, "because you think so well of me, though I don't deserve it. Well, the story I want to tell is this: there was a gentleman in my village who sent out an invitation, and he was a very rich and highborn man, because he was one of the Álamos from Medina del Campo, and he'd married Doña Mencía de Quiñones, who was the daughter of Don Alonso de Marañón, who was one of the Knights of the Order of Santiago until he was drowned in the port of Herradura, and he was the one we had that quarrel about, in our village, years ago, and as far as I remember my lord Don Quijote was involved in that — and Tomasillo, the wild son of Balvastro the blacksmith, came out of that quarrel wounded — and isn't this the strictest truth, my lord and master? Say so, for God's sake, so these noblemen and lady won't take me for a lying babbler."

"So far," said the priest, "I'd have to say you were more of a babbler than a liar, but from here on I have no idea what I'll think."

"You give us so much evidence, Sancho," said Don Quijote, "and so many proofs, that I could hardly say anything but that you were telling the truth. But go on, and cut the story short, because, the way you've begun, it might take you two days to get to the end."

"No, no, he's not to cut it short," said the duchess, "because I love to hear him. I'd rather he just told it the way he knows it, even if it takes him six days to finish, because if that's how long it takes they'll seem to me like the best days I've ever spent in my life."

"So, as I was saying, my lords," Sancho continued, "there was this gentleman, and I know him as well as I know my own hands, because it wasn't even a bowshot from his house to mine, and he sent out an invitation to a poor farmer, who was a very respectable man."

"Go on, go on, brother," the priest declared, "because the way you're going this story will only end in the next world."

"God willing," replied Sancho, "I'll stop before I'm halfway there. Anyway, as I was saying, this poor farmer came to the aforesaid rich man's house, and may his soul rest in peace, because by now he's dead, and they say he died an angel's death, though I wasn't there at the time, because just then I'd had to go do some mowing in Tembleque . . ."

"To save your life, my son, hurry back from Tembleque and please don't stop to bury this gentleman before you finish your story, if you don't want to see even more funerals."

"Well, then, it happened," said Sancho, "they were going to sit down at table, and I seem to see them right in front of me . . ."

The duke and duchess were delighted, watching how vexing Sancho's digressions and pauses were to the good priest, as the squire's tale slowly unfolded; Don Quijote, meanwhile, was almost wild with anger.

"So, as I was saying," said Sancho, "since they were getting ready to sit down at table, the farmer insisted that the nobleman take the seat of honor, and the nobleman insisted, for his part, that the farmer take it, because in his house people had to do what he told them to do, but the farmer, who considered himself courteous and well-bred, just wouldn't do it, until the nobleman, really annoyed, put his hands on the farmer's shoulders and forced him into a chair, and said to him: 'Sit down, you idiot, because as far as you're concerned wherever I'm sitting will be the head of the table.' And that's the story, and I really think it wasn't dragged in where it wasn't appropriate."

Don Quijote turned a thousand colors, which on his sundarkened skin produced a wonderfully speckled effect, while, to keep our knight from having an absolute fit, the duke and duchess hid their amusement, for they were quite aware how slyly Sancho had spoken, and so to change the subject (as well as to keep Sancho from launching into more foolishness), the duchess asked Don Quijote what news he had of his lady Dulcinea, and whether he had recently sent her any giants or scoundrels, for surely he could not have helped but conquer a good many of that sort. To which Don Quijote replied:

"My lady, although my misfortunes had their beginning, they will never have an end. I have conquered giants, and I have sent criminals and other scoundrels to her, but where could they have found her, since she is under an enchantment, transformed into the ugliest peasant girl one could possibly imagine?"

"I don't know," said Sancho Panza, "because to me she seemed the most beautiful creature in the world. As far as being light-footed, anyway, and being able to jump, I know she's as good as any acrobat. By God, My Lady Duchess, she can leap from the ground up onto a donkey's back as if she were a cat."

"Have you seen her in this enchanted state, Sancho?" whispered the duke.

"Have I seen her!" Sancho whispered back. "Who the devil but me was the first to figure out this whole business of her enchantment? My father's just as enchanted as she is!"

Hearing them talk of giants, criminals, and enchanted folk, the priest understood that their guest had to be Don Quijote de La Mancha, whose history the duke was always reading, something for which he had often scolded the nobleman, insisting that it was ridiculous to read such ridiculous stuff — and now, having proof of what he had previously suspected, the priest turned to the duke and said, with considerable heat:

"Your Excellency, My Lord, you will be responsible to Our Lord on High for this good man's actions. I doubt that this Don Quijote — or

Don Idiot — or whatever his name may be — can really be as empty-headed as Your Excellency would like him to be, giving him such opportunities to carry on with his nonsense and his idiocy."

And then the priest turned to Don Quijote, and declared:

"And you, you brainless wonder, how did you ever get it into your head that you were a knight errant, and a conqueror of giants and captor of criminals? Oh, you're a fine one, let me tell you: go home! Bring up your children, if you have any, and take care of your own property, and stop this wandering around the world, acting like an idiot and making everyone laugh at you, whether they know you or not. In the name of all that's holy, what makes you think there ever were or now are real knights errant? Where can you find giants here in Spain? — or criminals in La Mancha? — or enchanted Dulcineas? — or any of this pile of stupidities they've been writing about you?"

Don Quijote had listened carefully to everything the man of the cloth said, and when he saw the priest had finished he stood up — in spite of the fact that he was in the presence of the duke and the duchess — and, clearly upset and angry, said . . .

But his reply deserves a chapter of its own.

Chapter Thirty-Two

— Don Quijote's reply to the priest who had scolded him, along with other matters both serious and amusing

So rising to his feet, trembling all over, like a man half poisoned with mercury, his speech hasty and ill-controlled, Don Quijote said:

"The place in which I find myself, and the presence of those who sit here, and the respect I have always had, and have, for the holy order to which your grace belongs, all restrain and tie up the hands of my right and proper anger, and knowing also, as everyone knows, that those who wear an ecclesiastical gown employ the same weapon wielded by women, which is of course the tongue, I will engage mine in equal battle with your grace's, from which one might better have expected good counsel than black-tongued abuse. Saintly and well-intentioned censure requires and deserves a different sort of response but, surely, to have censured me in public, and in such harsh terms, exceeds the limits of any decent reprimand, for properly framed counsel better accords with gentleness than with severity, nor is it sensible, without full knowledge of the sin being censured, to simply label the sinner an out and out dolt and a fool. Please tell me, your grace, what foolishnesses you have actually seen and can condemn in me, and on account of which you command me to go home and take care of my property, and my wife, and my children, though you have no idea what property I own or whether I have a wife and children? Is it so easy, then, to come rushing into other people's houses and take charge of their owners, having yourself been raised within the confines of boarding schools and university dormitories, without having seen any more of the world than is contained in the forty or fifty miles of your parish, and then to proclaim yourself law-giver for all of knighthood, and judge of the ancient order of knight errantry? Is it, by any chance, entirely useless and a mere waste of time to roam through the world, not in search of its pleasures, but hunting only for those harsh experiences through which the good attain to immortality? If knights considered me a fool, and the great, and the liberal, and the highly born, I would be fatally insulted, but if someone whose nose has always been buried in books thinks me a fool, someone who has never so much as set foot on the pathways of knight-hood, I couldn't care less, for I am a knight, and I shall die a knight, if it so pleases God. There are those who travel down the broad highway of arrogant ambition; others who make their way by base, servile flattery and fawning; and others who employ hypocritical deceit; and there are some who take the way of true religion; but I, drawn by my star, travel down the narrow path of knight errantry, which profession leads me to scorn wealth, but not honor. I have set injuries and insults straight, righted wrongs, punished arrogance, conquered giants, and trampled on monsters; simply because knights errant are required to be lovers, I am a lover, yet not a depraved, but only a chaste and platonic one. In everything I do I strive toward the good, which means that I try to do good to everyone and evil to no one — and if the man who follows this path, and takes on these tasks, and so conducts himself, if he deserves to be called a fool, then call him so, Your Highnesses, Most Excellent Duke and Duchess."

"Bravo, by God!" said Sancho. "Don't say another word for yourself, my lord and master, because there's nothing else to say, and nothing else to think, and nothing else in the world to insist on. And what's more, when this gentleman denies, as he has, that there have ever been knights errant, and aren't any now, does he really know much about all these things, though he talks about them?"

"And are you, by any chance," said the priest, "that Sancho Panza they talk about, to whom your master has promised an island?"

"That's me," replied Sancho, "and I'm the one who deserves it just as much as anyone else; I'm someone who says 'stick with good people, and you'll be one yourself,' and who says 'it doesn't matter who you were born but who you become,' and one of those who says 'if you take shelter under a good tree, you'll sit in the cool shade.' I took shelter with a good master, and I've traveled with him a long time, months and months, and if it so pleases God I'll be another like him, and long live him and long live me, and may he not lack realms to rule or me an island."

"By God, no, Sancho my friend," the duke said at this point, "because acting in Don Quijote's name I hereby make you the governor of an island I just happen to have available, and not such a tiny one, either."

"Down on your knees, Sancho," said Don Quijote, "and kiss His Ex-cellency's feet for the favor he has bestowed on you."

Which Sancho did, and when the priest saw all this he got up from the table, absolutely furious, and said:

"By the holy garments I wear, I'd have to say Your Excellency is as great a fool as either of these sinners. Why shouldn't they be lunatics, when sane folk canonize their insanity? Well, you stay with them, Your Excel-lency, and as long as they remain in your house I will have to remain in mine, rather than reprove what I cannot repair."

Not saying another word or eating another morsel, he left, paying no attention to the duke and the duchess, who attempted to stop him — not that the duke, in particular, could say very much, because he was choking with laughter at the priest's insolent rage. When he finally stopped laughing, he turned to Don Quijote:

"You have made such a noble response, your grace, Sir Knight of the Lions, that nothing more remains to be done, to set this apparent injury straight, since it has been no injury at all, for as your grace knows perfectly well women cannot insult a knight, and neither can priests."

"That's true indeed," replied Don Quijote, "because anyone who cannot be insulted cannot insult anyone else. Women, children, and priests, who cannot defend themselves if they are offended, cannot ever, in the knightly sense of the word, be insulted. Because as Your Excellency knows, there is this difference between an offense and an insult: an insult must come from someone capable of giving it, who then gives it, and maintains it, while an offense can come from anyone and anywhere, without constituting an insult. For example: there's a man walking carelessly down the street, when ten armed men rush up and start beating him, so he draws his sword and does what he can, but there are too many against him and he can't do what he wanted to do, which is to avenge himself. Such a situation must be considered an offense, but not an insult. Yet another example will confirm this: a man's back is turned; someone comes up behind him and hits him with a stick, then turns and runs right away, and though the man who has been hit runs after him he cannot catch up; he who was struck has been offended against, but not insulted, because an insult must be maintained. If the man who did the hitting, even though he did it surreptitiously, afterwards drew his sword, and stayed where he was, with his face instead of his back toward his enemy, he who had been hit should be termed both offended against and insulted — offended against, because he was treacherously assaulted, and insulted, because the man who struck him stood behind what he had done, instead of turning his back and running.

"Thus, according to the accursed laws of dueling, in this case I can consider myself offended against, but not insulted, for children cannot be insulting, nor can women, and neither can they inflict a wound, or stand their ground, and those in holy orders are in exactly the same position, these three categories of people being incapable of either offensive or defensive weaponry, and even though they are of course obliged to defend themselves, as best they can, they cannot insult anyone. And even though, a moment ago, I said I might be offended, I will now unsay that, and very emphatically, since anyone who cannot be insulted is still less capable of insulting anyone else, for which reason I should not feel, nor should I have felt, injured by what that good man said to me; I only wish he had stayed a bit longer, to explain to him his error in imagining and actually saying that there never have been, and are not now, knights errant in the world, because if Amadís were to hear this, or any one of his numberless descendants, I suspect it would not go well with his grace."

"Oh, I'll swear to that!" said Sancho. "They'd have sliced him up like a pomegranate, from top to bottom, or maybe like a nice fat melon. They were too touchy to stand for nonsense like that! By all that's holy, I'll bet if Reinaldos de Montalbán had heard what that little fellow said, he'd have smashed in his face and your priest wouldn't have said another word for three whole years. Ha, just let him tackle *them*, and we'll just see how he comes off!"

The duchess half died of laughter, listening to Sancho, thinking him funnier as well as crazier than his master, nor was she by any means the only one who held that opinion. In the end, Don Quijote calmed himself, the meal was finished, and when the tablecloths were taken away four young women entered, one carrying a silver basin, a second with a water pitcher, also of silver, the third with two superb snow-white towels over her shoulder, and the fourth, her sleeves rolled halfway up her arms, and carrying in her white hands — and how white they indeed were! — a round cake of Neapolitan soap. The girl with the basin approached Don Quijote and, her manner as suave and easy as it was assured, held it directly under his beard, and he, silently watching this whole ceremony, though with some astonishment, assumed it was the usual custom of the house to wash diners' beards instead of their hands, so he proffered his beard as well as he could, at which the girl with the pitcher began to pour out water, and the girl carrying the soap rapidly lathered him up, creating waves of snow (not a bit less gleamingly white than the thick lather) not only on his beard but all over his face and even over the obedient knight's eyes, so he was obliged to squint them tightly shut.

The duke and the duchess, who had not been prepared for this, were attentively watching, to see how this extraordinary washing-up would end. The barbering girl, once she had him eight inches deep in lather, pretended that she'd run out of water, and directed the pitcher-carrier to fetch more, while my lord Don Quijote waited. The pitcher-carrier went off, leaving Don Quijote with the strangest, most laughable-looking face anyone could possibly imagine.

Everyone there (and there were a good many people in the room) watched closely, staring at our knight's half-yard of neck, considerably darker-skinned than usual, his tightly closed eyes and his beard all puffy with soap, and to keep their laughter under control required a good deal of tact. The four girls kept their eyes lowered, not daring to look at their master and mistress, who for their part felt gusts of laughter mixed with anger and did not know which to express: should they punish the four girls for their boldness, or reward them for the sheer pleasure of seeing Don Quijote in such a state?

The pitcher-carrier finally returned, and they finished washing Don Quijote and quickly fetched towels, cleaning and rinsing him very calmly and gently, after which all four of them bowed and curtsied most reverently and prepared to leave, but the duke, to keep Don Quijote from tumbling to the joke, called to the pitcher-carrier, saying:

"Now come and wash me — and make sure you don't run out of water."

Sharp-witted and careful, the girl hurried over and put the basin in front of the duke, exactly as she had with Don Quijote, and her master was quickly well soaped and washed, and then, having rinsed and dried him, they bowed and curtsied and left. They later learned that the duke had sworn to punish their boldness, had they not washed him exactly as they had Don Quijote, a matter they quite sensibly took care of by lathering him, too.

Sancho was watching this whole washing ceremony with great attention, and saying to himself:

"Mother of God! Could it be the custom around here not just to wash knights' beards but squires' too? Because by God I could certainly use it — and even more if they used a razor on me."

"What are you mumbling to yourself, Sancho?" asked the duchess.

"I was saying, my lady," he answered, "I've always heard that, at other princes' courts, when they take away the tablecloths they bring in water for washing hands, but not cakes of soap for washing beards, which is why it's a good idea to live as long as you can, so you can see a lot, even though sometimes they say the longer you live the more bad things happen to you — but a washing like this is more fun than punishment."

"Don't worry, friend Sancho," said the duchess, "I'll make sure my young ladies wash you — and I'll even have them go further than that, if you like."

"Taking care of my beard will be good enough for me," answered Sancho, "at least for now — and later on, God knows what might happen."

"Butler," said the duchess, "pay attention to my good Sancho's request, and make sure he gets exactly what he wants."

The butler replied that my lord Sancho would have everything he wanted, and then off went the butler to have his own dinner, taking Sancho with him, thus leaving the duke and duchess alone with Don Quijote; they discussed a variety of things, but all having to do with the professions of war and of knight errantry.

The duchess asked Don Quijote to describe and depict for her, since he seemed to have an excellent memory, the beautiful face and features of his lady Dulcinea del Toboso, for according to what was generally reported she must surely be the most beautiful woman in the world, and even in La Mancha. Hearing the duchess' request, Don Quijote sighed:

"Were I able to draw forth my heart and lay it in front of your highness' eyes, here on a plate, and on this table, it would spare my tongue the labor of trying to say what is almost unsayable, for then Your Excellency could see her exactly as she truly is, but how shall I now describe and depict for you my matchless Dulcinea's beauty, point by point, and feature by feature, for this is a burden better suited to other shoulders than mine, and a task which might employ the paint brushes of Parrhasius, Timantes, and Apelles, and Lysippus' chisel,[1] to paint and carve it on canvas, and in marble, and in bronze, as it would require Ciceronian and Demosthenian rhetoric to properly praise her."

"What do you mean, 'Demosthenian,' my lord Don Quijote?" asked the duchess. "That's a word I've never in all my life heard."

" 'Demosthenian rhetoric,' " answered Don Quijote, "means the same thing as 'the rhetoric of Demosthenes,' just as 'Ciceronian' refers to that of Cicero, these two being the best rhetoricians the world has ever known."

---

1. Three famous classical Greek painters and a sculptor [*Translator's Note*].

"Indeed," said the duke, "and the question reveals your ignorance. But all the same, my lord Don Quijote, it would give us great pleasure if you would describe her for us; surely even a sketch or the merest outline of her should be enough to make the most beautiful woman jealous."

"I should certainly oblige you," replied Don Quijote, "if the unfortunate accident I suffered, not long ago, had not utterly wiped her image from my mind, leaving me better able to weep for than to describe her — for your highnesses must know that, some time ago, while journeying to kiss her lovely hands and receive her blessing, her approval, and her permission to set out on this third expedition in search of adventure, I found something quite unlike what I was seeking: I found her enchanted, transformed from a princess into a peasant girl, changed from beauty into ugliness, from an angel into a devil, from a thing of scented loveliness into a thing of pestilential odors, from a well-spoken woman into a rustic bumbler, from a creature of calm and grace into a hopping, skipping wonder, from light into darkness and, last but not least, from Dulcinea del Toboso into a low peasant from Sayago."

"Lord help us!" the duke exclaimed violently. "Who can possibly have perpetrated such a foul deed? Who could have ripped from the world the beauty which so delighted it, the wit which so entertained it, and the virtue which so adorned it?"

"Who?" answered Don Quijote. "Who could it be, except one of those evil magicians who, motivated by the most intense jealousy of me, have long persecuted me? These cursèd creatures have been brought into the world for the sole purpose of blackening and wiping out the glorious deeds of good men, and raising the fame of, and casting bright light upon, the deeds of evil men. These enchanters have persecuted me; these enchanters continue to persecute me; and these enchanters will go on persecuting me, until they have cast me and all my feats of high knighthood into the bottomless pit of oblivion, for they stab and wound me where they see I am most vulnerable: to deprive a knight errant of his lady is to take away the eyes with which he sees, and the sun which shines down upon him, and the very stuff which keeps him alive. I have said this many times, and now I say it again: a knight errant without his lady is like a tree without its leaves, a building without its roof, and a shadow without any body that can cast it."

"That goes without saying," said the duchess. "But just the same, if we are to believe the history of My Lord Don Quijote which, not too long ago, has been given to the world (to very general approval and applause), we are assured, if I remember it rightly, that your grace has in fact never seen lady Dulcinea, and indeed that the world contains no such lady, for she is nothing more than a phantasm conjured up and born in your grace's brain, a vision to which you assigned whatever graces and perfections you preferred."

"A good deal might be said, on this score," replied Don Quijote. "God only knows if the world does or does not contain anyone like Dulcinea, or whether she is or is not a mere phantasm, nor are these issues which can be settled with absolute certainty. On the other hand, I've neither created nor given birth to my lady, although I meditate upon her as of course she simply must be, a lady who in every possible way can rightly be the most celebrated woman in the world — flawlessly beautiful, serious but never arrogant, loving but modest, courteously grateful (and courteous because bred to be so) and, finally, of noble birth, because in good blood beauty gleams and glows more gloriously, more perfectly, than it does in beauty which is humbly born."

"Indeed," said the duke, "but my lord Don Quijote must give me leave to observe, what I am compelled to observe after reading the history of his knightly deeds, that one must infer, whether there is or is not a Dulcinea, in Toboso or outside it, if she is indeed as beautiful as your grace says she is, then her lineage does not flow from such mighty sources as those of the Orianas, and Alastrajareas, and Madásimases,[2] and all the others of that sort, who throng through the histories your grace knows so well."

"As to that," replied Don Quijote, "one can say that Dulcinea is the daughter of her own deeds, and that virtue strengthens blood, for one must think better of someone humble but virtuous than of someone noble but vice-ridden. Moreover, there is a quality in Dulcinea which might well raise her to be a queen, with a crown and a scepter, because a modest, virtuous woman's merits can lead to still greater miracles even than that, and so in reality (even if not formally) she contains within herself the seeds of her own greater good fortune."

"Let me say, my lord Don Quijote," said the duchess, "that you are a man who speaks with great deliberation and caution — constantly sounding the depth of the water, as they say; and so from now on I shall believe, and I shall see to it that everyone in my household believes (and even, if I have to, my lord the duke), that there is indeed a Dulcinea del Toboso, and that she is a living woman, and beautiful, and nobly born, and worthy to have such a knight as Don Quijote in her service — for that is the highest praise of which I am capable, or which I know how to give. But, still, I cannot keep myself from experiencing a certain qualm, and having a certain grudge against Sancho Panza: and that qualm concerns what is written in that history about you, when said Sancho Panza, sent by you to bear her a letter, comes upon said lady Dulcinea sifting a sack of wheat — and, what's worse, the history records that it was *red* wheat, something which makes me very seriously doubt her lineage."

Don Quijote answered:

"My dear lady, your highness surely knows that everything — or at least most things — which have happened to me are not the usual sorts of thing encountered by other knights errant, whether that be a result of the inscrutable wishes of fate or the malice of some jealous magician, and as it has long since been shown that among all, or most, celebrated knights errant, one has the power of being immune to enchantment, another of possessing flesh which no point can pierce or wound (like the famous Roland, one of the Twelve Knights of France, of whom it was said that he could only be wounded in the sole of his left foot, and even then only with the point of a thick pin and not by any other sort of weapon in the

2. Oriana = beloved of Amadís of Gaul; Alastrajarea = wife of Don Falanges of Astra, in *Don Florisel of Nicea*; Madásimas = a number of characters so named, in *Amadís of Gaul* [*Translator's Note*].

world, so that when Bernardo del Carpio killed him, at Roncesvalles, having first found that he could not wound him with steel, he lifted Roland off the ground in his arms and smothered him, reminding us of how Hercules killed Antaeus, that ferocious giant who was said to be the son of Mother Earth herself). I would guess, from all of this, that I too might have some special gift, not of being immune to all wounds, because experience has repeatedly proven to me that I am made of distinctly pliant flesh, not in the least impenetrable, nor that I cannot be enchanted, because I've seen myself locked into a cage — something that no power in the world is strong enough to do to me, except by magic; but since I did in the end set myself free, I am obliged to believe that nothing else can hurt me. But then, when these magicians found they could no longer get at me with their wicked schemes, they took their vengeance on the things I love best, trying to deprive me of my life by mistreating Dulcinea, for whom I live, and so I believe that when my squire came to her, bearing my message, they transformed her into a low peasant woman, busily doing something as base and vulgar as sifting wheat. Yet as I have previously declared, that wheat was neither wheat nor red, but seeds of oriental pearls — in proof of which, let me explain to your highnesses that, not long ago, when I arrived in Toboso, I simply could not locate Dulcinea's palace, and on another day, after my squire, Sancho, had seen her as she truly is — the most beautiful sight in the world — she appeared to me like a coarse, ugly peasant girl and, though my Dulcinea is the wisest woman in the world, not even well-spoken, so that even though I am no longer enchanted, and can no longer be (so far as I can determine), it is she who has been bewitched, injured, and transformed, distorted and even more than distorted, and through her my enemies have avenged themselves on me, so that I will live for her, now, in eternal tears, until I can see her again as she truly is.

"I have explained all this, so no one need concern themselves with what Sancho reports about Dulcinea sifting wheat, since just as they changed her for me, it would hardly be surprising that they changed her for him, too. Dulcinea is highly and nobly born, of the best blood to be found in Toboso — and Toboso boasts many good families, ancient and excellent, though to be sure none can compare to my peerless Dulcinea, for whose sake her birthplace will be known and celebrated for all time to come, as Troy was made famous by Helen, and Spain by La Cava,[3] though Dulcinea's claims will be greater. I should also like your highnesses to understand that Sancho Panza is one of the jolliest squires any knight errant has ever had; he is sometimes so keenly plain and simple that it becomes great fun to see whether he is indeed plain and simple or actually quite keen; he has sly tricks that brand him as a rascal, and artlessnesses that make him out a fool; he doubts everything, but he also believes everything; just when I'm convinced he's turning into a complete fool, he comes out with wisdom that soars to the very heavens. In short, I would not trade him for any other squire, even if you threw in a city, but I don't know if I would send him to be the governor of the island your grace has granted him, for

3. Count Julián's daughter, seduced by King Rodrigo [*Translator's Note*].

even though I perceive in him a certain administrative aptitude, which with a bit of mental trimming and tucking might make him capable of governing as well as the king, for example, manages with his tax-collecting, especially since we all know, from experience, that one needs neither great skill nor much learning to be a governor, for we can find a hundred of them who, though they can barely read, can govern like high-flying hawks, the essential thing being that they mean well and wish always to do well: there is no shortage of people to advise them, to help them do what they need to do, as for example those gentleman governors, complete amateurs, who pass judgment only with a counselor at their side. I will advise him to take no bribes and corrupt no law, plus a few other things I have on my chest, which I will produce in good time, for Sancho's use and for the sake of the island he'll be governing."

The duke, the duchess, and Don Quijote had come to this point in their conversation when they heard loud voices and a burst of noise, and all of a sudden there was Sancho, frightened out of his wits, a coarse cloth tucked under his chin, and behind him a flock of boys — or, more accurately, scullions and kitchen boys and other such riff-raff, one of them carrying a small basin, full of water that, from its color and its general lack of clarity one could tell had been used for washing dishes, and chasing along after Sancho with this basin, trying as hard as he could to stick it in under his beard, while another kitchen boy showed signs of wanting to wash that same beard with said water.

"What's going on, brothers?" asked the duchess. "What is this? What do you want from this good man? Have you forgotten that he is a governor elect?"

To which the scullion barber replied:

"This gentleman doesn't want to get washed, the way everybody else has been, including my lord the duke and his own master."

"I will, I will," replied Sancho furiously, "but with cleaner towels, and better soap, and hands less filthy, because there's not so much difference between my master and me that they wash him with fragrant angel-water but me with dirty devil-water. The customs of different places, and of different princes' houses, are only good when they're not a pain in the neck, and the way they have of washing you, around here, is worse than being whipped. My beard's clean, I don't need this kind of comfort, and anyone who tries to wash me, or touches a hair on my head — I mean, in my beard — I've got to say, with all due respect, that I'll hit him so hard that my fist will look like a jewel set in his skull, because all these seerimonies and soaping-ups look more like they're having fun than taking care of guests."

The duchess was dying of laughter, seeing Sancho's anger and hearing Sancho's words, but Don Quijote was not pleased to see his squire so poorly outfitted in a dirt-spattered towel, and with kitchen boys swarming all around him, and so, bowing most reverently to his hosts, as if asking their permission to speak, he said to the ragged flock, his voice very calm:

"Now, now, gentlemen! Leave this young fellow alone, your graces, and go back where you came from, or anywhere else you feel like going, because my squire is quite as clean as anyone else, and these bowls and pots of yours will not do for him any better than flower vases. So take my advice, and leave him alone: neither he nor I have much fondness for these kinds of pranks."

Sancho then took the words right out of his master's mouth, and went on:

"No, by God, let them play games with this poor simpleton, because I'd just as soon deal with them now as later! Go get yourselves a comb, or anything you like, and come curry my beard, and if you can pull out anything dirty, go ahead and shave an X on my head."

Then the duchess declared, still laughing:

"Everything Sancho Panza has said is correct, as it always will be, whenever he speaks: he is clean, as he says he is, and there is absolutely no need to wash him, so if our ways don't suit him, he can pick his own stick — especially since you self-appointed cleaning men have been exceedingly lazy and careless, I might even say impudent, fetching wooden bowls and pans, and kitchen pots, for such a personage and such a beard, instead, as would have been proper, bowls and pitchers of pure gold and Holland towels. But then, you're wicked and low-born, and how can you help yourselves, scoundrels that you are, from showing the jealousy you feel toward the squires of knights errant?"

The roguish kitchen boys, and even the butler (who had come with them), thought the duchess was speaking seriously, so they took the cloth off Sancho's neck and, confused, almost running, left the room — and, finding himself saved from (to his mind) an exceedingly grave danger, Sancho fell on his knees in front of the duchess, saying:

"Great mercies can be expected from great ladies: what your grace has done for me, today, could only be repaid were I to wish myself dubbed a knight errant, so I could spend the rest of my life in the service of such a noble lady. But I'm a farmer, and my name's Sancho Panza; I'm married, I have children, and I serve as a squire; and if in any of these capacities I can be of service to your highness, it will take me less time to obey than it will take you to command me."

"It's very clear, Sancho," replied the duchess, "that courtesy itself has taught you to be courteous. It is clear, I mean to say, that you have been raised in the bosom of my lord Don Quijote, who is surely the very acme of politeness, as he is the soul and flower of ceremony — or, as you have said, *seerimonies*. Blessings on such a master and such a servant, the one the very north star of knight errantry, the other the shining star of all faithful squires. Rise, Sancho my friend: I will repay your politeness by making sure that my lord the duke fulfills, just as rapidly as possible, the pledge he has made you of a governorship."

Thus ended their conversation; Don Quijote went off to take his siesta; and the duchess invited Sancho, unless he was really longing for sleep, to come spend the heat of the afternoon in a very cool room with her and her ladies. Sancho answered that, though he did indeed usually sleep for four or five hours, in this summer weather, to oblige her highness he would try as hard as he could, today, not to sleep at all, but come in obedience to her call — and so he did. The duke renewed his orders that Don Quijote was to be treated like a knight errant, exactly and in every detail as knights errant were said to be treated, in all the old tales of chivalry.

Chapter Thirty-Three

— *the delightful conversation the duchess and her ladies had with Sancho Panza, well worth both reading and noting*

Our history records, then, that Sancho indeed gave up his sleep that afternoon, at her request paying the duchess a visit, and she, taking immense pleasure in his words, seated him on a low chair next to her, though Sancho, out of sheer good breeding, was disinclined to be seated at all, but the duchess explained that he should be seated like a governor and talk like a squire, for in both those capacities he merited the chair of Sid Ruy Díaz himself.[1]

Shrugging his shoulders, Sancho obeyed and seated himself, and all the duchess' maids and ladies in waiting gathered in an attentive circle, to hear what he might say, but it was the duchess who spoke first:

"Now that we're all alone, where no one can hear us, I should like you, my lord governor, to clear up some of my uncertainties about this book, now in print, which tells the story of our great Don Quijote, one of those uncertainties being that, since our good Sancho Panza has never seen Dulcinea — I mean, my lady Dulcinea del Toboso, nor did he actually deliver my lord Don Quijote's letter, which was left in the notebook, back in the Sierra Morenas, how on earth did he have the nerve to invent her reply, saying that he'd found her sifting wheat and all that, every bit of which was a joke and a pure fabrication, and also seriously damaging to the matchless Dulcinea's reputation, in addition to being unsuited to the nature and loyalty of all good squires?"

Hearing this, Sancho stood up, not saying a word and, bending low, stepping very softly, with his finger held to his lips, circled all round the room, raising the curtains,[2] and then, this accomplished, went back to his chair and said:

"My lady, now that I've made sure there's no one hiding out there, listening, and it's just us in here, I can answer your question without being afraid, and I'll tell you the whole story, and the first thing I have to say is that, in my opinion, my lord Don Quijote's hopelessly out of his head, although sometimes he says things that, to my mind, and even to everybody else who hears him, are so sensible and so right on the mark that the Devil himself couldn't say them any better, but just the same, really and truly and without any question whatever, I know he's crazy. Well, knowing that, you see, I can take the chance and make him believe in things that don't exist — like for example Dulcinea's answer to his letter, and what happened six or eight days ago, so it isn't in the book yet, I mean all that about my lady Dulcinea being enchanted, which I made him believe, though it's no truer than the cow jumping over the moon."

The duchess asked him to explain the joke about Dulcinea's enchantment, and Sancho told it to her, exactly as it had happened, much to the delight of all his listeners, and when he had done, the duchess said to him:

---

1. See *Poem of the Cid*, lines 3114–3119 [*Translator's Note*].
2. Closed, of course, to keep out the afternoon heat [*Translator's Note*].

"Now, from what our good Sancho's been telling me, another doubt pops into my head, and I hear a little voice whispering in my ears, telling me: 'If Don Quijote de La Mancha's crazy, a fool and a simpleton, and his squire, Sancho Panza, knows this, and yet still goes on serving him and waiting for him to keep his silly promises, then the squire has surely got to be even crazier and more of an idiot than his master, and if that's the case, as it is,' this little voice goes on, 'how can you, my lady duchess, let this Sancho Panza be governor of an island, because if he doesn't know how to take care of himself, how can he possibly know how to rule over others?' "

"By God, my lady," said Sancho, "your doubt has a lot to say for itself, but you can tell it, your grace, it doesn't have to whisper, because it can speak up as loud as it wants, and I know it's telling the truth, and if I were really sensible I'd have left my master a long time ago. But that was how it worked out for me, and just my bad luck; I couldn't do anything else; I've got to stay with him; we're from the same village, I've eaten his bread, I really like him, and he's grateful to me, he's given me donkey colts and, more than anything else, I'm loyal, so the only thing that could keep us apart is the pick and shovel. And if your majesty doesn't want to see me given this island, well, God made me without it, and it could be, if He doesn't let me have it, it'll be good for my conscience, because irregardless of being a fool, I know the old saw: 'when ants got their wings, they didn't do good things,' and yes, maybe it'll be easier for Sancho the Squire to get into Heaven than Sancho the Governor. The bread they make here is just as good as the bread they make in France — and all cats look alike in the dark — and the man who's really unlucky is the one who still hasn't had breakfast, even though it's two hours after noon — and nobody's stomach is better than anybody else's, so, just the way they say, you can fill them all with hay — and the little birds in the field look to God for their feed — and you'll stay warmer with four yards of Cuenca flannel than four of Segovia silk — and when we leave the world of the living, and they put us into the ground, a prince goes down just as narrow a path as a ditch digger, because the Pope's body doesn't need any more room than the man who sweeps out the church, even though one was more important than the other, and when they drop you into the pit you've got to make yourself fit, like it or lump it — and then it's lights out. So let me say once more: if your ladyship doesn't want to give me that island, because I'm a fool, I'm smart enough not to worry about it, because I've heard it said that just behind the Cross there's the Devil, and everything that glitters isn't gold, and farmer Wamba went right from his oxen and his yoke and his plow to being King of Spain, but Rodrigo went straight from his fun and his silks and his diamonds to being eaten by snakes — anyway, if the old songs are telling the truth."

"And how can you doubt it!" exclaimed Doña Rodríguez, the lady in waiting, who was one of those listening. "Because there's a song that says they put King Rodrigo, while he was still alive, down in a tomb full of toads, and snakes, and alligators, and two days later they heard his mournful voice coming up out of the ground, saying softly

They're eating me, they're eating me,
On the part that sinned the most,[3]

so this gentleman is absolutely right, saying he'd rather be a farmer than a king, if it comes to being eaten up by vermin."

The duchess couldn't keep from laughing at her lady in waiting's simplicity, any more than she could help being astonished at how words and proverbs bubbled up out of Sancho, to whom she said:

"Let our good Sancho understand that, once a gentleman has given his word, he does his very best to keep it, even if it costs him his life. My lord and husband, the duke, may not be a knight errant, but that doesn't mean he's not a knight and a gentleman, and he will keep his promise about the island, no matter what anyone thinks or says. Rest assured, good Sancho, that just when you least think it, you'll see yourself seated on your island throne, and in possession of your estate there, and the governorship will rest in your hands, and you won't want to trade it for anything else in the whole world. And I recommend that he be careful how he rules over his new subjects, for he should know they are all loyal and well-born."

"As for governing them well," replied Sancho, "you don't even have to warn me, because I'm naturally charitable, and I sympathize with poor people, because who'll let you steal a loaf when he's kneaded and baked it? Let me tell you, I won't take any wooden nickels; I'm an old dog, you don't have to whistle at me — I can lift up my nose and smell what's cooking, and no one's going to pull the wool over my eyes, because I know when my shoe's too tight, and, believe me, good people are going to be all right with me: it's the bad ones who'll have trouble. And, as far as I'm concerned, this is where government begins, and maybe once I've been a governor for two weeks I'll want to be a governor forever and — who knows? — I could even be better at that than at farming, even though I've been out in the fields all my life."

"How right you are, Sancho," said the duchess, "because nobody's born knowing anything, and they make bishops out of men, not stones. But let me go back to what we were just saying about lady Dulcinea's enchantment, because it seems to me absolutely certain — indeed, proven beyond any doubt — that the whole idea of Sancho's fooling his master, and making him think a farm girl was really Dulcinea, and Don Quijote couldn't recognize her because she'd been bewitched — that whole thing was a scheme invented by one of those magicians who are always persecuting your master, because I have it from a reliable source that, in fact, the peasant girl who jumped up on the donkey was and is Dulcinea del Toboso, and that our good Sancho, thinking he was the trickster, has really been tricked, nor is there any more reason to disbelieve this than there is to doubt anything else we've never seen for ourselves, for you must understand, my lord Sancho, that we have our own magicians, who love us dearly and tell us what's going on in the world, straight and simple, without playing any games or concocting any little schemes, so please believe me,

---

3. These lines allude to several verses from an old Spanish ballad in which King Rodrigo, whose seduction of Florinda (La Cava) led to the invasion of Spain by the Moors in A.D. 711, complains in octosyllables that a snake is eating his penis.

Sancho: that leaping peasant girl truly was and is Dulcinea del Toboso, and she really is as enchanted as the mother who bore her — and when we least expect it, we're going to see her as she really is, and after that Sancho will be free of the spells he's now under."

"It could be, it could be," said Sancho Panza, "and now I'm inclined to believe what my master said he saw, down in Montesinos' Cave, where he told us he saw My Lady Dulcinea del Toboso dressed just the way she was that day when I enchanted her just to please myself, and everything must be exactly the opposite, the way you, my lady, say it is, because with my dull wits I can't, and I mustn't, dare to think that, just like that, I could dream up such a clever hoax, and neither should I believe my master is so completely crazy that a thin, feeble brain like mine could make him swallow something so wildly impossible. But just because of something like this, my lady, your goodness shouldn't think I'm a bad man, because an oaf like me can't be expected to figure out what these terrible magicians are thinking and plotting, and I was pretending all that so I wouldn't have to argue with my lord Don Quijote, and not because I wanted to hurt him, and if it's turned out the other way around, well, God's in His Heaven, and He judges all our hearts."

"True," said the duchess. "But now tell me, Sancho, what's all this about Montesinos' Cave? I'd very much like to know."

So Sancho Panza told her, blow by blow, everything already written, here, about that adventure. And the duchess said, after listening to him:

"What we can conclude from all this is that, since our great Don Quijote says he saw, down there, exactly the same peasant girl that Sancho saw riding out of Toboso, that has certainly got to be Dulcinea herself, and that we're dealing with some pretty clever and exceedingly active enchanters."

"I say so too," said Sancho Panza, "because if My Lady Dulcinea del Toboso's really enchanted, so much the worse for her, because I'm not going to mess with my master's enemies — not me! — when there seem to be so many of them, and they're such bad customers. It may be true that the girl I saw was a farm girl, and I thought she really was a farm girl, and I never thought she was anything else, so if it turns out she was Dulcinea, that has absolutely nothing to do with me, it's not my fault, I've said what I've said. By God, they can't keep running to me all the time, claiming 'Sancho said it, Sancho did it, Sancho did this, and Sancho did that,' as if Sancho were just some who-knows-what and not the very same Sancho who's already known all over the world, in a book, according to what Samson Carrasco tells me (and he's a university graduate, he is, and from Salamanca, and people like him aren't allowed to tell lies, except when they feel like it, or when they have a very good reason), and nobody ought to mess with me, either, because I've got a good reputation and, from what I've heard my master say, a good name's worth more than piles of money, so just let me get my hands on this governorship and you'll see some wonderful things, because anyone who's been a good squire is bound to be a good governor."

"Everything you have heard our good Sancho say," pronounced the duchess, "is wisdom worthy of Cato the Wise — or, in any event, drawn from Micael Verino himself, *florentibus occidit annis* [dead in the flower of his youth].[4] To put it all in a nutshell, and also to put it in Sancho's own style, look under a patched-up coat and you'll find a good drinker."

"Yet it's the truth, my lady," replied Sancho, "that drinking's never been one of my vices; I do drink when I'm thirsty, yes, because I'm no hypocrite; I also drink when I feel like it, and sometimes when I don't, because I don't want to look like I'm finicky or badly bred — I mean, when a friend drinks to you, what kind of a stony heart would you have to have, not to do the right thing? But you can wet your whistle without drowning it — and especially squires who work for knights errant, because what they usually drink is water, being always out in the forests and the woods and the fields, and up mountains and cliffs, where you couldn't find a lifesaving drop of wine if you gave your eyeballs for it."

"And I believe that, too," said the duchess. "So now, let's send our Sancho off to rest; we'll have more to say about all these things later, and then we'll arrange it so, as he puts it, he can get his hands on that governorship as quickly as possible."

Sancho kissed the duchess' hands all over again, and begged her to be kind enough to make sure that his little dappled one was well taken care of, because he was the apple of his master's eyes.

"What little dappled one?" asked the duchess.

"My ass, my donkey," answered Sancho, "and to keep from having to call him 'my ass,' sometimes I call him my little dappled one, and I asked that lady in waiting of yours to take care of him, when I first came to this castle, and she got all excited, as if I'd said she was ugly or old, though it seems to me it'd be a lot more natural, and ladies in waiting would do a lot better, if they were thinking about donkeys and asses instead of just sitting around in waiting rooms and looking important. Oh Lord, but there's a gentleman back in my village who really has it in for these ladies!"

"He must be a low-born peasant," said Doña Rodríguez, the lady in waiting, "because if he were really a gentleman, and well-born, he'd be praising them to the skies."

"Enough of that," said the duchess. "Stop it: you be quiet, Doña Rodríguez, and you calm down, my lord Panza, and let me see to this little dappled one, because if he's the jewel of our Sancho's eyes, I'll watch over him as if he were the apple of *my* eye."

"The stable's more than good enough for him," answered Sancho, "because we're neither of us worthy of being the apple of your highness' eye, not for one single moment, and I'd just as soon let you do that as stick myself all over with knives, because even though my master says, in this politeness game, it's better to lose because you have a card too many, instead of a card too few, just the same, when it comes to donkeys and little asses we have to watch our step and not overdo it."

"Take him with you, Sancho," said the duchess, "when you become a governor, and then you can let him have as good a time as you like, and maybe even pension him off."

"Your grace, my lady duchess," said Sancho, "please don't think that

---

4. Micael Verino (1469–1487), Italian poet known and, like Cato, frequently quoted for his wise Latin verses; the quoted phrase is from a commemorative poem about Verino by Angelo Policiano [*Translator's Note*].

would be anything to write home about, because he wouldn't be the first ass I've seen sent to become a governor, and if I take mine with me it won't be anything new."

Sancho's comments made the duchess start laughing all over again; she sent him to his siesta and went, herself, to report what had been happening to the duke; after which the pair of them plotted out a joke to play on Don Quijote, which was both first-class comedy and in perfect knightly style — and this was something they did any number of times, each joke beautifully worked out and vastly amusing — indeed, some of the very best adventures to be found anywhere in this great historical account.

Chapter Thirty-Four

— which tells how they planned to disenchant our matchless Dulcinea del Toboso, an adventure which ranks among the most renowned to be found in this book

The duke and duchess took such infinite delight in Don Quijote and Sancho Panza's conversation, that it made them even more determined to devise a number of jokes, all in the manner and guise of adventures, and drawing on what Don Quijote had told them about Montesinos' Cave, they concocted a particularly fine one. All the same, what especially struck the duchess was Sancho's incredible innocence, for having himself been the magician and the instigator of that entire business, he was now quite prepared to believe in the absolute truth of Dulcinea del Toboso's enchantment. Having given their servants very careful instructions, six days later they took our knight on a great game hunt, employing such a show of huntsmen and beaters that they might have been escorting an emperor or a king. They gave Don Quijote a hunting outfit, and gave Sancho one, too, of the finest green cloth, but Don Quijote would not wear anything of the sort, explaining that he would soon have to return to the harsh profession of war and could not afford to carry along a wardrobe or any purely ornamental garb. Sancho accepted his, intending to sell it as soon as he could.

The long-awaited day finally came; Don Quijote put on his armor; Sancho decked himself out in his new finery and, climbing up on his dappled donkey (which he would not abandon, even though they offered him a horse), joined the company of mounted huntsmen. The duchess emerged, magnificently dressed, and Don Quijote, in sheer politeness and courtesy, took her palfrey's reins (though the duke did not want him to) and, after a time, they reached a wood, lying between two towering mountains; taking up their posts, hiding in their blinds and lookouts, and allocating all their people to positions here, there, and everywhere, they began the actual hunt with such a clamor, such a chorus of shouting and yelling, and a general uproar so immense that, what with the barking of the hounds and the sounding of the trumpets, they could not so much as hear one another.

Dismounting, a sharp spear in her hands, the duchess posted herself where she knew wild boars frequently emerged from the wood. The duke and Don Quijote also dismounted, and set themselves on either side of her; Sancho stayed well to the rear, still on his donkey, afraid to leave it for fear that, by some accident, it might be hurt. They were barely settled in their places, along with a whole row of ducal servants, when they saw running toward them, hounded by pursuing dogs and trailed by hunters, an enormous boar, foaming at the mouth, its huge teeth and tusks gnashing, and at the sight Don Quijote drew his sword and braced himself. So too did the duke, cocking his spear — but the duchess would have stood in front of them all, had the duke not pushed her back. But Sancho, seeing the great beast bearing down on them, deserted the little dappled donkey and ran for his life, first trying to climb to the top of a tall oak tree, and then, when he found himself partway up and unable to get any higher, in reaching desperately for a branch, to pull himself up, being unlucky enough to break the branch clean off and, falling toward the ground, getting caught on a protrusion lower down and just hanging suspended there, unable to move in any direction. Finding himself thus well hooked, his green hunting outfit ripped, and hanging low enough down so that the fierce beast, if it chose to, could easily reach him, he began to shriek and beg for help so wildly that everyone who heard but could not see him thought he was surely right in the teeth of the most savage of animals.

The sharp-toothed boar finally fell, run through by a host of spears which permitted him no escape, and when Don Quijote turned to look for Sancho, whose cries and screams he had long since recognized, he saw his squire hanging head down and feet up, and his donkey standing next to him, unable to let him suffer his calamity alone — for as Sidi Hamid records, one rarely saw Sancho without seeing the donkey, or saw the donkey without seeing Sancho, so close and warm was their friendship.

Don Quijote went over and unhooked his dangling squire, who, as soon as he found himself back on his feet and safe on the ground, took a good hard look at the damage done to his hunting suit and felt sick at heart, thinking it was worth a king's ransom. In the meantime, the powerful boar had been lifted onto a mule and covered with sprigs of rosemary and myrtle branches; then they carried him off, like some battle trophy, to a cluster of great field-tents, erected in the middle of the wood, where they found tables already set and food laid out, all in such sumptuous and magnificent style that it was easy enough to tell the wealth and grandeur of those who had provided the feast. Showing the duchess the rips in his ruined outfit, Sancho said:

"If we'd been hunting little birds or hares, you'd never see my clothes looking as bad as this. I don't understand what pleasure you get, hunting an animal that, if it can reach you with one of its tusks, can easily kill you. I remember hearing an old ballad that went

> May you be eaten by bears
> Like Favila the fierce."[1]

"He was a Gothic king," said Don Quijote, "who went hunting and got eaten by a bear."

"That's just what I was saying," answered Sancho, "because I don't want

---

1. From a sixteenth-century ballad, *Maldiciones de Salaya, hechas a un criado suyo que se llamaba Misanco, sobre una capa que le hurtó* [Salaya's curses, directed at one of his servants, named Misanco, because of a stolen cloak] [*Translator's Note*].

princes and kings putting themselves in danger like that, just for a pleasure that doesn't seem like pleasure to me, because it means you have to kill an animal that hasn't done anything wrong."

"But you're completely mistaken, Sancho," replied the duke, "because, especially for a king or a prince, hunting out in the forest is one of the worthiest and indeed most necessary practices he can possibly engage in. For hunting is the very image of war: it employs stratagems, tricks, and traps for safely defeating the enemy; you have to put up with enormous cold and intolerable heat; laziness and sleep are stripped away, your strength is built up, you become nimble with the exercise and, in a word, it's a sport you can partake of without hurting anyone, but giving pleasure to many — and, best of all, this kind of hunting is not for everyone, as are other kinds of hunting — except of course falconry and hawking, which are likewise reserved for kings and princes. And so, oh my Sancho! revise your opinion, and when you become a governor engage in hunting, and you'll see for yourself how worthwhile it will be."

"Not on your life," replied Sancho. "A good governor, he gets himself a broken leg and stays home. What a wonderful thing it would be, wouldn't it, if business people came and wore themselves out, looking for him, while he was loafing around up in the mountains! What a mess the governorship would be in! By God, my lord, hunting and playing around is stuff for loafers, not for governors. Me, at Christmas and Easter I'll have fun with a nice quiet hand of trump-your-penny, and then bowling on Sundays and holidays, because all this hunting and punting just doesn't go with being a governor — and, besides, my conscience wouldn't like it, either."

"May God let it be as you wish, Sancho, because there's a big difference between saying something and actually doing it."

"Let it be however it wants to be," answered Sancho, "because a man with good credit doesn't mind leaving a deposit, and it's the early worm that catches the bird, and it's the belly that feeds the feet and not the feet that feed the belly — what I'm trying to say, your grace, is that if God helps me, and I do what I'm supposed to do and He knows I mean well, then I'll be one hell of a good governor. I mean, if I just keep my tongue out of sight, they'll find out if my teeth can bite!"

"May the curses of God and all His saints fall on you, Sancho!" said Don Quijote. "I'll say it again, as I've said it many times before: may I live to see the day when you simply speak a straight sentence, without quoting proverbs! Don't trouble yourselves with this fool, your majesties, because he'll grind the life out of you, not just between a pair of these infernal proverbs, but between thousands of them, all dragged in as much to the point and proper as the good health God should give us both — but not me, if I have to listen to any more of them."

"Ah," said the duchess, "but even if Sancho Panza offers us more proverbs than our commanding Greek himself,[2] that's no reason not to respect their compressed wisdom. I must say, really, that I enjoy his proverbs far more than others, quoted much more appropriately."

---

2. A reference to the classical scholar Hernán Núñez de Guzmán and his massive collection of proverbs, published in Salamanca in 1555 [*Translator's Note*].

With such pleasant conversation, they left the tent and went back into the wood, spending the rest of the day, right up to nightfall, looking into assorted traps and snares and hunters' blinds, and when darkness came it was neither so straightforward nor so peaceful as might have been expected at that time of year (which was midsummer), because there was a certain *chiaroscuro*, an indefiniteness and contrast of light and dark, which, as it happened, was very useful for the duke and duchess' plans, for as the night began, just at twilight, the whole wood suddenly seemed to glow, as if it were burning, and then there began to be heard, first here, then there, then everywhere, a host of trumpets and other martial instruments, much as if a horde of cavalrymen were passing among the trees. The blazing firelight, and the blare of these warlike instruments, half blinded the eyes and deafened the ears of their entire party, and indeed of everyone who was anywhere in the wood.

And then they heard the ululating cries uttered by Moors, as they rush into battle; trumpets and bugles blew, drums beat, flutes and fifes twittered, and all this was so jumbled together, so rapid and unrelenting, that anyone in his right mind would have lost it in the confused blaring. The duke was stunned, the duchess amazed, Don Quijote surprised, Sancho Panza trembling, and even those who knew what was going on were frightened. Fear forced them into silence — and then a herald, dressed in devil's clothing, dashed in front of them, not blowing a trumpet but some sort of hollow, ghastly-sounding horn that emitted a hoarse, ragged noise.

"Hey there, huntsman!" called the duke. "Who are you, and where are you going, and whose are all these soldiers I seem to hear riding through this wood?"

The herald answered him in bold, terrifying tones:

"I am the Devil, and I am hunting Don Quijote de La Mancha; the hordes you hear are six troops of magicians, who have with them, in a triumphal chariot, the matchless Dulcinea del Toboso. They bring her enchanted, and with her that gallant Frenchman, Montesinos, and both of them come to tell the said Don Quijote what he must do, if he wishes to see the lady freed of her enchantments."

"If in fact you were the Devil," answered the duke, "as you say you are, and as you certainly seem to be, you'd surely have recognized that knight, Don Quijote de La Mancha, because here he is, standing right in front of you."

"By God and my conscience," responded the Devil, "I paid no attention to him, for my mind was so busy with so many things that, for the moment, I'd almost forgotten what I was up to."

"Clearly," said Sancho, "this devil must be both a good man and a good Christian, or he'd never have sworn 'By God and my conscience.' I begin to see that, even in Hell, there must be decent people."

Then the Devil, not bothering to dismount, looked straight at Don Quijote, and said:

"As for you, Knight of the Lions (and how I wish I could see you clutched in their claws!), it was that brave but unfortunate knight, Montesinos, who sent me here, commanding me on his behalf to tell you: stay and wait for him, wherever I find you, because he's bringing you the female they call Dulcinea del Toboso, and will explain to you what must be done to disenchant her. And that being what I came for, there is no need for me to linger any longer: may all the demons in Hell be with you, and all the angels in Heaven with these other gentlemen and ladies."

Having said which, he raised his huge horn and blew a blast, then turned and left them, waiting for no reply.

He left everyone, and especially Sancho and Don Quijote, even more astonished than before — Sancho, seeing that, no matter what the truth, they kept saying Dulcinea was really enchanted, and Don Quijote, because he still wasn't sure that what had seemed to happen in Montesinos' Cave had really happened. And as our knight turned this matter over in his mind, the duke said to him:

"Will you wait, then, my lord Don Quijote?"

"Why not?" answered our knight. "I will stand here, fearless and unflinching, even if all Hell comes attacking me."

"Well, if I see another Devil, and hear another horn like that one," said Sancho, "you're as likely to find me here as in Flanders."

The night began to darken around them, and all sorts of lights began to flicker through the wood, much like those cold fiery flashes that fall from Heaven and, to our eyes, seem to be shooting stars. And they also heard a fearful noise, like the massive groaning of huge oxcart wheels, which harsh and unremitting shrieking is said to frighten even wolves and bears, if they happen to hear it. And on top of all this tumult, swelling it still more hugely, all over the wood there burst forth fierce battle sounds, with frightful cannon exploding from one side, and volleys of muskets from another, with the combatants' cries seeming close beside them, and in the distance, once again, the ululating war-calls of the Moors.

The effect of all these bugles and cornets, these trumpets and horns and drums and cannon and muskets and, above all the rest, the horrible screeching of the cart wheels, mounting into a wildly jumbled cacophony, forced Don Quijote to summon up every bit of courage he could find in his heart, but both Sancho's courage and his consciousness deserted him, and he fell to the ground at the duchess' feet, the lady enfolding him in her skirts and quickly ordering water to be splashed onto his face. Which was done, and he came to, just as the cart with its groaning wheels finally arrived.

It was drawn by four huge oxen, draped, shrouded all in black; each of their horns bore a good-sized wax torch, burning brightly, and on top of the cart there stood a raised chair, in which a venerable old man was seated, his beard, which hung far down past his belt, whiter than the whitest snow; he was dressed in a black buckram robe — as it was easy enough to see, the whole cart being lit by more flaring torches than anyone could have counted. The cart was driven by two ugly demons, dressed in the same black buckram, their faces so hideous that Sancho, the moment he saw them, closed his eyes to keep from having to see them again. When the cart had drawn up in front of them, the venerable old man rose from his chair and, standing high above them, declared in a loud voice:

"I am the wise Lirgandeo."[3]

At which the cart moved on, without another word being spoken. Just behind it appeared another cart of exactly the same sort, bearing another enthroned old man who, gesturing for the cart to pause, declared in a voice no less somber than the first man's:

"I am the wise Alquife, famous friend of Urganda the Unknowable."

And he too passed on.

And immediately there appeared yet another cart, virtually identical, but the man seated high on its throne was not, like the others, old and venerable, but strong and singularly nasty-looking, and he too rose up on his feet and declared, in a voice even hoarser and more diabolical:

"I am Arcalaus the Magician, mortal enemy of Amadís of Gaul and of all his kith and kin."

And he passed on. But none of the carts went very far, all of them stopping close by, and the horrible noise of their wheels also stopped — only to be replaced, not by a noise, but by the gentle sounds of harmonious, well-played music, which cheered Sancho and seemed to him a very good sign, so he said to the duchess (from whose skirts he had not moved an inch):

"My lady, there can't be any bad things happening, when there's music like that."

"Nor where we have such lights and radiant brightness," answered the duchess.

To which Sancho replied:

"Fire produces light, and bonfires make things bright, as we can see all around us, and such things can also burn us — but music is always a sign of happiness and feasting."

"We'll see what we'll see," said Don Quijote, who had been listening to everything.

And indeed he was right, as the following chapter will prove.

Chapter Thirty-Five

— more about what Don Quijote was told, by way of disenchanting Dulcinea, together with other remarkable events

Next, moving in time to the pleasant music, they saw a triumphal chariot approaching, drawn by six brown mules, all draped in white linen, and a Penitent of Light[1] riding on each of them, every man completely clothed in white, every man carrying a burning wax torch in his hand. This chariot was twice, or perhaps even three times as large as those that had preceded it, and all around, and inside it, there stood twelve more penitents, every one of them garbed whiter than white, all carrying burning torches — a sight both astonishing and terrifying. High on a raised throne there sat a

---

3. Supposed to be the chronicler-author of the well-known chivalric tale *El Caballero del Febo* [*Phoebus' Knight*] [*Translator's Note*].

1. As opposed to penitents *de carne* [of flesh] or *de sangre* [of blood], who carried whips and scourged themselves as they marched [*Translator's Note*].

nymph, wearing a thousand filmy silvery veils, all glittering with innumerable silver sequins, making her seem, if not richly dressed, at least stunningly. She wore a gauzy, transparent veil over her face, scarcely hiding her from their sight, for they could easily make out a beautiful girl's features, and indeed the quantity of burning torches let them distinguish both her beauty and her age, which seemed no older than twenty, no younger than seventeen.

Standing next to her was a figure dressed in what is called a flowing or sweeping robe, reaching down to his feet; his head was swathed in a black veil. And just as the chariot came abreast of the duke, the duchess, and Don Quijote, the gentle music was hushed, and all at once harps and lutes sounded from within the chariot, and the man in the flowing robe rose, throwing off his veil and pulling the robe open with both hands, revealing the unmistakeable, unforgettable figure of Death himself, all skin and bones and ugly, a sight Don Quijote was not pleased to see and which absolutely terrified Sancho, and even the duke and duchess showed signs of being afraid. This living Death stood tall above them and, in a bored and sluggish voice, began to recite, as follows:

> — My name is Merlin. I am he who the histories
> Say had the Devil Himself for a father — a lie,
> But a lie grown healthy and hoary from much retelling.
> I am the King of Magic, monarch and treasure
> Chest of all Zorastrian learning, aped
> And envied down the ages and across all time —
> Time which tries to cover over the glorious
> Deeds of many brave knights errant, for whom
> I had, and have today, a great affection.
> For even if other enchanters and wise men, wizards
> And sages, magicians and Magi, persist in being
> Flinty-hearted, strong but harsh and severe,
> My nature is gentle, sweet and soft and loving,
> And forever fond of doing good to everyone.
>   Deep in Dis'[2] gloomy caverns, where my busy
> Soul was spinning rhombic shapes and circles,
> And polynomial wonders, and special signs,
> I heard the sad yet charming voice of the lovely,
> Matchless Dulcinea del Toboso.
> I knew of her enchantment and your misfortune,
> And how she'd been changed from a noble lady to a graceless
> Country girl; my heart was touched, and I dove
> Deep, scanning with all my powers the frightful
> Spells woven around her, wrestling in the darkness,
> And after consulting a hundred thousand books
> Of my sometimes indecent and rather devilish science,
> I found, at last, the secret cure for such
> A monstrous sadness, such a wicked wrong.
>   Oh you, Quijote, eternal honor and glory

---

2. Dis = god of the lower world, also known as Dis Pater [Father Dives], Pluto, etc [*Translator's Note*].

Of all who clothe themselves in adamant steel,
Light and flaming torch, symbol and sign
And guiding star for those who shake off sluggish
Dreams, and drop their lazy pens, and oblige
Themselves to learn the hard, unbearable ways
Of war, with all its rivers of blood and gore!
You, oh man owed such endless praise
That no time ever can forget you! You, brave
And wise Don Quijote, splendid Man
Of La Mancha, brilliant star in the Spanish sky,
For matchless Dulcinea del Toboso
To ever recover her true and original form,
Your squire, Sancho Panza, must first whip
Himself three thousand biting strokes, and then
Three hundred more, directly on both his fleshy
Buttocks, bared to the passing breeze, strokes
So smart that he burns, he stings at the bitter touch
Of the lash. This is the cure that will undo magic;
The wise enchanters who cast those spells have agreed,
And here I am, to solve your lady's need."

"Mother of God!" Sancho burst out. "Not three but three thousand
lashes: I'd just as soon stab myself, one, two, three! God damn this crazy
system for breaking spells! What the hell has my ass got to do with magic?
By all that's holy, if my lord Merlin can't find any better way of disenchanting lady Dulcinea del Toboso, she can stay enchanted until they
bury her!"

"You garlic-stuffed peasant," said Don Quijote, "I'll take you and tie
you to a tree, as naked as the day your mother bore you, and I won't give
you just three thousand and three hundred lashes — by God, I'll give
you six thousand and six hundred, and they'll fall on you so fast and hard
it will take three thousand and three hundred yanks on the whip to tear
it loose. Say just one word, damn it, and I'll rip out your heart."

At this, Merlin said:

"That won't do, because our good Sancho has to willingly accept these
lashes; they can't be forced upon him; and he has as much time as he
likes to take care of the business, because no specific final day has been
established — though he can stop whipping himself when he's halfway
through this flogging ordeal, if he's willing to let someone else administer
the remainder, even if, as may happen, the rest may be laid on with a
fairly heavy hand."

"No one else's hand, and not mine, and not a heavy hand, and not any
hand," answered Sancho, "because no one's going to lay any kind of anything on me. Did I go dreaming up this lady Dulcinea del Toboso, so my
rear end has to pay because she wasn't careful? Now, my lord and master
— sure, she belongs to him; every step he takes, he calls her 'my life, my
soul,' his support and his protection, so he can whip himself, and he ought
to, and he should do everything that has to be done to break the spell on
her — but me, whip myself? . . . Get thee beside me, Satan."

Sancho had barely finished when the silvery nymph, standing next to

Merlin's ghost, drew back her gossamer veil, revealing a face that struck every watching eye as almost impossibly beautiful, and boldly, even swaggeringly, her voice quite unladylike, spoke directly to Sancho Panza:

"Ah, you miserable squire, with your brittle soul, your wooden heart, your flinty, rock-hard guts! Had you been ordered, oh, you impudent thief! to throw yourself to the ground, from the top of a tall tower — had you been asked, oh you enemy of all human decency, to swallow a dozen toads, and two dozen lizards, and three dozen snakes — if they wanted you to murder your wife and children with some cruel, sharp sword — then who could wonder that you showed yourself finicky and cold? But just for a mere three thousand and three hundred blows, or as much as fall on every child learning his catechism, no matter how small or how frail he may be — ah, that must surprise, astonish, and stun to their pious hearts every pair of ears that hears you, as it will similarly shock all those who may learn of it, in time yet to come. Look! oh you vile and hardhearted beast! Look, I say, with your frightened little piggy eyes, look into these eyes of mine, which sparkle like stars in the sky, and see how they pour out endless tears, plowing furrows, lines, and paths across the lovely fields of my cheeks. Let the sight of my blossoming youth stir you, oh sly, wicked monster, for I am still in my teens, still only nineteen and not yet twenty, and yet this blooming youth finds itself wasted, withered under the crude outer covering of a low peasant girl — for if that is not how I appear to you, now, it is thanks to lord Merlin, here beside me, who has granted me this special favor specifically so I can move you with my beauty, for the tears of suffering beauty can turn the very cliffs into soft cotton, and make sheep out of tigers. Rise, rise, out of your corpulent sloth, you beast-soul, and draw upon that inner spirit which, now, moves you only to eat and then eat again, and set free my smooth skin, my gentle soul, and my lovely face — and even if I cannot soften that hard heart, or bring you to some just and reasonable decision, let it be done for the sake of that poor knight beside you — for your master, whose heart I can see, barely peeping from his throat, no more than a bare seven or eight inches from his lips, not knowing whether your answer will be harsh or mild, uncertain whether to leap from his mouth or fall back into the pit of his stomach."

Don Quijote felt his throat, hearing this, then turned to the duke and said:

"By God, my lord, but Dulcinea's telling the truth, because I can feel my heart stuck right here in my throat like the screw on a crossbow."

"And you, Sancho, what do you say to all this?" asked the duchess.

"What I say, my lady," replied Sancho, "is what I've said already: as far as those lashes are concerned, get thee beside me, Satan."

"Sancho, you should say 'get thee *behind* me, Satan,' " noted the duke.

"Leave me alone, your majesty," answered Sancho, "because right now I'm not in the mood for quibbling about a letter here or a letter there. This stuff about all the lashes I have to take, or I have to want to take, has me so upset that I don't know what I'm saying or what I ought to do. I'd just like to ask my lady Doña Dulcinea del Toboso where she learned how to beg people for favors, because here she is, wanting me to split my skin with a whip, and she tells me I have a 'brittle soul,' and I'm a 'vile and hard-hearted beast,' plus a whole long string of bad names she ought to save for the Devil. Does she think my flesh is made out of brass, or that I give a hoot whether she gets disenchanted or not? Is she coming with a basket of nice white clothes in her hands — shirts, handkerchiefs, socks (though God knows I don't wear them) — so she can talk me into it? No, she's loaded down with one insult after another, though she ought to know what they say around here, that a donkey loaded with gold goes leaping up a mountain, and gifts make pain bearable, and you should pray to God but nail with a hammer, and that one 'here, take this,' is worth two 'I'm going to give you'? And as for my lord and master, who ought to be soft-soaping me like mad, and trying to soften me up like wool and well-brushed cotton, well, he tells me he'll tie me to a tree, bare naked, and give me a double dose of lashes — and all these merciful magician gentlemen need to remember, too, that it's not a simple squire who's supposed to whip himself, but the governor of an island, which would really be like rubbing salt in my wounds. Like it or not, let them learn how to ask for favors, and let them learn how to beg and behave like well-bred people, because times change, and everyone isn't always in a good mood. Right now, for example, my heart's absolutely sick, seeing my green coat ripped, and this whole business of cutting loose and whipping myself feels about as important as becoming an Indian chief."

"But truly, my friend Sancho," said the duke, "if you don't show us you can be as meek as a lamb, you're not going to get that governorship. Good lord, how would it be to send my island a cruel governor, so hard-hearted that he couldn't be moved by the tears of unfortunate maidens, so stiff-necked that he couldn't be touched by the appeals of wise, powerful, venerable magicians and enchanters! Oh no, Sancho: either you have to whip yourself, or we have to whip you, or you can't be a governor."

"My lord," answered Sancho, "can't I at least have a couple of days, so I can make up my mind?"

"Absolutely not," said Merlin. "This business has to be settled right here and right now: either Dulcinea goes back to Montesinos' Cave, once again transformed into a rough country girl, or else, in the shape she has now been restored to, she will be carried off to the Elysian Fields, there to wait until all the stipulated number of lashes have been administered."

"Now, come on, my good Sancho," said the duchess. "Show that you've both eaten and properly appreciated the bread your master Don Quijote has given you — a knight we are all bound to serve and please, not only because of his kind nature but also for his extraordinarily chivalric deeds. Agree to this modest flogging, my son, and down with the devil and with mealy-mouthed fear, because, as you know perfectly well, bad luck can't break a stout heart."

To all of which Sancho replied, absurdly, by turning and asking Merlin:

"Tell me, your grace, my lord Merlin: when that herald devil appeared and gave my master a message from my lord Montesinos, he told Don Quijote to stay right here so lord Montesinos could come and tell him how to disenchant my lady Dulcinea del Toboso, but we still haven't seen hide nor hair of Montesinos, or anyone who even looks like him."

To which Merlin responded:

"Friend Sancho, the Devil is both a fool and the worst scoundrel who ever lived. I sent him in search of your master, yes, but with a message from me, not from Montesinos, because Montesinos is in his cave, longing — or I might better say hoping — for his own disenchantment, and that has to be done right, you can't skin a cat and forget about the tail. If Montesinos owes you anything, or if you have some business with him, I'll dig him out and set him down wherever you like. But right now, let's first settle this whipping business — and, trust me, it will be highly useful to you, quite as much for your soul as for your body; that is, it will be good for your soul because of the charity you'll show, performing it; and it will be good for your body because I see what a sanguine complexion you have and being bled a little won't do you a bit of harm."

"The world is full of doctors," replied Sancho, "and now even the magicians are doctors — but all right, you're all telling me to do it, though I can't see why, myself, so I'll agree and say, yes, I'll be glad to give myself three thousand and three hundred lashes, on condition that it's up to me to give each one how and when I want to, without anyone setting any limits to how fast I get it done, or how long I take doing it, but I'll try to pay off the debt as fast as I can, so the world can enjoy my lady Doña Dulcinea del Toboso's beauty, because although I didn't think so, it looks like I was wrong and she really is beautiful. And it also has to be agreed that I'm not obliged to draw blood with the blows, and any lashes that turn out like fly-swatting still count. Furthermore, in case I lose track of how many, my lord Merlin here, since he knows everything, has to be keeping careful count and has to let me know how many more I need or how many too many I've already had."

"There's no problem about too many," replied Merlin, "because the instant you reach the required number, Lady Dulcinea will be immediately disenchanted, and she will appear right here, anxious to thank you, my good Sancho, and reward you for your good deed. So there's no need to worry about there being either too many or too few — and Heaven forbid that I should deceive anyone by even so much as a single hair."

"All right, then! It's in God's hands!" said Sancho. "It's my misfortune, and I accept it — that is, I accept the whipping, but only on the conditions already noted."

Sancho had scarcely uttered these last words when the soft, harmonious music began once more, and a million muskets sounded, and Don Quijote threw his arms around his squire's neck, kissing his forehead and his cheeks a thousand times over. The duke and duchess, and everyone else present, seemed absolutely delighted, and the chariot began to move off — and as it passed, the beautiful Dulcinea bent her head to acknowledge the duke and duchess, and made a deep curtsy to Sancho.

By which time, too, happy, smiling dawn was upon them, revealing the little flowers of the fields, standing straight and tall; the liquid crystal of tiny streams went murmuring among smooth brown and white pebbles, hurrying to pay tribute to the waiting rivers. The whole earth was happy, the skies were bright and clear, the air pure, the light peaceful and calm, each and all indicating that this day, already treading on dawn's skirts, would be serene and untroubled. The duke and duchess, well satisfied with their night's hunting, and with how neatly and discreetly their plan had been carried out, went back to their castle, intending to continue amusing themselves, for there was nothing in all reality which could have pleased them quite so much.

Chapter Thirty-Six

— which narrates the extraordinary, unimaginable adventure of Lady Dolorida, otherwise known as the Countess Trifaldi, as well as Sancho Panza's letter to his wife

The duke's steward was an exceedingly jolly, fun-loving, witty fellow: it was he who had played the role of Merlin and arranged the entire apparatus of the previous evening, as well as writing the characters' lines, composing Merlin's poem, and persuading a young page to play Dulcinea. With his master's and mistress' help, he next concocted one of the funniest, wildest farces anyone could have dreamed up.

The duchess asked Sancho, the next day, if he had set to work, doing what needed to be done to disenchant Dulcinea. Sancho answered that he had, and that night had given himself a full five lashes. The duchess then asked what instrument he had employed, and Sancho replied that he had used his hand.

"Ah," replied the duchess, "but those are more like slaps than lashes. I don't think Merlin the Wise will be satisfied with such gentleness: our good Sancho must fashion himself a truly penitential whip, something weighty enough so it will really be felt, because this is a message which must be written in blood, nor can the freedom of such a great lady as Dulcinea be purchased at such bargain prices and at such a low cost. You must realize, Sancho, that lukewarm, slovenly charity is meaningless and worth nothing."

To which Sancho replied:

"Your grace, let me have some kind of handy whip, or a rope end — something I won't too much hurt myself with, because you've got to understand, your grace, that even if I am a peasant, there's more cotton in me than bramble bushes, and it wouldn't be a good idea to ruin myself on someone else's account."

"I'll be glad to help," the duchess answered. "Tomorrow I'll give you just the right kind of whip, one that will just suit your tender flesh, and treat it like its own brother."

To which Sancho said:

"You must know, your majesty, lady of my heart and soul, that I've had a letter written to my wife, Teresa Panza, telling her everything that's happened since I left. It's right here in my shirt, because all that's left to do is address it, and I'd like your wisdom to read it, because I think it sounds just the way a governor's letter ought to — I mean, it's written exactly the way governors ought to write their letters."

"And who dictated it?" asked the duchess.

"Who should have dictated it but me, sinner that I am?" answered Sancho.

"And did you write it yourself?" the duchess asked.

"I couldn't if I wanted to," replied Sancho, "because I don't know how to read or write, just how to sign my name."

"Let me see it," said the duchess, "because I'm certain that you've displayed in it your mind's true nature and high competence."

Sancho drew the letter out of his shirt, the duchess took it, and then read as follows:

SANCHO PANZA'S LETTER TO HIS WIFE, TERESA PANZA

Maybe I got a good whipping, but I rode like a real gentleman; if I got a good governorship, I paid for it with good lashes. Teresa, my wife, you won't understand all this, but in good time you will. What you've got to understand, Teresa, is that I'm determined to see you riding in a coach, because that's what really matters: any other way of riding is like walking on all fours. You're now a governor's wife: watch out they don't start talking behind your back! I'm sending you a green hunting outfit, given me by my lady the duchess: fix it up so it makes a nice skirt and blouse for our daughter. According to what I hear them saying, around here, my master, Don Quijote, is a crazy wise man and an elegant idiot, and I'm not far behind him. We've been in Montesinos' Cave, and Merlin the Wise has gotten hold of me for disenchanting Dulcinea del Toboso, who's called Aldonza Lorenzo, around where you are; with three thousand and three hundred lashes, minus five, which I've already given myself, she's going to be as disenchanted as the day her mother bore her. Don't tell anybody about this, because if you wash your linen out in public there'll be those who'll say it's white and those who'll say it's black. I'll be leaving here, in not too long, to become a governor, and I'm really anxious to get started because I want to make a lot of money, which is how they say all new governors begin; let me see how things go, and I'll let you know if you ought to come join me or not. The dapple donkey's doing fine, and sends you his warm regards; I wouldn't abandon him even if they were taking me to be the Grand Turk himself. My lady the duchess kisses your hands a thousand times, so send her back two thousand, because my master says there's nothing that costs less or is a better bargain than being polite. God didn't feel like letting me have another suitcase with another hundred gold pieces in it, the way He did before, but don't let that bother you, my Teresa, because whoever rings the bells comes out well, and it'll all come out in the wash, once I'm a governor, though it does worry me that, according to what they tell me, once you've tried governing you can't ever let it alone, and if that's the way it's going to be, then it won't be such a good bargain, but on the other hand cripples always think begging's the best job in the world, so one way or another you're bound to get rich and lucky. May God grant it to you, because He can, and may He preserve me to take care of you. From this castle here, on the twentieth of July, 1614,

Your husband the governor
SANCHO PANZA

Having read his letter, the duchess said to Sancho:

"Our good governor has made just two small mistakes, first of all in saying, or at least indicating, that he received this governorship in return for the whipping he had to give himself, because he knows, and surely cannot deny, that when the duke my lord promised it to him no one in the whole world had even dreamed of any lashes, and secondly because he shows himself to be very greedy, and that's not what I want him to be: greed breaks the bag, and a greedy governor makes for ungoverned justice."

"That isn't the way I meant it, my lady," answered Sancho, "so if your grace doesn't think this letter is what it ought to be, I'll just have to rip it up and get another one, and that one could be even worse, if it's left to a brain like mine."

"No, no," responded the duchess. "This one's quite good enough; indeed, I'd like the duke to see it."

So they went out to a garden, where they were to dine that day. The duchess showed Sancho's letter to the duke, who found it delightful. Then they ate, and after the tablecloths had been removed, and they'd been amused for some while by Sancho's savory conversation, suddenly they heard the piercingly sad sound of a flute and a raucous, discordant drum. Everyone seemed disturbed by the disordered, martial, mournful music, especially Don Quijote, who could not stay seated for sheer excitement — while, as for Sancho, it need only be said that fear led him to his usual hiding place, which was either next to or right in the duchess' skirts, because the sound they were hearing was really and truly as sad and mournful as it could possibly be.

And then, as they all waited, they saw two men in the very fullest mourning — so full that it hung down to the ground — enter the garden, playing two great drums, which were also completely draped in black. The flute-player walked beside them, as pitch-black as the others. These three were followed by an enormously large man, absolutely covered rather than merely dressed in a black robe, the skirts and folds of which were as immense as the man who wore it. A huge black sword belt was buckled all the way around this robe, and from it there hung a gigantic scimitar, its handle and scabbard all studded with black gems. His face was covered by a light veil, also black, through which one could see an incredibly long beard, as white as the whitest snow. He walked to the beat of the two drums, his steps slow, sombre, and assured. And his size, his walk, his black-enshrouded figure, and those who marched with him, might well have astonished, as indeed they did, all those who saw him but had no idea who he might be.

He approached the duke — who by this time, like everyone else, was standing and awaiting him — with this same deliberate, exceedingly solemn gait, and then sank to his knees, but the duke would not permit him to speak until he rose. The enormous apparition complied and, when he was back on his feet, drew the veil from his face, showing the most horrific, the hugest, the whitest, and the bushiest beard ever seen, to that moment, by human eyes, and, from the immense expanse of his broad chest, he produced a deep, sonorous voice, with which he addressed the duke as follows:

"Oh noble and powerful lord of lords, my name is Trifaldín the White-Bearded, and I am the Countess Trifaldi's squire, she who is also known as the Lady Dolorida [*dolorida* = of sorrows], from whom I bring Your Majesty a message, which is that Your Magnificence might be pleased to permit her to enter and tell you her troubles, which are surely the most novel and astonishing that even the most worried spirit in the world might have conceived. But first I am bidden to ask if, at this moment, your castle contains that brave and never vanquished knight, Don Quijote de La Mancha, for whom my mistress has come searching, on foot and never breaking her fast all the long way from the kingdom of Candaya to this your estate, a phenomenal journey which can and should be considered either miraculous or else the fruit of some enchantment. She stands outside this fortress, or country house, and only awaits your permission to enter. I have spoken."

And then he coughed and, with both hands, smoothed his huge beard from top to bottom, then stood calmly awaiting the duke's reply, which was as follows:

"Indeed, my good squire, Trifaldín the White-Bearded, it has been a very long time since we had news of my lady the Countess Trifaldi's misfortune, she to whom the magicians have given the name of the Lady Dolorida, so surely, oh magnificent squire, tell her she may enter, and tell her, too, that the brave knight, Don Quijote de La Mancha, is indeed here, and his generous nature can certainly promise her whatever help and protection she may require, and also tell her that, for my part, if my own assistance may be needed, it too will not be withheld, for being myself a knight I am bound to offer it to her, since knighthood necessarily involves the responsibility of coming to the aid of all womankind, but especially noble widows, sorrowful and in difficult straits, as your mistress would appear to be."

Hearing this, Trifaldín once more bent his knee to the ground and then, signaling the three musicians to begin playing, he left the garden exactly as he had first appeared, and at the same pace, much to the astonishment and wonder of all who had seen him. And then, turning to Don Quijote, the duke said:

"So, my famous knight, neither the darkness in which ill-will always dwells, nor ignorance itself, can hide or obscure the light of courage and virtue. I am obliged to say this, seeing how, though your goodness has been in my castle no more than half a dozen days, the afflicted and those in mourning come seeking you from faraway places — and not in carriages, or riding on camels, but on foot and fasting — trusting that, in your strong arm, they will find the cure for their sorrows and their struggles, and all this because of your great and noble deeds, word of which runs and fairly encircles the entire known world."

"I could wish, my lord duke," replied Don Quijote, "that the holy man could be here, he who at your table the other day showed such a fierce grudge against and such ill-will toward all knight errantry, so he could see with his own eyes whether or not the world truly needs such knights. At least, he might come to know at first hand that, in profoundly troubling situations and disasters of truly enormous proportions, it is not to the houses of learned men that the extraordinarily afflicted and miserable come, nor to the holy men who dwell in their villages, nor to the knight who has never gone beyond the boundaries of his own estate, nor to the lazy courtier who would rather hunt for news, so he can gossip and chatter about it, instead of hunting for deeds that he might do and which others would talk and write about — no, he who cures sorrows, and aids the needy, and shelters maidens in distress, and takes care of widows, is nowhere found more often than in the person of a knight errant, and I give endless thanks to Heaven which has made me one, just as I welcome with open arms any misfortune or struggle that may come to me, as I practice this magnificent profession. Let this lady come in and ask whatever her heart most desires, and the strength of my arm and the unconquerable determination of my brave spirit will provide her with what she seeks."

Chapter Thirty-Seven

— which continues the celebrated tale of Lady Dolorida

The duke and duchess were in seventh heaven, seeing how beautifully Don Quijote had reacted to their plan, but just then Sancho said:

"I don't want this lady messing with my governorship, because once I heard a pharmacist from Toledo, and he could talk like a bird singing, and he said that when this kind of lady gets involved in things, nothing good comes of it. My God, how that pharmacist hated them! Which makes me wonder, since all *dueñas* [ladies, ladies in waiting, matrons, chaperones] have big mouths and they're all a pain in the neck, no matter how well-born they are or what sort they seem to be, what the ones in trouble are going to be like, because this one's in trouble, this countess Truffle or Trifle or whatever her name is? Anyway, where I come from truffles aren't trifles and trifles aren't truffles."

"Be still, Sancho, my friend," said Don Quijote, "because if this lady from such a distant land comes seeking me, she can't be one of the kind your pharmacist was talking about, especially because she's a countess, and when countesses serve as chaperones or ladies in waiting it's only for queens and empresses, because in their own houses they're in charge and they have other ladies serving *them*."

And then Doña Rodríguez, who happened to be there, spoke up:

"My lady the duchess has other ladies serving *her*, and they too might be countesses, if Fate had so willed, but the people in charge of things are always kings, so let's not have anyone saying bad things about *dueñas*, especially those who happen to be both old and unmarried — not that any such description applies to me, but just that I understand and I can see pretty clearly the advantage an unmarried lady in waiting has over one who's a widow — still, whoever does the shearing has the shears in his hand."

"All the same," replied Sancho, "*dueñas* need a lot of shearing, my barber tells me — but if the rice is already boiling, don't stir it up, even if it's getting sticky."

"Squires," replied Doña Rodríguez, "have always been our enemies, and since they virtually haunt waiting rooms and keep their eyes on everything we do — when they're not saying their prayers, of course, which is most of the time — they waste hour after hour mumbling and gossiping about us, digging up our old skeletons as they bury our reputations. But I'd ship them all off to the galleys, because in spite of these pests we're going to live on in this world, and in the noblest of noble houses, even if we perish of hunger and have to wrap our delicate (or not so delicate) bodies in nothing more than black mourning cloth, the way you cover and hide a dungheap with a tapestry, the day of a parade. By God, if it were up to me, and I had the time, I'd explain to the whole world, not just those present here, there's absolutely no virtue you can't find in a *dueña*."

"I do believe my good Doña Rodríguez is right," said the duchess, "and very right indeed, but — on her own behalf, and for the sake of all *dueñas* — she'd do well to look for some better time to expose that evil-minded pharmacist's wicked opinions, and to cleanse their residue from the heart of our great Sancho Panza."

To which Sancho replied:

"The moment I began to feel governor's blood running in my veins, I stopped wasting time on squirely silliness, so I don't give a good god damn for all the *dueñas* in the world."

This debate about *dueñas* might well have continued, if they hadn't heard the drums and the flute returning, which told them that lady Dolorida was coming. The duchess asked the duke if he ought perhaps to go and welcome her, since she was a countess and highborn.

"On account of her being a countess," answered Sancho, before the duke himself could respond, "I think you both should go and welcome her, but nobody should move a step just because she's a *dueña*."

"Who asked you for your two cents worth, Sancho?" said Don Quijote.

"Who, my lord?" Sancho replied. "I stuck my own nose in, because I know what my two cents are worth, because I'm a squire who's learned the rules of politeness by going to school to you, your grace, you being the most courteous and well-behaved knight in the whole of knighthood — and in things like this, as I've heard your grace say, 'you lose just as much from having a card too many as from having a card too few,' and also 'a word to the wise is sufficient.' "

"You're quite right, Sancho, quite right," said the duke. "Let's go have a look at this countess, and then we can decide how much politeness she deserves."

Just then, the drums and the flute appeared, exactly as they had the first time.

And here, too, our author finished a very short chapter and began the next one, continuing this same adventure, clearly one of the most remarkable in this entire history.

Chapter Thirty-Eight

— the lady Dolorida's misfortunes, as narrated by the lady Dolorida

Behind the three mournful musicians came two files of *dueñas*, as many as a dozen in all, every one of them wearing flowing mourning robes (looking much like the fine wool serge worn by monks and nuns) and long white headdresses fashioned of shimmering Indian cotton, hanging so low that only the hems of the black robes peeped through. And behind them, led by the hand of Trifaldín the White-Bearded, came the Countess Trifaldi, garbed in the most delicate of black baize, the nap so thick that, had the cloth been tufted, each knob would have been fully as large as huge Martos chick peas. The trailing skirt (or train, or tail, or whatever you call it) was divided into three sections, each ending in a point, and each point held up by a page, and each page dressed in mourning, so that the three acute angles formed by pages and points and train traced out a neat geometrical shape, so that everyone who beheld the triangulated skirt could easily see why the countess' name had to be 'The Countess Trifaldi' [*tri* = three, *falda* = skirt], as if we were saying *la condesa de las Tres Faldas*, or 'The Three-Skirted Countess' — and indeed Sidi Hamid Benengeli records that the countess' real name was *la condesa Lobuna* [*condesa* = countess, *loba* = she-wolf or priest's cassock], because on the estate where she'd grown up there were a lot of wolves and, had they been vixen [*zorras*] rather than wolves, she'd have been known as *la condesa Zorruna* [*zorra* = vixen or prostitute], since it was the custom in those regions for lords of the manor to take their names from the thing or things most abundant on their estates. Just the same, in the interests of her skirt's novelty and high fashion, this countess dropped the title of Lobuna and assumed that of Trifaldi.

The lady and her twelve *dueñas* approached with the solemn slowness of a religious processional; all their faces were covered with black veils that were not transparent, like Trifaldín's, and in fact were so tightly woven that nothing whatever could be seen through them.

When the entire squadron of *dueñas* was visible, the duke, the duchess, and Don Quijote rose to their feet, along with the others who were watching the slow processional. The twelve *dueñas* came to a halt, then shaped a lane between them, down which came Dolorida, still holding Trifaldín's hand and, seeing this, the duke, the duchess, and Don Quijote came twelve paces forward, to welcome her. Kneeling before them, her voice more rough and hoarse than soft and delicate, Dolorida said:

"Your majesties need not do such honor to this your hand-servant — I mean, this your hand-maiden — but I am so overwhelmed with sorrow that I'll never be able to say what I ought to, because my strange and unheard-of misfortune has carried off my brains I don't know where, but it must be a very long way, since the more I look for them the less I can find them."

"Anyone who failed to recognize your importance, lady," replied the duke, "would indeed be witless, for you obviously show yourself worthy of the very cream of courtesy and the absolute flower of civilized ceremony."

Whereupon, raising her by the hand, he led her to a bench alongside the duchess, who similarly welcomed her most politely.

Don Quijote stayed silent, and Sancho was fairly bursting to see Countess Trifaldi's face, or the face of any of her numerous *dueñas*, though there was plainly nothing he could do about it until it pleased them to willingly reveal themselves.

Indeed, the silence was universal, as everyone waited to see who might first break it — which Dolorida did, speaking these words:

"I am confident, most potent potentate, and loveliest of ladies, and wisest and most sensible of all bystanders, that my infinite grief must surely find asylum in your bravest of all breasts (every bit as serene as they are magnanimous and sorrowful), because my misfortune should be sufficient to soften marble itself, as well as thaw the hardness of adamant and melt the most steely-hearted hearts in all the world — but before it finds room in your hearing, not to say in your ears, I would wish you to inform me whether there is to be found in this company, or group, or congregation, that purest of all pure knights, Don Quijote, the Mostest of La Mancha, and that Squire of all Squires, Panza."

"That Panza," answered Sancho, before anyone else could speak, "is right here, and that Mostest of La Mancha and Quijoteed of all Quijotes too, so all you have to do, oh most saddest of all most sorrowingest ladies, is to tell us what you most of all mostnesses would like, which we'll be the quickest of quicknesses and readiest of readinesses to be at your most service of servicenesses to do."

Don Quijote immediately addressed the sorrowing lady:

"If your grief, oh afflicted lady, can have any hope of remedy from the courage and strength of a knight errant, let me hereby offer you mine, and weak and limited as they are, they are entirely at your service. I am Don Quijote de La Mancha, whose task it is to help all those in need — and that being the case, my lady, as it most assuredly is, there is no need to woo my benevolence or hunt for introductory approaches, but simply tell your misfortune straight out, with no evasions, and those who hear you will at least have compassion, whether or not they can provide any remedy for such sadness."

Hearing this, Dolorida made as if to throw herself at Don Quijote's feet, and then did so and, while struggling to wrap her arms around his legs, declared:

"I cast myself down before these feet and these legs, oh invincible knight! for these are the pillars and foundations of knight errantry. I wish to kiss these feet, for from their steps will hang and dangle the only cure for my misfortune. Oh brave errant, whose glorious and factual deeds will cast into the shade and forever darken the famous doings of all the Amadíses, and the Esplandianes, and the Belianises!"

And then, suddenly abandoning Don Quijote, she turned to Sancho Panza and, gripping his hands, said:

"And you! The most loyal of all squires who ever served a knight errant, now or in any past century, you whose goodness is even longer than my faithful companion Trifaldín's beard, here you are! Well may you proclaim that, in serving the great Don Quijote, you in effect serve the whole mob of knights who have ever borne arms anywhere in the world. I entreat you, in the name of your own faithful goodness: intercede for me with your master, so he will come swiftly to the aid of this your most humble and most unfortunate of all countesses."

To which Sancho replied:

"My lady, as far as my goodness being as big and as long as your squire's beard, it doesn't seem to me very likely; I hope my soul, at least, will have a beard and whiskers when it comes to leaving this life, because that's what matters,[1] because whether I have a skinny beard or no beard at all, while I'm still here, isn't going to do anything for me, one way or the other, but you don't need to flatter me or beg me, because of course I'll intercede with my master to protect and help your grace in any way he can, since I certainly know he loves me, especially right now when he needs me for a certain business we have in hand. So you can cough up your grief and let us hear all about it, and then leave it to us, because we understand everything."

The duke and duchess were choking with laughter, hearing all this, and so too were the others who knew what was going on, and they were quietly congratulating Trifaldi on her wit and her acting ability. The sorrowful countess then returned to her seat and began her story:

"The queen of the famous kingdom of Candaya, which lies between the great Trapobana and the Southern Sea, seven or eight miles beyond Cape Comorín, was my lady Doña Maguncia, King Archipiela's widow, who had been her lord and her husband; their marriage produced the princess Antonomasia,[2] heiress to the throne, who was raised under my tutelage and care, because I was both the oldest and highest ranking of her mother's ladies in waiting. So time passed and little Antonomasia grew to be fourteen years old, and so utterly beautiful that Nature could not have created a greater perfection of loveliness. And let me tell you, she wasn't so dumb, either! She was as sensible as she was beautiful, and she was the most beautiful girl in the world — and still is, for that matter, unless the jealous and hard-hearted Fates have clipped the thread of her life. But no, they won't have, because Heaven wouldn't let them do such a wicked thing to the Earth, snatching away, still unripe and on the vine, such a budding blossom of beauty. My clumsy tongue can't praise her beauty as it ought to be praised, but an infinity of princes from all over the world were in love with her, and among all those who dared pray to Heaven that he might win such beauty there was, in particular, one gentleman at court who staked his claim on his youth, his gallantry, his many talents and charms, and the quick cleverness of his mind, because you've got to understand, your highnesses, if I'm not going on too much and too long, that when he played a guitar he made it talk, and what's more he was a poet, and a fantastic dancer, and he could make bird cages so well

---

1. Reference to a joke about a beardless man (a eunuch?) who hoped his soul had a moustache and beard, because his body didn't need any [*Translator's Note*].

2. *Candaya* = an imaginary name; *Trapobana* = old name for Ceylon; *Cape Comorin* = south of India, east of Ceylon; *Maguncia* = Latin name for the city of Mainz, in Germany; *Archipiela* = variation on "archipelago"; *Antonomasia* = name used as a generic epithet (e.g., a Hitler = a tyrant, a J. P. Morgan = fabulously wealthy and powerful man) [*Translator's Note*].

that, if he'd been forced to, he could have made his living doing just that
and nothing else, and talents and charms like this are enough to move a
mountain, not just a tender young girl. But all his gallantry and good
humor, and all his charms and talents, would have been of little or no
use in conquering my little girl, except that the shameless rascal was careful, first, to win *me* over. Cold-blooded scoundrel and good-for-nothing
that he was, he won my good-will and bought my affection, so that, wicked
watchman that I was, I handed over the keys to the fortress I was supposed
to be guarding. What I mean, he flattered me and conquered my will with
jewels and who-knows-what other gifts — but, even more than that, what
brought me to the ground was a poem I heard him sing, one night, while
standing near a window-grille that opens out on the street where he lived,
and unless I remember it wrong it went:

> She, my sweet, my beautiful foe,
> Has wounded my heart to the quick,
> And the sorest tormenting pain and sickness
> Is having to suffer but let no one know.[3]

To me, these verses seemed like pearls, as his voice was like the sweetest
syrup of honey — and from that moment on, let me tell you, after seeing
what wickedness could be worked by these and others of his poems, it has
seemed to me that sensible and well-ordered republics really ought to
banish all their poets, as Plato advised — or, at least, the lustful poets,
because what they write, unlike ballads about the Marqués of Mantua
(which make women and little boys weep), has a keen, biting edge to it,
piercing the heart like smooth-coated thorns, and like flashes of lightning,
inflicting inner wounds without leaving any outer marks. Another time,
he sang:

> Come, you dark and hidden Death,
> Creep so silent I never hear you,
> Give me no chance to love or fear you
> Lest, loving, I wish to draw more breath.[4]

There were other poems, too, enchanting when sung, and astonishing
when written. And then, when they take the trouble to write the kind of
poetry that was popular in Candaya, back then, the kind they call *seguidillas!*[5] Ah, then hearts go dancing about, laughter comes leaping, feet start
tapping and, finally, all your senses are on fire. So what I say, my lords, is
that such troubadors have earned the right to be banished, sent off to
tropical islands far from civilization. But the blame isn't really theirs: it's
the fools who praise and the idiots who believe them — and if I'd been
as good a *dueña* as I should have been, their hackneyed ideas would never
have affected me, nor would I have seen any truth in things like 'I live in
death, I burn in ice, I shiver in the flames, I hope without hope, I leave
and yet I remain', and all the other idiocies of that sort, with which their
writing is stuffed. And when they offer you the Arabian Phoenix, and

3. Translated from the Italian of Serafino dell'Aquila (1466–1500) [*Translator's Note*].
4. Adapted from a poem by Knight Commander Escrivá, of Valencia, published in 1511 [*Translator's
Note*].
5. A form associated with the driving, passionate music of flamenco [*Translator's Note*].

Aridiana's[6] crown, and the horses of the Sun, and an Ocean of Pearls, and all the gold in Tíbar plus all the balsam in Pancaya! That's when they really let their pens loose, because how much does it cost to promise what you know you can't possibly deliver?

"But why am I wandering so far from my tale? Ah me, how unlucky I am! What madness — what foolishness — drives me to talk of other people's mistakes, when there's so much to say about my own? And once again, ah me! Oh luckless woman that I am! Because it was not poetry that overcame me, but my own folly; it was not music that melted my heart, but my own fickleness: it was my profound stupidity and careless indifference that opened the road and cleared away the path down which Don Clavijo proceeded — for that is the name of the gentleman I've been speaking of — and thus it was, I being his intermediary, that claiming the rights of a husband he first came, and came thereafter many times, to Antonomasia's bedroom, for it was not he who was her deceiver, but me, even though, sinner that I am, I'd never have let him come close to the sole of her shoe, had it not been that he came as her husband. No, no, not like that! If I'm going to be involved in any business like this, marriage has to come first! But in this case there was an additional problem, which was that they weren't truly equals, because Don Clavijo was just an ordinary gentleman, and the Princess Antonomasia, as I've said, was heiress to the throne. Well, this whole mess was hidden for a while, because I was good at such sly tricks, but then I saw it wouldn't be long before everything was out in the open, because I saw a certain swelling in Antonomasia's belly, so fear led the three of us to take counsel together, and we decided that, before this unfortunate message grew fully clear, Don Clavijo should ask the court chaplain to make his marriage to Antonomasia official, according to the terms of a marriage contract I'd drafted for them myself, and I'd drawn it up so tightly that Samson himself couldn't have broken it. What had to be done was done, the chaplain saw the contract and heard the lady's confession, which was absolutely unconditional, so he sent her to stay at the house of a very respectable court judge — "

At this, Sancho suddenly said:

"So Candaya has court judges, as well as poets, and *seguidillas*, which makes me ready to swear that the whole world is all the same. But you'd better hurry up, my lady Trifaldi, because it's getting late and I'm dying to get to the end of this long story."

"Indeed, I'll hurry," replied the countess.

Chapter Thirty-Nine

— in which the Countess Trifaldi continues her stupendous, infinitely memorable tale

Every time Sancho spoke, the duchess was as delighted as Don Quijote was infuriated, but all the same she told him to be quiet, and Dolorida went on as follows:

6. Rural corruption of Ariadne [*Translator's Note*].

"To make a long story short, after all sorts of writs and replies, the chaplain ruled in favor of Don Clavijo, because the princess stuck to her guns and never varied even an inch from what she'd said the first time, so she was handed over to him as his legal wife, which was so upsetting to Queen Maguncia, the Princess Antonomasia's mother, that it wasn't three days before we buried her."

"She had to be dead, of course," said Sancho.

"That's for sure!" replied Trifaldín, "because in Candaya we don't bury live people, just dead ones."

"Well, Señor Squire," answerered Sancho, "I've seen them bury a man who'd fainted, thinking he was dead, and it seems to me that Queen Maguncia certainly had to faint before she died and, as long as you're still alive, as kinds of things can still be fixed up, because after all, what the princess did wasn't so wildly foolish that her mother had to be as offended as all that. If the lady had married one of her pages, or some other house servant, which often happens, as far as I've heard it said, then the damage would be past repairing, but after she'd married a gentleman as well-bred and clever as this one we've been hearing about, well, to tell the truth, it was foolish, but not so foolish as you might think, because according to what my master says about the law — and he's right here, and he won't let me tell a lie — if learned men can become bishops, it's easy to turn knights, especially if they're knights errant, into kings and emperors."

"You're quite right, Sancho," said Don Quijote, "because a knight errant, if he has even a little bit of luck, is always well positioned and placed to become the most powerful lord on earth. But let Lady Dolorida go on, because I venture to say she still has to come to the bitter part of this story, which to her has certainly been sweet enough."

"Oh how much bitterness is still to come!" replied the countess. "And such exceedingly bitter bitterness that, in comparison, an emetic seems sweet and hemlock delightful. So: the queen was dead when we buried her, yes, not in a faint, and the last shovelful of dirt had scarcely covered her over, and we had barely spoken our last *vale* [farewell], when

quis talia fando temperet a lachrymis?[1]
[Who, hearing this, could keep back his tears?]

For just then, directly over the queen's tomb, and mounted on a wooden horse, there appeared the giant Malambruno, Maguncia's first cousin, who in addition to his cruelty is also a magician, and in order to avenge his cousin's death, and to punish Don Clavijo for his boldness and daring, as well as out of annoyance at Antonomasia's audacity, he cast spells which reduced them both to figurines on the queen's tomb, she transformed into a bronze monkey, and he turned into a ghastly crocodile fashioned of some unknown metal, with a tall metallic column set between them, on which was recorded, in Syriac, an inscription which, translated first into Candayan, and afterwards into Spanish, contains the following sentence:

---

1. Virgil, *Aeneid*, II, 6–8 [*Translator's Note*].

These two rash lovers shall not be changed back to their original form until the brave Knight of La Mancha comes to meet me in combat, hand to hand, for the Fates have reserved this unparalleled adventure only for his great courage.

"And, having cast these spells, he unsheathed a monstrously broad scimitar, seized me by the hair, and made as if to slice right through my neck and cut my head off. I trembled; my voice seemed to be stuck in my throat; I was violently agitated; but just the same I took heart as best I could and, my words emerging shakily and with great sorrow, I told him, and kept telling him, such things that, finally, he abandoned so rigorous a punishment. Then he had all the *dueñas* in the palace brought before him, who were the ladies you see before you here, and after having vastly over-inflated our guilt, and reviled the characters of all ladies in waiting, their bad habits and even worse schemes and plots[2] — blaming everyone for what I alone was responsible — he declared that he did not wish us to suffer capital punishment, but rather to inflict more drawn-out penalties, which would amount to a kind of perpetual living death — and even as he spoke we could all feel the very pores of our faces opening, pricking at us like needle points. And when we raised our hands to our faces, we found them as, now, you shall see them."

Swiftly, Dolorida and the other *dueñas* lifted their veils and revealed their faces, which were all bearded, some red, some black, some white, and some splattered black and red — a sight which amazed the duke and duchess, dumbfounded Don Quijote and Sancho, and generally astonished everyone who was there.

The Countess Trifaldi went on:

"Thus has Malambruno punished our wicked idleness, covering over our soft, smooth faces with these rough, coarse bristles — and if only it had pleased Heaven, instead, that he cut off our heads with his wild scimitar, rather than darken the light of our faces by covering them with this goathair, because if you really think about it, gentlemen (and what I am going to say, now, I wish I could say with tears flowing from my eyes, except that meditating on our misfortune, and the oceans of tears we've already shed, has left us as empty and dry as chaff on the threshing floor — and thus, as I say, quite tearless), really think about it, where can a bearded lady-in-waiting possibly go? Since, even with a smooth complexion and a face tortured by a thousand varieties of cosmetic potions and creams, she can scarcely find anyone who will want her, how should it be when she's seen with a forest growing over her face? Oh my old friends, my fellow *dueñas*, we were born under an evil star, and our fathers were not at their best when they conceived us!"

And, as she said these words, she seemed about to swoon.

---

2. *Trazas* = schemes, plans, but it also means "looks, appearance." The pun is untranslatable [*Translator's Note*].

Chapter Forty

— certain matters relevant to this adventure and
to this remarkable history

Everyone who enjoys stories like this ought to be really and truly grateful to Sidi Hamid, our original author, for the care he has taken to report all these details to us, omitting nothing, no matter how small or minute, and shedding a clear light on everything. He has told us what people were thinking, how their minds worked, answered questions, cleared up doubts, and resolved disputes and, in short, given even the most inquisitive among us every speck of information he might want. Oh most justly famous author! Oh fortunate Don Quijote! Oh celebrated Dulcinea! Oh charming Sancho Panza! May each and all of you live down the infinite ages, for the pleasure and entertainment of those who shall live after you.

Our history then records that, seeing Dolorida falling over in a faint, Sancho said:

"I swear by my faith as a man of standing, and in the name of the generations of Panzas who came before me, that I've never heard nor seen, nor has my master ever told me about, nor has it ever crossed his mind to tell me of, an adventure like this one. May a thousand demons take you — not that I mean to curse you, Malambruno, you being both a magician and a giant — but couldn't you find some other kind of punishment for these sinners, without growing beards on them? Wouldn't it have been better, because it certainly could have been more to the point, to take away maybe the lower half of their noses, even though that might make them speak nasally, instead of giving them beards? I'll bet they don't even have enough money to get themselves shaved."

"Now that's true, my lord," said one of the twelve ladies in waiting, "because we haven't got the money to get this stuff cleaned off our faces, so, as a cheap way out, some of us have tried using sticking plasters and all kinds of gummy patches, and when we yank them off they leave us as smooth and even as the bottom of a grindstone, because even though Candaya has women who go from house to house, taking off hair and plucking eyebrows, and assisting women with other cosmetics, we've never been willing to let them in, as ladies in waiting to our señora, since most of them look like pimps, or whores past their prime,[1] so if my lord Don Quijote doesn't help us, we'll wear our beards to our graves."

"I'll peel my own beard off," said Don Quijote, "in the land of the Moors,[2] if I don't take care of yours."

Just then Trifaldi returned to consciousness, and said:

"The sound of that promise, oh brave knight, reached my ears even in the middle of my swoon, and helped me recover and regain my senses, so let me beg you, once again, illustrious errant and dauntless lord, to turn your gracious words into deeds."

"I shall not delay," replied Don Quijote. "Decide, my lady, what you wish me to do, for I am more than ready to serve you."

---

1. Another untranslatable pun: *terceras* = pimps, third parties; *primas* = prime, first [*Translator's Note*].
2. Many Moors let their beards grow long, because barbers were coarse rascals [*Translator's Note*].

"The fact is," answered Dolorida, "that the distance from here to Candaya, if one travels overland, is fifteen thousand miles, give or take a couple, but if you go through the air, and in a direct line, it's only nine thousand two hundred and twenty-seven. Now, you also have to know that Malambruno told me, when Fate should supply me with the knight meant to liberate us, he himself would send that knight a steed worth far more, and afflicted with fewer flaws, than any rented animal, because it would be the same wooden horse which bore the brave Pierres when he stole away the fair Magalona,[3] an animal that's steered by means of a peg set in its forehead, for this peg serves as its bit, and the horse flies through the air so easily and rapidly that it feels as if the Devil himself were guiding it. According to ancient tradition, this horse was created by the magician Merlin, who lent it to Pierres, his good friend; Pierres used it for long journeys and, as I've said, employed it to steal away the fair Magalona, who sat mounted behind him as it soared through the air, stupefying everyone who saw them from the earth below. Merlin only lent it to those he loved or who paid the highest fees, and from the time of the great Pierres to right now there is no record of anyone ever riding this horse again. Malambruno employed his magic arts to steal the animal from Pierres, and has kept it for himself, using it on the various journeys he's always making to this or that part of the world, so that today he's here, and tomorrow he's in France, and the next day in Potosí [Bolivia] — and the best part of it is that this horse neither eats nor sleeps nor wears out the shoes on its hooves, but just ambles along through the air so smoothly and calmly, though it has no wings, that whoever is riding on its back could carry a glass of water in his hand and never spill a drop, which made the fair Magalona really enjoy riding on it."

At this Sancho said:

"For a smooth, calm ride, I'll take my dapple donkey, even though he doesn't go through the air — but on the ground, I'll match him against any amblers anywhere in the world."

Everyone laughed, and Dolorida continued:

"And if Malambruno's really willing to see the end of our misfortunes, this horse should be here among us before this very night is half an hour old, because Malambruno explained that the signal he'd give me, if I'd really found the knight I was seeking, would be to promptly send me the horse, wherever I might be."

"And how many can ride on this horse?" asked Sancho.

Dolorida answered:

"Two people — one in the saddle, and the other behind him, on its haunches, and these two persons are usually a knight and his squire, except when there's a kidnapped maiden."

"My lady Dolorida," said Sancho, "I'd also like to know the name of this horse."

"It isn't the same," answered Dolorida, "as Bellerophon's horse, which was called Pegasus, nor the same as Alexander the Great's, which was

---

3. The wooden horse, Magalona, and Pierres all have a long literary history, beginning in the late thirteenth century with the French poet Adenet li Rois' *Thousand and One Nights* [*Translator's Note*].

called Bucephalus, nor the same as Wild Orlando's, which was called
Brigliador, and it isn't called Bayard, as was Reinaldo de Montalbán's
horse, or Frontino, which was Ruggiero's, and it isn't called Bootes or
Peritoa, which is what they say the horses of the Sun are called, nor is it
named Orelia, which was the name of the unfortunate Rodrigo's horse,
that last King of the Goths, when he rode into the battle where he lost
both his kingdom and his life."

"Since they haven't given it any of those famous horses' names," said
Sancho, "I'll bet they didn't borrow one from my master's horse, Rocinante, either — and it's a better name than any of those you've mentioned, because it really fits him."

"That's true," answered the bearded countess, "but they chose a very
appropriate one, anyway, because it's called Clavileño [little peg] the Fleet,
which is a suitable name because it's made of wood, and it has a peg in
its forehead, and it goes fast, so as far as names go it can certainly compare
with your famous Rocinante."

"I don't dislike that name," replied Sancho. "But is he steered by his
bit or by his halter rope?"

"As I told you," answered the countess, "it's with the peg, which you
turn this way or that, and then the knight who's riding on him can make
him go whichever way he wants, either high up through the air or skimming along just over the earth, practically sweeping the ground, or else
neither too high nor too low, which is what should be sought and is in
fact aimed for in all properly conducted flying."

"I'd like to see it," responded Sancho. "But if you expect me to ride on
this animal, sitting either in the saddle or behind it, you're asking for the
moon. Good Lord, I can barely stay up on my own donkey, and he's got
a packsaddle softer than silk — and you think I'm going to set myself on
bare wood, without a pillow or any kind of cushion! By God, I'm not
interested in getting all beaten up, just to take off anybody's beard! Let
everybody shave himself the best way he knows how, because I'm not going
on such a long trip with my master. Especially since I can't do anything
about this shaving off of beards, the way I can with disenchanting my lady
Dulcinea."

"But you can, my friend," said the countess, "and indeed, I know that
without your being there, there'll be nothing we can do."

"God help me!" said Sancho. "What business do squires have, messing
with their masters' adventures? Are they supposed to win all the fame,
while we take all the trouble? Mother of God! So let the chroniclers say:
'Such and such a knight accomplished such and such an adventure, but
without the help of so and so, his squire, the whole thing would have been
impossible.' But all they write is: 'The adventure of the six monsters was
performed by Don Paralipomenón of the Three Stars,' and they don't so
much as name his squire (who had to be there the whole time), just as if
he'd never even existed! So let me tell you again, my lords: my master can
go by himself, and much good may it do him, because I'm staying right
here, along with my lady the duchess, and maybe by the time he comes
back he'll find my lady Dulcinea's business a lot further along the road,
because when I'm not busy with other things, and I have some free time,

I plan to give myself such a lot of lashes that my hide will never be whole again."

"All the same, my good Sancho," said the duchess, "if your presence is necessary you have to go, because these ladies' faces can't stay covered with stubble just because of your silly fears: that would be very bad indeed."

"Oh God help me all over again!" replied Sancho. "If this were a charitable service for some modest, sheltered maidens, or a pack of little orphan girls, maybe it would be worth going to a lot of trouble, but to go through all this just to take the beards off some ladies in waiting? That's a hell of a business! I'd rather see beards on the whole lot of them, from the top all the way down, and from the most finicky to the most hypocritical!"

"You don't care for ladies in waiting, Sancho my friend," the duchess continued. "You stand right in line, directly behind the pharmacist from Toledo. But indeed you're quite wrong, for in my house I have ladies in waiting who could serve as models for all *dueñas* everywhere — like my lady Doña Rodríguez, who wouldn't let me say anything different if I wanted to."

"Say it, if you want to, Your Excellency," said Doña Rodríguez, "because God knows the truth, and whether ladies in waiting are good or bad, bearded or hairless, our mothers bore us the same as all other women, and since God put us in the world, He surely knows why, and I rely on His mercy, and not on anyone's beard."

"Well, my lady Rodríguez," said Don Quijote, "and my lady Trifaldi, and all those here present, I hope Heaven looks down on your afflictions with benevolent eyes. Let Sancho do what I tell him to do, and your magic horse appear, and I stand face to face with Malambruno, and I'm sure no razor can shave your lovely faces more readily than my sword will shave Malambruno's head from his shoulders, because even though God tolerates evil-doers, His patience is not infinite."

"Ah!" exclaimed Dolorida. "May all the stars in the high celestial regions smile kindly down at your highness, brave knight, and breathe into your heart all the good things, and the courage, to make you the shield and protector of the reviled and humiliated race of *dueñas*, loathed by pharmacists, gossiped about by squires, and cheated by pages, for woe betide the unhappy woman who, in the flower of her youth, has not chosen rather to be a nun than a lady in waiting. We are miserable unfortunates, all of us! Though we may be descended in a straight line, from one generation to the next, beginning with Hector the Trojan, our mistresses won't condescend to treat us like equals, because it makes them feel like queens! Oh you giant Malambruno, you may be a magician but you keep your promises! Send us your matchless magic horse, so our misery may be ended — because if we still have our beards, by the time the heat of summer arrives, woe is me for the trouble we'll have!"

Trifaldi said this with such emotion that everyone's eyes grew damp, even Sancho's, and he made up his mind to go with his master, even to the ends of the earth, if only he could help take the stubble off those venerable faces.

Chapter Forty-One

— the arrival of the magic horse, and the end of this long,
drawn-out adventure

Night fell, and then the hour when the famous horse, Clavileño, was supposed to appear, but the animal was late and Don Quijote was unhappy, imagining that, since Malambruno was taking so long about sending it, either Don Quijote de La Mancha was not the knight for whom this adventure had been reserved, or that Malambruno was afraid to face him in hand-to-hand combat. But hold! See, yonder, there come into the garden four wildmen, dressed all in green ivy leaves, carrying on their shoulders a huge wooden horse. They set it down on the ground, and one of the savages said:

"Let anyone who is brave enough mount this machine."

"Me," said Sancho, "I'm not mounting it, because I'm not brave enough, and besides, I'm not a knight."

The savage went on:

"And let the squire sit behind, if the knight has a squire, and you may trust the word of the brave Malambruno that no sword of his shall strike the squire, nor anyone else's sword, either, nor will any other harm be done him, nor any insult be offered. All you need do is turn this pin, here on the horse's neck, and the animal will carry you through the air, to where Malambruno awaits you; however, since the altitude and the sublime state of the road to be traveled might otherwise cause dizziness, the riders' eyes must be covered until the horse neighs, which will indicate that their journey has been completed."

Having said this, the four wildmen left Clavileño and, politely and gallantly, turned and went back from whence they'd come. Dolorida, almost in tears as soon as she saw the horse, said to Don Quijote:

"Oh brave knight, Malambruno's promises have been kept; the horse is here, our beards are growing, and each and every one of us, with each and every hair on our faces, implores you to shave and shear us, for all you need do, now, is to mount this beast, together with your squire, and happily begin your novel journey."

"As indeed I will, my lady Countess Trifaldi," said Don Quijote, "very gladly and with great good will, not pausing to pack a suitcase, nor put on my spurs, lest I delay any longer, so deeply do I yearn to see you, my lady, and all these other *dueñas*, with your faces smooth and well-trimmed."

"But I won't," said Sancho, "neither with bad will nor good, and not under any circumstances at all, and if this shaving can't get done unless I climb up behind, then my master can find himself another squire to go with him, and these ladies can think of a different way of smoothing their faces, because I'm no sorcerer who likes traveling through the air. Besides, what would my islanders say, if they knew their governor went riding around on the wind? And another thing: since it's nine thousand miles and more from here to Candaya, what happens if the horse gets tired, or the giant gets mad, and keeps us from coming back for half a dozen years, then I won't have an island or any islanders who might recognize me, and they always say that delay is dangerous, and when someone wants to give you a cow, get yourself a rope, these ladies' beards will just have to excuse me, because Saint Peter is off in Rome, by God — what I mean is that I'm perfectly happy right here, where I'm treated so well, and where I have high hopes the lord of the house will make me a governor."

The duke then said:

"Sancho my friend, the island I've promised you isn't going anywhere; it won't escape: its roots are so deep they reach all the way into the earth's very abysses, so they can't be pulled out or moved with a tug or two, and since you know quite as well as I do that you can't get any important post without some sort of bribe — maybe a big one, maybe a little one: whatever — what I want from you, in return for this governorship, is that you go with your master, Don Quijote, and put the finishing touches on this extraordinary adventure, so whether you come back on Clavileño, traveling as swiftly as his lightfootedness promises, or whether obstinate Fortune forces you to return on foot, traveling like a pilgrim, from one tavern to the next and from one inn to the one after it, whenever you get here you'll find your island exactly where you left it, and your islanders will be as happy to welcome you as their governor as they ever were, and my goodwill, too, will be unchanged, nor should you doubt a word of this, Señor Sancho, because that would be to seriously offend against my desire to be of service to you."

"Enough, my lord," said Sancho. "I'm just a poor squire, I can't handle all that polite talk, so let my master mount, then wrap up these eyes of mine and commend me to God — and tell me, please, if while we're flying through all those heights I can still pray to the Lord or ask the angels to come protect me."[1]

To which the countess answered:

"You can certainly pray to God, Sancho, or to anyone you like, because even though Malambruno is a magician he's also a Christian, and he performs his enchantments wisely and carefully, so he offends against nothing and no one."

"Now then," said Sancho, "may God and the Holy Trinity of Gaeta[2] help me!"

"Since our remarkable adventure with the hydraulic hammers," said Don Quijote, "I've never seen Sancho as afraid as he is now, and if I were as superstitious as most people, his cowardice would make my courage waver a bit. Please step over this way, Sancho: with these noble lords' and ladies' permission, I wish to speak a few words with you, in private."

Taking Sancho off among some trees, and grasping both his hands, he said:

"Seeing the long journey we have ahead of us, Sancho my brother, from which only God knows when we will return or what time and opportunities we will have, during this whole business, I suggest that, here and now, you retire to your room, as if going to hunt for something you'll

---

1. I.e., in accepting the fruits of magic, Sancho wonders if he has implicitly denied himself the grace of God [Translator's Note].

2. Italian monastery, traditionally invoked by sailors [Translator's Note].

need on the voyage, and, quick as a wink, give yourself a good dose of those three thousand three hundred lashes you're bound to lay on your back — say at least five hundred — because to have a job started, you know, is to have it half finished."

"Mother of God!" said Sancho. "You've really got to be out of your mind, your grace! It's like saying, 'You see me carrying a child, so you tell me to be a virgin!' Just when I have to go who knows where, and with who knows what, your grace wants me to whip my own ass? Oh, your grace, that really makes a lot of sense. Let's just go get these *dueñas* shaved, because when we get back, let me tell you right now, your grace, either my name isn't Sancho Panza or I'll finish that lashing business one, two, three quick, and you'll be satisfied, and I don't want to say anything else."

Don Quijote answered:

"I'll take comfort in that promise, my good Sancho, and trust you to do exactly as you say, because in truth, though you may be stupid, you're a veracious man."

"I'm not voracious," said Sancho, "just hungry — but even if I was, just a little, I'd still do what I said I would."

Then they went back to mount Clavileño and, as he was about to climb into the saddle, Don Quijote said:

"Just close your eyes, Sancho, and climb up, for anyone who sends for us, from such far-off lands, would not bother deceiving us, simply for the petty glory of tricking people who trust his word — and even should this whole adventure turn out exactly the opposite of how I imagine it, no malice in the world can dim the glory of having undertaken this great deed."

"Let's get going, my lord," said Sancho, "for the beards and the tears of these ladies have really pierced me to the quick, and I'm not going to enjoy a bite of food until I see them as smooth and clean-faced as they used to be. You get up, your grace, and let them blindfold you first, because it's plain that if I'm supposed to sit behind you, first you have to be in the saddle."

"Quite true," replied Don Quijote.

He drew out a handkerchief and asked Dolorida to tie it tightly across his eyes, but then, when this had been done, he lifted the handkerchief away and said:

"Unless I remember it wrongly, I've read in Virgil that the Palladium of Troy[3] was a wooden horse that the Greeks dedicated to the god Pallas Athena, and it was then stuffed full of armed knights who thereafter caused the total destruction of Troy, and so it would be good to have a look, first, to see what Clavileño here has in his stomach."

"That won't be necessary," said Dolorida, "because I know Malambruno, and I trust him, and there's nothing malicious or treacherous about him: you may mount, my lord Don Quijote, without the slightest fear — and indeed, should anything go wrong, you may hold me personally responsible."

---

3. The Palladium of Troy was in fact a sacred image of the goddess Pallas Athena, stolen from Troy by the Greek heroes Odysseus and Diomedes [*Translator's Note*].

Don Quijote felt that making an issue of his safety might well cast a shadow on his reputation for courage, and so, without any further discussion, he climbed up on Clavileño and took hold of the wooden peg, which he found moved quite easily; since he wore no spurs, and his legs therefore hung loose, he looked very much like a figure in a Flemish tapestry, painted or woven into the scene of a Roman triumph. Sancho inched his way up, grumpily, and settled himself as best he could on the animal's haunches, which he found hard and not a bit smooth, so he asked the duke, if at all possible, to furnish him with a cushion or a pillow, even if it had to be taken from the duchess' chair or some page's bed, because this horse's haunches seemed to him more like marble than wood.

But the countess informed him that no harness or any other kind of trapping or adornment could be put on Clavileño, and perhaps the best thing to do would be to sit sideways, like a woman, so he didn't feel the hardness quite so acutely. Murmuring, "It's God's will," Sancho did as she suggested, but even then he could be heard sighing; then he looked yearningly and tearfully at everyone in the garden, and said they could help him, in this hour of his difficulty, if they would say paternosters and avemarias for him, so that, should they themselves ever find themselves in a similar crisis, God would provide someone to pray for them, too. At which point Don Quijote said:

"You thief, do you really think you're up on the gallows, or facing the final moment of your life, and need to use such pitiful language? You worthless, cowardly creature, aren't you sitting in exactly the same place once occupied by the fair Magalona — who, when she descended from this horse's back, did not go down to her grave, but — if the histories tell us the truth — to the throne of all France? And I, whom you see at your side, am I not the equal of brave Pierres, who squeezed into this same seat I have now squeezed myself into? Cover your eyes, cover your eyes, you faint-hearted beast, and keep your fears to yourself, at least in my presence."

"Blindfold me," replied Sancho, "and since you don't want me to pray to God, or have anyone else pray for me, is it any wonder I'm afraid there's some brand[4] of devils around here, who'll carry us off to the firing squad?"

Once they were both blindfolded, and Don Quijote considered himself sufficiently settled in the saddle, he reached out for the wooden peg — and had barely touched it with his fingers when all the *dueñas* and everyone else present began to call out:

"May God guide you, oh brave knight!"

"God be with you, fearless squire!"

"Oh, how quickly you're flying through the air, tearing along faster than arrows from a bow!"

"Lord, now you're starting to astonish anyone who looks up and sees you so high in the sky!"

"Watch out, brave Sancho, and don't lean over! Be careful not to fall,

---

4. Sancho says *región*, "region," instead of *legión*, "legion"; the translation attempts to replicate this with "brand" for "band" [*Translator's Note*].

because it would be a worse tumble than that reckless boy took, when he tried to hold the reins of the sun chariot, the way his father did!"

Hearing these cries, Sancho grabbed hold of his master and wrapped both arms around him:

"My lord, how can they say we're going so high, if their voices come up this far and still sound like they're talking right next to us?"

"Pay no attention to that, Sancho, because none of these things, these flying expeditions, travel by ordinary paths, so even from a thousand miles away you can see and hear anything you want to. And stop holding me so tight, because you might make me fall — and, frankly, I can't understand why you're so upset and fearful, because let me tell you, and I can swear to this, I've never in all my life ridden on a horse with such a smooth gait: it almost seems as if we're not moving at all. So drive away your fears, my friend, because this magical beast is doing exactly what it's supposed to do — and we even have a stern wind blowing us on."

"That's true," answered Sancho, "because on this side, here, I feel a wind so strong it's like a thousand bellows puffing away."

Which was also true, because there were indeed some great bellows blowing air at them, the duke and his steward having arranged their adventure so carefully that nothing needed to bring it off to perfection had been omitted.

Feeling the wind, Don Quijote said:

"Clearly, Sancho, we must have risen into the second layer of the air, where hail and snow are born; thunder and lightning, and whirlwinds, come from the third layer and, if we keep going higher, as we've obviously been doing, we'll soon be up to the layer of fire, and I don't know which way to turn this peg, to keep us from going so high that we get burned."

Just then, by means of cotton wicks at the end of long poles, easy both to light and to extinguish, heat was blown against their faces. Feeling the warmth, Sancho said:

"May I die and be buried if we aren't already in that fiery place, or very near it, because a big chunk of my beard's just been scorched off, so I think, my lord, I'd better take off this blindfold and find out where we are."

"Do no such thing," replied Don Quijote. "Just remember the true story of that high university graduate, Doctor Torralba,[5] who was carried through the air by devils, mounted on a broomstick, with his eyes closed, and got to Rome in just twelve hours, and dismounted at Torre de Nona, which is a street in that city, and there he saw Rome being sacked and all the fighting and Charles, Duke of Bourbon, being killed, and then the very next day he was carried back to Madrid, where he told what he had seen, and he also reported that, while he was flying through the air, the Devil had ordered him to open his eyes, and when he did he saw himself so near, or at least thought he was so near, the moon that he could have reached out and touched it with his hand, and that he didn't dare look

---

5. Eugenio Torralba was prosecuted for witchcraft in 1528 and confessed to precisely what Don Quijote reports. Rome was in fact sacked by Charles, Duke of Bourbon (who was killed in the process), in 1527 [*Translator's Note*].

down at the earth, for fear of getting dizzy. And that, Sancho, is why it's not a good idea for us to take off our blindfolds, because he who has brought us here will take care of us — and who knows? Maybe we're swinging up higher just so we can swoop down into the kingdom of Candaya, the way a falcon drops right onto a heron, to make sure it catches it, no matter how high the heron may have flown, because even though it may seem to us not even half an hour since we left, I suspect we must have come a long way."

"I don't know anything about that," answered Sancho Panza. "All I can say is, if the lady Magallanes, or Magalona, or whatever, was happy sitting where I'm sitting, her flesh couldn't have been very tender."

All this conversation between the two brave men was of course heard by the duke and duchess, as well as by everyone else in the garden, and thoroughly delighted them all. Then, wanting to put the finishing touches to this extraordinary and extremely well fabricated adventure, they applied their torches to Clavileño's tail, and all of a sudden — since the wooden horse had been filled with thunderous skyrockets — these explosive rockets came flying out in all directions, to the accompaniment of an extraordinary roaring sound, and the horse leaped into the air, and both Don Quijote and Sancho were thrown to the ground, half scorched.

By this time, the squadron of bearded *dueñas* were all gone from the garden, Trifaldi and all, and everyone who was left was stretched out on the ground, as if in a swoon. Don Quijote and Sancho got up, somewhat the worse for wear, and when they looked around were astonished to see themselves in exactly the same garden they had flown away from, as also they were amazed to see so many people lying all over the place, and their astonishment was still greater when they saw, on one side of the garden, a huge spear thrust deep into the ground and, hanging from it, by a pair of green silken cords, a smooth white sheet of parchment, on which, in golden letters, was written the following:

By the very act of undertaking it, the illustrious knight, Don Quijote de La Mancha, has finished and completed the adventure belonging to the Countess Trifaldi — she who is also known as the lady in waiting, Dolorida — and to all her company.

Malambruno hereby declares himself fully satisfied in all respects, so that the dueñas' beards have already been completely shaved and cleaned away, and King Clavijo and Queen Antonomasia are now restored to their original shapes. And as soon as the whipping squire has whipped the full total required of him, the white dove will find herself free of the pestiferous falcons which have been persecuting her, and once again in the arms of her beloved admirer, all of this having been ordained by our lord Wise Merlin, the Enchanter who rules all other enchanters.

The moment Don Quijote read this proclamation, he understood perfectly well that it spoke of Dulcinea's enchantment, and he was immensely pleased that Heaven had allowed him to accomplish so great a deed, and restore the original complexions of so many venerable *dueñas*, all with so little peril to himself, so he went to where the duke and the duchess were lying, not yet quite recovered from their swoons, and grasping the duke's hand, declared:

"Ah, my good lord, take heart! Take heart, for all difficulties have now been surmounted! This adventure is over, without anyone being hurt in the slightest, as we can clearly read from what is written on this parchment."

Slowly, as if he were shaking himself awake after a singularly deep sleep, the duke returned to consciousness, as did the duchess and all the others lying about the garden, and each and all of them were so visibly astonished and even amazed that it really seemed as if the whole thing had actually happened, so beautifully executed was the entire farce. With eyes only half open, the duke read the placard, and then immediately, with arms spread wide, he embraced Don Quijote, exclaiming that his guest had to be the very best knight ever seen on earth.

Sancho went all around, looking for Dolorida, to see if her face was truly free of its beard, and if she was in fact as beautiful as her charming disposition promised, but they explained to him that, as Clavileño came flying down out of the clouds, and smashed into the ground, the entire squadron of ladies in waiting, along with the Countess Trifaldi, had all at once disappeared, instantaneously freed of every trace of beard and stubble. The duchess wondered how Sancho had enjoyed his long journey. Sancho replied:

"It felt to me, my lady, as if we were traveling — the way my master explained it to me — through the region of fire, and I wanted to uncover my eyes a little, and see for myself, but when I asked my master if I could, he said I couldn't, but anyway, since I was born curious and I always want to know everything about everything that gets in my way and makes things difficult, I sneaked a careful little look, without anyone noticing, right out between my nose and the edge of the handkerchief tied around my eyes, and that way I could see all the way down to the ground, and it seemed to me that everything looked like it wasn't any bigger than a mustard seed, and the men walking around weren't any bigger than hazelnuts, which will tell you how high we must have been flying, just then."

The duchess answered:

"Be careful what you say, Sancho my friend, because it seems as if you really didn't see the earth itself, but only people walking on it, which strikes me as perfectly clear when you consider that, if the earth looked like a mustard seed, and every human being like a hazelnut, then one man all by himself must have covered the entire earth."

"That's true," replied Sancho, "but just the same I did peek out a little, sort of through the side, and I saw everything."

"But remember, Sancho," said the duchess, "you couldn't possibly have seen all there was to be seen, just looking out through a little opening."

"I don't know anything about this looking at things," responded Sancho. "All I know is your ladyship ought to realize that, flying around by magic, by the same magic I ought to be able to see the whole earth and everyone on it, no matter which way I looked, and if you don't believe what I've been telling you, then your grace certainly won't believe that, peeking out just over my eyebrows, I saw myself so close to the sky that it was barely a foot away, and I can swear to your grace, my lady, that it's really big up there. And then we went through the part where the seven little goats are [the Pleiades], and by God and my very soul it was like when I was a little boy and herding goats, and when I saw them, hah! I had a real longing to fool around with them for a while . . . and I thought I'd just burst if I didn't. So I went and — what do you think I did? Without saying a word to anyone, not even to my master, I sneaked down from Clavileño, real quiet like, and I went and fooled around with the little goats — because they're really just like gillyflowers, you know, and other flowers like that — and I stayed with them three quarters of an hour, and Clavileño just stayed where he was and didn't move a bit."

"And while our good Sancho was amusing himself with the goats," asked the duke, "what was my lord Don Quijote up to?"

To which Don Quijote replied:

"Since everything that happened was extraordinary, and no part of the natural order of things, it's not surprising that Sancho says what he said. For myself, all I can say is that I did not uncover my eyes, neither at the top nor the bottom of the handkerchief, nor did I see the sky or the earth, or the sea and the deserts. I did really feel us passing through the air, and although we brushed the fiery regions I can't believe we really went through them, since that lies between the skies around the moon and the final layer of air, so without burning ourselves we couldn't have gotten to the skies where Sancho says he saw the seven little goats, and since we did not burn up, I must assume either that Sancho is lying or that he was dreaming."

"I'm neither lying nor was I dreaming," answered Sancho. "If I'm not telling the truth, just ask me what those little goats looked like, and then you can tell whether I really saw them or not."

"So tell us what they looked like, Sancho," said the duchess.

"Two of them," replied Sancho, "were green, two were red, two were blue, and one was all kinds of colors."

"That's a very new breed of goats," said the duke, "because at least around here we don't have any such colors — I mean, not any *goats* of such colors."

"That's absolutely right," said Sancho, "of course — because goats up in the skies have to be different from goats down here on earth."

"Tell me, Sancho," asked the duke, "among all these little goats you saw, were there any billy goats?"

"No, my lord," replied Sancho, "but I've heard it said that billy goats can't jump over the moon's horns."[6]

They did not want to ask him anything else about his journey, because it was clear that Sancho was ready to run all up and down the heavens, reporting on everything that went on up there, even though he'd never left the garden.

So that was how the adventure of *dueña* Dolorida ended, amusing the duke and the duchess not only right then, but all through the rest of their

---

6. Another untranslatable pun: *cabrón* = male goat or cuckolded husband, and *cuernos* = animal horns or cuckolded husbands [*Translator's Note*].

lives, and giving Sancho tales to tell for centuries still to come, should he happen to live that long — but Don Quijote came over to his squire and, bending low to his ear, said:

"Sancho, if you want me to believe what you think you saw up in the sky, you've got to believe what I think I saw in Montesinos' Cave. And that's all I have to say."

Chapter Forty-Two

— Don Quijote's advice to Sancho Panza, before his squire assumed the governorship of his island, along with a number of other carefully considered matters

The duke and duchess were so pleased and satisfied with Dolorida's adventure that, seeing what ready-made players they had at hand, for turning jokes into reality, they decided to stage more, and the next day (that is, the day after Clavileño's flight), after instructing their various servants and underlings how to deal with Sancho in his role as governor of an island, the duke told Sancho to ready himself for assuming his promised governorship, because his future subjects were looking forward to his arrival as to the showers of spring. Sancho made a reverent bow and said:

"Ever since I came back down out of the clouds, after seeing the earth from that great height and finding how tiny it looked, it no longer seems to me quite such a great thing, this becoming a governor, because what's so high and mighty about being the ruler of a mustard seed? And how much dignity and pride can a man take in being the governor of half a dozen men the size of hazelnuts? — which, so far as I can see, is about what the whole population of the earth amounts to. Now, if your majesty could let me have just a little slice of the sky, even if it's no bigger than a mile or two, I'd prefer that to the biggest island in the world."

"Look here, Sancho my friend," replied the duke, "I can't give any part of the sky to anybody, not even a piece the size of your fingernail, because that kind of gift comes only from God Himself. What I can give you is what I am giving you, and that is a whole island, round and well made, and overflowingly fertile — a place where, if you know what you're up to, you can use the earth's riches to earn yourself a share of Heaven's."

"All right," replied Sancho, "let's have this island, then, and I'll struggle and strive to be the kind of governor who, in spite of all the scoundrels on earth, gets to go to Heaven, nor will this be because I'm anxious to rise above my station, or to try to be better than I really am, but just because I want to find out what it's like to be a governor."

"Once you try it, Sancho," said the duke, "you won't be able to get enough of it, because the sweetest thing of all is to command and be obeyed. Certainly, once your master comes to be an emperor, as he clearly will, the way things are going for him, it won't be something he wants to give up — indeed, he'll be very sorry, his very soul will ache, for all the time he spent *not* being one."

"My lord," replied Sancho, "I suppose being in charge is a good thing, even if it is only a herd of cows."

"You're a man after my own heart, Sancho: you understand everything," responded the duke, "so I look for you to be exactly the kind of governor your good sense promises, and that's that. But remember: tomorrow's the day you'll have to go and take up your duties, so later on they'll be fitting you for the clothes a governor needs to wear and getting everything ready for your departure."

"They can dress me any way they like," said Sancho, "because I'm still going to be Sancho Panza, no matter what I'm wearing."

"True enough," said the duke, "but a man's clothing needs to be appropriate for his rank or profession, because it wouldn't be right for a consulting attorney to dress like a soldier, or a soldier like a priest. You, Sancho, will be dressed partly like a man of learning and partly like a commanding officer, because, on this island I'm giving you, weapons are as necessary as learning, and learning is as necessary as weapons."

"Learning," replied Sancho, "isn't something I have very much of, because I don't even know the alphabet — but all I have to keep in mind, to be a good governor, is the *Christus* [cross] all the alphabet books start with. As for weapons, I'll wield whatever they give me until I can't hold them any more, and after that it's up to God."

"Anyone who can give that good an account of himself," said the duke, "won't make any mistakes."

Don Quijote arrived and, since he knew what had been going on, and how quickly Sancho would have to leave to take up his governorship, with the duke's permission he took his squire by the hand and led him off, intending to counsel him on how to conduct himself in his new post.

So they went to Don Quijote's room, and closed the door behind them, and then, virtually forcing Sancho to sit beside him, Don Quijote declared, his voice calm:

"I am endlessly thankful to Heaven, Sancho my friend, that even before I met with good fortune, good fortune herself has come forward to greet and welcome you. Having thought that good fortune would repay you, on my behalf, for your services, I now find myself still waiting at the door, while you, before your time and in the teeth of all reasonable expectation, see yourself rewarded exactly as you desired. Now, some people will offer bribes, and harangue, and flatter, try all sorts of tricks, beg, keep coming back and back and back, without getting what they're after, and then others, not really knowing how or why, will suddenly find themselves in possession of the post and the responsibility that so many have sought in vain — and this is where the old saying applies: sometimes fortune smiles on ambition, and sometimes it doesn't. There isn't a doubt in my mind that you're a lazy fool, and yet without any effort, neither troubling yourself to rise early or get to bed late, you're touched by the merest breath of knight errantry and there you are, governor of an island, just as if that were a mere nothing. Oh Sancho, I say these things so you don't think you've been rewarded because you deserve it, rather than being thankful to Heaven, which quietly takes care of everything, and thankful, too, to the inherent nobility of knight errantry as a profession. With a heart prepared to accept, oh my son! listen to what I am about to tell you — I who thus serve as your Cato,[1] wanting only to advise you and be your Northern Star and guide to a safe harbor in this stormy sea into which you're about to sail, for indeed high offices and responsibilities are nothing but a deep abyss of uncertainties. And first, oh my son! remember to fear God, for wisdom lies in fearing Him, and if you are wise you can do no wrong. Second, be careful to watch yourself, seeking to know who you truly are, which of all knowledge is the hardest you could ever think of. Knowing yourself will keep you from becoming puffed up like the frog who wanted to be as big as an ox, and will serve you as the peacock's ugly feet help him to counterbalance the glory of his tail, for you will remember that once, in your birthplace, you had to take care of pigs."

"That's true," replied Sancho, "but only when I was a boy; afterwards, when I'd grown up a bit, I took care of geese instead of pigs. But I don't think any of that makes any difference, now, because you don't have to have the blood of kings to be a governor."

"And that too is true," answered Don Quijote, "and it is why those who are not of high birth need to temper the weight of their responsibilities with a gentle manner, for this, joined with wisdom and discretion, will preserve them from malicious gossip, although no one in high places ever truly escapes from that. Glory in your humble birth, Sancho, and never be too proud to say your ancestors were peasants and farmers, because when it's seen that you're not embarrassed no one will seek to embarrass you; value yourself as a humble honest man, rather than a proud sinner. Many, many people rise from low birth, even to the supreme heights of popes and emperors — as I could show you by so many examples that you'd weary of hearing me. Be careful, Sancho: if you choose the path of virtue, and value yourself for your virtuous deeds, you'll never need to be jealous of princes and other lords, because blood is inherited but virtue must be acquired, and virtue possesses an inherent worth that blood does not have. This being the case, as it is, if by any chance some of your kinfolk come to visit you, there on your island, neither scorn nor insult them, for you should by all rights welcome and entertain and treat them royally, for thus you will please Heaven, which wants to see no one scorn what it has made, and you will do what harmonious Nature requires of you. If you send for your wife (because those responsible for governing should not remain long separated from their families), teach her, school her, and smooth out her natural coarseness, because everything his good fortune allows a wise governor to acquire can be lost and thrown away by a clumsy, foolish wife. If you become a widower, which is something that can always happen, and decide that your higher position requires a higher-born wife, don't pick someone who will make a juicy bait to dangle on your hook and line, and who has a nice deep pocket, because, let me tell you, and it's true, that anything the judge's wife takes, her husband will have to account for in the hereafter, and in death he'll pay fourfold for what, while alive, he refused to be responsible for. Never rely on law you

---

1. I.e., "mentor"; derived from the popular schooltext *Dichos de Catón* [*Cato's Sayings*], originally a Latin anthology of proverbs and maxims erroneously attributed to Marcus Porcius Cato (234–149 B.C.) [*Translator's Note*].

invent to suit yourself, as ignoramuses so often do, thinking they're terribly clever. Let the poor man's tears move you more, though never to unfairness, than the rich man's writs and reports. Try to pick the truth out of the rich man's gifts and promises, just as you seek it in the poor man's sobs and prayers. When natural law can and should have a place in your judgments, don't press too hard on the guilty, for a hanging judge has no better reputation than a merciful one. If, now and then, you let the staff of justice bend, let it not be from the weight of a gift, but only with the weight of compassion. Should you have to judge your enemy's lawsuit, put aside all thoughts of your own grievance and think only of the truth of the case before you. Don't ever let your own strong feelings blind you, in someone else's case, because the errors you'll make are likely to be beyond repair — or, if you do set them straight, it will probably be at the cost either of your reputation or even your property. Should a beautiful woman come to beg justice from you, don't let your eyes see her tears or your ears hear her moans, and take the time to soberly consider what she is asking, lest her tears drown your reason and her sighs wash away your honesty. Speak gentle words to anyone whose body you need to punish, since the pain of torture will be quite sufficient, without adding unpleasant words to the poor man's burden. He who comes before you, and is guilty, should be seen as a miserable creature, in the grip of that natural depravity which afflicts us all, and so far as you can, decently and honestly, show him both pity and mercy, for although all aspects of God are one and the same, mercy and compassion reveal themselves and shine more brightly in our human eyes than does justice. Follow these rules and injunctions, Sancho, and your days will be long, your reputation eternal, your rewards bountiful, your happiness beyond any description; you'll marry your children well, and to your own satisfaction; they'll all have titles, as will your grandchildren; you'll live in peace, high in all men's opinion, and then the final steps of your life will lead you to death, after an easy, ripe old age, and the gentle, delicate hands of your great-grandchildren will close your eyes.

"What I have said, thus far, is all for your heart and soul. Now hear the words meant for your body."

Chapter Forty-Three

— Don Quijote's second set of counsels and injunctions for Sancho Panza

Who could have heard what Don Quijote just said, and not think him one of the sanest and best-intentioned of men? For as the progress of this great history has often shown, he only strayed off course when it came to matters chivalric: everything else he said revealed a clear, confident mind, his intelligence seeming, with every word, to quite discredit his actions, just as his actions discredited his words. In this second set of counsels and injunctions for Sancho, indeed, he showed himself immensely witty, raising to a new and higher level both his wisdom and his madness.

Sancho sat listening attentively, trying to fix in his memory everything he was hearing, like someone bent on closely following every bit of advice he was hearing, and thus helping the pregnancy of his governorship lead to a successful delivery and birth. Then Don Quijote went on as follows:

"As far as governing both yourself and your household, Sancho, the things you need to do are, first, make sure you keep yourself clean, and your nails trimmed, not letting them grow long, as some do, believing (in their ignorance) that long nails make hands handsome, as if these bodily excrescences and excesses they don't bother cutting are truly nothing but fingernails, and not, as in fact they are, the claws of a lizard-catching hawk and a rare and filthy abomination. Don't go about, Sancho, with your clothing slack and unbelted, because disorderly clothing indicates a slack and languid mind — unless sartorial disorder and indifference are a mark of sly cunning, as they were considered to be in the case of Julius Caesar. Evaluate most carefully what your post is likely to bring you and, if you can afford uniforms for your servants, provide them with decent and useful outfits, rather than attention-getting and gaudy ones, and then distribute uniforms both to your servants and to the poor — that is, if you're able to furnish outfits for six pages, put uniforms on three and then give three to the poor, thus supplying yourself with three pages for Heaven and three for this earth — a novel method for clothing one's servants that vainglorious folk will never understand. Eat neither garlic nor onions, so that their odor is not a walking advertisement for your low origins. Make sure you walk slowly; speak calmly — but not as if you're listening most attentively to your own words, for affectation is always bad. Eat lightly, and especially at dinner, for the body's health is born in the stomach. Learn how to drink moderately, remembering that too much wine betrays secrets and swears unreliable oaths. Be careful, Sancho, not to stuff your cheeks as you chew your food, and never eructate in front of anyone."

"I don't know what this *eructate* means," said Sancho.

Don Quijote informed him:

"*Eructate*, Sancho, means *belch*, which is one of the most unpleasant yet most important words in the whole Spanish language, so particularly scrupulous people who have studied Latin say *eructate* instead of *belch*, and *eructations* instead of *belches*, nor does it matter if people can't understand such terminology, because in time the polite usage will become customary and will then be readily comprehensible — which is how a language is enriched, for speech is governed by the majority and its usage."

"Honestly, señor," said Sancho, "one of your counsels and injunctions I'll have to be especially careful to remember is not to belch, because it's something I'm always doing."

"*Eructate*, Sancho, not *belch*," said Don Quijote.

"*Eructate*'s what I'll say from now on," replied Sancho, "and by God I won't forget it."

"In addition, Sancho, you shouldn't jumble up your speech with piles of proverbs, as you usually do, because even though proverbs pack a lot of wisdom into a short space, you often drag them in by the hair, so they seem less like sense than nonsense."

"God will have to take care of that," replied Sancho, "because I know more proverbs than any book, and they come jumping into my mouth whenever I open it to say anything, and then they fight with each other to see who can get out first, but my tongue just tosses out the first one it finds, even if it's not right on target. But from now on I'll try to stick to ones better suited to the dignity of my office, because when a house has a well-stocked larder, there's always something cooking, and the man who cuts the cards doesn't shuffle them, and the man who rings the alarm bell doesn't get caught in the fire, and if you're going to be a giver or a keeper, you'd better know what you're doing."

"That's exactly it, Sancho!" said Don Quijote. "Let them roar, let them rip, there's bound to be one that makes a fit — and who's going to stop you from pouring them out! My mother may catch me at it, but I'll keep on fooling her! Here I am, telling you to stay away from proverbs, and quick as a wink you trot out a whole troop of them, all about as relevant to what we're discussing as your great aunt's uncle. Look, Sancho: I'm not telling you there's anything wrong with a proverb, properly used, but to reel off cartloads of them, all helter-skelter, drains the life out of your speech and makes it worthless.

"When you're riding, don't let yourself slump and slide to the back of the saddle, and never hold your legs all stiff and rigid, pointing outward from the horse's belly; don't flop this way and that, so you look as if you were still on that dapple donkey of yours, because the way you sit on a horse makes some people look like gentlemen and others like stablehands.

"Be moderate in your sleep, because the man who does not rise early does not take full advantage of the day — and remember, oh Sancho! that hard work is the mother of good luck, just as laziness pulls you in the other direction and will never take you where you want to go.

"And now this last counsel I give you, though strictly speaking it does not concern bodily improvement, is nevertheless something I want you never to forget, because I think it every bit as important as anything I have told you thus far: never embroil yourself in arguments about family trees, at least not in making comparisons between and among them, since one will inevitably prove superior to another, and then the man whose lineage you disparage will loathe you, while you'll gain nothing from the man whose lineage you praise.

"Always wear full-length breeches, a long-sleeved jacket and, over it, a plain cape, somewhat longer still; never put on loose, Greek-style trousers, for they are unsuitable either to gentlemen or to governors.

"And, for now, this is the advice I can offer you, Sancho. In time to come, and as occasion dictates, I can supply you with more, provided you keep me informed about how your affairs are progressing."

"My lord," said Sancho, "it's obvious that you've told me nothing but good things, blessedly good and wonderfully useful — but how will any of it help, if I can't remember it? I can't possibly forget what you've told me about not growing my fingernails long, or about getting married again, if I get the chance — but all that other stuff, all those complications and the whole mess of it, I already can't remember any more than I can about the clouds that were up in the sky last year, so you'll have to give it to me in writing, and since I can't read or write I'll give it to the priest who hears my confessions, and whenever it's necessary he can sneak some in and make me think about it."

"Ah, how foolish of me!" replied Don Quijote. "And how bad it looks,

for a governor not to know how to read and write! Because you've got to
understand, oh Sancho! that when a man doesn't know how to read, or
when he's left-handed, it indicates one of two things: either he comes from
a very low, a very humble family, or else he's such a wicked rogue that
neither good models nor good teaching could have any effect on him.
This will be a very serious deficiency — so I want you to learn how to
sign your name."

"Of course I can sign my name," replied Sancho, "because when I was
an usher at union meetings, back home, I learned how to write some of
the letters of the alphabet — like the marks they put on bales and barrels
— and they said that was how my name was written and, anyway, I can
make believe my right hand's paralyzed, so somebody else has to sign
things for me, because there's a way around everything except death, and
when I'm in charge and the stick's in my hand I can do whatever I want
to, because, you know, when your father's the judge . . .[1] And I'll be the
governor, which is even better than being a judge — so come on, and
we'll see what we'll see! No, let 'em make fun of me and call me names,
because they can come after wool and go home fleeced, and when God
loves you, He knows where you live, and in this world a rich man's foolishness is called wisdom, and since I'm going to be both a governor and
generous (because that's what I'm planning), no one's going to criticize
me. No, just make honey and there'll be flies all over, because, as my
grandmother used to say, whatever you own, that's what you're worth, and
you can't sue city hall."

"Oh in the name of God, Sancho!" said Don Quijote after this outburst.
"May sixty thousand demons come and carry off you and your proverbs
too! You've been reeling them off for the last hour, and for me every single
one of them is sheer torture! They'll bring you to the gallows, some day;
on their account, your subjects will drive you out of your governorship, or
else you'll start a revolution. Tell me, you jackass: where on earth do you
find them, and what do you think you're doing with them, you idiot? For
me to say just one, in the right way and at the right time, I have to sweat
and struggle like a ditch digger."

"By God, my dear master," answered Sancho, "your grace is making a
big fuss about nothing. Why in the name of the devil are you getting mad,
just because I use something that belongs to me, since I don't own anything else, not a blessed thing except proverbs and more proverbs? Right
now I've got four of them, as right to the point as pears in a basket —
but I won't say them, because, as Sancho always says, silence is
golden."

"That must be some other Sancho," said Don Quijote, "because you
not only don't know how to hold your tongue, you also don't know how
to use it, and in addition you're as stubborn as a goat — and yet, in spite
of everything, I'd like to know which four proverbs your memory just
produced, each one of them right to the point, because I've been running
through my own memory, which I think a good one, and I can't find a
one."

1. "When your father's the judge, you can feel safe going to court" [*Translator's Note*].

"So what would be better," said Sancho, "than 'never let yourself get between two close relatives'? And there's no answer to 'get out of my house' or 'what do you want from my wife?' And how about 'whether the pitcher whacks the stone, or the stone whacks the pitcher, it's the pitcher that breaks'? That fits just right. Because nobody ought to pick a fight with the governor, or whoever's in charge, because he's sure to lose, just like the man who gets between two close relatives — and even if they're not close, but just relatives, that's good enough — and there's no answering the governor, just as in 'get out of my house' and 'what do you want from my wife?' And even a blind man can see the one about the stone and the pitcher. So what you have to do, to see the mote [speck] in someone else's eye, is see the beam in your own, because otherwise it's like the dead woman who was frightened by a corpse — and your grace surely knows that a fool knows more, in his own house, than a wise man knows when he's in someone else's?"

"That one won't work, Sancho," replied Don Quijote, "because a fool doesn't know anything either in his own house or in anyone else's, and you can't build a sensible building on a foolish foundation. But let's leave this where it is, Sancho, because if you govern badly the fault will be yours, but the shame will be mine: I have to take comfort in having done what I ought to do and given you the best, the soundest advice of which I'm capable, which releases me from both my obligation and my vow. May God guide you, Sancho, and may He govern you while you yourself govern, and may He deliver me from my nagging fear that you'll turn the whole island topsy-turvey, which is something I could prevent by telling the duke who and what you really are, explaining to him that, inside that fat and grubby little person, there's only a bag stuffed with proverbs and perversity."

"My lord," replied Sancho, "if your grace thinks I'm truly not fit for this governorship, I give it up right here and now, because one dirty fingernail of my soul means more to me than my whole body, and I can keep body and soul together on dry bread and onions just as well as I can being a governor and living off partridges and capons, and what's more, we're all one and the same, when we're asleep, important people and unimportant people, poor and rich alike — and if you think about it, your grace, you'll realize it was all your idea, this business of my being governor of an island, because I know as much about being a governor as a hawk does, and if there's any chance that being a governor will help the Devil get hold of me, I'd rather go to Heaven, being just plain Sancho,[2] than go to Hell as a governor."

"By all that's holy, Sancho," said Don Quijote, "with just these last words you've shown yourself worthy to be governor of a thousand islands: you're a naturally good man, and without that there isn't any knowledge worth a cent — so commend yourself to God, and try not to stray from your original plan: I mean, in whatever you do, always try as hard as you can to do right, because a good heart always has Heaven's help.

2. The pun on *Sancho* and *santo*, "blessed, holy," underlies much of this dialogue [*Translator's Note*].

"And now let's go have our dinner, because I suspect the duke and duchess are waiting for us."

Chapter Forty-Four

— how Sancho Panza was taken to his governorship, and the strange adventure experienced by Don Quijote in the duke and duchess' castle

It is said that, in the true original of this chapter, one can read how, when Sidi Hamid came to write this chapter (which his translator only partially rendered into Spanish), the Moor penned a kind of complaint against himself, for having undertaken such a dry and narrow history as Don Quijote's, because it seemed to Sidi Hamid that he was always having to write either about Don Quijote or about Sancho, without ever being able to spread himself more broadly, with other and more serious, not to say entertaining, diversions and incidents, and he recorded that, being obliged to constantly bend his mind, his hand, and his pen to writing on just this one subject, and to expressing himself through the mouths of so few characters, was an intolerable struggle of no great benefit to himself as an author, which was why, to extricate himself from such a difficult situation, he had in the first volume of this history used the device of quite separate and distinct stories, like *The Man Who Couldn't Keep from Prying* and *The Captive's Tale*, in addition to narrating those events which had happened to Don Quijote himself and so could not be omitted. It also seemed to him, he said, that there would be a lot of people so totally absorbed in Don Quijote's doings that, finding these other stories of little interest, they would simply skip over or just skim rapidly through them or, if they did read them, would do so only grudgingly, paying no attention to their considerable elegance and artistry, qualities which would be very well exhibited had they been published by themselves, rather than set next to Don Quijote's madness and Sancho's foolishness. And this, in turn, was why, in this second volume, he had decided not to introduce any separate, artful tales, but only such narratives as, to his mind, emerged out of the strictly historical facts, and to tell even these in narrow compass and at just enough length to make them clear; and thus, confining himself as he does to the narrow bounds of history, while having the talents, capabilities, and understanding to deal with the entire universe, he concludes his complaint by asking his readers not to look down on what he has here accomplished, and to praise him, not so much for what he has written, as for what he has refrained from writing.

The history then continues on its way, explaining that, after dinner on the day when he'd given Sancho so much advice, that very same evening Don Quijote gave his squire a written copy of all his counsels and injunctions, so Sancho could find someone to read them to him, but he'd hardly handed them over when Sancho lost them and the duke got hold of them, who shared them with the duchess, both of them astonished yet again by Don Quijote's madness and his cleverness — and then, so they could keep their joke going, they sent Sancho, along with a great train of followers, to the village which was to be his island.

Now, as it happened, the man who was in charge of Sancho's journey was one of the duke's stewards, a charming and very sensible man (because there can't be charm where there's no sense) who had played the role of the Countess Trifaldi, with all the wit and flair already noted — and having both this performance to his credit, and the ability to pay close attention to what his master and mistress wanted him to tell Sancho, he managed their scheme brilliantly. But as soon as Sancho saw this steward, he saw Dolorida's face, and, turning to his master, said:

"My lord, may the Devil pick me up and take me away on the spot, unless your grace admits that this steward's face, this man right here, is also Dolorida's face."

Don Quijote considered the steward carefully, and then replied:

"You don't need to be carried off by the Devil, Sancho, nor do you need to be one of his faithful believers, because, yes, Dolorida's face and this steward's face are one and the same, but that does not mean the steward actually is Dolorida, since that would imply a colossal contradiction — nor is this the right time to undertake any such inquiry, for it would drag us into a labyrinth of fearful complexity. Believe me, my friend, we must pray most earnestly to Our Lord to deliver us from both wicked witches and evil enchanters."

"This is no joke, my lord," Sancho answered, "because I heard him talking, before, and what I was hearing was exactly Countess Trifaldi's voice. All right: I won't say any more — but from here on I'm going to be on notice, and I'll be watching for anything that might either prove or disprove my suspicions."

"Which is what you should do, Sancho," said Don Quijote, "and let me know everything you find out about this business, as well as everything that happens to you as governor."

So Sancho left, at last, with a great retinue; he was as well dressed as a lawyer, wearing a light red raincoat, amply cut, and a cap of the same gleaming silk and camel's hair cloth, and riding, with short stirrups and his legs bent like a Moor, on a strong mule; behind him, as the duke had ordered, came his own dapple donkey, all decked out in brand-new silk trappings and a fine harness. Sancho kept turning his head, to look back at his little donkey, so happy to have the animal's company that he would not have changed places with the Emperor of Germany.

In saying farewell to the duke and duchess, he had kissed their hands, and been awarded Don Quijote's blessing, which was given tearfully, and received with damp cheeks and overflowing eyes.

And so, my dear reader, we will let our good Sancho make his departure in peace, and with the sun smiling down upon him: you can look forward to a couple of bushels chockfull of laughter, which will be yours once you hear how he managed his new responsibilities, and, in the meantime, turn your attention to what, that very same night, happened to his master — and if this doesn't make you laugh, surely it will at least spread your lips in a monkey grin, because Don Quijote's doings always deserve to be welcomed either with wonder or with laughter.

We're told, then, that Sancho had hardly gone when Don Quijote became aware of pangs of loneliness, and indeed, had it been possible for him to revoke Sancho's commission, and take away the governorship, Don

Quijote would have done so. Perceiving his melancholy, the duchess asked why he was sad, because, she said, if it were on account of Sancho, she had squires, and ladies in waiting, and maidens galore in her house, all of whom would be delighted to serve him in any way he might desire.

"You're right, my lady," replied Don Quijote, "that I am feeling Sancho's absence, but I don't think that's the primary cause of my sadness: of all the many offers Your Excellency has made me, pray let me choose and accept only the good will with which you've made them, and beg Your Excellency to allow me to withdraw to my room and there, quite alone, serve myself."

"Really, my lord Don Quijote," said the duchess, "it shouldn't be like that, for you can have four of my maidens to serve you, each of them as lovely as a flower."

"But for me," replied Don Quijote, "rather than flowers, they would be thorns piercing me to the heart. They, or anything or anyone like them, will as soon enter my room as spread their wings and fly. If Your Majesty wishes to continue favoring me, far beyond what I deserve, allow me to do as I wish and serve myself in my own room, for I keep a stout wall between my desires, on the one hand, and my modesty, on the other, and I do not want to give up this habit for the generous freedoms Your Highness would like to extend. And so, in short, rather than permit anyone to help me remove my clothes, I will sleep in them."

"Enough, enough, my lord Don Quijote," replied the duchess. "I shall personally order that not even a fly, much less one of my maidens, will trespass on your property, for I am hardly the one to rupture Don Quijote's modesty, because modesty, I would conjecture, stands first among the ranks of all his many virtues. By all means undress yourself, your grace, and you alone shall serve you according to your fashion, how and when you please, nor will there be anyone to interfere, for you'll find in your room all the vessels required by someone who sleeps behind closed doors, and no natural need will require you to open them. May the great Dulcinea del Toboso live a thousand years, and may her name be spread wide across the face of the earth, for she deserves to be the belovèd of such a brave and moral knight, and may the merciful heavens implant in the heart of Sancho Panza, our governor, a desire to quickly finish whipping himself, so the world may once again relish the beauty of so magnificent a lady."

To which Don Quijote replied:

"Your Highness has spoken like the great lady you are, for nothing immoral can ever come from the mouth of a virtuous woman, and my Dulcinea will be both blessed and better known for having received Your Highness' praise than for all the praises that might be heaped upon her by the most eloquent tongues on earth."

"Well then, my lord Don Quijote," answered the duchess, "dinner time is here, and the duke must be awaiting us: come and dine, your grace, so we may all find our way to bed early — for the journey you made to Candaya, yesterday, was not so short that it would not have been somewhat fatiguing."

"I feel no fatigue at all, my lady," answered Don Quijote, "for I can freely swear to Your Excellency that never in my life have I mounted a calmer and easier horse than Clavileño, nor can I understand what could have moved Malambruno to destroy such a light-footed and splendid steed, and simply burn him up, just like that."

"We might suspect," replied the duchess, "that, repenting the wrong he'd done to Trifaldi and her ladies, and also to others, as well as all the wickedness he surely must have committed, as an enchanter, he wanted to be done with all the tools of his craft, and since Clavileño was his primary means of transporting himself here and there, all over the earth, both causing and encouraging his restless spirit, Malambruno decided to burn his magical horse, the charred ashes of which, together with the triumphant parchment placard, offer eternal testimony to the courage of the great Don Quijote de La Mancha."

Don Quijote thanked the duchess yet again, and after dinner he retired to his room, alone, refusing to allow anyone to come serve him — a fair measure of how fearful he was of anything that might tempt or even oblige him to forsake the chaste propriety he had vowed to his lady Dulcinea, for he kept forever fresh in his mind the goodness of Amadís, flower and very model of all knights errant. He shut the door behind him and, by the light of a pair of wax candles, got undressed, and as he drew off one of his stockings — oh misfortune, unworthy of such a personage! — there popped out, not sighs or anything else that might sully the purity of his manners, but two dozen stitches, turning what had been smooth fabric into something rather more like lattice-work. Our good knight was sorely distressed, and more than willing to give a solid ounce of silver for just a bit of green silk thread — green silk, that is, because his stockings were green.

At this point Benengeli exclaimed, recording these events, "Oh poverty, poverty! I cannot understand why that great Cordoban poet[3] ever called you

divine blessing, so undivinely received!

For even I, though a Moor, can readily perceive (having been in contact with many Christians) that holiness is composed of charity, humility, faith, obedience, and poverty — but all the same, I must say that he who is happy, being poor, must be very close to godliness, unless it's the sort of poverty of which one of the greatest Christian saints[4] says: "Possess all things as though ye possessed them not," which is the kind of poverty they call spiritual — but you, you other kind of poverty, I'm talking about you: why do you impose on gentlemen and those of good families more than on other folk? Why do you make them struggle to keep their shoes shiny, and to have some of their jacket buttons made of silk, but others of twisted horsehair, and still others of glass? Why do their collars usually have to be ruffled and frilled rather than flat and open?" This of course shows us that, even in the old days, our ancestors used starch and open collars. And

3. Juan de Mena (1411–1456), in his *Laberinto de Fortuna* [*Fortune's Labyrinth*], a complex, highly worked Dantesque allegory [*Translator's Note*].
4. St. Paul, I Corinthians, 7:30–31; modern English translations are all more or less different, though the essential meaning is the same [*Translator's Note*].

then Sidi Hamid goes on: "Oh you miserable, well-born folk, forever stuffing your honor to the gills while sitting behind closed doors and feeding your own selves on little or nothing, play-acting at picking your teeth, afterwards, out in the street, even though you've eaten nothing needing to be cleaned away! Oh you miserable folk, I say once more, terrorized by honor, worried that someone two miles distant will see the patch on your shoe, the sweat-stains on your hat, the clumsy stitching that holds your cloak together, and the hunger burning in your stomach!"

The run in his stocking reminded Don Quijote of all this, once again, but he felt a bit better, noticing that Sancho had left him a pair of field boots, which he planned to put on in the morning. He lay down, at last, preoccupied and troubled, bothered equally by Sancho's absence and the irreparable accident suffered by his stocking, for, had he been able, he would even have sewn them up with different-colored silk thread — one of the plainest, most significant signals of misery any gentleman can display, as his tiresome poverty unfolds itself. He put out the candles, but it was a warm night and he could not sleep, so he climbed out of bed and gently pushed open a window set above a lovely garden, and as he opened it became aware that he could hear people outside, moving back and forth and talking. He was immediately all ears. The people down below raised their voices, and this is what he heard:

"Oh Emerencia! Don't insist that I sing, for you know full well that the very moment this newcomer entered the castle, and my eyes beheld him, I have forgotten how to sing, but can only weep — and you know, too, that my lady tends to sleep lightly, not deeply, and I would not for all the treasure in the world want her to find us here. And even were she already sleeping, and I did not wake her, my singing would be to no avail if this new Aeneas himself were asleep, and so could not hear me, he who has come here simply to make sport of me, and mock me."

"Don't think such things, my dearest Altisidora," came the reply, "for surely the duchess and everyone else in this house is asleep, though the lord of your heart and ravager of your soul may not be, because I can see, now, that the window to his room is open a crack, so he is certainly awake — so sing softly, you poor, suffering girl, to the gentle sound of your harp, and if the duchess becomes aware of us we can blame the uncomfortable heat of the night."

"That's not the point, oh Emerencia!" replied Altisidora. "It's just that I wouldn't want my singing to reveal my heart, and make people who don't understand love's power think me a capricious and flighty girl. But never mind: it's better to have your face show shame than let your heart bleed."

And, as she spoke, she ran her hands delicately down the harp's strings. Don Quijote was in a state of high and breathless excitement, hearing this, for he was remembering all the many, many adventures of this same sort, in which music, wooing, and love-choked swoons were played out, through windows, iron grilles, and gardens, in all the swooning tales of chivalry he had read. His mind leaped to the thought that one of the duchess' ladies had fallen in love with him, but modesty was forcing her to keep her desires secret, and he was immediately concerned that she might win him over, so he sought to set himself resolutely against being thus overcome, praying as hard and devoutly as he could to his lady, Dulcinea del Toboso, but determined all the same to listen to this unknown lady's singing — and, to let them know that he was in fact there, he pretended to sneeze, thus delighting the two girls, who wanted nothing more than that Don Quijote should hear them. So, having tuned her harp, Altisidora struck the strings and began this song:

> Oh you, asleep in your bed
> in soft and silken sheets,
> your legs flung out wide,
> lost in gentle sleep,
>
> the bravest, best of knights
> La Mancha ever bore,
> purer and better than Arabian
> gold, mined from Arabian ore,
>
> oh hear this sad-eyed maiden,
> well-born but unlucky in life,
> whose heart glows and burns
> in the light of your sun-bright eyes.
>
> You roam the world for adventures,
> helping unfortunate virgins;
> your sword is sharp, but ah!
> you never give in to your urgings.
>
> Tell me, oh valiant youth,
> as God may grant thee boons,
> were you born in the Libyan deserts
> or the mountains high on the moon?
>
> Were you nursed by venomous snakes
> or fed by the friendly breasts
> of harsh and horrid wolves
> roaming the rocky crests?
>
> Well may Dulcinea rejoice,
> that stocky, sturdy girl,
> at having conquered a tiger,
> fierce — wild — a pearl!
>
> They'll shout her name to the skies
> from Benares off to the Seine,
> from the Rhône across to the Rhine,
> from Shanghai down to the Thames.
>
> I'd gladly take her place
> and give her a petticoat fine,
> striped and bright and pleated,
> the best that I can call mine.
>
> And ah, to lie in your arms,
> or at least near your bed,

scratching away the dandruff
from the top of your itching head.

I ask too much, I want
far more than I deserve:
I'd be happy to rub your feet
if only I had the nerve.

What caps I'd love to give you!
What silver-buckled shoes!
What silken-spangled breeches!
What capes of many hues!

I'd love to give you pearls
as large and round as shells,
larger and rounder than walnuts,
louder and brighter than bells!

No need to stand like Nero,
watching my fire burn,
oh Nero-like Manchegan,
whipping the flames as I yearn.

I'm only a girl, a young one,
I haven't reached fifteen,
I've six months more to go,
if I were wood I'd be green.

My legs are sound, I'm not lame,
I haven't lost any fingers,
and when I walk my hair
down on the ground it lingers.

My mouth is a little bit big,
my nose is a little bit wide,
but my teeth are nice and straight
and my lips have nothing to hide.

And, hearing my voice, you know
it's as sweet and lovely as any,
and my figure, which you can't see,
is not as pretty as many.

But whatever I have is yours,
I'm a trophy yours for the taking;
I'm Altisidora, I live here,
I'm the love you've been forsaking.

And so the lovesick Altisidora's song ended, but Don Quijote's perplex-
ity, finding himself thus wooed, had just begun; with a deep sigh, he said
to himself:

"Oh, why do I have to be so unlucky a knight, that girls only have to
look at me and love sweeps them away! Why must my matchless Dulcinea
del Toboso's good fortune be thus threatened, and she prevented from
being the only one to relish my perfect fidelity! Oh queens of the world,

what do you want of her? Why do you persecute her, oh you empresses? Why do you harass her, oh you girls of fourteen and fifteen? Let the poor, miserable woman enjoy her triumph — leave her alone — let her boast of the happy Fate which led Love to bring her, in total subjection, my heart and soul. Oh you flocks of lovesick women, understand that only for Dulcinea am I soft as dough, as tender as sugar paste: toward all others I am like flint. For her I may be honey, but for the rest of you I am bitter fruit. In my eyes, Dulcinea alone is Beauty, Wisdom, Modesty, Elegance, and High-Birth; all others are Ugliness, Foolishness, Fickleness, and Low-Birth; Nature thrust me into the world only to be hers, and no one else's. You may weep, or you may sing, Altisidora; ah, you may well despair, damsel for whom I suffered myself to be cudgeled, in the castle of the enchanted Moor;[5] but I must be Dulcinea's — baked or roasted, but pure, faithful, and modest — and never mind all the wonder-working powers on earth."

And at this he slammed the window shut, feeling as peevish and unhappy as if he had experienced some great misfortune, and stretched himself out in his bed — where, for the moment, we will leave him, for we are summoned to the side of the great Sancho Panza, who is about to begin his celebrated reign as governor.

Chapter Forty-Five

— how the great Sancho Panza took possession of his island, and the way he began to govern it

Oh You who regularly explore the opposite ends of the earth, light and torch of the world, eye of the heavens, You who make men run to the sweet, refreshing coolness of wine — You, known here as Thymbrius, there as Phoebus Apollo, in this place a bowman, in that a physician, father of Poetry, creator of Music — You who rise up forever and, appearances to the contrary notwithstanding, never set! I address myself to You, oh Sun, with whose help man begets other men,[1] I call to You, who protect me, and brighten the darkness of my mind, enabling me to elaborate in all its detail this account of the great Sancho Panza's governorship, for without You I feel myself tepid, lifeless, and all uncertain.

Accordingly, then, let me say that Sancho and his retinue arrived at a town of perhaps a thousand inhabitants, one of the largest in the duke's realm. He was told it was known as Barataria Island, either because this chief center of population was known as Baratario, or perhaps because of the bargain price at which the governorship had been transferred.[2] There was a wall around the town, and when Sancho arrived at the gates the leading citizens came forth to greet him; the bells were pealing, and all

---

5. I.e., Maritornes: see I.16 [*Translator's Note*].
1. Aristotle, *Physics*, II, 2: "For both man and the Sun beget man"; meant only in the metaphysical sense of the sun as ultimately responsible for all life on earth [*Translator's Note*].
2. *Barato* = bargain price, gambler's tip; *baratero* = cheapskate; *baratería* = fraudulent sale [*Translator's Note*].

the inhabitants seemed extremely happy, conducting him in an ostenta-
tious procession to the town cathedral, there to give thanks to God for his
safe arrival, immediately after which, in a ceremony of exquisite silliness,
he was presented with the keys to the city and installed as permanent
governor of Barataria Island.

The new governor's garb, and beard, and girth, and how very short he
was, greatly surprised all those who were not in on the secret — and even
all those who were, of whom there were a lot. But they led him out of the
biggest church in town and brought him to the court and the governor's
throne, and seated him on it, and then the duke's steward explained to
him:

"The ancient custom of this place, lord governor, requires that he who
takes possession of this island is obliged to answer a question posed to him,
which question, further, must be distinctly complex and difficult, for it is
from his reply that the inhabitants are able to judge and understand their
new governor's mind, and thus either rejoice at or bemoan his coming."

As the steward was making this statement, Sancho sat looking at some
large, elaborate writing, inscribed on the wall opposite his throne, and
since he did not know how to read, he asked what had been painted up
there. The response was:

"My lord, what's there written and inscribed is the day on which Your
Lordship took possession of this island, and the epitaph declares: *Today,
in such-and-such month, and such-and-such year, our lord Don Sancho
Panza took possession of this island, which may he long enjoy.*"

"And who is this Don Sancho Panza," Sancho asked.

"You, Your Lordship," replied the steward, "because the Panza now
sitting on its throne is the only Panza who's ever come to this island."

"Then let me tell you, brother," said Sancho, "that I'm no *Don*, and
there's never been one in my family: my name is simply Sancho Panza,
and my father was just called Sancho, without any *Don* in front of it, and
so was my granddad, and they were all just Panzas, without any *Dons* or
Doñas, and maybe here on this island you've got more *Dons* than rocks
on the ground — but that'll do: God understands what I'm talking about,
and maybe, if my governorship lasts for four days, I'll get rid of all those
Dons, because if there's such a mob of them they must be worse than
mosquitoes. So, Mister Steward, go on and ask your question, and I'll give
you the best answer I can, whether it makes people unhappy or it doesn't."

Then two men came into the courtroom, one dressed like a farmer and
the other, who was carrying a pair of scissors, like a tailor, and the tailor
said:

"My lord governor, this farmer here and I appear before your grace
because, yesterday, this good man came to my shop (because, if nobody
minds my saying so,[3] I'm a licensed tailor, may the Lord be thanked) and
handed me a length of cloth and asked me: 'Mister Tailor, is this enough
to make me a cap [*caperuza* = pointed cap, hood, cowl]?' I had a look at
the cloth and told him, yes, and then, as I suspect, and I think I suspect
right, he thought I might be planning to cheat him out of some of the

---

3. The reputation of tailors was exceedingly bad [*Translator's Note*].

cloth, because he's a tricky fellow and also because he knows what most people think of tailors, so he asked if it looked like enough for two, but I knew what was on his mind and I said yes again, and then he, natural swindler that he is, kept trying to make trouble for me, asking if it would make three, and four, and five, and until he got to five I kept saying yes, and now he's come to fetch them, and I gave him all five, but he won't pay me for my labor and says I have to either pay him for the cloth or else give it back to him."

"Is that really what happened, brother?" Sancho asked the farmer.

"Yes, my lord," answered the man, "but let your grace make him show you the five caps he made for me."

"Gladly," said the tailor.

And he stuck out his hand, showing five caps on each of his five fingers, and said:

"Here are the five caps this good man asked me to make, and before God and my conscience there isn't a scrap of cloth left, and the official inspectors are welcome to check whether I did a good job."

Everyone laughed, seeing this abundance of little caps, and hearing such a novel lawsuit. Sancho sat pondering for a bit, then declared:

"I don't think I need to waste a lot of time on a case like this, but just sum it up like an honest man, so my decision is that the tailor loses his labor, and the farmer loses his cloth, and the caps go to the prisoners in the jail, and that's the end of it."

The judgment Sancho later pronounced, in the matter of the cattle dealer's purse, astonished everyone who heard it, but this decision made them all laugh — still, the decision stood as rendered, and was carried out as ordered.

Next, two old men appeared, one using a long staff as a cane, the other walking unaided, and the latter said:

"My lord, a while ago I lent this good man ten dollars in solid gold, just to make him happy and as a good deed, on condition he'd pay me back whenever I asked. I didn't ask for a long time, because I didn't want to get him into any more trouble than he'd been in when I lent him the money, but then I began to think he wasn't much interested in paying me back, so I did ask him, and more than once, but not only wouldn't he pay me, he said I'd never lent him a cent, and what's more, even if I did, he'd already paid me back. I haven't got any witnesses of the loan, and there aren't any of the return payment, because he never made one, so what I want your grace to do is put him under oath and, if he swears he really has paid me, I'll forgive him the debt right here and now, in God's own sight."

"So what do you say to this, you good old man with your staff?" said Sancho.

The second old man answered:

"My lord, I admit he lent me the money, so lower your staff of office so I can reach it, and swear on it, and since he says he'll rely on my oath, I'll swear that I've honestly and truly paid him back in full."

So Sancho lowered his staff of office and, as he did so, the old man with the staff handed it to the other old man, to hold while the oath was being administered — as if the long stick would get in his way — and then immediately set his hand on the cross of Sancho's staff and swore he had in fact borrowed the ten gold dollars but had already returned them, so the lender shouldn't keep pestering him for the money. At this, the noble governor asked the lender what he had to say to his opponent's testimony, and the lender replied he had no doubt at all that the borrower had spoken truly, because he was surely a good man and a good Christian, so he himself must have forgotten how and when the repayment had been made, so from now on he'd stop asking for the money. The borrower reclaimed his staff, bowed his head to the governor, and left the courtroom. But when Sancho saw this, and that the borrower went off without another word, and saw too how patient a man the lender was, he bent his head to his chest, put the index finger of his right hand on his nose, right across his eyebrows, and sat for a few moments as if lost in thought; then he raised his head and ordered that the old man with the staff, who had already left, be brought back. He was fetched before the governor, who said to him:

"Let me have your staff, my good man: I need it."

"Gladly," answered the old man. "I've got it right here."

So he handed it over to Sancho, who took it and gave it to the other old man, saying:

"God bless you, now you've been paid."

"Me, my lord?" responded the old man. "Is this stick worth ten dollars in gold?"

"It is," said the governor, "or, if it's not, then I'm the worst idiot in the world. So: let it be seen, now, whether I have the brains to govern a whole kingdom."

Then he directed that, right there in front of everyone, the staff be broken open. Which was done — and hidden inside it there were ten dollars in gold. Everyone was astonished, and thought the new governor a veritable Solomon.

They asked him how he had figured out that the ten gold dollars were hidden in the staff, to which Sancho replied that he had watched the old man, before he swore his oath, handing the staff to the other old man, then swearing the loan had really and truly been paid back, and finally, when he'd made his oath, turning and asking for the staff again, and it had popped into his mind that the payment just sworn to must in fact be hidden in the staff. From which it could be concluded, said Sancho, that though governors might be fools, God would sometimes lead them into the light — and, what's more, he had heard his parish priest tell of an incident much like this, and he had such an extraordinarily good memory that, if he didn't keep forgetting everything he wanted to remember, he'd have to say there wasn't anyone on the island with a memory to equal it. And so one old man went off, thoroughly ashamed of himself, and the other left, quite repaid, and all the bystanders were amazed — and he who was recording Sancho's words, deeds, and actions couldn't decide whether he ought to consider the new governor a fool or a wise man.

Once this case was disposed of, a woman came into the courtroom, screaming at the top of her lungs and holding on for dear life to a man who was dressed like a wealthy cattle dealer:

"Justice, my lord governor, justice! And if I can't find it, here on earth, I'll go seek it in Heaven. Oh my dear lord governor, this wicked man caught me out in the middle of a field, and made use of my body as if it were an unwashed rag, and, oh my misfortune! He took from me what I have guarded and kept for twenty-three years, protecting it against Moors and Christians, against neighbors and strangers — and I, always as tough as an oak tree, preserving myself as uncorrupted as a salamander in a fire, or wool laid out on a bramble bush, I to be pawed, now, by this man with his clean, clean hands!"

"Well, we still have to settle that question," said Sancho. "Are this gallant gentleman's hands clean or aren't they?"

Then he turned to the man and asked him what response he made to the woman's complaint. Considerably shaken, the man replied:

"Gentlemen, I'm a poor man who makes his living buying and selling pigs, and this morning I left this town to sell, please forgive me for mentioning them, four pigs, and what with paying taxes and being swindled, I sold them for a little less than they were worth; so then I turned around to come home, and I met this lady on the road, and the Devil, who makes a stinking mess out of everything, made us lie together, and I paid her what she was owed, but she wanted more, and she grabbed hold of me and she hasn't yet let go. She says I forced her, and she's lying, and I'll swear to that and to any oath you want, and this is the whole truth, and it isn't missing a single crumb."

Then the governor asked if he was carrying any money, in silver; the man answered that he had perhaps twenty silver ducats in a leather purse that he wore under his shirt. Sancho ordered him to take it out and hand over the whole thing, just as it was, to the complainant, which the man did, trembling. The woman took the purse and, to the tune of a thousand curtsies and bows to everyone, and prayers for the governor's good health and long life, because he took such good care of orphans in need and maidens in distress, she left the courtroom, clutching the purse in both hands — although she checked, first, to see if the coins really were silver.

She was hardly out of the room when Sancho told the pig dealer, who was already starting to weep, both his eyes and his heart following along behind his purse:

"Good man, go after that woman and take the purse away from her, whether she likes it or not, and then bring it back here."

He was not speaking to a fool or a deaf man, because the fellow shot out like a bolt and ran to do as he'd been told. The bystanders were all in a tizzy, waiting to see how this case would turn out; the man returned, soon enough, even more tightly glued to the woman than the first time, she with her skirt hiked up and the purse pressed inside it, and the man desperately trying to get it away from her — but he could not, the woman fought back so valiantly, screaming all the time:

"Justice! Before God and man! Your grace, my lord governor, just see what a shameless cold-blooded monster this is, and how utterly unafraid, because right in the middle of town, right in the middle of the street, he's been trying to take away the purse your grace ordered him to give me."

"But has he taken it?" the governor asked.

"What the hell are you talking about?" replied the woman. "I'd rather give up my life than this purse. What kind of a baby am I supposed to be? Maybe some other cat can run me up a tree, but not this miserable pig! Pliers and hammers, mallets and chisels, couldn't pry this thing out of my nails — not even a lion's claws! I'd sooner let him grab the soul right out of my body!"

"She's right," said the man, "and I might as well give up, and admit I can't get it away from her, because I'm just not strong enough, and that's that."

Then the governor said to the woman:

"Let me see this purse, oh brave and honorable woman."

She immediately gave it to him, and the governor returned it to the man, and told the strong, obviously inviolable woman:

"My dear sister, if you'd shown the same spirit and courage, or anything like it, in defending your body as you've just shown us, defending this purse, Hercules himself couldn't have raped you. So God be with you, if He feels like it, and goodbye and good riddance: don't show your face on this island, or anywhere within twenty miles of it, under penalty of two hundred lashes! Now get out of here, you liar, you faker, you shameless cheat!"

Frightened and unhappy, the woman left, her head low, and the governor said to the man:

"Good man, God be with you: go home with your money and, from now on, if you don't want to lose it, try to restrain yourself from lying around with anyone."

The man thanked him, not terribly cheerfully, and then left, and the bystanders were left admiring and astonished all over again by the new governor's cleverness and good sense. And all this, carefully noted by his chronicler, was immediately transcribed and sent to the duke, who was awaiting it with great interest.

And let us leave our good Sancho, at this point, for his master — much excited by Altisidora's music — requires our attention far more urgently.

Chapter Forty-Six

— Don Quijote's fearful shock, in the course of the lovestruck Altisidora's hang-the-bell-on-the-cat wooing

We left the great Don Quijote wrapped in all the thoughts summoned up by the lovestruck maiden Altisidora and her music. He put himself to bed with them and, just as if they had been fleas, they would allow him neither sleep nor rest — and the terrible shortcomings of his stockings lent them their support. But time travels on light-footed feet, nor is there any obstacle which can hold him back, so the hours came galloping on and very soon it was morning. And when Don Quijote saw it was light, he left his soft featherbed and, no sluggard he, put on his chamois-colored clothes and, to hide his stockings' misfortunes, his field boots; he wrapped himself in his scarlet cloak, set a green velvet cap, decorated all in silver, on his head; slung over his shoulder the belt from which hung his good, sharp sword, took up a large rosary that he always carried, and with a keen sense of his own importance and a carefully contained swagger to his walk, went out to the anteroom, where the duke and duchess, already dressed, awaited him. As he passed through an adjoining room, there were Altisidora and the other girl, her friend, lying in wait for him, and as soon as Altisidora saw him she pretended to swoon away, and her friend drew her to herself and, with incredible speed, began to unlace her bodice. Seeing this, as he approached them, Don Quijote said:

"Ah, I know what caused this."

"I don't," replied the girl's friend, "because Altisidora is the healthiest girl in the whole house, and I've never heard so much as a peep out of her, the whole time I've known her. The devil with all the knights errant in the world, if they're all so ungrateful! Go away, Don Quijote, your grace, because this poor child won't come to as long as you're still here."

To which Don Quijote answered:

"Madame, do me the favor of having a lute put in my room, tonight, so I can offer this poor girl what comfort I can, for when love has barely taken wing a prompt dash of cold water can often prove efficacious."

And then he left them, not wishing anyone to see him there. He had barely gone when the swooning Altisidora came to, observing to her companion:

"The lute must be put in his room, for surely Don Quijote means to give us some music — and indeed, being his, it won't be bad."

So they hurried off to report to the duchess and tell her that Don Quijote had asked for a lute, at which news the great lady, delighted, set herself to plotting, together with the duke and her maidens, a joke a good deal more likely to be funny than dangerous, and then they all happily awaited darkness, which arrived quite as promptly as had daylight; the duke and duchess spent the intervening hours pleasantly conversing with Don Quijote. And that same day, the duchess actually sent one of her pages — the one who, in the forest, had played the role of the enchanted Dulcinea — to Teresa Panza, bearing her husband's letter as well as the bundle of clothing Sancho had left to be sent to his wife, the duchess having instructed her page to bring her a careful account of everything Teresa said and did.

This done, and the clock having turned to eleven at night, Don Quijote found that a guitar had in fact been brought to his room, so he tuned it, adjusted the frets as well as he was able, then opened the window and, seeing people walking in the garden, spat and cleared his throat and promptly began, his voice hoarse, but his pitch true, to sing the following ballad, which he had composed that very same day:

> — Love leans his mighty weight
> on hearts, and bends them out of shape,
> whenever hands have nothing to do,
> and minds are full.
>   The only protection against this venom
> is womanly work, washing and sewing
> and all the bustle of busy lives

and no time for lingering.
　　Girls who live at home, and quiet,
who long for marriage as their best reward,
can bring their husbands as a happy dowry
　　their modest fame.
　　Both knights who practice errantry,
and knights who practice dancing at court,
will play with wild and wayward women,
　　but marry modestly.
　　Love lives East, and love lives West,
and traveling people meet, and love,
and soon are gone, both traveling on
　　to journey's end.
　　Love grows like a hothouse flower, brand new
and bright, but dies with the setting sun,
and even faces blur and fade
　　and are gone forever.
　　A picture of a picture will show you nothing,
mere meaningless lines, devoid of shape:
love rules with such exclusive laws
　　that no copies are made.
　　And this heart of mine is painted over
with Dulcinea del Toboso's face
gleaming so bright, in colors so clear,
　　they'll last forever.
　　And lovers who love, love that can't fade,
hearts that stay true, are worth double price,
and Love rewards them with eternal wonders
　　in lovers' heaven.

The duke and duchess, and Altisidora, and indeed everyone who lived in the castle, were listening to Don Quijote's song, which had just gotten to this point when, suddenly, from a passageway just above our knight's window, someone threw down a rope hung with more than a hundred bells, and then a huge sack full of cats with smaller bells tied to their tails. The jangling and clanging of the bells, and the mewing of the cats, made such an incredible noise that even the duke and duchess (who had planned the whole thing) were startled, and Don Quijote was so terrified that he could not move. Then two or three cats clawed their way in through his window and, leaping from one side of his room to the other, made him think a whole troop of devils had been let loose. The frenzied animals extinguished all his candles, then raced back and forth in the darkness, trying to find a way of escape. The rope from which the great bells hung kept jerking up and down — and most of the people in the castle, who had no idea what was going on, were absolutely dumb-struck.

Then, drawing his sword, Don Quijote leaped at the window, slashing away and shouting:

"Be gone, you cursed enchanters! Be gone, you bewitched scum — because I am Don Quijote de La Mancha, and your evil spells are utterly worthless against me!"

Spinning around, he began striking at the cats, which were still dashing from one side of the room to the other; they broke for the window and all jumped out except one, which was so closely hounded by Don Quijote's savage strokes that it leaped at his face, sinking its teeth and its claws into his nose, the pain of which made Don Quijote scream as loud as he knew how. Hearing this, and realizing what was probably happening, the duke and duchess rushed to his room and, opening the door with their master key, saw our poor knight struggling as hard as he could to pull the spitting, clawing cat away from his face. Candles in hand, they entered the room and saw exactly what sort of unequal combat was going on; the duke started to pull the cat off, but Don Quijote shouted:

"Let no one take him away! Let me fight this demon hand to hand, this wretched witch, this foul magician, and by God I'll teach him who Don Quijote de La Mancha is!"

The cat, indifferent to these threats, growled and hung on still harder, but finally the duke pulled it off and threw it out the window.

Don Quijote's face was pretty well slashed and clawed, and his nose was in rather bad shape, but he was furious at not getting to finish his fierce fight with that evil enchanter. They sent for curative oils, and Altisidora herself bandaged all his wounds with her own lily-white hands, murmuring to him, all the while:

"All these calamities, oh hard-hearted knight, are punishment for your sinful stubbornness, so may it please God that your squire Sancho will completely forget about whipping himself, and then your beloved Dulcinea will never be free of her enchantment, and you'll never enjoy her, bride and groom in bed together, at least while I, who adore you, am still alive."

Don Quijote's only response was a deep, mournful sigh, and shortly thereafter he stretched out on his bed, having thanked the duke for his help — not because our brave knight had any fear of those catlike scoundrels, those witches and their infernal bells, but simply because he wanted to acknowledge the duke's well-meaning attempts to come to his aid. The duke and duchess left him, and retired to their own beds, deeply unhappy at the turn their joke had taken, for they had never dreamed that Don Quijote would come out of this adventure so painfully wounded that, in fact, he was forced to spend five days shut in his room, and confined to his bed, during which time he experienced yet another adventure, even more delightful — but one which your historian cannot recount right now, because he must return to Sancho Panza, whose governorship was proceeding both very carefully and very amusingly.

Chapter Forty-Seven

— continuing the narrative of Sancho Panza's behavior as a governor

Our history records that, when he left the courtroom, Sancho Panza was conducted to a sumptuous palace, in one large room of which a feast fit for a king had been set out; as Sancho entered the room, flutes began to play, and four pages emerged, bringing him water for washing his hands, a ceremony which Sancho performed with great seriousness.

The music stopped, Sancho seated himself at the head of the table, that being indeed the only chair available, and no other place having been set. A personage, who turned out to be a doctor, came and stood at his side, holding a whalebone rod in his hand. A handsome white cloth, which had been covering all sorts of fruit and a host of different dishes, was lifted off; someone who appeared to be a student gave the blessing, and a page tied a protective bib, lace-trimmed, under Sancho's chin; another man, performing the duties of a butler, set a plate of fruit in front of the new governor; but Sancho had barely taken a bite when the man with the whalebone rod touched it to the plate and, with astonishing speed, the plate was removed; and then the butler replaced it with a different dish. Sancho began to taste this one, but before he could get at it, much less taste it, once again the whalebone rod reached out and, just as rapidly as with the plate of fruit, a page removed it. Seeing all of this, Sancho sat motionless, looking around him, then inquired if he was supposed to dine via some sort of magical disappearing act. To which the personage with the whalebone rod replied:

"My lord governor, this food must be eaten as, on other islands where there are governors, food is usually and customarily consumed. I, my lord, am a doctor, and I earn my living here on this island by serving its governors, watching far more zealously over their health than over my own, studying both night and day, scrutinizing the governor's complexion so that, should he fall ill, I will be able to cure him, and my chief charge is to assist him when he is eating, allowing him to dine only on foods I consider appropriate, and ensuring the removal of foods which I consider potentially dangerous or noxious to his stomach. Thus, I ordered the plate of fruit taken away, because it had far too much moisture, and that other dish I ordered removed because it was much too hot and contained a great many spices, highly likely to augment thirst, for he who drinks too much uses up and destroys that essential radical humor which comprises life itself."

"So," said Sancho, "I guess that plate of partridges over there, roasted and, it seems to me, quite nicely seasoned, won't do me any harm."

To which the doctor replied:

"While I am alive, the lord governor will never eat that."

"And why not?" said Sancho.

And the doctor answered:

"Because our Master, Hippocrates, North Star and Guiding Light of all medicine, declared, in one of his famous adages: *Omnis saturatio mala, perdices autem pessima.* Which means: 'Excessive consumption of food is always bad, but partridges are worst of all.'"

"If that's how it is," said Sancho, "if my lord doctor will just have a look at what's on this table, and determine which dishes are good for me and which will do least damage, then he can let me eat without banging on me with his rod, because by His Excellency the Governor's life, so long as God permits me to enjoy it, I'm dying of hunger, and denying me food, though it may disturb my lord the doctor, and he may say to me God only knows what, is more likely to kill me than keep me healthy."

"You're quite right, your grace, my lord governor," responded the doctor, "so I don't think your grace ought to eat that platter of rabbit stew, because it's a very dangerous dish. That veal, now, if it hadn't been roasted or pickled you probably could have tried that — but as it is, it's completely out of the question."

And Sancho said:

"That steaming bowl right in front there: it looks to me like Spanish stew, and they put so many different things in there, why, I can't help but find something I like and that's good for me."

"*Absit!* [Desist!]" said the doctor. "Suppress any such baleful thought, for there is nothing in the world less nourishing than a Spanish stew. May such concoctions grace the tables of cathedral priests, or the headmasters of schools, or even a peasant's wedding, but keep them off governors' tables, where everything that is served must be pure and most perfect, the reason for which is that everyone everywhere always prefers simple to compound medicines, for there is no possibility of error in those which are simple, while, in those which are compound, it is always possible to commit an error in how much of this or how much of that is added. It seems to me that what my lord governor ought now to eat, in order to preserve and fortify his health, is roughly a hundred dry crackers and some thin slices of ripe quince, which will settle his stomach and aid his digestion."

Hearing this, Sancho leaned back in his chair and stared hard at the doctor, and then, his voice somber, he inquired about his name and where he had studied. To which the doctor replied:

"My lord governor, my name is Doctor Pedro Recio de Agüero, and I come from a town called Tirteafuera,[1] which is between Caracuel and Almodóvar del Campo, on the right hand side, and I took my degree in medicine at the University of Osuna."[2]

To which Sancho replied, furiously angry:

"In which case, Mister Doctor Pedro Recio de Mal Agüero [ill-omen], graduate of Osuna, who comes from Tirteafuera, which is on the right hand side as we go from Caracuel to Almodóvar del Campo, get the hell out of here or, I swear by the sun on high, I'll take a club and, starting with you, beat the shit out of every doctor on this island, or at least those I think as stupid as you, though I'll reverence and honor, as men of divine standing, every wise, moderate, and sensible doctor I can find. So let me say it again, Pedro Recio: get the hell out of here or, by God, I'll take this chair I'm sitting on and smash it over your head, and when they ask me about that, at the Final Judgment, I'll explain that I was only serving God by killing a bad doctor, the scourge of the whole country. Now let me eat, or else take back this god damned governorship, because any job where a man can't eat isn't worth a pair of dried beans."

Seeing how furious the governor had become, the doctor was frightened and about to scurry out of the room, when at that very moment a post horn was heard out in the street; going to the window at once, the butler returned to his new master, explaining:

---

1. *Recio* = harsh, severe; *agüero* = omen, sign; *tirte afuera* = get the hell out [*Translator's Note*].
2. Again, Osuna, founded only in 1548 (by which point the University of Salamanca had existed for over three hundred years), was a minor and ill-regarded university [*Translator's Note*].

"There's a courier from my lord the duke; he must be bringing something very important."

The courier came in, all sweaty and anxious, and, taking a sealed document out of his shirt, put it in the governor's hands, at which Sancho turned and put it in the butler's hands, ordering him to read out the address, which was as follows: *To Don Sancho Panza, Governor of Barataria Island, to be delivered to him personally or to his secretary.* Hearing this, Sancho said:

"Which one of you is my secretary?"

And one of the men in the room said:

"Me, my lord, because I know how to read and write, and because I'm a Basque."[3]

"With that last addition," said Sancho, "you could certainly be secretary to the emperor himself. Unseal this document, and tell me what it says."

The newly minted secretary did as directed, but having read the document said that it was a matter to be dealt with in private. So Sancho ordered everyone out of the room, leaving only the duke's steward and his own butler, for all the others, including the doctor, had gone, and then the secretary read the letter aloud:

It has come to my attention, my lord Don Sancho Panza, that certain of my enemies, who are also enemies of your island, are planning a violent assault on you, although it is not known on what night they will attack; you must be vigilant and watchful, so you're not taken by surprise and unprepared. I am also informed, by reliable spies, that four disguised assassins are now in your city, intending to kill you, because they're afraid of your keen intelligence, so keep your eyes open, watch everyone who comes to visit you, and eat nothing that is set in front of you. I shall of course come to your aid, if you see yourself in any difficulty; I am confident you will act, in all of this, with your usual rare comprehension. Given here, on the 16th of August, at four o'clock in the morning,

Your friend,
THE DUKE

Sancho was astonished, and those with him looked as if they were, too; turning to the duke's steward, Sancho said:

"The very first thing we must do, and I mean right away, is lock up Doctor Recio, because if anyone's likely to kill me, it's certainly him — and it'll be a slow and painful death, the way starvation is."

"But also," said the butler, "I don't think your grace ought to eat anything on this table, because it came from the nuns, and, as they say, the devil stands right behind the cross."

"I can't deny it," replied Sancho, "so for now give me a chunk of bread and about four pounds of grapes, because you can't get any poison into that stuff — because, really, I can't carry on without eating, and if we have to be ready for these threatened battles, we've got to be well fed,

---

3. Because of their discretion and loyalty, Basques were especially valued as secretaries [*Translator's Note*].

because the guts hold up the heart, not the other way around. And you, Mister Secretary, write an answer to my lord the duke and tell him we're doing what he ordered, and exactly as he ordered it, down to the last detail, and tell him I send a kiss to the hands of my lady the duchess, and remind her not to forget to send a messenger to my wife, Teresa Panza, with my letter and that bundle I left her, because I'll be very grateful and forever careful to serve her the best I know how — and, just in passing, also put in a kiss on the hands for my lord Don Quijote de La Mancha, so he can see I'm downright grateful; and then, as a good secretary, and a good Basque, you can add whatever else you like and happens to come to mind. So: let's have them take away this tablecloth, and bring me my food, and then I'll take care of all the spies and assassins and enchanters who'll be coming after me and my island."

A page came in, at this point, saying:

"There's a farmer and trader wanting to speak to Your Excellency about something, he says, that's very important."

"Oh, this is craziness," said Sancho. "Can these businessmen really be so stupid? Can't they figure out these aren't times for paying such calls? Those of us who are governors and judges, aren't we still men of flesh and blood? Why do they have to come pestering us, when they ought to leave us alone and let us have the rest we need — unless maybe they think we're made out of marble? By God and my conscience, if this governorship lasts (and I'm starting to think it won't) I'll cool down a couple of these businessmen. So tell this good man to come in — but first make sure he's not one of these spies, or an assassin who's after me."

"No, my lord," answered the page, "because he looks like a pretty plain fellow, and unless I don't know anything about it, he's as dangerous as a loaf of bread."

"And there's nothing to be afraid of," said the steward, "because we're all here."

"Might it be possible, Mister Butler," said Sancho, "now that Doctor Pedro Recio's no longer with us, for me to eat something with a little weight and body to it — even just a loaf of bread and an onion?"

"At dinner, tonight," said the butler, "we'll make up for the nourishment you've been lacking, and Your Lordship will be fully satisfied, I guarantee it."

"May God be willing," replied Sancho.

In came the farmer-businessman, who carried himself so well that you could see, from a thousand miles away, he was in fact a good, honest man. And his first words were:

"Which one of you gentlemen is the lord governor?"

"Who do you think it would be," answered the secretary, "except the man sitting on the throne?"

"Then I humble myself in his presence," the fellow said.

And, falling to his knees, he tried to kiss Sancho's hand. Sancho refused to let him, ordering him to stand up and say what he wanted. The man did so, saying:

"My lord, I'm a farmer from Miguelturra, which is about seven miles from Ciudad Real."

"We've got ourselves another Tirteafuera!" said Sancho. "Let me tell you, brother, I know Miguelturra very well, because it's not very far from where I live myself."

"So this is what it's all about, my lord," the farmer continued. "Through God's mercy, and the way it's done in the Holy Roman Catholic Church, I got married; I have two sons, both students, one, the younger, studying for his bachelor's degree, and the other, the older, for his master's; I'm a widower, because my wife died, or, to put it more accurately, a bad doctor killed her for me, by giving her an enema when she was pregnant, and if God had seen fit to let the baby live, and if he'd been a boy, I'd have gotten him studying for a doctorate, so he wouldn't be jealous of his brothers for having, one a bachelor's degree, and the other a master's."

"So," said Sancho, "if your wife hadn't died, or hadn't been killed, you wouldn't be a widower?"

"No, my lord, not at all," replied the farmer.

"All right, now we've run *that* around the maypole!" said Sancho. "Go on, brother: you're doing more for bedtime than for business-time."

"So," said the farmer, "this son of mine who's studying for his bachelor's degree has fallen in love with a girl from our town, Clara Perlerina [the Paralytic or pearl-like], daughter of Andrés Perlerino, who's a rich farmer — not that they have any legal right to the name Perlerino: it's just that every one of them has some kind of paralysis, so Perlerino's a better name, though, to tell the truth, this girl's just like a pearl straight out of the Orient, and when you look at her from the right hand side she's a real flower of the field, though not so much if you look from the left hand side, because the eye on that side's missing on account of smallpox, and even though her face is pretty well pock-marked — lots of them, and big, and deep — her good friends say they're not pock-marks at all, but just the tombs where she buries her lovers' souls. And she's so fussy about her appearance that, to keep from messing up her face, she kind of tucks up her nose, you know, so it really looks as if it's trying to get away from her mouth, but all the same the effect's a good one, because she has a big mouth, and if she didn't have ten or twelve teeth missing, here and there, she could compare pretty well with the best-looking of them, and maybe beat out a few. I don't have to tell you anything about her lips, because they're so thin and delicate that, if wool yarn was wound around lips, instead of spools, you could get a real big length around hers, but hers are really something, anyway, because they're not the usual color — they've got blue streaks in them, and green, and a kind of purple eggplant color, so I hope, my lord governor, you'll forgive me for painting her in all this detail, because sooner or later she's going to be my daughter, and I love her, I do, and I don't think she looks all that bad."

"Paint her any way you like," said Sancho, "because I've been enjoying your painting and, in fact, if I'd been able to eat anything, I couldn't think of a better dessert."

"I haven't yet gotten that far," replied the farmer, "but we'll get there pretty soon, if we haven't already arrived. So let me tell you, my lord, if I could paint you her elegance, and how nice and tall she is, you'd be astonished, but I can't, because she's all doubled over and bent, so her

knees are level with her mouth, though all the same she'd really be something if only she could straighten herself out, and her head would reach
the ceiling, so she certainly would have given my son her hand in marriage, except she can't open it out, it's so knotted up, but anyhow you can
see how well-made a hand it is just from her big long fingernails, and all
the grooves in them."

"Fine," said Sancho, "so let it be noted, brother, that you've painted
her from head to foot. Now: what is it you want? And get to the point,
instead of going around in circles and up and down back alleys — no
more pieces of this and scraps of that."

"What I want, my lord," answered the farmer, "is for your grace to do
me the favor of letting me have a letter of recommendation for my son's
new father-in-law, asking him to please let this marriage take place, because he and I aren't badly matched, either in property or in nature, and
since, to tell the truth, lord governor, my son is absolutely possessed —
I mean, at least three or four times a day there are evil spirits tormenting
him, and because he fell into a fire, once, his face is all wrinkled up like
a piece of old paper, and his eyes are always running and watery, but he's
as good as an angel and if he weren't always hitting himself, punching
himself in the face and all, he'd be a true saint."

"And that's all you want, my good man?" replied Sancho.

"Well, there is one other thing," said the farmer, "except I'm afraid to
say it — but why not, let's see what happens, because I've got to get it
off my chest, whether it works or it doesn't. Well, what I want, my lord,
is to ask your grace to let me have three hundred dollars, or maybe six
hundred, so I can arrange my son's dowry — I mean, help him set up
house, because, after all, they'll have to live by themselves, and not have
to worry about the fathers-in-law bossing them around."

"You're sure that's all you want," said Sancho, "and you're not holding
anything back because you're shy or embarrassed?"

"Oh no, certainly not," said the farmer.

He had barely finished speaking when the governor rose up, grabbed
the chair on which he'd been sitting, and said:

"God damn it, you stinking peasant, if you don't get your ugly face out
of sight and take yourself the hell out of here, I'll smash your head open
with this chair! You tricky son of a bitch, you people-painter straight out
of hell, is this the time to come begging for six hundred dollars? And
where would I get it from, eh, you lousy skunk? And even if I had it, why
should I give it you, you crooked idiot? What the hell do I care about
Miguelturra, and the whole race of Perlerinos? Get out of here or, by the
life of my lord the duke, I'll do exactly what I told you I'd do. You're not
from Miguelturra, you're some shifty skunk the Devil sent up here to tempt
me. I haven't been governor for a day and a half, you monster, and you
think I've gotten six hundred dollars out of it?"

The butler signaled to the farmer to leave, which he did, head bowed
low, apparently terrified that the governor would wreak his anger on him
— because this was, in fact, a rascal who really knew how to play his
role.

But now let's leave our angry Sancho (may peace reign once again) and return to Don Quijote, whom we left with his face bandaged and healing, after his cat-inflicted wounds, though it took eight days for him to be whole again, and on one of those days he experienced something that Sidi Hamid promises to record for us with exactly the same care and accuracy he has employed in narrating the other events of this history, no matter how insignificant they might have been.

Chapter Forty-Eight

— what happened between Don Quijote and Doña Rodríguez, the duchess' lady in waiting, along with other matters worthy of being recorded and forever remembered

Our badly wounded Don Quijote was exceedingly gloomy and dejected, his face bandaged and marked, not by God's hand, but by a cat's claws, though these were but the sorts of misfortunes all knights errant had to deal with. He stayed out of sight for six days, and during one of those nights, as he lay on his bed, wide awake, restless, contemplating how badly things had gone, and how Altisidora was harrying him, he thought he heard a key turn in the locked door of his room, and immediately imagined the lovestruck girl had come to assail his chastity and force him to betray the faithfulness he owed to his lady, Dulcinea del Toboso.

"No," he said, sure he was right, and speaking in a voice loud enough to be heard, "the most beautiful woman in all the world could not keep me from adoring that vision of you, my lady, stamped and engraved deep in my heart and in the furthest recesses of my bowels, whether of you, magically transformed into a rough peasant girl or of you, a nymph out of the golden River Tagus, entwining threads of silk and gold together — whether and no matter where Merlin holds you captive, or Montesinos — because wherever you may be you are mine, and I, everywhere I have been, and everywhere I will be, am yours."

He spoke the last of these words just as the door opened. Then he stood erect on his bed, wrapping himself in a bedspread of yellow satin, on his head a nightcap that fitted over his ears, his face and even his moustache swathed in bandages (those on his face for the protection of his scratch wounds, those on his moustache to keep it from tumbling languidly down), and, in this weird garb, looking like the most extraordinary phantasmagorical figure anyone could have imagined.

He stared directly at the door, expecting to see Altisidora's humbled, pitiful figure entering his room, but saw, instead, an ancient, venerable *dueña*, enveloped in a white veil so long and flowing that it covered her from head to foot. Her left hand held a short candle, lit, and her right hand shielded her eyes (over which she wore huge spectacles) from the light. She was walking with great care, silently and softly.

Watching her from his vantage point, Don Quijote fancied, seeing how she was dressed, and observing how quietly she came, that she was a witch or sorceress bent on some evil deed, so he hurriedly began to cross himself. Reaching the middle of the room, the apparition raised her eyes and saw

Don Quijote, furiously crossing himself over and over, and was quite as terrified by the sight as he was, seeing her, for he was so immense and yellow (wrapped in the bedspread, and with his face bandaged), and seemed so frighteningly deformed, that she screamed:

"Oh Jesus! What is this?"

Terror made her drop her candle — and then, finding herself in utter darkness, she turned and started to run, but in her fright tripped over her own skirts and fell flat on the floor. Don Quijote called out, in dread:

"I conjure you, phantom or whatever you are, to tell me your name and what you want with me. If you are a spirit in torment, say so, and I will do for you everything I can, for I am a Catholic Christian and devoted to kindness toward all men and women, which is why I have dedicated myself to the order of knight errantry whose tenets I profess, which tenets even permit the performance of good deeds for souls in purgatory."

Staggered as she was, the lady in waiting understood, hearing herself thus addressed, that Don Quijote was just as terrified as she was, so in a soft, pained voice she said:

"My lord Don Quijote — if by any chance you, your grace, are indeed Don Quijote — I'm no phantom, nor an apparition, nor a soul from purgatory, as your grace seems to have thought, but just Doña Rodríguez, my lady the duchess' honored lady in waiting, who has come to your grace precisely because I'm in one of those difficulties your grace is always helping people out of."

"Then tell me, Doña Rodríguez," said Don Quijote, "are you by any chance acting as intermediary in some sort of amatory affair? For I am obliged to inform you, in that case, that your errand must be a fruitless one, thanks to the incomparable beauty of my lady, Dulcinea del Toboso. Accordingly, Doña Rodríguez, if your grace puts aside and totally omits all amatory dealings, you're welcome to light your candle once again, and come back, and we can discuss everything you desire and whatever I can best do to make you content — excepting, as I have said, anything of a provocative nature."

"I someone else's message-bearer, my lord?" replied the *dueña*. "How little you know me, your grace, for I'm hardly old enough to involve myself in such silliness — since, God be praised, I'm still as lusty as a spring chicken, and all the teeth I was born with are still in my mouth, except for a few stolen from me by the chills and fevers we have so much of, here in Aragón. But just hold on a little, your grace; I'll go out and get a light for my candle, and then I'll come right back and tell you my troubles, since you're a help and comfort to the whole world."

She left the room, not pausing for any reply, and Don Quijote, calm but still exceedingly thoughtful, awaited her return; then a thousand ideas about this new adventure suddenly surged into his mind, and he fancied it would be a mistake, and a very bad plan, to let himself be placed in danger of breaking the faith he had plighted to his own lady, at which realization he said to himself:

"Who knows whether or not the Devil, sly and cunning as he is, is trying to use a *dueña* to accomplish what could not be effected by empresses, queens, duchesses, marquissas, or countesses? For I've often heard it said, and by men of much wisdom, that, if he can, he prefers to make use of some snub-nosed hussy, rather than a true aristocrat. And who knows, too, whether this loneliness, this time and place, and even this deep silence, may not combine to wake my sleeping desires and make me stumble and fall, here toward the end of my days, as I have never tripped and fallen before? At such times, flight is safer than waiting for combat to be joined. But I must be out of my mind, thinking such things, for it's impossible that a big tall *dueña* wrapped in a great white veil, and wearing spectacles, could rouse lascivious thoughts in even the most ferociously callous of hearts. Can there possibly be a lady in waiting in the entire world who's worth looking at? Could there be a *dueña* in the entire universe who's not insolent, squeamish, and a mincing fraud? So get thee gone, you *dueña*-ish hordes, incapable of any human delight! Ah, how well she knew what she was up to, that lady who is supposed to have kept two statues of ladies in waiting next to her sofa, with their spectacles and their pin cushions, just as if they were plying their needles, and who found these statues every bit as effective in preserving the tone of her drawing room as any real ladies in waiting could ever be!"

And then he rose from his bed, intending to shut the door and not let Doña Rodríguez back in, but just as he was about to close it, the lady returned, carrying a lit wax candle — and seeing Don Quijote from closer up, wrapped in his bedspread, with all his bandages and his strange nightcap, she was frightened all over again, and, taking two steps backward, said:

"Am I quite safe, sir knight? Because it doesn't seem to me a very proper sign that your grace has gotten out of bed."

"I might well ask you exactly the same question, madame," replied Don Quijote, "and indeed do let me ask if I, in my turn, am safe from being assaulted and violated?"

"Sir knight, from whom, or to whom, do you address this request for such a guarantee?" replied the lady.

"To you, and from you," replied Don Quijote, "because I am made neither of marble nor of brass, and right now it's not ten o'clock in the morning but midnight — and even a bit after, I suspect — and in a place more isolated and private than the cave must have been, where the bold and treacherous Aeneas took possession of the lovely and devout Dido. But give me your hand, madame, for I need no greater protection than my own continence and modesty, as well as that offered by your most sanctified of all veils."

Saying which, he raised his right hand to his lips, and she did exactly the same thing, after which they shook hands.

Now, at this point Sidi Hamid indulges himself in a parenthesis, noting that, in the name of Mohammad, he'd have given the very best of the two cloaks he owned, could he have been able to see these two, their hands clasped and joined, walking from the door to Don Quijote's bed.

So Don Quijote climbed back into bed, and Doña Rodríguez seated herself in a chair, not too close to the bed, removing neither her spectacles nor her veil. Don Quijote curled up under the blankets, only his face uncovered; once they were both reasonably calm, it was Don Quijote who first broke the silence:

"Now, Doña Rodríguez, if your grace would care to bring into the open and reveal everything hidden in your sorrowful heart and care-worn bosom, I shall hear you with chaste ears and help you with compassionate deeds."

"I believe you will," answered the lady in waiting, "because, from your grace's gallant and cordial bearing, one could expect nothing but such a Christian response. Now it happens, my lord Don Quijote, that although your grace sees me seated here on this chair, right in the middle of the kingdom of Aragón, dressed as a worn-out old lady in waiting, I am in fact a native of Asturias de Oviedo,[1] and from a family widely connected among the better people in that province, but because of my own ill luck, and my parents' carelessness (for they had no idea how it all happened), we were quite suddenly impoverished, so they brought me to the court in Madrid, where, to prevent even worse calamities, my parents found me a place as a seamstress for a highborn lady, and I should like to inform your grace that no one who has ever lived can surpass me at hemstitching or linen embroidery. My parents left me in service and returned home, and not many years thereafter ascended to Heaven, for they were exceedingly good and Catholic Christians. So I was left orphaned and dependent on the miserable wages and paltry rewards such serving maids usually receive, in palaces. At about this time, without any assistance from me, a squire serving in the same house fell in love with me — a mature man, full-bearded and respectable and, above all else, as fine a gentleman as any king, for his was a mountain family. We did not particularly conceal our love, and so my mistress, to prevent any difficulties, had us openly married, according to the laws of our Holy Mother Roman Catholic Church, and to this union there was born — to kill off any good fortune I may have had — a daughter, and I say this, not because I died giving birth, for in fact everything went exactly as and when it was supposed to, but because, not long after, a certain violent shock killed my husband — and if I took the time, now, to explain how that happened, your grace would surely be astonished."

She began to weep bitterly, at this point, and then said:

"Forgive me your grace, my lord Don Quijote, because every time I remember my dear departed, so untimely taken, I can't control myself and my eyes fill with tears. Mother of God! How nobly he rode on that big strong mule, as black as jet, with my mistress up behind him! Because in those days they didn't use coaches, or carry people around in sedan chairs, the way I'm told they do now, and ladies rode everywhere, sitting behind their squires. But I must just tell you this, so you can see how scrupulously well-bred my good husband was. As he started down Santiago Street, in Madrid, where it's rather narrow, a court magistrate drove out, preceded by two constables and, the moment my good squire of a husband saw him, he turned his mule full around, indicating that he too would escort the judge.[2] My lady, sitting behind him, whispered:

" 'What on earth are you doing, you faint-hearted wretch? Have you forgotten I'm here?' "

"The judge, out of politeness, pulled up his horse and said:

1. I.e., western Asturias; the eastern part is Asturias de Santillana [*Translator's Note*].
2. As custom and law required he do, to properly honor so important a personage [*Translator's Note*].

" 'Go on your way, sir, for it's I who should escort my lady Doña Casilda,' that being my mistress' name. But my husband insisted, his hat in his hand, that he would be pleased to escort the judge, and my mistress, wild with anger at the sight, pulled a heavy pin from her sewing box — more like a kind of punch, or an awl — and drove it right into his back, which made my husband shout and so abruptly twist his body about that my lady fell to the ground. Her two footmen hurried to pick her up, as did the judge and the two constables; there was great excitement all around the Guadalajara Gate, among all the riffraff who congregate there; my mistress walked away, and my husband ran into a barber's house, crying that the thing had gone clean through his entrails.[3] My husband's courteous behavior was much talked about, even by the boys out in the street, and for that reason, and also because he was a little short-sighted, my lady[4] dismissed him — a source of such sorrow, I am convinced, that without the slightest doubt it brought on the sickness which killed him.

"So I was left widowed and alone, with a daughter to care for — a daughter whose beauty grew like foam on the waters of the sea. In the end, because I had such a reputation as a seamstress, my lady the duchess, who had only recently married my lord the duke, decided to bring me with her to this kingdom of Aragón, and my daughter with me, and as time went on my daughter grew up and developed all the charm in the world: she sings like a lark; is so light on her feet, dancing, that she seems to move like a thought, whirling and spinning like a lost soul; she reads and writes like a schoolteacher; and she handles numbers like a miser. I need say nothing of her purity: the water she drinks is no purer than she is; and by now she's, let me see, sixteen years old, plus five months and three days, give or take a little. So, finally: this girl of mine has fallen in love with a rich farmer's son, living in one of the duke my master's villages, not very far from here. And then, I don't know how, he tricked my daughter, telling her they'd be married, and got into bed with her, but now he won't live up to his promise, and even though my lord the duke knows all about it — because I complained to him, not just once, but many times, begging him to force this farmer to marry my daughter — he won't pay any attention, and barely so much as listens to me, because this trickster's father is filthy rich and lends the duke money, and always bails him out when he gets into debt, so the duke doesn't want to annoy or upset him in any way at all. So I'd like you, my lord, to see if your grace can fix all this up, either by peaceful means or at swordspoint, because everyone says your grace came into this world to undo wrongs, and set them right, and to protect the unfortunate, and just think, your grace, my poor orphaned daughter has no one else to take care of her — and she's so refined, she's so young — and she has all the good qualities I've said she has, and by God and my conscience, out of all the girls who serve my lady, there isn't one who can hold a candle to her, and the one they call Altisidora, who they think is the most self-possessed and elegant and grace-

---

3. "Barber" and "surgeon" were virtually synonymous terms [*Translator's Note*].
4. Cervantes calls the mistress "my lady duchess" (the duchess is not referred to for another quarter of a page); I have quietly corrected a minor but obvious error [*Translator's Note*].

ful, doesn't come within five miles of my daughter. So I want your grace to know, my lord, that all that glitters isn't gold, because this little Altisidora is more arrogant than beautiful, and she's bold rather than decently reserved, and she's also not very healthy, and she has bad breath, so you can't stand to be near her very long. And even though my lady the duchess . . . but I'd better hold my tongue, because, as they say, the very walls have ears."

"By my life," asked Don Quijote, "Doña Rodríguez: is there something the matter with the duchess?"

"Since you implore me so feelingly," answered the *dueña*, "I am obliged to answer your question both fully and truthfully. My lord Don Quijote, you've seen how beautiful my lady the duchess is, what a complexion she has, as smooth as a polished sword blade, and her cheeks — like milk and red roses, with the sun in one, and the moon in the other — and the grace with which she moves, as if too light to bother touching the ground? Well, please understand, your grace, that for all this she has to be thankful to God, in the first place, and then to two manmade ulcers in her legs, which are draining off the negative humors her body is full of, according to the doctors."

"Mother of God!" said Don Quijote. "Can my lady the duchess really need that kind of medical treatment? I wouldn't have believed a word of it, even had barefoot friars told me — but since Doña Rodríguez says so, it must be true. Yet such openings in the skin, made in such a place, can't really flow with bad humors, but only with liquid perfume! I am fully persuaded, finally, that when doctors make these incisions, they must in fact powerfully improve a person's health."

Don Quijote had hardly spoken when the door of the room blew open, sending such a burst of air across the room that Doña Rodríguez's candle fell from her hand and, as the saying goes, everything turned as dark as a wolf's mouth. The poor *dueña* felt two hands close suddenly around her throat, gripping so tightly that she could not breathe, and then immediately someone else, in absolute silence, turned up her skirts and, with what seemed to be a slipper, began to whack at her so vigorously that it was truly pitiful — and they even laid hands on Don Quijote, who hadn't budged out of his bed and, not knowing what on earth to do, was lying quiet and still, worried that it might be his turn next. Nor was that an idle fear, because once they'd given the lady in waiting a good whipping (she not daring to make the slightest protest), they turned their attention to Don Quijote, rolling him out of his bedspread and sheets and pinching him so vigorously that he couldn't help punching out at them, in self defense — the whole affair going on in utter silence. It was a battle that lasted fully half an hour, and then the phantasmic figures rushed out, Doña Rodríguez straightened her skirts and, bemoaning her misfortune, went out the open door, not saying a word to Don Quijote, who was thus left alone, unhappy and well-pinched, bewildered and lost in thought — and there we will leave him, trying to understand which wicked enchanter, this time, had done all these things to him. But that too will be revealed, in good time, because Sancho Panza (not to mention the proper telling of our tale) is calling us elsewhere.

Chapter Forty-Nine

— what happened to Sancho Panza, as he patrolled his island

When we left our great governor, he was furious at the rascally portrait-painter farmer, who had been instructed by the steward, as the steward had been instructed by the duke, to make fun of Sancho, but no matter how silly and coarse and fat he might be, Sancho hadn't let anyone roll over him, informing all those around him (including Doctor Pedro Recio), who had come back into the room once the duke's confidential communication had been taken care of:

"Ha! Now I see just how smart judges and governors have to be — and maybe they ought to be made of brass — to keep from being bothered by all these pesky businessmen, who want to be listened to and waited on, in season and out, all day long, just worrying about their own affairs, come hell or high water, and if the poor judge doesn't give them a hearing, and take care of them, even if it's not something the judge can do, or it just isn't the right time for handling those things, then they curse him, and tell stories about him, and start gnawing at his bones, and even make fun of his ancestors. Well, you pigheaded idiots, you stupid fools, just you keep your pants on, and wait for the right time and the right occasion for conducting your business. Don't show up when it's dinner time, or bed time, because judges are made out of flesh and blood, and they have to yield to Nature just the way all men do — except me, that is, thanks to my lord Doctor Pedro Recio Tirteafuera, who's standing right here, who wants to starve me to death and insists his kind of dying is really living, so I hope God grants him, and all those like him, exactly that kind of life — and of course I'm talking about bad doctors, because the good ones deserve prizes and laurel wreaths."

Those who knew Sancho Panza were astonished, hearing him speak so well, and didn't know what was responsible, except perhaps that serious posts and professions can either improve the mind or utterly ruin it. In the end, Doctor Pedro Recio Agüero from Tirteafuera promised to let Sancho have his dinner, that night, even if it violated all the maxims of Hippocrates. And this promise satisfied the governor, who then began to eagerly, even somewhat desperately, anticipate the coming of night and his dinner time, and despite the fact that, to him, time seemed to have stopped in its tracks, never moving from one minute to the next, the hour he so longed for did in fact arrive, and he dined on pickled beef and onions and boiled calves' feet (by no means fresh). He consumed it all, and with a better appetite than if he'd been given black quails from Milan, pheasants from Rome, veal from Sorrento, partridges from Modón, or geese from Lavajos. And, while he was eating, he turned to the doctor and said:

"Listen, Mister Medical Man: from now on don't fix me any fancy things to eat, or any special dishes, because that would just throw my stomach out of kilter, because what it's used to is goat meat, and plain old beef, and bacon, and pickled meat, and turnips and onions, and if we feed it palace food we're going to make it unhappy, and even upset. What the butler can do is just bring me those, you know, Spanish stews (and the longer they've been sitting around, the better they smell), and they can toss in anything they feel like, as long as it's edible, and I'll appreciate him doing that, and pay him back some day — and let's not have anybody fooling around with me, because, you know, to be or not to be: as long as we're all alive, let's all of us eat in peace and harmony, because when God sends the daylight He sends it for everyone. I'm going to govern this island without giving up anything I'm entitled to, and without taking any bribes, and everybody had better watch their step, because they've got to understand this: if they want a fight, I'm their man; just give me an excuse, and I'll show them things that'll make their eyes pop. It's like this: if we don't make honey, the flies won't eat any."

"Most certainly, my lord governor," said the butler, "what your grace is saying makes a lot of sense, and I can assure you, in the name of all the inhabitants of this island, that we'll serve your grace to the hilt, with good will and affection, because the easy-handed way you've begun your governorship, your grace, can't make us do or think anything likely to make trouble for you."

"That's what I think, too," said Sancho, "and they'd be stupid to think or do otherwise. So let me repeat: take care of my food, and my little donkey's, because that's what's really important in this whole business — that's what really counts. And when it gets to be time, let's patrol around this island, because I plan to get rid of dirty, indecent people, which means bums, and loafers, and anyone who doesn't want to work, because I want you to understand, my friends, that shiftless, lazy folk do the same thing in a country that drones do in a beehive, which is: they eat the honey the worker bees make. I intend to protect farmers and peasants, help well-bred people keep what they've got, reward all those who are virtuous and, above all else, preserve respect for religion and honor those who belong to the Church. How does that strike you, my friends? Am I on to something, or am I just shooting off steam?"

"You're saying a great deal, your grace, my lord governor," said the steward, "so much so that I'm astonished to find a man as uneducated as your grace (because I don't think you've had any schooling at all) speaking words so full of wisdom and good sense — words so different from anything anticipated about your abilities, either by those who sent you here or those who came with you. The world shows us new things, each and every day: jokes turn into truths, and jokers find that they're the ones being fooled."

Night fell, and the governor had his supper (with Doctor Recio's permission). He got ready to go on patrol, and sallied forth with the steward, his secretary, the butler, and the chronicler responsible for keeping a record of the new governor's actions, as well as enough constables and scribes to constitute a fair-sized squadron. Sancho walked in the center, carrying his staff, and was a fine sight to see, and they hadn't gone very far when they heard the sound of blade meeting blade, so they followed the noise and found a fight between two solitary men, who, seeing the forces of the law approach, stopped their combat and stood still, one of them calling out:

"In the name of God, and the king! How can you let people be robbed in this town, right out in public, and attack people in the middle of the street?"

"Gently, my good man," said Sancho, "and tell me what caused this quarrel, because I am the governor here."

The second combatant said:

"My lord governor, I'll tell you the whole thing in a nutshell. Let me inform your grace that this charming fellow has just won over a thousand dollars, in the gambling house over there, and God only knows how. And since I was there myself, I settled more than one dispute in his favor, although my conscience told me I shouldn't. So he collects his winnings, and I expected him to give me a generous tip, you know the way it's always done, because I'm a respectable man, who comes there to help with supervising things, and lend a hand when someone's being cheated, and keep people out of fights, and he just puts his money in his pocket and leaves the establishment. That annoyed me, so I followed him, and speaking nice and polite I asked him to give me something like eight dollars, because he knows I'm an honorable man, but I don't have a job or a profession, because my parents neither taught me nor left me one, and this rascal, who's a worse thief than Cacus and a bigger swindler than Little Andrada, wouldn't give me more than four dollars, so you can certainly see, your grace, my lord governor, that he has no shame and even less conscience! But by God, if you hadn't come walking up, I'd have made him vomit up his winnings and taught him how to settle his accounts."

"And what do you say to all this?" Sancho asked the first man.

He answered that his opponent had spoken the plain truth, and he didn't want to tip him more than four dollars because he'd had to tip him so many times before, and people who lived off tips had to be obliging and take with a smile whatever they were given, and not start drawing up accounts with the winners who tipped them, unless they know for a fact there's been cheating and the winners don't deserve what they won, and the best proof that he himself was an honest man, and no thief, as his opponent claimed, was precisely that he hadn't wanted to give a larger tip, because cheaters always have to pay off the spectators who know what they've been doing.

"That's true," said the steward. "Now let's see, your grace, my lord governor, what you're going to do with these two fellows."

"This is what I'm going to do," replied Sancho. "You, Mister Winner, I don't care if you're good, or bad, or half one and half the other, but you hand this quarrelsome fellow a hundred dollars, and then give us another thirty for the poor people in jail — and you, who don't have any job or profession, and just loaf around this island, you take your hundred dollars and sometime tomorrow you leave this island, under sentence of exile for ten years — and if you come back before then, you'll finish your exile in the next world, because I'll hang you on the gallows (or, anyway, the hangman will, on my orders), and don't either one of you answer me a word, or you'll feel the weight of my hand."

The first man opened his purse, the second man took his money, and then the latter left the island and the former went home, and the governor said:

"So: either I'm not worth much, or we should get rid of these gambling houses, because it seems to me they do a lot of harm."

"But this one, anyway," said one of the scribes, "your grace won't be able to get rid of, because it's owned by a very important person, who without any question loses a lot more, every year, than he ever earns from these games. Your grace can show your power against other, lesser gambling houses, and indeed they're the ones that do the most harm and harbor the worst excesses, because, in houses owned by highborn gentlemen, truly celebrated swindlers don't dare show their hands, and given that the vice of gambling has become so common, it's better to have it done in highborn rather than in lesser houses — where, after midnight, if they catch some unfortunate fellow, they just skin him alive."

"All right, mister scribe," said Sancho. "There's a lot to be said about all this."

A bailiff suddenly appeared, with a young fellow on whom he had a good grip:

"My lord governor, this young man was walking toward us, and the minute he saw we were policemen he turned and ran like a deer, which shows he has to be guilty of something. I ran after him, but if he hadn't tripped and fallen I'd never have caught him."

"So why were you running?" Sancho asked.

The boy replied:

"My lord, to keep from having to answer all the questions these cops ask."

"What business are you in?"

"Weaver."

"And what do you weave?"

"With your grace's permission, iron spearheads."

"You're being funny with me? You think you're a real comedian? Fine! And where were you going?"

"For a breath of air, my lord."

"And where do you find a breath of air, here on this island?"

"Wherever the wind blows it."

"Fine! You've told me exactly what I wanted to know. You're a smart young fellow, but now let's pretend I'm the air, and I'm blowing on your back, and you're going to jail. You: take him away! For tonight, I'll make sure you don't sleep out in the air!"

"By God," said the boy, "your grace can no more make me sleep in jail than make me king!"

"And why can't I make you sleep in jail?" replied Sancho. "Don't I have the power to arrest you and let you go whenever I feel like it?"

"Whatever power you may have, your grace," said the boy, "it won't be enough to make me sleep in jail."

"And why not?" answered Sancho. "Take him away right now, so he can see the truth with his own eyes — and even if the magistrates want to treat him with their usual greedy generosity, suppose I fine them two thousand dollars if they let you take one step out of that jail?"

"That's a laugh," replied the boy. "The fact of the matter is, all the men on earth won't be enough to make me sleep in jail."

"So tell me, my little demon," said Sancho. "Do you have a guardian angel who'll set you free, and pull off the chains I think I'll have them put on you?"

"Ah now, my lord governor," said the boy good humoredly, "now let's be reasonable and get to the heart of it. Your grace imagines you'll have me carried off to jail, and they'll put all kinds of chains and shackles on me, and they'll throw me in a dungeon, and you'll threaten the magistrates with big fines if they let me go, so they'll do exactly as you tell them to — but, in spite of all that, if I don't want to sleep, and stay awake all night — not sleeping a wink! — does your grace think all your power is enough to make me sleep, if I don't feel like it?"

"No, certainly not," said the secretary. "The fellow has established his point."

"But," said Sancho, "if you won't sleep, it's just because you yourself don't want to, and not because I said you should?"

"Oh no, your grace," said the boy. "I wouldn't dream of such disobedience."

"So go home in peace," said Sancho. "Go sleep in your own bed, and may God let you sleep well, because I don't want to deprive you of it. But let me give you some advice: from now on, don't play games with policemen, because maybe you'll meet up with one who'll break the joke right over your head."

The boy went off, the governor continued on his rounds, and not too long afterward they met two constables with a man they were holding fast, and the policemen said:

"My lord governor, this may look like a man, but it isn't, it's a woman, and not a bad-looking one, who's going around dressed like a man."

They held two or three lanterns up to her face, the light showing them a woman's face, perhaps sixteen years old, or a bit more, with her hair caught up in a silken net, colored gold and green, as lovely as a thousand pearls. They inspected her from head to foot, and found she was wearing red silk stockings, with white taffeta garters, fringed in gold and small seed pearls; her breeches were green and gold, as was her loose jacket, under which she wore a vest of the very finest white and gold cloth, and on her feet she wore white men's shoes. She wore no sword at her waist, but carried an exceedingly ornate dagger, and her fingers displayed a good many extremely fine rings. She seemed pretty to all who looked at her, but no one knew who she was, nor could the local people even begin to identify her, and those who were in on the various jokes played on Sancho were the most astonished of all, because this was not a discovery they had planted, and so they were extremely concerned to see what might happen.

Sancho, stunned by the girl's beauty, asked her who she was, where she was going, and what could have caused her to be dressed as she was. Her eyes directed at the ground, in modesty and acute embarrassment, she replied:

"My lord, I cannot say in public what it so much matters to me must be kept a secret. Please do understand this one thing, however: I am neither a thief nor a criminal, but just an unfortunate girl, obliged by the power of jealousy to violate the decorum owed to modesty."

The steward, hearing these words, said to Sancho:

"My lord governor, let all these people stand back, so the lady can tell you, with less embarrassment, what you want to know."

The governor directed that this be done, and everyone except the steward, the butler, and the secretary drew back. Seeing that they were alone, the girl went on:

"Gentlemen, I am Pedro Pérez Mazorca's daughter, and he collects the wool tax, and he often comes to visit my father."

"That can't be true, my lady," said the steward, "because I know Pedro Pérez very well indeed, and I know he has no children, either male or female — and what's more, how can you say he's your father and then immediately say that he often comes to visit your father?"

"I'd noticed that," said Sancho.

"I'm all upset, gentlemen, and I don't know what I'm saying," replied the girl. "But the truth is I'm Diego de la Llana's daughter, and all you gentlemen surely know him."

"Now that could be true," said the steward, "because I know Diego de la Llana, and I know he's a highborn gentleman, and rich, and he has both a son and a daughter, and ever since he's been a widower no one in this entire town can say they've ever seen the daughter's face, because he keeps her so shut in that the sun himself never catches a glimpse of her, but just the same rumor has it she's wonderfully beautiful."

"It really is true," replied the girl, "and that daughter is me; except whether or not rumor is lying, when it talks of my beauty, you will have discovered for yourselves, gentlemen, since you have now seen me."

Then she began to weep bitter tears, and the secretary, seeing this, said to the butler, very softly:

"Something of real importance has surely happened to this poor girl, she being the well-born lady she is, to lead her out of her house in such clothing, and at such an hour."

"Who could doubt it?" replied the butler. "And, what's more, her tears simply confirm your suspicion."

Sancho comforted her as best he could, asking her not to be the least bit afraid of telling him what had happened, and then they'd all try as hard as they could to help her in any way they could.

"What has happened," she answered, "is that my father has kept me shut away for ten years, or the whole time since the earth swallowed up my mother. The house has a richly furnished chapel, where mass is said, and during these years all I've seen has been the sun in the sky, during the day, and at night the moon and the stars, without ever a glimpse of streets, plazas, churches, and not a man except my father, and my brother, and Pedro Pérez, the tax collector, who often comes to our house, which is why I suddenly thought of saying he was my father, so I wouldn't have to tell you my real name. Shutting me away like this, denying me any opportunity ever to leave the house, even to go to church, has for a long time been making me extremely unhappy; I wanted to see the world — or, at least, the town where I was born, nor did it seem to me that such desires were a violation of the decorum which young women of good birth are supposed to observe. When I heard it said there were bullfights, or they were staging mock battles — men on horseback, using canes instead of spears — or putting on plays, I asked my brother (who's a year younger than me) to describe all these things, and many others I'd never seen, and he told me about them as best he could, but his explanations only made me burn the more fiercely to see for myself. Well, to shorten this tale of ruin and damnation, let me just tell you I begged and pleaded with my brother, as I never, never had done before . . ."

And then she fell to sobbing once again. The steward told her:

"Continue, your grace, my dear lady, and tell us what happened, for your words and your tears astonish and perplex us."

"There's not much left to say," the girl answered, "although there are lots of tears still to be shed, because misplaced longings can only produce misplaced consequences."

The butler, deeply affected by the girl's beauty, lifted his lantern once more, to see her again, and it seemed to him she was not weeping tears, but dew on the meadows, or seed pearls — or lovelier things still, like true oriental pearls — and he hoped passionately that her misfortune was not so immense as, by her tears and her sighs, she seemed to indicate. The governor, however, was growing weary, seeing how long it was taking the girl to tell her story, so he told her not to prolong matters, because it was getting late and they had a great deal of the town still to patrol. So she said, her words broken by sobs and half-swallowed sighs:

"My misfortune, and my misery, is simply that I begged my brother to let me dress as a man, wearing some of his clothing, and then, while our father slept, to take me to see this whole town, and, because I kept pestering him, he finally agreed, and lent me this costume I'm now wearing, while he put on one of mine, which fit him as if he'd been born to wear it, for he's too young to have a beard and looks like an extremely pretty girl, and then earlier tonight, not much more than an hour ago, we left the house and, impelled by our wild, childish idea, we went all over town, and then, when we were about to return home, we saw a great troop of people and my brother said:

" 'Sister, this must be the official patrol, so lighten up your feet, and put wings on them, then run right behind me so we can keep them from finding out who we are, which wouldn't do us any good.'

"So he turned and ran — no, not run: he flew. But I'd gone barely six steps when I fell, because I was so frightened, and then the policeman came and carried me before you gentlemen, and here I am, in front of so many people, shamed by own wickedness and silly whims."

"Are you telling us," said Sancho, "that this is the only misfortune you've met with, and it wasn't jealousy that made you leave your house, even though that's what you said it was, when you started to tell us all this?"

"Nothing else happened to me," replied the girl, "and it wasn't jealousy, it was just wanting to see what the world looked like, and to me that meant the streets of this town."

And, as if to nail down the truth of her story, constables appeared with her brother in their grip, one of them having chased him down when he ran away from his sister. And he was all dressed up in a richly woven skirt and a short cape of blue damask, fringed with fine gold lace; he wore no veil, and all that decorated his head was his own hair, wound in golden ringlets, wonderfully blond and curly. The governor, along with the steward and the butler, took him aside and asked how he happened to be dressed like that, and the boy, no less ashamed and embarrassed, told exactly the same story his sister had told, which the lovestruck butler was delighted to hear. So the governor said to them:

"What you've surely done, you two, is play a very foolish prank, which doesn't justify such big tears, or anything like this much weeping and sighing, because if you'd just said, 'We're a boy and a girl, who left our father's house like this, just because we were curious, and for no other reason at all,' that would have been the end of it, without any of these sobs and tears."

"You're right," said the girl. "But you gentlemen have to understand I was so very upset I couldn't think straight."

"No harm done," replied Sancho. "Let's go: we'll bring you back to your father's house, and maybe he hasn't even noticed you were gone. But from now on don't do such silly things, and don't be so anxious to see the world, because a modest woman stays home, as if she had a broken leg, and women and hens both suffer, when they go roaming, and a woman who wants to see, also wants to be seen. I'll say no more."

The boy thanked the governor for his graciousness in returning them to their home, which was where they indeed went, and it wasn't very far away. When they got there, the boy threw a pebble at a window grating, and a maid quickly came down (for she had been waiting for them) and opened the door, and they went back in, leaving the governor's party as struck by her charm and beauty as by her longing to see the world — in the darkness, and without going any farther abroad than the streets of their town. But their youth and inexperience explained everything.

The butler, however, felt as if his heart had been pierced right through, and he vowed to go to her father, first thing tomorrow, and ask for her hand in marriage, feeling sure his suit would not be rejected, since he was one of the duke's servants — and even Sancho was wondering if he could marry the boy to his daughter, Sanchica, and planning to do something about that, when he had time, assuring himself that no one could refuse to marry a governor's daughter.

And then they finished their rounds, that night, and two days later his governorship was finished, too, which destroyed and utterly wiped out all his plans, as you will see, when you read on.

Chapter Fifty

— wherein it is explained just who the enchanters and scourges who spanked the dueña and pinched Don Quijote were, plus what happened to the page, when he brought Sancho Panza's letter to Sancho's wife, Teresa Panza

Sidi Hamid, devoted investigator of the very atoms of this truthful history, records that, when Doña Rodríguez left her room, intending to visit Don Quijote, her roommate heard her going, and since ladies in waiting universally hunger for knowledge, understanding, and the general sniffing out of everything as yet unknown, the roommate followed after her, and so silently that Doña Rodríguez never knew she was there, and then, not being deficient in the universal characteristic of ladies in waiting, namely gossip-mongering, the moment she saw Doña Rodríguez actually entering Don Quijote's room, she hurried off to let her mistress the duchess know what was going on.

The duchess promptly informed the duke, asking his permission to take Altisidora and go see what the elderly *dueña* wanted with Don Quijote, to which the duke assented; cautiously and quietly, step by step, the two ladies sneaked to the door of our knight's room, coming so close, indeed, that they could virtually smell what was being said inside, and when the duchess heard how Doña Rodríguez had been broadcasting the news of the artificial ulcers in her legs, she couldn't bear it, and neither could Altisidora, so the two of them, furiously angry and fairly lusting for vengeance, burst into the room and harassed Don Quijote, and thrashed Doña Rodríguez, in the style we have already narrated — for any insult aimed directly at a woman's beauty (and vanity) fans a wild fire of anger and a burning desire for revenge.

The duchess told the duke what they had done, which much amused him, and then, continuing with her plan to amuse and entertain herself at Don Quijote's expense, she sent the page who had played Dulcinea, in the famous disenchantment farce (every aspect of which, by the way, had now fled right out of Sancho Panza's mind, what with his duties as governor), to pay a visit to Teresa Panza, Sancho's wife, bringing her husband's letter as well as other things, plus, as a present, a rich and beautiful coral necklace.

Our history records, accordingly, that this was a sensible and very keen-witted page, most anxious to be of service to his lady, so he rode cheerfully off to Sancho's village, and just before he arrived he saw a number of women, washing clothes in a stream, of whom he asked if this was the village in which he would find Teresa Panza, wife of a certain Sancho Panza, squire to a knight named Don Quijote de La Mancha. Hearing this question, a girl who'd been washing clothes stood up and said:

"This Teresa Panza is my mother, and that Sancho is my lord father, and that knight is our master."

"Then come on, girl," said the page, "and bring me to your mother, because I'm carrying both a letter and a present from your father."

"I'll be very glad to do that, my dear sir," replied the girl, who looked to be roughly fourteen years old.

Leaving the clothes she was washing for another girl to take care of, neither putting anything on her head nor on her feet (for she remained shoeless and disheveled), she ran off in front of the page's horse, saying:

"Come, your grace, because our house is right at the entrance to the village, and that's where my mother is, and she's been worried sick for news of my father."

"Well," said the page, "the news I'm bringing her is so good that she'll be thanking God to have it."

Hopping and skipping, running and jumping, the girl led them to the village, and before she was even in the house she called loudly from the very doorway:

"Come on out, Mama Teresa, come on, come on, because there's a gentleman here, bringing a letter and other things from my father, bless him."

And at this her mother, Teresa Panza, did indeed come out, busily spinning a tuft of cotton. She was wearing a grey skirt, cut so short that it almost looked as if she was being publicly shamed, a grey bodice, and a sleeveless blouse. She was not terribly old, although she seemed distinctly the wrong side of forty, but she was strong, muscular, vigorous, with a dark, sun-browned complexion; seeing first her daughter, and then a man on horseback, she said:

"Girl, who is this? Who is this gentleman?"

"A servant to my lady, Doña Teresa Panza," answered the page.

And, matching his deeds to his words, he jumped off his horse and, with great humility, knelt before the lady Teresa, saying:

"Let me kiss your hand, your grace, my lady Doña Teresa, as the duly espoused and sole wife of My Lord Don Sancho Panza, lawful Governor of Barataria Island."

"Oh, my lord, get up from there! Don't do that," replied Teresa, "because I'm nobody in particular, but just a poor peasant woman, daughter of another country humpkin[1] and wife of a knight errant's squire, who's no governor at all!"

"Ah," said the page, "but your grace is indeed the infinitely dignified wife of an immensely dignified governor — in proof of which, please accept, your grace, both this letter and this small gift."

And he whipped out of his pocket a coral necklace, with gold clasps, then put it around her neck, saying:

"The letter I bring you is from my lord governor, and this coral necklace is from my lady the duchess, who sent me here to your grace."

Teresa was stunned, as was her daughter, who said:

"May I live and die if our master, Don Quijote, hasn't gone and gotten Daddy that governorship he kept promising him."

"He has indeed," replied the page, "because it is on my lord Don Quijote's account that my lord Sancho is now governor of Barataria Island, as you can see by this letter."

"Your grace, my dear gentleman, please read it to me," said Teresa, "because even though I know everything there is to know about spinning, I can't read at all."

"Neither can I," added Sanchica, "but just a minute: I'll go fetch someone who can read, maybe the priest himself, or that college graduate, Samson Carrasco, and they'll be glad to come, seeing as how it's news of my father."

"You don't need to call anyone," answered the page, "because even though I don't know anything about spinning, I do know how to read, and I'll read it for you."

---

1. She corrupts *destripaterrones*, "country bumpkin," into *estripaterrones*, meaning something like "grooved bumpkin" [*Translator's Note*].

And he did, in its entirety, but since it has already been set out in these pages there is no need to set it out again. Then he drew out another letter, this one from the duchess, which went as follows:

My Dear Teresa: The talents and wit of your husband Sancho so affected me that I was absolutely forced to ask my lord, the duke, to give him one of the many island governorships my lord has at his disposal. I've been informed that your Sancho has taken to governing as a falcon to its wings, which pleases me very much, as also it does the duke, my lord, and I am truly thankful to Heaven it was no mistake to choose your Sancho for a governorship, for you must understand, my lady Teresa, that good governors are hard to find, in this world of ours, and may God deal with me as well as Sancho does in his governing.

My dear lady, I send you herewith a coral necklace with gold clasps; I need hardly say I would be happier, were it of pure oriental pearls; but, as they say, "He who gives you a bone does not wish you to be a skeleton." We will come to know each other better, in the days to come, and we will tell each other things — and who but God knows what will happen? Please convey my good wishes to your daughter, Sanchica, and let her know that I want her to be ready, because I plan to fix up a first-rate marriage for her, just when she least expects it.

I'm told that your village boasts giant acorns: could you send me a dozen or two, for which I would be very grateful, coming directly from your hand, and do please write to me at length, letting me know how you are and whether you are comfortable — and if there is anything you need, you have only to ask, and whatever you need will be heaped up for you. And may the Lord keep you.

From this place,
Your friend who loves you well,
THE DUCHESS

"Oh!" said Teresa, after hearing the letter, "what a good, what a plain-talking, what a humble lady! I'd like to be buried with ladies like that, not with the stuck-up kind around here, who think just because they're somebody the wind blows on other people, but not on them, and they come parading into church with all the vanity of queens and empresses, and they think it's beneath them even to look at a peasant woman — and here you see this good lady, even though she's a duchess, calls me her friend and treats me as if I were her equal — so may I live to see *her* as lofty as the tallest bell tower in all La Mancha! And as far as those acorns are concerned, my dear sir, I'll send your ladyship a gallon bucketful, and they'll be so big you can cluck over them like a prize pig. And for right now, Sanchica, you take good care of this gentleman: make sure his horse is comfortable, and fetch some eggs out of the stable, and cut us a big chunk of bacon, and we'll let him eat like a prince, on account of the good news he's brought us, and the handsome face he has, which deserves all of it — and while you're at it, I'll go tell all my neighbors around here how well we're doing — and I'll tell the priest, and Master Nicolás, the barber, who are and always have been such good friends of your father's."

"I'll take care of it, Mama," replied Sanchica. "But you're going to have to give me half of that necklace, because I don't think my lady the duchess is such a fool that she'd send it all just to you."

"It's all for you, my daughter," answered Teresa, "but just let me wear it around my neck for a few days, because, honestly, it seems to really cheer me up."

"And you'll also feel good," said the page, "when you see the package I've got for you in this suitcase, because it's an outfit of the very finest fabric, and the governor wore it just once, when he went hunting, and now he's sent it expressly for my lady Sanchica."

"May he live a thousand years," exclaimed Sanchica, "and also he who brought it, no more and no less — but maybe two thousand, if that's better."

Then Teresa left the house, carrying the two letters, and wearing the necklace, and as she walked she strummed on the letters as if they were a tambourine; then, meeting up with the priest and Samson Carrasco, she began to dance, crying out:

"By God, we're not poor relations any more! We've got ourselves a nice little government! No sirree, just let the best painted lady mess with me, and I'll take care of her!"

"What's going on, Teresa Panza? What kind of craziness is this? And what are those documents?"

"The only craziness around here is these letters from duchesses and governors, and this thing I've got around my neck is fine coral — I mean, the little beads are coral, but the big ones are hammered gold[2] — and me, I'm a governor's wife."

"By God or the Devil, Teresa, we can't understand you — we don't know what you're talking about."

"Then here, see for yourselves," answered Teresa.

And she gave them the letters. The priest read them out loud, for Samson Carrasco to hear, and then the two men looked at one another as if stunned by what they'd heard, and the college graduate asked who had brought her these letters. Teresa replied that they should come to her house and see the messenger, who was a young fellow every bit as elegant as a piece of gold jewelry — and he'd brought her a present which was worth even more than that. The priest took the necklace, and looked at it, then looked at it again, and finding that it was genuine was stunned all over again:

"By the holy habit I wear," he said, "I don't know either what to say or what to think about these letters and this present of yours, because, on the one hand, I can see and feel what good coral this is, but, on the other, what I read here is that this is a duchess writing to you, and requesting that you send her two dozen acorns."

"What can you say, or think, about stuff like that!" said Carrasco. "Well now, let's just go and have a look at the bearer of these documents, and perhaps he can help us solve our problem."

Which they did, and Teresa returned with them. They found the page

___

2. That is, the beads for saying "ave marías" are coral, and those for "pater nosters" are gold [Translator's Note].

sifting a bit of barley for his horse, and Sanchica slicing bacon, to cook it, with eggs, for the page to eat, and the page's bearing as well as his garb much pleased them, so, after greeting him courteously, as he did them, Samson asked him to tell them news of both Don Quijote and Sancho Panza, for having just read Sancho's letter, and my lady the duchess', they found themselves distinctly confused, quite unable to understand what all this about Sancho's governorship might mean, and especially the governorship of an island, since all or at least most Spanish islands were to be found in His Majesty's Mediterranean Sea. To which the page replied:

"There can be no question that My Lord Sancho Panza is indeed a governor; as to whether or not it is an island that he governs, I have nothing to say, but perhaps it will be sufficient to tell you that it's a place with more than a thousand inhabitants. As far as acorns are concerned, I can say that my lady the duchess is so straightforward and humble that not only," said he, "might she ask a peasant to send her acorns, but she has been known to borrow a comb from one of her neighbors. You must understand, gentlemen, that the noble ladies of Aragón, no matter that they're just as well-born, are neither as finicky nor as full of themselves as are Castillian ladies; they deal with everyday folk in everyday terms."

Sanchica returned, as he was in the middle of these remarks, with her skirt full of fresh eggs, and asked the page:

"Tell me, sir: since my father's become a governor, does he by any chance wear those long stockings?"

"I'm afraid I haven't noticed," replied the page, "but he probably does."

"Ah, Lord in Heaven!" answered Sanchica. "That I should ever see my father wearing garters! Isn't it funny — because, ever since I was born, I've always wanted to see my father in those long stockings!"

"Your grace may be able to see him in all sorts of things, if you live long enough," said the page. "By God, he may end up wearing a rich man's hood, if he can just last two more months as a governor."

The priest and the college graduate could easily see how sly the page was being, but the undoubted genuineness of the necklace, and also of the hunting outfit which Sancho had sent, undercut that perception, for Teresa had already shown them the garment in question. But they couldn't help laughing at Sanchica's lifelong yearning, and even more when Teresa said to the priest:

"Father, keep an eye out, around here, for someone going to Madrid, or Toledo, who can buy me a big hoopskirt, the whole real thing, and one that'll be in the latest fashion, too, because, really and truly, I've got to show my respect for my husband's governorship the best way I know how, and even if it's a pain in the neck I may decide to go visit this royal court, and make a splash in a coach, the way they all do, because a woman who's got a governor for a husband can certainly afford to keep a coach."

"And why not, Mama!" said Sanchica. "I just wish to God all this had already happened, instead of having to wait for it, even if there'll be people, seeing me sitting next to my Mama in that coach, who'll say things like: 'Just have a look at that one, will you? Her father's nose is stuffed with garlic, and there she goes, lying around in a coach, as if she was the Pope!'

But the hell with those mud sloggers, because I'm sure going to ride in my coach, and *my* feet won't have to touch the ground. The devil with all those mumblers, because their mouths can run if I have my fun, and isn't that the way it is, Mama?"

"That's just exactly the way it is, daughter!" replied Teresa. "My good Sancho told me to expect all this fine fortune, and even more, and you'll see, daughter, he won't stop till he's made me a countess, because you have to start somewhere, if you're going to be lucky, and many's the time I've heard your good father say (because he's your father, but he's the father of all proverbs, too): 'If they want to give you a heifer, come running with a halter; if they want to give you a government, take it; if they want to give you a countship, grab it; and if they come with something nice in their hands and call you over, here pup, here pup! just gulp it right down.' Unless you're asleep, how do you keep from opening the door, if good luck's standing right out there and calling you!"

"So what do I care," added Sanchica, "if they see me strutting around and showing off, and they say, 'Oh, look at that mutt in fancy clothes,' and all that sort of stuff?"

And, hearing this, the priest said:

"It's hard not to believe every one of these Panzas wasn't born with a bag of proverbs inside them. I've never seen one of them who didn't spout proverbs no matter who was saying what, or when."

"Indeed," said the page, "my lord governor Sancho says them all the time, and even if they're not particularly relevant, they're always fun, and my lady duchess, and the duke, too, really like them."

"Nevertheless, my dear sir," said Carrasco, "you do affirm that Sancho is now a governor, and that there is a genuine duchess sending him presents and writing him letters? Because even after touching the presents, and reading the letters, we don't believe in them, and we wonder if these are the kinds of things our countryman Don Quijote is always talking about, which are worked by magic, so that I almost feel it necessary to touch and feel you, your grace, to make sure you're not some kind of fantastic ambassador rather than a creature of flesh and blood."

"Gentlemen, all I know about myself," replied the page, "is that I'm a real live ambassador. And my lord Sancho Panza is a lawfully appointed governor, his being a post which their highnesses, the duke and duchess, can legitimately dispose of, and I've heard that your Sancho Panza has been conducting himself extremely well, in this new post of his. As to whether or not any of this is due to magic, you gentlemen will have to settle that for yourselves, for I know no more than what I have now told you, and I'll swear to that on my parents' lives, both of whom are in fact still alive and exceedingly dear to me."

"That's all very well," replied the college graduate, "but *dubitat Augustinus* [Augustine doubts it]."[3]

"He who doubts is entitled to his doubt," replied the page. "The truth is as I have spoken it, and truth will always rise above lies, as oil floats over water — and, in any case, *operibus credite, et non verbis* [believe in

---

3. Traditional academic expression [*Translator's Note*].

the deeds and not in the words],[4] so if either of you gentlemen would like to come with me, you will be able to see with your eyes what your ears refuse to believe."

"Oh no, that's a trip I'm making," said Sanchica. "You can take me, sir, riding behind you on your horse, because I'd be very happy to go see my father."

"Governors' daughters," said the page, "must not travel the highways by themselves, but in a procession of great coaches and litters and many, many servants."

"By god," answered Sancha, "I can travel on a she-ass just as well as in a coach! What kind of a finicky Phoebe do you think I am!"

"Be quiet, girl," said Teresa, "because you don't know what you're talking about, and this gentleman is absolutely right. You've got to go the way the wind blows: if he's just plain Sancho, you're just plain Sancha, but when he's a governor, you're 'my lady,' and that's that."

"My lady Teresa speaks even better than she knows," said the page. "So: let me eat and then let me hurry back, because I'd like to be home by dark."

And at this the priest said:

"Please come and dine with me,[5] your grace, because, for such a guest, Madame Teresa's good will runs deeper than her larder."

The page tried to refuse, but was finally forced to yield, for his own good, and the priest carried him off very cheerfully, knowing that, now, he would have the opportunity to question him at length about Don Quijote and his doings.

Samson Carrasco offered to transcribe Teresa's reply letter for her, but she was reluctant to let him get involved in her affairs, thinking him rather a sarcastic fellow, so, instead, she gave a roll and a couple of eggs to an altar boy who knew how to write, and he wrote out both her letters, one for her husband and the other for the duchess, and both dictated straight out of her own head — and, as we will see, they're by no means the worst letters to be found in this great history.

Chapter Fifty-One

— how Sancho Panza's governorship progressed, along with other matters just as interesting

Dawn broke, the morning after the governor's nocturnal patrolling, but the butler did not close his eyes, that night, his mind possessed by thoughts of the girl in disguise and her face, her charm, her beauty, and the steward spent what was left of the night recording for his lords, the duke and duchess, exactly what Sancho Panza had said and done, quite as astonished by the new governor's actions as by his words, for in both there was a simultaneous blending of wisdom and foolishness.

---

4. John 10:38 [*Translator's Note*].
5. Literally, "Come and do penance with me": a traditional formula for inviting someone to dine [*Translator's Note*].

My lord governor woke up, finally, and by Doctor Pedro Recio's orders made his breakfast on a bit of fruit preserves and four swigs of cold water, though Sancho would have been glad to trade all this for a crust of bread and some fried eggs, but though his heart ached, and his stomach along with it, he accepted his fate, seeing that it involved force more than it did volition — and, besides, Pedro Recio had persuaded him that lean portions of delicate foods heightened the mind's powers, which was the most important thing for persons placed in positions of command and high importance, positions which called for mental exertions rather than physical ones.

So Sancho endured his hunger, for the sake of this sophistry, but he was longing for food so piercingly that, secretly, he was beginning to curse the governorship and he who had given it to him, but nevertheless — hunger and fruit preserves and all — he set himself to judge court cases that day, and the first problem he had to deal with came from a stranger, and was presented in the presence of the steward and all the other attendants:

"My lord, a broad river separates the two parts of a single domain (and please, your grace, follow me closely, because this is an important case, as well as a rather complex one). Now, there's a bridge over this river, and at one end there stands a gallows and a court building, in which four judges usually preside, applying the law formulated by the lord of this river, this bridge, and this entire realm, which ran as follows: 'Anyone passing over this bridge, from one section of this domain to the other, must first declare under oath where he is coming from and where he is going, and if he swears truly, he shall be allowed to pass, but if he lies, he shall be hanged from the gallows standing nearby, without any appeal or reprieve allowed.' This law, and its rigorous application, was well known; many people used the bridge and, since it was obvious they were telling the truth, the judges would let them cross over. Well, it happened, one day, that a man came and swore the required oath, saying among other things that he had come to be hanged on that gallows, and for no other purpose. The judges considered his oath, saying: 'If we simply let this man cross the bridge, his oath will be a lie, and then, according to the law, he ought to die, but if we hang him, the oath he swore about being hanged on this gallows will be true, and then the same law decrees that he be allowed to cross over in peace.' Please consider, my lord governor, your grace, what the judges should do with this fellow, for even now they remain anxious and unsure how to proceed, and, having been made aware of your grace's keen mind and sublime understanding, they have sent me here to implore your grace to tell them how you view this singularly complicated and puzzling case."

Sancho replied:

"Surely, these honorable judges didn't have to send you to me, because I'm a lot better known for dull wits than for sharp ones — but, anyway, tell me this business once more, so I can get a handle on it, and then maybe I'll be able to figure it out."

The question was posed a second time, and then a third, exactly as at first, and Sancho said:

"As far as I can see, it shouldn't take long to sum up this whole business: if this man swears he's to die on the gallows, and he does, then he's swearing the truth and, according to the law, he ought to be allowed to cross the bridge in peace, but if he's not hanged then he's swearing falsely, and according to the same law he ought to be hanged."

"Exactly as my lord governor says," said the messenger. "You couldn't ask for a better summary of the whole case, with nothing left out and nothing left unclear."

"So what I'd say," answered Sancho, "is that whatever part of the man swore truthfully should be allowed to cross the bridge, and whatever part swore to a lie should be hanged, and then what happens to him will fit right to the letter of the law."

"But, my lord governor," said the questioner, "the man will then have to be divided into two parts, one lying and the other truthful, and if he's divided, then of course he'll be dead, and that won't fit the letter of the law at all, and the law has to be followed."

"Look here, my good friend," replied Sancho. "Either it would be just as reasonable to kill this man we're talking about, as it would be to let him live, or I'm a complete idiot, because if the truth saves him, the lie just as clearly condemns him, and that being the case, as plainly it is, I think you ought to tell the gentlemen who sent you to me that there's a perfect balance here, as between condemning him or saving him, so let him cross over in peace, because it's always better to do good than evil, and I'd write this out and sign my name under it, if I knew how to sign my name, nor am I just making all this up out of my own head, because I remember a rule — one among many I got from my master Don Quijote, the night before I came here to be governor of this island — which says: Any time justice is doubtful, lean toward compassion and take shelter in mercy, and it's God's will that I remember that rule right now, because it fits this case as if it had been made for it."

"True," replied the steward, "and I think even Lycurgus himself, who gave the Greeks their laws, couldn't give a better judgment than the great Panza has just done. Now, let us conclude this morning's session, and I will arrange for my lord governor to dine exactly as he pleases."

"That's all I want," said Sancho, "turn about is fair play: let me eat, and then I'll tackle cases, and doubts, and go right through them, like a hot knife through butter."

The steward was as good as his word, convinced it would burden his conscience, should so wise a governor be starved to death — especially since he planned, that same night, to stage the final joke he'd been commissioned to play on Sancho.

Accordingly, having dined in direct violation of Doctor Tirteafuera's rules and regulations, the moment the tablecloth was removed Sancho received a messenger, bearing a letter for the Governor of Barataria, from Don Quijote. Sancho ordered his secretary to first read it to himself, and then, should there be nothing in it requiring secrecy, to read it aloud in a clear voice. The secretary complied; reviewing the document silently, he said:

"This can certainly be read aloud, for what my lord Don Quijote here writes to your grace is as if engraved and inscribed in letters of gold, and goes as follows:

LETTER FROM DON QUIJOTE DE LA MANCHA TO SANCHO PANZA,
GOVERNOR OF THE ISLAND OF BARATARIA

Sancho, my friend, even though I expected to hear news of your negligence and bumbling, what I have in fact heard speaks only of your wisdom and good sense, for which I am especially grateful to High Heaven, which knows how to raise the poor from the dungheap and make the foolish wise. They tell me you are governing like a man, and that you are a man in the same way, once, you were an animal, so marked is the humility with which you treat others, so I want to warn you, Sancho, that maintaining the authority and dignity of your office will quite frequently require you to go against your heart's true humility, because proper attire in a person charged with grave responsibilities must correspond to what such responsibilities demand, and not to the standards toward which a humble person's nature may incline him. So you must dress yourself well: a handsomely dressed stick does not look like a stick. I'm not saying you ought to deck yourself out in jewelry and flowers, nor that, serving as a judge, you should look like a soldier, but simply that you adorn yourself in the style your office requires, as long as what you wear is clean and neat.

To win the good will of the people over whom you govern, you must do many things, but two in particular: first, you must be well-mannered toward everyone (and yes, I know this is not the first time I've said such things to you), and second, try to make sure that food is always plentiful, for there is nothing that wears on a poor man's heart more than hunger and scarcity.

Don't promulgate a lot of laws, and if you do, try not only to make them good laws but, above all else, try to be sure they are observed and obeyed, because laws which are not obeyed are like laws which never existed, but create the impression that the prince who has the wisdom and the authority to make them, in the first place, lacks the courage to ensure their enforcement, and laws which merely threaten, but never actually do anything, come to be like the great beam which was the king of frogs: they terrify, for a while, but in time they are despised and people walk all over them.

Be like virtue's father but vice's stepfather. You should not be invariably harsh or invariably kind, but rather, choose the midpoint between these two extremes, which in this matter is both the goal and the height of wisdom. Visit the jails, the butcher shops, and the town squares, for the governor's presence in such places is of great importance: it offers comfort to those who have been arrested, providing hope that they may be soon released; it serves as a bogeyman for the butchers, and — at least for a while — they let their scales show true weights, and it scares the market women, for exactly the same reason. Don't let yourself be seen, even if by any chance you actually are — and I do not believe you are — greedy, a skirt-chaser, or a glutton, because if those you govern over and deal with come to know any such fixed propensity in you, it will be precisely there that they will tend to attack you, and ultimately throw you down to the depths of the abyss.

Consider, and then reconsider — study, and then study all over again

— *the advice and counsels I wrote out for you, before you left here to become a governor, and you'll realize that what you there have, if you heed them, is a ready support which can help you bear the trials and tribulations which confront a governor at every step. Be sure to write to your own superiors, and show them your gratitude, for ingratitude is pride's own daughter and one of the worst sins I know of, and the person who demonstrates his gratitude to those who have done him a good service thereby indicates that he will be grateful to God, who has done him infinite kindnesses and will grant him many more.*

My lady the duchess sent one of her people to your wife, Teresa Panza, bearing your hunting outfit and another present; for the moment, we are still awaiting his return.

I have been a bit ill, on account of a certain cat-clawing which did not exactly improve my nose; but it wasn't much of anything; and if there are magicians who mistreat me, there are also those who protect me.

Let me know if the steward who's gone there with you turns out to be, as you suspected, the person you saw as Countess Trifaldi; and let me know, too, everything which happens to you, for the road between us is not a very long one — and especially since I'm thinking of soon abandoning this lazy existence in which I find myself, because it is not what I was born for.

Something has come up which, I think, will likely put me in disfavor with the lords of this place, and although I care deeply about their good opinion, I can't really care about it at all, since, when it comes right down to it, I must fulfill my vows rather than my personal desires: as they say, amicus Plato, sed magis amica veritas *[I am Plato's friend, but even more a friend to the truth].*[1] *I say this to you in Latin because I imagine that, since you've become a governor, you've learned it.*

May God be with you, and may He keep you from requiring anyone's pity,

Your friend,
DON QUIJOTE DE LA MANCHA

Sancho listened most attentively to this letter, which was praised and labeled wise by those who heard it, then immediately got up from the table and, summoning his secretary, went off and shut himself in his rooms and, without any delay whatever, set out to reply to his master, Don Quijote, telling his secretary to write down, without the slightest addition or subtraction, exactly what Governor Sancho Panza said, which was exactly what the secretary did, and what resulted was the following letter:

SANCHO PANZA'S LETTER TO DON QUIJOTE DE LA MANCHA

My job keeps me so busy that I haven't even got time to scratch my head, nor to cut my nails, either, and they've grown so long that God Himself will have to help me with them. I tell you this, my most beloved lord, so your grace will not be surprised that, until now, I haven't given you any news of

---

1. An adage put in this form by Erasmus; earlier, the reference had usually been to Socrates [*Translator's Note*].

how things are going with me, for good or for bad, in this governorship, in which I'm experiencing fiercer pangs of hunger than when we were traveling together through all those forests and deserted places.

My lord the duke wrote to me, the other day, warning me that certain spies have come to this island, with instructions to kill me, but to this point all I've found is a certain doctor, who's paid to kill every governor who might ever come to this place: his name is Doctor Pedro Recio, and he comes from Tirteafuera — and with a name like that, your grace can see why I'm afraid of dying at his hands![2] What this doctor says of himself is that he doesn't simply cure diseases, as and when they occur, but stops them so that they don't occur at all, and the medicine he uses is dieting and then more dieting, until he turns you into skin and bones — as if being starved wasn't a lot worse than any fever. In the end, he'll kill me with hunger, and I can already see myself dying of frustration, because when I thought about coming to this governorship I thought about eating hot, and drinking cold, and relaxing my body between sheets of Holland silk, on feather mattresses, but what's happened is that I'm doing penance, as if I were a hermit, and since this isn't either my idea or anything I like, I think I'll end by going straight to the Devil.

To this point I haven't laid hands on any taxes or fees, and I haven't taken any bribes, either, and I can't imagine what this is all about, because what they've told me, around here, is that, before the governors who usually come to this island ever show up, the people either give them, or loan them, lots of money, and that's usually the way it is with everyone who gets to be a governor, not just governor of this island.

Last night, when I was out on patrol, I bumped into a very beautiful girl dressed like a man, and her brother, who was dressed like a woman; my butler is in love with the girl, and — in his own mind — he tells me he's picked her for his wife, and I've picked the boy for my son-in-law. We're both going to try out our ideas on their father, today, he being a certain Diego de la Llana, both a gentleman and as Old a Christian as you'll ever find.

I've gone and visited the town squares, as your grace advised me to, and yesterday I found a woman selling hazelnuts, and learned that she'd mixed a load of dried-up old nuts with the fresh ones, so I took the whole lot for the children at the charity school, because they know how to tell the difference, all right, and I've ordered her to stay out of the square for two weeks. They say this was a good idea; all I can tell you, your grace, is that in this town there's no one with a worse reputation than these lady vendors, because they're all completely shameless, utterly cold-blooded, and as bold as brass, and I believe it, after what I've seen in other towns.

I am very happy to hear that my lady the duchess has written to my wife, Teresa Panza, and sent her the present your grace talks about, and when I have the chance I'll try to show her my gratitude. Please kiss her hands for me, your grace, and tell her I said she hadn't been tossing things into any broken bags, as she'll see when I do whatever I'll do.

---

2. Again, *recio* = harsh, severe; *agüero* = omen, sign; and *tirte afuera* = get the hell out [*Translator's Note*].

I wish your grace wouldn't get into any nasty quarrels with these lords of mine, because it's clear that, if your grace gets angry at them, it won't do me any good, and it won't be worth anything for you to advise me to be grateful, if you yourself, your grace, aren't, when you consider how good they've been to you and how well you've been treated in their castle.

I don't understand what you mean about cat-scratching, but I imagine it's got to be still more wicked deeds, like the ones those evil enchanters are always doing to your grace. I'll find out whenever we get to meet.

I wish I could send your grace something, but I don't know what I could send, except maybe some nice enema tubes — interesting things you use with bags — that they make, here on this island, but if I last in this job I'll see if I can find some fees or maybe some bribes to send.

If my wife, Teresa Panza, writes to me, would your grace please pay the postage charges and send her letter on to me, because I'm really anxious to know what's going on, back home, with my house, and my wife, and my children.

So, with that, may God free your grace from these evil magicians, and may He let me get out of this governorship in peace, and without too much trouble, though I don't think He will, because I suspect, the way Doctor Pedro Recio treats me, I'll only leave here feet first.

> *Your grace's faithful servant,*
> SANCHO PANZA, THE GOVERNOR

His secretary sealed the letter, and immediately sent it via the courier, and then those who were in charge of all the jokes being played on Sancho sat down together and began to arrange how they would get him out of the governor's chair. Sancho spent the afternoon working out laws for the better government of what he still thought was an island; he decreed that no one was to go around hawking food at fancy prices, not anywhere in the whole country, and that anyone could bring in wine from anywhere they felt like, as long as they made clear where it came from, so the price could be fixed according to how it had been appraised, and how good it was, and what its reputation might be, and then anyone who watered it or changed its name would be executed.

He lowered the price of all footwear, especially shoes, because those prices struck him as exorbitant; he set a limit on servants' wages, which he thought were absolutely running wild, out of sheer self-interest; he established truly serious penalties for anyone caught singing rude or lascivious songs, whether by night or by day. He decreed, too, that blind men were forbidden to sing ballads about miracles, unless they had reliable evidence that such things had indeed happened, because it seemed to him that the miracles most blind men sing about were imaginary, and this was harmful to those which were in fact true.

He created and set up the machinery for a poor people's constabulary, so they could be tested to see if they really were poor or not, because strong-armed thieves and healthy drunkards often hid under cover of a pretended physical handicap and some fabricated wound or disease. In short: he decreed such wonderful things that, to this very day, his laws are still observed there, and are known as *The Great Governor Sancho Panza's Legal System.*

Chapter Fifty-Two

— in which is narrated the adventure of the second doleful or anguished dueña, *otherwise known as Doña Rodríguez*

Sidi Hamid records that, being now healed of all his scratches, it seemed to Don Quijote that the life he was leading in that castle was almost the direct opposite of what his oath of knight errantry required, so he decided to ask the duke and duchess if he might leave them and go to Zaragoza, where feast days were drawing near and the suit of armor awarded for victory in such tournaments might well be his.

At table with his hosts, one day, and just about to put his plan into effect, he suddenly saw two women (as they later proved to be) entering the great dining room, draped in mourning from head to foot, and then one of them, approaching Don Quijote, threw herself face first on the ground, her mouth pressed against his feet and emitting such misery-wracked moans, so wrenching and deep, that they upset everyone who could see and hear her, and even the duke and duchess at first fancied this was some joke being played on Don Quijote by the servants, but then, seeing how the woman, now kneeling, sighed and moaned and wept, the noble pair were confused and uncertain, until, at last, Don Quijote mercifully raised the woman from the ground and made her uncover herself, removing the mantle from her tear-stained face.

The woman did so, and revealed what no one could have expected, for the features she uncovered were those of Doña Rodríguez, lady in waiting to the duchess, and when the other mourner's identity was made known, she was seen to be Doña Rodríguez's daughter, the girl who had been deceived by the rich farmer's son. All those who knew the *dueña* were astonished, and especially the duke and duchess, who considered her a dolt, pleasant enough, but characterless and certainly not the sort who indulged in such wild pranks. After a moment, Doña Rodríguez turned toward her mistress and the duke, and said:

"May it please Your Excellencies to allow me some words with this knight, for it will not take long to conclude a matter in which, because of the insolence of a wickedly motivated peasant, I happen to be concerned."

The duke replied that she had his permission, and indeed she might say as much to Don Quijote as she cared to. Turning to our knight, she declared:

"Brave knight, some days ago I told you of the injustice and treachery perpetrated against my dearly beloved daughter by a wicked peasant. This is she, standing right here, and you have promised me to be her champion and to right the wrong done her, but now I learn you plan to leave this castle, searching for whatever good adventures God may be pleased to bring you, and so, before you are lost to our sight, down those endless roads, I beg you to issue a challenge to this proud rustic and force him to marry my daughter, fulfilling the pledge he gave, before he lay with her, that he would be her husband, because I believe that to expect justice in this matter from my lord the duke is to ask for the moon, as I have previously, and in complete secrecy, explained to your grace. May our Lord on high grant you good health, your grace, and keep you from abandoning us."

Don Quijote answered her, soberly and with great seriousness:

"Moderate your tears, my good *dueña*, or perhaps I should say, wipe them away and cease your sighs, for I undertake to help your daughter, though she herself would have done better not to so readily believe lovers' promises, which are for the most part easily given and very hard to keep, and so, with the permission of my lord the duke, I will as soon as I am able leave in search of this hard-hearted young man — and I will find him, and challenge him and, if he does not fulfill his pledge to the letter, I will then and there kill him, for a knight errant's primary concern is to forgive those who are penitent but punish those who are proud — in short, to aid those in distress and destroy those who would crush others."

"There'll be no necessity," responded the duke, "for your grace to trouble yourself, hunting up the country person of whom this good *dueña* speaks, nor does your grace need my permission to issue this challenge, for I hereby consider him to have been fully and properly challenged and take it upon myself to so notify him, and to ensure that he accepts it and thereafter comes to this castle of mine to answer for it, on an absolutely impartial field which I guarantee will be fair to you both, according to all the rules and regulations usually and appropriately imposed in such matters, as I and all princes are bound to do, when we give a free field in our realms to those who engage in combat."

"With this guarantee, then, and with your highness' permission," replied Don Quijote, "I hereby declare that, expressly and solely for this occasion, I renounce my status as a nobleman and lower and accommodate myself to the level of the wrongdoer, making myself no more than his equal, thus empowering him to engage in lawful combat with me, and on these terms and conditions I do hereby challenge him, on the grounds that he has done wrong in cheating this poor maiden, who by reason of his default is alas no longer a maiden, and because he is obliged either to fulfill the promise he gave her and become her lawfully wedded husband, or else to perish for his refusal."

And quickly peeling off a glove, he threw it in the middle of the room, and the duke, picking it up, declared that, as he had already explained, he accepted this challenge in his vassal's name and designated the date of their combat to be in another six days; the place of their combat to be the courtyard of his castle; and the weapons to be those in customary knightly use, namely, spear and shield, and a full set of armor; no kind of trickery or magic to be employed, as certified by the judges of said field.

"But before anything goes a step further," the duke went on, "this good *dueña* and this bad maiden must solemnly place their cause in the hands of my lord Don Quijote, for until and unless this has been done, nothing else can follow, nor can this challenge have any force and effect."

"I so place my cause," replied the lady in waiting.

"And I," added her daughter, weeping pitifully for shame, and in no very cheerful mood.

This having been duly noted, and the duke having decided what he himself had to do, the two mourners left the hall and, the duchess having ordered that from then on they were not to be treated like her servants, but as ladies errant who had come to her house in search of justice, mother and daughter were given a room of their own, and served as if they had been strangers to the house, which much annoyed the other servants, who wondered where the foolishness and brazenness of Doña Rodríguez and her miserable daughter would end.

This having been taken care of, who should we see coming into the room — to brighten the party and properly round off the comedy — but the page who had brought letters and presents to Teresa Panza, wife of Governor Sancho Panza, and his return delighted the duke and duchess, who were anxious to know how his expedition had turned out and, when they inquired of him, the page replied that he couldn't possibly answer in public, nor in just a few words, and so, if their excellencies would be pleased to wait until they were alone, he might in the meantime entertain them with some letters. Thereupon, he drew out two letters and handed them to the duchess. On one, the superscription read: *Letter for my lady the duchess such-and-such, of I-don't-know-where,* and on the other: *To my husband Sancho Panza, Governor of Barataria Island, and may God send him more years of prosperity than He sends me.* The duchess did not wait for the bread to be well baked, as the saying goes, but read her letter at once, first opening it and reading it to herself, and then, seeing that it might be read out, so the duke and the others might hear it, she read as follows:

TERESA PANZA'S LETTER TO THE DUCHESS

The letter your excellency sent me, my lady, made me very happy, for indeed it was just what I could have wanted it to be. The coral necklace is wonderful, and my husband's hunting suit is every bit as good. This entire village is very glad that your highness has made Sancho, my consort, a governor, although no one here really believes it, and especially our priest, and Master Nicolás, our barber, and Samson Carrasco, our college graduate, but that doesn't matter a bit to me, because as long as it is the way it is, as it is, they can each and all say whatever they like — though, to tell the truth, if you hadn't sent the necklace and the hunting suit, I wouldn't have believed it either, because everyone here thinks my husband is a fool and, except for governing a herd of goats, they can't imagine what kind of governing he could be good at. May God work His will, and guide my Sancho in whatever path He sees that our children truly need.

I have decided, lady of my heart and soul, with your grace's permission, to take advantage of this opportunity and present myself at Court, so I can lie back in a coach and let the thousand jealous eyes already watching me really get a workout, so let me beg your excellency to have my husband send me some money, and more than just a little some, because it's expensive to be at Court: I mean, bread costs a dollar, and meat thirty cents a pound, which is crazy, but if my husband doesn't want me to go, then he ought to let me know before I leave, because my feet can't wait to start down the road, and all my friends and neighbors tell me my husband can get to be better known on account of me than me on account of him, if me and my daughter come to Court all puffed up and really grand, and lots of people have to ask: 'Who are those ladies in that coach over there?' And then one of my servants will tell them: 'That's Sancho Panza's wife and daughter, and he's Governor of Barataria Island,' so that way they'll all get to know Sancho, and really respect me, and right on to Rome we go!

I feel about as bad as I can feel that, this year, there haven't been any acorns in this town, in spite of which I'm sending your majesty almost half a bucketful that I went up on the mountain and picked for you, by hand, but I couldn't find any bigger ones: I wish they were regular ostrich eggs!

I hope your magnificence won't forget to write to me, because I'll be very careful to answer you, telling you all about my health and everything else that's worth talking about, in this town, where I remain, praying to Our Lord to watch over your greatness, and not to forget about me, either. My daughter Sancha, and my son too, kiss your grace's hands.

She who'd rather see your ladyship than write to her, your servant,

TERESA PANZA

This recitation of Teresa Panza's letter was received with great delight, especially by the duke and his duchess, and then the duchess asked Don Quijote if it would be proper to open the letter Teresa had sent to her husband the governor, which she expected would be all kinds of good fun. Don Quijote replied that, to please themselves, they ought indeed to open the letter, which they did, and what they saw was the following:

TERESA PANZA'S LETTER TO HER HUSBAND, SANCHO PANZA

I have received your letter, Sancho of my heart and soul, and let me tell you, on my oath as a Catholic and a Christian, I've been just an inch away from going crazy with happiness. Look, my brother: when I first heard you'd become a governor, I thought I'd just drop dead of pure pleasure, because they say, you know, that sudden joy can kill you just as easily as great sorrow. Your daughter, Sanchica, leaked all over herself without knowing it, just for pure joy. With the hunting suit you sent right in front of me, and the necklace sent by my lady the duchess around my neck, and both letters right in my hands, and the bringer of all these things standing there too, it still seemed to me what I was actually seeing and touching was really only a dream, because who would ever think a goatherd could come to be a governor of islands? You know, my mother used to say, my friend, that you had to live a lot to see a lot; I say this because, if I live more, I think I'll see more, because I don't plan to stop until I see you a landlord or a tax collector, because even if those are jobs that can send you right to the Devil, if you don't do them right, just the same, they always make money, and they keep it, too. My lady the duchess will tell you how anxious I am to be at Court; think about it, and let me know your pleasure, so I can try to do you honor by going around Court in my coach.

The priest, the barber, the college graduate, and even the sacristan, can't any of them really believe you're a governor; they say the whole thing is a trick, or maybe something magical, like all those things that always happen to Don Quijote, your master, and Samson Carrasco says he's got to go and hunt you up and pull all this governor stuff right out of your head, and take all the craziness out of Don Quijote's, and I just laugh and look at my necklace and work out a design for the dress I think I'll make for your daughter, out of that hunting outfit.

I sent some acorns to my lady the duchess; I wish they'd been made of gold. Send me some pearl necklaces, if there are any on that island.

What's new here is that Old Lady Berrueca married her daughter to a worthless painter, who came here to paint whatever he could find; the town council hired him to paint His Majesty's coat of arms over the town hall doors, and he said it would cost two dollars, so they paid him in advance, and he worked for a whole week, but he hadn't painted anything the whole time and said he couldn't be bothered painting such geegaws and knick-nacks, so he gave them back the money and, somehow or other, he's still gotten the reputation of a reliable workman; anyway, I admit he's put down his paint brush and picked up a shovel, and now he works in the fields like a gentleman. Pedro de Lobo's son has taken minor orders, and his head's been clipped, and he means to become a priest; Minguilla, Mingo Silvato's niece, found out about it, and she's hauled him into court on a breach of promise charge; there are wicked tongues saying he's gotten her pregnant, but he denies the whole thing.

There are no olives, this year, and you can't find a drop of vinegar any-where in town. A troop of soldiers came through; when they left, they took three girls away with them, but I don't want to tell you who they are; maybe they'll come back, and there won't be any shortage of men who'll marry them, flaws and all, good or bad.

Sanchica is making needlepoint lace; she's clearing about twenty-five cents a day, and locking it up in a money box to help with her dowry; but now that she's a governor's daughter you'll just give her a dowry, and she doesn't have to work for it. The fountain in the town square has gone dry, and lightning hit the gallows — and it can hit it again and again, as far as I'm concerned.

I will look forward to hearing from you, and finding out whether I'm supposed to go to Court or not; so, may God let you live longer than me — or at least as long, because I don't want to leave you alone in the world, without me.

Your wife,
TERESA PANZA

Teresa's letters were made much of, laughed over, appreciated, and wondered at — and then, as a finishing touch, the courier came in, bringing the letter Sancho had sent to Don Quijote, and that too was read aloud, which reading raised a good deal of doubt about the governor being truly a simpleton.

Then the duchess left them, in order to find out from her page what had happened in Sancho's home town, which narrative was given to her at great length, omitting no relevant detail. The page gave her the acorns and, what's more, a cheese Teresa had sent, saying it was particularly good, and even better than the cheeses to be had from Zaragoza. The duchess was delighted to have it — and there we will leave her, in order to relate the last hours of Sancho Panza's governorship, he who was the flower and very model of island governors.

Chapter Fifty-Three

— the weary finale of Sancho Panza's governorship

To expect stability from our life in this world is a waste of time — indeed, it seems to me things tend to go around in circles, and around and around and around: spring takes us into early summer, which blossoms into full summer, which brings us into autumn, and autumn takes us to winter, and then winter back to spring once more, which is how time perpetually turns around and around in its circle.[1] But our human life runs giddily out, long before time does, and there is no hope for renewal except in the next world, which is eternal and without any end. Or so says Sidi Hamid, Muhammadan philosopher, for there are many who, without the light of true faith to show it to them, nevertheless fully comprehend the fickleness and instability of this mortal life, and the endless reach of eternity toward which it looks — though what our author is talking about, here, when he refers to the speed with which things come to an end, and are consumed, and lie totally undone, is how Sancho's governorship vanished into shadows and smoke.

And on the seventh night of the seventh day of his reign, as Sancho lay in his bed, not bloated and weary from either bread or wine, but from formulating judgments and giving opinions and drawing up laws and regulations, and just as sleep was beginning to close his heavy eyelids, in spite and defiance of hunger and all its pangs, he heard an immense noise, bells ringing and men shouting until it seemed as if the whole island must be sinking. He sat up in bed, attentive and alert, trying to imagine what might be the cause of such a huge uproar, yet not only was that impossible, but now, in addition to the cries and the bells, he heard endless blasts of trumpets and banging of drums, leaving him still more confused but also shocked and afraid. He got out of bed, put on his slippers (lest the ground be damp) and, not bothering with a bathrobe or anything even resembling it, went to the door of his room, just in time to see more than twenty people, with burning torches and unsheathed swords in their hands, rushing down the corridor, crying at the top of their lungs:

"To arms, to arms, my lord governor! To arms! Enemy hordes have invaded the island and, if your skill and courage don't save us, we're lost!"

And with such frenzied cries and wild clamoring they ran up to Sancho,

---

1. Sidi Hamid describes the North African schema, which has five rather than four seasons, "spring" and "summer" being replaced by *primavera*, *estío*, and *verano*, with more or less the meanings used in the text, above [*Translator's Note*].

who stood astonished and stupefied by what he was seeing and hearing, and as they reached him one of them said:

"To arms, your lordship, if you don't want to be lost — and this whole island lost!"

"What have weapons got to do with me?" replied Sancho. "What do I know about war or saving people? You'd better leave such stuff to Don Quijote, my master, who'll take care of it in two shakes of a cat's tail and save everybody's neck, because, by God, sinner as I am, I don't know a damned thing about all this skirmishing up and down."

"Ah, my lord governor!" said another man. "Are you pulling our legs? To arms, your grace, because we've brought all you'll need, for offense or defense, so come out to the square and be our leader and our general, as by right you ought to be, since you're our governor."

"Arm me, then," said Sancho, "and much good may it do you."

So they showed him the two big shields they'd come prepared with, and without letting him stop to get on any other clothing, clamped them both on him, over his shirt, one in front and the other behind, then pulled his arms through holes they'd cut, and tied them so firmly into place that he was virtually walled in and boarded over, wound tightly around with rope like a stiff, straight bobbin, unable to bend his knees or take a step in any direction. They put a lance in his hands, against which he leaned, to hold himself up. Once he was all ready, they told him to come out and lead them, and spur them all on, for with him as their North Star, their Flaming Lantern and Guiding Light, surely everything would turn out well.

"How am I supposed to walk, oh miserable me," replied Sancho, "when I can't even wiggle the joints in my knees, with these boards you've clamped on my hide? You'll have to lift me up and set me at a gate or a window or something, whether lying down or standing up, and then I can stand guard either with my spear or with my body."

"Hurry, lord governor," came the reply, "because what's holding you back is more fear than shields. Come on, let's go, because it's getting late, the enemy is all over the place, and the shouting's growing louder, and the danger's getting worse."

Such pushing and scolding propelled the governor into attempting movement, but he immediately toppled over with such a crash that he thought he'd broken himself into pieces. And there he lay, like a giant turtle hidden in its shell, or half a side of bacon laid out between two great troughs and ready for salting, or even like a boat pulled bottom up on the beach, and all those who were having their noisy fun felt not the slightest pity for him, but rather, snuffing out their torches, they began to shout still louder, urgently repeating the call of 'To arms! To arms!' and tramping back and forth on top of Sancho, bashing away so vigorously at his covering shields that, if he hadn't pulled and shrunk himself deep down into his protective shell, it might have gone rather badly for the poor governor, shut all sweating and dripping in such narrow quarters, and praying as hard as he could for God to save him from that sore peril.

Some of them stumbled over him, some of them slipped and fell, and one man stood on him for quite a while, as if Sancho had been a watchtower, and directed the troop movements, shouting:

"Our men over here — charge the enemy from this side! Watch that gate over there! — get that door shut! — those stairs are blocked! Hurry up, bring on the pitchpots and resin! Where's the boiling oil? Barricade the streets with mattresses!"

In a word, with incredible zeal he ran off the names of every gadget and device and instrument of war used in defending cities from assault, and our ground-down, exhausted Sancho, hearing and suffering through the whole long list, said to himself:

"Oh Lord, please let this island be lost and gone, and me either dead or out of this pain and anguish!"

And then Heaven heard his pleas, and, just when he least expected it, he heard cries:

"Victory! Victory! Our enemies have been beaten! Come on, lord governor, get yourself up, your grace, and come enjoy the victory, and hand out the treasures we've taken from our enemies, all through the strength of that invincible arm!"

"Lift me up," said Sancho, his voice low and afflicted.

So they lifted him up, and set him on his feet, and he said:

"I've defeated as many enemies as I've driven nails into my forehead. I don't care about dividing up treasures — all I want is to beg some friend, if I still have any, to let me have a swig of wine, because I'm parched, and wipe all this sweat off me, because I'm melting."

They cleaned him off, and brought him wine, and untied the shields, and he sat down on a bed and, what with the fear and the shock and the struggle, fainted dead away. Those who'd been playing the trick on him were sorry, now, they'd worked him over quite so hard, but then Sancho came back to himself and eased their chagrin at his having passed out. He asked what time it was; they told him it was already dawn. Without another word, he began to get dressed, buried in a profound silence, and they watched him, waiting to see what this haste to clothe himself was all about. Finally, he was dressed and then, slowly, very slowly, because he'd been well beaten and bruised and could not move swiftly, he went to the stables, everyone trailing along after him and, going over to his little donkey, hugged him and solemnly kissed him on the forehead, then said, with tears in his eyes:

"Come to me, my friend, my companion, my helper in all my trials and tribulations, for when you and I were together, and all I ever worried about were the problems of repairing your harness and keeping your little body fed and well, oh what a happy time it was, every day and every year! But since I've gone away from you, and set myself to climbing the towers of pride and ambition, my heart has been afflicted with a thousand miseries, a thousand hardships, and four thousand fears and anxieties."

And as he was saying all this, he set about saddling the donkey, no one else speaking a word. The saddle finally in place, Sancho mounted, slowly and with great difficulty, and then, directing his words to the steward, to the secretary, to the butler, and to Doctor Pedro Recio and all the many others who were there, he said:

"Out of my way, gentlemen, and let me return to my former freedom; let me go hunt for the life I used to lead, and resurrect myself out of this living death. I was not born to be a governor, nor to defend islands and cities from enemies who wish to attack them. I know a lot more about plowing and digging, about pruning and tending vines, than I do about making laws and defending provinces or kingdoms. Saint Peter belongs in Rome — which means that each of us should do the work we were born to do. A scythe fits my hand better than a governor's scepter; I'd rather stuff myself with plain ordinary *gazpacho*[2] than fall victim to the stinginess of an arrogant doctor who'd just as soon kill me with hunger, and I'd rather stretch out in the shade of an oak tree, in the summer, and wrap myself in a coat made of two sheepskin hides, in the winter, but a free man, than lie down at night between Holland silk sheets, or dress myself all in sables, and be subject to any government's control. My blessings on all of you, your graces, and tell the duke my lord that, just as I was born naked, so I find myself naked again; I've neither lost anything nor gained anything; what I mean is I came to this governorship with my pockets empty, and I leave it the same way, which is certainly the reverse of how most governors of islands leave office. So step back, please, and let me go, because I have to find myself some mustard plasters: I think every one of my ribs is cracked, thanks to all the enemies who were walking up and down on me, tonight."

"It doesn't have to be like this, my lord governor," said Doctor Recio. "I can give your grace a drink that cures both falls[3] and beatings, and pretty soon you'll be as healthy and strong as you ever were, and as far as food is concerned, I promise your grace I'll change my ways, and I'll let you eat as much as you want of anything you want."

"You got there too late!" replied Sancho. "I'd just as soon turn myself into a Turk as stay here. These jokes aren't funny, the second time around. By God, I'd just as soon stay here or take on another governorship, even if they handed it to me on a silver platter, as I would fly up into the clouds without any wings. I am a Panza, and we're a pig-headed bunch, and once they call 'odds!,'[4] it's got to be odds, even if it's evens, and in spite of the whole world. Right here in this stable I leave the ant's wings that carried me up into the air, so the swallows and the swifts could eat me, because I'm going back to walking on the ground with my own flat feet, because if they're not decorated with fancy shoes and fancy leather, at least they have hemp sandals with leather straps. Birds of a feather should flock together, and nobody ought to stretch out his legs without worrying how long the sheet is, so please let me go, because it's getting late."

The steward replied:

"My lord governor, we'll gladly let your grace leave us, but we deeply regret the loss, because your wit, and your Christian ways, have made us want you. Still, you know that all governors, before they leave their posts, must render their accounting, so let your grace do that for the ten days you've been governor, and then you may go with God's blessing."

"No one can ask that of me," answered Sancho, "except someone so

---

2. *Gazpacho* = a cold tomato-, onion- and garlic-based soup common and ordinary enough in Spain (and South America) but fairly exotic in less exuberant climates [*Translator's Note*].
3. *Caídas,* "falls," can also mean "witticisms, witty remarks" [*Translator's Note*].
4. *Decir nones* = "to call odds or evens," and "to say no, to refuse" [*Translator's Note*].

designated by my lord the duke, and since I'm going to see him, I'll give it to him exactly as it ought to be — but remember: the fact that I'm leaving here empty-handed, as I am, makes it unnecessary to produce any other evidence that, without any question, I have governed like an angel."

"By God," said Doctor Recio, "the Great Sancho is absolutely right, and I think we should let him leave, because the duke will be delighted to see him."

Everyone agreed, and so they let him depart, but offering him, first, an escort, and second, anything he might want or need either for his pleasure or for the greater comfort of his journey. All he needed, Sancho said, was a bit of barley for his donkey and half a cheese and half a loaf of bread for himself, the journey being such a short one that he needed nothing more and no larger a larder. They all embraced him and he, weeping, embraced them, and left them astonished and admiring, not only at what he'd said but also because of the firm and eminently sensible decision he'd come to.

Chapter Fifty-Four

— dealing with matters relevant to this history and to no other

The duke and duchess had made up their minds that Don Quijote's challenge to their vassal, given on the grounds already narrated, should be permitted to proceed, but since the young man in question was in fact in Flanders, where he had fled to preserve himself from Doña Rodríguez as a mother-in-law, they directed that a Gascón footman of theirs, named Tosilos, take the true culprit's place, first instructing him, most carefully, as to everything he had to do.

Two days later, the duke informed Don Quijote that in four days more his opponent would meet him on the field of battle, armed as a knight and maintaining that the girl had lied in her teeth (and in the rest of her mouth, too)[1] if she insisted she'd been given a vow of marriage. This news delighted Don Quijote, who silently vowed to perform miracles in this matter, thinking it great good luck that such an occasion had offered itself, allowing this great lord and his wife to see just what his mighty arm could do; virtually singing and dancing, he waited for the four days to pass — and, measured in terms of his desires, they dragged on for four whole centuries.

Let us leave those long days passing, as we let other things pass too, and go keep Sancho company while, sometimes sad, sometimes happy, he jogs along on his little donkey, hunting for his master, whose companionship meant more to him than being governor of all the islands in the world.

And so it happened, before he'd traveled very far from the island where he'd been governor — though he'd never been sure whether it was really an island, a city, a town, or a village he was governing — he saw coming

---

1. Literally, "she'd lied right down the middle of her beard (and even through the whole of her beard)" [*Translator's Note*].

toward him along the road a group of six pilgrims with staffs, foreigners who sing and beg for alms as they go, and when they reached him they ranged themselves in a line and, singing in close harmony, began to sing, in their own language, a song Sancho could not understand, except for the single word, very clearly pronounced, "alms," which told him all he needed to know of the substance of their song, and since, as Sidi Hamid has often told us, he was extremely charitably inclined, he took out of his saddlebags the half loaf of bread and the half cheese his late subjects had given him, and gave them to the pilgrims, explaining to them with gestures that he had nothing else he could give. They accepted his gift most gladly, saying:

"Geld! Geld!"[2]

"Good folk," replied Sancho, "I don't know what you're asking me for."

Then one of them pulled out a purse and showed it to him, which let Sancho know it was money they were after, so he put his thumb on his throat and fanned out his empty fingers above it, thus explaining that he didn't have a red cent, then spurred his donkey and started to ride past them. But one of the pilgrims, who had been regarding him attentively, reached out and, winding his arms around Sancho's waist, said in a loud voice, and in very good Spanish:

"Mother of God! Who is this? Can I possibly be holding in my arms my dear old friend, my good old neighbor, Sancho Panza? By God, I think I am, because I'm not asleep and, at the moment, I'm not drunk, either."

Sancho was startled, finding himself thus named and embraced by a foreign pilgrim, but after a long, silent, and extremely careful look, he could not recognize anyone he knew, and the pilgrim, seeing his uncertainty, exclaimed:

"Sancho Panza, my brother, is it possible you don't recognize your neighbor, Ricote the Moor, who kept shop in your very own village?"

So Sancho looked at him still harder and, beginning to slowly conjure up an almost forgotten face, finally did indeed recognize his old friend. Without climbing down from his donkey, he threw his arms around the other's neck and said:

"Who the devil could have recognized you, Ricote, dressed like some carnival clown? Tell me: who turned you into a god damned Frenchy — and how can you dare come back to Spain, because if they ever catch you and realize who you are, oh, they'll really hand it to you?"

"If you didn't know who I was, Sancho," the pilgrim replied, "I'm damned sure that, in this outfit, nobody's going to recognize me. But let's get off the highway and into that woody grove over there, where my friends are planning to eat and rest a little, and you can eat too, because they're easygoing fellows. I can tell you everything that's happened to me, since I had to leave our village, by His Majesty's decree threatening such harsh punishment of my people — as you well know."[3]

Sancho complied, Ricote spoke to the other pilgrims, and then they all

---

2. German for "money" [*Translator's Note*].
3. Expulsion of the Moors dates from 1609 to 1613; the Moors of Ricote (a valley in Murcia, along the River Segura) were among the last to be expelled. Murillo notes that "Ricote, like Sancho Panza, is a prototypical name with folkloristic resonances" [*Translator's Note*].

retired to the woody grove, well away from the highway. The pilgrims threw down their staffs, pulled off their hoods (emblems of their profession), and in their shirtsleeves could be seen to be young and handsome fellows — except for Ricote, who was well on in years. They all carried knapsacks, each and every one of them (as far as could be seen) singularly well stocked, at least as far as items capable of provoking and inviting thirst, from distances up to four or five miles off.

They stretched out on the ground and, using the grass as their tablecloth, set out bread, salt, knives, nuts, chunks of cheese, and well-chewed ham bones that, perhaps past gnawing, could at least still be sucked. They also laid out a kind of black dish known, they said, as *caviar*, explaining that it was made of fish eggs and wonderfully useful at building up a thirst. There were plenty of olives, and though they were dry and more or less pickled, they were still tasty and filling. But what truly stood out, on the green field of this banquet, were six bottles of wine, one having emerged from each pilgrim's knapsack, and even old Ricote (who had transformed himself from a Moor into a German, or a Dutchman) pulled out a bottle, and his could have competed, in size, against all five of the others.

With great gusto they began their meal, dining very slowly and expansively, savoring every bite, which they nipped off the point of their knives, taking only a little at a time — and then, all together, as if at some sudden signal, they lifted their arms, and their wine bottles, set the open ends against their waiting mouths and, their eyes turned toward Heaven (as if aiming artillery in its direction), stayed in that posture for a long time, decanting the contents of their bottles down into their bowels, their heads slowly wagging from side to side in witness to the pleasure they were experiencing.

Sancho watched it all, and none of it bothered him in the least;[4] indeed, to fit his actions to the old proverb, which he knew perfectly well, stipulating that "When you're in Rome, do as the Romans do," he borrowed Ricote's bottle and aimed just as high, and took quite as much pleasure, as any of the others.

The bottles were tilted back four times, but the fifth try was a failure, every container suddenly drier than a blade of dry grass — a development which tended to wither the sense of general happiness. From time to time one of the pilgrims would take Sancho's right hand in his own, declaring:

"Spanish people and German people, all one: good friend."

And Sancho would answer:

"Good friend, I swear God!"

And then he'd howl with laughter, for an hour or so, never once thinking of anything that happened during his governorship, because troubles have very little power over us, when we're eating and drinking. Finally, the wine used up, they fell asleep, sprawling out on the same grass they'd been eating on, only Ricote and Sancho still awake and alert, because

---

4. A popular old song about Nero, which declared *Gritos dan niños y viejos, Y él de nada se dolía,* "Children and old people screamed, But nothing bothered him a bit" [*Translator's Note*].

they'd eaten more and drunk less, so they walked away a bit and seated themselves under a beech tree, leaving the pilgrims buried in a sweet sleep, and Ricote, never once slipping into his own Moorish speech, spoke what follows in the purest Spanish:

"Oh Sancho Panza, my neighbor and my friend! How well you know that the proclamation against my people, ordered by His Majesty, shocked and terrified every one of us; it certainly had that effect on me, at least, because even before the time came for us to leave Spain, I had felt the harshness of the punishment fall both on me and on my children. It seemed to me only sensible (just like someone who must provide himself another house to live in, once he knows that by such-and-such a day he must leave the house he now occupies) to leave our village first by myself, without my family, and hunt comfortably and without the undue urgency other Moors would later be feeling, for a place to take them, because I believed, as did all the older men among us, that these proclamations were not mere threats, as some considered them, but carefully thought-out laws that, when the time came, would be fully enforced, and I was driven to this conclusion by what I knew of the vicious, crazy plans hatched by some of our people, so wild, indeed, that it seemed to me that nothing less than divine inspiration could have led His Majesty to promulgate such a courageous decree — not that all of us were equally guilty, some Moors having become firm and reliable Christians, but most were, and the minority among us could not have successfully opposed the vast majority, and why nourish a viper in your bosom, and let your enemies lodge in your house? Truly, the penalty of perpetual exile fell upon us for good cause, and though some may think it a mild and gentle punishment, to us it was the most terrible we could have received. Wherever we are, we weep for the Spanish homeland where, after all, we were born and raised, nor have we found, anywhere else, the welcome our miserable hearts long for, and even in Algeria and Morocco and all the places in North Africa where we hoped and expected to be eagerly and joyously and bounteously received, there above all else we have been most reviled and mistreated. We had not known our good fortune until we lost it, and virtually every one of us has such a burning desire to return to Spain that those among us who know the language as I do — and there are many, many who do — in fact make our way back, abandoning our wives and children in all those other places, for that is how intensely we love Spain, and now, indeed, I know and have experienced the common saying: The love of your country is sweet.

"Well, I left our village, as I said, and went to France, and though we were well received there, I wanted to see more of the world. So I went on to Italy and then to Germany, where I thought it most possible for us to live freely, the Germans not being an exacting people, letting everyone live as they choose, and most of that country enjoying religious freedom. So I set up house in a town near Augsburg, and then I joined up with these pilgrims, most of whom make regular annual trips to Spain, visiting its shrines and holy places, which they regard as their golden Indies, and a source of absolutely certain, tried-and-true profit. They go almost every-where, and nowhere do they leave without being wined and dined, as the saying goes, and without at least a dollar in their pocket, and by the time they turn homeward they have more than a hundred dollars in hand, which they change into gold and manage to smuggle back into their own country, in spite of the customs guards and the official control points, either hidden in the hollow parts of their staffs, or sewn into the patches on their cloaks, or by using other tricks they know about. So it's my plan, Sancho, to go dig up the treasure I buried — and since it's well outside the village, I should be able to get it without taking any risks — and then I'll either write to my wife and daughter, from Valencia, or cross over from there to Algeria, because I know that's where they are, and then I'll figure out how to get them to some French port, and from there I'll bring them to Germany, where we will await God's will — because in a word, Sancho, I know perfectly well that my daughter and Francisca my wife are good Catholic Christians, and even if I'm not quite what they are, all the same I think I'm more Christian than Moor, and my constant prayer to God is that He will open the eyes of my mind and show me how I can serve Him. What absolutely baffles me, Sancho, is why my wife and daughter went to Algeria rather than to France, where they could have lived as Christians."

To which Sancho replied:

"Remember, Ricote, it may not have been up to them, because it was Juan Tiopieyo, your wife's brother, who took them and, surely, being a cunning Moor, he went down the easiest road he could find. And I know something else I can tell you: I think you'd be wasting your time, going to look for whatever you buried, because I heard your wife and your brother-in-law were caught trying to sneak a lot of pearls and gold coins out of the country, and it was all taken away from them."

"That may well be, Sancho," answered Ricote, "but I know they never laid a hand on what I buried, because I never told them where it was, because I was afraid of some kind of disaster — so, if you'd like to come with me, Sancho, and help me dig up what I've buried, I'll pay you two hundred dollars, which would help you get some of the things you need, and who knows better than I do how much that is?"

"I'd do it," replied Sancho, "but not because I'm greedy. If I were, I wouldn't have tossed up the job I quit just this morning, which would have let me build the walls of my house out of gold, and it wouldn't have been six months before I was eating off solid silver plates, which is why I wouldn't go with you, and do something that looks to me like helping my king's enemies, even if, instead of promising me two hundred dollars, you promised me four hundred."

"So what job did you quit, Sancho?" asked Ricote.

"I gave up being governor of an island," Sancho answered, "and one the like of which you won't easily find."

"And where's this island?" asked Ricote.

"Where?" answered Sancho. "Five or six miles from here, and it's called Barataria Island."

"Oh, that's really something, Sancho," Ricote said, "because you find islands out in the ocean, not on dry land."

"Why not?" answered Sancho. "Let me tell you, Ricote my friend, I just left there this morning, and yesterday I was governor for as long as I wanted to be,[5] but I quit just the same, because it seemed too dangerous."

"What good did it do you, being a governor?" asked Ricote.

"I learned," answered Sancho, "that I'm not cut out to govern, except maybe a flock of sheep, and that the riches you can pile up in that kind of job come at the expense of giving up peace and losing sleep — and even food, because the governors of these islands aren't allowed to eat much, especially when they have doctors watching out for their health."

"I don't know what you're talking about, Sancho," said Ricote, "but it seems to me everything you're saying is crazy — because who on earth gave you an island to govern? Is there a shortage of people better qualified for governorships than you? Snap out of it, Sancho, and be yourself, and think good and hard if you want to come with me, as I said, and help me dig up the treasure I buried, because there's so much of it you can really call it 'treasure,' and I'll give you something you can live on, as I said I would."

"Ricote," Sancho replied, "I've already told you I don't want to; be satisfied that I won't turn you in; and go your way happily, and let me go mine; I know things you've earned can be lost, but when things you haven't earned get taken away, they can take you with them."

"I don't want to insist, Sancho," said Ricote. "But tell me: were you there when they left, my wife and my daughter and my brother-in-law?"

"I was there," answered Sancho, "and I can tell you that when that beautiful daughter of yours left, everyone in town came to see her off, and they all said she was the loveliest creature in the world. She was weeping and hugging all her girl friends, and all the women she knew, and asking everyone to pray to God for her, and to His Blessed Mother, and with such feeling that she made me cry myself, and I'm not usually much of a weeper. And there were a lot of people, I can also tell you, who wanted to hide her, or even follow her down the road and steal her away, but fear of breaking the king's law stopped them. The one who was most upset was Don Pedro Gregorio, that rich young heir you know as well as I do, who swore he loved her like crazy, and after she left he was never seen around there again, and we all think he went after her, to kidnap her, but nobody knows what's happened."

"I was pretty sure that young gentleman was after her," said Ricote, "but knowing what kind of daughter I had, his feelings about her never bothered me, because surely you've heard it said, Sancho, that very few Moorish women, or even none at all, ever fall in love with Old Christians, and since I think my daughter cared a lot more about being Christian than about being loved, this rich young man wouldn't have been able to woo her."

"May it be God's will," replied Sancho, "because it wouldn't have done either of them any good. And now let me leave, Ricote my friend, because I'd like to reach my lord Don Quijote tonight."

---

5. Sancho adds, *como un sagitario,* "like a _____," but what *sagitario* means, here, is not known [*Translator's Note*].

"God go with you, Sancho my brother, and I see my companions start-ing to stir, and it's time we went on our way, too."

Then they embraced, and Sancho climbed back on his donkey, and Ricote picked up his pilgrim's staff, and they parted.

Chapter Fifty-Five

— what happened to Sancho along the way, together with other unsurpassable matters

Having lingered with Ricote, Sancho could no longer hope to reach the duke's castle that day, but he got within about a mile and a half of it before a rather dark and cloudy night descended upon him, but since it was summertime he wasn't much concerned, and left the road, intending to wait for daylight to return — but it was his dim-witted and unlucky destiny that, just as he was hunting around for somewhere he could be most comfortable, he and his little donkey both fell into a deep, dark pit between some rickety old buildings. He tumbled down, praying to God as hard as he could that he might not have fallen into that pit which has no bottom. Nor had he, for the donkey hit bottom about twenty feet down, with San-cho, totally uninjured or hurt in any way, still mounted on his back.

He felt himself all over, and took a deep breath, to see whether he was truly undamaged or had been punctured somewhere, and finding himself sound, healthy, and in good condition, he poured out thanks to Our Lord God for the mercy He had shown him, because he had certainly expected to be broken into a thousand little pieces. He also groped around with his hands, testing the sides of the pit, trying to see if it might be possible to get out without aid, but all he found was smooth walls and nothing to get a grip on anywhere, which much distressed Sancho, especially when he heard his little donkey whimpering softly and sadly — and no wonder, nor was the complaint unreasonable, for truly the donkey had not come out of their fall very well.

"Oh!" Sancho exclaimed, "what unexpected things are always happen-ing, over and over, to those who live in this miserable world! Who could have predicted that a man who, yesterday, saw himself the enthroned gov-ernor of an island, giving orders to servants and subordinates, would find himself, today, buried in a pit, with absolutely no one to help him, no servant, no subordinate to come to his aid? My donkey and I will have to die of hunger, down here, if we don't die even sooner, he from being banged and smashed about, and I of pure sadness. Anyway, I don't expect to be as lucky as my master, Don Quijote de La Mancha, was, when he went all the way down into that enchanted Cave of Montesinos and found people who treated him better than he lived at home, because they ap-parently had a table all laid for him, and a bed all ready. Gentle, beautiful phantoms presented themselves to him, down there, but what I see here, as far as I can tell, are spiders and toads. Ah, how unlucky I am, and how all my foolishness and fantasies have ended! They'll drag my bones out of here, whenever Heaven may be pleased that they be found, all picked clean, all white and bare, and my little donkey's bones with them, which may well let them know who we were, anyway, at least to those who knew that Sancho Panza was never separated from his donkey, nor his donkey from Sancho Panza. I'll say it again: how miserable we are, prevented by our cruel destiny from dying in our own country, surrounded by our own people, because even if they couldn't find a way of helping us, there would at least have been people to mourn over us, and to close our eyes at the last moment, when we left this earth! Oh, my friend and beloved companion, how terribly I've paid you back for all your wonderful service! Forgive me, and implore Fortune, however you know how, to get us out of this miserable mess in which we both find ourselves, and I promise I'll put a laurel wreath on your head, and you'll look exactly like a triumphant poet, and I'll give you double rations, too."

Thus Sancho Panza went on lamenting, his donkey listening and never saying a word in reply, which showed in what distress and affliction the poor beast found himself. In the end, Sancho having spent the entire night in moaning and weeping, daylight finally returned, and in its clear, shining light he could see exactly how impossible it would be to escape from that pit unaided, so he began to moan and call out, to see if anyone would hear him, but it was as if he were a lonely voice crying in the desert, because there was absolutely no one near enough to hear him, and so he resigned himself to death.

His donkey had been lying face down, so Sancho helped him get to his feet, which the little animal could barely manage, and then his master opened the saddlebags, which had of course tumbled down with them, and took out a crust of bread, which he fed to the donkey, who was glad to have it, and Sancho told him, exactly as if the animal understood:

"No matter how much it hurts, food makes it feel better."

And then, suddenly, he saw there was a hole in the side of the pit wall, just large enough for a man to fit through, if he bent very low and made himself as small as he could. Sancho went over, crouched down, squeezed himself through, and found the inside broad and spacious, as he could see perfectly well because there was sunlight coming through what might be called the roof. He also saw that it widened out and got longer on the far side, which led him to turn and go back to the donkey, then begin widening the opening with a stone, so that soon there was a gap quite wide enough for the animal to go through, as he did, after which, leading him by the halter, Sancho went walking through the cavern, trying to see if, somewhere along the way, there might be an exit. It was frequently dim, and sometimes entirely dark, but Sancho was continuously afraid.

"May God Almighty help me!" he kept repeating to himself. "To my master, Don Quijote, this whole unlucky business would be a wonderful adventure. He'd see these deep dark dungeons as flowering gardens, and Galiana's[1] palaces, and he'd think he was sure to emerge from this tight-fitting gloom out onto some bright meadow, but I, having neither luck, nor anyone to advise me, and without anything like his courage, expect

---

1. Legendary Moorish princess, supposed to have been the wife of Charlemagne and the ruler of fabulously rich palaces near Toledo [*Translator's Note*].

that at every step I'll find opening out beneath me another and even deeper abyss, in which I'll be utterly swallowed up. Well, let evil come, if it comes by itself."

Walking and thinking like this, it seemed to Sancho as if he had traveled a mile or more, at which point he saw a kind of uncertain light that seemed to be daylight, filtering in from somewhere and indicating that his path, which felt to him like the road leading into the next life, would end in some sort of opening.

Sidi Hamid Benengeli leaves Sancho, at this point, and goes back to deal with Don Quijote, who, excited and happy, was looking forward to his combat with the man who'd stolen away Doña Rodríguez's daughter's honor, for he fully expected to righten the outrageous wrong done her.

It happened, accordingly, that when he sallied forth, one morning, to calculate and test the tactics to be used in this combat, which would take place in only one more day, he was running Rocinante through a rapid, short maneuver, and the horse's feet came so close to a deep opening in the ground that, had Don Quijote not pulled him up very sharply, he could not have helped but fall in. He managed to stop without taking a fall, but then edged a little closer, not dismounting, to see just what this aperture might be, and as he was staring down he heard shouts coming from inside the pit and, by listening most attentively, was able to decipher what was being said:

"Hello up there! Are you a Christian listening to me, or some compassionate gentleman who'll take pity on a sinner buried alive, or on a miserable ungovernored governor?"

It seemed to Don Quijote he was hearing Sancho Panza's voice, which astonished and confused him, so in as loud a voice as he could manage he called back:

"Who's down there? Who's that moaning and groaning?"

"Who could it be — who has such good reason to moan and groan," came the response, "but the careworn Sancho Panza, for his sins and wicked deeds governor of Barataria Island, and once the squire of that famous knight, Don Quijote de La Mancha?"

Hearing this, which doubled his wonder and more than doubled his amazement, Don Quijote thought that Sancho Panza must have died and his soul was doing penance down there, and this thought led him to declare:

"I conjure you, by everything which can have power over a Catholic Christian, that you tell me who you are, and if as I suspect you are a soul in purgatory, tell me what you wish to be done for you, because being sworn to help and protect the needy of this world, I can also protect and help those in the next life, who are unable to help themselves."

"So you," came the response, "who are speaking to me, you, your grace, must be my lord Don Quijote de La Mancha, and you must be speaking in your own voice, for it can be no one else's."

"I am indeed Don Quijote," Don Quijote answered, "he who is sworn to aid and assist, when they are in need, both the living and the dead. Tell me, then, who you are, who thus astonish and amaze me, because if you are my squire, Sancho Panza, and if you are dead and, through the mercy of God, in purgatory (since the devils have not carried you else-where), then our Holy Mother, the Roman Catholic Church, has ways and means more than sufficient to help draw you out of the torment in which you now lie, and I, who will intervene with her on your behalf, will urge her as hard as my limited wealth will permit, so name yourself, and tell me who you are."

"In the name of God!" came the response, "and by the birth of anyone you like, your grace, I swear, my lord Don Quijote, that I am your squire, Sancho Panza, and that I've never died in all the days of my life, but having given up my governorship on account of things and for reasons it would take too long to tell you, right now, last night I fell into this pit in which I'm buried, and my little donkey with me, who wouldn't let me tell a lie and, to prove it, here he is, right here."

And what's more, it must have seemed the donkey understood what Sancho was saying, because just then he began to bray so loudly that the whole cave boomed and echoed him.

"What a witness!" Don Quijote exclaimed. "I recognize his bray as well as if I'd given birth to him, and it is indeed your voice I'm hearing, my dear Sancho. Wait right here: I'll go to the duke's castle and bring back people who can take you out of that pit, into which it surely must have been your sins which placed you."

"Go on, your grace," said Sancho, "and hurry back, in the name of the One God, because I can't stand being buried alive down here, and I'm dying of fear."

Don Quijote left him, and went to the castle to tell the duke and duch-ess what had happened to Sancho, and greatly astonished they were to hear it, although they were not in the least surprised that he had fallen into that cave, for it had been there since time immemorial; nor could they understand how he had managed to give up his governorship without their having been notified. In a word, as they say, they ordered ropes and cables to be brought,[2] and although it took a lot of time for a lot of people, they pulled the donkey, and Sancho Panza too, out of that darkness and back into the light of the sun. Seeing which, a student observed:

"All bad governors should have to leave their governorships just like this, exactly as this sinner emerges from the depths of the abyss, half dead of hunger, pale as a ghost and, as far as I can tell, with their purses empty."

Sancho heard this, and said:

"Brother gossip, eight or ten days ago I became governor of the island they gave me, and in all that time I never even got enough to eat. I was persecuted by doctors; enemies crushed my bones; I had no chance either to take bribes or collect fees; and that being the case, as it is, I don't think I do deserve to come back into the world like this; but man proposes and God disposes, and God knows best, and what's best for all of us, and you've got to take things as they come, and nobody ought to say, 'I'll never be forced to drink out of *that* cup,' because just when you think you've got the bacon you're likely to get a licking; and God knows what I'm talking

---

2. In old ballads, one of which reads *Toman sogas y maromas / Por salvar del muro abajo*, "They bring ropes and cables / To climb the castle walls . . ." [*Translator's Note*].

about, and that's enough for me, so I won't say any more, though I could."

"Don't be angry, Sancho," said Don Quijote, "and don't be upset by what you hear, or there'll never be an end to it: if you're secure in your own conscience, let them say whatever they want to, because restraining slanderous tongues would be like putting gateways on the open fields. When a governor leaves his post rich, they say he's been a thief, and when he leaves it poor, they say he's been a numbskull and a fool."

"For sure," replied Sancho, "what they'll have to call me is a fool, not a thief."

And then, chatting like this, they came to the castle, and were surrounded by boys and many others, and on one of the balconies the duke and duchess stood waiting for them, but Sancho would not go to them without first getting his donkey into the stables, because, he said, the little animal had spent a very bad night in their lodgings. But he soon went to them and, kneeling, said:

"Because it was your wish, Your Majesties, rather than because of any merit of mine, I became Governor of your Barataria Island, a post I took up with an empty purse, and from which I return in the same state: I have lost nothing, and I have gained nothing. Those who have seen me there will have to tell you, however they may please, whether I governed well or ill. I resolved difficulties, I judged lawsuits, and the whole time I was dying of hunger, at the express wish of Doctor Pedro Recio, a citizen of Tirteafuera, and medical officer to both the island and to its governor. Enemies attacked us under cover of darkness, and things were pretty chancey for a while; the people down there said we came out victorious, on account of the strength of my sword arm, and may God reward them with health that matches the truth in those statements. Anyway, all that time I was trying to calculate just what a governor's responsibilities are, and what he's required to do and be, and the way I figure it they're nothing my shoulders can bear, nor any kind of weight I can carry, nor any arrows I can fit in my quiver, so rather than letting the governorship turn me upside down, I decided to turn it upside down, and yesterday morning I left the island exactly as I found it: the same streets, the same houses, the same roofs that were there when I arrived. I haven't borrowed anything from anybody, nor did I try to squeeze out any profits for myself; and although I did think about promulgating some useful laws, I didn't, because I was worried they wouldn't be obeyed, which would be the same thing as if they didn't exist. So, as I say, I left the island, accompanied only by my little donkey, and I fell into a pit, and kept walking along down there until this morning, when by the light of the sun I saw the way out, but it wasn't an easy way, and if Heaven hadn't sent me my lord Don Quijote, I'd have stayed down there till the end of the world. And that is the tale, my lord duke and duchess, of your governor, Sancho Panza, who stands here, having learned from only ten days of being a governor that I don't ever want to be a governor again — and not just governor of an island, but governor of anything in the whole world — so, with that in mind, I kiss your highnesses' feet, and just the way little boys say 'You jump over me, and then I'll jump over you,' so I jump away from being a governor and jump right back into the service of my lord Don Quijote, because even though, with him, I may salt my food with fear, I at least get enough to eat, and as long as my belly's full, it doesn't matter to me whether I eat carrots or partridges."

Sancho thus concluded his long speech, during the whole length of which Don Quijote was worried that his squire was going to say millions of stupid things, but seeing that, by the end, he had said very little that was not wise and sensible, our knight gave silent thanks to Heaven, and the duke embraced Sancho, and said he was sorry the governorship hadn't lasted longer, but he'd arrange for Sancho to be given some other post on his estate, something more useful and less onerous. And the duchess embraced him as well, and ordered that he be wined and dined, because he showed signs of having returned exhausted and not at all in good shape.

Chapter Fifty-Six

— the colossal, absolutely unique battle between Don Quijote de La Mancha and the footman, Tosilos, in defense of the dueña Doña Rodríguez's daughter

The duke and duchess had no regrets about the joke they'd played on Sancho Panza, pretending to make him a governor, and regretted it still less when, later that day, the steward arrived and told them in great detail virtually everything Sancho had said and done, all during that time, ending with a joyful account of the attack on the island, and Sancho's fear, and his departure, all of which was listened to with great pleasure.

Our history records that, thereafter, the day appointed for the battle came around, by which point, having over and over again drilled the footman, Tosilos, as to how he ought to manage a victory over Don Quijote, without killing or even wounding our knight, the duke further stipulated that no iron points were to be left on their lances, explaining to Don Quijote that true Christianity, which he so treasured, would not permit this combat to involve such great risk and danger to human life, and that Don Quijote should be satisfied that the duke had freely granted him a battlefield on his lands, even though he thereby went directly contra to the Sacred Council of Trent's [1545–1563] decree prohibiting such challenges and duels, for which reason it was better not to carry this fierce combat to the absolute limits.

Don Quijote replied that it was for His Excellency to arrange the details of this business as he thought best, and all such terms and conditions would be carefully observed. So the fearful day arrived and, the duke having ordered a spacious wooden shelter erected, on the square in front of the castle, in which he placed the battlefield judges, and the two ladies in waiting and plaintiffs in the case, mother and daughter, a vast crowd assembled from villages and towns all around, to watch this novel battle — a phenomenon never seen in that neighborhood either by the living or by the dead.

The first to appear on the field of battle was the master of ceremonies, who made a thorough examination of the entire marked-off area, ensuring that there were no tricks or cheating devices, and that all was level and firm, with no hidden holes to stumble and fall over. Then the ladies in waiting made a prompt entrance, taking their assigned seats with a show of considerable emotion; they wore veils covering their eyes and falling down to their bosoms. Don Quijote made his appearance, and soon, to the blare of trumpets, the big footman Tosilos appeared on the other side of the square, eclipsing everything else in sight, sitting tall and stiff on a huge, powerful horse, his visor lowered across his face, his armor heavy and gleaming. The horse, it could now be seen, was an immense Frisian, wide-beamed and dapple gray in color, twenty-five pounds of wool dangling from each of his monstrous legs.

This worthy warrior made his appearance, as we have said, well-schooled by his master the duke as to how he was to deal with the courageous Don Quijote de La Mancha, having been warned that under no circumstances was he to kill our knight, and, indeed, was to try to dodge away, on their first encounter, because to plunge directly at Don Quijote would certainly be to kill him. He came across the square and, as he passed the two ladies in waiting, paused for a moment, staring at the young woman who wanted him to marry her. The master of ceremonies asked Don Quijote, who had earlier made his appearance, to join with Tosilos and himself, and then made formal inquiry of Doña Rodríguez and her daughter, asking if they accepted Don Quijote de La Mancha as their duly constituted legal representative. They both said they did, and that whatever he might do was well and truly done, and valid and binding on them both.

The duke and duchess had now come out on a balcony, overlooking the field of battle, which was by this point packed closely around by enormous numbers of people, anxious to glimpse so unique a conflict. The terms of this combat were that, should Don Quijote prevail, his opponent would be obliged to marry Doña Rodríguez's daughter, and should Don Quijote be vanquished, his opponent would be deemed freed of any such pledge and obligation, and would bear no further responsibility of any kind.

The master of ceremonies carefully positioned the combatants, to keep either from having an advantage with respect to the glare of the sun, leading each man to his assigned position. Drums began to beat, trumpets sounded everywhere, the very earth under their feet trembled; the spectators' hearts beat fast, some of them fearing and some hoping for a successful or an unsuccessful outcome to the challenge. Finally, Don Quijote, praying with all his heart to God Our Lord, and to his lady Dulcinea del Toboso, stood waiting for the signal to attack; but our footman's mind was filled with very different thoughts, for he was thinking what I shall now describe for you:

It seems that, when he stood staring at his lady enemy, she struck him as the most beautiful woman he had ever seen in his life, and that blind little boy known up and down these streets as Love saw his chance to trample on a footmanish heart and dangle it on the long list of his trophies — and so, skipping over to Tosilos, quite unseen, he drove an arrow two yards deep into his left side and right through his heart, all of which he accomplished in perfect safety, because Love is invisible, and comes and goes as he pleases, never accounting to anyone for anything he does.

When the signal to attack was given, accordingly, our footman was in a state of utter rapture, dreaming of the beauties of she who he had made mistress of his freedom, so he paid no attention to the trumpet call, unlike Don Quijote who, the very instant it sounded, came charging down at his opponent as fast as Rocinante could go, at which sight his good squire Sancho began to shout:

"May God guide you, flower and cream of knight errantry! May God grant you the victory, because you fight for the right!"

But though Tosilos could see Don Quijote coming straight at him, he did not move a step; instead, raising his voice, he called to the master of ceremonies, and when that functionary approached, to see what he wanted, he asked:

"Sir, the reason for this battle is, is it not, that I either marry or do not marry that lady?"

"Exactly so," was the response.

"In that case," said the footman, "my conscience troubles me, and would trouble me more if I carried on with this combat, so I hereby declare that I consider myself conquered and that I want to marry that lady as soon as possible."

The master of ceremonies was struck dumb by Tosilos' statement, and since he was in on the entire scheme, he couldn't think of a word to say in reply. Don Quijote pulled up, right in the middle of his charge, seeing that his opponent was not coming at him. The duke could not understand why the battle had been interrupted, but the master of ceremonies came over and told him what Tosilos had said, which both baffled and utterly infuriated the footman's master.

While these things were going on, Tosilos went over to Doña Rodríguez and declared, in a loud, clear voice:

"Madame, I wish to marry your daughter, nor do I wish to accomplish by fighting and arguments what I can achieve peacefully and without any risk of death."

Our brave Don Quijote, hearing this, said:

"This being the case, I am free and released from my promise: now marry her and be happy, and since God Our Lord has given her to you, may Saint Peter add his blessing."

The duke had by now walked out on the field of battle and, coming over to Tosilos, he said:

"Is it true, my dear sir, that you have declared yourself vanquished and, impelled by your tender conscience, you now plan to marry this lady?"

"Yes, my lord," replied Tosilos.

"He's doing the right thing," Sancho Panza remarked, "because why not just give the cat what you were going to give the mouse, and save yourself the trouble?"

Tosilos set about unlacing his visor, and asked the others to help him, because he was having trouble breathing, shut up as he was in such a cramped space. They quickly got it off him, and there for all to see was the footman's face. And when Doña Rodríguez and her daughter saw this, they began to scream:

"It's a trick, it's a trick! We've got Tosilos, my lord's footman, instead of the true husband! Justice, before God and the King, for such wickedness — for such a swindle!"

"Ladies, don't be upset," said Don Quijote, "for this is neither wickdness nor a swindle, but if it is, it's not the duke who's done it but those evil magicians who persecute me: jealous that I should receive the glory of this conquest, they have transformed your husband's face into this, which you say belongs to the duke's footman. Listen to me and, in spite of my enemies' wickedness, marry him, for without a doubt he is truly the man you wanted for your husband."

Hearing this, the duke was so wracked with laughter that his anger disappeared, and he said:

"Such exceedingly strange things happen to my lord Don Quijote, that I'm tempted to believe this footman of mine is really someone else; but let's try this way of getting around the problem: let the wedding wait for two weeks, if that's agreeable, and let's keep this person about whom we're so unsure under lock and key, and we'll see whether or not he turns back into who he really is, because I don't imagine these magicians' ill-will toward Don Quijote will last quite that long, especially once they see how little good all these tricks and transformations have done them."

"Oh my lord!" said Sancho, "these scoundrels are always changing one thing into something else, when it comes to my master. A knight my master conquered, a while ago, called the Knight of the Mirrors, was turned into Samson Carrasco, the college graduate, who lives in our village and is our great friend, and for me they turned my lady Dulcinea del Toboso into a plain country girl, and so I guess this footman will have to live and die a footman, the rest of his life."

To which Doña Rodríguez's daughter said:

"Whoever this is who's asked me to marry him, I thank him, because I'd rather be the legal wife of a footman than the rejected lover and deceived victim of a gentleman — and the man who seduced me is no gentleman."

In the end, everything that had been said and done ended in Tosilos being locked up, to see how his transformation turned out; Don Quijote's triumph was universally hailed, though most of the audience were sorely disappointed, because the combatants they'd so eagerly awaited had not smashed each other to pieces, just as little boys are disappointed when the man they've come to see hanged never makes his appearance, either because the judge or the prosecuting attorney has pardoned him. Everyone went home; the duke and Don Quijote went into the castle; Tosilos went to be locked away; and Doña Rodríguez and her daughter were happy, seeing that, one way or another, their suit would end in marriage — a consummation for which Tosilos was every bit as eager.

Chapter Fifty-Seven

— which deals with Don Quijote's farewell to the duke and what happened with the wise but bold Altisidora, the duchess' maid

Don Quijote had long since decided to break away from the idleness in which he was living, there in the castle, for he thought himself mightily missed, being thus lazily shut away among all the endless comforts and pleasures furnished him, as a knight errant, by the duke and duchess, and he considered himself bound to give a close accounting to Heaven for all such idleness and sequestering of himself, so one day he begged to be permitted to leave. Permission was granted, though both royal folk gave him clear evidence that they regretted his departure. The duchess put his wife's letters into Sancho Panza's hands, who wept over them, saying:

"Who could have thought that such grand expectations, brought swirling into my wife's breast by the news of my governorship, would have to end with me returning to my master Don Quijote de La Mancha's miserable adventures? All the same, it makes me feel good to see my Teresa being exactly who she really is, and sending acorns to the duchess, because if she hadn't sent them I'd have been sorry, and she'd have been ungrateful. What consoles me is that there's no way this gift could possibly be called a bribe, because I was already a governor when she sent them, and it's only right and proper for those who've been given jobs, even if they're foolish jobs, to show they're grateful. Anyway, I came to the governorship naked, and I left it the same way, so I can safely say, and with a good conscience, 'I came into the world naked, and naked is how you find me: I've lost nothing, and I've gained nothing.'"

Sancho said this to himself the day they left. Before they rode off, Don Quijote, who had made his farewells to the duke and duchess the night before, appeared in the castle courtyard, the next morning, fully armed. Everyone was watching, from windows and from balconies, and the duke and duchess, too, came out to see him. Sancho was mounted on his donkey, with his saddlebags, and his suitcase, and all his supplies, happy as a lark because the duke's steward (the same fellow who'd played the role of Countess Trifaldi) had handed him a purse containing two hundred dollars in gold, to take care of whatever they might need on the road, a gift that Don Quijote as yet knew nothing about.

Suddenly, as everyone stood watching, the voice of the bold and witty Altisidora arose from among the crowd of ladies in waiting and maids, pitifully singing:

> Oh listen, wicked knight,
> pull in your eager reins;
> keep those sharp spurs
> from your wild horse's veins.
>   Think, you thief, how you're running
> not from some fiery snake,
> but a helpless, half-grown lamb,
> little more than a maid.
>   You awful monster, you've cheated

the prettiest girl — and so good! —
Diana ever saw in her mountains,
or Venus saw in her woods.
Vireno — Aeneas[1] *— what shall I call you?*
Barrabas go with you, evil befall you!

In your bloody, dripping paws
you're carrying off, oh liar!
the heart, the liver, the soul
of a girl who loved like fire.
　You're carrying three of my 'kerchiefs,
and some garters (accustomed to limbs
whiter than marble, and just
as smooth) in colors fairly dim.
　You're carrying two thousand sighs
that could each have burned a thousand
Trojans, if that many Trojans
were anywhere still to be found.
Vireno — Aeneas — what shall I call you?
Barrabas go with you, evil befall you!

May your squire Sancho's heart
be turned as hard and cold
as your own, and may Dulcinea
ne'er be as she was of old.
　May your guilt to me produce
her punishment, pain, and sadness;
you sinners rarely pay,
but the good must pay with madness.
　May all your best adventures
be turned to useless dust;
may dreams be your only pleasure,
and your courage be gnawed like a crust.
Vireno — Aeneas — what shall I call you?
Barrabas go with you, evil befall you!

May everyone all over Spain
know you for a thief, and untrue,
and people all over the world
know what you'd stoop to do.
　May you lose at cards, and be trumped,
may your aces fall to a trey,
may your tricks fail as you take them,
may your losses last all day.
　If you cut the corns on your feet
may the blood flow from your blade;
if a dentist pulls your teeth
may their roots be yanked from the shade.
Vireno — Aeneas — what shall I call you?
Barrabas go with you, evil befall you!

---

1. Vireno deserts Olympia, in *Orlando Furioso*; Aeneas deserts Dido, in the *Aeneid* [*Translator's Note*].

While the pitiful Altisidora was thus singing her mournful song, Don Quijote stared back at her and did not say a word, but when she was done he turned to Sancho and said:

"In the name of your ancestors, oh Sancho, I implore you to tell me the truth. Tell me, do you by any chance actually have the three 'kerchiefs and the garters of which this lovestruck maiden speaks?"

And Sancho answered:

"I've got the 'kerchiefs, yes, but not the garters — that's way off the mark."

The duchess was stunned by Altisidora's brazenness; she knew the girl was bold, witty, and daring, but she'd never thought her capable of anything quite this extreme, and not having been told of this joke beforehand, she was all the more startled. Wanting to keep the jest going, the duke said:

"Sir knight, it doesn't seem to me quite right, having received here in this castle of mine so warm a welcome as you have had, that you should dare to carry off — at the very least — three 'kerchiefs, and perhaps also a number of garters, all belonging to this maid of mine. These are truly signs of wickedness that do not square with your reputation. Now return those garters — or else, I shall have no choice but to challenge you to mortal combat, and without the slightest fear that rascally magicians will transform me, or change my face, as they did to Tosilos my footman, who was supposed to meet you in hand to hand combat."

"May it not be God's wish," replied Don Quijote, "to see me unsheathe my sword against your most illustrious person, after having received so many signs of your favor. The 'kerchiefs will be returned, now that Sancho has told me he has them; but this business of the garters simply cannot be possible, because neither I nor he have ever had them, so if your maid will please look in those places where she keeps such things, I'm sure she'll find them. My lord duke, I have never been a thief, nor do I expect ever to be one, so long as I live, so long as God may choose to hold me in His hand. This girl speaks, as she herself says, like someone lovestruck, for which I bear no blame whatever, so I do not think I need beg pardon either of her nor of Your Excellency, though I do beg you, please, to have a better opinion of me — and, again, give me your permission to follow my road away from here."

"May God arrange it so well, my lord Don Quijote," said the duchess, "that the news we hear of your deeds be forever good. So go with God, for the longer we detain you, the hotter burns the fire in the breasts of all the damsels who behold you — and this one I will punish, and in the future she will not stray, either with her eyes or with her tongue."

"Hear me just once more, oh brave Don Quijote!" Altisidora said at this point. "And this time only to beg your pardon about the stolen garters, because by God and my soul I'm wearing them right now, and I've been as careless as that man who went looking for his donkey, even while he was sitting right on it."

"Didn't I tell you?" said Sancho. "Catch me covering up a robbery! If that was my style, by God, I'd have had lots of chances when I was a governor."

Don Quijote bent his head, bowing to the duke, the duchess, and to all those present, then swung Rocinante's reins around and left the castle, starting down the road to Zaragoza, with Sancho on his donkey riding behind him.

Chapter Fifty-Eight

— which tells how so many adventures came piling up on Don Quijote, and so fast, that none of them could catch their breath

Finding himself out on the open road, freed from Altisidora's clinging compliments, Don Quijote felt he was once again where he truly belonged; renewing his quest for knightly adventure made his heart soar, and, turning to Sancho, he declared:

"Freedom, Sancho, is one of the most precious gifts Heaven gives us; no treasure buried in the earth can compare to it, nor any covered by the oceans; in the cause of freedom, as in the cause of honor, one can and should risk life itself, just as freedom's opposite, captivity, is the worst evil a man can experience. I say this, Sancho, because, now, you have observed the luxury, the flowing abundance with which we were treated, in that castle, and yet in the very midst of all those mouth-watering banquets and snow-cooled drinks I felt myself cramped by the fiercest pangs of hunger, because I could not freely savor any of it as I could had it been mine: the obligation to requite those who do us such kindnesses and favors is like a chain that cannot keep from being a restraint on the free spirit. Happy the man to whom Heaven gives a crust of bread, without making it necessary that he thank anyone but Heaven for what he receives!"

"All the same," said Sancho, "and despite everything your grace has said, it wouldn't be right for us not to be grateful for the two hundred dollars the duke's steward gave me, in gold, just for dealing with things that can happen: it's in a little purse, and I'm carrying it next to my heart, like a poultice or a tonic, because we won't always be able to find castles where they'll wine and dine us, and then we'll have to deal with inns where, without money, they might beat us."

Our travelers, knight and squire, went along, chatting on these and other subjects, and had gone perhaps three or four miles when they saw, stretched out in the green grass of a little meadow, lying on their cloaks and eating their dinner, perhaps a dozen men, dressed like farmers. Next to them, under what looked like white sheets or altar cloths, lay some hidden objects, here protruding up, there smoothed down flat. Don Quijote rode up, greeted them most courteously, and then asked what was under those cloths. One of the men answered:

"My lord, under these cloths there are some bas-relief carvings, and also support boards for an altar-decoration we're making, in our village; we carry them covered up so they don't get dirty, and on our shoulders, so they don't get broken."

"If you don't mind," replied Don Quijote, "I should be very pleased to see them, for carvings carried so carefully surely must be good ones."

"Are they ever good!" said the other. "They'd better be, when you realize how much they cost, because I don't think there's one of them that's not worth more than five hundred dollars — and so you can see that's the plain truth, your grace, you just wait a minute, your grace, and you'll see for yourself."

And he got up, left his dinner and went to pull the cover off the first carving, which turned out to be Saint George on horseback, with a dragon writhing at his feet and a spear thrust down its throat, a scene depicted in all its usual savage ferocity. The whole carving glittered, as they say, like gold. And after looking at it, Don Quijote said:

"This was one of the divine army's best knights errant; his name was Don Saint George, and he was a zealous defender of maidens. Let's see this other one."

The man uncovered it, and they saw Saint Martín, also on horseback, giving half his cloak to a beggar, and no sooner had Don Quijote seen this image when he said:

"This knight, too, was a great Christian Adventurer, and I think he was even more generous than courageous, as you can easily see here, Sancho, for he's sharing his cloak with the poor man and giving him half of it, and it was surely winter at the time, or else he'd have given away the whole thing, he was so charitable."

"That doesn't have to be it," said Sancho, "because maybe he was just keeping in mind the proverb, which says: Giving it away but still keeping it — that's the way to go."

Don Quijote laughed, and asked that the third cloth be removed; underneath it there lay a carving of the patron saint of all Spain, mounted, his sword bloody, trampling down Moors and riding over their severed heads; and Don Quijote said, the moment he saw it:

"Now this is a true knight in Christ's holy army! His name is Don San Diego Matamoros, one of the bravest saints and most courageous knights the world has ever seen or Heaven ever held, to this very day."

Then the next cloth was pulled back, and they saw it was Saint Paul falling from his horse, along with all the usual details of his conversion. And it looked so lifelike that you would have said Christ was speaking to him, and Paul was answering.

"In his day," said Don Quijote, "this was the worst enemy the Holy Church of God Our Lord ever had, and then the best protector and defender it will ever have; a knight errant in life, and a barefoot saint in death, and a tireless laborer in the vineyards of the Lord; teacher of the Gentiles, himself schooled by Heaven, and his own teacher and master no less than Jesus Himself."

There were no more carvings, so Don Quijote directed that they be covered over again, and then he said to the men who were bearing them:

"I think it a very good omen, brothers, to have seen what I have seen, because these saints and noble knights lived by the same faith and the same principles that I too follow, which is war — the difference between us being that they were saints and fought in God's wars, while I am a sinner and fight in humanity's. They conquered Heaven by force of arms, for Heaven does not reject force and violence,[1] and I do not know, so far,

---

1. "The kingdom of heaven suffereth violence": Matthew 11:12 [*Translator's Note*].

what my own struggles may have conquered, but if my Dulcinea del Toboso could only be released, my fortunes might be improved, and my mind
strengthened, and it might well be that I could direct myself down some
better road than the one I now follow."

"May God hear you, but the Devil be deaf," said Sancho promptly.

The farmers were struck both by Don Quijote's appearance and by his
words, though they did not understand even half of what he had said.
They finished their food, loaded up their burdens and, bidding Don Quijote farewell, went on their way.

But Sancho was left feeling, once again, that he'd never truly known
his master, absolutely amazed at how much Don Quijote knew, for it
seemed there was no tale ever told, nor any deed ever done, that his lord
did not carry fixed in his mind and forever ready at his fingertips.

"Really, master," he said, "if this could be called an adventure, it's been
one of the gentlest and nicest we've ever run across in all our wanderings.
We've gotten out of it without being beaten, and without anything scary
happening, and we haven't had to draw our swords or been hammered
into the ground — and we're not even hungry! May God be blessed,
Who has allowed me to glimpse this with my very own eyes."

"That's well said, Sancho," said Don Quijote, "but you have to realize
that things aren't always the same, and don't always work out in the same
way, so what are commonly called omens, which are not based on any
kind of natural logic, will simply be considered good fortune by those who
have the wisdom to properly appreciate them. A superstitious man gets up
in the morning, walks out of his house, meets a barefooted friar of the
Blessed Order of Saint Francis, and promptly turns around and goes
home,[2] as if he'd met some mythical monster. Another man, whose name
happens to be Mendoza,[3] spills salt on his tablecloth and feels as if he's
spilled melancholy all over his heart — just as if Nature was bound to
give us an advance warning, before misfortune could strike, and convey
its message by means of such trivia as this. A wise man and good Christian
will not quibble with Heaven: it will do what it will do. When Scipio
arrived in Africa, and jumped onto dry land, he stumbled, and his soldiers
thought it a bad omen, but Scipio reached down and embraced the
ground, saying: 'You'll never get away from me, Africa, now that I've got
you in my arms.' So as far as I'm concerned, Sancho, coming across these
carvings has simply been a happy accident."

"I agree with you," replied Sancho, "and I wish your grace would explain to me why the Spanish, before they go into battle, always call on
Santiago Matamoros: 'For Santiago, and shut up, Spain!'[4] Is Spain's mouth
supposed to be open, so they have to shut it, or what's all that about?"

"You're too simple-minded, Sancho," answered Don Quijote. "Remember that this great Knight of the Red Cross was given to Spain by God
Himself, to be its patron saint and protector, especially in its fierce struggles

2. Morning meetings with friars were considered very bad luck [Translator's Note].
3. People with this name were considered so superstitious that *mendocino*, "one of the Mendozas,"
   could be used to mean "superstitious" [Translator's Note].
4. The Spanish battle cry during their centuries-long war against the Moors was ¡*Santiago y cierra
   España!*, "For St. James and close ranks, Spain!" St. James was known as "Santiago Matamoros,"
   i.e., the Moorslayer.

with the Moors, so he's invoked and called on in all our battles, and he's frequently been seen, visibly present on the battlefield, humbling and trampling, destroying and murdering, those Squadrons of Hagar [Moors], a truth of which I could give you many citations from the works of our truthful Spanish chroniclers."

Sancho then changed the subject, saying:

"I was astonished, my lord, at how brazen the duchess' maid, Altisidora, was acting: that little fellow we call Love must have really wounded her, run her right through, because they say he may be a blind hunter, all bleary-eyed or, better yet, without any eyes, but all he has to do is aim at a heart and, no matter how small it is, he drives his arrows right through, from one side to the other. I've also heard it said that a girl's modesty and virtue can blunt and weaken his amorous darts, but in this Altisidora they seem to have been sharpened rather than dulled."

"You need to remember, Sancho," said Don Quijote, "that Love never pays any attention to reason, or worries about its limits, being very like Death in nature, attacking a king's high palace walls just as it attacks a shepherd's hovel, and the very first thing it does, once it's taken possession of someone, is take away every trace of fear or shame, so Altisidora announced her passion shamelessly, and what I felt was more embarrassment than compassion."

"But how cruel that is!" said Sancho. "It's incredibly ungrateful! Me, I'd have surrendered at her very smallest, first breath of passion. Son of a bitch! What a marble-hard heart — what brass-lined bowels — what a stony soul! Still, I can't imagine what this girl saw in you, your grace, to overpower and conquer her like that: I mean, what particularly choice part, what special charm, what display of wit, what feature of your face — which one of these, or what mixture of them all, made her fall in love with you? Because, truthfully, I often stop and look your grace over, from the point of your shoes to the very last hair on your head, and I see more things to frighten than to fire up love, and since I've also heard you say that beauty is the primary and chief reason for falling in love, and you don't have any beauty, your grace, I don't know what the poor girl fell in love with."

"Remember, Sancho," replied Don Quijote, "that there are two kinds of love: there's spiritual love, and then there's bodily love; spiritual love walks, and shows itself, in the mind, in virtue, in honorable behavior, in generosity, and in good breeding, and these are all qualities that can occur and be found in an ugly man, so that when we're talking about this sort of beauty, and not the bodily kind, love usually swirls up impetuously, like a whirlwind. I am very well aware that I'm not handsome, Sancho; but I also know that I'm not deformed, and a good man only has to be something other than a monster, to be well loved, if that is he possesses the gifts I've been talking about."

As they were thus conversing, they wandered off the road and into a wood, and suddenly, without any warning whatever, Don Quijote found himself tangled in a number of nets woven of green cord, stretching between and among the trees; unable to understand what was going on, he said to Sancho:

"Sancho, it strikes me that these nets must belong to the most unusual adventure imaginable. Mother of God, if these magicians who keep persecuting me aren't trying to tangle me up in these things, to keep me from going on, as though in vengeance for my severity to Altisidora! But I can assure them that, even if these ropes were spun of the hardest diamonds, or were stronger than the chains the jealous God of Forges [Vulcan] wrapped around Venus and Mars, I'd still smash them as I would nets fashioned of seaweed or of light cotton thread."

And, intending to ride on and smash every one of them, he suddenly saw in front of him, emerging from behind some trees, two of the most beautiful shepherd girls he'd ever seen — or, at least, they were dressed like shepherd girls, except that their jackets and skirts were of fine brocade, the skirts short and elaborately decorated with golden silk. They wore their hair loose over their shoulders, and it gleamed as if in competition with the sun's own rays; garlands of green laurel plaited with crimson amaranth encircled their heads. They did not look younger than fifteen or any older than eighteen.

This sight astonished Sancho, totally stunned Don Quijote, caused the sun to stop in its tracks, in order to watch, and imposed a wonderful silence on all four of the human beings. Finally, the first to break that silence was one of the shepherdesses, who said to Don Quijote:

"Hold, sir knight, and do not break our nets, which have not been hung here to do you any harm but only for our pleasure, and since we know you'll now have to ask us why they're there, and who we are, we wish to quickly and briefly explain.

"In a village about seven miles from here, inhabited by many high-born folk and rich gentlemen, a group of men arranged that they, along with their sons, wives, and daughters, their neighbors, friends, and relations, should take their holiday in this place, which is one of the pleasantest for miles around, thus constituting themselves a new and pastoral Arcadia, the girls all dressing as shepherdesses, the boys as shepherds. We've been rehearsing two eclogues [pastoral poems], one by the great poet Garcilaso, and the other by the illustrious Camoens,[5] written in his native Portuguese tongue, neither of which we have as yet performed. We came here, indeed, only yesterday; we've pitched our dwellings, better known as 'field tents,' among these branches, and along the borders of a swift-flowing river that feeds all these meadows; last night we stretched these nets across these trees, hoping to catch silly little birds that our noise might frighten into them. Should it please you, señor, to be our guest, we will feast you freely and courteously, because — at least for now — no sorrow or melancholy can be allowed in this sanctuary."

She stopped, and said no more, and Don Quijote answered:

"Surely, most beautiful lady, even Actaeon himself, stumbling onto Diana as she bathed, could not have been more astonished than your loveliness astonished me. Nor could I more heartily approve of such entertainment as you have chosen, as also your kind and gracious invitation. If I can be of any service to you, please command me, and be assured of

5. Luis de Camoens, 1524–1580, of partly Galician ancestry; most famous for *Os Lusíadas* [*The Lusiads*], an epic poem on Portugal's history [*Translator's Note*].

my obedience, for my sole profession and charge is to show myself grateful and well disposed toward all manner of people, and in particular those of high-birth, among whom you are so clearly included. Even if these nets, which only occupy a very tiny space, stretched all the way around the earth, I should search for new worlds, to keep from having to break them as I pass. And to lend credit to these perhaps exaggerated expressions of mine, note that he who makes these vows to you is none other than Don Quijote de La Mancha, if by any chance that name has ever reached your ears."

"Oh, my dear dear friend!" said the other shepherdess. "What wonderful luck we've had! Do you see this gentleman right here in front of us? Well, rejoice — for he's the bravest, the most passionate, the most courteous in the whole world, unless the history which records his deeds is lying and deceiving us, because I've read it. And I'll bet this good man with him is a certain Sancho Panza, his squire, who says the funniest things!"

"That's true," said Sancho, "because I'm that witty fellow and also that squire your grace spoke of, and this gentleman is my master, and he's precisely the Don Quijote de La Mancha the book is written about."

"Ah!" said the first shepherdess. "My dear friend, let's ask him please to stay, because our fathers and brothers will enjoy that tremendously, and I've heard just what you said about his courage and the funny things he says and, more than everything else, that he's the most faithful, loyal lover anyone's ever heard of, and his lady's a certain Dulcinea del Toboso, who's said to be the most beautiful woman in all Spain."

"And they say rightly," declared Don Quijote, "unless, to be sure, your own matchless beauty casts doubt on their judgment. But please, do not tire yourselves, ladies, with trying to detain me, because the requirements of my profession, which are absolutely clear, do not under any circumstances allow me to rest."

At this point, they were joined by a brother of one of the girls, dressed, like them, in shepherd style, and with the same opulent elegance; the shepherdesses told him that one of the men with whom they were talking was the brave Don Quijote de La Mancha, and the other was his squire, Sancho Panza, "and you know who *he* is, because you've read the book about him!" The gallant shepherd introduced himself and asked, most politely, that they visit his tent and, unable to refuse such a request, Don Quijote consented.

Just then, the game-beating began, and the nets were filled with all sorts of birds, who, tricked by the safe-seeming green, flew into precisely the danger from which they meant to flee. More than thirty people had now joined the group, all of them dressed like gallant shepherds and shepherdesses, and they were immediately informed just who Don Quijote and his squire were, which news delighted them, because they already knew about him, from the published history. And when they reached their tents, fully set tables were awaiting them, the food being elegant, abundant, and well laid out; they pressed the place of honor upon Don Quijote, all of them watching him intently, astonished to be actually seeing him.

Later, when the tables had been cleared, Don Quijote rose and, with immense calm, proceeded to say:

"The greatest sin a man can commit, some will say, is pride, but I say it is ingratitude, for as they say: Hell is full of ingrates. From the moment I first learned the use of reason, I have tried as well as I knew how to avoid this sin, and if I cannot repay in kind all the kindnesses done me, I can at least offer the desire to do so, and when that desire, too, is not enough, I can make those kindnesses public, for he who openly declares and proclaims the good deeds done him would, in fact, repay them in kind, if he could, since those who receive are usually of lower standing than those who give, and God, Who stands highest of all, is indeed the giver of everything, nor can man's gifts be in any way compared to God's, though to some extent this very difficulty can augment our merely human gratitude. Thus, my gratitude for the favor you have shown me, here, though it cannot conform in kind or quality to what I have received, is still I think satisfactory, because it is the best I am able to do, and so let me offer you what I have to offer, which is this: I hereby declare that, here in the middle of this highway, I will proclaim, and am prepared for a period of two days to defend the proposition, that these lovely but counterfeited shepherdesses are the most beautiful and most gracious damsels in all the world, with the sole exception of my matchless Dulcinea del Toboso, sole lady of my thoughts, which amendment I make with God's good grace to any and all who may hear me."

Sancho, who had been listening closely, suddenly called out, in a very loud voice:

"Would anyone in the world dare affirm that this master of mine is mad? Tell me, your graces, gentlemen shepherds all: is there a village priest, no matter how wise and scholarly he may be, who could possibly have made the statement just uttered by my master? Is there a knight errant, no matter how famed for his courage and bravery, who could present you with a gift like that my master has offered?"

His face red with anger, Don Quijote turned toward Sancho:

"Is there anyone in the whole universe who would *not* say that you're a fool, inside and out, brushed with I know not what colors of sly wickedness? Who asked you to meddle in my affairs? — to determine whether I am a wise man or a nuisance? Be silent, don't say a word, but just saddle Rocinante, if he is not already saddled. We will now put my proposition to the test, and, with reason and justice at my side, you may all consider that anyone who dares contradict me is as good as rolling in the dust."

In a high rage, and showing it very clearly, Don Quijote rose from his chair, astonishing all those around him and making them wonder, indeed, whether he ought to be considered mad or sane. In the end, after they had tried to dissuade him from issuing such a challenge, the truth of which, they said, they freely admitted, and there being no need whatever to prove his courage, for it was quite sufficient that they had read the history of his deeds, he still insisted on fulfilling his pledge and, mounting Rocinante, he took up his shield and his spear and set himself directly in the middle of a road that ran just beside the green meadow. Sancho trailed after, on his little donkey, along with the whole flock of pastoral vacationers, anxious to see what might come of our knight's arrogant and quite incredible proclamation.

There was Don Quijote, as I've said, right in the middle of the road, and he made the air fairly ring with his words:

"Oh gentlemen! Passersby! Travelers! Knights! Squires! Pedestrians, and you who come riding down this road! Know that here stands the knight errant, Don Quijote de La Mancha, ready to defend the proposition that the lovely nymphs who now dwell in these fields and woods are the most beautiful, and the most courteous, in all the world, with the sole exception of the lady of my heart, Dulcinea del Toboso! Let anyone who thinks differently come forward; I await him."

He made this declaration twice more, and no venturesome voice was raised in opposition, there being no one to hear him — but Fate, which had begun to direct his affairs more and more carefully, arranged that, suddenly, not far off, there appeared a whole crowd of mounted men coming down the road, many of them with spears in their hands, riding close together and riding very fast. Don Quijote's audience no sooner saw them than, turning right around, they moved a fair distance away from the road, well aware that, if they stayed where they were, it might become dangerous. But Don Quijote, as ever fearless, remained exactly where he was, though Sancho Panza took shelter behind Rocinante's hind quarters.

The troop of lance-carrying cowhands rode up, and one of them, riding in front, began to shout at Don Quijote:

"Get out of the road, you son of a bitch, or these bulls will smash you into little pieces!"

"Hah, you scum!" replied Don Quijote. "I don't give a damn about your bulls, even if they're the fiercest ever bred on Jarama's banks! Scoundrels! Admit, here and now, that what I have here proclaimed is the truth — and, if not, prepare to do battle with me."

The cowhand had no time to reply, nor did Don Quijote have a chance to get out of the way, even had he wanted to, for the herd of wild bulls and gentle oxen, along with all the cowhands and others who were driving them to where, the next day, there would be a bullfight, simply rode right over Don Quijote, and Sancho, and Rocinante, and the little donkey, flattening them out and rolling them along the ground. Sancho was left battered, Don Quijote stunned, the donkey miserable, and Rocinante in not terribly good shape — but eventually they managed to get to their feet, and Don Quijote, slipping here and tumbling there, started running after the herd, shouting:

"Stop, wait, you wicked scoundrels! One knight, all alone, still awaits you here, and he's not one of those who cry after a fleeing enemy, 'Let them cross on a bridge of pure silver!' "

But the fast-moving riders would not stop on his account, paying no more attention to his threats than to the rain in last year's clouds. Weariness soon halted Don Quijote who, more enraged than avenged, sat down on the roadway, waiting for Sancho, Rocinante, and the donkey to catch up to him. They arrived; master and man mounted their steeds; and without going back to bid farewell to the imitation Arcadians, feeling a good deal more embarrassment than pleasure, they rode on their way.

Chapter Fifty-Nine

*— which narrates an extraordinary thing that happened to Don
Quijote, quite possibly to be considered an adventure*

Don Quijote and Sancho Panza let a clear, clean stream, which they
found flowing in a cool grove, wash away the dust and dirt and weariness
of their encounter with the rude bulls: after turning Rocinante and the
donkey loose, without halter or bridle and bit, master and man seated
themselves along the bank. Sancho dipped into his saddlebag larder, producing what he always called "eats"; Don Quijote wiped his mouth and
washed his face, which refreshed and reinvigorated his sagging spirits as
well. But sorrow and regret would not let him take a single bite, and
Sancho did not dare touch the food spread out in front of them, out of
pure respect and courtesy, waiting until his master had first tasted it. But
then, seeing Don Quijote lost in his own world, not deigning even to
bother with food, Sancho without comment trampled on every rule of
good breeding, beginning to cram the bread and cheese that were lying
there into his stomach.

"Eat, Sancho my friend," said Don Quijote. "Life must be sustained,
that being far more important to you than to me; leave me to die, murdered by my thoughts and my misfortunes. I was born to live dying, Sancho, and you to die eating, and if you want to see how truly I speak, just
consider me, printed in books, celebrated in war, a man of courtesy and
honor, respected by princes, pursued by lovely girls — and at the end of
it all, when I look forward to acclaim, to triumphs and crowns, to the
spoils and rewards of my brave deeds, I find myself, this morning, trampled
and kicked and beaten by the hooves of filthy, vulgar beasts. Just thinking
of this enfeebles my jaws, befuddles my molars and numbs my hands,
depriving me of all interest in food, so that I think about letting myself
die of hunger, the cruelest death of all."

"Then I guess," said Sancho, not interrupting the vigorous motion of
his own jaws, "your grace doesn't approve of the old proverb, 'if the body
has to die, let it be with a full stomach.' Anyway, I don't expect to kill
myself that way; I think I'll be like the shoemaker, who keeps stretching
his leather with his teeth, until he finally gets it to the size he wants; I'll
keep eating and pulling my life along until it gets as far as Heaven wants
it to go — and let me tell you, señor, there's nothing crazier than to sink
down into despair the way you're doing, and believe me, once you have
something to eat, and lie down and take a little nap on the green pillows
of this grass, you'll see, after you wake up, everything will feel better."

Don Quijote took his advice, for it seemed to him that Sancho spoke
more like a philosopher than a fool:

"And if you, oh Sancho! will do for me what I will now ask of you, my
consolation will be more certain and my sorrows will not seem so immense, and what I ask is that, while I sleep, obediently following your
advice, you go a little way from here and, using Rocinante's reins, expose
your flesh and give yourself three or four hundred of those three thousand
and some lashes that you need to administer, in order to break the spell

on Dulcinea, for it causes me no small sorrow that the poor lady remains enchanted only through your carelessness and neglect."

"There's a lot to say about all that," said Sancho. "Let's both go to sleep, right now, and leave the rest to God. Your grace must realize that a man whipping himself in cold blood is a hard business, especially when the blows fall on a malnourished, ill-fed body. Let My Lady Dulcinea be patient and, when she's least expecting it, she'll see me skinned alive, I'll take so many lashes, and anyway, where there's life, there's hope — what I'm trying to say is that while I'm still alive, I still want to do what I promised to do."

Don Quijote thanked him, and ate a bit, and Sancho ate a good deal, and then they both stretched out to sleep, leaving those two eternal companions and friends, Rocinante and the little dapple donkey, as free as they pleased, without any restraint whatever, grazing on the thick green grass that covered the meadow. The two men slept late, then hurriedly remounted and rode down the highway, trying to reach an inn that seemed to them no more than two or three miles further along. And I call it an inn, reader, because that was what Don Quijote called it, departing from his habit of labeling every inn he saw a castle.

They reached it, finally, and asked the innkeeper if he had a room. He assured them he did, and with all the luxuries and comforts they could find in Zaragoza itself. They dismounted, and Sancho locked up his larder in a room to which the innkeeper gave him the key; then he brought their animals to the stable, gave them their fodder, and went to see what Don Quijote (who was sitting on a bench) might want of him, particularly thanking Heaven that his master had not seen this inn as a castle.

The dinner bell tolled; they went up to their room, and Sancho asked the innkeeper what there might be for supper. The innkeeper assured him it was his choice entirely; he had only to ask and he would have what he wanted, for this inn could provide the birds that flew through the air as well as those that strutted on land, and offered, also, the fish that swam in the sea.

"We don't need all that," replied Sancho. "A couple of roast chickens will do the trick, because my master has a weak stomach and doesn't eat a lot, and I'm not that much of a glutton."

The innkeeper answered that he had no chickens, because the hawks had gotten every one of them.

"Then roast us a pullet, if you please," said Sancho, "as long as it's tender."

"A pullet? Oh Lord!" replied the innkeeper. "As a matter of fact, just yesterday I shipped more than fifty to the city, so ask for anything you want, except for pullets."

"You're not out of veal or kid, are you?" said Sancho, "and for the same reasons?"

"As it happens, just right now," answered the innkeeper, "we don't have either, because we've used everything all up, but we'll have more than enough in another week."

"That'll do us a lot of good!" said Sancho. "I suppose what all these shortages add up to is a lot of bacon and eggs?"

"Mother of God!" replied the innkeeper. "He's got a sense of humor, this guest of mine! I tell him we have no chickens, and we have no hens, and he asks if we have eggs? Try some other delicacies, if you please, and stop chasing after chickens."

"By God," said Sancho, "why don't you just get down to it and tell me what you've really got, and stop all this scurrying around."

The innkeeper said:

"What I've really and truly got are some cow's feet that look like calves' hooves, or a couple of calves' hooves that look like cow's feet, and they've been cooked up with chick peas, onions, and bacon, and they just sit there, saying 'Eat me! Eat me!' "

"Mark them as mine, right this minute," said Sancho, "and don't let anyone else lay a hand on them, because I'll pay you more than they will: I couldn't ask for anything I'd like better, and I don't give a damn whether they're calves' hooves or cow's feet."

"They're yours," said the innkeeper, "because my other guests, all of them highborn people, bring their own cook, and their own steward, and their own food."

"If it's highborn you want," said Sancho, "you won't find anyone higher than my master, but his job doesn't let us carry what we eat or drink — we stretch out in the middle of a meadow and root out acorns and nuts."

And that was all Sancho said to the innkeeper, because it was all he wanted to tell him, for there had already been a lot of questions about just what Don Quijote was and what he did.

When it was time to eat, Don Quijote withdrew to his room, the innkeeper plucked the stew pot off the stove and brought it in, and our knight sat down and began. From the next room, meantime, which was separated from his by no more than a thin partition, our knight heard the following:

"Your grace, my lord Don Gerónimo, while they're bringing in our dinner why don't you just read us another chapter of that *Don Quijote de La Mancha: The Second Part?*"[1]

Don Quijote jumped to his feet, the moment he heard his name mentioned, and listening carefully to see what else they might say, he heard the person addressed as Don Gerónimo reply:

"Ah, my lord Don Juan, why would your grace want to hear nonsense like that? No one who's read the First Part of the History of Don Quijote de La Mancha could possibly enjoy reading this second part."

"Just the same," said Don Juan, "it would be fun to read, because there isn't a book so awful that it hasn't got *something* good in it. What bothers me most about it is how it paints Don Quijote as no longer in love with Dulcinea del Toboso."[2]

Hearing this, Don Quijote's wrath flared, and he thundered out:

"Anyone who says that Don Quijote de La Mancha has forgotten, or possibly could have forgotten, Dulcinea del Toboso, will have to learn from me, in equal combat, that he's a liar, for the matchless Dulcinea del

---

1. That is, the false volume 2, written by Avellaneda [*Translator's Note*].
2. True: Aldonza Lorenzo having threatened reprisals for what had been said of her, Avellaneda's Don Quijote calls himself *el caballero desamorado*, "The Knight Who's Fallen Out of Love" [*Translator's Note*].

Toboso is unforgettable, nor is Don Quijote capable of forgetting, for constancy is his very motto, and he has sworn himself to preserve it with gentle hands and let no violence disturb it."

"Who is it that thus answers us?" came a voice from the other room.

"Who *could* it be," replied Sancho, "but Don Quijote himself, who will prove anything and everything he's said and may still say? He who pays his debts, doesn't mind giving guarantees."

Sancho had barely finished speaking when two men who seemed to be gentlemen appeared at the door to Don Quijote's room, and one of them threw his arms around our knight's neck, saying:

"Your appearance surely vouches for your name, as your name vouches for your appearance: you, my dear sir, you are without question the one and only Don Quijote de La Mancha, North Star and Shining Light of knight errantry, in spite and quite regardless of the fellow who has tried to steal your name and nullify your great deeds, writing such a book as this, which I herewith hand you."

And he took a book which his companion bore, and presented it to Don Quijote, who took it without a word and began to glance through it, but after turning the pages a bit he handed it back, saying:

"I've already seen, in just this short time, at least three things for which this author should be taken to task. First of all, there are the nasty things he says about Miguel de Cervantes, in his Prologue; second, the grammatical mistakes he makes, in his use of definite articles; and third, which more than anything else proves his ignorance, he wanders off track and tells lies about the most important parts of my history, because he says that my squire Sancho Panza's wife is named Mari Gutiérrez, which isn't her name at all, but Teresa Panza[3] — and anyone who is wrong about such important matters is very, very likely to be wrong about everything else."

Sancho burst out:

"Oh, there's a learned historian! He's really got to know a lot about us, to say my wife's name is Mari Gutiérrez and not Teresa Panza! Have another look at that, my lord, and see if I'm in there, and whether he's changed my name, too."

"From what I've just heard you say, my friend," said Don Gerónimo, "you must surely be Sancho Panza, my lord Don Quijote's squire."

"That's me all right," replied Sancho, "and proud of it."

"Well, I can tell you," said the gentleman, "that this new author doesn't paint you as you really are: he turns you into a glutton, and a fool, and not in the least funny, and, in short, totally unlike the Sancho depicted in the first part of your master's history."

"May God forgive him," said Sancho. "He should have just left me alone, and not bothered at all, because you shouldn't pick up a guitar if you don't know how to play it, and Saint Peter's doing fine, in Rome where he belongs."

The gentlemen invited Don Quijote to come to their room and dine with them, for they knew very well, they said, that nothing to be had in

---

3. As Riquer says, however, "Cervantes assigns a variety of names to Sancho's wife," one of them being, in fact, Mari Gutiérrez [*Translator's Note*].

this inn could be worthy of him. As ever polite, Don Quijote agreed to join them, though Sancho remained at home with the stew pot, which now belonged solely and completely to him; making himself thoroughly at home, he took his seat at the head of the table, and dined along with the innkeeper, who was just as fond as he was of hooves and feet.

As dinner progressed, in the next room, Don Gerónimo asked Don Quijote what news he'd had of Dulcinea del Toboso: was she married? did she have a child, or was she pregnant? or, were she still a virgin, how did she feel — having thus kept her modesty and delicacy intact — about Don Quijote's amorous thoughts of her? To which Don Quijote replied:

"Dulcinea remains a virgin, and my thoughts of her remain as steady as they ever were; our relationship too remains as barren as it was; and all her beauty is still transformed into the coarse vulgarity of a common peasant."

And then he explained to them, blow by blow, how lady Dulcinea had been enchanted, and everything that had happened in Montesinos' Cave, and told them, too, what Merlin the magician had commanded done, in order to disenchant her, which was of course the whipping Sancho was supposed to give himself.

Both gentlemen were wonderfully pleased to hear Don Quijote tell the strange events of his history, and quite as struck by the nonsense he narrated as by the elegant way he spoke it. One minute he sounded like a man of good sense, the next he slid down into foolishness, nor were they able to find the slope that led him from the one to the other.

Sancho finished his meal and, leaving the innkeeper half seas over, went into the next room, where his master was.

"What kills me, gentlemen," he said as he came in, "is that the author of this book doesn't even want us to have a crumb to eat; from what your graces tell me, he's already called me a glutton, but I hope he doesn't call me a drunkard, too."

"He does," said Don Gerónimo, "and though I don't remember exactly how he puts it, I do recall that it's offensively worded — and untruthfully, too, as I can see perfectly well from the face of the good Sancho I'm actually looking at."

"Take it from me, gentlemen," said Sancho. "The Sancho and the Don Quijote in that book have got to be different people from the ones in Sidi Hamid Benengeli's book, because the ones in *his* book are us: my master is brave, and wise, and madly in love, and I'm just a plain fellow with a good sense of humor, and no glutton and no drunkard."

"I believe you," said Don Juan, "and if it were possible, it ought to be made illegal for anyone but Sidi Hamid, the original author, to write about the great Don Quijote and his doings, just the way Alexander ordered that no one but Apelles[4] might dare paint his portrait."

"Let anyone paint me, if he wants to," said Don Quijote, "so long as he doesn't mis-paint me, because patience can break down, if you pile enough insults on its back."

---

4. Fourth century B.C.; antiquity's greatest painter, and a particular favorite of Alexander the Great [*Translator's Note*].

"No one," said Don Juan, "can insult my lord Don Quijote without having to pay for it, unless Don Quijote's patience shields him from vengeance — and, so far as I can tell, that patience is truly both broad and strong."

They spent much of the night discussing these and other similar matters, and although Don Juan wanted Don Quijote to read more of the book, to see what sorts of counterpoint our knight might compose on it, he couldn't persuade him to pick the thing up again: it should be considered thoroughly read, said Don Quijote, and completely stupid, and he had no interest in giving its author the gratification of thinking that, just because he had briefly held the book in his hands, he had also read it; he needed to keep his mind, and even more his eyes, free of all indecency and ugliness.

They asked him where he was intending to go. He replied, Zaragoza, to compete in that city's annual tournaments. Don Juan told him that this new book had Don Quijote — or whoever he was — in Zaragoza, competing for the prize, but although its pages were full of foolishness they were pallidly imagined, poorly written, and painfully presented.

"And in that case," replied Don Quijote, "I will not set foot in Zaragoza, and thus expose for all the world to see how this purported second part of my history is all lies, and also let everyone see that I am not the Don Quijote he's talking about."

"An excellent idea," said Don Gerónimo. "And there are other tournaments in Barcelona, where my lord Don Quijote can truly demonstrate his valor."

"As I will," said Don Quijote. "And if you gentlemen will excuse me, it is now time for me to seek my bed. Consider me, please, among your warmest friends and servants."

"And me too," said Sancho. "Maybe I'll be good for something."

So they said their goodnights, and Don Quijote and Sancho retired to their room, leaving Don Juan and Don Gerónimo both astonished at the mixture of wisdom and madness of which our knight was composed, and also truly believing that these were indeed the real Don Quijote and Sancho, not those described by our Aragonese author [Avellaneda].

Don Quijote made an early start, the next morning, saying farewell to his hosts of the previous night by knocking on the partition between the two rooms. Sancho paid the innkeeper magnificently, but suggested that he either say less about how sumptuously his inn was supplied or else in fact supply it better.

Chapter Sixty

— what happened to Don Quijote, on the way to Barcelona

It was a cool morning, and promised to be a cool day, as Don Quijote went forth from the inn, having first found out which would be the most direct road to Barcelona, without so much as passing through Zaragosa — so determined was he to show that this new historian, who apparently had so many nasty things to say about him, was in fact a liar.

And then, as it turned out, for the next six days and more nothing happened to him worthy of being recorded, after which time, night overtook him just as he was leaving the road and riding into a dense grove of oak trees — or perhaps they were cork trees, for Sidi Hamid is not quite so careful, on this point, as he usually is about such matters.

Master and man dismounted and, when they were settled with their backs against the tree trunks, Sancho, having filled his belly very well, that day, let himself roll right through the gates of sleep, but Don Quijote, kept awake by his mind more than by his stomach, found it impossible to close his eyes: his mind kept rushing this way and that, now here, now there. He thought he was back in Montesinos' Cave; then he was watching Dulcinea, transformed into a peasant girl, skipping and hopping about on her she-ass; then he was hearing the Magician Merlin's words once again, reciting the terms and conditions that had to be met if Dulcinea were ever to be disenchanted. He was disappointed and discouraged, seeing Sancho's laziness and indifference, for so far as he was aware his squire had given himself no more than five hundred lashes — a mere trifle, compared to how many were still to come — and this thought made him so darkly angry that he said to himself:

"If Alexander the Great cut the Gordian Knot, saying: 'What difference does it make if it's cut or untied?', and it made him the ruler of all Asia, exactly the same thing might happen with Dulcinea's disenchantment, right now, if I whipped Sancho in spite of himself, because if the condition of this cure is that Sancho receive his three thousand and some lashes, what difference does it make to me if he gives them to himself, or if someone else administers them, since what matters is that he gets them, not who deals them out?"

With this idea he went over to Sancho, having first removed Rocinante's reins and fixed them for whipping rather than riding, and began to loosen his squire's belt (for it is thought that Sancho wore but the one to hold up his breeches), but he had barely touched the sleeping man when Sancho sat bolt upright, saying, like a man very wide awake:

"What's going on? Who's that monkeying with my belt?"

"It's me," answered Don Quijote, "coming to make up for your deficiencies and ease my own troubles: that is, I propose to whip you, Sancho, and thus discharge, at least in part, the debt you owe. Dulcinea is dying, but you, indifferent, live on, while I, lovesick, am dying too, so undo your belt yourself and here in this lonely place I will give you two thousand lashes, or perhaps a bit more."

"Oh no you won't," said Sancho. "You stay right where you are, your grace, or by the God in Heaven the very dead will hear us. These have to be lashes I volunteer for, not lashes anyone forces on me, and right this minute I'm not a bit interested in being whipped. You'll have to be satisfied, your grace, with my promise to thrash and flog myself when I happen to feel like it."

"I can't wait for you to be chivalrous, Sancho," said Don Quijote, "because you're not only a hard-hearted, rude peasant, but you're a soft-skinned one, to boot."

He went on struggling, trying to undo his squire's belt, and, seeing this,

Sancho stood up and threw himself at his master, first grabbing him with his bare hands, then knocking his legs out from under him and throwing Don Quijote flat on his back, after which he set his right knee on his master's chest and pinned both Don Quijote's hands to the ground, holding him so he could neither roll over nor breathe.

"What, you traitor?" said Don Quijote. "You show yourself thus disrespectful of your master and natural lord? You dare do this to the hand that feeds you?"

"I'm not knocking a king off his throne, or putting anybody up on one,"[1] answered Sancho. "I'm just helping myself, because I'm my own lord. Promise me you you'll keep your hands to yourself, and you won't try to whip me, and I'll set you free as the breeze. Otherwise,

> Traitor, Doña Sancha's foe,
> Here is where you die."[2]

Don Quijote gave his word, swearing by the life of the lady of all his thoughts that he wouldn't touch even a thread of Sancho's clothing, and that his squire would be left to decide, entirely for himself, when he felt like having his whipping.

Sancho then stood up and walked a fair distance away, but, as he was settling himself against a different tree, he felt something touch his head, and when he raised his hands found it was two human feet, wearing stockings and shoes. He shook with fear, went to another tree, and found exactly the same thing. He called to Don Quijote to come help him. Don Quijote came, asked what had happened and why he was afraid, and Sancho told him that all these trees were full of human feet and human legs. So Don Quijote felt them, quickly realized what they had to be, and said to Sancho:

"There's no need to be afraid, because these feet, and the legs you feel but can't see, surely belong to bandits and outlaws who have been hanged in these trees, since that's the way the police do it, around here, hanging twenty or thirty at a time, when they catch them — and this makes me think we must be getting close to Barcelona."[3]

And the truth was exactly as he had suspected.

Dawn was breaking and, lifting their eyes, they saw great clusters, which were the bodies of dead bandits, dangling from the trees. And if the corpses shocked them, they were no less affected by the sight of forty or more living bandits, who suddenly surrounded them, telling them, in Catalan, to stand still and stay where they were, until their commander arrived.

Finding himself on foot, his horse unbridled, his lance leaning up against a tree and, in a word, absolutely defenseless, Don Quijote thought it best to say and do nothing, but merely bow his head and wait for some better opportunity.

---

1. The words said to have been spoken, either by Bertrand Duguesclin or by Claquín, when, by tripping him, in 1379 one or the other helped Henry of Trastamara kill his brother, Peter the Cruel [*Translator's Note*].
2. Final lines of the well-known ballad "*A cazar va don Rodrigo*" [Don Rodrigo goes hunting] [*Translator's Note*].
3. Barcelona = capital city and center of Catalonia, which had in earlier times been a separate kingdom and, then and now, had strong separatist leanings [*Translator's Note*].

The bandits went over the donkey with a fine tooth comb, leaving absolutely nothing either in the saddlebags or the suitcase, and Sancho was lucky that the duke's gold coins, plus those he had brought with him from La Mancha, were in a moneybelt around his waist — and lucky, too, that just then their commander arrived, for these fine folk would certainly have dug around between skin and flesh, and weeded out whatever they might have found hidden there. The commander was a man of about thirty-four, strong, fairly tall, with a somber, swarthy face. He rode up on a powerful horse, and was wearing chain-mail armor, with four pistols — called flintlocks, in that part of the country — at his sides. He saw that his squires (which is what they call those who follow this particular profession) were about to strip Sancho Panza, and ordered them to hold off, which they very obediently did, which was how the moneybelt survived. He was astonished, seeing a lance leaning against a tree, and a shield lying on the ground, and Don Quijote, armed and withdrawn, his face as sad as sorrow could make it. So he went over to our knight, saying:

"Don't be so mournful, my good man, because you haven't fallen into the hands of some savage Osiris,[4] but into those of Rocque Guinart,[5] which hold more compassion than brutality."

"I don't regret having fallen into your hands, oh brave Rocque," replied Don Quijote, "for your fame extends everywhere on earth! But only that my own carelessness let your soldiers catch me with my horse unbridled, for according to the rules of knight errantry, to which I am sworn, I am bound to be perpetually on the alert, and my own sentinel, twenty-four hours a day — and you need to know, oh great Rocque! that had they come on me when I was on horseback, and with my lance and my shield, I would not have been quite so easy to conquer, for I am Don Quijote de La Mancha, whose deeds the whole world knows so well."

Rocque Guinart could tell at once that it was Don Quijote's mind, and not his courage, which was weak; he had often heard our knight's name, but never thought he truly existed or, indeed, been able to make himself believe that anyone could really be driven by such motives, so that actually meeting Don Quijote vastly delighted him, for now he could find out for himself, at first-hand, what before he had only heard about from a distance.

"Brave knight," he said, "save your resentment; don't think things have gone so badly for you, for who knows? Perhaps these very obstacles will let your winding Fate set itself straight, for Heaven can follow strange and unheard of paths, which we humans cannot even imagine, when it chooses to raise the fallen and enrich the poor."

Don Quijote was about to thank him when, from behind them, they heard what at first sounded like a troop of cavalry, but turned out to be only one horse, ridden by what seemed to be a young fellow of about twenty, wearing green Damascus silk, gold ornamented, and breeches, and a florid hat with a turned-up brim and Dutch-style plumes, his boots tight and well-waxed, his spurs, dagger, and sword all gilted, a small rifle in his

---

4. Egyptian king (actually named Busiris) who sacrificed all foreigners to his gods [*Translator's Note*].
5. Pedro Roca Guinarda (1582–?), Catalan bandit and popular hero, later pardoned and made a captain in the Spanish army [*Translator's Note*].

hands and two pistols at his sides. Turning his head, Rocque noted this handsome figure who, reaching him, called out:

"It's you I'm looking for, oh brave Rocque! because even if you can't cure it, at least you'll make my misfortune easier to bear — and, so I don't keep you in suspense, since you've never seen me before, please let me tell you who I am: I am Claudia Jerónima, Simón Forte's daughter, he who is both your good friend and especially hated by your mutual enemy, and your political opponent, Clauquel Torrellas. This Torrellas has a son, as you know, named Don Vicente Torrellas — at least, that was his name until about two hours ago. Let me make a long story of misfortune shorter, and quickly tell you what this Don Vicente did to me. He saw me, he wooed me, I listened, I fell in love — all, alas, without my father's knowledge, for no woman, no matter how secluded or how modest, can be kept from acting on her impulsive longings. Finally, he promised to be my husband, and I said I would be his wife, though nothing more than that took place. And then yesterday I heard that, forgetting what he owed me, he meant to marry someone else, and the ceremony was to be this morning, and the news drove me wild, and my patience snapped and, since my father wasn't home, I got myself into this clothing, and by galloping this horse I caught up to Don Vicente about three miles from here, and without complaining or waiting to hear any excuses I fired this rifle, and then, just to make sure, these pistols, and I must have lodged more than two bullets in his body, thereby opening doorways to set my honor free, steeped in his blood. I left him there, with his servants, none of whom dared to defend him. And I came looking for you, so you could smuggle me into France, where I have relatives I can live with, and also to beg you to protect my father, to keep all Don Vicente's relatives from wreaking their wild vengeance on him."

Struck by the beautiful Claudia's spirit, and her courage, and her fine figure, and what she had done, Rocque said to her:

"Come, señora, and we'll see if your enemy is indeed dead, and after that we'll see what we can do for you."

Don Quijote, who had been listening closely to everything Claudia said, and how Rocque Guinart had answered her, said:

"No one need trouble himself to defend this lady, because I will assume that responsibility. Let me have my horse and my weapons, and then wait for me here, and I will find this gentleman and, dead or alive, I will make him honor the promise he gave to so beautiful a creature."

"Don't anybody think he won't," said Sancho, "because my master's a first-class matchmaker, and just a few days ago he married off another fellow who'd gone back on his word to another lady, and if it weren't for all the magicians who keep persecuting him, and who changed the man into a footman, instead of what he really was, by now that maiden wouldn't have been a maiden."

More concerned with what happened to the lovely Claudia than with anything said by either master or man, Rocque didn't hear a word. He ordered his men to give Sancho back everything they'd taken, and also ordered them to go back where they'd lodged, the night before, and then immediately rode off with Claudia, at full speed, to find either a

wounded or a dead Don Vicente. When they reached the spot where
Claudia had found him, there was nothing to be seen but freshly spilled
blood, but looking this way and that they spied a group of people going
up a hill and, assuming that this must be Don Vicente's party, as indeed
it was, and that his servants were carrying him off, alive or dead, either to
cure or to bury him, they hurried after them, and since those they pursued
were moving very slowly, it did not take long.

They found Don Vicente in his servants' arms, begging them, his voice
weary and weak, to let him die right where he was, because his wounds
were so painful he could not allow them to carry him any farther.

Claudia and Rocque jumped down from their horses and went over to
him, the servants terrified by Rocque's presence, Claudia moved by the
sight of Don Vicente; half tenderly, half harshly, she took his hands in
hers and said:

"If you'd given me your hand, as you promised, none of this would have
happened."

The wounded man opened his eyes; recognizing Claudia, he said:

"I see perfectly well, oh lovely but mistaken lady, it's you who have
killed me, a punishment I neither deserved nor should have earned, for
neither in intention nor in deed have I ever wanted or been able to offend
you."

"And isn't it true," replied Claudia, "that just this morning you were on
your way to marry Leonora, rich Balvastro's daughter?"

"Certainly not," answered Don Vicente. "My evil Fortune must have
brought you such news, which made you, oh jealous one, take my life —
but since I depart from this life in your hands, and in your arms, I think
myself lucky, after all. And to show you this is the truth, squeeze my hand,
if you want to, and welcome me as your husband, for what better satisfaction can I offer you for the injury you think I've done you?"

Claudia squeezed his hand and, her heart constricted, fainted away on
his bloody breast, and he shuddered into death. Rocque, sorely perplexed,
did not know what to do. Don Vicente's servants ran for water to sprinkle
on their faces, and brought it back, and sprinkled it on them. Claudia
returned from her swoon, but not Don Vicente from his, for his life was
over. And Claudia, seeing that her sweet husband lived no longer, pierced
the air with her cries, wounding Heaven with her moans, tearing out her
hair and casting it to the winds, raking her face with her nails, along with
all the other signs of misery and sorrow that a sorrowing heart could possibly conceive.

"Oh cruel, rash woman!" she exclaimed. "How quickly you led yourself
into the evil your mind only imagined! Oh wild fury of jealousy, what
hopeless things you make us do, once we let you into our hearts! Oh my
husband, my husband, your miserable fate has taken you from the marriage bed to the grave, and all because you pledged yourself to me!"

Such mournful laments poured out of Claudia that they brought tears
to Rocque's eyes, where tears had never been seen. Don Vicente's servants
wept, and Claudia swooned at every step, and everything and everyone
there seemed to belong to a field of mourning and a place of misery.
Finally, Rocque ordered the servants to bring Don Vicente's body home

to his father, who lived nearby, so it could be prepared for burial. Claudia informed Rocque that she would enter a convent, where her aunt served as abbess, and there spend the rest of her life with that other, better Husband and endlessly enduring Companion. He praised her for so fine a goal, offering to take her wherever she meant to go, and to protect her father from Don Vicente's family and the whole rest of the world, should anyone think to attack him. But Claudia did not want him to escort her and, thanking him as warmly as she knew how, she left there, weeping as she went. Don Vicente's servants picked up the corpse, Rocque turned and went back to his men, and that was the end of Claudia Jerónima's love affair. But should anyone be surprised, since her pitiful story was woven on jealousy's harsh, uncaring loom?

Rocque Guinart found his men where they had been ordered to wait for him, and Don Quijote, mounted on Rocinante, right in the middle, trying to talk them out of a way of life as dangerous for the soul as it was for the body, but most being Gascons, country fellows and wild, they paid very little attention to his words. Riding up, Rocque asked Sancho Panza if all the valuables taken from the donkey had been given back to him. Sancho said yes, except for three 'kerchiefs, worth as much as three whole cities.

"What are you talking about, man?" said one of the soldiers. "I've got them, and they aren't worth three *dollars*."

"Indeed," said Don Quijote. "But my squire values them as he does, knowing who gave them to me."

Rocque Guinart ordered them handed over, at once, and then had his men fall into line, and everything that they'd stolen since the last sharing-out brought forth — all the clothing, jewels, and money — and, quickly adding it all up, swapping back and forth what couldn't be expressed in dollar terms, he divided everything among the lot of them, so carefully and sensibly that it all came out perfectly even and no one was in any way cheated. Once this was accomplished, and everyone visibly satisfied with the results, Rocque turned to Don Quijote and said:

"If I were not this careful with these fellows, there'd be no living with them."

At which Sancho remarked:

"From what I've just seen, justice is so important that it even matters among thieves."

One of the soldiers heard him and, raising the butt-end of his rifle, would have smashed open Sancho's head, had not Rocque Guinart shouted at him to stop. Dumbfounded, Sancho decided to keep his lips pressed tightly together, as long as they were with these people.

Just then, one of the soldiers posted as sentinels along the roads, watching to see and report to their chief who came by, came running up:

"My lord, there's a whole bunch of people on the road to Barcelona, and not far off, either."

To which Rocque replied:

"Can you tell whether they're the kind we're not looking for, or the kind who are looking for us?"

"They're the kind we're looking for, all of them," said the soldier.

"Then go get them all," responded Rocque, "and bring them here right away, and make sure nobody escapes."

The man ran off again, leaving Don Quijote, Sancho, and Rocque alone, waiting to see what the soldiers brought in, and during this interval Rocque said to Don Quijote:

"These adventures of ours, and the things we're up to, and the dangers we deal with, must seem to you, my lord Don Quijote, like a whole new way of life, nor does that surprise me, because I have to admit there is no way of life more unsettling and even frightening than ours. What got me into this was an indefinable thirst for revenge, which can easily turn even the calmest and most peaceful of hearts quite upside down; I am compassionate and well intentioned by nature, but, as I said, a longing to be revenged for a wrong done me has simply swept away all my good intentions and kept me where I am, no matter what my understanding tells me, and just as one abyss calls to another, and one sin to the next, I've gone on spinning out my revenge until it's not just mine I'm satisfying any more, but other people's as well — and yet it's God's will that, for all the labyrinth of uncertainty in which I find myself, I've never lost hope of finding my way out and landing in some safe port."

Don Quijote was indeed surprised, hearing Rocque speak so logically and in such a well-thought-out fashion, having always thought that those who led lives of stealing, killing, and highway robbing were incapable of clear thought, and he answered:

"Señor Rocque, the beginning of health lies in diagnosing the sickness, and in the sick man being prepared to take the medicines the doctor prescribes for him: you, your grace, are sick, and you know the disease very well indeed, and Heaven — or, more accurately, God Himself, doctor to us all — will furnish you with healing medicines that, little by little, neither all of a sudden nor miraculously, will cure you, and cure you even more certainly, for wise and knowing sinners are far more likely to amend their ways than are foolish ones and, your grace having already shown such wisdom, all you need do is lift your heart and pray that the sickness in your conscience be made whole, and should your grace long to save time and set yourself quickly and easily on the road to salvation, come with me, and I will teach you to be a knight errant, and you will experience so many trials and tribulations that, taken together with your penitence, you'll be in Heaven before you know it."

Smiling at Don Quijote's advice, Rocque changed the subject and told Claudia Jerónima's tragic story, which sorely upset Sancho, who had not thought badly of the girl's beauty, boldness, and fiery spirit.

Then Rocque's troops arrived, bringing with them two gentlemen on horseback, two pilgrims on foot, and a coach full of women, accompanied by perhaps six servants, who had been riding and walking behind the vehicle, plus a pair of young mulehands who were with the gentlemen on horses. The soldiers set their captives in the center of a ring, surrounding them on all sides, both conquerors and conquered preserving an absolute silence, all waiting for the great Rocque Guinart to speak. He proceeded to ask the gentlemen who they were and where they were going, and how much money they were carrying, and one of them responded:

"My lord, my colleague and I are captains in the Spanish infantry; our companies are in Naples and we plan to embark on four galleys, which we understand are now in Barcelona, with orders to sail for Sicily; we have with us between two and three hundred dollars, which seems to us a rich and satisfying treasury, for the poverty of soldiers does not allow us to accumulate more."

Rocque asked the same questions of the pilgrims, who answered that they were headed for Rome and had, between them, perhaps seventy dollars. Rocque then asked who was traveling in the coach, and how much money they had with them, and one of the mounted servants said:

"My lady, Doña Guiomar de Quiñones, wife of the chief magistrate of the Ecclesiastical Court in Naples, and her little daughter, and a maid and a lady in waiting, are traveling in the coach; they have six servants with them, and six hundred dollars."

"And thus," said Rocque Guinart, "we have a total of nine hundred and seventy dollars; I think my troops number about seventy; so let someone who's a better hand with figures than I am figure out how much each man is supposed to get."

Hearing this, the bandits shouted:

"Long live Rocque Guinart, and damn all the *lladres*[6] who try to bring him down!"

The infantry officers looked gloomy, the magistrate's wife was on the verge of tears, nor did the pilgrims look particularly happy, seeing how their property was being taken from them. Rocque let them hang in the wind a bit, but did not wish to keep prolonging their agony, which anyone could have spotted from a hundred feet away, so he turned to the two officers and said:

"Your graces, would you mind, as officers and gentlemen, lending me the sum of seventy dollars? And you, Mistress Magistrate, perhaps another eighty, to keep this squadron of mine happy, for the abbot has to live by singing for his supper? And then you can all go your merry way, free and unhindered, for I will furnish you with a safe conduct, to protect you in case you meet up with any more of the assorted squadrons I have in these parts, because it is not my intention to injure either soldiers or ladies, and especially ladies of high birth."

Both officers thanked Rocque profusely, and in singularly well-turned phrases, for his courtesy and generosity — for so they took it — in letting them keep their own money. Doña Guiomar de Quiñones wanted to throw herself out of her coach, to kiss the great Rocque's hands and feet, but he would not let her, begging her pardon, instead, for the injury he was doing her, obliged as he was to fulfill the requirements of his unpleasant post. The lady then ordered one of her servants to immediately hand over the eighty dollars assigned as their share, the two officers having already disbursed their seventy-dollar portion. The pilgrims were about to hand over their entire pittance, but Rocque told them to stay where they were and, turning to his men, said:

"Two dollars apiece for every one of you, which leaves twenty over.

---

6. *Lladres* = "thieves" or "crooks"; a Catalan word.

Give these pilgrims ten, and then ten more to this good squire [Sancho], so he can say good things about this adventure."

Ordering writing materials to be brought (he never traveled without them), he wrote out a safeconduct, addressed to the leaders of his various bands, then bid them all farewell, letting them go on their way, struck by his nobility, his gallant manner, and his odd behavior, and thinking him more like Alexander the Great than a notorious thief.

In his motley language, half Gascón, half Catalán, one of the soldiers muttered:

"This our captain more better for friar than for bandit: let he be generous with own money, not ours."[7]

But the unlucky fellow did not speak so softly that Rocque could not hear him, and drawing his sword, he split the man's head almost in half, saying:

"This is how I punish those who talk too much and too boldly."

The rest of them were silent, no one daring to say a word, so absolute was the obedience he enforced.

Then Rocque withdrew a bit, and wrote a letter to one of his friends, in Barcelona, explaining that he had with him the famous Don Quijote de La Mancha, that knight errant about whom everyone was talking, and he, Rocque, had to admit that Don Quijote was the most charming and best intentioned man in the world, and would his friend please advise all his other bandit friends (so they could amuse themselves, if they cared to) that in four more days he meant to set our knight on the city's sea shore, in full armor and with all his weapons, mounted on his horse, Rocinante, and together with his squire, Sancho, riding on a donkey. Rocque would have preferred that the bandits in the faction opposed to theirs do without this good fun, but knew that was impossible, because Don Quijote's mixture of madness and sense, and the funny things said by his squire, Sancho Panza, simply could not help delighting everyone in the whole world. He sent this letter via one of his soldiers, who took off his bandit's uniform and dressed himself like a peasant, and then went off to Barcelona to make his delivery.

Chapter Sixty-One

— what happened to Don Quijote, when he went to Barcelona, along with other matters truer than they are clever

Don Quijote stayed with Rocque for three days and three nights, and had he remained for three centuries he would not have ceased to watch and wonder how the bandit chieftain lived: he would wake in one place, breakfast in another; sometimes they would flee, not knowing from whom, and sometimes they would lie in ambush, not knowing for whom. They slept standing up, their sleep constantly broken as they moved from one place to another. They were always posting spies, and sentinels, and care-

---

7. Many "Gascón" bandits of the day were French Huguenot refugees [*Translator's Note*].

fully wiping off the fuses on their rifles (though they did not have many, all of them carrying flintlock pistols). Rocque never slept in the same place as his men, and they never knew where he might be, because the Viceroy of Barcelona's frequent edicts, condemning him to death, kept him restless and afraid, unable to trust anyone, fearful even of his own soldiers, who might either try to kill him or else hand him over to the authorities: truly a miserable, grinding existence.

And finally, on the fourth day, Rocque, Don Quijote, Sancho, and six of Rocque's men left for Barcelona, traveling on little-used roads, and taking hidden shortcuts and paths. They reached the city's sea shore in the darkness, on the eve of the Feast of Saint John the Baptist [24 June], and Rocque embraced our knight and his squire (giving Sancho the promised ten dollars he had not till then received), and left them, all of them freely exchanging farewell compliments and assorted other civilities.

Rocque rode off, and Don Quijote remained, exactly as he was, mounted, in full armor, waiting for daylight to come, nor was it long before the fair face of Dawn began to appear on the balconies of the East, gladdening the grass and the flowers, although perhaps not the ear — though just then the ear was quickened and cheered by the sound of a host of flutes and drums, and the ringing of bells, and cries (which seemed to be coming from the direction of the city proper) of 'Step lively! Out of the way, out of the way!' Dawn yielded to the Sun, his face rounder and fatter than a shield, rising inch by inch above the low line of the horizon.

Don Quijote and Sancho stood looking all around them — and they saw the sea, which neither of them had ever seen before, and it seemed to them immense, stretching in all directions, broader by far than the lakes of Ruidera, which they'd seen in La Mancha; they saw all the galleys pulled up near the beach, and watched as their canvas awnings were rolled down, and their pennants and streamers flapped in the wind, sweeping across, even brushing, the waves; and they heard trumpets and bugles and flutes sounding from the decks, wafting forth both gentle and warlike melodies. They watched the galleys beginning to move on the calm waters, executing something like a mock battle — and saw this maneuver being matched, in wonderfully similar fashion, by troops of cavalry, mounted on gorgeous horses and wearing fine uniforms, who came pouring out from the city. Infantrymen on board the ships fired volley after volley, answered by those stationed on the city's walls and its forts, and then heavy artillery boomed and fractured the air, and was answered by the galleys' shrapnel-firing cannon. The bright sea, the joyful earth, the clear air, streaked with smoke from the great guns, seemed to fill everyone with an unexpected, swelling happiness.

Sancho could not understand how those huge boats, moving this way and that across the water, could have so many feet. And then, to the sound of Moorish war cries, the uniformed riders swept up to where Don Quijote, uncertain and astonished, sat awaiting them, and one among them, who was in fact the man to whom Rocque had written, called to our knight, in a loud voice:

"Our city bids welcome to the very model, shining light, and bright North Star of knight errantry, so far as knight errantry may be thought to have reached. We bid welcome, I say, to the brave Don Quijote de La Mancha — not the counterfeit, not the false and fictive, the apocryphal Don Quijote, brought before us, recently, by lying histories, but the true, the lawful, and the real Don Quijote drawn for us by Sidi Hamid Benengeli, flower of all historians."

Don Quijote did not answer with a word, nor did the horsemen wait for a reply, but wheeling and galloping back to their fellows, they began to execute a swift spiraling maneuver around and around our knight, who turned to Sancho and said:

"These good people know who we are. I dare say they have read our history — and perhaps have even read the one put into print, recently, by that Aragonese scribbler."[1]

Then the gentleman who had spoken to Don Quijote rode up once more:

"Your grace, my lord Don Quijote, please come with us, for we are all your servants, as we are great friends of Rocque Guinart."

To which Don Quijote replied:

"If courtesy gives rise to more courtesy, then yours, sir knight, is either child or at least some close relative to that of the great Rocque Guinart. Take me where you will, for I have no will but yours, especially should there be any service I can perform for you."

The rider replied in terms no less elaborately civil, and then, carefully surrounding Don Quijote, they set out toward the city, flutes piping and drums drumming. But at the city gate the Devil, who is in charge of all the evil on earth, and the boys of the city, who are even wickeder than the Wicked One Himself, arranged for two youngsters to push and wiggle their way through the crowd, and one of them lifted Rocinante's tail, and the other the little donkey's, and each shoved in handfuls of prickly brambles. The poor animals immediately felt their new spurs and, by pressing down their tails, succeeded only in adding to their discomfort, and finally, hunching and bucking, they threw both their masters to the ground. Embarrassed and humiliated, Don Quijote quickly pulled the plumes from under his old nag's tail, and Sancho did the same for the little donkey. Those who were conducting Don Quijote into the city would have liked to punish the boys for their insolence, but how could they? — the two youngsters simply melted into the thousands of others following the procession.

Don Quijote and Sancho remounted and, to general applause and the same music, they arrived at their guide's house, which was large and imposing, as a rich gentleman's house ought to be — and there, for the moment, we will leave them, because Sidi Hamid wants us to.

---

1. An allusion to Avellaneda, who published, in 1614, a spurious sequel to *Don Quijote*, Part I. The Prologue to this forgery is included in the "Backgrounds and Contexts" section of this edition.

Chapter Sixty-Two

— the adventure of the enchanted head, along with other foolishness that simply cannot be omitted

Their host was Don Antonio Moreno, a rich and sensible man, and very fond of decent, pleasant amusement. Having Don Quijote in his house, he set out to find ways of leading our knight to display his madness, but without hurting himself, for anything painful can hardly be considered funny, nor are entertainments worth a thing if they hurt others. His first step was to get Quijote out of his armor and bring him, in his tight, chamois garments — many times described in these pages — out on a balcony overlooking one of the city's main streets, where the people and the little boys could stare at him, as they would at a monkey. The uniformed riders galloped past once more, as if for his eyes alone and not as part of the general festivities of the day, and Sancho was in seventh heaven, feeling as if he had somehow found himself yet another Camacho wedding, yet another house like that of Don Diego de Miranda, yet another castle like the duke's.

Some of Don Antonio's friends dined with him, that day, all of them careful to honor Don Quijote as a notable knight errant, and he, feeling puffed up and rather pompous, almost could not contain himself for happiness. Sancho's clever remarks flew so thick and fast that all the servants, and indeed everyone who heard him, crowded around for more. At table, Don Antonio asked him:

"We have heard, my good Sancho, that you're so fond of custard pudding, and of meat balls, that if you have any leftovers you carry them in your shirt, for some other day."[1]

"No, sir, I don't," replied Sancho, "because I'm a lot cleaner than I am greedy, and as my lord Don Quijote, who's sitting right here, knows very well, a handful of acorns, or some nuts, sometimes lasts us for a whole week. Now it's true that, if they offer me a heifer, I come running with a halter — I mean, I eat what they give me, and I take things the way I find them, but anyone who says I'm a guzzling glutton, and an unclean one to boot, I just have to say he's wrong — and if I didn't respect the honorable men around this table, I'd put that in different words."

"Certainly," said Don Quijote, "Sancho's moderation, like his table manners, could be recorded and engraven on bronze tablets, to make them an eternal memory in centuries to come. It is true, indeed, that when he gets hungry he may seem somewhat over-eager, because he eats hurriedly and chews with his cheeks well-filled, but he always preserves absolute cleanliness, and while he was serving as a governor he learned to dine so fastidiously that he'd eat grapes with a fork, and even pomegranate seeds, too."

"What!" exclaimed Don Antonio. "Sancho's been a governor?"

"Yes," answered Sancho, "and I was governor of an island named Barataria. I governed it for ten days, and did everything exactly the way it ought

---

1. As Sancho is made to do, in chapter 12 of Avellaneda's book [*Translator's Note*].

to be done — and in those same ten days I also lost my peace of mind, and learned to despise every governorship in the whole world, so then I ran away, and I fell into a cave, and gave myself up for dead but, by a miracle, I got out of there alive."

Then Don Quijote told them, in detail, the whole story of Sancho's governorship, and his audience listened with great pleasure.

The tablecloths were removed, and Don Antonio took Don Quijote's hand and led him into another room, furnished with nothing but a table, apparently made of marble from top to pedestal base, on which there stood what seemed to be a bronze bust, much like those of the Roman emperors. Don Antonio took Don Quijote around the entire room, going around and around the table, until at last he said:

"And now that we're alone, my lord Don Quijote, in a locked room where no one can hear anything we say, I want to recount to your grace one of the strangest adventures — or, more accurately, to describe to you one of the greatest novelties — anyone could possibly imagine, but only on condition that what I tell your grace must remain forever hidden away and secret."

"Consider me sworn to the secrecy of the grave," replied Don Quijote. "And then let me place a headstone over that grave, for absolute security — for I should like your grace to know, my lord Don Antonio" (he had by now learned his host's name), "that you are talking to someone who, though he has ears to hear with, has no tongue to speak, so your grace may safely transfer whatever you may have in your heart to mine, and rest assured that you have thereby cast it down into the very depths of silence."

"In reliance on that promise," replied Don Antonio, "let me now astonish you with what you will see and hear, and thereby provide myself with some relief for the difficulty I am in, knowing I cannot talk about these secrets of mine, for not everyone can be trusted with such things."

Don Quijote was puzzled, wondering where such precautions might be leading. Just then, Don Antonio took his guest's hand and passed it over the bronze head, and the whole table top, and then down the marble base on which it rested.

"This head, my lord Don Quijote, has been designed and shaped by one of the greatest magicians and wizards the world has ever known, a man who was, I believe, a Pole, and a disciple of the celebrated Escotillo,[2] of whom so many marvelous tales have been told. That Polish wizard was here in my house, and I paid him a thousand dollars to construct this head, which possesses the power to answer any question asked in its ear. He plotted lines, drew magic signs, consulted the stars, calculated degrees and, after a time, brought it to the perfection which we will see tomorrow — for on Fridays this head stands mute and, today being Friday, we are obliged to wait until tomorrow. But you can make use of the time, your grace, to plan what questions you'd like to ask — because I have learned from experience that this head of mine always speaks the truth."

---

2. *Escotillo* = "little Scot" — but whether or not this refers to the thirteenth-century theologian Michael Scotus is doubtful. Murillo notes that "Escoto was the name of many wizards and practitioners of black magic" [*Translator's Note*].

Don Quijote was astonished, hearing the head's powers and capabilities, though he was inclined not to believe Don Antonio, but knowing he would soon be able to see for himself, he decided to say only that he was grateful for having been entrusted with so great a secret. They left the room, Don Antonio locked the door behind them, and then they rejoined the others. In their absence, Sancho had been recounting many of his master's adventures.

That afternoon, they took Don Quijote out for a ride,[3] in street clothes rather than in armor, and wearing a heavy cassock of tawny yellow wool, which — in that season — could have made ice itself drip with sweat. Don Antonio ordered his servants to entertain Sancho, to keep him from getting out of the house. Don Quijote did not ride on Rocinante, but on a huge, well-equipped beast with an even, ambling gait. When they helped him into the heavy cassock, they secretly hung across its back a placard, on which was written, in large block letters: *This is Don Quijote de La Mancha*. From the moment he set out, accordingly, this inscription caught the eye of everyone passing by, and when they read out loud, "This is Don Quijote de La Mancha," our knight was astonished to find how many people knew him by name, and turning to Don Antonio, who rode alongside, he said:

"Plainly, the privileges of knight errantry are large and numerous, making those who profess it known and even famous all across the earth — or else why, my lord Don Antonio, would even the boys of this city, who have never seen me, know who I am?"

"Quite true, my lord Don Quijote," replied Don Antonio, "for, just as fire cannot be hidden away, so too virtue cannot help but be known, and he who achieves it by the bearing of arms outshines all others."

And then it happened that a Castilian, seeing Don Quijote passing, and all the attention being paid to him, read the inscription on his back and called out, in a loud voice:

"The hell with Don Quijote de La Mancha! How can you still be alive, after all those beatings? You're crazy, that's what you are, and if you were quietly crazy, and kept it all to yourself, it wouldn't be so bad, but you have the knack of making lunatics and fools of everyone you meet — just look at those gentlemen with you! Go home, you fool, and take care of your estate, and your wife and your children, and stop all this nonsense, because it's rotting your mind and using up your brain!"

"Brother," said Don Antonio, "just go your own way, and stop giving advice to people who don't ask for it. My lord Don Quijote de La Mancha is perfectly sane, and we who ride with him are no fools: virtue must be respected, no matter where it's found — and so, the devil with you, and don't meddle where you're not wanted."

"By God, your grace is absolutely right," replied the Castilian, "because giving this good man advice is like pouring water into a sieve — still, just the same, it makes me damned sad, seeing that keen brain he's supposed to have (in just about everything else) washed down the sewer with all this stupid knight errantry stuff. Well, may the devil you sent me to, your grace,

---

3. *Sacaron a pasear* = "took out for a ride" or "took out on exhibition" [*Translator's Note*].

come and get me, from here on, and all my descendants, too, even if I live as long as Methuselah, if I ever give advice to anyone, whether they ask for it or not."

So the advice-giver went away, and the ride continued, but there was such a pushing and shoving, boys and grownups alike, trying to see and read the placard, that Don Antonio was finally forced, pretending he was removing something else, to take it off Don Quijote's back.

Darkness came; they rode back to the house, where there was a ladies' soirée, that evening, Don Antonio's wife — a gay, fun-loving lady of high birth, beautiful and sensible — having invited some of her women friends to come and pay their respects to her guest (and also to relish his unheard of madness). They came, had a splendid dinner, and at ten o'clock began their little party. Two of the ladies, in particular, were mischievous wags, completely chaste but also, when it came to playing harmless jokes, sometimes a bit wild. They kept pressing Don Quijote to dance with them until he was exhausted — not simply in body, but in spirit as well. It was quite something to see Don Quijote — tall, lean and lanky, pale, wearing tight-fitting garments — dancing clumsily on his remarkably non-twinkling toes. The ladies flirted with him, sneakily, and he just as slyly dismissed their attentions, until, hard-pressed, he finally raised his voice a bit, declaring:

"*Fugite, partes adversae!* [Be off with you, evil ones!]⁴ Ah, leave me in peace, you unwelcome thoughts. Hold back your desires, ladies, because she who is queen of mine, my peerless Dulcinea del Toboso, allows only her own wishes to subdue and conquer me."

Saying which, he sat down on the floor, right in the middle of the room, worn out and utterly defeated by so much dancing. Don Antonio had his servants lift him right up and carry him off to his bed, and Sancho, the first to take hold of him, said:

"Damn it, my lord, you've been dancing up a storm! Do you think all brave men are gazelles, and all knights errant are ballerinas? Well, if you think so, you're wrong, because there are men who'd rather go killing giants than do a single pirouette. Now, if it was heel and toe stamping, I could have taken your place, because I can do those dances like a lord, but I'm worthless when it comes to this formal stuff."

Babbling on like this, Sancho made everyone laugh, and then he put his master to bed, covering him warmly so he could sweat off a chill, if he'd caught one while dancing.

The next day seemed to Don Antonio a good time for the experiment with the talking head, so with Don Quijote, Sancho, and two of his own friends, plus the two ladies who'd worn Don Quijote out, on the dance floor (and who had stayed the night with Don Antonio's wife), he shut them into the room where the head was kept. He told them what it could do, charged them to keep the information secret, and explained that this was the very first time he had ever tested the head's magic powers; other than his two friends, no one knew the head's true secret, and so well

---

4. Official Church exorcism: *Ecce crucem Domini, fugite, partes adversae,* "Here is the cross of God; be off with you, evil ones" [*Translator's Note*].

managed and arranged was the trick that, had he had not told them about it, in advance, they would have been every bit as astonished as the others.

Don Antonio himself was the first to bend his mouth to the magic ear, and he murmured, though not too low to be heard by everyone:

"Tell me, head, by the powers vested in you, what I am thinking about right now?"

Without moving its lips, and in a clear and distinct voice that all could understand, the head answered him:

"I have nothing to do with thoughts."

Everyone was struck dumb, especially since they could see that nowhere in the room, nor anywhere around the table, was there any human being who could have given that response.

"How many of us are there?" asked Don Antonio next.

And he was answered, exactly as before:

"You and your wife; two of your friends, and two of hers; and a famous knight, Don Quijote de La Mancha, and his squire, whose name is Sancho Panza."

How they were astonished once again! How the hair on their heads stood up, in sheer fright! Then Don Antonio moved away from the head, saying:

"I am satisfied, oh wise head, oh talking head, oh question-answering head, oh marvelous head! that he who sold you to me was no cheat. Now let someone else come and ask him whatever they please."

And, since women are usually quick-moving, as well as anxious to know everything, the first to approach was one of the lady friends of Don Antonio's wife, and what she asked was:

"Tell me, head: what should I do, to become very beautiful?"

And she was answered:

"Be perfectly chaste."

"I'll ask you nothing else," she said.

Then the other lady friend asked:

"What I should like to know, head, is whether or not my husband loves me?"

And she was answered:

"Consider how he treats you, and you will know."

The lady stepped back, saying:

"There's no need to ask a question, to get an answer like that, for surely what someone actually does is enough to tell you how that person feels."

Then one of Don Antonio's friends approached, asking:

"Who am I?"

And he was answered:

"You already know."

"I didn't ask you that," replied the gentleman. "Just tell me if *you* know who I am."

"I know you," was the reply. "You're Don Pedro Noriz."

"I have no other questions, since this one is enough to assure me, oh head, that you know everything!"

He stepped back, and Don Antonio's other friend approached, asking:

"Tell me, head, what my oldest son is after?"

"I have already told you," came the reply, "that I have nothing to do with desires and thoughts — but, all the same, I can tell you that what your son wants is to bury you."

"He does indeed," the gentleman said. "And it's so easy to see, you can point to it with your finger!"

And he asked no more questions. Don Antonio's wife approached, asking:

"I don't know, head, how to ask this — but all I want to know is, will I enjoy my husband for many years?"

And she was answered:

"Yes, you shall, for his health and his temperate ways are such that he should live a very long time, for it is intemperance that cuts so many lives short."

And then Don Quijote approached, saying:

"Tell me, you who give these answers: Is my account of what happened to me in Montesinos' Cave the truth or merely a dream? Will my squire Sancho ever accomplish all his whipping? Will Dulcinea ever be disenchanted?"

"As to the cave," came the reply, "there is much to be said on both sides: it's some of this, and some of that. Sancho's whipping will take a long time. Dulcinea's disenchantment will occur, in due course."

"I wish to know nothing more," said Don Quijote, "because once I see Dulcinea disenchanted, it will seem to me that all the good fortune I could ever want has suddenly come to pass."

The last questioner was Sancho, and what he asked was:

"By any chance, head, will I ever be a governor again? Will I always remain a poor squire? Will I ever see my wife and children again?"

And he was answered:

"You will govern in your own house; if you go home to her, you will see your wife and your children; and when you cease to serve your master, you will no longer be a squire."

"That tells me a lot!" said Sancho. "I could have told myself as much: you couldn't have said it better, if you were the prophet Perogrullo himself."[5]

"Idiot!" said Don Quijote. "What do you want it to tell you? Isn't it good enough for you that this head gives you answers that fit the questions?"

"It's enough, yes," said Sancho, "but I would have liked it to tell me more, and really say something."

That was the end of the questions and answers, but not of the amazement of all present (except for Don Antonio and his two friends). And Sidi Hamid thought it best to explain at once, so no one would be left in suspense, thinking that this head embodied some witchcraft and strange mystery, that having seen a head like it in Madrid, where it had been made by an engraver, Don Antonio Moreno had this one made right in his own house, to fool and entertain the ignorant, and its construction was as follows: the table top was wood, painted and varnished to look like marble, and the base too was of wood, with four eagle claws jutting out,

---

5. A popular prophet whose replies were all obvious truisms [*Translator's Note*].

to hold it more firmly in place. The head, which looked like the bust of a Roman emperor, and was bronze-colored, was in fact completely hollow, as was the table top, and the head had been so precisely fitted into the table top that there was no sign of any jointure whatever. The base, which was connected to the bust's throat and chest, was equally hollow, and in its turn was connected to another room, directly below. A tin-plated tube ran through this entire apparatus, from table base through table top to the bust's chest and throat, nicely fitted and, once again, invisible. In the room just below stood the person who gave the responses, his mouth at the end of the tube, very much the way one speaks into an ear-trumpet, so what was said above and what was said below both came through clearly and well-articulated, and it was impossible to see through the trick. Don Antonio's nephew, a keen-witted student, spoke on the head's behalf, and having been told by his uncle who would be in the room, that day, it was easy enough to frame a quick, accurate answer to the first question, and then to calculate highly probable and sensible responses to all the rest. And Sidi Hamid notes that this wonderful device lasted for ten or twelve days, until word went round the city that Don Antonio had a magical head in his house, capable of answering any and all questions, and Don Antonio, worried that the tireless upholders of our faith might hear of it too, informed the gentlemen of the Inquisition himself, whereupon they ordered him to dismantle and never use it again, to keep from scandalizing common, ignorant folk. But both Don Quijote and Sancho Panza remained convinced that the head was enchanted and really did answer questions, though Don Quijote was more satisfied with what he heard than was Sancho.

To oblige Don Antonio, and entertain Don Quijote (while also giving him an opportunity to exhibit his foolishness), the gentlemen of the city ordered that, in six days, a knightly tournament should be held — though, for reasons which will be explained in due course, it never in fact took place.

It pleased Don Quijote to just wander around the city — on foot, however, because he was worried that, on horseback, he would be pestered by boys — so he and Sancho, accompanied by two servants sent along by Don Antonio, would regularly stroll the streets. And so it happened, one day, that Don Quijote spied, written above a doorway, in very large letters: BOOKS PRINTED HERE. This delighted him, because he had never been in a printer's shop and much wanted to know how they operated. They went in, he and his entire entourage, and observed how, in one corner, men were printing off sheets, proof reading them in another, setting type here, and over there making corrections, and, in a word, doing all the things that are done in large print-shops. Don Quijote went over to one stall and asked a workman what he was doing; he was informed, was properly astonished, and walked on. Then he approached a workman in yet another stall, and again asked what he was doing. He was told:

"Sir, that gentleman over there," and the workman indicated a well-dressed, handsome man of a rather serious appearance, "has translated a book from Italian into our Spanish tongue, and I'm setting type for it, so it can be printed."

"What's the book's title?" asked Don Quijote.

To which the writer himself replied:

"Sir, in Italian the book is called *Le Bagatele*."[6]

"And what does that mean in our Spanish?" asked Don Quijote.

"*Le Bagatele*," said the writer, "would be 'trifles,' or 'trivialities,' in Spanish, but even though its title is extremely modest, the book deals with excellent and truly substantive matters."

"I have some knowledge of Italian," said Don Quijote, "and I can boast of being able to recite some stanzas of Ariosto. But tell me, your grace, my dear sir — and I ask this strictly out of curiosity, and not with any desire to test your knowledge — have you ever run across the Italian word *pignatta*?"

"Often," replied the writer.

"And how would you translate that into Spanish, your grace?" asked Don Quijote.

"How else," answered the writer, "but 'pot'?"

"Mother of God," said Don Quijote, "how well your grace knows Italian! I'd be willing to bet that, when the Italian reads *piace*, your grace translates 'pleases,' and when the Italian has *più*, you say 'more,' and that you turn *su* into 'above' and *giù* into 'below.'"

"That certainly is what I do," said the writer, "because that's what the words mean."

"And now I'd be willing to bet," said Don Quijote, "that your grace has no very great reputation, because the world never likes to reward brilliance or indeed anything really worth doing. What talents it manages to bury! What keen minds it ignores! What true virtue it scorns and despises! It seems to me, all the same, that translating from one language to another, except from those queens of all languages, Greek and Latin, is rather like looking at Flemish tapestries on the wrong side, because even though you can make out the figures, they're partially hidden behind this thread and that thread, and you can't ever see them as clearly and with all the detail you can find on the right side, and translating from easy languages requires neither wit nor eloquence, like someone who simply transcribes or copies from one document to another. Not that I mean to say translation can't ever be worthwhile, because, after all, a man could occupy himself with worse and even less profitable things. I make an exception for two famous translators: one, Doctor Cristóbal de Figueroa, and his *Pastor Fido*, and the other, Don Juan de Jáurigui and his *Aminta*, both of which are so well done that it's hard to tell which is the translation and which the original.[7] But tell me, your grace: are you printing this book at your own expense, or have you sold the rights to a publisher?"

"I'm printing at my own expense," answered the writer, "and I expect to make at least a thousand dollars on this first printing, which will be of two thousand volumes, which I'm sure will sell one, two, three quick at sixty cents a copy."

"You certainly know your arithmetic!" replied Don Quijote. "But I'm afraid you don't know the ins and outs of publishing, and how all these

6. This seems to be an invented title; no such Italian book is known [*Translator's Note*].
7. Battista Guarini's *Il Pastor Fido* [*The Faithful Shepherd*] (1590), translated by Cristóbal Suárez de Figueroa in 1602; Torquato Tasso's *L'Aminta* (1580), translated by Juan de Jáurigui in 1607 [*Translator's Note*].

people work together. I can promise you that, when you find yourself with two thousand books on your hands, your hands will be hurting so hard you won't believe it, especially if your book is something a bit different from usual, and not at all spicy."

"So what am I supposed to do?" exclaimed the writer. "Is your grace suggesting that I give it to a publisher, who'll pay me three cents for the rights and even think he's done me a favor, paying that much? I'm not printing my books to become famous, because the world's already familiar with my work; I want to make some hard cash, because without money fame isn't worth a cent."

"May God grant your grace good luck," replied Don Quijote.

Then he moved on to another stall, where he could see they were proofreading a sheet from a book entitled *Light of the Soul*,[8] and he remarked:

"These are the sorts of books that need to be printed, even though there are lots like them, because we also have lots of sinners, and there are so many living in darkness that we need an infinity of light."

He walked on and saw they were simultaneously proofreading another book, and when he asked for the title, they told him *The Second Volume of That Ingenious Gentleman, Don Quijote de La Mancha*, written by someone from Tordesillas.

"I've heard of this book," said Don Quijote, "and truly, on my conscience, I thought it had long since been burned and reduced to ashes, since it serves no purpose, but pigs are slaughtered every Saint Martin's Day [11 November], and its turn is bound to come, because historical imitations are better, and better liked, the closer they come to the truth, or some semblance thereof, and true histories are always at their best when they're the most truthful."

He exhibited a certain displeasure, as he made these remarks, and then left the print-shop. And it was that same day that Don Antonio arranged for him to visit the galleys, anchored off the sea shore, which idea delighted Sancho, for he'd never been on board any such boat in his life. Don Antonio informed the fleet commander that his guest, that afternoon, would be the celebrated Don Quijote de La Mancha, of whom the commander and indeed everyone in Barcelona was already well aware, and what happened when Don Quijote made this visit will be told in the next chapter.

Chapter Sixty-Three

— *Sancho Panza's misfortune, on his visit to the galleys, and the novel adventure of the beautiful Moorish girl*

Don Quijote spent a great deal of time thinking about the enchanted head's response to his questions (though none of his thoughts touched on the fact that it was all a trick), all of it focused on the promise, which

---

8. Felipe de Meneses (a Dominican friar), *Luz del alma cristiana contra la ceguedad y ignorancia* [*Light of the Christian Soul Facing Blindness and Ignorance*], 1554 (reprinted eleven times, though never in Barcelona, and last printed in 1594) [*Translator's Note*].

seemed to him absolutely certain, that Dulcinea would be freed from her enchantment. Everything led to that one conclusion, to which he returned over and over, and always contentedly, believing as he did that this was a promise soon to be fulfilled, while Sancho, even though he had hated being a governor, nevertheless longed to once again give orders and see them obeyed — the curse and affliction that comes from being in command, even in jest.

So that afternoon their host, Don Antonio Moreno, and his two friends went to the galleys with Don Quijote and Sancho. The fleet commander having been informed of his good fortune, the knight and his squire being incredibly famous visitors, the moment Don Antonio's party arrived at the harbor, canvas awnings came rolling noisily down on every single one of the ships, and on-board flutes piped up; a skiff was launched, virtually lined with rich tapestries and crimson cushions and, as Don Quijote stepped in, the flagship fired its shrapnel-cannon, and the other galleys did the same, and when our knight came up the starboard ladder the entire crew saluted him, in the style usually reserved for singularly distinguished visitors, calling in unison, three times, "Hoo! HOO! Hoo!" The high-born gentleman from Valencia who served as commander — shall we call him an admiral? — gave Don Quijote his hand and embraced him, declaring:

"This will be a day for flying flags and banners — one of the greatest occasions I expect ever to experience — for now I have seen with my own eyes lord Don Quijote de La Mancha; these fluttering pennants will mark the time when we were privileged to meet the man who embodies and encapsulates in his own being all the bravery and courage of knight errantry."

Don Quijote answered him with equal civility, utterly thrilled to find himself treated in such lordly fashion. They proceeded to the raised stern of the ship, which had been very nicely decorated in his honor, and seated themselves along its benches; the officer in charge of the galley-slave rowers, who had piped the party up the runway, then whistled to the galley-slaves to pull off their shirts,[1] which they immediately did. Sancho was dumbfounded, seeing so many half-undressed men, but even more stunned when they rolled up the awning so rapidly that, to him, it seemed as if all the devils in Hell had suddenly gone to work — but all of this was child's play, compared to what I'll tell you next. Sancho had been sitting on the great beam from which the awning was hung, just to the right of the lead rower[2] and, having been told beforehand what he was to do, this man took hold of Sancho, lifted him in his arms, and then all the rowers, ready and waiting, began to pass him down the starboard side, rolling him from one bench to the next like a barrel, spinning him so fast that poor Sancho could no longer see where he was (thinking, no doubt, that those same devils had now carried him off), nor did they stop until he'd traveled all the way down the line and back up on the larboard side and been deposited, at last, back on the stern. The poor fellow was so

---

1. As Riquer notes, this is "to prepare themselves for rowing" [*Translator's Note*].
2. The rowers face to the stern; the lead rower faces the bow, with his back to the others [*Translator's Note*].

tumbled about, so sweaty and out of breath, that he still could not understand what had happened to him.

Seeing Sancho flying along, but without wings, Don Quijote asked the admiral if these were usual ceremonies, regularly performed for people boarding the galleys for the first time, because if they were, and having no intention of taking to the sea as a new profession, he was not interested in doing anything of the sort and, should anyone try to take hold of him, with such flying in mind, he swore he'd kick the living soul out of him — and, so saying, he stood up and put his hand on his sword.

Just then they rolled out the awning once more, and swung down the long lateen yard, and the noise was immense. Sancho thought the sky had come loose from its moorings and was about to fall on his head; terrified, he ducked low, his face between his legs. Nor was Don Quijote entirely sure what was going on, for he too shivered and hunched his shoulders, and his face went pale. The crew hauled up the lateen yard just as fast, and with just as much noise, as they had lowered it, but without saying a word, as silent as if they possessed neither voices nor breath. The lead rower gave the signal for hoisting the anchor, then leaped to the middle of the gangway and, cowhide whip in hand, began lashing the men's shoulders, so that, bit by bit, slowly, they eased out to sea. Seeing so many red feet moving all at once (for that was what he thought the oars were), Sancho said to himself:

"These are truly enchanted things, not the stuff my master talks about. What have these miserable fellows done, for them to be whipped like that, and how can this one man, walking around with his whistle, dare lash out at so many men? This is Hell, I say — or, at least, it's Purgatory."

Seeing how closely Sancho was watching, Don Quijote said to him:

"Ah, Sancho my friend, how quickly, and at what small cost, might you, should you care to, strip to the waist and place yourself with those gentlemen, and thus bring Dulcinea's enchantment to an end! For among so much pain and misery, you'll hardly feel your own — and what's more, it may well be that the magician Merlin would count each of these lashes, which are so well laid on, as equaling ten of those you're sooner or later going to have to give yourself."

The admiral meant to inquire what lashes they were discussing, and what sort of disenchantment Dulcinea might require, when a sailor called out:

"Monjuí[3] signals there's a galley off the western coast."

The admiral immediately jumped onto the gangway, crying out:

"Ah ha, boys! Don't let her get away! The watchtower must have spotted an Algerian pirate brig."

The other three galleys came over to the flagship, to see what their orders were. The admiral commanded two to come to sea with him, and the third to sail along the coast, because that way the barque could not escape them. The slaves dug in their oars, pulling the galleys through the water so rapidly that they seemed to be flying. And the three whose work was out at sea hadn't gone two miles when they saw a ship, looking as if

3. Watchtower castle to the south of Barcelona [*Translator's Note*].

it had fourteen or fifteen banks of rowers, which turned out to be the case; when it spied the admiral's fleet, this ship turned tail and ran, plainly intending to use its speed to get away, but the plan misfired, the flagship being one of the lightest, fastest ships sailing the sea, and as it was closing on the brig the Moorish captain, clearly seeing he could not escape, stopped running and shipped oars, to keep from angering the captain of our boat. But Fate, which was guiding things according to a different plan, arranged that as the flagship was pulling up close, and the men on the brig could hear the cries of "Surrender!" two of the dozen or so Turks they had on board, quite drunk, discharged their rifles and killed a pair of the soldiers stationed, in boarding position, in the gunwales of our ship. Seeing this, the admiral swore that no one on the brig would be left alive; he had the flagship launch a furious attack, but the brig slipped past us, under our oars, and our galley went a good way past. While our boat was swinging back toward them, those on the brig hoisted their sails, knowing they were beaten, and once again tried to flee, using both sail and oars, but their skill helped them less than their boldness hurt them, because in not much more than half a mile the flagship caught up to them, flung its oars over the brig's sides, and captured every one of them alive.

Our other two galleys came up, and our three ships, with theirs in tow, swiftly returned to shore, where a crowd was waiting, anxious to see what we had brought. Close in, the admiral dropped anchor, and saw that the governor of the city had come, too. He despatched the skiff to bring the governor on board, and then ordered the lateen yard lowered at once, so he could hang the brig's captain immediately, along with everyone else captured on board, amounting to thirty-six men, good-looking fellows and most of them Turkish infantrymen. The admiral asked who was the captain, and one of the captives, who afterwards turned out to be a renegade, answered him in Spanish:

"This young fellow, sir, is our captain."

And he pointed to one of the handsomest, most elegant looking young men the human mind could ever have imagined. He looked less than twenty years old. The admiral asked him:

"Tell me, you stupid dog, why on earth you killed my soldiers, seeing you couldn't possibly escape? Is that the kind of respect to show a flagship? Don't you know the difference between rashness and courage? Doubtful expectations ought to make men daring, but not reckless."

The brig's captain was about to reply, but for the moment the admiral was unable to listen to him, having to welcome on board the governor, who had just arrived, along with his servants and some townspeople.

"That was good hunting, my lord admiral!" said the governor.

"And just how good," answered the admiral, "Your Excellency will now see from the game hanging on this yard arm."

"How so?" replied the governor.

"Because," answered the admiral, "contrary to all the laws and rules and customs of war, they've killed two of the very best soldiers I had, and I've sworn to hang every one of them I could catch, and especially this young fellow, who is their captain."

And he indicated the young captain, standing with his hands tied and a rope already around his neck, awaiting death.

When the governor looked at him, and saw how handsome he was, and how well he carried himself, though not at all arrogantly, it was as if, in that instant, his beauty wrote him a letter of recommendation and made the governor want to spare him, so he asked:

"Tell me, captain, are you a Turk, or a Moor, or a renegade?"

The young man replied, in equally good Spanish:

"I'm neither a Turk, nor a Moor, nor a renegade."

"Then what are you?" replied the governor.

"A Christian woman," the young fellow answered.

"A woman, and a Christian, dressed like that, and in such straits? But this is too much to believe."

"Oh gentlemen!" said the young fellow, "postpone my death for a moment, for your vengeance will not suffer much, waiting while I tell you my life story."

How hard would a heart have had to be, not to be softened by these words — or, at least, to wait and hear what the unfortunate, miserable youngster wanted to say? The admiral told him to say what he had to say, but not to expect any pardon for his obvious guilt. Given this permission, the youth began as follows:

"I was born into that race more unfortunate than it is wise, and on which a whole sea of miseries has rained down: my parents were both Moors. In the course of my unhappy existence I was brought to Barbary, by my aunt and uncle, for it did me no good to say that I was, as indeed I am, a Christian — and not a feigned or only nominal Christian, but a true and Catholic Christian. It did not help me a bit, with those who were in charge of our unhappy banishment, to honestly and truthfully tell them this, nor did my aunt and uncle themselves believe me, thinking it was simply a lie invented to let me remain in the country where I was born, and so they took me with them, more by force than of my own free will. But I had a Christian mother, and a wise and Christian father: that's the plain and simple truth. I drank the Catholic faith with my mother's milk; I was taught good habits; neither in speech nor in manners, so far as I am aware, was there anything Moorish about me.

"Along with these virtues, as I think them, I also acquired whatever beauty I possess, and although I was both modest and well secluded, my way of life was not so rigid that a young gentleman named Gaspar Gregorio, oldest son of a gentleman who owned a village near ours, happened to see me. Just how he saw me, and we began to talk, and he fell wildly in love with me, and I equally with him, would all take a long time to tell, and especially when I fear this harsh and threatening rope may at any moment cut between my tongue and my throat, so let me say only that Don Gregorio longed to go into exile with me. He joined the Moors leaving from other nearby villages, for he knew the language well, and in the course of our journey he became friendly with the aunt and uncle who were taking me away with them — which was because my sensible, far-seeing father, the moment he heard the first edict of our banishment, left our village and went to find some foreign country where we might take refuge. He left, secretly buried, and in a place that I alone know, a great horde of pearls and immensely valuable gems, along with gold coins of all sorts. And he ordered me not to so much as touch the treasures he had left behind, if we were sent into exile before his return. I obeyed him and, as I've said, together with my aunt and uncle, and other relatives and connections, we went to Barbary and settled in a town in Algeria, which was like going to live in Hell itself. The king became aware of my beauty, and rumor informed him that I was rich, which was to some extent lucky for me. He summoned me to appear before him, asked from what part of Spain I had come, and what money and gems I had brought with me. I told him my birthplace, and that the jewels and money were buried there, but that I could easily get them if I myself were to return. I told him all this, worried that he might be blinded by my beauty, if not by his own greed.

"And as we were discussing these matters, the king was brought word that there had arrived from Spain, along with me, one of the most elegant and beautiful young men imaginable. I understood at once that they meant Don Gaspar Gregorio, whose beauty had indeed grown beyond praise. And I was worried, because I knew the danger Don Gregorio was in, because these barbarous Turks much prefer a handsome boy, or young man, to the most beautiful woman alive. The king then commanded that Don Gregorio be brought before him, asking me if what they said about him was true. And I replied, almost as if warned by Heaven, that yes, it was, but that he must understand that we were not talking about a young man but a woman, like me, and I asked him, most earnestly, to let me go and dress her in her proper clothing, so she might appear in his presence in all her natural beauty and with less embarrassment. He told me to go right ahead, and afterward we would talk about the best way for me to return to Spain, to dig up the hidden treasure.

"I spoke to Don Gaspar, explaining the danger he'd be in, showing himself as a man, then dressed him like a girl and, that same afternoon, brought him before the king, who was struck with admiration and decided to keep Don Gregorio there, in order to present 'her' to the Sultan, but in order to avoid the dangers to which 'she' might be exposed, among the women in his harem, and also to keep himself from temptation, he ordered Don Gregorio sent, then and there, to the home of a highborn Moorish woman, where 'she' would remain, for the time being, in that lady's service. How this made us both feel — for I cannot deny that I love him — may be left to the understanding of those who have had to be parted from their loved ones.

"Then the king worked out a plan for me to return to Spain in this brig, accompanied by the two Turks who killed your soldiers. This Spanish renegade came with me," and here she motioned to the man who had first spoken, "because I know perfectly well he's a Christian in disguise and would far rather remain in Spain than return to Barbary. All the others on board the brig are Moors and Turks, serving strictly as rowers. As for the two Turks, an arrogant and greedy pair, instead of following their instructions to land this renegade and myself in the first Spanish soil we reached, both of us dressed as Christians (in clothing we brought with us), decided to first have some fun, cruising along this coast and, if they could, capturing some booty, because they were worried that, if they just set us on shore, and by some accident we were captured and we let on that the brig had brought us and was still in these waters, and there were galleys on patrol, the Spaniards might send them to sea and then the Turks would be the prize. We spotted this shore, last night, but did not see these four galleys, and the rest of what happened you've seen for yourselves. To make a long story short, Don Gregorio has been left in women's clothing, and surrounded by women, and he's clearly in very great danger, and here I am, with my hands tied, and waiting — no, I should say *fearing* — to give up this life of mine, of which I am long since weary. And that, gentlemen, is the end of my pitiful history, every bit as true as it is miserable. All I ask of you is that you let me die as a Christian, for as I have told you I am not in the slightest degree guilty of the crime others of my race have committed."

And she fell silent, her eyes brimming with tears (like many of those who were listening to her). The governor, who was a compassionate and emotional man, went over to her and, not saying a word, took off the rope tied around her hands.

But while the Moorish Christian had been telling the tale of her wanderings and troubles, an old pilgrim who had boarded the galley with the governor had been fixedly staring at her, and she had barely finished when he threw himself at her feet and, embracing them, his words broken, sobbing and moaning, said:

"Oh Anna Félix, my miserable daughter! I am your father, Ricote, who came back to hunt for you and cannot live without you, oh my living soul!"

Sancho's head had been drooping, remembering the miserable experience he himself had endured, but at these words his eyes opened wide and his head straightened and, staring at the pilgrim, he recognized the selfsame Ricote he'd bumped into, the day he'd abandoned his governorship, and he recognized Ricote's daughter — and she, unbound, threw her arms around her father, her tears blending with his, as Ricote said to the admiral and the governor:

"Gentlemen, this is my daughter, whose life has been less happy than her name, she being called Anna Félix [*felix* = happy], her surname being Ricote, and she herself as well known for her beauty as for her father's wealth. I left home to search through foreign lands for somewhere to shelter and settle my family, and having found such a place in Germany I came back to Spain, dressed as a pilgrim and in the company of Germans, to find my daughter and dig up the great treasure I had hidden. I did not find my daughter; I did find the treasure, which I have with me — and now, by the strange turnings you yourselves have seen, I have also found a treasure which still more enriches me, my beloved daughter. If our innocence, and her tears, and mine, given the honesty of Spanish justice, can somehow open the doors of your compassion, oh extend it to us who have never once thought of injuring you, nor have in any way been part of, or been in sympathy with, the plots of our people, who have rightly been banished."

At which Sancho said:

"I know Ricote very well, and he's speaking the truth about Anna Félix being his daughter; as for all this other stuff about coming and going, and good plots, and bad plots, I don't know a thing."

Everyone was struck by this strange case, and the admiral said:

"One by one, your tears have washed away my vow: you shall live, beautiful Anna Félix, for as long as Heaven wants you to, and the greedy and arrogant men who committed the crime shall suffer for it."

And he gave the order to hang on the yard arm the two Turks who had killed his soldiers, but the governor warmly urged that they not be hanged, for what they'd done smacked more of lunacy than of boldness. The admiral granted the governor's request, vengeance being difficult to carry out in cold blood. And then they immediately set themselves to thinking how best to rescue Don Gregorio from the peril in which he'd been left; to save the young man, Ricote offered more than two thousand dollars in pearls and other gems. They talked of many different methods, but none matched that proposed by the Spanish renegade, which was that he return to Algiers in some small boat with not more than six banks of oars, manned by Christian rowers, because he knew just where, and how, and when to land, and also knew the house where Don Gregorio had been lodged. The admiral and the governor doubted the renegade's good faith, worried about trusting him with Christian rowers, but both Anna Félix and her father were sure the man was trustworthy, and Ricote offered to pay the Christians' ransoms, if for any reason they were captured.

This settled, the governor went back to Barcelona, and Don Antonio Moreno carried off both the Moorish girl and her father, the governor having requested that they be entertained and treated as well as possible, and indeed offering to entertain them in his own home — such being the kindness and charity with which Anna Félix's beauty had filled his heart.

Chapter Sixty-Four

— the gloomiest of all the gloomy adventures ever experienced by Don Quijote

Our history records that Don Antonio's wife was wonderfully happy to have Anna Félix in her house. She welcomed the girl with great good will, as much struck by her beauty as by her good sense, for the Moorish girl was profoundly blessed in both respects, and everyone in Barcelona came to see her, as if summoned by the sound of clanging bells.

But Don Quijote told Don Antonio their idea for freeing Don Gregorio was a bad one, far more dangerous than it ought to be, and it would have been better to set him down in Barbary, with his horse and armor, for he would find the young man in the face of every Moor on earth, just as Don Gaiferos had found his wife Melisendra.

"Your grace should remember," said Sancho, hearing this, "that Don Gaiferos rescued his wife by land, and took her directly into France, whereas here, even if we rescued Don Gregorio, there'd be no way to bring him to Spain, because the sea lies between here and there."

"But there is a way around everything," replied Don Quijote, "with the single exception of death, for if the boat approached the shore, we could get on board, and let the whole world try to stop us."

"You make it all sound well and easy, your grace," said Sancho, "but, as they say, there's many a slip 'twixt cup and lip, and I trust the renegade, who seems to me a very good man, with his heart in the right place."

Don Antonio said that, if the renegade couldn't do the job, they'd certainly try sending the great Don Quijote into Barbary.

Two days later, the renegade sailed off in a small boat, with six banks of rowers, manned by a brave crew, and two days after that the fleet of galleys set sail for the Middle East, the admiral having asked the governor to let him know how things went with Don Gregorio's freedom, and with Anna Félix, and the governor having agreed to honor that request.

One morning, Don Quijote having set out for the sea shore, wearing full armor (for, as he often said, this was his proper costume, just as combat was his true consolation; he was not often seen, dressed less than fittingly), he saw a knight coming toward him, also in full armor, and with a shining moon painted on his shield, and as soon as he came within hailing distance he called to Don Quijote, in a loud voice:

"Oh renowned knight, and never sufficiently praised Don Quijote de La Mancha, I am the Knight of the White Moon, of whose unheard of deeds you may perhaps have heard; I come to do combat with you, and test the strength of your arm, by making you acknowledge that my lady, whoever she may be, is incomparably more beautiful than your Dulcinea del Toboso; if you will unambiguously affirm this truth, you will not need to die, and I will be spared the trouble of killing you; but if you choose to fight, and I defeat you, the only satisfaction I desire is that you put off your armor and abstain from any seeking of adventures, withdrawing and retiring to your home for the space of one year, during which time you are not to touch your sword but live peacefully, in beneficial calm, and thereby both increase your estate and improve your soul; and if you defeat me, you may if you like cut off my head, and my armor and my horse will belong to you, and whatever fame I have acquired from my deeds will also be transferred to you. Consider what course you think it best to take, and give me a swift reply, for on this day I have begun and on this day I must finish this entire business."

Don Quijote was both perplexed and astonished, quite as much by the Knight of the White Moon's arrogance as by the nature of his challenge, and immediately answered him, calmly but with a grim face:

"Knight of the White Moon, whose deeds have, to this moment, never been brought to my attention, I think I can safely avow that you have never seen the illustrious Dulcinea, for, if you had, I know perfectly well you would have tried to avoid making this challenge, the very sight of her making you realize that there neither has been nor ever could be any beauty comparable to hers, and so, though I do not affirm you a liar, I say only that you are wrong, and I accept your challenge on the terms you have stated, and I accept it here and now — for there is no need to let the appointed day pass — with only one exception, which is that the fame of your deeds shall not be transferred to me, for I do not know what they are or of what merit: I am satisfied with my own, such as they may be. Take whatever part of the field you like, and I will do the same, and to whomever God gives the victory, may Saint Peter add his blessing."

The people of Barcelona had seen the Knight of the White Moon, and the governor had been advised that said knight was in conversation with Don Quijote. Believing this to be some new adventure concocted by Don Antonio Moreno, or other city gentleman, the governor came down to the sea shore, along with Don Antonio and a host of others, just at the very moment when Don Quijote was preparing to wheel Rocinante around and measure off the space he would need for his charge.

Seeing that they were both preparing for battle, the governor set himself between them, asking what had impelled them into this sudden combat. The Knight of the White Moon replied that it was a question of beauty's precedence, explaining tersely what he had already said to Don Quijote, as well as the terms of the challenge to which both parties had agreed. The governor went over to Don Antonio and inquired, quietly, if he knew who this Knight of the White Moon was, and whether this was some joke being played on Don Quijote. Don Antonio answered that he neither knew who this knight was nor whether his challenge was a joke or for real. The governor was perplexed, hearing this, not knowing whether he should allow this combat to take place, but finding it hard to believe that this could be anything but a joke, he took himself off the field of battle, saying:

"Knights, if the only solution is to yield or die, and my lord Don Quijote stands firm, and your grace of the White Moon stands even firmer, the question must be decided by God on high, so carry on."

He of the White Moon thanked the governor, in courteous, sensible terms, for granting his permission, as did Don Quijote, and then our own knight, commending himself with all his heart both to God and to his Dulcinea — which was the usual custom, before engaging in combat — turned and measured off a still longer distance for his charge, because he saw that his opponent was doing exactly that, and without the sound of a trumpet or any other warlike instrument to signal the charge, at just the same point they both swung their horses around, and attacked, and since he of the White Moon rode a faster horse he had covered a full two-thirds of the ground when he encountered Don Quijote, and charging into our knight with immense force, but not so much as touching him with his spear — for he seemed to deliberately keep his weapon from making any contact — he brutally hurled both Rocinante and his rider to the ground. And then he immediately approached our knight, set the point of his lance against the fallen Don Quijote's visor, and declared:

"You have been defeated, knight, and, if you do not concede the terms of our challenge, you may be dead as well."

Bruised and stunned, Don Quijote replied, not raising his visor, and speaking like someone from inside a tomb, his voice weak and sickly:

"Dulcinea del Toboso is the most beautiful woman in the world, and I am the most miserable knight on earth, nor is it fitting that my weakness should detract from this truth. Grip your lance, knight, and, having taken my honor, now take my life."

"That I most certainly will not do," said he of the White Moon. "May the fame of Lady Dulcinea del Toboso's beauty live in all its fullness, and live long, for I am satisfied if only the great Don Quijote retire to his home for one year, or until whatever intervening date I may direct, exactly as we agreed before beginning this combat."

The governor and Don Antonio heard every word of this, as did the many other people who were there, and they all heard Don Quijote say, too, that so long as he was not commanded to do anything in prejudice of Dulcinea, all the rest would of course be fulfilled, as befitting a true and honorable knight.

This having been acknowledged, he of the White Moon swung round his horse, bowed his head to the governor, and rode off into the city at a half gallop. The governor ordered Don Antonio to follow after him and, however he could, find out who he was. They lifted Don Quijote up and raised his visor, revealing a face damp with perspiration and chalky white. The shock had been too much for Rocinante, who for the moment could not move at all. Completely saddened, utterly depressed, Sancho did not know what to say or what to do: it seemed to him that the whole thing had been a dream, and every bit of it was the doing of some enchanter. He saw his master defeated, and sworn not to take up arms for an entire year; it seemed to him that the glorious light of Don Quijote's great deeds had been darkened, and all the expectations roused by his new promises totally undone, swept away like smoke in the wind. He was afraid Rocinante had been maimed for life, and Rocinante's master knocked half to pieces, though it would do no harm if Don Quijote had been shaken out of his madness.[1] And then, once the governor had sent for a sedan chair, they carried Don Quijote back into the city, to which also the governor turned his steps, wondering who this Knight of the White Moon might be, who had rendered Don Quijote so desolate and stricken.

Chapter Sixty-Five

— which explains who the Knight of the White Moon was, and recounts Don Gregorio's liberation, as well as other matters

Don Antonio Moreno followed after the Knight of the White Moon, and a crowd of boys followed him too, pell-mell and harassingly,[1] until they finally cornered him at an inn in Barcelona. Don Antonio went in, determined to find out who the man was. A squire came out to welcome the unknown knight and help him off with his armor, and both withdrew to a closed room — but Don Antonio followed right after, unable to rest until he had learned the knight's identity. And seeing that this gentleman was resolved to stick to him like glue, he of the White Moon said:

"I am quite aware, sir, of your errand, which is to learn who I am, and since I have no reason to deny my identity, let me proceed to tell you everything you need to know, omitting no relevant details, while my servant continues to remove my armor. Know then, sir, that my name is Samson Carrasco, and I am a graduate of Salamanca; I come from the same place as does Don Quijote de La Mancha, whose madness and foolishness saddens and moves to pity all those who know him, and one of those most affected has been me, and so, believing that his health

---

1. Don Quijote is *deslocado*, "shaken up," but *deslocar* = to cease being crazy [*Translator's Note*].
1. *Seguir* = to follow; *perseguir* = to follow or to persecute, harass [*Translator's Note*].

depended on his being calm and at rest, and that he belongs in his own village and his own house, I worked out a scheme for putting him there, and three months ago I rode out in the guise of a knight errant, calling myself the Knight of the Mirrors, intending, without hurting him, to do battle with and vanquish him, setting as the terms of our combat that the conquered would be subject to the will of the conqueror, and what I planned to demand of him, because I thought he was as good as already defeated, was that he would return home and not sally forth for the period of one year, during which time, perhaps, he might be cured of his madness, but Fate arranged matters differently, because in fact he won the battle, defeating me and tumbling me off my horse, so my plan never went into effect: he went on his way, and I limped home, beaten, embarrassed and bruised by my fall, which had been a distinctly nasty one — but this was not enough to take away my desire to come hunting for him once more, and defeat him, as you saw me do today. Being, as he is, punctilious about following all the rules of knight errantry, there is no doubt whatever that he will keep his word, and fulfill the pledge he made. And this, sir, is what has happened, and there is nothing more I can tell you: I must ask that you not reveal my identity, especially to Don Quijote, so that my good intentions may be put into effect and a man of excellent good sense may be returned to sanity, once the foolishness of this knighthood business is abandoned."

"Ah, sir," said Don Antonio, "may God forgive you for the damage you've done to the whole rest of the world, in trying to cure the wittiest lunatic ever seen! Don't you see, my dear sir, that, whatever utility there might be in curing him, it could never match the pleasure he gives with his madness? But I suspect that, despite all your cleverness, sir, you cannot possibly cure a man so far gone in madness, and, if charity did not restrain me, I would say that Don Quijote ought never to be rendered sane, because if he were we would lose, not only his witticisms, but those of Sancho Panza, his squire, any one of which has the power to turn melancholy itself into happiness. Nevertheless, I will stay silent and say nothing, to see whether or not I am correct in thinking that, for all his cleverness and hard work, Señor Carrasco has in fact accomplished nothing."

The college graduate answered that he thought things had already gone very well indeed, and he was hopeful of success. Don Antonio then offered to do whatever he was asked to, and they bade each other farewell. Carrasco had his arms and armor tied onto a jackass and immediately, riding the same horse he'd ridden into battle, earlier in the day, rode out of the city and returned home, meeting along the way nothing which needs to be recorded in this truthful history.

Don Antonio did of course tell the governor everything he'd learned from Carrasco, nor was the governor much pleased to hear it, for Don Quijote's withdrawal would deprive them of the pleasure so freely provided by his wild doings.

Don Quijote was in bed for six days, depressed, sad, yearningly thoughtful and generally in no very good mood, working around in his mind, over and over, the events of his miserable defeat. Sancho comforted him, saying, among other things:

"My lord, lift your head and rejoice, if you can, in the kindness of Heaven, which, though you were thrown to the ground, kept you from breaking a single bone, for you know very well that combat is all give and take, and just because you see a fence doesn't mean there are pigs on the other side of it, and the hell with the doctor, because we don't need him to cure this disease: we'll just go back home and stop hunting for adventures in all these strange places — and if you really think about it, I've lost a lot more than you have, even though it was you, your grace, who took a beating. I may have given up wanting to be a governor, when I gave up being one, but I'd still like to be a count, which will never happen if your grace leaves off being a knight and gives up on being a king, and so my dreams have been turned into so much smoke."

"Be still, Sancho, because after all I only have to withdraw and retire for a year, and afterwards I can go back to this honorable profession of mine, and maybe I won't lose out on winning a kingdom and making you a count."

"May God be listening," said Sancho, "and the Devil be deaf, because I've always heard it said that a good bird in the bush is worth two bad ones in hand."

And at this point Don Antonio came in, saying with every sign of great satisfaction:

"Good news, my lord Don Quijote! Don Gregorio and the renegade who went after him have reached our shores! What did I tell you, that day? He's at the governor's house, and he'll be here any minute."

Don Quijote was somewhat cheered by this news, and said:

"But after all, I can almost say it would have been nice, had things gone the other way, because then I would have been obliged to cross into Barbary, where the strength of my arm would have freed not only Don Gregorio, but all the Christian captives held in that whole country. But, ah me, what am I saying? Am I not the one who was defeated? Am I not the one who was thrown from his horse? Am I not the one who cannot take up arms for an entire year? So what am I proposing? Why am I singing my own praises, if, now, I'm better fitted for the spinning wheel than the sword?"

"Stop that, my lord," said Sancho. "Long live the hen, pip and all! Today it's your turn to suffer, but tomorrow maybe it'll be mine. Don't worry about all this fighting and banging business, because if you fall down today you can stand up again tomorrow, unless you'd rather just lie around in bed — what I mean is, he who gives up, can't summon the spirit for new battles. So get up, your grace, and welcome Don Gregorio, because everything seems to be in an uproar around here, so he must be here already."

Which was true, because having given the governor an account of the voyage out and back, Don Gregorio wanted to see Anna Félix, so he and the renegade hurried to Don Antonio's house; when he'd fled from Algeria he'd been dressed like a woman, but once on board the ship he'd exchanged clothes with another prisoner who escaped with him; still, whatever he might be wearing, he showed himself as someone to be sought after, and served, and appreciated, for he was a surpassingly handsome youngster of perhaps seventeen or eighteen. Ricote and his daughter came out to welcome him, the father weeping, the daughter shy and bashful. The two young people did not embrace, for when love is deep and real, modesty usually prevails. But their beauty, side by side, was noted and admired by all who saw them. It was silence that spoke for these two lovers, and the happy, honest thoughts their eyes revealed.

The renegade explained the scheme he had concocted, and the means he had employed, to free Don Gregorio, and Don Gregorio told them of the dangers and difficulties he had experienced, among the women with whom he'd been living — not saying a great deal, but speaking briefly, and showing wisdom far beyond his years. Ricote generously rewarded both the renegade and those who had done the rowing, and they were all well satisfied. The renegade made his peace with the Church, becoming again one of the faithful, and transforming himself, with penitence and repentance, from a rotten limb to a pure and healthy one.

Two days later, the governor and Don Antonio discussed how best to arrange for Anna Félix and her father to stay in Spain, thinking it ought not to be difficult for such a thoroughly Christian daughter, and a father, so far as one could tell, so extremely well intentioned. Don Antonio volunteered to bring the matter up at Court, where he had other urgent business, explaining that, with a certain amount of patronage, and some greasing of the wheels, difficult things could definitely be accomplished.

"No," said Ricote, who was also present, "I don't think we can trust either patronage or presents, because the great Don Bernardino de Velasco, Count Salazar, to whom His Majesty has given the responsibility for our expulsion, will not be moved by pleas, or promises, or presents, nor pitiful tears, for though it may be true that he blends mercy with justice, he sees that the whole body of our nation is contaminated and rotting, and so he has chosen to apply a burning cauterization rather than some merely soothing salve; sensibly, wisely, diligently, as well as by the fear he inspires, he has taken on his own broad shoulders the whole weight of carrying into effect this grand scheme, and none of my people's tricks, or stratagems, or petitions, or deceits have been able to blind his Argus-like[2] eyes, always open and alert to ensure that not one of us remains hidden, like some unseen root that, in time, will bring forth venomous fruits here in Spain, which he has cleansed and completely freed of the fear engendered by our so numerous presence. Phillip the Third's courageous decision was heroic indeed, and he displayed an unheard-of wisdom, entrusting the execution of that decision to Don Bernardino de Velasco!"

"All the same," said Don Antonio, "I intend, while I'm in Madrid, to do everything I can, and then Heaven may do as it thinks best. Don Gregorio will have to come with me, to ease the pain and suffering his absence must have caused his parents; Anna Félix will stay here in my house, with my wife, or else in a convent, and I know our lord governor will be glad to keep Ricote in his house, while we wait to see what I can do in this business."

The governor was in complete agreement, but when Don Gregorio was informed of the plan, he said that he neither could nor would abandon

---

2. The prototypical watchman, Argus had eyes all over his body [*Translator's Note*].

Doña Anna Félix; still, since he intended to visit his parents, to arrange how best to plan for her final return, he accepted the proposal. So Anna Félix remained with Don Antonio's wife, and Ricote stayed on with the governor.

Don Antonio's departure date arrived, and then, two days later, Don Quijote's and Sancho's, our knight's brutal fall making it impossible for him to travel any sooner. Don Gregorio's parting from Anna Félix was accompanied by tears, moans, sobs, and fits of fainting. Ricote offered Don Gregorio a thousand dollars, if he'd take it, but he would not, though he borrowed five dollars from Don Antonio, promising to pay him back when they got to Madrid. So Don Antonio and Don Gregorio left, and then, as we've said, so did Don Quijote and Sancho, our knight dressed like a traveler, and neither wearing armor nor carrying any weapons, and Sancho being forced to walk, because the little donkey was loaded with his master's tools of war.

Chapter Sixty-Six

— which deals with what any reader of these pages will see for himself, and anyone who has this read to him will hear

As they were leaving Barcelona, Don Quijote turned to look at the spot where he had been tumbled from his horse, saying:

"This was my Troy! Here my misfortune, but not my cowardice, carried off all my glory; here Fortune toyed with me, as she turns this way and that; here my great deeds were covered in darkness; and here, in a word, my hopes and my happiness fell, never to rise again!"

Hearing this, Sancho said:

"My lord, brave hearts must learn to bear their suffering, in times of misfortune, just as they deal with their happiness, when things go well, and I can tell this from my own experience, because if I was happy, as a governor, I'm not sad now, even though I'm a squire and on foot, because I've heard it said that this creature we call Fortune is a drunken, fickle female and, worst of all, a blind one, to boot, so she doesn't see what she's done, or who she's knocked down and who she's raised up."

"You're truly philosophical, Sancho," replied Don Quijote, "and you speak very wisely. I don't know who taught you such things. But all I can say is that, in this world, there is no Fortune, nor does anything that happens to us, whether good or bad, happen by accident, but by the special providence of Heaven, from which we may derive the common saying: we are all the architects of our own fortunes. I have fashioned mine, but not with the wisdom I should have shown, and so I have had to pay in spades for my vanity, because I ought to have understood that my feeble Rocinante could never withstand a horse so immensely strong as the Knight of the White Moon's. I gambled, in short, and did the best I could, but I was tumbled in the dust, and though I lost my honor I neither lost, nor could I have lost, the virtue of keeping my word. When I was a knight errant, brave and bold, both my actions and my hands could guarantee what I did, and now, having become a mere country squire, my words must guarantee that my promise will be kept. So let's just go on, friend Sancho, and we'll keep a quiet year in our own homes, and in that seclusion we can find new powers and thereby restore ourselves to the unforgettable profession of bearing arms."

"My lord," replied Sancho, "this business of traveling on foot isn't such fun that I feel like making any long journeys. Let's just put all this weaponry and armor in a tree, like someone being hanged, and let me get back up on my donkey's shoulders, with my feet off the ground, and then we'll make this trip any way your grace wants, because it's a waste of time to think I'm going to stay on my feet a long time and make this trip."

"Well said, Sancho," replied Don Quijote. "We'll hang my armor and weapons as a trophy, and down below them, or around them, we'll carve into the tree what was written on the trophy they made of Roland's war tools:

Let no one move this
Who shrinks from combat with Roland."

"That would suit me just fine," responded Sancho, "and maybe, if we didn't need him on the road, we ought to hang Rocinante up there, too."

"But no, we won't hang him, and we won't hang the armor and weapons, either," said Don Quijote, "so no one can say: Bad pay for good services!"

"You're absolutely right, your grace," said Sancho, "because what sensible people say is that, when the donkey makes a mistake, the packsaddle shouldn't have to pay for it, and since in all this the fault is yours, your grace, you ought to punish yourself, instead of venting your anger on this armor, because it's already broken and bloody enough, and you shouldn't blame it on Rocinante's meek, mild ways, or even on the softness of my feet, when we try to make them march longer than they can."

They rode along, talking like this, all that day, and for the next four, without anything happening to interfere with their journey, but then, on the fifth day, as they approached a village, they found a crowd of people gathered at the door of an inn and, since it was a holiday, having themselves a very good time. As Don Quijote rode up, a peasant called out, loudly:

"One of these two gentlemen over here, neither of whom knows the parties, will tell us what to do about this bet of ours."

"I'll certainly be glad to tell you," replied Don Quijote, "and with complete honesty, if I can grasp what it's about."

"Well, my good sir, this is how it is," said the peasant. "One of the men around here, so fat that he weighs almost three hundred pounds, challenged another fellow, who only weighs a hundred and twenty-five, to a race. They agreed to run a hundred paces, carrying equal loads, and when they asked the challenger how they were supposed to make the weights equal, he said that the other man, who weighs only a hundred and twenty-five, should put six big iron bars on his back, and that would make him weigh almost three hundred pounds, and they'd be all even."

"No, no," Sancho said at once, before Don Quijote could answer. "Let me take care of this, because I just gave up being a governor, not long ago, and a judge, as everybody knows, has to render opinions in all kinds of cases."

"Go right ahead, Sancho my friend," said Don Quijote, "because right now I'm not good for a thing, my mind is so confused and turned every which way."

The peasants were standing there, mouths agape, awaiting the decision, and so, once he'd obtained his master's permission, Sancho told them:

"Brothers, what the fat man wants is wrong — it doesn't have any color of justice — because even if it's true, as he says, that the challenger gets to choose the weapons, still, it's not fair to let him pick weapons that keep the other fellow from having any chance of winning, so it seems to me the challenger has to slim himself down, prune and chop, snip and cut, until he's gotten rid of a hundred and fifty pounds — from whatever part of his body he thinks best, it's entirely up to him — and then, when he weighs just a hundred and twenty-five, he and his opponent will be exactly even and they can run on equal terms."

"Mother of God!" said one of the peasants, hearing Sancho deliver this judgment. "This gentleman has spoken like a saint, and given a judgment like a canon lawyer! But just the same, it doesn't look as if this fat fellow wants to lose an ounce off his bones, much less a hundred and fifty pounds."

"Let them forget about running," replied another, "so the thin fellow doesn't kill himself with all that weight, and the fat one doesn't have to peel off any flesh. Spend half the bet on wine, and let's take these gentlemen to the best tavern in town, and if there's any problem, well, let the raincoat be on me if it starts raining!"[1]

"Gentlemen," replied Don Quijote, "I thank you, but I cannot let myself be delayed for even a moment, for sad events and sad thoughts force me to seem discourteous and travel on as fast as possible."

Saying which, he spurred Rocinante and rode on, leaving them as astonished at the sight of his strange appearance as at the wisdom of his servant, which was what they took Sancho to be. And one of the other peasants said:

"If the servant is as wise as that, what must the master be! I'll bet if he went to study at Salamanca, they'd have to make him a magistrate right off the bat, because it's all just fooling around, except for studying, and then more studying, and having a patron, and having luck, and before you know what's happening you find you've got a magistrate's staff in your hand or a bishop's hat on your head."

Master and man spent that night in the middle of a field, under the open sky, and the next day, as they traveled on, they saw a man walking toward them, a mail bag over his shoulder and a kind of javelin or pike in his hand, and as soon as he drew near Don Quijote (who was of course mounted on Rocinante) he started walking faster, almost running and,

---

1. "A humorous tag-line [*salida*], since one expects he'll say something like, 'if there's any problem, let it be/fall on my head.' " — Riquer [*Translator's Note*].

embracing our knight's right thigh, which was as high as he could reach, he said with evident delight:

"Ah, my lord Don Quijote, how happy my master's heart will be, when he knows your grace is returning to his castle, where he and the duchess have both remained!"

"But I don't know you, my friend," replied Don Quijote, "nor who you are, unless you choose to tell me."

"I, my lord Don Quijote," said the courier, "I am Tosilos, footman to my lord the duke, who didn't want to fight with you, your grace, about marrying Doña Rodríguez's daughter."

"Mother of God!" said Don Quijote. "Can you possibly be the man my enemies, the magicians, transformed into a footman, to deprive me of the glory of that battle?"

"Don't be silly, my good sir," replied the mailman, "because I haven't been enchanted or transformed or anything like that, because I was Tosilos the footman when I rode into the arena, and I was Tosilos the footman when I rode out again. I hoped I could get married without having to fight at all, because the girl really looked good to me, but it worked out just the opposite, because, as soon as your grace left our castle, my lord the duke had me given a hundred lashes for disobeying the orders he gave me, before the fight, and all that's happened is the girl's gone into a nunnery, and Doña Rodríguez's gone back to Castile, and right now I'm going to Barcelona, with a sack of letters my master's sending to the governor. If you'd like a swig of the best stuff going, your grace, though it's a little warm, I've got a gourd of it right here, and I don't know how many chunks of good Tronchón cheese, which will do very nicely for whipping and waking up your thirst, if it happens to be still asleep."

"I'll take you up on the offer," said Sancho, "and never mind any more politeness, so serve out that best stuff, Tosilos, and the hell with all the enchanters in the Indies."

"In short, Sancho," said Don Quijote, "you're the worst glutton in the world and the most ignorant man on earth, since you can't understand that this mailman is enchanted, and Tosilos nothing but a fake. Stay here with him, and stuff yourself, but I'll go on, slowly, and wait for you to catch up."

The footman laughed, pulled out his gourd, took out his chunks of cheese and a small loaf of bread, and then he and Sancho sat down on the green grass and, peacefully and companionably, ate their way right to the bottom of the mailman's saddlebags, and with such gusto that they even licked the envelopes, just because they smelled of cheese. Tosilos said to Sancho:

"Your master, Sancho my friend, has got to be a lunatic."

"Why must he?" answered Sancho. "He doesn't owe anything to anybody,[2] and he pays for everything, and he pays even more when madness is the coin of the realm. I see it, all right, and I tell him so, but what's the use? And especially now, when he's finished off, because the Knight of the White Moon beat him."

---

2. *Debe de ser un loco* = must be a lunatic — but *debe* also means "to owe," as in *No debe nada a nadie*, "He doesn't owe anything to anybody" [*Translator's Note*].

Tosilos asked to hear the whole story, but Sancho said it would be impolite to leave his master waiting for him, and some other time, if they bumped into each other again, he'd be sure to tell Tosilos everything. So he brushed the crumbs off his coat, and the last bits of cheese out of his beard, and got up, took the little donkey by the halter rope, said goodbye to Tosilos, and went to catch up to his master, who was waiting for him in the shade of a tree.

Chapter Sixty-Seven

— Don Quijote's decision to become a shepherd and live in the fields while he waited for his promised year to pass, along with other events both pleasant and cheering

If the thoughts running through his head had wearied Don Quijote, before he'd been tumbled off his horse, after his fall they troubled him still more. He was, as I have said, in the shade of a tree, and there, as flies go after honey, he picked and pecked around in his mind: sometimes he reflected on Dulcinea's disenchantment, and sometimes on the life he would have to lead, in his enforced retirement. Sancho came up and praised Tosilos' generous nature.

"Sancho, Sancho," said Don Quijote, "do you still think he's a real footman? How can you? It has slipped your mind, apparently, that you saw Dulcinea transformed into a peasant girl, and the Knight of the Mirrors turned into our friend, Samson Carrasco, all accomplished by the magicians who keep hounding me. But tell me: did you ask this Tosilos, as you call him, what has happened with Altisidora? Has she wept over my departure, or has she already forgotten all those lovelorn thoughts that, when I was there, so afflicted her?"

"What was on my mind," replied Sancho, "kept me too busy to worry about nonsense. My God, my lord! Is this the time for your grace to start examining other people's thoughts, especially the amorous kind?"

"Now look here, Sancho," said Don Quijote, "there's a great deal of difference between what you do for love and what you do because you're grateful. A knight can certainly be unreceptive but, strictly speaking, it's not possible for him to be ungrateful. So far as I can tell, Altisidora honestly loved me; she gave me those three 'kerchiefs, as you know, and she cried when I left, and she cursed me, she scolded me, she complained about me, and in spite of modesty she did these things openly and in public, all of which clearly indicates that she truly adored me, for lovers' anger usually ends in curses. I cannot offer her any hope, nor have I any treasures to give her, because everything I possess has been surrendered to Dulcinea, and besides, if a knight errant has any treasure, it's as much an illusion and a deceit as fairy treasure,[1] so that all I can offer her are these memories of her I still retain, without prejudice, to be sure, to my memories of Dulcinea, who you continue to wrong by not carrying out the whipping and punishment of your flesh — and how I wish I could see it eaten by

1. Which was said to turn into carbon soot, when a human found it [*Translator's Note*].

wolves! — which would far rather save itself for the worms and maggots than offer any help to that poor lady."

"To tell you the truth, my lord," answered Sancho, "I can't convince myself that whipping my rear end has anything to do with disenchanting anyone who's been enchanted, because that's like saying: 'If your head hurts, rub some salve on your knees.' And I dare say, in all the histories of knight errantry you've read, your grace, you've never once come across a magic spell that was broken by whipping anybody — but be that as it may, I am going to do it, but only when I feel like it and it seems to be a good time for beating on myself."

"May God bring it to pass," replied Don Quijote, "and Heaven grant you grace and let you understand and appreciate your obligation to help my lady, who is yours as well, since you belong to me."

They rode along, talking in this fashion, until they suddenly arrived at the spot where they'd been trampled by bulls. Don Quijote recognized the place, and said to Sancho:

"This is the same meadow where we bumped into those highborn shepherdesses and gallant shepherds, who were trying to renew and re-create a bucolic Arcadia, an idea as novel as it is sensible, and in imitation of which, if it seems good to you, I should like us, oh Sancho, to change ourselves too into shepherds, at least for as long as I need to cloister myself away. I'll buy us some sheep, and everything else necessary for a pastoral existence, and I'll be 'The Quixotic Shepherd,' and you can be 'The Panzaic Shepherd,' and we'll wander over mountains and woods and meadows, in one place singing, in another mourning, drinking the rivers' crystal liquid, or perhaps the clear, clean streams', or perhaps that of the bountiful lakes. The oaks will scatter down their sweet fruit on us, with generous hands, and the hard trunks of cork trees will serve us as couches, the willows will let us have their shade, and the roses will lend us their perfume, and the wide meadows will give us carpets of a thousand hues; our breath will be drawn from the pure, clear air; the moon and the stars will give us their light, in spite of night's darkness; songs will quicken us to delight, rain will pour down happiness, Apollo himself will give us verses, love will fill our minds with such thoughts that we will make ourselves eternally famous, not simply in this time of ours, but for all ages to come."[2]

"Oh boy," said Sancho, "that kind of life sounds fantastic, and more than fantastic[3] — and what's more, as soon as Samson Carrasco, our college graduate, and Master Nicolás, our barber, get a good look at what we're doing, they're going to want to do it, too, so they'll come and be shepherds with us — but I hope God doesn't put it into the priest's head to come and join us, because he's a cheerful fellow and likes to have fun."

"That's very well said," replied Don Quijote, "and if our college graduate, Samson Carrasco, does come with us, as he surely will, we could call him 'The Corruscating Shepherd,' and the barber could be 'Micu-

---

2. Having tried to imitate life as it appeared in his cherished romances of chivalry, Don Quijote is now ready to imitate the lives of the pseudo-shepherds who populate pastoral romances. See the selection from Jacopo Sannazaro's *Arcadia* in the "Backgrounds and Contexts" section of this volume.
3. Literally, "It not only hits me square on [*cuadrado*], but gets me on all sides [*esquinado*]" [*Translator's Note*].

loso,' the way, once upon a time, Garcilaso called the poet Boscán 'Nemoroso' [sylvan], but I'm not sure what name to give the priest, except maybe one derived from the name we use when we speak to him, something like 'The Shepherd Curiambro.' For the shepherdesses, who of course have to be the ones we love, we can pick names the way you pick pears, but since my lady's name fits a shepherdess just as well as a princess, I don't have to give myself the trouble of finding anything better, and you, Sancho, can call yours whatever you like."

"I don't think I'd call her anything but 'Teresona' [big Teresa]," said Sancho, "which goes better with how fat she is and also with her real name, which is Teresa, so when I sing songs about her, and get to talking about my chaste desires, it won't look as if I'm hunting for better bread in other people's houses. It wouldn't be good for the priest to have a shepherdess, because that would set a bad example, but if the college graduate wants one, that's his business."

"Ah, my Lord!" said Don Quijote, "and what a life we'll lead, Sancho my friend! What soft flute sounds will come to our ears — what Zamoran bagpipes — what drums and tambourines — what timbrels — what lutes and violins! And just suppose, among all these other instruments, we hear the sound of cymbals [*albogues*]! Ah, then we'll have virtually everything that produces pastoral music."

"What are these symbols?" asked Sancho. "I've never heard of them, in all my life, and I've never seen them, either."

"Cymbals," answered Don Quijote, "are flat sheets of metal, and they're used like brass candlestick holders, banging one against the other, on the hollow parts, to produce a sound which, though it may not be terribly pleasing or harmonious, is nevertheless not displeasing, and goes well with the rustic quality of the bagpipes and tambourines. The name *albogues* comes from Arabic, like all the words in Spanish that start with *al*, namely *almohaza* [curry comb], *almorzar* [to lunch], *alhombra* [carpet], *alguacil* [policeman, bailiff, magistrate], *alhucema* [lavender], *almacén* [warehouse], *alcancía* [money box], and others of the same sort, though there are not too many more; our language has only three words we've borrowed from the Moors and which end in *i*, and these are *borceguí* [half boot], *zaquizamí* [garret, attic], and *maravedí* [old coin]. The words *alhelí* [gillyflower, carnation] and *alfaquí* can be seen to be from the Arabic, as much because of the *al* at the beginning as the *i* at the end.

"I've told you all this, in passing, because mentioning the name *albogues* reminded me of it.

"It will be extremely useful to us, in bringing all this to perfection, that I am something of a poet, as you know, and our college graduate, Samson Carrasco, is even more of one. I can't say anything about the priest, but I'd be willing to bet he's tried his hand at poetry, and so has Master Nicolás, I'm sure, because all barbers — or most of them, anyway — play the guitar and sing ballads [*copleros*]. I can sing the sorrows of absence; you can praise steadfast love; our Carrascón shepherd can sing about rejection; and our priest Curiambro can sing about whatever he wants to — and there you have it, the whole thing will go as well as you'd ever want."

Sancho replied:

"But I'm so unlucky, my lord, that I can't believe the day will actually come, and I'll really be a shepherd like that. Ah, what shining spoons I'll make when I get to be a shepherd! What nice fried breadcrumbs, what good rich cream, what garlands, what little pastoral thises and thats! And even if these things don't make me famous for being wise, they can still earn it for me, on account of being clever [*ingenioso*]! My daughter Sanchica will bring our meals to our shepherds' hut. But wait a minute! She's good looking, and there are shepherds who are sly and wicked, rather than innocent, and I don't want her to come for wool but go back shorn, because there are just as many lovers, and there's just as much lust, out in the fields as in the cities, and there's no difference between shepherds' huts and royal palaces, and if you take away the cause you stop the sin, and when the eyes don't see anything, the hearts don't break, and you're better off getting away from good men than asking them for help."

"Please, no more proverbs, Sancho," said Don Quijote, "because any single one of those would have been enough to explain what you meant, and as I've so often advised you, don't be so free with your proverbs, but hold yourself back, and in any case this seems to me to be preaching in the desert, and 'my mother may catch me at it, but I'll keep on fooling her.' "

"It seems to me, your grace," replied Sancho, "that what applies here is the old saying about the pot calling the kettle black. Here you are, scolding me for using proverbs, and there you go, your grace, reeling off a pair of them."

"But consider, Sancho," answered Don Quijote, "that I use proverbs when they're appropriate, and when I recite them they fit like a ring fits your fingers, but you just drag them in by their hair, you haul them in by the bucketload instead of ushering them on stage — and, unless I remember it wrong, I've already told you that proverbs are compressed wisdom, drawn from the thought and experience of our old wise men, and also that an irrelevant proverb sounds more like foolishness than wisdom. But let's leave this, and since I see it's getting to be night, let's go off the highway a bit and find a place to spend the night, for God knows what will come tomorrow."

They left the road, and they dined — late, and badly, and very much against Sancho's better judgment, for he kept thinking what a hard life knights errant lived, in the woods and the mountains, even though, in castles and rich houses, they sometimes experienced the pleasures of plenty, as at Don Diego de Moreno's, and at the wealthy Camacho's wedding. But he also reflected that it couldn't always be either day or night, and then he spent that night sleeping, while his master spent it wide awake.

Chapter Sixty-Eight

— *Don Quijote's bristly adventure*

The night was rather dark, even though there was a moon, for it was not visible, since sometimes the Lady Diana takes a walk down to the

Antipodes, leaving the mountains dark and the valleys dim. Don Quijote followed Nature's lead and slept his first sleep, but never descended into the second, quite the opposite of Sancho, who never knew a second sleep, because his rest extended from night until morning, all of which could be seen in his clear complexion and his freedom from care and worry. But Don Quijote's cares kept him so sleepless that he woke Sancho, saying:

"I am amazed, Sancho, at what self-assurance you feel: I suspect you must be made of marble, or of hard bronze, untroubled by any sentiment or any emotions. When you sleep, I lie awake; when I weep, you're singing; when I'm faint from fasting, you're lazy and breathless from too much food. But good servants should share their masters' suffering, and feel what they feel, even if they only seem to feel it. Look at this peaceful night, the solitude in which we find ourselves, fairly inviting us to break into our sleep with some vigil. Get up, by God, and go off a bit, and with good spirit and courageously, gratefully, and give yourself three or four hundred lashes toward the total necessary to disenchant Dulcinea, and I simply beg this of you, because I have no desire to be clutched in your grip, like the last time, because your arms are mighty ones. And after you've done this, we can spend the rest of the night singing, I of my absence and you of your faithfulness, starting to lead, here and now, the pastoral life we intend to live when we reach home."

"My lord," replied Sancho, "I'm not some monk who can get up in the middle of my sleep and whip myself, and I'm even less able to go from the extreme pain of whipping right into making music. You've got to let me sleep, your grace, and not plague me about this whipping business, because you're going to make me vow never to touch a hair on my coat, much less my skin."

"Ah what a flinty-hard heart! Oh merciless, merciless squire! Ah the wasted bread I've given you, and the ill-considered favors I've granted you, and still plan to grant you! You've been a governor, because of me, and because of me you can see yourself close to becoming what you want to be, a count or some title of the same sort, nor will the fulfillment of those pledges have to wait longer than the passing of this single year, since *post tenebras spero lucem* [After the darkness, comes the light]."[1]

"I don't understand that," answered Sancho. "All I know is that while I'm asleep, I'm never afraid, and I have no hopes, no struggles, no glories — and bless the man who invented sleep, a cloak to cover over all human thought, food that drives away hunger, water that banishes thirst, fire that heats up cold, chill that moderates passion and, finally, universal currency with which all things can be bought, weight and balance that brings the shepherd and the king, the fool and the wise, to the same level. There's only one bad thing about sleep, as far as I've ever heard, and that is that it resembles death, since there's very little difference between a sleeping man and a corpse."

"I've never heard you speak so eloquently as that, Sancho," said Don Quijote, "which tells me the proverb you like to cite, sometimes, is true: 'It's not where you're born that matters, but where you eat'."

1. Job 17:12 [*Translator's Note*].

"Oh god damn it, my lord and master!" replied Sancho. "Now it's not me who's stringing together proverbs, because they're dropping out of your mouth faster than they ever drop out of mine, except there's this difference between your proverbs and mine: your grace brings them in when they ought to come, and I bring them in here, there, and everywhere — but, just the same, they're still proverbs."

They were thus occupied when, suddenly, they felt a muffled rumble and heard a harsh noise that seemed to spread all over that valley. Don Quijote jumped up and grasped the hilt of his sword, and Sancho crouched down under his donkey, putting the bundle of armor and weapons on one side of him, and the donkey's packsaddle on the other, as shaking with fear as Don Quijote was excited and alert. The noise kept growing louder and louder, and coming ever closer to the two terrified men — or, anyway, to one terrified man, because everyone knows the other's bravery.

What it was, as it happened, was more than sixty pigs being driven to market at a fair, and the drovers had set out at that hour; the animals were making such a din, grunting and snorting, that Don Quijote and Sancho were deafened, and could not understand what was going on. The rambling, wide-ranging herd reached them and, without the slightest respect for Don Quijote's authority, or for Sancho's, went right over both of them, tumbling down Sancho's hasty trenches, and not only knocking over Don Quijote, but Rocinante, to boot. The wild rushing this way and that, the grunting, and the rapidity with which the filthy beasts came and went, left everything and everyone strewn across the ground — saddlebags, armor and weapons, the little donkey, Rocinante, Sancho, and Don Quijote.

Sancho got up as best he could, asking his master for his sword, and saying he wanted to kill half a dozen of those fat, rude pigs — for he by now realized what they were. Don Quijote replied:

"Let them be, my friend, for this humiliation is punishment for my sins, and is righteous chastisement from Heaven for a vanquished knight errant, letting jackals consume him, and wasps sting him, and pigs trample on him."

"Then it must also be punishment from Heaven," responded Sancho, "that the squires of such defeated knights be bitten by flies, eaten by lice, and attacked by hunger. If squires were sons of the knight they served, or very close relatives, it would be no wonder for the punishment to reach unto the fourth generation, but what have the Panzas got to do with the Quijotes? Never mind: let's turn over and settle down and sleep for what little is left of the night, and then God will give us the dawn, and we'll do better."

"You sleep, Sancho," answered Don Quijote, "because you were born to sleep — and I, who was born to keep a vigil, in what time is left between now and daylight I will let my thoughts roam, and I'll let them pour off in a song which, without your knowing it, I wrote in my head last night."

"As far as I'm concerned," replied Sancho, "thoughts that lead you to writing poetry can't amount to very much. You poeticize as much as you like, your grace, and I'll sleep as much as I can."

And then, stretching out on a properly sized piece of ground, he dropped into an easy sleep, undisturbed by commitments or doubts or the slightest sadness. Don Quijote, leaning up against the trunk of a beech, or perhaps it was an oak tree — again, Sidi Hamid Benengeli doesn't tell us what kind of tree it really was — and to the sound of his own sighs sang the following song:

> — Love, whenever my mind turns
> to the evil you've done me, terrible and harsh,
> I hurry toward Death's own darkness,
> hoping to finish your burning.
>
> But as I reach the gates
> of this harbor in my sea of torment,
> it seems so Heaven-sent
> that life seems lovely, and I stop and wait.
>
> Thus life remains my murderer,
> for Death returns me waking.
> Ah, what a novel fate,
> life and death together: unheard of![2]

Each of these stanzas was set to many sighs and no small number of tears, as if he were truly one whose heart had been pierced by his defeat, and by Dulcinea's absence.

At this point, daylight returned, and the sun's rays shone into Sancho's eyes, and he woke up, and stretched, and shook himself, and moved his sluggish limbs; he considered the ruin wreaked on his stores by the herd of pigs, and cursed (and even worse) the whole lot of them. Finally, they got back on the highway, and toward the end of the afternoon saw roughly ten mounted men coming toward them, along with four or five on foot. Don Quijote's heart leaped, and Sancho's beat harder, because these people were carrying lances and shields, and were marching like disciplined men of war. Don Quijote turned to Sancho, saying:

"Were I able to wield my weapons, Sancho, and my arms had not been tied by my promise, this troop marching toward us would be like child's play — but this just might be something different from what we fear it to be."

Just then the mounted men rode up and, silently raising their lances, surrounded Don Quijote and leveled their weapons at him, front and back, not saying a word but threatening him with death. One of those on foot, putting his finger to his lips (signaling to their captive, too, to be silent), took hold of Rocinante's bridle and drew him off the road, and then the others gathered up Sancho and the little donkey, all the while preserving a wonderful stillness, and went following after those who were carrying off Don Quijote — and though our knight wanted, several times, to ask where they were taking him or what they wanted, each time he opened his mouth they immediately closed it with the points of their lances, Sancho being treated in exactly the same style, for he too had barely begun

---

2. Translation of a madrigal set by Pietro Bembo (1470–1547) [*Translator's Note*].

to speak when one of the men on foot jabbed him with a spear-point, and obviously would have done the same to the little donkey, if he had tried to say anything. Night closed down on them and they quickened their pace — which worried the captives, especially when they heard occasional mutterings:

"Get going, you troglodytes!"

"Shut up, barbarians!"

"You'll pay for this, anthropophagians [cannibals]!"

"No complaining, Scythians!"

"Keep your eyes closed, you Polyphemian assassins!"

"Bloodthirsty lions!"

And other epithets just like these kept afflicting the ears of the miserable pair, master and man. Sancho said to himself:

"We're troggy lights? We're berberens — we're ants and profanians? We're little sitinens — the kind you call to, here sitty, here sitty? I don't like these names — this is a bad wind blowing across our threshing floor, and bad things come in bunches, like blows on a dog's back — dear God! Don't let all this go from bad to worse!"

Don Quijote felt himself totally at sea, unable to comprehend what all these savage names were supposed to signify, except that they did not seem to indicate anything good, and perhaps a good deal of evil. And then, about an hour after midnight, they came to a castle, which Don Quijote immediately recognized as the duke's, where not long before they had been guests.

"Mother of God!" he murmured, after recognizing the place. "What is all this? It's all politeness and fine living, here in this house — except once you've been defeated in combat the good turns to bad, and the bad turns to worse."

They rode into the castle's main courtyard, and found it readied and prepared in a fashion that only heightened their astonishment and doubled their fear, as the next chapter will make plain.

Chapter Sixty-Nine

— the strangest and most unusual thing that happens to Don Quijote in the whole of this great history

The captors who'd been on horseback dismounted and, together with the men on foot, picked up both Sancho and Don Quijote and carried them bodily into the courtyard, lit by the flaring light of almost a hundred torches set in holders, as well as by more than five hundred lamps in the balconies and galleries, so that even though it was the middle of the night (and a rather dark night), you could not have known it was not daytime. A tomb had been erected in the middle of the courtyard, about two yards off the ground, covered with a huge canopy of black velvet, and on its steps, all around, burned white wax candles set in silver candelabra; at the very top of the tomb there was the dead body of a beautiful girl, so excruciatingly beautiful, indeed, that she made even death look like loveliness.

Her head, garlanded with all sorts of braided, sweet-scented flowers, rested on a brocade pillow; her hands were crossed on her breast, holding, between them, a triumphant yellow palm branch.

To one side of the courtyard there was a platform, on which stood two chairs, and seated in them were two figures which, because they wore crowns on their heads and carried scepters in their hands, seemed to be kings, perhaps real, perhaps feigned. Beside this platform, and reached by a number of steps, there were two more chairs, and on these they deposited Don Quijote and Sancho, still preserving the same absolute silence and gesturing to their captives to do likewise — though our knight and his squire would have been silent even without these instructions, so struck with wonder that their tongues might as well have been tied.

Then two persons of importance, accompanied by a good many attendants, ascended the platform, and Don Quijote immediately recognized his host and hostess, the duke and duchess, who proceeded to seat themselves on two richly decorated chairs just alongside the two king-like figures. Who would not have been struck dumb by all this, especially when we add that Don Quijote had also recognized the body on top of the tomb as that of the lovely Altisidora?

As the duke and duchess came up the stairs to the platform, Don Quijote and Sancho rose and made them a deep bow, and the noble pair, slightly inclining their heads, returned the sign of recognition and acknowledgment.

At this point, an official of some sort came across the platform, walked over to Sancho, and draped over him a long, stout robe, completely black and painted all over with flickering flames, then took off Sancho's cap and placed on his head a cone-shaped cardboard hat of the sort worn by those whom the Holy Inquisition is punishing, and, bending to Sancho's ear, whispered that he was not to open his mouth or they would have to gag him, or perhaps kill him on the spot. Looking himself up and down, Sancho saw that he was being consumed by fire, but since the flames did not burn him he wasn't worried about them. He took off the cardboard hat, looked it over too, saw that it was painted with devils, and then put it on again, saying to himself:

"So far, anyway, that fire hasn't burned me, and those demons haven't carried me off."

Don Quijote too examined his squire and, though fear had dulled his senses, he couldn't help laughing at Sancho's appearance.

Soft and gentle flute music began to sound, at this point, apparently from underneath the tomb, and, not being overshadowed by a human voice (the silence being still unbroken), it seemed gentle, even loving. Then suddenly, alongside the apparently dead woman's pillowed head, there appeared a handsome young man dressed, like an antique Roman, in a toga, who proceeded to sing the following stanzas, to the sound of a harp which he himself played:

> — While Altisidora, her life cut short
> by Don Quijote's cruelty,
> comes back to life, and this magic court

sees ladies dressed in mourning mufti,
and my lady duchess dresses her maids
in heavy flannels and serge,
I'll sing this beauty, and the price she paid,
in verses worthy of Orpheus' urge.

— Nor does my song speak only of life,
for I also sing the language of death,
and my frozen tongue, thus shorn of breath,
still pours out praise for her loving strife,
as my soul, set free from its narrow prison,
rises across the Stygian lake,
and flying above the hellish chasm
hails your beauty, and death's hold breaks.[1]

"Enough," pronounced one of the king-like figures, "enough, divine singer, for there can be no end to rehearsing the matchless Altisidora's charms or the tale of her death — yet not death, as the ignorant world knows it, but still living on Fame's warm tongue and in the suffering which Sancho Panza, who has now come here, must experience, to return her to the light she has lost, and so, oh dread Rhadamanthus, since you and I together sit in judgment, deep in the gloomy caverns of Lethe,[2] and you well know all that the inscrutable shades have declared necessary for returning this damsel to life, speak! Tell it, now, so we need wait no longer for that blessing to which, with her return, we look forward!"

Minos had barely finished speaking when his companion and fellow judge, Rhadamanthus, rose to his feet and said:

"Now, servants of this house, high and low, great and small! Now, come one and all and administer twenty-five full slaps to Sancho Panza's face, plus twelve pinches and six pinpricks on his arms and back, for this is the ceremony on which Altisidora's life depends!"

Sancho, hearing this, broke his silence:

"The hell with this! I'd just as soon turn myself into a Turk as have my mug slapped and pawed! Mother of God! What has manhandling my face got to do with resurrecting this lady? Let the old lady enjoy her spinach![3] They put a spell on Dulcinea, and I'm supposed to whip myself, so they can take it off again; Altisidora dies from who knows what God-given sickness, and to bring her back to life they have to give me twenty-five slaps and stick me full of holes and, Mother of God, turn my arms black and blue with bruises! Go find somebody's brother-in-law and play these games with him, because I'm an old dog, by God, and you're not going to play 'nice doggy, nice doggy' with me!"

"Then die!" said Rhadamanthus sternly. "Or else calm yourself, you bloodthirsty tiger! Make yourself humble, oh arrogant Nimrod! Suffer, and be silent, for nothing impossible is demanded of you, nor is it for you to

---

1. Stanza 2 is by Garcilaso de la Vega [*Translator's Note*].
2. Minos (mythical king of Crete) and Rhadamanthus, brothers who in life had quarreled, became two of the judges in antiquity's Hell [*Translator's Note*].
3. Proverbial saying: *Regostóse la vieja a los bledos, ni dejó verdes ni secos*, "The old lady loved her spinach, and every bit of it [i.e., whether green or dried out] got finished" [*Translator's Note*].

question the obstacles that must now be surmounted. You must be slapped. You must be riddled with holes. You must groan as you are pinched. Now then! Come, servants of this house, and do my bidding — or else, in the name of an honest man, we shall have to see just why you were born!"

At this, six ladies in waiting came across the courtyard, walking one directly behind the other, four of them wearing spectacles, and all of them with their right hands raised on high, showing three inches of bare wrist (as fashion now decrees) to make their hands look larger. Sancho had no sooner seen them, than he bellowed like a bull:

"Maybe I could let the whole world manhandle my face, but let *dueñas* touch me? Never! Go on and scratch me up, the way you did my master, right here in this very castle! Pierce my body with sharp daggers! Tear the flesh off my arms with red-hot tongs! I'll bear it all, and patiently, just to please the duke and duchess over here. But though the Devil carry me off, I won't let any *dueñas* touch me!"

And then Don Quijote too broke his silence, saying to Sancho:

"Patience, my son, and do what these gentlemen ask of you, and give thanks to Heaven for having granted you such power that your martyrdom can disenchant the enchanted, and even resurrect the dead."

Then the ladies-in-waiting closed in on Sancho, and he, calmer and convinced, now, of what he had to do, sat down in his chair once more and lifted his face and his beard to the first of the women, who let him have a royal slap, and immediately afterward bowed to him, low and reverently.

"Try a little less courtesy, *señora dueña*," said Sancho, "and less cosmetic stuff, too, because, by God, your hands smell of vinegar!"[4]

All the ladies in waiting came and delivered their slaps, and a horde of others from the household pinched him — but it was the pinsticking he couldn't bear, so he rose up from his chair, visibly angry, and seizing a lighted torch that was blazing away, nearby, took out after the *dueñas* and all his other executioners, crying:

"Away with you, you instruments of the devil! I'm not like a man made out of brass, who wouldn't feel this torture!"

Just then Altisidora, who must have been getting tired, after lying on her back, absolutely still, for such a long time, turned over on her side, and when those who were watching saw this, they began to cry as if with one voice:

"Altisidora's alive! Altisidora's alive!"

Rhadamanthus commanded Sancho to purge himself of his anger, for he had already accomplished what he'd set out to do.

The moment Don Quijote saw Altisidora move, he went down on his knees in front of Sancho, saying:

"Oh son of my heart and no more my squire, now is the time to give yourself those lashes you must give, for Dulcinea to be disenchanted! Now is the time, now when you're brimming with magical power, and can truly accomplish the blessed work we await from you."

---

4. Vinegar was used, cosmetically, to whiten both hands and faces [*Translator's Note*].

To which Sancho replied:

"To me, that looks like piling one trick on another, not pouring honey on pancakes. Lashes after pinches and slaps and pinsticking — oh, that would be real fun. Why not just take a big rock, and tie it around my neck, and drop me into a well? — because that wouldn't be so bad, if I have to cure the world's problems by being everybody's scapegoat. Leave me alone — or else, by God, I'll knock over this whole Punch and Judy show."

At which moment, Altisidora sat up on the tomb, and instantaneously pipes began to sound, accompanied by flutes and by the voices of everyone there, calling out:

"Long live Altisidora! Long live Altisidora!"

The duke and duchess rose to their feet, as did Kings Minos and Rhadamanthus, and all of them, Don Quijote and Sancho too, went to welcome Altisidora and take her down from the tomb, and she, as if newly recovered from a long fainting fit, bowed to the duke and duchess and, looking at Don Quijote out of the corner of her eye, said to him:

"May God forgive you, loveless knight, because your cruelty has caused me to be in the other world, as nearly as I can tell, for a thousand years or more. And you, oh you, most merciful squire in the world! I owe my life to you, only you. Accept, oh Sancho my friend, to have and to hold from this day on, six chemises which I hereby promise you, from which you can have six shirts made, and though they may not be completely new, they are certainly very clean."

Sancho kissed her hands, kneeling, pointed hat in hand. The duke ordered that he be relieved of the pointed hat and given his proper cap, and that they take away his robe with all its flames and give him his own jacket. Sancho asked the duke to let him keep both the robe and the pointed hat, for he wanted to bring them home with him, as tokens and memorials of this incredible event. The duchess answered that indeed he should have them, for he already knew how great a friend of his she was. The duke then directed that they clear the courtyard, and that everyone go back to their rooms, and Don Quijote and Sancho be given the quarters they already knew so well.

Chapter Seventy

— which follows chapter sixty-nine, and deals with matters that, for the understanding of this whole history, must be clearly understood

That night, Sancho slept on a cot in Don Quijote's room, something he would have just as soon gotten out of, had he been able, because he knew perfectly well that his master would keep him awake with questions and answers, and he didn't feel particularly like talking, because the pain through which he had suffered had not yet gone away, and he had no inclination to set his tongue wagging: it would have done him more good to sleep all alone, in a tiny hut, rather than in that rich apartment, but with his master for company. And his concern was so justified, and his suspicion so accurate, that Don Quijote had barely climbed into his bed before he asked:

"What do you think, Sancho, of what happened tonight? The force of amorous disdain, clearly, is immense, because you have seen with your own eyes Altisidora dead, not pierced by real arrows, nor by some sword, nor by any instrument of war, nor by any mortal poison, but simply because of the harsh disdain I have so consistently displayed toward her."

"She could have died whenever she wanted to, and however she wanted to," replied Sancho, "and let me stay home, because in all my life I've never made love to her or rejected her. I haven't the least, faintest idea how the good health of a girl like Altisidora, who's not as wise as she is fickle, could possibly, as I've said before, have anything to do with Sancho Panza's suffering. I'm beginning to understand pretty clearly and distinctly, all right, that there are enchanters and enchantments in the world, but may God keep me away from them, because I don't know how to do it for myself, and now, all the same, let me beg your grace to please let me go to sleep, and not to ask me any more questions, unless you want me to throw myself down out of a window."

"Sleep, Sancho my friend," replied Don Quijote, "if the pinpricks and the scratches and the slaps you got will let you."

"The slaps weren't painful," replied Sancho, "except that they came from *dueñas*, god damn them, so let me again ask your grace to let me sleep, for sleep lightens the miseries we feel when we're awake."

"So be it," said Don Quijote, "and may God be with you."

They both fell asleep — and, while they were sleeping, the author of this great history, Sidi Hamid, wanted to set down and explain what prompted the duke and duchess to create the whole scheme just narrated. He writes that Samson Carrasco, our college graduate, was unable to get his defeat out of his mind, after Don Quijote had tumbled the Knight of the Mirrors off his horse and defeated him, thus wiping out and undoing all the plans he'd made, so he wanted to try his hand at it once more, hoping for a better result the second time around, and when the page who'd brought the letters and the duchess' present to Teresa Panza, Sancho's wife, told him where Don Quijote was, he hunted up new armor and a new horse, and painted a white moon on his shield, then loaded the whole apparatus on a jackass, led by a peasant, this time, and not by his former squire, Tomás Cecial, to keep either Sancho or Don Quijote from recognizing him.

When he got to the duke's castle, he was told Don Quijote's destination and the route our knight was following, intending to enlist in the jousting tournaments at Zaragosa. The duke also informed him of the joke about disenchanting Dulcinea, and how it was likely to be painful to Sancho's rear end. He heard about Sancho's joke on his master, too, making Don Quijote think Dulcinea had been enchanted and turned into a peasant girl, and then the duke told him how his wife, the duchess, had persuaded Sancho that it was he himself who was under a spell, because Dulcinea was really and truly enchanted, and all of this amused and considerably astonished the college graduate, struck by Sancho's combination of keenness and simplicity, as well as by the extent of Don Quijote's madness.

The duke asked Samson Carrasco, whether or not he defeated Don Quijote, to come back to the castle and tell him how things had gone. Carrasco agreed; rode off in search of our knight; did not find him in Zaragosa; rode on and did what has already been narrated.

Our college graduate then went back to the castle and told the duke what had happened, and the terms under which the battle had been fought, and that Don Quijote was already on his way home, like a good knight errant, to fulfill his pledge about retiring for a year, during which time, Carrasco said, it might be possible to cure him of his madness, this having been his own reason for undergoing these assorted knightly transformations, because it seemed to him a pitiful affair, seeing a gentleman with as fine a mind as Don Quijote so out of his senses. Whereupon he took his farewell of the duke and set out homeward, expecting that Don Quijote, who was coming along behind him, would soon be there as well.

Which was when the duke decided to cook up the joke about Altisidora's death, for he took immense pleasure in everything Sancho and Don Quijote said and did, so he sent many of his people, mounted and on foot, up and down all the roads, near and far, that Don Quijote might have taken, so that if they found him they could bring him, one way or another, back to the castle. They did find him, the duke was notified and, he having already arranged all the things that had to be done, immediately ordered the torches lit, and all the lights set around the courtyard, and Altisidora laid on her tomb, and all the rest of the apparatus (of which so lively an account has been given) set in motion, all of it so very well managed that between farce and reality there was remarkably little difference.

Sidi Hamid also records that, in his opinion, those who concocted the joke were quite as crazy as those who were obliged to experience it, and that in working so hard to make fun of fools, the duke and duchess had come within an inch of looking like fools themselves. As for the fools in question, one of them slept like a rock, while the other kept vigil over his disordered thoughts, until daylight returned and, with it, the desire to rise once more, for laziness was never to Don Quijote's liking, whether he woke as winner or loser.

Altisidora — now, as Don Quijote believed, returned from the dead — suddenly swept into Don Quijote's room, as her master and mistress had instructed, leaning on a walking stick of fine black ebony, still wearing the garland set on her head while she'd been on her tomb, and garbed in a flowing tunic of white taffeta, embroidered with gold flowers, her hair loose down her back. Her presence so unsettled and upset him that he shrank virtually all the way down under the covers, struck utterly dumb, neither greeting her nor uttering a single courteous word. Altisidora seated herself on a chair, near the head of his bed, and after giving a long, langorous sigh, spoke to him in a soft and feeble voice:

"When wellborn women and modest maidens ride roughshod over honor, letting their tongues break free of every proper restriction and making public the secrets hidden deep in their hearts, they find themselves in singular difficulties. And I am one such woman, my lord Don Quijote de La Mancha, hard-pressed, vanquished, and lost in love — and yet, for all that, I remain long-suffering and modest, and so much so that my soul silently burst and I lost my life. And I have spent two days lying dead, oh hard-hearted knight! and all because of the harshness with which you have treated me:

> Oh you, set harder than marble against my sighs![1]

Or so they tell me, who saw me so, and had Love not taken pity on me, and entrusted my salvation to your good squire's sufferings, it is in that other world where I would have remained."

"Love might have done better," said Sancho, "to entrust it to my donkey's sufferings, and I would have been much obliged to him. But tell me, my lady (and may Heaven provide you with a tenderer lover than my master), what did you see, there in that other world? What goes on, down in Hell? Because of course that's where those who die of despair have to go."

"To tell you the truth," replied Altisidora, "I must not have been completely dead, because I never went to Hell; if I had gone there, truly I could never have left, though I would have wanted to. What did happen was that I came to a gate, where a dozen or so devils were playing ball, all of them dressed in jackets and breeches, with Vandyke collars trimmed in Dutch lace and an edging of the same material, which served them as cuffs, three inches of wrist being left exposed, to make their hands seem longer, and in those hands they held rackets made of fire, instead of wood — but what most astonished me was that, instead of balls, they were using what looked to me like books, all puffed up with hot air and trash, which was indeed a wonderful and novel sight. But this didn't surprise me so much as seeing that, though those who win are usually happy, in the games we play here, and those who lose are unhappy, there all the players were grunting and growling and muttering and cursing."

"There's nothing surprising about that," said Sancho, "because devils can't be happy whether they're playing or not, or winning or losing."

"I suppose so," replied Altisidora. "But there was something else that surprises me, too — I mean, that surprised me, back then — which was the very first time one of those balls got hit, that was the end of it, they could never use it again, so they had to keep changing books, old ones and new ones, it didn't matter, and it was really something to behold. There was one of them, absolutely brand new and nicely bound, and they gave it such a whack that they spilled out its guts and scattered all its pages. One of the devils said to another: 'Hey, what book is that?' And the second devil answered: 'That's the so-called second part of Don Quijote de La Mancha's history, not written by Sidi Hamid, the original author, but by some Aragonese fellow who's supposed to come from Tordesillas.' 'Get it out of here,' said the first devil, 'and throw it down into the very deepest pit of Hell: I don't ever want to see it again.' 'Is it really that bad?' asked the second devil. 'It's so bad,' the first one said, 'that even if I myself tried to write a worse one, I couldn't do it.' And so they went on playing, whacking away at other books, while I, having heard them speak of Don

---

1. Adapted from *Égloga I* [First Eclogue] of Garcilaso de la Vega (1501–1536), whose pastoral hero Salicio (a partial anagram for the poet himself) addresses the absent Galatea: "¡O más dura que mármol a mis quejas . . . !"

Quijote, for whom I feel such mad passion, did my best to fix this vision in my memory."

"It surely must have been a vision," said Don Quijote, "because I'm the only Don Quijote in the world, and though this so-called history has for some time been making the rounds, going from hand to hand, it doesn't stay anywhere, because everyone kicks it out. I'm not sorry to hear that I'm wandering through the darkest depths of Hell, nor even in the clear light of earth, in such a fantastic embodiment, because I'm not the person that history is about. Had it been any good, faithful and truthful, it could have lived for centuries, but since it's so very bad, it won't have much of a journey from the cradle to the grave."

Altisidora was just about to go on complaining about Don Quijote, when he said to her:

"I've often told you, my lady, that it pains me to find myself in your thoughts, since all they can ever expect from my own thoughts is gratitude, and not any help whatever, for I was born to belong to Dulcinea del Toboso, and the Fates, if there be such creatures, have irrevocably dedicated me to her, and even to contemplate that some other beautiful lady can take the place she holds in my heart is to imagine the unimaginable. And this, I think, should be sufficient disillusionment for you to retreat behind the barriers of your modesty, for nobody can be obliged to do what cannot be done."

At this, Altisidora flared up and grew angry, and said:

"In the name of the Lord, you dried-up old fish, you mouldy, metallic soul, you're colder and harder than some pigheaded peasant who's been asked for a favor he's determined not to give! I'll rip out your eyes, if I ever get hold of you! Do you really think, you born loser, you beaten-up hulk, that I died for *you*? Everything you saw last night was all a fake, because I'm not the kind of woman who needs to let the dirt at the end of one of my fingernails suffer, much less kill myself, just for a camel like you!"

"Now *that* I can certainly believe," said Sancho, "because all this stuff about people dying for love just makes me laugh. They can talk about it, all right, but as for doing it, try telling that to Judas."

In the middle of this light conversation, the musician, singer, and poet who had sung the two stanzas, quoted earlier, came into the room, and bowing low to Don Quijote, said:

"Sir knight, your grace, I count myself one of your most devoted servants, for I have been drawn to you for a very long time, as much for your reputation as for your glorious deeds."

Don Quijote responded:

"Please tell me who you are, your grace, so my heart can reply to you as you properly deserve."

The young fellow answered that he was last night's musician and poetic celebrant.

"Ah," said Don Quijote, "clearly your grace possesses a remarkable voice, but what you sang did not strike me as entirely fitting, for what has Garcilaso's poem got to do with this lady's death?"

"You should not be surprised at that, your grace," replied the musician, "because the uncouth poets of this age of ours are quite accustomed to writing and stealing exactly as they please, no matter whether it has any relevance, for they can write off whatever nonsense they care to sing or scribble as mere poetic license."

Don Quijote wanted to respond, but he was prevented by the duke and duchess, who just then came to see him, and there followed a long and delightful conversation with them, during which Sancho said so many witty things, and so many wicked ones, that the duke and duchess, when they left, were astonished all over again, as much by his foolishness as by his keen mind. Don Quijote asked their permission to leave the castle that very day, since defeated knights like him were better lodged in a pigsty than in a royal palace. They freely granted him permission to leave; the duchess asked if Altisidora was still in his good graces. He answered:

"My lady, Your Highness ought to know that whatever may be wrong with this young woman comes solely from not being kept busy, and the cure for her disease is good, hard work. She told me, right here in this room, that they wear lace in Hell, and since she surely knows how to make it, let it be constantly in her hands, because if she's busy plying her needle, then her mind won't be conjuring up images of anyone she thinks she loves: that I think is the truth, and it is my firm opinion and the advice I give you."

"Me too," added Sancho, "because in all my life I've never seen a lacemaker who died of love, and girls who are working hard think a lot more about getting their tasks done than about their love affairs. And I know what I'm talking about, because when I'm digging a ditch I never think about my wife, my Teresa Panza, even though I love her more than my own eyelashes."

"Well said, Sancho," said the duchess, "and I will make sure that, from now on, my Alisidora is kept busy doing linen embroidery, because she does it extremely well."

"You won't need to resort to any such measures, my lady," said Altisidora, "because the very thought of how cruelly this monster of perversity has treated me will wipe him out of my memory, without the need for any other device. And with your permission, Your Majesty, I wish now to leave this room, so I need never again see before my eyes — not his sad face, but his horrible, ugly face."

"I am reminded," said the duke, "of what they often say:

> Whoever's hurling insults
> is almost ready to forgive."[2]

Altisidora pretended to be wiping her eyes with her handkerchief, then she curtsied to her master and mistress and hurried out of the room.

"Tough luck, you poor girl," said Sancho, "and it's tough, I say, because, worse luck, you hit on a Spartan soul and an oak-hard heart. Now if you'd come after me, by God, a different cock would have crowed for you!"

Which ended the conversation; Don Quijote rose and dressed, dined with the duke and duchess, and left the castle that same afternoon.

2. A common ballad verse, used often and with many variations [*Translator's Note*].

Chapter Seventy-One

— what happened to Don Quijote and Sancho, his squire, as they were traveling back home

A defeated and exhausted Don Quijote jogged along, thinking extremely gloomy thoughts, in one regard, but very happy ones, in another. His sadness stemmed from his defeat, and his happiness from remembering how wonderfully well Sancho had behaved, in Altisidora's resurrection, though he retained some doubt about the lovelorn damsel having really been dead. Sancho walked along most unhappily, for it deeply saddened him that Altisidora had not kept her word about the six chemises, and as he chewed this around and around in his mind, he finally said to his master:

"Really, my lord, I've got to be the unluckiest doctor anywhere in the world, because there are lots of doctors who cure people by killing them, but still want to be paid for their trouble, when all they really did was sign a prescription for some medicine that the druggist, and not the doctor, has to fix up, and the swindle's complete, but I have to shed real drops of blood, to cure these people, and I have to get slapped and pinched and stuck with pins and whipped, and nobody pays me a cent. Well, I swear to God, let them bring me one more sick man, and they'll have to grease my palms before I'll cure him, because the abbot earns his dinner by singing, and I'm not ready to believe Heaven gave me these powers I have, just so I can give them away, strictly for free."

"I think you're absolutely right, Sancho my friend," replied Don Quijote, "and Altisidora has done a very bad thing in not giving you those promised chemises, and though these powers came to you *gratis data* [given for free] and cost you no study or effort whatever, suffering personal pain amounts to more than merely studying. I can tell you, for myself, that if you'd wanted to be paid for those lashes which will disenchant Dulcinea, I'd have long since, and very gladly, given you the money, though I am not entirely sure that payment would not interfere with the potency of the remedy, and I would not want payment to interfere with the medicine's efficacy. Just the same, it seems to me there's not a great deal to be lost in trying the experiment: just consider, Sancho, what you might want, and then do the whipping and pay yourself, because you are guardian of my money."

At this offer, Sancho opened both his eyes and his ears a full foot or more, and assured himself that, on these terms, he'd be delighted to whip himself.

"So now, my lord," he said to his master, "I'd like to make use of myself, to make your grace happy, if you make it worth my while, because love of my wife and children requires me to be interested. So tell me, your grace: how much will you pay me, per lash?"

"Were I obliged to pay you, Sancho," replied Don Quijote, "what the magnitude and immensity of this remedy truly deserves, all the treasure of Venice, plus that in the mines of Potosí, would not be sufficient. Add up what money you have of mine, and then put a price on each lash."

"There are supposed to be three thousand and three hundred and some lashes," replied Sancho, "of which I've already given myself five, and all the rest are still left. Stick those five in with the others, and we have a total of three thousand and three hundred, and, at a quarter of a dollar per lash (and I wouldn't take less, even if the whole world told me to), that adds up to three thousand and three hundred quarters of a dollar, so let's first take three thousand quarters, which make a thousand and five hundred half dollars, which make seven hundred and fifty whole dollars, and then we take the three hundred quarters, which makes a hundred and fifty half dollars, which makes seventy-five whole dollars, and if we add the seven hundred and fifty to that, we get a total eight hundred and twenty-five dollars. So I'll separate this much from your grace's money, which I have in my possession, and I'll go back to my own house rich and happy, though well-whipped, because you won't get what you want[1] . . . but I won't say any more."

"Ah, blessed Sancho! Ah, warm-hearted Sancho!" replied Don Quijote. "How grateful both Dulcinea and I will be to you, all the rest of our lives, as Heaven sees fit to grant them to us! If she becomes who she was (which she can't be, until she does), her misfortune will have been fortunate, and my victory will be the happiest of triumphs! So tell me, Sancho, when you want to begin, because if you do it soon, I'll add in another hundred dollars."

"When?" replied Sancho. "Tonight, and no mistake about it. Make sure that we're out in the fields, your grace, right out under the open sky, and I'll whip myself to the bones."

Don Quijote could not have longed for nightfall with greater anxiety and, by the time it actually arrived, it seemed to him that the wheels of Apollo's golden chariot must have been broken, and daylight stretched out far beyond its usual bounds, just as it happens to lovers, for whom time moves to the measure of their desires. And so, finally, they went into a pleasant grove of trees, just a little off the highway, and took off Rocinante's saddle, and the little donkey's saddlebags, and stretched out on the green grass and ate the supper Sancho supplied, and then Sancho, having made a powerful, flexible whip out of the donkey's halter and harness ropes, stepped some twenty paces away from his master, into a grove of beech trees. Seeing him march off, boldly and with a light step, Don Quijote said:

"Be careful, my friend, not to cut yourself to pieces; take your time, stroke by stroke; don't rush and, halfway through, find you're out of breath; what I mean is, don't whip yourself so hard that, before you reach the required number, you leave this life behind. And so you keep an exact count, neither too much nor too little, I will stand over here and use my rosary beads to count the lashes you give yourself. May Heaven smile on you, as your good intentions deserve that it should."

"A man who pays his debts doesn't mind depositing some security," replied Sancho. "I plan to lay it on, without killing myself, so I do really suffer, because that's got to be the heart of this miracle."

---

1. *No se toman truchas, a bragas enjutas*, "You won't get what you want if you just sit on your ass" [*Translator's Note*].

Then he pulled off his shirt, picked up the rope, and began to whip himself, and Don Quijote began to count the strokes.

Once Sancho had given himself six or eight good strokes, the game stopped being funny, and the price began to seem far too low, so he stopped for a moment and told his master he'd made a bad mistake, because lashes like these deserved to be paid for at the rate of a whole dollar apiece, not just a quarter of a dollar.

"Go on, Sancho, and don't give up," Don Quijote told him, "because I'll double my bid."

"In that case," said Sancho, "I'll leave it to God, and let it rain lashes!"

But the rascal stopped laying them on his own shoulders, and began whipping the trees, sighing from time to time as if every stroke was ripping out his soul. This moved Don Quijote and, afraid that Sancho might actually kill himself, and through such negligence keep his master from attaining the goal he so longed for, he said:

"For your own sake, my friend, let's stop this business for the time being, because this medicine seems to me somewhat too severe, and it would be better to accomplish things one step at a time. Zamora[2] was not won in an hour. You've given yourself more than a thousand blows, unless I've counted wrong. Let that be enough for now, because, to put it crudely, the donkey can manage the load, but not the overload."

"No, no, my lord," replied Sancho. "No one's going to say about me, 'They paid him to work well, but he shirked his work like hell.' You just go back where you were, my lord, and let me give myself at least another thousand, because just a couple of flourishes like these and your business will be done, and a little more."

"Since you're so much in the mood," said Don Quijote, "Heaven help you, and whip on, while I stand aside."

Sancho went back to work with such enthusiasm that he stripped the bark from a good many trees, so vigorously did he ply his whip; and once he called out, giving a beech trunk a particularly savage stroke:

"Here you will die, Samson, and everyone else with you!"

His pitiful voice, and the fierce, biting thud of his whip, brought Don Quijote on the run, and, seizing the twisted rope being used as Sancho's lash, he exclaimed:

"Sancho, my friend, Fate will not let you give up your life, just to please me, for you are your wife's and your children's support. Dulcinea can wait for a better opportunity, and I will keep myself within the bounds of hope soon to be satisfied, and wait till you have recuperated and recovered your strength, and then we can finish this business to everyone's satisfaction."

"If that's the way you want it, my lord," replied Sancho, "fine: that's the way we'll do it. So throw your cloak on this back of mine, because I'm sweating and I don't want to catch cold, because people who aren't used to scourging themselves run that risk."

Don Quijote obliged him and, leaving himself in his shirt sleeves,

2. Refers to the long siege of Zamora by King Sancho II of Castile, during the war of succession caused by the division of the kingdom of Fernando I (1035–1065). A Spanish equivalent for "Rome wasn't built in a day."

wrapped Sancho in his cloak; Sancho slept till sunrise, and then they continued their journey, breaking it — for the time being — at a village six or seven miles down the road. They dismounted at an inn, which Don Quijote recognized for what it was, not taking it for a castle with a great moat, tall towers, iron portcullises, and a drawbridge that went up and down — and indeed, ever since his defeat in combat, he had spoken more rationally on all manner of subjects, as we shall see in a moment. He was lodged in a room on the ground floor, which was decorated with old tapestries, of the sort usually found in little towns and villages, instead of the more usual painted leather hangings. One of these tapestries, very crudely executed, showed Helen being carried off, dashing Paris stealing her away from Menelaus; another depicted the story of Dido and Aeneas, with her up on a high tower, waving something like half a bed-sheet to her fleeing guest, who was on the high seas in a frigate or brig.

He noted that, in these representations, Helen was hardly being forced to leave her husband, for she was shown laughing slyly and craftily, but the lovely Dido was shedding tears the size of walnuts. Don Quijote remarked, seeing this:

"These two ladies were extremely unfortunate, not having been born in our time, and I am supremely unfortunate, not having been born in theirs, for had I dealt with those gentlemen, Troy would not have been burned, nor Carthage destroyed: all I would have had to do was kill Paris, to avoid all those tragedies."

"I'll bet," said Sancho, "that before too long there won't be a restaurant, or a tavern, or an inn, or even a barber shop that doesn't have a painting of our great doings. But I'd like them to be painted by someone better than the fellow who did these."

"You're right, Sancho," said Don Quijote, "because this painter reminds me of Orbaneja, from Úbeda, because when they asked him what he was painting, he'd answer: 'Whatever comes out,' so if by chance he painted a rooster, he'd write underneath it: 'This is a rooster,' so no one would think it was a fox. I feel the same way, Sancho, about the painter, or writer (and they amount to the same thing), who gave the world this new Don Quijote who's going around: the man must have just painted or written whatever came out, or else he was like a poet named Mauléon, who used to be at Court and, when they asked him a question, he'd answer anything that came into his head, and someone asked him what *Deum de Deo* [God from God] meant, and he answered: 'Let him hit me anywhere he can' [*Dé donde diere*]. But leaving that subject, Sancho, tell me: do you plan on giving yourself another whipping tonight, and if so, do you prefer doing it inside or out in the open air?"

"By God, sir," answered Sancho, "for what I plan on giving myself, I can manage inside or out — but, just the same, I think I'd rather do it where there are trees, because they kind of keep me company, and they really help me bear the pain."

"Well, we can't hurry things like that, Sancho my friend," said Don Quijote, "because you have to get yourself strong again, so it will have to keep until we get home, because we'll be there, at the latest, the day after tomorrow."

Sancho answered that it was entirely up to his master, but he himself would prefer to get the whole business over and done with, while his blood was still up and he was ripe for the picking, because there was always a risk in waiting, and 'Man proposes, but God disposes,' and 'A bird in the hand is worth two in the bush,' and 'one of "I'll take that" is worth two of "I'll give you." ' "

"No more proverbs, Sancho, please, in the name of God," said Don Quijote. "You seem to be *sicut erat* [returning to what you were]; just speak straightforwardly, plainly, and don't complicate things, because as I've often told you, and you'll find out it's true, 'one good loaf of bread is worth a hundred fancy cakes.' "

"I don't understand why I'm like that," replied Sancho, "because I can't say anything without using proverbs, and every proverb I think of seems to me right on target — but I'll try to do better, if I can."

And, for the moment, that was the end of their conversation.

Chapter Seventy-Two

— *how Don Quijote and Sancho came home*

Don Quijote and Sancho spent the entire day right where they were, and in the same inn, waiting for nightfall, the one so he could finish, out in the open air, the flogging he'd begun, and the other longing to see the same task completed, for it was his heart's very desire. A traveler on horseback arrived at the inn, accompanied by three or four servants, one of whom said to his master:

"You can take your siesta here, your grace, Don Alvaro Tarfe:[1] the inn seems clean and cool."

Hearing this, Don Quijote said to Sancho:

"Look, Sancho: when I leafed through that book, the one about the second part of my history, I think I remember seeing that name, Don Alvaro Tarfe."

"That may be," answered Sancho. "Let's let him dismount, and then we can find out."

The gentleman got off his horse, and the innkeeper gave him a room exactly opposite Don Quijote's, decorated with different tapestry paintings, but of the same sort. Having changed into light summer clothing, the newly arrived gentleman walked out to the inn's spacious, cool front hall, where Don Quijote was strolling, and asked him:

"My dear sir, in what direction might your grace be heading?"

Don Quijote answered:

"To a village near here, of which I am a native. And you, your grace, where are you headed?"

"I, sir," replied the gentleman, "am going to Granada, which is where I come from."

"And a very good place to be from!" replied Don Quijote. "But please

---

1. A character invented in the false version of volume 2 by Avellaneda [*Translator's Note*].

tell me your name, your grace, because I suspect it might be more important for me to know than I can readily explain."

"My name," said the other guest, "is Don Alvaro Tarfe."

To which Don Quijote responded:

"Then I believe your grace must certainly be the same Don Alvaro Tarfe who appears in the second part of *The History of Don Quijote de La Mancha*, recently printed and given to the world by a new author."

"I am he," replied the gentleman, "and the said Don Quijote, principal figure in that history, is my very great friend, and indeed it was I who took him away from his village — or, at least, was responsible for his so doing — to attend some jousting tournaments in Zaragoza, where I myself was going, and furthermore I have done him no end of kindnesses, including saving him from a good hiding by the public executioner, when he was far too daring for his own good."

"But tell me, your grace Don Alvaro Tarfe, do I resemble this Don Quijote of whom you speak?"

"No, not in the least," replied the other guest.

"And this Don Quijote," our knight continued, "did he have with him a squire named Sancho Panza?"

"He did indeed," replied Don Alvaro, "and although he has the reputation of being quite a wit, I never heard him say anything in any way humorous."

"I can certainly believe that," said Sancho, at this point, "since it's not for everyone to be witty, and this Sancho Panza you're talking about, my dear sir, must be some sort of monstrous rascal, and all in all a nobody and a thief — because the real Sancho Panza happens to be me, and I think I create a lot more smiles than I do tears, and if you don't think so, make the experiment, your grace, and follow along behind me for a year or so, and you'll see it keeps happening to me, no matter what, that without my even knowing, sometimes, what I'm saying, everyone who hears me starts laughing — and the real Don Quijote de La Mancha, the famous one, brave and wise, the great lover, the undoer of wrongs, the guardian of wards in chancery, and of orphans, the protector of widows, who bowls over pretty girls but has for his one and only lady the matchless Dulcinea del Toboso, is, in fact, the man you see right here, who is my master, and any and all other Don Quijotes, and any and all other Sancho Panzas, are just bad jokes and figments of the imagination."

"By God, I believe you," replied Don Alvaro, "because you, my friend, have said more funny things in four sentences than I've ever heard that other Sancho Panza say, and I've heard him say a lot! He prefers good eating to good talking, and he's more foolish than funny, and it seems clear that those enchanters who persecute the good Don Quijote have felt like persecuting me with the bad one. But what can I say? I could swear I left Don Quijote locked up in the great lunatic asylum in Toledo, so they could make him sane again, and now I seem to have found another Don Quijote, right here, who's not in the least like the one I know."

"Whether I am good or not," said Don Quijote, "I have no idea, but I certainly can say that I'm not the bad one, and to prove that, your grace, my dear Don Alvaro Tarfe, I'd like you to know that I've never in my life been in Zaragoza. Indeed, precisely because I was told this chimera of a Don Quijote had entered the tournaments in that city, I decided not to go there myself, so I could show him up for the fraud he is, so I went straight on to Barcelona, source and storehouse of true chivalry, refuge of strangers, asylum of the poor, mother of brave men, avenger of the injured and insulted, home of staunch friendships, and unique both for location and beauty. And although what happened to me, there, was not particularly pleasant, but distinctly sorrowful, I endured it without sorrow, simply because I had seen that great city.

"And to make a long story short, my lord Don Alvaro Tarfe, I am that same Don Quijote de La Mancha of whom fame speaks — not the unlucky wretch who has tried to steal my name, my honor, and even my thoughts. I must beg your grace, on your honor as a gentleman, to swear an affidavit before the magistrate of this town, testifying that, till now, your grace has never in all your life so much as laid eyes on me, and that I am not the Don Quijote who appears in that so-called second part of my history, just as this Sancho Panza, my squire, is not the one you know."

"I'll be delighted," replied Don Alvaro, "though it's quite astonishing to see two Don Quijotes and two Sanchos at the same time, identical in name but totally different in behavior. Let me repeat and reaffirm that I can't have seen what I saw, nor can I have experienced what I experienced."

"Clearly," said Sancho, "you must be enchanted, your grace, like my lady Dulcinea del Toboso, and if Heaven were pleased to work your disenchantment by having me give myself another three thousand or so lashes, the way I'm doing for her, I'd do it without any payment whatever."

"I don't know what lashes you're talking about," said Don Alvaro.

Sancho answered that it would take a long time to explain, but if they happened to be traveling the same route he'd be glad to tell the whole story.

Dinner time came, and Don Quijote and Don Alvaro ate together. The town magistrate happening to come in, along with a notary clerk, Don Quijote made a formal request that, as a matter of law, Don Alvaro Tarfe, then present, might swear before his grace the magistrate that he had no knowledge of Don Quijote de La Mancha, also present, and that said Don Quijote was not the person of the same name who appeared in a printed book entitled *Second Part of the History of Don Quijote de La Mancha*, written by one Avellaneda, a citizen of Tordesillas. The magistrate set all this in proper legal language; the affidavit was sworn to, according to all the forms and procedures required in such cases; and Don Quijote and Sancho were deeply pleased, as if such a declaration meant a great deal to them and their very words and actions did not clearly demonstrate the difference between the two Don Quijotes and the two Sancho Panzas. Don Alvaro and Don Quijote exchanged innumerable pledges and politenesses, which still further demonstrated to Don Alvaro the great Manchegan's wisdom and the serious error into which he himself had fallen — indeed, he was convinced he really must have been enchanted, to have encountered two Don Quijotes of such opposite natures.

That afternoon they all left, and in barely two miles the road forked, one way leading to Don Quijote's village, the other being the route Don Alvaro had to follow. In the brief time they rode together, Don Quijote explained his unfortunate defeat and how Dulcinea had been put under a magic spell and was to be disenchanted, all of which astonished Don Alvaro all over again. Then, embracing both Don Quijote and Sancho, he went on his way and Don Quijote on his, spending that night in a grove of trees, so Sancho could complete his penance, which he did in the same fashion he'd begun the night before, and for which birch-tree bark rather than his shoulders paid, for he was so careful of his hide that, had a fly settled down, none of the lashes would have disturbed it.

Completely taken in, Don Quijote kept careful count of every stroke, making the grand total for both nights three thousand and twenty-nine. Then the sun appeared, apparently to witness Sancho's great sacrifice, and by his light they went on their way, discussing how Don Alvaro had been deceived and what a wonderful stroke it had been to have that gentleman make his statement before both a magistrate and a notary.

That day, and the night that followed, they journeyed on without anything worth telling about, unless it might be that, during this time, Sancho finally completed his task, to Don Quijote's vast delight: he could not wait for daylight, in case he might meet his now disenchanted lady Dulcinea, and as they jogged homeward there was not a woman who came along the road that he did not investigate, to see whether she might be Dulcinea del Toboso (for how could the infallible promises of a magician like Merlin possibly be a lie?).

Their minds and hearts thus occupied, they suddenly rode up a slope and, from where they were, could see their own village, and at the sight Sancho went down on his knees, declaring:

"Open your eyes, beloved homeland, and see that your son, Sancho Panza, has come home to you, and if he isn't coming home particularly rich, he's certainly coming well whipped. Open your arms and welcome, at the same time, your son, Don Quijote, who may be returning after a defeat in battle but who has won the battle with himself, and that, according to what he's told me, is the greatest victory anyone could want. I bring money, and maybe I got a good whipping, but at least I rode like a real gentleman."

"Enough of this foolishness," said Don Quijote, "and let's go down to our village and think what we're to do next, and how we're to live shepherds' lives, as we mean to."

And so they walked down the slope and into their home town.

Chapter Seventy-Three

— the omens Don Quijote encountered, as he came home to his own village, along with other events that adorn and validate this great history

And as they were about to enter the village, according to what Sidi Hamid tells us, Don Quijote saw two boys fighting, rolling around on the communal threshing floor, and one of them suddenly said to the other:

"If you don't give up, Periquillo, you'll never see it again as long as you live."

Hearing which, Don Quijote said to Sancho:

"Didn't you notice, my friend, what that boy said? 'You'll never see it again as long as you live'."

"So what?" replied Sancho. "Who cares what this boy says?"

"Good Lord!" said Don Quijote. "Don't you see how, if you apply that to my own longing, it means I'll never see Dulcinea again?"

Sancho was about to reply but stopped himself, seeing a hare come running across the field, pursued by a horde of hunters with greyhounds; terrified, the animal tried to hide, crouching under the donkey. It wasn't hard for Sancho to pick him up and present him to Don Quijote, who was muttering:

"*Malum signum! Malum signum!* [A bad omen! A bad omen!] A hare comes running, with greyhounds coming after, so Dulcinea will not come!"

"You're very strange, my lord," said Sancho. "Let's suppose this hare really is Dulcinea del Toboso, and these greyhounds chasing after her are the wicked magicians who turned her into a peasant girl. She runs, I pick her up and hand her over to your grace, and you hold her in your arms and make her feel good — and what kind of bad omen is that? And what kind of bad sign can you find in these boys?"

The two boys who'd been fighting came over to see the hare, and Sancho asked one of them what they'd been quarreling about. And the boy who'd said 'You'll never see it again as long as you live' told him he'd taken a cricket cage from his friend, and didn't intend ever to give it back. Sancho pulled four quarters out of his purse and gave them to the boy, in payment for the cage, then took the cage and handed it to Don Quijote, saying:

"Here you are, my lord: now these signs and omens of yours are smashed to pieces and all gone — and, anyway, it seems to me, fool though I may be, these things have no more to do with what happens to us than last year's clouds. And unless I misremember, I've heard our priest say that good Christians and sensible people shouldn't pay any attention to foolishness like this, and even you yourself, your grace, have told me the same thing, explaining that Christians who do believe in omens are idiots. But we don't need to stand here and quarrel about it: let's go right into the village."

The hunters came up and asked for their hare, and Don Quijote gave it to them; master and man went on, and in a small meadow just outside the village they bumped into the priest and Samson Carrasco, saying their prayers. It must be understood that Sancho Panza had taken the long robe painted with flickering flames, in which he himself had been draped, the night at the duke's castle when Altisidora had returned from the dead, and thrown it over both his little donkey and the bundle of arms and armor the donkey was carrying. The donkey was also wearing the same cone-headed hat his master had worn — all of which surely decorated and transformed him about as strangely as any donkey in the world.

The priest and the college graduate recognized them at once, and hurried over with their arms open. Don Quijote dismounted, and warmly embraced them both, while the little boys, who always have lynx-sharp eyes, spotted the hat on the donkey's head and came rushing to see it, saying as they ran:

"Hey, fellows, come and see Sancho Panza's donkey, all dressed up fit to kill, and Don Quijote's horse, even leaner than the day he set out."

Then, surrounded by boys, and accompanied by the priest and the college graduate, Sancho and his master went to Don Quijote's house, where the housekeeper and Don Quijote's niece were standing at the door, waiting, for they had already been told about the homecoming. Teresa Panza, Sancho's wife, had also been given the news and, disheveled and not quite fully dressed, tugging her daughter Sanchica by the hand, had also come to see her husband, and seeing that he was nowhere near so well dressed as she expected of someone so recently a governor, she said:

"What kind of homecoming is this, husband, coming back on foot and all dusty, and looking more like a man totally ungoverned than one who's been a governor?"

"Shut up, Teresa," answered Sancho, "because lots of times there's a fence but no bacon, so let's just go home and I'll tell you marvelous things. I'm carrying home money, and that's what matters, and I worked hard to earn it, and nobody got hurt."

"Then bring home your money, my good husband," said Teresa, "and who cares how you came by it? Whatever you did, you won't have been the first man in the world to do it."

Sanchica hugged her father, and asked if he'd brought her anything, because she'd been as anxious for his return as for the spring rains, so off they went to their own house, Sanchica holding onto her father's belt, on one side, and also leading the little donkey, while her mother, on the other side, held Sancho's hand, leaving Don Quijote in his own house, taken in charge by his niece and his housekeeper, with the assistance of the priest and the college graduate.

Without worrying about the time or any other restrictions, Don Quijote immediately shut himself up in his room with the college graduate and the priest, giving them a succinct account of his defeat in battle, and his commitment to remaining at home for an entire year, which pledge he meant to honor to the letter, not trespassing against it in any way whatever, exactly as befitted a good knight errant, bound by the scrupulous rules and regulations of knight errantry, and informing them, also, that he had been thinking of spending this year as a shepherd, passing his time in the solitude of the fields, an easy existence in which he could indulge his thoughts of love, while serving in that honorable pastoral calling, and in which, provided they had no pressing obligations, and were not involved in more important matters, he would like to ask them to join him, for he would buy enough sheep and cattle for them to legitimately call themselves shepherds, and then he added, finally, that the most significant part of the whole enterprise had already been taken care of, for he had assigned them all names, which fitted them like gloves. The priest asked to hear them. So Don Quijote explained that he himself would be known as 'The Quixotic Shepherd,' the college graduate as 'The Corruscating Shepherd,' and the priest as 'The Shepherd Curiambro,' while Sancho Panza would be 'The Panzaic Shepherd.' "

They were dumbfounded at Don Quijote's new madness, but to keep him from leaving home again, chasing after knightly experience, and because they hoped he could be cured during that year, they agreed to his new plan, approved of his madness as if it had been good sense, and volunteered to be his companions in the project.

"What's more," said Samson Carrasco, "since I am, as everyone is aware, a very well-known poet, always composing pastoral or courtly verse, or whatever other kinds of poetry I happen to feel like, we can all be suitably entertained along the paths and byways we will need to tread — and, even more important, gentlemen, we will each of us choose the name of some shepherdess to extoll in our verses, nor will we leave a tree trunk, no matter how tough and hard it may be, on which we have not engraved and carved her name, which is the usual custom of lovelorn shepherds."

"Oh, that's exactly it," exclaimed Don Quijote, "but although I'm free to choose the name of some imaginary shepherdess, my choice will be the peerless Dulcinea del Toboso, the wonder of our rivers and streams, the glory of our meadows, the very guardian of beauty, the cream of all graces and, indeed, a woman for whom any and all praise is appropriate, no matter how hyperbolic it may be."

"That's true enough for you," said the priest. "But we'll still have to hunt up some willing shepherdesses, because if they don't suit us just right, we'll have to make them fit."

Samson Carrasco added:

"And if our poetic veins run dry, we can name them after the shepherdesses in books, for the world is full of them: Phyllises, Amaryllises, Dianas, Fleridises, Galateas, Belisardas — and since they're for sale everywhere, we can certainly buy them and use them as our own. So if my lady — or, more accurately, my shepherdess — happens to be named Anna, I can celebrate her as 'Anarda,' and if she's Francisca, as 'Francenia,' and if she's Lucía, as 'Luscinda,' because everything works wonderfully that way, and Sancho Panza, if he's going to join our little club, can celebrate his wife as 'Teresaina.' "

Don Quijote laughed at this fooling about with names, and the priest praised to the skies his just and honorable decision, promising once again to keep our knight company, for whatever time a busy cleric could spare from his own rigorous obligations. At which point they said their goodbyes, advising him not to neglect his health and to take good care of himself.

Now Fate had arranged it so that Don Quijote's niece and his housekeeper heard every word the three of them had said, so as soon as the visitors were gone they both went into our knight's room, and his niece said to him:

"What's going on, uncle? Just when we think your grace means to stay in your own home, and lead a quiet, honorable life, are you planning to get yourself into more trouble, playing at:

Little shepherd, little shepherd, are you coming?
Little shepherd, little shepherd, have you gone?[1]

But, Lord! Those reeds are too old to make into shepherds' pipes!"
And the housekeeper added:
"And do you think your grace could stand the hottest parts of summer, or the cold winter nights, out in the open fields, with all the wolves howling? Not a bit of it, because this is work for strong men, tough and raised for the job almost since they were in swaddling clothes. My God, when you weigh one evil against the other, you'd be better off as a knight errant than a shepherd! So look, my lord: take my advice, because I'm not giving it to you after a lifetime of stuffing myself on bread and wine, but after lots of fasting, and with a full fifty years behind me: stay home, take care of your property, keep going to confession, be kind to the poor, and let it be on my soul if anything bad comes of it."

"Be still, my daughters," Don Quijote answered them, "I know perfectly well what I'm supposed to do. Take me to my bed, because I don't feel at all well, and just remember: whether I'm a knight errant, as now, or a shepherd, later on, I'll never stop doing for you whatever needs to be done, as you will see in the event."

And his good daughters — as they most assuredly were, his housekeeper and his niece — took him off to bed, where they gave him something to eat and made him as comfortable as they could.

Chapter Seventy-Four

— *how Don Quijote fell sick, and the will he made, and his death*

Since human things — and most especially human lives — are never eternal, falling forever away from their starting points, down to their final end, and since Don Quijote did not have Heaven's permission to hold back the course of his life, it reached its end and was over just when he least thought that might happen, for whether because of the sadness he felt, seeing himself defeated in combat, or simply because Fate, being so inclined, had decreed it, a fever settled on him, sending him to bed for six days, during which time he received many visits from his friends the priest, the college graduate, and the barber, and his good squire, Sancho Panza, never left his bedside.

They all tried as hard as they could to cheer him, convinced that what had brought on this unlucky turn was the combined sorrow of seeing himself defeated and being unable to finally disenchant and set free Dulcinea. Samson Carrasco urged him to take heart, to rise up and begin his shepherdly work, in honor of which the college graduate had already composed an eclogue that would guarantee oblivion for all the eclogues ever written by Sanazaro,[1] and he had also bought, from a Quintanaran shep-

---

1. Verses from a Chistmas carol [*Translator's Note*].
1. Jacopo Sannazaro (1458–1530), Italian author of the pastoral novel in both verse and prose, *Arcadia*, widely read and much imitated in Spain [*Translator's Note*]. See selection from the *Arcadia* in the "Backgrounds and Contexts" selection of this volume.

herd, and with his own money, two wonderfully celebrated sheep dogs, one named Brindle and the other called Pit-Bull. But still, Don Quijote could not shake off his sadness.

His friends called in the doctor, who took our knight's pulse and was not much pleased by what he found, advising them that, whether Don Quijote lived or died, they needed to be concerned about the state of his soul, for his body was in serious danger. Don Quijote listened to this quite calmly, but not so his housekeeper, his niece, and his squire, for they began to shed mournful tears, as if he already lay in front of them, dead. It was the doctor's opinion that he was dying of sadness and regret.

Don Quijote asked to be left alone, for he wanted to sleep a bit. They obliged, and he slept, as they say, six hours at a stretch — sleeping so long, indeed, that his housekeeper and niece thought he would never wake again. But after six hours he did wake up, calling in a loud voice:

"Blessed be Almighty God, Who has offered me such grace! Truly, truly, His mercies have no end, and we human sinners can neither obstruct nor abbreviate them."

His niece, listening to him closely, thought his speech suddenly more sensible than it had been, at least since his illness, so she asked:

"What do you mean, your grace? Is there anything wrong? What mercies are you talking about, and what human sins?"

"My niece," replied Don Quijote, "I mean the mercies granted me, this very moment, by Our Lord, who has, as I said, not been checked by my sins. I am in my right mind, now, clear-headed and free of the murky darkness of ignorance, brought down upon me by my continual, bitter reading of those abominable books of chivalry. Now I understand their stupidity and their deceptions, and all that troubles me is that, the realization having come to me so late, I no longer have time to make any recompense, reading other books which might illuminate my soul. I am at the point of death, my niece, and I should like to die in such a way that no one will think my entire life has been nothing but a disease, and my name not remembered as that of a madman, for even though that is indeed what I have been, I do not want my death to still further verify and strengthen that reputation. My dear, send for my good friends, the priest; Samson Carrasco, the college graduate; and Master Nicolás, the barber; for I wish to confess and make my last will and testament."

But his niece was saved the trouble, for just then the three of them entered the room. He had no sooner seen them when Don Quijote declared:

"My dear gentlemen, congratulate me, for I am no longer Don Quijote de La Mancha but Alonso Quijano, whose way of life made people call me 'the Good.' I am now the determined enemy of Amadís of Gaul and all his infinite herd of descendants; all those blasphemous stories of knight errantry are odious and hateful to me; I recognize my foolishness and the danger in which I placed myself, reading these books; by God's infinite mercy, I have finally learned from my mistakes, and now I loathe them."

Hearing this, the three men surely believed that some new madness had seized him. Samson Carrasco said:

"My lord Don Quijote, now that we've been advised of Lady Dulcinea's disenchantment, how can you say such things? And now that all of us are so ripe and ready to be shepherds, and spend our lives in song, like princes, does your grace plan to become a hermit? Be still, for God's sake, and be yourself, and stop all this story-telling."

"The story-telling that, until now, has truly put me in danger," replied Don Quijote, "I hope, with Heaven's help, my death will turn to my good. Gentlemen, I feel myself descending rapidly into death; no more joking, please, but bring me someone to hear my confession, and a scribe to record my last will and testament, for at critical moments like this a man cannot afford to jest about his soul, and so I beg you, while the priest hears my confession, please fetch the scribe."

They stared at one another, shocked by what Don Quijote had said, and, though they were not completely sure, they were inclined to believe him, for one of the signs by which death's coming could be foretold was the ease with which he had gone from being a lunatic to being sane — for, in addition to what he had already said, he went on to speak so many good, sensible, Christian things that none of them doubted any longer, but all believed that he had truly been cured.

The priest sent the others out of the room, and remained alone with Don Quijote, and heard his confession.

The college graduate went after the scribe, and soon returned with him and also with Sancho Panza (to whom Samson Carrasco had explained his master's condition), and finding the housekeeper and the niece weeping, Sancho's face screwed up and his tears too began to fall. Then, the confession finished, the priest emerged, saying:

"He is indeed dying, and truly, Alonso Quijano the Good has been cured; we can now go in and hear him make his last will and testament."

This news gave a terrible impetus to the housekeeper's and the niece's and to our good squire Sancho's brimming eyes, which fairly exploded with tears, and their breasts heaved with a thousand sighs — for truly, as has been said before, whether Don Quijote was just plain Alonso Quijano the Good, or whether he was Don Quijote de La Mancha, he was always a mild-mannered and pleasant man, for which reason he was beloved not only in his own house but by everyone who knew him.

The scribe had come in with the others, and once the formal opening of the will had been completed, and Don Quijote, employing all the requisite Christian terminology, had set his soul in proper order, they came to his bequests, and he declared:

"*Item*, I direct that certain moneys, given to Sancho Panza while, in my madness, he served as my squire, shall be retained by him; inasmuch as he and I have had certain dealings, credits and debits alike, I wish him to make no accounting whatever, and should there be anything left over, once my just debts have been paid, that remainder shall be his, little though it be, and may it serve him well, for if when I was mad I had a share in procuring him the governorship of an island, I now wish, being sane again, that I could give him an entire kingdom, since the simple honesty of his nature, and his perfect loyalty, well deserve it."

And, turning to Sancho, he said:

"Forgive me, my friend, for having made you seem as mad as I was, by making you fall into the same error into which I had fallen, namely, that there were, and still are, knights errant in the world."

"Oh!" exclaimed Sancho, weeping. "Don't die, your grace, my lord, but take my advice and live a long, long time, because the worst madness a man can fall into, in this life, is to let himself die, for no real reason, without anybody else killing him or any other hands but those of sadness and melancholy taking his life. Don't be lazy, but get up from your bed, and let's go out into the fields, dressed as shepherds, the way we decided we would: who knows if maybe we'll find My Lady Doña Dulcinea behind some bushes or trees, just the way she used to be. If you're dying because you got defeated in that battle, just blame it all on me, and say you fell because I didn't buckle up Rocinante tight enough, especially since your grace knows from your books of chivalry how knights are always knocking each other off horses, and the one who's beaten today will be the winner tomorrow."

"That's true enough," said Samson Carrasco, "and our good Sancho Panza is certainly telling how it really happens."

"Not so fast, gentlemen," said Don Quijote, "not so fast, for now there are no more birds in last autumn's nests. I was mad, and now I am sane; I was Don Quijote de La Mancha and now, as I have said, I am Alonso Quijano the Good. I pray that my repentance, and my honesty, may return me to the good opinion your graces once held of me — and now, señor scribe, let's get on with it.

"*Item*, I direct that everything I possess, whether expressly or implicitly, shall pass to my niece, Antonia Quijana, here present, having first subtracted from whatever funds lie closest to hand the moneys necessary to fulfill my other bequests — and I wish the first payment she makes to be to my faithful housekeeper, for the wages owed her, plus an additional twenty gold pieces to buy herself a dress.

"I wish my executors to be the priest and Samson Carrasco, the college graduate, also here present.

"*Item*, I wish that, should my niece, Antonia Quijana, desire to marry, she marry a man who first declares that he has no idea what books of chivalry might conceivably be about, and in the event that he says he does know such books, and if in spite of that fact my niece still wishes to marry him, and does so, she is to be deprived of everything I have left her, and my executors shall distribute it to such pious and charitable causes as they shall think proper.

"*Item*, I ask of the aforesaid gentlemen, my executors, that should they ever have the good fortune to know the writer responsible for that history known by the title of *The Second Part of the Exploits of Don Quijote de La Mancha*, to beg him to forgive me, as earnestly as he can, for having been as responsible as I suspect I am for his having written such highflown nonsense, because I leave this life sadly conscious that it was indeed I who gave him cause to write at all."

Don Quijote's will ended here, and he fell into a faint, stretching out on his bed. Everyone ran about, trying to help him; for the three days he lived, after having made his last will and testament, he fell into many fits of unconsciousness. The house was in a perpetual uproar — but, all the same, the niece ate, and the housekeeper drank, and Sancho Panza was joyful, because, for the man who inherits, the business of inheriting softens and moderates the memory he rightly retains of the pain and suffering which gave rise to his inheritance.

And so Don Quijote came to his end, having received all the sacraments, and having roundly and pungently cursed all tales of chivalry. The scribe was present, and remarked that in none of the books of chivalry *he* had read had there ever been a knight errant who died in his bed, so peacefully and in such Christian fashion as had Don Quijote, who, amid universal sympathy and tears from everyone who was with him, surrendered his spirit — that is to say, he died.

Seeing which, the priest asked the scribe to witness that Alonso Quijano the Good, commonly known as Don Quijote de La Mancha, had departed from this life, dying of natural causes, and that he, the priest, was asking the scribe to bear this witness in order to prevent any writer other than Sidi Hamid Benengeli from falsely resurrecting Don Quijote and turning out endless tales of his exploits.

Thus the Ingenious Gentleman of La Mancha came to his end, Sidi Hamid never clearly indicating just where in La Mancha our knight came from, so he could leave all the towns and villages free to quarrel among themselves and claim him as their own, just as the seven cities of Greece fought to claim Homer.

Sancho's lament for Don Quijote, like the housekeeper's and the niece's, are here omitted, as well as the new epitaphs placed on his tomb, though it is recorded that Samson Carrasco placed thereon the following lines:

> Here lies a strong-hearted nobleman,
> so wonderfully brave
> that even Death, opening the grave
> beneath him, could savor
> no triumph.

> The world never worried him;
> it thought him mad, it thought him wild,
> but he, like some innocent child,
> was granted God's mercy and mild
> forgiveness, and, living insane,
> he died like a man.

And the exceedingly wise Sidi Hamid said to his pen:

"Now you can rest, oh my pen, hung from this hook by a copper wire, and though I may never know whether you wrote well or badly, you will live through the centuries, unless arrogant and wicked writers pluck you out and desecrate you. But before their hands ever touch you, warn them off, and tell them, as best you can:

> Wait, wait! you good for nothings!
> Hands off! For oh, good king,
> These printed words, these pages,
> Belong to me, and the ages.

And Don Quijote was born only for me, as I for him; he knew how to act, and I how to write; only we two are a unity, in spite of that fake Tordesillan scribbler who dared — and may dare again — to record with his fat ostrich-feathered quill such badly drawn adventures for my brave knight, who is far too weighty for his shoulders to bear, and is a subject his frozen brains could never take on — so warn him, if you happen ever to meet, that he'd better let the weary, powdered bones of Don Quijote rest in their tomb, and not even think of raising them up, against all Death's laws, and carrying them off to Old Castile,[2] yanking them out of that eternal resting place where, really and truly, they now lie stretched in moldering peace, incapable of making more journeys or sallying forth yet again, because in the cause of mocking knight errantry, as he has done, the two journeys he made are more than enough, and they gave immense pleasure and satisfaction to all who read them, whether here in Spain or abroad. And, in so doing, you will live up to your obligation as a Christian, giving good advice to someone who wishes you ill, and I will remain pleased and proud, having been the first writer to fully relish, as deeply as anyone could ever want, the fruit of his own work, for all I ever wanted was to make men loathe the concocted, wild-eyed stories told as tales of chivalry, nor can there be the slightest doubt that this truthful history of my Don Quijote has already begun to pull those books to the ground, just as surely as it will bring down every last one of them.

"*Vale* [Farewell]."

---

2. As in fact, in the false Part Two, Avellaneda had said he would do [*Translator's Note*].

BACKGROUNDS AND CONTEXTS

Cervantes in His Own Voice

[Fear of Publishing]†

* * *

Human difficulties are at once so alike and so different, and the aims and actions of human beings so various, that some writers, desiring glory, will risk everything; others, fearing infamy, won't dare to publish anything that, once in print, may suffer the judgment of the masses, dangerous and almost always deceptive. I, with little reason to be presumptuous, have shown signs of daring with the publication of this book, if only because I've not been able to determine which is the greater of two evils: that of the writer who, wishing to communicate a God-given talent, rashly ventures to offer its fruits to his friends and homeland, or that of the writer who, being too scrupulous — lazy, belated, never satisfied with what he produces, only content with what is out of reach — can never decide to disclose and circulate his writings. Just as the boldness and confidence of the one can be condemned for excessive license, the product of his self-esteem, so the fearfulness and tardiness of the other is an error, given that he will too late or never enrich, with his genius and application, those who desire help and models in order to advance in their own endeavors. Fleeing from these two polarities, I've not published this book until now, but neither did I wish to keep it locked up any longer, since my understanding composed it for more than my own personal gratification. I'm well aware that people tend to condemn any excess in the matter of prescribed style, for the prince of Latin poetry himself [Virgil] was slandered for making some of his eclogues sound more elevated than others. So I'll not worry too much if someone condemns my having mixed philosophical discourse with the amorous talk of shepherds, who seldom rise above country matters, and this with their customary simplicity. But if we make clear — as is sometimes done in this text — that many disguised shepherds are so only in dress, the objection is not valid. Any other objections must be directed to the creativity and the disposition of this work, which the discreet reader may forgive, remembering that the author's intention is only to please, attaining to whatever he could in this book.[1] And if it does not live up to his wishes, the author will offer other books in the future, of more pleasure and wit.

---

† From Miguel de Cervantes, Prologue to *La Galatea* (1585), ed. Juan Bautista Avalle-Arce, 2 vols. (Madrid: Espasa-Calpe, 1968), pp. 7–9. Translated by Diana de Armas Wilson.
1. In I. 6 of *Don Quijote*, Cervantes will look back on this book, his first publication, with a critical eye. (See p. 39 of this edition.)

749

[Portrait of the Artist as an Old Man]†

I would have preferred, had it been possible, Dearest Reader, not to write this Prologue: the one I put in my *Don Quijote* was not such a success that I am anxious to follow it with another. The blame lies with a friend of mine, one of many I have acquired over the years, more by luck than judgment, who could well have engraved my portrait on the title-page of this book, as is the custom, since the celebrated Juan de Jáuregui had given him my likeness. With that, my ambition would have been satisfied, as too would the desire of anyone keen to know what he looks like, this man who dares to display his inventions and submit them to public gaze in the market-place of the world. All he had to do was write under the portrait:

"This man you see here, with aquiline face, chestnut hair, smooth, unwrinkled brow, joyful eyes and curved though well-proportioned nose; silvery beard which not twenty years ago was golden, large moustache, small mouth, teeth neither small nor large, since he has only six, and those are in poor condition and worse alignment; of middling height, neither tall nor short, fresh-faced, rather fair than dark; somewhat stooping and none too light on his feet; this, I say, is the likeness of the author of *La Galatea* and *Don Quijote de la Mancha*, and of him who wrote the *Viaje del Parnaso*, after the one by Cesare Caporali di Perusa, and other stray works that may have wandered off without their owner's name. He is commonly called Miguel de Cervantes Saavedra. He was many years a soldier, five and a half a prisoner, when he learned patience in adversity. He lost his left hand in the naval battle of Lepanto, from a blunderbuss wound, which, although it looks ugly, he considers beautiful, since he collected it in the greatest and most memorable event that past centuries have ever seen or those to come may hope to see, fighting beneath the victorious banners of the son of that glorious warrior, Charles V of happy memory."

And if the memory of my friend, of whom I complain, had failed to come up with anything more to say about me than the above, I would have put together a couple of dozen testimonials and passed them to him on the quiet so that he could extend my renown and bear witness to my inventiveness. For it is foolish to imagine that such eulogies tell the exact truth, as praise and vituperation have no fixed abode.

In the event, for that opportunity was lost and I have been left blank and unillustrated, I shall have to make do with my tongue, which, though tied, will be quick enough to tell home truths, which are wont to be understood even in the language of signs. And so I say again, Gentle Reader, that you cannot make a fricassée with these novels I now offer you, for they have no feet, nor head, nor entrails, or anything of the kind; by which I mean that the sweet nothings you will find in some of them are so proper and so seasoned with reason and Christian discourse, that

---

† From Miguel de Cervantes Saavedra, "Prologue to the Reader" (1613), *Exemplary Novels* (Warminster: Aris & Phillips Ltd., 1992), Vol. 1, pp. 3–5. Trans. B. W. Ife. Reprinted by permission of the publisher and translator.

they could not provoke anyone who might read them, careless or otherwise, into evil thoughts.

I have called them *Exemplary*, and if you look closely, you will see that there is not one from which you cannot extract some profitable example; and if it were not for the fact that it would make this over-long, perhaps I would show you the delicious and wholesome fruit which could be pulled both from the collection as a whole and from each one alone.

My intention was to set up in the main square of our society a billiard table, where anyone could come and have fun without snookering anyone else; that is, without harming body or soul, for honest and agreeable exercise is of benefit rather than harm.

After all, we cannot always be in church; the oratories are not always occupied; we cannot always be doing business, no matter how important it is. There is time for recreation, when the tormented spirit can rest.

That is why poplar groves are planted, springs are made into fountains, slopes are levelled and gardens created in wonderful designs. One thing I will venture to say, and that is that if by any chance it should happen that the reading of these novels might lead my readers into evil thoughts or desires, I would rather cut off the hand with which I wrote them than have them published. At my time of life I cannot afford to mess around with the hereafter, for at fifty-five I might have nine years left, and I could still beat them to it.

So I have applied my imagination to the end to which my natural inclination leads me. And there is one more thing I would make clear, and that is that I am the first to write novels in Castilian, for the many novels which have appeared in print are all translated from foreign tongues, and these are my very own, neither imitated nor stolen; they were conceived in my imagination, given birth by my pen, and are being nurtured in the arms of the printing press. After them, if life does not abandon me, I will offer you the *Trabajos de Persiles*, a book which dares to compete with Heliodorus,[1] if, indeed, it does not overreach itself and fall on its face; and first you will see very shortly the further exploits of Don Quixote and more quips from Sancho Panza, and then the *Semanas del jardín*.

This is a lot to promise with strength as weak as mine; but who can put a rein on desire? I would only wish you to consider this: that since I have been bold enough to dedicate these novels to the Count of Lemos, they must contain some hidden mystery which elevates them to that level.

Enough, except to say may God keep you and give me patience to suffer sharp remarks and starchy comments. Vale [Farewell].

---

1. Heliodorus of Emesa (in Syria) composed the *Ethiopica* sometime between A.D. 250–380. This Greek novel, which navigates readers through a polyglot and racially mixed world, was highly esteemed in sixteenth-century Spain.

[Cervantes's Self-Critique]†

With *Don Quijote*, I've given cause for joy
  to the melancholy and the fretful soul
  at any time of day or night or year.
With my *novelas* there is now a way
  the Spanish tongue can speak quite properly
  of crazy deeds and actions out of joint.
I am that man who through invention goes
  beyond most men, who, lacking in this skill,
  fall far behind requirements of fame.
From my first youth I've loved the art
  of sweet, harmonious, rhythmic poetry,
  And in it I have always tried to please.
My humble pen has never flown across
  the field satiric, never sunk so low
  as to deserve the prize of ill-repute.

[Cervantes's Last Words]‡

It so happened, dearest reader, as two friends and I were coming from
the famous town of Esquivias, famous for a thousand reasons, one of them
being its illustrious families and another its even more illustrious wines,[1]
that I perceived someone behind me spurring his mount on in a great
hurry. He apparently wanted to overtake us and soon made that clear by
calling out for us not to spur on so urgently. We waited for him, and on
a she-ass up came a drab student, drab because he came dressed all in
rustic brown with leggings, round-toed shoes, a sword in a chaped scabbard, and a starched lace collar with its matching ties; the fact of the matter
is that he had only two of these ties to hold it on, so every other minute
the collar kept falling over to one side and he was at great pains to keep
it straight.

Catching up to us he said, "You, sirs, must be on your way to court to
obtain some office or benefice — for his Most Illustrious Grace of Toledo
and His Majesty themselves are doubtless there — judging by the hurry
with which you're traveling, since even my ass, which has been praised
more than once for her speed, couldn't catch you." To this one of my
companions replied, "It's the fault of Señor Miguel de Cervantes's nag,
which is somewhat long-stepping."

Scarcely had the student heard the name Cervantes when he dis-

---

† Elias L. Rivers, who has published the definitive critical edition of Cervantes's *Viage del Parnaso*
[*Voyage of Parnassus* (1614)] (Madrid: Espasa-Calpe, 1991), provided the above translation of
chapter 4, lines 22–36, especially for this edition.
‡ From Miguel de Cervantes, Prologue to *The Trials of Persiles and Sigismunda, A Northern Story*
(1617). Trans. Celia Richmond Weller and Clark A. Colahan (Berkeley: University of California
Press, 1989), pp. 15–16. This Prologue — from Cervantes's posthumously published last novel
— is reprinted here by the kind permission of the translators. Some notes have been omitted.
1. Esquivias, located in the province of Toledo in central Spain, was the hometown of Cervantes's
wife, Catalina de Salazar y Palacios. The couple was married there in 1584.

mounted from his pack animal, sending his saddlebags flying in one direction and his valise in another — he traveled so completely outfitted — and rushed up to me, seizing my left hand and saying, "Yes, yes, this is the complete cripple, the completely famous and comic writer, and lastly, the delight of the muses!"[2]

I, who in so short a space of time saw such great compliments in my praise, felt it would have been discourteous not to respond to them. And so, embracing him around the neck, whereby I destroyed his collar altogether, I said to him: "That is an error into which many of my uninformed admirers have fallen. I, sir, am Cervantes, but not the delight of the muses or any of the other foolish things that you mentioned. Round up your ass, mount up, and let's pass the brief remainder of our journey in pleasant conversation."

The obliging student did just that, we reined in slightly, and then resumed our trip at a more leisurely pace. As we traveled we talked about my illness and the good student immediately diagnosed me a hopeless case, saying: "This sickness is dropsy, incurable even if you were to drink all the waters of the Ocean Sea made sweet. Señor Cervantes, sir, you should limit your drinking and don't forget to eat, for thereby you will recover without any other medicine."

"That's what many have told me," I replied, "but I just can't give up the pleasure of drinking all I want, for it almost seems I was born to it. My life's race is slowing at the rate of my pulse and by this Sunday at the latest it will complete its course and with it my life.[3] You, sir, have made my acquaintance at a difficult moment, for there isn't enough time left to express my gratitude for the goodwill you've shown me."

At this point we arrived at the Toledo bridge where I crossed into the city and he rode off to enter by the Segovia road. As to what may be said of this incident, fame will take care to report it, my friends will take pleasure in telling it, and I even more pleasure in hearing it. Once again we embraced each other, he spurred his mount and left me just as ill at ease as he was in trying to be a gentleman on that ass. He had afforded my pen a great opportunity to be witty, but you can't always make of one moment what you can of another. A time may come, perhaps, when I shall tie up this broken thread and say what I failed to here and what would have been fitting. Goodbye, humor; goodbye, wit; goodbye, merry friends; for I am dying and hope to see you soon, happy in the life to come!

---

2. These phrases in praise of the author reflect his very real fame in Spain following the publication of *Don Quijote*. The novel's humor and the fact that he had lost the use of an arm in the famous naval battle of Lepanto explain the specific tongue-in-cheek epithets used here by Cervantes to describe himself.

3. Cervantes actually died not on Sunday, but on *Saturday*, April 23, 1616.

Sources and Influences

JACOPO SANNAZARO

From Arcadia†

Chapter One

[Various episodes in *Don Quijote* — the hero's Golden Age speech to the goatherds (I.11), the contrasting stories of Marcela (I.12–14) and Leandra (I.51), and the failed bucolic "sabbatical" preceding Don Quijote's death (II.73) — demand a familiarity with the codes of the pastoral. A literary convention in which aristocratic pseudo-shepherds play their oaten flutes while lamenting the coldness of their mistresses, the pastoral has focused much of its machinery on lost, unrequited, or frustrated masculine love. Although the pastoral's origins are in antiquity, with Theocritus and Virgil its prime practitioners, Sannazaro's *Arcadia*, written during the 1480s, became a seminal text for sixteenth-century Europe. The eclectic *Arcadia* exploited not only Graeco-Roman bucolics but also the Petrarchan love lyric. Part of Sannazaro's pastoral legacy, the formal interlacing of verse eclogues and prose, informed Cervantes's *Galatea* (1585), an unfinished work slyly self-evaluated in *Don Quijote* (I.6). But Cervantes rejected another part of the arcadian legacy: the representation of women as inaccessible objects rather than as desiring subjects. Sannazaro's "unbending" and "unpitying" shepherdess who remains "colder than ice" qualifies as a literary foremother of Cervantes's Marcela. But unlike the conventionally mute women found in the *Arcadia*, the females in the pastoral episodes of *Don Quijote*, whether invoked or represented, are both more assertive and more subversive. Reprinted below is part of Ergasto's complaint during a gathering of shepherds near the top of Mt. Parthenius.]

There lies on the summit of Parthenius, a not inconsiderable mountain of pastoral Arcadia, a pleasant plateau, not very spacious in extent, since the situation of the place does not permit it, but so filled with tiny and deep-green herbage that, if the wanton herds with their greedy nibbling did not pasture there, one could always find green grasses in that place. There, if I am not mistaken, there are perhaps a dozen or fifteen trees of such unusual and exceeding beauty that any who saw them would judge that Mistress Nature had taken special delight in shaping them. These trees, standing somewhat apart and arranged in non-artificial order, with their rarity ennoble beyond measure the natural beauty of the place.

* * *

† From Jacopo Sannazaro, *Arcadia and Piscatorial Eclogues*, trans. Ralph Nash (Detroit: Wayne State University Press, 1966), pp. 30–34.

In this so lovely a place the shepherds with their flocks will often gather together from the surrounding hills and exercise themselves there in various strenuous contests, such as hurling the heavy stake, shooting with bows at a target, and making proof of their skill in light leaping and stout wrestling, full of rustic trickery: and most often in singing and in playing the shepherd's pipe in rivalry one with another, not without praise and reward for the victor.

But at one of these times, when almost all the neighboring shepherds with their charges were gathered together in that place, and each one seeking various forms of amusement, they had a wonderful holiday. Ergasto alone was lying, without saying or doing anything, at the foot of a tree forgetful of himself and of his flocks, not otherwise than if he had been a stock or stone, although in former days he was wont to be pleasant and gracious in greater degree than the other shepherds. Selvaggio, moved to compassion of his piteous state, in order to give him some comfort began to address him in a friendly fashion, singing in clear tones thus.

ECLOGUE I SELVAGGIO AND ERGASTO

Sel.
Ergasto mine, why do I see you meditating
   solitary and silent? ay me, that unhappily
      your flocks are allowed to wander at their pleasure.   *   *   *

Erg.
Selvaggio mine,   *   *   *
How can you wish that my prostrate heart should rise
   to fix its care on my poor and humble flock,
      since rather I fear that it will be scattered among the wolves?
Amid my griefs I find no other remedy
   than that of sitting alone at the foot of a maple,
      of a beech, of a pine, or of a cork tree.
For thinking of her who has lacerated my heart
   I become an icicle and care for no other thing,
      nor feel the pain from which I grow lean and waste away.

Sel.
With wonderment I grow harder than a stone,
   hearing you speak so much the malcontent;
      and in making demand of you I somewhat reassure myself.
Who is she that has a heart so wayward
   that she has made you change your appearance and habit?
      Tell me, for I will never breathe it to another.

Erg.
One day leading my lambs beside a river,
I saw in the midst of those waves a lovely light
that bound me then with two golden locks
and painted in the middle of my heart a face
that far outdid for color cream and roses:
then it hid itself in such manner within my soul
that weight of other burden does not oppress me.
Thus I was taken; from which I have such yoke on my neck

that I make proof of it and know it more than did ever man of flesh;
so that in thinking of it all lofty thought is vanquished.
I saw first one and then the other eye;
skirts raised to the knee as it seemed to me
she stood in midstream under the hot sky:
she was washing out a garment, singing in a clear voice.
Alas that when she saw me, she fell silent,
cutting off her song in haste:
and it displeased me that, for my greater troubling,
she let down her garments, and covered herself completely:
then she immersed herself there within up to the waist;
so that overcome I fell stunned on the earth:
and to give me comfort then she ran up
and succored me, weeping so with her outcries
that the shepherds who were round about the region
came running to her screams,
and for pity made trial of a thousand arts.
But my scattered senses at last returned to me
and made defense of my life hanging in doubt.
Repentant she, when I had recovered myself,
turned then away, and burned my heart the more
all by showing herself at once piteous and cruel.

Unbending and unpitying my shepherdess,
　　though night and day I call her to my aid,
　　　　and she remains proud, and colder than ice;
well do they know, these woods, how much I love her,
　　rivers, mountains, beasts and men they know it,
　　　　how weeping and sighing every hour I need her.
How many times a day I call her name
　　my flock knows, that hears me all the time,
　　　　whether it is grazing in the woods or ruminating in the fold.
Echo resounds, and often returns again to me
　　the words that sound so sweetly in the air,
　　　　and in my ears her lovely name reverberates.
Constantly these trees converse of her
　　and show her written on their bark,
　　　　so that often they spur me to weeping and to singing.

GARCI RODRÍGUEZ DE MONTALVO

From Amadis of Gaul†

[The Penance on Poor Cliff]

[In his famous Defence of Poetry (1595), Sir Philip Sidney — the English
godson of Spain's King Philip II — claimed to have known men who by the

† From Amadis of Gaul: A Novel of Chivalry of the 14th Century Presumably First Written in
Spanish. Revised and reworked by Garci Rodríguez de Montalvo prior to 1505. Trans. Edwin B.
Place and Herbert C. Behm. 2 vols. (Lexington: The University Press of Kentucky, 1974),
Vol. 2, Bk. 2, pp. 461–67; 483–86; and 493–98. Reprinted by the permission of The University
Press of Kentucky. The Place and Behm translation does not use an accent in Amadis.

act of reading *Amadís of Gaul* had "found their hearts moved to the exercise of courtesy, liberality, and especially courage." Don Quijote is one of these men. He is moved not only to the exercise of all the above virtues, but also to an avowed imitation of the fictional character of Amadís. Most impressive for Don Quijote is Amadís's self-imposed penance in the wilderness for the love of Oriana (I.25–26).

About a century before *Don Quijote* appeared in Spain, Garci Rodríguez de Montalvo had revised and reworked a fourteenth-century narrative of chivalry into the Spanish text known across Europe as *Amadís of Gaul.* Published in 1508, it was the first of its kind in a long series of sixteenth-century runaway bestsellers. For almost a century, the Books of Chivalry (*libros de caballerías*) enthralled readers of all classes, from kings to kitchenmaids, and in all climes, from Spain's metropolis to its American colonies. Although many humanists reviled these books — Juan Luis Vives characterized them as "scorpion oil" — their role in the production of Castilian cultural identity was pivotal. The genre propped up the ideology of Spain's ruling class, reaffirming its chivalric ideals, its social hierarchies, and even its imperial longings.

Montalvo's revision of *Amadís* would find its way into Don Quijote's library where, among a host of sequels and imitations, it was responsible for "drying out" the hero's brains. During the "inquisition" of the hero's library — when his books are scrutinized as if they were heretics to be condemned or pardoned — the priest and barber spare *Amadís* from the bonfire on the grounds of its being "the very best book of chivalry ever composed" (p. 35). This judgment would have gratified the exorcist-hero of Gabriel García Márquez's *Love and Other Demons* (1994) — a theologian "demonized" by love and haunted by his youthful reading of *Amadís.* Below are reprinted various selections from Amadís's penance on "Peña Pobre" (which this translation renders as "Poor Cliff," but Raffel's as "Barren Mountain"), the abode of an elderly hermit.]

*   *   *

"Good sir," said Amadis, "I do not ask of you advice in this matter, for I do not need it, but I ask of you counsel for my soul and that you be pleased to take me with you; and if you do not do this, I have no other remedy but to die on this mountain."

And the good man began to weep with the great sorrow that he had, so that the tears were falling on his beard, which was long and white; and he said:

"My son, sir, I dwell in a place very forbidding and difficult to live in, which is a hermitage located a good seven leagues out to sea on a very high cliff, and this cliff is so narrow that no ship can reach it except in summer, and there I have dwelt for thirty years, and anyone who dwells there must leave worldly delights and pleasures; and my sustenance is from alms that those of the land give me."

"All of this," said Amadis, "is to my taste, and I should like to live thus with you during the short lifetime that remains to me, and I beg you, for the love of God, to grant it to me."

The good man agreed to it much against his will, and Amadis said to him:

"Now command me, father, what to do, for I shall be completely obedient to you."

The good man blessed him and then said vespers, and bringing out a bag of bread and fish, told Amadis to eat, but he did not do so, although three days had already gone by during which he had not eaten; and the priest said:

"You will have to give obedience to me, and I order you to eat; if not, your soul would be in great danger if thus you should die."

* * *

The good man kept gazing at him, noting how handsome and well proportioned he was and the great distress in which he was; and he said:

"I wish to give you a name that will be in conformity with your person and the anguish in which you are, for you are young and very handsome and your life is in great bitterness and in darkness: I want you to have the name Beltenebros."

Amadis was pleased with that name, and considered the good man understanding in having given it to him so rightly; and by this name he was called as long as he lived with him, and for a long time afterward he was no less praised under that name than under the name of Amadis, in accordance with the great feats that he performed, as will be told later.

Then talking about this and other things, they reached the sea, it being already nightfall, and they found there a boat in which the good man was to be transported to his hermitage. And Beltenebros gave his horse to the sailors, and they gave him an old cloak and a tabard of heavy brown wool; and they got in the boat and went toward the cliff, and Beltenebros asked the good man what his dwelling place was called and what his name was.

"The dwelling place," said he, "is called the Poor Cliff, because no one can dwell there except in extreme poverty, and my name is Andalod, and I was a well educated cleric, and I spent my youth in many vanities; but God, through his mercy, set me to thinking that those who are to serve Him have great difficulties and obstacles in communicating with the people — for in accordance with our weakness, we are inclined to evil rather than to what is good — and therefore I decided to withdraw to this very solitary place, where thirty years have already passed during which I never had left it until now, when I came to the burial of a sister of mine."

Beltenebros was very fond of the solitude and ruggedness of that place, and when he thought about dying there, he received some surcease. Thus they went sailing in their boat until they reached the Cliff. The hermit said:

"Go back."

And the sailors returned to land with their boat; and Beltenebros, thinking about that austere and holy life of that good man, with many tears and groans, not from devotion but out of great despair, thought that along with the hermit, he would endure everything while he lived, which to his way of thinking would not be long.

* * *

Just as you hear, Beltenebros was doing his penance with much grief and great misgivings, which he had continually, believing that if God through His pity did not help him with the favor of his lady, he would have death nearer than life, and most nights he spent the whole night under some trees with heavy foliage, which were there in an orchard near the hermitage, in order to grieve and weep without the hermit's or the youths' being aware of it. And recalling the loyalty he always had maintained to his lady Oriana and the great deeds he had performed to serve her, and her having given him such a bad reward, without cause or his having deserved it, he composed this song out of the great rage he had, as follows:

> Since victory is denied me
> Where rightly it was owed to me,
> There where glory dies
> It is glory for life to die.
>
> And with this death of mine
> Will die all my hurts
> My hope, my striving,
> Love and its deceits.
> But there will remain in my memory
> A lament never lost,
>
> For in order to kill my glory
> My glory and life have been slain.

* * *

The maid of Denmark * * * arrived at the foot of the Poor Cliff, where Beltenebros was, which was immediately recognized by those of the ship, for some of them knew that Andalod the holy hermit was there living in the hermitage above. This they had told the maid of Denmark, and she, as one who had escaped from such danger, being returned thus from death to life, gave orders that she be taken up to the Cliff, in order that while hearing mass from that good man, she might thank the Virgin Mary for that favor that her Glorious Son had rendered them.

* * *

The maiden entered alone the room where Beltenebros was; who, on thinking what he might do, was unable to make up his mind; for if he made himself known to her, he would be violating the command of his lady; and if not, if that woman, who was the whole restorative of his life, were to go from there, no hope remained for him. Finally, believing it would be much harder for him to anger his lady than to suffer death, he decided by no means to let her recognize him. Then the maiden coming close to his bed, said:

* * *

"This your lady sends you, and through me informs you if you are that Amadis that you were wont to be, whom she loves so much, that forgetting what is past, be with her at once in her castle of Miraflores, where with great pleasure amends will be made for the pain and anguish that the boundless love she has for you, has caused."

He took the letter and after kissing it many times, placed it on his heart, and said:

"Oh, afflicted heart, which for so long a time with such great anguish, shedding so many tears, have been able to sustain yourself even unto the straits of cruel death, receive this medicine, for none other could have sufficed for your good health; take away those clouds of great gloom with which until now you were covered, take courage with which to be able to recompense that lady of yours for the favor she does you in freeing you from death."

Then he opened the letter to read it, and it read thus:

(LETTER FROM ORIANA TO AMADIS)

If the great mistakes that are done through hatred, when transformed into humility are worthy of being pardoned, then what will become of those that are caused by great excess of love? Nor on that account do I deny, my true beloved, that I deserve much punishment, because one must consider that in prosperous and happy situations Fortune lies in wait in order to render one wretched, and rightly I ought to have considered your discretion and your uprightness which have not erred in anything up to now; and especially the great surrender of my sad heart, which came to it only from that subjection, for in it yours is confined; for if by chance some portion of its burning flames had been cooled, and my heart sensing it, some rest for its mortal desires they would have been the cause of bringing about. But I erred like those women who, being very fortunate and very sure of those they love, not being able to contain so much good, through suspicions conceived more willfully than reasonably from the words of innocent or slanderous persons — words of little truth and less virtue — want to obscure that great joy with a cloud of scant tolerance; thus, my loyal lover, as from a guilty person who recognizes her error with humility, may this maid of mine be received, who better than the letter will make known to my lover the extremity that my life is in, for which, not because it deserves it, but for the restoration of yours, one should have pity.

The letter having been read, the joy of Beltenebros was so excessive that just as with his past sadness, so with joy he was swooning with tears falling down his cheeks without his feeling them. Immediately by those present he was brought back to consciousness so that making known to all those who were coming there that the maiden, in God's service was taking him from that place, where there was no provision for his good health, and that within the hour, having returned to the ship, they should reach the mainland, thus this was done. But first, bidding farewell to the hermit, letting him know how that maiden through God's compassion, by great good luck was carried there for his salvation; and begging him earnestly to take charge of reorganizing the monastery which he had promised to build at the foot of the Cliff of the Firm Island, and this having been agreed to by him, Beltenebros put out to sea, without being recognized by anyone except only by the maiden.

*   *   *

LUDOVICO ARIOSTO

From Orlando Furioso†

Canto 23

[Various episodes in *Don Quijote* function as parodies of events in Ariosto's *Orlando Furioso*, a poem generically related to the Charlemagne legends. Published in its complete form in 1532, the *Furioso* takes its place, along with Boiardo's *Orlando Innamorato* (1494) and Tasso's *Gerusalemme Liberata* (1581), as one of the famous triad of Renaissance Italian romance epics. The most memorable episode in Ariosto's chivalric narrative — and the one that gives the poem its name — represents Charlemagne's nephew Orlando (in English, Roland) in the act of going *furioso*. Orlando's murderous madness is triggered by the discovery that his beloved Angelica has been sleeping with the enemy, a wounded Moorish foot soldier called Medoro, with whom she elopes to Cathay. At the entrance to a grotto, Orlando discovers a carved inscription in Arabic, in which Medoro reveals that the beauteous Angelica has lain within his arms. This knowledge drives Orlando into the forest, where he goes berserk. Before undertaking his own crazy antics in the Sierra Morena (I.25–26), Cervantes's latter-day knight references the jilted Orlando as a possible model for imitation. When Don Quijote catalogues all the madnesses perpetrated by "Roland, or Orlando, or Rotolando" — "and all the wild things he said, and all the furious thoughts he contemplated" — Sancho sensibly reminds his master that he has no evidence for believing that Dulcinea "has committed any kind of stupidity with anyone, Moor or Christian" (I.25) (p. 151)].

* * *

CXXV

Never from tears, never from sorrowing,
He paused; nor found he peace by night or day:
He fled from town, in forest harbouring,
And in the open air on hard earth lay.
He marvelled at himself, how such a spring
Of water from his eyes could stream away,
And breath was for so many sobs supplied;
And thus ofttimes, amid his mourning, cried

CXXVI

"These are no longer real tears which rise,
And which I scatter from so full a vein.
Of tears my ceaseless sorrow lacked supplies;
They stopt when to mid-height scarce rose my pain.
The vital moisture rushing to my eyes,
Driven by the fire within me, now would gain

---

† From Ludovico Ariosto, *Orlando Furioso* (1532). Trans. William Stewart Rose; ed. Stewart A. Baker and A. Bartlett Giamatti (Indianapolis: Bobbs-Merrill, 1968), pp. 244–45.

A vent; and it is this which I expend,
And which my sorrows and my life will end.

CXXVII

"No; these, which are the index of my woes,
These are not sighs, nor sighs are such; they fail
At times, and have their season of repose:
I feel, my breast can never less exhale
Its sorrow: Love, who with his pinions blows
The fire about my heart, creates this gale.
Love, by what miracle dost thou contrive,
It wastes not in the fire thou keep'st alive?

CXXVIII

"I am not — am not what I seem to sight:
What Roland was is dead and under ground,
Slain by that most ungrateful lady's spite,
Whose faithlessness inflicted such a wound.
Divided from the flesh, I am his sprite,
Which in this hell, tormented, walks its round,
To be, but in its shadow left above,
A warning to all such as trust in love."

CXXIX

All night about the forest roved the count,
And, at the break of daily light, was brought
By his unhappy fortune to the fount,
Where his inscription young Medoro wrought.
To see his wrongs inscribed upon that mount,
Inflamed his fury so, in him was nought
But turned to hatred, phrensy, rage, and spite;
Nor paused he more, but bared his falchion[1] bright;

CXXX

Cleft through the writing; and the solid block,
Into the sky, in tiny fragments sped.
Wo worth each sapling and that caverned rock,
Where Medore and Angelica were read!
So scathed, that they to shepherd or to flock
Thenceforth shall never furnish shade or bed.
And that sweet fountain, late so clear and pure,
From such tempestuous wrath was ill secure.

1. A broad curved sword with the edge on the convex side.

CXXXI

For he turf, stone, and trunk, and shoot, and lop,
Cast without cease into the beauteous source;
Till, turbid from the bottom to the top,
Never again was clear the troubled course.
At length, for lack of breath, compelled to stop,
(When he is bathed in sweat, and wasted force,
Serves not his fury more) he falls, and lies
Upon the mead, and, gazing upward, sighs.

CXXXII

Wearied and woe-begone, he fell to ground,
And turned his eyes toward heaven; nor spake he aught.
Nor ate, nor slept, till in his daily round
The golden sun had broken thrice, and sought
His rest anew; nor ever ceased his wound
To rankle, till it marred his sober thought.
At length, impelled by phrensy, the fourth day,
He from his limbs tore plate and mail away.

CXXXIII

Here was his helmet, there his shield bestowed;
His arms far off; and, farther than the rest,
His cuirass; through the greenwood wide was strowed
All his good gear, in fine; and next his vest
He rent; and, in his fury, naked showed
His shaggy paunch, and all his back and breast.
And 'gan that phrensy act, so passing dread,
Of stranger folly never shall be said.

CXXXIV

So fierce his rage, so fierce his fury grew,
That all obscured remained the warrior's sprite;
Nor, for forgetfulness, his sword he drew,
Or wonderous deeds, I trow, had wrought the knight:
But neither this, nor bill, nor axe to hew,
Was needed by Orlando's peerless might.
He of his prowess gave high proofs and full,
Who a tall pine uprooted at a pull.

CXXXV

He many others, with as little let
As fennel, wall-wort-stem, or dill, up-tore;
And ilex, knotted oak, and fir upset,
And beech, and mountain-ash, and elm-tree hoar.
He did what fowler, ere he spreads his net,
Does, to prepare the champaigne for his lore,

By stubble, rush, and nettle-stalk; and broke,
Like these, old sturdy trees and stems of oak.

CXXXVI

The shepherd swains, who hear the tumult nigh,
Leaving their flocks beneath the greenwood tree,
Some here some there across the forest hie,
And hurry thither, all, the cause to see.
— But I have reached such point, my history,
If I o'erpass this bound, may irksome be;
And I my story will delay to end,
Rather than by my tediousness offend.

ALONSO FERNÁNDEZ DE AVELLANEDA

Prologue to the *"False Quijote"* †

[In 1614, almost a decade after the appearance of the first part of *Don Quijote* (1605), an apocryphal sequel to Cervantes's novel appeared on the literary scene. Licensed and printed in Tarragona by Felipe Roberto, a bookseller no longer in business, this spurious continuation was issued by a writer who styled himself, on the title page, as "the licentiate Alonso Fernández de Avellaneda, born in the village of Tordesillas." The mysterious Avellaneda may have been a pseudonym for Lope de Vega, whose squabbles with Cervantes were well known, or for Jerónimo de Pasamonte, an Aragonese soldier who may have been writing in the service of Lope. To this day, the authorship remains murky. Dedicating his volume to the Mayor, Councilmen, and Nobles of "the Illustrious town of Argamasilla, fortunate native land of the hidalgo Knight Don Quixote de La Mancha," Avellaneda tried to defame Cervantes even as he pirated his work, producing a wretched novel that chronicled the slapstick and mechanical adventures of two puppets impersonating as Cervantes's main characters, Don Quijote and Sancho Panza. This pseudonymous forgery, however, prompted Cervantes to finish his own second part of *Don Quijote* (1615), whose Prologue includes some vitriolic words about the so-called *False Quijote*.[1] A translation of Avellaneda's earlier Prologue — whose *ad hominem* attack against Cervantes contains a litany of virulent abuses — is printed below.]

Since the story of Don Quixote de la Mancha is almost a play, it cannot nor should it fail to have a prologue. Therefore, at the beginning of this second part of his exploits there appears this one, less boastful and offensive to its readers than the one Miguel de Cervantes Saavedra placed before his first part, and more humble than the one he wrote for his *Novelas*, satirical rather than exemplary, although quite ingenious.

---

† From Alonso Fernández de Avellaneda, *Don Quixote de La Mancha (Part II): Being the spurious continuation of Miguel de Cervantes' Part I.* Trans. and ed. Alberta Wilson Server and John Esten Keller (Newark, DE: Juan de la Cuesta, 1980), pp. 3–5. Reprinted by the permission of the publisher. Some notes have been omitted.
1. On this whole thorny issue, see E. T. Aylward, *Towards a Revaluation of Avellaneda's "False Quixote"* (Newark, DE: Juan de la Cuesta, 1989).

He will not consider as such the accounts in this story, which is continued as authoritatively as he began it, with a copy of the faithful records which came into his hand (and I say "hand" because he himself admits he has only one,[2] and while we are talking so much about everybody we should say of him: "As a soldier as old in years as he is youthful in courage, he has more tongue than hands"). But let him complain about my work because of the profits I take away from his second part. At least he cannot refuse to admit that we both have one aim, which is to banish the harmful lesson of the inane books of chivalry so commonplace among rustics and idle people. However, we differ in method: he took that of offending me, one so justly praised by the most distant nations, one to whom our nation owes so much because of his having for so many years decorously and richly entertained the theaters of Spain with innumerable stupendous plays, with the artistic strictness the world demands and with the assurance and purity to be expected from a minister of the Holy Office.

My purpose has not been only to bring the stupidities of Sancho to the present comedy, avoiding offending anybody or making a display of learned synonyms (although I could do the latter well but the former poorly); I only say that nobody need be startled that this second part comes from a different author, for there is nothing new about different persons pursuing the same story. How many have spoken of the love affairs of Angélica and what happened to her? Various *Arcadias* have been written, and the *Diana*[3] is not all by one hand. Since Miguel de Cervantes is now as old as the Castle of Cervantes,[4] and is so hard to please because of his years that he is annoyed by everybody and everything, he therefore so lacks friends that when he wished to adorn his books with pompous sonnets he had to attribute them (as he says) to Prester John of the Indies or the Emperor of Trebizond, perhaps not finding a titled person in Spain who would not be offended if his name were mentioned, so many having permitted their names to appear at the beginning of books by the author he backbites — please God may he stop this, now that he has taken refuge in the sanctuary of the Church. Let him be content with his *Galatea* and prose plays, for that is what most of his novelettes are; let him not vex us.

* * *

Saint Thomas * * * teaches us that envy is sadness because of another's good fortune and prosperity, a doctrine he took from John of Damascus. In book 31, Chapter 31, of the moral exposition he made for the story of Saint Job, Saint Gregory says that the children of this vice are hatred, gossip about and defamation of one's neighbor, joy over his troubles, and regret about his good fortune; and well is this sin called envy: *a non videndo, quia invidua non potest videre bona aliorum.*[5] All are effects as

---

2. Cervantes was wounded and maimed in his left hand during the naval battle of Lepanto in the Gulf of Corinth, 1571, when the united Christian fleets defeated the navies of Islam.
3. Versions of the story of Angélica appeared in 1586 and 1602, the latter by Lope de Vega; the Italian Sannazaro's *Arcadia* (1504) was revised in Spanish by the same Lope (1598); Jorge de Montemayor's *Diana* was continued by two different authors, both of their works appearing in 1564.
4. A ruined fortress in Toledo, built in the eleventh century!
5. From the *Etymologies* of St. Isidore: ". . . from not seeing because the envious man is unable to bear the good of others."

infernal as their cause, so contrary to Christian charity, of which Saint Paul said in I Corinthians: 13: *Charitas patiens est, benigna est: non emulatur, non agit perperam, non inflatur, non est ambitiosa . . . congaudet veritati*, etc.[6] But on this subject he excuses the errors in the First Part by the fact that it was written among people in prison:[7] because of this he could not avoid being smirched by them, nor could he help coming out other than complaining, gossipy, impatient, and short-tempered, as prisoners are. This part varies somewhat from his First Part because my disposition differs from his, and in matters of opinion about anything historical, and as authentic as this is, each can strike out in the direction he pleases. This is truer when one has such a wide field as the multitude of papers I have read to compose this story, not to speak of the equal amount of those I have failed to read.

Let nobody complain because printing of such books is permitted, for this one does not teach lewdness but rather not to be crazy. When so many *Celestinas*, mother and daughter,[8] are now in permitted to roam about the public squares, a Don Quixote and a Sancho Panza may well be allowed into the fields, for they were never known to have any vice:

> rather, they had the commendable desire to right
> injustices done to orphaned girls,
> undo wrongs,
> etc.

PATRICIA FINCH AND JOHN J. ALLEN

Don Quijote across the Centuries†

"How do they talk about me, around here?" Don Quijote asks Sancho, at home after their first sally together. "What do ordinary people think of me? — and gentlemen? and noblemen? What do they say about my courage, and my great deeds, and about my gallantry? What do they say about my taking it on myself to resurrect and bring back to the world the forgotten order of knighthood?" . . . "As far as your courage, your grace," Sancho replies, "your gallantry, your great deeds, and the burden you've taken on yourself, there's a variety of opinions. Some say, 'He's crazy, but funny,' and others say, 'He's brave, but unlucky,' and still others, 'He's gallant, but he's got a lot of gall.'" (II.2) [362–63].

---

6. Verses 4–6, which read: "Love is patient; love is kind and envies no one. Love is never boastful, nor conceited, nor rude; never selfish, not quick to take offense. Love keeps no score of wrongs; does not gloat over other men's sins, but delights in the truth." Avellaneda's memory seems imperfect.

7. Cervantes suggested in the Prologue to Part I that his work was *of the type* that "might be engendered in a prison," but he never said it was *really* written there. Avellaneda, like innumerable others, has been too narrow in his reading.

8. *La Celestina* is one of the pinnacles of Spanish literature. Its original version (1499) was written by Fernando de Rojas, and was continued by four different authors; the last version, *The Daughter of la Celestina*, was published in 1612.

† This essay is a revised version of a paper delivered at Yale University, at a symposium in honor of Manuel Durán, on November 1, 1996. Quotations from *Don Quijote* are cited by part and chapter number. Norton Critical Edition page numbers follow in brackets.

These three local reactions to Part One of *Don Quijote* anticipate all of the major strains of interpretation of Cervantes's masterpiece over the past four hundred years. For those readers during the first hundred and more years after its publication whose responses have come down to us, and for a few influential twentieth-century critics, Don Quijote is "crazy, but funny"; for the Romantics, and for most readers who came after them, he is "brave, but unlucky"; for others who have found an important moral lesson in the book, he is "gallant, but he's got a lot of gall." Although the interpretations vary — as of course they must in a work of this complexity — testimony to the preeminence of *Don Quijote* and evidence of its pervasive influence are everywhere.[1]

Witnesses to the novel's power came early in England. "Of all the books of invention," wrote John Locke (1632–1704), "I know of none that equal *Don Quixote* in utility, humor, and consistent decorum."[2] A generation later, during an attack on the "foolish Writer" who "spoke of *the Quixotism of R. Crusoe*," Daniel Defoe (1660–1731) felt obliged to classify "the famous History of *Don Quixot*, a Work which thousands read with Pleasure" as a satire "upon the Duke *de Medina Sidonia*." For Defoe's near-contemporary, Alexander Pope (1688–1744), Don Quijote was "the most Moral and Reasoning Madman in the World." Cervantes's moral madman served as a model for Henry Fielding (1707–54). After publishing a play called *Don Quixote in England* (1734), Fielding explicitly acknowledged, on the title page of *Joseph Andrew*, that his work was "Written in Imitation of The Manner of Cervantes, Author of *Don Quixote*." Samuel Johnson (1709–84), who regarded *Don Quijote* as the greatest book of entertainment in the world "after Homer's *Iliad*," numbered it among the few books he was sorry to finish. "Was there ever yet anything written by mere man that was wished longer by its readers, excepting *Don Quixote, Robinson Crusoe*, and the *Pilgrim's Progress*?" Johnson also noted that very few readers of Cervantes's novel, "amidst their mirth or pity, can deny that they have admitted visions of the same kind . . . When we pity [Don Quijote], we reflect on our own disappointments; and when we laugh, our hearts inform us that he is not more ridiculous than ourselves, except that he tells what we have only thought." A different philosophical approach to Don Quijote was taken by one of Dr. Johnson's contemporaries, the philosopher David Hume (1711–76), who invoked the story of Sancho's judgment in wine — a quality inherited from two extraordinary winetasters in the Panza family — to illustrate what the Hume called "*delicacy of taste*." Writing more ecstatically about Don Quijote than perhaps anyone in his age, Laurence Sterne (1713–68) praised him as "the peerless knight of La Mancha, whom, by the bye, with all his follies, I love more, and would actually have gone further to have paid a visit to, than the greatest hero of antiquity."

The English Romantics also found much to admire in Cervantes. William Wordsworth (1770–1850) represented himself in Book 5 of *The Pre-*

1. See John J. Allen, *Don Quijote. Hero or Fool?* (Gainesville: University Presses of Florida, 1969 and 1979), Part II.
2. A list of sources for all citations, in alphabetical order, follows this essay [*Editor's Note*].

lude as "seated in a rocky cave / By the sea-side, perusing, so it chanced, / The famous history of the errant knight / Recorded by Cervantes. . . ." As a reader, Wordsworth claimed he felt more reverence than pity for Don Quijote, thinking that, "in the blind and awful lair / Of such a madness, reason did lie couched." Wordsworth's collaborator and sometime friend, Samuel Taylor Coleridge (1772–1834), canonized four writers — Dante, Shakespeare, Rabelais, and Cervantes — as "the greatest creative genuises of the modern world" — but then halved the list on the following grounds: "to combine the permanent with the individual, is one of the highest creations of genius, and has been achieved by Cervantes and Shakespeare, almost alone." *Don Quijote* was, for Coleridge, a book which "you read *through* once or twice only, but which you read *in* repeatedly." Lord Byron (1788–1824), it would seem, read in *Don Quijote* repeatedly. Not only did he use a cluster of stanzas in *Don Juan* to analyze the narrative — "Of all tales 'tis the saddest — and more sad, / Because it makes us smile" — but also, after considering Socrates himself as "Wisdom's Quixote," Byron concluded, in a fit of witty hyperbole, that "Cervantes smiled Spain's chivalry away; / A single laugh demolished the right arm / Of his own country; seldom since that day/ Has Spain had heroes. . . ."

Response to Cervantes from France also came early, and it has been particularly impressive in the 20th century. Sainte-Evrémond[3] (1613–1703) claimed that *Don Quixote* was the one book he would most like to have written. Montesquieu[4] (1689–1755) wrote in his *Persian Letters*, somewhat grudgingly, that the only good book the Spanish had produced was one that showed how ridiculous all the others were. In a mocking response to a sentry who challenged his arrival at the German city of Hertford, Voltaire (1694–1778) identified himself as "Don Quichotte." Over a century later, when Napoleon Bonaparte (1769–1821) was reading aloud from *Don Quijote* during his exile in St. Helena, one of his chroniclers recalled that he "stopped at several jests, and, putting down the book, remarked that it surely took courage to laugh in that moment at such trivialities." Stendhal (1783–1842) enlisted himself in the ranks of French novelists who admired *Don Quijote*. "The discovery of this book is perhaps the greatest epoch of my life," he wrote. Eugene Delacroix (1798?–1863) noted in his *Journal* that some men "have, after a long and almost dark career, shone with an incomparable splendor, as was the case with Cervantes." The enthusiastic critic Sainte-Beuve (1804–69) not only called *Don Quijote* "the Bible of Humanity" but also identified the human race with Cervantes's main characters: "Everyone is Don Quijote sometimes, and sometimes Sancho. . . . One goes to sleep Don Quijote and wakes up Sancho Panza." For Flaubert (1821–80), Cervantes's novel towered over all other books, including his own. "I read Rabelais and *Don Quijote* every Sunday . . . and never tire of them," he wrote. "What overwhelming books! The more one contemplates them the bigger they grow, like the

---

3. Charles de Saint-Denis Saint-Evrémond was a French critic who spent much of his life as an exile in England [*Editor's Note*].
4. Charles-Louis de Secondat Montesquieu was a French social and political philosopher [*Editor's Note*].

pyramids, and in the end they almost frighten you. What is prodigious about Don Quijote is the absence of art, and that perpetual fusion of illusion and reality which makes the book so comic and so poetic. All others are dwarfs beside it! How small one feels, oh Lord, how small one feels!" And while rereading *Don Quijote*, Flaubert wrote in another letter. "What a giant of a book! Is there anything more splendid?" His own *Madame Bovary* is, for many readers, as splendid a book. Emma Bovary arrived to fill the gap lamented by the Danish philosopher Soren Kierkegaard (1813–55), who had found it "remarkable" that the whole of European literature lacked "a feminine counterpart to *Don Quixote*."[5] André Gide (1869–1951) allowed that he had managed "to remain insensitive until these past few years to the authority of Cervantes," whom he did not consider a comic writer. "If I admire him today as much as the greatest, I should nevertheless say that he doesn't make me *laugh*, and that that is all the same to me and does not diminish at all, in my eyes, his outstanding merits." In a similar challenge to "hard" readings of *Don Quijote* — largely by critics who regard the text as a "funny book" — André Malraux (1901–76) claimed after World War II that "only three books, *Robinson Crusoe*, *Don Quijote*, and *The Idiot* are truly meaningful to the survivors of prisons and concentration camps." Michel Foucault (1926–84) — whose remarks on Cervantes are reprinted in the present volume [pp. 792–95] — called *Don Quijote* "the first modern work of literature" because "it marks the point where resemblance enters an age which is, from the point of view of resemblance, one of madness and imagination."

In Germany, Goethe (1749–1832) responded enthusiastically to his reading of *Don Quijote* during the summer of 1782: "Cervantes is my life-jacket in a sea of official papers." For both Hegel (1770–1831) and Schopenhauer (1788–1860), Cervantes's knight and squire embodied "the everlasting dilemmas of metaphysics." The German Romantics made Cervantes one of their most exalted figures. Trying to account for the "glory and admiration" that "all the nations of Europe" accorded to Cervantes's masterpiece, Schlegel (1772–1829) spoke of its "excellent style" and "perfect exposition"; its supremacy, among works of genius, "in invention and inspiration"; and, finally, its "vivid epic depiction of Spanish society and of the Spanish national character." Schelling (1775–1854) outdid Schlegel's panegyrics in one sentence: "To understand what is meant by the idea of a mythology created by the genius of a single individual, one has only to remember Cervantes." Heinrich Heine (1797–1856) claimed that "Cervantes, Shakespeare and Goethe form a triumvirate of poets that have brought forth the best in the three genres of poetic presentation, that of the epic, the dramatic, and the lyric." Instead of praising *Don Quijote*, Nietzsche (1844–1900) noted, in his *Genealogy of Morals* (1887), that it

> leaves a bitter taste in our mouths today; we almost quail in reading it. This would have seemed very strange to Cervantes and to his contemporaries, who read the work with the clearest conscience in the world, thought it the funniest of books, and almost died laughing over it.

---

5. *The Female Quixote* (1752) by Charlotte Lennox (1720–1804) had already provided English readers an early female version of Cervantes's hero.

About a decade after Nietzsche's anxious response, Sigmund Freud (1856–1939), the future creator of psychoanalysis, would confess to his fiancée Martha Bernays that he was frittering away much of the summer of 1883 by concentrating more on *Don Quixote* "than on brain anatomy." Freud's efforts to become a neurologist were thwarted by an increasing curiosity about psychopathological issues, and his recollection of this generative period has a distinctly quixotic ring: "We were all noble knights passing through the world caught in a dream." Years later, Freud would explain how Cervantes first captivated him. "As a young student, the desire to read the immortal *Quijote* in the Spanish original led me to learn, without teachers, the beautiful Castilian language." A great admirer of both Cervantes and Freud, Thomas Mann (1875–1955) made an ocean "voyage with *Don Quijote*" in 1939, which he recounted in a vivid memoir to which he gave that title.

Russian commentary on Cervantes came to the fore with Ivan Turgenev (1818–1883), whose essay on "Hamlet and Don Quixote" portrayed Cervantes's hero as a nobler and less egoistic character than Hamlet. In an even more encomiastic vein, Dostoevsky (1821–81) wrote that "if this world ended and people in some other world were asked whether they understood their life on earth and what conclusion they had come to about it, a man could just present the volume of *Don Quijote* and say: 'Here is my conclusion on life. Can you condemn me for it?' " The great disseminator of the polyphonic Dostoevsky, Mikhail Bakhtin (1895–1975), called *Don Quijote* "the classic and purest model of the novel as genre . . . , which realizes in itself, in extraordinary depth and breadth, all the artistic possibilities of heteroglot and internally dialogized novelistic discourse." The Russian who most notoriously popularized Cervantes, however, was the expatriate Vladimir Nabokov. Remembered as the fastidious author of *Lolita* and *Pale Fire*, the latter novel visibly influenced by Cervantes, Nabokov delivered, in the 1950s, a series of quirky lectures to Harvard undergraduates on *Don Quixote*, which he read as a cruel "fairly tale."

Peninsular Spanish writers have of course lived most in Cervantes's shadow. Although countless Spaniards have paid tribute to him down the ages, perhaps his most eloquent admirers belong to the twentieth century. Unamuno (1864–1936) wrote often of Cervantes and Don Quijote, and one of his books, *The Life of Don Quijote and Sancho Panza*, is a chapter-by-chapter commentary on the novel. "Is Cervantes joking?" asks Ortega y Gasset (1883–1955) in his provocative *Meditations on Don Quijote* — "and what is he making fun of? In the distance, alone on the open Manchegan plain, the tall figure of Don Quixote bends, forming a question mark."

A number of Eastern European writers have entered the Cervantine circle of influence, one of them focusing on that very question mark. The Hungarian marxist Gyorgy Lukacs (1885–1971) — whose work inaugurates serious twentieth-century theorization on the genre of the novel — considered *Don Quijote* "the first great novel of world literature." The Czech novelist Milan Kundera (b. 1929) — who celebrated Cervantes for teaching us "to comprehend the world as a question" — was unstinting in his admiration: "The novelist need answer to no one but Cervantes." Kundera concluded that Cervantes, whom the phenomenologists "neglected to take into consideration in their judgment of the Modern Era," is one of the founders of that era. "By that I mean, if it is true that philosophy and science have forgotten about man's being, it emerges all the more plainly that with Cervantes a great European art took shape that is nothing other than the investigation of that forgotten being."

That "great European art" has been having, since the early seventeenth century, a visible impact on North American writers. In the 1630s, for instance, Cervantes's hero was tilting at windmills in the New England colonies — metaphoric windmills that John Morton and Cotton Mather located in the figures of Miles Standish and Roger Williams, respectively. A century later, the sixteen-year-old Benjamin Franklin (1706–90) wished that some "great genius" would describe the actions of certain ecclesiastics or "*Saint-errants*" just as the great Cervantes had done of knights-errant "in the *Life and Actions of Don Quixote*, who spent his Time in *Adventures* to free the World of Monsters, and to tame Gyants." Unlike the majority of his countrymen, who read Cervantes in translation, Thomas Jefferson (1743–1826) passed the time during a summer crossing to England "drinking light wines and reading *Don Quixote* in Spanish." A generation later, Herman Melville (1819–91), writing a parody of chivalry in *The Piazza Tale*, represented Don Quijote as "that sagest sage that ever lived." Mark Twain (1835–1910) advertised his own debt to Cervantes through Tom Sawyer's pert response to Huck Finn's inability to see "elephants," "A-rabs," and other such exotica in a Sunday-school picnic: "He said if I warn't so ignorant, but had read a book called 'Don Quixote,' I would know without asking." William Faulkner (1897–1962) claimed to have read *Don Quijote* "every year, as some do the Bible." Walker Percy (1916–1990) said that the book he would most like to have written was *Don Quijote*. Major American critics such as Lionel Trilling (1905–75) and Harold Bloom (b. 1930) have nothing but panegyrics for Cervantes's work. While Trilling claims that "all prose fiction is a variation on the theme of *Don Quixote*," Bloom considers Cervantes to be "the only possible peer of Dante and Shakespeare in the Western Canon."

As for Latin American writers, one of the best-known stories by the Argentine writer Jorge Luis Borges (1899–1986) — "Pierre Menard, Author of the *Quixote*" — is reproduced in this volume [847–53]. Apart from various other short fictions about Cervantes's creations, Borges wrote these lines about Cervantes himself in a poem called "A Soldier of Urbina": "He thought he was finished, alone and poor, / not knowing the music he had mastered; / crossing the depths of a dream, / Don Quijote and Sancho rode within him." The Mexican novelist and essayist Carlos Fuentes (b. 1928), who wrote a long influential essay called *Cervantes, or the Critique of Reading*, may be numbered among the Latin-American Magic Realists — writers such as Alejo Carpentier and Gabriel García Márquez — who loudly advertise their "quixotic roots."[6]

Perhaps the voice that most forcefully sums up this survey of responses — whose coverage pretends to be neither inclusive nor conclusive —

---

6. See Edwin Williamson, "The Quixotic Roots of Magic Realism. History and Fiction from Alejo Carpentier to Gabriel García Márquez," in *Cervantes and the Modernists. The Question of Influence*, ed. Edwin Williamson (London: Tamesis, 1994), pp. 103–20.

belongs to the Nigerian poet and novelist Ben Okri (b. 1959): "I found that, as I read *Don Quijote*, I was reading almost every important Western text of the last two or three hundred years."

Works Cited

Bakhtin, Mikhail M. *The Dialogic Imagination. Four Essays*, ed. Michael Holquist, trans. Caryl Emerson and Michael Holquist (Austin: U of Texas Press, 1981), p. 324.
Bloom, Harold. *The Western Canon* (N.Y.: Harcourt Brace, 1994), p. 127.
Bonaparte, Napoleon. Cited in Comte Emmanuel Auguste Dieudonné de Las Cases, *Le Memorial de Sainte-Hélene*. (Paris: G. Barba, 1852).
Borges, Jorge Luis. *Obra poética*, 1923–1977 (Madrid: Alianza. Emecé, 1981), p. 199.
Byron, George Gordon, Lord. *Don Juan*, ed. Leslie A. Marchand (Boston: Houghton Mifflin, 1958), Canto XIII, stanzas 9–11, p. 358.
Clemens, Samuel Langhorne (Mark Twain). *Adventures of Huckleberry Finn*, ed. Sculley Bradley et al. 2nd Norton Critical ed. (N.Y.: Norton, 1977), p. 16.
Coleridge, Samuel Taylor. *Inquiring Spirit*, ed. Kathleen Coburn (London: Routledge & Kegan Paul, 1957), p. 189; *Coleridge's Miscellaneous Criticism*, ed. Thomas M. Raysor (London: Constable & Co., 1936), p. 103.
Defoe, Daniel. "Preface to Volume III of *Robinson Crusoe*," from *Serious Reflections during the Life and Surprising* Adventures *of Robinson Crusoe*. London, 1720. Cited in the Second Edition of the Norton Critical Edition of Defoe's *Robinson Crusoe*, ed. Michael Shinagel (New York: Norton, 1994), pp. 240–41.
Delacroix, Eugène. *The Journal of Eugène Delacroix*, trans. Walter Pach (N.Y.: Grove Press, 1961), p. 721.
Dostoevsky, Fyodor. *Selected Letters of Fyodor Dostoevsky*, ed. Joseph Frank and Darrel Goldstein, trans. Andrew R. MacAndrew (New Brunswick, 1987), p. 272, n. 72.
Faulkner, William. *Writers at Work*, ed. Malcolm Cowley (N.Y.: Viking, 1958), p. 136.
Fielding, Henry. *Joseph Andrews, with Shamela and Related Writings*, ed. Homer Goldberg, Norton Critical Edition (New York: Norton, 1987), p. 2.
Flaubert, Gustave. *The Letters of Gustave Flaubert 1830–1857*, Vol. I, ed. and trans. Francis Steegmuller (Cambridge: Belknap Press of Harvard UP, 1982), p. 173; and *The Letters of Gustave Flaubert 1857–1880*, Vol. II, ed. and trans. Francis Steegmuller: (Cambridge: Belknap Press of Harvard UP, 1982), p. 128.
Foucault, Michel. *The Order of Things* (N.Y.: Vintage, 1973), pp. 48–49.
Franklin, Benjamin. Cited in James Parton, *Life and Times of Benjamin Franklin*, Vol. I (N.Y.: Mason Bros., 1864), p. 67.
Freud, Sigmund. The letter to Martha Freud of 22 August 1983 is in *The Letters of Sigmund Freud, 1873–1939*, trans. Tania Stern and James Stern (New York: Basic Books, 1961). The "noble knights" passage is cited by Ernest Jones, *Sigmund Freud. Life and Work*. 3 vols. (London: Hogarth Press, 1953), 1.191. Freud's memory of learning Castilian is in *Standard Edition of the Complete Psychological Works* (London: Hogarth Press, 1961), p. 289.
Fuentes, Carlos. *Don Quixote, or The Critique of Reading* (Austin: University of Texas Press, 1976).
Gide, André. *Journal 1939–1949. Souvenirs* (Paris: Gallimard, 1954), p. 1191.
Goethe, Johann Wolfgang von. *Letters from Goethe*, trans. M. Von Herzfeld and C. Melvil Sym (Edinburgh U. Press, 1957).
Hegel, Georg Wilhelm Friedrich, and Arthur Schopenhauer. J. J. A. Bertrand, *Cervantes et le Romantisme Allemande*. 1914. p. 459ff; cited by Harry Levin, *The Gates of Horn* (N.Y.: Oxford UP, 1963), p. 100.
Heine, Heinrich. From the Introduction to the German translation *Der Sinnreiche Junker "Don Quixote von la Mancha"* (Stuttgart: Verlag der Classiker, 1837–38); English translation cited here is from *A Critical Trajectory*, ed. Raymond Barbera (Boston: Mirage Press, 1971).
Hume, David. "Of the Standard of Taste" [1757], *Literary Criticism in England, 1600–1800*, ed. Gerald Wester Chapman (N.Y.: Alfred A. Knopf, 1966), p. 294.
Jefferson, Thomas. John Dos Passos, *The Head and Heart of Thomas Jefferson* (Garden City, N.Y.: Doubleday, 1954), p. 253.
Johnson, Samuel. From Hester Lynch Piozzi, *Anecdotes of . . . Samuel Johnson* (London, 1786), 281; and from *Rambler*, No. 2, in *The Rambler*, Vol. 1 (Boston: M. & F.E. Cotton, 1811), p. 66.
Kierkegaard, Soren. *Either/Or* (Princeton: Princeton UP, 1944), I, 210n.
Kundera, Milan. *The Book of Laughter and Forgetting*, trans. Michael Henry Heim (NY: Penguin, 1981), p. 237; *The Art of the Novel*, trans. Linda Asher (N.Y.: Grove, 1986), pp. 144 and 4–5.
Locke, John. *Essay on the Human Understanding. Some Thoughts Concerning Reading and Study for a Gentleman*. London. Printed by Elizabeth Holt for Thomas Bassett, 1690.
Lukács, Georg. *The Theory of the Novel*, trans. Anna Bostok (1971; reprinted. Cambridge, Mass.: MIT, 1977), p. 88.

Malraux, André. *Les Noyers d'Altenburg* (Paris, 1948), pp. 119–121. Cited by Ian Watt, *The Rise of the Novel* (Berkeley: U of California P, 1962), p. 133.

Mann, Thomas. "Voyage with Don Quixote." [1934]. From *Essays of Three Decades*, trans. H. T. Lowe-Porter (NY: Alfred A. Knopf; London: Martin Secker & Warburg Ltd., 1965), pp. 429–464.

Melville, Herman. *The Piazza Tales*, ed. Harrison Hayford et al., Vol. 9 (Evanston: Northwestern-Newberry, 1987), p. 6.

Montesquieu (Charles Louis de Secondat, Baron de la Brède et de Montesquieu). Charles Agustin Sainte-Beuve, *Les Nouveaux lundis*. Vol. 8. (Paris: Michel Lévy Frères, 1864), p. 61.

Morton, John. Cited in Wilson's Introduction to this volume, p. xiv.

Nabokov, Vladimir. *Lectures on Don Quixote*, ed. Fredson Bowers (N.Y.: Harcourt Brace Jovanovich, 1983).

Nietzsche, Friedrich. *The Birth of Tragedy and The Genealogy of Morals*, trans. Francis Golffing (Garden City, N.Y.: Doubleday & Co., 1956), p. 198.

Okri, Ben. Mike Dibb, Dibb Directions. *The Further Adventures of Don Quixote de la Mancha* (BBC-TV, 1995).

Ortega y Gassett, José. *Meditaciones del Quijote* (Madrid: Revista de Occidente, 3rd. ed., 1956), p. 75. [Author's translation].

Percy, Walker. *New York Times Book Review* (December 6, 1981); cited in *Walker Percy. A Life* (N.Y.: Farrar, Straus, Giroux, 1997).

Pope, Alexander. *Correspondence*. Ed. George Sherburn, 5 vols. (Oxford: Clarendon, 1956), IV, 208.

Sainte Évremond, Ch. M. Saint-Denys de. Charles Augustin Sainte-Beuve, *Les Nouveaux lundis*, vol. 8 (Paris: Michel Lévy Frères, 1864), p. 60.

Sainte-Beuve, Charles Augustin. *Les Nouveaux lundis*, vol. 8 (Paris: Michel Lévy Frères, 1864), p. 37.

Schelling, Friedrich Wilhelm von Schelling. *Realen und Idealen in der Natur* (Hamburg 1806); cited by Leopoldo Rius y Llosellas, *Bibliografía crítica de las obras de Miguel de Cervantes Saavedra* (N.Y.: Burt Franklin, 1970) ([originally published in 1904]), III, 218.

Schlegel, Friedrich von. *Geschichte der alten und neuen Litteratur. Vorlesungen gehalten zu Wien im Jahre 1812*, Vol. II, pp. 108–111; cited by Leopoldo Rius y Llosellas, *Bibliografía crítica de las obras de Miguel de Cervantes Saavedra* (N.Y.: Burt Franklin, 1970 [originally published in 1904]), III, 228.

Stendhal (Marie Henri Beyle). *De L'amour*, ed. Henri Martineau (1927), II, 179; cited by Levin, *Gates of Horn*, p. 100.

Sterne, Laurence. *The Life and Opinions of Tristram Shandy, Gentleman*, ed. Ian Campbell Ross (N.Y.: Oxford UP, 1983), I, x, 10.

Trilling, Lionel. *The Liberal Imagination* (N.Y.: Viking, 1950), p. 203.

Turgenev, Ivan. "Hamlet and Don Quixote," trans. W.A. Drake, in *The Anatomy of "Don Quixote*," ed. M.J. Benardete and Angel Flores (Port Washington, N.Y.: Kennikat Press, 1969).

Unamuno y Jugo, Miguel de. *Vida de don Quijote y Sancho Panza* (Madrid: Espasa-Calpe, 1956 [3rd and final author's edition, 1930]).

Voltaire, Francois Marie Arouet de. Cited in Haydn Trevor Mason, *Voltaire* (N.Y.: St. Martin's, 1975), p. 123.

Wordsworth, William. *The Prelude; Or, Growth of a Poet's Mind* (1850). Reproduced in Wordsworth, *Poetical Works*, ed. Thomas Hutchinson, in the revision by Ernest de Selincourt (Oxford, 1969), pp. 5, 60–61, 143–52.

CRITICISM

General Essays on *Don Quijote*

CARLOS FUENTES

Foreword†

When I was a young student in Latin American schools, we were constantly being asked to define the boundary between the Middle Ages and the Modern Age. I always remembered a grotesquely famous Spanish play in which a knight in armour unsheaths his sword and exclaims to his astonished family: "I'm off to the Thirty Years' War!"

Did the modern age begin with the fall of Constantinople to the Turks in 1453, the discovery of the New World in 1492 or the publication by Copernicus of his Revolutions of the Spheres in 1543? To give only one answer is akin to exclaiming that we are off to the Thirty Years' War. At least since Vico,[1] we know that the past is present in us because we are the bearers of the culture we ourselves have made.

Nevertheless, given a choice in the matter, I have always answered that, for me, the modern world begins when Don Quixote de la Mancha, in 1605, leaves his village, goes out into the world, and discovers that the world does not resemble what he has read about it.

Many things are changing in the world; many others are surviving. *Don Quixote* tells us just this: this is why he is so modern, but also so ancient, so eternal. He illustrates the rupture of a world based on analogy and thrust into differentiation. He makes evident a challenge that we consider peculiarly ours: how to accept the diversity and mutation of the world, while retaining the mind's power for analogy and unity, so that this changing world shall not become meaningless.

Don Quixote tells us that being modern is not a question of sacrificing the past in favour of the new, but of maintaining, comparing and remembering values we have created, making them modern so as not to lose the value of the modern.

This is our challenge as contemporary individuals and, indeed, as present-day writers. For if *Don Quixote*, by its very nature, does not define the modern world but only an aspect of it, it does, I believe, at least define

---

† From "Foreword" by Carlos Fuentes to *The Adventures of Don Quixote de la Mancha* by Miguel de Cervantes, trans. Tobias Smollet, introduction by Carlos Fuentes. (New York: Farrar, Straus & Giroux, 1986), pp. xi–xiii. Introduction copyright © 1986 by Carlos Fuentes. Reprinted with the permission of Farrar, Straus & Giroux, Inc.

1. Giambattista Vico (1668–1744), an Italian philosopher and classical scholar, wrote *Principles of a New Science of Nations*, in which he developed his theory of historical change as a cycle of phases — barbarism, heroism, and reason — each with its corresponding linguistic, political, and cultural modes [*Editor's Note*].

777

the central problems of the modern novel. I remember discussing the matter over luncheon one cold day in 1975 with André Malraux: he chose Madame de Lafayette's *La Princesse de Clèves* as the first modern novel because, he said, it was the first psychological, interior novel, constructed around the reasons of the heart. Anglo-Saxon criticism would perhaps prefer, along with Ian Watt, to establish "the rise of the novel" in connection with the appearance of a middle class of affluent readers in England, politically emancipated and psychologically demanding of novelty in theme and characterization: Richardson, Fielding, Smollett.

Yet I shall not travel the road of Quixote's modernity alone. After all, as Lionel Trilling once wrote, "All prose fiction is a variation of the theme of *Don Quixote*: . . . the problem of appearance and reality." This all-encompassing fictitiousness in Cervantes is not at odds with Harry Levin's vision of its modernity: *Don Quixote* is seen by Levin as "The prototype of all realistic novels" . . . for it deals with "the literary technique of systematic disillusionment." And its universality is not in contradiction to Alejo Carpentier's discovery in Cervantes of the imaginary dimension within the individual: Cervantes invents a new I, says the Cuban novelist, much as Malraux said of Mme de Lafayette.

Wayne Booth's self-conscious narrator in *Don Quixote*; Marthe Robert's conception of *Don Quixote* as a novel in search of itself; Robert Coover's vision of *Don Quixote* in a world divided between reality and illusion, sanity and madness, the erotic and the ludicrous, the visionary and the eschatological; all of these highly articulate and penetrating discussions on the modernity and relevance of Cervantes accompany me in my own search for *Don Quixote*. But it is, perhaps, Michel Foucault who has best described the dis-placement that occurs in the dynamic world of Cervantes: *Don Quixote*, writes Foucault in *The Order of Things*, is the sign of a modern divorce between words and things. *Don Quixote* is desperately searching for a new coincidence, for a new similitude in a world where nothing seems to resemble what it once resembled.

This same dynamic dis-placement, this sense of search and pilgrimage, is what Claudio Guillén calls the "active dialogue" in *Don Quixote*. A dialogue of genres, in the first place: the picaresque, the pastoral, the chivalric, the byzantine, all the established genres stake their presence and have their say in *Don Quixote*. But the past and the present are also actively fused and the novel becomes a critical project as it shifts from the spoken tale to the written narrative, from verse to prose and from the tavern to the printing shop.

Don Quixote, it is true, bears all of the marks of what it leaves behind. If it is the first modern novel, its debt to tradition is enormous, since its very inception, as we all know, is the satire of the epic of chivalry. But if it is the last Medieval romance, then it also celebrates its own death: it becomes its own Requiem. If it is a work of the Renaissance, it also maintains a lively Medieval carnival of games, puns and references not far from Bakhtin's definition of festive humour in the novel, breaking down the frontiers between actors and audience. And finally, if it opens for all the adventure of modern reading, it remains a book deeply immersed in the society and the history of Spain.

Miguel de Cervantes was born in 1547 and died in 1616. He published the first part of *Don Quixote* in 1605, and the second part in 1615. So that everything I have said up till now happens historically within a contradiction. Cervantes' work is one of the great examples of Renaissance liberation. But his life occurs within the supreme example of the negation of that same liberation: the Spanish Counter Reformation. We must judge Cervantes and *Don Quixote* against this background if we are to understand his achievement fully.

*   *   *

HAROLD BLOOM

Cervantes: The Play of the World†

We know more about Cervantes the man than we do about Shakespeare, and doubtless there is still much to be learned about him, because his life was vivid, arduous, and heroic. Shakespeare was an immense financial success as a playwright and died affluent, his societal ambitions (such as they were) fulfilled. Despite the popularity of *Don Quixote*, Cervantes received no royalties on it and had little luck with patrons. He had few realistic ambitions, beyond supporting himself and his family, and he failed as a playwright. Poetry was not his gift; *Don Quixote* was. Shakespeare's contemporary (they died, it is thought, on the same day), he has in common with Shakespeare the universality of his genius, and he is the only possible peer of Dante and Shakespeare in the Western Canon.

One thinks of him in conjunction with Shakespeare and Montaigne because the three of them are wisdom writers; there is no fourth so sane, temperate, and benign unless it be Molière, and in some sense he was Montaigne born again, but in another genre. In one respect, only Cervantes and Shakespeare occupy the highest eminence; you cannot get ahead of them, because they are always there before you.

Confronting the strength of *Don Quixote*, the reader is never lessened, only enhanced. That is not true in many moments of reading Dante or Milton or Jonathan Swift, whose *Tale of a Tub* always impresses me as the best prose in the language after Shakespeare's and yet reproves me incessantly. It is also not true of the experience of reading Kafka, the central writer of our chaos. Shakespeare is again the nearest analogue to Cervantes; we are sustained by the dramatist's well-nigh infinite capacity for disinterestedness. Although Cervantes is ceaselessly careful to be faithfully Catholic, we do not read *Don Quixote* as a pious work. Presumably Cervantes was an Old Christian, not descended from Jewish *conversos*[1] or New

---

† Excerpts from Harold Bloom, *The Western Canon: The Books and School of the Ages* (New York: Harcourt Brace & Co., 1994), pp. 127–35.

1. Ethnically defined as "New Christians of Jewish origins," *conversos* were forcibly baptized Catholic Christians who often lived outwardly as such while secretly practicing Judaic rites and customs [*Editor's Note*].

Christians, yet we cannot be certain about his origins, just as we cannot hope to surmise his attitudes precisely. Characterizing his ironies is an impossible task; missing them is also impossible.

Despite his heroic war service (he permanently lost the use of his left hand at the great sea battle of Lepanto against the Turks), Cervantes had to be very wary of the Counter-Reformation and the Inquisition. Quixote's modes of madness grant him, and Cervantes, something of a fool's license, akin to that of the Fool in *King Lear*, a work staged simultaneously with the publication of the first part of *Don Quixote*. Cervantes was almost certainly a disciple of Erasmus, the Dutch humanist whose writing on Christian inwardness appealed greatly to the *conversos*, caught between a Judaism they had been forced to abandon and a Christian system that made them second-class citizens. Cervantes' ancestral family was crowded with physicians, a popular Jewish profession in Spain before the expulsions and forced conversions of 1492. A century later, Cervantes seems subtly haunted by that terrible year, which did much harm to Jews and Moors, as well as to Spain's well-being as an economy and a society.

No two readers ever seem to read the same *Don Quixote*, and the most distinguished critics have failed to agree on most of the book's fundamental aspects. Erich Auerbach thought it had no rival in the representation of ordinary reality as a continuous gaiety. Having just finished rereading *Don Quixote*, I blink at my inability to find what Auerbach called "so universal and multi-layered, so noncritical and nonproblematical a gaiety." "Symbolic and tragic terms," even when employed to categorize the hero's madness, seemed false to Auerbach. Against that claim I set the most poignant and Quixotic of all critical agonists, the Basque man of letters Miguel de Unamuno, whose "tragic sense of life" was founded upon his intimate relationship with Cervantes' masterpiece, which for Unamuno replaced the Bible as the authentic Spanish Scripture. "Our Lord Don Quixote," Unamuno called him, a Kafkan before Kafka, because his madness comes from a faith in what Kafka was to name "indestructibility." Unamuno's Knight of the Sorrowful Countenance is a quester for survival, whose only madness is a crusade against death: "Great was Don Quixote's madness, and it was great because the root from which it grew was great: the inextinguishable longing to survive, a source of the most extravagant follies as well as the most heroic acts."

In this view, the Don's madness is a refusal to accept what Freud called "reality testing," or the reality principle. When Don Quixote makes friends with the necessity of dying, he dies soon enough, thus returning to a Christianity conceived as the cult of death — and not just by Unamuno among Spanish visionaries. For Unamuno, the book's gaiety belongs solely to Sancho Panza, who purges his *daimon*, Don Quixote, and thus pleasurably follows the sad knight through every outrageous misadventure. This reading is again very close to Kafka's extraordinary parable, "The Truth about Sancho Panza," in which it is Sancho who has devoured all the romances of chivalry until his imagined demon, personified as the Don, departs upon his adventures with Sancho tagging along. Perhaps Kafka was making *Don Quixote* into one long and rather bitter Jewish joke, but that may be more faithful to the book than reading it with Auerbach as unalloyed gaiety.

Probably only *Hamlet* spurs as many variant interpretations as *Don Quixote* does. No one among us can purge Hamlet of his Romantic interpreters, and Don Quixote has inspired just as numerous and persistent a Romantic school of criticism, as well as books and essays opposing such a supposed idealization of Cervantes' protagonist. Romantics (myself included) see Quixote as hero, not fool; decline to read the book primarily as satire; and find in the work a metaphysical or visionary attitude regarding the Don's quest that makes the Cervantine influence upon *Moby Dick* seem wholly natural. From the German philosopher-critic Schelling in 1802 down to the Broadway musical *Man of La Mancha* in 1966, there has been a continuous exaltation of the supposedly impossible dream-quest. The novelists have been the major proponents of this apotheosis of Don Quixote: exuberant admirers have included Fielding, Smollett, and Sterne in England; Goethe and Thomas Mann in Germany; Stendhal and Flaubert in France; Melville and Mark Twain in the United States; and virtually all modern Hispanic American writers. Dostoevsky, who might seem the least Cervantine of writers, insisted that Prince Myshkin in *The Idiot* was modeled on Don Quixote. Since Cervantes' remarkable experiment is credited by many as having invented the novel, as opposed to the picaresque narrative, the devotion of so many later novelists is understandable enough; but the enormous passions evoked by the book, in Stendhal and Flaubert in particular, are extraordinary tributes to its achievement.

I myself naturally gravitate to Unamuno when I read *Don Quixote*, because for me the heart of the book is its revelation and celebration of heroic individuality, both in the Don and in Sancho. Unamuno rather perversely preferred the Don to Cervantes, but there I refuse to follow, because no writer has established a more intimate relation with his protagonist than Cervantes did. We wish we could know what Shakespeare himself thought of Hamlet; we know almost too much about how Don Quixote affected Cervantes, even if our knowledge is often indirect. Cervantes invented endless ways of disrupting his own narrative to compel the reader to tell the story in place of the wary author. The wily and wicked enchanters who supposedly work without ceasing to frustrate the magnificently indomitable Don Quixote are also employed to make us into unusually active readers. The Don supposes the sorcerers to exist, and Cervantes pragmatically realizes them as crucial components of his language. Everything is transformed through enchantment, is the Quixotic lament, and the wicked sorcerer is Cervantes himself. His characters have read all of the stories about one another, and much of the novel's second part concerns itself with their reactions to having read the first. The reader is educated into considerably more sophistication of response, even when Don Quixote stubbornly refuses to learn, though that refusal has more to do with his own "madness" than with the fictive status of the chivalric romances that have crazed him. The Don and Cervantes together evolve toward a new kind of literary dialectic, one that alternates in proclaiming both the potency and the vanity of the narrative in its relation to real events. Even as the Don, in part one, gradually comes to understand the limitations of fiction, so Cervantes grows in his pride of authorship and in the particular joy of having invented the Don and Sancho.

* * *

* * * A loving but quarrelsome duo, Sancho and the Don are united by more than their mutual affection and their authentic respect for each other. At their best, they are companions in the order of play, a sphere with its own rules and its own vision of reality: Unamuno is again the useful Cervantine critic here, but the theoretician is Johan Huizinga in his subtle book, *Homo Ludens* (1944), which barely mentions Cervantes. Huizinga begins by asserting that his subject, play, is to be distinguished from both comedy and folly: "The category of the comic is connected with *folly* in the highest and lowest sense of that word. Play, however, is not foolish. It lies outside the antithesis of wisdom and folly."

Don Quixote is neither a madman nor a fool, but someone who plays at being a knight-errant. Play is a voluntary activity, unlike madness and foolishness. Play, according to Huizinga, has four principal characteristics: freedom, disinterestedness, excludedness or limitedness, and order. You can test all of these qualities upon the Don's knight-errantry, but not always upon Sancho's faithful service as squire, for Sancho is slower to yield himself to play. The Don lifts himself into ideal place and time and is faithful to his own freedom, to its disinterestedness and seclusion, and to its limits, until at last he is defeated, abandons the game, returns to Christian "sanity," and so dies. Unamuno says of Quixote that he went out to seek his true fatherland and found it in exile. As always, Unamuno understood what was most inward in the great book. The Don, like the Jews and the Moors, is an exile, but in the mode of the *conversos* and *moriscos*,[2] an internal exile. Don Quixote leaves his village to seek his spirit's home in exile, because only exiled can he be free.

Cervantes never tells us explicitly why Alonso Quijano (the book gives the name several variant spellings) was first driven to craze himself by reading chivalric romances, until at last he went out upon the roads to become Don Quixote. A poor gentleman of La Mancha, Alonso has only one vice: he is an obsessive reader of the popular literature of his day, which crowds reality out of his mind. Cervantes describes Alonso as a pure case of the unlived life. He is single, close to fifty, presumably without sexual experience, confined to the company of a housekeeper in her forties, a nineteen-year-old niece, a field hand, and his two friends: the village curate and Nicholas the barber. Not far away lives a peasant girl, the robust Aldonza Lorenzo, who has unknowingly become the ideal object of his fantasies, renamed in them as the great lady, Dulcinea del Toboso.

Whether she is truly the object of the good man's quest is unclear. One critic has gone so far as to suggest that Quijano is impelled to become Don Quixote because of barely repressed lust for his own niece, a notion nowhere in Cervantes' text, but an indication of the desperation to which

---

2. *Moriscos* were Christianized Muslims. See footnote on the *morisco* translator of *Don Quijote* (I.9) on p. 51 of this text [*Editor's Note*].

Cervantes has been known to drive his scholars. All Cervantes tells us is that his hero has gone mad, and we are given no clinical details whatsoever. Unamuno's reaction seems to me the best one on the Quixotic loss of his wits: "He lost them for our sake, for our benefit, so as to leave us an eternal example of spiritual generosity." That is to say, Don Quixote goes mad as a vicarious atonement for our drabness, our ungenerous dearth of imagination.

Sancho, a poor peasant, is persuaded to go along as squire on the knight's second sally, which turns into the glorious affair of the windmills. The inducement for the good and ostensibly slow-witted Sancho is that he will govern an island, which the knight will conquer for him. Cervantes is inevitably ironic when he first introduces us to Sancho, whose wit is extraordinary and whose true desire is to gain fame rather than wealth, as a governor. More fundamentally, an element in Sancho desires the order of play, uneasy as the rest of Sancho is with some of the consequences of Quixotic play. Like the Don, Sancho searches for a new ego, an idea that Alejo Carpentier, the Cuban novelist, believes Cervantes first invented. I would say that Shakespeare and Cervantes came at it simultaneously, the difference between the two being the modalities of change in their principal characters.

Don Quixote and Sancho Panza are each other's ideal conversationalist; they change by listening to each other. In Shakespeare change comes from self-overhearing and from pondering the implications of what one has heard. Neither the Don nor Sancho is capable of overhearing himself; the Quixotic ideal and the Panzaesque reality are too strong for their upholders to doubt, so they cannot absorb their own departures from their standards. They can speak blasphemies but not recognize them when they emerge. The tragic greatness of the Shakespearean protagonists extends to comedy, history, and romance; only in climactic recognition scenes are the survivors able to listen fully to what others are saying. Shakespeare's influence, and not just in English-speaking countries, has overcome that of Cervantes. Modern solipsism stems from Shakespeare (and from Petrarch before him). Dante, Cervantes, Molière — who depend on interchanges between their personae — seem less natural than Shakespeare's gorgeous solipsism, and perhaps they are indeed less natural.

Shakespeare has no parallel to the exchanges between the Don and Sancho, because his friends and lovers never quite listen to one another. Think of Antony's death scene, in which Cleopatra hears and overhears mostly herself, or the attempts at play between Falstaff and Hal in which Falstaff is forced into defense because the prince so perpetually attacks. There are gentler exceptions, like Rosalind and Celia in *As You Like It*; but they are not the norm. Shakespearean individuality is matchless, but it exacts enormous costs. Cervantine egoism, exalted by Unamuno, is always qualified by the free relationship between Sancho and the Don, who grant one another space for play. Both Cervantes and Shakespeare are supreme in the creation of personality, but the greatest Shakespearean personalities — Hamlet, Lear, Iago, Shylock, Falstaff, Cleopatra, Prospero — at last wither gloriously in the air of an inward solitude. Don Quixote is saved by Sancho, and Sancho, by the Don. Their friendship is canonical and changes, in part, the subsequent nature of the canon.

*   *   *

JAVIER HERRERO

Who Was Dulcinea?†

Don Alonso Quijano was an exceedingly absent-minded gentleman. When he first sallied forth in quest of adventures, he forgot that he had not been dubbed a knight and consequently, following the rules of chivalry, he was not allowed to enter into combat. He tried to remedy his oversight by stopping into the first castle he encountered and having himself dubbed by the courtly Castilian, lord of the castle. He was lucky; he soon found a most elegant fortress, ladies dallying by the moat, other knights dressing their palfreys and, finally, the elegant lord who received him with the civility owed to a comrade in arms. The fact that the castle was an inn, the Castilian a scoundrel, the knights muleteers and the palfreys mules, the damsels whores that they hired to enliven their tiring journey, these highly complex characteristics of a world that does not fit into the bookish mold of his beloved romances, escaped him; this lack of awareness of the distance between romance and *La Mancha* got him into a dangerous scrape and to his first victory (he almost killed one of the muleteers who rudely interrupted the sacramental holiness of the dubbing ceremony). He also forgot that a knight needs a squire, that wounds need medicine, and that sweaty shirts must be changed. But among so much oblivion there is one act of forgetfulness that is almost unforgivable and that could have brought with it the direst consequences, had he not put brilliant remedy to it in the very last moment: on the brink of leaving his home in search of glory and adventures Don Quijote suddenly realized that he had forgotten to fall in love.

This is no minor oversight. As Don Quijote himself will tell Vivaldo later in the story,

> I say that it is impossible that there could be any knight errant without a lady. For it is as right and proper for them to be in love as for the sky to have stars: I can vouch for it that there has never been a knight errant without a lady in any history whatsoever. For the very fact of his having no lady would show him to be no legitimate knight, but a bastard who has entered the fortress of chivalry not through the gate but over the fence, like a thief and a robber. (99–100) [70]

We can see, then, the abyss of shame into which Don Quijote's absent-mindedness almost threw him: without a lady his battles and deeds, instead

---

† From Javier Herrero, *Who Was Dulcinea?* (New Orleans: The Graduate School of Tulane University, 1985), pp. 1–11. Reprinted by permission of the author. Quotations are from Miguel de Cervantes Saavedra, *The Adventures of Don Quijote*, translated by J. M. Cohen (London: Penguin Books, 1974; 1st printed 1950). Page numbers from Cohen's translation appear in parentheses. Norton Critical Edition page numbers appear in brackets.

of being the adventures of a knight, would become the exploits of a bandit! Fortunately, though, he remembered on time and proceeded immediately to search for a lady with whom to fall madly in love. He remembered a good looking, peasant wench, whom he had admired at a distance, in the past, whose name was Aldonza Lorenzo. Since Aldonza was a rather vulgar and lowly name, he decided to change it to a princely and melodious one, worthy of the elegant gentlewoman who deserved to be the queen of his fancy. He, then, christened her "Dulcinea del Toboso." I qualified this invention as brilliant, and so it is. Not only is Dulcinea an inverted acronym of Aldonza, but * * * the semantic wealth of the name Dulcinea is almost inexhaustible. It is a name of chivalry and pastoral roots, binding into one both sources of romance; it has religious undertones, giving to the knight's love (and to his call) the sense of sacred quest which Don Quijote often claims; and finally by meaning "the sweet one" Don Quijote overreaches himself and falls into a comic trap. He, and all his fellow knights, whose beloved ones are called Phyllis, Belisa, or Amaryllis, become slightly sugary, somewhat ridiculous. Ridiculous, that is, with a comic force that makes of their lofty passion a parody of love itself, a stylized contraption that belongs to a genre (and a world) that is going away and that Cervantes is helping into the grave with a final blow: laughter.

But, then, who is Dulcinea? Certainly not Aldonza, since she is neither a lady, not does she seem to possess any of the canonic qualities required by the romances for the source of knightly valour and gentleness. Dulcinea del Toboso certainly is fully qualified for this noble task, but she does not seem to exist. But doesn't she? Or does she? That is the question. * * *

* * *

Dulcinea's enchantment and her metamorphosis are a rather complex affair. The enchantment proper, her final transformation into the uncouth peasant, takes place in the chapter X of the second part, but Cervantes develops in it the split that he had already established in the first part between a lady of light and a woman of darkness. I shall carefully follow each of the stages of this evolution, and, hopefully, through a close look at the texts, we shall be able to follow the progressive decadence of our heroine. Cervantes depicts this fall into darkness with so much irony, enveloping his narrative in complicated games of deceptions, jokes, and outright lies, twisting, as he himself says, the thread of the narrative in such a way, that the unravelling of his deliberately labyrinthian tissue becomes a rather exacting task. Fortunately, I think, we can follow a short-cut. We know that Cervantes puts together in *Don Quijote* the world of the romances and another world to a certain extent new in literature: the everyday Castilian landscape of inns, dusty roads, the vagrants who roam through them, windmills, peasants, and whores. This new world had never been fully absent from artistic representation, and had already emerged with aggressive violence in some European classics (especially in Spanish ones such as *La Celestina* and *El Lazarillo de Tormes*) but the great novelty of Cervantes is, not only to maintain them together, but, by doing so, to play them against each other. *Don Quijote's* world doubles: reality appears split and sardonically confronted: inn/castle; giant/windmill; lord of the castle/*pícaro*; magical helmet/barber's basin; and, finally, beautiful princess/uncouth peasant. This confrontation aims to produce an Erasmian laughter that, like the one of the *Praise of Folly*, would blow to pieces a dying world.

To make what could be a very long matter short, I shall succinctly state here that I believe that this split of the novel's world implies the confrontation of two artistic codes, and the eventual replacement of one by the other. The world of castles, giants, forests, palfreys, and damsels is replaced by the one of inns, dusty roads, windmills, silk merchants, sweaty, fat farmers, and uncouth, ill-smelling peasant girls. These literary images are, as such, signifiers, the expressive elements of artistic codes whose signified, their sense, is the task of the critic to find out through literary analysis.

* * *

* * * Dulcinea is a deliberate creation of Don Quijote who knows that it is essential for a knight to have a lady whom he can worship religiously, endure hardship for, send her the knights he vanquishes, and if necessary, die for. All this is commonplace and does not require special comment. But it is important to sum up the characteristics of the ideal Dulcinea. She stands above all other women because of her *beauty*, her *chastity*, and *her elegance and refinement*: "and for my part, I think of her as the greatest princess in the world . . . in beauty she has no rival, and few can equal her in good name" (210) [157]. In the remarkable Chapter XXV, where Don Quijote gives us a surprising insight into the workings of his mind, we hear him assert that he is aware that Dulcinea is in a certain way a creation of his will in order to make possible the world of adventure.

* * *

* * * In Chapter XXV Don Quijote's squire expresses his surprise at finding out that Dulcinea is Aldonza Lorenzo, and proceeds to give us a description of her as a sturdy, lusty lass. Two facts diminish the trustworthiness of this picture: we see here Aldonza through Sancho's eyes, and Sancho later denies knowing her. But since he exclaims spontaneously on hearing her name, "I know her well," we can assume that his words convey some truth. Her parents were Lorenzo Corchuelo and Aldonza Nogales. Sancho is particularly impressed by what we could call her rather virile characteristics: "She pitches a bar as well as the strongest lad in the whole village, praise be to God! She is a brawny girl, well built and tall and sturdy, and she will know how to keep her chin out of the mud with any knight errant who ever has her for his mistress." Her powerful voice can be heard from "nearly two miles away." She is always ready for a good laugh, and mocks everything and everybody: "There is a good deal of the courtesan about her too, for she has a crack with everybody, and makes a joke and a mock of them all." Her strength and vigor might be partly explained by the fact that she works the land like any other peasant. Sancho cannot see much point in knights going to visit her since she might be at the time "dressing flax or threshing in the barn" (209) [156]. He will also tell us later she is illiterate: "she couldn't read or write" (269) [204].

A very important aspect of Sancho's description regards her sexual mores. If anything, Dulcinea is the very incarnation of chastity. But, was Aldonza chaste? Everything seems to point to the contrary. When in Chapter XXV Don Quijote informs Sancho of his desire to do penance for the rigors of Dulcinea, he explains that there are two models he could choose, Orlando (who made such a terrible fuss when he found that Angelica had "dishonored herself" with Medoro), or Amadís.

* * *

* * * We have seen that in Chapter XXV Don Quijote had decided, imitating Amadís, to do penance in the loneliness of Sierra Morena as a proof of his devotion to Dulcinea. He sent Sancho to *El Toboso* with a message to his lady communicating to her his purpose. Sancho never arrived at *El Toboso*, but, upon his return, he lied to Don Quijote and gave to him an imaginary description of his visit. This description is significant for two reasons. Although what Sancho says is imaginary, his picture of Dulcinea is obviously based in what he knows of Aldonza Lorenzo. Because he is annoyed with Don Quijote (he has just been given a heavy blow by his master) Sancho obviously exaggerates the uncouth features of Aldonza, giving a caricature of a farm-girl; but this caricature is undoubtedly the basis for the invention, in Chapter X of part II, of the peasant/Dulcinea, through which he finally enchants the lady.

The Dulcinea described by Sancho in Chapter XXXI preserves and brings to grotesque extremes the main features of the Aldonza we already know. When Sancho arrives at *El Toboso* she was "winnowing a couple of bushels of wheat in her back yard"; she is, says Sancho, "a good hand's breadth taller than I am"; when he approached her, he "got a sniff of something rather mannish. It must have been because she was running with sweat from the hard work" (268–70) [203–04]. Tall, sweaty and stinking, working on rude farming tasks, Aldonza is here, indeed, a far cry from the elegant princess of *La Mancha*.

* * *

ANTHONY J. CASCARDI

Personal Identity in *Don Quixote*†

* * *

With regard to personal identity, Don Quixote's death at the end of the novel, and his defeat at the hands of Sansón Carrasco which anticipates his death, are not spiritual failings. Don Quixote may be weak of body, unable physically to attain the full heroic potential which he imagines for himself, but even in defeat he is resolute on affirming that he knows who

† From Anthony J. Cascardi, *The Bounds of Reason: Cervantes, Dostoevsky, Flaubert* (New York: Columbia UP, 1986) 64–72. Copyright (c) 1986 by Columbia University Press. Reprinted with permission of the publisher. All notes are the editor's.

he is. This tenacious adherence to the idea of personal identity, more than to any one role, in the face of physical defeat, endows Don Quixote with a sense of moral and ethical commitment. * * * The adherence to the word of honor, the knight's sacred promise, is not just a hollow invocation of an outmoded chivalric code. It is evidence that Don Quixote must be an exemplar, in his actions, of the knowledge of who he is. To be the product of one's own works, the architect of one's own fortune, and to win identity in this way, means that it is up to us to invest our lives, to take an interest in them and to reap the profit therefrom. The claim that he is the maker of his fortune echoes the Counter-reformation debate over faith and good works; but in Cervantes' text it has more the ring of a challenge than of an admonition. Of the characters in the book, it is only Sancho who responds to the call. That money should be one of his motives is an appropriate enough sign of the value he places on the enterprise, and of the interest he takes in it. It does not mean that money will necessarily be enough to wake people up to their lives; the Knight of the Green Greatcoat is as well-off as any of the characters in the *Quixote*, but he has not sallied forth, he has not ventured and risked as Don Quixote and Sancho have. Likewise, simply dressing up as a knight-errant is no proof of a real investment in living; Sansón Carrasco can disguise himself as a knight, but he is not the product of his works in the way that Don Quixote is; the true investment in living is funded only by ethical commitment.

The economic metaphors which the *Quixote* suggests to explain personal identity highlight the ethical individualism which underlies Cervantes' evaluation of his characters. But I want to emphasize that these are metaphors primarily representative of value and worth, not wealth. In *The Rise of the Novel*, Ian Watt saw a more literal parallel between novelistic characterization and the socioeconomic conditions which prevailed during the period of the novel's rise in England. Watt identified economic individualism and the advent of capitalism together as factors central to the triumph of the genre. Particularly in Defoe — in Moll Flanders, in Roxana, in Captain Singleton, in Colonel Jacque, and above all in Robinson Crusoe — we have characters whose lives are directed by financial pursuits. Their ability to make their own lives is dependent on their ability to seek and determine their fortunes in the world. They are not bound to the static, feudal order of things; and they are virtually free from the limitations of family structures. They are thus able to accept the basic principles of capitalism — of investment, profit, and growth — and find in these principles the necessary resources to create their own lives. By its very nature, capitalism works a continuous transformation on its objects; it fiercely resists economic stasis; when the "objects" involved are novelistic characters and their world, it can provide conditions favorable to personal growth.

In certain ways, the socioeconomic circumstances of Spain at the height of her Golden Age match those which prevailed during the time of the rise of the novel in England. Cervantes wrote the *Quixote* in advance of the serious economic decline, at a time when the caste values of medieval Spain were being eroded by the ascendant values of class. Because of economic expansion in America and wars in Europe, a nation with a feudal economy was being pulled into capitalistic economic circumstances; caste life among Christians, Moors, and Jews had become disrupted and grew intolerant because of the gradual advances, and now the effective dominance, of the Christians. Even before the *Quixote*, in the romances of chivalry on which Cervantes drew, there is a visible spirit of adventure which drives the heroes; and in actuality, from the first encounters with the New World — in the diaries of Columbus, for instance — there is an economic fire, a material acquisitiveness, which approximates those actual adventures to the fictional paradigms which Cervantes had in mind when writing the *Quixote*.

Yet Don Quixote purifies these motives; his spirit of adventure is not driven by dreams of wealth. In Cervantes's novel, the economic interest shows up more literally in Sancho than in Don Quixote. It is Sancho who forsakes his family, who seeks financial reward and economic independence; he is moved to follow Don Quixote by the promise of social gain, the governance of an island. In this regard, Sancho is more typical of later novelistic heroes than Don Quixote is. Certainly he is prototypical of the bourgeois class of readers who saw their own desires for financial and social independence mirrored in the novel. This is not to condemn Sancho; it is simply to say that the *Quixote* stands apart from the English novelistic tradition because the *hero* dissociates himself from such motives. Cervantes sees that the enterprising spirit may promote individual responsibility, as for Sancho; the desire for financial and social independence may instill a certain personal autonomy. But if Sancho embodies the bourgeois wish to be free of economic constraints and class limitations, then Don Quixote represents that wish fulfilled; he seeks to transcend, to go beyond the boredom which follows on the financial independence that characterizes his idle condition at the opening of the book. He leaves the relatively secure surroundings of his library to strike out in the world. His individualism is of an ethical sort, which means that it entails actions which transcend material circumstances or causes. Don Quixote is a character struck with the idea of self-knowledge and self-determination in an instinctual way; he knows who he is and he is able to determine his existence and his fortune apart from considerations of estate or class. If his identity is a function of the models he imitates, the roles he plays, then that must be taken as a sign of the nearly religious nature of his self-knowledge. His penitence in Sierra Morena, his self-imposed asceticism, the ritual of having himself dubbed a knight are clues that his role-playing and heroism are matters of moral import; they cannot be limited to purely financial concerns.

The natural danger for the man of bourgeois circumstances is that the same factors which prompt his aspirations to independence may prove liabilities and may compromise him ethically. Because of the way in which he takes his roles upon himself, because he transcends the given economic conditions of life, Don Quixote is free from those dangers. Again in this way, the *Quixote* distinguishes itself from the European novel of the eighteenth and nineteenth centuries and the moral dilemmas of the surrounding bourgeois culture. As Alasdair MacIntyre wrote in regard to Henry James (*The Portrait of a Lady*), Diderot (*Rameau's Nephew*), and Kierkegaard (*Either/Or*):

The unifying preoccupation of that tradition is the condition of those who see in the world nothing but a meeting place for individual wills, each with its own set of attitudes and preferences and who understand that world solely as an arena for the achievement of their own satisfaction, and who interpret reality as a series of opportunities for their enjoyment and for whom the last enemy is boredom . . . the problem of enjoyment arises in the context of leisure, in which large sums of money have created some social distance from the necessity of work.[1]

As a consequence of these material conditions, the economic individualism which may have prompted the first growth of the novel has become little more than moral emotivism, an attitude which takes the subjective self as the highest court of appeal in ethical decisions and in which the world is, as a consequence, a "meeting place for individual wills" rather than as a place for public agreement and dissent. Superficially, the scenario that MacIntyre describes might seem to match that of the *Quixote*. Cervantes' knight is in certain ways like Kierkegaard's "A," who is rich, or Rameau, who is a parasite on his patrons and clients. But Don Quixote's individualism is not limited to the possibilities or opportunities supplied by wealth or free time; and, as I have discussed, the general conditions of knowledge in the book are public and communal rather than private. Those romantic characters often lose their moral integrity and capacity for ethical choice because the leisured social and economic environment in which they flourish, which demands them to seek or protect personal status, mandates ethical and moral subjectivism to the disadvantage of ethical individualism. Unlike Don Quixote, they easily degenerate into what Kierkegaard called the aesthetic stage of life, forsaking altogether the responsibility of choosing right and wrong except as such decisions will foster their private comfort; Flaubert's Emma Bovary will offer such a case. As if in response to this tradition *avant la lettre*, Don Quixote fashions an identity for himself, wins his self, achieves his individuality, without forsaking moral choice; conversely, he is able to act ethically without sacrificing his personal autonomy. For these reasons, Cervantes' conception of personal identity as reflected in his hero offers an important window on larger moral problems, problems which are in the end far greater than the novelistic tradition itself.

The staunchly individualistic characters of that tradition, like the aesthetes MacIntyre describes, are not immoral or amoral characters, at least not ostensibly so. But they are likely to base their choices on the values set by the individual's subjective consciousness, apart from concern for the larger social good or even for the public (communal, political) contexts in which choice and action necessarily occur; their ethical lives are ruled by the vagaries of personal choice. They may take themselves to be the products of their own works, but they fail to place their "works" in any interpersonal, public sphere. Cervantes breaks the patterns of moral subjectivism into which ethical individualism can so easily degenerate because he bases the moral aspect of his hero's identity on the socially derived

---

1. From Alasdair MacIntyre, *After Virtue: A Study in Moral Theory* (Notre Dame: University of Notre Dame Press, 1978), p. 24.

category of *role*. In this, Cervantes registers his greatest distance from Descartes. In the *Quixote*, the hero can play many roles and still not be compromised by the contradictions among them; roles are social structures through which the individual engages values responsibly, thus transcending purely subjective concerns. For Descartes, as for any thinker espousing a subject-centered understanding of personal identity, the very possibility of multiple roles is inconceivable. Indeed, the subject of the *Meditations*, the thinker committed to rigorous self-doubt, is bound to slough off all roles as inauthentic or self-deceptive; he seeks a stable point of personal identity, in order to define his personal essence (in Descartes's case on the basis of the *cogito*, of his status as a *res cogitans*)[2] rather than in terms of social function. The private, isolated conditions in which the thought of the *Meditations* takes place are designed to insure such a monistic conception of personal identity.

Because we have, as a post-Enlightenment culture, largely forgotten what role-playing means and what value it has, we are surprised by the fact that Don Quixote shapes an identity of profound moral integrity through his imitations and that his role-playing in turn gives him a self-knowledge which lies beyond the claims or the caveats of rational thought. Contemporary philosophical and popular thinkers alike view role-playing with a substantial degree of circumspection. * * * Certainly, the vulgarized interpretations of Don Quixote in our century run directly counter to the sense of Cervantes' novel: they make Don Quixote a champion of selfhood *over and above* the self's roles, of "sincerity" over virtuous action. But all the evidence of the novel suggests that Don Quixote gains personal identity and value through the role, not the "self." One of the immediate advantages of Alasdair MacIntyre's *After Virtue* in this regard is that it revives the notion of role-playing in a positive moral sense, one which is able to account for personal identity as we see it in the *Quixote*. In what he rightly calls "heroic" societies (which would be an apt description of the setting that Don Quixote imagines for himself), individual value is judged in conjunction with the values of a social group. The self is responsible, to itself and to the group interdependently, but is not the "center of a world" as a Cartesian subject is. Action is unmediated by self-consciousness and is spawned by the heroic virtues. As Don Quixote demonstrates in his valorous response to defeat by Sansón Carrasco, his principles of action are congruent with this way of being; he is bound to keep his word of honor even though there may be other possible paths of action which might gain him more immediate personal benefit or pleasure.

To consider the virtues that Don Quixote exhibits is to give a descriptive portrait of his identity and role. As a character, he is a focus for the engagement of an ethos, that of chivalric knighthood. What Don Quixote is and, moreover, *who* he is, depend on his practice of the virtues; these cannot remain abstract, theoretical paradigms or categories. Especially in the episodes where Cervantes shows Don Quixote in the foreground —

---

2. The *cogito* refers to the famous Cartesian argument, *Cogito ergo sum* [I think therefore I am]. The status of the subject is that of a *res cogitans* or "thinking thing."

where he fights the army of sheep, or attacks the "giants" (windmills) — Cervantes maps out the profiles of his character in terms of a code of traditional behavior. Don Quixote is courageous; he is a gentleman of honor, who keeps his promise; he is temperate; he is just; and he is the character defined by these virtues because he practices them, engages them, puts them into play. * * * Don Quixote is virtuous, and unlike the lesser townspeople he is a "character" because he applies the moral knowledge inherent in the virtues. The minor figures in the book all have roles in the society — the Barber, the Curate, the Renaissance Gentleman of the Green Greatcoat, the Duke and the Duchess; each has a certain identifiable status. But none of them makes his role the focus of moral concern; none engages his social position ethically. Don Quixote strikes out to practice the virtues. Of him it could be said what Marx challenged in his eleventh thesis on Feuerbach, that he is not content simply to interpret the world; he knows that the time has come to change it, regardless of the fact that the project may be hopeless and thankless. Seen in this way, the *Quixote* raises serious doubts about the conventional notion that a novelistic character is someone who is unique and inimitable, someone who knows himself subjectively, as Descartes did. Self-knowledge and personal identity in Cervantes's novel at least are not founded on the fruits of a mind's project of pure enquiry but on the ethical and moral bases of character and role.

*　*　*

MICHEL FOUCAULT

[Don Quixote as Hero of the Same]†

With all their twists and turns, Don Quixote's adventures form the boundary: they mark the end of the old interplay between resemblance and signs and contain the beginnings of new relations. Don Quixote is not a man given to extravagance, but rather a diligent pilgrim breaking his journey before all the marks of similitude. He is the hero of the Same. He never manages to escape from the familiar plain stretching out on all sides of the Analogue, any more than he does from his own small province. He travels endlessly over that plain, without ever crossing the clearly defined frontiers of difference, or reaching the heart of identity. Moreover, he is himself like a sign, a long, thin graphism, a letter that has just escaped from the open pages of a book. His whole being is nothing but language, text, printed pages, stories that have already been written down. He is made up of interwoven words; he is writing itself, wandering through the world among the resemblances of things. Yet not entirely so: for in his reality as an impoverished hidalgo he can become a knight only by listening from afar to the age-old epic that gives its form to Law. The book is not so

---

† From Michel Foucault, *The Order of Things: An Archaeology of the Human Sciences.* Trans. of *Le Mots et les choses* (New York: Vintage Books, 1973), pp. 46–50. Reprinted by permission of Georges Borchardt, Inc.

much his existence as his duty. He is constantly obliged to consult it in order to know what to do or say, and what signs he should give himself and others in order to show that he really is of the same nature as the text from which he springs. The chivalric romances have provided once and for all a written prescription for his adventures. And every episode, every decision, every exploit will be yet another sign that Don Quixote is a true likeness of all the signs that he has traced from his book. But the fact that he wishes to be like them means that he must put them to the test, that the (legible) signs no longer resemble (visible) people. All those written texts, all those extravagant romances are, quite literally, unparalleled: no one in the world ever did resemble them; their timeless language remains suspended, unfulfilled by any similitude; they could all be burned in their entirety and the form of the world would not be changed. If he is to resemble the texts of which he is the witness, the representation, the real analogue, Don Quixote must also furnish proof and provide the indubitable sign that they are telling the truth, that they really are the language of the world. It is incumbent upon him to fulfill the promise of the books. It is his task to recreate the epic, though by a reverse process: the epic recounted (or claimed to recount) real exploits, offering them to our memory; Don Quixote, on the other hand, must endow with reality the signs-without-content of the narrative. His adventures will be a deciphering of the world: a diligent search over the entire surface of the earth for the forms that will prove that what the books say is true. Each exploit must be a proof: it consists, not in a real triumph — which is why victory is not really important — but in an attempt to transform reality into a sign. Into a sign that the signs of language really are in conformity with things themselves. Don Quixote reads the world in order to prove his books. And the only proofs he gives himself are the glittering reflections of resemblances.

His whole journey is a quest for similitudes: the slightest analogies are pressed into service as dormant signs that must be reawakened and made to speak once more. Flocks, serving girls, and inns become once more the language of books to the imperceptible degree to which they resemble castles, ladies, and armies — a perpetually untenable resemblance which transforms the sought-for proof into derision and leaves the words of the books forever hollow. But non-similitude itself has its model, and one that it imitates in the most servile way: it is to be found in the transformations performed by magicians. So all the indices of non-resemblance, all the signs that prove that the written texts are not telling the truth, resemble the action of sorcery, which introduces difference into the indubitable existence of similitude by means of deceit. And since this magic has been foreseen and described in the books, the illusory difference that it introduces can never be anything but an enchanted similitude, and, therefore, yet another sign that the signs in the books really do resemble the truth.

Don Quixote is a negative of the Renaissance world; writing has ceased to be the prose of the world; resemblances and signs have dissolved their former alliance; similitudes have become deceptive and verge upon the visionary or madness; things still remain stubbornly within their ironic identity: they are no longer anything but what they are; words wander off on their own, without content, without resemblance to fill their emptiness; they are no longer the marks of things; they lie sleeping between the pages of books and covered in dust. Magic, which permitted the decipherment of the world by revealing the secret resemblances beneath its signs, is no longer of any use except as an explanation, in terms of madness, of why analogies are always proved false. The erudition that once read nature and books alike as parts of a single text has been relegated to the same category as its own chimeras: lodged in the yellowed pages of books, the signs of language no longer have any value apart from the slender fiction which they represent. The written word and things no longer resemble one another. And between them, Don Quixote wanders off on his own.

Yet language has not become entirely impotent. It now possesses new powers, and powers peculiar to it alone. In the second part of the novel, Don Quixote meets characters who have read the first part of his story and recognize him, the real man, as the hero of the book. Cervantes's text turns back upon itself, thrusts itself back into its own density, and becomes the object of its own narrative. The first part of the hero's adventures plays in the second part the role originally assumed by the chivalric romances. Don Quixote must remain faithful to the book that he has now become in reality; he must protect it from errors, from counterfeits, from apocryphal sequels; he must fill in the details that have been left out; he must preserve its truth. But Don Quixote himself has not read this book, and does not have to read it, since he is the book in flesh and blood. Having first read so many books that he became a sign, a sign wandering through a world that did not recognize him, he has now, despite himself and without his knowledge, become a book that contains his truth, that records exactly all that he has done and said and seen and thought, and that at last makes him recognizable, so closely does he resemble all those signs whose ineffaceable imprint he has left behind him. Between the first and second parts of the novel, in the narrow gap between those two volumes, and by their power alone, Don Quixote has achieved his reality — a reality he owes to language alone, and which resides entirely inside the words. Don Quixote's truth is not in the relation of the words to the world but in that slender and constant relation woven between themselves by verbal signs. The hollow fiction of epic exploits has become the representative power of language. Words have swallowed up their own nature as signs.

Don Quixote is the first modern work of literature, because in it we see the cruel reason of identities and differences make endless sport of signs and similitudes; because in it language breaks off its old kinship with things and enters into that lonely sovereignty from which it will reappear, in its separated state, only as literature; because it marks the point where resemblance enters an age which is, from the point of view of resemblance, one of madness and imagination. Once similitude and signs are sundered from each other, two experiences can be established and two characters appear face to face. The madman, understood not as one who is sick but as an established and maintained deviant, as an indispensable cultural function, has become, in Western experience, the man of primitive resemblances. This character, as he is depicted in the novels or plays of the Baroque age, and as he was gradually institutionalized right up to the advent of nineteenth-century psychiatry, is the man who is *alienated* in *analogy*. He is the disordered player of the Same and the Other. He takes things for what they are not, and people one for another; he cuts his friends and recognizes complete strangers; he thinks he is unmasking when, in fact, he is putting on a mask. He inverts all values and all proportions, because he is constantly under the impression that he is deciphering signs: for him, the crown makes the king. In the cultural perception of the madman that prevailed up to the end of the eighteenth century, he is Different only in so far as he is unaware of Difference; he sees nothing but resemblances and signs of resemblance everywhere; for him all signs resemble one another, and all resemblances have the value of signs. At the other end of the cultural area, but brought close by symmetry, the poet is he who, beneath the named, constantly expected differences, rediscovers the buried kinships between things, their scattered resemblances. Beneath the established signs, and in spite of them, he hears another, deeper, discourse, which recalls the time when words glittered in the universal resemblance of things; in the language of the poet, the Sovereignty of the Same, so difficult to express, eclipses, the distinction existing between signs.

This accounts, no doubt, for the confrontation of poetry and madness in modern Western culture. But it is no longer the old Platonic theme of inspired madness. It is the mark of a new experience of language and things. At the fringes of a knowledge that separates beings, signs, and similitudes, and as though to limit its power, the madman fulfils the function of *homosemanticism*: he groups all signs together and leads them with a resemblance that never ceases to proliferate. The poet fulfils the opposite function: his is the *allegorical* role; beneath the language of signs and beneath the interplay of their precisely delineated distinctions, he strains his ears to catch that 'other language', the language, without words or discourse, of resemblance. The poet brings similitude to the signs that speak it, whereas the madman loads all signs with a resemblance that ultimately erases them. They share, then, on the outer edge of our culture and at the point nearest to its essential divisions, that 'frontier' situation — a marginal position and a profoundly archaic silhouette — where their words unceasingly renew the power of their strangeness and the strength of their contestation. Between them there has opened up a field of knowledge in which, because of an essential rupture in the Western world, what has become important is no longer resemblances but identities and differences.

✳   ✳   ✳

Essays on Selected Episodes of *Don Quijote*

ELIAS L. RIVERS

[Cervantes's Revolutionary Prologue]†

The first problem that faces us as readers of Part One of *Don Quixote* is where does the text actually start: is the beginning Chapter I, or is it the prologue to the reader? There is no doubt as to the order in which they were written: Cervantes started with Chapter I, wrote until he reached the last chapter of Part I (number 52), and then he added the prologue to the beginning. That is where he wants us to start, as readers; there he addresses each of us in the singular, with the words "desocupado lector": "idle reader". He knows that it is a long book and that only a person with a certain amount of free time at his disposal can think of settling down to read it. But he does not want the reader to plunge in without first having been made aware of the writer, or better the narrator, the story-telling voice which will mediate between the reader and the story, that complicatedly interwoven set of texts which brings the reader into various degrees of verbal proximity to Don Quijote and his world. Cervantes does not want us to ignore the narrator, to forget that it is he the writer who has woven a plot of texts in which we will soon become enmeshed. He is presenting me, the reader, with a printed book, but he wants to talk to me first, to establish fictitiously that intimate relationship between an "I" and a "thou," a relationship which really exists only when two persons talk face-to-face. (The special nature of this relationship has been emphasized not only by religious figures such as Martin Buber and Fr. Ong, but also by a great Indo-European linguist, Emile Benveniste, who has argued convincingly that the first person singular and the second person singular are the only true persons in grammar; that the third person singular is essentially an unmarked form, a non-person, excluded from the dialogue.)[1]

The prologue to Part I of *Don Quixote* is a literary *tour de force*, with a complicated interplay of discourse, dialogue and narrative. We see this at

---

† From Elias L. Rivers, "Talking and Writing in *Don Quixote*," *Thought* 51 (September 1976). Selections reprinted from pp. 299–301. Reprinted by permission of the publisher (New York: Fordham University Press), Copyright 1976. All notes are the editor's.
1. The Jewish theologian Martin Buber wrote *I and Thou*, trans. Ronald Gregor Smith (New York: Scribner's, 1937). Walter J. Ong is a contemporary Jesuit scholar famous for his studies on orality, rhetoric, and technology, as well as for his editions of Peter Ramus (1969, 1970). Emile Benveniste's essays are collected in *Problems in General Linguistics* (Coral Gables: University of Miami Press, 1971).

the very beginning of the first sentence: "Desocupado lector, sin juramento me podrás creer que quisiera que este libro, como hijo del entendimiento, fuera el más hermoso . . . que pudiera imaginarse." "Idle reader: without my swearing to it, you can believe me when I tell you that . . ." (When two persons talk face-to-face, they cannot lie to one another without losing face, that is, feeling ashamed * * * .) The vocative "lector," or "reader," with an epithet, and the use of the "tú," or "thou," form of address, were established literary conventions of the prologue. But Cervantes chooses a very unconventional epithet: "desocupado . . .," "idle reader," implying that I, the reader, have nothing better to do than to waste my time reading a strange sort of worthless book. An ironic conversational relationship is immediately established, drawing the reader into the writer's confidence. But the writer's attitude toward the book that he has written, or the personality that he has begotten (for the words "Don Quijote" refer to both of them simultaneously) — the writer's attitude is ambiguous: he says that he feels less like a proud father than like an indifferent or even hostile stepfather; that the act of literary procreation has taken place, not in the Muses' *locus amoenus*, but in a noisy prison, without amenities of any kind. Since this is such a strange, or original, sort of book, the author tells the reader that he is quite free to praise it, or condemn it, as he sees fit, for Aristotle had nothing to say about this peculiar sort of fiction, which turned out to be the modern novel.

But at this point the author has a problem that is more immediate than the story itself: it is the problem of how to write a prologue. This is a digression from the proper subject, the book being presented, to the act of presentation itself, which is a simultaneous act of trying to write and of reading; Cervantes refers to "esta prefación que vas leyendo," "this preface which you are now in the process of reading," but it is a preface that he is simultaneously struggling to write. Now other learned authors, he says, have no such problems: they know how to write proper prologues. On the other hand, he, Cervantes, is a lazy man (like the idle reader, perhaps) and has not had a good education. So he does not know how to write a prologue. He has tried many times in vain. But one day, while he is sitting there with the blank paper in front of him and with his pen behind his ear, his elbow on his desk and his hand on his cheek, trying to think of what to say, that is what to write, an anonymous sociable friend just happens to drop into his study. We see here how the supposedly discursive prologue is converted into a narrative: the present-tense monologue in which the writer (in the first person) addresses the reader (in the second person) has become a past-tense narrative about a third person, or non-person, and what he said.

This fictitious friend provides the substance of the prologue by laughing at the writer's problem. He tells him that it is very easy to write a prologue and to publish a book: all you have to do is to decorate it with a few familiar quotations in Latin, and everybody will think you are a learned and industrious author, a real authority. If your purpose is to attack the false romances of chivalry, all you have to do is attack them in a straight-forward way. (We realize at this point that the friend is actually telling Cervantes how to write, not the prologue, but the book itself, a book which incidentally has already been written, but which we have not started to read yet. Or have we?) In any case, to write this prologue, all Cervantes has had to do is transcribe his friend's advice as to how to write one: before our very eyes the prologue is written, a masterpiece of prestidigitation. In order to write something, one simply writes about the problem of writing: nothing could be more apparently simple and profoundly complicated, as Borges[2] continues to demonstrate in the 20th century.

RUTH ANTHONY EL SAFFAR

In Marcela's Case†

The case of Marcela, a woman who declares her right to live beyond the confines of the patriarchally constructed world into which she was born, has stirred a storm of critical controversy, much of it surprisingly — or perhaps not so surprisingly — gender-inflected. * * *

* * *

The first of five interpolated tales in Don Quixote, part I, the story that involves Marcela so intensely draws those who want to know more about her into a thicket as forbidding and impenetrable as that into which she herself disappears. Like Gelasia of Cervantes's pastoral romance La Galatea, Marcela is a woman who is loved but does not love. In contrast to the "elusive woman" of the Spanish comedia, Marcela succeeds in eluding the usual alternatives of marriage or the convent prescribed for women of her social class.[1] Declaring her refusal to submit ("I have no wish for subjugation" [I.14] [78]), Marcela justifies, on the grounds of her right to freedom, her rejection of all suitors, including the shepherd Grisóstomo, who has died for love of her. After her ringing speech in her own defense at his funeral, she returns to her preferred dwelling deep in the mountains, never to be heard from again.[2]

The rough sierras which Marcela makes her home are inhospitable to

2. Jorge Luis Borges (1889–1986), an Argentinian writer, is best known for his collections of short stories: Ficciones (1945), El Aleph (1949), and Labyrinths (1953). His well-known story "Pierre Menard, Author of the Quixote" is included in this volume (pp. 857–63).

† From Ruth Anthony El Saffar, "In Marcela's Case," in Quixotic Desire: Psychoanalytic Perspectives on Cervantes, ed. Ruth Anthony El Saffar and Diana de Armas Wilson (Ithaca: Cornell University Press, 1993) 157–78. Reprinted by permission of Cornell University Press. This essay has been condensed. Spanish citations have been omitted, and the original footnotes have been reduced and edited. El Saffar's own translations are cited by part and chapter number. Norton Critical Edition page numbers follow in brackets.

1. For a sense of how rare it was for a young maiden to escape from a marriage she sought to avoid, see Melveena McKendrick's study of the mujer esquiva tradition in the Spanish comedia in Woman and Society in the Spanish Drama of the Golden Age (Cambridge: Cambridge University Press, 1974). The elusive woman, a favorite theme in Spanish theater, serves only to heighten the excitement of a drama that centers on the inevitability of the woman's eventual defeat.

2. Criticism on Marcela's speech divides fascinatingly along gender lines. Herman Iventosch is alone among male critics in reacting favorably to Marcela's claim for freedom. See his "Cervantes and Courtly Love: The Grisóstomo-Marcela Episode of Don Quijote," PMLA 89 (1974):71. All other studies supporting Marcela are by women. * * * Adrienne Munich reads Marcela as an escape from a system designed to capture and silence women in "Notorious Signs, Feminist Criticism, and Literary Traditions," in Making a Difference: Feminist Literary Criticism, ed. Gayle Green and Coppelia Kahn (New York: Methuen, 1985), 138–59. Yvonne Jehensen sees Marcela's speech as undercutting all the conventional expectations, turning her from "an object of their [the male characters'] imagination" to "absolute subject," in "The Pastoral Episode in Cervantes' Don Quijote: Marcela Once Again," Cervantes 10 (1990): 26.

the men who enter them to seek her out. Drawn to a beauty that is at home only in the wilds, the men who desire Marcela meet, in the places where she lives, not her receptivity but their own madness and death. Any analysis of her case must take into account not only Marcela's refusal to mirror back the desire men express for her but also their desperate insistence that she do so. For Grisóstomo is not alone in desiring Marcela. The narrator describes a kind of bedlam in the mountains where she seeks freedom: "Here one shepherd sighs; there another moans; from the distance you can hear songs of love; from near at hand dirges of despair" (I.12) [66]. The number of men afflicted by desire for Marcela suggests that Grisóstomo represents only the most extreme case of a general cultural phenomenon.

Marcela thrives where madness, outlawry, desire, and rage, repressed in approved social discourse, find their home.[3] Her realm proves dangerous and disorienting to the men who follow her there.[4] The exclusively female space Marcela occupies ("I enjoy the modest company of the village shepherdesses" [I.14] [78–79]) and its implied harmony with nature ("My desires are bounded by these mountains; and if they extend beyond them, it is to contemplate the beauty of the sky, a step by which the soul travels to its first abode" [I.14] [78]) have proved exasperating not only to shepherds desperate to gain access to Marcela but to critics as well.[5]

Issues of sexual politics, as well as of deep psychological pain are clearly stirred in the image of a female figure who claims an autonomy that requires no support from men or from the social order. Pursuing Marcela's case means entering into a territory hedged around with silence and repression, as she opens us up into an area poorly described by classical psychoanalysis and avoided by the prescriptions that define feminine behavior. In order to approach Marcela and the deep-seated conflicts between men and women which her presence evokes, it is necessary to begin with an excursus into mythology. * * *

* * *

The archetypal perspective with which I begin this inquiry into the nature of Marcela is intended to reveal a psychic pattern that has a history deeper than that of the particular individual. To insist on Marcela's individuality or pathology would be to miss the echoes of her character type

---

3. Part I of *Don Quixote* abounds in examples. In the sierras the shepherds clamor for Marcela (I.12); Grisóstomo commits suicide (I.14); Rocinante attempts a sexual encounter with some mares (I.15); galley slaves escape their chains (I.22); Cardenio lives as a savage (I.23); Don Quixote strips from the waist down and does somersaults to prove his love for Dulcinea (I.25); the curate imagines dressing as a damsel in distress (I.28); and the seduced and abandoned Dorotea, dressed as a man, kills the servant who tried to rape her as she pursues her false lover (I.28).

4. Many of the critics who condemn Marcela do so because of the disturbance her allure produces. See, for example, Peter Dunn, who notes: "We might say that for man to indulge his nostalgia for the state of nature is to desert the state of grace. Or, on a less purely theological plane, that those men and women who became shepherds and shepherdesses for the sake of love, abandoning their husbandry and social ties and duties, forgot the true relation of art to life," in "Two Classical Myths in *Don Quijote*," *Renaissance and Reformation* 9 (1972): 3–4.

5. Renato Poggioli, for example, accusing Marcela of self-love, argues that Marcela "treats her far less carnal but no less profane passion as if it were a form of sacred love," in *The Oaten Flute: Essays on Pastoral Poetry and the Pastoral Ideal* (Cambridge: Harvard University Press, 1975), 174.

present in figures already outlined in Greek and Roman mythology.[6] The Marcela who prefers the "conversation of the shepherdesses," like the Grisóstomo who experiences a psychic dismemberment by inner wild beasts when Marcela rejects him, have counterparts in the figures of Diana and Actaeon as Ovid portrayed them in book 3 of the *Metamorphoses*. In Ovid's telling, Actaeon on the hunt strays into the area where Diana is bathing with her nymphs. Infuriated by his uninvited gaze, Diana flings water in his face. Where the drops fall, horns emerge, and soon Actaeon has been transformed into a stag whom his hounds attack. Both Cervantes and Ovid disguise the murderous nature of the desired woman by linking the lovers' deaths to their own destructive qualities. The Greek goddess Artemis from whom Diana descends, however, much more obviously combines attributes of beauty with an active desire to kill. It is worth exploring in a little more detail the characteristics of Artemis because a sense of her complexity sheds light on what has so confounded critics when approaching Marcela.

Artemis, goddess of the moon and twin of the sun god Apollo, is associated with hunting, chastity, and childbirth. Only a few hours old, Artemis helped her mother, Leto, give birth to her twin brother, Apollo. Although the moon goddess herself remained fiercely virgin, the stories of her infancy made her the patroness of midwives in the popular imagination. That "strange, disquieting savagery" that Karl Kerenyi finds in Artemis has to do with her role not only in helping but also in killing women in childbirth.[7] In the Homeric hymn to her, Artemis' bloodlust is even more evident. While presenting Artemis as capable of enjoying with Apollo "the grass country," Delphi, where she goes and "arranges a chorus of Graces and Muses," the poet also shows her at home "in the wind on mountaintops," where "she darts in and out everywhere . . . killing all kinds of animals."[8] Artemis, like Diana, clearly has a dual aspect that involves death as well as beauty.

Cervantes's Marcela, who appears as "a marvelous vision" (I.14) [76] atop the very peak at the bottom of which lies Grisóstomo's dead body, belongs to the same constellation of psychic energies that informed the Greek conception of Artemis and Ovid's depiction of Diana. Like her Greek and Roman antecedents, Marcela represents a dual goddess whose beauty is associated with death. Her very name, as Dominique Reyre points out in her onomastic study of *Don Quixote*, supports the "homicidal shepherdess" (I.13) [67] epithet the shepherds have attached to her.[9]

Marcela's coldheartedness has received ample commentary. Echoing the condemnation of the goatherds, Grisóstomo's friend Ambrosio asks,

---

6. A criticism often made of archetypal psychology is that in its recourse to mythology it supposes eternal personality types that are impervious to the shaping factors of personal history and the impact of time, place, and economic and social factors. My references to Artemis and the Great Mother are intended to show a conditioning that is a response to the pervasive impact of father god and sky god rule on the lives of women and on the patterns of female response.

7. Karl Kerenyi, *Goddesses of the Sun and Moon* (Dallas: Spring Publications, 1979), 42.

8. *The Homeric Hymns*, trans. Charles Boer (Dallas: Spring Publications, 1970), 4–5.

9. Associating the prefix *mar-* with the god of war, Mars, Dominique Reyre adds that "ce prénom est toujours porté par des femmes génératrices de conflit [this pronoun is always used for women who generate conflict]," in *Dictionnaire des noms des personnages du 'Don Quichotte' de Cervantes* (Paris: Editions Hispaniques, 1980), 91. Since Artemis is, among other things, a warrior goddess, the name that affiliates her female surrogate with Mars is especially appropriate.

when Marcela appears at the funeral, "Have you come here, perhaps, fiery basilisk of these mountains, to see if the wounds of this wretch, whom your cruelty killed, will bleed at the sight of you?" (I.14) [77]. Critics have tended, as I have already noted, to follow suit in blaming Marcela for Grisostomo's demise.

      * * * Unless Marcela is recognized as the expression of a pattern long since familiar in depictions of female behavior, however, much of the richness of her appearance gets lost in gender-based responses that perpetuate the atmosphere of conflict that has long characterized relations between men and women. Marcela's connections to the moon goddess are surprisingly well developed, and are not simply limited to her associations with beauty and death. To trace those connections, it is necessary to amplify on images of Artemis present in Greek sources. The huge statue of Artemis in the Temple of Diana at Ephesus shows her with many breasts, as the mother who feeds all, suggesting an early affiliation of Artemis with the Great Mother. In this guise her triple nature — maiden, mother, and crone — corresponds with the three phases of the moon. In the time of Homer, however, the more archaic aspects of Artemis' Great Mother characterization gave way to her more sisterly, virginal aspects.

      Artemis' independence allies her with the Amazons. The stories of the Amazons may hark back to a period of struggle between sky god and earth goddess cults, as some have contended, or they may simply reflect periods when the oppression of women or the inner feminine provoked a retaliative movement in an effort to restore balance.[1] Generally, as with the story of Achilles and Penthesilea, Diana and Actaeon, or Artemis and Orion, the gendered battles for dominance that the Amazon archetype evokes end in the death of one partner or the other. In classical Greek and in western Christian re-evocations of the Amazons, it is the women who are generally depicted as either being defeated by or submitting to their male conquerors.[2] The important point for this study is that the defeat or submission of the goddess always entails a breakup of the original triplicity of her nature, dividing the maiden from the mother, the mother from the crone, and the "good" qualities from the "bad." Traces of the original unity can still be found, however, in the beauty-death amalgam that clings to the figure of Artemis. It is an amalgam much more clearly evident in non-European female goddesses such as Isis and Kali, who remain powerful as givers of both life and death.[3] That Cervantes would include in Don Quixote a figure of female power who is not forced to submit suggests that he is

1. René Malamud says of the Amazon myth that it was "an 'answer' from the central Mediterranean archetype of the Great Mother to the arrival of the Zeus-religion of the Indo-European invaders"; see "The Amazon Problem," in Facing the Gods, ed. James Hillman (Dallas: Spring Publications, 1980), 55.
2. Herodotus, in book 4 of The Histories, ed. Walter Blanco and Jennifer Tolbert Roberts (New York: W. W. Norton, 1992), 123–26, imagines a form of marriage between Scythian warriors, who move from their homeland and take up Amazonian nomadic ways, and their Amazon lovers. His is one of the few stories that seek to depict a relationship between Amazonian women and warrior men, and in it the men, in order to live with the women, leave their habitual ways and their society of origin.
3. Isis, the most famous of the Egyptian goddesses, was the sister-wife of Osiris and supreme in magical power, knowledge, and cunning. She was goddess of the earth, the sea, the Nile, the underworld, love, magic, and healing. Kali or Kali Mai (dark mother) dates from late Epic Hindu mythology, although the origins of her worship are obscure. Widely regarded as a goddess of death and destruction, she is depicted as black, four-armed, blood-stained, with matted hair and a necklace of skulls [Editor's Note].

introducing into his works a myth that counters the Christian orthodoxy that prevailed in his time.

To support the notion that throughout the pastoral episodes of which Marcela forms a part we are in the realm of the Great Mother, we have only to refer to chapter 11, which immediately precedes the Marcela-Grisóstomo episode. There Don Quixote delivers his Golden Age speech, which reveals him as enveloped in a fantasy of the all-good mother. Although he clearly yearns for a time before the era of father dominance, Don Quixote strips the Great Mother whom he evokes of her dark side. She is all-giving but not all-powerful. Like Dulcinea, Don Quixote's maiden version of the Great Mother, she retains only those qualities that are desirable and attractive to men.[4] The mother and the maiden whom Don Quixote extols bring only peace and satisfaction, having none of the terrifying attributes of Kali, or even Artemis.

An image symptomatic of the disturbed relations between the sexes that the presence of Marcela will later stir, the mother of Don Quixote's Golden Age fantasy bears a startling resemblance to the idealized image of the mother in the mother-son dyad to which Freud sometimes alludes in his own version of paradise lost. Don Quixote says of his picture of a bygone time of plenitude: "All was peace then, all amity, all concord" (I.11) [59]. The mother, then, was still a virgin: "The crooked plough had not yet dared to force open and search the kindly bowels of our first mother with its heavy coulter" (I.11) [59]. Her creative energy was turned entirely to the feeding and pleasure of her sons, to whom she was exclusively devoted: "For without compulsion she yielded from every part of her fertile and broad bosom everything to satisfy, sustain, and delight the children who then possessed her" (I.11) [59].

Expressions of this yearning for the all-good mother appear again at the end of part I, when Don Quixote unfolds the fantasy of the Knight of the Lake. In that fantasy he imagines himself in a magical place, surrounded by beautiful women whose sole object is to gratify him. The tendency to split the feminine image into all-good and all-bad parts also becomes evident when Sancho fails to attach to Don Quixote's ethereal princess Dulcinea the split-off earthiness of an Aldonza Lorenzo, who knows how to salt pork and call in the hogs (I.25) [156]. In figures such as Maritornes, the innkeeper's wife, the Duchess, and Altisidora, Cervantes offers images of the dark, sexual, and sometimes cruel side of the feminine which Don Quixote seeks to expunge from his consciousness.

*   *   *

The fact that Marcela appears and disappears so mysteriously, leaving no trace, distinguishes her from most of the other characters in the novel. Her speech, however rhetorically complete, also lacks the quality of feeling that would align her as a character among characters.[5] Other hints deepen

---

4. Arthur Efron, in *Don Quixote and the Dulcineated World* (Austin: University of Texas Press, 1971), has been the most explicit among critics of *Don Quixote* in seeing in Dulcinea a figure that represents the life- and body-denying aspects of culture.

5. Thomas Hart and Steven Randall, responding to Mary Mackey's study in praise of Marcela's speech, note that "the *ethos* projected by Marcela, far from disposing her audience to find her innocent, tends to confirm the charge that she is cruel and insensitive, a proud, cold creature incapable of sympathy with others," in "Rhetoric and Persuasion," 292.

the sense that, through Marcela, Cervantes was invoking Artemis, and beyond her the Great Mother. The goatherd Pedro, through whom the story of Marcela and Grisóstomo first comes to notice, tells his listeners that Marcela's mother died giving birth to her. From the very beginning death in childbirth is linked with Marcela. So also is beauty. Pedro insists that Marcela's mother's beauty was surpassed only by that of Marcela herself.

Peculiarly, unless we have the myth of Artemis and Apollo in the back of our minds, Pedro illustrates his notion of Marcela's mother's beauty by reference to the sun and moon: "I can just see her now, with that face of hers, the sun on one side, as you might say, and the moon on the other" (I.12) [64]. The Artemis who combines the solar attributes of her twin, Apollo, with her own lunar qualities is surely hiding under the surface of this description, as is the Artemis of Bauron, whose priestesses inherited the clothes of women who died in childbirth.[6] Further underscoring the death-giving qualities of the moon goddess is the fact that Marcela's father, Guillermo, when deprived of the radiance of his wife's beauty, also dies. Much as Grisóstomo will later do, Guillermo lives when the woman with the sun and moon in her face shines on him, and he dies when it is eclipsed.

Already, with only this much detail, echoes of Artemis' disguised presence can be heard by the listener attuned for her. Further details show up like Freudian slips, pushing their way into the rustic narrator's accounting of Marcela and Grisóstomo through a series of lexical errors. Don Quixote's corrections highlight the errors, all of which call attention to elements constellated in the moon goddess in her triple aspect, that is, with the sun and the moon, life and death, and old age.

In the first case Pedro refers to solar or lunar eclipses, using the word *cris*, instead of *eclipse*; speaking of Grisóstomo's knowledge of astrology, he says "he could always give accurate notice of the *crisis* of the sun and moon" (I.12; emphasis added) [63]. The darkening of the sun and the moon, associated with the death of Marcela's mother and with all kinds of disaster, is in fact *both* an eclipse and a crisis.

When Pedro goes on to confuse *estil* (summer) with *estéril* (sterility), Don Quixote again interrupts, slowing the narration to highlight another key aspect of the moon goddess — her ability to confer or withhold reproductivity. When the goddess of the moon was not properly worshiped, not only women but also land became barren. To refuse the goddess was to dam up the energies of life and death associated with her. Finally, the conflation of *sarna* (the itch) for *Sarra* (Sarah) brings to light the aging aspect of the moon goddess, who is still capable of reproduction. Sarah, as a mother goddess of the Abraham tribe, again takes us into the purview of Artemis' realm.[7] The "negative" aspects of the goddess include darkness (eclipse), death in birth (sterility), and birth in old age (Sarah). As these

6. Kerenyi, *Goddesses*, 42.
7. Much more has been passed down through the Hebrew tradition about Abraham than about his wife, Sarah. Yet it is well known that Sarah was, at the time of her marriage to Abraham, more powerful than he, an issue discussed by Barbara Walker in *The Woman's Encyclopedia of Myths and Secrets* (San Francisco: Harper and Row, 1983), 890.

are repressed in the effort to reserve of the goddess only that which pleases and supports "man," they enter discourse by "mistake," in this case as the errors of an illiterate narrator. The Great Mother, who is autonomous, indifferent to the ego and its concerns, and deeply connected to all aspects of the life course, makes her appearance in Cervantes's novel through the beautiful, death-giving Marcela, to whom men in the wilderness cry out as an infant cries out to its mother.

ROBERT TER HORST

Sex and the Chain Gang†

Chapter 22 of Part One of *Don Quijote*, the episode in which the knight unwisely sets twelve galley slaves free, is justly celebrated for its indeterminacy. On the practical level there seems to be no problem, for each condemned person more or less confirms his guilt. And once they all are liberated, taking their lead from Ginés de Pasamonte, they refuse to reconstitute themselves as a small new society or state of freedmen that would obey Don Quijote's injunction to seek out the city of Toboso and there present themselves collectively before Dulcinea. Instead, in fear of the Santa Hermandad or Holy Brotherhood — the highway police patrol created by the Catholic monarchs Ferdinand and Isabella — they disperse as individuals, but not before stoning down Don Quijote, Sancho, and their mounts. Nonetheless, on the theoretical level, this same chapter raises some truly troubling issues in connection with power. The word *fuerza* (perhaps best Englished as the obsolete "main," as in "by main force" or "by might and main"), throughout a whole range of acceptations, is the leitmotif of the episode as it addresses the strengths of monarchy, the state, the criminal justice system, the police, individuals, and human sexuality. The central philosophic issue appears to be compulsion, not its reality (for in the chain gang and the highway patrol that reality is manifest), but its licitness and its efficacy.

By misunderstanding Sancho straight off, Don Quijote questions the royal use of power. Sancho describes the chained men as, literally, "people under royal restraint, on their way to the galleys" ["gente forzada del rey, que va a las galeras"] [127]. The key term here is *forzada* — "under compulsion" — and Don Quijote interprets Sancho's use of the word in the sense of the legalistic *hacer fuerza*, i.e., to attack, to violate, to abrogate the lawful remedies of another. Consequently, as a believer in a just monarchy and judicial system, he inquires of Sancho, "Is it possible that the king actually enslaves ["haga fuerza"] anyone?" [127]. Sancho at once understands how he has been misunderstood and most lucidly amplifies

† From Robert ter Horst, a revised and abridged version of "The Sexual Economy of Miguel de Cervantes," in *Bodies and Biases: Sexualities in Hispanic Cultures and Literatures*. Hispanic Issues. General Editor, Nicholas Spadaccini. Ed. David William Foster and Roberto Reis (Minneapolis: University of Minnesota Press, 1996), pp. 1–23. Copyright © 1996 by the Regents of the University of Minnesota. Reprinted by permission of the University of Minnesota. Norton Critical Edition page numbers appear in brackets.

his original statement, explaining — and here I translate literally — that these men are "people condemned for their crimes to serve the king in his galleys under compulsion" [127]. One must admire Sancho's legal precision in the choice of his terms: "crimes," "condemned," "under compulsion" ("delitos," "condenada," "de por fuerza"). But his argument is unavailing as Don Quijote insists upon framing the situation on the basis of an opposition between free will and constraint, without allowing for occasions when it is just to deprive a person of her or his freedom, a possibility of which Sancho is well aware: "Your grace must realize . . . that Justice — which means the king — is neither compelling nor injuring people like this, but only punishing them for their crimes" [127].

There is, moreover, a strong sexual undercurrent in the flow of this chapter. The Spanish word *fuerza*, to begin with, denotes rape, *stuprum*, in a legal context. But here sexuality emerges jocosely when the first prisoner examined by Don Quijote declares that "love" has brought him to his present condition of servitude. The object of the prisoner's affection, however, was no lady; rather it was a basket of household linens embraced so steadfastly that it required the police to make him turn it loose. The sly humor of the statement beautifully includes a periodic rhetoric that opposes compulsion ("por fuerza") to the free expression of desire ("de mi voluntad"). That opposition produces the binary structure of the episode and also goes to the roots of its sexuality, in which Don Quijote comes to be included through his seeming misapprehension of the prisoner's use of the term "love," for in the courtly sense, he himself is a lover (*enamorado*), and if being a courtly lover is grounds for being sent to the galleys, then Don Quijote allows that he has been a candidate for quite some time: "If lovers are to be thrown into the galleys, I would have been rowing in one of them a long time ago" [128]. Yet, rhetorically speaking, this is no misunderstanding at all, for in some of the finest poems of the period lovers are indeed sent "to the galleys."

By representing the caitiff lover of the poems in a prose burlesque, Cervantes curiously liberates a remarkable quantum of sexual energy that overflows into forbidden zones. This is the case with the prisoners questioned by Don Quijote just before he confronts Ginés de Pasamonte. One of these prisoners — the fifth to be questioned and the one who intervenes in Don Quijote's interrogation of the elderly man — explains his own captivity: "I'm here because I fooled around too much with a couple of my cousins, plus two other girls ["hermanas"] who weren't my sisters ["hermanas"], and I had so much fun with all of them that we ended up with a family tree the devil himself couldn't have straightened out" [130]. Cervantes achieves a pronounced comic effect with the several forms of the Spanish verb *burlar* — to mock, to trick, to deceive, but above all for a man to take advantage of his superior position in society in order to induce a woman to have sex with him on the basis of false assurances, usually a pledge to marry her. This trickster or *burlador* fully avows sexual relations and illegitimate offspring, both with his cousins and with several nuns ["hermanas"]. He seems to have established an incestuous extended family in which all the blood lines are hopelessly blurred.

It is, however, in the interview with the fourth prisoner that Cervantes introduces radically new material. All the conversations that surround this interview are with individuals who are wise guys; but the exchange with the elderly man shows no sign of the complex of ironies that infects the rest of this episode. This aged man is sympathetically described by Cervantes as having a "white beard down to his chest, and a venerable face" [129]. His interpreter — the incestuous fifth prisoner mentioned above — explains that the old man's crime is to have been both a pimp and a black magician. But as a typically Cervantine wiseacre, this interpreter cannot resist having his bit of a joke, so that he first characterizes the fourth prisoner as sentenced for having been a "broker of the ear and even of the entire body" ["corredor de oreja y aun todo el cuerpo"] [129]. In the realm of commerce, a *corredor de oreja* is a middleman who brings buyer and seller together in the credit market and is, according to the *Diccionario de autoridades,* synonymous with the broker of letters of credit, or *corredor de cambios,* who "solicits letters of credit for foreign parts, or loans for businessmen, as well as collateral ad guarantees." I would guess that this kind of agent is designated *de oreja* because he scurries from client to client speaking confidentially in the ear of each. Moreover, this kind of brokerage is completely contaminated with the sexual, from the more or less acceptable activities of the *corredor de matrimonios,* or matchmaker, to the work of the pimp. Thus, in the fifth prisoner's amusing synecdoche, the ear represents the whole body. In addition, the casting of spells has left its mark on the older prisoner, who "shows signs of being a black magician," as well as a pander [129]. As in the opposition between whoremongering and witchcraft, everything in this chapter is binary, including Don Quijote's reaction to these dual activities. He lauds the work of the pimp but denounces the efforts of the caster of spells. Indeed, one wonders how his eulogy of the pimp's profession — which I read as altogether un-ironic although embedded in a maze of ironies — got past the censor: *Dormitabat bonus censor* [The good censor was sleeping].

In an eloquent little speech, Don Quijote, whom one thinks of as retired from the sexual arena himself, links commerce to sex through semantics. But he also adds to the mixture an unexpected dose of politics and power, for he declares that one who is "purely" a pimp — the "purely" is not without ironic reverberation — hardly deserves a sentence as one of the oarsmen in the galleys, but rather should be sent to command and be admiral over them. Don Quijote exalts this profession, commonly held to be vile, saying that it is vital to a well-constituted state and that only savvy people ("discretos") should practice it. He adds that it should be regulated like any other branch of commerce, but be open only to a good class of persons who would have their designated inspectors and examiners, just as stockbrokers do. Regulation of the business of sex would, the knight asserts, remedy many of the ills that stem from its being in the hands of young, stupid, and inexperienced males who freeze when they are confronted with a crisis. His concluding remarks cause one to realize that this proposed reform is at least as wild as the one he will later advance for destroying the Turkish powers (II.1), but the present proposal is made somewhat firmer by the actual existence of the activity and of persons who profess it. Nor is Don Quijote able to leave the matter without rehearsing

Cervantes's familiar dicta as to the inefficacy of love potions, which, he argues, cannot compel desire.

One of Cervantes's greatest discoveries as a novelist, perhaps his greatest, is his revelation and exploitation of the sexual marketplace, surely a fundamental factor in all human systems of value and exchange, but one so far left unexplored even in this age of economics. In the examination of the condemned pimp (*alcahuete*) in the galley slave episode, we catch a sort of Adam Smithian glimpse of how untrammeled transactions in the field of desire might operate. The major premise here is that, for the proper price, any desire can be gratified. Regulation would be introduced not to impede exchange but to assure efficient functioning of the whole sexual economy. No manner of purchase or sale is privileged. All expressions of want and every move to satisfy it are equal, and the regulators are umpires who guarantee the fairness of the game by preventing fraud and deceit and all artificial advantages, such as those of gender. The mode of the system is egalitarian and adverbial. It works voluntarily, *de grado*. But what impedes the free play of market forces is power, *fuerza*, especially in the male. Often the female is introduced into the field of desire only to be imprisoned in a tiny lyric segment of it. Dispossession in Cervantes frequently leads to repossession, but such infractions of sexuality's drive to achieve gratification through leveling help define the arena of struggle as might defends its privilege against free exchange. Cervantes's address to power is various, including an inquiry into the paradoxical freedom found in oppression. Combining unhappy personal experience with poetic and literary models, Cervantes extensively explores the realm of what one might call the vanquished. The most condensed expression of this situation is to be found in the galley slave episode (I.22). But owing to the inevitable link between the Mediterranean galley and the Ottoman Empire, the Islam of Cervantes is a very great extension of the conditions of powerlessness that obtain among the captured or condemned rowers. Of course, the sexuality of warfare is a sexuality of inequality, of victors over vanquished. Greek pederasty, with its insistence on rigid definition of role, *erastés*, the senior partner, dominating *erómenos*, the junior male beloved, surely is the product of a culture designed for triumph in battle, whether domestic or foreign. Indeed, in their subjection boys and women are alike, for *erastés* indifferently designates the male possessor of both.[1] The very few references in Cervantes to overt male homosexuality occur in the context of warfare at sea in galleys, for example, in *The Captive's Tale* (I.39–41) and, later, in the episode of Ana Félix (II.63–64).

In *The Captive's Tale*, Ruy Pérez de Viedma describes the career of his master Tiñoso in positive terms, explaining how he came to be bey of Algiers "relying on the indecent methods and schemes used by most of the Great Turk's confidantes [sic]" [271]. But sex was precisely the means of advancement for Viedma's next owner, the monstrously cruel Azán Agá, "who'd been captured while a ship's cabin boy, and of whom Uchalí was so fond that he became one of the man's pampered favorites" [271]. Toward the end of Part Two of *Don Quijote*, when the hero is in Barcelona,

---

1. Kenneth Dover, *Greek Homosexuality* (Cambridge: Harvard UP, 1978), p. 16.

Ana Félix recounts, in her wonderfully implausible tale, how the bey of Algiers, upon her arrival there, learned of her remarkable beauty, as well as of that of her faithful lover, Gaspar Gregorio, who had accompanied her into exile. In the bey's presence she hears Gaspar described as "one of the most elegant and beautiful young men imaginable" [698]. In Golden Age Spanish the adjectives "elegant" (*gallardo*) and "beautiful" (*hermoso*) apply to either gender. The true sense is something very like the Shakespearean "gallant" or "brave." Ana Félix herself describes the youth's desirability as a "beauty . . . indeed grown beyond praise" [700], and she is terribly worried, for "these barbarous Turks much prefer a handsome boy, or young man, to the most beautiful woman alive" [700]. To save her lover from becoming such a love object, Ana dresses him as a Moorish female. She herself is captured in male dress and is about to be executed as a man when her gender is discovered.

The episode of the galley slaves (I.22) functions as a tuning fork for these later theatrics of power. Here Don Quijote cunningly represents the king as a despot: the reference is logically to Philip II, monarch during the fictional time of *Don Quijote*, Part One, although the charge of despotism could easily embrace Philip III, that *roi fainéant* [lazy or idle king] who reigned during the publication of Cervantes's novel. In any case, royal tyranny erases the distinctions that come from lesser-allowed degrees of might, especially those of man over woman. And even though Cervantes represents Turkish sexuality in general, and Turkish pederastic homosexuality in particular, as alien and uncouth, one of his great strokes of genius in fiction, in anticipation of Montesquieu's *Lettres persanes*, is at once to expatriate the domestic and to repatriate the foreign.

Just as Don Quijote can base a theory of sexual economy on the despised figure of the pimp (*alcahuete*), so Cervantes can found a novelistics of cultural exchange on the renegade, who moves with shameless ease between Islam and Christianity.[2] Expatriation is the first move as an individual, usually but not always female, comes on the sexual market by being torn from home and family and cast into a seemingly strange environment where power and money alone determine gratification. But this is the cruel pleasure of the overlord in which the person, male or female, who is possessed endures violation of his flesh in the hope of replacing the oppressor one day — the history, in short, of Azán Agá — a sadomasochistic process in which the masochist ultimately comes to replace the sadist. S-M is Cervantes's macroeconomics since its reversible hierarchy encompasses all sexual orientations. Yet, his outlook also involves an ineradicable domestic ideal of sexual equality and intersubjectivity. Such an ideal derives from the pastoral, where denial and passivity create not only a fragile equality, but also a potent vision. And such an ideal, which haunts his writings from the beginning to the end of his career, validates the claim that Cervantes — perhaps unique among male Golden Age authors — is something of a feminist. His fiction's desire to be a fiction

---

2. For more on this renegade, see Paul Julian Smith, "The Captive's Tale: Race, Text, Gender," in *Quixotic Desire: Psychoanalytic Perspectives on Cervantes*, ed. Ruth Anthony El Saffar and Diana de Armas Wilson (Ithaca: Cornell UP, 1993), pp. 230–32.

of equality is greater than any other desire in his writings. However, since this goal is shared by only a very few obsessed individuals, it works as a microeconomics.

In *Don Quijote* — by no means the end of its author's creative history — Cervantes takes on the go-between's role as regulator of the sexual economy with mixed, or relatively little, success. The great difficulty is this novel's poetic and parodic aversion to power, to confrontation with it. It is a poem of and to the powerless that is nonetheless drawn to the seats of power. So Don Quijote and Sancho prudently but also somewhat cravenly turn off the high road, fearing the arrows of the highway patrol once it is discovered who released the chain gang. For all the aversion to power in *Don Quijote*, however, the episode of the galley slaves — with its haunting configurations of sexuality and coercion — begins to question what Cervantes presciently regards as an outworn poetics of dominance and submission.

EDWARD DUDLEY

[Rescuing Dorotea]†

*   *   *

The history of women's discourse is a difficult topic to extract from the formulations of male rhetoric and literary genres. Mostly women's language has been created by men and put in the mouth of heroines of the sort Dorotea is about to play. *   *   *

*   *   *

*   *   * Her betrayal by Fernando has led to her social and spiritual isolation in the Sierra Morena. Contrary to the vestal-like Marcela, who chooses to live at the margins of society, Dorotea has been forcibly excluded from human discourse. Hence her lament about her lack of access to a viable language with which to re-insert herself into the society of her time.

In the same way, Dorotea is inevitably caught within the male horizon of expectations: She will either die or be reconciled to Fernando. Within the discourse of the abandoned woman either resolution is possible, but it is difficult to imagine Fernando undergoing the fundamental character change necessary for a convincing reconciliation. In fact most modern criticism has failed to produce a believable reading of his repentence. From the viewpoint of a modern psychological reading, his acceptance of Dorotea at the inn seems contrived or at best temporary. It is just a matter of time until he will again be back to his old tricks. The practicing Don Juan makes a poor risk as a husband. In this light Dorotea will have to make do with him because she has no other social choice. For this

† From Edward Dudley, *The Endless Text: "Don Quixote" and the Hermeneutics of Romance* (Albany: State University of New York Press, 1997), pp. 258–63. Reprinted with the permission of the publisher. All notes are the editor's.

reason the story proves to be an unsatisfying example of compromised expectations.

An intellectually more acceptable hermeneutic is provided by Joaquin Casalduero's venerable but durable *Sentido y forma en el "Quijote."* There he successfully argues that Fernando is presented as the ideal Baroque hero, the man who rationally overcomes his passions for the sake of a Christian ideal of marriage. This reading is in its own way "correct" but nevertheless emotionally unsatisfying for the modern reader who does not accept the hierarchy of values of the Counter Reformation. This is probably accurate in itself: this reading consigns the story to the literary trash bin of history. Even if Cervantes did conceive the reconciliation of Dorotea and Fernando as a satisfying exemplum of Counter Reformation sophistry, later readers are under no obligation to buy into an archaic value system. From this point of view the episode needs a new validity.

At the same time the alternative reading of the conventional happy ending for a Romance is not any more satisfactory. Even the powerful analysis of Northrop Frye succumbs in this instance to the modern belief that Romance leads to positive resolutions. At their sources, however, the Celtic ur-Romances obey no such imperative. The classic example of Deirdre,[1] whose name means "sorrow," suffices to make this expectation unreliable. While Romance sometimes does, as say in *La Traviata* or *Madama Butterfly*, offer an emotionally satisfying unhappy ending,[2] that also is a nineteenth-century convention alien to the mythmaking power of Celtic narrative. So too we find in Chrétien an ambivalence about the emotional expectation of human happiness. Even though *Li Contes del Graal* remains unfinished, it is difficult to program a Romance ending in which Perceval walks off into the sunset hand in hand with Blancheflor. As later sequels added layer upon layer of interpretation to the enigma of the grail procession, nothing of that sort was envisioned. While it is always acceptable for a later age to re-interpret a story, it is often not always possible to entirely undo earlier meanings. At first sight this impasse seems to remain as an enigma at the heart of the story of Dorotea and Fernando. However, once Fernando's repentence is recognized as logocentrically "unreadable," the reader is alerted to the existence of other unreadable items in the story and a different hermeneutic begins to emerge.

Among the unreadable items we have elaborated, a Romance landscape for Dorotea is already in place. From a woman without a place or name, she moves into a Romance geography of indeterminant specificity. From Guinea, Ethiopia, the Black Sea, she moves into a garbled Spanish scenario where she presents Osuna as a seaport and has to be rescued by the priest's stratagem as re-presenting Osuna as the place where she first heard Don Quixote's name. The priest's hermeneutic cover-up has been noted as an item suggesting that the model for Dorotea is to be found in an

---

1. Deirdre was a mythic Irish heroine who escaped from her suitor, the King of Ulster, in order to marry her young lover. The King later appeared to forgive the couple and invited them back to Ireland. Once there, he ordered the murder of Deirdre's husband and arranged to have her live with the murderer. She committed suicide by throwing herself from the King's chariot.
2. In tragedy or grand opera, the story usually ends with the death of the protagonist(s), but, along with this resolution, the evil forces leading to these deaths are overcome.

historically recorded instance of a girl who was seduced by the scion of the house of Osuna (Márquez Villanueva). The evidence for this missing patronymic is inscribed in the opening line of Dorotea's story to the priest where she is careful not to reveal her full name and in fact situates her lack of name as part of her lack of place. The missing place name of Osuna hangs in the air as she begins: "En Andalucía hay un lugar de quien toma título un duque." "In Andalusia there is a place from which a duke has taken his title" (pt. 1, ch. 28). * * *

Given this context of circumscribed rhetorical and narrative tropes, Dorotea's situation does not seem promising. The role of the damsel-in-distress is the most limited and conventional of heroine paradigms for a woman to assume. In this situation all the woman has to do is provide the hero with a challenge situation. Once this is defined, she has no active role in her own redemption. Her narrative function is complete, and emotionally she vanishes from the narrative horizon. In spite of these severe prescriptions Dorotea overturns the convention by creating a radically subversive feminist re-constitution of the language of chivalric Romance. To do this she utilizes, as already noted, the feminist resources of both the pastoral and Byzantine novels as well as the unpredictable improvisations of the commedia dell'arte[3] theatrical tradition. The result is inevitably theatrical and manneristic but unexpectedly serious and powerful. To achieve this she also taps into the earlier suppressed matriarchal energies of chivalric Romance itself. She sets up camp in the heart of the enemy enclosure and proceeds to destroy Fernando's destructive advantage. In this endeavor she is dead serious, despite what surface gestures indicate to the contrary.

We have observed that one of the causes of the historical rise of Romance in Western culture was the suppression of the originary matriarchal situation of Celtic women. Both in the traditional tales as they come down to us from the monastic scribes and as further re-worked in twelfth-century France the role of women is inscribed as excluded from political and intellectual discourse but at the same time curiously powerful in the domain of emotions. Since men were proscribed from expressing their emotions, they were left particularly vulnerable to the powers of "unscrupulous" (i.e., persons not committed to the establishment) enchantresses. This situation produced an endless succession of *belles dames sans merci* [merciless beautiful women] who took the forms of archetypal "evil women": Morgan le Fay, Eve, Isolde, Lorelei, and so forth. Even Guinevere's capricious sexual adventures with Lancelot result finally in the destruction of Camelot. The blame is entirely hers, however, and not Lancelot's or Arthur's. This interpretation of the love triangle is the result of intricate attitudinal forces constructed to circumscribe women outside the centers of societal power. At the same time, the setting aside of the matter of Britain as a literature dedicated to women readers provided a marginal space for feminist concerns. After all, men were not supposed to read this "vain" literature. The fact that they did shows the power inscribed in its articulation.

---

3. An Italian dramatic form in which the actors and actresses, once told the plot, are left free to make up their own lines.

In the *Quixote* this male fascination with Dorotea is undoubtedly erotic at its source but is nevertheless intensified by men's limited access to their own repressed emotions. This phenomenon may be as old as civilization itself and works its spell on all of Dorotea's male listeners: Cardenio, the priest, the barber, Sancho, Don Quixote. Only Fernando seems resistant, and that is because as a Don Juan his male erotic responses are conditioned by his greater fear of women. At the same time Don Juan is a known male type that threatens society's concern with safeguarding its property and genetic arrangements. Thus, like Dorotea, Fernando also has a "wild" status. Their incorporation into the prevailing societal structure is problematic but achievable within the rhetoric of Romance norms. No other literary mode of the time would comfortably accommodate them, and Cervantes attempted this same goal in both his "romance" novelas and in the *Persiles*. Therefore, the Dorotea/Micomicona configuration is central to the total agenda of Cervantes' art, and it is his best example of a subversive story decked out in conventional trappings. That it is neither conventional nor acceptable to the social conventions of his era provides the underlying cause of its unreadable features. As is always the case when the Romance story seems to provide a "pointless" episode, it is in fact engaged in serious underground activity. The result is that what is really going on is kept out of sight and the episode may seem out of place. The very fact that it appears awkward within the apparent agenda of the work is the sign of its real power.

Fortunately, Romance narratives accommodate this type of action while it fits poorly into the decorum of realism. This situation is what obtains in the Dorotea/Fernando story. What is happening is not acceptable to either the fictional norms or the referential social reality in question. Hence both the numinous appeal of its self-conscious theatricality. These features, instead of trivializing its discourse, are the signs of its unacceptable seriousness. Most readers, then and now, are not ready for what it reveals about the human condition. This in part accounts for the critical neglect the episode has suffered and the unwillingness to accept the Dorotea factor as central to the textual discourse of the *Quixote*. Instead she has been treated as an embarrassing failure of the master and relegated to the external interpolative rhetoric of the text rather than seen as the central climax of part 1. What I am positing is that this narrative component is part of the radical if disconcerting energies of the work as a whole. Our embarrassment with it and our need to "explain" Dorotea alerts us to the importance of our discomfort. Instead of being trivial, the Romance unreadability indicates our unwillingness to know what is going on. In fact the stress on the comic importance of the *Quixote* helps accommodate our unease. This may indicate that it is the reader and not Dorotea who needs to be rescued by Romance.

*   *   *

NICOLÁS WEY-GÓMEZ

Anselmo's Eating Disorder†

I wish to illustrate the usefulness of psychoanalytic concepts in understanding the mechanisms of Cervantes's poetics. To this end, I shall forego the usual procedures of invoking psychoanalysis to understand the author, as did Sigmund Freud in his works on Leonardo and Dostoevsky, or the author's fictional characters, as did Carroll Johnson in his more recent work on Alonso Quijano's mid-life crisis.[1] Freud's theoretical discussion of jealousy offers an insight into Cervantes's own complex — perhaps unconscious — understanding of substitute fictions and metaphors in his treatment of jealous characters.[2] Indeed, Freud's explanation of jealousy sheds light on Cervantes's conception of the activity he called "to novelize" (*novelar*). Freud himself may well have found in Cervantine fiction echoes of the work he was developing during the early years of his career. His reading of Don Quijote at the time he began his research on hallucinatory psychosis (1883) — together with his extensive correspondence in Spanish with his school friend Eduard Silberstein under the pseudonyms of the talking dogs Cipión and Berganza in Cervantes's "Colloquy of the Dogs" — has led scholars in recent years to pose some intriguing questions: to what degree did Cervantes's work influence either Freud's discovery of wish fulfillment or his invention of the dialogical drama enacted between the analyst and the analysand?[3] Although the evidence to support such a strong claim for the origins of psychoanalysis remains slim, I explain by way of illustration why Cervantes ought to be further studied in connection with Freud. My exemplum is the interpolated tale of "The Curious Impertinent" [translated in this volume as "The Story of the Man Who Couldn't Keep from Prying"], a story read aloud by the priest from a manuscript left behind at Juan Palomeque's inn by an unnamed itinerant hand (I.33–35).

An easily accessible aspect of the relationship between literature and psychoanalysis, usefully discussed by Peter Brooks, concerns the similitude

---

† This is a revised section of a longer essay in *Cervantes and His Postmodern Constituencies*, ed. Anne J. Cruz and Carroll Johnson (New York: Garland Press, 1998). By permission of Garland Press. Unless it is specified otherwise, English passages are taken from the present translation by Burton Raffel, subsequently cited by part and chapter number. Norton Critical Edition page numbers follow in brackets.

1. I am referring to Freud's *Leonardo da Vinci and a Memory of his Childhood* (1910) and "Dostoevsky and Parricide," both in *The Standard Edition of the Complete Psychological Works of Sigmund Freud*, 24 vols, trans. James Strachey (London: The Hogarth Press and the Institute of Psychoanalysis, 1957), 11:57–137 and 21:173–204, respectively. Further references to *The Standard Edition* appear as year, *SE*, volume, and page number. See also Carroll B. Johnson, *Madness and Lust: A Psychoanalytical Approach to "Don Quixote"* (Berkeley: University of California Press, 1983).

2. I cite mainly "Some Neurotic Mechanisms in Jealousy, Paranoia, and Homosexuality" (1922 *SE* 18:221–32).

3. For recent views in this regard, see the work by León Grinberg and Juan Francisco Rodríguez, "Cervantes as Cultural Ancestor of Freud," in *Quixotic Desire: Psychoanalytic Perspectives on Cervantes*, ed. Ruth Anthony El Saffar and Diana de Armas Wilson (Ithaca: Cornell University Press, 1993), 23–33. See also the more cautious article by E. C. Riley, " 'Cipión' Writes to 'Berganza' in the Freudian Academia Española," *Cervantes* 14.1 (1994): 3–18.

between the task of the reader and that of the analyst: "[t]exts, like analysands, offer resistances, which must be progressively semanticized."[4] What Brooks means by this can be better understood by bearing in mind that the key concept behind his analogy is repression: storytellers, like analysands, effect on their stories a series of meaningful substitutions that bar immediate access (hence the term "resistance") but systematically refer to a story which their listeners or readers, like analysts, must reconstruct or at least intuit (hence the term "semanticize"). Perhaps the spell that literary texts wield over readers resides precisely in the controlled revelation of, or allusion to, repressed material.

In the work that first invited the elaboration of this analogy, "Creative Writers and Day-Dreaming," Freud argues that "hardly anything is harder than for a man to give up a pleasure which he has once experienced. Actually, we can never give anything up; we only exchange one thing for another. What appears to be a renunciation is really the formation of a substitute or surrogate."[5] The formation of a substitute or surrogate participates in what Freud, in his discussion of repression, refers to as the economy of a psychic operation involving the "turning something away, and keeping it at a distance, from the conscious."[6] This economy prescribes that the psychic energy directed toward the satisfaction of the particular impulse that must be suppressed be withdrawn and reinvested in an acceptable substitute. Because this substitute is both associated with and sufficiently remote from the original impulse, it escapes repression.[7]

It is not difficult to imagine, then, that in literary texts (and oral storytelling), metaphor is the precipitate of the repressive economics of the psyche. Literary tropes — and substitute fictions, if one considers the multitude of Cervantine characters, mad and otherwise, who invent fictions that parody their own and each others' predicaments — tell from a distance the story, or most likely, the multitude of stories, behind the story. True, psychoanalysis has produced a handful of master narratives out of the broken accounts of analysands. Yet, these narratives are not necessarily the fallout of perverse reductionism (interpretation is essentially a form of reduction), but the result of close attention devoted to repetition in individual and collective (not universal) storytelling. Theoretical frameworks need not be graves for the stories we read. Cervantes the master of ambiguity and polysemy — perhaps not the moralist in him — would most surely have abhorred the potential tyranny of hermeneutic ultimacy posed by theoretical frameworks. My present use of psychoanalytic concepts as a privileged lens on jealousy in Cervantes is based on the modest notion that there are psychic structures sufficiently shared by the members of a human community so as to become the explicit or implicit subject matter of the stories they tell about themselves. And, in the case of Cervantes, these structures are precisely the storehouse he plundered in his own treat-

4. Peter Brooks, *Psychoanalysis and Storytelling* (Cambridge, MA: Blackwell, 1994), 61.
5. 1908 *SE* 9:145.
6. See "Repression" (1915 *SE* 14:147); and "The Unconscious" (1915a *SE* 14:180–85), further cited as 1915a *SE* 14, and page number. A brief explanation of both concepts may be found in J. Laplanche and J.-B. Pontalis, *The Language of Psycho-analysis*, trans. Don Nicholson-Smith (New York: W. W. Norton & Co., 1973).
7. 1915a *SE* 14:182.

ment of the jealous character. Sufficient linguistic and cultural continuity exists between Cervantes and ourselves to justify the further exploration of his treatment of jealousy in terms that Freud made explicit in later history.

So what does jealousy tell in Cervantine fiction? Let us turn to Anselmo's predicament in this tale of "curious impertinence." Freud's conception of jealousy is clearly useful in lending support to the idea that homosexuality lies at the core of Anselmo's impertinent curiosity. Freud conceived of jealousy as a substitute affect for a libidinal impulse that has been repressed. Jealousy entails the jealous subject's identification with both a real or imagined rival and with the loved one he or she imagines to be in danger of losing.[8] Freud understood this libidinal impulse to be bisexual in nature: its substitute affect, jealousy, takes in the male the form of "pain about the woman he loves and hatred of the man who is rival, but also grief about the man, whom he loves unconsciously, and hatred of the woman as his rival." In some cases, the jealous male even consciously imagines himself to be in the position of the faithless woman.[9] The substitute formula of the jealous male, particularly of the male who suffers from what Freud termed delusional jealousy, is this: " 'I do not love him, she loves him!' "[1] Indeed, Cervantes prefaces Anselmo's fabrication of a "labyrinth" of jealousy by mentioning the protagonist's dismay at the fact that, following his wedding to Camila, his discreet friend Lothario has, out of respect for Anselmo's honor, made himself scarce from the newlyweds' house. Camila's role as intruder or true rival is eloquently marked by Anselmo's peculiar statement that he never would have married Camila "had he realized his marriage would have the effect of thus diminishing their friendship." Anselmo's statement, coupled with his exhortation to Lothario to become again "master of his house" ("señor de su casa")[2] is consequent with an established philosophico-literary tradition in the Christian West that revered male bonding while denying female subjectivity. Anselmo's response to his friend's restraint in effect construes Lothario as the protagonist's primary consort.

Cervantes then tells us that the two friends spent a good part of their days together quarreling over Lothario's reluctance to visit the newly wed Anselmo. This lovers' quarrel carries on until Anselmo decides to confess to Lothario his irrepressible wish to test Camila's fidelity by asking his own friend to court her in secret. Anselmo prefaces his confession thus: "I am the most peevish and disagreeable man on the face of the earth, and because I can no longer say just when this mood came over me and I found myself gripped by such a strange, outlandish desire, I am astonished by myself, and when I'm alone I scold and argue, trying to stifle this desire and keep it hidden even from my own mind" (I.33) [216]. Cervantes's choice of a character who claims to have suffered for an uncertain period of time from an impulse so unseemly that he secretly scorns himself and

8. 1922 SE 18:16.
9. Ibid., 223.
1. Ibid., 225.
2. Translation mine (I.33) [215]. All my own translations are from *El Ingenioso Hidalgo Don Quijote de la Mancha*, ed. Francisco Rodríguez Marín, 10 vols. (Madrid, 1947–49). Cited parenthetically in this essay by volume and chapter number of *Don Quijote*.

struggles to hide it from his very own thoughts could not speak more eloquently of the author's prescient, intuitive understanding of the Freudian unconscious, or of the scene of analysis. For in Anselmo we have an insightful neurotic (the analysand) who not only alludes vaguely to the time of the onset of this compulsion and diagnoses his own illness, but also warns his interlocutor that he may not be a reliable speaker insofar as he is aware that there are impulses so hideous as to merit hiding them from one's own thoughts. Having undermined his authority as a speaker, he proceeds to hold Lothario to secrecy, consecrating him as the only agent with the power to free Anselmo from the anxiety that this strange impulse is causing him. Lothario is to be, as Anselmo states later in their colloquy, "the instrument carving out this work of my whim."[3]

A perplexed Lothario urges Anselmo to stop "beating around the bush" and to reveal to him his most hidden, innermost thoughts. Anselmo's curious self-diagnosis and prescription is indeed reminiscent of what Freud, in referring to "Dora's" first account of herself, called "an unnavigable river whose stream is at one moment choked by masses of rock and at another divided and lost among shallows and sand banks."[4] Anselmo is unable to tell the story straight "insofar as the history of [his] life coincides with the history of [his] illness."[5] Freud could hardly have expressed more neatly that the scene of analysis is founded upon this problematic conflation, and that to reconstruct its etiology, the analytic process entails the understanding and practice of narrative poetics.

Insofar as Anselmo is ill, that is, insofar as his account of himself can offer only the topography of a wish which he misidentifies as a compulsion to persuade himself of Camila's virtue, the cure he suggests for his illness is suspect. In this intimate fiction, Lothario is to pretend to court Camila so that, if she succeeds in resisting Lothario's advances, Anselmo will find his cure: "I will be able to declare that the hollow emptiness of my desires is now filled to the brim" (I.33) [217]. Anselmo's string of metaphors, his roundabout speech, and the suspect fiction by which he intends to put an end to his plight are indeed the result of a psychical economics in which the energy initially invested in the satisfaction of an unthinkable impulse has been reinvested in a substitute that speaks from a distance the very contents of Anselmo's wish. One might say that Anselmo's theatrics both miss and hit their target: in the phantasized scene of Camila's repudiation of Lothario, Anselmo encrypts his own triumph over the callings of the flesh, and in that of his wife defiled by his accomplice friend, the fulfillment of this desire so strange. Anselmo's disease lies in the dislocation between an original impulse and its visible symptoms. Anselmo unwittingly suffers from what has been called a disease of representation.[6]

In the extended colloquy that follows between the two friends (the text reifies them as *Los Dos Amigos*), a baffled Lothario offers his delusional

3. Translation mine (*Don Quijote* I.33 [217]).
4. "Fragment of an Analysis of a Case of Hysteria" (1905 *SE* 7:16).
5. Ibid., 16. Supplementation mine.
6. On this disease, see Diana de Armas Wilson, " 'Passing the Love of Women': The Intertextuality of *El curioso impertinente*," *Cervantes* 7.2 (1987): 26.

friend an exquisite string of elliptical exempla, which, like a liturgical sermon, is meant to show Anselmo that his request in effect bids Lothario to rob him of his very honor and life. Lothario's disquisition culminates with an exemplum so graphic that it nearly drives his delusional friend into a frenzy. Lothario relates no other than the passage in the Book of Genesis recounting the creation of Eve from Adam's rib (I.33 [222]). Lothario's climactic exemplum does more than illustrate the metaphorical reciprocity between a woman's fidelity and her husband's honor. It literalizes this interdependence by tracing its origin to a parthenogenitive myth which models the structural subordination of woman in patriarchal society by making her flesh of Adam's flesh ("caro de carne mea" [Genesis 2:21–25]). Its effect, however, is to call Anselmo's attention to a body imagery ("flesh of my flesh") that conjures the very thought he cannot bear: that he himself is, by extension, the Camila of his suspect fiction. Anselmo's reaction to the unbearable thought lurking behind this imagery is to issue a final plea to Lothario explaining the "reason" behind his extraordinary petition: "[Y]ou must realize that what I'm suffering from, now, is the same disease that often afflicts women when they have a longing to eat dirt, or plaster, or charcoal, or still worse things, nauseating even to look at, but worse to swallow. So something must be concocted to bring me to a cure, which indeed is easily managed, for all you need to do is start, no matter how tepidly, no matter how falsely, your attempt to seduce Camila, who is not likely to be so approachable that she'll surrender at the very first assaults on her virtue" (I.33 [223]).

While society is the domain in which the obsessive neurotic enacts his or her "diseased" metaphors and fictions, the stage of the hysteric is the body. Freud referred to hysterical attacks as a type of representation in which "phantasies are translated into the motor sphere, projected on to motility and portrayed in pantomime."[7] Anselmo's "eating disorder" is the result of a phenomenon which Freud, in one of his earliest reflections on hysteria, referred to as "conversion," in which an impulse has been divested from its original object and has been "transformed into something somatic."[8] Anselmo's body becomes not just the locus of affliction, but also the very site from which meaning is broadcast.

What is Anselmo attempting to communicate by means of this pantomime? Anselmo's illness was diagnosed in modern times by one of Cervantes's most notable editors, who referred to it as an "appetitive perversion" that caused women in Cervantes's time, particularly young virgins, to eat the clay of which certain drinking vessels were made.[9] The ingestion of clay caused "opilación," an obstruction of the arteries and other body conduits through which the humors were believed to flow.[1] The medical

7. "Some General Remarks on Hysterical Attacks" (1909 [1908] SE 9:227–234).
8. The first mention of this phenomenon appears in "The Neuro-Psychoses of Defence" (1894 SE 3:49). I have also consulted "The Aetiology of Hysteria" (1896 SE 3:187–221). Particularly useful in gaining further insight into the projective character of Anselmo's malady is "Hysterical Phantasies and Their Relation to Bisexuality" (1908 SE 9:155–66).
9. Francisco Rodríguez Marín's note to this effect appears in vol. 3 of the above-mentioned Spanish edition of Don Quijote (I.33:47–48).
1. This blockage is described in Sebastián de Covarrubias's popular Tesoro de la Lengua Castellana, 1611 (Barcelona: Editorial Alta Fulla, 1989), and the standard Diccionario de Autoridades, 1737, 3 vols. (Madrid: Editorial Gredos, 1990).

source from which Cervantes took his inspiration for Anselmo's illness is a popular Renaissance treatise that the author appears to have treasured, namely, the *Examen de ingenios* by the physician Juan Huarte de San Juan.[2] Huarte calls this malady "malacia" (also known as "pica"), a humoral imbalance that he describes as having predatory effects on the rational, sensitive, and generative faculties of the human soul.[3] Anselmo's hysterical reasoning and compulsive eating quite explicitly echo the symptoms described by Huarte. The Cervantine text, however, stops short of making explicit reference to the symptoms that revealed "malacia's" predation on the generative faculty of the soul. If we are to believe that Cervantes was well acquainted with Huarte's treatise, and that he was the exacting reader that he proves to be throughout his works, we must also believe that Cervantes would not have failed to notice Huarte's words on this matter: "If we consider the generative faculty, in it we shall find as many other appetites and as much variety. For there are men who crave an ugly woman and despise a pretty one; others prefer the foolish one over the wise one; they are bored by the fat one, and they love the slim one; they are offended by silks and ornaments, and they lose themselves to a wretch in rags. This occurs when their genitals are in good health: but if they fall prey to the stomach illness we call malacia, they then crave to commit unspeakable abominations ["bestialidades nefandas"]."[4] Cervantes's explicit interest on Anselmo's hysterical reasoning and compulsive eating is significantly contiguous with his silence regarding the least palatable symptom of malacia. In Cervantes's omission we have found the very object of this tale's poetics, that is, of Anselmo's pantomime. Anselmo's hysteria, this disease of representation, could not have chosen a more appropriate substitute for the sodomitical impulses mentioned by Huarte than the unrestrained consumption of unsuitable materials once hidden from sight in the earth's very bowels (i.e., clay, plaster, coal) or, worse yet, of repulsive substances that speak their origin in the entrails of the human body.

Anselmo's belief that he suffers from a "female" malady, his compulsion to eat things that will precipitate an obstruction of the body's conduits — his wish to fill "the hollow emptiness" of his desires by having Lothario be "the instrument carrying out this work of [his] whim" — could not express more clearly his resolution to occupy the place of the beloved Camila whom he wishes both exalted and defiled, and to perpetrate "unspeakable abominations" with Lothario. Anselmo's eating disorder, his compulsion to harden his entrails through the consumption of mineral substances, stands in significant complicity with his projective mineralization of Camila, that is, with his insistence that his malady will not be cured "unless I find some way to test her which will reveal just how good she actually is, the way we test gold by fire" (I.33) [217]. Anselmo's ambivalent desire to have Camila fall prey to the eating disorder from which

2. See Harry Sieber, "On Juan Huarte de San Juan and Anselmo's Locura in 'El Curioso Impertinente,'" *Revista Hispánica Moderna* 36.1–2 (1970–71): 1–8.
3. See Huarte's *Examen de ingenios para las ciencias*, 1578 (Madrid: Ediciones Cátedra, 1989), 480–81. Subsequently cited by author and page number.
4. Huarte 480. Translation mine.

he suffers is cleverly encoded in the fact that he himself is to give Lothario "two thousand gold crowns" to offer — and even give — to Camila, "and another such amount to buy jewels with which to fatten her."[5] Could this phantasized scene of seduction, in which Anselmo imagines Camila accepting gold crowns and jewels, speak more clearly of his desire to relinquish his own patrimony in order to take possession of Lothario's treasure?

The text abounds in images that liken Camila to the hard substances of the earth. Lothario's warning to Anselmo not to put to the test what might be broken describes Camila as "a superb diamond, the quality and worth of which had been abudantly attested to" (I.33) [220]. He also calls Anselmo's impertinent wish "a desire to take this diamond and put it between an anvil and a hammer, so that by pure force you could find out if it was as hard and as fine as everyone said" (I.33) [220]. Even the narrator calls our attention to Anselmo's projective mineralization of Camila by asking the protagonist: "For if the rich mine of her honor, and her beauty, and her modesty, and the care of her spirit is freely offered to you, and this gift brings you everything you long for, why should you wish to dig still deeper, hunting for new lodes of ore and treasures no man has ever seen, but risking the collapse of everything you already have, since, in the end, it's all propped up by nothing more than the fragile timbers of her natural weakness?" (I.33) [226].

If the text's mineralization of Camila speaks from afar Anselmo's identification with his beloved wife, the transaction of hard substances between Los Dos Amigos, namely, gold and jewels, denotes Anselmo's unwitting surrender of masculinity, his submission to a rival/consort who is then meant to "fatten" or "stuff" ("cebar") the beloved and despised bride/self with the relinquished treasure. It is a tribute to Cervantes's skill as a storyteller — his understanding of the purpose and power of metaphor — and to his intuitive apprehension of the unconscious, that the revelation of Camila's fall should come to Anselmo when he least expects it. Anselmo's epiphany takes him by surprise, when, unaware that Camila and Lothario have eloped to evade his wrath because they imagine themselves to have been given away by Camila's corrupt maid, he returns to Camila's bedroom to find her coffers empty (I.35) [245]. It is the sight of the stolen treasure that reveals Camila's fall to Anselmo. In effect, this scene of castration simultaneously speaks to the loss of bride and rival, the symbolic loss of honor and worldly goods, and the phantasized fulfillment of a dreaded wish that dare not speak its name. As we well know, the wound caused by this loss is, in Anselmo's case, lethal. I shall not expand further upon what one might call the coprology of treasure in this Cervantine tale and will note only that, in Freud's numerous references to the symbolics of anal eroticism, he establishes significant connections between the handling of "gifts" and "money" (gold) and the "retention" or "release" of the contents of the bowels by means of which children rehearse eventual control over their genitalia. Like male genitalia, the contents of the bowels are detachable parts of the body which participate in a symbolic circuitry

5. Translation mine (*Don Quijote* I.33) [225].

connected to the "castration complex."[6] Anselmo's compulsion to stuff himself with "dirt, or plaster, or charcoal, or still worse things, nauseating even to look at, but worse to swallow" could not speak more eloquently to the contents of his impertinent curiosity.

MARÍA ANTONIA GARCÉS

[Cervantes's Veiled Woman]†

A veiled woman in Arab dress arrives at a Spanish Inn, accompanied by a man in the attire of those recently returned from Barbary. When she hears her name described as Lela Zoraida, she exclaims "No, not Zoraida: María, María," to which she hastily adds "Yes, yes, María; Zoraida macange" — which means "not Zoraida" [251]. Puzzled by these uncertainties, Dorotea asks the Captive whether "this lady is a Christian or a Moor? Because by her clothing and her silence we have been led to believe that she is, in fact, what we wish she were not" [251]. The question regarding the character of Zoraida in *The Captive's Tale* (I, 37–42) has long baffled the critics. Zoraida's motives vis-a-vis the Captive and her conversion to Christianity are as shrouded as her entrance into the Inn, her face covered with a veil. Indeed, the mystery that surrounds the peculiar couple is emphasized by the narrator, who describes Zoraida as the "veiled" (muffled) woman [250], while focusing on her conspicuous, distinctive silence. That the narrator himself is a Moor who belongs to Zoraida's world makes her case more ambiguous, since it is Sidi Hamid Benengeli, the Morisco "author" of *Don Quijote*, who attempts a first reading of the mysterious young woman in terms of the metaphor of the veil.

The Captive's Tale is divided into three sections, the last of which relates the Captain's liberation at the hands of his Moorish savior Zoraida, their adventures at sea, and final deliverance onto Spanish soil. Zoraida's story reveals a similar three-fold organization: beginning with the narrator's introductory description of the couple's arrival at the inn, it is concluded by his remarks on the resolution of the interpolated episodes which criss-cross each other continuously in the novel (I, 46). Accordingly, the body of a Moorish woman — a foreign text, paradoxically read by a Christian soldier — lies wedged between the preamble and concluding observations of the Arab historian. It is Captain Ruy Pérez de Viedma who paints his and the Moorish woman's story with the skill of a master story-teller.

A captive behind the closed windows of her father's house, Zoraida is

6. *Three Essays on the Theory of Sexuality* (1905 SE 7: 186–87). See also Freud's "Character and Anal Erotism" (1908 SE 9: 173–75); his "On Transformations of Instinct as Exemplified in Anal Erotism" (1917 SE 17: 125–33); and his analysis of the relationship between anal erotism and the "castration complex" in his study of the "Wolf Man," "From the History of an Infantile Neurosis" (1918 [1914] SE 17: 1–123).

† A longer version of this essay, "Zoraida's Veil: The 'Other' Scene of *The Captive's Tale*," appeared in *Revista de Estudios Hispánicos* 23, 1 (January 1989): 65–98, published by Washington University in St. Louis. Printed with the permission of the journal. Part and chapter numbers appear in parentheses. Norton Critical Edition page numbers follow in brackets.

also a writer. She writes the corpus of her own story in the three letters addressed to the Spanish soldier, whom she has chosen among other captives seen in the prison courtyard. Composed in Arabic, which the Captain cannot read, the letters are finally translated by a bilingual Spanish renegade who offers to render their meaning word by word. In this way, the story of Zoraida's life stands as a Spanish translation of an Arabic text, retold by the Captive Captain as part of the "true discourse" of his life. Zoraida's story consequently recalls the complex underlying structure of *Don Quijote*. The history of the Spanish knight was originally written in Arabic by the Moorish historian Sidi Hamid Benengeli who, in turn, gathered it from various chroniclers of La Mancha. Later found by the unnamed editor of the work in the market of Toledo, this account is transposed into Spanish by a Morisco (Arab Christian), who translates the text neither "omitting nor adding a thing" [46]. Zoraida's story thus repeats the pattern of translations and interpretations which constitute *Don Quijote* as novel: a preliminary draft, created by various "authors," is later reconstructed in Arabic by Zoraida herself, who composes the letters delivered to the Christian Captive. These messages are successively deciphered and rendered into Castilian by a bilingual Spanish renegade — an inversion of *Don Quijote* I, 9 — and reinterpreted and edited by the Christian soldier, who presents Zoraida's story woven into his own story to the audience at the inn. The Captive's "reading" of this "body of text," however, is complicated by the opening and closing observations of the Arab narrator, which function as marginal commentaries on the Spaniard's reading of a Moorish text.

The Captive begins the tale of his rescue immediately after mentioning the presence of Cervantes — "a Spanish soldier named Saavedra" — in the scenario of his captivity in Algiers [272].[1] Significantly, Zoraida makes her entrance into the Captive's story after this authorial intrusion, as if the hand which marked a cleavage in the text at the mention of Saavedra's name were magically transformed into the enigmatic female hand which appears and disappears at the window over the prison's courtyard, where the captives are held. The ambiguity posed by the presence of Cervantes's name as a character in the fiction that he writes is further enhanced by the cryptic portrayal of Zoraida as sign: a sign which fluctuates between history and fiction, between the Spanish and the Arab cultures, between the Castilian and the Arabic languages, between the economic language of power and the unspoken language of desire, in the indeterminacy which is best expressed by Dorotea's question to the Captive: "is this lady a Christian or a Moor?"

This undecidability regarding Zoraida's identity is enhanced by the symbols which mark her appearance at the window over the prison courtyard. These are, on the one hand, the small cross made of reeds, which was

---

1. The importance of the theme of captivity in Cervantes cannot be stressed enough. Depicting the overwhelming reality of sixteenth-century Spain and its wars against the Turks, *The Captive's Tale* reflects, in its historical and autobiographical details, crucial aspects of Cervantes's life and captivity in Algiers. For an elegant biography, consult Jean Canavaggio's *Cervantes*, trans. J. R. Jones (New York: W. W. Norton, 1990), especially 48–96. On Cervantes's captivity, see Donald P. McCrory's fine introduction to his translation of *The Captive's Tale* (Warminster, England: Aris & Philips, 1994), 1–58.

shown and immediately withdrawn from the half-closed window and, on the other, the ten *cianiís* — coins used among the Moors — which were dropped in a bundle at the Captain's feet [273]. Embodying the maximum value of Christianity and a clear representation of Moorish economic supremacy, these symbols arise as images of two conflicting symbolic systems which clash against each other. The vacillation between these contradictory systems is emphasized by the Captive's description of the hand peeking through the window, a white hand which seems to be, at first, that of a Christian captive, but then, according to the bracelets that adorn it, that of a Moorish woman. The uncertainty posed by these signifiers is transposed unto the first letter delivered to the Captive. This happy deliverance arrives "unsigned" — that is, signed with a Christian cross. Yet the equivocal signatures are again sabotaged by the Arabic characters of the text, in an escalating confusion of signs that reaches its apex in the emergence of the forty gold Spanish doubloons that accompany Zoraida's first letter.

The ambiguity which marks Zoraida's entrance into the Captain's tale notably recalls her arrival at the inn, covered by a veil. Ostensibly, the presence of the Moorish woman is not directly revealed but mediated by the variety of signs that serve both to defer her advent and to announce her proximity. Her face remains concealed, framed and yet screened by the clandestine window which veils her figure. Furthermore, if Zoraida's introduction at the inn is characterized by the veil which camouflages her features, her appearance in *The Captive's Tale* is similarly "veiled" by the silence that personifies her in the story. In addition, if Zoraida's first letter to the Captive withholds her name, the revelation of her identity will be also deferred by the narrator, who delays naming the woman "whom you now know as María" [276].

In her first letter, Zoraida states that, as a child, her father had a slave who taught her to say the Christian prayers in Arabic and to worship Lela Marién [the Virgin Mary], whom she wants to see in the Christian land — Spain. Declaring that she is young, beautiful, and rich, Zoraida offers to marry the Captive once they have escaped to Spain because, although she has seen many Christians, he is "the only one who's looked like a gentleman" [274]. Nevertheless, the young woman adds that, once in Spain, if he does not wish to marry her, Lela Marién will find her another husband. These equivocations are emphasized by her curious advice to the Spaniard: "Don't trust a Moor, because they are all liars" [274]. More pertinently, the Moorish woman closes her missive with an allusion to the language of "signs" which should be used between them, which Lela Marién will help her understand.

If Zoraida is a Moor, her adoption of Castilian beliefs in regard to the Arabs redoubles the ambiguities of her letter, conveying a mysterious quality to her text. Contrast the use of her own (Arabic) language with her pejorative views of her fellow countrymen, whom she calls "liars," a stance that reinforces the undecidability of her position concerning her Christian/Moorish identity. Likewise, the constant oscillation between the Arabic and the Castilian languages — highlighted by Allah, Lela Marién, and the "Christian prayers" recited in Arabic — underlines the fluctuating movements of the narrative from one cultural code to another. These oscillations suggest a crisis in signification and a collapse in the signifying function of Zoraida/María as text.

Zoraida consequently surfaces as a dislocation, an explosion of signification that ruptures the civilized order of speech, that is, in Lacanian terms, the socio-symbolic order which involves the inscription in a system of signs and the recognition of the paternal function.[2] No other episode exemplifies better this function of Zoraida as a disrupter of the signifier than the scene at Hadji Murad's garden, where the Captive sees the beautiful Moorish woman face-to-face for the first time [279–80]. Zoraida emerges here both as a speaking subject and an underminer of the Law (the father's word). In turn, her father serves as interpreter, conversing with the soldier in the lingua franca used all over Barbary between captives, Moors, and Turks. This language that is not Moorish nor Spanish, "but a jumble of all languages" [279] exemplifies the type of "language" that Zoraida speaks and writes.[3] Consequently, if the Captain refers to this language as "the bastard tongue" [281] — a tongue that sabotages the grammatical legitimacy of the signifier — his allusion also serves to describe the rhythmic, fragmented "style" that distinguishes Zoraida's discourse. Moreover, even though she is fluent in Arabic and the lingua franca of Barbary, Zoraida speaks more eloquently "with signs than words" [281].

The scene in her father's garden precisely illustrates Zoraida's "style." Her voluble conversation with the Captive in her father's presence exposes her discursive abilities, even while enhancing the artful double-entendres with which she questions the Spaniard about his plans to leave Barbary. Similarly, during a momentary absence of her father, Zoraida reveals a different angle of her personality, by asking the Captive with her eyes full of tears, whether he is finally departing: "Amexi, oh Christian, amexi?" [281]. Lastly, when the "quick and clever" Zoraida [281] pretends to have fainted in the Captive's arms soon after her father discovers her embracing him, the young woman demonstrates an audacity and astuteness that challenges her previous characterization as a paradigm of Christian virtues. Some questions, then, are bound to arise in reference to Zoraida, and they recall Dorotea's opening question: is Zoraida a "true" Christian — in the language of the novel — or is she as dishonest and duplicitous as a Moor?

Such questions refer back to the religious and ethnic conflicts that had long agitated the Iberian peninsula, finding their climax with the establishment of the Inquisition in fifteenth-century Spain. From the seven hundred years of conquests and reconquests in which Christians and Moors fought or coexisted with each other, two distinct ethnic representations emerged: that of the Castilians and that of the inhabitants of al-Andalus.[4] Significantly, when the Captive begins his long soliloquy before

2. Jacques Lacan, "Function and Field of Language in Psychoanalysis," *Ecrits: A Selection*, trans. Alan Sheridan (New York: W. W. Norton, 1977), 67.

3. On the multicultural society of early modern Algiers, see John B. Wolf, *The Barbary Coast: Algiers Under the Turks, 1500 to 1830* (New York: W. W. Norton, 1979).

4. For these relations, see *Convivencia: Jews, Muslims, and Christians in Medieval Spain*, ed. Vivian B. Mann, Thomas F. Glick, and Jerrylin D. Dodds (New York: George Braziller and the Jewish Museum, 1992). On al-Andalus, see Richard Fletcher, *Moorish Spain* (Berkeley: University of California Press, 1992).

the audience at the inn, he distinguishes himself as a true Castilian by placing his origins "in a village in the León mountains" [264]. It is precisely from this area of Spain that the march of the Reconquest [Reconquista] began in the early Middle Ages. The process, which had been completed with the victory of the Catholic monarchs over Granada in 1492, culminated in the dramatic expulsion of the Moriscos from Spain in 1609.

This radical opposition between Christians and Moors is highlighted by *The Captive's Tale*. While Zoraida speaks of her fellow countrymen as liars and the Arab author Sidi Hamid Benengeli is assumed to be a falsifier — "since it is very natural for the people of that race to be liars" [52] — Captain Pérez de Viedma presents himself as a model of truthfulness, announcing that his account is a "true tale" [264], one that presumably differs from other stories in *Don Quijote*. This issue is again highlighted by the Captive's insistence on belonging to the caste of Old Christians, in opposition to the advocates of false credences: the conversos, Jews, or Moors. The question of Christian truthfulness versus Moorish deceit is again underlined by the letter-contract in which the Captive promises "as a good Christian" to marry Zoraida, for "Christians keep their promises far better than the Moors do" [275].

The problem of truth, as it turns out, appears to be linked to the inclination for sensual pleasure, ascribed to the Arabs by other cultures even before the advent of Islam. As registered by the fourth-century historian Ammianus Marcellinus, the Arabs were characterized by the passion with which both sexes abandoned themselves to the pleasures of love. Other scholars later claimed that Venus — a sign notorious for its concupiscence — reigned over the peoples of Islam. This view was endorsed by Medieval astrologers and philosophers who posited that the Arabs — including the inhabitants of al-Andalus — were governed by Venus, while the Jews and Christians were dominated by Mercury and Jupiter.[5] Such notions allude to the glorification of love and sexual fulfillment found in the Qur'an, considered as joyful gifts which signal the Providence of God.[6]

The recent publication of an anonymous erotic treatise, written in Spanish by a Morisco exiled to Tunis in 1609, confirms the persistence of these beliefs among the Moorish population of early modern Spain. This remarkable Spanish Kāma Sūtra proposes the compatibility of sexual love with the highest form of spiritual life.[7] Yet beyond its combination of a religious vision with an explicit depiction of coitus, the most astonishing aspect of this Hispano-Muslim study is its reiterated defense of a woman's right to express her sexuality freely.[8] This inspired glorification of sexuality

5. See the commentaries of the Jewish commentator and astrologer, Abraham ibn 'Ezra, in Luce López-Baralt, *Islam in Spanish Literature; from the Middle Ages to the Present*, trans. Andrew Hurley (New York: Brill; San Juan: Editorial de la Universidad de Puerto Rico, 1992), 61–62.
6. Abdelwahab Bouhdiba, *Sexuality in Islam*, trans. Alan Sheridan (London: Routledge & Kegan Paul, 1985), 88–95.
7. Title given to the unnamed manuscript by its editor, Luce López-Baralt, *Un Kāma Sūtra español* (Madrid: Siruela, 1992).
8. For instance, the maximum virtue of the perfect wife consists in joyfully making love with her husband: "Washing herself after the act with her husband is more than slaying a thousand sheep and giving them to the poor. . . . And a day of marriage . . . is better than praying for a hundred years" (*Kāma Sūtra*, 366).

is obviously contrary to the dogmas of Christianity, a civilization built on chastity and celibacy which teaches ascetic renunciation of the flesh. A profound hostility toward sexuality is revealed in the works of St. Paul, who accepts marriage only as a remedy against sin: "It is good for man not to touch woman" (1 Corinthians 7:1). In the same way, he bids the Thessalonians to renounce sexual pleasure: "For this is the will of God . . . that ye should abstain from fornication" (1 Thessalonians 4:3). Expanding St. Paul's notions on the evils of the flesh, St. John Crysostom asserts that sexual desire and sexual intercourse — including marriage — were not naturally implanted in man at his creation, but were caused by the Fall.[9] Such blatant differences regarding sexuality made the Christians assimilate Islam to the temptations of the flesh that the Fathers of the Church so harshly deprecated. Hence, the Muslims not only represented a fundamental hedonism which Christianity radically condemned, but their religion was regarded as a farce, worked by the devil.[1] In fact, various Castilian legends attributed the Arab invasion of Spain to a punishment for the sexual sin committed by the Visigoth king Rodrigo and the Cava Florinda. The story of this invasion was retold in the thirteenth-century *History of Spain*, compiled by King Alfonso X the Wise, who described the Moors as a barbarous and deceitful people. Likewise, the Qur'an was commonly denounced for exciting people to sensual rather than spiritual pursuits, while Muhammad was accused of being an impostor, identified as either an heretic Christian or a malicious Jew. The raging conflict between Arabs and Christians found its apex in the Revolts of the Alpujarras which ravaged Spain during 1568–1570, ending with the brutal repression and massacre of thousands of Moorish men, women and children, and the forced exile of the Moriscos from Granada.

Beyond the Christian stereotype of Moors as untruthful beings dominated by lasciviousness, the Moorish woman was assimilated to the subhuman world of witches and prostitutes — a link that Cervantes himself often makes in his work. It was the Moorish woman, then, particularly the Morisca, who was invested with the occult powers of darkness and evil and reviled as a witch. In contrast to these images, Spanish folklore establishes that the greatest enemy of the witch is the Virgin Mary, who represents the maximum symbol of chastity for the female gender. This takes us back to the subject of the veiled Zoraida, who wavers flirtatiously between the limits set by her two names: Zoraida/María. The Captive's attempt to define her within a Christian framework — "She is dressed like a Moor, and her body is that of a Moor, but her soul is that of a very genuine Christian, for she has an immense desire to be one" [258] — alludes to the conflict that Zoraida represents for his ascetic Christian soul. If she is a true Moor, she must conform to the pattern of lasciviousness and sensuality that is ascribed to Moorish women. Like the rest of her fellow Arabs, Zoraida would be placed under the sign of Venus, a sign conflicting with that of Mary, who presumably governs the young woman's

9. See Peter Brown, *The Body and Society: Men, Women, and Sexual Renunciation in Early Christianity* (New York: Columbia University Press, 1988).
1. Anwar G. Chejne, *Muslim Spain: Its History and Culture* (Minneapolis: University of Minnesota Press, 1974), 125–27.

dreams. The menace represented by Venus seems to be imminent, for the soldier averts his gaze in the garden scene in which he meets Zoraida face to face for the first time, apparently disavowing what he sees: that is, the conspicuous physical charms of "the most beautiful woman in all Barbary" [276]. In fact, the Captive attempts to "veil" Zoraida's body by focusing on her adornments. His description transforms the young woman into an inventory of gold and precious stones: "More pearls hung from her lovely neck, her ears, and her hair than she had hairs on her head; on her [bare] ankles . . . she wore two *carcajes* . . . of the purest gold, set with so many diamonds that she told me . . . they were worth ten thousand doubloons, . . . and the ones she had on her wrists were worth just as much more" [279–80].

Reinscribed in a lapidary economy, Zoraida disappears as a human being. Only her bare feet protrude out of this avalanche of gold, diamonds, and pearls, which threatens to entomb her forever. The image perceived by the Captive is certainly one of striking brilliance, a blinding glow which appears to radiate from Zoraida's face and ornaments, confirming the symbolism of her name: pleiad, cluster of stars. Ironically, as his reading transforms Zoraida into an allegorical representation of virtue, the Captive is able to see her, this time not as a Moorish body but rather as a (dis)embodied celestial apparition: "She appeared before me like some heavenly goddess, descending to earth to aid and delight me" [280]. The phrase establishes the significant connection between the representations of Zoraida and Mary, Queen of Heaven, in her apotheosis at Christ's side, as recounted by the Apocalypse: "A great wonder in heaven; a woman clothed with the sun, and the moon under her feet, and upon her head a crown of twelve stars" (Revelations 12:1). As early as the fifth century, the "woman clothed with the sun" was understood to be the Virgin Mary, an idea that was progressively woven into the Assumption iconography which depicts Mary arrayed in the sun and adorned with gold, pearls, and priceless gems. This radiant image of the Virgin as "the Woman of the Apocalypse" was especially popular in the Spain of the Counter-Reformation, where a new form of veneration for Mary's Immaculate Conception emerged.[2] Two centuries later, the dogma which proclaimed the Virgin to be free from original sin was finally established by Rome (1854). In early modern Spain, however, representations of Mary's Immaculate Conception by artists such as El Greco, Velázquez, Zurbarán, and Murillo already attest to the efforts to depict her as the heavenly apparition that transcends death. Indeed, for Christianity, the Virgin Mary stands as a negation of the female body, a repression of the physical charms that the Captive does not want to see.

As it turns out, Mary's apocalyptic depiction is linked to that of the saint resurrected by Spanish legends to lead the war against the Moors. The name of the mounted hero Santiago the Moorslayer [Santiago Matamoros] served as the national battle cry which contested the war cry of the Arab legions. In 1573, Pope Pius V instituted the feast of Our Lady of Victory

---

2. On the cult of the Immaculate Conception, see Marina Warner, *Alone of All her Sex: The Myth and Cult of the Virgin Mary* (New York: Knopf, 1976), 236–54.

to commemorate the defeat of the Turks at the Battle of Lepanto (1571) by the Holy League under Don Juan of Austria. Both the memory of this battle, in which Cervantes participated as a soldier, and the image of Mary, Goddess of Victory against Islam, subtend *The Captive's Tale*. In fact, this tale is not only constructed around the sacred crusade against the infidel but also propped up by the image of the Virgin Mary, often paraded amidst battles as a "charm" against the threat of the Moorish (Turkish) invasion.[3] Presiding over war and peace, the Virgin not only represented the most refined Christian construct regarding femininity and sexuality, but also, like the legendary Santiago Matamoros, the maximum opposition to the dark menace epitomized by the Arab invaders for the Christians of Medieval and Renaissance Spain.

If at the scenario of the inn Zoraida presents herself as María, subverting her role as the "veiled woman," it is the Captive himself — her reader and interpreter — who seems to be especially interested in emphasizing the Marian attributes of his Moorish savior. Recall the numerous allusions to either Lela Marién or the Virgin Mary that traverse the Captive's narrative, especially in regard to Zoraida's Christian qualities. Indeed, the Marianization of Zoraida is notably highlighted in the moment in which the Captive renames her with a Christian surname: "Lady of our liberty" (I, 41). The new appellation evokes one of the titles given to Mary — "Our Lady of Liberty" — as special protector of the captives held by the Turks. This characterization of Zoraida suggests that her conversion into María was determined long before her arrival at the Spanish inn.

No other creature in the Cervantine world, except for the mythic Dulcinea, is portrayed in such lofty terms as Zoraida. Encrusted with gold and diamonds, she is fetishized, deified, and even "mineralized" by the reading performed by the Captive. Beyond his fixation with Zoraida's jewels, however, the Captive is obsessed with the specter of her virginity, which he allegorizes as "the jewel that was worth more than all others" [288]. Such images accentuate Zoraida's symbolic transformation in the Captive's eyes into a bastion of purity as removed from a mortal's touch as her poetic name: stars.

The uncanny representation of Zoraida in terms of an object of fantasy — a fantasy that finds its subtext in the register of the imaginary — transports us into the mysterious realm of desire. Indeed, Zoraida's phantasmatic depiction situates the Captive's imaginary construction in an economy of the unconscious, an economy that projects us into the present age, when psychoanalysis has undertaken the reading of fantasy (and of desire) according to the topology and laws of the Other. The tools of psychoanalysis, then, handily open *The Captive's Tale* to Other meanings arising from the text itself.[4] By focussing on Zoraida as an emblem of desire, I am appealing to a notion of sexuality that finds its register in the complex network of fantasies and symbolizations which constitute the human subject. What the Captive rejects through his idealized representation

---

3. On the battles presided over by the Virgin Mary, see Warner, 303–08.
4. On the role of the Other in the constitution of the subject, see Bruce Fink, *The Lacanian Subject* (Princeton: Princeton University Press, 1995), especially 1–23.

of Zoraida, I would argue, is the obscure threat significantly characterized by Freud as the "dark continent" of female sexuality. In regard to idealization, Freud states that "the objects to which men give most preference, their ideals, proceed from the same perceptions and experiences as the objects which they most abhor and that they were originally only distinguished from one another through slight modifications." It is possible for the "original instinctual representative to be split in two, one part undergoing repression, while the remainder, precisely on account of this intimate connection, undergoes idealization" (SE 14: 150). That which is idealized, therefore, is always closely related to its obverse image — the split image which underwent repression. This mechanism may help us understand the Captive's idealization of Zoraida.

Recalling the operations of the fetishist, who repels the horrible "scar" of the female genitalia by erecting, as it were, a substitute construction which will compensate the woman for her "lack," the Captive endows his woman with the compensatory characteristics which will make her, to use Freud's words, "tolerable as a sexual object" (SE 21:154). By asking Zoraida to conform to the paradigm of Mary, the Captive is also asking her to model herself after an impossible dream, for the Virgin represents a painful contradiction — one which accepts the biological destiny of women (as mothers) and yet denies the conditions required by all women to fulfill this destiny.[5] As for the Captive, his horror of sexuality seems to be close to that of Don Quijote and his contemporaries, the austere Castilian knights who defined themselves against the Arab invaders, exposing erotic love as the sin which brings forth all sorts of disasters. The Captive's escape will function as a flight towards light, away from the "darkness" that stains Zoraida's body, far from the "abyss" that marks sexual difference.

In "The Taboo of Virginity," Freud adduces that the fear of something "uncanny" may attach itself to the first sexual encounter with woman and even to sexual life as a whole, taking the form of a "generalized dread of woman," perhaps based on the fact that "woman is different from man," forever mysterious, strange: "The man is afraid of being weakened by the woman, infected with her femininity and of then showing himself incapable" (SE 11: 198–99). Freud's words seem curiously pertinent to Captain Pérez de Viedma's sensual apprehension, a fear comparable to Don Quijote's *terror feminae* [horror of woman] in the novel. They may also explain why the brave protagonist of *The Captive's Tale* becomes more and more morose as the dramatic moment of his marriage approaches. This reading might also reveal why his relation to Zoraida, in which he has acted "as her father and her squire, not her husband" [291], represents a "love deferred."

Whether *The Captive's Tale* is a "love story" or not remains unanswered. It may be relevant, however, to conclude with the Moorish narrator's final commentaries on Zoraida. His views complete the tale, bringing to an end the interpolated episodes in the First Part of *Don Quijote*. Sidi Hamid tells us that Zoraida, not understanding Spanish, "swung from sadness to excited pleasure, according to what she thought was happening . . . , and

5. Warner, 336.

particularly what she could tell from her Spaniard, whom she watched closely and on whom her soul fairly hung" [315]. Reinscribing Zoraida into the unspeakable yet vivid economy of desire, the Moorish narrator implicitly questions the Captive's specular appropriation which negates the possibility of Zoraida's desire. As for the heroine, whether she attempted to escape in search of a maternal paradise, or, in a Quixotic manner, in order to run away with the man she loves, is irrelevant. What is relevant is the enigma that lurks behind Zoraida's veil — that is, the enigma of desire, which escapes language, eluding representation.

In the end, Zoraida remains veiled, a signifier in the chain of desire that perpetually oscillates between one and another signified, like the cane which signaled her proximity at the window of Agi Morato's house. Her silence represents her (veiled) truth — that is, what remains unsaid, what is "masked" or "muffled" in the marginal discourse of woman: "the veiled one." But if woman is the other of language, her silence, as Julia Kristeva suggests, is also the other of truth, the Other truth which attempts to fracture the symbolic order.[6] The force of this eruption shatters the order of representation (the order of language), in the same way as Zoraida's bare feet, peeking out of the "script" of gold and precious stones that attempts to entomb her forever, threaten to demolish the Captive's construction. As the other side of language, Zoraida represents a "truth" that is outside time, that is neither true nor false, neither here nor there, one that erupts, like her rebellious feet or her disorderly discourse, in a "bastard tongue" which ruptures the legitimacy of the signifier.

HENRY W. SULLIVAN

[The Duke's Theatre of Sadism]†

* * *

* * * Don Quixote and Sancho are rarely out of the spotlight in Part II. During the telling of stories in Part I, the two had often been reduced to the status of passive listeners, virtually disappearing from view, while other characters took up center-stage (during the *Tale of Foolish Curiosity*, for example, or the *Captive's Tale*, or the narrated tribulations of Cardenio, Lucinda, Dorotea, and Ferdinand). But, in Part II, even when an adventure centered on someone else arises (such as Camacho's wedding, dealing with the loves of Basilio and Quiteria), Knight and Squire become directly involved in the adventure's development and outcome. But their centrality comes through most of all in the torments contrived and inflicted on them in a series of incidents that focus pertinently on the temperament of the two protagonists.

6. Julia Kristeva, "About Chinese Women," trans. Séan Hand, *The Kristeva Reader*, ed. Toril Moi (New York: Columbia University Press, 1986), 153.
† From Henry W. Sullivan, *Grotesque Purgatory: A Study of Cervantes's "Don Quixote," Part II* (University Park, PA: Pennsylvania State UP, 1996), pp. 56–57; 59–60; 65; 147–49. Reprinted by permission of the publisher. Quotations from *Don Quijote* are cited by part and chapter number. Norton Critical Edition page numbers follow in brackets.

Their sufferings at the ducal estate, we may say, are person-specific, measured out with a certain semicriminal intelligence. Don Quixote's celibate resolve is tortured in the flesh and in the spirit by the blandishments of Altisidora, and by the perhaps innocent attentions of Doña Rodríguez. When the duenna enters his bedroom at night, he believes she is a soul in Purgatory wandering abroad, though she explicitly denies this (chapter 48). But, while a woman's aggressive sexual attention would be exciting to some men, to the chaste and faithful Knight it is a source of horror. * * *

The bon vivant and roly-poly Sancho is tormented in the flesh during his governorship of Barataria through being deprived of food and drink by the bogus diet of Doctor Pedro Recio de Agüero, and also by being starved of sleep. He is crushed and bruised in the pseudo-attack on the island; and later punished with slaps (*mamonas*), pinches, and pinpricks on his arms and loins in the bogus resurrection of Altisidora (chapter 69). The 3,300 lashes that Sancho is supposed to inflict on himself for the disenchantment of Dulcinea are also a violent penitential sentence, but with a purportedly talismanic efficaciousness. It would probably be true to say, furthermore, that these torments are not simply interchangeable. The ascetic Don Quixote, long used to physical injury, vigils, hunger, and denial of the body, would not have been unduly afflicted by the physical toils imposed on Sancho. Sancho, by the same token, would not have been repulsed by the attention of women; he would have been perplexed perhaps, but charmed that ladies of a higher social rank forced themselves on him.

So both are systematically compelled to suffer in ways tailor-made to fit the nature of each's vulnerability. Indeed, the whole sojourn on the Duke's estate is a kind of theater of sadism that encloses the two protagonists, while not making them privy to the true nature of their roles. Their situation is almost comparable to a kind of "persecuted innocence," which lends a refined psychological dimension of cruelty to the whole. The comparison with a bullfight (where all participants except the bull know what is going to happen) might be appropriate, except that Don Quixote and Sancho — unlike animals — possess human discourse and self-awareness, but are the dupes of aristocratic prestige and carefully constructed lies. Such a comparison is not exactly appropriate for another reason: Don Quixote and Sancho are not entirely innocent either.

* * *

* * * The vale of woe through which the two pass is a "grotesque Purgatory"; that is to say, its dimensions of distortion and fantastic ugliness are the vehicle by which laughter may be provoked, while the underlying seriousness of the narrative may also be maintained. I refer deliberately to the grotesque as a mode; not as a genre or an artform. Comedy can assume a grotesque mode (Ionesco, Pinter); and so can tragedy (Hamlet's ravings in Shakespeare's play); so normally can a lampoon (political cartoonists). Painting and drawing can be grotesque (Goya's etchings known as *Los disparates* [Absurdities]); and so can music (the rickety timpani theme from

the scherzo of Beethoven's Ninth Symphony; some of the enfant terrible
works of Prokofiev). * * *

* * *

When we consider the Purgatory through which Don Quixote and Sancho arguably pass in Part II, it is striking how much of their suffering is
related to the body and clothing, and to the soul as an indirect outcome.
Indeed, they are not aware of direct spiritual torment, or they would revolt
in some fashion. The mocking of Don Quixote's celibacy is a taunt to his
private parts; Altisidora pretends the parting pair have stolen her garters;
Don Quixote's face is scratched by cats; his hose is full of holes; he is
trampled by bulls, by a herd of swine, lampooned with a sign on his back
in Barcelona, thrown from his horse on the beach, deluded with fake,
speaking heads, "speaking" monkeys, carved wooden bodies of puppets,
the firework-filled body of a wooden horse, and so on. Sancho is starved,
kept thirsty, kept awake, trampled, slapped, pinched, pricked with pins,
cajoled to flagellate himself, and thrown around like a ball and battered
by the oarsmen of a galley.

The difference between these torments and the knockabout humor of
Part I lies in their contrived, pseudoformal framework. In Part I, Don
Quixote's injuries arose from attacks he undertook of his own free will,
however ill-advised, and punishment was meted out to him by rightly
outraged persons. The same is true of the scrapes into which Sancho is
unwillingly dragged. But virtually everything that befalls Knight and Squire
in Part II is offered up by jokers as if it were a true public ceremony or
honorific event. In other words, a Symbolic-order context is created for
these cruel japes and jests, however bogusly, while those in the know look
on with tongue-in-cheek. When the physical intrusions occur, it is into
this falsely public and official setting, thus producing what we have defined
as the essence of the grotesque: body parts detached and thrown in incongruous fashion into the coherence and formality of the Symbolic order.

* * *

* * * Altisidora forms part of the jocose cruelty to which Don Quixote
is subjected at the Duke's castle, particularly after the departure of Sancho.
It is his affective vulnerability, when bereft of the humor and companionship of his squire, which the erotic charades of Altisidora are designed to
exacerbate. The text records the Knight's reaction to her seductive harp
ballad as "fright [asombro]" and "some great disaster [alguna gran desgra-
cia]" (DQ II. 44, [593]). But, from a wider perspective than the Knight's
own immediate psychological discomfort, Altisidora does indeed function
as an arm of Providence, or a gift of the Most High: she is trying, virtually
in the role of therapist, to displace Don Quixote's feelings of infatuation
for Dulcinea toward herself. If she can succeed in this and then break the
spell of any so-induced infatuation by declaring her own love for Don
Quixote to be a sham, then she might show his own infatuation with
Dulcinea also to be a sham.

Altisidora, moreover, continues the movement begun at the end of the
dream in the Cave of Montesinos. Like the Dulcinea who demanded

children and grandchildren, or the impregnated Princess Antonomasia, Altisidora is a real woman. That is to say, she is a sexual being who, in the words of her ballad sung from the gardens at night, wants to lie in his arms and offer her young body to him. Her forward sexual offer is dramatized in a new emblem, when the tricks for the following night are set up: the lute in Don Quixote's room, the rope draped with bells, and the sack of cats. When the cats are dropped at his balcony, some enter the room in panic and one jumps onto his face to counterattack Don Quixote's swordthrusts. Now in European folklore and also in modern slang (English "pussy"; French *la chatte; la chatoune; le minet; le minou;* Spanish calque of Guaraní in Paraguay, *la gatita*), the female cat commonly symbolizes the female genitalia. The jest, though it misfires in the eyes of the Duke and Duchess, drives home the point that Altisidora is thrusting her "pussy" in the Knight's face just as he thrusts it away with jabs of his "sword." It is she who, after he is freed of the animal, bandages his wounded face and especially his nose, another common symbol or displacement for the male genitalia.

So the sexual attentions of Altisidora are harrowing in the extreme. They attack the very heart of Don Quixote's difficulties with sexuality and conjure up the terrifying prospect of a sensual, desiring woman. Nor does she let this sexual pressure up. As they leave the castle, she accuses the itinerant pair falsely of having purloined her intimate apparel, her garters, a new piece of flagrancy unauthorized by her employers. In the reprise of the visit to the ducal castle, as Knight and Squire are on the way home to La Mancha, Altisidora merges herself completely with the enchanted Dulcinea. She feigns that she has finally died of grief thanks to Don Quixote's stout indifference. It is now up to Sancho to revive her.

The clearly intended parallel between Dulcinea in the thrall of enchantment, and Altisidora in the thrall of suspended animation, comes through in the fact that it is only Sancho who has the "virtue" (*virtud*), through his martyrdom, to transform the women whom Don Quixote as "lover" has stricken in such strange fashion. So his penitential actions appear to rouse Altisidora from death, leaving the deluded Don Quixote in no doubt about the reality of her love for him, its desperate quality, or the miraculous gifts that Sancho possesses to resuscitate the dead or to disenchant the entranced. It is with all the more force, then, that her exasperated rebukes to him at the end of chapter 70 produce an "effect of truth," *and the disenchantment of Don Quixote.* * * *

* * * She prepares the way for the ultimate disenchantment of the hero when he realizes that, despite Sancho's apparent completion of his penance, his "virtue" is no more effective in the disenchanting of Dulcinea than it was in reviving a corpse that was not really dead in the first place. So the reader should perhaps not judge Altisidora so harshly as he has been taught to do. She is a helper of Don Quixote on the road to recovery. She plays her appointed role adroitly and lives up to her name as proof that God moves in mysterious ways and that her gifts of the Most High are a genuine instrument of Providence.

*   *   *

CARROLL B. JOHNSON

[Dreaming in the Cave of Montesinos]†

* * *

The struggle over the control of Dulcinea's creation is the central theme of Don Quixote's dream in the cave of Montesinos, which he recounts to Sancho and a character known only as the "cousin of the Licenti-ate," * * * who has guided them to the place. This episode (II, 23–24) is a most important one in the evolution of our hero's relationship both to Sancho and to Dulcinea, and its disquieting, almost surreal features have made it one of the most studied sequences in the novel. It deserves our careful attention.

I should first insist that Don Quixote's experience in the cave of Mon-tesinos is in fact a dream, a perfectly normal function in a verisimilar literary character such as our hero, and not some kind of allegorical non-sense referable only to some inverisimilar literary tradition. I should also insist that Don Quixote's dream is a plausible — that is, a verisimilar — one and that it responds to the analysis of dreams as normally practiced in psychoanalysis. * * *

Mere plausibility, however, does not guarantee any integration into the total personality of the literary character or into the total aesthetic system of the work. Norman N. Holland has provided both an excellent ex-ample and a splendid methodological caveat in his analysis and interpre-tation of Romeo's three-line dream about being awakened from death and then transformed into an emperor by his lover's kiss.[1] Holland considers it essential first to establish the context in which the dream was dreamed and the chronology of day residue that may appear in it. Second, although we lack the dreamer's associations to his dream — a powerful tool in real dream analysis in the clinical situation — we can still provide an interpretation of the symbols and the analyst's associations to them. Finally — and this is most important — we must ask, Of what use is the analysis of the dream to our comprehension of the work? In order to transform our observations from the status of psychological curios to valid critical insights, Holland proposes a simple test: "To see whether the psychological description of the character (or event) can be phrased in words that apply to the total work, be they ordinary critical language or the technical terms of psychoanalysis." The dream must be placed in the context of everything we know about the dreamer's life. Only in this way can a literary dream — or a real one, for that matter — yield any insights.

---

† From Carroll B. Johnson, *Madness and Lust: A Psychoanalytical Approach to "Don Quixote"* (Berkeley and Los Angeles: University of California Press, 1983), pp. 154–168. Reprinted and condensed by permission of the author. References to *Don Quijote* are cited by part and chapter number. Norton Critical Edition page numbers follow in brackets.
1. Norman N. Holland, "Romeo's Dream and the Paradox of Realism," *Literature and Psychol-ogy* 13 (1963): 97–103. This dream from Shakespeare's *Romeo and Juliet* (V.1.6–8) occurs while Romeo is in exile in Mantua [*Editor's Note*].

Let us turn to the dreamwork and consider those features of it which allow us to identify Don Quixote's experience in the cave as a dream. By the term *dreamwork* is meant the experience of the dream itself plus the secondary elaboration grafted onto it as it is recalled and narrated by the dreamer. The dreamwork is what Don Quixote tells Sancho and the [cousin]. First, we may observe that Montesinos as Don Quixote reports him is dressed not in the garb of chivalry but, incongruously, as a scholar. This is an example of what is termed the "day residue" — recollections left over from our experiences during the hours of wakefulness — and of their effect on the creation of the dream: Don Quixote dresses Montesinos like the [cousin], with whom he has spent the day. In addition we can note the presence of a number of anomalies of the kind we can all agree are possible only in dreams. The controversy over whether a dagger or a dirk was the weapon used to remove Durandarte's heart, the fact that Montesinos had the heart salted down so it would not smell as he transported it, Durandarte's totally anachronistic and inappropriate expression, "Have patience and deal the cards again," and finally the mention of Belerma's lack of menstrual periods are all examples of the kind of incongruous details that populate our dreams.[2]

Don Quixote narrates a plausible dream, a message not from beyond but from within. Its theme, logically, is a matter with which our hero has been wrestling since II, 10: the fact that the Dulcinea now operative in his life (at least his conscious life) is the new, enchanted Dulcinea invented by Sancho and "transformed" into a coarse farm girl. At the time he could not afford to argue with Sancho because Sancho's Dulcinea was the only one available, and to destroy her would have been disastrous for Don Quixote. So she exists, precariously, in his consciousness, but if he is to regain some semblance of authenticity in his own existence he must internalize Sancho's Dulcinea — come really to believe in her — and he must regain control of her continued evolution. That part of the dreamwork in which he narrates her presence, along with her two companions, in the enchanted nether world of Montesinos's cave is therefore of paramount importance. It is a great victory in the sense that she is there, below the level of consciousness, in that preconscious zone where dreams are made. She has percolated down at least to this level of our hero's psyche, and he has assumed the task of her continued evolution. She is needy, she approaches him for a loan, she refuses to talk to him, and the like. Sancho is dismayed by what to him is proof of his master's accelerating flight into more aberrant forms of madness, since he knows that this new Dulcinea was in fact his creation. Sancho does not yet grasp the full significance of the fact that the new Dulcinea now exists independently of

2. I am by no means the first to call attention to these anomalies. Their presence has been pointed out by *inter alios:* T. E. Hamilton, "What Happened in the Cave of Montesinos?" *Proceedings of the Comparative Literature Symposium*, 2 vols. (Lubbock, Texas: Texas Tech College, 1968), 1: 3–18; Manuel Durán, *La ambigüedad en el Quijote* (Jalapa, México: Universidad Veracruzana, 1960), pp. 210–228; Helena Percas de Ponseti, "La cueva de Montesinos," *Revista Hispánica Moderna* 34 (1968): 379–393; Avalle-Arce, *Don Quijote como forma de vida*, pp. 187–213. Most critics are concerned with the dream as a revelation of our hero's unconscious attitudes toward the chivalric ideal and its realization. Here I shall be concerned with what the dream can tell us about his attitudes toward women.

her original creator. The duke and duchess will make it painfully clear to him beginning in II, 33.

* * *

There are, alas, some not entirely positive aspects to the presence of Sancho's Dulcinea in our hero's dream. Don Quixote's encounter with her is generally unsatisfactory. She refuses to see him, preferring to work through an intermediary; she is needy; she asks for a loan against collateral in the form of a more or less intimate item of feminine apparel; and worst of all, Don Quixote is unable to satisfy her needs. The obvious interpretation of this last is that the money stands for sexual needs (hers) and prowess (his) and that his failure to produce the six *reales* requested is indicative of his fear of impotence.[3] This is a perfectly plausible interpretation and probably correct. It is also possible to interpret Dulcinea's need not as that for sexual gratification but as a need for being. She is incomplete, still Sancho's creation, and needs Don Quixote's active participation to make her whole. He literally "gives it everything he has," not the six reales requested but the four he has.

Thus, in the dream, he "invests" everything he has in the new Dulcinea, in both the obvious financial and the metaphysical psychic senses. That is, the money may be interpreted not simply as sexual prowess but as a metaphor for the psychic energy Don Quixote has at his disposal for the maintenance of the myth of Dulcinea. His total resources fall short of the amount requested. This raises a nagging doubt to the effect that perhaps our hero just does not have it in him to accept completely a Dulcinea who is the product of someone else's imagination. If Don Quixote's all is not enough, then Dulcinea comes apart. She is no longer available to serve as a displacement for Don Quixote's real desires, and he is plunged again into an intolerable situation, except that now his psychic resources are depleted if not exhausted. In order to prevent this from happening he will have to invest massive amounts of psychic energy — as he does here — in an effort to make Sancho's Dulcinea truly his own. This in turn means that he will have less energy at his disposal to deal with whatever new crises may present themselves later.

At the end of this episode we can see more clearly the paradoxical effects on Don Quixote of Sancho's enchantment of Dulcinea in II, 10. On the one hand it frees him from the need to come face-to-face with her, with its concomitant of having to admit she is only a figment of his imagination. On the other hand, because she is now also the figment of someone else's imagination, his psychic efforts to accept her and make her his own threaten his relationship with Sancho and have a debilitating effect on our hero. In a very real sense *Don Quixote, Part II* is the story of the accumulation of such debilitating effects, until the will to sustain life itself is finally overcome and Don Quixote dies.

Identifying the main theme of our hero's dream and underscoring its

---

3. John G. Weiger is among several critics who offer this interpretation. See *The Individualed Self* (Athens: University of Ohio Press, 1979), p. 61. See also Louis Combet, *Cervantès ou les incertitudes du désir*, pp. 380–381.

importance for the evolution of Dulcinea — and indeed of the remainder of the novel — does not begin to exhaust its content or its interpretive possibilities. If we stay with it a while longer we may be able to make some discoveries, or at least some reasonable inferences, about other, related aspects of Don Quixote's psychic life.

*   *   *

* * * I should note that what I identified as the major theme — the internalization of Sancho's Dulcinea — consumes much less space than the rest of the dreamwork, which is concerned with Montesinos, Durandarte, and Belerma. We should therefore pay some attention to the major portion, if not the most obvious theme. We shall be concerned with the "chivalric" characters Don Quixote encounters (Montesinos, Durandarte, Belerma) and their relation to him.

Before we start it might be well to recall the processes by which a dream's latent content is transformed into the manifest content, the dreamwork reported by the dreamer. Briefly, these are distortion, displacement, symbolization, condensation, and secondary elaboration.[4] Of these, the least obvious, but still important for purposes of our analysis of Don Quixote's dream, is that of condensation. By condensation is meant simply that a number of facts, or persons from the dreamer's childhood, recent past, and contemporary experience, may be condensed into one, so that a single character in the dreamwork may in fact represent two or more individuals from the dreamer's life, including perhaps himself. * * *

Armed with this knowledge, let us examine the characters, beginning with Montesinos. His scholarly appearance suggests he knows the answers to the questions Don Quixote brings to his cave, but in fact he does not. He cannot recall whether he used a dagger or a dirk, he does not know if Don Quixote is the one called upon to disenchant him, and he does not recognize Dulcinea. He appears to be at once a projection of Don Quixote's own uncertainties and, in all probability, a representation of his father or some other influential adult man from his childhood. Dreams about old people frequently involve a return to the dreamer's past, and an old man is most frequently the dreamer's father. If in Montesinos our hero conjures up his father, the father so constituted is not everything a father should be. He does not have the answers to Don Quixote's questions, and his principal achievement is the removal of Durandarte's heart with some kind of a knife.

In the case of Durandarte two facts stand out. First, he shares with Don Quixote the profession of knight. Second, Durandarte's hand is described by Don Quixote in his dream in a way that recalls his earlier description of his own hand to Maritornes and Palomeque's daughter in I, 43. Durandarte's hand is "somewhat hairy, with prominent nerves, a sign of the great strength of its owner" (II, 23) [480–81]. Don Quixote calls attention in his own hand to "the contexture of its nerves, the articulation of its muscles, the breadth of its veins, all signs of the strength of the arm behind

4. See Emil A. Gutheil, M.D., *The Handbook of Dream Analysis* (New York: Liveright, 1951; 2d ed., New York: Washington Square Press, 1966), p. 94.

it" (I, 43) [301]. In brief, Durandarte is easily identifiable with Don Quixote himself. Indeed, it has already been suggested that in his encounter with Durandarte our hero sees a prefiguring of his own death.[5]

*   *   *

Having observed the presence of Guinevere and Quintañona, who are merely mentioned in passing, we should devote some attention to the other "real" (that is, visualized) woman Don Quixote evokes in his dreamwork, the noble lady Belerma. Like Montesinos and Durandarte, she is unknown in French literature, and like them also, her physical appearance is described by our hero in some detail. She is, in brief, old and not as beautiful as tradition depicts her. Her description is a catalog of the ravages of time: she is postmenopausal; she has dark circles under her eyes; her complexion is sallow; she has lost many of her teeth. Her red lips, in marked contrast, suggest a more youthful sensuality. It is reasonable to suggest that she represents all the older women in Don Quixote's life — his mother, grandmother, and perhaps an aunt or two. The combination of advanced age and sensuality suggests an oedipal attraction in our hero's past. Now, the only older female relative he has mentioned in the text is his paternal grandmother, in I, 49, where he associates her with the dueña Quintañona. We also know, from his nocturnal fantasy in I, 16, that he considers Quintañona an erotic object along with Guinevere. These associations suggest in turn that the grandmother is the particular older woman from our hero's childhood most readily identifiable with Belerma in his dream.

This identification does not exhaust Belerma's importance, however. Her first identity, after all, is that of Durandarte's lady. She has his heart but not his body. We have already observed the identification of Durandarte with Don Quixote. Belerma is to Durandarte as Dulcinea is to Don Quixote. * * * This evocation, moreover, in the form of an older but still interesting woman suggests that more archaic material, from Don Quixote's childhood, may also have been present in the need to create Dulcinea at the beginning. In turn this suggests a clue to whatever it was in his early life that incapacitated him for normal relationships with women. The point of all this, we must keep in mind, is not to dredge up Don Quixote's childhood ourselves — an impossible task since he exists only in a book that begins when he is already fifty — but to insist on the fact that his behavior at age fifty-plus is so astonishingly verisimilar that it allows us to conceive of "early childhood" and "adolescent" experiences for him. Cervantes's genius projects Don Quixote's prehistory behind and beneath the moment we meet him in I, 1. It is this archaic, oedipal aspect of Belerma which explains Don Quixote's violent reaction to Montesinos's comparison of her beauty with Dulcinea's. It is not simply that Belerma is old and not as beautiful as tradition depicts her, for Montesinos is careful to ascribe her appearance to the effects of enchantment and grief. It is rather the idea that Belerma and Dulcinea have in common an identity as erotic objects. Don Quixote experiences their sudden rapprochement, the blurring of the differences between them, as intolerable because it

5. Percas, "La cueva de Montesinos," p. 390.

brings the hidden relationship between them dangerously close to the surface.

Finally, Belerma is reminiscent of Don Quixote himself, in spite of the difference in their sexes. There are several points of contact. First there is the abandonment of at least a part of normal sexual functioning. Don Quixote is impotent, Belerma post-menopausal. There is also the matter of teeth or their lack. Belerma's are "sparse and ill-placed." Some of Don Quixote's are missing as well, as Sancho observed when he dubbed his master "the Knight of the Sad Countenance" in I, 19 [108]. Both Belerma and Don Quixote have sallow complexions. We have noted hers already, and Don Quixote himself mentions his to Don Diego de Miranda in II, 16, where he tells him not to marvel at "my armor, nor at the yellowness of my complexion" [438].

Of what use is it to note that Don Quixote and Belerma share certain relatively minor physical characteristics and to conclude that she is a projection by him of himself? The identification of Belerma with Don Quixote leads to a larger one, namely, the fact that all three of the chivalric characters are projections of different aspects of our hero himself. He projects in Montesinos a number of more or less intellectual insecurities, in Durandarte his fears of castration and impotence, and in Belerma his concern for age and aging. All three have in common with Don Quixote their ages and the fact that their lives cannot go forward even though they are nominally alive. The enchantment suffered by the chivalric characters is the perfect analogue of Don Quixote's own arrested psychosexual development. It would be more accurate to say that the characters' enchantment is Don Quixote's projection of his unconscious realization of that most basic fact of his own situation.

* * *

* * * The manifest content of the dreamwork — the chivalric characters and the institution of chivalry, together with Don Quixote's attitude toward it — does not begin to exhaust the importance of the dream. Analyzable by the criteria of psychoanalysis, Don Quixote's dream correlates amazingly well with what is revealed about him through his waking thoughts, words, and actions. It is truly a tribute to his creator.

ANNE J. CRUZ

Don Quijote's Disappearing Act†

Alonso Quijano's mad readings of chivalric novels propel the middle-aged squire toward a series of adventures that begin with his metamorphosis into the self-appointed knight, Don Quijote. Yet his transformation,

† From Anne J. Cruz, "Don Quijote's Disappearing Act: Structural Unity and Character Transformations in *Don Quijote*." Originally appeared in *Indiana Journal of Hispanic Literatures* 1 (1992): 83–99. Revised by the author and reprinted with the permission of the publisher, the Department of Spanish and Portuguese, Indiana University. Quotations from *Don Quijote* are cited by part and chapter number. Norton Critical Edition page numbers follow in brackets.

at the end of *Don Quijote*, into the moribund figure of Alonso Quijano the Good neither leads to the heroic attainment of a transcendent state of wisdom, as "soft" critics would have it, nor results from the knight's folly, as "hard" critics have averred.[1] Rather, Don Quijote's final disappearing act confirms his irrevocable subsumation into his own text, an act that binds the two volumes (1605, 1615) into one readerly whole.

The novel's two volumes come together in the confrontation of the character, Don Quijote, with the text, *Don Quijote*:

> "Not so fast, gentlemen," said Don Quijote, "not so fast, for now there are no more birds in last autumn's nests. I was mad, and now I am sane; I was Don Quijote de la Mancha and now, as I have said, I am Alonso Quijano the Good. I pray that my repentance, and my honesty, may return me to the good opinion your graces once held of me." (II.74) [744]

Don Quijote regains his sanity and rejoins his friends; his life, however, is not sacrificed for any grand cause. The knight's death is instead tautological, since he dies to end the narrative. In turn, the death of Alonso Quijano the Good signifies the end of the novel because, emptied of reference, he has been replaced by his text.

Accepting his inability to assume a self-invented role in his own story, Don Quijote refuses to continue his portrayal of a knight-errant. As his long tale of madness draws to a close, however, he no longer holds the slightest interest for the other characters. Writing his text one last time, Don Quijote dictates his will only to be repaid by the cold self-interest of his heirs in his impending death:

> The house was in a perpetual uproar — but, all the same, the niece ate, and the housekeeper drank, and Sancho Panza was joyful, because, for the man who inherits, the business of inheriting softens and moderates the memory he rightly retains of the pain and suffering which gave rise to his inheritance. (II.74) [744–45]

As we shall see, Don Quijote's loss of reference ensues precisely through the coherence of the narrative's two volumes. The transformations from Alonso Quijano to Don Quijote and, finally, to Alonso Quijano the Good, as well as the transformations undergone by the other characters, may be traced through the text's narrative structure.

Michel Foucault reminds us, in *The Order of Things*, that the intrinsic order of a literary work is found in its simplest unit of narration: "Order . . . is established without reference to an exterior unit . . . one cannot know the order of things 'in their isolated nature,' but by discovering that which is the simplest, then that which is the next simplest, one can progress invevitably to the most complex things of all."[2] If we separate *Don Quijote*'s different narrative strata — adventures and interpolated narrations — what remain exposed are the static moments between actions.

---

1. For the rival schools of "soft," "hard," and "perspectivist" Cervantes criticism, see John J. Allen, *Don Quixote: Hero or Fool?* I; II (Gainesville: U of Florida P, 1969; 1979).
2. *The Order of Things* (New York: Vintage Books, 1973), p. 53. Further references to this text will be parenthetically documented.

Supplying the text's narrative unity, the inns in Volume One and the
Duke's castle in Volume Two are the substrata upon which Don Quijote
evolves from madman to poet.

It is at just such moments that Don Quijote and Sancho experience the
transformations that effectively destroy their image as the so-called eternal
antithesis. Don Quijote's first stay at the inn (I.2, I.3) [17–26] is the static
moment from which the adventures of Volume One take off. Don Quijote
as a character first comes alive at the inn: there he is knighted, there he
names himself, and there he invokes Dulcinea for the first time. A well-
known convention of picaresque literature, the inn is the locus of initiation
where the young and presumably innocent boy receives his first lesson in
what is to be the hostile world. It functions, then, as a microcosm of society
in which the boy is deceived and from which he departs to deceive others.
There is no disparity between the *pícaro* and the inn's other guests — all
form part of the same debased milieu. In contrast, the distance between
the characters at the inn and Cervantes's hero is morally incommensur-
able.

Don Quijote reverses the picaresque formula: rather than leaving the
inn a deceived man, Don Quijote leaves his mark on the innkeeper. In
the conflict with his host, Don Quijote experiences the first clash between
his innocent idealism and external reality. Labeled a thief ("as accomplished a thief as Cacus" I.2) [19], the innkeeper mockingly initiates Don
Quijote's investiture "to have some fun" (I.3) [22]. Yet by forfeiting his
pay rather than keeping the knight as guest, the innkeeper ultimately ends
up the butt of his own joke. The tension between interiority and external
reality may be regarded as a "motif," the theme of an irreducible part of
the narrative.[3] Georg Lukács attributes this tension to the particular historical moment, "a period of the demons let loose, a period of great confusion of values in the midst of an as yet unchanged value system."[4] He
observes, however, that the struggle between the two opposing points of
view results in the contamination of the victor:

> *Don Quixote* is the first great battle of interiority against the prosaic
> vulgarity of outward life, and the only battle in which interiority suc-
> ceeded, not only to emerge unblemished from the fray, but even to
> transmit some of the radiance of its triumphant, though admittedly
> self-ironising, poetry to its victorious opponent. (Lukács 104)

Yet the poetry is ultimately written at the expense of the poet: Don Quijote
does indeed leave behind the trace of his idealism, but he must finally
disappear from the text — by becoming the text — in order to do so.

While the events at the first inn register Don Quijote's initiation into
public life, the second inn witnesses Sancho Panza's formal introduction
to his role as squire. On approaching the inn, he first identifies the sight:
"Sancho argued stubbornly that it was an inn, and his master insisted
equally stubbornly that no, it was a castle, and the debate lasted so long

---

3. Boris Tomashevsky, "Thematics," *Russian Formalist Criticism, Four Essays* (Lincoln: U of Ne-
braska P, 1965), p. 67.
4. *The Theory of the Novel* (Cambridge, Mass.: MIT P, 1994), p. 104. Further references to this text
will be parenthetically documented.

that, before it was ended, they had in fact reached the place" (I.15) [86]. Although Don Quijote's delusion is great enough to transform real inns into imaginary castles, Sancho is caught between his desire and reality. He has already been sufficiently influenced by Don Quijote to believe in the possibility of ruling an island. His transformation is symbolized by the mock ritual blanketing which initiates him into his role as squire, as well as by his increased victimization by his master.

Don Quijote and Sancho's stay at the second inn in Volume One comprises only two days in the chronology of the narrative, but takes up fifteen chapters of the text and includes two interpolated stories. This stay introduces the first of Don Quijote's displacements that will culminate in his disappearance in Volume Two, as he becomes further and further removed from the narrative. Since he has returned to the inn, we expect him to resume his role as protagonist; he is, however, strangely absent from the action. He pays no attention to the public reading of "The Man Who Couldn't Keep from Prying," and at the outcome of the story regarding Dorotea, Fernando, Cardenio, and Luscinda, we find Don Quijote fast asleep, dreaming of another chivalric adventure. This time, though, the adventure is not shared by others but is contained privately in his own mind.

When the reading of the interpolated story is interrupted by Don Quijote's battle with the wineskins, the incident appears totally gratuitous and the reader is anxious to return to the story. Later, when the innkeeper, the priest, and the barber continue their discussions, Don Quijote is no longer the topic of their conversation but is instead replaced by the romances of chivalry. Although this conversation continues the same discussion begun at Don Quijote's library, the innkeeper has now superseded Don Quijote as the defender of romances. We begin to see here how Don Quijote's influence over others is already being supplanted by the influence of another text.

The interpolated stories now assume central importance in the narrative. When Don Quijote is about to decide whether to intervene in the struggle between the innkeeper and Maritornes against the guests, the narrator interrupts to continue the story of Don Luis and Doña Clara: "But let's leave the poor fellow there, for surely he'll find someone to help him, or maybe not . . . and let us move some fifty feet off, to see what Don Luis told the judge" (I.44) [307]. Although this passage recalls the abrupt interruption in the middle of the Basque episode in Volume One, its purpose here is not to arouse the reader's interest in the following chapter. It is, rather, a tacit admission that the interpolated tale may be more engaging than Don Quijote's own adventures.

The stay at the inn allows for the reunion of all the characters of the interpolated stories within the principal narrative. Until now, Don Quijote's influence on the lives of others had provided the catalyst that united and reunited brothers, lovers, and friends; but by the end of Volume One, his power over them has weakened considerably. As Lukács asserts, the humiliating departure from the inn in a cage presages Don Quijote's imminent fall from his innocent idealism: "The purest heroism is bound to become grotesque, the strongest faith is bound to become madness, when the ways leading to the transcendental have become impossible; reality does not have to correspond to subjective evidence, however genuine and heroic" (104). The sojourns at the inns in Volume One have laid the groundwork for the other characters' transformations, all the while detracting from Don Quijote as the main protagonist.

This process of displacement becomes the dominant theme in Volume Two, as Sancho's role expands at his master's expense. In Chapter Five, despite the narrator's assertions that, given Sancho's customary character, the episode must be apocryphal, Sancho appropriates don Quijote's usual superior tone to berate his wife. In Chapter Ten, Sancho takes advantage of the knight's paranoid fear of enchanters to convince him of Dulcinea's enchantment — ironically applying to Don Quijote the imaginative powers that had earlier been his alone.

Nor is Sancho the only one to affect Don Quijote. Although the players in the "Parliament of Death" finally reveal their identity to Don Quijote, this episode marks the moment at which his imagination begins to lose control: "By my faith as a knight errant," replied Don Quijote, "when I saw this cart I thought I was about to have some grand adventure, but now I must say that a man needs to touch mere appearances with his hand, to keep from being deceived" (II.11) [414]. The episode of the Knight of the Wood also involves Don Quijote's imagination, but this adventure has been deliberately planned by others in an attempt to influence Don Quijote. After conferring with the priest and the barber in order to force Don Quijote's return home, Samson Carrasco masquerades as the Knight of the Wood accompanied by his "squire" Tomé Cecial. The episode is divided into Don Quijote's encounter with Carrasco and Sancho's dialogue with the knight's supposed squire. It is no coincidence that Sancho's account is narrated first: "They divided themselves, accordingly, into two groups, one of knights and one of squires, the former retelling their loves, the latter their lives, but our history first narrates the squires' conversation" (II.13) [422].

By now as deluded as his master, Sancho ignores the squire's insistent pleas that they both abandon the search for chivalric adventures and return to their families. Don Quijote, in the meantime, after defeating the Knight of the Mirrors and observing his uncanny resemblance to Samson, again blames the enchanters for the delusion. This time, Sancho, who had recognized the squire as Tomé Cecial, agrees with his master. The episode differs from past adventures in its effect upon the other participants. Rather than laughing at Don Quijote's antics as others had previously, Carrasco vows to take vengeance (II.15) [435]. Don Quijote is no longer protected by his "madness" from those whom he has offended. Proudly announcing that "thirty thousand volumes of my history have been printed, and thirty thousand thousand more are likely to be printed, unless Heaven puts an end to it" (II.16) [438], he has become accessible through the publication of Volume One and is now as vulnerable to public opinion as any published text.

In contrast to the control wielded by chivalric novels in Volume One, external reality exerts more and more power over Don Quijote's will. Instead of opposing his imaginative excesses, his fellow characters work to ensure that he continue to believe them. But the less opposition there is to his fantasies, the more lucid Don Quijote becomes, his judgment improving in direct proportion to his loss of imagination. Don Quijote's stay at the inn in Chapter Twenty-Five evinces the changes that he has undergone. For the first time, he does not imagine the inn a castle (II.24) [491]. The puppet show episode in particular illustrates the manner in which Don Quijote is now influenced by those around him. Although it is not Maestro Pedro's intention to trick him, Don Quijote is nevertheless seduced by the synthesis of the tale's two elements — vocal and visual — external to himself: the boy's narration and the puppets' actions. Both sound and sight combine to make him susceptible to the representation of Melisendra's story. This incident, which parallels the windmill episode in its ridicule of Don Quijote's battle with inanimate objects, serves as a metaphor for Don Quijote's reading of chivalric novels. While warning of the dangers posed by the literal interpretation of a fictional text, the Maestro Pedro episode underscores the uselessness of any attempt through censorship to eradicate fiction's potentially pernicious influence. Yet, while the earlier episode had originated entirely in the knight's imagination, the incident of the puppet show relies on the fusion of predetermined external elements with Don Quijote's skewed judgment.

Like Don Quijote's stay at the inns in Volume One, the sojourn at the Dukes' castle forms the basic unit of narration for Volume Two. But while the inn's episodes revealed Don Quijote's ability to influence those around him, the incidents at the castle consistently undermine his imaginative powers. As Don Quijote succumbs to outside forces, he ceases to be the principal actor and becomes just another bit player, with less and less control over the succeeding events. Ironically, Don Quijote's power to influence others in Volume One has resulted in his own loss of power in Volume Two. Having read his exploits, the Duke and Duchess now usurp his role. The stay at their castle permits a series of heavyhanded jokes that arrest the episodic thrust of Volume One, creating in its stead an unexpectedly static period.

The Dukes' jokes demonstrate yet another form of control over Don Quijote's imagination. As each adventure narrated from the castle increasingly reduces Don Quijote's imaginative power, each enhances Sancho's importance in the narrative. From Chapter Thirty-Two on, when the Duke and Duchess replace Don Quijote as the donors of the island, Sancho becomes, in the words of the Duchess, "funnier as well as crazier than his master" (II.32) [530]. By inventing the farce of Merlin the Magician, the Duke and the Duchess, as authors, control the continuation of Volume One, whose readers they have been. They thus exercise as much power over Don Quijote as they do over Sancho, convincing the former of his knighthood ("it was the first time he was ever fully convinced that he was a real rather than somehow an imaginary knight errant" II.31 [521]), while instilling doubts in the squire about what actually took place (II.33) [538].

Although both Don Quijote and Sancho participate in the adventures concocted by the Duke and Duchess, it is Sancho who becomes the principal player. In the Clavileño episode, Sancho's imagination substitutes for the knight's so effectively that Don Quijote immediately compares the adventure to his own most highly imaginative moment: "Sancho, if you want me to believe what you think you saw up in the sky, you've got to believe what I think I saw in Montesinos' Cave" (II.41) [578]. The endowment of the island follows the Clavileño incident, dividing the narrative into two parts which in turn distract the reader's attention from the pair as a unit to each as a separate protagonist: Don Quijote, occupied with his adventures at the castle, and Sancho, busily governing the island. Such a separation turns the narrative into a veritable duel in which the two compete with one another for the attention of the reader. Since Don Quijote's character had already been delineated in Volume One, his role in Volume Two remains subject to similar adventures. The Altisidora episode (II.44) [590–93], however, underscores Don Quijote's lack of any direct involvement in Volume Two, as his imagination alone can no longer be blamed for any misunderstanding. While Don Quijote's infatuation with Maritornes was thoroughly unsuspected by her, Altisidora deliberately pretends to be in love with him. He is as victimized by her as by the Duke and Duchess, who first thought up the deceit.

Sancho's new persona develops without any interference from Don Quijote. Even to the critical eyes of his master, Sancho seems to have risen in stature while governor (II.55) [655]. Don Quijote, in contrast, suffers numerous reversals which culminate in his defeat by the Knight of the White Moon. And despite Don Quijote's challenge, Tosilos refuses to do battle with him; nor, much to Don Quijote's chagrin, does he marry Doña Rodríguez's daughter. The only "real" opportunity Don Quijote has to save a damsel in distress, and thus conduct himself in the manner befitting a knight, is ultimately thwarted by the Duke and Duchess. They not only control Don Quijote's fictive adventures, but also those of all their retainers.

By the end of Volume Two, the dispirited Don Quijote has developed a contentious relationship with Sancho. The pair's role reversal is marked by the stylistic inversion of their speech. Don Quijote's archaic expressions reflected his readings of chivalric novels; the abrupt change from this archaic, private *parole* to the shared *langue* of everyday utterance reveals the failure of his enterprise.[5] However, it also signals Don Quijote's return from madness. To Foucault, the initial transformation undergone by Don Quijote in Volume One corresponds to his alienation as a madman. The differences of an "other," non-literary reality are indistinguishable to the knight, since he subsumes all differences: "the madman fulfils the function of homosemanticism: he groups all signs together and loads them with a resemblance that never ceases to proliferate." As Foucault explains, "This character . . . is the man who is alienated in analogy. He is the disordered player of the Same and the Other. He takes things for what they are not, and people for one another" (49). Don Quijote's actions are propelled syntagmatically from Volume One to Volume Two. Himself a human grapheme, he cannot privilege the adventures in Volume One; instead, as

---

5. According to Ferdinand de Saussure, a linguist and the "father of semiology," the term *langue* stands for the whole of the linguistic system, while *parole* addresses individual speech events. See his *Course in General Linguistics* (London: Peter Owen, 1960). (Originally published in French in 1916) [Editor's Note].

Foucault explains, he is condemned to repeat them, thereby becoming their sign (48).

Foucault, however, sees no difference in Don Quijote's character as portrayed in the novel's two volumes. Yet, what saves *Don Quijote* from being merely the proliferation of linear adventures is the ironic disappearance of its character, Don Quijote, subsumed as he is by the text. In Volume Two, Don Quijote is neither alienated nor mad: he has assumed the characteristics of Volume One as a book of chivalry to be read only to fall victim to his own creative act. Don Quijote's poetization occurred, according to Lukács, when the hero became universal, at the "time . . . when man became lonely and could find meaning and substance only in his own soul" (103). Because it is allegorical, the poet's function is the opposite of the madman's. Unlike the madman, the poet recognizes difference in order to seek resemblance. Or in Foucault's words, "the poet is he who, beneath the named, constantly expected differences, rediscovers the buried kinships between things, their scattered resemblances" (49).

In its episodic format of continuing adventures, the narrative of Volume One is metonymic. As the adventures of Don Quijote become the adventures of *Don Quijote*, the first volume becomes the paradigm of the second. Volume Two's protagonist must behave according to his printed image in Volume One. Don Quijote is replaced paradigmatically by *Don Quijote*. Poeticized into Alonso Quijano the Good, who strains to resemble the others, he integrates finally into society, but at the cost of his own life. The novel's processes of transformation come full circle: the romances of chivalry act upon Alonso Quijano, converting him into Don Quijote, who is in turn acted upon and reified by his own romance, *Don Quijote*, which then transforms him into Alonso Quijano the Good.

Paradoxically, Don Quijote's salvation from madness comes about only through his loss of imaginative powers and corresponding inability to influence others. Don Quijote is thus split into the written character in Volume One who is read by all, and into the "real" character in Volume Two who, inevitably, must die. No longer mad, he is rejected by those characters who wish to see him remain as Don Quijote, that is, as an alienated poetic text. Instead, in his sanity and sameness, Don Quijote disappears silently from the text to become one of them.

Ficciones on *Don Quijote*

JORGE LUIS BORGES

Pierre Menard, Author of the *Quixote*†

[At the beginning of this complex story, Pierre Menard, a fictional French Symbolist who wrote between 1899 and 1934, is already dead. The story itself is narrated by one of Menard's self-styled "true friends," an anonymous toady patronized by various titled society ladies. The narrator's fastidious catalogue of his dead friend's "visible work" — monographs, prefaces, invectives, sonnet sequences, and "definitions" of Countesses and Baronesses — gives the impression that Menard, as a literary figure, was a frightful lightweight. But the story itself focuses on Menard's "invisible" work, the "heroic, peerless, unfinished" work of writing *Don Quijote*, specifically two chapters of Cervantes' novel and a fragment of a third.

Menard's act of "authorship" attempts to abolish the distance between writing and reading, to link them together in a single signifying process. What the narrative implies is that *Don Quijote* belongs as much to Menard as to Cervantes. Just as Menard "authors" the novel he is reading, accessing it through the contingencies of his French Catholic culture, later readers of Cervantes — ourselves included — will construct a different *Don Quijote*, finding new elements to value or devalue in the text. All literary works, Borges' story suggests, are "authored" anew by different cultures and different readers. Borges is here fictionalizing a process that would become a major tenet of poststructuralist discourse, namely, the supremacy of reading over writing. Whether or not we accept this theory, we can still enjoy the audacity of the author of "Pierre Menard." A similar kind of outrageousness informs Borges' account of his own transactions with Cervantes' novel: "I first read *Don Quijote* in English. When I reread it in Spanish, it seemed to me a poor translation."

The three footnotes in "Pierre Menard" are Borges' own, in Irby's English translation. I see no need to crowd them with further editorial footnotes in order to clarify Borges' intentionally opaque, and richly transnational, style. If portions of "Pierre Menard" remain ambiguous, we might recall its own narrator's claim that "ambiguity is richness."]

The *visible* work left by this novelist is easily and briefly enumerated. Impardonable, therefore, are the omissions and additions perpetrated by Madame Henri Bachelier in a fallacious catalogue which a certain daily, whose *Protestant* tendency is no secret, has had the inconsideration to inflict upon its deplorable readers — though these be few and Calvinist,

† From Jorge Luis Borges, *Labyrinths*, trans. James E. Irby. Copyright © 1962, 1964 by New Directions Publishing Corp. Reprinted by permission of New Directions Publishing Corp.

if not Masonic and circumcised. The true friends of Menard have viewed this catalogue with alarm and even with a certain melancholy. One might say that only yesterday we gathered before his final monument, amidst the lugubrious cypresses, and already Error tries to tarnish his Memory . . . Decidedly, a brief rectification is unavoidable.

I am aware that it is quite easy to challenge my slight authority. I hope, however, that I shall not be prohibited from mentioning two eminent testimonies. The Baroness de Bacourt (at whose unforgettable *vendredis* I had the honor of meeting the lamented poet) has seen fit to approve the pages which follow. The Countess de Bagnoregio, one of the most delicate spirits of the Principality of Monaco (and now of Pittsburgh, Pennsylvania, following her recent marriage to the international philanthropist Simon Kautzsch, who has been so inconsiderately slandered, alas! by the victims of his disinterested maneuvers) has sacrificed "to veracity and to death" (such were her words) the stately reserve which is her distinction, and, in an open letter published in the magazine *Luxe*, concedes me her approval as well. These authorizations, I think, are not entirely insufficient.

I have said that Menard's visible work can be easily enumerated. Having examined with care his personal files, I find that they contain the following items:

a) A Symbolist sonnet which appeared twice (with variants) in the review *La conque* (issues of March and October 1899).

b) A monograph on the possibility of constructing a poetic vocabulary of concepts which would not be synonyms or periphrases of those which make up our everyday language, "but rather ideal objects created according to convention and essentially designed to satisfy poetic needs" (Nîmes, 1901).

c) A monograph on "certain connections or affinities" between the thought of Descartes, Leibniz and John Wilkins (Nîmes, 1903).

d) A monograph on Leibniz's *Characteristica universalis* (Nîmes, 1904).

e) A technical article on the possibility of improving the game of chess, eliminating one of the rook's pawns. Menard proposes, recommends, discusses and finally rejects this innovation.

f) A monograph on Raymond Lully's *Ars magna generalis* (Nîmes, 1906).

g) A translation, with prologue and notes, of Ruy López de Segura's *Libro de la invención liberal y arte del juego del axedrez* (Paris, 1907).

h) The work sheets of a monograph on George Boole's symbolic logic.

i) An examination of the essential metric laws of French prose, illustrated with examples taken from Saint-Simon (*Revue des langues romanes*, Montpellier, October 1909).

j) A reply to Luc Durtain (who had denied the existence of such laws), illustrated with examples from Luc Durtain (*Revue des langues romanes*, Montpellier, December 1909).

k) A manuscript translation of the *Aguja de navegar cultos* of Quevedo, entitled *La boussole des précieux*.

l) A preface to the Catalogue of an exposition of lithographs by Carolus Hourcade (Nîmes, 1914).

m) The work *Les problèmes d'un problème* (Paris, 1917), which discusses, in chronological order, the different solutions given to the illustrous problem of Achilles and the tortoise. Two editions of this book have appeared so far; the second bears as an epigraph Leibniz's recommendation "*Ne craignez point, monsieur, la tortue*" and revises the chapters dedicated to Russell and Descartes.

n) A determined analysis of the "syntactical customs" of Toulet (*N. R. F.*, March 1921). Menard — I recall — declared that censure and praise are sentimental operations which have nothing to do with literary criticism.

o) A transposition into alexandrines of Paul Valéry's *Le cimitière marin* (*N. R. F.*, January 1928).

p) An invective against Paul Valéry, in the *Papers for the Suppression of Reality* of Jacques Reboul. (This invective, we might say parenthetically, is the exact opposite of his true opinion of Valéry. The latter understood it as such and their old friendship was not endangered.)

q) A "definition" of the Countess de Bagnoregio, in the "victorious volume" — the locution is Gabriele d'Annunzio's, another of its collaborators — published annually by this lady to rectify the inevitable falsifications of journalists and to present "to the world and to Italy" an authentic image of her person, so often exposed (by very reason of her beauty and her activities) to erroneous or hasty interpretations.

r) A cycle of admirable sonnets for the Baroness de Bacourt (1934).

s) A manuscript list of verses which owe their efficacy to their punctuation.[1]

This, then, is the *visible* work of Menard, in chronological order (with no omission other than a few vague sonnets of circumstance written for the hospitable, or avid, album of Madame Henri Bachelier). I turn now to his other work: the subterranean, the interminably heroic, the peerless. And — such are the capacities of man! — the unfinished. This work, perhaps the most significant of our time, consists of the ninth and thirty-eighth chapters of the first part of *Don Quixote* and a fragment of chapter twenty-two. I know such an affirmation seems an absurdity; to justify this "absurdity" is the primordial object of this note.[2]

Two texts of unequal value inspired this undertaking. One is that philological fragment by Novalis — the one numbered 2005 in the Dresden edition — which outlines the theme of a *total* identification with a given author. The other is one of those parasitic books which situate Christ on a boulevard, Hamlet on La Cannebière or Don Quixote on Wall Street. Like all men of good taste, Menard abhorred these useless carnivals, fit only — as he would say — to produce the plebeian pleasure of anachronism or (what is worse) to enthrall us with the elementary idea that all epochs are the same or are different. More interesting, though contradictory and superficial of execution, seemed to him the famous plan of Daudet: to conjoin the Ingenious Gentleman and his squire in *one* figure, which was Tartarin . . . Those who have insinuated that Menard dedicated his life to writing a contemporary *Quixote* calumniate his illustrious memory.

1. Madame Henri Bachelier also lists a literal translation of Quevedo's literal translation of the *Introduction à la vie dévote* of St. Francis of Sales. There are no traces of such a work in Menard's library. It must have been a jest of our friend, misunderstood by the lady.
2. I also had the secondary intention of sketching a personal portrait of Pierre Menard. But how could I dare to compete with the golden pages which, I am told, the Baroness de Bacourt is preparing or with the delicate and punctual pencil of Carolus Hourcade?

He did not want to compose another *Quixote* — which is easy — but *the Quixote itself*. Needless to say, he never contemplated a mechanical transcription of the original; he did not propose to copy it. His admirable intention was to produce a few pages which would coincide — word for word and line for line — with those of Miguel de Cervantes.

"My intent is no more than astonishing," he wrote me the 30th of September, 1934, from Bayonne. "The final term in a theological or metaphysical demonstration — the objective world, God, causality, the forms of the universe — is no less previous and common than my famed novel. The only difference is that the philosophers publish the intermediary stages of their labor in pleasant volumes and I have resolved to do away with those stages." In truth, not one worksheet remains to bear witness to his years of effort.

The first method he conceived was relatively simple. Know Spanish well, recover the Catholic faith, fight against the Moors or the Turk, forget the history of Europe between the years 1602 and 1918, *be* Miguel de Cervantes. Pierre Menard studied this procedure (I know he attained a fairly accurate command of seventeenth-century Spanish) but discarded it as too easy. Rather as impossible! my reader will say. Granted, but the undertaking was impossible from the very beginning and of all the impossible ways of carrying it out, this was the least interesting. To be, in the twentieth century, a popular novelist of the seventeenth seemed to him a diminution. To be, in some way, Cervantes and reach the *Quixote* seemed less arduous to him — and, consequently, less interesting — than to go on being Pierre Menard and reach the *Quixote* through the experiences of Pierre Menard. (This conviction, we might say in passing, made him omit the autobiographical prologue to the second part of *Don Quixote*. To include that prologue would have been to create another character — Cervantes — but it would also have meant presenting the *Quixote* in terms of that character and not of Menard. The latter, naturally, declined that facility.) "My undertaking is not difficult, essentially," I read in another part of his letter. "I should only have to be immortal to carry it out." Shall I confess that I often imagine he did finish it and that I read the *Quixote* — all of it — as if Menard had conceived it? Some nights past, while leafing through chapter XXVI — never essayed by him — I recognized our friend's style and something of his voice in this exceptional phrase: "the river nymphs and the dolorous and humid Echo." This happy conjunction of a spiritual and a physical adjective brought to my mind a verse by Shakespeare which we discussed one afternoon:

> Where a malignant and a turbaned Turk . . .

But why precisely the *Quixote*? our reader will ask. Such a preference, in a Spaniard, would not have been inexplicable; but it is, no doubt, in a Symbolist from Nîmes, essentially a devoté of Poe, who engendered Baudelaire, who engendered Mallarmé, who engendered Valéry, who engendered Edmond Teste. The aforementioned letter illuminates this point. "The *Quixote*," clarifies Menard, "interests me deeply, but it does not seem — how shall I say it? — inevitable. I cannot imagine the universe without Edgar Allan Poe's exclamation:

Ah, bear in mind this garden was enchanted!

or without the *Bateau ivre* or the *Ancient Mariner*, but I am quite capable of imagining it without the *Quixote*. (I speak, naturally, of my personal capacity and not of those works' historical resonance.) The *Quixote* is a contingent book; the *Quixote* is unnecessary. I can premeditate writing it, I can write it, without falling into a tautology. When I was ten or twelve years old, I read it, perhaps in its entirety. Later, I have reread closely certain chapters, those which I shall not attempt for the time being. I have also gone through the interludes, the plays, the *Galatea*, the exemplary novels, the undoubtedly laborious tribulations of Persiles and Segismunda and the *Viaje del Parnaso* . . . My general recollection of the *Quixote*, simplified by forgetfulness and indifference, can well equal the imprecise and prior image of a book not yet written. Once that image (which no one can legitimately deny me) is postulated, it is certain that my problem is a good bit more difficult than Cervantes' was. My obliging predecessor did not refuse the collaboration of chance: he composed his immortal work somewhat *à la diable*, carried along by the inertias of language and invention. I have taken on the mysterious duty of reconstructing literally his spontaneous work. My solitary game is governed by two polar laws. The first permits me to essay variations of a formal or psychological type; the second obliges me to sacrifice these variations to the "original" text and reason out this annihilation in an irrefutable manner . . . To these artificial hindrances, another — of a congenital kind — must be added. To compose the *Quixote* at the beginning of the seventeenth century was a reasonable undertaking, necessary and perhaps even unavoidable; at the beginning of the twentieth, it is almost impossible. It is not in vain that three hundred years have gone by, filled with exceedingly complex events. Amongst them, to mention only one, is the *Quixote* itself."

In spite of these three obstacles, Menard's fragmentary *Quixote* is more subtle than Cervantes'. The latter, in a clumsy fashion, opposes to the fictions of chivalry the tawdry provincial reality of his country; Menard selects as his "reality" the land of Carmen during the century of Lepanto and Lope de Vega. What a series of *espagnolades* that selection would have suggested to Maurice Barrès or Dr. Rodríguez Larreta! Menard eludes them with complete naturalness. In his work there are no gypsy flourishes or conquistadors or mystics or Philip the Seconds or *autos da fé*. He neglects or eliminates local color. This disdain points to a new conception of the historical novel. This disdain condemns *Salammbô*, with no possibility of appeal.

It is no less astounding to consider isolated chapters. For example, let us examine Chapter XXXVIII of the first part, "which treats of the curious discourse of Don Quixote on arms and letters." It is well known that Don Quixote (like Quevedo in an analogous and later passage in *La hora de todos*) decided the debate against letters and in favor of arms. Cervantes was a former soldier: his verdict is understandable. But that Pierre Menard's Don Quixote — a contemporary of *La trahison des clercs* and Bertrand Russell — should fall prey to such nebulous sophistries! Madame Bachelier has seen here an admirable and typical subordination on the part of the author to the hero's psychology; others (not at all perspi-caciously), a *transcription* of the *Quixote*; the Baroness de Bacourt, the influence of Nietzsche. To this third interpretation (which I judge to be irrefutable) I am not sure I dare to add a fourth, which concords very well with the almost divine modesty of Pierre Menard: his resigned or ironical habit of propagating ideas which were the strict reverse of those he pre-ferred. (Let us recall once more his diatribe against Paul Valéry in Jacques Reboul's ephemeral Surrealist sheet.) Cervantes' text and Menard's are verbally identical, but the second is almost infinitely richer. (More ambig-uous, his detractors will say, but ambiguity is richness.)

It is a revelation to compare Menard's *Don Quixote* with Cervantes'. The latter, for example, wrote (part one, chapter nine):

> . . . truth, whose mother is history, rival of time, depository of deeds, witness of the past, exemplar and adviser to the present, and the fu-ture's counselor.

Written in the seventeeth century, written by the "lay genius" Cervantes, this enumeration is a mere rhetorical praise of history. Menard, on the other hand, writes:

> . . . truth, whose mother is history, rival of time, depository of deeds, witness of the past, exemplar and adviser to the present, and the fu-ture's counselor.

History, the *mother* of truth: the idea is astounding. Menard, a contem-porary of William James, does not define history as an inquiry into reality but as its origin. Historical truth, for him, is not what has happened; it is what we judge to have happened. The final phrases — *exemplar and adviser to the present, and the future's counselor* — are brazenly pragmatic.

The contrast in style is also vivid. The archaic style of Menard — quite foreign, after all — suffers from a certain affectation. Not so that of his forerunner, who handles with ease the current Spanish of his time.

There is no exercise of the intellect which is not, in the final analysis, useless. A philosophical doctrine begins as a plausible description of the universe; with the passage of the years it becomes a mere chapter — if not a paragraph or a name — in the history of philosophy. In literature, this eventual caducity is even more notorious. The *Quixote* — Menard told me — was, above all, an entertaining book; now it is the occasion for patriotic toasts, grammatical insolence and obscene de luxe editions. Fame is a form of incomprehension, perhaps the worst.

There is nothing new in these nihilistic verifications; what is singular is the determination Menard derived from them. He decided to anticipate the vanity awaiting all man's efforts; he set himself to an undertaking which was exceedingly complex and, from the very beginning, futile. He dedi-cated his scruples and his sleepless nights to repeating an already extant book in an alien tongue. He multiplied draft upon draft, revised tena-ciously and tore up thousands of manuscript pages.[3] He did not let anyone

3. I remember his quadricular notebooks, his black crossed-out passages, his peculiar typographical symbols and his insect-like handwriting. In the afternoons he liked to go out for a walk around the outskirts of Nîmes; he would take a notebook with him and make a merry bonfire.

examine these drafts and took care they should not survive him. In vain have I tried to reconstruct them.

I have reflected that it is permissible to see in this "final" *Quixote* a kind of palimpsest, through which the traces — tenuous but not indecipherable — of our friend's "previous" writing should be translucently visible. Unfortunately, only a second Pierre Menard, inverting the other's work, would be able to exhume and revive those lost Troys . . .

"Thinking, analyzing, inventing (he also wrote me) are not anomalous acts; they are the normal respiration of the intelligence. To glorify the occasional performance of that function, to hoard ancient and alien thoughts, to recall with incredulous stupor that the *doctor universalis* thought, is to confess our laziness or our barbarity. Every man should be capable of all ideas and I understand that in the future this will be the case."

Menard (perhaps without wanting to) has enriched, by means of a new technique, the halting and rudimentary art of reading: this new technique is that of the deliberate anachronism and the erroneous attribution. This technique, whose applications are infinite, prompts us to go through the *Odyssey* as if it were posterior to the *Aeneid* and the book *Le jardin du Centaure* of Madame Henri Bachelier as if it were by Madame Henri Bachelier. This technique fills the most placid works with adventure. To attribute the *Imitatio Christi* to Louis Ferdinand Céline or to James Joyce, is this not a sufficient renovation of its tenuous spiritual indications?

Miguel de Cervantes: A Chronology

1547   Miguel de Cervantes born in Alcalá de Henares, on September 29(?).
        First *Index* of prohibited books in Spain.
        First Purity-of-Blood statutes in Spain.
1568   Studies under the humanist Juan López de Hoyos.
1569   In Rome under the service of Julio Acquaviva, who becomes a Cardinal in 1570.
1570   Wounded while fighting the Turks at Battle of Lepanto.
1575   Captured by Barbary pirates en route to Spain. Begins five years of captivity in Algiers, including four escape attempts.
1580   Ransomed from captivity by Trinitarians and returns to Spain.
1582   First failed attempt to secure a post in the Indies.
1584   Acknowledges a natural daughter, Isabel de Saavedra, born of his union with Ana Franca de Rojas. Later that year marries Catalina de Salazar in Esquivias.
1585   Publishes *La Galatea*, an unfinished pastoral novel.
1587   Secures job commissioning supplies for the Spanish Armada.
1589   Unsuccessfully petitions Council of the Indies for a post in the New World.
1590   Briefly jailed at Castro del Río for a business failure.
1595   Works as a tax collector across Kingdom of Granada.
1597   Jailed in the Prison of Seville, thanks to bankruptcy of a banker with whom he had deposited state funds.
1598   Philip II of Spain dies, and Cervantes writes a sonnet to his tomb.
1605   Publication of First Part of *Don Quijote*.
1607   Francis Beaumont's *The Knight of the Burning Pestle*, derived from *Don Quijote*, appears on the London stage.
1612   Thomas Shelton translates *Don Quijote*, Part I, into *The History of the valorous and wittie Knight-Errant, Don Quixote of the Mancha*.
1613   Publishes the *Exemplary Novels*.
        A lost play titled *Cardenio*, possibly composed by Fletcher and Shakespeare after Cervantes's character Cardenio, is enacted at the English court.
1614   Publishes the *Voyage of Parnassus*.
        Avellaneda publishes a spurious continuation of *Don Quijote*.
1615   Publication of Part Two of *Don Quijote*.
        Publication of *Eight Plays and Eight Interludes*.
1616   Death of Cervantes.
1617   Posthumous publication of Cervantes's *Persiles and Sigismunda*.

Selected Bibliography

The following list offers readers of English a brief selection of books on or related to Cervantes and *Don Quijote*, as well as individual articles included in this Norton Critical Edition. For other articles on *Don Quijote*, too numerous to cite here, readers may consult the *Cervantes International Bibliography Online*, ed. Eduardo Urbina, at: http://www.csdl.tamu.edu/cervantes

•Indicates works included or excerpted in this Norton Critical Edition.

Allen, John J. *Don Quixote: Hero or Fool? A Study in Narrative Technique.* 2 vols. Gainesville: University of Florida Press, 1969, 1979.
•Ariosto, Ludovico. *Orlando Furioso.* Trans. William Stewart Rose. Ed. Stewart A. Baker and A. Bartlett Giamatti. Indianapolis: Bobbs-Merrill, 1968.
•Bloom, Harold. *The Western Canon: The Books and School of the Ages.* New York: Harcourt Brace & Co., 1994.
———, ed. *Cervantes: Modern Critical Views.* New York: Chelsea House, 1987.
•Borges, Jorge Luis. *Labyrinths.* Trans. James E. Irby. New York: New Directions Publishing Corp., 1962.
Byron, William. *Cervantes: A Biography.* London: Cassell, 1979.
Canavaggio, Jean. *Cervantes.* Trans. J. R. Jones. New York: W. W. Norton & Company, 1990.
•Cascardi, Anthony J. *The Bounds of Reason: Cervantes, Dostoevsky, Flaubert.* New York: Columbia University Press, 1986.
•Cervantes, Miguel de. Prologue to *La Galatea.* Ed. Juan Bautista Avalle-Arce. 2 vols. Madrid: Espasa-Calpe, 1968. 7–9.
•———. Prologue to *Persiles and Sigismunda, A Northern Story.* Trans. Celia Richmond Weller and Clark A. Colahan. Berkeley: University of California Press, 1989. 15–16.
•———. Prologue to the Reader to *Exemplary Novels.* Trans. B. W. Ife. Vol. 1. Warminister: Aris & Phillips Ltd., 1992. 3–5.
•———. *Viage del Parnaso y Poesías varias* [Voyage of Parnassus]. Ed. Elias L. Rivers. Madrid: Espasa-Calpe, 1991. Chap. 4, ll. 22–36.
Close, Anthony. *The Romantic Approach to "Don Quixote": A Critical History of the Romantic Tradition in "Quixote" Criticism.* Cambridge: Cambridge University Press, 1977.
•Cruz, Anne J. "Don Quixote's Disappearing Act: Structural Unity and Character Transformations in *Don Quixote.*" *Indiana Journal of Hispanic Literatures* 1 (1992): 83–99.
•Dudley, Edward. *The Endless Text: "Don Quixote" and the Hermeneutics of Romance.* Albany: State University of New York Press, 1997.
Eisenberg, Daniel. *A Study of "Don Quixote."* Newark, Del.: Juan de la Cuesta, 1987.
El Saffar, Ruth. *Beyond Fiction: The Recovery of the Feminine in the Novels of Cervantes.* Berkeley: University of California Press, 1984.
———. *Critical Essays on Cervantes.* Boston: G. K. Hall, 1986.
———. *Distance and Control in "Don Quixote": A Study in Narrative Technique.* Chapel Hill: University of North Carolina Press, 1975.
•———. "In Marcela's Case," in *Quixotic Desire: Psychoanalytic Perspectives on Cervantes.* Ed. Ruth Anthony El Saffar and Diana de Armas Wilson. Ithaca: Cornell University Press, 1993. 157–78.
•Fernández de Avellaneda, Alonso. Prologue to *Don Quixote de La Mancha (Part II): Being the spurious continuation of Miguel de Cervantes' Part I.* Trans. and ed. Alberta Wilson Server and John Esten Keller. Newark, DE: Juan de la Cuesta, 1980. 3–5.
•Finch, Patricia, and John J. Allen. "*Don Quijote* across the Centuries." Paper presented at symposium in honor of Manuel Durán, November 1, 1996, at Yale University, New Haven, CT.
•Foucault, Michel. *The Order of Things: An Archaeology of the Human Sciences.* New York: Vintage Books, 1973.

Fuentes, Carlos. *"Don Quixote," or the Critique of Reading*. Austin, Tex.: Institute of Latin American Studies, 1976.

•———. Foreword to *The Adventures of Don Quixote de la Mancha* by Miguel de Cervantes. Trans. Tobias Smollet. New York: Farrar, Straus, Giroux, 1986. xi–xiii.

•Garcés, María Antonia. "Zoraida's Veil: The 'Other' Scene of *The Captive's Tale*." *Revista de Estudios Hispánicos* 23, 1 (January 1989): 65–98.

Gerli, E. Michael. *Refiguring Authority: Reading, Writing, and Rewriting in Cervantes*. Lexington: The University Press of Kentucky, 1995.

Gilman, Stephen. *The Novel according to Cervantes*. Berkeley: University of California Press, 1989.

•Herrero, Javier. *Who Was Dulcinea?* New Orleans: The Graduate School of Tulane University, 1985.

ter Horst, Robert. *The Fortunes of the Novel*. New York: Peter Lang, 1999.

•———. "The Sexual Economy of Miguel de Cervantes," in *Bodies and Biases: Sexualities in Hispanic Cultures and Literatures*. Ed. David William Foster and Roberto Reis. Minneapolis: University of Minnesota Press, 1996.

Hutchinson, Steven. *Cervantine Journeys*. Madison: University of Wisconsin Press, 1992.

Johnson, Carroll B. *"Don Quixote": The Quest for Modern Fiction*. Boston: G. K. Hall, 1990.

•———. *Madness and Lust: A Psychoanalytical Approach to "Don Quixote."* Berkeley: University of California Press, 1983.

Lezra, Jacques. *Unspeakable Subjects: The Genealogy of the Event in Early Modern Europe*. Stanford: Stanford University Press, 1997.

Mancing, Howard. *The Chivalric World of "Don Quixote": Style, Structure, and Narrative Technique*. Columbia: University of Missouri Press, 1982.

Mariscal, George. *Contradictory Subjects: Quevedo, Cervantes, and Seventeenth-Century Spanish Culture*. Ithaca: Cornell University Press, 1991.

McGaha, Michael D., ed. *Cervantes and the Renaissance*. Easton, Pa.: Juan de la Cuesta Press, 1980.

McKendrick, Melveena. *Cervantes*. Boston: Little, Brown, 1980.

Murillo, Luis A. *A Critical Introduction to "Don Quixote."* New York: Peter Lang, 1988.

Ortega y Gasset, José. *Meditations on Quixote*. Trans. Evelyn Rugg and Diego Marín. New York: W. W. Norton & Company, 1963.

Parr, James A. *"Don Quixote": An Anatomy of Subversive Discourse*. Newark, Del.: Juan de la Cuesta, 1988.

Percas de Ponseti, Helena. *Cervantes the Writer and Painter of "Don Quijote."* Columbia: University of Missouri Press, 1988.

Riley, Edward C. *Cervantes's Theory of the Novel*. Oxford: Clarendon Press, 1964.

———. *Don Quixote*. London: Allen & Unwin, 1986.

•Rivers, Elias L. "Talking and Writing in *Don Quixote*." *Thought* 51 (September 1976): 296–305.

•Rodríguez de Montalvo, Garci. *Amadis of Gaul*. Trans. Edwin B. Place and Herbert C. Behm. 2 vols. Lexington: The University Press of Kentucky, 1974.

•Sannazaro, Jacopo. *Arcadia and Piscatorial Ecologues*. Trans. Ralph Nash. Detroit: Wayne State University Press, 1966.

Spadaccini, Nicholas, and Jenaro Talens. *Through the Shattering Glass: Cervantes and the Self-Made World*. Minneapolis: University of Minnesota Press, 1993.

•Sullivan, Henry W. *Grotesque Purgatory: A Study of Cervantes's "Don Quixote," Part II*. University Park: Pennsylvania State University Press, 1996.

•Wey-Gómez, Nicolás. "The Jealous and the Curious: Freud, Paranoia, and Homosexuality in Cervantes's Poetics," in *Cervantes and His Postmodern Constituencies*. Ed. Anne J. Cruz and Carroll Johnson. New York: Garland Press, 1998.

Williamson, Edwin. *The Halfway House of Fiction: "Don Quixote" and Arthurian Romance*. Oxford: Clarendon Press, 1984.

———, ed. *Cervantes and the Modernists: The Question of Influence*. London: Támesis, 1994.